CW01560922

Lectures on the physiology of plants

Julius Sachs

Nabu Public Domain Reprints:

You are holding a reproduction of an original work published before 1923 that is in the public domain in the United States of America, and possibly other countries. You may freely copy and distribute this work as no entity (individual or corporate) has a copyright on the body of the work. This book may contain prior copyright references, and library stamps (as most of these works were scanned from library copies). These have been scanned and retained as part of the historical artifact.

This book may have occasional imperfections such as missing or blurred pages, poor pictures, errant marks, etc. that were either part of the original artifact, or were introduced by the scanning process. We believe this work is culturally important, and despite the imperfections, have elected to bring it back into print as part of our continuing commitment to the preservation of printed works worldwide. We appreciate your understanding of the imperfections in the preservation process, and hope you enjoy this valuable book.

LECTURES

ON THE

PHYSIOLOGY OF PLANTS

SACHS

London

HENRY FROWDE

OXFORD UNIVERSITY PRESS WAREHOUSE

AMEN CORNER, E.C.

LECTURES

ON THE

PHYSIOLOGY OF PLANTS

BY

JULIUS VON SACHS

TRANSLATED BY

H. MARSHALL WARD, M.A., F.L.S.

FELLOW OF CHRIST'S COLLEGE, CAMBRIDGE, AND PROFESSOR OF BOTANY IN
THE FORESTRY SCHOOL, R. I E. COLLEGE, COOPER'S HILL

WITH 455 WOODCUTS

Oxford

AT THE CLARENDON PRESS

M DCCC LXXXVII 1887

[*All rights reserved*]

PREFACE.

AFTER the fourth edition of my 'Text-Book of Botany' (1874) had nearly passed out of print, I received from the publishers, as well as from botanical friends, repeated invitations to prepare a fifth edition. It is, however, an old experience that while one works up with pleasure a second and even a third edition of a comprehensive work, frequent repetition eventually becomes inconvenient or even painful to the author. Having experienced this sufficiently with the fourth edition, I was unable to make up my mind to a fifth. Apart from other circumstances, I was driven to this to an important extent by the progressive development of my scientific convictions. My mode of comprehending important questions of the Physiology of Plants had undergone changes in various directions, particularly in consequence of my compilation of the 'History of Botany'; like others, more or less subject to the prevailing opinions of the present, I had held as important matters which I was gradually impelled to recognise as insignificant and transitory, higher stand-points and freer prospects opened out to me in the course of time, and the form of my text-book would no longer adapt itself to the advanced view. The artist may touch up his composition here and there with a few strokes of the pencil, or even make greater alterations; but that is not sufficient when the composition itself has ceased to be the expression of his idea. This is the position in which I find myself with respect to my text-book, since the chief thing in it to me is the composition, the form of the exposition as a whole

Moreover for several years past the wish had been taking a more and more definite form in my mind, to set forth the most important results of the physiology of plants in such a manner that not only students, but also wider circles, should be interested in them. That object, however, is only to be attained by a freer form of exposition, and I believe I have found it in the choice of lectures. It is not only the right but also the duty of any one who lectures, however, to place in the foreground his own mode of viewing the matter, the audience wish to know and should know how the science as a whole shapes itself in the mind of the lecturer, and it is comparatively unimportant whether others think the same or otherwise.

I would have the present book criticised from this point of view It is intended to introduce students and cultivated readers generally to the study of the Physiology of Plants, free from the trammels of learned descriptions of apparatus which of course could not be dispensed with in a text-book or hand-book for specialists.

Perhaps no other branch of Natural Science is so unknown to the educated public as the Physiology of Plants; because, in spite of the important progress which has been made in it during the last twenty years, and in spite of the uses to which it may be applied, no one has undertaken to publish its established results in a convenient and intelligible form This really serious want in our literature I wish to supply by means of my 'Lectures,' and this is of course only possible by the contents being strictly scientific; only the form of the exposition is to differ from that hitherto customary, in running in phrases which are universally intelligible. The object indicated, however, requires also that much which is apparently self-evident to the specialist must here be expressly brought forward and explained, so that a certain prolixity of description is often unavoidable, while, on the other hand, some questions of the day important to the Botanist are entirely passed over or can only be briefly touched upon. Again, having regard to the super-abundance of material, a suitable selection must be made, for, as is well known, the secret of being tedious lies in trying to say all one knows.

The notes on the literature attached to the separate lectures are only intended for those readers who may be by any chance stimulated by my book to wish for further direction along the untrodden grounds of our literature.

The publishers were of opinion that a new edition of the systematic part of my 'Text-book' might conveniently be attached to my 'Lectures.' Since I have myself neither the time nor the inclination to undertake such a new working-up of this domain of Botany, I have made arrangements with Professor GOEBEL, and he is to compile the systematic portion of my Text-book independently, and according to his own judgment, and publish it as a separate Book, which the reader may employ as a supplement to my 'Lectures.'

D<small>R</small> J v. SACHS

WÜRZBURG, *June 27th,* 1882

PREFACE TO THE ENGLISH EDITION.

THE work of translating Professor Sachs' 'Vorlesungen über Pflanzen-physio-logie' has been carried on during intervals between scientific duties of other kinds, and some delay has resulted from the pressure of certain of these duties of late

To put the graphic language of the original into English, which should be as widely read in this country as the German lectures have been on the Continent, has been a distinct wish and aim on my part; but it is well known that difficulties often arise in the attempt to render a German scientific sentence into simple English intelligible to the general reader, and that the force of many expressions may be readily injured or destroyed by displaying too much fear of their foreign form. That it has not always been possible to reproduce the living ideas of the author with their full force in the new language, I am only too well aware, but it is hoped that the faults are venial: they would have been more numerous but for the kindness of Dr. S. H. Vines, F R S, of Christ's College, Cambridge, who has been so good as to look over the proofs before I finally revised them for the press. I am also indebted to the courtesy of Mr. W. T. Thiselton Dyer, F R S., C.M G., the Director of the Royal Gardens, Kew, and to Dr. Bayley Balfour, F.R S., Professor of Botany in the University of Oxford, for several suggestions

The index is the only real departure from the original: this I have greatly extended, in the hope that it will be correspondingly useful to students and teachers. With regard to the bibliography, I have not added to the notes selected by Professor Sachs; but it may be pointed out that further references to the literature connected with special points are available in the English editions of De Bary's 'Comparative Anatomy of the Ferns and Phanerogams,' by Professor Bower and Dr. Scott, Goebel's 'Outlines of the Classification and Special Morphology of Plants,' by Professor Bayley Balfour and the Rev H E. F. Garnsey; De Bary's 'Comparative Morphology and Biology of the Fungi, Mycetozoa and Bacteria,' by the same; and in the 'Lectures on the Physiology of Plants,' by Dr S H Vines

H. MARSHALL WARD.

FORESTRY SCHOOL,
    COOPER'S HILL.

CONTENTS.

PART I.—Organography.

PART I.

ORGANOGRAPHY

LECTURE I.

INTRODUCTORY REMARKS ON THE

PHYSIOLOGICAL ORGANOGRAPHY OF THE VEGETATIVE ORGANS.

In the vegetable, as in the animal kingdom, we find extremely simply organised forms, in which all the processes necessary for the maintenance and reproduction of the individual are carried on in the limited space of microscopically small cells, in a scarcely ponderable mass of vegetable substance. In such cases as the Yeast-fungi and many very small Algæ, the body of the plant appears therefore, at least from the exterior, of very simple construction, in the form of a cell, globular or ellipsoidal, discoid, tubular, or of some other shape. In such cases nothing is to be seen of a segmentation into different organs distinct from one another externally. With increasing perfection of organisation, however, parts of various form, organs with different functions, make their appearance as segments of the body of the plant, the life-functions of which supplement one another; and this end is attained the more completely the more each individual organ discharges but one function. With this division of physiological labour, the perfection of organisation of a living being increases.

The most important division of physiological labour consists in this, that in addition to the organs which serve for the maintenance of a plant already existing, reproductive organs, i.e such as have the sole object of producing new plants of like kind, also arise. We may class together the former as vegetative organs in contradistinction to these reproductive organs.

Apart from quite isolated phenomena in plants of simple organisation, it is the vegetative organs alone which constitute the whole body of a plant that strikes the eye · the reproductive organs in the narrow sense of the word, the spores, oospheres, antherozoids, pollen-grains, are always of microscopic minuteness, although larger parts, which belong, strictly speaking, to the vegetative body, may assume special forms and functions, by means of which they are enabled to act as accessory organs in reproduction To this category belong, for example, the parts of the flowers of phanerogamous plants.

Only later, when we are concerned more in detail with the physiology of the reproductive phenomena, shall we examine closely also the forms of the reproductive organs. As a preparation for the theory of nutrition, of growth, and of the phenomena of irritability, however, it suffices for the present to make ourselves acquainted with the most important characteristics of the vegetative organs   In this I do not aim in any way at setting forth, in the sense of descriptive or morphological Botany, all possible varieties of form of homonymous organs in the whole vegetable kingdom; the point in question here is rather to show the beginner, proceeding from physiological points of view, the most important modifications of form, since the purely formal morphological contemplation of the organs of the plant customary hitherto has left their physiological relations entirely out of account   Any one who has been exclusively concerned with the formal morphology of the vegetable kingdom prevalent during the last thirty or forty years, can scarcely conceive the importance which the vegetative organs possess physiologically

Considering the grand variety of forms in the vegetable kingdom, which commences with simple spheroidal organisms only visible with the microscope, and ascends to such forms as we meet with in phanerogamous trees and shrubs, it is not easy to state in a few words the correspondences in nature of similar organs, and their essential differences.   We know, it is true, that from the lowest stages of vegetable organisation up to the most highly developed plants, the same plan of organisation is always adhered to in all essential points.   It is found, however, that very often organs which are in their nature of the same kind, may be endowed with not only very different forms, but also with different physiological functions.   Since we assume from the standpoint of the theory of descent that the more highly organised forms have been developed from the simpler, the most varied shapes from the same primary form, it becomes clear that very different organs may nevertheless be of like original nature; but that, in the course of changes which the whole organisation of the vegetable kingdom has undergone in time, they have been able to obtain new qualities, and to lose older ones.   Thence follows, however, that we are not in a position to say in a few words which properties of an organ are essential, and correspond originally with the general plan of construction of the vegetable kingdom; in other words, it is not possible to express organographical ideas clearly and exhaustively by means of simple definitions.

We adopt, therefore, a totally different mode of consideration   Without concerning ourselves in any way with definitions, we regard first the various organs where they present themselves in the highest perfection in their typical character, and then seek to establish which organs, in other regions of the vegetable kingdom, present also the same essential peculiarities more or less modified.   In doing this, however, we place in the foreground the physiological properties, which very often correspond but little with the relations of outward form which constitute the subject-matter of morphology I believe, however, that this comparative physiological method of consideration of the organs apprehends their true nature in a more fundamental manner than morphology has done hitherto

Above all, physiological organography has to do, not merely with the incidental visible forms of organs, but more especially with their functional importance for the life of the plant, these functional activities, however, are nothing but reactions to external influences, even where the case appears to be otherwise.   Each reaction of an organ to external influence is, however, what is usually termed irritability, as will be shown more fully later on, all the organs of the plant, without exception, are in some one sense irritable, and the essential differences and agreements of the various organs depend especially upon their irritability, i.e. upon the manner in which they react to external influences. In what follows, the organs of vegetation will be characterised from this point of view.

Departing from the customary mode of view, we divide the body of the more highly developed plants into two groups of organs,—Root and Shoot. In accordance with its original signification, the root is that part of a plant which becomes fixed on or in a substratum as an organ of attachment, and in the latter case serves for the absorption of nutritive matters contained in the substratum. The shoot, or, to express it more generally, the system of shoots of a plant, is on the other hand originally that part which, becoming developed outside the substratum, produces and increases the substance of the plant, and brings forth, in addition, the reproductive organs, which never appear on a root.

That both fulfil their characteristic functions depends upon their different reactions to the universal forces of nature, gravitation, light, contact, &c. That, as we shall see later, there are roots which grow forth above the substratum like shoots, that there are also numerous shoots which penetrate into the substratum like roots, does not alter their original nature ; and only proves, as has been mentioned already, that with progressive development of the vegetable kingdom, with progressive adaptation of various organs to special requirements of life, some peculiarities may be lost, whilst new ones on the other hand may arise. This, however, will become clear only in the further course of our investigations.

In the first place, it will be advisable to illustrate more fully, by a few examples, the difference between root and shoot.

If we allow an Almond, for example, to germinate in moist earth, we find after a few weeks that the young plant already contained in the seed becomes further developed (Fig. 1): the primary root (w) has grown down into the earth, and numerous thin filiform lateral rootlets (w') spring forth from it, growing obliquely or horizontally.

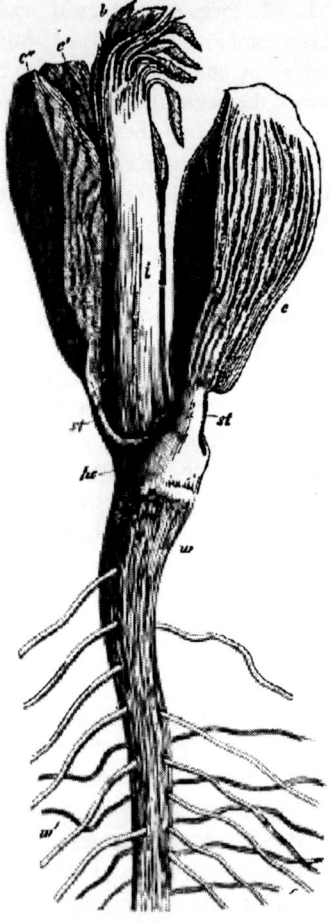

FIG. 1.—Seedling of the Almond (*Amygdalus communis.* w primary root; w' secondary roots; *hc* hypocotyledonary (first) segment of the seedling shoot ; *c* cotyledons (first leaves) ; *st* their stalks ; *i* first internode of the shoot-axis of the seedling ; *b* its young leaves (nat. size).

Language has not waited for Botany to recognise this portion of our plant extended in the substratum, as a special and peculiar organ, and to distinguish it from the remaining parts by the name of Root.

On the other hand, there rises from the germinating Almond, above the substratum, that part of the plant which will later on develope in the air and in the presence of light as the Almond-tree: it consists, in the first place, of a cylindrical part (*i*) tending upwards, which we recognise immediately as the future main stem of the young Almond-tree, and at the upper portion of which the young leaves (*b*) are already visible. The two bodies, densely filled with nutritive matters marked (*c*) in our figure (the Cotyledons), are also to be regarded as leaves which spring from the seedling stem. We comprehend the whole of this structure under the name of Shoot, as opposed to Root, and distinguish on it two categories of parts, viz. the leaves (*b* and *c*), and the Shoot-axis (*i*). However sharply the leaves are here and in other cases separated off from the shoot-axis, an extended comparison of different forms of plants leaves no doubt that they are nothing but portions or outgrowths of the shoot-axis, and must be taken together with this as one whole. Our plant is thus in the first instance segmented into root and shoot, as the two chief forms of vegetative organs.

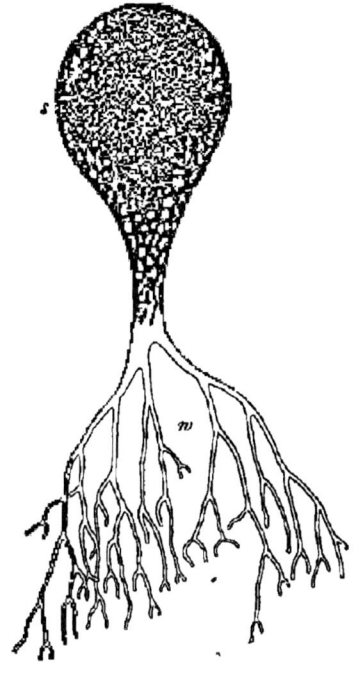

If, in contradistinction to this highly organised seedling, which developes into a tree, we now contemplate a small plant of extremely simple nature, growing even without cell divisions, as *Botrydium* (Fig. 2), we here again find the two parts, Root and Shoot. The first, consisting of thin, branched tubes, has penetrated into the substratum (wet clay), it fixes the entire plant, and at the same time absorbs mineral nutritive materials from the soil, and it does both by virtue of a series of properties which it shares with the highly organised root of the Almond plant; it is only by the external form and visible internal structure that it is distinguished from it; the function, performed in virtue of special irritability, is in all essential points the same in both. The other portion of our *Botrydium* plant is a globular swelling of the vesicle of which the whole plant consists: this part, however, comes forth above the substratum, and meet-

FIG 2.—*Botrydium granulatum*　An Alga, magnified about 30 times　*w* root, *s* green shoot (after Rostafinski)

ing the light, the usual green colouring matter of plants is produced—viz., chlorophyll; by means of this, it is enabled to decompose carbon dioxide, and, with the aid of the mineral substances absorbed by the roots, to produce organised plant-substance. In this point the globular shoot, in spite of its extremely simple organisation, corresponds to the highly developed germinal shoot of the Almond. It does so also in a second point; the reproductive organs arise in it sooner or later, though in a much simpler form than is the case with the Almond-tree, on which the reproductive bodies (oospheres and pollen-grains), also microscopically small, only arise after some years—when the germinal shoot is strongly developed and much branched—in the interior of the flowers, which are simply altered shoots. A detailed exposition of these matters would present a thousand examples, which, even on a purely external examination, would exhibit all possible transitional forms between the organisation of the germinating Almond and the *Botrydium*; but for a physiologically correct comprehension of the actual state of affairs we scarcely require this aid, since we can prove that that part of either plant which penetrates into the substratum, and equally that rising above the substratum, undertakes in both cases essentially the same functions for the whole plant, in spite of all difference of form, and is to this end endowed with the same kinds of irritability.

In order to obtain at once more general points of view for physiological organography, we will take into consideration yet a third example, a plant of structure equally simple to that of *Botrydium*, which also consists simply of a single, branched, tubular cell, a mould-fungus of the *Mucor* group, which is represented in Fig. 3. The part (*m*), with its thousands of branches, has arisen from the germinating spore, and has extended in the substratum (e. g. moist bread, the flesh of an apple, &c.) After some time, there grow forth from the main arms of this branch-system thicker simple tubes, which rise above the substratum, swell up in a globular manner at their ends, and develope reproductive organs in these sporangia. Our whole *Mucor* plant is devoid of chlorophyll, and is therefore unable to produce organic vegetable substance by decomposition of carbon dioxide; on the contrary it absorbs it for its development out of the substratum, that is, by means of the portion *m* (contained in the substratum) which, in spite of its different organisation, behaves itself, physiologically, exactly as the root of the

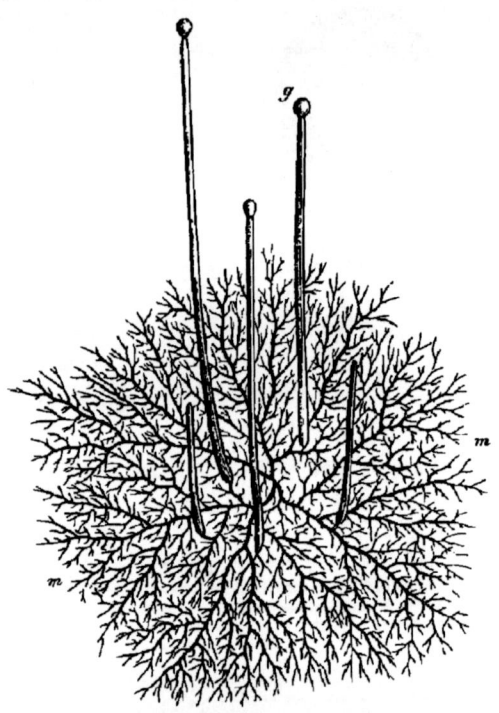

FIG 3.—*Phycomyces nitens* *m* mycelium (root) grown in gelatine, *g* conidiophores, rising above the substratum.

Botrydium and of the Almond, since it penetrates into the substratum, urged by the same kind of irritability, and absorbs water and nutritive matters from it. We are therefore completely justified in regarding this portion of our fungus, distinguished by botanists as the mycelium, as its root, and accordingly the fruit-bearing portions, protruding above the substratum, appear as shoots; it is true they show, as already said, an essential difference from the forms of shoot hitherto considered, inasmuch as they are devoid of the capacity of producing vegetable substance from carbon dioxide, since they contain no chlorophyll; instead of this, however, the other property of the shoot—to bear reproductive organs—has been preserved to them.

We have started in our organographical consideration, as also appears in the history of science, from a highly developed plant, from a plant the roots of which every one knows as such, the essential root-properties of which are developed in the highest perfection   The germinal shoot of the Almond is likewise that which language has all along distinguished as a shoot.   I name such organic forms which present the essential peculiarities in great perfection, and from which therefore a clear scientific consideration best proceeds, *typical forms*, and believe myself in this use of the word to be completely in accordance with the original sense of the word Type. When we now, proceeding from typical forms of organs, compare abnormal forms with them, we find two different categories of these   For, on the one hand, we meet in the lower regions of the vegetable kingdom with such forms of organs, especially of roots and shoots, in which the organic differentiation generally is not yet so far advanced as in the typical ones ; we have to do with feeble beginnings, which have not yet attained to the typical standard   In this sense, we may term the roots of our *Botrydium* and *Mucor* rudimentary roots, in so far as the word rudiment signifies a state of beginning which has not yet attained to completeness.   In strong contrast to these rudimentary forms, we have to distinguish further the degenerate or reduced forms.   As it is to be assumed, from the standpoint of the theory of descent, that the more perfect have gradually developed from the simple organisms, we are also driven to the further assumption, that, in consequence of special modes of life, more simply organised forms have again arisen from those more highly organised, and this process we term degeneration, or reduction   This process is strikingly exhibited when plants, which we must regard as originally always containing chlorophyll, become parasitic.   Since through parasitism they come into the condition of absorbing organic material from without, they cease to form it by decomposition of carbon dioxide , under these circumstances the chlorophyll is superfluous as an instrument of assimilation, and in consequence of this, the whole remaining organisation becomes simplified, so far as it is connected with the activity of the chlorophyll; and since it is especially the shoots which are the bearers of the assimilating organs, these lose, in parasites, together with the loss of chlorophyll, all those peculiarities which arise from the activity of the chlorophyll, viz , the larger development of surface, and the external segmentation connected therewith, and so on   There then remains to the shoot only the second primary peculiarity, viz., to be a bearer of fructification, and such we find to be the case in the third plant considered above, the *Mucor*, as with most of the other fungi, and the phanerogams devoid of chlorophyll.   To recapitulate what has been said, we have, as the typical forms, the highly organised ones which first offer themselves for consideration.   Comparison with these brings into notice, on the one hand, the rudimentary organs which have not yet come up to the typical standard , and on the other hand, we regard those organs as degenerated, or reduced, which have been developed from typical forms by simplification of their functions.

It is, however, always very difficult so to form our general conceptions, that they shall comprehend all the cases occurring in nature. So it is also here. For very often organic forms are met with, with regard to which one knows not in which of these categories they should be placed   For example, it is certain that the flowers of phanerogamous plants belong to the category of leafy shoots ; from a purely æsthetic point of view, one might be led to consider them as the most highly developed form of shoot, whereas the systematic or phylogenetic mode of consideration leads us to the conclusion, that the flower shoots are to be considered as altered leaf shoots, of which the capacity for assimilation has ceased, because they take part in the function of fertilisation. They are in this sense, therefore, reduced forms of shoot In the same way, we may assume that the tendrils of the Vine, in spite of their containing chlorophyll, yet scarcely come into consideration in the assimilation of the whole plant; whilst they serve it as climbing organs, and in so far contribute to the green leaves being able vigorously to carry on their function of assimilation. Again, we may regard the numerous subterranean forms of shoot as derived from green leafy shoots, which, however, on their part, assist in the performance of the processes of nutrition by the latter in this or that manner. It is against common sense to regard those kinds of organic forms, which have it is true only been derived later from the typical ones but which contribute to the greater perfection of the entire organism, simply as degenerations. In order to express this objection adequately in language, I shall designate these kinds of organs, derived or metamorphosed forms, a flower, a vine-tendril, a subterranean runner, &c. are thus, for us, derived or metamorphosed shoots; and in the same way, roots which serve the function of nutrition either not exclusively or not at all, but rather do duty as climbing organs, reservoirs of reserve material, and so forth, are not necessarily to be termed reduced, but more generally as derived or metamorphosed forms of root

In this setting forth of the ideas of rudimentary, typical, derived and reduced organs, we also find at once the reason why it is in general quite impossible to characterise correctly by means of short, precise definitions, a comprehensive category of organs: thus, in comparison with the typical forms of a group, various characters may yet be wanting to the rudimentary forms of the same group, on the other hand, certain characters may become lost by degeneration, and it is obvious how very difficult it is, under such circumstances, to have regard to all these various cases in a definition.

It is therefore, in my opinion, the best, as well for research as for my exposition, to find out first by careful comparison of very many cases, what organic forms present themselves as typical within a category; these are precisely those organs where the forms concerned are developed in the highest degree. one has then only yet to establish, whether and how far other forms are to be looked upon as rudimentary or derived. The setting up of a typical form supplies in a certain manner the ideal towards which the rudimentary forms are striving, and from which the derived forms have fallen away again[1].

---

[1] The usual division of all organs of the plant into root, stem, and leaf, no longer comes up to the present state of science—at best it might hold good exclusively of the vegetative organs. Nevertheless, it will, as I believe, clearly result from what has already been said in the text, as well as from the following lectures, that there is no meaning in considering stem and leaves separately from one another, as two groups co-ordinated with the roots, that, rather, both together are to be co-ordinated with the root, as shoot Since what is necessary has been said in the text, it is superfluous to attempt any further demonstration here.

Yet a few words in anticipation on the reproductive organs, to which I shall, however, return in the last part of this book That the reproductive organs in the first place of the phanerogams were regarded as leaves, or as appendages of such, in the sense of the doctrine of metamorphosis, was only justified so long as the stamens and carpels of the phanerogams were considered as the true sexual organs. No attempt was made to arrange the archegonia and antheridia under one of

It is however necessary yet to refer to some other points of general significance.

We seek the characteristic properties of organs, from our point of view, not in their outward form, not even especially in their visible anatomical structure, but, as already stated, in their manner of reacting to external influences, or of being irritable; and this depends, as we shall yet see in what follows, less upon the external form and anatomical structure, than upon those invisible relations of structure which are usually termed molecular, and in the sense of chemistry, atomic. This implies, however, that the characteristic similarities and differences of organs depend upon their material constitution. From general scientific principles, we must assume that to each visible external difference of the organ, there corresponds also a difference of its material substance, exactly as we regard the form of a crystal as an expression of the material properties of the crystallising substance. In our time of advanced scientific knowledge, it might appear, strictly speaking, scarcely necessary to lay special stress upon this principle; but the thoroughly scholastic way of thinking, which, coming from former centuries, has been kept alive up to the most modern times in the region of botanical morphology, makes it seem still advisable to devote a few words to the matter. As late as the year 1880 one of the most renowned German botanists, from the stand-point of these antiquated views, used the following words in an academical address: "The figure of the entire organism, which will only be realised in a material form in the future, already operates virtually in the present, as a motive cause, before and during the development of the parts, just as does the plan according to which the builder places his blocks." Such a mode of looking at organic forms

---

the general, so-called morphological conceptions, and yet nobody ventured to form of them a special category of organs, in contradiction to the obsolete doctrine of metamorphosis.

In the present state of our knowledge, however, we have without doubt to take as the typical reproductive organs of the whole vegetable kingdom, on the one hand sporangia, on the other the archegonia and antheridia of the Mosses and Vascular Cryptogams. It would be ridiculous to wish to arrange these under the morphological conception, leaf or stem; we have here to do, rather, with two groups of organs, well characterised physiologically and morphologically, viz. sporangia and sexual organs. In the comparison of the Algae and Fungi with the Muscineæ and Vascular Cryptogams, it is shown at once, not only that the proper spores of both groups correspond to one another, but also that the so-called oogonia of the Thallophytes, are rudimentary simpler archegonia, and the same holds good with respect to the antheridia. On the other hand, following up the sporangia and sexual organs of the Vascular Cryptogams into the classes of the Gymnosperms and Angiosperms, progressive degenerations of them, and a remarkable combination of the sexual organs with the spores are found. That the pollen-grains correspond to the male microspores, the embryo sacs to the female macrospores of the higher Cryptogams, is now generally accepted, after this relation had long been established by Hofmeister and myself. Numerous more recent works bearing on the history of development, especially those of Goebel, leave no doubt that the anthers, as well as the ovules, are true though reduced sporangia, &c.

Since I shall return to these matters later on, what has been said is only to serve to emphasize, in connection with the division of the vegetative organs into root and shoot, that two peculiar groups of organs stand opposed to them, viz. the sporangia and sexual organs, in their typical form as archegonia and antheridia. We have thus to distinguish five categories of organs (I) the vegetative organs—(1) root and (2) shoot; (II) the reproductive organs—a asexual sporangia and spores (3), b the sexual archegonia (4) and antheridia (5). All other forms of organs are rudimentary or reduced organs of these groups.

I have good reason for entirely discarding the term *thallus*. In the first place, the Greek word θάλλος means simply shoot; and, secondly, the thallus of the Algæ and Fungi, taken purely as a matter of fact, according to the customary view, is simply characterised by the want of leaves, although the morphologists are by no means able to say what a leaf really is.

and their existence, to which I replied at the time[1], is only possible if, as has happened hitherto, the organic form is regarded as something existing *per se*; as if the organs of the plant themselves by no means consisted of real matter, with its forces and reactions to external influences, but, like platonic ideas, existed only in the abstract, but were nevertheless able to operate upon the actual matter of plants

If now the outward form and internal structure, and the functional capacity of an organ resulting therefrom, constitute the necessary expression of its material substance, then a very simple consideration leads us to the perception, that this material substance of an organ is itself again the result of the physiological activity of preceding organs of the same plant. The first organs of the seedling arise from materials or chemical compounds, which the mother-plant has produced and apportioned to them; the later organs arising after germination, the shoot and its parts, roots and so forth, however, are constructed from the materials which the organs of the seedling have taken up from without, and then further altered according to the specific nature of the plant; each subsequent organ is the result of the constructive activity of preceding organs. Thence it follows that the construction of organs, their developmental history and growth, is also a subject-matter of vegetable physiology, and that, as one may say, not only the most important but also the most difficult part of it. Vegetable physiology has thus to do not merely with the functions of organs already existing, but also with the origination of the organs themselves, which is itself a function of preceding organs. In reproduction we must assume that certain particles of matter pass over into the reproductive cells, which have been previously produced and their nature determined by the organs of the mother-plant, and now possess the capability, whilst appropriating to themselves new matter from without, of imprinting upon this the same series of material differences as had already declared themselves in the mother-plant[2]. This repetition of the formative processes which depend on chemical processes is, as a rule, a very exact one in each organic form, so that the descendants resemble the progenitors in all points It is this process which is termed Heredity. It is at once perceived that Heredity is simply a fact of experience, the cause of which we do not know, and nothing more. It can therefore only lead to more complete confusion in science, if, as often happens in these days, Heredity is treated in a very thoughtless manner as a force of nature, by which it is imagined to be possible to explain all manner of things.

But this constant repetition of the peculiarities of the ancestors in the descendants is not without exception; sometimes, as cultivated plants especially show in a thousand ways, more or less extensive deviations from the peculiarities of the parents appear in the descendants, which, under certain circumstances, may become more and more intensified in the following generations, by further propagation. This fact is expressed by the term 'formation of varieties.' Its cause is in general unknown, in any case, however, we are correct in assuming that the changes, perceptible externally in variation, consist in material alterations in the parents, during procreation or

---

[1] Compare my treatise '*Stoff und Form der Pflanzenorgane*' in the Arbeiten des botan Instituts in Wurzburg, 1880, Bd II, p 453.

[2] I have explained in my two treatises on '*Stoff und Form*' in the Arbeiten des botan Instituts in Wurzburg, Bd II, that the 'gemmules' in Darwin's Pangenesis are not meant here, but matter in the sense of chemistry and physics

immediately after it, most probably in a change of the proper generative substances. This is not the place to go into these matters more in detail, we ought rather to emphasise only that the theory of descent has been developed from the consideration of variation in reproduction, from the fact of the accumulation of new peculiarities in the varieties. These facts, in combination with the observation that from the simplest forms of plants up to the most highly organised there is an unbroken series of transitional or intermediate forms, have led to the hypothesis, as daring as fruitful, that the most highly developed organisms have been gradually developed from the simplest, by means of the progressive formation of varieties. This is essentially the meaning of the theory of descent, which has during the last twenty years produced so great a revolution in the views of naturalists. We also cannot dispense with it in our organographical considerations, simply for the reason that the understanding of any organic form whatever is only possible if one looks upon it as the result of the ever progressing organising tendency of the substance of the plant, i. e of the variation of other preceding organic forms; or in other words, every organic form is the outcome of a history, which is as old as the organic world itself. This principle asserts itself far less in the consideration of the specific functions of given organs, than in the comparison of their external forms, and the natural system is the attempt to state clearly this historical relationship of all plants to one another. Like all new and comprehensive hypotheses, the theory of descent has also caused confusion and devastation in weak minds, and perhaps done as much harm as good. We shall be on our guard against laying any value whatever upon the excrescences of the theory of descent, without casting aside the good and helpful which is contained in its scientific nucleus. Even the above statements concerning typical, rudimentary, reduced and metamorphosed forms, have a clear, actual meaning only on the basis of the theory of descent, and so I shall, in our further considerations, have recourse to the theory where the facts require it.

Concerning one point I should wish to anticipate · viz. the use of the word Purpose, a word which many fanatics of the theory of descent would, if possible, banish entirely from the language. But the fact that, formerly, Purpose in the mechanism of organisms was referred to causes other than now, is no reason for robbing our language of a pregnant term. By the expression, This or that mechanism has a Purpose in an organism, one understands really nothing more than that this contributes to the ability of the organism to exist. It is now obvious, however, without further discussion, that all properties of any organism must necessarily be so arranged, that they at least do not call in question its existence under the circumstances of life natural to it. 'To the purpose' means, therefore, in general, the same as 'capable of existence,' and it would be foolishness to waste even a word as to whether one may use the term in this sense or not. This implies, however, that there is absolutely no scientific merit in maintaining of any organic mechanism whatever, that it is in general to the purpose, or contributes to the capability of existence; since that is self-evident. On the other hand, it is in certain circumstances very important and profitable to demonstrate how far, and under what conditions, a given mechanism in the organism is of purpose; in what way this contributes, in combination with other mechanisms, to the capability of existence of a given organism; and strictly speaking, the whole of physiology is essentially occupied with such demonstrations.

LECTURE II.

THE TYPICAL ROOTS OF VASCULAR PLANTS

It has been already remarked in the first lecture, while considering the differences between roots and shoots, that the primary and essential character of the root consists in that it becomes, first of all, developed as an organ of attachment on or in a substratum, and, when the latter is the case, it is at the same time the medium of absorption of nutritive matters contained in the substratum. Since, moreover, assimilation—i. e. the production of organic vegetable substance—is foreign to its physiological purpose, the instrument of assimilation, chlorophyll, is also wanting to it; though it is not thereby precluded that in certain rare cases, when the roots are developed in air or water and thus exposed to light, chlorophyll may also arise in them. However I shall return to the physiological properties of roots afterwards. Meanwhile, it will be to the purpose to consider the relations of organisation, and we will concern ourselves, according to the scheme of comparative organography given above, first with the typical, and then with the rudimentary and reduced forms of roots.

We find typical, and at the same time very highly organised roots, in the large majority of vascular plants, the phanerogams and higher cryptogams: botanists for about the last forty years have accustomed themselves to term these organs exclusively roots, which is from a purely formal point of view but half justifiable, and from the standpoint of physiological organography must be entirely rejected.

In vascular plants with upright main stems, as the Sunflower, Tobacco, Hemp, and others, we meet with a root-system developed completely in the earth, and composed of long, cylindrical fibres of varying thickness, which is in ordinary language simply termed the root, in scientific language it is however more to the purpose to call each one of these fibres a root. In many cases the first root, already present in the embryo of the plant, becomes vigorously developed, penetrating perpendicularly into the earth (*w*, Fig. 4): from it spring, radiating laterally in two, three, or more directions, numerous new roots (*n*) which grow horizontally or obliquely downwards, and in their turn again produce new root-fibres, and in such a way that the new, young roots always arise behind the growing end of what is the mother-root for the time being. In the case here considered, which is realised especially in trees and annual erect plants, the whole root-system of a plant thus arises from the embryonic root (radicle): this is the oldest, grows most vigorously, and penetrates deepest into the earth.   It is, however, more frequently the case, that the first root of the seedling, with its ramifications, soon ceases to grow, and new, more vigorous roots are then formed from the lower parts of the shoot-axis, which likewise, although they arise above the ground, penetrate into the earth

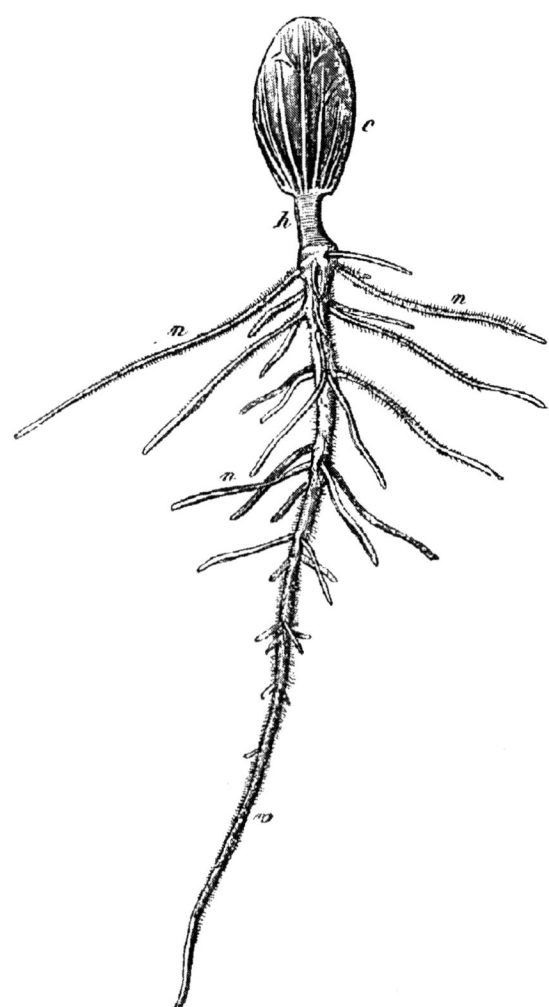

and become branched there. In such a case, more vigorous roots may go on continually appearing higher up the stem, so that the root - system ramifying in the ground, arises, not as before from a tap-root but from the main stem of the plant.   The Palms and the Maize furnish excellent examples of this.   In creeping plants—e.g. the Gourd — more especially when the stem creeps forward beneath the earth, roots usually spring from the under side of the shoot-axis along its whole length, in many cases even close behind the bud, and these may branch also in their turn. In subterranean creeping stems, the root-system originally formed on the seedling may then die off, and rot away, together with the hinder part of the stem itself, new roots being continually produced behind the apex of the growing bud. But even when the primary root-system remains preserved, but the stem climbs, it frequently happens that new roots are continually

FIG. 4—Seedling of Gourd (*Cucurbita Pepo*). *w* primary root; *n* secondary roots; *h* the hypocotyledonous segment of the shoot-axis; *c* the cotyledons (nat. size).

produced below the bud; these then cling to solid bodies as climbing organs, as in the Ivy and many tropical Aroids.   Roots of this kind are commonly termed aërial roots; they may also grow down from a considerable height in the form of thick, cylindrical cords several metres long, and finally penetrate into the ground, there to become branched (tropical Aroids).   But even in stems growing upright, it happens frequently enough that roots arise immediately beneath the growing point, and even that the whole root-system of the plant consists of them, as occurs in many Ferns, particularly the Marattiaceæ and many tree ferns. In several species of Cactus, moreover, the tendency also exists to put forth roots close beneath the growing point of the shoot; finally, roots may even spring out of leaves, as occasionally happens in a fortuitous manner, but occurs quite normally in our common large Fern, *Aspidium Filix-mas*, where the shoot-axis is so densely beset with leaves, that it generally shows no proper surface at all; all the numerous roots of this plant spring from the basal parts of the leaves.

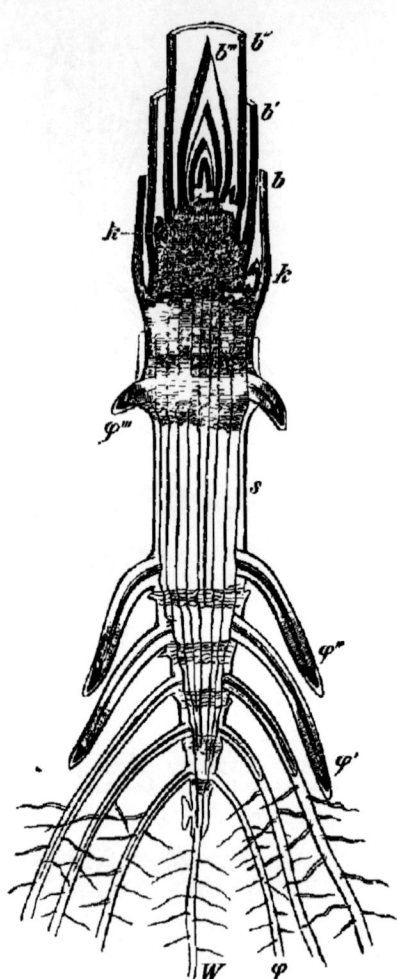

Since the roots developed in the earth especially absorb water and nutritive matters dissolved in it, their number and ramifications, and thus the whole formation of the root-system, are the richer, the more vigorously the green, transpiring and assimilating leaf-surface of the aerial shoots is developed. In time, in proportion as the assimilating foliage increases in surface, the subterranean root-system becomes larger, and fresh portions of the soil are penetrated by it. The number of root-fibres, and the space which they traverse in all directions within the soil, is much larger than one usually supposes It is certainly not put too high if we assume this space to be more than a cubic metre in the case of a well-developed Sunflower, Hemp, or Gourd plant; and in the case of large trees we may estimate it even at hundreds of cubic metres This space then is so traversed in all directions by thousands of fine roots, that scarcely a cubic centimetre of it remains exempt By this means the plant, abundantly provided with foliage, succeeds in extracting from the soil the very large quantities of water which are transpired from the leaves, together with the nutritious matters contained in it. S. Clark has taken the trouble to

FIG 5 —Diagrammatic longitudinal section through a young Maize plant (Zea Mays) *w* primary root, φ φ' φ''', the roots springing from the shoot axis (*s*), *b* leaves, *k* buds The growing points are represented black the elongating parts grey , the portions left white are fully grown

measure the length of all the roots of a large Gourd plant, and found that it amounted to twenty-five kilometres. This relation between root-formation and leaf-surface makes itself evident again in that, in floating aquatic plants (*Hydrocharis*, *Stratiotes*, *Lemna*), the number and length of the roots are generally inconsiderable, since they find the nutritive fluid in abundance, while the leaves, floating on the water or surrounded by the damp air, use up but little water; plants living in humus and root-parasites which have no green foliage leaves, as *Neottia, Lathræa, Orobanche*, have also but an insignificant root-system in proportion to their body-weight, because in the absence of green leaves the most important transpiratory surface is wanting. In general the root fibres are the thinner, the more numerous they are in the root-system; since, in the formation of roots, it is essentially a matter of a large surface, with least possible

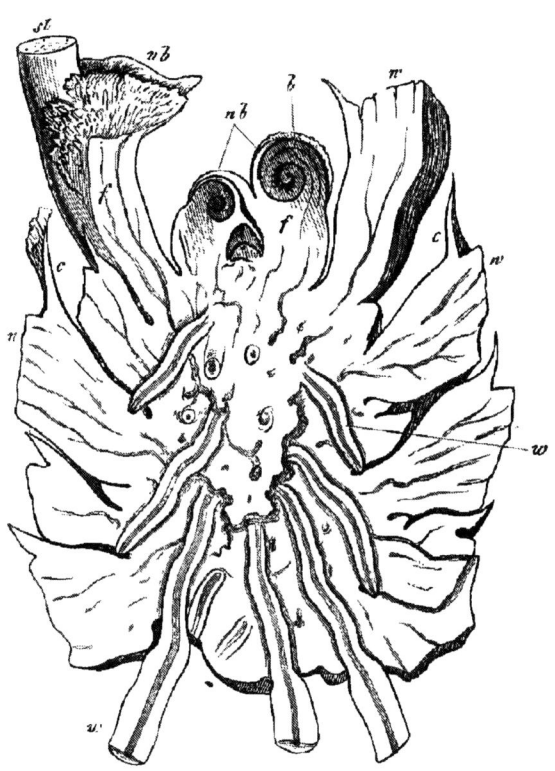

FIG. 6.—Vertical longitudinal section of the stem of a young *Angiopteris evecta*. Above, the youngest leaves (*b*) are still completely enveloped in the stipules (*n b*); *st* stalk of an unfolded leaf, with its stipules *n b*; *n* everywhere the leaf-scars on the basal portions *ff* from which the leaf-stalks have been separated; *cc* the commissures of the stipules in longitudinal section; *ww* roots (nat. size).

mass of the organ. Hence the less numerous, short roots of plants devoid of chlorophyll, as well as of water-plants, are remarkably thick and fleshy; while the young absorbing roots of large trees and shrubs very often scarcely attain the thickness of a horse-hair. If we now examine a single root fibre more closely, we have at its free end the growing point, out of which the whole cellular tissue of the fibre becomes developed. This growing point is moreover encased with a cap of firmer permanent tissue. The fore end of the root is, in fact, destined to be pushed forwards in the earth, much as the point of a nail which is driven into a board. It is obvious that the solid root-cap, with its smooth slippery surface and its conical form, facilitates the progress forwards, and at the same time protects the delicate tissue of the growing point. In aërial and aquatic roots, which we may regard as derived or even reduced forms, the root-cap is feebler, and is only in general an organ of protection against the drying up of the growing point, or against its immediate contact with water. The anatomical relations need only be briefly referred to: each root-fibre consists of a central or axial vascular bundle, or fibro-vascular cord, and a soft cortex of exceedingly thin-walled parenchyma cells surrounding it. The axial cord, the histological constitution of which differs considerably from the vascular bundles of the shoot, is at its posterior end connected with the vascular bundles of the organ bearing it; it runs through the whole length of the root, and terminates in the growing point, from which it, as well as the cortex, obtains the elements for its further growth in length. Through this cord, and particularly through the non-lignified elements of it, the formative matters, especially such as are of proteid nature, are conducted to the growing point from the mother-organ Since the roots have to absorb water and the nutritive matters dissolved in it, and do not need protection against evaporation in the soil, they are devoid of the resistant epidermis of the shoot-axis, the outer wall of the cells is not at all or very slightly cuticularised, and obviously the stomata are wanting, since in roots there is no question of a rapid interchange of gases with the environment.

When a new root-fibre is about to arise, there is formed in the interior of the tissue of the mother-organ, for instance inside a root, or a shoot-axis, or even a leaf, in the first place a new growing point, which usually consists of small-celled embryonic tissue, which becomes at once clothed on the outside with the root-cap. These new growing points generally arise on the outer side of the vascular bundles of the mother-organ, and when the young roots begin to grow, they must first break through its cortical tissue, as may easily be observed in fresh roots. the lateral roots of these protrude from slits, the edges of which are often raised up in a lip-like manner. As a rule, a root, and likewise a shoot-axis, gradually produces a large number of root-fibres, which on their part generally act in the same manner In this the rule holds good which prevails generally in the formation of organs in the vegetable kingdom, that the roots appear in acro-petal succession—i. e. the youngest roots are always nearest the growing point of the mother-root, or of the root-forming shoot, and the further they are removed from the growing point of the mother-organ, the older and longer they are. Since the

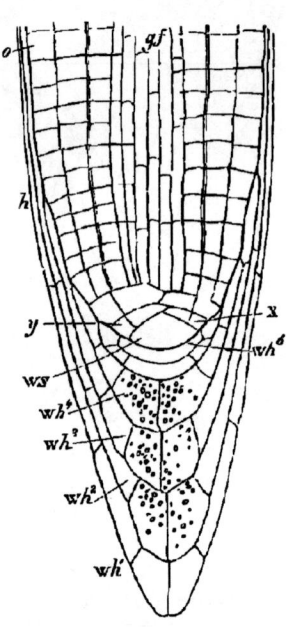

FIG. 7 —Longitudinal section through the root-apex of *Marsilia salvatrix* *ws* the apical cell, *xy* its last segments, *o* the epidermis, *gf* the axial vascular bundle of the root, *wh* layers of the root-cap, *h* the parts of the root-cap extending further back on the root (highly magnified)

young roots arise on the outer side of the vascular bundles, or at any rate in definite relation to the vascular bundles of the mother-organ, and these run more or less parallel to one another, it follows obviously that the roots which spring from an organ are arranged in longitudinal rows. This arrangement appears much clearer in the branching of the root itself, than in root-forming stems; we find here the lateral roots arranged in 2, 3, 4, 5 or more longitudinal rows, or orthostichies In general, however, the arrangement of the roots on their mother-organ is not so strictly regular as, for example, the arrangement of leaves on their shoot-axes. It is also to be insisted upon that the young roots always appear first at some distance from the advancing growing point of the mother-root or mother-shoot, even though they have been previously developed from the embryonal tissue of the same; a root beset with numerous lateral roots, therefore, usually possesses a naked end some or several centimetres long.

I now pass on, finally, to a short description of the proper physiological peculiarities of the root. I confine myself again in so doing to the typical forms, more especially as we meet with them as subterranean roots in the land plants with green leaves. The main purpose of these is, as already insisted upon, in addition to the fastening of the plant into the ground, the absorption of fluid nourishment out of it; and this must be kept in view in judging of all the physiological properties of the root. Above all, it of course depends upon this that the roots really penetrate into the substratum: to this end the tap-roots, of seedlings especially, as well as those roots springing from stems and destined to become further developed in the ground, are endowed with

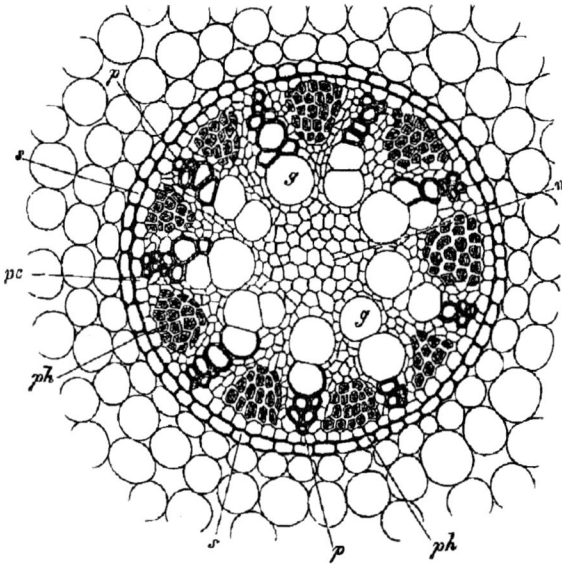

geotropism; that is, the growing portion, some millimetres long, lying behind the growing point, reacts to the influence of the gravitation of the earth in such a manner, that the growing point becomes directed downwards exactly vertical. This, if the root had previously another direction, is effected by a corresponding curvature behind the growing point. If such a root is placed in the light first, it may be also heliotropic, i e it becomes curved at the same place in such a way that the growing point is directed away from the source of light; and both kinds of

FIG 8 —Root of *Acorus calamus* Transverse section of the axial cylinder, with surrounding cortical tissue, *s* endodermis, *p* pericambium *ph* phloem, *g* groups of vessels (strongly magnified)

reaction work therefore, in general, to the same end—that the apex of the root penetrates into the ground. The same result is yet further secured, by the growing end of the root being sensitive to slight pressure and to moist surfaces; the growing end becomes concave on the pressed and on the moister side, and it is obvious that, under ordinary conditions of life, these two irritabilities also will act like the geotropism and heliotropism of the root, and contribute to give the root-apex that direction by which it penetrates into the substratum

Concerning the origin of roots from shoot-axes, it is frequently to be observed that the place of origin of the growing points is already determined by external influences alone, or together with others. it is either the side lying towards the centre of the earth which alone produces roots, in consequence of an effect of gravity, or, in climbing stems, it is the shaded side turned away from the light, which is also in general at the same time moister, from which alone new roots arise.

A root having in this way penetrated into the earth, and grown forwards perpendicularly within it, lateral roots arise progressively from above downwards, in the order stated. These also are geotropic, and sensitive to contact and to moisture, but in a different degree from the tap-root their geotropism especially is different, the lateral roots are caused by the influence of gravitation to grow, not vertically downwards, but obliquely, or even horizontally. However difficult it may be to conceive this varying sensitiveness of the different roots of a system, thus much is obvious, that the entire root-system is compelled to grow into the earth in all directions by it At a later period, when we are particularly concerned with the irritability of plants, I can speak in detail concerning the properties of roots here mentioned: the point now is simply to establish the existence of these properties, and to insist upon their purpose for the life of the plant.

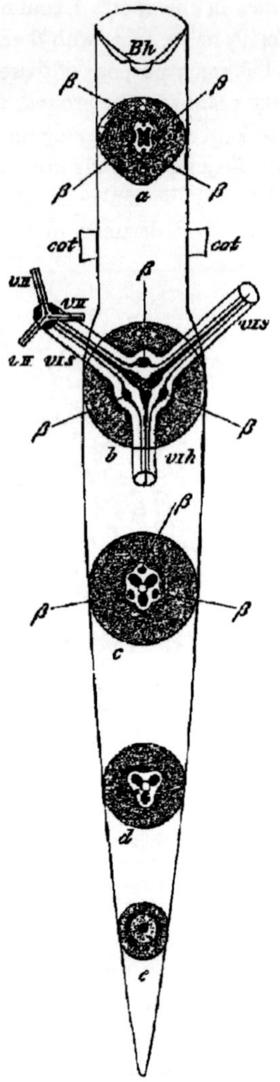

In this connection, however, there are yet a few points of special interest in the first place stress is to be laid upon the fact, that in roots growing into the earth, the portion which is becoming elongated behind the growing point is very short, even in vigorous tap-roots only 8–10 mm. long, and in thin lateral roots often only 2–3 This appears remarkable, when one considers that in aerial leaf-shoots and flower-scapes the elongating portion is commonly many centimetres long. In the shortness of the root, however, an arrangement is afforded which renders the progress of the apex of the root within the earth considerably easier, since the whole force of the push by which the growing point is driven forward is concentrated immediately behind it. In the long aerial roots of tropical Aroids, and others, where this mechanical arrangement is unnecessary, I found, accordingly, a much more considerable length of the elongating region.

Fundamentally, however, the roots, as we have hitherto learned to understand them, are only the bearers of the proper organs for the absorption of food, namely, the root-hairs. These are exceedingly delicate-walled,

FIG 9 —Diagram of the primary root and lower part of the shoot axis of a seedling of *Pisum sativum* (Pea) *Cot* cotyledons, *a b, c d, e* transverse sections at the various heights, *B* (everywhere) the phloem of the vascular bundles, *vih* a secondary root (behind), *vis* secondary roots at the sides of the seedling, *Bh* the first leaf (behind), *vii* tertiary roots

narrow tubes, some millimetres in length and a few $\frac{1}{100}$ ths of a millimetre in diameter, which grow forth from the surface of the roots in very large numbers If roots become developed in moist air, they appear to be covered with a brilliant white velvety pile, which consists of the densely crowded root-hairs. These tubes are simple protuberances of the outermost cortical cells of the root; they arise on the recently developed part, and therefore behind the elongating region. In a root about 12–20 centimetres long, they cover, however, by no means the whole surface, but only a piece of a few centimetres in length; the root-hairs in fact die off again after a few days, and completely disappear. It is therefore always only a young, but completely elongated portion of the root, which is covered with vigorous hairs. If we thus picture to ourselves a root as it grows longer, the posterior

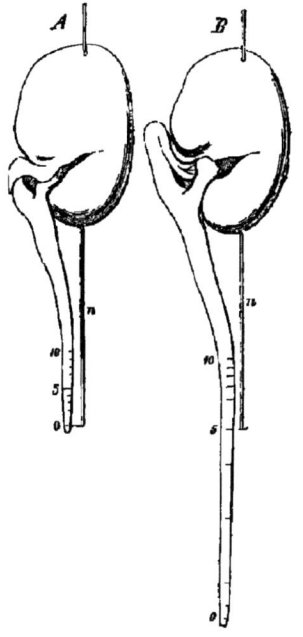

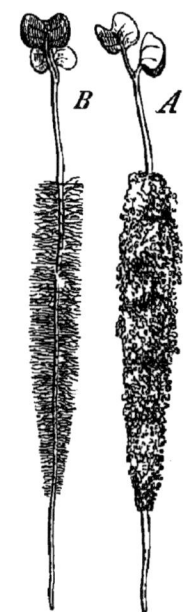

FIG. 10.—A seedling of *Vicia Faba*, fastened by means of a needle (*n*) into a cork (not figured) to show how the apex of the root (*o*) grows beyond the point of the needle The marks 5 and 10 are to be observed Comparing *B* with *A*, point 10 is not displaced at all, and 5 but little The growth has taken place chiefly between *o* and 5

FIG. 11 —Seedling of *Sinapis Alba* (white mustard) *A* with the particles of soil clinging to the root hairs, *B* after their removal by washing in water

hairs die off, in proportion as new ones arise behind the growing apex; thus the part of the root provided with hairs moves forward. If this takes place in the earth, it is obvious that the portion beset with vigorous root-hairs continually comes in contact with such particles of soil as have before remained untouched Now, it is the root-hairs by which the roots become capable of actually taking up the water and the nutritive matters of the soil. As these fine tubes grow in between the particles of soil, they apply themselves here and there to them so intimately and firmly, that they cannot be separated again without injury. How necessary this is, I shall be able to make quite clear in the theory of nutrition; so much, however, is understood without further remark, that by means of this arrangement, particles of earth which we may imagine to ourselves in the form of a cylinder of 6–10 mm thick around the root (about ½ mm. thick), are called into requisition in nutrition. We can demonstrate this at once in a neat and instructive manner, if fresh, vigorously growing roots are carefully lifted out of the loose earth. the particles of earth cling so fast to the tract which is beset with root-hairs, that they cannot be shaken off, whereas the growing end of the root is quite smooth and clean, and the particles of earth also fall off from that part of the root which lies behind the hairs, because the hairs have there died off and disappeared. A clear representation of the activity of the roots in the earth is only to be obtained when we picture to ourselves the richly branched root-system of a large, vigorous land-plant, and reflect how the thin root-fibres travel through the soil in all directions, and that each thin fibre exhausts a cylinder of earth several millimetres in diameter, and how the absorbing part of each root-fibre penetrates continually from day to day into new, fresh portions of soil, while the hairs disappear from the older parts of the fibres, because there is nothing more there for them to seek. It may be added, that only by the intimate growing together of the root-hairs with the earth particles is it possible for transpiring land-plants still to take up large quantities of water from a soil apparently almost dry, in order to transmit it to the green leaves.

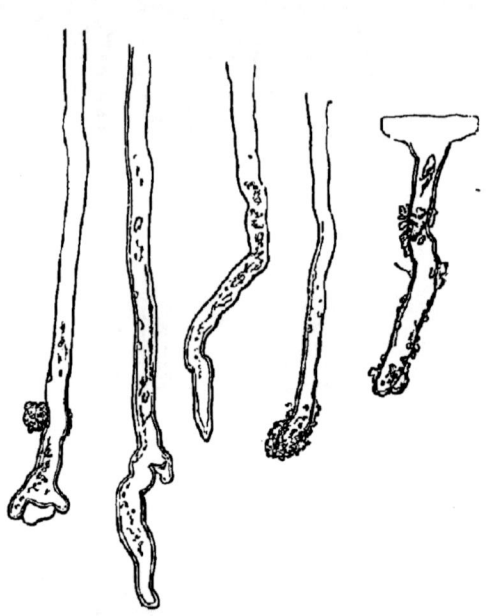

FIG 12.—Root-hairs of a *Selaginella*—some with particles of soil clinging to them The outlines show the impressions of the particles of soil to which the tubes had closely applied themselves (strongly magnified)

To the most remarkable properties of roots belongs the shortening of the tract of a root-fibre, already grown to its full length [1] It begins immediately behind the place where the elongation has ceased, and may then continue for a long time in the older parts. This shortening, which may amount to 10, or even 25 per cent. of the original length, is brought about by the parenchymatous cortex, and the axial fibro-vascular cord becomes passively drawn together, so that its vessels assume a serpentine course, while the outer layers of the cortex, also passive, develope transverse folds, which can be easily seen with the unaided eye, especially in

---

[1] The shortening of roots at the termination of the growth in length was discovered by Fittmann (Flora, 1819, Bd. II. p 651), again found later by myself (Arbeiten des botan Inst Würzburg. I. p 419), then brought forward anew in its biological bearing by Irmisch (Beitr zur vergl Morph. 5 Abtheilung, Aroideæ, Halle XIII 1 1874 p 11) Hugo de Vries has furnished a detailed investigation of the mechanics of this shortening, from the point of view of more recent knowledge (Bot Zeitung, 1879, p. 650)

the roots of bulbous plants, but also on other thick root-fibres. It is clear that, from the place where a root-fibre has closely applied itself to the soil by means of its root-hairs, this shortening of the older tract of fibre must tend forcibly to draw its point of attachment back to the mother root, or to the part of the stem

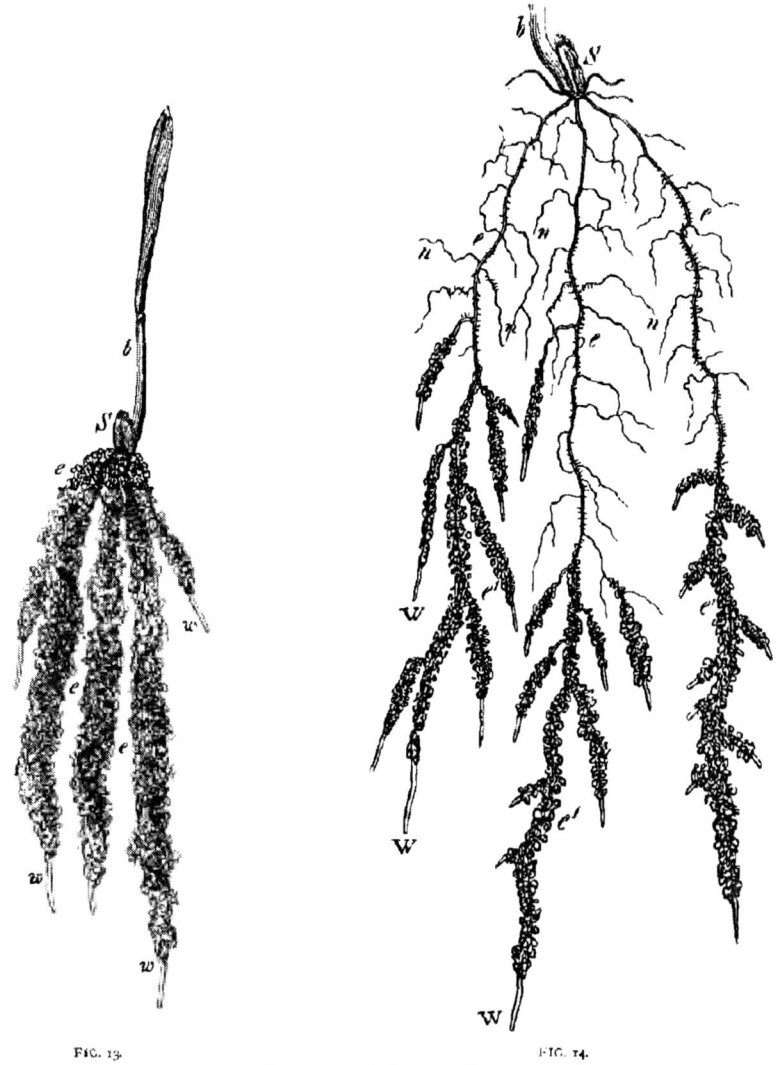

FIG. 13.   FIG. 14.

A wheat plant during germination. Fig. 14 four weeks older than Fig. 13. *S* the seed (or, properly, the fruit) ; *b* first leaf ; *WW* apices of roots not yet covered with root-hairs ; *ee* in Fig. 13 parts of root the hairs of which are attached to particles of soil—in Fig. 14 these portions (*e*) are older and the root-hairs have perished—younger parts (*e′ e′*) have own become attached to the soil.

whence it rises. A vertical tap-root will thus be drawn tight in various directions by its numerous side rootlets, very much as the mast of a ship is strained and made fast in different directions by the cordage. This tension, arising from subsequent shortening, shows itself especially in the aërial roots of many fig-trees, which grow vertically downwards; these hang down slack until they penetrate into the earth, as soon, however, as the lower end becomes fixed and branched within the earth, the part of the aerial root which is in the air appears tightly stretched, like the string of a piano, in consequence of the after-shortening. It is easily understood that the horizontal branches of the Indian fig-trees, from which such aerial roots grow down into the earth, must obtain by this mechanism a very firm hold, which becomes enhanced still more by the roots referred to growing thicker later on, and becoming woody. Much more general, however, is the effect which is produced through the shortening of the tap-roots in herbaceous plants. If, for example, the seeds of Umbelliferous plants or Composites, or others, are allowed to germinate, thinly covered with earth, the seedling shoot at first rises 1 to 2 c.m. above the earth, after several days, however, we remark that the part of the seedling shoot beneath the first leaves is quite sunk into the earth, so that the primary leaves lie on the surface of the earth This change can only have been effected by the tap-root, the under part of which is fast anchored in the earth by the root-hairs, shortening in the ground, and drawing the stem of the seedling into the earth In many cases, indeed, this shortening of the tap-root appears to proceed steadily even for years. For only by means of this assumption can it be explained how the rosettes of radical leaves, in plants with so-called polycephalous main-roots, remain close to the surface of the earth, instead of becoming gradually lifted up. We have a very instructive example of this kind in the common Dandelion (*Taraxacum officinale*). From the upper part of the fleshy and strong tap-root spring several shoots, which continue to grow for years, and annually bear a rosette of leaves close to the surface of the earth. These shoots grow upwards, though slowly, and yet the leaf-rosette, renewed annually, always remains close to the surface of the earth The phenomenon can certainly not be explained otherwise than by the assumption that the tap-root always creeps in the soil, and draws down the shoots just as deep as they have become elongated above. The case appears to be the same in the species of *Verbascum*, in *Gentiana lutea*, and others, accordingly, the tap-roots of older plants of this kind also present deep transverse folds.

The creeping of a root in the earth may thus, in some degree, be compared with the mode in which an earthworm bores into it the anterior part becomes pushed in forcibly between the particles of earth, while the posterior becomes drawn after it by shortening

Finally, we may mention the fact that the roots of vascular plants frequently appear as organs of regeneration, since they produce shoots which, growing up in their turn into the air, constitute new plant individuals. To the best known examples in this connection belong the common Acacia (*Robinia pseudacacia*) as well as *Ailanthus glandulosa*, from the horizontally spreading roots of which young trees grow forth out of the earth In a perennial species of cucumber, *Thladiantha dubia*, the annual regeneration is, in fact, confined to such root-born shoots. On the very long thin root-fibres of this plant roundish tubers become developed, from the upper side of which numerous shoot-buds arise, which grow forth the following year above the earth, independent of the mother plant, and represent new plants. I regard it as simply a modification of this process when leaf-forming shoots spring not laterally from roots, but direct from their growing points, of which, however, but few examples are known as yet.

This fact has been longest known in *Neottia Nidus Avis*, an orchid of our woods, the leaves of which are not green, of the numerous and short, stout roots of its subterranean stem, some produce leaf-buds from their growing points, the root-cap becomes torn and pushed aside, and the root apex forthwith transformed into a shoot Goebel has described the same fact in the root of an Aroid (*Anthurium longifolium*) in our gardens[1], and apparently the fact is just the same in a fern cultivated here (*Platycerium Willingkii*) In this category we may also place the transformation of the roots of Selaginella into leaf-shoots[2]. In these plants, belonging to the class Lycopodiaceæ among the Vascular Cryptogams, the leaf-shoots become branched in a forked manner, and at the points of branching appear filiform structures, also dichotomously branched, which in many species are at once possessed of the properties of roots, in other species, however, are somewhat different from common roots, and are then called *Rhizophores*, because they assume the form of ordinary roots only on penetrating the soil. In some species of Selaginella (*S. Martensii, inæqualifolia, lævigata*), these rhizophores may acquire the form of leafy shoots.

---

[1] Compare Goebel, Bot Zeit 1878, p 645.

[2] Compare Pfeffer, in Hanstein's botanischen Abhandlungen, Bonn, I p. 67, and Sachs, Lehrbuch, IV Aufl pp. 171, 470.

LECTURE III.

ROOTS (continued).

METAMORPHOSED AND REDUCED ROOTS OF THE VASCULAR CRYPTOGAMS, RUDIMENTARY ROOTS OF THE MOSSES AND THALLOPHYTES

In the last lecture, I kept in view only the typical forms of roots of the vascular plants, and their most important peculiarities. According to the mode of life of the plants concerned, however, more or less extensive deviations from the typical form of root may appear even in vascular plants. These deviations are to be distributed chiefly in three categories; thus, we have in the first place roots which, originally quite typical, only modify their form and properties at a later period of life, in order to serve special objects for the plant; then are to be noticed the aërial and aquatic roots which, from the first, undertake a function more or less departing from the normal, and possess accordingly an abnormal organization, thirdly, we find in parasites among vascular plants a continuous series of degenerations, through which their roots, in consequence of more and more pronounced parasitism, finally lose all the anatomical peculiarities of typical roots, though the most important physiological properties remain preserved to them. And finally we shall consider, in addition to these metamorphoses, the roots of Mosses, Algæ, and Fungi, especially pointing out that the so-called rhizoids of these plants are in fact nothing more than simply organised roots, different, it is true, in their anatomical structure from those of vascular plants, but agreeing with them completely in physiological relations.

The first category named above comprehends the lignified older roots of Conifers and other trees, the soft, perennial, turnip-shaped roots of many vegetables, true subterranean root-tubers, as well as some aërial roots. They have all the common peculiarity of being, fundamentally, typical roots, which eventually acquire other properties   This is perceived most plainly in perennial woody roots. The tap-root of the seedling of a tree with its first ramifications is, in the beginning, thoroughly typical, even with reference to those peculiarities which stamp it as a nutritive organ. When, however, the young tree becomes larger, it requires a firmer hold in the ground, and the roots become thicker and more solid, by the formation of wood; as they become surrounded with a cork layer, they cease entirely to take up nutritive matters and water from the earth: they are now simply organs of attachment, and the function of nutrition is restricted to the younger fibres of the root system In tap-roots thickened to a turnip shape, which, especially by cultivation, swell up to huge, soft masses of tissue, a tissue, anatomically similar to the wood but not lignified, also becomes formed in the ordinary thin root-fibres by the activity of a cambial layer this causes the upper part of the tap-root, with occasionally the lower part of the stem, to swell up in a napiform manner. Common examples are Beet-root, Radish, Carrot, Chicory root, &c. In this case the object is not only to attain greater solidity, these kinds of roots are, rather, reservoirs of reserve materials, in which sugar, starch, or inulin become stored together with proteid substances, which are employed in the next period of vegetation for the production of new shoots. Here, also, the function of absorbing nutritive matters remains to the lateral roots, which are attached as fine threads to the large tap-root. Lateral roots may also swell up to tuberous reservoirs of reserve material, as happens in the Dahlia, Hop, and conspicuously in *Ipomœa purga* and *Thladiantha dubia.* In many other root-tubers, the facts are otherwise; the stout, round or lobed tubers of the *Ophrydeæ*, which furnish salep, and the napiform tubers of the Monks' hood (*Aconitum napellus*) and others, as well as those of *Ranunculus Ficaria*, are formed at the base of a subterranean bud of the stem, and appear forthwith as thick, fleshy, short swellings, the root nature of which is indeed not doubtful, which, however, together with the other filiform roots of these plants, have essentially the purpose of serving as reservoirs of reserve material for the shoot-buds connected with them. In the species named, in fact, the whole plant disappears after the ripening of the fruit, with the exception of these tubers, out of each of which a new plant arises in the next period of vegetation.

Of aërial roots, many may be regarded as quite ordinary typical roots, the full development of which, however, becomes prevented by accidental outward circumstances. Thus, the aërial roots of the Ivy, which arise densely crowded and in rows on the shaded side of the shoot axis, are capable, when supplied with earth, of growing out into long, typical, branched roots, because darkness and moisture favour their development; usually, on the other hand, where they become too much dried up in the air and hindered in growth by the light, they remain simple, short threads However, being sensitive to touch and at the same time negatively heliotropic, they cling fast to the trunks of trees, rocks, and walls, on which the shoots climb up, and so serve as clasping organs. Very instructive, with reference to the capacity of the roots to adapt themselves to outward conditions of life, are also the long aërial roots of some tropical Aroids (e g. *Monstera*). These roots, arising in the bud of the climbing stem, are vigorous, often 6–8 mm. and more thick, and will develope into ordinary, branched, absorbing roots, if a shoot is cut off and stuck into the earth If, on the other hand, they are compelled to grow down through the air, which sometimes occurs for several meters, they remain quite simple and unbranched, until the apex finally penetrates into the earth, and there produces a much-branched root system If these aërial roots have the opportunity of clinging to a wall, a thick stem, &c., the apex soon becomes closely applied to it, and root-hairs and lateral roots arise behind it, which also cling to the support. The rhizophores of some Selaginellas, already mentioned, behave in a manner fundamentally quite similar : in them also, the true root-nature only appears when they penetrate into the earth On the other hand, the aërial roots of many tropical orchids, which live on the branches of high trees, are specially organised for life in the air. The aërial roots are here in the first place clinging organs stimulated by contact with the cortex of the tree, they wind round and become applied fast to it, at the same time, however, they possess the function of conveying water to the plant, and, where possible, of absorbing soluble matters. The latter is attained by their putting forth root-hairs where they come into contact with a solid body, to which they cling fast. The absorption of water is favoured in these aerial roots by the so-called *velamen* arising from the outer layer of tissue behind the growing green end . it is several cell-layers thick, and appears as a white spongy covering, since its cells contain air The cell-walls are capable of imbibing, and are able to absorb not only rain and dew, but even the vapour of the atmosphere The aerial roots of some tropical Aroids also behave similarly, e. g. species of *Anthurium, Philodendron, Rhaphidophora, Monstera,* and others.

As parasitism acts generally in a degrading manner on organisms, and causes degeneration of organs, so also in roots; the more decidedly parasitism makes itself evident in phanerogamous parasites, the more do their roots lose their ordinary typical structure, and at last only amorphous masses of tissue or even isolated cells remain, which have still in common with true roots only the property of penetrating into the substratum, and absorbing food By botanical authors such roots are termed *haustoria*. A few examples may further illustrate what has been said [1].

In our Mistletoe (*Viscum album*), which, as is known, lives on the stems and branches of apple-trees, horse-chestnuts, pines, poplars, and other plants, the roots penetrate, it is true, into the cortex and wood, but chiefly, as one may assume, only to absorb water and minerals dissolved in it, i e. the so-called crude sap, which is being conveyed in the wood of the tree to the leaves, whether the roots of the mistletoe, losing themselves in the cortex, possibly extract organic matters also from the tree, is uncertain. So much is at any rate established, that the shoots of the mistletoe, unusually well supplied with chlorophyll, produce organic materials independently, even the roots flourishing in the wood and cortex are rich in chlorophyll, and green; the parasitism of the mistletoe, as regards its nutrition, is in any case only partial and, accordingly, also the degrading influence of the parasitism but insignificant.

If a viscid mistletoe berry sticks to a young branch of a tree, covered with a thin cork layer, the somewhat large embryo, very rich in chlorophyll, germinates.

---

[1] The most important treatises concerning phanerogamous parasites are Franz Unger, *Beitrage zur Kenntniss der parasitischen Pflanzen* , Eichler, *Die Balanophoreen,* in Flora Brasiliensis, Heft 47, 1869 , Graf zu Solms-Laubach, *Ueber Bau und Entwicklung der Ernahrungsorgane parasitischer Phanerogamen,* in Jahrb. f Wiss. Bot VI p 509 , the same, *Ueber den Thallus von Pilostyles,* Bot Zeit 1874, Nov. 4 and 5 , the same, *Die Entwicklung der Bluthe bei Brugmansia,* Bot Zeit 1876, p 449 , Ludwig Koch, *Die Klee und Flachsseide,* Heidelberg, 1880 , Robert Hartig, *Uber Viscum* Zeitschr f Forst und Jagdwesen, Bd. VIII

Its root-apex becomes turned away from the light to the branch, the radicle bores through the cortex, and makes its way through the cambium to the wood; if its apex is situated deep in the wood, later on, this is the result of the new woody layers of the branch growing round the base of the root, while this becomes elongated a little to a corresponding extent. Later on, as it seems, roots arising from the base of the stem grow within the soft living cortex, and from these again lateral roots arise on the side turned towards the wood of the host: they penetrate through the cambium layer to the wood, are then surrounded by the younger, growing, woody layers, becoming meanwhile elongated to a corresponding extent at the base, and now constitute the so-called suckers of the mistletoe. Of these three forms of root, only those which grow in a sinuous manner within the cortex, apparently, have a root-cap, which, however, even here is not well developed. The anatomical structure of the *Viscum* root allows little to be recognised of the structure so distinctive of true roots;

FIG. 15.—Lower portion of the stem (*a*) of the Mistletoe (*Viscum album*). *h* the wood of the shoot-axis; *i* primary root; *ff* roots growing in the cortex of the host-branch (*c*); *g* two buds arising from these; *ee* so-called *Haustoria*, roots which penetrate through the cambium into the young wood, and become surrounded by it later; *bb* wood of host-branch (half cut across at *dd*) showing the annual rings (nat. size).

even the characteristic axial vascular bundle is considerably reduced, and the adaptive peculiarity of the sucker is especially striking—its growing point is converted into permanent tissue, while the growth in length, inconsiderable it is true, is carried on at the part which lies in the cambium layer of the branch of the tree. In spite of all this, no unbiassed person will hesitate to regard these green organs of the mistletoe, even though devoid of a cap and anatomically abnormal, as reduced roots, and this is so far of some importance, since here we have one of the first stages of reduction produced on roots by parasitism. Finally, it may be mentioned that the *Viscum* roots losing themselves in the cortex of the host, represent very active organs of multiplication: from them spring shoots, which, breaking through the cortex of the tree, come forth into the light, and from these, new roots then again run into the cortex, so that as occasionally occurs on old apple-trees the whole tree, from crown to root, is infested with the mistletoe.

Like the mistletoe, so also are the species of *Cuscuta* parasitic on the aërial green shoots of woody plants. their parasitism is, however, complete, since they not only possess no roots fastening them into the soil, but they also completely lack chlorophyll, and are necessitated to take the whole of their nourishment from the host. This they do by means of *haustoria*, which arise within the twining stem of the *Cuscuta* only where this closely surrounds the host-plant, and it is apparently the pressure hereby exercised which induces the origin of the *haustoria*. That these latter are to be regarded as reduced roots can hardly be doubtful from all the researches before us, as well as from our figure. Not only the place and the occasion of their origin, but also the primary young stages of these organs, correspond with those of typical roots. In the further development, however, a striking deviation from these appears. The tissue of the *haustorium*, corresponding to the body of the

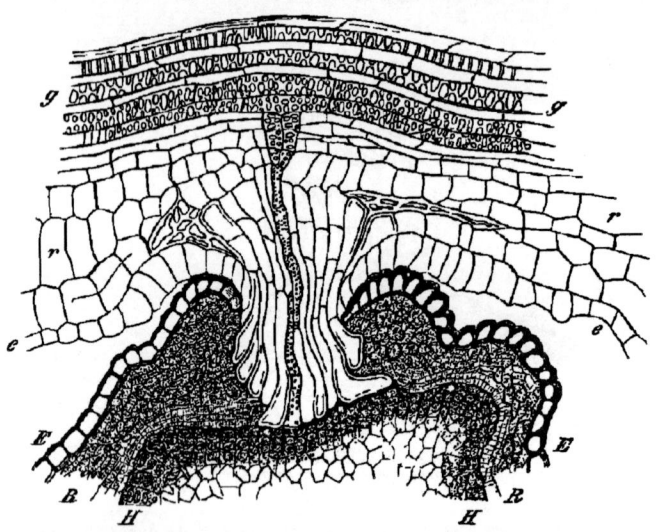

FIG 16.—*Haustorium of Cuscuta epilinum* on the axial vascular bundle (*g*), beneath the cortex (*rr*) of the shoot axis of the *Cuscuta* *ee* epidermis of latter , *L* epidermis of *Linum* stem , *R* its cortex , *H* its wood The axis of the *Cuscuta* and its *haustorium* in longitudinal section , stem of *Linum* in transverse section (magn)

root, becomes arranged into a bundle of rows of elongated cells, which, growing forward at the end, break through first the cortex of the *Cuscuta,* and then the cortex of the host-shoot, to penetrate to the woody body of the latter, or even to break through into its pith Hereupon, indeed, the cell-rows of the body of the root may become isolated as separate threads, which grow into the tissues of the host. In the axis of the *haustorium,* the axial cord of vascular bundles is also still to be recognised, and the vessels of this become fused with the vessels in the wood of the host-plant This intimate union of the *haustorium* of the *Cuscuta* with the stem of the host-plant becomes aided yet more by an outgrowth of the tissue of the *Cuscuta,* which surrounds the *haustorium* in the form of an annular wall, and becomes closely applied to the shoot of the host.

Similar *haustoria,* departing still further from the type of true roots, become developed on the otherwise typical roots, branching in the earth, of *Thesium* and

Rhinanthus, green-leaved plants which are parasitic only by-the-way, and fasten themselves to the roots of neighbouring plants by some of their root-fibres. We find the last stage in the reduction of the root-formation in phanerogamous parasites, finally, in the *Balanophoreæ* and *Rafflesiaceæ*, in which, as has been mentioned before, the vegetative body, seen apart from the flower-shoots, no longer allows the differentiation into shoot and root to be recognised. In the *Rafflesiaceæ* the root presents amorphous masses of cells, which become extended in the tissue of the host, and in the *Balanophoreæ* their parasitism brings about out-growths of tissue on the

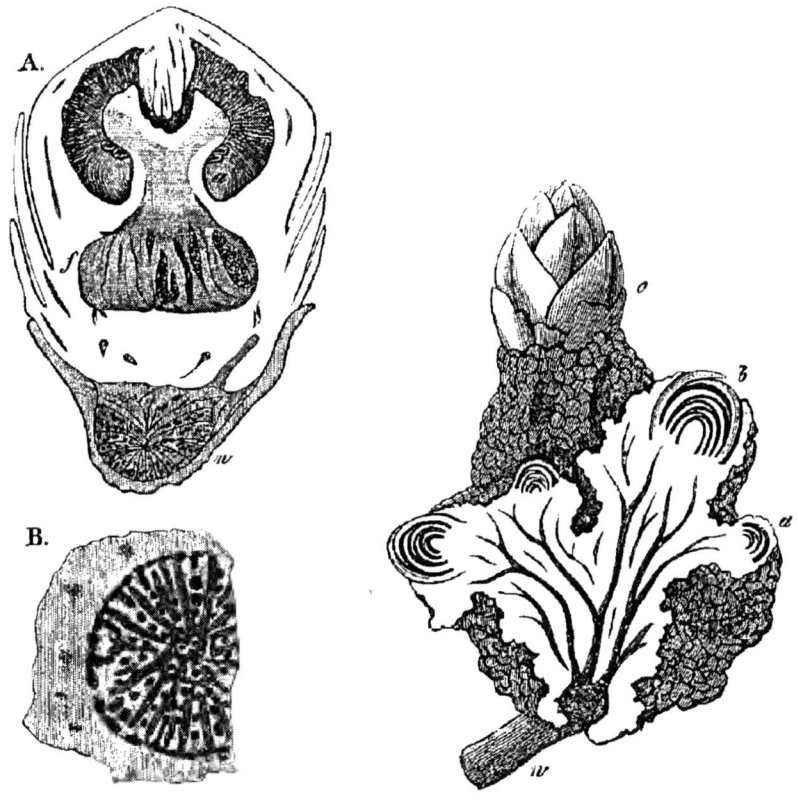

FIG. 17.—*A* Longitudinal section of the flower of *Brugmansia Zippelii*, the vegetative body of which is parasitic in the root (*w*) of a *Cissus. f* ovary, represented in transverse section at *B* (nat. size, after Solms-Laubach).

FIG. 18.—*Balanophora fungosa. w* root of host plant, out of which the tuberous part of the parasite grows; the woody bundles of the host-root (represented as dark streaks) penetrate into the latter; *a, b, c* young inflorescences (nat. size).

affected roots of the host-plant, which make the union of the parasite with this yet closer, and call to mind in many respects the gall-formations produced by insects (cf. Figs. 17 and 18).

From what has been said concerning parasites, it follows that the typical roots of vascular plants may lose their external form and anatomical structure completely, under certain circumstances, so that their chief physiological properties alone are maintained.

If we now turn to the more simply organised plants, to the Mosses and Algæ, we there find, in correspondence with the simpler organisation of the whole, roots also of simpler structure—rudimentary forms of root in which, however, the essential physiological properties of true roots appear quite as evident as in them; it is therefore, though unimportant in itself, a logical error to distinguish these organs of the Mosses and Algæ with a special term as *Rhizoids*, since it must be the aim of comparative organography to name alike organs which are alike in their nature

Meanwhile, with regard to this matter also a few examples must suffice Let us turn first to the true Mosses[1], which come so near to the vascular plants in their shoot formation. From the asexually produced reproductive cell (the spore) of a moss, there arises not immediately the proper moss-plant, but a much simpler plantlet, consisting of jointed and much-branched cell filaments, the so-called Protonema. Already in the germination, and yet more in the further growth of this, the contrast of shoot and root comes out distinctly. While at the one end of the germinating spore a filament containing chlorophyll becomes developed, ascending above the substratum or creeping on its surface, with branches which in many respects remind us of leaves, there appears from the other end of the spore a thread devoid of chlorophyll, which bores forthwith into the substratum, in certain respects comparable to a tap-root, and producing, like this, a branch-system of roots

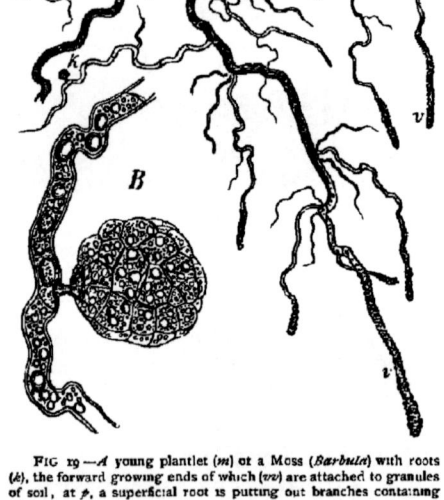

As, however, even in the vascular plants the primary root usually remains feeble, and becomes replaced by later ones arising from the stem, so also on the protonema of the moss, roots arise here and there from the creeping shoot-

FIG 19 —*A* young plantlet (*m*) of a Moss (*Barbula*) with roots (*k*), the forward growing ends of which (*vv*) are attached to granules of soil, at *p*, a superficial root is putting out branches containing chlorophyll (i e *protonema*), at *k* a tuberous bud is situated on a subterranean root, *B* the latter more strongly magnified (*A* × 20, *B* × 300)

axes, as from the creeping shoots of vascular plants At the same time there arise from the protonema-shoots the proper moss-stems furnished with leaves; a process which corresponds to the formation of flowering leaf-shoots from the rhizomes and stolons of vascular plants Out of the shoot-axes of this moss-stem, fresh root-fibres now arise, either from the basal parts only, just as in the Maize

---

[1] Compare Schimper, *Recherches anatomiques et physiologiques sur les Mousses*, Strassburg, 1848, Sachs, Lehrb d Bot Cap *Laubmoose*, Hermann Muller, in Arbeiten des Bot Inst Wurzburg, I p 475

and other Monocotyledons, or close beneath the growing point of the stem, so that this is finally covered by a dense feltwork of roots, like the stems of many tree-ferns. If the foliage shoot of the moss under consideration is dorsiventral, and expanded in an oblique or horizontal position, with the upper and under side differently organised, root-fibres arise only in acropetal succession from the shaded side turned towards the substratum. In all these points, the rhizoids of the moss completely resemble the typical roots of vascular plants; the abnormality consists only in that, in keeping with the simple cellular structure of the moss, they consist not of

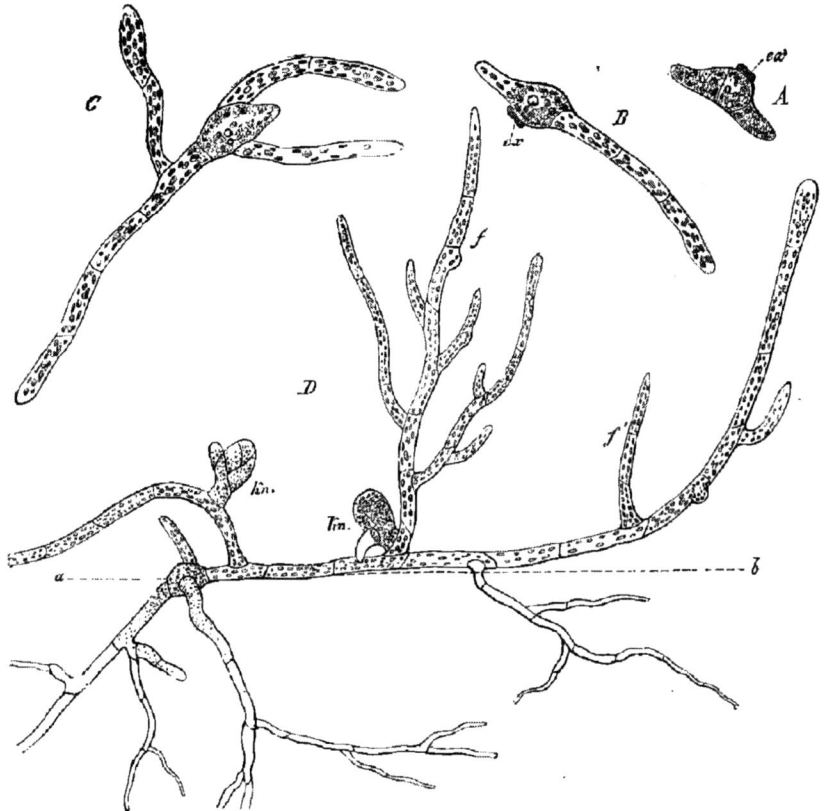

FIG 20.—*A, B, C* germination of *Funaria hygrometrica* (a Moss); *D* older seedling creeping on the surface (*a, b*) of the soil. From the creeping protonema, which branches at *ff*, and forms leafy shoots at *kn*, arise roots which penetrate into the soil. (After Müller; highly magnified.)

masses of tissue, but of jointed cell filaments. However, so far as this anatomical structure admits, the relations of growth agree also with those of true roots: a long cell occupying the end of the root-fibre of the moss corresponds to the growing and cell-forming end of a phanerogamous root, and the growth in length takes place only in this one cell; its free end corresponds to the growing point, and further backwards it represents the portion of a root which is becoming elongated. New segments are added to the root-fibre by obliquely placed walls, and lateral root-fibres arise from them with properties like those possessed by the lateral roots of vascular plants. As the younger part only of a true root attaches itself to the soil by its root-hairs, so in the roots of mosses a similar connection appears at the young end only, further backwards from this, the cell-wall becomes thicker, and takes on more or less the solidity, resistance, and dark colour found on the older root-fibres, e. g. of Ferns and Horse-tails. Although the geotropism, heliotropism and the sensitiveness to pressure and moisture in the roots of mosses have not been hitherto directly investigated, it may nevertheless be concluded with certainty, judging from their whole biological behaviour, that they completely resemble true roots in all these respects.

Still more simply organised are the roots of the Liverworts, especially those with flat, extended, ribbon-like shoots, e. g. of *Marchantiæ* From the shaded underside of their dorsiventral shoots, thin-walled, narrow, but very long tubes appear, simply as protuberances of certain epidermis cells, which penetrate deep into the earth without becoming branched. In the simplicity of their anatomical structure, they resemble apparently only the root-hairs of the vascular plants, with which, in fact, they agree in so far that they, like those, are immediately concerned with the function of nutrition These simple tubes, however, possess in addition the essential physiological peculiarities of typical roots, as is to be concluded with certainty from their whole behaviour, their sensitiveness to light and moisture, and their origin under the influence of gravitation and pressure, are beyond doubt. We have before us, in the root-hairs of the *Marchantiæ* and other flat-shooted Liverworts, organs of the simplest structure, in which are united all the physiological peculiarities of the root-hairs and root-bodies of the more highly organised vascular plants, as further proof that these physiological properties are quite indepen-

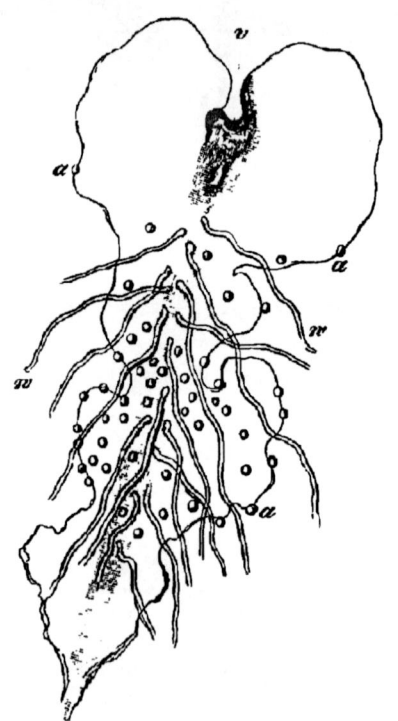

FIG 21.—Pro embryo (*Prothallus*) of a Fern (*Osmunda regalis*) seen from the under side *a* antheridia , *w* root-hairs, *v* the growing point (magnified)

dent of the cellular structure of the higher plants The prothallia of Ferns agree with the Liverworts, as regards the formation of roots, so completely, that it is sufficient to refer to Fig. 21 for the elucidation of both

If we now turn to the Algæ, we meet with great variety both in the root formation, and with respect to all other relations of organisation But the Algæ, with rare exceptions, live entirely in water, and can absorb this and the food-matters dissolved in it with their whole surface; and their roots must thus be of very subordinate importance in the absorption of food, whereas the second main function of roots, to be organs of attachment, asserts itself prominently.

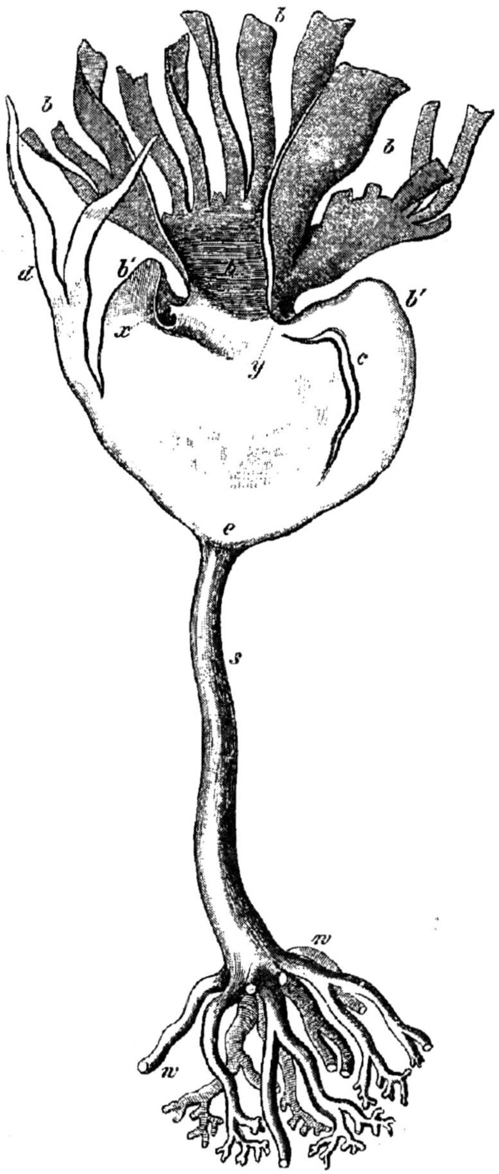

FIG. 22.—Entire plant of *Laminaria Claustoni.* *w* root; *s* shoot-axis; *bb* old leaf divided up; *b' b'* newly arising leaf, the tissue of which originates from the growing point *e*; *y* boundary between new and old (perished) leaf. At *c,* the new leaf is beginning to split; at *x* another split portion (*d*) torn off. (⅓ nat. size).

We may first consider the genera *Fucus* and *Laminaria,* including large plants which are also highly organised anatomically; here we find the base of the whole plant anchored fast to stones, rocks, &c., by means of a much-branched root. The attempt to penetrate into a nutritive substratum is hardly made, since it is superfluous, as has been said; it suffices here that the roots cling as organs of attachment to any solid body, since the whole surface of the plant takes up food, but is also exposed to the brunt of the waves. If the student has made himself sufficiently acquainted with the peculiarities of the typical roots described, there cannot be the slightest doubt that these organs of attachment of the large sea-wracks are roots, in which the function of nutrition is a secondary matter. Their anatomical and cellular structure corresponds with the whole character of the plant; these roots consist of masses of tissue as do those of the vascular plants, and they are branched dichotomously like those of the *Lycopodiaceæ.*

If we then proceed to Algæ of simpler structure, we meet among others with the group Characeæ, the roots of which agree in most essential peculiarities with those of the Mosses—simple cell-filaments with oblique cross-walls, which penetrate into the substratum and become branched there. Finally are to be mentioned here the roots of the non-cellular Algæ, with which we have become acquainted already in the genus *Botrydium* (cf. p. 4). It is obvious that in these essentially non-cellular plants, the much-branched roots are not divided into cell-chambers; but it has already been pointed out that this simple non-cellular structure nevertheless does not prevent them from exhibiting all the essential physiological properties of a typical root.

In those Algæ the shoots of which are simple segmented filaments, or rows of cells, as in the genera *Œdogonium, Cladophora,* and others, the root is usually very small in proportion to the green shoot, since this small size, with very simple organisation, suffices to supply an organ of attachment, the mechanical action of which, considering the mode of life of these plants, is very little called into play. In the genus *Spirogyra* we meet even with the extreme case in this connection, that in the germination of the spore the shoot portion becomes vigorously developed, while the root end is only indicated, as it were, and no longer used even as an organ of attachment, the simple unbranched filaments of this alga float, in fact, quite free in the water. Nevertheless the ability to form roots is not wanting in *Spirogyra*, if its long filaments are cut up, and the pieces laid on wet peat, some of their cells put out branched colourless tubes, which behave like roots. In this connection we find similar cases also in highly developed plants, on the one hand, the rooting of severed portions of shoots in many vascular plants, on the other hand, the effect which continued contact with a solid body exerts on the development of new roots, as e. g. in *Cuscuta*, and the gemmæ of *Marchantia*.

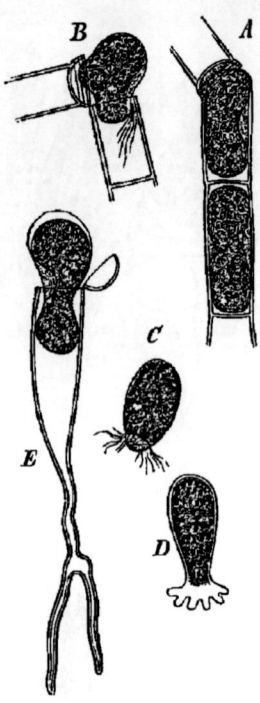

FIG 23 —Development of zoospores of *Œdogonium* (after Pringsheim × 350) *AB* zoospores arising from an old filament, *C* free zoospore (motile), *D* the same beginning to germinate, *E* a zoospore formed from the entire contents of a germinated swarm-spore, root and shoot are to be distinguished in the latter

Passing over finally to the Fungi, it has already been mentioned in the first lecture (p 5), that the mycelium of these resembles

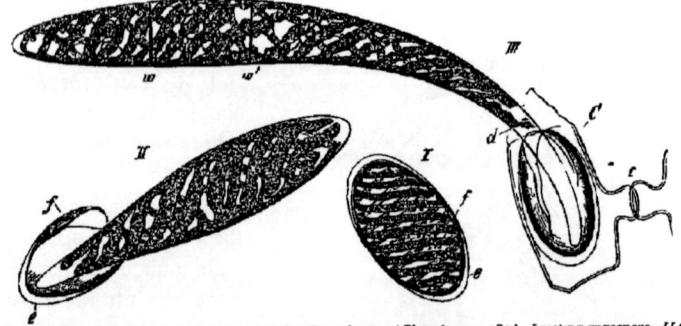

FIG. 24.—Germination of *Spirogyra fugalis* (after Pringsheim in 'Flora' no 30 1859) *I* resting zygospore, *II* the same beginning to germinate, *III* further developed (the zygospore was enclosed in the cell *C* of a filament on which the conjugating apparatus is still visible), *e* outer cellulose wall of spore, *f* yellowish brown membrane, *g* the third innermost membrane of the spore, which forms the germinal tube, *w w'* first septa of a germinal tube, the posterior end (*d*) of which grows out as a narrow root process.

typical roots from the physiological point of view; it has, however, to take up not merely water and dissolved salts, but also organic food-matters. Apart from certain special cases of complex formation of tissue, the mycelium consists of much-branched tubes, which are unsegmented in the *Phycomycetes*, but in all other cases divided by transverse walls. From the manner in which these cell-filaments penetrate into the substratum, become branched there, and, under certain circumstances, again come forth from the substratum, and so on, it follows that the mycelium of the Fungus agrees entirely with typical roots in respect to geotropism and heliotropism, and in

FIG. 25 —A portion of the foliaceous thallus o *Peltigera horizontalis* *a* apothecia, *r* roots (nat size)

FIG 26 —*Usnea barbata* a fruticose lichen *a g* fructification , *f* organ of attachment, which becomes firmly fixed on the bark of a tree

its sensitiveness to moisture and contact. The mycelium, it is true, possesses the property of producing fruit-bearing hyphæ, which we have already distinguished. as the formation of the shoot in Fungi. This is not an essential deviation from the typical roots, since in many phanerogams and vascular cryptogams the tendency exists in a very prominent degree to produce shoots out of roots ; and we meet further with the formation of shoots out of roots in the Mosses. It cannot therefore be urged against the root-nature of the mycelium of the Fungi, that the fruit-bearing portions ordinarily spring out of it as shoots. This happens in fact even in *Monotropa*—a phanerogam devoid of chlorophyll—in a quite similar manner.

Among the Fungi, the group of Lichens is distinguished by a very remarkable form of parasitism. The fungus tissue, in fact, surrounds the Algæ containing chlorophyll which nourish it, so that the latter behave like a histological constituent of the Fungus, which has now become in a certain sense a plant containing chlorophyll In accordance with this, the shoot-formation of the Lichens is also often far more complete than in other Fungi, and thence follows, again, that in them the contrast between shoot and root is more sharply expressed than in other Fungi.

Here too, again, the root may act not merely as an organ of attachment only, but also at the same time as an organ of nutrition. The first is the case in many so-called fruticose lichens, which are attached by a narrow base to the dry bark of trees, e g. the genus *Usnea*. The roots of the so-called foliaceous lichens, the shoots of which are extended as flat dorsi-ventral plates on the earth, or on tree trunks, as in the large genus *Peltigera*, appear not only as organs of attachment, but also as organs of nutrition. From these highly organised forms of Lichens down to the so-called crustaceous Lichens, the vegetative body of which grows in the interior of the dry bark of trees, on dry earth, or even on hard stones, we find a series of transitional forms, ending in cases in which a proper formation of shoot and root are hardly to be spoken of[1].

---

[1] The reason why I term all these organs roots, will follow sufficiently from the connection of the text If the prejudice against descriptive botany, still frequently existing even in scientific circles, is ever to cease, it will be well entirely to get rid of the superfluous nomenclature exemplified by the words *Rhizoids, Rhizines,* &c Where would Zoology be if the feet of insects, as well as their eyes and wings, were distinguished by such names? Yet the mania for inventing names has gone so far of late years, that the root of vascular plants has been termed a thallus, simply because it has no leaves

LECTURE IV.

THE TYPICAL FORMS OF SHOOT OF THE VASCULAR PLANTS

We distinguish, generally, as the shoot, the vegetative organ standing in opposition to the root   There are, it is true, derived (metamorphosed) forms of shoot which live hidden in the substratum, as there are indeed derived forms of root also, which, abandoning their primitive characters, become developed outside the nutritive substratum   The primary and most prominent peculiarity of the shoots, however, is that they raise themselves above the substratum, in order to fulfil their most important vital function in the air (occasionally in water) under the influence of light, that is, to decompose carbon dioxide by means of their chlorophyll, and to produce organic substance, from which new shoots and new roots may be formed A second function of the shoots, perhaps as essential, consists in that earlier or later they bear the proper reproductive organs, viz the sporangia and sexual organs, which are never formed on roots

The mode of life, outward form, and internal structure of the shoot depend upon the way in which, according to circumstances, these two main problems, assimilation and the development of reproductive organs, are solved. In many cases, it suffices that the shoot containing chlorophyll simply rises above the substratum to the light; it then assimilates, and subsequently developes the reproductive organs Generally, however, a further division of labour appears within a shoot or shoot-system; some branches, as subterranean shoots, store up the products of the assimilation of those above ground, and become transformed into reservoirs of reserve material, while, very often, certain branches are specially entrusted with the formation of reproductive organs   That roots also may arise on the shoots, according to their mode of life, has already been mentioned several times ; they represent, therefore, the proper body of the plant, on which all other organs appear, as the limbs on the trunk of an animal

These deviations from the primitive nature of the shoot, and its metamorphoses and reductions, go much further, and are far more various than in roots, and it is not so easy as with the latter to express the fundamental physiological character clearly and exhaustively. It will be the object of later lectures to give clear ideas of this enormous variety of the development of shoots, by a series of examples. To-day, however, we shall confine ourselves exclusively to the peculiarities of typically developed shoots, as they occur in the great majority of vascular plants   What the non-botanical student sees and knows of the vegetable world, apart from the larger flowers of phanerogams, are the shoot-formations which we have here in view. They are the so-called stalks or stems, with the leaves situated upon them, and, in order to avoid any misunderstanding, I may add that I shall consider first exclusively those shoots the leaves of which contain chlorophyll. Such leaves are called foliage-leaves, and accordingly the shoots are called foliage-shoots. We have at first to do with these only. A Palm-stem with its huge crown of leaves is thus

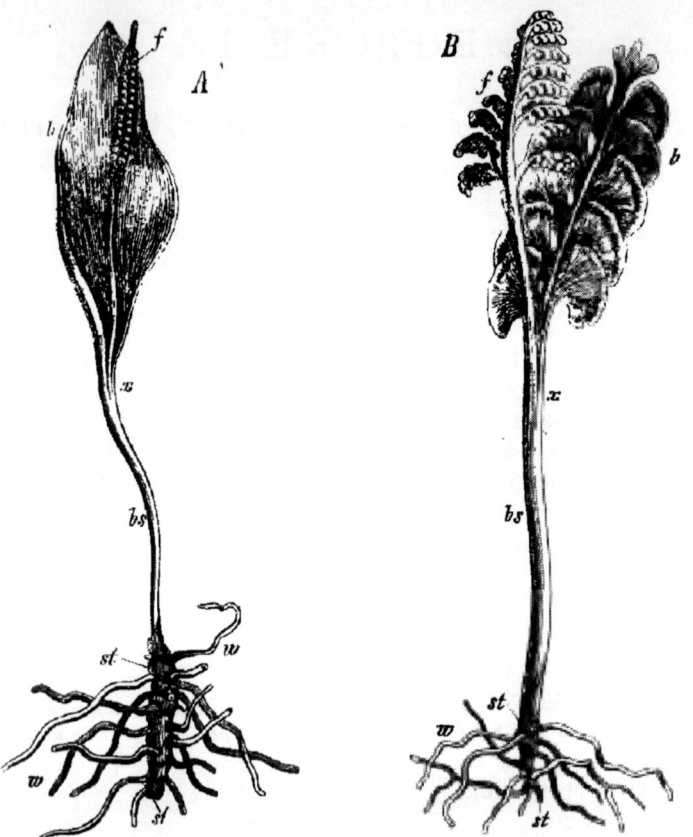

FIG. 27.—*A Ophioglossum vulgatum; B Botrychium Lunaria.* (Both natural size.) *w* roots; *st* stem; *bs* leaf-stalk; *x* point of branching of the leaf, where the sterile lamina (*b*) separates from the fertile one (*f*). The shoot axis remains in the earth; only its leaves (one each year) come forth to the light.

a foliage-shoot, as is also the upright stem, furnished with large leaves, of a tobacco plant. The foliage-shoot generally becomes branched, i.e. a foliage-shoot produces new shoots at definite points, which in their turn do the same, and so there arises from one shoot step by step a shoot-system, on which every single member is to be distinguished as mother-shoot or daughter-shoot, according as its relation to a preceding or following shoot is to be indicated. Mother- and daughter-shoots may be like or unlike between themselves. The Coniferæ, e.g. Firs and Pines, as well as other forest trees, and a great number of annual plants, e.g. Thorn-apple, Hemp, &c., are in their aërial parts branch-systems which have become developed from the original germinal shoot (Plumule) of the seed.

As already indicated above, a typical shoot consists of the leaves and the shoot-axis, which are, however, in the first place not properly to be considered as different organs, but essentially only as portions of one organ, although, by peculiar development and further formations later, the leaves as well as the shoot-axes may assume distinctive characters. Essentially, and as the history of development shows, the leaves are however, strictly speaking, nothing more than protuberances or out-growths of the shoot-axis, which, by means of their large development of surface, are qualified to present the chlorophyll contained in them to the light, and to the air containing carbon dioxide, in the most appropriate manner, so that the process of assimilation, the production of organic substance for the whole plant, may take place with the greatest possible energy. In this connection, the shoot-axis appears first only in the simple character of a support, on which these organs of assimilation are suitably arranged in large numbers. The products of assimilation are also conducted upwards as well as downwards in it, while at the same time water and nutritive matters are conveyed from the roots to the leaves through it. The whole structure of a higher plant is only to be understood if these matters are kept in view.

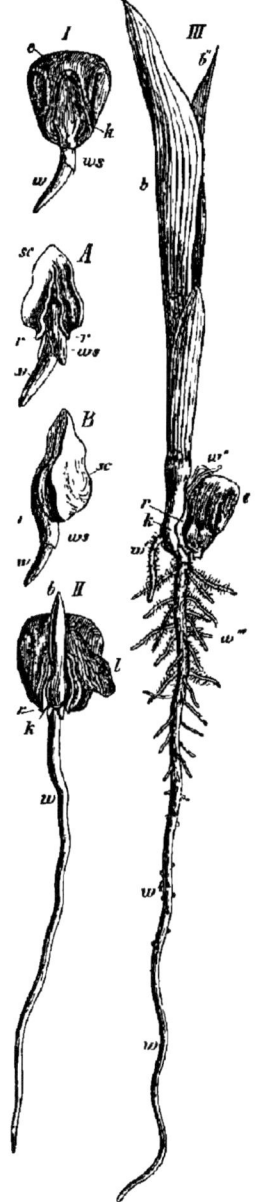

FIG 28.—Germination of Indian corn (*Zea mais*) successive ages, *I*, *II*, *III A* and *B* the seedling removed from *I*, with its scutellum *sc* Everywhere, *w* primary root, *ws* root sheath, *w'*, *w''* secondary roots, *b* first leaves, *k* first segment of shoot axis, *r* edge of scutellum, *e* endosperm, surrounded by the pericarp (nat size Cf. I ig 5)

The interdependence of the leaves and their shoot-axes is made especially clear at the growing point of the shoot, where it is easy to see that the leaves are, fundamentally, only protuberances of the substance of the shoot-axis itself; outer and inner layers of the tissue of this form protuberances, the tissues of which

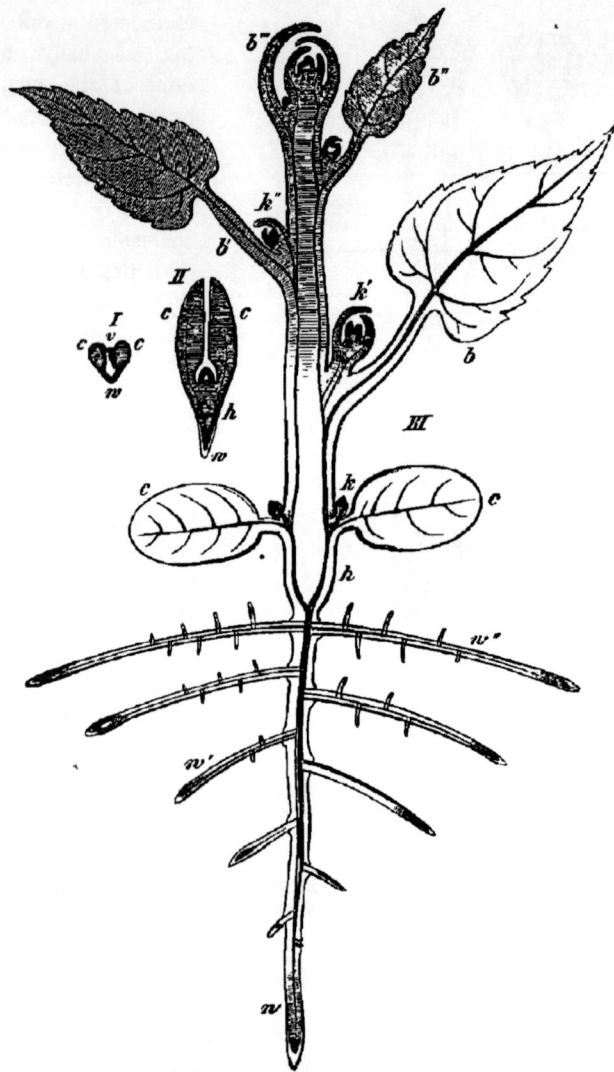

FIG 29.—Diagram of a dicotyledonous plant. *I* and *II* embryonic stages, *III* after germination *c c* cotyledons; *w, w'* roots, *h* hypocotyledonous segment of shoot axis, *b—b'''* leaves, *k k'* buds The growing points are shaded black, the parts becoming elongated grey

are from the first, and during the whole duration of life of the leaf, in complete continuity with the tissue-systems of the shoot-axis. A root is connected with its mother-root, or with the stem from which it arises, as something extraneous, like a parasite which has first to establish its connection with the mother-organ. The leaves

stand in quite a different relation towards the shoot-axis: the epidermis of the latter
passes over to the leaf without visible interruption, and the cortical tissue of both
is also in complete continuity, and, apart from a few cases, the vascular bundles
of the stem or shoot-axis are really nothing more than the lower ends of the
vascular bundles which curve out above into the leaves, and produce in these the
so-called venation. In its original condition, indeed, the shoot-axis has generally
no surface of its own at all, since the leaves come forth so closely one upon another at the growing point, that no free surface of the shoot-axis remains. If the
growth in length of the latter is very slight, even the completely formed shoot-
axis has no free surface; it is quite covered with leaves, as in our wood-fern,
Aspidium Filix-mas, and in such stems of phanerogams as bear their leaves in
so-called radical rosettes, and in many other cases. But even where a more vigorous
growth in length of the shoot occurs, the bases of the leaves may grow with it, in
such a manner that the whole surface of the shoot-axis is nevertheless clothed with

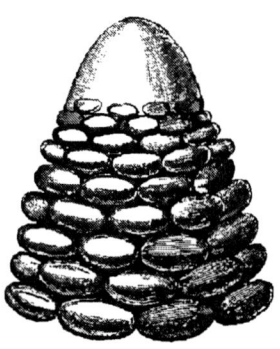

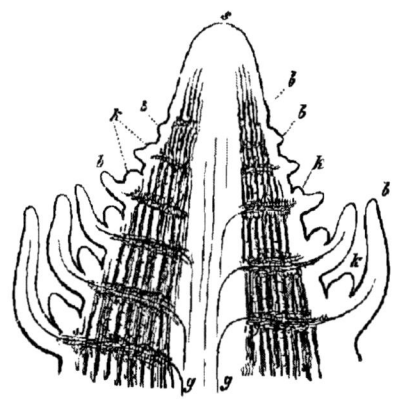

FIG. 30.—Upper end of a shoot-axis of
Hippuris vulgaris, after removal of the
surrounding older leaves. Above is the
naked growing point, from which arise the
young leaves visible lower down (magnified).

FIG. 31.—Longitudinal section through the apex
of an erect shoot of *Hippuris vulgaris*. *s* apex of
shoot; *b, b, b* leaves (in whorls); *k, k,* their axillary
buds, which become flowers; *g, g* primary vessels.
The dark parts indicate the cortex, with its intercellular spaces.

leaf-substance, as occurs especially with very small leaves, e. g. in the *Selaginellæ*
and many *Cupressineæ*, such as *Thuja*. In the typical development of a shoot,
however, the growth of the shoot-axis proceeds in such a manner that the bases
of the leaves, at first closely crowded, become separated, since between each two
superimposed leaves of the growing point, a piece of the shoot-axis is as it were
intercalated, and then attains a more or less considerable length. Such a portion
of the axis is then called an *internode*, or inter-foliar part of the shoot-axis.
Only among the vascular cryptogams are single cases known (*Salviniaceæ*) where,
immediately on the development of the leaves at the growing point, such interfoliar parts of the axis with free surfaces are present. One of the most striking
phenomena in shoots, viz. the position of the leaves on their axis, can be in part
explained causally from the fact that the youngest leaves arise at the growing point,
as said, so close above and by the side of one another, that the whole surface of
the shoot-axis is covered by them, so that with the growth of the leaves mutual
pressure must necessarily occur.

Yet another, and much more striking phenomenon, however, is produced by the crowded position of the youngest leaves at the end of the shoot-axis, in connection with a further fact, viz. the much quicker growth of the leaves, as contrasted with the elongation of the shoot-axis This is the formation of Buds. By the word bud, we distinguish generally the young condition of a shoot. either the whole young shoot, or the young portion at the free end of a shoot already further developed, is a bud. Shortly put, the bud is the growing point of a shoot, surrounded by its leaves We can thus only speak of buds in connection

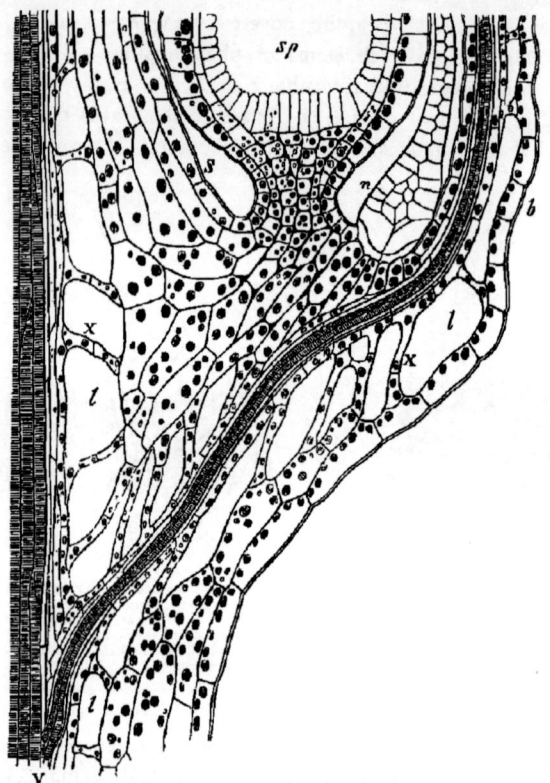

FIG 32.—*Selaginella inæqualifolia* longitudinal section through the right side of the fertile spike *b* base of leaf, *i* ligule, *sp* sporangium, *v* point of connection of the cauline and foliar bundles, *l* air cavities, *x* series of cells traversing the cavities (× 120)

with leaf-forming shoots. in contrast to them, stand the naked growing points of the leafless shoots of Algæ and Fungi, to which I shall refer later.

The development of every new plant individual begins with the production of a young shoot; in leaf-forming plants, therefore, with the formation of buds Thus there arises, even in the embryo of the vascular plants as soon as any organs become recognisable on them, a bud (the plumule), and in the same way the development of any new shoot, after a growing point has been formed, consists in the development of a bud, which then grows out further, at once or later. While the growing point itself, just as the youngest parts of the shoot-axis on which leaves are already situated, only grows very slowly in length, the growth of the young leaves is on the other hand much more vigorous; as each older leaf lying further back from the

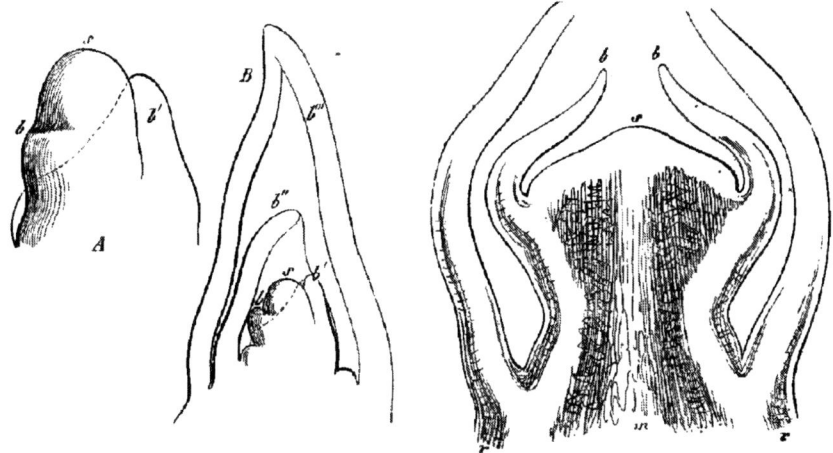

FIG. 33.—Apical regions of two primary shoots of *Zea Mais.* Apex of the very small-celled growing point, from which the leaves *b, b', b'', b'''* arise as multicellular protuberances, which soon surround the stem, and envelope it and the younger leaves like sheaths. In the axil of the third youngest leaf *b',* the very young rudiment of a branch is visible as a roundish protuberance (cf. Fig. 9).

FIG. 34.—Longitudinal section through the apical region of the primary stem of *Helianthus annuus,* immediately before the development of the flowers. *s* apex of the broad growing point; *b, b* youngest leaves; *r* cortex; *m* pith.

growing point has a start of all the younger ones, and as, at the same time, each older leaf is arched concave inwards and envelopes the younger more or less,

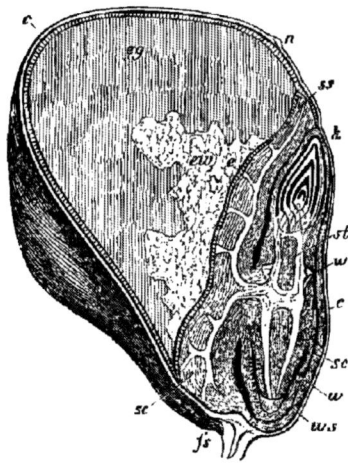

FIG. 35.—Longitudinal section of the fruit of *Zea Mais* (× 6). *c* pericarp; *n* remains of stigma; *fs* base of the fruit; *eg* dense yellowish portion of endosperm; *cw* whiter, less dense portion of endosperm; *sc* scutellum of embryo; *ss* its apex; *e* its epithelium; *k* plumule; *w* (below) primary root; *ws* its root-sheath; *w* (above) secondary roots arising from the first internode (*st*) of the embryonal stem (cf. Fig. 27).

leaf thus lying on leaf, a bulb-like body, the young shoot, is formed. If this now becomes further unfolded, the leaves expand according to their succession in age, attain their complete development, and become thrown outwards, while at the same time the corresponding segments of the shoot-axis are further developed. Sometimes the bud consists only of a few very young leaves, as in the climbing-buds of the Ivy; in other cases, however, dozens of leaves and internodes are found in the bud state. If the period of vegetation is interrupted by the winter, the bud may maintain its form, simply because the further development of the parts is discontinued, until, with favourable weather, the older parts of the bud again begin to grow, and new ones are formed at the growing point; e. g. in our so-called Acacia (*Robinia pseudacacia*) and the Arbor vitæ (*Thuja*). In the majority of trees and shrubs, however, peculiarly organised winter-

buds are formed, which are situated at the end or at the sides of the branch as special
organs   When a winter-bud is about to be formed at the end of a leaf-shoot,
e. g. of a Fir, Oak, Horse-chestnut, &c., the development of foliage-leaves suddenly
ceases, and a number of corresponding leaf-rudiments assume the form of scales,
which tightly surround the younger parts, and are often glued together with resin or
balsam. Very commonly, it is the lateral shoots of woody plants which on their origin
assume at once the form of winter-buds, and commence with the formation of scale-
leaves. In some special cases, as in the Fir and Pine, the apex of the shoot which
becomes developed in the next period of vegetation into the leaf-shoot, is already
present in a quite embryonic state, enveloped by the bud-scales   In other cases,
again, as in the Horse-chestnut and our fruit trees, we find already in the autumn,
within the winter-bud, not only the end of the young shoot, but a branch-system,
with flower buds and more or less developed foliage leaves, and all these parts
already so far formed, that the first warm days of spring suffice to bring them to
complete development, after the bud-scales
have opened.

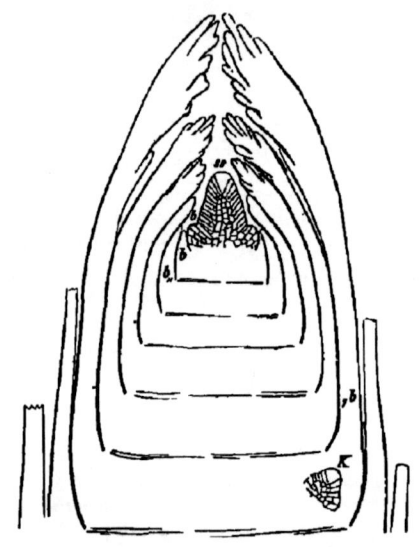

In herbaceous plants it often occurs
that all the organs produced in one
period of vegetation—root, shoots, and
flowers—completely disappear, and that only
a few buds, with or without enveloping
scales, remain over the winter; and, developing in the next spring and forming
new roots, represent a new transitory
plant individual. So it is in many water
plants, as *Aldrovanda vesiculosa* and *Utricularia*, and many land plants, where
the bud, remaining behind in connection
with a reservoir of reserve material, represents a tuber, capable of germinating, as in
our species of *Ophrys*, in the Arrow-head
(*Sagittaria*), *Crocus vernus*, and in *Ficaria
ranunculoides*, &c. Strictly speaking, bulbs
also are only peculiarly developed persistent
buds, the outer leaves of which are thick,

FIG 36.—Longitudinal section through the apical region o
a bud of *Equisetum arvense*. *ss* apical cell, *b—b*₅ the sheath-
like leaves (magnified)

swollen, and filled with reserve materials, the substances which are used in the
beginning of the period of vegetation for the development of the young shoot-
rudiments in the interior of the bulb   One need only cut through a common
kitchen onion (*Allium Cepa*), in the direction of its length, or a Hyacinth or Tulip
bulb, in autumn or winter, in order to recognise the state of affairs at once.

Entering now more closely upon the study of the organisation of the shoot,
it is better to consider the shoot-axis and leaves separately   No one will wish
to compare the organisation of the leaves with that of the root, but the typical
form of the shoot-axis, with its cylindrical or prismatic figure, suggests a comparison
between it and the root. In spite of this external similarity, however, the organisation
of the leaf shoot-axes is very strikingly different from that of the roots. If the fully

developed shoot-axis possesses inter-foliar parts, as is usually the case, these are usually clothed with a well-developed epidermis, which is in its turn covered by a cuticle, and perforated by stomata. Hairs also of the most varied form, prickly, woolly, or glandular, are very common appendages. If the typical leaf-shoots are destined to last several or many years, their epidermis becomes sooner or later replaced by a uniform cork layer, a so-called periderm, which carries on the main function of the epidermis (viz. the prevention of the loss of water by evaporation), more completely than the epidermis itself.

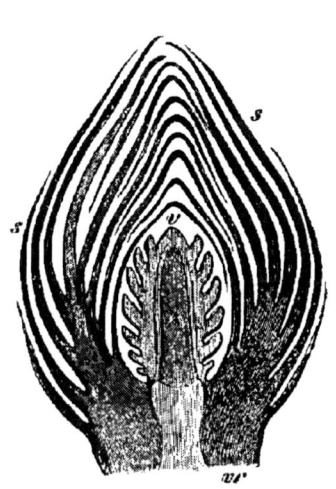

FIG. 37.—Median longitudinal section through a small winter bud of *Abies pectinata. ss* scale-like enveloping leaves, which arise from a cup-like outgrowth of the cortex (*vr*) of the preceding year; *z* pith of the new rudimentary shoot; *v* its growing point.

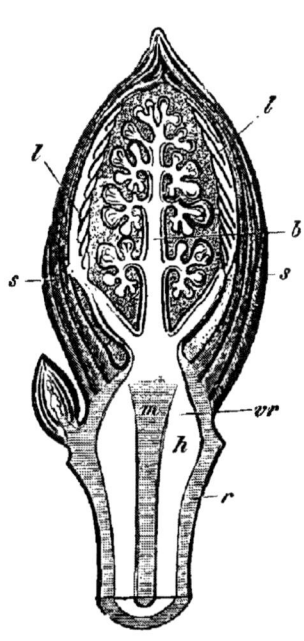

FIG. 38.—Median longitudinal section through a vigorous winter bud of the Horse-chestnut (*Æsculus hippocastanum*). *m, h, r* pith, wood, and cortex of shoot-axis (*vr*) of the preceding year; *ss* bud scales; *ll* young foliage-leaves; in the middle is the young inflorescence—the dotted space is filled with woolly hairs.

In the interior, the young shoot-axes consist of a basis of succulent parenchymatous tissue, in which run a few or very many vascular bundles, often also sclerenchymatous cords. While in the roots the vascular bundles are united into a single axial strand, surrounded by the parenchymatous cortex of the root, the vascular bundles of the shoot-axes on the other hand run, primarily at least, as isolated filaments, the upper ends of which curve out into the leaves, while their lower ends attach themselves to the middle parts of the preceding bundles. Only in rarer cases, e. g. in some water plants (*Hippuris*) and a few Cryptogams (*Marsilea, Pilularia*, &c.), is the shoot-axis traversed by an axial strand of vascular bundles, a so-called cauline bundle, to which the bundles of the leaves become attached. Thus, in contrast to the roots, each single vascular bundle of the shoot-axis is surrounded by parenchymatous ground tissue. If the shoot-axes, however, form true wood later on, which in fact only occurs in the Coniferæ and Dicotyledons, then a so-called Cambium-layer arises, which is developed in part in the vascular bundles, in part in the parenchyma between these, and from which true wood-tissue is produced towards the inside, and so-called secondary cortex towards the outside. In this way, the originally tender shoot-axes of the plants named become transformed into solid, persistent, woody stems and branches, from which the leaves fall later on, and which serve henceforward only as supports for the shoots existing for the time being. In the stems of Palms and Ferns, such a secondary formation

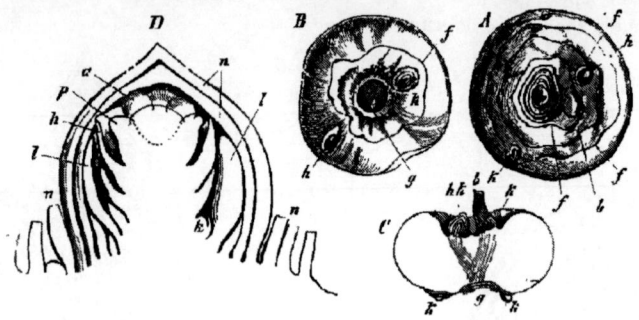

FIG. 39.—*Crocus vernus:* A corm seen from above, B from below, C from the side, and in longitudinal section. The ring-like lines of insertion of the cataphyllary leaves are seen at *f, f, f,* and at *k, k* the axillary buds belonging to them ; *b* base of decayed flower- and leaf-stem, by its side *hk* (in C), the bud which will replace it, from which a new corm and flower-stem will arise. D longitudinal section through this bud; *n, n* its cataphyllary leaves; *l, l* foliage-leaves; *k* bract; *p* perianth ; *a* anthers; *k* a bud in the axil of a foliage-leaf.

of wood and cortex by means of a cambium does not take place. In them, the shoot-axis is at once from the beginning so thick, and so penetrated by bundles and layers of elastic fibres, that it is able, with progressive elongation of the stems, to bear the burden of the leaves arising at the apex. It would carry us much too far to go more closely into the anatomical and exceedingly various relations of organisation of shoot-axes. The main point for physiological consideration is, that, as supporters of the leaves, and, later on, of entire and often huge branch-systems, they must possess not only the necessary solidity, which is afforded by true wood or by numerous bundles of elastic fibres; but provision must also be made, that the water taken up by the roots, ascending in the woody parts, is not evaporated on its way through the stem and the shoot-axes. This is sufficiently provided against in younger shoots by the epidermis, in older

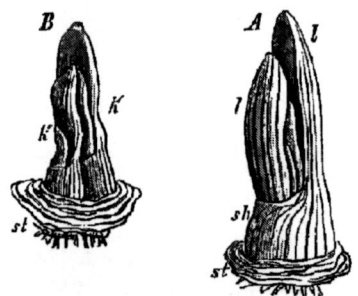

FIG. 40.—Bud in interior of bulb of *Allium Cepa*, after removal of the scales. *st* broad, short part of stem on which the scales are inserted; *l* (in A) lamina; *sh* the still short sheath of foliage leaves. In B the outer leaves have been removed, and an axillary bud (*k''*) comes into view in addition to the terminal bud *k'*.

ones by the cork-periderm, and in the very old ones by the solid bark. Another function of the shoot-axes is, finally, to convey the substance assimilated by the foliage-leaves, on the one hand to the root, and on the other to the buds and shoots ; this is accomplished in part by means of the so-called phloëm (soft-bast) of the vascular bundles, or the secondary cortex, in part by the parenchymatous fundamental tissue.

If the variety of form of the shoot-axis makes itself evident especially in

its anatomical structure and in its formation of wood and cortex, in the leaves
of the shoot, on the other hand, it is especially the outward form which
exhibits in astonishing variety the unbounded formative tendency of vegetable
substance. I may well expect from my readers that the ordinary external forms

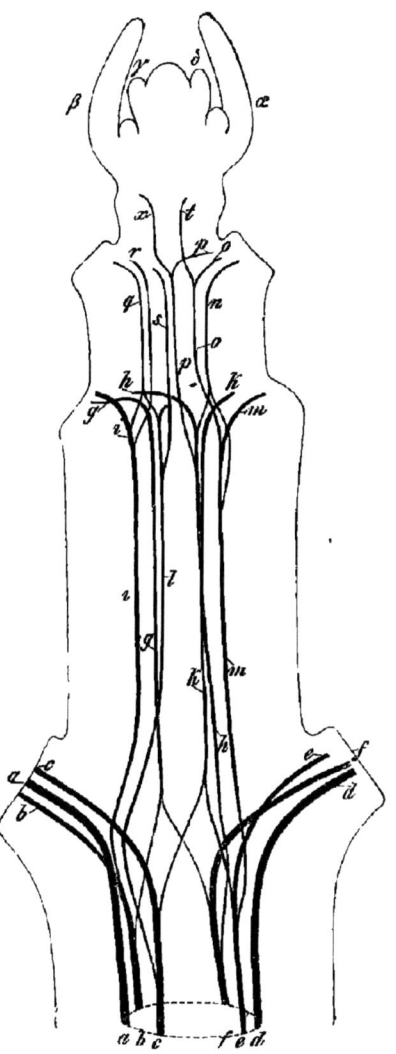

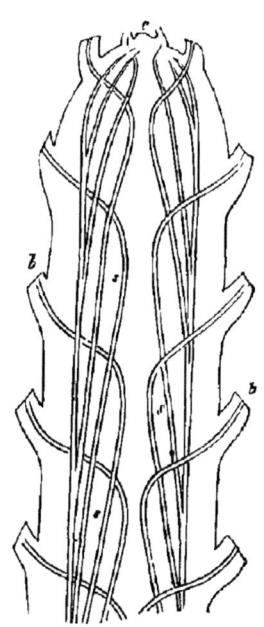

FIG. 41—*Clematis viticella* (after Nägeli) End of the
shoot rendered transparent, to show the course of the
vascular bundles (leaf traces), which curve out above into
the (removed) leaves

FIG. 42.—Course of the vascular bundles in a
monocotyledonous shoot of the Palm type *r*
growing point, *ss* shoot-axis, *bb* bases of leaves.
(After Falkenberg)

of foliage leaves are to some extent familiar to them; that they know the chief
division of the same into *lamina*, *petiole* and *sheath*; that the term *stipule*, and,
further, the terms *entire*, *divided*, *lobed*, *pinnatifid*, *compound* leaves, &c., are not
quite strange to them. On the other hand, it accords with the main object of this

lecture to turn our attention to some other points in the organisation of the foliage-leaves.

The physiologically important part of any foliage leaf is the blade (*lamina*), a lamella, consisting of several layers of tissue, in the typical case however always very thin, a few tenths of a millimeter thick, in which the cells containing chlorophyll, the so-called mesophyll, play the chief part. Upon the activity of this layer containing chlorophyll the structure of the foliage-leaves depends.

All other arrangements in a foliage leaf have as their object the presenting of this very thin layer of tissue, extended flat, to the light, of moderating and regulating according to requirement the too rapid evaporation of the water out of it, of bringing about the flow of new assimilable matters to the cells containing chlorophyll, and making possible the return flow of the products of assimilation

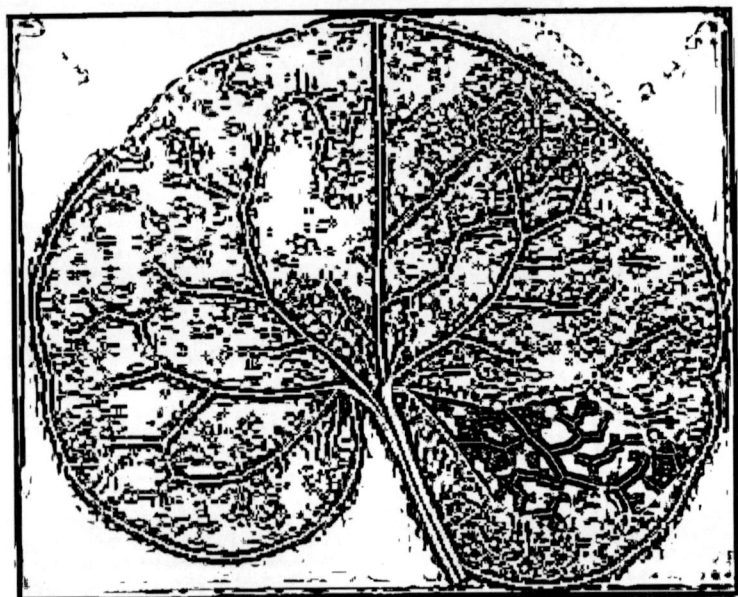

FIG. 43.—Venation of the foliage leaf of *Asarum Europæum* (after Ettinghausen)

to the shoot-axis, as well as, finally, of protecting these thin lamellæ of tissue against being torn under the influence of the wind. All the relations of organisation of the foliage leaves are intelligible from this point of view.

The epidermis of foliage leaves is the most completely organised which is found on plants. On their upper and lower sides, it envelopes the thin lamella of tissue containing chlorophyll. it protects it by means of its elasticity and solidity: its strongly developed cuticle prevents a too rapid evaporation of the water flowing to the mesophyll: its innumerable stomata, the openings of which widen or close according to need, allow to the watery vapour arising in the inter-cellular spaces of the mesophyll a passage out into the atmosphere, regulated according to need, and at the same time facilitate the entrance of the carbon dioxide, and, after its decomposition, the exit of the oxygen. Hairy coverings of the most varied kind—prickles, stinging hairs, woolly hairs, and glandular hairs—protect the leaves against too intense sun-light, against too strong cooling, and against numerous attacks of insects, &c., according to the biological relations of the plants concerned Of great importance to the function of the foliage leaves, and consequently to the existence of the whole plant, is the so-called *venation* The essential parts of this are the vascular bundles, which, bending out from

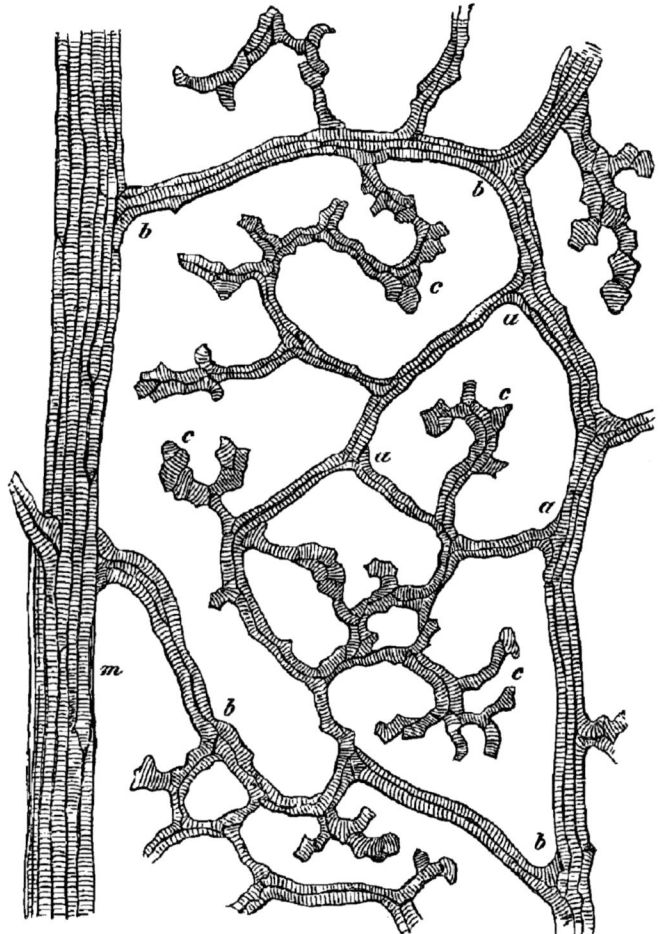

FIG. 44.—Several meshes from the leaf of *Anthyllis vulneraria* *m* midrib , *b, b* secondary cross veins radiating from it, *a a* a closed mesh , *c, c* endings of the finest veins. The figure shows only the spiral cells of the veins , but the phloem of the vascular bundles runs with these, and the meshes are filled with the parenchymatous mesophyll (Strongly magnified.)

the shoot-axis into the base of the leaf, and running through the petiole when it is present, become branched in the leaf-blade or lamina. It depends solely and simply upon the nature of the leaf what the form and importance of its venation shall be. In the first place, the vascular bundles of the leaf venation have the duty of conveying the water, laden with nutritive matters, to the assimilating mesophyll, and of conducting back a part of the products of assimilation into the shoot-axis.

If the leaves are small, and already rendered sufficiently stiff by means of their epidermis, the vascular bundles lose themselves within the mesophyll to fulfil the functions named, and little or nothing of the venation is to be remarked externally. The venation is the more prominent, however, the larger the leaf surface and the thinner the leaf tissue. For in this case it is no longer merely a matter of the con-duction of water and the carrying away of the products of assimilation, as in small, thick and stiff leaves, it is now, rather, an important function of the venation to keep the thin lamina of the leaf expanded flat, much as the ribs of an umbrella extend its thin covering. This purely mechanical office falls essentially to the mid-rib and to its stronger ramifications in the leaf. the vas-cular bundles of these are surrounded by more or less thick layers of succulent and tightly stretched parenchyma, and their epidermis is further supported by elastic tissue These so-called primary veins of the leaves project on the under-side as strong ribs, their rigidity (upon which almost everything depends), is due to strong tensions between the succulent parenchyma and the epidermis. By their growth in length, the veins strive to obtain greater linear dimensions than the thin lamina of mesophyll stretched between them; hence they hold the latter tightly extended, exactly as the ribs of an umbrella hold the silk. From these mechanically effective primary veins which project on the underside of the foliage leaf, arise further, as lateral branchings, thinner vascular bundles, by means of which the spaces between the primary veins become so con-nected, that the lamina of the leaf is divided up into a large number of small and still smaller fields or areolæ Out of these anas-tomoses, finally, in the highly organized thin leaves of the Dicotyledons, ramifications of

FIG 45 —Venation of the leaf-like shoot of *Ruscus hypoglossum*, a Monocotyledon (after Ettingshausen)

vascular bundles arise which become branched within the smallest areolæ of the venation, and at length terminate blindly (Fig. 44).

The venation of thin and large foliage leaves has thus two chief functions First, a mechanical one, with the object of keeping the thin lamina stiff and extended flat; and secondly, it has the object of promoting the processes of nutrition in the leaf, since the finer ramifications of the venation permeate the leaf much in the same way as the smaller furrows of a well-designed irrigation system run through a meadow in all directions, in order to bring and carry off water Even in large foliage leaves, the space is so closely permeated by the ends of veins, that every square millimeter of mesophyll possesses its canals for bringing and carrying off· these all run into the primary veins of the leaf, and thence into the petiole, or into the shoot-axis.

In ordinary very thin leaves, the venation has, however, yet a second purely mechanical end to fulfil, in addition to the stretching of the green lamina, namely, to protect the leaf from rupture. This problem is not satisfactorily solved in all leaves: the large, sometimes gigantic leaves of the Banana (*Musa*), *Strelitzia*, *Ravenala*, &c, are provided with so inadequate a venation, that not only in our inclement climate, but even in their milder native home, they become torn by the currents of air; so that the broad leaf surface (3–6 m. long and 0 5 to 1 m. wide) is regularly slit into a number of lobes and shreds, still held together only by the powerful mid-rib From this, innumerable lateral veins proceed, close to one another, and parallel, and directed perpendicularly towards the margin of the large leaf, to end there without adequate connection. When the wind whips the large leaf surface, it tears from the margin inwards, like an unhemmed flag, and the slits go parallel to the lateral veins up to the mid-rib. The large majority of leaves, on the other hand, and especially very thin

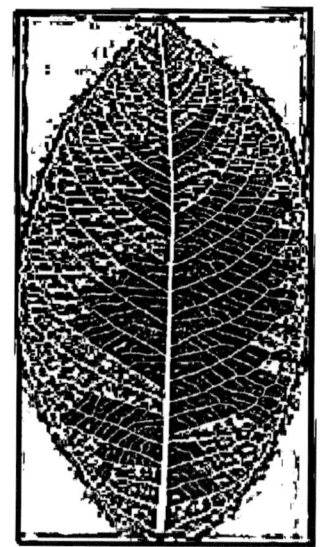

FIG 45.—Venation of the leaf of *Salix grandifolia* (after Ettingshausen)

ones, are protected by the mode of distribution of their veins, in a remarkably efficient manner, against the so-called shearing action of the wind, i.e. against the tearing from the margin inwards. First, it is to be remarked that the epidermis at the leaf margins generally undergoes considerable strengthening, and that the cuticle especially, and perhaps elastic fibres as well, usually form a thick, and often very solid border at the margin of the leaf. The resistance to incision is again strengthened by the course of the leaf-ribs in the neighbourhood of the margin of the leaf. Without entering into too much detail, or into an exhaustive survey of all the cases occurring, the subject is still sufficiently interesting to bring forward some at least of the most important examples. In this I commence with the most complete arrangements known to me, such as we find in the large thin and entire leaves of dicotyledonous plants.

The commonest case appears to be this Starting from the strong mid-rib of the leaf, each of the primary lateral ribs, which alternate right and left, runs forwards and outwards at an acute angle towards the apex of the leaf, to become joined finally, in a curve convex towards the leaf margin, on to the rib next in front. There thus arises a series of arches, which run immediately within the leaf margin (*Ficus acuminata, religiosa*) If the leaf margin is compared say with a bridge, the lateral ribs, with their arch-like marginal connections, represent the piers with their arches. In very large and delicate leaves, this arrangement is strengthened by the formation of a second system of smaller arches, convex outwards, the piers of which rest on the primary lateral ribs, or there is even a third system of still smaller pier-arches, with their convexities lying towards the margin. The leaf margin is then comparable to a railway viaduct, constructed of two or three storeys of arches, a comparison which is by no means a merely superficial or formal one, but completely describes the fact itself, since this mechanical arrangement of the venation has a similar mechanical significance to that of the arch-piers of a bridge We find this double or triple arch system perfectly evident in the leaves of Tobacco, *Catalpa*, and the Tulip-tree; less evident in those of the Rhubarb, and in *Asarum* (Fig. 43), and *Salix grandifolia* (Fig. 46). This arrangement is also well seen in the individual leaflets of the Walnut-tree, as well as in the large leaves of *Nymphæa alba*, floating on the surface of water · and it is expressly to be remarked here, that leaves floating on or in water must be insured against being torn by the shock of its waves, in the same manner as aerial leaves are protected against the wind.

In the large thin leaves of the Dicotyledons we find, however, besides the arrangement named of a single, double, or triple arch system, quite another form of distribution of the ribs, in that the side ribs spreading from the primary rib run out straight to the margin, and terminate there. Out of these spring secondary and tertiary lateral ribs, which behave in exactly the same way; so that the leaf margin is met by a very large number of ribs coming from the interior of the leaf and terminating in it, which are supported beneath the margin by feeble cross-connections. It is obvious that this arrangement offers less guarantee for the solidity of the leaf margin than that described above Nevertheless, it is often enough very distinctly developed, e.g. in the foliage leaves of the common Bottle Gourd, in those of *Corylus colurna* and *maxima*, and in the floating aquatic leaves of *Euryale ferox*. This form of venation asserts itself much more distinctly in many Ferns with dichotomously (forked) branched ribs (*Scolopendrium, Aspidium spinulosum, Osmunda regalis*, &c). Mixed systems, according to both the principles named, are also frequently to be observed.

A much rarer form of distribution of the ribs for protection against incision is found in the magnificent leaves of *Cyanophyllum formosum*, and also in a monocotyledonous plant—*Smilax sarsaparilla* In the lanceolate lamina, close to the right and left margin, and proceeding from the base of the mid-rib, a thin rib runs on each side, which is again united with the mid-rib at the apex of the leaf. Further removed from the right and left leaf margin, a strong rib then rises on each side, also springing from the base to the apex of the mid-rib. Starting from the mid-rib, numerous ribs pass across right and left through the leaf-substance to the two last named, and in like manner from these over to the marginal ribs; and the fields of the leaf-surface so formed are reticulately penetrated by numberless water-veins. This venation, also occasionally occurring in Dicotyledons, leads us to the majority of the broad monocotyledonous leaves, e.g. of *Potamogeton natans, Alisma plantago, Majanthemum bifolium, Convallaria latifolia,* and others, where, proceeding from the base of the mid-rib, two, three, four, or more lateral ribs arise, which run in an arch-like manner to the apex of the leaf, approximately parallel to the leaf margin. Feebler cross veins then often divide the longitudinal bands of the lamina thus arising into smaller fields. In the commonest form of monocotyledonous leaves, however, where the lamina forms a long narrow band, as in the Grasses, Lilies, and *Dracænas*, a number of weak ribs run parallel with the leaf margin and the mid-rib to the apex of the leaf—an arrangement which thoroughly satisfies the requirements in the face of the danger of transverse and longitudinal tearing.

If we now return to the broad dicotyledonous leaves, we find, first, those the margin of which is coarsely toothed, or variously incised and lobed. In such cases as the leaf of the Vine, *Petasites albus*, and many others, the course of the ribs resembles the second case described above, e. g. that of *Cucurbita*. The lateral ribs spreading from the mid-rib, as well as their secondary ramifications, run direct to the leaf margin, and generally end in a prominent tooth of the same: this occurs also in small toothed leaves, e. g. of *Viburnum lantana*. Inside the depression between the teeth, in this case, a smaller vein generally ends; or two

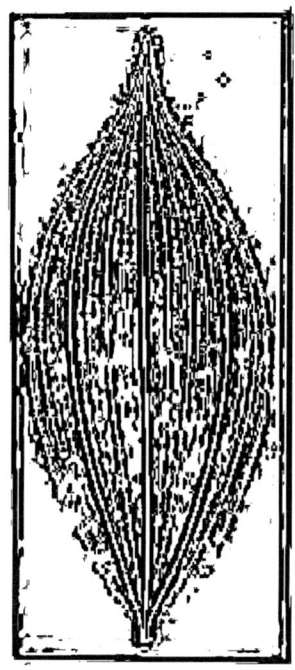

small lateral veins meet here at an obtuse angle. With this arrangement, also, the arch-like marginal connection of the lateral veins may again be mixed

If we now pass to the divided and compound leaves, the important question is whether the different parts of the lamina have each a considerable extent of surface, as in the Walnut, or whether they are small and narrow. In the first case, the venation has the same mechanical function as in large, entire leaves, in the second case, on the other hand, as in the finely divided, doubly and triply pinnatisected leaves of many Umbelliferæ (*Conium, Anthriscus*), in the Milfoil and others, a connected leaf-surface, and a tearing of it from the edge inwards, are hardly to be spoken of, and the corresponding arrangements of the venation do not exist. The same is the case also in the great majority of the finely divided leaves of Ferns; where, moreover, the leaf tissue already possesses considerable solidity on its own account.

FIG 47—Venation of the leaf of *Convallaria latifolia* (after Ettingshausen)

If the mechanical principles of leaf-venation here made evident are kept in view, it is always easy to understand the distribution of the coarser leaf-ribs, even in cases not here considered. It is further obvious that in very small leaves, as those of the Lycopodiaceæ, most Coniferæ, and many Dicotyledons, the mechanical arrangements described would be quite superfluous, and consequently they are not present In the same way it is clear that in very stiff leathery leaves, as those of the *Oleander*, the mechanical aspect of the venation becomes wholly insignificant in contrast to its importance in connexion with the carrying to and fro of nutritive substances; and that finally, in the so-called succulent plants, the foliage leaves of which are very thick, and sufficiently solid besides, nothing at all is to be noticed of the mechanical venation. These considerations, however, teach us at the same time how fruitful is every conception of organic forms based on the principle of causality, as contrasted with the merely formal comparison of the same. Ettingshausen has in the latter sense described thousands of leaf-venations, without arriving at any important result whatever; while our simple principle, according to which the leaf-venation fulfils, on the one hand, the carrying to and fro of nutritive matter, and, on the other, the mechanical office of keeping the lamina tightly extended and protecting it from rupture, affords a very clear insight into the variety of forms here prevalent.

As regards the mechanical arrangements, however, we have yet to refer to one point hitherto not touched upon. It is quite a common phenomenon that small narrow leaves are situated immediately upon the shoot-axis, while the majority of large, thin leaves of aërial plants, as well as of aquatics, are fastened on more or less long and thin stalks. I see in this disposition a further expression of the mechanical principle in the organization of the leaves: for it is at once obvious, that the described arrangements of the venation against rupture by the wind, or the wave-shock of water, are necessarily aided when the large thin leaf-surfaces swing on elastic movable stalks. Storm and wave-shock hardly affect the lamina when it is situated on an elastic stalk which yields readily to the pressure of the wind or water current, and turns so that the leaf resembles a weather-cock rather than a common flag. If, on the other hand, the leaf is situated on the axis without a stalk, all depends upon whether the axis itself is flexible and elastic. If we now reflect, that an extremely important feature in the general appearance of plants consists in whether their leaves are small or large, whether they are entire or divided, whether

FIG 48 —Venation of the leaf of a Fern (*Adiantum*)

they are stalked or sessile, &c., it is obvious that we obtain by means of the mechanical principle here expounded, a right understanding of one of the most striking and widely extended phenomena of the vegetable world. And if we ask, finally, why it is just in the case of the foliage-leaves that this mechanical principle is so clearly manifested, the answer is already given above it is simply a matter of presenting the chlorophyll cell-tissue of the plant to the light in the form of a very thin lamina, and at the same time of providing that by means of a regulated evaporation of water out of this lamina the food-materials taken up by the root also flow to the leaf[1]

---

[1] In accordance with the purpose of the present book, I must refrain from the treatment of the venation of leaves more in detail, although there is much temptation to attempt to refer these relations of organization, so obvious but hitherto not understood, to a principle so simple as that indicated in the text. Schwendener (*Das mechanische Princip im anat Bau der Monocotylen* Leipzig, 1879) has also concerned himself, it is true, with the rigidity of leaves, so far as it is based on the anatomical structure of the transverse section, but has scarcely noticed the relations pointed out by me in the text. Compare also Haberlandt in Jahrb. für wiss Bot. Bd XIII pp. 160, &c. I hope later to establish further the short notices given in the text, in a detailed exposition.

LECTURE V.

METAMORPHOSED AND REDUCED FORMS OF SHOOT OF THE VASCULAR PLANTS   THE SHOOTS OF MOSSES, ALGÆ, AND FUNGI

THE further, with progressive division of labour in the body of a plant, the particular biological *rôle* assigned to a shoot becomes removed from that of the typical leaf-shoot, the more its external form, internal structure, and irritability also are modified. A deeper study of these metamorphoses and degenerations of the shoot might easily lead to a very long series of monographs of the most various plants; we must content ourselves, however, with a condensed survey of the more common cases.

Let us first consider some modified forms of sub-aerial shoots, among which those of the so-called Succulents are distinguished in that, while they possess massive shoot-axes or leaves, a surprisingly small extension of the surface is produced: in contrast with the slender, graceful structure of the typical leaf-shoot, we have thus to do here with stout, massive forms. By means of this constitution, the succulent plants are enabled to live, even in hot dry air, with a small supply of water from the earth, of course at the expense of their increase in body-weight, since the small development of surface allows such plants only a relatively inconsiderable superficial extension of the chlorophyll, and accordingly a less plentiful production of organic substance.

Confining ourselves first to the very decided cases of succulence, this may appear either in the shoot-axis or in the leaves.

In the succulent shoot-axes, the leaves, although formed at the growing point, usually become partly or wholly arrested later; the developed shoot then consists only of the leafless axis. This is the case in the true Cactus forms, *Echinocactus,* *Mamillaria, Cereus, Opuntia,* &c., the shoot-axes of which resemble either roundish tubers or thick prismatic bodies, on the surface of which the places whence the leaves have disappeared are marked by tufts of hairs and prickles, situated on projecting cushions or ridges. Occasionally, the shoot-axes of *Cacti* also assume flat, leaf-like forms (*Phyllocactus,* &c.). In other families, succulent leafless shoot-axes are found in individual species, the habitats of which are favourable to such an arrangement. Thus we have Cactus-like forms in the family of the Asclepiadaceæ in the African genus *Stapelia;* and in the genus *Euphorbia* in a series of species likewise

African, as *Euphorbia canariensis, globosa, Caput medusæ,* &c. The assimilating tissue containing chlorophyll is, in these leafless succulents, extended in the form of a very thin layer beneath the epidermis of the shoot-axis.

We find weak, thin shoot-axes, with very succulent leaves, in the family of the Crassulaceæ, and in the genus *Mesembryanthemum;* among the Monocotyledons especially in the genus *Aloe,* and here and there also in other plants. The leaves in these cases entirely give up their usual expansion as thin laminæ; they become thick, tuber-like, or prismatic, and so forth. The parenchyma containing chlorophyll forms also in them only a thin layer extending beneath the epidermis, while the main mass of such leaves consists of colourless, succulent, slimy tissue.

In contrast to the Succulents, there are also plants the shoot-axes of which remain thin, and possess abundant chlorophyll beneath the epidermis, while the leaves are all arrested as small scales, so that here also, as in the Cactus-like succulent plants, the shoot-axes themselves undertake the function of assimilation Such plants are found in various families of Phanerogams, among the Papilionaceæ, e. g *Spartium junceum,* and among the Scrophularinæ, *Russelia juncea,* &c. The whole Cryptogamic class Equisetaceæ (Horsetails) also belongs here, as well as the genus *Psilotum* included in the Lycopodiaceæ

Especially instructive, with reference to the relations between axis and leaf, are the plants which produce so-called Cladodes. These are shoots, the leaves of which are arrested as very small scales, while the shoot-axes themselves assume the flat form of ordinary leaves, to such an extent that an unpractised observer would undoubtedly take shoot-axes of this kind for ordinary foliage leaves. Among the Monocotyledons the genus *Ruscus* from the family of the Asparagineæ, among the Coniferæ the genus *Phyllocladus* from the family of the Taxineæ, and among the Dicotyledons the genus *Phyllanthus* from the family Euphorbiaceæ, require special mention.

FIG 49 —*Ruscus aculeatus* (after Duchartre) *a* main shoot of the usual form, *cld* the leaf-like lateral shoots (cladodia) on which the flower shoots *(fl)* are situated.

In such cases, it is generally only lateral shoots of the main axis which assume the form of thin foliage leaves, it may also occur, however, that all the shoots, even if not exactly leaf-shaped, are flattened, broad, and abound in chlorophyll, and so replace the arrested foliage leaves, as in *Muhlenbeckia platyclada* (Polygonaceæ), and in *Carmichaelia* (Papilionaceæ).

In the cases of metamorphosed shoots mentioned hitherto, it is essentially a question of the distribution of the assimilating tissue containing chlorophyll, either in the leaves or in the shoot-axis itself. The climbing shoots, on the other hand, belong to quite another category of metamorphoses, in which the relation of the foliage leaves to the shoot remains essentially undisturbed; where, however, arrangements exist by means of which the feeble, thin, shoot-axes, which are not able to bear the weight of the leaves, flowers, and fruit, are enabled to climb up foreign bodies, usually other plants   In the Ivy, for example, and *Ficus scandens*, this takes place simply by the shoot-axes attaching themselves firmly to tree trunks or walls, and fastening themselves by means of clinging roots.   Much more perfect is the arrangement for climbing, however, in the foliage shoots of twining plants, where, in the long drawn shoot-axes, a tendency to spiral curvature is combined with the irritability for the geotropic influence of gravitation [1], by which shoot-axes of this kind are caused to wind themselves spirally close around upright poles, stems, or branches, and so push their leaf-forming buds continually higher

FIG. 50.—Apex of a shoot of *Akebia quinata*, growing out beyond the supporting rod, four free spiral turns have been produced

Well-known examples of such twining plants are the Hop, Bindweed (*Convolvulus*), Bean (*Phaseolus*), and *Dioscorea.*

We find the most perfect mechanism of climbing shoots, however, in the tendril-plants; the leafy shoot-axes of which are likewise so thin and flexible, that they are not able to support the weight of leaves, flowers, and fruits   Such plants, therefore, just as true twining plants, must climb upon shrubs and similar supports, since, if they find no opportunity of doing this, they become arrested   The climbing organs, now, are simply the tendrils   These are long, thin, filiform organs, which, by the continual contact of a thin solid body, are induced to wind fast around it, so that at the same time the whole leaf shoot is caused to elevate its apex higher and higher.   Such sensitive tendrils may be developed in very different ways: sometimes it is the long thin stalks of the proper foliage leaves themselves, which wind around their supports, as in the Spanish cress (*Tropæolum*), *Clematis*, *Maurandia*, *Fumaria*, *Solanum jasminoides*, &c.   In other cases, it is the elongated midrib of the foliage leaf, with or without ramifications, as in *Nepenthes*, *Cobea scandens*, *Pisum sativum* (Pea), and species of Vetch (*Vicia*)   Finally, also, metamorphosed shoot-axes, with entirely arrested leaflets, may occur as irritable tendril filaments; thus, the tendrils of the Vine and the Virginian Creeper (*Ampelopsis*) are metamorphosed lateral shoots on the normal leaf shoots of these plants.   They may in fact be considered as flower shoots degenerated to climbing organs.   To the same category belong, probably, the extraordinarily sensitive tendrils of the Gourd-like plants and the Passion-flowers (*Passifloreæ*); while in the genus *Smilax* (Monocotyledons) the tendrils are outgrowths of the leaf stalks.   I shall return later to the highly

---

[1] That the theory of the twining of climbing plants proposed by Darwin is wrong, has been shown by H de Vries   Compare Arb. des Bot Instit. I p. 317, and II. p 718.

remarkable phenomena of irritability of the tendrils, and shall only mention here that these climbing organs may arise by metamorphosis of very different parts of the shoot, and this either at the expense of the development of leaves, or without the latter being essentially affected.

In a certain sense the so-called thorns stand in contrast to the tendrils; they agree with them, however, in that they arise from various parts of the shoot, generally with suppression of the leaf-formation. As thorns we distinguish certain hard pointed, simple or branched bodies, which serve the plants concerned either as a protection against the attacks of larger animals, or as climbing-organs.

Frequently, thorns arise from the metamorphosis of foliage leaves, as in the Barberry (*Berberis*); or they are remnants of fallen foliage leaves, as in *Isoetes hystrix, Astragalus tragacantha;* or the end of a foliage shoot becomes transformed into a thorn, as in *Ramnus cathartica,* or an entire branched shoot, furnished with small leaflets, at first delicate and soft, eventually hardens to a system

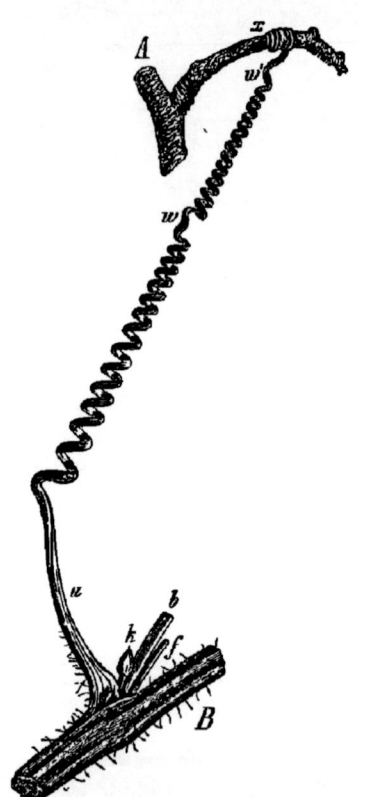

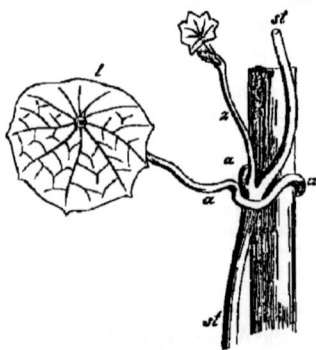

FIG 51.—*Tropæolum minus* The long petiole (*a, a, a*) of the leaf (*l*) is sensitive to continued contact, and has so wound itself round a support and its own stem (*st*), that the latter becomes firmly fixed to the support, *x* the axillary shoot of the leaf.

FIG 52.—*Bryonia dioica B* a portion of the stem from which the tendril arises, together with the leaf-stalk (*b*) and the bud (*k*), the lower part of the tendril (*u*) is stiff (not tendril like), the upper portion (*x*) has coiled round a branch. The long intermediate part of the tendril, between the rigid basal portion (*u*) and the point of attachment (*x*), has become spirally coiled, and thus raised the stem *B*, *w w'* the points where the direction of the coil is reversed

of thorns, as in *Gleditschia ferox, triacanthus,* &c Thorns of this kind are shoot-axes, on which the development of leaves ceases, while the tissue, and even that of the growing point, is changed into hard, woody, permanent tissue The older nomenclature has hitherto carefully avoided classing together with thorns the prickles, which agree with them physiologically. These are hard, pointed, short or long bodies, developed from various places on the shoot-axes, or even from leaves, and which cannot be looked upon as metamorphosed shoots or leaves In the Roses and Brambles they are known to every one; among the American species of *Solanum,* many are remarkable for conspicuous brightly coloured prickles, e. g *Solanum pyracantha* and *atro-sanguineum ;* many Palms, on the other hand, have very long and hard ones resembling those of a porcupine.

Among sub-aërial shoots the filiform, often very long runners, which usually spring from the base of an upright leafy shoot and bear a few inconspicuous leaf-scales on their long internodes, deserve even if only passing mention here.

FIG 53.—A potato plant grown from seed   *r* primary root, *ct* cotyledons , *ff* foliage leaves , *b b* lateral shoots, with leaf scales *c' c'* , *t b* the tubers at the ends of these shoots (after Duchatre)

These produce, at some distance from the mother-plant, a rosette of foliage leaves, from which spring, downwards, a tuft of roots, and upwards, flower shoots. The Strawberry affords a very good example. Runners of this kind are fundamentally organs of multiplication, since from each rooted tuft of foliage leaves at the end of a runner, the filiform part of which perishes later, a new independent plant arises. Very many other plants behave in a similar manner; their runners or stolons grow forth as horizontal fibres beneath the surface of the earth, and produce from their terminal bud a new rooted plant, often far removed from the mother-plant. This is the case for example in the Umbellifer *Ægopodium podagraria,* in the common Valerian (*Valeriana officinalis*), and in many labiate plants

(*Stachys, Mentha*). With these forms are connected those in which the end of a subterranean runner does not develope into a sub-aërial leaf shoot at once and in the same period of vegetation, but swells up as a thick tuber, on which, in the axils of very small arrested leaflets, buds (eyes) are situated, from which rooted sub-aërial leafy shoots arise in the next period of vegetation from these again arise tuber-producing subterranean runners. We find an example of this, as well known as instructive, in the Potato, and the Jerusalem artichoke (*Helianthus tuberosus*).

Many bulbs also arise at the end of subterranean runners, e. g. those in young tulip plants. Bulbs are distinguished from tubers, however, in that, in them, not the shoot-axis, but the leaves enveloping the leaf-bud become thick, succulent, and fleshy, and filled with reserve materials like the tubers. In the majority of bulbs, however, the buds arising in the axils of the bulb-scales are transformed at once into new bulbs, which are not removed by far-reaching runners from the parent bulb. This is the case, for example, in our common kitchen Onion, the Garlic, Crown Imperial, and many others. It is evidently an advantageous arrangement when tubers and bulbs, from which new plants arise in the next year, are formed at the end of more or less long runners; since the newly arising individuals are thus developed far from the mother-plant, in a soil which has not yet been exhausted by the latter.

It is clear that all plants with runners (above ground or below, forming tubers and bulbs or simply bearing leaf-shoots at the end) are constantly travelling, and consequently they appear each year in places further distant. If such plants are particularly well adapted for the soil and prevailing climate, they may at length

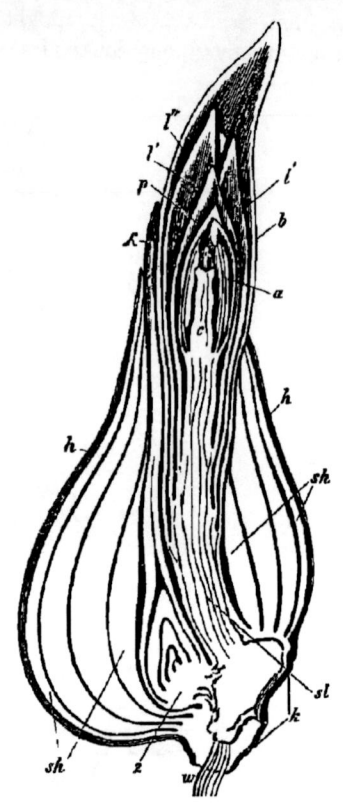

FIG. 54.—Longitudinal section through a germinating bulb of *Tulipa præcox* *h* brown membrane covering the bulb, *k* the part of the stem bearing the bulb-scales (*sh, sh*), *s l* the elongated portion of stem bearing the foliage leaves (*l' l'*) which ends above in the terminal flower, *c* ovary, *a* anthers, *p* perianth, *z* a lateral bud (young bulb) in the axil of the youngest bulb scale, *k* the apex of the first leaf of this lateral bud. The lateral bud developes as the bulb of next year *w* the roots which arise on the fibro vascular bundles of the base of the bulb.

completely occupy wide stretches of ground, since they dispossess all other plants Such is the case with the Couch Grass (*Triticum repens*) and with many Sedges (*Carex*), and particularly with the Horsetails (*Equisetum*): *Equisetum limosum*, and *palustre*, for example, are able, by means of their subterranean runners creeping in the mud. to occupy large stretches in bogs and the margins of ponds and lakes, to the exclusion of other plants. Plants provided with subterranean runners play an important part in nature; and the dense grass of meadows, as well as the ineradicable weeds, owe their existence in great measure to the mode of life described.

In plants provided with runners, the main shoot for the time being, with its foliage leaves and flower-stalks, is developed chiefly above ground. It occurs, however, not rarely that the whole shoot-system of a plant consists of subterranean creeping shoot-axes, from which only the foliage leaves appear above the earth, in order to form products of assimilation in the light, these are carried down through the leaf-stalks, and deposited as reserve material in the subterranean thick shoot-axes. A very perfect example of this occurs in our Bracken fern (*Pteris aquilina*), from the subterranean shoot-axes of which only a single large foliage leaf from each bud comes forth each year above ground; similarly also in the Fern *Lygodium*, where likewise only the foliage leaves live above ground, and their mid-ribs climb like the stem of a twining plant. It is indifferent, from a physiological point of view, whether the system of subterranean perennial shoot-axes forms a Monopodium or a Sympodium. Thus, a Monopodium arises when the growing points of the

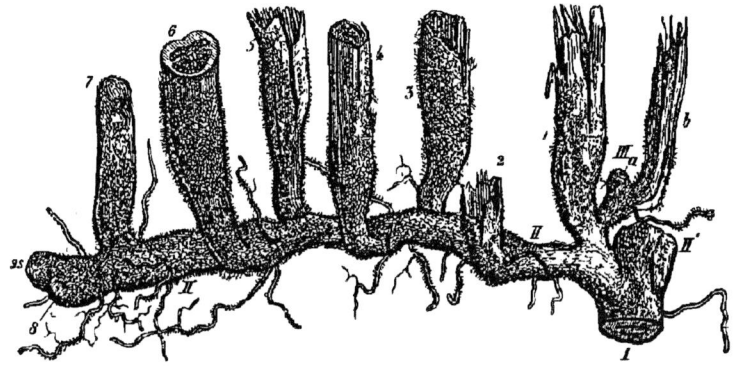

FIG 55.—Rhizome of *Pteris aquilina*. *I, II, III* the subterranean creeping shoot axes, *ss* the apex of one of them, *1, 2* to *6* the basal portions of the leaf stalks, *7* a young leaf, *b* a rotted leaf stalk, the still living basal portion of which bears a bud *a III*. The fibres covered with hairs are roots, which develope behind the forward growing apex of the stem

subterranean system continue to grow, while the annually renewed sub-aërial shoots bearing leaves and flowers spring from lateral growing points of the subterranean system, e. g. Herb Paris (*Paris quadrifolia*). A subterranean Sympodium occurs, on the other hand, when from the growing point of a subterranean creeping shoot there finally arises a sub-aërial foliage shoot or flower stem, which then again disappears; only the subterranean creeping piece of the shoot-axis still remains, and a subterranean lateral bud, growing further in the direction of the previous subterranean bud, again developes at its end into a transitory leaf-shoot. The subterranean system of shoot-axes then consists of numerous basal pieces of different shoot-generations, the apical portions of which have come forth year by year above the earth, and then disappeared. We find an excellent example of this in the so-called Solomon's Seal (*Polygonatum*).

To these aphoristic remarks concerning subterranean shoots, I have to add finally that these shoots are distinguished as Rhizomes, when, creeping horizontally or

obliquely from the shoot-axes, as is generally the case, they produce numerous roots.
I could scarcely mention a more illustrative example of Rhizomes or Root-stocks
than those of the genus *Iris*, the Flag (*Acorus calamus*), and especially the common
Asparagus (*Asparagus officinalis*). The examples named, moreover, offer only
a small selection from the great variety of subterranean forms of shoot. It is for
our purpose, however, quite superfluous to enter further into particulars, since any
one who has rightly understood what has been said will, on careful observation
of any subterranean shoot, easily comprehend the true state of the matter. Concerning this, I may simply remark that one has to guard occasionally against
confounding subterranean shoots with roots; since the former very often assume
externally the aspect of roots. Above all, they contain no chlorophyll: the subterranean shoot-axes are white, brown, or yellow, instead of green. The decisive
point always lies, however, in that subterranean shoot-axes possess leaves, and bear

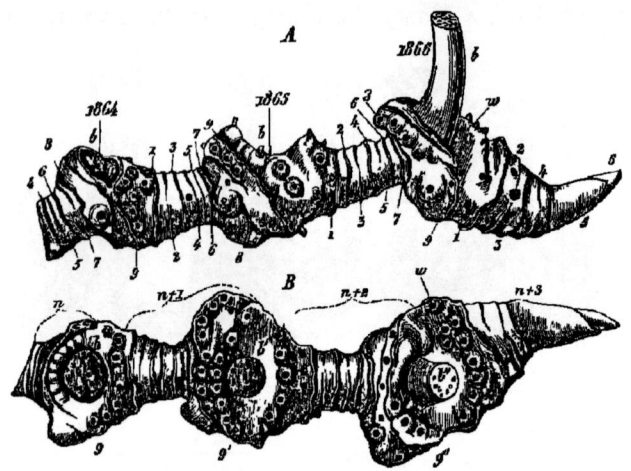

FIG. 56.—*Polygonatum multiflorum.* The anterior piece of a much longer rhizome, consisting of
four annual growths, *A* seen in profile, *B* from above, all the adventitious roots have been cut off, their
position being indicated by the roundish scars. The numbers 1864, 1865, 1866, indicate the years in
which the respective pieces of the sympodium have been produced.

a leaf-forming bud at the end. Of course the leaves of runners and rhizomes are
usually small, inconspicuous, membranous, or scale-like, and arrested generally,
since the true leaf-nature can only appear when the leaf rudiments develope under
the influence of light as green foliage leaves. That these inconspicuous subterranean leaves, like the scales of sub-aerial winter buds, are only arrested
foliage leaves, may be in part experimentally demonstrated[1]; since it is possible,
by proper interference with the normal conditions of vegetation, to produce true
foliage leaves from such scales. With respect to Bulbs, it may finally be mentioned
that their stout, soft scales are also leaves, according to their developmental history
—generally entire metamorphosed leaves, as in the Crown Imperial and Tulip.

---

[1] That the leaf-scales are only foliage leaves prevented from their normal development, but do
not represent a so-called leaf formation in the sense of the Braunian Morphology, has been
experimentally demonstrated by Goebel, Bot. Zeitg. 1880, pp. 753, &c

Sometimes, however, the body of the bulb is composed of the subterranean basal portions of leaves, the sub-aërial parts of which possess the properties of green foliage leaves : our common kitchen Onion presents the most familiar example. As may be readily supposed, subterranean shoots may resemble true roots not only in their form but also in their functions ; since they, like the latter, take up food from the earth, and are endowed with irritabilities by means of which they grow through the substratum in all directions like true roots. We find subterranean shoots of this kind sometimes covered with absorbing root-hairs, e. g. in the Horsetails. Besides the horizontal creeping runners, there are others which penetrate obliquely or vertically downwards into the earth, and behave also in other respects like primary roots. This

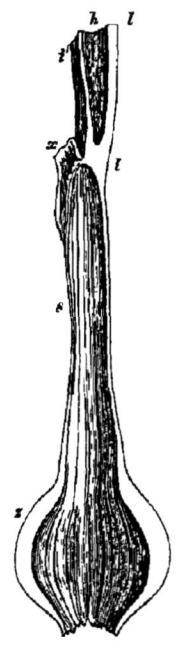

occurs to a very marked extent in the subterranean shoots of the genus *Dracæna ;* and from the subterranean shoot-system of *Equisetum* spring single branches, which grow down 2–3 m. perpendicularly into the earth. Since, consequently, shoot-axes can undertake the functions of roots, the development of true roots may be entirely wanting in such cases. There is a whole series of examples known in this connection

The genus *Psilotum*, belonging to the *Lycopodiaceæ*, developes a subterranean system of shoots, the leaf rudiments of which are only to be traced by careful microscopic research ; while they behave in other respects exactly like roots. Completely rootless are, further, some Orchideæ devoid of chlorophyll (*Corallorhiza, Epipogum*), the subterranean shoots of which may in truth be recognised as such at once, but nevertheless completely undertake the function of roots. I take this opportunity of remarking that the genus *Salvinia* is also completely rootless, in a manner, however, quite different from the plants hitherto named. *Salvinia* is,

FIG 57 —A leaf of *Allium cepa* divided lengthwise *s* the thickened base of the sheath, which remains behind as a bulb scale after the upper part of the leaf has died down , *s* the membranous part of the sheath , *i* the hollow lamina , *k* cavity, and *i* inner side of the lamina , *x* ligule

in fact, a plant floating horizontally on the surface of water, and provided with broad aerial leaves, from the shoot axis of which long root-like fibres hang down into the water : the latter are, however, neither true roots nor metamorphosed shoots, but, according to the history of development, peculiarly modified leaves, which have thus here undertaken the function of roots.

In all the cases considered hitherto, we have been concerned with derived or metamorphosed forms of shoot of those vascular plants in which at least the main shoots either produce green assimilating leaves, or are abundantly provided with chlorophyll in their stems The departures from the type are in these cases brought about by division of the physiological labour The deviations from the typical forms of shoot proceed much further in plants devoid of chlorophyll, which either take up organic food from the remains of other plants that are becoming decomposed, or obtain it directly from other living plants, to which they are parasitically attached. To the first category, which are usually distinguished as Co-prophytes, but which I, however, prefer to name Humus-plants (saprophytes), belong as well-known examples some of our native Orchids—*Neottia*, *Epipogum*, *Corallorhiza*, and also *Lathræa* and *Monotropa*. In these the consequence of the want of chlorophyll is that the leaves, which are otherwise numerously developed, remain small and scale-like; since large leaves have only a meaning and object when they abound in chlorophyll, and serve as organs of nutrition. Since, thus, the function of assimilation is absent, so also is the conveyance of mineral nutritive matters, dissolved out of the earth in corresponding quantities of water, wholly or in part superfluous. Accordingly, such plants have but few roots; and, likewise, a vigorously developed woody body in the shoot-axes is wanting. The same is also the case with many Parasites, particularly in the genus *Orobanche*, very rich in species, which though parasitic on the roots of other plants, nevertheless developes some roots in the earth, for the flower stem shooting up above the ground must needs have a certain supply of water, since it loses at least small quantities of vapour for months. The species of *Cuscuta* possess after their germination no roots whatever in the earth: by means of the numerous haustoria, which penetrate into the tissue of the host-plant from the long filiform shoot-axes winding around it, they extract not only all food matters, but also the necessary water, the quantity of which is of course extremely small, since the leaves are reduced to minute membrane-like scales   Much more complete than in these cases is the degradation of the shoot-formation in those parasites

FIG 58.—*Balanophora fungosa.* *w* the root of the host plant on which it is parasitic, the darker veins are woody bundles which run from the root into the tissue of the parasite, *a, b, c* young flower shoots (natural size)

the whole vegetative body of which developes in the tissue of the host-plant until the production of flowers, or, after taking its origin in these, grows forward below ground. This is the case in the *Balanophoreæ*, the *Hydnoreæ*, and *Rafflesiaceæ*, of which I have already mentioned that the organs penetrating into the nutritive substratum entirely lose the root-form common in the vascular plants   Up to the time when the flower buds arise, one can scarcely distinguish the vegetative body of such plants as a shoot. That we have to do with plants from the group of Phanerogams, is only to be recognised when the flowers or inflorescences arise; and these, in their turn, are to be regarded even in the typical plants containing chlorophyll as highly metamorphosed shoots. But even the parts of parasites of this kind which protrude from the substratum have, in comparison with the typical shoots of the vascular plants, something uncommonly strange about them. They sometimes resemble in their whole aspect the fructifications of large Fungi, in a very striking manner, for instance, in the genus *Scybalium*. That in all the saprophytes and parasites hitherto mentioned, it is in fact only the want of chlorophyll by which the degradation of all the vegetative organs has been brought about, is clear at once, if we compare with them the Misletoe and the whole family of the *Loranthaceæ*. These plants also are parasitic by their roots, as has already been shown, on the tissues of their host-plants. They are, however, abundantly provided with chlorophyll, and accordingly their shoot-formation leaves nothing to be desired. Their broad, dark green foliage leaves, on green, sharply segmented axes, possessing the anatomical structure of highly organized vascular plants, show that the strange aspect of the saprophytes and parasites devoid of chlorophyll is simply to be ascribed to the want of chlorophyll; for the Loranthaceæ, with their little altered roots, absorb in the main only water and mineral food-matters from the wood of the trees inhabited by them, and they are able, by means of their shoots containing chlorophyll, to produce organic substances by the decomposition of the carbon dioxide of the atmosphere. In accordance with this, the woody body of the shoot-axis is strongly developed, the water provided with mineral matters being conveyed through this to the assimilating leaves. From the comparison of the Saprophytes and Parasites with normal plants possessing green leaves, we gain the conviction that the whole vegetative segmentation, the distinction of root and shoot, the differentiation of the shoot into leaf and axis, and the production of wood and other anatomical elements, have

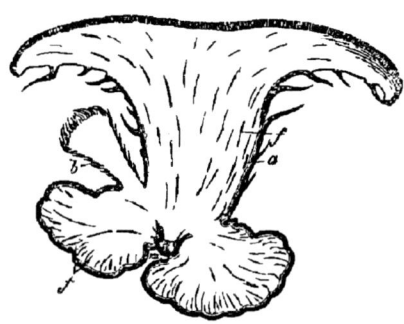

FIG 59.—*Scybalium fungiforme* ⅞n (between the two lobes) the root of the host plant, *a* a flower shoot, which bears numerous small flowers densely crowded on its flat upper surface, *b* young shoot, *f f* fibro-vascular bundles (after Eichler)

essentially been called forth by the activity of the chlorophyll in nutrition. In proportion as plants strive to present to the light and the air flat plates of tissue rich in chlorophyll (i.e. leaves) from their shoot-axes, the shoot-axes must also develope those forms of tissue which serve for the conveyance of nutritive materials into the leaves and back from them; and, in proportion as this happens, the roots contained in the substratum must also be capable of absorbing the water lost at the evaporating leaves, together with the mineral matters necessary to assimilation. The richer in chlorophyll and the larger the leaves (or the shoot-axes themselves, as in the Cacti and cladodia), the more perfect also must the roots thus be. It is, therefore, easily intelligible, that with increasing parasitism,—with the decrease, and, finally, the entire disappearance of the chlorophyll-contents of the shoots, the formation of roots also becomes simplified, and finally ceases altogether; and that when parasitism is carried to the highest degree, even the differentiation of root, shoot, and leaves in the vegetative body finally ceases, till, at last, the relation of plants of this kind to highly organised phanerogams is recognised only in the development of the flowers or inflorescences. Similar degradations are also met with in animal parasites.

Firmly fixed on or in the animal host, and relatively incapable of movement, the animal parasite requires only feebly developed feeding and motile organs, or even none at all, and accordingly no organs of sense. In animal parasites also, with increasing parasitism, the external segmentation and the anatomical structure proper to the parasite as a member of a highly organised group disappear more and more; and here in general, just as in plants, the reproductive organs succumb less than the vegetative organs to the destructive action of laziness. It is, in fact, in both cases inactivity—laziness, which distinguishes parasitism, and effects the degeneration of organs. As an animal which clings by means of suckers during its

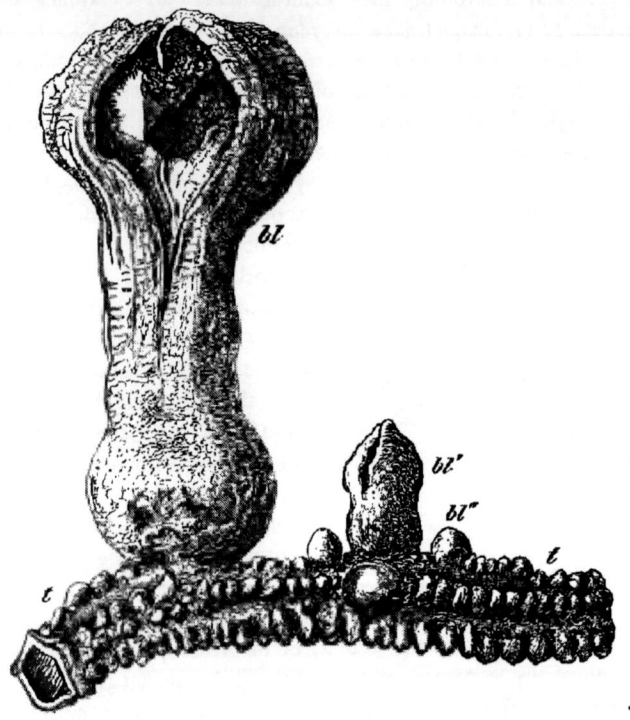

FIG. 60.—*Hydnora Africana.* *t t* a small piece of the subterranean vegetative body of the host-plant; out of this spring a mature flower *bl* and flower buds *bl' bl''* (⅔ natural size).

whole life on or in another animal can dispense with the various activities which other animals require for the seizing of their food, and the corresponding movements and use of the sense-organs; so a plant loses, with the loss of chlorophyll, the necessity for raising itself above the substratum to the light and of developing all those adaptations which subserve this purpose.

If we now turn to the more simply organised plants, the Mosses and Algæ, we find, the lower we descend, continually simpler forms of shoot: we have to regard these, however, not as reduced, but rather as rudimentary—as not yet typically developed. Numerous transitional forms, however, indicate the passage from the typical leaf-shoots of vascular plants down to the simplest beginnings of shoot-formation; where, finally, there still remains of the shoot-nature only the rising above the substratum, the production of the generative organs, and the capacity for assimilation with the irritabilities necessary thereto.

We shall here refer only to some important points and give a few examples, since these matters have been already spoken of.

In the true Mosses, and, in the subdivision of the Liverworts, in the foliose Jungermanniæ, we find quite typical shoots, differentiated into leaves and axes, but anatomically much simpler than those of the vascular plants. We have here

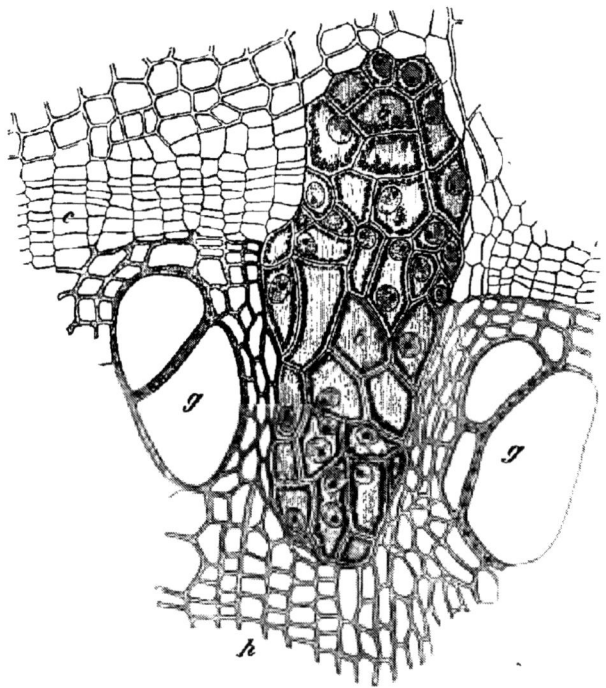

FIG. 61.—Portion of transverse section of root of *Cissus. c* cambium; *h* wood; *g* large vessels. The tissue *b b* belongs to the vegetative body of *Brugmansia Zippelii*, parasitic in the *Cissus* root: its thin fibres creep in the cortex of the *Cissus* root, and swell up here and there into thick cushions (as in the figure), from which flowers are developed, which then appear externally as in Fig. 17 *A* (strongly magnified; after Solms-Laubach).

always to do with small plantlets, usually growing together in dense swards, which only vegetate in moist air, and make use of a dried-up condition as a period of rest. Accordingly, the necessity for the formation of wood and the conduction of water, and the arrangement of those anatomical points which bring about the solidity of large land plants—all those arrangements generally which are only necessary to large land plants—are wanting. In particular, the foliage leaves of the Mosses, considering their small size and the life-conditions mentioned, do not need to form a network of ribs and veins, as we found to be the case with the large leaves of land plants: or, to express the causal relations more correctly, since the formative forces in the class of Mosses tend neither to the formation of wood, vascular bundles, and elastic fibres, nor to a great extension of the assimilating surface, the plants remain relatively small—their mass is insignificant in comparison with the majority of the more highly organised plants. Moreover, the most various metamorphoses may occur in the shoots of Mosses, as in those of the vascular plants. They produce runners with small leaves, which

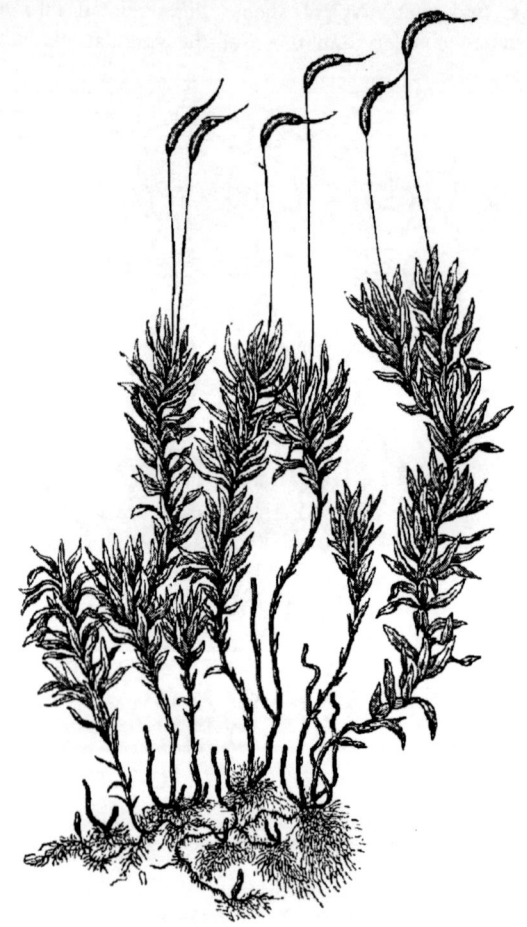

FIG. 62.—*Catharinea undulata*, a moss. From the creeping rooted rhizomes are developed upright leafy shoots, the older of which bear the long-stalked sporogonia (natural size; after Schimper).

sooner or later become rooted again and form upright leaf shoots, or they produce tubers, rhizomes, &c.; these all very small, and of simple cell-structure. A special peculiarity of the true Mosses, however, lies in the production of a system of shoots consisting merely of cell-filaments, the so-called protonema; which possesses in all essential points the nature of a shoot, without developing the typical perfection of the moss-shoot. From this protonema are developed, as lateral outgrowths, not only roots but also the proper shoots of the Moss, which in their turn are the bearers of the sexual organs; the protonema may thus be looked upon as a simple preliminary stage of the whole vegetative body of the Moss. The leaf-like plates of tissue, abounding in chlorophyll, which sometimes occur on the

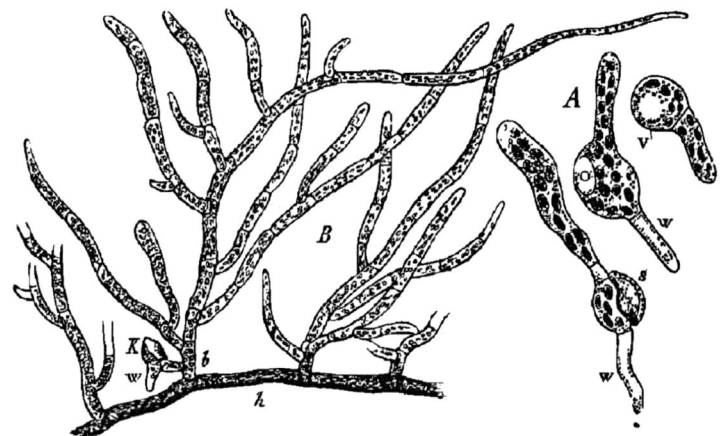

FIG 63.—*Funaria hygrometrica   A* germinating spores, *v* vacuole, *w* root, *s* exosporium, *B* part of a developed protonema, about three weeks after germination, *h* a prostrate main shoot, with brown walls and oblique septa, from which erect branches proceed, *K* rudiment of a leaf shoot, with root *w* (*A* X 550, *B* X about 90)

protonema, but which cannot be regarded as leaves in the narrower sense of the word (*Tetraphis*), also deserve special mention. Like numerous similar structures in the Algæ, Liverworts, and even the prothallia of the Ferns, we have here to do with shoot-formations which, like the cladodes of vascular plants, serve essentially

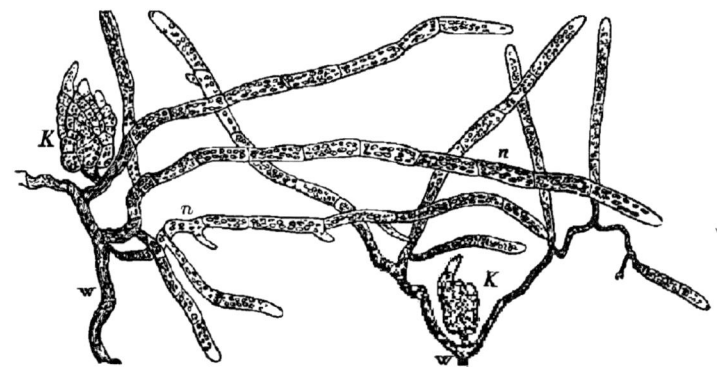

FIG 64.—Protonematous outgrowth from the root of *Mnium hornum*, with leaf-forming buds *K   w w* the roots of an inverted sod, from which the protonema filaments (*n n*) shoot forth (X90)

only the purpose of presenting a larger quantity of chlorophyll to the light, and so aid nutrition.

In some subdivisions of the Liverworts we meet with flat broad shoot-axes, which, provided with rhizoids on their under sides, either possess leaf-like membranes or entirely dispense with them · this, however, from our point of view, does not affect the shoot-nature of these kinds of structure. We have here to deal simply with flat shoots; which by means of their chlorophyll contents, their rising above the substratum, and their ability to form reproductive organs, make their shoot-nature sufficiently evident. Nothing can be more superfluous than the morphological hair-splitting, which sees in organs of this kind anything essentially different from the leaf-shoots of other plants, simply because the external segmentation into axis and leaf is wanting, a want which is compensated by the flat extension and the abundance of chlorophyll.

In the endless variety of forms of the Algæ, any one who is accustomed to the great constancy of the typical form of shoot of the vascular plants and higher Mosses, is struck by the fact that here, even in closely allied subdivisions, the development of shoots containing chlorophyll, so far as their segmentation into leaf and axis is concerned, is extremely various. Nature, one might almost say, has here given free play to the formative forces of vegetable substance, under the simpler conditions of life which water presents; while for the higher development under more difficult relations, such as the life of the land-plant brings with itself, the typical form of leaf-shoot has evidently proved itself to be most to the purpose, and with progressive development of the vegetable kingdom has been retained almost without exception Where in the Algæ a sharper segmentation appears, there the difference between parts usually extended flat and rich in chlorophyll, and thin stem-like parts—that is, the main difference of leaves and axes—makes itself evident. This occurs in a very peculiar, and, in comparison with the vascular plants and Mosses, very strange form, in the Laminariæ. The whole of the perennial plant (Fig. 66) consists of a shoot

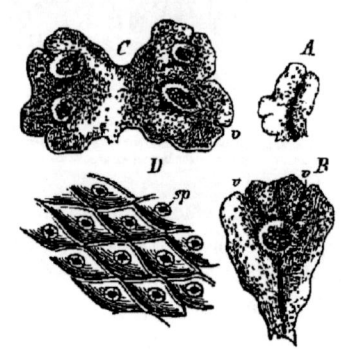

FIG 66.—*Marchantia polymorpha* (slightly magnified) *A B* young shoots, *C* the two shoots, with cupules and gemmæ, which arise from a gemma, *v v* the depressed apical region, *D* a portion of epidermis seen from above, *sp* stomata on the rhomboid areolæ (more strongly magnified)

rooted below, the lower part of which (*s*), like a leaf-stalk, bears at its upper end (*b*) a lamina, which may be compared to a large foliage leaf The growing point of this remarkable shoot is situated at the boundary of the stalk and lamina (at *e*); it produces annually, to a certain extent by intercalation, a new lamina (*b′*), upon which the older one (*b*) decays away

Thus, although a great difference exists formally between a shoot of this kind and a leaf-shoot of the higher plants, it is nevertheless clear that, by means of the segmentation indicated, the same physiological advantages are attained on the whole as are provided by the ordinary segmentation into leaf and axis. The physiological similarity is exhibited still more in the throwing off of the flattened leaf-like portion, and in the replacement of it by a new organ of a similar kind. In another also highly organised genus of Algæ, *Sargassum*, we find forms of shoot which deviate but little from those of vascular plants. From the growing point of a thin axis arise flat leaves (*b*), separated by internodes; and, in addition, portions of the shoot serve as swim bladders (*l*), and sexual organs (*f*) are exclusively formed on others—a division of labour which is elsewhere met with only in highly organised plants. In the species of *Fucus*, on the other hand, there is generally no segmentation into leaf and axis, and the branched shoots are themselves flat, or even band-shaped, like the cladodes of many Phanerogams. In many other genera of Algæ are found richly branched shoots without any flat tissueplates whatever; the assimilating chlorophyll lies beneath the surface of the cylindrical body of tissue (Fig. 68), the physiological behaviour of which may very well be compared with the shoot system of *Spartium junceum* or of *Psilotum*. Again, in other cases the whole shoot consists of a short rooted basal portion, on which are situated leaf-like, thin plates of tissue (Fig. 69), from the margin of which similar organs often grow forth, like the segments of an *Opuntia*. I must unfortunately deny myself in this superficial survey, from going more deeply into the variety of forms prevailing here; since just those organographical relations which are most important for us could only be rendered clear by means of numerous drawings and detailed descriptions. On account of their importance, however, mention must finally be made of those Algæ the growth of which is not accompanied by cell-division, and which thus, as one is accustomed to say, only consist of one cell: this, however, does not prevent these plants occasionally attaining considerable magnitude, and, in addition to the formation of roots, the most varied segmentation of their shoots also. In this sense the genera *Caulerpa*, *Botrydium*, *Vaucheria*, and others (cp. p. 4) have already been referred to.

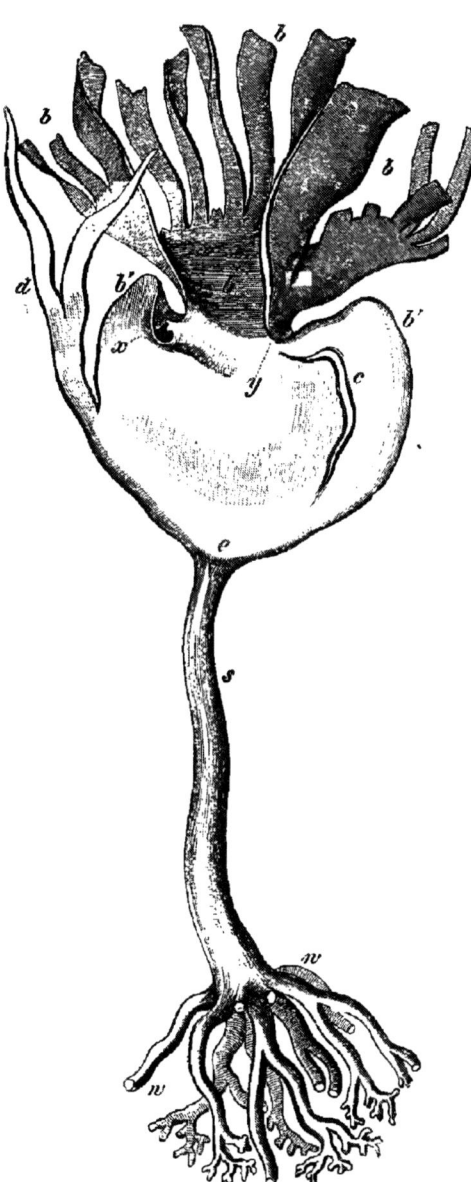

FIG. 66.—*Laminaria Cloustoni.*

I have previously insisted upon the fact that in the simplest Algæ, as in the simplest Fungi, the segmentation of the vegetative body into root and shoot does not occur. It has already been mentioned, also, that the accepted description of the segmentation of more highly developed Fungi into mycelium and fructification, signifies essentially, from our point of view, nothing further than the segmentation into root and shoot; only, we have here to do with plants devoid of chlorophyll, in which, as in all other plants devoid of chlorophyll, the shoot is no

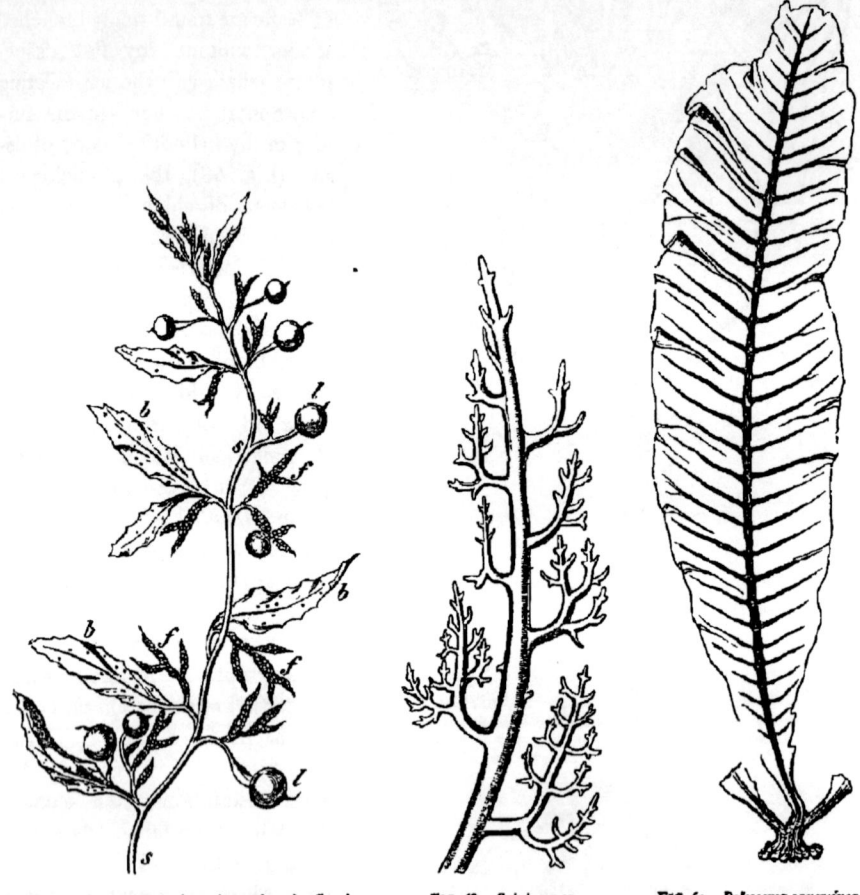

FIG. 67.—*Sargassum vulgare* (natural size) Cp the text

FIG. 68.—*Gelidium* sp

FIG. 69.—*Delesseria sanguinea*; leaf like shoot, with anchoring root below

longer an organ of assimilation, but only the bearer of reproductive cells, as which, with few exceptions, it also protrudes above the nourishing substratum. In the large common Mushrooms and Toadstools of the woods and fields, the stalked pileus, on the under side of which the spores arise, is thus the fructification, or, according to our view, the shoot reduced to a mere fructification; the proper root-system being extended in the earth as the mycelium. That we are here again concerned with innumerable varieties of form, is evident in the richness in species of the Fungi, and in the great variety of their modes of life.

In this condensed treatment of comparative organography, I have aimed essentially at bringing forward only those points which may serve for the understanding of subsequent general physiological expositions. To this end we have regarded the different parts of plants simply as organs, i e as instruments for definite physiological functions, and in particular, only those which, in contrast to the Reproductive organs, have been distinguished as the Vegetative organs. This physiological treatment of organography, hitherto unduly repressed in Botany under the sway of the morphological school, is moreover by no means intended to exclude the purely formal comparison, as it has hitherto been conducted under the name of morphology; its effect on the latter is only to be that of explaining and enlightening. That the comparison of organic forms from purely physiological points of view, which are exclusively concerned with the functions of the organs, can exhaust *one* side only of the subject, and that, besides the functional signification of the organs, phylogenetic relations also exist, which, quite independently of the mode of life of organisms, concern their relationship and their descent, requires in our time no proof. The whole of systematic botany and morphology, so far as they have any meaning at all, have to do exclusively with this; and it is just because this morphological and phylogenetic mode of consideration of plants has always prevailed in Botany, and now threatens to overgrow every other interest in plants, that I have considered it to the purpose to

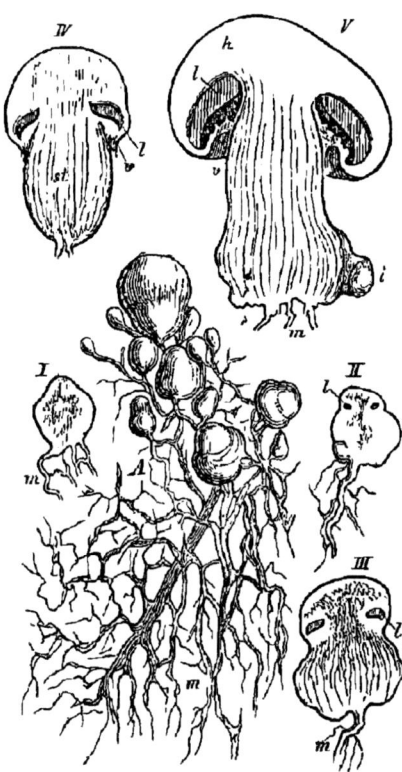

FIG 70.—*Agaricus campestris A* shows the mycelium (*m*) beset with fructification, *I—V* development of the fructification (natural size)

obtain, by means of the preceding lectures, a more fitting basis for our physiological considerations

Only this one point I would yet emphasise here. According to my view, progress in the department of Botany lies in the physiological direction, and sooner or later, starting from physiological points of view, we shall also come to understand the proper morphological hereditary properties of the organs, and the causes of their variations. The purely formal relations of organisms among themselves also, chiefly disclosed by the history of development, must sooner or later be expressed as the effects of physiological causes which can be definitely stated.

LECTURE VI.

ON THE CELLULAR STRUCTURE OF PLANTS. PROTOPLASM.
NUCLEUS. CELL-WALL

THAT plants consist of cells is now known to every well-informed man; yet the true meaning of the word Cell may be quite clear to but few, the less so since biologists themselves, even now, hold and discuss the most different opinions upon it. To many, the cell is always an independent living being, which sometimes exists for itself alone, and sometimes 'becomes joined with' others—millions of its like, in order to form a cell-colony, or, as Häckel has named it for the plant particularly, a cell-republic. To others again, to whom the author of this book also belongs, cell-formation is a phenomenon very general, it is true, in organic life, but still only of secondary significance, at all events, it is merely one of the numerous expressions of the formative forces which reside in all matter, in the highest degree, however, in organic substance.

Such being the case, it is certainly best to leave every theory aside for the present, and confine ourselves to the most immediate experience, and to the consideration of a few objects which, without any controversy, consist of cells.

Let us first turn for this purpose to Fig. 71, which represents the transverse section of the flower-stalk of a plant closely allied to our common kitchen Onion. We see at once that its area is occupied by a mesh-work, or is divided into numerous closed chambers. The walls of the latter consist, as is perceived at once, of solid, and, as further experience will show, even of extraordinarily solid substance. the spaces bounded by these contain fluid, and, as we shall see later, other constituents still more important. The size of the chambers is very various, and so is their form. From our figure it is at once observed, however, that the chambers resembling one another in size and form are aggregated in layers or groups, arranged on the transverse section of the organ of the plant

The individual mesh-like spaces or chambers are the cells: the groups of similar cells are the various forms of tissue.

An equally thin longitudinal section through the same flower stalk would present a less evident, and apparently less orderly picture. Careful consideration would, however, even on the longitudinal section, again enable us to recognise chambers closed on all sides, and bounded by a net-work of solid walls; only in this case the chambers appear more extended in the longitudinal direction (especially those marked (*g*) in the figure) in the form of very long narrow tubes

A careful comparison of the two figures—i. e the transverse and longitudinal sections—leads to the conclusion that the various linear networks of the longitudinal and transverse sections are due to the presence of chambers closed on all sides, the cavities of which are separated from one another by solid walls, just like the rooms in a large building   The transverse section of a portion of a plant thus corresponds to the ground-plan of a building; the longitudinal section to the elevation of the same.

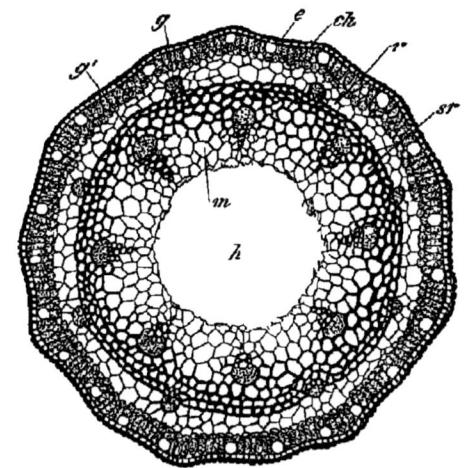

FIG 71 – Transverse section of the flower scape of *Allium Schoeno-prasum* (x 30)   *e* epidermis, *ch* cells containing chlorophyll, *r* colourless cortical parenchyma, *m* pith parenchyma, *g g'* vascular bundles, *sr* ring of sclerenchyma

Apart from those Algæ and Fungi which we have already learned to recognise as non-cellular plants, we find in all plants and parts of plants this chamber-like structure; and we still designate the single chambers by the same term which their discoverer, Robert Hooke (1667), employed for them, because he was struck by the similarity of the chambers with the cell-structure of a honeycomb. We shall of course see that this similarity is an extremely superficial one, although in the cells of plants, as in those of a honeycomb, living contents become formed, and formative nutritive materials are stored up

If we regard the longitudinal or transverse section of a very young portion of a plant, such as a growing point (Fig. 72) or the transverse section through ordinary wood or cork, we remark that all the cells fit closely into one another on all sides, since between any two neighbouring cells there is always only *one* solid wall, like a simple wall between two chambers of a house   This kind of cellular structure originally exists in every cellular plant, and accords with the origin of the cells during growth   But very often it happens that in the course of the further development, the chambers separate partly or entirely from one another, the simple primary partition walls becoming more or less split; and each single chamber thus becomes bounded by a wall of its own, at certain places, or over its whole circumference   This case is observed very generally in the tissue of green leaves, especially in the lower half of the thin lamina   The cells, at first fitting closely on all sides, have separated from one another during the growth of the leaf, and are now connected only at isolated points.   The case is similar also in the seed-coat of the Gourd, of which Fig 73 represents a transverse section.   The inner layer of this seed-coat consists of cells which have eventually become separated from one another, since through growth they have assumed various irregular forms.   In such cases empty spaces exist between the now independent chambers or cells, which are termed intercellular spaces, or lacunæ. In the ordinary succulent tissues of Stems, Roots, Fruits, etc., these intercellular spaces are relatively very small, since the cells of these portions of the plant, at first fitting closely on all sides, separate a little from one another only here and there. It often happens, however, especially in aquatics and bog-plants, that the large cells of the succulent tissue (parenchyma) become separated from one another in layers, so that large chamber-like cavities arise, which are separated from one another by simple layers of cells An excellent example of this, easily perceptible even with the unaided eye, is presented by the leaf-sheaths of the species of *Musa*.

This mutual isolation of cells, resulting spontaneously during growth, may under certain circumstances be produced artificially, especially when the partition-walls are thick; either simply by means of continued boiling in water, or by long maceration in a mixture of chlorate of potash and nitric acid, or even by slow rotting. In the excrement of plant-eating animals, also, we find the undigested cells often completely isolated from one another under the influence of the gastric and

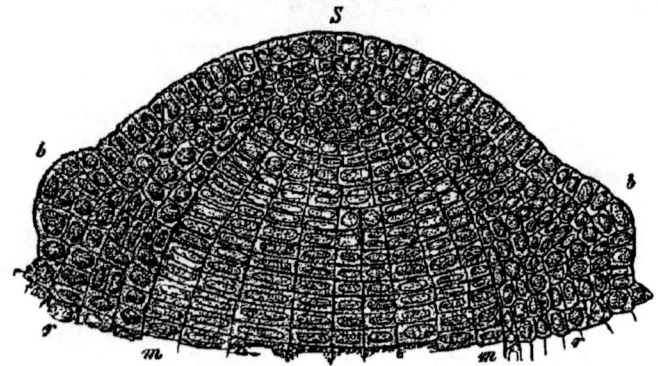

FIG. 7a.—Longitudinal section through the growing point of a winter bud of *Abies pectinata* (× about 200). *S* the apex of the growing point, *b b* youngest leaves, *r* cortex, *m* pith

intestinal juices. In such cases, a splitting of the originally simple partition wall of neighbouring cells is effected by external influences; or a thin layer, the so-called middle lamella, lying in the thick partition wall, is dissolved However, even in the normal course of vegetation, and especially in the formation of reproductive organs, a complete isolation of the cells occurs in such a manner that, finally, they become emptied out of the reproductive organs in the form of a more or less fine dust The pollen from the opened anthers of the stamens of flowering plants, for instance, consists of such isolated cells; and occasionally, as in the Pines and many Nettle-like plants, these are carried away in great quantities by the wind. The spores of most Cryptogams are further examples The fine heavy dust, bought in the apothecaries' shops under the name of *Lycopodium*, consists entirely and simply of such spores; and similarly we can shake out of any moss capsule, or blow away from a tuft of the commonest mould (*Penicillium glaucum*), a still finer powder. If the unfolded pileus of a ripe Mushroom or Toad-stool is laid with the lower side on paper, it is found, after some hours, that a picture of its lamellated or tubular underside has been formed,—a figure in dust, which has arisen by millions of small cells (i. e. spores) having become loosened from the Fungus, and fallen on to the paper beneath.

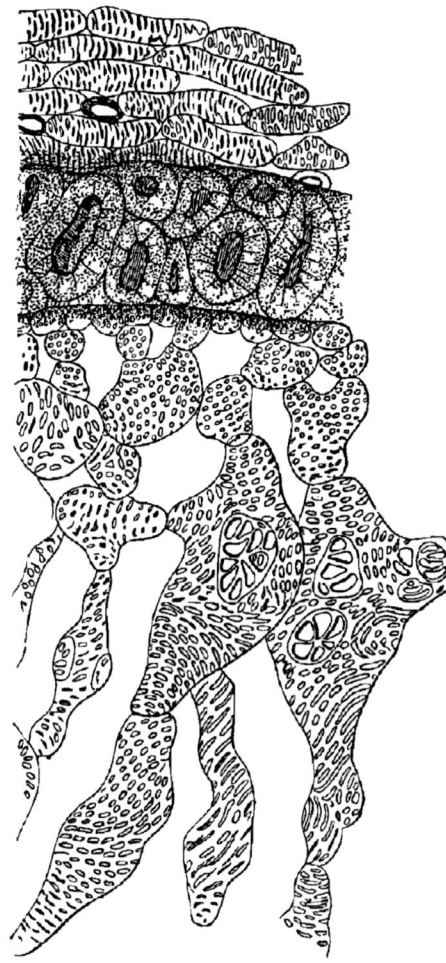

FIG. 73.—Portion of a transverse section through the testa of the seed of a Gourd.

FIG. 74.—Ripe pollen grain of *Cichorium Intybus.* The almost globular cell membrane is beset with ridges connected in a net like manner, each of which bears pectinate series of spines

In the first place, then, and especially when we investigate anatomically the more highly developed plants, the cells appear as chambers, or as a framework in the substance of the plant. We see, however, that these chambers may also become separated in part or wholly from one another, so that they finally appear as independent bodies. In many Algæ and Fungi, (e. g. the Yeast fungus) indeed, all the cells arising during growth become separated from one another. Finally I may again refer to the non-cellular plants or *Cœloblastæ.* We have found examples of these already in the genera *Caulerpa, Botrydium,* and *Vaucheria,* and have seen that their substance is not divided up into cell-chambers. But every such plant arises primarily by the growth of an isolated cell, which may assume the most various forms later on. A fully grown plant of this kind may thus, in a certain sense, be considered as a single cell; on the other hand, however, it appears in comparison with ordinary plants as a non-cellular plant, because in it the formation of chambers during growth, on which the cellular structure depends, is suppressed.

It follows from what has already been said, and will become still more evident subsequently, that we must not imagine the cellular structure of a plant to be due to cells previously independent becoming united with one another to form an aggregate, but we must regard the cells as small portions of the growing plant-substance, which either remain united to one another, as is usually the case, or eventually become separated from one another. According as we keep the one or the other case in view, the cells appear as mere chambers and parts of the growing plant-body, or as independent living organisms from which new plants arise by growth. It depends, therefore, entirely upon our mode of consideration, and upon the point of departure of our consideration, whether we regard the cells as independent so-called elementary organisms, or merely as parts of a multi-cellular plant.

Our consideration of cells has hitherto been particularly concerned with their external boundary, which is afforded by the solid cell-wall or cell-membrane; and in a larger cellular plant these walls or membranes form the solid framework, within which, in the cell-chambers and partly in the framework itself, the fluid sap moves and all other substances of the plant are contained. It now concerns us to make ourselves more closely acquainted with the matters which are contained in the chambers—in the cells. In very many cases, e.g. ordinary wood, cork, bark, or even old dried-up pith from shoot-axes (Elder pith), or the tissue of fallen leaves, &c., we find the cell-chambers empty, i.e. they contain either merely air, or at most clear water or a few granules. The same is the case also with the integuments of seeds and dry pericarps. We have become accustomed to consider such parts of plants as dead or perished; since experience teaches, without exception, that when the cell-chambers are empty in the manner stated, the parts grow no more, that no more metabolism occurs in them, and that no new cells are formed in them. They are in these respects inactive, physiologically dead, but they may be nevertheless of great use in the general economy of the plant, as we shall learn subsequently with respect to wood, elastic fibres, and cork. It is, moreover, a peculiarity of the more highly developed plants, especially of the so-called vascular plants, that masses of such dead cells (contributing to the life of the plant however) become accumulated. In the Mosses, Algæ, and Fungi this occurs only incidentally. In every living plant, however, are found layers, strands, and other aggregates of living cells; i.e. such in which further growth, cell-multiplication, and chemical processes of life take place. In highly organised plants, it is the soft cortex of older parts, the succulent shoot-axes and leaves, the growing points of the shoots and roots, the flowers, unripe fruits and seeds, which consist of such living cells. In Mosses, Algæ, and Fungi the whole living body of the plant generally is composed of them.

The contents of the cell-chambers in such living parts of the plant, in the narrower sense of the word, may be exceedingly various. Very generally there are found together with a watery fluid, the cell-sap, more or less numerous starch-grains, drops of fat, small crystals, and in ripe seeds so-called aleurone-grains. In green leaves, and in other green parts of the plant, green roundish or polygonal granules of soft substance are particularly conspicuous: these are the chlorophyll granules, which in many Algæ are replaced by green bands, plates, and the like. All these contents of the living cells when sufficiently magnified attract the attention at once, and up to about the year 1840 they were almost the only contents which were noticed in the cell. But on more careful observation of the interior of the cell-chambers, especially when the granular structures named are not present in too great quantity, there is perceived in every living vegetable cell another substance of a very peculiar kind, which generally presents itself as a slimy, or occasionally gelatinous, or sometimes more or less solid mass, and either completely fills the cavity of the cell, or only clothes the wall as a thin layer, or traverses the sap cavity of the cell in the form of a network

This is the universally known and yet essentially unknown protoplasm, that substance which, according to the researches of the last forty years, represents the proper living body of every cell; and which, as has been gradually proved, is the actual basis of life of all organisms, both of animals and of plants, and the investigation of which therefore, in our time especially, is the object of the Zoologist and Botanist. In the protoplasm itself, again, is found the nucleus of the cell, which generally presents itself as a definitely formed part of the protoplasm Only one nucleus is usually present; but in large, and especially in elongated cells, several or many nuclei may be distributed in the protoplasm More-over, particularly in the non-cellular plants among the Algæ and Fungi, hundreds, or even thousands of nuclei may be found in the protoplasm, where formerly, up to the year 1878, their presence had been alto-gether overlooked

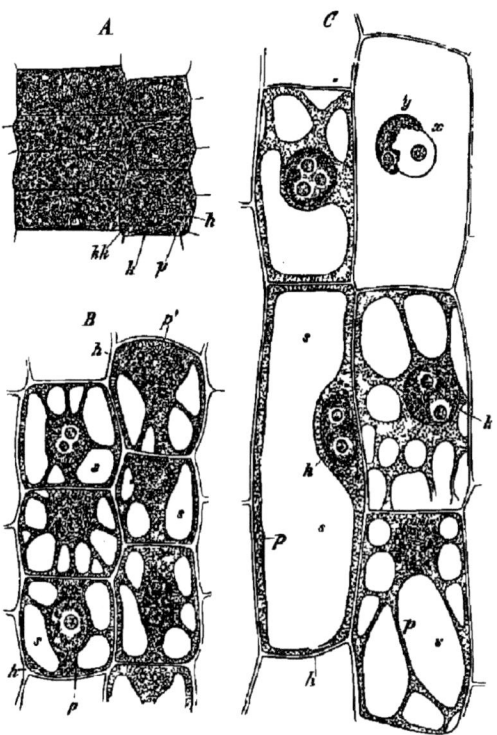

FIG 75.—Parenchyma cells from the middle layer of the root cortex of *Fritillaria imperialis* [longitudinal section × 550] *A* very young cells still devoid of cell sap, lying close to the apex of the root, *B* cells of the same description about 2 mm. from the apex of the root, the cell sap (*s*) forms isolated drops In the protoplasm (*p*), plates of protoplasm separate these drops *C* cells of the same description about 7—8 m m from the apex of the root, the two cells to the right below are seen from the front, the large cell to the left below is in optical section The cell to the right above is opened by the section, the cell-nucleus shows a peculiar appearance of swelling under the influence of the penetrating water (*x y*)

From what has been stated, the protoplasm, with its nucleus, and the cell-membrane or cell-wall, appear as the essentials of every vegetable cell. The other visible substances are temporary structures, nutritive materials, products of metabolism, or refuse matters and the like, to which we shall return in detail when we are considering the theory of nutrition.

For the present, however, we will keep to the essential constituents of the vegetable cell—the protoplasm, nucleus, and membrane; and these we will now study more in detail

The Protoplasm, the fundamental significance of which for the whole life of the plant has been already indicated, consists of albuminous substances, i.e. of chemical compounds which behave essentially like common egg-albumen, or the casein of milk, or like the coagulable substance of blood, &c. These chemical compounds are composed of the elements carbon, hydrogen, oxygen, nitrogen, and sulphur. they are the most complex of all organic chemical combinations, and, as the result of their decomposition a large number of simpler organic carbon compounds are formed. The statement that protoplasm consists of albuminous substances is, however, not to be understood to mean that proteid and protoplasm are identical. For by the former is meant only the chemical compound of the elements mentioned; whereas the protoplasm composed of this possesses a definite organisation, which is foreign to the chemical compound as such. The case is similar to that of the chemical compound of chlorine and sodium (common salt) on the one hand, and, on the other hand, of the crystals of common salt. It is, moreover, only an abbreviation to say that protoplasm consists of proteids. This is only its essentially distinctive character; but, as a matter of fact, living protoplasm always contains a larger or smaller quantity of water, and if this is withdrawn up to a certain minimum it loses its vital activity, and on the withdrawal of more water even its ability to live. The water belongs to the molecular structure of the living protoplasm in the same sense as the water of crystallization is necessary to the structure of very many crystals, which lose their crystalline form on the withdrawal of the water of crystallization.

On examination we find, moreover, that in the protoplasm mineral constituents are further contained, which, after its combustion, remain over as incombustible ash, a series of salts

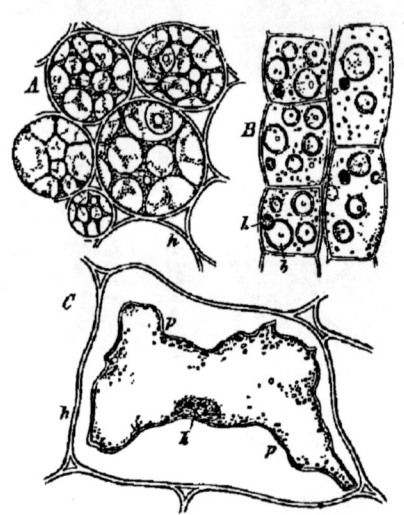

Fig 76.—Forms of the protoplasm enclosed in cells *A* and *B* of *Zea Mays A* cells from the first leaf-sheath of a seedling, *B* from the first internode of the same, *C* from the tuber of *Helianthus tuberosus*, after the action of Iodine and dilute Sulphuric acid, *k* cell wall, *k* nucleus, *p* protoplasm.

in which alkalies, lime, magnesia, phosphoric acid, and sulphuric acid predominate. Even so far, the protoplasm appears to be a mixture of numerous chemical compounds, and we have cause to believe, in addition, that continual chemical changes are connected with the vital processes in it, the products of which remain, at least for a time, between the molecules of the protoplasm. The substance of the protoplasm here described appears quite homogeneous under the microscope, even with very strong magnifying powers. In actively vegetating cells, however, this substance, in itself homogeneous and transparent, is thickly set with very numerous small granules (microsomes), these appear even with the strongest magnifying powers as dots, the true nature of which, from a chemical point of view, and the importance of which for the life of the protoplasm, are still doubtful, although we may assume as probable that they are very finely divided nutritive matters which are employed in the vital processes.

In the tissue of growing points and embryos, the protoplasm usually fills up the entire space enclosed by the thin cell-walls, and shares it as yet only with the relatively large nucleus (compare Fig. 72). As Fig 75 shows, however, the protoplasm assumes different forms with the growth of the cells As the cells become larger, the protoplasm does not increase in an equal degree, but there are formed in it cavities, filled with fluid, i.e with cell-sap. The protoplasm itself then assumes the form of plates and threads, united in a net-like manner, which radiate from a central clump investing the nucleus, to the periphery of the cell, there to pass over into a more or less thin layer of protoplasm, which here clothes the cell-wall like a hollow sac. The more the cells enlarge with progressive growth, the larger the sap-vacuoles in the protoplasm become, until, very often, there remains of the latter only a thin lamella lying on the cell-wall, somewhat as a wall-paper on a chamber wall. The elongation of the cells, as we see, is essentially connected with the absorption of water, without a corresponding increase of the protoplasm. In very succulent parts of plants it is therefore by no means easy to see the protoplasm with the microscope: in the large

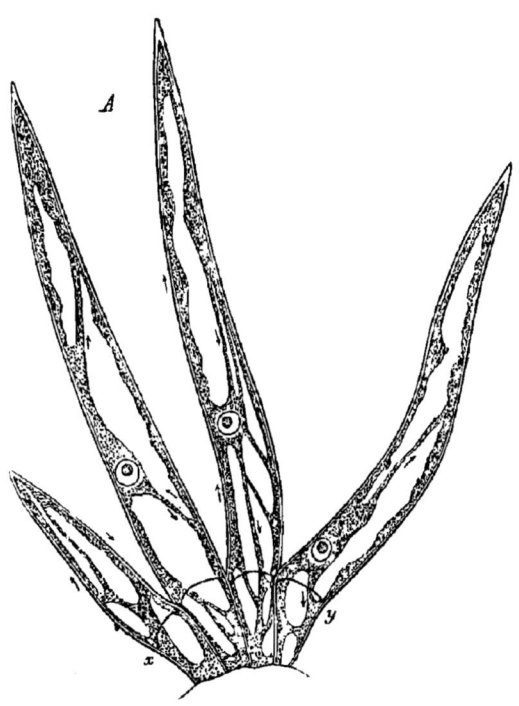

FIG 77.—Stellate hair on the calyx of the young flower bud of *Althæa rosea*

parenchyma cells of the root-cortex, the pith and the cortex of vegetating shoots, in leaves, fruits, and so forth, it often requires special methods of investigation to bring into view the exceedingly thin protoplasmic utricle which encloses the large sap-cavity of the cell, and lies close upon the cell-wall. This is accomplished by means of various contracting media, e g dilute solutions of iodine, alcohol, glycerine, &c., by which the protoplasm is killed, and compelled to separate from the cell-wall in the form of a pellicle, sometimes exceedingly thin

It often happens, however, that, with vigorous growth of the cells, and therefore with considerable enlargement of their cavities, the protoplasm also becomes highly nourished and increased in mass. In such cases there are found, even in large cells, considerable quantities of protoplasm, usually so distributed that a thicker or thinner layer of it clothes the inner side of the cell-wall, while a more or less massive clump envelopes the nucleus, from which threads or bands of protoplasm pass out to the wall. This arrangement of the protoplasm is very easily seen under the microscope, without disturbance to its life, in the hairs on the epidermis of many plants. If we observe such a living cell attentively and for a long time, the substance of the protoplasm is seen to be in continual movement—one of the most remarkable of phenomena, which allows of the

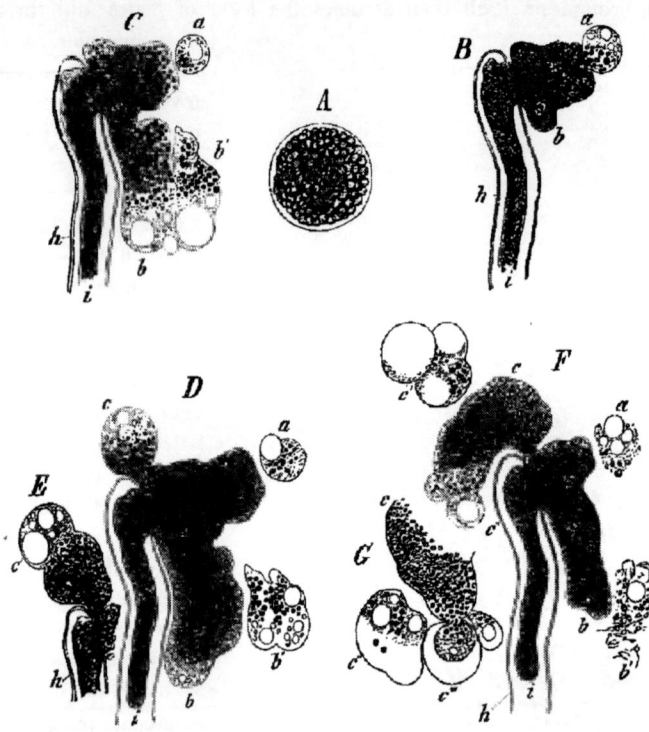

FIG. 78.—*B* to *G* protoplasm from a ruptured filament of *Vaucheria terrestris*, slowly emerging in water, and in various successive conditions, at intervals of about five minutes. *h* cell-membrane of the ruptured filament; *i* the portion of protoplasm still in the filament; *a* (in *B, C, D, F*) a sphere of protoplasm becoming detached, forming. vacuoles, and then becoming deliquescent (in *F*); *b* a branch of the protoplasm from which the mass *b'* separates off. This is isolated in *D*, and then becomes deliquescent in *F*; *c* and *c'* behave similarly. *G* shows the further changes of the portion *c''* in *F*; *A* a recently escaped clump of protoplasm, rounded off into a sphere, the chlorophyll granules lying all together inside, and hyaline protoplasm enveloping the whole as a skin.

immediate recognition of the internal disturbances of equilibrium taking place in the protoplasm. These movements are rendered visible by means of the finer or coarser granules distributed in the protoplasm. These are seen to travel from the cell-wall in the strands of protoplasm towards the nucleus, returning thence by the same or other strands to the peripheral layer; and here gliding onwards again, sooner or later to be carried once more through other threads of protoplasm to the nucleus, and thence to turn back as before. In many water-plants the movement of the protoplasm is simpler: it forms a relatively thick layer on the inner side of the cell-wall, and is very watery, therefore resembling a fluid, and moves as a flowing stream along the cell-wall, while with it float the nucleus and the chlorophyll corpuscles, and incidentally small crystals of calcium oxalate. This form of movement has been distinguished as rotation of the protoplasm from that first described, which is termed circulation

Circulation and Rotation, however, are only special forms of the movements of protoplasm within closed cells. If cells rich in protoplasm, especially those of the Cœloblastic Algæ, are ruptured under the microscope, the protoplasm gushes forth out of the opened cell-membrane as a viscid mass, which may assume the most various forms. these are by no means simply those of a viscous fluid body, but are produced by peculiar movements within the protoplasm An

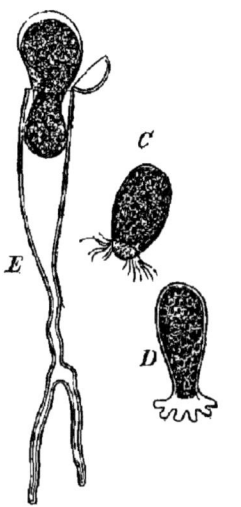

FIG 79 —*C* swarm spore of *Œdogonium* free and motile, *D* the same after it has become fixed and has formed the organ of attachment, *F* exit of all the protoplasm of a germinating plant in the form of a swarm-spore (X 350. After Pringsheim *Jahrb f wiss Bot* i Taf i)

example of this is illustrated in Fig 78 Here may be noted the remarkable fact that separated portions of the exuded protoplasm, provided they contain one or more nuclei, may become surrounded after some time with a cell-membrane, grow, and form a new plant Such is the case not only with the *Vaucheria* represented in the figure, but, according to Schmitz, also with some other non-cellular Algæ (*Siphonocladium* and *Vallonia*) What happens in such cases by means of external accidental influences, is constant in the reproduction of very many Algæ. Either the whole mass of protoplasm of their cells becomes loosened from the surrounding wall, and emerges through an aperture in the latter, or the protoplasmic body is first broken up into a large number of individual nucleated portions, which are then expelled from the parent cell-membrane. Such free protoplasmic bodies — the swarm-spores of the Algæ — are furnished with more or less fine cilia, by the aid of which they swim about in water, just like *Infusoria*, until they become fixed in some place, surround themselves with a cell-membrane, and begin to grow. The movement of such protoplasmic bodies, which are generally ovoid in shape, is two-fold, they revolve round the axis, and at the same time travel forward in the water, a motion similar to that of a planet in space, or of a shot fired from a rifled cannon

To the most remarkable phenomena in the life of protoplasm belong the processes observed in a subdivision of the Fungi, the *Myxomycetes* During their vegetative condition, before they develope their spores, these organisms consist entirely of naked protoplasm (i e not surrounded with a cell-membrane) which occasionally creeps forth in large quantities out of the nourishing substratum of foliage or tan on to the surface, and is found for hours in active movement from place to place as a so-called plasmodium. This phenomenon is easily observed in the so-called 'flowers of tan' On moist, sultry summer mornings, there issues from old tan in the pits, or in greenhouses and hot-beds, a bright yellow, apparently liquid substance, which collects in the form of large flat cakes, occasionally pounds in weight and some centimetres thick, and the surface of which is sometimes smooth, sometimes covered with numerous branched excrescences. In greenhouses it may happen that this substance (*Æthalium septicum*) creeps up the stems of plants a metre high and more, in the form of thin threads, and becomes collected above on large leaves as thick cakes the size of the hand. If large quantities of tan, in which the yellow clumps of *Æthalium* are already recognisable, are placed on a dish early in the morning, and covered with a bell-glass and

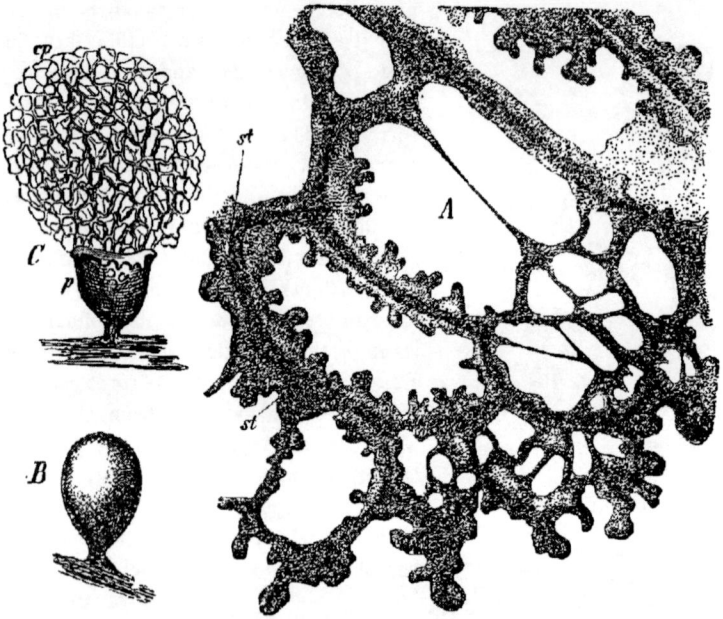

FIG. 80.—A plasmodium of *Didymium leucopus* (after Cienkowsky, × 350). *B* fructification of *Arcyria incarnata*, still closed ; *C* the same after rupture of the wall *p* and extension of the capillitium *cp* (after De Bary, × 20).

allowed to stand in a room, the movements of the *Æthalium* may be observed for days together. Occasionally it creeps over the edge of the dish on to the table, and spreads on this, forming threads and broad cakes with undulating or moss-like surfaces, until it finally becomes rigid and breaks up into innumerable small cells. If wet glass slips are placed vertically in the tan already containing the *Æthalium*, it creeps up upon these ; and if brought under the microscope the form and movement of the substance may be more exactly observed (Fig. 80). There remains no doubt whatever that we have here to do with a structure which resembles in every detail the circulating protoplasm in living plant-cells, only its mass is relatively extraordinarily large.

Besides the internal mobility of these free masses of protoplasm, by means of which they are enabled to creep upwards, they present the striking phenomenon that sooner or later, when the active external movement ceases, they assume definite forms (often in the highest degree characteristic, and resembling those of mushrooms, etc.) and then become rigid, solid substances are secreted on the surface, and partly also in the interior, while the remainder breaks up into innumerable round cells   The plasmodium of the *Myxomycetes* may be considered as the simplest type of a growing plant; a plant which during its growth produces no cell-walls at all, even at its outer surface, but is at the same time able to assume certain simple and characteristic forms.   From these relations of form of the plasmodia up to the processes of growth of the Cœloblastæ, or non-cellular Algæ and Fungi, there is practically only one step; for if we imagine a plasmodium externally surrounded by a cell-membrane, the latter not essentially hindering the configuration of the protoplasm, we have somewhat the same process as in the growth of a plasmodium, only with the difference, that by means of the solid outer membrane, less dependence upon the external world and a greater individuality of the configuration are attained.   If we imagine further that within a Cœloblast, such as a *Caulerpa, Vaucheria, Bryopsis*, etc, with progressive growth, a cleaving of the protoplasmic mass takes place in the interior by partition walls placed transversely and longitudinally, we obtain an ordinary plant, consisting of cell-chambers   The continuation of our description will show that the ordinary structure of the plant can in fact be understood according to this scheme.   Fundamentally, every plant, however highly organised, is a protoplasmic body coherent in itself, which, clothed without by a cell-wall and

FIG 81—*Didymium farinaceum* a Myxomycete The whole structure at first consists of protoplasm, from which the solid fabric here figured is separated out later, while the remainder (inside the capsule) breaks up into spores (after Rostafinski) The stellate bodies on the capsule are crystals.

traversed internally by innumerable transverse and longitudinal walls, grows; and it appears that the more vigorously this formation of chambers and walls proceeds with the nutrition of the protoplasm, the higher also is the development attained by the total organisation   It is perhaps impossible to make the significance of the protoplasm for the life of the plant clear in any other manner than this; although to those not yet familiar with the facts it certainly cannot be easy to apprehend the true meaning of the matters here stated.   Nevertheless it was an ingenious thought of Hofmeister's to put down the apparent creeping motion of the plasmodia of the *Myxomycetes*, and their later transformation into fructification, as the simplest type of growth, even for more highly organised plants.

In spite of its internal mobility and apparently viscid or slimy consistence, the protoplasm exhibits occasionally, besides the coarser structure already described, a still finer organisation, which is only to be detected by means of strong magnifying powers. This consists in reticulated fibrillæ, or in a system of very small chambers, the walls of which appear to be relatively more solid and the contents more fluid · as yet, however, but little is certainly known concerning this very fine structure.

We may regard the chlorophyll-bodies as a constituent of the protoplasm. These generally appear in the form of roundish or polygonal granular structures of soft consistence; in many lower Algæ they occur also in the form of bands or plates with similar properties. The chlorophyll-bodies, whatever form they possess, always lie embedded in the substance of the protoplasm, and usually in a middle layer of the peripheral protoplasm; so that they are separated from the cell-wall itself as well as from the sap-cavity of the cell, by a layer of colourless protoplasm If parts of plants containing chlorophyll are placed in strong alcohol, the green colouring matter becomes dissolved in the latter, and imparts to it a magnificent colouration, which in transmitted light appears green, and in reflected sunlight blood-red This green colouring matter, distinguished by the fluorescence just indicated and by other optically remarkable properties, is, however, only a very small part of the chlorophyll-granule relatively to its mass, for in cells extracted with alcohol the latter are found still of their original size and form, but now colourless It is easily recognised that the proper substance of the chlorophyll-granules is a colourless mass, which was homogeneously permeated, wholly or in part, by the colouring matter The colourless matrix remaining behind after the extraction, exhibits towards chemical reagents the essential properties of proteid substances, and the origin of the chlorophyll-granules in young cells, as well as the fact that in many lower plants the whole protoplasmic body of a cell, or the greater part of it, behaves like a chlorophyll-body, leaves no doubt that a chlo-

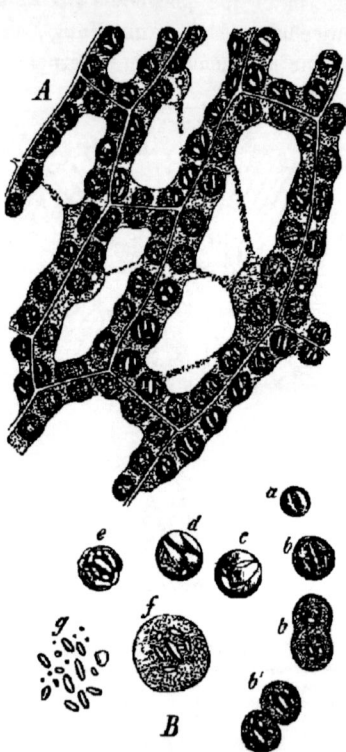

FIG 82.—*Funaria hygrometrica* (a moss) *A* cell of a leaf with protoplasm and chlorophyll-grains embedded in it. *B* chlorophyll grains with their enclosed starch, *b, b', b''* a chlorophyll-grain dividing, *f, g* a chlorophyll grain disorganised by water

rophyll-granule is practically a portion of the protoplasm tinged with chlorophyll colouring-matter. This, however, does not interfere with the fact that the chlorophyll-granules conduct themselves in many respects like individual independent organisms inside the protoplasm: for they can not only grow and under certain circumstances change their form, but they divide also, becoming constricted in the middle until the two halves separate entirely from one another. By means of such divisions into two—which are easy to discover and to follow in the leaves of the Mosses, in the cells of the *Characeæ*, and in the prothallia of Ferns, and which appeal to occur very commonly also elsewhere in the vegetable kingdom—the number of the chlorophyll-granules increases somewhat proportionally to the increase in surface of the growing cell-membrane.

It may be reserved for other opportunities to treat of the properties of the

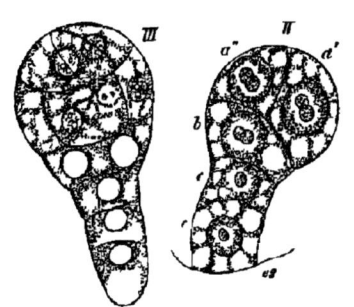

FIG 83 —Embryos in the embryo sac of *Allium cepa* they contain very large cell nuclei, each with two nucleoli

chlorophyll colouring-matter, and of the grand part which the chlorophyll-bodies play in the vegetable kingdom as instruments of assimilation; and, finally, of the small starch-granules commonly arising in them in consequence of assimilation. Here it was only proposed to state preliminarily the most necessary facts concerning the external appearance of the chlorophyll-bodies

The cell-nucleus occurs, as already stated, in the ordinary cells of the higher plants, only singly in each cell as a rule. In very long vesicular cells, and in the latex-tubes and bast-cells, on the other hand, nuclei are present in larger numbers; and in Algæ and Fungi it happens, when the cells are spacious or very long, that two, several, or even hundreds and thousands of nuclei (which are then usually very small and difficult to observe) exist in a cell[1] In accordance with its general behaviour, the cell-nucleus may always be considered as a peculiarly individualised and substantially somewhat distinct part of the protoplasm, from which it is commonly sharply separated in the form of a globular or ovoid mass, often lens-shaped later, or rarely in the form of a more band-like or vermiform body. In older, still living, vigorous cells, it commonly appears in the form of a vesicle, or a sphere filled with granular substance, in which is almost always to be detected a so-called nucleolus, or two, or even several So far as the discussion (vigorously

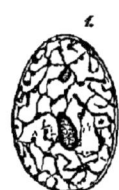
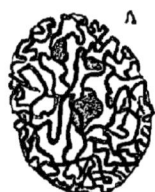

FIG 84.—Cell nuclei of *Nothoscordon fragrans* (after Flemming) 1 resting nucleus, 2 the nuclein of the nucleus arranged in a filamentous coil, 3 optical section of the coil, where apparently only granules are visible.

revived of late) concerning the nature of the cell-nucleus allows the forming of an opinion, the nucleus consists of two kinds of substances. the main mass,

---

[1] More details concerning what has been stated in the text are found in my 'Text Book of Botany' With regard to what specially concerns the multi-nuclear cells, at that time (i e up to 1874) still unknown, cf Schmitz, *Beobachtungen uber die vielkernigen Zellen der Siphonocladiaceen* Festschrift der Naturforsch Gesellsch, Halle, 1879 The same in Sitzungsber. der niederrhein. Gesellsch fur Natur- und Heilk., Bonn, 1880, June 7, and 1879, August 4. Treub, *Sur les cellules végétales à plusieurs noyaux*, Archives néerlandaises t. xv. Johow, *Untersuchungen uber die Zellkerne in den Secretbehaltern und Parenchymzellen der Monocotylen*, Bonn, 1880.

a watery proteinaceous substance, differs apparently not very essentially from the surrounding protoplasm. Within this is present, however, a second substance in the form of granules or filaments, which, according to certain statements, is distinguished by containing phosphorus [1], and appears in a more definite form especially when, at the commencement of cell-division, the cell-nucleus itself prepares to divide. These two substances may perhaps be distinguished most advantageously by the terms *nucleoplasm* and *nuclein.* The latter is especially remarkable in that with colouring media, and particularly with Hæmatoxylin, it stains more quickly and deeply than the *nucleoplasm;* whence this reagent is also employed to make the nuclei evident, and indeed generally in very large numbers, in cells where no nuclei at all were detected formerly. In the larger fully grown cells of the higher plants, the nucleus appears generally as an inactive mass; in cells poor in protoplasm usually lying on the wall. Its prominent significance is clear, on the other hand, in two cases. First, in the growing point (Fig. 72), where the nuclei almost entirely fill up the space of the otherwise small cells, so that the mass of a growing point consists to a very great extent of nuclear substance. Yet more striking, however, appears the nucleus as an essential element of the cell during cell-formation itself: there results at this time a more definite separation of its two constituents, the nucleoplasm and the nuclein, to which I shall return later.

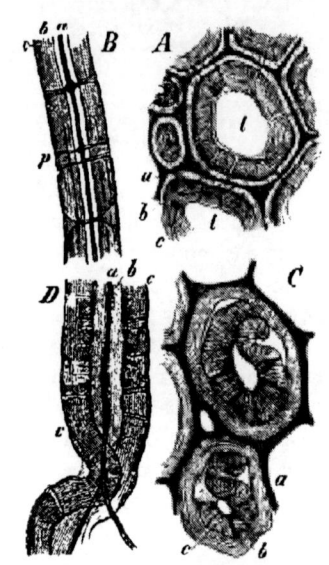

FIG. 85.—*Pteris aquilina:* structure of the brown sclerenchyma in the stem (× 550). *A* a fresh thin transverse section; *B* the longitudinal wall between two cells (fresh), a twisted pit-canal at the lower end; *C* transverse section in concentrated sulphuric acid; *D* longitudinal section of the wall in sulphuric acid; *a* the middle lamella of the wall; *b* second shell; *c* third, innermost shell of the wall; *p* pore canals; *l* lumen of the cell.

The third essential constituent of a vegetable cell, the cell-membrane or cell-wall, forms, as already mentioned, the external solid boundary of the cell. In its primitive state it consists of a peculiar chemical compound, cellulose, which is composed of Carbon, Hydrogen, and Oxygen. This substance is remarkable for its great resistance to the most various chemical solvent reagents; and its extra-ordinary solidity and elasticity are of especial importance for the plant. The sharp outline and impressive form of the parts of plants, and their great solidity, though containing enormous quantities of water, depend essentially upon this property of cellulose. Nevertheless, only the very thin cell-membranes in the young parts of plants, and perhaps in older parenchyma, consist of true cellulose, which is moreover always mixed with water and incombustible mineral substances. With increasing age, and according to the physiological work which the

---

[1] Zacharias, *Über die chemische Beschaffenheit des Zellkerns,* Bot. Zeitg. 1881, p. 170.

cells concerned have to fulfil in the life of the plant, both the chemical and the physical properties of the cell-wall become changed   In the great variety here met with, there may be distinguished three chief cases of metamorphoses of the substance of the cell-wall as of especially frequent occurrence · these are lignifica-tion, suberisation and the conversion into mucilage   Lignification, which we find in the typical form in the empty cells of ordinary wood, but also in many other cases, is usually associated with a considerable thickening of the otherwise very thin cell-walls   It is due to the formation of a peculiar chemical compound, which is soluble in potash solution and also in a mixture of potassium chlorate and nitric acid, and which causes the lignified cell-wall to become highly coloured when treated with iodine solution and various other substances (e.g with aniline sulphate a bright yellow)   It is to this woody substance, the so-called *xylogen*, apparently, that the peculiar properties of the lignified cell-walls are to be as-cribed.   It is distinguished above all by its great hardness and elasticity, so that it absorbs relatively but little water, and consequently increases but little in

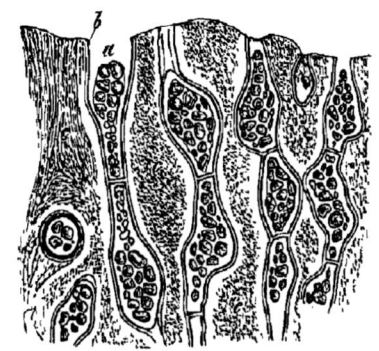

FIG 86 —Transverse section of the endosperm of *Ceratonia siliqua*. *a* granular cell contents , *b* solid walls surrounding them , *c* the so called intercellular substance—*i e* the middle swollen portion of the wall between each two cell cavities strongly magnified)

volume when thoroughly wetted, and on drying up loses but little in volume—properties upon which the endless varieties of uses of wood in the arts especially depend, and which in like manner come into consideration for the life of the plant itself   Among the most prominent peculiar-ities of lignified cell-walls (to which, more-over, I shall return in detail at a later period) is its capacity of allowing im-bibed water to move with facility between the molecules of the substance; upon which, as we shall see, depends the physiological significance of wood as an organ for con-ducting water in transpiring land plants   If the *xylogen* is extracted by means of proper solvents from the cell-wall, a skeleton of the wall of similar form remains behind, which then exhibits the ordinary reactions of cellulose

In a certain sense the suberisation of the cell-wall forms the contrast to its lignification; it consists in that in the basis of cellulose another substance, *suberin* or cork substance, is deposited   Such suberised cell-walls of which common bottle-cork, the skin of potatoes, the outer cortex or periderm of most young branches of trees, &c consists, may be somewhat thick ; they are generally, however, relatively thin, upon which depends in part the compressibility of common cork   The *suberin*, together with which are often found considerable deposits of silica and other mineral substances in addition, confers upon the cell-wall the property of being able to absorb water only in very small quantities ; and of hindering with great energy the passage of watery vapour and other gases through the cell-wall   In a word, the suberised cells have essentially the properties to which common bottle-cork owes its varied uses, because it allows the vapours of fluids to pass through it so exceedingly slowly   On this account also every part of a plant the fluids of which require to be protected against evaporation, is surrounded by suberised cell-tissue ; as the stems and older branches of woody plants, in the wood of which the current of water moves.

In like manner the outside of leaves and of young shoot-axes is clothed with a pellicle, generally exceedingly thin, the so-called cuticle, the substance of which possesses all the essential properties of suberised cell-walls. While lignification

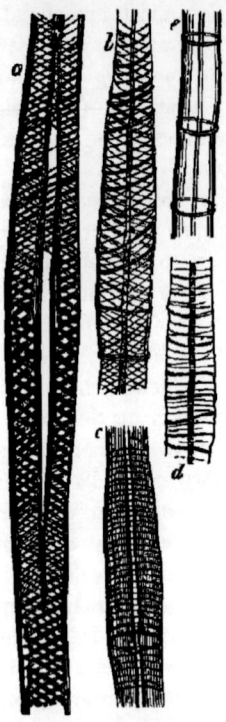

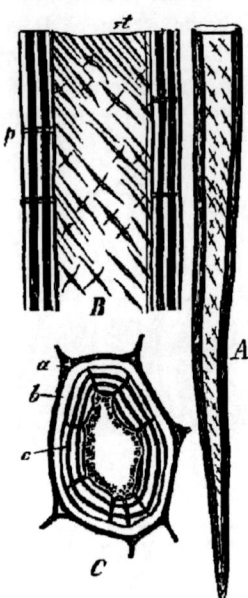

FIG 87—Cells from a leaf of *Hoya carnosa* (X 800), showing the striation, though far less strongly marked in nature, the striæ are quite as evident *a* optical longitudinal section of the crossed annular striation ; *b* external view of the side where the annular striæ cross, *c d* external view of the side where they do not cross, *e* a portion of cell-wall where only isolated annular striæ are evident

FIG 88.—Cells with brown walls in the stem of *Pteris aquilina* *A* half a cell, isolated and decolorised by Schulze's maceration, *B* a piece more highly magnified (X 550)—the fissure-like pits are crossed i. e. the fissure becomes twisted with increase of thickening, *p* lateral view of a fissure, which here appears as a simple canal, since it exhibits the narrow section

makes the cell-walls predominantly hard and rigid, they gain by means of suberisation in extensibility and elasticity.

The third common form of metamorphosis of the cell-wall, the conversion into mucilage, consists in a chemical alteration of the cellulose, in consequence of which it obtains the property of absorbing large quantities of water, and of swelling up in a corresponding degree, in many cases so strongly that the volume increases a hundred-fold or more. According as this property is more or less developed, the mucilaginous change of the cell-wall makes itself evident in a more or less gelatinous consistence; and it may even be converted into a liquid slime with water. As a further metamorphosis, we may consider the formation of Bassorin, and finally that of soluble gum-arabic. This mucilaginous change of the cell-walls may, under certain circumstances, occur as a diseased condition, as in the gum-formation of Plums and Cherries; in other cases, on the other hand, especially when the mucilaginous change is associated with only a slight alteration of the original cellulose, it appears as a normal change serving definite purposes of life. Numerous seeds and dry indehiscent-fruits possess within their epidermis mucilaginous layers of cell-membrane, which, on being moistened with water, break through the cuticle and surround the seed or the fruit as a gelatinous envelope. This is the case for example with the seeds of the Quince, the Flax, *Plantago psyllium*, &c.; if a large quantity of the small grains is moistened with water, a viscid paste is formed, the swollen-up mucilaginous layers forming a coherent mass.

In the economy of the Algæ and many Fungi (especially certain Gasteromycetes), and some Lichens (e. g. the Collemaceæ), the mucilaginous change of the

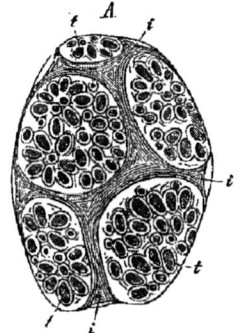

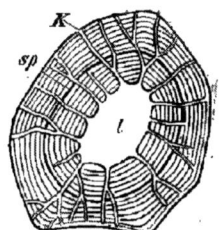

FIG. 89.—A parenchyma cell from the cotyledon of *Phaseolus multiflorus* isolated by maceration. *i, i* the rounded corners bounding intercellular spaces; *t, t* the walls in contact with neighbouring cells, and provided with pits.

FIG. 90.—Transverse section of a sclerenchyma cell from the root-tuber of *Dahlia variabilis* (× 800). *l* the lumen of the cell; *K* pit-canals which penetrate the stratification; *sp* a fissure by which an inner system of layers has become separated.

cell-walls plays a very prominent part; so much so, indeed, that the form and mode of life of such plants are to a certain extent determined by it.

These chemical alterations of the cell-walls, here briefly described, need by no means always invade the entire thickness of a cell-wall. It is often only definite layers or shells of it which are affected by the changes named. The suberisation or cuticularisation frequently takes place only at the exterior, especially in the case of isolated cells; whereas lignification tends to affect the middle layers of strongly-thickened cell-walls; while the formation of mucilage may affect either the middle lamella or any other layer of the cell-wall.

The extremely thin walls of young vigorously growing cells usually appear quite homogeneous, even with strong magnifying powers. In thicker, and especially in very thick cell-walls, on the other hand, a concentric stratification is recognised on the transverse section, to which a corresponding marking is again found also in the longitudinal section. With particularly clear objects it is perceived that this concentric stratification of thickened cell-walls depends upon the alternation of lamellæ, some poor in water and hard, others richer in water and soft, which together make up the cell-wall.

Besides these concentric layers there is to be recognised, however, in very many cases in thick cell-walls, occasionally also in thinner ones, the so-called striation, which is perceived best with very strong magnifying powers when the cell-walls are seen in surface-view. The striation appears then in the form of parallel lines, which generally run obliquely across the object, or travel round the cell-wall in the form of a spiral, or even in closed circles. In the first case are recognised occasionally,

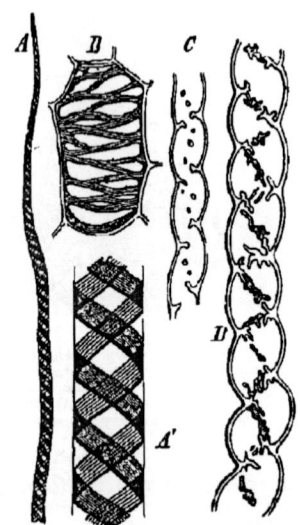

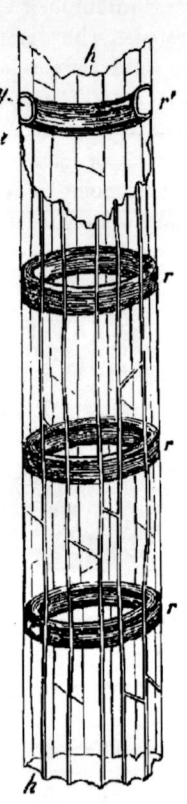

FIG. 91 —Forms of cells of *Marchantia polymorpha* (a Liverwort) with thickenings projecting inwards *A* half an elater from the sporogonium, with two spiral bands, *A'* a portion more highly magnified, *B* a parenchyma cell from the middle portion of the thallus, with reticulate thickenings projecting inwards, *C* a fine root-hair with thickenings projecting inwards—these are arranged on a spiral constriction of the cell-wall, *D* a thicker root hair—the projections are thicker and branched and the spiral arrangement still more evident.

FIG. 9e —Portion of an annular vessel from the fibro-vascular bundle of *Zea Mays* (× 550) *h h* the thin cell wall of the vessel, on which are clearly to be seen the boundary lines of the neighbouring cells, *r, r* the annular thickenings of the wall of the vessel, *y* the inner substance of one of the rings cut through transversely, *t* the denser layer which extends over the ring on its inner side projecting into the lumen of the cell.

with sufficient magnifying power, two systems of striation crossing one another. Nageli has also referred the striations of the cell-wall to the existence of layers, alternately richer and poorer in water, which traverse the cell-wall from without inwards. The whole cell-wall, according to this view, resembles a crystal cleavable in three directions, the intersecting lamellæ of which are alternately richer and poorer in water.

In addition to this very fine structure of the cell-wall, we have to consider, however, a far more conspicuous coarser structure in the same cells. this is visible with weaker magnifying powers, and makes itself chiefly evident by individual parts of a cell-wall being much thinner or much thicker than accords with the common thickness. We are here concerned with what may be termed the sculpture of the surface. The commonest form of this sculpture consists in that, on cell-walls not excessively thick, single or grouped roundish areas remain thin during the growth in thickness of the whole wall, or do not take part in the growth in thickness generally. We term such areas pits, and the cell-wall itself pitted. If the parts of the wall lying between the pits grow very much in thickness, the pits appear no longer merely as thin areas, but as canals running through. the thickness of the wall from the cavity of the cell, and closed exteriorly by a very thin membrane. The pits lie in the partition wall between two neighbouring cells of a tissue, and the pit-canals run on both sides so as to meet one another. The thin membrane which closes the pit of one side forms also at the same time the closure for the pit of the other side. If, therefore, we imagine the cells not isolated, but in connection as usual, like the chambers of a house, and separated by their walls, the pits and pit-canals appear like holes, through which the neighbouring chambers communicate; in such a manner, however, that a very fine membrane is always still present in the middle, by means of which the neighbouring cell-cavities are in fact separated from one another. It is easy to see, and is to be insisted upon still

FIG 93—Ripe pollen grain of *Cichorium Intybus* The almost spherical cell wall is beset with reticulately connected thickening ridges, each of which supports comb like series of spinose thickenings, projecting still more prominently

more in detail later on, that the exchange of sap between neighbouring cells must be facilitated by means of the pitting; especially when the partition-walls are of considerable thickness, whereby of course the diffusion movements from cell to cell would be rendered very difficult without the presence of numerous pits.

Another form of sculpture of the cell-wall, also very frequent, shows itself in that not thin areas, as in the pitting, but strongly thickened areas stand out as peculiarly formed parts of the wall, which otherwise remains very thin. Sometimes the thickened areas appear as cones projecting inwards, or they form massive rings, which often become loose and fall out on cutting succulent stems and leaves, yet more frequently, the thickened part of the cell-wall forms a spiral band, running on the inner side of the thin wall, somewhat like a spirally-wound wire fitted in a glass tube of suitable width. Very often two or three such spiral bands with parallel windings are present, and, like the rings, these also often become loosened on cutting or tearing off leaves and stalks, and may then be perceived even with the unaided eye as threads of extreme fineness but considerable length. these are very distinct for example in the leaves of *Agapanthus* when torn across. Finally, a common form is the so-called reticulate thickening, which we may suppose to be derived from the spiral by connections or anastomoses being established between the parallel spiral bands, so that a mesh-work arises. If we suppose the meshes of this net-work very narrow, and the thick bands relatively broad, then the meshes appear as pits, as is clearly seen in the so-called pitted vessels.

In these cases of sculpture the thicker portions of the cell-wall necessarily project inwards, when the cells are tightly closed in on all sides by other cells. In isolated cells, on the other hand, as the pollen-grains of the Phanerogams and the spores of the Cryptogams, the thicker parts of the cell-wall project towards the exterior, and present the most various forms of knobs, cones, prickles, combs, ledges united into net-works, and so forth Generally the whole outer surface of such cell-walls is cuticularised, and the sculptured parts mentioned consist also of cuticular substance.

LECTURE VII.

DEVELOPMENT OF CELLS

WE have hitherto considered the cells in the condition in which they immediately present themselves in the living parts of plants under the microscope The organs, however, at first themselves microscopically small, grow up later to a considerable size. This growth must necessarily also affect the cells of which the organs consist; and thus, with increasing growth of the organs, the cells also would have to attain a considerable size if, during the growth itself, a diminution and at the same time multiplication of them did not take place by division. In general, the growth of the organs of the plant, especially in its first stages, is associated with multiplication of the existing cells, and only in the final processes of growth, where the organs attain their definitive form and size, does the multiplication of the cells in them cease, and the cells themselves attain their ultimate form and size

Thus, to observe the formation of new cells we must not make use of organs already fully grown, we must rather examine the growing points and the parts which are becoming elongated. However, although there is no doubt that cell-divisions are constantly taking place in the growing points, it is still very difficult to observe this process there On the other hand, it is relatively easy to see the multiplication of the cells further distant from the growing points in the parts becoming elongated, and moreover, as experience has shown, it is particularly in the development of the organs of reproduction that the processes of cell-formation may be easily seen.

Above all, it is to be premised that the multiplication of cells is always brought about by the division of cells already existing; and that new cells at no time shoot forth like crystals out of a fluid Each newly arising cell originates by division of one already existing; and very generally this division is a bipartition, i. e. two daughter-cells arise from a mother-cell from the substance of the former becoming divided into two equal halves

Before I enter more in detail into the processes which take place in the bipartition of a cell, it will be advisable to consider the more obvious facts.

Since the cells generally appear as chambers in the substance of the plant, their new formation or division may also be represented, especially during growth, as a progressive formation of chambers or compartments. Within the cells already existing and dividing, new partition walls arise, somewhat as if the chambers of a house were each divided into two smaller rooms, by putting in partition walls The formation of cells in growing organs where the existing cells increase in size, gives therefore the impression of each cell being only able to attain a definite size; and, when it passes beyond this, a division wall appears by means of which the cavity becomes divided generally into two equal halves. In most cases these new partition walls can be recognised in the framework of the older cell-walls on transverse and longitudinal sections as thin lines, which are usually set at right angles on the older walls, as the accompanying figure clearly shows The cells already present grow; and as they grow and the chambers formed by them become larger, partition walls arise, by means of which the increasing size of the cells is to a certain extent again equalised, so that in a given plant, in spite of the progressive growth, the cell cavities never exceed a certain dimension. The man-

ner in which the new partition walls are inserted in the growing cells, gives in a certain sense the impression of the latter being, so to speak, cut through, and so divided each into two portions The cell-division appears therefore (and this should be especially insisted upon) as a diminution in size of the chambers into which the living plant substance is divided, following upon growth and conditioned by growth. This mutual relation of growth and cell-division is particularly clear if one examines from this point of view plants of simple construction, such as the *Characeæ* Fig 95 represents a longitudinal section through the

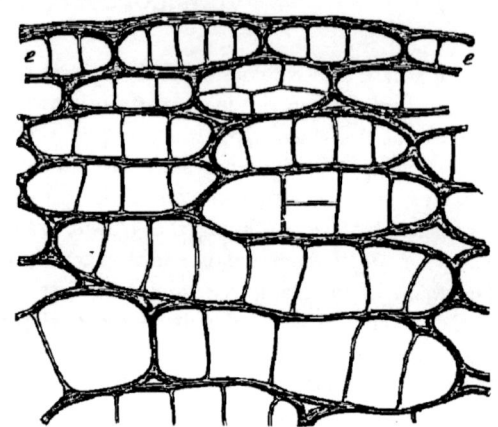

FIG. 94.—Epidermis and adjacent cortical parenchyma of the hypocotyl of *Helianthus annuus* which rapidly increases in thickness at the conclusion of germination the darker thicker cell walls are the original ones, the thinner radial ones those recently developed The vigorous tangential growth of the epidermis cells and the cuticle is especially interesting

apex or terminal bud of such a plant, which is preeminently suited, on careful consideration, to render clear the relation of cell-division to growth and the whole external and internal configuration of a plant. From the so-called apical cell (*v*) found at the end of the stem, each time this attains a certain height by growth, a lower transverse disk is cut off, and thus a new cell, a so-called segment, is formed This is again divided by means of a transverse wall into two cells lying one above the other; a lower lenticular one, and an upper one which resembles a biconcave lens. The former is no more divided on further growth; and gradually assumes the forms *i''*, *i''*, *i''''*, by which, as seen, it becomes transformed into a cylinder, continually increasing in length, and constitutes a joint or interfoliar part of the axis of the *Chara*. The upper biconcave daughter-cell of the segment developes, on the other hand, a number of outgrowths around the axis of the stem, from which the leaves originate ; while the middle portion becomes the node between two interfoliar parts.   These leaves and nodes now continually undergo repeated divisions during their growth, which follow a quite definite and exactly known law, both as regaids their direction in space and also their sequence one upon the other in time.

It is not necessary here to enter more particularly into these matters. We shall be able to apprehend in the main the relation between growth and the repeated division of the cells into two, if we observe that in our figure the parts

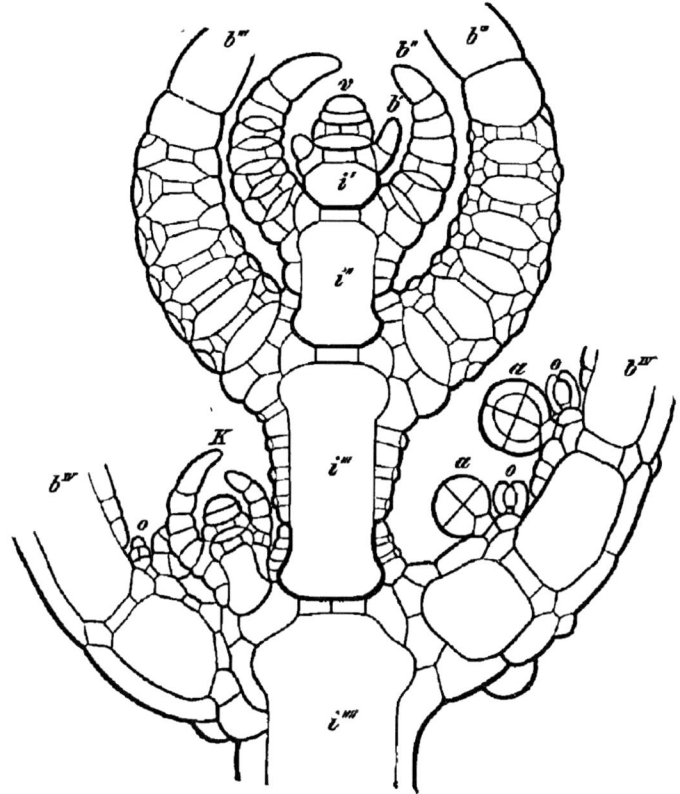

FIG 95 —Longitudinal section through the apex of *Chara*. Each portion of tissue bounded by a thick contour has originated from a segment, i e from a cell immediately segmented off from the apical cell (Partly diagrammatic)

distinguished by *i*, *b*, respectively, always proceed from a segment of the apical cell ; and that with the increasing growth of the same the number of division walls contained in them increase also   If we compare, for example, the portion *i″ b″* included by the thick contours, with the younger portion *i′ b′*, we easily perceive how with the growth of the former, which previously possessed exactly the form and size of the latter, the cell-divisions have proceeded ; and if, further, we take into consideration the portion *i‴ b‴*, in like manner enclosed by thick contours, we again recognise how, with progressive growth, the cell-divisions have proceeded in definite order also.

The development of the stomata in the epidermis of a leaf (Fig. 96) may serve as a second example showing how the division of cells already existing proceeds with their growth In Fig. *A* are represented a number of epidermis cells of a very young leaf, seen from the outer surface The chambers (*s*) are those from which the two guard-cells of a stoma are formed later. These, as well as the surrounding epidermis cells, grow, become enlarged, and change their form, thereupon new cell-divisions appear, as in figure *B*, where the older cell-walls are indicated by thick lines, those most recently formed with thin ones. It is observed that around each mother-cell of a stoma (*s*) a number of new cell-walls have appeared, by which pieces have become, as it were, cut out of the neighbouring epidermis cells; so that each mother-cell of a stoma (*s*) is surrounded by a group of new cells Fig. *C* shows a mother-cell now divided into two guard-cells (*s s*), with the group of adjoining cells and neighbouring epidermis cells surrounding

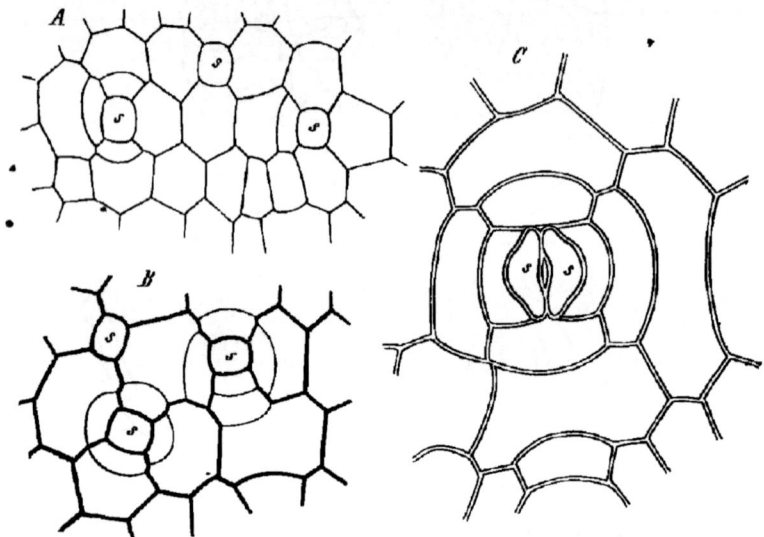

FIG 96.—Development of stomata on the leaf of *Commelyna cœlestis* *A* and *B* very young, *C* nearly mature, *ss* (in *A* and *B*) mother cells of stomata, *ss* (in *C*) guard cells In *A* and *B* is shown the formation of the neighbouring cells

them: all the cells already indicated in *B* have grown further, i. e. they have enlarged and changed their form, and the cell-walls have become thicker. By means of the further growth, which now proceeds without cell-divisions, they finally become fully developed

It is evident from what has been hitherto said concerning the division of cells, that each newly produced cell is not only a portion of the mother-cell, but that even its original form depends upon what form the mother-cell possessed at the moment of division, and in what direction the division wall was formed. Very generally the latter happens in such a manner that the division wall is set at right angles on the walls already existing, and, when necessary to this end, it presents a corresponding curvature. The newly arising division walls are therefore commonly not flat plates, but in most cases more or less, though it may be almost imperceptibly, curved, as seen in the figures. The figures also

[3]   H

show at once that a certain relation exists between the form of the organ in which growth and cell-division are taking place, and the direction, curvature, and general arrangement of the newly arising cell-walls—a relation of which we shall speak more in detail later on, when considering growth in its relation to cell-formation.

The relations just mentioned are partly or entirely wanting in the develop-

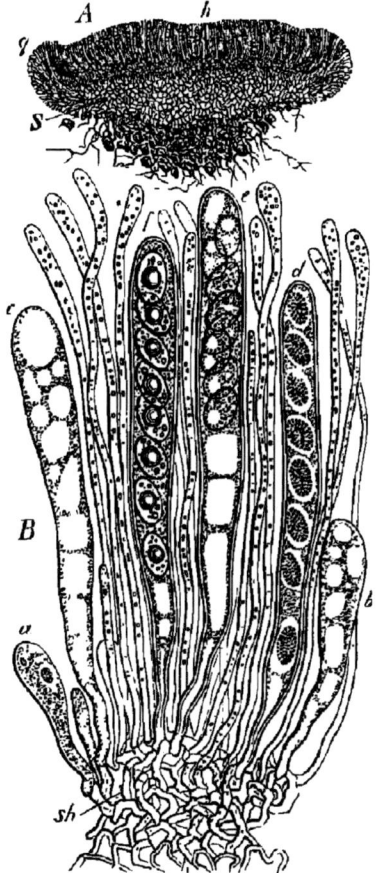

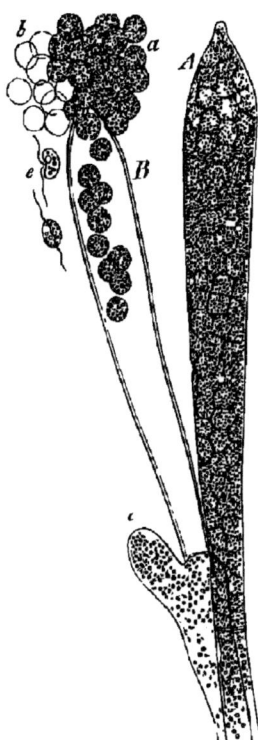

FIG 97 —*Peziza convexula* *A* vertical section through the whole Fungus (× 20), *h* Hymenium, *e* the layer in which the spore producing asci are situated, *s* the tissue body which surrounds the hymenium at the margin (*g*) like a cup Fine filaments proceed from the base and penetrate into the soil *B* Small portion of hymenium (× 550), *sh* sub hymenial layer of densely interwoven hyphæ, *a—f* asci, with spores in various stages of development, between are thinner filaments—paraphyses—containing red granules

FIG. 98 —Zoosporangia of *Achlya* (× 550) *A* still unopened, *B* the zoospores are escaping, *a* zoospores just emitted, *b* membranes left behind, from which the swarming zoo spores (*e*) have escaped, *c* a lateral bud.

ment of reproductive cells, such as oospheres, spores, and pollen-grains · for, in the majority of such cases, the formation of new cells appears as if it did not depend upon a mere cutting-through by means of a new partition wall. The cell-formation gives here the impression of being not a mere division into chambers or compartments of the chambers already present; the new cells appear rather from the very beginning as more or less rounded, independent bodies, isolated from the sister-cells.

This difference is especially conspicuous where a large number of rounded daughter-cells are formed inside a mother-cell, in such a manner that a portion

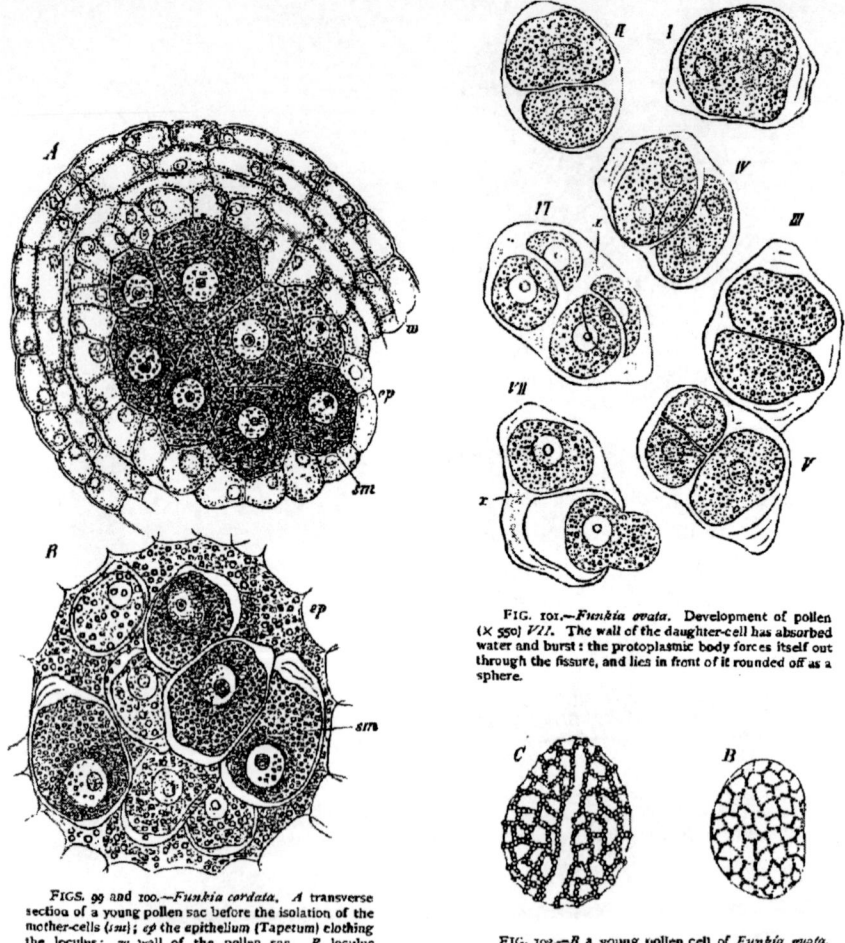

FIG. 101.—*Funkia ovata.* Development of pollen (× 550) *VII.* The wall of the daughter-cell has absorbed water and burst : the protoplasmic body forces itself out through the fissure, and lies in front of it rounded off as a sphere.

FIGS. 99 and 100.—*Funkia cordata.* *A* transverse section of a young pollen sac before the isolation of the mother-cells (*sm*); *ep* the epithelium (Tapetum) clothing the loculus; *w* wall of the pollen sac. *B* loculus after isolation of the mother-cells (*sm*); *ep* remains of Tapetum (× 550). For further development cf. the following figs.)

FIG. 102.—*B* a young pollen cell of *Funkia ovata.* The externally projecting thickenings are still small (in *C* they are larger) and arranged as lines connected into a network.

of the existing protoplasm of the mother-cell remains unemployed, as in Fig. 97. This mode of cell-formation has long been distinguished from the cell-division previously described as an essentially different process, as free cell-formation : more recent researches have shown, however, that between these apparently very different modes of cell-formation the most various intermediate stages occur, which

make a fundamental distinction impossible. It is more a matter of an external
difference concerning the form of the daughter-cell, than an essential difference
in the process of formation itself.   The chief difference between the so-called
free cell-formation and ordinary cell-division lies especially in that, in the former,
the developing daughter-cells appear not as mere segments of the mother-cell,
but as rounded off individuals; and whether in this a part of the protoplasm
of the mother-cell remains unemployed or not, may be considered as unessential
for the cell-formation itself, although specifically important for its purpose at the
time.   We have, for example in Fig. 98, a case of cell-division where numerous
daughter-cells, at first polyhedral but subsequently rounded off, are developed from

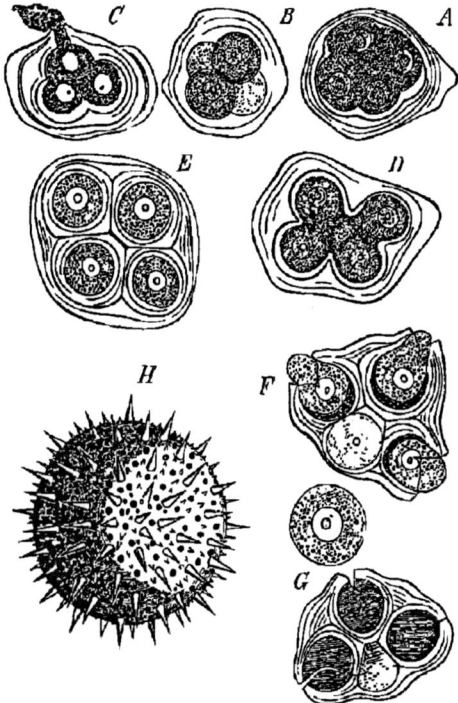

FIG. 103.—*Althæa rosea.*—Division of the pollen mother-cells into four, *A—E, F* and *G* a tetrad.   The membrane
of the 'special mother cell' has burst under the influence of water, and allowed the protoplasmic body of the young
pollen cells to escape   *H* a fully developed pollen grain seen from without, and magnified to the same extent

the protoplasm of a relatively large mother-cell; here the first processes come under
the same category as ordinary cell-division, while the later ones resemble free cell-
formation   On the other hand, we find in the origin of the pollen grains in Fig. 101,
in the ordinary repeated bipartition of a mother-cell, with the simultaneous secretion
of a cell-membrane and rounding off of the mother-cell itself, a case in which the cell-
division presents itself in the form previously described as a development of chambers
inside chambers already existing; only that the chamber-walls, as they rapidly
grow in thickness, round off the cavities enclosed by them.   To be sure, there
appears later a very conspicuous difference from the ordinary bipartition of
cells in vegetative growing organs, in so far, that in this case the walls formed in

the division are destroyed, and each protoplasmic body becomes enveloped in a new specially formed cell-wall, so that finally only these newly formed cell-walls remain after the destruction of the older ones, while the whole complex of cells, produced by repeated bipartition, now consists of individual pollen grains entirely separated from one another, each of which, from its origin and organisation, however, must nevertheless be regarded as a cell. We may here perceive clearly how cells, appearing inside a growing organ as mere chambers, arise in connection with reproduction as individual bodies entirely separated from one another. This process is still more conspicuous in the formation of the pollen grains of most dicotyledonous plants, of which an example is represented in Fig. 103. Here the four daughter-cells of a pollen mother-cell arise (at least apparently and so far as concerns the development of the wall) simultaneously, and not by means of a repeated bipartition of the existing cell-cavity. After the preparatory stages to be described later, in which also we can still recognise the principle of bipartition, the protoplasmic body of the pollen mother-cell becomes so constricted around the four nuclei produced by repeated bipartitions, that it assumes in the first place a four-lobed form, and the relatively very thick wall of the mother-cell growing towards the centre in the form of ledges so projects, that four chambers closed off from one another result (*E*), in which the nucleated masses of protoplasm lie Here then the rounding off of the developing daughter-cells is particularly clear. It becomes still more so in that now, inside each of the chambers of the mother-cell (the so-called special mother-cell), a new cell-wall is secreted by each protoplasmic body, which it retains during further growth, while the chamber-walls arising before and during the division dissolve and disappear[1]

The more recent researches in the province of the cell theory have shown that at the foundation of all these different forms of cell-formation there lies a common principle, that especially the first preparatory stages, which are particularly clear in the behaviour of the cell-nucleus, are everywhere essentially the same; that it always depends originally upon a bipartition of the substance of the cell-nucleus, and a corresponding grouping of the protoplasm around the centres so arising; the process being completed by the formation of a new cell-wall

What has been hitherto stated especially concerns the external appearances, which are to be recognised clearly enough even with relatively low powers of the microscope Only recently, with very strong magnifying powers and new micro-chemical reagents and methods, a series of processes have been shown to take place in the interior of the cell-nucleus and the protoplasm, which afford a deeper insight into the behaviour of the living cell contents during the formation of new cells. We owe especially to the researches of Strasburger, Flemming, Schmitz, and others, a very thorough knowledge of the most minute details in the changes of the protoplasm and nucleus during division[2] From the statements of the former, as well as from those of a number of zoologists, moreover, the very important fact results that the

---

[1] More details concerning what has been said in the text up to this point are found in my 'Text Book,' the fourth edition of which appeared before the new researches on cell-division

[2] Of Strasburger's many works on cell-division, mention need be made only of his last book, '*Zellbildung und Zelltheilung*,' Jena, 1880 Further important are Flemming, '*Beitrage zur*

processes during the cell-formation of plants and animals are in all essential points alike

The following description is taken chiefly from the statements of Strasburger, with which my own observations agree, at least in the points which appear important to me · the questions still under discussion between the specialists in this province may here be avoided as much as possible

The first preparations for the division of a vegetable cell are noticeable in the changes of the cell-nucleus; and it is in fact in the visible elements of the nuclein that the first indications and further course of the division of the nucleus are to be traced.

'In general,' says Strasburger, 'the contents of the nucleus (the nuclein) become coarsely granular: hereupon the granules fuse with one another into shorter or longer

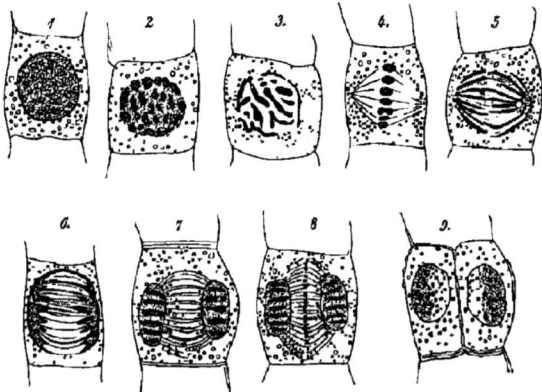

FIG 104 —Changes in the cell nucleus during the division of the mother cell of a stoma of *Iris pumila* (1) In 9 the division is completed and the two guard cells have been produced The dark portions are nuclein (× 880—after Strasburger)

filaments, curved in all directions. The nucleoli often remain preserved in vegetable cells for a long time, much longer than in animal cells: finally they too enter into the formation of filaments, and the wall of the nucleus also becomes concerned in the process. In the rare cases where this does not happen, they disappear, at least at the poles of the nucleus. When the wall of the nucleus has become, as is usual, completely absorbed, the filaments lie immediately in the surrounding protoplasm of the cell, and may in many cases be dispersed somewhat widely in it The nuclear filaments (filiform arrangement of the nuclein) are, particularly in round cell-nuclei, nearly equally distributed through the entire space of the nucleus, in elongated cell-nuclei they follow more or less the longitudinal axis They begin later in all cases to place themselves parallel to one another. If an elongation of the cell-nucleus in a definite direction has taken place meanwhile, the filaments become elongated in the same direction. Two poles become plainly distinguishable in the cell-nucleus. The

Kenntniss der Zelle und ihrer Lebenserscheinungen,' I and II; in Archiv für mikroskopische Anatomie, Bonn, Bd. XVIII and XX, 1880–81, and Schmitz, '*Struktur des Protoplasmas und der Zellkerne,*' in Sitzungsber. der niederrhein Ges. für Nat und Heilk zu Bonn, 13 July, 1880

more or less linear extended filaments are usually connected at their ends, now and again they become connected also at other points by cross bridges Later, in cell-nuclei poor in contents (i. e. containing little nuclein), the individual filaments become drawn together in such a manner, that they form a simple layer of rodlets or granules in the equatorial plane. If the filaments were fused at their polar ends, this connection is first loosened In cell-nuclei rich in contents (i. e. rich in nuclein) the filaments also maintain a considerable length in the stage now treated of, and they may even reach from the one pole of the nucleus to the other. In nuclear figures with equatorial bridges, the loops open, not only in the filaments turned towards the poles but also in those lying equatorially. The equatorial connecting filaments hereupon resolve themselves chiefly into V-shaped figures placed radially with the free legs directed outwards. The filaments directed towards the poles become more or less drawn towards the equator and at the same time shortened, or they maintain their original lengths. They converge somewhat towards the poles, or run almost parallel to one another, or curve, even spreading strongly outwards from one another In the formation of the nuclear figure described, the whole stainable substance (the nuclein) of the cell-nucleus is demonstrably employed[1]'

Strasburger distinguishes this everywhere as thenuclear disc. This consists therefore in the simplest case of a simple layer of granules or of straight parallel rodlets These elements are visibly separated from one another, and, looked at from one of the nuclear poles, a radial arrangement is sometimes to be discovered, sometimes not. The rodlets of the nuclear disc (the nuclein rodlets) may, however, also be of more considerable length, and at the same time be curved in an irregular manner, spreading very much towards the exterior. On both sides of the nuclear disc, in the great majority of cases, delicate fibrillæ are visible which (with colouring media such as hæmatoxylin) are generally stained only faintly or not at all. These are the so-called spindle striæ or fibrillæ of Strasburger.

'These form together with the nuclear disc (the described arrangement of the nuclein) the nuclear spindle The spindle fibrillæ show themselves most beautifully and plainly when the nuclear disc is limited to only one equatorial layer of granules or rodlets. They are so much the less visible the greater the extension of the nuclear disc (i e again the nuclein rods) towards the poles' The so-called spindle fibrillæ of Strasburger are, according to his view, formed from the substance of the surrounding protoplasm, or they belong, as we may well assume, to the ground substance of the cell-nucleus, the *nucleo-plasma.* 'Since now the formation of the spindle fibrillæ,' says Strasburger, 'starts from the two poles of the cell-nucleus and proceeds towards the equator, the continuous spindle fibrillæ, which can be traced between the elements of the nuclear disc (the rodlets of nuclein) from one pole to another, can only have originated by fusion of the ends meeting one another. Other spindle fibrillæ join the elements of the nuclear disc (the nuclein rodlets) on both sides.

---

[1] The staining of the nuclein is brought about especially by means of haematoxylin, with the aid of picric-acid, alum, and other reagents Compare the works mentioned in note 2, p. 101.

'The division of the nuclear disc (which consists of nuclein rodlets) is accomplished in the equator, and both halves separate from one another   Elements which lie in the equatorial plane, or run through it, undergo division   With granules, rods, and rodlets, this takes place simply by constriction. If the nuclear disc consists of accumulated granules or rodlets, one part goes over on the one side, the other part on the other.   The process is more complicated in nuclear discs which present filaments placed equatorially   These form mostly two or more legged figures, with the ends of the legs turned outwards.   The figures become doubled

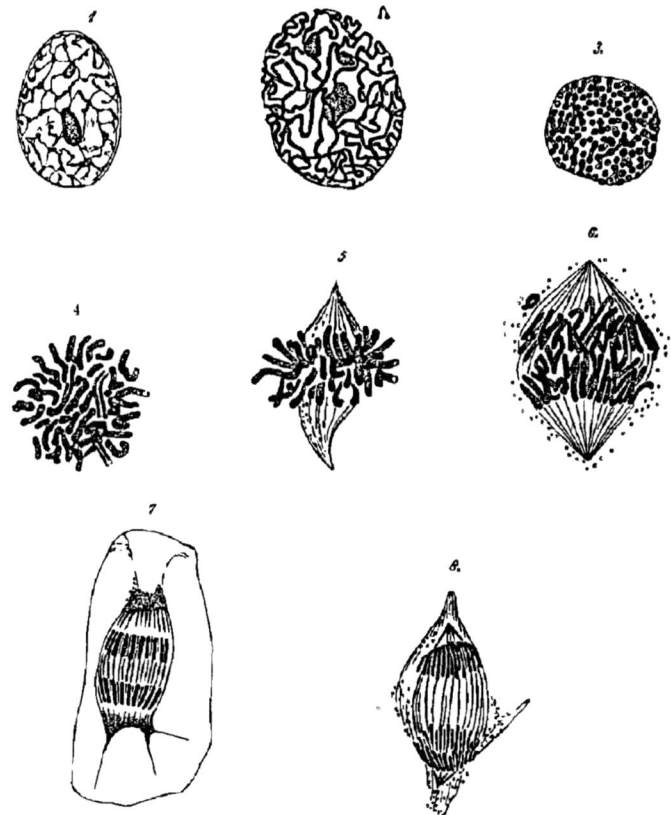

FIG. 105.—Changes of the cell nucleus during division   1—3 from the endosperm of *Nothoscordon fragrans*, 4—8 from *Allium odorum*.   The dark portions are the Nuclein (after Flemming strongly magnified)

into two similar ones, or now pass over to the corresponding daughter-nuclei in such a manner that their fused ends are directed towards the pole, their free ends towards the equator'

'During the development of the daughter-nuclei,' proceeds Strasburger, 'they are usually nourished at the same time from the surrounding protoplasm, that they may grow up to the size of the mother-nucleus. This may be followed very well in *Spirogyra*, on account of the free suspension of the nucleus in the cell.   All the protoplasm collected at the polar side of the daughter-nucleus, and here forming a layer of considerable thickness, is finally consumed by the young daughter-nuclei, which increase in size accordingly.   An absorption of the protoplasm of the cell, collected together at the poles of the nucleus, can also be clearly made out in the staminal hairs of *Tradescantia*.'

After these changes have occurred in the nucleus and protoplasm, the formation of the new partition walls begins, and I will describe this also according to Strasburger's statements. 'That may be regarded as the commonest form of cell-division in the vegetable kingdom,' he says, 'which is accomplished by means of a partition wall originating in the connecting fibrillæ between the nuclei   The few filaments which finally remain behind between the separating halves of the nuclear disc, and which are to be referred to spindle fibrillæ, become elongated and increased in number by the deposition of new cell protoplasm, which becomes like them differentiated into filaments   The newly added filaments are not to be distinguished from those originally present : they react like these, and consequently again support the view that the spindle fibrillæ are cell protoplasm'   Strasburger understands by the expression 'cell-plate,' a plate-like arrangement of small granules from which the new partition-wall arises.   He says it is difficult to decide as to the chemical nature of these granules

'So much is certain,' says Strasburger, 'they enter directly into the formation of the cell-wall.   There is thus probably not a layer formed of protoplasm, which subsequently becomes split up and secretes cellulose at the separating surfaces, but the cellulose wall probably originates directly from material conveyed to the spot   I have been able to establish in the living *Spirogyra* that the granules destined for the formation of the partition-wall wander as such to the place where they are employed.   In other (the most numerous) cases, on the contrary, the granules appear to be formed at the spot, there and then.

'It is especially striking that they are at first small, gradually becoming larger   The connecting fibrillæ usually become laterally extended so far, that they spread over the entire transverse section of the cell.   Where this has happened, the cell-plate also extends across the whole cell   The cellulose wall is formed simultaneously from this, and fits close on the wall of the mother-cell at the periphery. Where the complex of connecting fibrillæ is not able to extend completely across the cell, it attaches itself first to one side wall of the cell, and, fitting close to this, the formation of the partition-wall out of the cell-plate begins.   From the developed wall, however, the complex of fibrillæ becomes slowly withdrawn, growing at the same time at its free edges by the continual formation of new connecting fibrillæ, and within this the cell-plate becomes completed, until it extends completely across the cell   These differences are conditioned by the size of the lumen of the cell, in relation to the mass of the protoplasm   In the cases where the cell-plates at once traverse the lumen of the cell, or at least but few movements are executed to this end, the cell-nucleus also lies approximately in the middle of the cell· where, however, the cell-plate has to extend across the lumen progressively, the cell-nucleus lies on one side wall of the cell, and becomes divided in this parietal position   Only after the foundation of the cell-wall is a connected layer of protoplasm produced on both sides of it.   In this numerous 'granules are often found still embedded, which have not been used up in the formation of the cellulose wall   The connecting fibrillæ hereupon become indistinct, they sink together to a structureless mass of plasma, which is withdrawn to the wall of the cell, or they fuse to several coarser fibres, or they simply disappear in the surrounding protoplasm.'

The processes of cell-division hitherto described may be considered as typical: but, under certain circumstances, more or less deviating forms occur.

Passing over isolated cases, we may turn at once to the processes which have hitherto been distinguished as essentially different from those above described, under the name of 'free cell-formation.' Apart from the cases already mentioned in cryptogamic plants, it is especially in the formation of the endosperm in the embryo-sac within the ovule of the Phanerogams that the so-called free cell-formation occurs.   The opinion was for a long time held, that in the protoplasm of the embryo-sac a great number of cell-nuclei arise simultaneously and independently of one another, as it were like crystals out of a mother-liquor, and that around each of these a portion of protoplasm collects which then becomes enveloped with a cell-membrane.   According to Strasburger's publications, however, the numerous cell-nuclei visible in the protoplasm of the embryo-sac, also arise by the division of one originally existing nucleus; and these nuclei then multiply rapidly by bipartition.   'Between the freely multiplying nuclei,' says the observer mentioned, 'connecting fibrillæ are visible in the usual manner.   In some cases these disappear very quickly, without increasing, in others they grow but imperfectly, in yet others, however, the

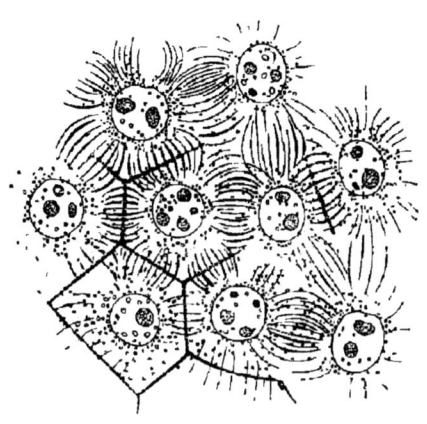

FIG 106.—Commencing development of partition walls between the nuclei produced by successive divisions in the embryo sac of *Agrimonia eupatorium*   (After Strasburger—very highly magnified)

connecting fibrillæ are seen to become considerably increased as in ordinary cell-division, and a cell-plate appears in them.

'Between the formation of free endosperm and the formation of numerous coherent cells, a distinction no longer exists.   If, for instance, numerous spores are to be developed in a sporangium (cf. Fig. 98), or numerous oospheres in an oogonium, or, finally, numerous spermatozoids in an antheridium, the nuclei in most cases are seen in the first place multiplying freely by bipartition, and arranging themselves at approximately regular distances, and then separating layers appear, by means of which the mass becomes cut up into as many divisions as there are cell-nuclei.   Each nucleus then occupies the middle of a cell.   Connecting threads are here not to be observed.'

The departures from the above described typical form of cell-division, and especially of nuclear division, go still further in many Algæ and Fungi   Thus, Schmitz observed in the older cells of the *Characeæ*, in which the most various kinds of nuclear division are to be found, that the nucleus breaks up into two nuclei by an annular constriction; or there is formed in the interior of the nucleus a fissure, which extends towards the exterior, and so leads to the division of the old nucleus It is not necessary here to enter further upon other cases of division of the cell-nucleus described by Strasburger and Schmitz; however, the fact discovered by the former, that a fusion into one of previously distinct nuclei occasionally occurs, may be mentioned here On the other hand, according to the statements of Schmitz, it may also happen in very simply constructed filamentous Algæ (*Chroococcaceæ, Oscillariæ, Nostocaceæ,*) that a properly defined nucleus is not to be demonstrated at all in the protoplasmic bodies of the small cells. Granules, which are characterised as nuclein by their reactions towards hæmatoxylin, are found distributed in the whole mass of the protoplasm of the cell

When the cell-division runs its course in the typical manner above described, the behaviour of the cell-nucleus easily gives the observer the impression that the impulse to cell-formation proceeds from it; and that the division of the protoplasmic body and the later origin of the cell-wall are caused by the activity of the nucleus There are, however, facts which show that, on the one hand, cell-nuclei may be repeatedly divided without a corresponding division of the cell ensuing, as is the case in the large-celled Algæ with very many nuclei on the other hand, again, cell-divisions (i.e. divisions of the protoplasmic body with subsequent formation of partition walls) may also appear in the same plants quite independent of the division of one or several nuclei The above described typical process of cell-division is thus only the ordinary case, and occurs in higher plants almost without exception. It must not be concluded from this, however, that the described changes of the cell-nucleus are the cause of the division of the cell itself. we have here rather a coincidence of two processes, which in other cases may appear separately—the division of the nucleus, and the cell-division itself

There are yet a few other remarks of general importance to be added here. Above all, is to be mentioned the fact that the whole protoplasmic body, with the nuclear substance contained in it, may, under certain circumstances, begin a new life. This, again, happens more frequently in the Algæ The protoplasm &c, becoming loosed from the already existing cell-wall, contracts by driving out water, rounds off, and leaves the cavity of what had hitherto been the cell to swim about for a longer or shorter period as a swarm-spore, in the form of a naked protoplasmic body: finally it becomes fixed, and. after the formation of a new cell-wall, developes into a new plant. Also the case must be mentioned where, by the union of two cells hitherto foreign to one another (or at least completely separate from one another), a single new cell is formed, two protoplasmic bodies containing nuclei fuse together, and represent a single body, which now becomes surrounded with a cell-wall, and sooner or later grows forth into a new plant. If the two fusing cells are of equal size, and generally similar, the process is termed 'conjugation': this is the normal form of reproduction in many Algæ and some Fungi Conjugation is, however, only the simplest form of sexual reproduction, the essence of which consists in that two nucleated masses of protoplasm which are not in themselves capable of any further development, furnish by their fusion a product which is capable of development. In its typical form, however, this sexual act consists in a relatively large cell, formed only of protoplasm and nuclein but without a cell-wall—the oosphere, taking up into itself very small movable corpuscles, the spermatozoids, and being thereby impelled, by the secretion of a cell-wall, to constitute itself into a true cell surrounded with a membrane, from which a new plant now proceeds   This is the case in all Mosses, many Algæ, and all Vascular Cryptogams.   In the Phanerogams, however, the oosphere is incited to further development by a substance passing over into it from the fertilising pollen-tube   According to Strasburger's statement it appears that this fertilising substance is essentially the nuclein of the pollen tube.   Zacharias and Schmitz are of opinion that in the Cryptogams the fertilising spermatozoid originates from the nucleus of its mother-cell, so that fertilisation appears to be essentially a matter of the transference of the substance of the cell-nucleus, especially of the nuclein, out of the

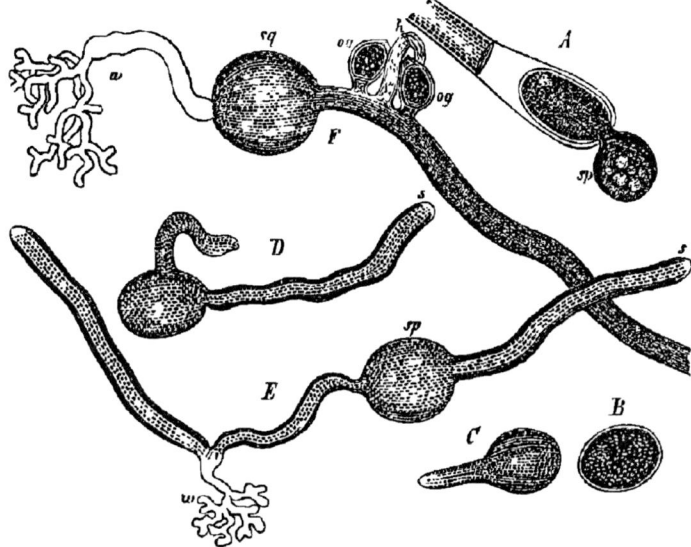

FIG. 107.—*Vaucheria sessilis* (× 30)   *A* exit of a swarm spore (*sp*). *B, C* its germination,
D germinating plant devoid of a root. *E, F* older plants with roots (*w*), *sp* the original spore
still visible as a swelling , *og* and *h* (in *F*) sexual organs

male organ into the oosphere[1]. A further pursuit of this topic, however, belongs to the theory of sexual reproduction, to be treated of later

Finally, with reference to the facts presented hitherto, we have still to cast a glance at the non-cellular plants, the *Cœloblastæ*.   These plants are often of considerable size, and develope roots and shoots, even leaf-forming shoots, fructification, and sexual organs, without their internal substance being converted by cell-division into a system of chambers   A plant of this nature, as we have already learnt from several examples (*Caulerpa, Bryopsis, Vaucheria, Mucor*), is a much branched vesicle, the various protuberances of which represent the different organs , roots, shoots, leaves, sexual organs, sporangia, and so forth.   The wall of the vesicle is a cell-membrane, and its contents protoplasm and cell-sap , and, with reference solely

[1] On the nature of the spermatozoa, see Zacharias, Bot Zeitg 1881, Nos. 50, 51.

to this condition of affairs, the whole plant may be considered as a single cell, or as a uni-cellular plant   It affects the fact little, that under certain circumstances, at particular places of such a plant, transverse septa arise in the vesicle.   The main point is, that growth, i.e the increase in volume and external configuration, is not here accompanied by corresponding cell-divisions as in other plants.   So much the more remarkable appears now the fact, established by Schmitz since 1878, that in the protoplasm of these *Cœloblastæ* numerous, even hundreds and thousands of cell-nuclei are contained, which, with the advancing growth of the plant, are multiplied by division, and obtain a definite arrangement within the protoplasm, thus behaving in a certain measure as if it were simply that the corresponding partition-walls are not formed.   This impression obtains in importance still more in that, according to Schmitz, the cell-nuclei are most numerous at the growing point of the vesicle, thus behaving as in the growing point of a cellular plant   Nevertheless, it is not at all probable that the *Cœloblastæ* are degraded or reduced forms—i.e. we cannot well assume that they have arisen from proper cellular plants by the cell-division, assumed as formerly existing, having ceased to develope partition-walls   Be that, however, as it may, the fact remains for physiological consideration that in the protoplasm of these plants a certain quantity of nuclear substance (especially the nuclein characteristic of it) is distributed in formed portions and at small intervals, and is especially aggregated in the growing points.   From this fact, we obtain once more, as we have already obtained from other sides, a certain insight into the true significance of the cellular structure of plants   We need only imagine in a not too complex cellular plant (a higher Alga, a Moss, or even a vascular plant) that in the substance enveloped by the outer walls of the epidermis, the cell-walls are simply wanting; whereas the protoplasm, with the cell-nuclei distributed in it, behaves essentially just as if these cell-walls were present.   Thus we have, on the whole, the structure of a *Cœloblast*   On the contrary, we need only imagine the inner cavity of such a *Cœloblast* to be divided up by numerous transverse and longitudinal partition-walls into very numerous small chambers, each of which encloses one or several of the cell-nuclei present, and we should thus have an ordinary cellular plant.   It is however very easily intelligible that not only the solidity, but also the shutting off of various products of metabolism, the conduction of the sap from place to place, and so forth, must attain greater perfection if the whole substance of a plant is divided up by numerous transverse and longitudinal walls into cell-chambers sharply separated off from one another.

LECTURE VIII.

FORMS AND SYSTEMS OF TISSUE   EPIDERMAL TISSUE AND VASCULAR BUNDLES.

By the term 'cell-tissue' is designated in general the cellular structure of plants   In particular, however, we understand by a form of tissue a layered, fibriform, or other mass of cells, which, in their growth and other physiological relations, present a certain agreement, and are distinguished from the other neighbouring masses of tissue.   It commonly happens that several forms of tissues are again connected with one another ; so that they constitute a whole of definite physiological character   Such a union of tissues is termed a 'system of tissues.'   Before entering more closely into the description of tissues and systems of tissues, however, it is perhaps desirable to learn how the expression 'tissue' in general has been introduced into vegetable anatomy, and later also into the histology of animals.   In this expression we have in fact to do with a historical curiosity ; since it is clear from what has been already stated, that the cellular structure of plants possesses very little resemblance to what are usually called tissues, such as linen, cloth, or Brussels lace, &c.   Nevertheless, the expression cell-tissue depends upon an erroneously assumed resemblance of cellular structure to the things mentioned.   One of the first founders of vegetable anatomy,

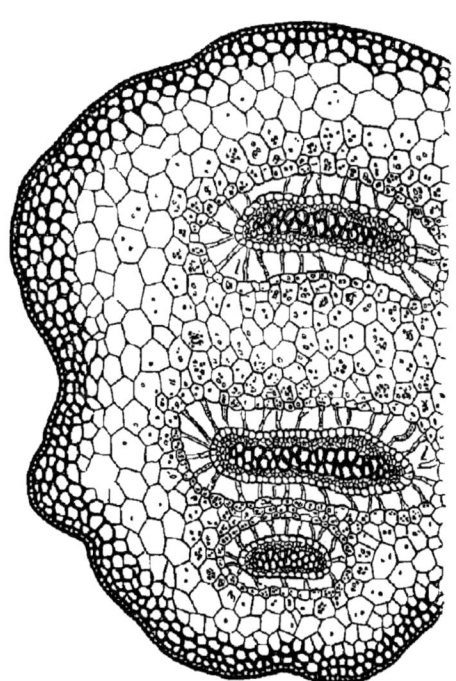

FIG 108 —Transverse section of the shoot axis of *Selaginella inaequalifolia*   The epidermis and several layers of external tissue possess dark coloured thick cell walls, the fundamental tissue, with thinner walls, envelopes three fibro vascular bundles, which are separated from it by large intercellular spaces (*l*)

Nehemiah Grew (1682), believed that he had discovered that the cell-wall framework of plants consists of exceedingly fine fibres; and that the cellular structure itself is to be compared to a great number of pieces of Brussels lace arranged upon one another in layers. In this sense he spoke of a cell-tissue (*contextus cellulosus*) of plants. Although the erroneous character of this view has long been known, the name has still been preserved, and even transferred from vegetable anatomy to animal histology. This need not be wondered at, since a very great number of other scientific terms date likewise from early erroneous conceptions.

I shall in this lecture only attempt to expound the most general principles of tissue formation; and in doing this, I shall again first deal with the typical forms of tissue, leaving many abnormal tissue structures to be mentioned later.

As will be remembered from what was said in the last lecture, the cells of a cellular plant arise by the intercalation of new partition-walls in the cell-cavities already existing, and as the cellular bodies grow, new partition-walls are repeatedly intercalated in the cell-cavities, in various directions, and in definite order as regards time It follows immediately from this, however, that it is utterly incorrect to regard the cells of a growing plant as structures originally free, and only fusing with one another later. This erroneous view, which phytotomists entertained in earlier decades, must necessarily lead to the further, but also unfounded

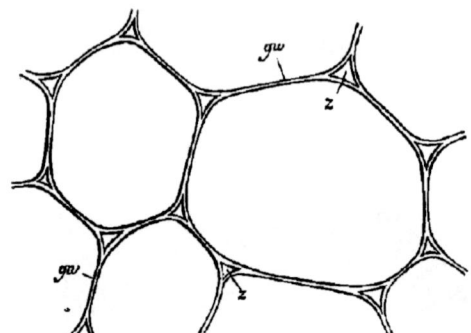

FIG 109 —Transverse section through the soft parenchyma of the stem of *Zea Mays* *gw* partition wall common to each of the two cells, *z* intercellular spaces produced by the splitting of this wall

assumption, that the partition-wall between each two neighbouring cells consists from the beginning of two separate lamellæ, and accordingly a cement was further believed to be necessary, by means of which these wall-lamellæ of neighbouring cells were stuck fast together. This cement was called the intercellular substance. The organisation of the partition-walls, especially in cells with thick walls, appeared thoroughly to confirm this view. This has long been given up, however, since we now know that each new partition-wall between two neighbouring cells of a tissue appears as an immeasurably thin solid membrane; and that, from the mode of origin of the latter, as described previously, not the remotest reason exists for considering this membrane—the new partition-wall—as consisting of two lamellæ. If later on, with progressive growth of the tissue-cells, the thickened partition-wall nevertheless presents itself as a double lamella, or as already mentioned becomes split into two lamellæ so that spaces arise between the cell-chambers, this is simply due to a subsequent splitting of the originally simple partition-wall into two lamellæ, and is not a proof that the partition-wall was composed, in the first instance, of two such lamellæ.

If the partition-walls between neighbouring cells attain a considerable thickness by means of subsequent growth, we observe between each two chambers (as Fig 110 shows) not a double wall, but three layers. The cavity of each one of the neighbouring cell-chambers is in fact enclosed by a more or less thick layer; while between the two lies a middle layer, which usually behaves differently towards chemical reagents This is either capable of swelling to a great extent, or is very strongly lignified or cuticularised. I distinguished this layer fifteen years ago, in order to exclude every theoretical explanation as to its origin, as the middle lamella of the thickened partition-wall of adjoining cells.

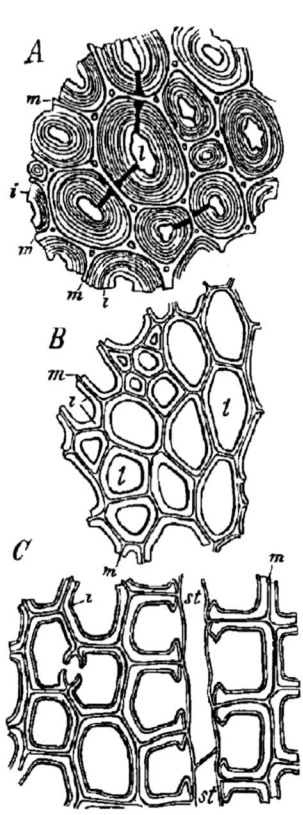

FIG 110.—Transverse sections of thickened cells, showing the middle lamella (*m*), *i* the whole mass of cellulose lying upon this middle lamella, *l* lumen of the cell from which the contents have been removed *A* from the cortical tissue of the stem of *Lycopodium chamæcyparissus*, *B* wood cells from the inner wood of a young fibro vascular bundle *of Helianthus annuus C* wood of *Pinus sylvestris*, *st* a medullary ray

As one of the most general results of the histological researches of the last four or five decades, it is remarkable that the whole internal structure even of the most highly organised plants arises from cells in the manner described. The older phytotomists were by no means of opinion that all the histological elements of highly organised plants could be considered as cells: they distinguished, rather, three chief forms, viz. cell-tissue, fibres, and vessels. Fibres are the long-drawn elements of the bast and wood running to a point above and below; vessels, again, are long prismatic or cylindrical tubes which run particularly in the wood It was one of Mohl's greatest services to demonstrate that the fibres, as well as the vessels and all other elements of the plant, arise by the progressive growth and changes of form of primitive ordinary cells For as, according to what has been already said, the leaves, roots, and such organs are constructed in the form of outgrowths from the growing-points of the higher plants; so also all the various forms of tissues arise from the embryonal-tissue of the growing-point. In this we find, in fact, very small thin-walled cells, all alike, and entirely filled with protoplasm and cell-nucleus: these cells are constantly multiplied during their growth by the intercalation of new partition-walls The youngest organs which grow forth from the growing-points themselves consist of such embryonal tissue; and in proportion as the young organs increase externally in size and complete their configuration, the embryonal tissue in the interior also undergoes further changes. The tissue, quite homogeneous at first, becomes differentiated into layers and strings of various nature, and with the growth of the organ itself, this internal differentiation into various forms and systems of tissues proceeds also, until in the fully grown organs the typical tissue forms have attained complete development. It is not my object to describe in detail this progressive differentiation of the forms of tissue out of the homogeneous embryonal tissue of growing-points and embryos; it suffices for our purpose to understand the forms and systems of tissues in their developed condition. Even in this, however, I confine myself to the most necessary points It only concerns . us at first to describe the tissues and systems of tissues generally distributed in the vegetable kingdom: the description of all those histological matters which subserve special physiological functions may be deferred until I have to speak of the latter themselves. We might otherwise at this period easily deteriorate into a dry formalism and a wearisome systematic arrangement, which will best be avoided by treating of the various points when discussing their physiological significance.

If we imagine any plant whatever consisting of cell-tissue, and living in water,

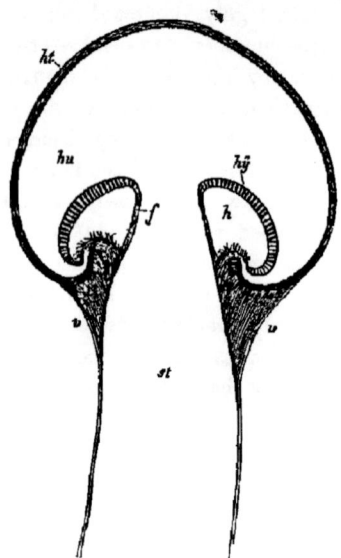

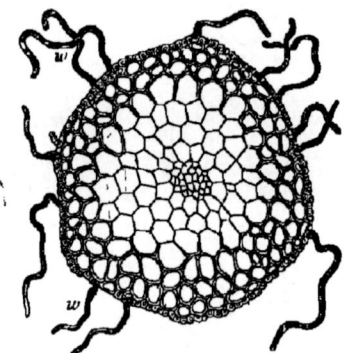

FIG. 111 —Fructification of *Boletus flavidus* in lon gitudinal section, and slightly magnified *st* stipes, *hu* pileus, *hy* hymenium, *v* velum, *h* the cavity beneath ' the hymenium, *f* continuation of the hymenial layer on the stipes, *ht* the removable yellow skin of the pileus.

FIG 112 —Transverse section of the stem of *Bryum roseum* (× 90) *w* root hairs, produced by the out growths of single cells of the external layer

earth, or air, the first thing demanded of its organisation is an efficient shutting off of the tissue-masses from the surrounding world: an external layer of cells, or according to circumstances several such layers, obtains greater solidity and other peculiarities, by means of which this shutting off is effected. Thus there arises in the first instance the differentiation of an epidermal tissue as distinguished from the inner mass of tissue, and it need hardly be added that the contrast between the two is the more marked the more important is the actual shutting off from without In the roots of land-plants and in the shoots of submerged water-plants, where the whole surface subserves the absorption of nutritive matters, the formation of epidermis will obviously be less conspicuous than in shoot-axes and leaves which live in the air, and have to be protected above all against the loss of water by evaporation; and if true roots here and there come into the same position, as is the case with the aërial roots of epiphytal Orchids and many Aroids, in these also the development of epidermis is more pronounced than in ordinary roots.

If a plant consisting of cell-tissue attains a certain size, and a sharper differentiation of root and shoot, and of assimilating leaf-like portions in contrast to the shoot-axes results, the demand arises in the plant for channels through which, on the one hand, the matters absorbed by the roots may be conveyed to the organs of assimilation, and, on the other hand, the organic substance there produced may be conducted to the remaining parts of the body of the plant,

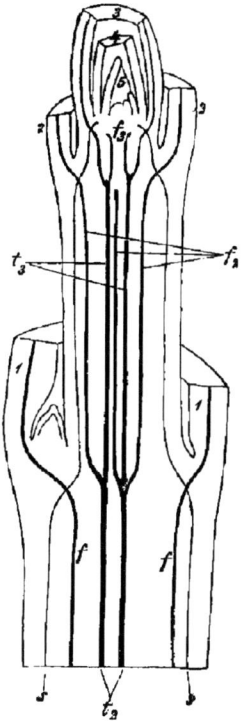

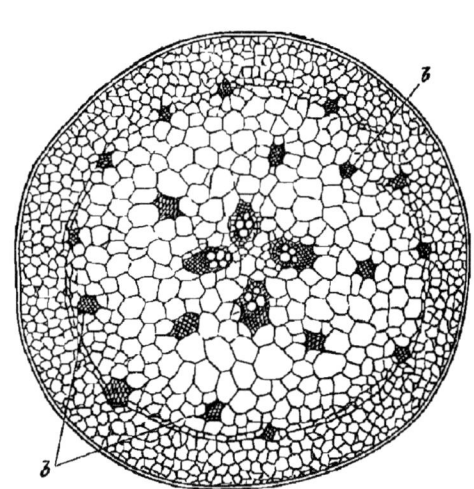

FIG. 113.—Apex of the shoot of *Tradescantia albiflora* rendered transparent in order to show the course of the vascular bundles. 1, 2, 3, the cut off leaves. {After De Bary.}

FIG. 114.—Transverse section through a young internode of the shoot axis of *Tradescantia albiflora*. *b, b* vascular bundles. The large cells are parenchyma of the fundamental tissue. {After De Bary.}

This is usually accomplished by means of fibriform arrangements of elongated cells, running from the roots through the shoot-axes to the organs of assimilation. In lower stages of organisation, as in the Algæ (e. g. many *Floridea*) and Mosses, this stops short with the differentiation of elongated cells, which differ otherwise but little from the surrounding tissues. In higher stages of organisation, on the contrary, i. e. in all vascular plants (the higher Cryptogams and Phanerogams), however, these undergo a very peculiar and complicated development, as strands of tissue serving as channels for the sap, and constitute the vascular bundles or fibro-vascular strands.

Thus, with a little consideration, and bearing in mind the most general vital conditions of the plant, we find that there is a triad of tissue-systems which compose the bodies of highly organised plants; or, put better, three systems of tissues arise in these plants by differentiation. These are the epidermal tissue, the fibro-vascular strands or vascular bundles, and the remaining tissue, which I have already distinguished from the other two as the fundamental tissue. It has recently been attempted, it is true, to resolve these three systems of tissues into a greater number of different forms of tissues; in this, however, either quite subordinate physiological points of view, or even purely formal morphological considerations have been started from. I find, after all that has been said in this direction in the literature of the last six or eight years, no ground whatever for giving up the classification into the three systems of tissues named, which is, moreover, almost universally accepted; and so much the less, since all other histological considerations can be harmonised with these three systems in a perfectly unconstrained manner This is possible on the one hand even with very highly organised vascular plants, where, at least in the young states of the organs, epidermal tissue, vascular bundles, and fundamental tissue are at once prominent as the three essential systems; on the other hand, I do not know how this triple division is to be evaded in the Mosses, especially in the more highly organised true Mosses, as well as in the more highly developed Algæ The last named subdivisions of plants present, rather, very fine examples of rudimentary forms of the three systems of tissues. If we take into consideration, finally, the forms reduced or degraded from the highly developed types, such as phanerogamic water-plants and parasites, it again results that all other differentiations of tissues fall completely into the background as secondary matters in contrast to those here brought forward.

As in the consideration of the external segmentation of plants, I shall here also introduce in the first place the typical highly developed forms, in their most important relations of configuration, and then come back to some rudimentary and derived or reduced forms.

We find the typical forms of the three systems of tissues, however, developed chiefly in the axes and leaves of aerial shoots, and the following statements are in the first place intended to refer to these.

The Epidermis is the superficial tissue of the younger shoot-axes and leaves, not yet altered by the requirements of an advanced age; since in true roots a specially organised epidermis can but rarely be spoken of, and even in submerged water-plants the outer layer of tissue is often scarcely to be distinguished from those lying deeper In its typical form, the epidermis is thus found on the leaves and shoots exposed to air and light, and is but little modified even on those underground. Physiologically understood, the epidermis is, as already mentioned, the layer of tissue sharply marking off the organ concerned from the exterior, and its essential properties chiefly amount to this,—to hinder the evaporation of the fluids contained in the cell-tissue, and to prevent injurious influences entering from without; while, on the other hand, through more or less numerous stomata, a means is afforded of discharging the aqueous vapour formed in the interior, according to need, and at the same time of facilitating the entrance and exit of carbon dioxide and oxygen gas We may regard this as the proper function of the epidermis; though it is by no means gain-said that the most various other functions are required of it according to circum-stances.

Let us first consider the arrangements of the epidermis serving for exclusion[1]. It consists usually of a single layer of tabular, or more rarely of columnar cells, the lateral walls of which are in close contact on all sides; so that the layer usually constitutes a very thin but, in relation to its thickness, extremely firm membrane formed of cells, which on leaves and young shoot-axes can in many cases be stripped off over wide areas. The external wall of the epidermis cells is usually of considerable thickness, and is occasionally so thickened that the cavity is relatively insignificant. In rarer cases it is the wall of the inner side which presents the strong thickening. The contents of the epidermis cells are usually devoid of chlorophyll grains, even on leaves and shoot-axes abounding in chloro-phyll; yet not unfrequently, especially in Ferns and some Phanerogams, and particularly those growing in the shade, the protoplasmic lining of the wall also contains chlorophyll grains, and in submerged water-plants the chloro-phyll contents of the external cell-layer (repre-senting the epidermis) may be even particu-larly abundant. The shutting off, already more or less completely ensured by the thickening of the outer walls, is however considerably promoted by means of a pellicle, usually very thin but sometimes thicker, which runs continuously over the outer surface of all the epidermis cells, and is distinguished as the Cuticle. The substance of this thin pellicle, the properties of which agree essentially with those of cork, differs from cellulose: it is dissolved by alkalies, but withstands concentrated sulphuric acid (which liquifies cellulose), and its most important property consists in that it is permeated only with difficulty by water, thus hindering the entrance and exit of that liquid. Hence the cuticle is especially thick in leaves and shoot-axes which have need of considerable protection against the evaporation of the water of the cells, as on the leaves of ever-green plants and of succulents (e. g. *Agave, Aloe*, Firs, and species of *Cactus*). Very frequently the protection afforded by the cuticle is enhanced by the cutin or cuticular substance being also deposited in the outer walls of the epidermis cells themselves, and forming in these the so-called cuticularised layers of the walls of the epidermis cells. As a further step towards the shutting off from the outer world, and especially against the entrance of rain-water and dew, we may regard the formation of wax, partly in the sub-

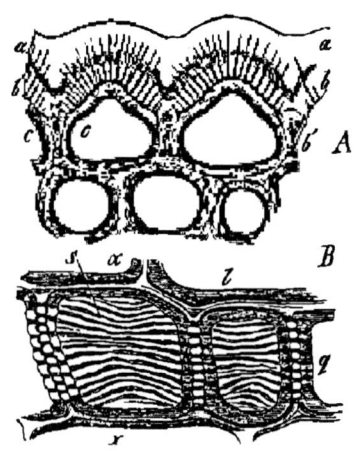

FIG. 115.—Epidermis of the midrib of the leaf of *Ilex aquifolium. A* transverse section, *B* surface view from without. *a, b* the very thick cuticle, with its processes *b'*, *c* wall of the cells of the epidermis.

---

[1] The most thorough description of the epidermis is found in De Bary's classical work, '*Ver-gleichende Anatomie der Vegetations-organe der Phanerogamen und Farne*,' Leipzig, 1877.

stance of the outer wall of the epidermis and the cuticle itself, partly on the outside of the latter. These waxy deposits, first exactly investigated by De Bary, appear in the form of exceedingly small granules on the surface of the cuticle, or as fine rodlets, or lastly as continuous, occasionally very thick, crusts of wax, which, in virtue of their fatty nature, do not allow water to adhere to the epidermis; so that rain and dew hanging on the shoots usually form round drops. If such leaves clothed with wax are dipped in water, they exhibit in it a silvery-glancing layer of air, and after withdrawal, it is found that they have not been wetted by the water, but are dry.

By means of this arrangement, the internal tissue is protected against the loss of those substances which would diffuse out through surfaces coming directly in contact with water — a point to which I shall return at another opportunity. It is obvious, by the way, that the arrangements just described are wanting in subterranean and submerged shoots which absorb water and nutritive materials from without

Although the leaf-surfaces are protected in the manner stated against the entrance of water from without, as well as against the unlimited evaporation of the water of the cell-sap; there yet remains on the other hand the necessity of letting aqueous vapour escape according to circumstances from the assimilatory surfaces into the atmosphere, in order that fresh water containing nutritive materials absorbed by the roots may follow on into the organs of assimilation, and it is likewise necessary to provide passages for the entrance of carbon dioxide as well as

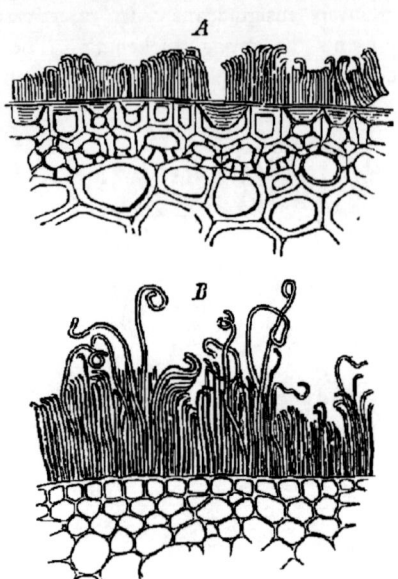

FIG 116.—Epidermis and layers of tissue immediately subjacent of the haulm of *Saccharum officinarum* (Sugar cane). *A* internode , *B* node—showing wax formations on the surface (De Bary.)

the exit of the oxygen gas produced by its decomposition. We find these in the so-called stomata of the epidermis. The more vigorous the transpiration, and, consequently, the more copious the absorption and decomposition of carbon dioxide by means of the chlorophyll-corpuscles, the more numerous in general are the stomata. Hence it is pre-eminently on the surfaces of the green organs of assimilation, the foliage-leaves, that they occur in enormous numbers; while they are always wanting at the roots, and are only found on subterranean and submerged shoots incidentally and in small numbers. On the sub-aërial shoot-axes and other organs they are more or less numerous according to circumstances. The extraordinary minuteness of the stomata, in connection with the properties of the cuticle which clothes them, prevents water under ordinary circumstances from entering by capillarity, and likewise prevents dust, fungus-spores, &c., from penetrating their openings; while an adequate exchange of gases and discharge of aqueous vapour can always be provided for by a corresponding increase in the number of these fine openings, and by the plant at the same time possessing the power of enlarging or diminishing the width of the stomata according to requirement

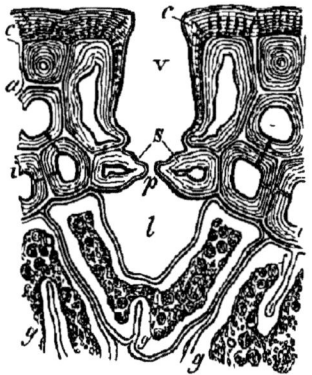

FIG 117 —Transverse section of the leaf of *Pinus Pinaster* (×800)   *s* guard cells of a stoma (*p*), under which is the air cavity *l*, *v* entrance surrounded by the epidermis cells, the cuticle (*c*) of which is very thick, *a* the middle lamella, and *t* the thickening layers of the sclerenchyma cells, *g* cells of the leaf parenchyma, with the contents contracted

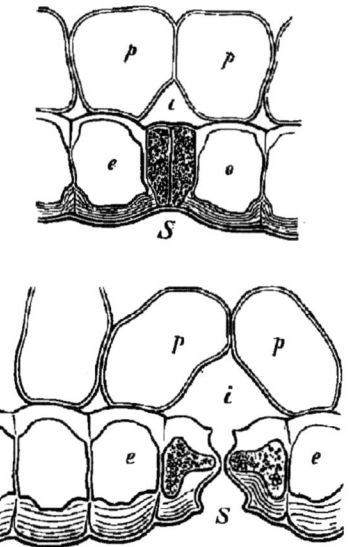

FIG 118, young, and (FIG 119) fully developed stomata of the leaf of the Hyacinth *s* stoma in transverse section, *i* air-cavity, *e, e* neighbouring cells of the epidermis, *p, p* parenchyma of the leaf

The extreme narrowness of these openings, even at the maximum, is shown by the statements of Mohl, according to which the very large stomata of various species of *Lilium* may be widened up to $\frac{1}{170}$ mm at most, and those of Indian corn (*Zea Mays*) up to $\frac{1}{178}$ mm at most; while Unger gives the size of the open fissures of *Agapanthus umbellatus* as 0 000047 sq. mm. This extraordinary minuteness is compensated by the large number of the stomata. On the foliage leaves, they amount per sq. mm in the most frequent cases to 40–100, very often 100–300, occasionally even 600–700 and more, so that the epidermis of a foliage leaf of any considerable size is penetrated by many millions of these fine openings —In accordance with the object of the stomata above indicated, they are fundamentally nothing but the mouths of the intercellular spaces of the internal tissue which are developed pre-eminently in the organs rich in chlorophyll; and the stomata are also again only intercellular spaces between peculiarly formed cells of the epidermis, the so-called guard-cells. Every stoma, where it penetrates the epidermis, is surrounded by two peculiarly formed cells, the guard-cells, the partition-wall of which, originally simple, has become split, and so formed the intercellular space or pore of the stoma The figures here annexed show the condition of things sufficiently for our purpose. If we strip off the epidermis from a foliage-leaf, and spread it out beneath the microscope, the peculiarly formed pairs of cells which have proceeded from one mother-cell, and have produced the proper stoma by the splitting of their partition-wall, and thus surround it, are easily recognised. Very often, especially in the highly organised Phanerogams, another group of peculiarly placed and formed epidermis cells are found around the pair of guard-cells, these have arisen, before or after the development of the proper guard-cells, from neighbouring epidermis cells by the corresponding formation of partition-walls, and further growth. Our figures show several cases of such accessory cells of the stomata. As a peculiarity of the guard-cells, it is moreover to be added, that

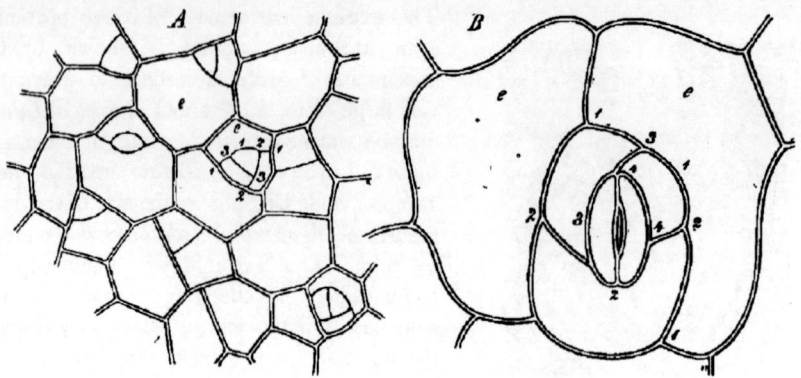

FIG. 120 —Development of stomata on the leaf of *Sedum purpurascens* *A* very young, *B* nearly mature, *e, e* epidermis cells. The numbers denote the order of succession of the divisions

they always contain chlorophyll-grains in somewhat large quantity, even when the rest of the epidermis is devoid of them.

There is no doubt that the stomata are originally destined for the exchange of gases of the assimilating organs, and for the regulated discharge of aqueous

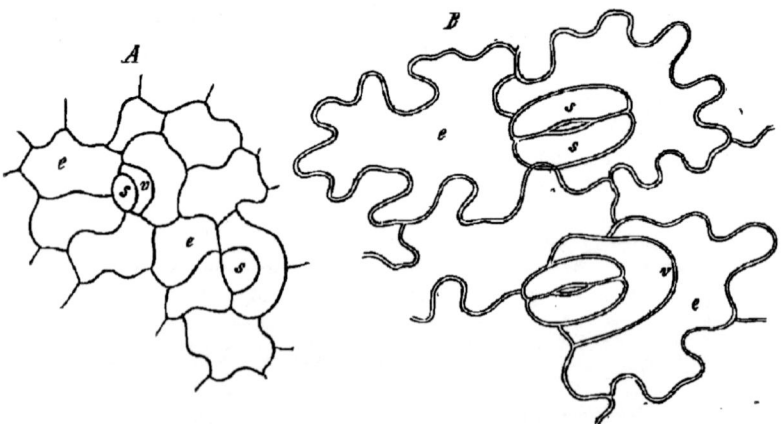

FIG. 121 —Development of stomata of *Pteris flabellata* (a Fern) *A* very young, *B* almost mature, *e* cells of the epidermis, *v* preparatory divisions, *s* (in *A*) mother cell, which forms the two guard cells (*ss*) in *B*

vapour Nevertheless, these organs, as occurs so often elsewhere, may also be made serviceable for totally different purposes; and thus we find in many cases, especially in the highly organised Phanerogams, that stomata, but little modified in other respects, are employed for the purpose of conducting to the surface water excreted from the internal tissues. Such stomata, which are generally situated on the margins of the foliage leaves or on the teeth of the leaf-margin, or more rarely at definite points on the surface of the leaf, are distinguished from the ordinary air-stomata as water-stomata. beneath them are the terminations of fibro-vascular bundles which convey the water. Later on, when the movements of water in the plant is being treated of, we shall return to these modified stomata. If, proceeding from the vascular plants down towards the more simply organised groups, we trace the formation of epidermis, we often find, especially in the *Muscineæ*, that where it is a matter not of simple tissue-layers but of solid masses of tissue containing chlorophyll, a completely typical epidermis, even with stomata, is present In the true Mosses, the spore-forming capsule, also histologically complex in other respects, possesses stomata in

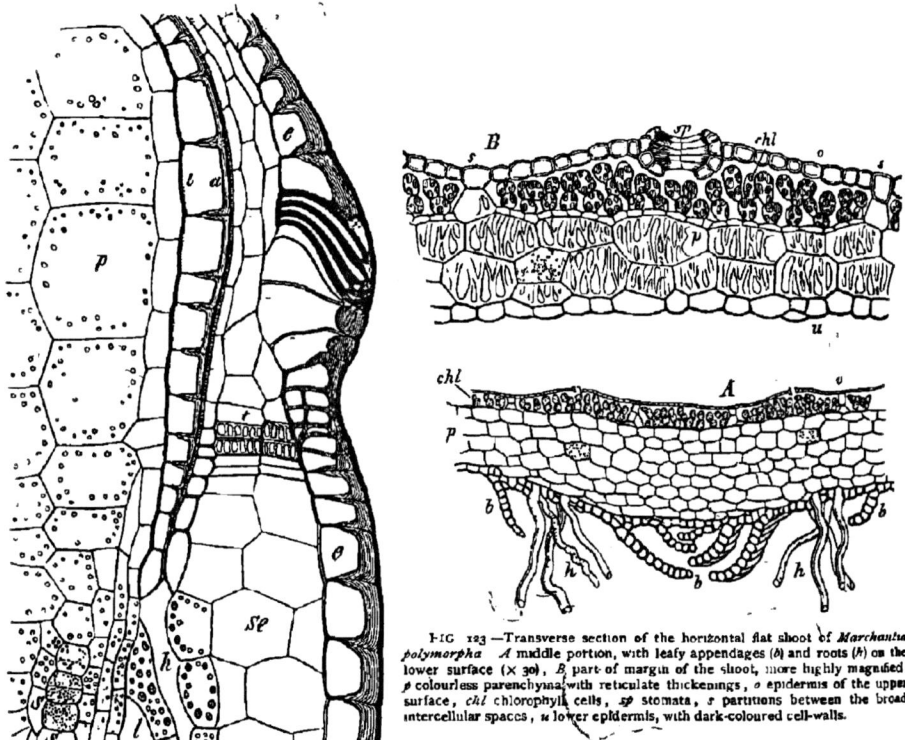

FIG 123 —Transverse section of the horizontal flat shoot of *Marchantia polymorpha* A middle portion, with leafy appendages (*b*) and roots (*h*) on the lower surface (× 30), *B* part of margin of the shoot, more highly magnified, *p* colourless parenchyma with reticulate thickenings, *o* epidermis of the upper surface, *chl* chlorophyll cells, *sp* stomata, *s* partitions between the broad intercellular spaces, *u* lower epidermis, with dark-coloured cell-walls.

FIG. 122.—*Funaria hygrometrica.* Portion of a longitudinal section of the immature capsule, *e* epidermis, *p* parenchyma, *i, a* thickened walls which develope later the inner and outer peristome.

a highly organised epidermis; and among the flat-shooted Liverworts, the shoot, composed of several layers of cells, exhibits on the surface conspicuously large stomata, deviating from the typical structure, and also differing in their development. In all Algæ and Fungi, on the other hand, these organs are completely wanting; and in most cases, the superficial tissue of these plants cannot well be termed epidermis, in the narrower sense of the word, although wherever the tissue of a plant consists of several layers, the outer layer, formed of one or more strata of cells, is so organised that it sharply shuts off the internal tissue from the external world. The cells of the outer layer especially fit together without inter-spaces, and are, like the epidermis cells of the higher plants, generally somewhat smaller than those of the internal tissue, and cuticularised on the outer side, or clothed by a cuticle : and even

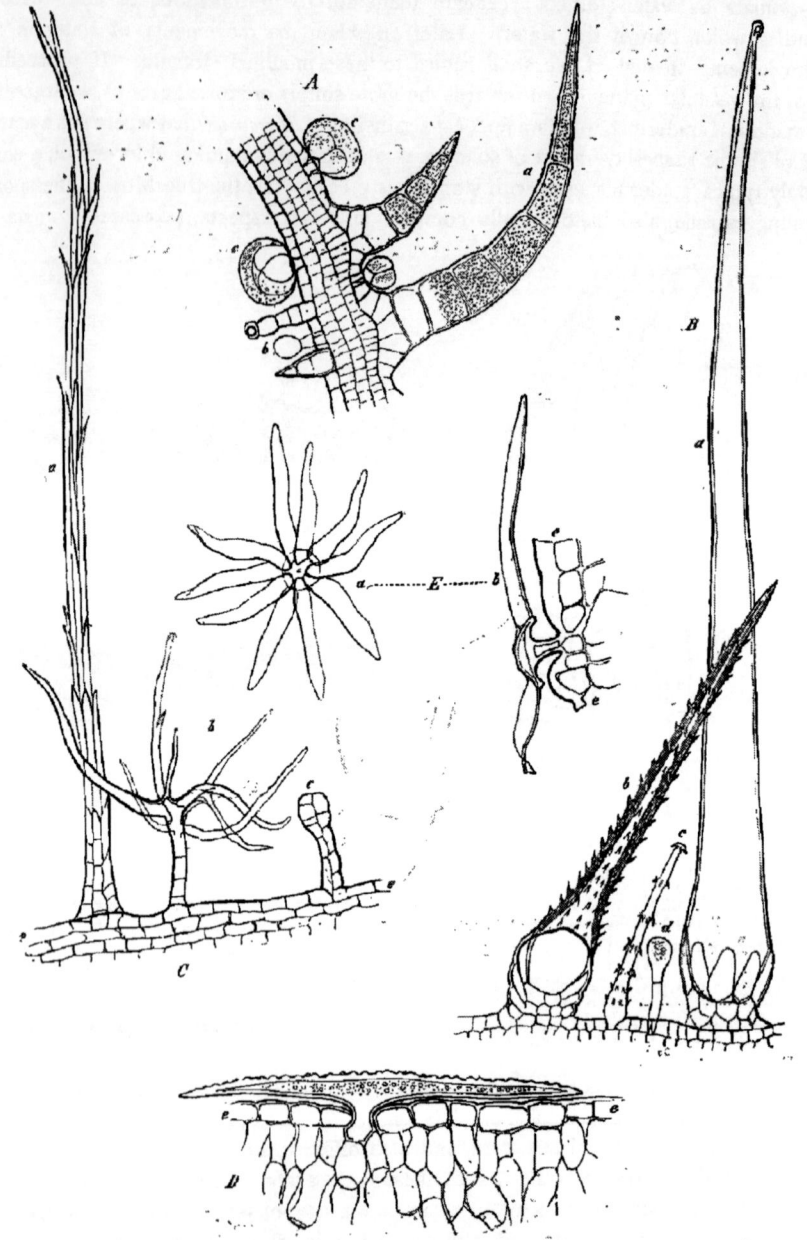

FIG. 124.—Examples of the forms of hairs. *A* of *Plectranthus fruticosus; B Cajophora lateritia; C Hieracium piliferum; D Cheiranthus Cheiri.* (After De Bary.)

in organs where a single layer of cells constitutes the tissue—as in the prothallia of Ferns, the leaves of Mosses, and in many Algæ,—and where the vegetative body consists only of septate filaments, or even only of isolated cells, as in many Algæ, we still find at the surface, at least cuticularised outer layers of the cell-wall, or even an actual cuticle; and this is not wanting even on the isolated cells of vascular plants, e.g. spores, and pollen-grains,—and indeed is often strongly developed on them.

To the characteristic peculiarities of the epidermis, especially of vascular plants, belong the structures known as hairs. In the narrower sense of the word, hairs are outgrowths of individual epidermis-cells, which however, by means of their growth and physiological adaptations, may assume the most various forms. According to circumstances, these outgrowths of the epidermis cell are wart-like projections, vesicles, elongated tubes, shield-like outspread scales, prickly outgrowths, or soft

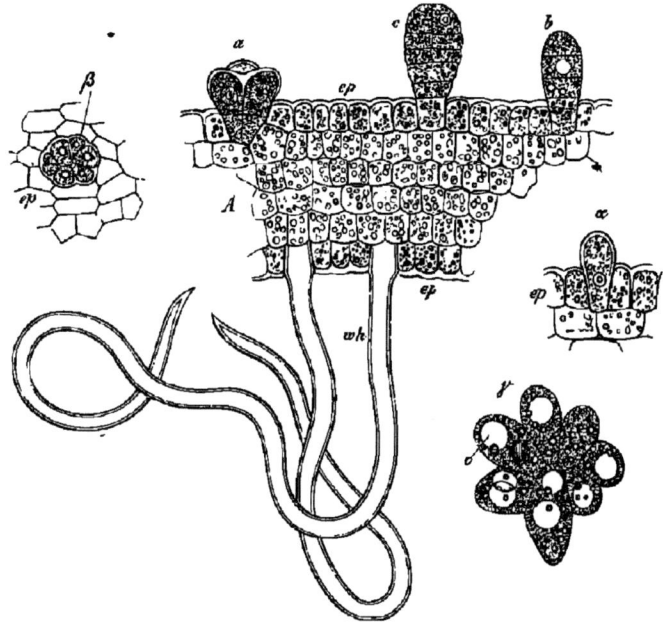

FIG 125 —Development of the hairs on the calyx of a flower-bud of *Althæa rosea* (× 300), *wh* (in *A*) woolly hairs on the inner surface, *b* and *c* glandular hairs in various stages of development, *a* (to the right) rudiment of a glandular hair, *ep* everywhere, the (still young) epidermis The figures *a* in *A*, *β* (to the left) and *γ* (to the right, lower figure) first stages of development of the stellate (or rather tufted) hairs, of which later stages may be compared in Fig 126 In *A*, *a* shows the hair in longitudinal section, *β* and *γ* seen from above The cells are rich in protoplasm, in *γ* the development of vacuoles (*v*) is beginning

woolly coverings, and so forth. Moreover, these outgrowths may remain simple tubes, or, as they grow further, become transformed by means of more or less numerous transverse and longitudinal divisions into multicellular organs. Among the vascular plants, there are only few, as the aerial shoots of Equisetums, Conifers, and Duckweeds (*Lemnaceæ*), where the formation of hairs generally is wanting. Usually, indeed, one and the same plant is furnished with various kinds of hairs, often so densely that hardly anything else is to be seen on the surface of the organ

There is scarcely any other organ in the vegetable kingdom where the two different principles—on the one hand the mere formative force of organic substance, and on the other hand the adaptation to definite life-purposes—come so clearly into view as in the hairs. For on the one hand we find them peculiar and constant in form in nearly whole families—e g. the large bristle hairs of the *Boragineæ*, the stellate hairs of the *Cruciferæ*, the tufted hairs of the *Malvaceæ* and so forth—without our being able to assign any use for them to the plant concerned. On the other hand, we find a great variety of forms of hairs, the biological significance of which can scarcely be doubtful, and the presence of which varies within closely allied groups. Among the simplest, and yet most important forms of hairs, are the root-hairs, already mentioned; these are mere protuberances

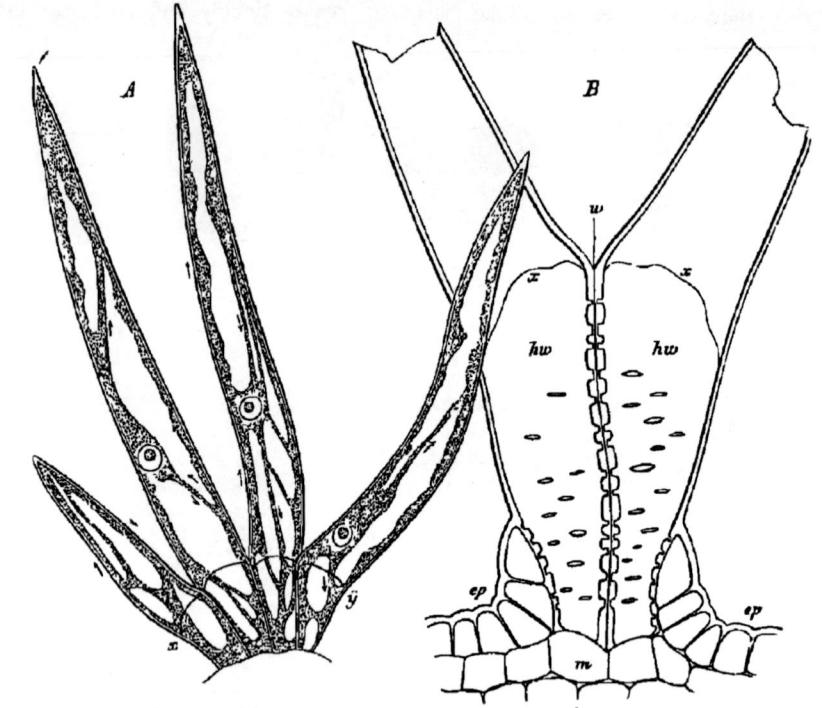

FIG 126.—*A* stellate hair on the calyx of a young flower bud of *Althæa rosea* thicker projections of protoplasm lie on the wall of each cell, and are in 'streaming' motion (indicated by the arrows), *B* epidermis (*ep*) with the basal portion of a fully developed stellate hair, showing the structure of the wall (× 550)

of the superficial cells of the roots which grow out into long tubes, and which, as has been already shown, play such a very important part (in the land-plants especially) in the taking up of water and mineral nutritive matters Much more various are the physiological uses of hairs on the aerial shoots, on leaves as well as shoot-axes There we find in the first place hairs of the simplest structure, as long, twisted, thin-walled vesicles very soon losing their fluid contents,—the woolly hairs, which form woolly coverings on the young parts of shoots before their complete development, and are thus to be looked upon as means of protection for the parts of the bud against injurious external influences; such hairy coverings are found, for example, on the unfolding buds of the Horse-chestnut, Alpine-rose, various Aralias, etc.

These become loosened from the epidermis on the complete unfolding of the bud-parts, so that later on no trace remains of their former existence   In other cases, on the contrary, these woolly hairs, which contain air and which are occasionally branched, multicellular, etc , and devoid of sap, remain even on the completely formed parts of the shoot the latter then appear in the fuller developed condition covered as with a white glistening wool—e. g. the leaves of the Mullein (*Verbascum*), of *Stachys germanica*, and so forth   A very common form of hairs is the glandular hair ; these are generally formed of a short or long stalk, with a little head situated upon it.   Ethereal oils, resin, gum, strong-smelling matters, &c. are secreted in the latter, which we therefore relegate to the category of organs of secretion, to be considered more closely later   To this category of organs belong also the so-called *Colleters* ,   These are usually multicellular, very variously formed hairs on the young bud-parts of widely different plants (e g *Rumex, Ribes, Alnus, Syringa*), out of which, on contact with water, a bal-

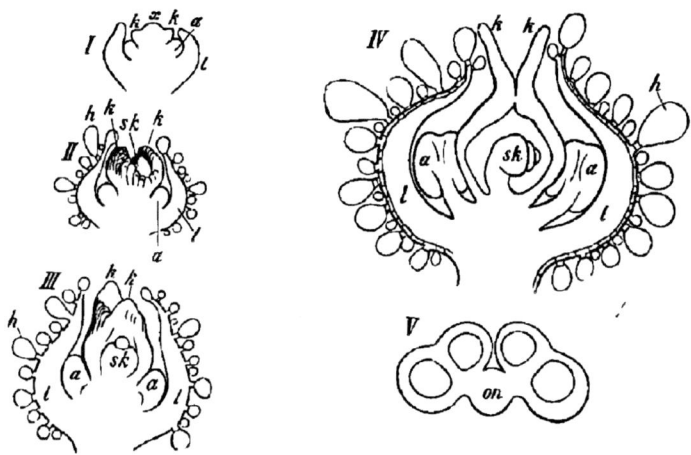

FIG 127 —*Chenopodium quinoa. I—IV* development of the flower (longitudinal sections), *l* the calyx, beset with glandular hairs , *a* anthers, *k, k* carpel, *sk* ovule, *x* apex of floral axis. *V* transverse section of an anther showing four pollen sacs and the connective (*on*) highly magnified

samic mixture of gums and resins exudes, which clothes the surfaces of the unfolding bud-parts, and subsequently disappears.   Commonly intermingled with such secreting hairs in very many Phanerogams are stinging hairs, of the most various form: long, conically projecting, pointed out-growths, the wall of which is usually strongly silicified, and among which the stinging hairs of the nettle-like plants (*Urticaceæ*), the *Loasaceæ* and others, are especially to be mentioned.   The tissue of the shoot-axes and leaves usually forms cushion-like outgrowths at the base of such hairs, as is also the case with the climbing hairs of twining stems (e g. of the Hop) ; these develope, from a short base sunk into the epidermis, on one, or two, or more sides, hook-shaped or needle-like, thick-walled, very hard outgrowths, which apparently contribute to increase the friction of the climbing stems on their supports.   In many insectivorous plants, the glandular hairs secrete peptonising digestive juices, and by this means indeed contribute to the nourishing of the plant (*Pinguicula, Drosera*).   On the other hand, again, the peltate or scale-like hairs (as in *Elæagnus*) springing from a narrow base in the form of a radially constructed shield, closely appressed to the surface of the leaf, as well as the stellate or tufted hairs proceeding from a single epidermis cell—e.g the Rose-mallow (*Althæa*)—are organs of quite unknown function. On the seeds and small fruits of very many Phanerogams are found hairs containing air, which appear in part as soft, twisted, woolly hairs (e.g. on the seeds of Cotton), or as stiff bristles (seeds of *Asclepias Syriaca*). They serve, as organs of flight, for the distribution of the seeds and small fruits, and they are especially well developed as the so-called Pappus of many *Compositæ* and *Valerianeæ*. Proceeding from the stinging hairs, we find, further, a series of stronger outgrowths of the epidermis, consisting of hard, lignified tissue, and, under the name of prickles, clothing the shoot-axes and occasionally the leaf-ribs of many phanerogamous plants. Some of these, which serve either for protection against the attacks of larger animals or as climbing organs, are, like the hairs, mere outgrowths of the epidermis—e.g. the prickles of the Bramble; more frequently, however, the deeper tissue also takes part with the epidermis in the formation of prickles, and even vascular bundles may terminate in them. Finally may be mentioned the flat, outspread, often relatively large hairs of many Ferns, empty of sap in the complete state, which clothe the leaf-stalk and occasionally the leaf-ribs of these plants with a dense 'ramentaceous' covering.

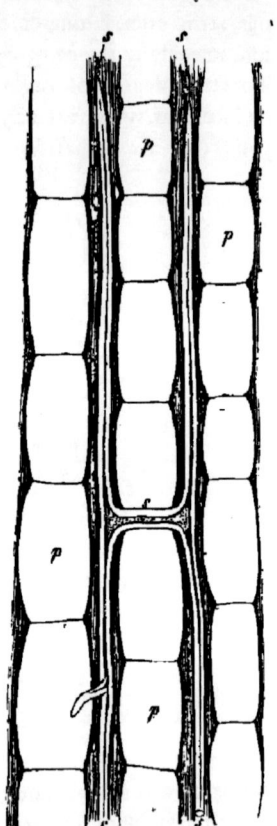

FIG 128.—Part of a longitudinal section of the leaf stalk of *Monstera deliciosa* (an Aroid) *p, p* parenchyma, *s, s* a sclerenchyma cell or internal hair in the form of the letter H

The hair-like structures certainly owe their existence and great variety to the circumstance that they are able to grow forth unhindered from the free surface of the plant. Hence cells and tissue-bodies which possess exactly the aspect of ordinary hairs are found generally in such places where free space for their formation exists; thus, single cells are developed in the form of hairs in internal tissues which are traversed by large, roomy, intercellular spaces. To the most conspicuous of such objects belong the stellate hairs in the leaf-stalks of the *Nymphæaceæ*, traversed by large intercellular spaces, and those in many tropical *Aroideæ*, the tissue of which indeed obtains, by means of such internal hair-like structures, a tenacious stringy texture. According to the principle stated (which regards the epidermis as the place of origin of the hairs less than the space free for the development of long outgrowths), hairs, often of considerable length, occur even on those very simple Algæ and Fungi where a true epidermis, or even indeed a distinct superficial layer, cannot be said to exist the hairs are in such cases simple outgrowths of the free surfaces of flat single-layered masses of tissue, as in the Alga *Coleochæte sculata*, or they are formed at the apex of a filament consisting of cells,

From the exceedingly various structure and biological significance of the hairs indicated above, it is self-evident that they present the greatest possible differences even in their material constitution. It is therefore hardly possible to say anything general concerning them, except that they are all, in their young states, simple cells, or portions of cells, or aggregates of cells, and that their membrane consists originally of cellulose, and their contents of protoplasm and cell-sap. With the further functional development the most various alterations may take place : the protoplasm and cell-sap may either completely disappear, and the hairs thus represent empty vesicles, as in cotton, and many other woolly hairs; or, on the other hand, the cell-contents are not only preserved, but the protoplasm is even very strongly nourished, and is then distinguished by circulatory movements and other vital peculiarities, as in the stinging hairs of the Nettle, the stellate hairs of *Althæa*, the jointed hairs on the stamens of *Tradescantia*, and in many other cases. According to circumstances, and corresponding to its biological importance, the cell-wall remains thin and pliant, or it becomes thickened, silicified, or stony—a process which may be extended to the tissue at the base of the hair (especially well seen, for instance, in the Gourd plant); or in contrast to this, certain layers of the cell-wall of the hair become mucilaginous, and swell up in contact with water, or a balsamic substance (ethereal oil, resin, etc.) is deposited between its fine cuticle and the inner layer of the cell-wall; or, finally, the capitula of the hairs become covered with waxy threads, as on the underside of the leaves of the Fern, *Gymnogrammè calomelanos*, and others.

In contrast to the numerous forms of hairs which can be distinguished as organs with definite functions, the frequent occurrence of hairs of which a biological significance is neither perceptible nor probable is of special interest. We find, for example, in some water-plants an uncommonly thick covering of hairs, especially on the young parts of the shoot, e g. in the Water-lily (*Nuphar*); while in other water-plants again with a very similar mode of life, this hairiness is wanting.

The second of the above systems of tissue are the Vascular bundles, or Fibro-vascular strands. I have already pointed out that the simplest rudimentary forms of these are observable already in some Algæ consisting of masses of tissue, as well as in the more strongly developed shoots of Mosses, where they are constituted in general as filiform bundles of thin-walled cells, distinguished from the rest of the tissue by their length. The typical form of vascular bundle, however, is so essential a characteristic of the higher Cryptogams and Phanerogams, that these two subdivisions have been placed from of old, under the name of vascular plants, in contrast to the *Muscineæ* and Thallophytes as the so-called cellular plants. The typical vascular bundles run in the form of thin filaments, often of considerable length, through the soft fundamental tissue of the roots, shoot-axes, and leaves In the roots, as already mentioned, there always runs but one strand, which lies in the axis, and with which the strands of the lateral roots are joined. It is however questionable whether these root-strands are not rather to be regarded as composed of two, three, four, or more proper vascular bundles.

Much more various are the relations in the shoot-axes. Only in some water-plants does a single strand of vascular bundles traverse the interfoliar part up to the growing-point; and with reference to its morphological nature the same probably holds good of it as of the axial root-strands. The vascular bundles of the leaves are

connected with this so-called cauline strand.   Usually, however, a larger number of
six, eight, ten, or even of hundreds of single thin vascular bundles run in a shoot-
axis; and each single vascular bundle generally belongs in its lower course to the
shoot-axis, but curves outwards into a leaf with its upper limb, in such a manner

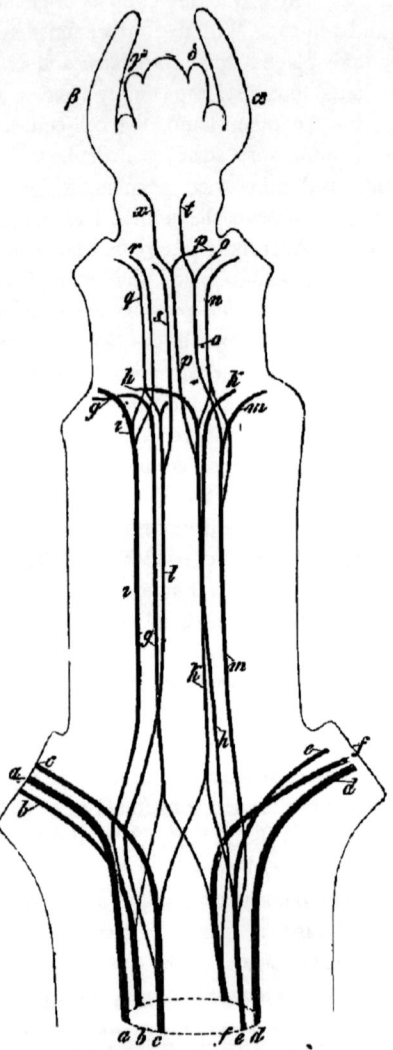

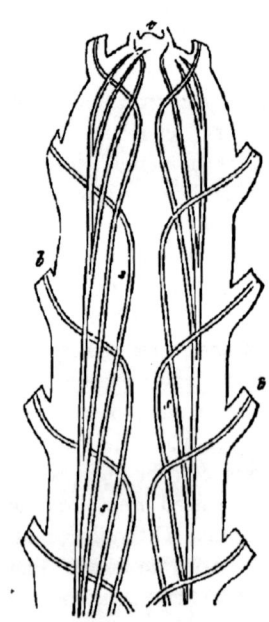

FIG. 109,—*Clematis viticella* (after Nageli)   Apex of
a shoot rendered transparent in order to show the course
of the vascular bundles, the upper ends of which curve outwards into the leaves.   The youngest leaves (a–δ) possess
as yet no vascular bundles

FIG 130,—Diagram showing the course of the vascular
bundles in a Monocotyledon of the Palm type (after Fal
kenberg).   b, b bases of the leaves, v growing points of
the shoot.

that each leaf takes up into itself one, two, three, or many such terminations of
the vascular bundles of the shoot-axis.   In the interior of the latter, however,
the single bundles are joined together so that the lower end of each becomes
fitted somewhere on the course of an older strand curving into a leaf situated

lower down.   As for the rest, great variety prevails in the other relations of the strands in the shoot-axes as well as in the leaf-stalks; and the cross connections of the strands at those parts of the shoot-axes which, as so-called nodes, represent swollen places close to the leaf-insertions, or occur as diaphragms at the corresponding places inside hollow stems (particularly evident in the Grasses), are especially to be alluded to.   Besides these common (to the axes and leaves) bundles, however, cauline bundles may also be found, the upper ends of which, growing further in the growing-point of the shoot-axis, do not curve out into leaves   In the leaf itself, especially in the lamina of green foliage leaves, the vascular bundles run in the leaf-ribs described previously, where they are surrounded by a special parenchymatous envelope.   Their generally very

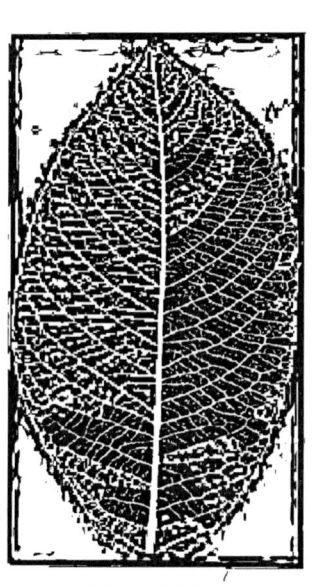

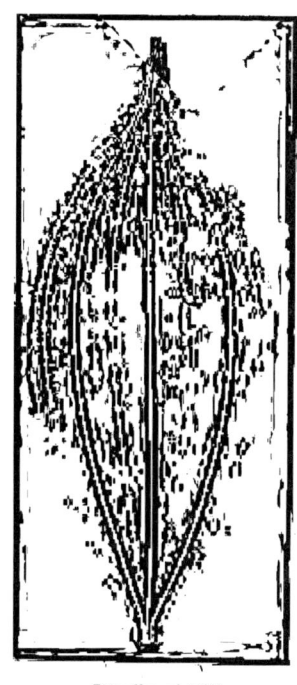

Salix grandifolia   *Convallaria latifolia.*

FIC 131 —Course of the vascular bundles (venation) in leaves

fine terminations however lose themselves, without projecting exteriorly, in the green leaf parenchyma itself, and there form the fine network of veins by which the broad ,dicotyledonous leaves especially are distinguished, or they branch there in a dichotomous manner, as in many Ferns, or extend in open curves, or almost straight lines in the leaves of the Monocotyledons,—relations which we have considered previously from another point of view, and shall yet treat of later on

The vascular bundles are generally very thin   In succulent shoot-axes, thinner roots, and in the venation of the leaves, they are often scarcely so thick as a human or horse hair; but occasionally they attain the thickness of a common thread, or thicker   'Only in the stems of the Tree-ferns, where they are broad and band-like, and form a coarse net-work, do they reach more considerable dimensions in transverse section. In general, they are just to be distinctly perceived with the unaided eye on transverse and longitudinal sections of the organs, especially by transmitted light. When they contain strongly lignified elements, which of course

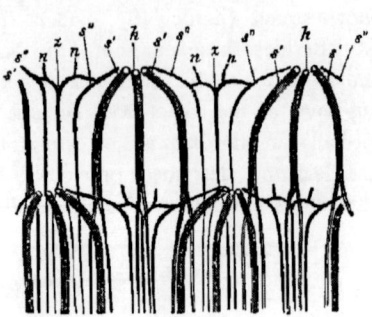

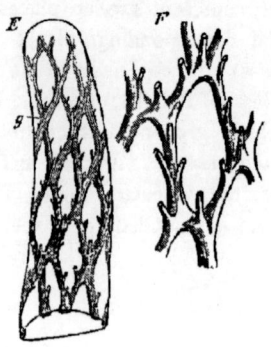

FIG. 132.—*Sambucus Ebulus:* the leaf-traces in two internodes. They are arranged in a cylinder, which is here flattened out in one plane. Each internode bears two opposite leaves, and each leaf receives from the stem a median bundle (*h*), and two strong lateral bundles (*s's'*). The descending bundles split below, and the limbs so formed are inserted into the spaces between the lower bundles. In addition to these, finer bundles (*s''x''*) exist, which are connected by horizontal branches from which bundles (*nn*) ascend into the stipules. (After Hanstein.)

FIG. 133.—*Aspidium filix-mas. E* network of vascular bundles (*g*) in the stem. *F* a single mesh, with the basal portions of fiber bundles which pass into the leaves.

only occurs in land-plants, and when, in consequence of this, they are tough and hard, they may often be drawn out from the tissues to considerable distances, in the form of extensible elastic threads (leaf-stalks of *Plantago major, Primula sinensis*); or

they may be laid bare in large pieces by scraping off the soft fundamental tissue, as in numerous Ferns, e.g. the stem of the Bracken, *Pteris aquilina,* and in our common male fern (*Aspidium filix mas*). After taking away all the leaf-stalks, it is possible by means of careful pressure, and bruising and washing, to obtain even the whole vascular bundle system of the stem, as a hollow cylindrical net-work. Particularly fine objects, very instructive for physiological purposes, are obtained as so-called vascular bundle skeletons, when

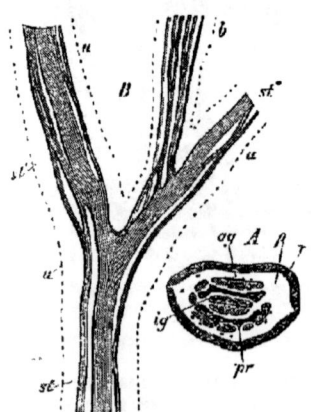

FIG. 134.—*Pteris aquilina. A* transverse section of the subterranean stem (natural size); *r* hard, brown sub-epidermal tissue; *p* soft, slimy parenchyma, rich in starch; *pr* dark walled sclerenchyma forming two broad bands traversing the stem; *ag* fibro-vascular bundles which run externally to these bands of sclerenchyma; *ig* bundles running internally to the same bands—*B* the fibro-vascular bundle *ag* (in *A*) isolated by scraping off the parenchyma: it divides and branches. The dotted lines (*u*) show the outline of the stem (*st*) and its branches (*st'* and *st''*) and a leaf-stalk (*b*).

suitable organs (parts of stems, foliage-leaves, fruits, &c.) are exposed to slow rotting under water, by which all the softer tissue is destroyed. Fine vascular bundle skeletons are often produced spontaneously in the open by frequent

[3]   K

freezing and thawing, and washing out in the rain. Of course such skeletons can only be obtained if the vascular bundles are lignified, or surrounded with lignified sheaths; since these, however, are found in the most various subdivisions of vascular plants, it is easy to make a collection of vascular bundle skeletons, certainly among the most instructive objects that can be preserved in a botanical museum. The careful and repeated study of successful vascular bundle skeletons of the most various leaves and shoot-axes, as *Œnanthe phellandrium*, *Zea Mais*, or old withered stems of Palms and *Dracænas*, as well as the fruits of the Thorn-apple (*Datura Stramonium*), old Banana fruits, and the like, is a most attractive occupation, provided that the observer is to a certain extent familiar with the physiological significance and origin of these structures. Only to one possessing

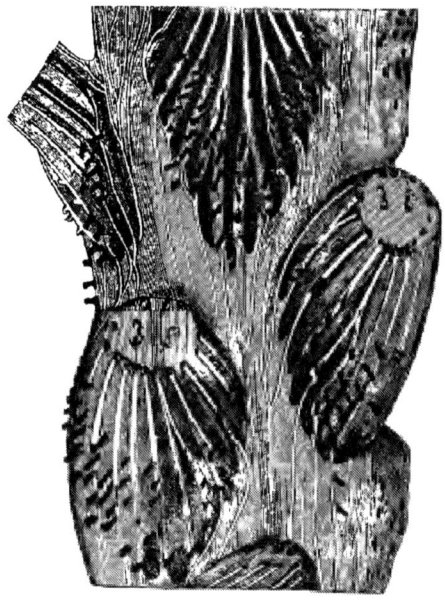

a sufficient knowledge of these microscopic relations can the microscopic structure of the vascular bundles be intelligible; and in order to arrive at clear conceptions concerning the conduction of materials which devolves upon the vascular bundles, and their co-operation in ensuring the solidity of the plant, the study of vascular bundle skeletons is indispensable. Their significance in teaching is even in our time much too little appreciated.

It is not very easy, in the short space at our disposal, to give a clear insight into the microscopical structure of vascular bundles: this, as need hardly be mentioned, undergoes great variations in the different subdivisions of plants. Only the most necessary points will be mentioned here, since I must repeatedly refer in detail to more special matters

FIG. 135.—*Cyathea Imrayana* (a Fern). Portion of a stem with the bases of four leaves, after the removal of the cortex, and showing the course of the vascular bundles. The dark bodies are roots. (After De Bary.)

subsequently, when we are concerned with physiological functions. In the first place, it is to be observed that a bundle by no means maintains the same structure through its entire course; the lower and upper ends are generally thinner than the middle parts, and therefore more simple in structure. As the thickness—i.e. the surface of the transverse section—grows, not only the number but also the variety of cell-forms increases. Thicker bundles may exhibit hundreds of cells on the transverse section, while the thinnest (e. g. in the venation of the leaves) consist of a few cells only.

It may also be pointed out that the microscopic picture of the vascular bundle in transverse section is generally extremely characteristic, and easily impresses itself on the imagination; whereas, in consequence of the great length, frequent thinning out, and oblique course of the individual elements, the picture of the longitudinal section of the vascular bundle often presents a confusing chaos of lines (contours of the cell-walls). In order to obtain a clear insight into the microscopic structure of the bundles, it is necessary carefully to compare transverse and longitudinal sections; since the characteristic forms of the cells are generally visible only in the lateral view (and therefore in the longitudinal section), while the arrangement and grouping of the elements are more evident in the transverse section. In addition, however, it happens that it is just in the study of the vascular bundles that the relations of symmetry prevailing in the anatomical structure of the plant, which we shall bring under general consideration later on, are particularly conspicuous; so that a longitudinal section through a bundle, carried in the radial direction from the outside inwards, affords a view quite different from that obtained when the knife meets the bundles parallel to the surface of the organ, or in any other direction. As

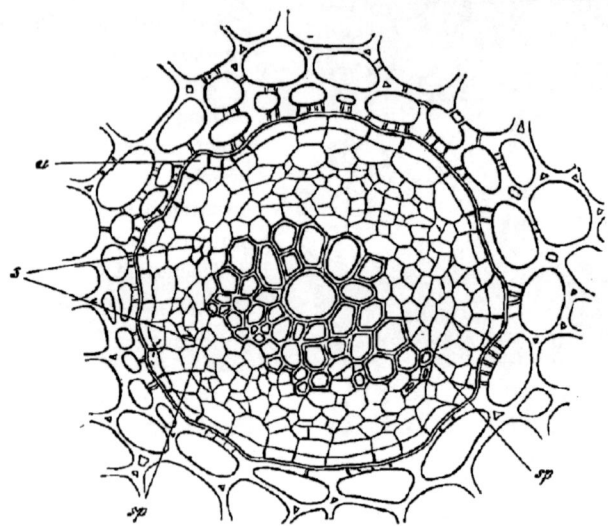

FIG 136.—Transverse section of a feebly developed vascular bundle from the rhizome of *Polypodium vulgare* (a Fern) *s* phloem, *sp* narrow spiral tracheides—the wider lumina belong to the broad scalariform tracheides. *n* endodermis (After De Bary)

a guide to the structure of a vascular bundle, always somewhat complicated, the distinction (first given by De Bary[1]) of the total mass of its cells into two subdivisions, the Bast-portion (*Phloëm* of Nägeli) and the Wood-portion (*Xylem* of Nägeli), is especially serviceable. Both groups consist in general of elongated, often very long, vesicular or tubular cells, narrow, or very narrow in transverse section, so that on a transverse section through an organ the vascular bundles usually come into view at once as groups of cells with peculiarly narrow lumina, situated in the large-celled parenchyma of the fundamental tissue. Individual elements, especially

---

[1] De Bary, *l c* p 330   I here bring forward De Bary's subdivision of the tissue of the vascular bundles into *Gefasstheil* and *Siebtheil*—the earlier subdivision into Wood and Bast (*Xylem* and *Phloëm*),—because by Schwendener's misusage of the word ‘Bast,’ by which he distinguishes all possible sclerenchymatous tissues not belonging to the vascular bundles, a confusion pernicious to the beginner has been introduced into the good old nomenclature

certain forms of vessels, may occasionally be very large, however, in transverse section. The phloem and xylem likewise agree in that, apart from rare exceptions and later transformations, they possess no intercellular spaces of any kind: the cells of a bundle all fit together closely on every side; and in this they differ conspicuously from the parenchyma of the fundamental tissue, which is interrupted by intercellular spaces.

The xylem, as well as the phloëm, consists of various forms of cells; and we may say, for the purposes of a rapid survey, that in each of these two groups, vascular,

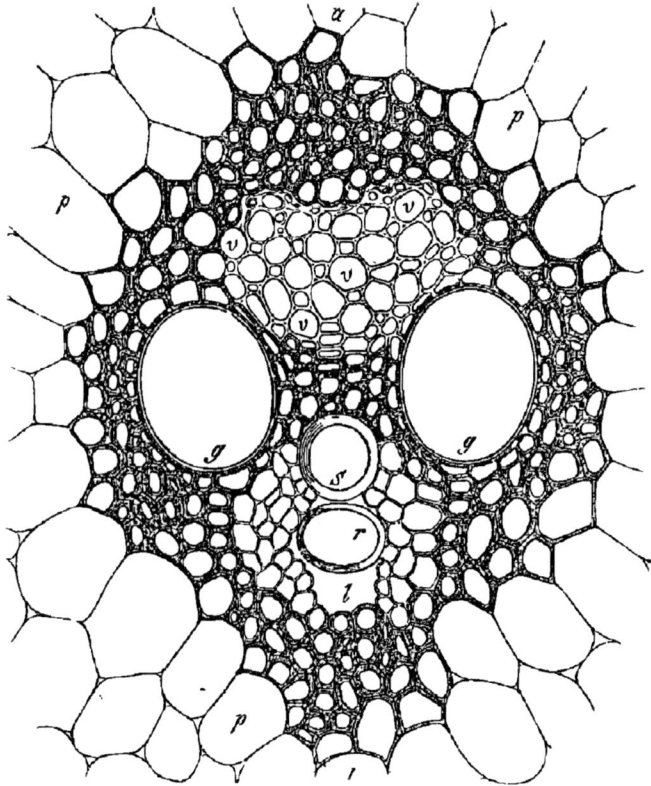

FIG. 137 —Transverse section of a closed fibro vascular bundle of the stem of *Zea Mays* (× 550) It consists of xylem (*g, g, S, r, l*) and phloem (*v, v*). The surrounding thick walled tissue is the bundle sheath, belonging to the fundamental tissue *p, p* thin-walled parenchyma of the fundamental tissue, *a* outer side, *i* inner side (facing the axis of the stem), *g g* two large pitted vessels, *s* spiral vessel, *r* isolated ring of an annular vessel, *l* air cavity produced by rupture during growth

fibrous, and parenchymatous elements occur. The homologous, and especially the vascular, elements of the one group, however, are different from those of the other group. In the more highly developed fibro-vascular bundles of terrestrial plants, the cell-walls in the xylem are either totally, or at any rate to a great extent, lignified; especially the walls of the vessels and woody-fibres. When the lignification in the xylem is reduced to a minimum, as occurs in very succulent tubers, tuberous roots, and aquatic plants, the lignification is not unfrequently confined to the walls of the vessels. In the phloëm, either no lignification of the cell-walls occurs at all, or it follows only late in the thick-walled fibres—the proper bast-cells: these, however, often also remain entirely unlignified.   The pliability of true bast, e. g. of Flax- and Hemp-fibres, simply depends upon their being not lignified at all, or only to a very slight extent.   The other elements of the phloem are remarkable for their soft, pure cellulose walls.   Difficult though it is, however, to separate phloem and xylem sharply from one another by words, the difference of their aspect under the microscope is nevertheless usually conspicuous.   It is especially characteristic for

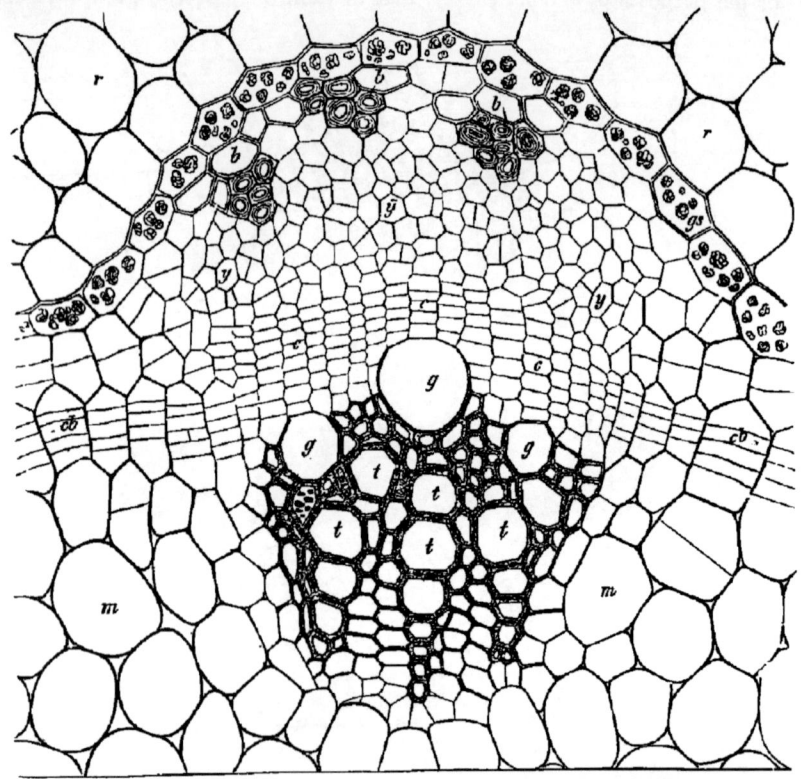

FIG. 138.—Part of a transverse section of the completely extended hypocotyledonous portion of the stem of *Ricinus communis*. *r* parenchyma of the primary cortex and *m* pith, both belonging to the fundamental tissue. Between *r* and *b* is the simple vascular bundle sheath (containing starch), which also belongs to the fundamental tissue. The bundle consists of phloem (*b*, *y*), xylem (*g*, *t*), and cambium (*c*, *c*) and is therefore an open bundle   The cambium (*c*, *c*) extends into the fundamental tissue situated between the bundles as interfascicular cambium (*c*, *b*), which arises by subsequent division of the large parenchyma cells   *b*, *b* bast fibres , *y*, *y* soft bast (partly parenchyma, partly sieve tubes) , *t*, *t* narrow, and *g*, *g* wide, dotted vessels, with wood prosenchyma between.

the xylem, that at least some air-conducting vessels are present; while the vascular elements of the phloem, the sieve-tubes, are filled with slime containing albuminous matters, or clear sap, and never contain air.   So far as we have yet succeeded in obtaining an insight into the physiological significance of the vascular bundles, the xylem appears to be the tissue which provides chiefly for the conveyance of the water taken up by the roots, and the mineral nutritive matters contained in it, to the organs of assimilation: however the true function of the cavities of the vessels, which, as we shall see later, contain very rarified air, and are only filled with water in special cases, still remains doubtful. On the other hand, we may regard the phloëm, in the main, as the form of tissue in which albuminous substances containing nitrogen are produced, and by which they are distributed for long distances in the organs: the elements of the phloem may also serve for the transport of products of assimilation. The vascular bundles of simpler structure, especially in water-plants, are probably confined to these functions; while in cases where, with the increase of the assimilating foliage, a more rapid bringing of water and carrying away of products of assimilation are necessary, greater complexities in structure occur. In land-plants especially the tendency prevails to produce elastic fibres within the vascular bundle itself; that is, wood-cells in the xylem, and true bast-fibres in the phloem. In other cases the vascular bundle is enveloped, on one side or all round, with such elastic fibres: this contributes to the solidity of the organs, especially of the shoot-axes and leaves, and as I hope to show later, the conduction of water is facilitated at the same time.

The arrangement of the xylem and phloem in a vascular bundle presents many noteworthy differences, according to the organ and the class of plant. it is not possible however, apart from details, to establish a relation between them and definite physiological principles. It may therefore suffice, with the help of the accompanying figures, simply to point out here a few of the most important differences in this connection. Thus, we find in the Ferns, as Fig. 139 shows, the xylem enveloped all round by a more or less thick layer of phloem. In the Monocotyledons,

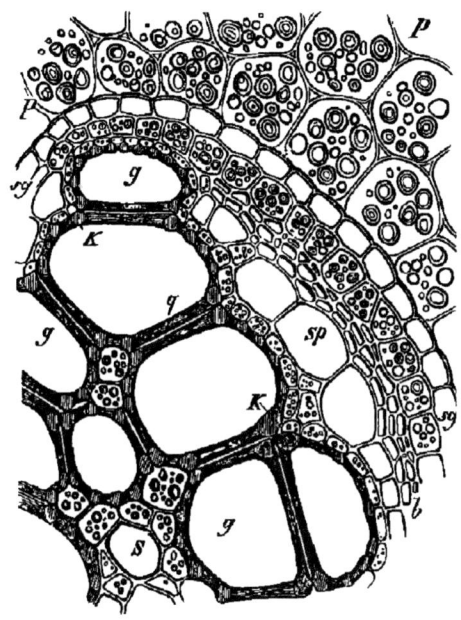

FIG 139.—Portion of the transverse section of a large vascular bundle from the stem of *Pteris aquilina*, with some of the surrounding parenchyma (*P*) the latter is filled (in winter) with starch *s* spiral vessel in one focus of the elliptical transverse section, this is surrounded by thick-walled wood cells, containing starch *g, g* scalariform vessels and *sp* sieve tubes Between these and the xylem is a layer of cells bearing starch in winter *b* bast cells with thick soft walls, *sg* vascular bundle sheath Between *sg* and *b* is a layer of cells containing starch.

on the other hand, and particularly in the Grasses, the latter forms a strand, which is accompanied on its inner-side (i e. the side turned towards the axis of growth of the organ) by the xylem, which also envelopes it more or less laterally {Fig 137). Fig. 138 gives an approximate representation of the ordinary structure of the vascular bundle of the Dicotyledons. With respect to details I may refer to the explanations of the figures, with the remark that in the monocotyledonous bundles (Fig. 137) the thick-walled cells, forming a sheath surrounding the whole proper vascular bundle, do not belong to the bundle itself, but represent one of the frequently occurring arrangements to ensure solidity appertaining to the fundamental tissue, to which I shall come back later. It would carry us here much too far to enter more in detail into the relations indicated: moreover this would be superfluous, since their physiological significance, as already explained, are either not known, or, where it is possible, will be brought forward subsequently as opportunity serves

Strikingly different from the vascular bundles of the shoot-axes and leaves are the fibro-vascular strands of all true roots; and they are usually so characteristic that it is recognised at once on a transverse section whether a root-strand is under observation or not   The most striking feature is that the xylem and phloem-bundles are so placed in groups at the periphery of the axial cylinder, that they alternate with one another laterally; the phloem-bundles being situated chiefly on the surface of the strands, and the xylem, radially placed, forming plates proceeding from the periphery towards the inside, between the phloem - bundles, as shown in the accompanying figures. One of the most striking pecu-liarities of the root-strand is that the narrowest, thinnest vessels lie on the outer cir-cumference, and are those first formed: further towards the interior of the strand, vessels with continually wider lumina become de-veloped. Only when the root-strand possesses a more considerable thickness, is its axial space occupied by a kind of pith—i. e paren-chymatous tissue : in very thin root-strands this is en-tirely wanting, and, indeed, a vessel, or a group of vessels may run in the axis of the strand. Moreover, between the vascular plates and phloem-bundles are

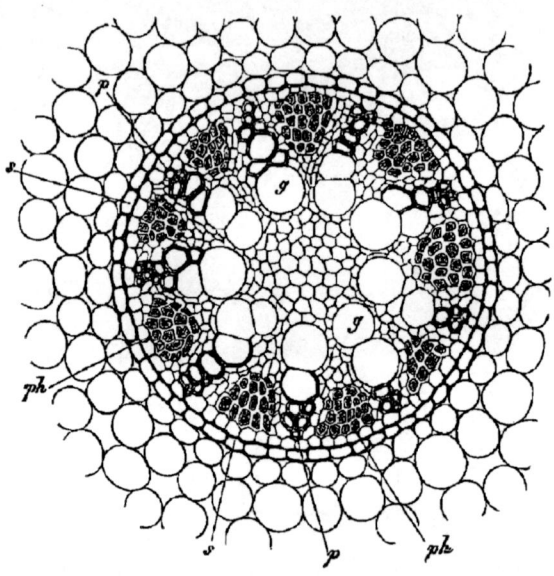

FIG 140.—Root of *Acorus Calamus*   Transverse section of the axial cylinder with surrounding cortical tissue   *s* Endodermis , *p, p* narrow, peripheral (oldest) vessels , *g* wide, inner (younger) vessels , *ph* phloëm

formed small quantities of parenchymatous tissue, filling the interspaces to a certain extent; as in the bundles of the shoot, parenchymatous elements are present in addition to the vascular and fibrous elements.

If we now, finally, take into consideration the cell-forms of the vascular bundles themselves, already mentioned, the vascular elements are most prominent in both parts.   Those in the xylem are generally termed, shortly, vessels; while those of the phloëm, corresponding to them, are named sieve-tubes

As vessels in the wider sense, and thus comprehending both the forms men-tioned, are to be distinguished longitudinal rows of cells, the cavities of which communicate directly with one another by the transverse septa being either com-pletely absorbed, or perforated by pores.

The vessels (wood-vessels) appear in relatively thick, vigorous bundles in various forms, as annular vessels, as spiral vessels with one or more spiral bands, or as

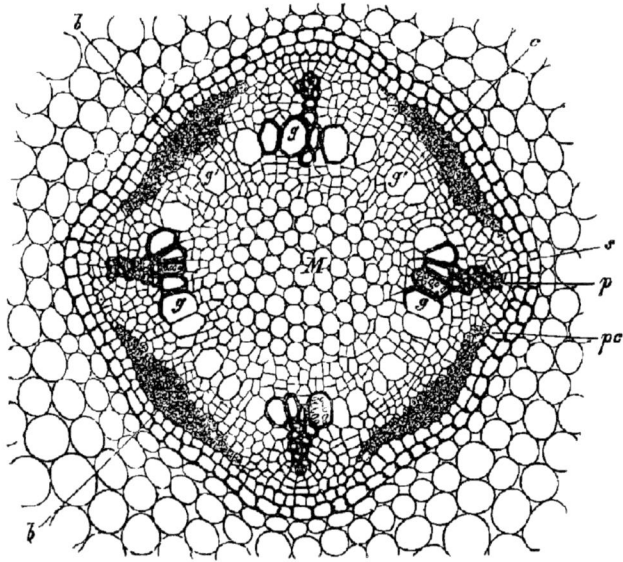

FIG. 141.—Transverse section of a primary root of a seedling of *Phaseolus multiflorus* taken from the upper swollen portion, at the time when the first leaves and lateral roots are already developed. *b* bast and phloem, *s* endodermis—vascular bundle sheath, *pc* pericambium inside the endodermis, *p* primary and *g* secondary vessels, *m* pith, *c* cambium.

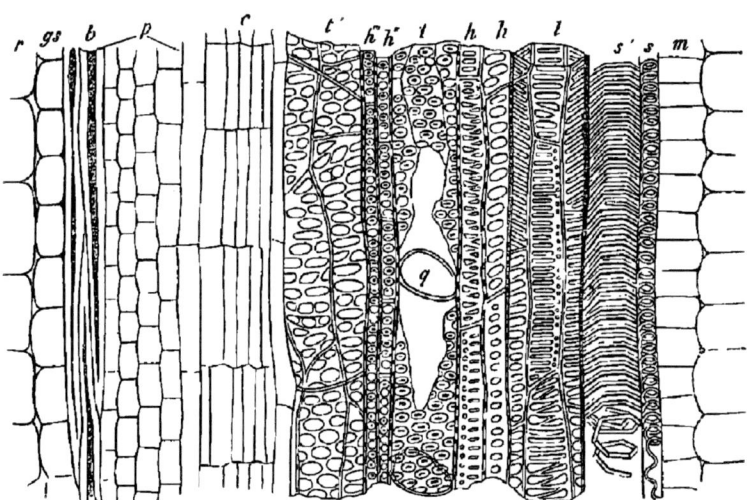

FIG. 142.—Longitudinal section of the vascular bundle of *Ricinus* (cf. transverse section in Fig 138). *r* cortical parenchyma, *gs* vascular bundle sheath, *m* parenchyma of the pith, *b* bast fibres, *p* phloem parenchyma, *c* cambium. The cells between *c* and *p* eventually form a sieve-tube. In the xylem the elements are gradually developed from *s* to *t*: *s* primary, narrow, and very long spiral vessel, *t'* wide spiral vessel—both with unrollable spirals, *i* scalariform—in part reticular—vessel, *h* and *h'* wood cells; *t* pitted vessel, with a resorbed septum at *q*, *h''*, *h'''* wood-cells, *t'* young pitted vessel—the borders of the pits develope first, and then the pore arises inside. At *l*, *t*, *t'*, the boundary lines of the adjoining cells—now removed—are observed on the walls of the vessels.

reticulately thickened vessels, and finally as so-called dotted vessels or vessels provided with bordered pits. In the development of a vascular bundle from the embryonal tissue of the youngest organs, these vessels are gradually constructed in the order here mentioned, and in general their breadth increases in the same sequence, while the length of the individual segments, or cells, of which the vessels are composed, decreases at the same time and in the same order. Hence the first formed, narrow, annular and spiral vessels, which have to take part in the whole growth in length of the organ, are in the completed state very long tubes, whereas in the last formed, pitted vessels, the individual segments, especially when they only attain completion after the termination of the growth in length of the organs, appear short and barrel-shaped. These also may occasionally however, as in roots, form very long tubes.

The nature of the sculpture on the walls of the vessels has already been explained (in lecture VI). Here is still to be added, that the vessels with bordered pits owe their striking aspect on the surface view to the circumstance that the pits are here not only very closely crowded, and are thus separated fundamentally only by thickening ridges; but the thickening ridges become arched, growing forth from the primary thin cell-wall into the interior of the cell, laterally and on all sides over the spaces between the meshes, so that each pit is connected with the inner cavity of the cell only by means of a very narrow pore or slit We may also say, a bordered pit is a short canal, leading out from the interior of the cell, and suddenly becoming widened at the primary cell-wall. In the surface view of a bordered pit, therefore, a roundish pore or slit is perceived in the middle, which is

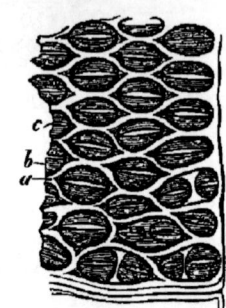

FIG 143.—Part of the longitudinal wall of a pitted vessel *a* the primary thickening ridges, which become arched over the areolæ (*b*), and only leave the slit (*c*) exposed

surrounded by a circular or polygonal border, corresponding to the outer circumference of the pit. In the Ferns (as Fig. 144 shows), where the segments of the pitted vessels are situated upon one another with very oblique septa, the bordered pits are so extended in breadth, that the thickening ridges between them often appear like the rounds of a ladder, hence the old name, ladder-like (scalariform) vessels. In addition to these proper vessels, there are found in the xylem of thicker strands other more fibrous elements, with the upper and lower ends obliquely cut off, or drawn out to long points, the finer structure of the walls and pits of which is similar to that of the true vessels. These, therefore, have been termed tracheïdes, in contradistinction to the true vessels, which are named tracheæ. All these tracheal elements lose their protoplasm, together with the cell nucleus, completely, as soon as their wall-structure is fully developed; so that later not the smallest remnants of them are to be perceived. Even the cell-sap disappears completely, and the vascular tubes only contain air; and indeed it is not improbable that they occasionally become even empty of air.

The resemblance of the vascular constituents of the phloëm, the sieve-tubes, to the tracheal elements of the xylem is very slight. The latter, with their ligni-fied cell-walls devoid of contents, are conspicuous on account of the sculpture of their wall; while the sieve-tubes, on the contrary, are provided with soft, supple, mostly thin walls, and, at least in the younger organs, are filled with slimy proteid. matter. The transverse septa, which lie closer to one another the older the part of the plant had already become before the formation of the sieve-tubes, are also of a soft, or even gelatinous consistence; and they are never entirely, or to any great extent absorbed; but by absorption taking place at isolated spots, they become transformed into a network of ridges, in the meshes of which lie the canals

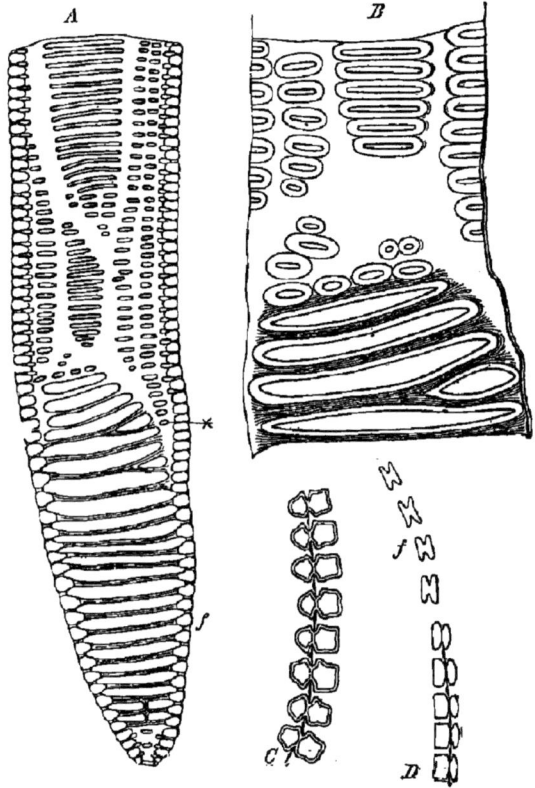

FIG 144.—*A* A third portion of a vessel from the rhizome of *Pteris aquilina.* The oblique scalariform eod (*f*) and a portion of the lateral wall in surface view   the areas not pitted correspond to the angles of neighbouring vessels   *B* is the part *x* (in *A*) more highly magnified (× 375)   *C* and *D* very thin longitudinal sections perpendicular to the lateral wall of two neighbouring vessels, showing the thin primary wall, on which are situated the sections of the thick projections between the pits   (After De Bary)

by means of which the segments of a sieve-tube, situated one over the other, communicate, and through which the slimy contents can be pressed. Where sieve-tubes border immediately on one another laterally, so-called sieve-plates may also be formed on their side-walls, the structure of which resembles that of the sieve-like transverse septa.

Amongst the tracheal structures of the xylem, and still more between the sieve-tubes, is found more or less abundant, parenchymatous, mostly thin-walled tissue: this consists of more or less elongated, soft cells, which contain fluids of various kinds, and frequently starch

Finally, as to the elastic fibres of the vascular bundle already mentioned. These occur in the phloëm as true bast-fibres, in the xylem as wood-fibres. the latter have been distinguished from the fibre-like tracheïdes more particularly as the libriform fibres of the wood. At another opportunity we shall see how, in cases where subsequent growth in thickness of the shoot-axes occurs (i.e. in the proper development of wood) the libriform fibres contribute to the formation of the true wood, and, so far as the true bast-fibres are concerned[1], it

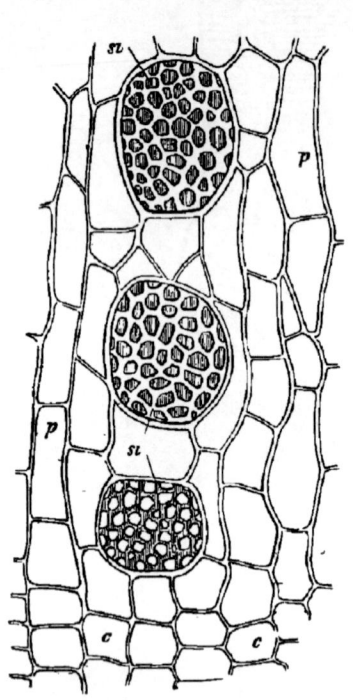 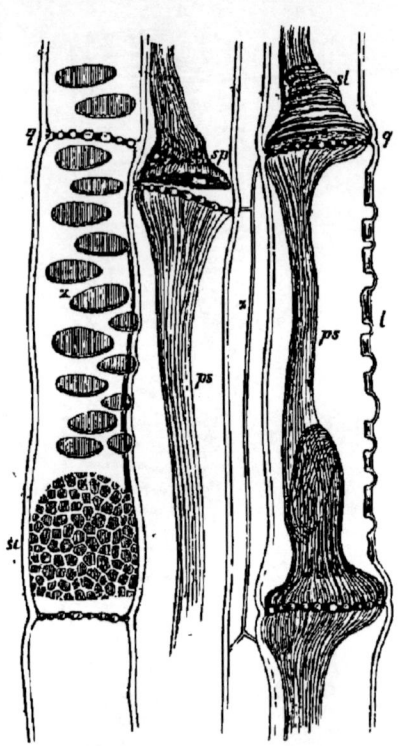

FIG. 145.—Transverse section of the phloem of a fibro-vascular bundle in the stem of *Cucurbita Pepo* (× 550) *si* septa of young sieve tubes showing areolæ—the pores not yet developed, *p, p* phloem parenchyma, *c, c* cambium. There are no bast fibres here, the whole phloem consisting of soft bast.

FIG. 146.—Longitudinal section of the phloem of *Cucurbita Pepo* showing three sieve tubes, the transverse septa (*q, q*) of which are not yet perforated. The slimy mass (*si* and *ps*) contained in them is contracted *si* a young sieve plate on the lateral wall pores will also be found later at *s* and *l* *z* narrow parenchymatous cells between the sieve-tubes.

may here be pointed out simply that they are wanting in many vascular bundles, and in other cases appear more isolated; in others, again, they exist in the form of layers or thick strands on the outside of the phloem

The peculiar characteristics of the vascular bundle lie, according to my view, which agrees with that of De Bary, in the presence of tracheal elements in the xylem, and of sieve-tubes, or of tissue-elements similar to them, in the phloem.

---

[1] It will be clear from the text and from note 2, that by 'bast-fibres' are not to be understood here the *Stereom elements* distinguished as 'bast' by Schwendener.

By the presence of these two groups of tissue, even when each of them only asserts itself by a few characteristic elements in the transverse section, the vascular bundles may always be distinguished from the strand-like structures, occurring frequently enough elsewhere, which run in the fundamental tissue of many shoot-axes and leaf-stalks in a similar manner to the vascular bundles; but which are essentially different from these, being merely special forms of fundamental-tissue. As the true nature of leaves and roots through the whole series of the vascular plants, though the structural relations are the most different possible, is always to be recognised; so also the vascular bundles of all vascular plants, even when they depart far from the typical structure, as in many water-plants and parasites, yet always appear as tissues of essentially the same nature. I interpolate this remark, because it has recently been attempted to confound these characteristic and constant constituents of the anatomical structure with other strand-like arrangements of tissue, which may be present or be wanting according to purely biological requirements; and this to the great injury of Phytotomy, which only loses thereby in clearness and scientific depth. One might just as well name any given filiform organ a root, or any flat structure a leaf, as place the vascular bundles on a level with other haphazard strand-like masses of tissue[1].

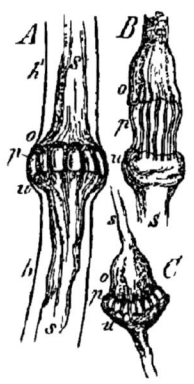

FIG. 147.—Parts of sieve tubes where the segments unite, showing the perforation of the septa after solution of the cell wall by sulphuric acid *A* and *B* from the petiole of *Cucurbita*, *C* from the stem of *Dahlia* In *A* the cell wall *h, h'* is not yet dissolved *s* slimy contents, *o* and *u* accumulation at the upper and under side of the septum, *p* the threads of slimy substance which connect these accumulations, and pass through the pores of the sieve plate

---

[1] The attempts repeatedly made of late to place the vascular bundles, as a subordinate form of tissue, approximately on an equal footing with mere sclerenchyma strands, only shows how little the younger botanists have succeeded in comprehending the province of vegetable anatomy, cultivated with such great results by Mohl, Nageli, and De Bary

LECTURE IX.

THE SYSTEMS OF TISSUES (*continued*).

FUNDAMENTAL TISSUE; RUDIMENTARY DIFFERENTIATIONS OF TISSUE.

I class together all the masses of tissue which are enclosed by the epidermal tissue, and traversed by the vascular bundles, under the term *fundamental tissue*[1]. In the younger and still succulent organs, covered only by the epidermis, and the vascular bundles of which have not yet been altered by subsequent growth in thickness, and in organs generally in which the formation of true wood and secondary cortex has not yet commenced, the main mass of the entire substance consists of fundamental tissue. This is perhaps best seen in an Apple, the whole edible substance of which consists of it. The succulent mass of tissue in the leaf of an Aloe, again, apart from the very thin vascular bundles and the epidermis, is formed entirely of fundamental tissue.

The most widely spread, and, as may well be assumed, the primitive and typical form of fundamental tissue, is the ordinary thin-walled parenchyma; in which we

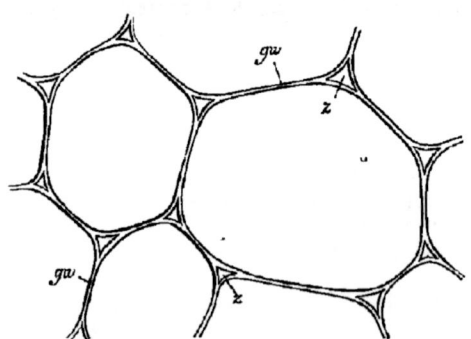

FIG. 148.—Transverse section through the soft parenchyma of the stem of *Zea Mays*. *gw* common wall between each two cells, *x* intercellular space produced by splitting of the wall.

may at the same time perceive the typical form of all true cell-tissue. The parenchyma cells are usually the largest in the body of the plant; and are either roundish, polyhedral, or elongated and prismatic, or more rarely pointed above and below. Very commonly, although not quite generally, small, or often very capacious intercellular spaces run between them. The contents consist of living protoplasm with a nucleus; the former, usually small in quantity, forming

---

[1] I first characterised the fundamental tissue as a system of tissue co-ordinated with the epidermis and vascular bundles in the first edition of my 'Text Book' (1868)

a thin clothing to the cell-wall   The remaining space is filled with watery sap; and the parenchyma cells may contain in addition the most various products of assimilation and metabolism.   It is chiefly in these cells that such substances are stored temporarily, or even up to the next period of vegetation and longer, to be dissolved and used up later for the purposes of growth.   In this form we find the parenchymatous tissue as a succulent envelope surrounding the axial strand of the young root, as pith, and primary cortex, and to a certain extent as the mass surrounded by the epidermis, and filling up the parts between the vascular bundles, in the shoot-axes and leaf-stalks, and in the leaves themselves, as well as in the coverings of the fruit.   Even the endosperm of seeds and the cotyledons of embryos may be classed under this head.

However, this parenchymatous cell-tissue is by no means the only form in the system of the fundamental tissue; for the parenchyma itself undergoes

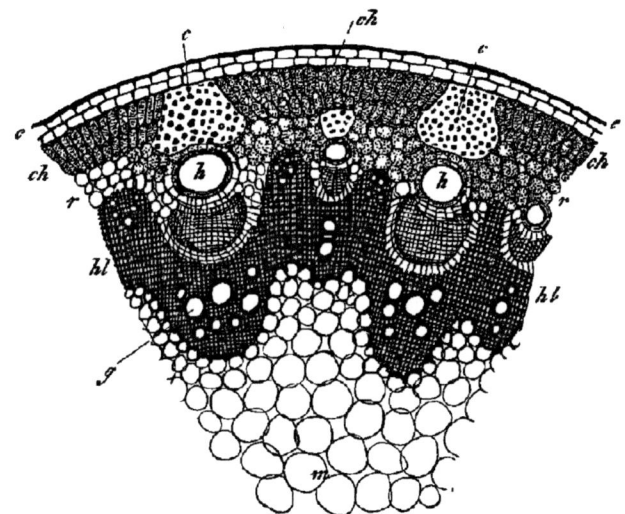

FIG 149 —A portion of the transverse section of the flower stem of *Faniculum officinale* slightly magnified. *e* epidermis, *hl* wood, *h* resin passages   All the rest is fundamental tissue—*m* parenchyma of the pith, *r* parenchyma of the cortex, *ch* parenchyma containing chlorophyll, *c* collenchyma.

more or less extensive differentiations, without losing its essential peculiarities, and, very frequently, cells and forms of tissue of the most various kind appear in it besides.

A differentiation within the parenchymatous fundamental tissue is very generally exhibited, firstly, in so far that the intercellular spaces towards the epidermis, as well as at the borders of the vascular bundles, disappear, and the sizes of the cells, and especially their diameters, diminish, and, generally, alterations in the thickness, substance, and pitting of the walls occur also.   These changes not rarely proceed so far that the layers of tissue concerned entirely lose their parenchymatous character   they then have different names assigned to them.

Thus, it is a very common phenomenon that beneath the epidermis of the shoot-axes, petioles and thicker leaf-ribs of dicotyledonous plants, the cells of the fundamental tissue are developed as *Collenchyma* (Fig. 150); the longitudinal walls exhibit pad-like projecting thickenings deposited in the angles of the cells, which swell up strongly in water, and still more in dilute potash solution, and give to the transverse section an uncommonly characteristic appearance. In the leaves of Conifers, Cycads, and in many other cases, the collenchyma is replaced by very thick-walled, prismatic, and even fibrous cells, in part lignified; these, as in Figs. 149 and 151, run close beneath the epidermis, and are grouped together in strands or layers. These, and similar so-called *Hypodermal* structures, serve to render the organs concerned elastic and solid; since, by means of their own stiffness, they increase, or, in the case of collenchyma, aid the elastic resistance which the epidermis opposes to the expansion of the succulent, turgid parenchyma.

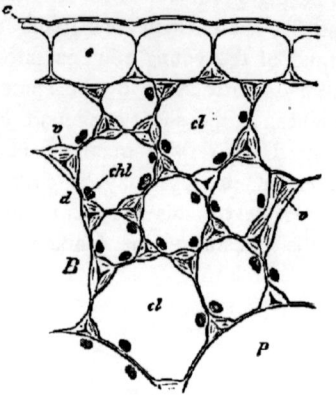

FIG. 150.—Epidermis (*e*) and Collenchyma (*cl*) from the petiole of *Begonia.* The outer walls of the epidermis cells are equally thickened; where they adjoin the collenchyma the thickening only occurs at the angles where three cells meet. These thickenings have a great capacity for swelling. *chl* chlorophyll grains; *p* parenchyma-cell.

Where the fundamental tissue bounds the vascular bundles, there are always formed layers, commonly sharply marked, which may be distinguished generally as vascular bundle-sheaths; these however, like the hypodermal layers, are, according to circumstances, of very different constitution. The commonest form of these vascular bundle-sheaths is usefully distinguished by De Bary as *Endodermis.* It is particularly well marked in the roots of all vascular plants, at the circumference of the axial strand, in the form of a simple layer of small cells, the walls of which are more or less suberized, cf. Fig. 8 *s.* In the shoot-axis

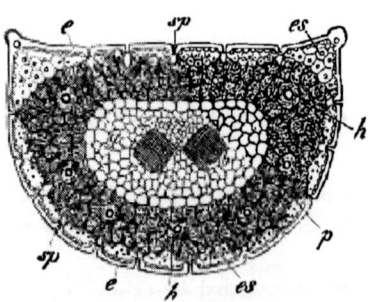

FIG. 151.—Transverse section of the leaf of *Pinus Pinaster* (× 30). *e* epidermis; *es* hypodermal prosenchyma; *sp* stomata; *h* resin-passages; *p* parenchyma containing chlorophyll; *g, b* colourless internal tissue enclosing two fibrovascular bundles.

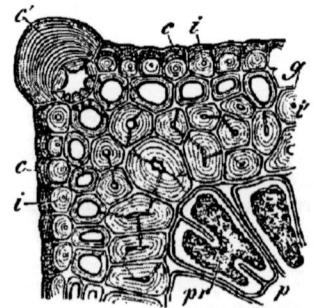

FIG. 152.—The left-hand corner of the previous figure (× 500). *c* cuticularised layer of the epidermal cells; *i* inner layer of the same, not cuticularised; *c′* very strongly-thickened outer wall of the epidermis cell lying in the corner; *g, i′* hypoderm cells; *g* middle lamella; *i′* stratified thickening mass; *p* parenchyma containing chlorophyll; *pr* contracted contents.

also a very similar endodermis is frequently found, enveloping all the leaf-traces as a hollow cylinder, and therefore appearing on the transverse section as a continuous ring, by which the whole tissue is separated into a cortex, lying outside the endodermis, and an internal core of tissue (plerome), cf. Fig. 138. Such plerome-sheaths are very distinct in the rhizomes of many Monocotyledons, as *Iris, Acorus*, and so forth, and also in the sub-aërial shoot-axes of many Dicoty-ledons. More frequently, a layer of tissue similar to the endodermis is present in sub-aërial shoot-axes and leaves, either only on the outside, or also on the inside of each single vascular bundle, or each individual bundle may be entirely sur-rounded by such a layer of tissue, as in Fig 153 In many other Ferns, this vascular bundle-sheath is distinguished by a strong thickening of the longitudinal walls turned towards the bundle, and often also by a dark brown colour (cf. Fig 136). In other cases, particularly in the upright shoot-axes and leaves of many Monocotyledons, especially of the Grasses, Palms, *Dracænas*, etc., which require

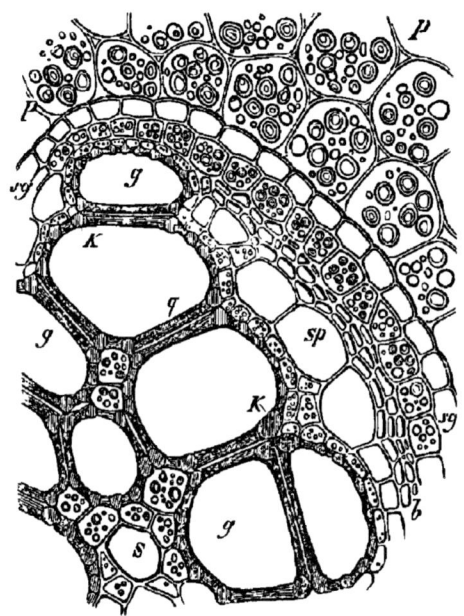

greater elasticity and rigidity, the vascular bundle-sheath consists of a more or less thick, often (especially in Palms) extraordinarily thick layer of very thick-walled, lignified, long, spindle-shaped fibres, which fit to-gether without intercellular spaces. While the function of the ordinary endodermis is apparently only to render slow the exchange of sap be-tween the parenchymatous fundamental tissue and the vascular bundles, these large lignified fibrous strands (Sclerenchyma) not only serve this purpose, but upon them depends, in plants not properly forming wood otherwise, the rigidity of the shoot-axes, since the vascular bundles of such Monocotyledons, and some

FIG 153.—Portion of the transverse section of one of the large vascular bundles of the stem of *Pteris aquilina*, with surrounding parenchyma *P* the latter is filled (in winter) with starch *s* spiral vessel in the focus of the elliptical transverse section, this is surrounded by thin walled wood cells containing starch *gg* the scalariform vessels, *sp* sieve tubes. *b* bast cells with thick soft walls, *sg* bundle sheath Between *b* and *sg* is a layer of cells containing starch

similarly constructed Dicotyledons, in themselves very thin and feeble, are not at all calculated to give the necessary rigidity to the stems and shoot-axes. These sclerenchyma-sheaths, moreover, do not always surround the entire vascular bundle, as in Fig. 154; frequently they accompany it only on its outer or inner side, or on both. Moreover, such layers of sclerenchyma, which belong to the fundamental tissue, do not always immediately accompany the vascular bundles, but very frequently are quite independent from these, as layers and strands running in the parenchyma of the fundamental tissue. They are particularly well seen as stout, dark brown, hard bands in the stem of the Bracken-fern (Fig. 134, *A, pr.*) as well as in the stems of Tree-ferns, where they not rarely form a hard protective coat, both under the epidermis and around each of the large vascular bundles. In the long, thin, and yet very elastic and firm flowering scapes of Rushes (*Juncus, Scirpus, Cladium*, etc.), lignified sclerenchymous strands either run close beneath the epidermis, or a closed ring of that tissue lies in the neighbourhood of the periphery, and gives the slender column the necessary rigidity. Schwendener, who first called attention to the significance of these sclerenchyma layers and strands with reference to the elasticity and rigidity of the organs concerned, distinguished their cells as bast-cells. This nomenclature, however, has not been accepted by botanists: the name bast was given long ago to the elastic fibres in the

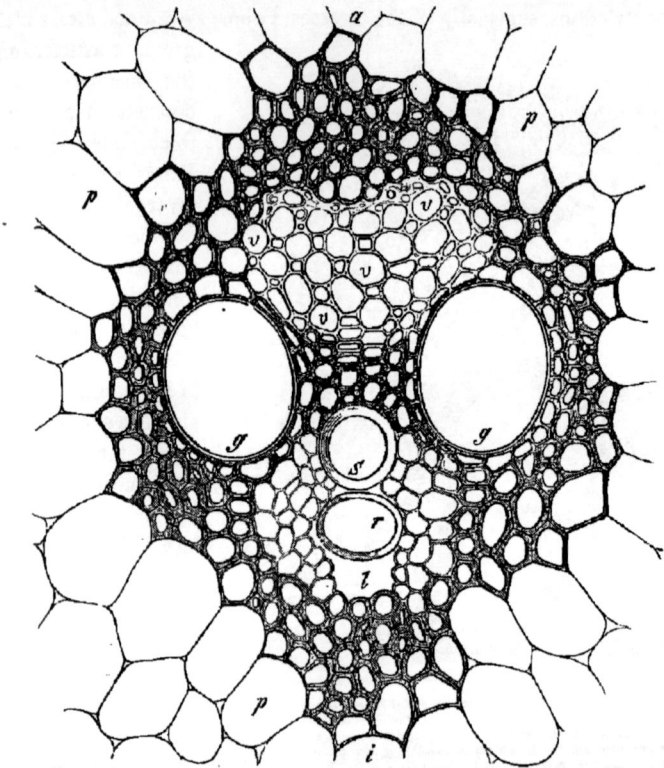

FIG. 154.—Transverse section of a fibro-vascular bundle from the stem of *Zea Mays* (Indian Corn) surrounded by its sheath of sclerenchyma: *a* is towards the exterior, and *i* towards the centre of the stem. *pp* large-celled parenchyma of the fundamental tissue. Only the parts *v* (sieve-tubes), *g* (pitted vessels), *s* (spiral vessels), *r* (annular vessels), and the elements lying between these constitute the vascular bundle—the thick-walled shaded tissue is the sclerenchymatous sheath.

phloëm of the vascular bundle and the secondary cortex. Generally speaking, this true bast is not lignified, its long fibres being rather distinguished in fact by their flexibility. Besides, plenty of examples occur where the sclerenchyma layers described consist of cells which cannot be in any way compared externally with bast-fibres: the sclerenchyma cylinder in the flowering scape of species of *Allium* (Fig. 155 *sr.*), for instance, consists of cells transversely or obliquely truncated above and below, the relation of which admits of no doubt whatever that the entire sclerenchyma ring is only a layer of narrower cells of the parenchymatous fundamental tissue, which is distinguished from the rest of the fundamental parenchyma by possessing much smaller intercellular passages, or none at all, and by the walls being strongly lignified   The same is the case with the brown strands of the Bracken-fern, which are prosenchymatous, it is true, but in part contain starch.   The stem of *Lycopodium chamæcyparissus* (Fig 157) shows that under certain circumstances the main mass of the fundamental tissue may assume the sclerenchymatous condition. the very thick-walled

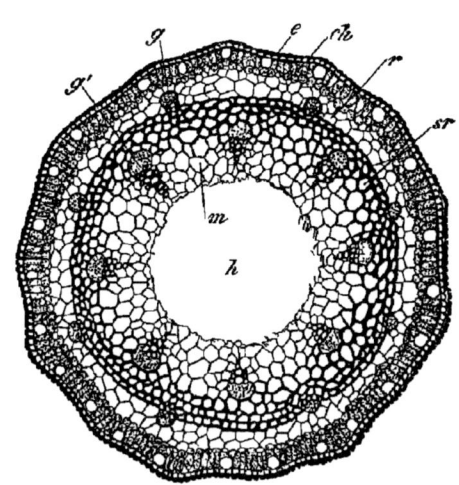

FIG 155.—Transverse section of the flower scape of *Allium Schoeno prasum* (× 30)   *e* epidermis, *ch* chlorophyll cells, *r* colourless cortical parenchyma, *m* pith parenchyma, *g g'* vascular bundles, *sr* ring of sclerenchyma, *h* central cavity

cells, figured in transverse section, are pointed above and below, and are arranged in prosenchymatous layers.   Not rarely, however, sclerenchyma cells occur isolated, or arranged together in small roundish groups, or even forming loose layers in the fundamental tissue   Thus, the hard concretions, about the size of a grain of sand, in the soft flesh of the Pear, consist of groups of very thick sclerenchymatous cells, which are apparently nothing further than peculiarly developed parenchyma cells.   The same holds good of the layers or groups of so-called stone cells, beneath the layer of cork in the cortex of dicotyledonous woody plants (e g in the Poplar).   In other cases, these isolated sclerenchyma cells exhibit more characteristic forms, as in Fig. 157 *b*, which represents a many armed, large sclerenchyma cell from the leaf of a Camelia   Similar forms are found in the cortex of some Conifers, very fine and numerous, for example, in the Fir (*Abies pectinata*).   In the hard stiff leaves of the *Proteaceæ* and some other evergreen plants, sclerenchymatous cells of the most various form are to be met with.   Also in the pith of

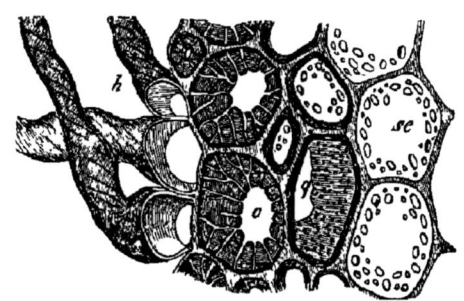

FIG. 156.—Transverse section from the rhizome of *Pteris aquilina*   *h* root hairs, *c* strongly thickened brown walled cells beneath the epidermis, *q* a more deeply situated cell, less thickened—part of the wall seen *en face* *se* cells of deeper layers containing starch, passing over to the internal colourless parenchyma of the fundamental tissue

some wood plants, isolated or grouped, lignified sclerenchyma cells occur, mostly however of simple form

If possible, yet more various than in the shoot-axes and leaves, are the forms of fundamental tissue developed in the fruits and seeds of the Phanerogams.   To select only a few examples from the almost endless variety, it may be mentioned that the

Plums and Cherries owe their name—stone fruit—to the circumstance that the fundamental tissue of the pericarp, at first homogeneous and parenchymatous, becomes separated into two layers, of which the outer, enclosed by a solid epidermis, forms the edible flesh of the fruit, and the inner one the so-called stone. Each consists at first of thin-walled large parenchyma cells filled with sap containing sugar, while the cells of the tissue of the stone become exceedingly thick-walled, and finally, on ripening, are very strongly lignified. Especially various are the cell-formations in dry fruits, capsules, and indehiscent fruits, as well as in the testa of many seeds. It is, however, difficult to give a survey of these forms at all comprehensive, since a comparative study of them is still wanting; and we have here to do everywhere with specific adaptations to definite biological relations of individual species of plants. In the tissue-formations of the coats of seeds and fruits it is sometimes simply a matter of solidity and mechanical protection; sometimes of arrangements which, on the ripening of the capsule, bring about its dehiscence and the scattering of the seeds. Berries and stone-fruits by means of nourishing masses of tissue attract animals to eat them, and the latter then scatter the hard-shelled seeds at other places. In other cases again, wings or parachute-like outgrowths (Pappus of the Compositæ) arise on seeds or dry fruits; and many other such arrangements exist, which are naturally connected with peculiar developments of the portions of tissue concerned.

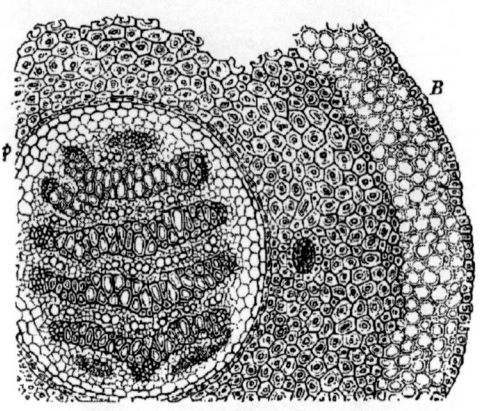

FIG. 157.—Transverse section of the stem of *Lycopodium chamæcyparissus*

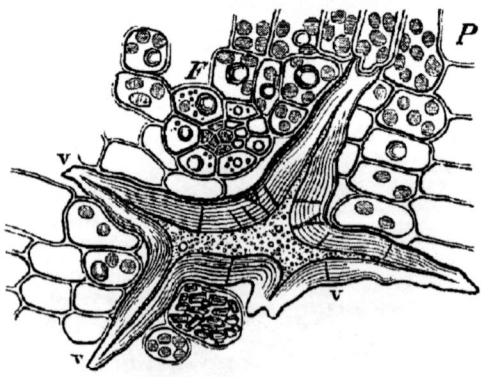

FIG. 157 b.—Part of the transverse section of a leaf of *Camellia japonica*. *P* parenchyma cells with chlorophyll grains and oil drops; *F* a very thin vascular bundle; *v v* a large branched sclerenchyma cell, the arms of which are inserted between the parenchyma cells.

Among the various forms of fundamental tissue is also to be included one which is the most widely spread and physiologically by far the most important, viz. the chlorophyll parenchyma of the green parts of plants, and especially of the foliage leaves. With reference to the forms of the cells and the formation of intercellular spaces, the absence of suberisation and lignification, and the usually thin walls and soft contents, the assimilating tissue does not differ essentially from ordinary parenchymatous fundamental tissue, which may also be termed nutritive tissue in the wider sense. The distinctive point—not only because the green colour of the plant is caused by it, but much more on account of its fundamental significance for the whole nutrition of the plant—lies in the presence of the chlorophyll-grains, which we may shortly distinguish as green-coloured portions of the protoplasm of these cells. Since, as I shall show later, the chlorophyll cells of the assimilating parenchyma, the typical forms of which are found in the green foliage leaves, must maintain a vigorous exchange of gases for the purpose of assimilation; and since, at the same time, the nutritive water of the soil is conducted to them, which they exhale into the air in the form of aqueous vapour, it is intelligible why the assimilating parenchyma in general possesses a spongy character. Its cells separate from one another until nearly isolated, often supporting one another only at single, narrow, circumscribed places, and forming numerous, large intercellular spaces, which usually communicate in all directions, and in which carbon dioxide, oxygen, and aqueous vapour can move from place to place. Since the assimilating tissue can perform its function only under the influence of light, we find it always in the form of thin layers immediately accessible to the light. Thick layers of chlorophyll would have no purpose, since thin layers of even 0 1 to 0 5 mm. thick absorb

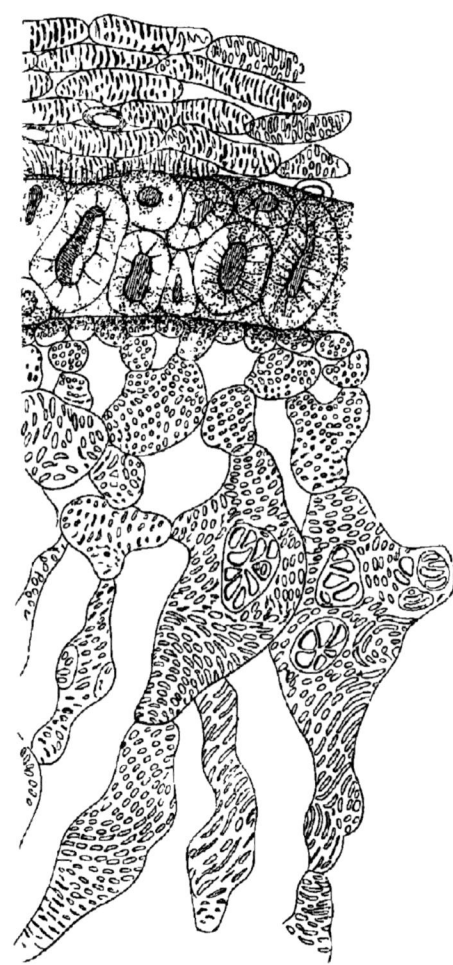

FIG. 157 c—Small portion of a transverse section through the testa of the seed of a Gourd

the useful light rays, layers lying deeper would thus obtain no more useful rays Hence the assimilating tissue generally occurs in the form of plates, which are very thin but extensive in surface, and which in ordinary thin foliage leaves are covered only by an epidermis, abundantly supplied with stomata. For the reasons named, moreover, even in the very thick leaves of succulent plants and the Crassulaceæ, species of *Aloe, Agave,* &c., only a thin lamella of green assimilating tissue is present close beneath the epidermis ; and the same is the case in the green shoot-axes of *Equisetum*, and still more evidently in the species of *Cactus*, the huge shoot-axes of which possess a thin green lamella only at the circumference. However, this is not the place to enter more closely into detail respecting the important physiological properties of the assimilating parenchyma, since this can be done in a proper manner only in connection with the theory of the nutrition of plants to be expounded later

In what has been said concerning the epidermis, the vascular bundles, and the fundamental tissue, we have a description, superficial though it be, of the typical histological structure of vascular plants, i e the Phanerogams and Cryptogams. According to the requirements of the mode of life, the most various deviations from the forms of tissue mentioned may occur; of these we do not propose to treat further, since what has been stated suffices as a basis for further physiological considerations As in the treatment of the external segmentation of plants, I shall, in connection with the three typical systems of tissue, again allude to the corresponding differentiations of tissue in the simply organised plants; where we find, according to the nomenclature introduced earlier, the rudimentary beginnings of the three systems of tissues If it were here proposed to exhaust all the various histological relations of the lower plants, the material for several volumes would present itself, it suffices however for my purpose to confine ourselves to a few short remarks, simply to serve for the guidance of the reader.

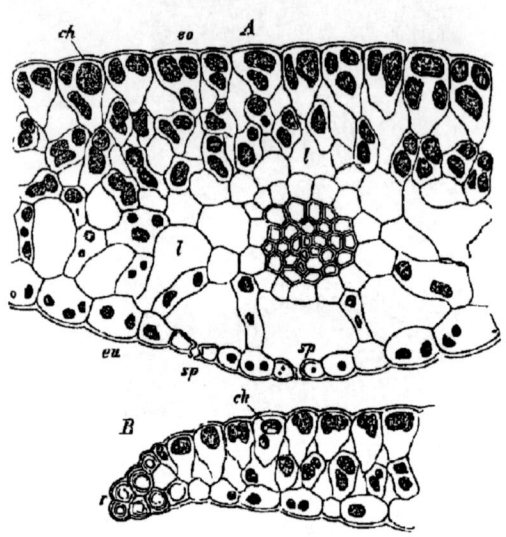

FIG 158.—Transverse section through the leaf of *Selaginella inaequalifolia* (550) *A* in the middle , *B* at the margin , *ch* chlorophyll grains—the small dots in them are starch grains , *eu* epidermis of lower side, *eo* that of upper side , *l* inter cellular spaces containing air , *sp* stomata.

It is already known from the first lectures, that in the Mosses, Algæ, and Fungi, many organs which in the vascular plants consist of multicellular masses of tissue, are constructed only of single cells, jointed filaments, or simple cell-layers In such cases, it is obvious that a differentiation into epidermis, fundamental tissue, and vascular bundles cannot be spoken of Where, however, the organs of the lower plants consist of several or numerous layers of tissue, we always meet with a more or less evident differentiation, which then presents itself as a rudimentary form of the three systems of tissue adopted by us. This is to be seen particularly clearly in the true Mosses, which are nevertheless highly organised. The spore-forming capsule (the sporogonium or moss-fruit) shows, especially in the highly developed typical Mosses, a sharply differentiated epidermis, which may even be provided with stomata, marked off from an inner mass of tissue, chiefly parenchymatous fundamental tissue, and which is generally differentiated into a compact colourless portion, and chlorophyll-tissue traversed with numerous intercellular spaces. Of special interest in this respect is the segmenting off of a portion of the epidermis as the deciduous cover of the moss-fruit, and, in the more highly organised forms, the formation of the so-called peristome. This consists of four, eight, sixteen or more so-called teeth, which on their part arise from peculiarly differentiated rows of cells beneath the cover mentioned, by the strong thickening and lignification of the cell-walls: this is illustrated in part by Fig. 122, and the accompanying Fig. 160. It has been already pointed out that in the filiform thin shoot-axis of the true Mosses, a strand, consisting of narrow, elongated cells, and which is undoubtedly to be regarded as a rudimentary vascular bundle, runs within a well-marked fundamental tissue, which is surrounded

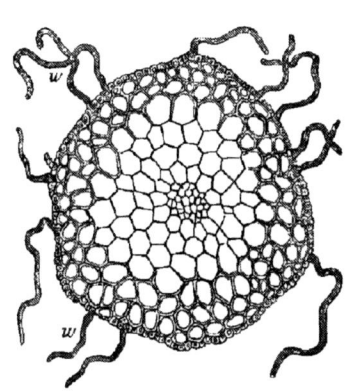

FIG. 159*a.*—Transverse section of the stem of *Bryum roseum* (× 90). *w* root-hairs produced by the outgrowth of single cells of the outermost layer.

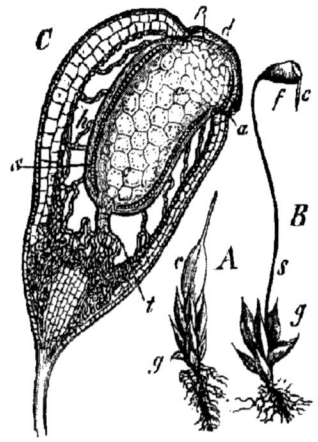

FIG. 159*b.*—*Funaria hygrometrica. A* a small leafy shoot (*g*) with the calyptra (*c*); *B* a plant (*g*) with the almost ripe sporogonium; *s* the seta; *f* the capsule; *c* the calyptra; *C* a longitudinal section through the middle of the capsule; *d* operculum; *α* annulus; *p* peristome; *c c'* columella; *h* air cavity; *s* mother-cells of spores. At *t* the loose tissue of the columella presents the appearance of confervoid filaments.

by a more or less sharply defined epidermal layer; and when the leaves of the Moss, elsewhere consisting of a simple cell-layer, possess a mid-rib, in this also a rudimentary vascular bundle runs, joining that of the shoot-axis. Since the roots of the Moss only consist of jointed cell-filaments, such tissue differentiations obviously cannot exist in them.

Much simpler are the forms assumed by the tissues in the majority of the Liverworts; which, however, in their most highly organised forms, the Marchantiæ, nevertheless attain a very considerable degree of organisation. The ribband-like foliar shoots of these plants, lying flat on the substratum, produce root-hairs on the lower side, as well as leaf-like outgrowths; while the upper side of the shoot developes into an organ of assimilation. A sharply marked epidermis invests an inner mass of tissue consisting of several layers, which is to be distinguished as fundamental tissue. Corresponding to the doisi-ventral structure spoken of, the under side dispenses with stomata these however are so much the more numerous on the upper side, and are developed in a form deviating from that usual elsewhere, as is shown in Fig. 161 *sp*. The piedominating parenchymatous fundamental tissue of the Marchantia shoot is also differentiated in accoidance with its ventral and dorsal side. It consists of a large-celled parenchyma, in which, according to Goebel, there are forms of cells which may be looked upon at any rate as feeble indications of vascular bundles; beneath the epidermis of the upper side of the shoot lies a spongy assimilating tissue, which is divided up into sharply bounded areolæ, each opening on to the exterior thiough a stoma

From these highly organised true Mosses and Liverworts, where the most essential relations of the typical systems of tissue are still to be recognised, a series of forms lead by imperceptible stages down to the simplest representatives of these two classes of plants, in the histological structure of which scarcely any traces of differentiation are to be found.

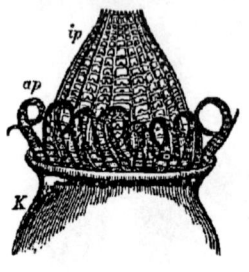

FIG 160.—The mouth of the cap sule (*k*) of *Fontinalis antipyretica* (×50) *ap* outer and *i* inner peristome (after Schimper)

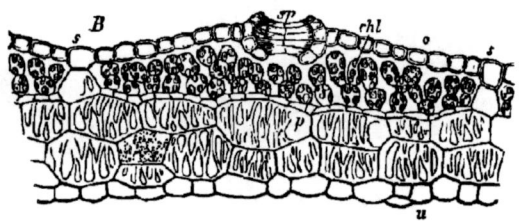

FIG 161 —Transverse section of the flattened shoot of *Marchantia poly morpha u* epidermis of lower surface, *o* that of the upper surface, *sp* stoma, *chl* chlorophyll tissue within an areola (bounded by *ss*), *p* colourless parenchyma

I have already, in the intioduction to the systems of tissue, mentioned by the way that in the Algæ and Fungi, when they consist of solid masses of tissue (which is, of course, a necessaiy condition), a differentiation into epidermal and fundamental tissue takes place, in which not rarely there runs a rudimentary vascular bundle consisting of long cells, and here the additional remark suffices, that stomata are always wanting to the epidermal tissue, even when it is otherwise sharply marked off.

In the consideiation of the external segmentation of the Algæ and Fungi, it was necessary to allude to the fact that instances of organisation occur, which often depart so completely from the typical relations of the Mosses and vascular plants, that we must look upon them no longer as rudimentary forms of the latter, but as quite peculiar. The same holds also with reference to the differentiation of tissue of many Algæ and Fungi. Here, again, it must however suffice to illustrate by a few examples what has been said, and indeed it is chiefly a matter of establishing the fact that even when the histological relations are entirely abnormal, the differentiation into a firmer, more resistent, epidermal layer, contrasted with an inner mass of tissue corresponding to the fundamental tissue, still recurs; and that where the relations of form otherwise admit of it, a bundle formed of parallel, elongated elements runs in the fundamental tissue, which again is to be regarded as the rudiment of a vascular bundle.

Apart from the Mucorini and a few other non-cellular Fungi, the hypha, or jointed fungus filament, is maintained with striking consistency as the elementary form of histological structure in the Fungi. The hypha is a filament segmented by transverse septa, mostly very thin, growing forward at its end, and often much branched. In the so-called Mould-fungi, the mycelium, as well as the fructification, consists of single hyphæ; where, however, the vegetative body is more massive, as in the fungi commonly known as Truffles, Mushrooms and Toad-stools, Gasteromycetes, etc., the mass of tissue, often variously differentiated, is likewise composed entirely of such hyphæ. The tissue of these plants is thus constructed, not, as in the majority of Algæ and all Mosses and vascular plants, by means of bi-partition and a corresponding forma-tion of chambers, commencing ori-ginally in the unicellular embryo and proceeding with the growth; but the internal structure of the Fungus gives the impression of very numerous hyphæ, each one of which strictly speaking leads an independent exist-ence, having become united into a colony, the single individuals of which —that is, the hyphæ—are subordi-nate, however, to a common plan of configuration. Instead of detailed explanations, the consideration of

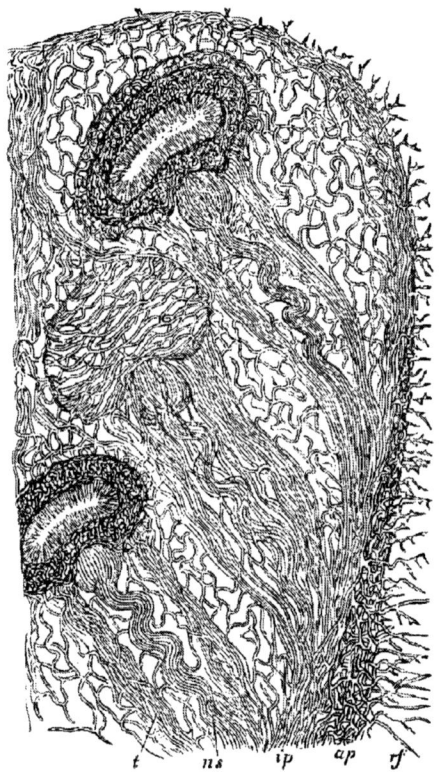

FIG. 162.—Half of a longitudinal section through the fructification of *Crucibulum vulgare* (a Gasteromycete). *ap* the so-called outer. *ip* the inner peridium; these together constitute the skin; *rf* hairs. The figure is diagrammatic in so far that the hyphae are represented far too thick.

the half diagrammatic Fig. 162 may give an idea of the facts indicated. In spite of this structure, entirely deviating from the usual histological type, here again a sharply marked differentiation of tissue nevertheless results: in Fig. 162 this is expressed chiefly by the closely packed (and, as it seems, lignified or other-wise altered) hyphæ running on the surface of the tissue-body, representing an epidermal tissue, to which even hair-like outgrowths are not wanting. Moreover, we perceive how in the internal mass of tissue the hyphæ bound certain spaces; of which the darker roundish portions enclose hollow chambers, in which the

reproductive cells (spores) are produced.
differentiated, however, as in the fruits
of Phanerogams, at the ripening of fructification. The previously slimy internal
hyphal tissue then dries up completely,
and the dense portions containing the
spores then appear as peculiar organs,
which remain free in the cavity of the
entire Fungus: this now, enclosed by
the firm epidermal layer, has somewhat the shape of an ordinary flower-
pot.

The fruticose Lichen, represented
in Fig. 163, may serve as a second example of hyphal tissue. The Lichens
are, as we now know, true Fungi,
which have the peculiar habit of enclosing in their tissue their host-plants
which contain chlorophyll (that is small
Algæ) without interfering with their reproduction : these appear in our drawing as dark granules. These elements,
serviceable, it is true, to the proper
body of the Lichen, but foreign in
other respects, behave within the hyphal tissue just as if they only constituted a special layer of tissue, corresponding to the assimilating parenchyma of a green plant; and this to
such an extent, that up to sixteen years
ago, when De Bary first perceived the
true nature of Lichens, these enclosed Algæ were considered as a
special form of tissue of the body of the
Lichen itself. Apart, however, from
these remarkable facts, Fig. 163 shows
with all requisite clearness the differentiation of the hyphal tissue into three
systems. The outermost of these may
be at once designated epidermal tissue ;
and in the interior is a strand separated
from the epidermal tissue. Thus again
we meet with the three forms, which we
have to regard as the most rudimentary
indication of the three typical systems of
tissue of the higher plants.

The tissues in this case are only fully

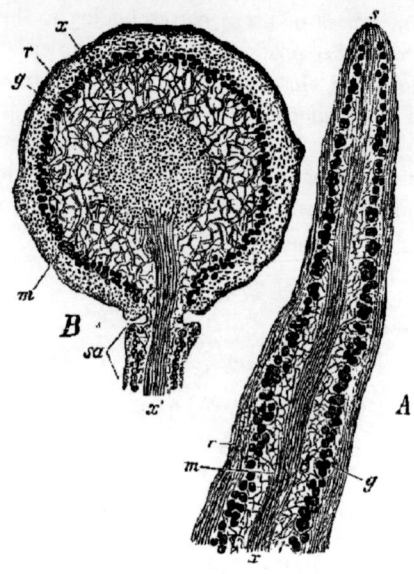

FIG. 163.—*Usnea barbata*, a fruticose Lichen. *A* optical longitudinal section of a thin branch, in potash ; *B* transverse section of a
thicker branch ; *g* the *Algæ* (so-called Gonidia) ; *r* epidermal layer ;
m fundamental tissue ; *x* the axial strand.

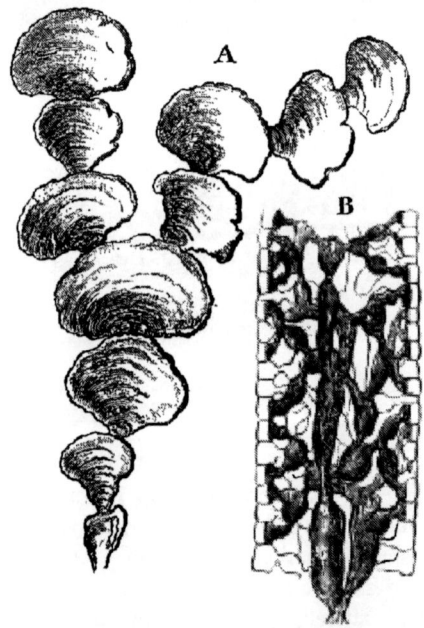

FIG. 164.—*Halymeda opuntia*. *A* a shoot—natural size ; *B* longitudinal section of a segment (slightly magnified) perpendicular to the
plane of the paper. The segments of *A* are flat.

A similar internal differentiation results, however, even in the case where a plant from the subdivision of the Cœloblastæ only consists of a single vesicle, the growth and branching of which is not accompanied by cell divisions at all. Among the Cœloblastæ in this connection are especially to be mentioned the marine Algæ *Codium* and *Halymeda.* These are plants of considerable size, variously segmented, and apparently composed of masses of tissue ; a transverse or longitudinal section, slightly magnified, presents apparently an ordinary plant tissue, resembling that of many other Algæ, until closer inspection shows that the apparent cell tissue consists of the ramifications of a tubular cell in itself continuous, the thousand-fold repeated outgrowths of which are more or less segmented by constrictions Here also the comparison of Fig 164 will show the true state of the case. One has only to observe that Fig *B* represents the longitudinal section of *A,* perpendicular to the plane of the paper, and indeed only through a small portion of the length of one of the Opuntia-like segments of the shoot It is perceived at once, that the vesicles form at the periphery of the shoot a dense layer, representing to a certain extent an epidermis ; and that in the axis the vesicles run longitudinally and are long-jointed, representing a looser vesicular system traversed by interstices, between the epidermal tissue and the axial strand, which however, corresponding to the form of the shoot, is to be imagined broad and flat.

LECTURE X.

THE SECONDARY GROWTH IN THICKNESS OF SHOOT-AXES AND ROOTS

HAVING started with the typical three systems of tissues, and traced the anatomical differentiation to its most rudimentary beginnings in the Mosses, Algæ, and Fungi, we may now pass to the consideration of the highest stage of development which the formation of tissue undergoes in the vegetable kingdom. We find this chiefly in true woody plants, the trees and shrubs of the natural classes Gymnosperms (especially the Conifers) and Dicotyledons. But in many species of both these sub-divisions, not generally considered as woody plants, exactly the same processes of tissue-formation take place as in perennial woody plants; in fact much of what is to be said concerning the formation of wood and the processes accompanying it is often especially evident in annual and biennial plants. In anticipation, however, it may be mentioned at once that the phenomena of growth to be treated of here do not, as a rule, occur in water-plants; since the biological relations connected with subsequent growth in thickness have in general a meaning and purpose only in transpiring land plants. We may comprehend the phenomena here concerned under the idea of the secondary growth in thickness of shoot-axes and roots.[1]

As the whole process of growth in length and the origin of new organs is referred to the growing point of the roots and shoots, so the entire growth in thickness springs from the functional activity of a thin layer of tissue of similar character—i. e. from the cambium. Where this remains active for a long time, as it does occasionally even for centuries, the originally thin root-fibres and shoot-axes gradually develop into those huge thick bodies met with as old tree-trunks and their branches, and napiform roots and tubers. Although these organs originally (i.e immediately after the conclusion of their growth in length) are composed, as already described, of epidermis, fundamental tissue, and vascular bundles; later, when the growth in thickness by means of the cambium has continued long enough, but little remains of that original structure, the whole of the thick stem, branch, or root, consisting, apart from insignificant remnants of the primary pith and vascular bundles, entirely of the products of the cambium. With the

---

[1] The extensive subject of the secondary growth in thickness, and especially the numerous abnormal cases not touched upon in the text, are thoroughly and accurately treated in De Bary's '*Vergl Anat der Vegetationsorgane*,' 1877

increasing age of such plants, the assimilating leaf-surface enlarges; and accordingly there gradually arises the necessity for a larger and more extended root-system, the parts of which, as well as the shoot-axes, gradually grow in thickness The thickened roots, stems, and branches present not only the necessary solidity of structure, but they are also essentially adapted to meet the increased requirements of the large leaf-surface. In the first place, it is necessary to convey from the earth to the leaves large quantities of water and dissolved salts: this is attained by the woody body, which is the organ for conducting water, continually increasing in thickness In addition, large quantities of products of assimilation are elaborated in the crown of foliage, these must, at least in part, be conveyed to the subterranean roots and lower portions of the stem Accordingly a so-called secondary cortex (secondary phloem), gradually increasing in thickness, becomes developed from the cambium, and in this secondary cortex, sieve-tubes and parenchyma form the chief conducting organs. At the same time masses of parenchymatous tissue in the cortex, as well as in the wood, are employed for the storing up of reserve materials. If, however, we consider the distances which the ascending as well as the descending nutritive sap traverse in the roots, stems, and branches, it is evident that the ordinary thin epidermis could not afford sufficient protection against injurious evaporation during this movement. In many cases, therefore, in woody plants, the epidermis becomes further developed Generally, however, it is replaced by a stronger layer—on the parts still young by typical cork-tissue, which possesses in an enhanced degree the properties of the epidermis, on older parts by the formation of bark, which in its turn affords protection not merely against prejudicial drying up of the sap-passages in the cortex and wood, but also against mechanical injuries which might occur in the course of time These remarks may serve to indicate simply the meaning of all the structural arrangements which are the result of the activity of the cambium In true water plants, which transpire but little, or not at all, the necessity of a vigorous supply of water from the roots is of course entirely wanting, and accordingly no subsequent formation of true wood takes place, consequently the increase in circumference of stem and root is unnecessary; and all those adaptations accompanying the formation of the secondary cortex, and of the cork and bark of the woody land-plants, are also wanting. Of course nature employs yet other means for the attainment in land plants of a considerable size of the body, and for ensuring a long continuity of life to the roots and shoot-axes. Among the Palms and palm-like Liliaceæ, for instance, as well as among the Ferns, plants of large dimensions are found, in which great solidity of the older roots and shoot-axes is necessary, and where practically the same remarks hold good as to the conduction of the sap. The circumstances here, however, are entirely different, in so far that in such plants the stem supporting the huge crown of leaves soon obtains its final thickness beneath the growing point The tissues serving as passages for the sap, and as elastic masses, are developed equally from the beginning, without any subsequent enlargement in diameter, and this again is connected with the circumstance that the assimilating crown of foliage, although continually renewed, does not annually increase in size as in true dicotyledonous trees.

I will now, in the first place, attempt to characterise as shortly as possible the tissue formations proceeding from the cambium and caused by the growth in thickness. In this, however, I shall again keep in view only the commonest or typical cases That in the great variety of the woody plants, innumerable more or less extensive deviations from this type occur, hardly needs mention. What is to follow concerns, in the first place, the growth in thickness of the shoot-axes; deviations in the roots (always insignificant) may be mentioned with them as occasion arises.

The whole growth in thickness is connected, as stated, with the functional activity of the cambium. The origin of the latter, however, is itself again dependent upon the original nature of the vascular bundles. Here are concerned only those parts of the bundles which run as so-called leaf-traces in the interfoliar parts, the upper ends being cast off in the leaves at their death. In the plants in question, these leaf-traces are seen, on the transverse section of the shoot-axis, to be arranged in a circle; and their longitudinal course is in general parallel to the surface, as represented in Fig 129. The phloem-portions of these usually not very numerous bundles are all turned towards the surface of the shoot-axis, the xylem-portions being directed towards the centre of the transverse section. From the very first, even before the origin of the cambium ring, the elements of the vascular bundles are arranged in radial rows

The first indication of the commencing growth in thickness consists in that a layer of cells, lying in the vascular bundle between the phloem and xylem, grows in the radial direction, and accordingly becomes divided by tangentially placed partition-walls. Thus originates the fascicular cambium The cells of this, arising by continually repeated divisions, when they lie towards the phloem side develope into elements of the secondary cortex (secondary phloem), and when they arise on the inner side of the cambium constitute new elements of the wood. In many cases, the growth in thickness progresses in such a manner that this cambium layer, lying in each individual vascular bundle, causes the phloëm as well as the xylem of the bundle to increase in the radial direction, so that the primitively rounded transverse section of the bundle becomes gradually elongated radially, and widened outwards into a wedge shape. The fundamental tissue lying between these vascular bundles which are growing in thickness, developes at the same time, by repeated cell-divisions. In this manner, however, a closed mass of wood is not formed; nor is a continuous layer of secondary cortex formed around the wood (e.g stem of Gourd).

In the typical case of growth in thickness, there is formed, after the production of a cambium layer in each leaf-trace, a similar layer also in the fundamental tissue between each two neighbouring bundles (see Fig 165, *B*); and this always in such a manner that the parenchyma cells of the fundamental tissue are elongated in the radial direction, and divide by means of tangentially placed longitudinal walls Thus arises the interfascicular cambium, which becomes joined on to the fascicular cambium, and together with this constitutes a continuous cambium layer. This appears on the transverse section as a ring, but of course it is really a hollow cylinder, running in the tissue of the shoot-axis. On the inside of this cambium-ring lie the xylem-portions, and on its outside the phloëm-portions of the leaf-traces; and since the cambium-ring produces wood progressively on the whole of its inner side, a woody ring or hollow cylinder of wood is produced, enclosing the pith or inner portion of fundamental tissue On the outside of the cambium-ring arises in like manner a hollow cylinder of secondary cortex. It may be mentioned here that with this mode of growth, certain differences between the arrangement and form of the secondary cortex and that of the secondary wood necessarily arise. The cambium-ring increases progressively in diameter, and the wood-elements arising from it, and which grow but little in transverse section, need only be deposited so to speak by apposition on the wood-elements already present; hence the transverse section of the wood comes to present a very evident arrangement of its elements in radial rows, and in layers concentric with the periphery. On the outside of the cambium-ring, on the other hand, it by no means suffices that the layers of cortex already existing receive new deposits on the inside; for the continually progressing increase in circumference of the cambium-ring necessitates a further growth in the peripheral direction of at least a part of the existing elements of the cortex. In consequence of this, subsequent alterations of the tissue-elements in the cortex take place, by means of which, under certain circumstances, their radial arrangement is much disturbed: the arrangement in concentric layers, on the other hand, is usually more marked. Finally, however, the peripheral growth frequently ceases in the most external (i.e. the oldest) cortical layers; and then, in consequence of the formation and growth of internal layers, longitudinal cracks arise on the exterior, or other distortions of the outermost, oldest layers of tissue take place.

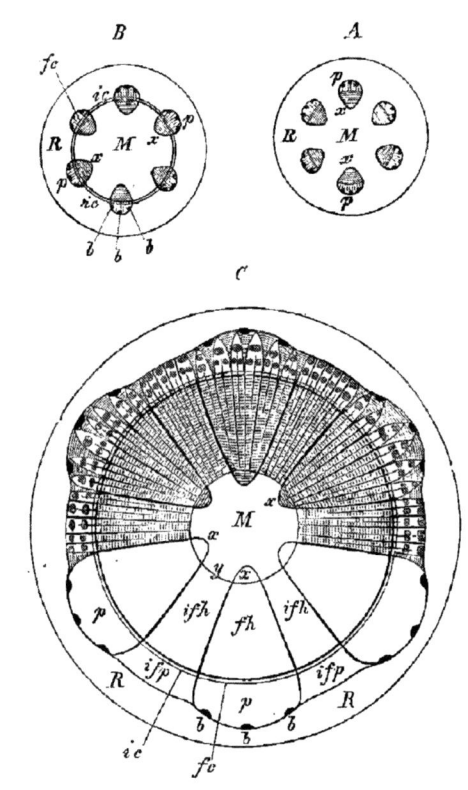

FIG. 165.—Diagram of ordinary growth in thickness, with the development of a compact woody mass. *A*, *B*, *C* the same transverse section at different stages in order of age. *A* before the origin of the interfascicular cambium ; *B* after its production ; *C* after the cambium has been active for some time. Everywhere, *R* primary cortex ; *M* pith ; *p* phloëm ; *x* xylem of the vascular bundles ; *b b b* three groups of bast-fibres in the phloëm. N.B. these are widely separated in *C* ; *fc* fascicular cambium ; *ic* interfascicular cambium ; *fh* the wood developed from the fascicular cambium ; *ifh* the wood developed from the interfascicular cambium ; *ifp* the secondary cortical tissue developed from the interfascicular cambium—the diagram is based on drawings of sections of the hypocotyl of *Ricinus communis*.

When the terms wood and cortex are employed in what follows, the secondary wood and secondary cortex developed from the cambium-ring are always to be understood. We will now consider somewhat more closely the anatomical constitution of these tissues.

The wood, as well as the cortex, consists of two systems of tissue, the origin of which is already to be seen in the cambium. First, of elements which are elongated longitudinally, and generally deposited together in the form of bundles or groups of fibres with a sinuous course. The meshes of the network which thus arise, forming longitudinally elongated slits between the bundles named, are filled up by horizontally elongated parallel rows of cells, running in the radial direction from the interior to the outside ; these are the so-called medullary rays, which, according as they run in the wood or in the secondary cortex, are to be distinguished as xylem-rays (the "silver-grain" of the carpenter) or cortex-rays (phloem-rays) It is to be noted, however, that each cortex-ray is simply the outer continuation of a xylem-ray, formed by the cambium This coarser structure of the product of the cambium is to be seen very plainly in the decomposed stems of *Brassica* (Cabbage), *Carica papaya*, and other plants, and still more conspicuously in the woody skeletons of various species of Cactus—e g *Cereus*, *Opuntia*, and others, where the meshes between the wood- and bast-bundles are unusually distinct. In like manner, the broad bands of the somewhat strongly lignified (an exceptional occurrence) commercial bast of the Lime illustrate what is here said. In these cases the radial tissue of the rays, which fills up the meshes between the wood- and bast-bundles as they undulate tangentially, becomes destroyed by rotting and the action of the weather in general, because it consists of soft non-lignified cells ; in the true woody plants, on the other hand, as may frequently be observed in the decomposed stems of the Red Beech in woods, the substance of the xylem-rays is occasionally more resistent than that of the wood bundles, and while the latter become destroyed by rotting, the former remain behind, constituting to a certain extent a skeleton of radially disposed plates On a tangential section, moreover, as well as on radial split surfaces of ordinary wood, the larger rays are perceived as bands running horizontally, which traverse the woody mass from within outwards ; the smaller and very small ones are only to be seen with the microscope Moreover only the first few rays, already existing at the beginning of the growth in thickness, run from the pith through the whole thickness of the wood into the cortex : they break up the mass of wood (seen on the transverse section) into a small number of wedge-shaped portions, with the broad side outwards. The rays subsequently developed with the progressive growth in thickness are much more numerous, and the later they arise, the further they are removed from the pith in the wood. They break this up, as seen on the transverse section, into continually finer, radially disposed portions, arranged in a fan-like manner. It is always to be understood, however, that this breaking-up apparent on the transverse section, is only the expression of the longitudinally elongated meshes in the undulating course of the wood, and that the rays themselves only represent the filling up of these meshes. I may take this opportunity of remarking, as to the principle lying at the base of all the tissue formation of the higher plants, that, apart from certain organs of secretion and isolated idioblasts lying in the tissue, similar tissue-elements of a plant stand everywhere in contact with one another As the epidermis, the vascular bundles, and the fundamental tissue, as well as the individual cells of the two latter are all in continuous connection throughout the entire plant ; so with the elements of the wood and cortex, now to be described more in detail, so far as concerns tissue-elements of the same kind. This principle comes out particularly clearly in the case of the medullary rays, inasmuch as these run as parenchymatous nourishing tissue continuously from the wood into the cortex, and in their turn are connected with the parenchymatous elements of the wood-bundles as well as with those of the cortex

As in the primary vascular bundles, on the existence of which the formation of the cambium-ring and the entire growth in thickness depends, we can also distinguish two main groups of tissue-elements in the products of the cambium   The whole of the secondary cortex arising on the outer side of the cambium-ring is in the main a continued development of the phloëm of the vascular bundle ; and the wood-mass arising on the inner side of the cambium-ring is in like manner a further development of the xylem of the original vascular bundle.   We here neglect the medullary rays for the moment. In

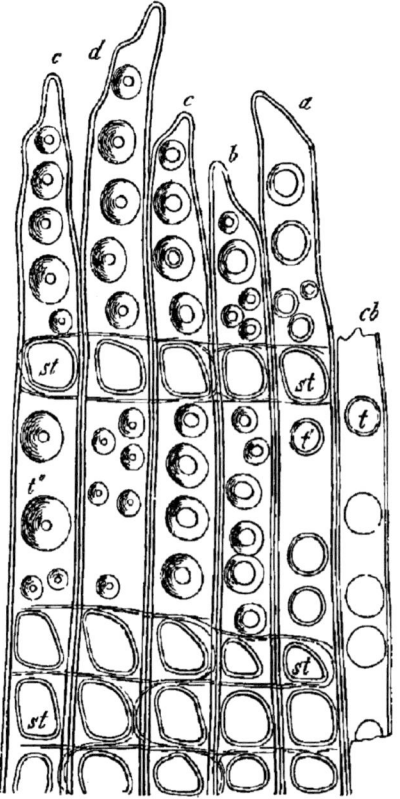

FIG. 166 —*Pinus sylvestris*   Radial longitudinal section through the wood of a vigorous branch , *cb* cambial wood cell , *a—t* older wood cells , *t t' t''* bordered pits of the wood cells in order of age , *st* large pits where cells of the medullary rays are in contact with the wood cells (× 550)

the cortex, as well as in the wood, we have again, in addition to vascular elements (sieve-tubes and wood vessels respectively), also parenchymatous tissue (xylem- and phloem-parenchyma) and elastic fibres (wood and bast-fibres).

We will, in the first place, consider the composition of the wood arising from the cambium-ring. In the Conifers, this consists entirely of elongated tracheides, or with a very small admixture of parenchyma. These are long fibres, pointed above and below, on the radial side walls of which are remarkably large, isolated, bordered pits, which produce a very characteristic appearance (Fig. 166) In the Dicotyledons, on the other hand, such tracheides usually enter, it is true, into the composition of the wood, together with these, however, three other elements occur. First the wood-vessels, which traverse the wood-bundle as continuous tubes, isolated or in groups, and usually with bordered pits. More rarely they are reticulately thickened (annular and ordinary spiral vessels do not occur in the secondary wood, though the Cactaceæ possess tracheides with the walls thus sculptured), and then follow parenchymatous cells—the wood-parenchyma.   These cells occur either in the form of spindle-shaped fibres pointed above and below, but with living contents , or they resemble these but are chambered by several transverse septa. Sometimes forming the main mass of the wood, sometimes less conspicuous in the mass, are the proper wood-fibres, or libriform fibres.   These are narrow, thick-walled, elongated cells, obliquely pointed above and below , the wall-structure of which may exhibit all transitions from that of tracheides with bordered pits to that of bast fibres.   Of these histological elements of the wood, the one or the other may predominate, or exist in small quantity, or be wholly wanting.   Generally they are all present, and their relative quantity and mode of grouping determine the character of the wood; which appears accordingly as a loose porous mass abounding in vessels and tracheïdes, or even chiefly parenchymatous, or, on the contrary, as a firm, dense mass of tissue chiefly composed of libriform fibres. Libriform fibres, tracheïdes, and wood-parenchyma form in ordinary cases the dense matrix of wood in which the vessels run; these usually possess far wider lumina, and are often recognisable on the transverse section even by the unaided eye as

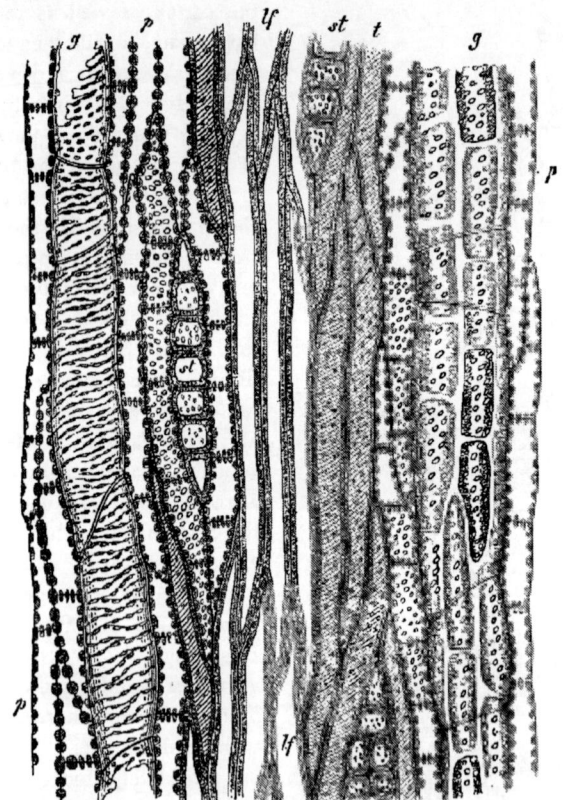

FIG. 167.—Tangential longitudinal section through the wood of *Ailanthus glandulosa*. *g g* vessels; *st* medullary rays cut across; *p* wood parenchyma; *t* tracheïdes.

punctate openings, and on the longitudinal section as more or less evident narrow canals.

The vessels, tracheïdes, and libriform fibres of the wood, as soon as they are fully developed, contain air, and their walls are usually strongly lignified; only the parenchymatous fibres (*Ersatz-fasern* and proper wood parenchyma) contain protoplasm and products of assimilation, and possess thin walls, which are pitted in the usual way and are often feebly or not at all lignified.

Apart from a few still doubtful exceptions, the woody mass arising from the cambium in the course of years is composed of concentric layers, which appear

[3]   M

on the transverse section as rings; and, since one of these is formed each year, they are distinguished as annual rings. These are, of course, in reality hollow cylinders disposed one around the other. Each annual ring is the product of the wood-forming activity of the cambium-ring during one period of vegetation. That these appear, even to the unaided eye, as layers of the wood-body sharply separated from one another, depends upon the fact that within any one period of vegetation (i. e. in the time during which an annual ring is formed), the formation of wood itself varies periodically. It is evident that the inner portion of any one annual ring is the first to be developed in the period of vegetation—that is, it is formed in the spring; while the outer portion of the same annual ring has arisen towards the conclusion of the wood-forming activity in the same period of vegetation. At the boundary of successive annual rings, therefore, the spring-wood of the following ring is always deposited on the autumnal wood of the preceding next inner ring; so that the usually different wood formations of two periods of vegetation lie immediately adjoining one another. Owing to this, the separation of two neighbouring annual rings is more clearly marked. Put quite generally, the spring wood is composed of elements with wide lumina and thin walls; the autumn wood last formed in a period of vegetation consists, on the contrary, of elements with narrow lumina, and often also thick walls. This difference comes out very clearly in the simple wood of the Conifers, which

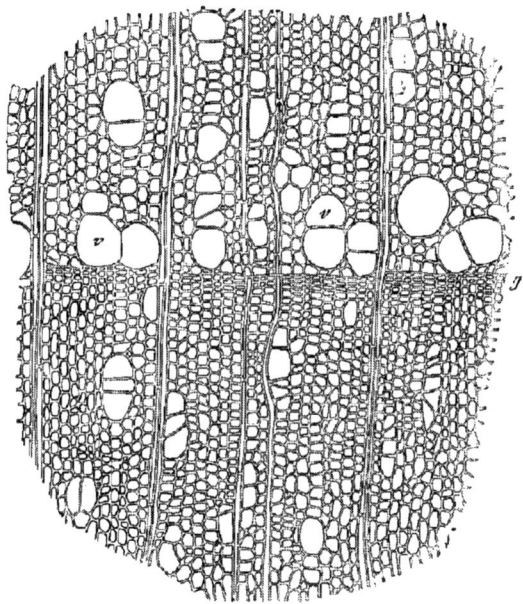

FIG. 168.—Transverse section of the wood of *Rhamnus frangula*. *g* the autumn-wood of an older annual ring; *vv* vessels in the spring-wood of a younger ring (after Rossmann).

consists, as stated, entirely of tracheïdes. The transverse sections of these are nearly square in the spring wood; in the autumn wood, on the contrary, they are narrow and rectangular, so that the cells appear compressed in the radial direction to one-third or one-fourth the diameter of those of the spring wood.

Apart from the stronger thickening of the walls, the autumn wood is also richer in wall-substance and poorer in cavities than the spring wood. In the dictyledonous woods there is associated with these differences affecting the parenchyma, tracheïdes, and libriform fibres, a corresponding difference in the vessels, so that in general the vessels lying in the spring-wood are far larger in transverse section than those formed in the summer and autumn. Frequently, the relative number of vessels in the rings of wood also diminishes with the advancing season. Thus, taken all together, the spring wood is more porous, looser, and poorer in substance than the autumn wood. The transition from the one to the other in the same annual ring may be gradual or sudden; and it is to be added that the middle part of an annual ring, between the spring and autumn wood, is often especially rich in libriform fibres.

On the transverse and longitudinal section of the older stems and branches of trees, the difference between the so-called splint (alburnum) and the heart-wood (duramen) is usually very marked. The alburnum is a pale, more or less thick zone of wood lying under the cortex, and in which two, three, or many annual rings may be recognised; the wood which lies within this zone is generally dark-coloured (red, yellow, brown, or black), and formed of a much harder mass. This is the duramen, alone employed in the arts. Since the thickness of the alburnum remains practically the same, while the duramen increases in thickness year by year, it is obvious that an inner layer of alburnum becomes transformed annually into a new outer layer of duramen. This difference between the alburnum and the duramen is not always evident in the colouring and hardness—in the Fir, for example; and indeed it is stated of the Box-tree and some kinds of Maple, that this difference does not exist at all, but that the entire wood of an older stem consists of alburnum. The alburnum is the wood in the condition in which it has arisen in a period of vegetation, by the development of the various wood elements from the cambium. it is the normal wood, which comes immediately and alone into consideration for the vital activity of the plant. The water absorbed by the roots ascends in it, and reserve materials are deposited in its medullary rays and other parenchymatous cells. The wood which has passed over into the condition of duramen, on the contrary, takes no more direct part in the vital activity of the plant; it is to be regarded as a mass of tissue passing over into decomposition, and perhaps also destined for the deposition of excretions. The duramen owes its darker hue, as well as its increased hardness and resistance to destruction, to the infiltration of dark-coloured substances, often soluble in water as colouring matters (Red-wood, Blue-wood, Yellow-wood); or of resinous bodies (*Guaiacum*, Conifers); or occasionally even of silica (*Tectona*, Iron-wood), and other substances which, like these, in extreme cases not merely impregnate the walls, but partly, or even entirely, fill up the cavities of the fibres and vessels.

In contrast to the resistent, elastic woody mass, the secondary cortex (secondary phloem) appears on the outside of the cambium-ring, generally as a softer mass of tissue composed chiefly of active living cells, in this tissue, however, bast-fibres, singly or in groups, produce a conspicuous fibrous structure of great toughness. As already mentioned, the sieve-tubes are to be regarded as the characteristic main element of the secondary cortex; in addition to which a larger or smaller quantity of thin-walled, elongated, soft parenchyma is never wanting. It is usual to distinguish both these together as the soft bast, in contradistinction to the proper bast-fibres. The latter are generally very thick-walled, often very long (but occasionally short) tough fibres; which in some cases are completely wanting in the secondary cortex, and in others are scattered as isolated elements in the soft bast. Frequently, however, these predominate throughout the structure of the secondary cortex, in the form of more or less thick bundles, or even layers. Like the various elements of the wood, those of the secondary cortex may also be present in very different quantities and variously arranged.

M 2

The whole structure of the secondary cortex is influenced by the horizontal tissue of the medullary rays to an extent even greater than is the case in the wood. To mention two extreme cases only; the medullary rays, when they traverse the cortex in great numbers, may cause the whole of the remaining tissue to appear arranged chiefly in radial rows on the transverse section (*Cinchona*); and when bast fibres are present, these also appear on the transverse section to be arranged chiefly in radial rows. In the other extreme case, on the contrary, individual medullary rays become much wider as they proceed from the cambium to the exterior; since their parenchyma cells grow very strongly in the tangential direction, in correspondence with the increase in circumference of the stem, and become chambered by radial longitudinal walls, thus constituting a parenchymatous mass of concentrically arranged layers of cells, in which lie thicker bundles of soft bast, traversed under certain circumstances by bast-fibres. In the Conifers the arrangement in radial rows

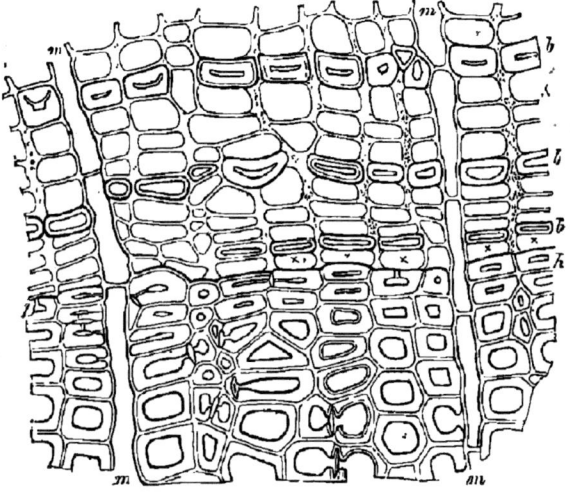

FIG 169 —Transverse section of the stem of *Juniperus communis*   *xx* Cambium, *hh* autumn wood of the youngest annual ring, *bb* bast fibres of the secondary cortex, in peripheral rows and with sieve tubes between them , *m* medullary rays (De Bary)

as well as that in concentric layers is usually evident, and Fig. 169 shows at once how the thick-walled bast fibres are here disposed in layers within the soft bast.

Observed on a tangential section, the secondary cortex, like the wood, is composed of sinuous or undulating bundles of elongated elements connected in a net-like manner, the meshes of which, likewise elongated longitudinally, are filled up by the parenchyma of the medullary rays. This structure is to be seen even by the unaided eye when the bundles abound in bast-fibres

The activity of the cambium is generally less energetic towards the exterior than on the inside; i.e. the formation of cortex proceeds in the radial direction much more slowly than the formation of wood. This is obvious at once, on comparing the cortex in the transverse section of a large Beech stem, where it is only a few millimeters thick, with the huge mass of wood; both of them being of the same age

In shoot-axes which eventually proceed to perennial growth in thickness, the formation of periderm occurs before the commencement of the growth in thickness, or simultaneously with it, or later. By periderm is understood a layer of tissue consisting of cork-cells, which in normal cases surrounds the whole of the shoot-axis or root as a continuous envelope. In most cases it is of inconsiderable thickness; occasionally, however, as in the Cork-Oak, it forms a layer (bottle-cork) several centimeters thick. We have in the peel of the potato a very instructive example of the formation of simple periderm. In some cases, as in the Elm, the cork-periderm grows out in the form of isolated longitudinal ridges. Thicker periderm may consist of alternate layers of thick-walled and thin-walled cork-cells; and the individual thin layers of cork not rarely become stripped off from one another, as on

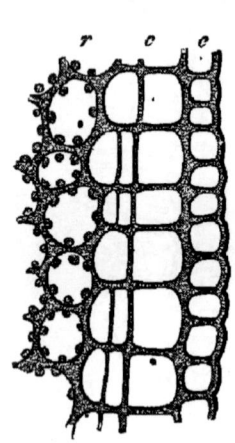

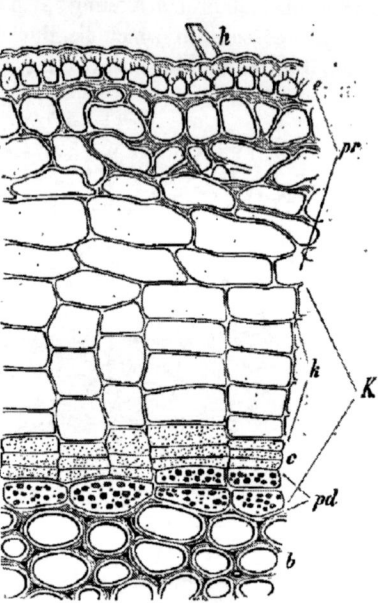

FIG. 170.—Commencing development of periderm in the shoot-axis of *Anona cheirimolia* (transverse section). *e* epidermis; *cc* cells dividing to form cork; *r* cortical parenchyma containing chlorophyll.

FIG. 171.—Cork formation in a first year's branch of *Ribes nigrum*; part of transverse section. *e* epidermis; *h* hair; *b* bast-cells; *pr* cortical parenchyma, distorted by the growth in thickness of the branch; *K* the total product of the phellogen (*c*); *k* the radial rows of cork-cells, developed from *c* in centrifugal order; *pd* phelloderm—parenchyma containing chlorophyll, and arising centripetally from *c* (× 550).

the older branches and younger stems of the Birch, and especially in many species of *Melaleuca*. The periderm is a strengthened substitute for the epidermis. The suberised cell-walls fit together on all sides without intercellular spaces, and possess the properties of the cuticle and the cuticularised outer cell-walls of the epidermis. The protection which they afford to the inner tissues against the evaporation of their fluids is increased by the cork-cells dying and losing their sap immediately after becoming fully developed; while granular or amorphous matters not rarely fill up the cavities in part or entirely (Birch). The origin of the periderm is due to a formation of tissue similar to the cambium. This cork-cambium or *Phellogen* either (and more rarely) originates in the epidermis itself, or in the layer of primary cortical tissue immediately beneath it; or in a layer lying somewhat deeper. The cells referred to grow first in the radial direction, and then become divided by tangential longitudinal walls. Of the two daughter-cells so produced, the outer developes into a cork-cell; while the inner one, continuously increasing in width radially, again divides. Of the two daughter-cells now existing, the outer one is again transformed into a cork-cell; while the inner one remains active, and repeats the same process. This layer of cells which continually become regenerated is the phellogen; the similarity of which to the cambium is increased yet more by the fact that layers of tissue often originate from the phellogen on the inner side also. These, as the so-called *Phelloderm*, strengthen the parenchymatous living cortex (cp. Fig. 171). The arrangement in radial rows and at the same time in concentric layers (which immediately results in part from the origin of the cork-cells mentioned above, and in part from their quickly terminated growth) are almost universally characteristic of cork-tissue.

As in many cases (*Viscum, Acer striatum,* species of *Cornus,* &c.) the epidermis itself follows the growth in thickness of the organ for many years, so also the periderm (and this is oftener the case) may for years follow the increase in circumference of a branch or stem by passive stretching and growth.

Sooner or later, however, where the growth in thickness persists for a long time, a repeated changing of the peripheral tissues usually results—Bark is formed. In rarer cases this occurs as so-called ring-bark. This arises from the development of new layers of periderm in the deeper cortex, some cell-layers distant from the preceding periderm; and the older layers thus become exfoliated across the stem (*Vitis, Clematis,* Cupressineæ, according to De Bary). Scale-bark, of which we find the simplest and most instructive example on the stems of *Platanus,* is however commoner. As is well known, there peel off from these stems in the summer larger or smaller plates of tissue, often as large as the hand and 1–2 mm. thick; and a somewhat rough surface, beset with corky warts, is left behind on the stem after their fall. If we now suppose that, at the same places in the cortex, such scales gradually die, and do not fall off, but remain suspended and clinging to one another on the stem, the latter would, after some years, become surrounded with a scaly layer of dead masses of tissue, deposited one over the other. These together constitute scale-bark; and at the same time, in consequence of the progressive increase in circumference of the stem, these dead packets of scales become more and more separated from one another by means of longitudinal clefts running between them. This process is to be recognised very clearly on close observation of the bark of old Pine stems. The origin of these scales of bark is brought about by the repeated formation of thin lamellæ of cork within the living cortex; these do not however run all round the organ, but their edges come to the surface at circumscribed places, so that a portion is cut out of the cortex, so to speak, as if with a gouge. Not only the phellogen-layer concerned, but also the whole of the cortical tissue lying on its exterior dies off and dries up; whereupon the same process is again repeated towards the interior. Since now these cork-lamellæ cut out indiscriminately the most various forms of tissue from connection with the living parts, the bark-scales consist of all the different cell formations which occur in the cortex generally; and it is clear that, since by the progressive development of bark a thicker and thicker coat grows around the stem, the living cortex itself, whilst being regenerated in its turn by the cambium, always represents only a relatively thin layer of the tissues produced from the cambium. After the primary cortex has been removed by the processes mentioned, the older layers of the secondary cortex gradually take part in the formation of bark, and as the inner older wood is transformed into heart wood, and the original pith and the primary vascular bundles surrounding it have likewise long ceased to take part in the vital processes, the organ concerned (an older shoot-axis or root) now consists only of such living masses of tissue (secondary cortex and alburnum) as owe their existence entirely to the activity of the cambium. The varying hardness and other material peculiarities of the bark (and especially the way in which it gradually becomes split up by means of continually deeper longitudinal cracks, often connected in a net-like manner) depend on the properties of those masses of cortical tissue which provide the material for the development of bark. If large quantities of elastic fibres are formed in it, the bark also exhibits a fibrous fracture; if, as very often happens, numerous stone-cells (*scleroblasts*) are present in the parenchymatous cortical tissue, these are found again in the bark-scales. The latter will also be rich in calcium oxalate when this has been accumulated previously in large masses in the secondary cortical tissue, as is commonly the case.

As in the epidermis the stomata exist as passages of communication between the atmosphere and the air contained in the intercellular spaces; so also in the periderm, and later in the bark, peculiar organs occur by means of which, it is assumed, a certain communication between the atmosphere and the interior of the cortical tissue is established. These organs are the *Lenticels*. They arise even in the first period of vegetation of lignifying shoot-axes, and project from the smooth periderm of annual and perennial shoots usually as pale coloured roundish warts. With the increase in circumference of the organ they become widened, and at length appear as transversely elongated masses of tissue, which swell up in moist weather like cushions, their number increasing with the advancing age of the branch or stem. The lenticels may be considered as peculiar localised growths of the periderm. Where the periderm is developed in the epidermis or close beneath it, the lenticels arise before it or simultaneously with it beneath the not very numerous stomata of the shoot-axis. In the tissue lying under a stoma, a phellogen, convex inwards, is formed; and from this, serially arranged cork-tissue is developed externally, and phelloderm internally. This phellogen is immediately continuous with the rest of the periderm-forming tissue of the shoot-axis, only its activity in developing cells is more vigorous, especially towards the outside. Moreover the cells originating from the phellogen externally are distinguished from those of the ordinary periderm, in that they possess intercellular spaces, and that the external mass of the lenticel forms a very loose powdery tissue, broken up into its individual cells. This may be termed lenticel-tissue, and is plainly shown in Fig 172. The cells of this lenticel-tissue remain thin-walled and for a long time living, and, on contact with water, capable of swelling and even of growth. At the conclusion of the period of vegetation a dense layer of cork, not traversed by intercellular spaces, is formed in the lenticel;

---

[1] What is here said concerning the Lenticels is taken from De Bary's '*Vergl Anat der Vegetations-organe*,' § 179.

by means of which the communication of the cortical intercellular spaces with the atmosphere during the period of rest is interrupted. At the beginning of the new period of vegetation, however, new looser lenticel-tissue arises from the phellogen of the lenticel, which splits the closing layer of cork and opens the lenticel during the period of vegetation. The origin of the lenticels is not always connected with the

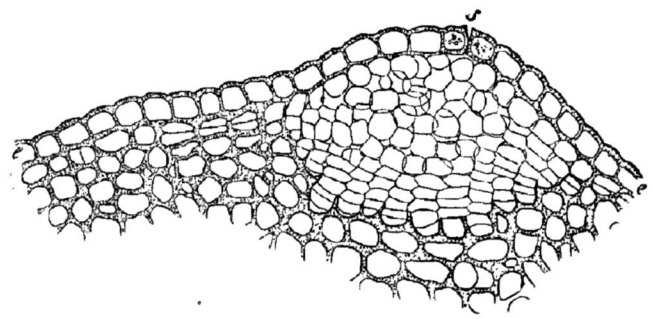

FIG. 172.—Transverse section through a lenticel of *Betula alba, e* epidermis ; *s* a stoma. Beneath this is the loose tissue of the lenticel, and further inwards the phellogen ; at the margin of the lenticel the development of periderm is beginning (after L e Bary).

existence of stomata, however. In the formation of internal layers of periderm, lenticels are developed quite independently, but to a certain extent as local growths of the new layer of periderm ; and since internal layers of periderm are necessarily connected with the formation of bark, lenticels thus arise within the bark. This is particularly clear after the fall of the bark scales in *Platanus*, on the fresh exposed surface of the cortex, which is now beset with corky warts.

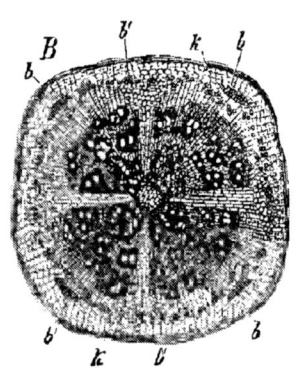

FIG. 173.—Transverse section through the upper swollen portion of the primary root of *Phaseolus multiflorus*—less magnified than Fig. 141. On comparing the two figures, the corresponding position of the primary bast (*b b*) is observed.

What has hitherto been said concerning growth in thickness, is true especially of the shoot-axes. As already mentioned, however, the roots of woody plants also undergo a subsequent growth in thickness, which only differs in a few points from that of the shoot-axes. Here, as there, the first origin of the cambium is connected with the vascular bundles. These, as we know already, form an axial cylinder in the roots ; in which the phloëm-portions are placed at the periphery, alternating with the xylem. The cambium arises therefore as an annular layer with sinuosities, so running that here again the phloëm comes to lie on the outside, and the xylem on the inside of the cambium. The formation of secondary wood and cortex then follows exactly as in the shoot-axis ; except that, in general, the peculiarity prevails in the root that the secondary wood springing from the cambium-ring (seen in transverse section) does not fit on to the xylem-portions of the axial string, but is developed between them,—i.e. on the inside of the primary phloëm-portions. In the growth in thickness of the root, also, the production of parenchymatous tissue very commonly predominates. In roots which grow in thickness, the formation of periderm usually occurs at an early period, and this always takes its origin deep in the internal tissue. Inside the endodermis before mentioned, which envelopes the entire axial cord, lies a layer of parenchyma, the so-called pericambium, and it is in this (according to De Bary) that the periderm of the root arises. Thus the whole of the cortical tissue of the root dies off, and a new cortical layer—i. e a phelloderm— is produced by the activity of the phellogen, on the outer side of which is formed at the same time a periderm, consisting of cork

Mention may here be made, finally, of the peculiar growth in thickness of many napiform roots, e g. Radish, Turnip, &c., as well as of the tuberous swellings of some shoot-axes, such as the Potato, Turnip, &c. These parts of the plant, edible on account of their soft, thin-walled, non-lignified masses of tissue, owe (since they too are thin and filiform at first) their later thickness and massiveness to the subsequent

growth in thickness brought about by means of a cambium - layer. Essentially, and considered purely formally, the processes are the same here as in the ordinary cases where the cambium produces true wood, only here, in place of the development of tracheïdes and libri-form fibres, the formation of paren-chyma predominates, and the ligni-fication of the cells produced on the inner side of the cambium-ring is entirely suppressed, or affects in a slight degree only the not numerous vessels which traverse the secondary wood consisting entirely of non-lig-nified parenchyma. Occasionally, as is known, Turnips and Potato-tubers become woody: they are then tra-versed by tough inedible fibres—i. e. by actually lignified strands.

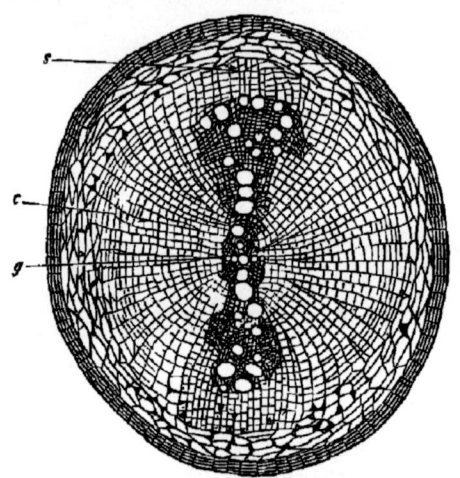

FIG 174—Transverse section of a thin root on the rhizome of the Nettle (*Urtica dioica*) *g* the series of primary vessels arranged right and left The secondary wood forms two groups—lying above and below in the figure *c* the cambium The primary cortex has been thrown off, the periderm is developing at the circumference (after De Bary).

Passing over the very numerous cases of abnormal growth in thickness[1] in dicotyledonous woody plants (since these, in spite of considerable deviations from the type, nevertheless differ in no way essentially from it), I may still say a few words as to the growth in thickness of a small group of monocotyledonous plants—Monocotyledons not elsewhere exhibiting this process Here are concerned a sub-division of the Liliaceæ, to which the well-known genera *Dracæna*, *Yucca*, and a few others belong. These plants, palm-like in advanced age, possess when young a thin stem, scarcely as thick as a finger, which may subsequently attain a considerable thickness. This occurs of course by growth in thickness; and this extends also into

---

[1] The essential facts on abnormal growth in thickness are found in De Bary's '*Anat der Vegetations-organe*,' Cap XVI

the roots   Now the young, thin stem is traversed, as in Monocotyledons generally, by isolated closed vascular bundles, which, originating near the surface, ascend within the stem in a radially oblique direction, reach about to the centre, and then curve out somewhat suddenly into the leaves (cp. Fig 130)   The paths of the numerous bundles arising at various heights and curving in and out, thus cross; and it is scarcely conceivable how, under these circumstances, a cambium

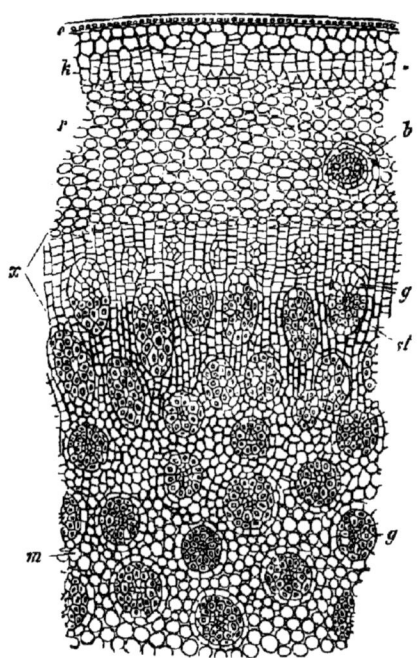

FIG 175 —Part of transverse section of a stem of *Dracæna* (*reflexa?*) about 13 mm thick and 1 m high, taken about 20 cm beneath the apex *e* epidermis, *k* cork (periderm), *r* cortical fundamental tissue, *b* transverse section of a fibro vascular bundle which bends out into a leaf, *m* the primary fundamental tissue (pith), *g* the primary bundles *x* the zone of meristem in which are young vascular bundles—older ones *g* have already, partly or wholly, emerged from the zone, its inner portion being transformed into radially arranged fundamental tissue (*sl*).

layer, connected as in the true wood plants, and at the same time running through the vascular bundles, could come into existence. As a matter of fact, the growth in thickness of these plants is initiated and carried forward in a somewhat different manner. A zone of the fundamental tissue, annular in transverse section, outside of which there lies a thin cortical tissue, becomes transformed by radial growth and the appearance of tangential partition-walls into a tissue capable of division—a meristem; the activity of which certainly possesses great similarity to that of the cambium   Some considerable differences, however, are apparent. Apart from the fact that the development of secondary cortex from this meristem is generally very inconsiderable, no mass of wood, homogeneous and compact as in the Coniferæ and Dicotyledons, is deposited on the inner side of the continually widening meristem circle; but the products of the layer of meristem are secondary vascular bundles, consisting of sieve-tubes and tracheides.   These secondary vascular bundles exhibit a sinuous undulating course, anastomose radially and tangentially, and thus form a dense network, the meshes of which are filled with radially elongated parenchyma which originates from the zone of meristem, and, as is easily observed, corresponds to the medullary rays of true wood.   With this growth in thickness is also connected a development of periderm at the surface of the organ; this, however, is usually confined to the production of a thin cork membrane, which, like the epidermis, completely envelopes the whole organ as a smooth layer.

LECTURE XI.

LATICIFEROUS VESSELS AND RECEPTACLES FOR SECRETIONS.

THE epidermal tissue, the vascular bundles, and the fundamental tissue may be traced from their most rudimentary beginnings in the Thallophytes, through the Muscineæ and Vascular Cryptogams up to the most highly developed Phanerogams as structures phylogenetically identical. In them is expressed an essentially similar plan of organisation of the whole vegetable kingdom, and even in the product of the cambium of the woody plants we discover nothing essentially new, but only a further development of these tissue-differentiations.

The fact is quite otherwise with the laticiferous vessels and organs of secretion, which allow no such phylogenetic continuity to be recognised. At the most various stages of development of the vegetable kingdom, we meet with organs of this kind in isolated small subdivisions; while they are wanting in other groups, often very extensive, or appear only here and there in them. In general, we have always to recognise in their existence, however, a sign of further advanced physiological division of labour, only the matter is especially one of chemical problems, which are to be solved by means of these relations of organisation Since the division of physiological labour is most distinctly expressed in the Phanerogams generally; so, too, the forms of tissue here to be considered occur in them more frequently and in greater variety than in the Cryptogams, though they are by no means wanting to the latter

It is especially characteristic of the laticiferous vessels and organs of secretion that, while similar in nature in other respects, they are not exclusively peculiar to any one of the three systems of tissue, but are curiously independent in their occurrence. We find laticiferous vessels and organs of secretion sometimes, though more rarely, in the epidermal tissue, at others in the fundamental tissue, or in the vascular bundles In this connection the most that can be said is that they particularly affect the fundamental tissue.

We may first consider the Laticiferous Vessels[1].

In a large number of families, and genera within certain families, or even species within certain genera (e. g. in the Euphorbiaceæ, Urticaceæ, Asclepiadeæ, Papaveraceæ, Campanulaceæ, Lobeliaceæ, Cichoriaceæ, etc), it is remarkable that from any wound, however small, there exudes at once a thick drop, or even a stream

---

[1] In so far as the description here given differs from that in my 'Text-book,' it is founded on De Bary's '*Vergleichende Anat. der Vegetations-organe,*' Cap. VI

(the larger Euphorbiaceæ) of milk-like fluid. This is usually white, like animal milk, more rarely yellow (*Chelidonium*) or orange-coloured (*Bocconia*); and the outflow ceases very soon after the injury. This milk-like fluid (the latex), as will be shown more clearly later on, is contained in narrow tubes, generally much-branched or anastomosing. These are the laticiferous vessels, which permeate all the organs of the plants concerned (in some cases perhaps with the exception of the roots) in such a manner that any puncture or cut, however insignificant, opens some of them, and occasions the outflow of the latex. The latex itself consists of two chief constituents, a watery fluid, and granules or drops, generally exceedingly small, suspended in it, which, as in animal milk, produce the opaque, milky appearance. In the watery fluid are usually dissolved, in addition to the mineral salts which occur in all the fluids of the plant, small quantities of sugar, gum, starch, and proteid-like substances, and, according to circumstances, peculiar alkaloids or vegetable acids and their salts. The substances which cause the latex when drawn off from the plant to form, on mere contact with air, water, alcohol, ether, or acids, flocky coagula which become more or less clumped together and separated from the watery fluid, are still unknown. The small corpuscles suspended in the fluid, which cause the opacity and cloudiness, appear when strongly magnified as round bodies, often almost immeasureably small, in other cases larger   In the latter case, especially in the Ficus-like plants, the corpuscles exhibit a concentric stratification, but are at the same time soft and sticky   These emulsified substances generally show a tendency to cohere among themselves in the latex drawn from the plant; and so form coherent masses, which after the evaporation of the watery constituent present themselves as dense unctuous mixtures like Opium, or as brittle resins like Euphorbium, or finally as elastic caoutchouc or India-rubber. In dried latex are also found small quantities of wax and fat. The most important product of the laticiferous vessels besides the Opium from *Papaver somniferum* (which contains Morphia) is perhaps Caoutchouc : this is obtained chiefly from a subdivision of arborescent Brazilian Euphorbiaceæ (*Hevea*), Indian species of *Ficus*, as well as from Apocynaceæ and some Asclepiadeæ.

The medicinal employment of a variety of kinds of dried latex shows that besides the predominant substances already mentioned, smaller quantities of narcotically active alkaloids or other peculiar matters are contained in them. The occurrence of bodies resembling ferments is of especial interest for vegetable physiology   Among these, besides the peptonising ferment in *Ficus carica*, the Papayotin contained in the latex of *Carica papaya* is particularly well known; and, according to the most recent researches, it is not improbable that ferments are distributed in many, or perhaps in most kinds of latex.

It appears that the laticiferous vessels play a part similar to that of the blood-vessels, and especially the veins of animals   They contain on the one hand matters which find immediate employment in growth, and, on the other hand, secretions and excretions which accumulate in them, and are of no further use. When they contain ferments, their physiological significance is still further enhanced. Of particular interest in this relation also is the existence of starch grains in the latex of many Euphorbiaceæ, since, with respect to these, we know that, after being dissolved and undergoing further chemical changes, they play a most important part in the metabolism of the plant. As however the occurrence of laticiferous vessels themselves is very variable, even within narrow circles of alliance; so also the chemical composition appears to be variable in the highest degree, from species to species and from genus to genus even within the families concerned. The substances mentioned as contained in the latex may be present or wanting, or one or another of them may predominate or be reduced to a minimum.

The laticiferous vessels themselves are always so narrow that they can never be seen on a transverse section of the organ with the unaided eye. The microscope, however, shows that they may be of very different diameter in the same plant. In the roots, shoot-axes and nerves of the leaves, run thicker tubes, from which thinner and yet thinner ones arise. The substance of the walls of the tubes always consists of soft cellulose, sometimes capable of swelling: they are never lignified, suberised, or otherwise essentially altered by infiltration. One of the most prominent characteristics of the laticiferous vessels is their continuity throughout the whole plant, or at any rate over wide areas. This may obviously, even if not in every point, be closely compared with the vascular system of an animal. This continuity is also the reason why a relatively considerable quantity of sap flows from a small injury at any part of the plant, in spite of the narrow diameter of the laticiferous vessels; for their walls are under high pressure on all sides, which is brought about by the turgescence of the surrounding tissues On the injury of any tube, therefore, the sap is pressed forward even from distant parts towards the opening.

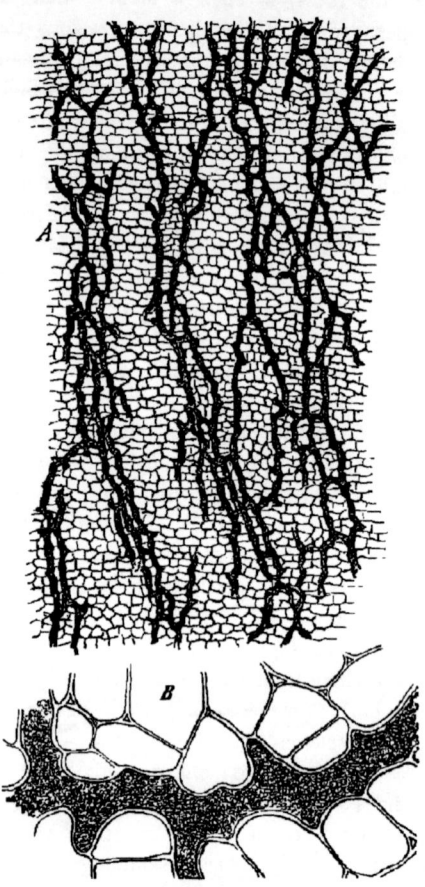

FIG 176 —*A* Tangential longitudinal section through the root of *Scorzonera hispanica.* In the parenchymatous tissues run numerous laticiferous vessels anastomosing laterally *B* small portion of a laticiferous vessel with adjacent parenchyma, more highly magnified.

According to their origin and form, two kinds of laticiferous vessels are to be distinguished—the segmented and the unsegmented.

The segmented laticiferous vessels, which occur in the Cichoriaceæ (particularly fine in the cortex of *Scorzonera*), in the Papaveraceæ, Campanulaceæ, etc, originate in the embryo, and in the embryonal tissue of the growing point, in the following manner. In certain series of cells which are previously distinguishable by their peculiar contents, the transverse septa become entirely, or in rarer cases (*Chelidonium*) partially absorbed, so that an actual vessel is formed; at the

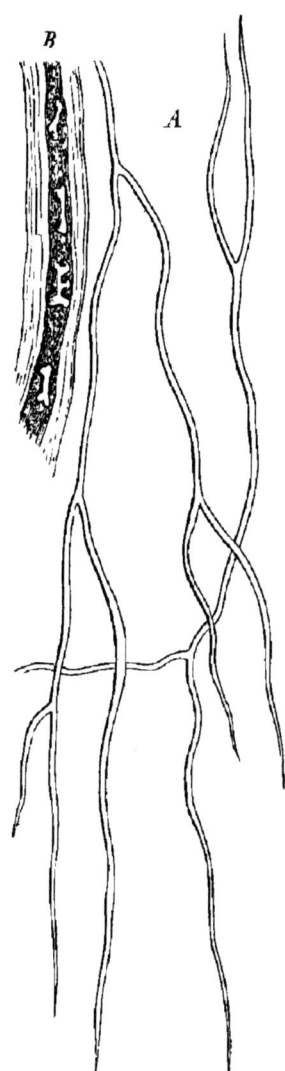

FIG. 177—Latex cells (unsegmented laticiferous vessels) of *Euphorbia splendens*, prepared free from the apex of a shoot by rotting *A* ramifications ending blindly, *B* a piece more strongly magnified, with 'bone shaped' starch grains.

same time, in many cases, lateral anastomoses are developed, the segments of these vessels sending forth protuberances between the cells of neighbouring tissues, which end blindly, or communicate directly with other protuberances of the same kind[1]. Thus the laticiferous vessels form a reticular system which extends up to the youngest leaves and growing points If in such plants a subsequent growth in thickness takes place, laticiferous vessels may gradually arise, singly or grouped in layers, as elements of the secondary cortex between the previously mentioned constituents of the latter (these are particularly abundant in the roots of *Taraxacum officinale*).

The unsegmented laticiferous vessels, which are at present only known in the Euphorbiaceæ, Asclepiadeæ, and Ficus-like plants (Moraceæ), arise in quite another way Schmalhausen showed some years ago that in the young embryo of these plants, at the place where the cotyledons spring from the axis of the seedling, some few (4—6) cells, recognisable by their contents, are present, which in the further development of the embryo put forth protuberances into the root as well as into the plumule (its axis and leaves). These much branched tubes now penetrate as far as the growing point of the root and shoot, grow continually with these, and become branched with the organs arising from the growing points, just as in the shoot-axes themselves; so that thus, in a vigorously developed plant of this kind, the whole system of unsegmented laticiferous vessels consists of a few multifariously branched and very long tubes, which were originally simple cells. If it were feasible by any means to destroy all the other tissues of such a plant as a large *Euphorbia* or *Asclepias*, the entire form of the plant would still be preserved as a mass of very fine threads of various thickness, representing the ramifications of the original latex-cells; just as the injected vascular system of a vertebrate animal after the removal of all other tissue allows the whole

---

[1] With respect to these anastomoses of the segmented laticiferous vessels, and the origin of the latter, see W H Scott's paper '*Zur Entwickelungsgeschichte der gegliederten Milchrohren*,' in '*Arbeiten des bot Inst in Würzburg*,' II 648.

organisation of the body to be recognised. Like the segmented laticiferous vessels, these unsegmented tubes may also send forth branches from the cortex across through the vascular bundles and secondary wood into the pith, in which they ramify all over or chiefly in the outer part. By maceration it is possible to free the ends of their branches in the growing points and leaves, and to convince oneself of the fact that we have here to do with continuously growing free ends of individual tubes, and not with the fusion of originally separated cells, as in the segmented laticiferous vessels. The walls of the thicker, older latex tubes, especially of the Euphorbiæ, may attain a very considerable thickness

While the finer ramifications of both kinds of laticiferous vessels are inserted between the most various tissues within the organs, the tendency prevails for the main stem of the tubes to accompany the vascular bundles, and especially to run in the neighbourhood of the sieve-tubes, or even to replace them. This is especially striking where the laticiferous vessels in the secondary cortex arising from the cambium are the more numerous the fewer the sieve-tubes, or *vice versa* (*Papaver Rhoeas, Argemone mexicana, Chelidonium majus*, and *Glaucium luteum*, according to De Bary).

The laticiferous vessels contain, as stated, two essentially different groups of substances, those which are again utilised in metabolism (proteids, carbo-hydrates, fats, ferments), and those which must be regarded as excreta useless in metabolism (resins, gums, caoutchouc, alkaloids, etc)

The Receptacles of Secretions, now to be considered, and which should more properly bear the name of excretory organs, contain on the other hand exclusively such matters as find no further use in the metabolism of the living plant This may be concluded with certainty from the fact that when these matters have once arisen in a given receptacle, they remain there, and are not again dissolved and used for the purposes of growth. It is not implied that these matters produced as bye-products in metabolism are completely useless to the plant, like the refuse in chemical works; they may, rather, according to circumstances, be of use for the well-being of the plants concerned in this or that sense. This is particularly well seen in many epidermal glands, to be described later. It is only to be insisted on here that the matters referred to are not further concerned in the nutritive processes and metabolism accompanying growth Since such substances, as already mentioned, also accumulate in the laticiferous vessels and become withdrawn from the processes of interchange of fluids, it is intelligible that, with few exceptions, the plants provided with laticiferous vessels possess none of the receptacles for secretion here to be described; and also that the presence of the latter generally precludes that of laticiferous vessels (De Bary)

The refuse matters collected together in the receptacles for secretions are, from a chemical point of view, of very various nature. Calcium oxalate, in the form of beautifully constructed crystals or crystalline granules, occurs very commonly, especially in Phanerogams. More confined to single orders and families are found resins and ethereal oils, both usually combined into a so-called balsam, mucus, swelling in water, and various kinds of gums also occur, and these, when they are accompanied in the receptacles for secretions by resins and ethereal oils and form emulsions in water, resemble latex. From the presence of these substances in laticiferous vessels, in the narrower sense, it cannot yet be concluded whether a sharp distinction exists between segmented laticiferous vessels and serially arranged secretion-vesicles. Very widely distributed are, further, certain tannins, often mixed with a red colouring matter. These are found in special individualised cells or in rows of cells, and are not again employed in metabolism, and are therefore to be considered as excreta; whereas in other cases (*e. g.* the plumule of the Oak) tannins of another kind are to be recognised, from their origin and disappearance, and by their behaviour in growth, as special forms of reserve-materials, which find further employment in metabolism, and are therefore to be excluded from our present considerations

It would, however, be in vain to attempt a thorough classification of the organs of secretion according to the chemical nature of their excreta; and a purely histological classification would lead just as little to a satisfactory result We will confine ourselves in what follows, therefore, chiefly to the general characters of the organs concerned, without attempting a rigid sifting according to this or that point of view. It may be mentioned in anticipation, however, that the receptacles for secretion[1] present anatomically the greatest possible variety. Very often they are individual cells, lying in the tissues, which contain calcium oxalate, mucus, resin, tannin, etc.. or such cells are arranged in long rows, which then usually follow the vascular bundles, or lie in the soft bast. Or the receptacles for secretion are intercellular spaces, which become filled with the secretion from the cells bounding them; and these intercellular spaces may either be long, more or less narrow canals, or form roundish or elongated sacs. Or serially arranged or roundish cell groups become disorganised, and the cavity thereby arising (according to De Bary a lysigenous intercellular space) remains filled with the products of decomposition of the cells. Finally, secretions may arise in the wall separating neighbouring cells, or even between the cuticle and the proper cell wall in the epidermis and hair-like structures, as is often the case with the numerous epidermal glands in the Phanerogams.

The fact that the receptacles of secretions, as well as the laticiferous vessels, with rare exceptions, make their appearance in the very youngest state of the organs, at the beginning of the differentiation of their embryonal tissues, throws light on their physiological signification. They are already sketched out or developed when the tissues of the vascular bundles and the fundamental tissue first commence to obtain their characteristic structure. Apparently the developing tissue rids itself during nutrition of certain products of decomposition even thus early; and these remain lying in the receptacles of secretion as such without further use

Here also the higher degree of organisation of the shoot, in comparison with the root, makes itself evident, in that receptacles of secretions, which appear in the shoot-axes and leaves, are not rarely wanting to the roots, or are more feebly developed in them; whereas they usually appear very abundantly in the flowering shoots of the Phanerogams. Families which possess no receptacles of secretions at all are relatively rare among the Phanerogams—e. g. the *Gramineæ* and *Cyperaceæ,*

---

[1] De Bary's description ('*Vergl Anat*' Cap III) of the receptacles for secretions is the only satisfactory one hitherto.

Cruciferæ, Ranunculaceæ; and *Taxus,* among the Conifers otherwise rich in secretions.

I now pass to a somewhat more detailed description of the most important forms of receptacles for secretions, and shall confine myself here also to the more common cases

The commonest of all the receptacles for secretions are the vesicles containing crystals (Lithocysts) in which calcium oxalate is accumulated as refuse matter. More rarely this occurs—as in many *Solaneæ,* some species of *Amaranthus,* in the pith of *Sambucus nigra,* etc.—in the form of exceedingly small crystalline particles, which are deposited in countless multitudes in individual cells, and fill these entirely. More frequently the oxalate of lime appears in the form of very thin needles, pointed at both ends, which lie parallel to one another and form bundles of so-called raphides, often filling up the entire cavity of elongated vesicles. This is to be observed in many Monocotyledons (Aroideæ, Liliaceæ); as well as in some Dicotyledons (the Vine and its allies, Cinnamon, *Impatiens,* etc.). In many Monocotyledons (species of *Allium,* Irideæ, Amaryllideæ) and in the great majority of Dicotyledons (particularly abundant and well developed in the bark of *Guiacum officinale*), the calcium oxalate appears in the form of single crystals, well formed on all sides, which are contained in the cells as simple individuals, or as twin crystals, or as clusters of crystals. The great variety of forms in which this salt appears is partly explained from the fact that, according to the rapidity of its separation, it crystallises either with two molecules of water of crystallisation in the klino-rhombic system, or with six molecules of water of crystallisation in the quadratic system. The much more frequent klino-rhombic forms in the plant are referred to the ground form of the hendyohedron, and develope as prisms, tables and twins with truncated angles of the most various kinds. The raphides also apparently belong here. The fundamental form of the calcium oxalate crystallising in the quadratic system is the quadrate-octahedron, the main axis of which is sometimes extremely short, so that the crystal assumes the form of a letter cover; in other cases combinations of the quadratic prism with the corresponding pyramid occur, and so forth[1]. As a rule the crystal-vesicles contain a slimy substance if the crystals are very large, the slime is less abundant

In some cases, on the other hand (tubers of Orchids), the cell is chiefly filled with slime, and contains only a small group of crystals. Where the crystals of oxalate appear as well-formed individuals or clusters, they often stand in relation with the cell-wall, and are embedded in cellulose projections, or in the cell-wall itself (pith of *Kerria, Ricinus,* in the vascular bundles of the petiole of various *Aroideæ,* leaf parenchyma of *Hoya carnosa,* leaves of *Citrus,* cortex of *Salix, Populus, Celtis, Fagus* and others). In other cases also a relation of this kind is at least not improbable. Very small crystals of calcium oxalate—their form no longer distinctly recognisable, but rendered evident by means of polarised light—are also found occasionally deposited in thickened cell-walls. These are particularly common in the bast of Coniferæ, and in a few Dicotyledons (leaves of *Sedum, Mesembryanthemum*).

---

[1] As regards the crystals of calcium oxalate, the chief work is that of Holzner, 'Flora,' 1864, p 273, and 1867, p 499 Further, Rosanoff, 'Bot Zeitg.' 1865 and 1867 Graf Solms-Laubach, 'Bot. Zeitg' 1871, and Pfitzer, 'Flora,' 1872, p 97, are also important.

[3]   N

Among the Gymnosperms, *Welwitschia mirabilis*—so very remarkable in other respects also—has thousands of well-developed oxalate crystals contained in the substance of the very thick walls of the schlerenchymatous cells (Fig. 178).

The quantity of oxalate of lime may occasionally be enormous. According to Schleiden, the dry substance of *Cereus senilis* contains more than 85 per cent. of its weight of it. This substance is also generally abundant in the parenchyma of foliage leaves, as well as in the secondary cortex and pith of dicotyledonous woody plants, and occasionally in the medullary rays also (*Camellia, Vitis*) Sometimes, however, the crystals are entirely wanting, as in the Equisetaceæ, and most Ferns and Grasses, and even in families of Phanerogams which are otherwise rich in calcium oxalate it is absent in single species, e. g. in *Petunia nyctaginiflora* (Solanaceæ), in *Tulipa silvestris, Lilium martagon*, and *Lilium candidum* (De Bary).

With regard to its distribution in the tissues, we may notice the frequency of crystals of oxalate in rows of cells which accompany the vascular bundles, or run in the secondary cortex, or which, on the other hand, occur in groups or rows beneath the epidermis Many Monocotyledons are especially remarkable for the serially arranged large vesicles, containing slime and raphides, in the petioles, leaves, and bulb-scales — e. g the Commelynaceæ, Amaryllideæ, and Palms.

In many crustaceous Lichens, and to a less extent in some other Fungi, calcium oxalate is excreted in large quantities on the exterior of the cells Although oxalate of lime is occasionally met with in the form of small crystals suspended in the protoplasm, in living cells rich in protoplasm, and even in those containing chlorophyll, this does not affect its being a useless secretion, since even in living cells — e. g. in hairs rich in protoplasm—such an excretion may obviously result without the life of the cell itself being endangered.

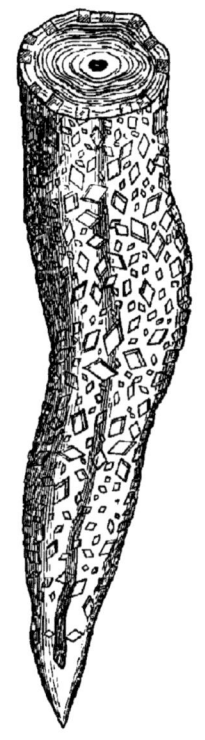

FIG 178 —Half of a sclerenchyma cell from *Welwit schia mirabilis* with numerous crystals of oxalate of lime embedded in the outer layer of the very thick wall

In comparison with the exceedingly common occurrence of calcium oxalate, the excretion of calcium carbonate in solid masses is rare. Among the Phanerogams there are two families especially—the Urticaceæ in the wider sense, and the Acanthaceæ—which are remarkable for the presence of so-called Cystoliths; in the first family in connection with the epidermal system, in the others in the interior of the fundamental tissue. Cystoliths are massive bodies, often resembling a bunch of grapes, attached by a thin short stalk to the wall of the cells in which they are contained. The substance of this body consists of cellulose, which is permeated by a large quantity of exceedingly fine granules of carbonate of lime, so that the whole represents a mass of stony hardness, from which the calcium salt may be dissolved out by weak acids, with the formation of carbon dioxide gas. Among the lower Cryptogams also cases of calcification are found—i. e deposits of calcium carbonate in the substance of the cell wall—so that the whole plant is of stony hardness, as in the Corallineæ and Melobesiaceæ among the Florideæ, and even in single species of *Halymeda*, as well as in *Acetabularia* among the Siphoneæ (Cœloblastæ).

If we now turn to those receptacles for secretions which contain fluids, we find the contents in the form of gummy mucus, or of latex like emulsions, which may flow out in abundance on wounding, or of solutions of tannin, balsams and the like We here meet with tissue-formations which, at the one extreme, pass almost imperceptibly into segmented laticiferous vessels, as in the so-called tannin-bearing laticiferous vessels of many *Aroideæ* and species of *Musa*; while the other extreme is exhibited in the occurrence of roundish cells, scarcely differing from the surrounding parenchyma, and isolated or grouped in all kinds of ways, in which the substances mentioned are contained, usually as mixtures We may term these structures collectively secretion-vesicles, and speak in more special cases of gum-vesicles, resin-vesicles, latex-vesicles, tannin-vesicles, and so forth. By this means the characteristic constituents of the contents are indicated. Apart from the laticiferous vessels of the *Aroideæ* and species of *Musa*, from their nature still somewhat doubtful, there are found in the most various subdivisions of the Monocotyledons, Dicotyledons, and some Ferns,

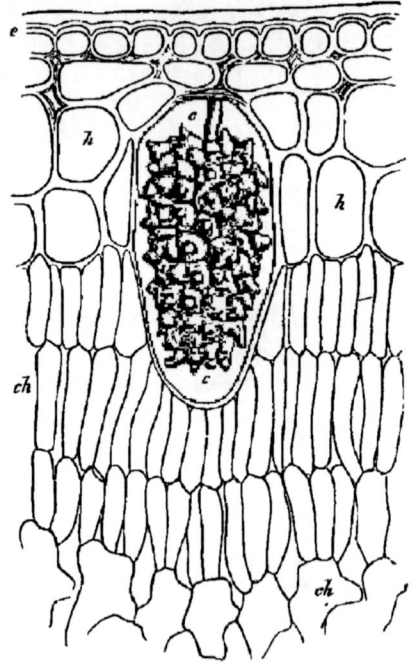

FIG 179 —Cystolith (*c c*) in a cell of the hypoderm (*h*) of the upper side of the leaf of *Ficus elastica* *e* epidermis, *ch* chlorophyll tissue

secretion-vesicles which are formed of thin-walled more or less long, often very long tubular cells, standing one over the other in rows, and accompanying the vascular bundles on the outer side, or at the circumference of the pith: or, as is the case with the rows of vesicles in *Phaseolus*, running in the soft bast of the vascular bundle itself. Among the most remarkable forms belonging here are the vesicles abounding in tannin which run in the internodes of *Sambucus nigra*, both in the cortex and in the circumference of the pith, these, according to De Bary, probably extend through the entire length of an internode (20 c. m.), and are at the same time remarkable for their breadth (0 1 mm and more). The so-called utricular vessels also, occurring in the Leeks, and especially in the bulb scales of *Allium Cepa, A. fistulosum*, etc., deserve mention ; they run somewhat close beneath the epidermis, and consist of serially arranged, rather broad vesicles, the ends of which communicate with one another by means of broad, pitted, transverse septa, and they contain a granular coagulable latex, which flows out in some quantity when a bulb is cut through at the base. The erroneously so-called laticiferous vessels of the Maples (well developed in *Acer platanoides*) are similarly constituted ; they run at the boundary between the phloëm of the vascular bundle, and the sclerenchyma strands accompanying it. The resin of the *Convolvulaceæ*, partly used in medicine (e. g. Scammony from the roots of *Convolvulus Scammonium*, Jalap resin from the root of *Ipomea purga*), and others, are obtained, like the dried latexes of the druggists' shops, by mere inspissation of the contents which flow out in the form of latex from the serially arranged more or less elongated secretion-

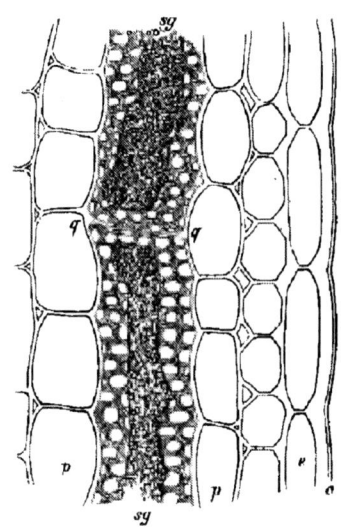

FIG. 180.—Longitudinal section through a scale of the bulb of *Allium Cepa. e* epidermis ; *c* cuticle ; *p* parenchyma ; *sg* the latex of the utricular vessel coagulated in potash solution ; *q q* septum of the vessel. The longitudinal wall is pitted, and separates the utricular vessel from one lying behind.

vesicles of these plants. Like the true laticiferous vessels, the rows of utricles mentioned may also be repeated in continually increasing numbers in the secondary tissue, originating from the activity of a cambium ring. The same holds good of the short resin and gum-resin vesicles found singly or in small groups in the cortex ; and which are distinguished by their refractive contents, and occasionally by their considerable size, in the Ginger-like plants, and in *Calamus* (*Acorus*), Piperaceæ, Laurineæ and Magnoliaceæ, and also in some Euphorbiaceæ (Cascarilla bark) and Aristolochiæ. To these forms are to be added the mucus-vesicles in the parenchyma of the Malvaceæ, Tiliaceæ, Laurineæ, Ulmeæ, and species of *Cactus*, and in the tubers of *Orchis* and the cortex of the Pines. They are generally distinguished from the cells of the surrounding parenchyma by their larger size ; and are filled with a gum-like mucus, which dissolves in water. This latter is in the majority of cases (according to De Bary) nothing more than strongly swollen cellulose, which fills up the lumen of the cell, and arises from alteration of the cell-walls, still showing in part the layering and pitting of the latter. The mucus in the tubers of *Orchis* (Salep) arises however, according to Frank, in the interior of the protoplasm in the form of a vacuole, which grows up together with a small bundle of raphides and presses the remaining contents aside. When, as in *Althea rosea*, peculiarly grouped mucus-cells of this kind become completely disorganised, there arise lacunæ in the parenchyma of various shapes and sizes, filled with this translucent mucus. Such gum-reservoirs are distinguished from the cases of proper Gummosis, where large groups of tissue in the older organs are changed into basorin and other kinds of gum (Cherry gum, Tragacanth, etc.),

in that they assume their characteristic condition at the beginning of the differentiation of the tissues in the very young organs. Further are to be mentioned the
tannin-vesicles of many plants. These are isolated parenchyma cells, often hardly
distinguished in any other way, which are filled with a concentrated solution of tannin,
frequently accompanied by a red colouring-matter Exquisite examples of them are
found in the cortex of the stem of the seedling of *Ricinus* and many other germinating woody plants, where they attract the attention of the microscopist either directly
by the red colour, or by forming ink on the addition of solutions of iron salts.

A group of receptacles for secretions, well characterised anatomically, are the
resin-passages and gum-passages; these arise by the separation of the walls of
neighbouring rows of cells, and thus constitute cellular passages filled with secretions. In the Cycadeæ, some Lycopodiæ, Marattiaceæ, and species of *Canna*,

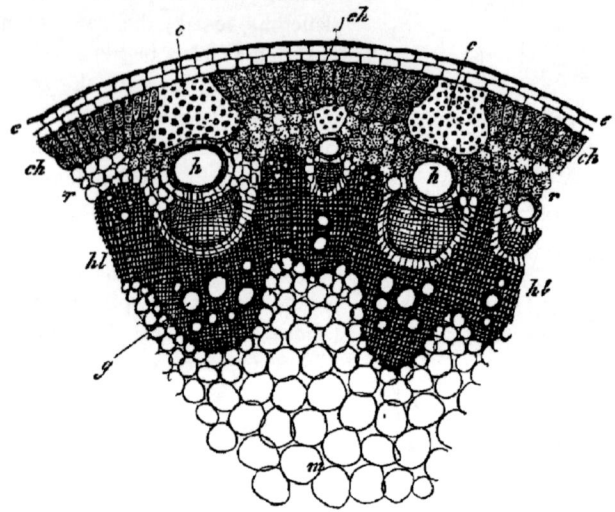

FIG. 181 —Part of the transverse section of the stem of *Fœniculum officinale* (Fennel) slightly magni
fied   *e* epidermis , *ck* green, and *r* colourless parenchyma of the cortex, *cc* bundles of collenchyma , *kh*
resin canals, *hl* wood , *g* vessels , *m* pith

Opuntiæ, and Araliaceæ, these passages contain mucous substances; in the Coniferæ
(with the exception of *Taxus*) the contents are mixtures of ethereal oil and resin
(balsam), and the same also occurs in the Terebinthaceæ, Umbelliferæ and those
Compositæ which possess no laticiferous vessels. These intercellular canals are
generally elongated, and often penetrate the whole of the organs of the plant,
or they may be wanting in the roots, but are then so much the more abundant
in the primary and secondary cortex of the shoot-axes, and occur also in the
foliage leaves. The length of these canals, and apparently also their occasional
lateral communications, explain why trees which produce resin gradually exude
such large quantities of balsam from local wounds, which then generally stiffens
to pasty resinous masses in the air (resins of Coniferæ, e.g Sandarach, Mastic
derived from *Pistacea terebinthus*, etc.) In other cases, again, as in the Alismaceæ,
Butomaceæ and the Aroideæ among the Monocotyledons, and in the Clusiaceæ, species
of *Mamillaria*, and Umbelliferæ, among the Dicotyledons, such intercellular passages

contain latex-like emulsions of resinous and gummy substances (De Bary). Occasionally these secretion-bearing intercellular passages only form short gaps in
the tissue, as in the small leaves of the Cupressineæ and in the seed-coats of some
plants of the same group.

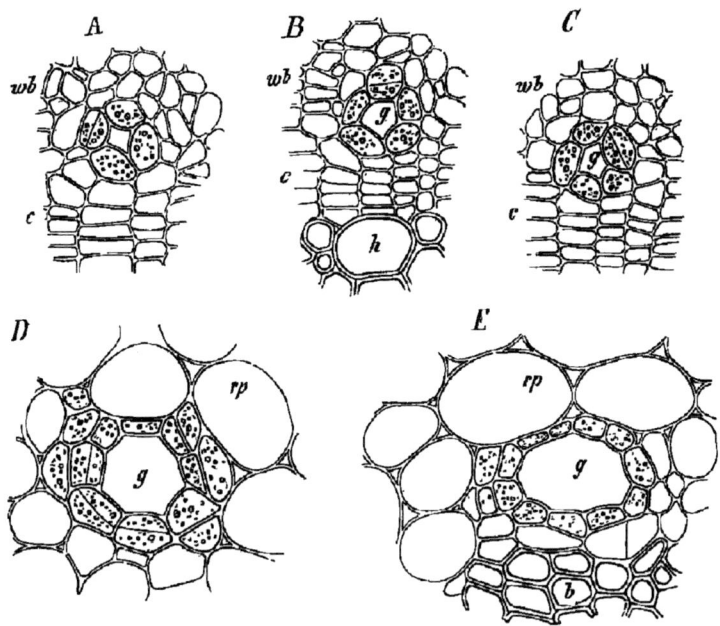

FIG 187.—Resin canals in the young stem of the Ivy (transverse section)   *A, B, C* young canals (*g*) at the
boundary of the cambium (*c*) and soft bast (*wb*), *h* wood   *D* and *E* larger and older canals (*g*) lying at the
boundary between the bast (*b*) and the cortical parenchyma (*rp*)

The intercellular secretion-passages arise early in the tissue-differentiation in
young organs; and may also be repeatedly formed in the secondary tissue-layers
produced from the cambium, especially in woody plants. It is generally by the
separation of the angles of four neighbouring longitudinal series of cells that the
passage is produced: this becomes filled at once with the secretion. If the passage
remains narrow in diameter, the cells surrounding it either remain undivided, or,
growing slightly, they undergo a single division only, so that the secretion-passage
is only bounded by a few cells on the transverse section. If, on the other hand, the
organ referred to increases in circumference generally, the secretion-passages running
in it may also be considerably extended in width, the cells surrounding them grow
to a corresponding degree with it, and become divided by radial as well as by
tangential walls (taken with regard to the passages), so that the passage is now
surrounded by two, or even by several layers of a special tissue, the epithelium of
the passage, the granular contents and delicate wall of which distinguish it from
the surrounding tissue. In the leaves of species of *Pinus*, the bordering of the
epithelium of the passages by a closed sheath of schlerenchyma cells is very
characteristic. As regards the source of the secretion, there can be no doubt
that it originates from the epithelium; although it is not quite certain that the

characteristic contents of the passage itself are already recognisable as such in the epithelium cells. Possibly the substance of the wall of the epithelium itself becomes chemically altered and concerned in the formation of the secretion.

All receptacles for secretions not consisting of long vesicles, series of vesicles, or long intercellular passages, were formerly collected together under the name of Glands. We shall employ this expression quite arbitrarily for a special kind of receptacles for secretion, which chiefly contain ethereal oils and resins dissolved in them; and we shall at the same time distinguish two subdivisions of these structures—the

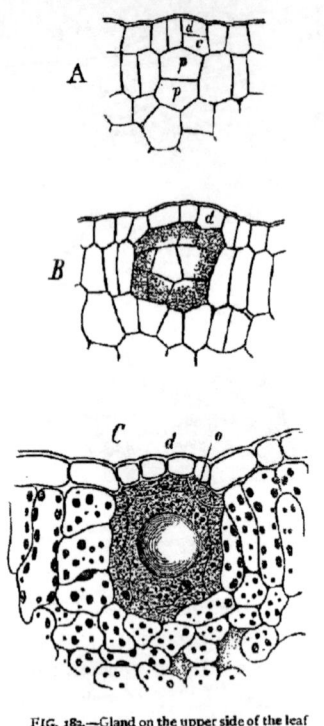

FIG. 183.—Gland on the upper side of the leaf of *Dictamnus Fraxinella* (after Rauter). *A, B*. early stages of development; *C* mature gland; *d* the covering layer forming a continuation of the epidermis; *c* and *p* mother-cells of the gland-tissue; *e* a large drop of ethereal oil.

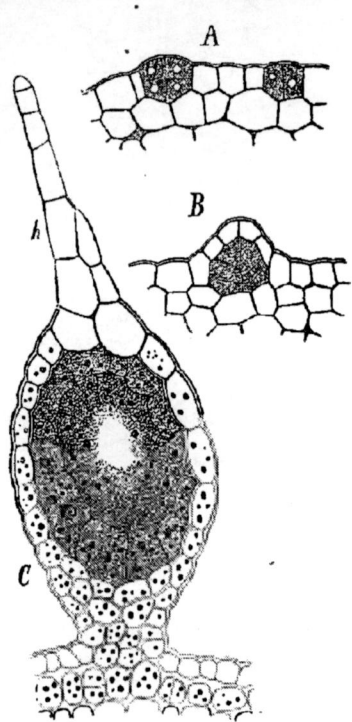

FIG. 184.—Gland with hair, from the inflorescence of *Dictamnus Fraxinella* (after Rauter). *A, B* early stages of development; *c* mature gland with the hair (*h*) at its apex.

internal glands, i.e. those situated under the epidermis, on the one hand; and the so-called epidermal glands, which belong to the epidermis and its hairs, on the other.

The internal glands are often perceptible to the unaided eye as bright, translucent dots in the tissue of foliage leaves or stems, e.g. in the leaves of the Citrons and Oranges, many species of *Hypericum*, *Lysimachia*, etc.; or they are contained in protuberances of the outer surface, as in *Dictamnus Fraxinella*. The internal glands in the skin of the fruit of the Orange are very conspicuous and large; they abound in ethereal oils, and appear in transverse and longitudinal sections as roundish cavities, from which the inflammable ethereal oil spurts on the application of pressure. Such glands originate, so far as investigation extends, from a single mother-cell, which, as it slowly developes, undergoes many divisions in all directions, so that a multicellular mass of tissue of roundish form arises, the cells of which subsequently become remarkable as containing very granular, apparently dead protoplasm. Later on, the thin cell-walls dissolve; the process commencing in the middle of the spheroidal group and proceeding outwards There thus arises a roundish cavity, filled partly with watery sap, partly with drops of ethereal oil or balsam—the products of solution of the mass of cells. The layers of tissue surrounding this cavity fit closely on all sides, without intercellular spaces, and thus form a kind of wall to the receptacle for the secretion (well seen in the leaves of *Citrus*). These processes will be sufficiently understood on comparing figures 183 and 184; the relations there illustrated appear with few deviations to be exactly the same in the internal glands of the Myrtaceæ, other Rutaceæ, and in *Hypericum, Gossypium* (Cotton), *Lysimachia* and species of *Oxalis*.

Very many plants[1], particularly among the Dicotyledons, owe the more or less

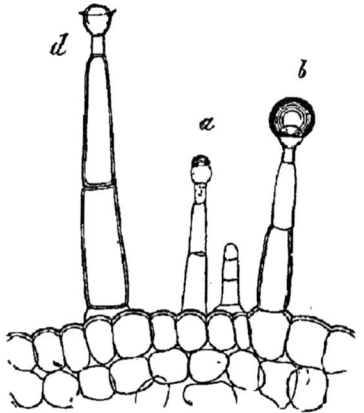

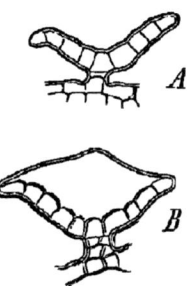

FIG. 185.—A portion of the epidermis with glandular hairs, from the petiole of *Primula sinensis a* commencement of the development of secretion, *b* a large bubble of secretion, *d* after the bursting of the bubble (De Bary).

FIG 186.—Lupulin gland of the Hop. *A* young, before the secretion separates, *B* older, the cuticle raised up by the secretion (De Bary).

sticky condition of the surfaces of the leaves and young shoot-axes to epidermal glands, as is easily perceived by passing the fingers over the surface of such plants As a rule, the secretion at the same time possesses a strong specific odour, as in the glands before mentioned The glandular condition of the epidermis proceeds in many cases from secretions developed by the epidermis cells themselves, as is very conspicuous under the nodes of the stem of *Lychnis viscaria*, on the young shoot-axes of the White Birch (*Betula alba*), on the teeth of the leaf of *Prunus* and species of *Salix*, and on small areas on the underside of the leaf of *Prunus laurocerasus* and others The viscid secretion appears here on the epidermis cells (which are otherwise intact, but sometimes distinguished by being particularly small and peculiar in shape) between the proper cell-wall and the cuticle situated upon

---

[1] Cp Johannes Hanstein, ' *Ueber die Organe der Harz- und Schleimabsonderung*,' 'Bot Zeitg.' 1868, p 697, and also the much better description in De Bary's ' *Vergl. Anat.*' § 19.

it. As the secretion increases, the cuticle becomes more and more raised up from the underlying cellulose wall (De Bary) The balsamic secretion between the cellulose wall and cuticle in the hair-glands or glandular hairs appears in exactly the same way. It is usually the so-called capitate hairs, i e. hairs consisting of a pedicle-like support and a roundish or broad shield-shaped capitulum, which show this peculiarity; and it is practically indifferent whether the whole hair consists of a single cell, or a cell series, or a mass of tissue. The secretion appears, as a rule, first at the apex of the capitulum, or, where none is present, at the apex of the cell series, between the wall and the cuticle; and, as the secretion extends from that point, the thin cuticle becomes gradually raised up in the form of a vesicle, the cavity of which is filled with the secretion. An unusually good example of this process is presented in the glandular hairs of *Primula sinensis* (Fig. 185). The so-called Lupulin also, a pulverulent strongly smelling substance which may be shaken from the ripe, cone-like, female inflorescences of the Hop, consists of glandular hairs, which, as Fig. 186 shows, are short, stalked, cup-shaped plates of tissue, the cuticle of which is raised up by the bulky secretion as a hemispherical vesicle, while the cells themselves die. The so-called Hashish arises similarly, in the long-stalked, many-celled capitate hairs of the female plant of the Indian Hemp. In very many other cases, e g. in the Patschouli plant (*Pogostemon patschouli*), in the Thyme (*Thymus vulgaris*), in *Cistus, Pelargonium* etc., and also in the Fern *Aspidium*, the processes are essentially the same. In other cases again the balsamic secretion appears in multicellular glandular hairs, within the generally radially arranged

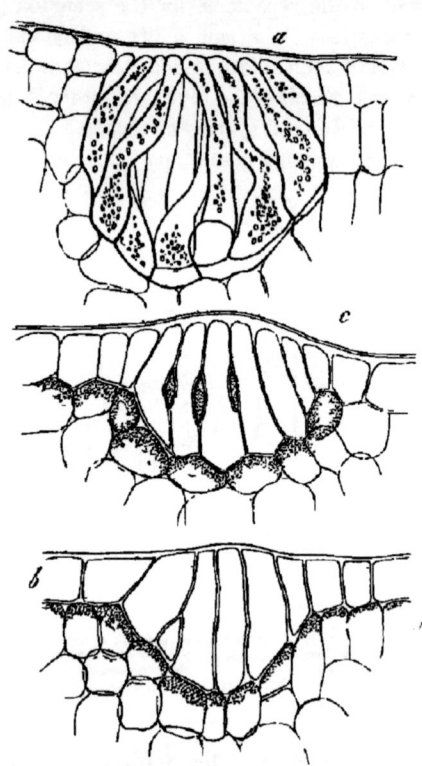

FIG 187 —Vertical section of the surface of the leaf of *Psoralea hirta* (Papilionaceæ) *a* an almost mature gland after the removal of the secretion from between the walls by alcohol, *c* commencing formation of secretion between the cell walls, *b* very young gland, before secretion It is seen that the glandular cells are only elongated epidermal cells (De Bary)

septa of the peltate short-stalked capitulum of the hair itself: the septa split into two lamellæ, and the intercellular space thus produced becomes filled with the secretion. Such 'schizogenous glands' are found on the under surface of the leaves of *Rhododendron ferugineum* and elsewhere. But schizogenous glands may also arise in the epidermis itself, as in the Papilionaceous plant *Psoralea hirta* (Fig. 187), where, by the division of one epidermis cell, a roundish group of cells is developed which extends deep into the tissue beneath and presents an almost globular aggregate, surrounded by the leaf-parenchyma The septa of this aggregate stand perpendicularly to the surface of the leaf, and first exhibit the splitting and separation of the secretion mentioned in the middle : this proceeds so far later on, that the individual cells of the complex appear to lie quite separate in the mass of secreted substances (De Bary).

Johannes Hanstein distinguished as Colleters certain massive multicellular hairs, the secretion of which consists of resin and gum, or gum alone, and effects the sticking together of the parts of the bud in many plants.　This secretion is very conspicuous on the just opening buds of the Horse-chestnut, Poplar, and *Syringa ;* and is evident in a less degree in very many other woody plants (*Ribes, Corylus, Carpinus, Lonicera, Sambucus*), and also in many herbaceous plants (*Helianthus, Datura, Salvia, Viola,* &c.).　In the Polygoneæ, especially the Docks and Rhubarbs, it is chiefly mucilage, which becomes diffluent in water and fills up the spaces between the folded parts of the bud and covers the developing leaves and buds　These secretions, which make their appearance in the very young parts of the bud, are lost on the complete unfolding of the leaves and internodes, and appear to be a means of protection for the young organs against drying up, and other injurious influences.　These substances are excreted from the hairs or colleters mentioned, which are developed especially at the edges · of the young stipules, and elsewhere on the parts of the bud.　They may present the most various forms, but the secretion always takes place between the cuticle and the outer cell-wall of the body of the hair : the cuticle, as in other cases, is raised up in a vesicular manner by the secretion, until it finally bursts (especially on the admission of water) by the swelling of the slime, and the mass spreads over the surface of the organ.　Examples of schizogenous glands occur here also ; and occasionally the epidermis itself is concerned in the formation of the secretion between its cuticle and cell-wall.

In connection with the glandular hairs may be briefly mentioned here the mealy, dust-like, capitate hairs, described by De Bary, to which the under surface of the leaf of the so-called Gold and Silver Ferns (*Gymnogramme, Nothochlaena, Cheilanthes*) owe their white or golden yellow (*Pteris aurata*) meal-like covering. The same is true of the mealy-dusted foliage leaves of many Primroses, e.g. *Primula marginata, farinosa, auricula.*　The mealy covering is exclusively produced by the round capitula of shortly-stalked hairs ; from all points of the surface of these capitula are developed very thin, but relatively long rodlets or threads of an apparently resinous substance, which dissolves in alcohol, ether, acetic acid, and alkalies, and (it is said) again crystallises out from the solutions.　This mode of excretion appears to be only another form of the excretion of balsam occurring elsewhere between the cuticle and cell-wall of the hair ; since, according to De Bary, the vesicular glandular hairs previously described may occur in place of these dusty hairs on the leaves of the same or allied plants.

Physiologically the most remarkable of all external glands are the digestive glands of the insectivorous plants.　I contemplate treating of these later, however, when dealing with the theory of nutrition.

PART II.

THE GENERAL CONDITIONS OF VEGETABLE LIFE, AND THE PROPERTIES OF PLANTS

LECTURE XII.

THE GENERAL EXTERNAL CONDITIONS OF PLANT-LIFE.

THE vital activity of plants is, like that of animals, the result of the co-operation of two factors, the internal structure, or inherited disposition, and the influences operating from without, or stimuli.

It is of the greatest importance to be perfectly clear on this point; therefore it may be permitted to make the nature of the two factors mentioned more intelligible, where possible, by the comparison of an organism with a machine.

The work done by a steam-engine, for example, depends in like manner upon two factors namely its structure, and the energy which is supplied to it. Upon the form and combination of its individual parts depends what kind of work it can perform—whether, as a locomotive, it will be in a position to draw a train; or, as an engine, to plough an arable field; or, as a spinning machine, to spin yarn out of thread, or whether it puts a loom in motion, or planes the iron parts for another machine, and so forth. But be the machine constructed as you will, it performs the work intended by the constructor only if it be set in motion; and this, as is well known, is accomplished by the tension of the steam which moves the piston to and fro in the cylinder

Moreover, it is not enough merely that the steam is evolved in the machine, since, so long as it possesses too slight a tension, not sufficient to overcome the friction of the parts of the machine, these latter do not move. The performance of work will only be attained if, by the supply of sufficient quantities of heat, the tension of the steam reaches a magnitude which gives to the parts of the machine the quickening energy by means of which it can perform the work in view.

The case is similar with the work performed by an organised body, particularly of a plant, or part of a plant. The work which it is able to perform depends essentially upon its structure—upon the combination and chemical nature of its smallest parts. Whether these parts will be set in motion, however, and whether in accordance with their nature and combination they will actually accomplish that which they are able to perform, depends entirely upon whether they obtain from without the energy in virtue of which they are put into those forms of movement, the co-operation of which we distinguish as the vital activity of the organism.

After these considerations, it is clear that the investigation of the phenomena of life—i. e. Physiology—has to do with two problems: on the one hand, with the investigation of the internal structure of the organs, and, on the other hand, with the exposition of those external influences by means of which this internal structure is impelled to the movements and performance of work specifically peculiar to it.

As an engineer who wishes to criticise a steam-engine must know exactly, on the one hand its structure, and, on the other, the properties of heat and of steam, so it is the aim of the physiologist to explain the phenomena of life from the internal structure of the organs, and the nature of the external influences acting upon them. Only he meets, of course, with far greater difficulties than the engineer; since the organism is an incomparably more complicated machine than any, however perfect, constructed by man. In the first place, the structure of the latter is relatively easy to comprehend; and it is set in motion by the well-understood activity of heat and steam. On the other hand, our knowledge of the actual internal structure of the organs of a plant is still in the highest degree incomplete, since in these matters it concerns the coarser visible portions far less than the molecular structure and atomic composition. This, since it depends upon invisible parts, can only be known by indirect methods, and by means of conclusions slowly obtained. Moreover, it is shown that the structure of the organism is not simply sensitive to one kind of external influence, as is that of a steam-engine; but that all known natural forces may affect the living machine. Plants do not re-act only to the motion which is communicated to them as heat, but also to the movements of the æther which our eye perceives as light. They are, at the same time, sensitive to electrical changes, and they re-act in a manner not yet understood to the influence of gravitation, and even slight contact may produce very great effects. But above all—a matter which does not come into consideration at all in a machine constructed by man—the organism nourishes itself—i e. it absorbs material into itself from without, and itself joins this to the substance of the organs already present. Here, also, it again depends upon the substance already existing, and its structure, that the nutrition in a given organism takes place in a certain manner, and not otherwise. When a seed or a bud becomes detached from a plant, in order to begin an independent life, the course of the latter is already traced out beforehand. The nature and combination of the smallest particles in the seed are specifically determined by the nature of the mother-plant—they are established beforehand The question is only whether the germ will develope; whether it will, as a matter of fact, perform all that which it can perform according to the laws prescribed for it by the mother-plant; and this 'whether' depends upon the external influences of heat, light, gravitation, electricity, nutrition and respiration, the contact of solid and fluid bodies, and so forth.

The difficult part of physiological investigation always lies in the explanation of the structural relations of the organs, by which the latter, in consequence of the influence of external forces, are put in motion in the way specifically determined, and, unfortunately, experience shows that the coarser visible structural relations only play a more subordinate part in the matter, and that physiological investigation is compelled to go back to the invisible, smallest particles of matter, the mutual relations of which, again, can only be inferred from the entire working of all the visible organs We may therefore reserve until we enter upon the consideration of the individual phenomena of vegetation, a detailed study of the corresponding structural relations of the organs.

Much, however, may be stated generally with reference to the influence of external causes on the phenomena of life; since here it is only a matter of proving, by means of observation and experiment, what kinds of vital phenomena appear when certain alterations are produced in the environment of the living plant. In this way it has been shown, even in the still very imperfect condition of our knowledge in this respect, that a far greater portion of the phenomena of life are called forth by external influences than one formerly ventured to assume; and that what the living organism performs of itself, by reason of its inherited structure, always concerns only the specific nature of the performance Whether and with what intensity this takes place depends, however, entirely upon the play of external influences.

What I would here emphatically lay down, is the fact that every phenomenon of life arises from two factors: on the one hand, from the structure transmitted from the mother organism, and, on the other, from external forces working on this structure. Every phenomenon of life is the product of these two factors, neither of which is at all effective by itself. The one factor, the external influences, which we may also distinguish as the external conditions of life, we will now take into view somewhat more closely in its most general outlines.

The life of the plant is a coherent chain of the most various motions of the smallest particles, the atoms and molecules of its substance, from which arise in the plant mass-motions of the entire organs, which, however, are slow and mostly difficult to perceive. The most general and important source of vital force through which the life-motions in the bodies of plants are called forth is, however, Heat[1]. As is well known, heat is to be imagined as a motion of the smallest particles of matter, which is transmitted from one substance to another. The intensity of this motion, or the force with which the smallest particles vibrate, is called the temperature, which in its turn is measured by means of the thermometer. Experience shows now that the vital motions in the interior of the plant do not occur until the temperature of the environment, which by degrees becomes communicated to the plant, reaches a certain height—a definite degree of the thermometer, i e. the heat-motion imparted to the plant must effect a certain intensity of the vibrations of its smallest particles, in order that those further motions of the atoms and molecules may take place by which the various chemical processes of nutrition, and all the various molecular motions of which the life of the plant consists, are called forth.

Numerous, but by no means final researches[2] have shown that temperatures

---

[1] I have given a comprehensive description of the effects of heat on vegetation, with detailed references to the literature up to the year 1865, in my '*Handbuch der Experimental-physiologie der Pflanzen*' (Leipzig, 1865), pp. 47–68, and supplied more details concerning freezing in my '*Lehrbuch der Botanik*,' 1868, p 562 Cp also the succeeding editions of the latter book

[2] Concerning the upper and lower limits of temperature of vegetation, cp my treatises in the 'Regensburger Flora,' 1863—'*Die vorübergehenden Starre-zustände periodisch beweglicher und reizbarer Pflanzenorgane*,' pp. 449, &c , and 'Flora,' 1864, '*Über die Temperaturgrenzen der Vegetation*,' p 8, and further, p 497, '*Über den Einfluss der Temperatur auf das Ergrünen der Blätter.*' More details in this connection are to be found in my treatise, '*Physiologische Untersuchungen über die Abhängigkeit der Keimung von der Temperatur*,' Jahrb für wiss Bot B II, 1860, p 338

between the freezing-point of water, on the one hand, and about 50° C. on the other, indicate those intensities of heat-motion at which plant life generally is still possible. It is quite conceivable, and even occurs occasionally, that certain phenomena of vegetation may still occur even below the freezing-point of water, because from various causes the water contained in the cells only begins to crystallise at a few degrees below zero. However, these are isolated cases: in the great majority the vital movements in general only begin at a few or several degrees above the freezing-point. On the other hand, the temperature of 50° C. also denotes the upper limit only quite generally, since the majority of the vegetative processes are brought to a standstill below this temperature; and temperatures of 45° to 50° persisting for a long time are simply fatal to most plants. It depends here essentially upon the abundance of water or the succulence of the parts of the plant concerned whether they freeze[1] at lower temperatures, or perish at too high a temperature below or above 50° C. Parts containing little water as the majority of ripe, dry seeds and winter buds, are exceedingly resistent even to low degrees of cold, and the former even resist temperatures of 60° to 80° for a long time; whereas very succulent organs often freeze even at temperatures in the neighbourhood of the freezing-point (this, however, is a specific peculiarity of certain plants), and are killed at 50° or even under.

Within the specified range of temperatures there lies for each individual vegetative function a certain degree of temperature at which it developes its greatest activity. We call this the optimum temperature; thus distinguishing that point of the thermometer at which any one vegetative phenomenon exhibits its maximum activity. At every degree of temperature above or below this optimum, the vegetative phenomenon in question will be less active. Exact investigation shows also that, proceeding from the lower limit of temperature, at each higher constant degree of temperature already mentioned, the activity of the phenomena of vegetation is greater, until at the specific optimum temperature itself the maximum activity is attained; and if the temperatures rise still higher, the activity decreases step by step, until on attaining the upper limit of temperature, it ceases entirely. If this high temperature acts for a short time only, the vegetative phenomenon may be renewed when a lower temperature recurs; if, however, the high temperature mentioned has continued too long, death ensues.

In this case especially, where it is a matter of the dependence of the life of the plant upon the temperature, we may again take the example of the steam-engine already employed. We may compare the lower zero-point with that condition where the tension of the steam just suffices to overcome the friction of the machine, and to bring about a slow movement, which with increasing tension of the steam

---

[1] Concerning the freezing of plants, cp Sachs, '*Krystallbildungen bei dem Gefrieren und Veränderung der Zellhaute bei dem Aufthauen saftiger Pflanzentheile*,' in the 'Berechten der kgl. sachs Gesellsch. der Wiss,' Febr. 1860, where I first described the separation of crystalline water from cells. In the '*Untersuchungen über das Erfrieren der Pflanzen*' in H 5 of the periodical, 'Die landwirthschaftlichen Versuchsstationen' (Dresden, 1860), I gave a theory of freezing on which all more recent researches in this direction have been based. This was improved in my '*Lehrbuch der Botanik*' (1868–74) Muller (Thurgau) made valuable further researches, 'Landwirthschaftliche Jahrbucher,' pub Thiel (Berlin, 1880).

becomes accelerated, until the machine works not only with a certain velocity, but also in such a manner that all the individual movements work together in the most advantageous manner, this would correspond to the behaviour of the plant at the optimum temperature. If the tension of the steam is increased by supplying more heat to the machine, dangers arise with the increasing velocity of its motion individual parts are heated and expanded too much, and others are strained until they rupture, increased centrifugal force may cause the fly-wheel to break, and the machine shortly becomes destroyed by its own motion. We may compare these processes in a certain sense with the death of the plant from heat

By the establishment of the three cardinal points of temperature (which expression includes the lower and higher temperatures as well as the optimum), it is seen that each single vegetative phenomenon in any one species of plant in general possesses its particular cardinal points In other words, the lowest temperature at which perceptible growth takes place, does not necessarily suffice for the development of chlorophyll, or for assimilation, or for the irritability of motile organs, and so forth; and when this is determined for one species of plant, the lower zero-points of these functions in another species are by no means necessarily the same. This is likewise the case with reference to the optimum temperatures and the upper limits of temperature In general it is shown, however, that most plants flourish best at certain medium temperatures, somewhere between 15° and 30° C, because within these limits the various phenomena of vegetation take their course with sufficient energy and work harmoniously together The diversity of the lower zero-points of the various functions may, however, bring it about that at certain lower temperatures, somewhere between 5° and 10° C, the various functions no longer work harmoniously together, so that pathological conditions are induced. It is observed, for instance, that in the spring time the young leaves of cereal plants grow, it is true, but in spite of bright illumination they remain yellow, because the lower limit of temperature for growth is not so high as that for the development of chlorophyll. Similarly, it is occasionally observed during the regularly recurrent cooling of the air about the middle of June, that plants which require a relatively high temperature, e. g. Beans (*Phaseolus*), Maize, Gourd, Buckwheat, etc., unfold new leaves, it is true, during such periods of cool weather, but for the reasons given above they remain yellow, until at a higher temperature the development of the chlorophyll is rendered possible.

No object would be served by bringing forward here all the numbers which various observers have to a certain extent established as to the limits of temperature and the optima of the various vegetative phenomena. Better opportunities for this will occur later on, when considering the individual phenomena of vegetation themselves. Yet it may in some measure contribute to the explanation of what has been said hitherto if a few numbers at least are mentioned as examples The growth of the seedling in its dependence upon temperature has been most frequently observed[1],

---

[1] In my treatise, '*Physiologische Untersuchungen uber die Abhangigkeit der Keimung von der Temperatur*,' in the Jahrb für Wiss Bot (1860), I first showed that the growth of roots and shoots above an optimum temperature is again retarded, and may thus be represented by a curve which first ascends from the abscissa and then returns to it, while up to that time, even by Boussingault, simple proportionality between temperature and growth had been assumed That the form of a curve

and it has been established that the seeds of cereals, for example, can still germinate
—i. e. develope their roots and seedling shoots—at a temperature very near to
the freezing-point of water, whereas the Maize and the Kidney-bean (*Phaseolus
multiflorus*) require at least a temperature of about 9° C ; and Date-stones, as it
appears, only germinate at 15° C. The optimum temperatures at which the quickest
growth of the organs of the seedling results, appears in our cereals to be 28° or 29°
C.; in the other plants mentioned, however, it seems to lie above 30° C. At a
continued temperature above 40° C. the germination of all these plants is abnormal,
or they perish.

Of the other most general vital phenomena of the plant, may be mentioned, in the first place, the streaming of the protoplasm In the hairs of
the Gourd-plant this movement appears only to begin when the temperature
reaches 10–11° C., the optimum temperature of the streaming of the protoplasm
may lie between 30° and 40° C ; and towards 50° it decreases more and more, to
cease entirely if the exposure continues sufficiently long.

The relations which we have so far explained between the vegetative processes
and the temperature may also be graphically represented If we suppose a straight
line drawn horizontally, and its length divided into a number of equal parts, which,
proceeding from left to right, are marked like a thermometer scale, 0°, 1°, 2°, 3°, and
so forth to about 50°; and if we then further suppose the growth in length of roots
or shoots attained at the temperatures named, and in equal times, to be denoted by
lines of corresponding lengths, erected perpendicularly on our horizontal line (the
so-called abscissa) at the places where the temperatures belonging to it are recorded,
these vertical lines represent ordinates of a curve obtained by connecting their upper
ends together by a continuous line. It is clear that this line, usually curved, as already said, attains its highest point above the optimum temperature of the abscissa
line, and from thence again sinks down to the latter. This curved line we term
simply the temperature curve of the growth in length; and to any one at all
familiar with these matters, such a curve presents the easiest guide to the relations
of law between temperature and growth established by investigation In like
manner the velocity of the protoplasmic movements may of course also be represented by vertical ordinates on a temperature abscissa, and thus in the form of a
curve; and, in general, each function of the plant dependent upon the temperature
may be so represented

So far as we at present understand the dependence of growth, of the movements of protoplasm, the formation of chlorophyll, assimilation, and of the various
other irritabilities upon temperature, light, electricity, and external influences in
general, all these relationships may be likewise expressed in the form of curves,
in each case the external influences being registered according to their intensity
on an abscissa line, and the corresponding effects on the plant being expressed by
ordinates. Everywhere, so far as sufficiently strict investigations are to hand,
the curves of function so constructed show the main property of temperature

---

ascending from the abscissa and returning to it may also be employed for other relations of
dependence of the plant upon external influences, was further established subsequently by myself
and other observers This law is, however, expressed generally for the first time in the present
lecture

curves *i.e.*, they begin at a certain intensity of the external influence, and thus at a definite place on the abscissa line, then ascend more and more until a maximum of the effect appears above a given point of the abscissa line, which is always to be distinguished as the optimum point, from whence onwards the curves again sink down to the abscissa. In order to illustrate this generalisation of our law of curves more clearly by an example, I may cite the dependence of the evolution of oxygen from the organs containing chlorophyll, under the influence of light of various colours; for the evolution of oxygen effected by the chlorophyll is a function of the wave-lengths of light, in so far that only light the wave-length of which amounts to at least 0 0003968 mm, and does not exceed 0 0006866 mm., effects the separation of the oxygen Starting from both extremes, this effect of the light increases, and reaches the maximum at an optimum

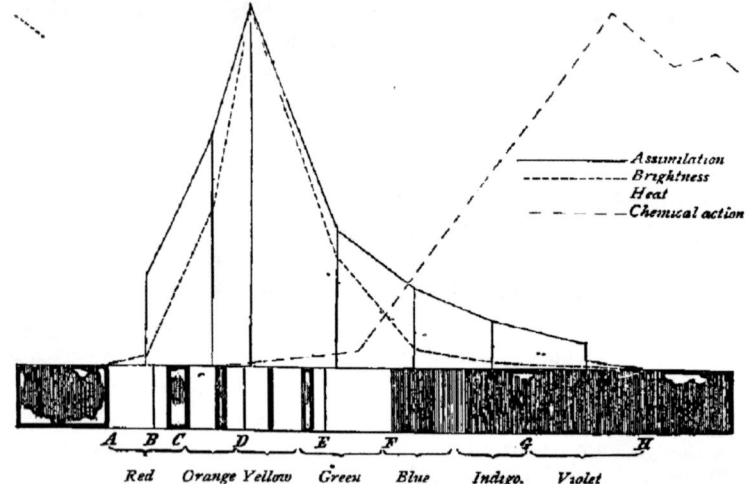

FIG. 188.—The band *A—H* denotes the absorption spectrum of a solution of chlorophyll. The lines *A, B—H* are Fraunhofer's lines. The spectrum is employed as the abscissa line for the curves explained in the figure (after Pfeffer)

wave-length of 0 0005889 mm. As is well known, the various wave-lengths of light produce in our eyes the sensation of the various colours of the spectrum, and since the number first mentioned represents the wave-length of the blue, and the second that of the red, while the third—the optimum—denotes the wave-length of yellow light, we may also say that the evolution of oxygen begins in the blue light, ascends thence through the green of the spectrum up to the middle of the yellow, and there reaching its highest point again descends in the orange-coloured rays, to cease within the red portion of the spectrum. Thus if we have a sufficiently large solar spectrum, and a green leaf is placed during equal times in the various coloured regions of the spectrum, the quantity of oxygen evolved each time is expressed by the curve of which the cardinal points were specified above[1].

---

[1] With reference to the effect of various coloured lights on assimilation, cp my treatise in ' Bot Zeit ' 1864, pp 353, &c , where the older literature, up to that time scarcely noticed at all, is

Indeed, it is not going too far to say that every dependence of a physiological function upon any one external influence assumes the form of a curve,
first ascending and then again descending; and that we have here one of the
fundamental laws of physiology Since now we may term each dependence of
a vegetative phenomenon upon external influences irritability, the form of curve
mentioned represents the fundamental law of irritability. This, expressed in words,
would run thus,—If the intensity of an external influence (*i. e.* of a stimulus) increases
more and more, the effect of the stimulus, or the corresponding function of the
plant also rises, but only up to a certain degree, the optimum of the former, if
it exceeds this optimum, the effect on the plant is diminished, until at a certain
most intense influence the functional capability of the plant ceases And further.
as the influence of the temperature only stimulates the plant when it attains
a certain height, so also every other external force or stimulus only then appears
to exert a perceptible effect when it has attained a certain intensity, sufficient to
overcome the resistances existing in the plant.

The law of the dependence of the phenomena of vegetation upon external
influences, which I have here attempted to make clear, gives, as is ever the case
with natural laws, the relations between cause and effect in the most general
and therefore abstract form possible Thus, even the simply formulated law of
gravitation is only a quite general abstract formula for an endless variety of
events The path described by a stone thrown into the air, as well as the
arrangement of the planetary system, the apparent irregularity of the movement
of comets, as well as the flowing of water from the continents towards the ocean,
and the ebb and flow of the latter, are ruled by the abstract proposition that
bodies attract one another in proportion to their mass, and in inverse proportion
to the square of their distances. or, to select yet another example, the endless
variety of natural phenomena produced by the reflection of rays of light, the
ordinary reflected image of our own person seen in the mirror, the focus of
a concave mirror, the Fata Morgana, and the signals of the Heliograph, all
come under the abstract natural law that rays of light are reflected from the
surface of a body at the same angle as that at which they meet it. Just as
little as we regard the fact that this geometrical expression underlies this endless
variety of figures and phenomena, so little do we regard the above-described
curves as representing in endless variety the relations between plants and the
external world. Since it is the object of this lecture to give an account as clear
and general as possible, and not merely abstract but also concrete, we will now
pause again at a sketch, though slight, of those phenomena of vegetation which
illustrate the dependence of the life of the plant upon external influences in a
particularly impressive and intelligible form

---

collected Pfeffer gave further investigations, made in my laboratory, in Arbeiten des bot Inst.
in Wzbg, B I p I   I referred to the errors of other observers on this question in the same (B I
p. 276), in the treatise ' *Die Pflanze und das Auge als verschiedene Reagentien fur das Licht* ' Here
I have still to remark that the expression for the dependence of the evolution of oxygen upon
coloured light—namely, a dependence upon the wave-length—correctly employed in the text, was
first established by me in the third edition of my ' Text Book ' (1873) and in the fourth edition
(1874), p 718. which Pfeffer has not quoted in his ' *Pflanzenphysiologie,*' p 212

There is, in the first place, the striking contrast of the winter rest of vegetation, as opposed to the vitality which the unfolding of the shoots and flowers in spring and summer presents. In the main it is the lower temperature of winter which renders the vital phenomena of the plant impossible, only when the temperature of the air and of the earth rises several degrees above the freezing point of water, with a higher position of the sun, do the buds of trees, subterranean rhizomes, bulbs, and tubers begin to be active and grow. At first, this is hardly perceptible, and very slow, but with the appearance of the first warm spring days, the shoots come forth into the light with striking rapidity, and in a few days the whole aspect of nature is changed. The surface of the earth is brilliant with vivid green, flowers make their appearance, and in a few weeks one hardly remembers how bare and lifeless the winter landscape was. The contrast appears no less conspicuous when, coming from the hot air of the plains, in the middle of summer, we ascend into the cool climate of Alpine heights, or journey towards the far north, we then leave a fully developed vegetation, to go towards a delayed spring. When our trees and fields are preparing for the autumn, vegetable life is just beginning on the mountains, and in high northern latitudes. If closely allied forms of plants are compared, of which the one is native with us and the others are at home between the Tropics, we very often find the former small, succulent herbs and shrubs, while the latter develope into woody bushes or huge trees—a difference which depends chiefly upon the fact that our summer is cool and short, while that of the Tropics is hot and long. Any one, finally, who has to cultivate plants of different climates on the same spot, e g. in a botanical garden, knows with what great cost and trouble this is done. The construction of greenhouses and the costly labour are chiefly, if not exclusively, caused by the different requirements of warmth of plants coming from different climates.

Still more various, if possible, are the phenomena due to the dependence of the life of the plant upon Light[1]

If, for example, we lead the terminal bud of a vigorous leafy shoot into the dark cavity of a box with opaque walls, a system of shoots, leaves, flowers, roots, tendrils, and even ripe fruits with seeds capable of germinating, develope on it. The whole, however, presents an exceedingly strange appearance; the shoot-axes and leaf-stalks are quite white, the laminæ of the leaves are small, and coloured yellow instead of green, and generally are not extended flat; and the entire substance of these so-called etiolated parts is richer in water, more delicate, and more sensitive to injurious influences than normal ones developed in the light. The flowers developed in the dark, however, attain their full beauty of colour and size If now a bud of this shoot-system, grown in the dark, is conducted through another narrow opening of the box out into the light again, normal, green, flat-extended and large leaves are produced once more, and the shoot, growing forward in the light, again obtains its normal peculiarities in every respect This experiment, as simple as it is instructive, shows that the growth of all the organs can take place, even in deep

---

[1] I published the first detailed investigation on the so-called etiolation of plants in my treatise ' *Ueber den Einfluss des Tageslichts auf Neubildung und Enfaltung verschiedener Pflanzenorgane,*' in Bot Zeit. 1863, and further in the treatise, ' *Wirkung des Lichts auf die Bluthenbildung unter Vermittlung der Laubblatter,*' Bot Zeit, p 117.

darkness, though with some inconsiderable abnormalities; that, however, the organs which are coloured green in the normal condition remain yellow or even colourless in the dark, whilst flowers, fruits and seeds are developed in the normal manner. The most important point here, however, is that such vigorous growth in the dark is only possible when the etiolated shoot is nourished by normal green leaves exposed to the sunlight [If these latter are shut off from the light, or are even much shaded, by which means their assimilation is destroyed or injured, the growth of the parts in the dark box also ceases, or becomes in a high degree abnormal Stated generally, the phenomenon described follows from the fact that the nutrition of the plant is a function of the chlorophyll in the green leaves; and that this chlorophyll is only formed under the influence of light, and is enabled by means of the latter to decompose the carbon dioxide of the air, and thereby to produce organic vegetable substance, which becomes transferred from the assimilating leaves into the buds, there to produce new organs even in the dark cavity. From the same fact is to be explained why the culture of plants in dwelling-rooms in general yields such unsatisfactory results. Even when provided with the best soil they remain small and inconspicuous, the older leaves fall off prematurely, and flowers, or it may be fruits, appear only in small numbers or not at all, because the influence of the light through the window on the green nutritive organs is too feeble to bring about a vigorous nutrition. [These evils of chamber-culture only come forward the more actively the warmer the plants are maintained; since the higher temperature forces them to vigorous growth, for which, however, in the feeble light, the corresponding production of constructive materials is wanting. The plants here grow themselves to death, so to speak It may be allowed here also to interpolate the rule, based on physiology, for the practical culture of plants in green-houses, that so far as plants are concerned warmth chiefly signifies growth, while light, on the other hand, brings about nutrition. Much light with a low temperature usually produces a superfluity of nutritive matters, which the plant bears without injury; a high temperature with feeble illumination brings about growth without the corresponding nutrition, and is highly injurious to the plant, and in extreme cases even fatal. The too short continuance of daylight also accounts for the fact that in hot, tropical countries many of our native cultivated plants do not flourish; because, although the high temperature stimulates them, it is true, to vigorous growth, the short tropical days do not allow of a sufficiently energetic nutrition. The larger the green surfaces, especially of the leaves, the greater is the number of rays of light by which the plant is stimulated to active nutrition. Careful observations have shown that a square metre of the green leaf surface of a vigorously growing plant produces, in ten sunny hours, 3-8 grams of dry plant-substance by the decomposition of carbon dioxide [1]. If one reflects how many square metres of leaf-surface a large tree possesses, and that the nutritive activity in one period of vegetation continues with us for about 150 days, it is clear that a tree forms many kilograms of organic substance in the course of a single summer, affording the material for the development

---

[1] The investigation *Uber specifische Assimilationsenergie* ('Arbeiten des bot. Inst in Wzbg, B II p 346) made by Karl Weber in my laboratory, may be consulted on this subject. See also Sachs, *'Ein Beitrag zur Kenntniss der Ernahrungsthatigkeit der Blatter'* in 'Arb. des Bot Inst.' 1884, B III p. 1, where it is shown that very much more than this may be produced.

of buds and flowers which takes place usually in the next spring This vegetable substance produced in the green organs is constructed from carbon dioxide and water, with the separation of a very considerable quantity of oxygen, it is therefore a substance poor in oxygen. Plants, as is well known, are combustible, i. e. their substance, poor in oxygen, is again converted, as it burns in the air, into the compounds rich in oxygen (carbon dioxide and water) from which it was originally produced in the cells containing chlorophyll. Just as much heat as is set free in the burning of a tree, must have been fixed during the production of its organic substance. This heat of combustion of a plant, however, represents a definite amount of energy which can be made useful—in a steam-engine, for instance an amount of mechanical work exactly as great, only in another form, was performed in the cells of the plant containing chlorophyll during the production of the organic combustible substance in them, from water and carbon dioxide with the separation of oxygen. Or, in other words, the energy which is produced by the combustion of vegetable substance existed originally in the form of luminous vibrations of the ether, the energy of which has been employed in the cells containing chlorophyll for the separation of the oxygen.

This work of the organs containing chlorophyll also changes with the alternation of day and night, but the resulting daily periodicity in vegetable life is made evident in many other phenomena. In the first place, in a periodical growth of the young organs, which may be accelerated by the darkness of night, unless the temperature sinks too low, and brings about, on the contrary, a retarding of the growth; thus, the rapidity of growth during the night may be greater or less than during the day[1], according to circumstances To the daily periodic changes most easily recognisable belong the so-called sleep-movements of leaves; these are particularly conspicuous in the compound leaves of the Leguminoseæ, e g. *Robinia* and the Oxalideæ; they take place in such a manner that the parts of a leaf fold themselves together in the evening, either upwards or downwards, and open out again on the following morning. But even simple foliage leaves move. In July and August one need only look around a garden after sundown to perceive the altered position of the leaves of almost all the plants; the large foliage leaves of the Sun-flower (*Helianthus annuus*), for instance, all bend downwards, so that the upper ones in part cover the lower, while the foliage-leaves of the large Balsam (*Impatiens glandulifera*) all stand upright at night. These are only examples, however, since these movements are quite general Still better known are the so-called sleep-movements of flowers, many of which close before sundown to open again next morning—phenomena which we shall consider in detail later on, and which depend upon the diurnal changes of intensity of the light and temperature I shall also have to speak more in detail later on of the heliotropic curvatures of the growing parts of plants, and of the influence of light on the hitherto unexplained swimming movements of the so-called swarm-spores of the Algæ. The manner in which light operates as a stimulus on plants is exceedingly various, and by its periodic daily alternations it leads consequently to daily periodical changes in plants

---

[1] I criticised, and corrected by my own observations, the older views (in great part quite wrong) on the daily periodicity of growth in length, in my treatise, '*Über den Einfluss der Lufttemperatur des Tageslichtes auf die stundlichen und taglichen Aenderungen des Langenwachsthums*' in Sachs' ' Arbeiten des bot Inst. in Wzbg,' B. I, p. 99

Of the cosmic forces universally operating on the plant, I have still to mention Gravitation. Plants possess an irritability—one might almost say a perception—with respect to the angle which their organs make with the perpendicular where they grow [1] They are irritable as to the direction in which gravitation acts on each of their organs, and this independently of their weight, or of any pressure. They possess a sensitiveness to gravity, as we do to light or heat, while a direct perception of gravitation is completely wanting to us, since we perceive it only through the effect of weight and pressure. If a plant in full growth, the roots of which have developed in a flower-pot, is brought from the ordinary erect position into some other—e g laid horizontally—it is noticed after several hours, or, according to circumstances, after some days, that all the growing organs, and some apparently already fully grown, have been caused to move by means of this change of position: the apices of the roots, the growing shoot-axes and leaves, flower stalks, etc., describe the most various curvatures, until the free moveable parts of the organs have again assumed those directions with respect to the horizon which they possessed before the change of position of the whole plant Those previously directed vertically upwards or downwards become curved until their apices are again directed upwards or downwards; and parts previously growing obliquely or horizontally become curved, after the change of position, until they can again grow forward obliquely or horizontally in the same manner We shall see later on that these movements are called forth by an effect of gravitation on those organs of a plant which are capable of growing Stimulations are produced so that the organs respond to every change of position with respect to the direction of gravitation, and these only cease when the organs have again attained their original direction. This phenomenon is termed Geotropism The influence of gravitation makes itself felt, however, in another and quite different manner, in that growing points arise at definite places, the position of which is determined by the direction of gravitation. To this point also we shall return subsequently It may here be mentioned, in anticipation, that the influence of gravitation on the direction of the position of equilibrium in which the various organs of the plant grow onwards undisturbed can also be established with certainty without special experiments, it suffices to observe [2] that the perpendicular stem of a Fir-tree or Palm stands vertical at every place on the globe where it grows—i e has exactly that direction which, continued downwards, leads to

---

[1] My views on Geotropism, presented in this book, are based on the following treatises by me— ' *Längenwachsthum der Ober- und Unterseite horizontal gelegter such aufwartskrummender Sprosse* (Arbeiten des bot Inst in Wzbg, B. I p 193), and ' *Über das Wachsthum der Haupt- und Nebenwurzeln* ' (ibid pp 385 and 584) where I also first showed that organs growing obliquely to the horizon are geotropic like lateral roots this was afterwards also demonstrated by Elfving for horizontal subterranean stolons I wrote on the Geotropism of shoot-axes in ' Flora ' (1873) the essay, ' *Über Wachsthum und Geotropism aufrechter Stengel,*' a short notice on a very long investigation In addition are to be compared on this subject my treatises, ' *Über Ausschliessung der geotropischen und heliotropischen Krummungen,*' and further, ' *Über orthotrope und plagiotrope Pflanzentheile,*' in ' Arbeiten des bot Inst in Wzbg', B. II. I specially refer to the concluding remarks in the essay last mentioned

[2] I first showed in my ' *Handbuch der Experimental-physiologie* ' (1865), p 100, that the demonstration of the influence of gravitation on plants by means of rapid rotation—undoubtedly first given by Knight in 1806—was not needed, since the same conclusion is to be drawn with the same certainty from every day observations, as I have pointed out in the text

the centre of gravity of the earth.   The terminal bud of such a stem grows away from the centre of the earth here just as it does at our antipodes, while the apex of the primary root tends towards it; and no other force than the gravitation of the earth is conceivable which could bring about this behaviour of the growing parts of plants.   Further consideration also shows that this is true for all parts of the plant, no matter under what angle they grow with respect to the horizon or the radius of the earth.   Each organ of a plant has its specific irritability as to the direction in which it is met by gravity; and this in such a manner that it only obtains a definite position of equilibrium or rest when it is intersected by the vertical at a certain definite angle.   It would be simply impossible for any one acquainted with this fact to imagine how the vegetable world could be formed, or exist in general without this effect of gravitation on the processes of growth, if we were not in a position entirely to neutralise the effect of gravitation on a living plant, by means of a simple instrument—the Klinostat   It suffices to fasten the plant in any position whatever on an exactly horizontal axis, and to keep it slowly rotating, so that the growing organs continually change their direction with respect to the horizon, and come into reversed positions during equal periods.   In this case the stimuli act in opposite directions on the same organ, and the angles under which the various organs grow forth from their mother-organs are only determined by internal forces   In a similar manner, moreover, the so-called heliotropic curvatures effected by light can also be set aside by continual rotation opposite the source of light.

Relatively little is as yet known concerning the influence of Electricity on the life of the plant[1]   Experiments have been made chiefly on the action of induction shocks on protoplasm, and on the irritable and motile foliar structures of many plants, but the results obtained have not afforded a deeper insight into the nature of plants. In general, all that can be said is that very feeble constant currents or induction shocks during short periods produce no visible effects on protoplasm, but that, on the other hand, with a certain strength of the currents, disturbances appear in the protoplasm which resemble those brought about by a high temperature, and that with still further increase of strength of the current the protoplasm is killed.   Feebler induction shocks act on the irritable organs of the leaves of *Mimosa*, the stamens of *Berberis, Centaurea*, etc, like shaking or contact—i. e the organs perform the corresponding movements.   I found that constant currents proceeding outwards from the pistil in the flowers of *Berberis* stimulate the anthers to irritable movements, whereas similar currents in the opposite direction are without effect.

That electro-motive mechanisms are present also in the normal life of the plant itself may be in part directly demonstrated, in part presumed on general grounds.   It has been established, for instance, that every movement of water in a tissue, even in the woody mass, is connected with slight electric disturbances; and that these even appear when displacements of water are caused by the mere passive bending of a portion of a plant, or by movements of irritability on its part—processes of which we shall treat still more in detail in the proper place.   In addition, however, we may assume

[1] I collected what was known up to the year 1865 on electrical mechanisms and effects in plants in the '*Experimental-physiologie*' (1865), p 74   Kunkel made more recent researches in my laboratory, and at my suggestion, on the electrical action and conductivity of the living parts of plants—'Arbeiten des bot Inst in Wzbg,' B II, p. 1 and p 333.

that the chemical processes in nutrition, continually going on in the plant, and the molecular movements during growth and the passage of fluids from place to place, are all connected with electrical disturbances of various kinds, although it has not been possible hitherto to demonstrate this experimentally. We may also suppose that in the ordinary life of land-plants especially, during the continually altering differences of electrical tension between the atmosphere and the soil, equalisations take place through the bodies of the plants themselves. The land-plant rooted in the soil offers a large surface to the air by means of its branches, and the roots are still more closely in contact with the moist earth, while the whole plant is filled with fluids which conduct electricity and are decomposed by currents. Such being the case, it can scarcely be otherwise than that the electrical tensions between the atmosphere and the earth become equalised through the plant itself. Whether this acts favourably on the processes of vegetation, however, has not yet been scientifically investigated, since what has been done here and there in the way of experiments in this sense can scarcely lay claim to serious notice.

We possess, on the other hand, more exact and deeper knowledge, reaching into the very essence of the matter, as to the action of Chemical forces in the plant Among the very numerous chemical elements of the earth, there are but few which enter from without into the body of the plant (either in the condition of an element, as the oxygen of the air, or in the form of very simple compounds, as carbon dioxide and water, or, finally, in the form of salts) and there undergo decompositions producing new chemical combinations, from which the organisable substance of the plant itself proceeds. It is the object of the theory of nutrition to study these processes in detail. Mention is made of them here only in so far as they constitute external conditions of the life of the plant If only a single element of those necessary to nutrition is by any chance absent, or is present in too small quantity, a plant cannot be nourished at that place, and thus cannot even live for long. The well-being of any plant, therefore, depends upon all the elements contributing to life being present in suitable chemical combinations and available to the plant. That nearly the whole surface of the earth is covered with vegetation, and that even the waters and the sea abound in plants, results simply from the fact that the few materials subserving life are almost universally present in the necessary combinations. Or, we may say, plants are constructed from those chemical compounds which are present in quantity almost everywhere on the surface of the globe Apart from oxygen, carbon dioxide and water, there are a small number of salts—potassium nitrate, potassium chloride, calcium and magnesium sulphates and phosphates, and compounds of iron—which, as we know, suffice for the nutrition of every plant, and which are, moreover, absolutely indispensable. These chemical compounds, however, are found together nearly everywhere, though mingled in the most various relative quantities: this influences the thriving of the plant for good or ill, and therefore co-operates in determining its distribution. To mention only a few examples in this connection: there are certain species of plants which flourish in fresh water only, and others which do so only in sea water. A certain large number of land-plants grow only in the neighbourhood of the sea, or around salt springs or on the saline soil of dried-up seas in places abounding in common salt, which places, however, other plants avoid as unsuited to them The presence or absence of water at a given spot is quite decisive as to the possibility of vegetation. The deserts of Asia and Africa owe their paucity of plants essentially to the drought prevailing there; since around every spring by chance occurring even in the desert, a luxuriant oasis of vegetation becomes developed, simply because all other nutritive materials are present in the sand of the desert and the water of the spring. Water also affects the whole organisation of the plant in a definite manner That submerged and floating aquatic plants in general present a different aspect from land-plants, and are of a more delicate and simpler structure, strikes every observer at once To lay stress on one point only, it is obvious that land-plants, the large green leaf-surfaces of which are extended in dry air for the purpose of producing vegetable substance under the influence of sunlight by assimilation, are necessitated not only to absorb the salts of the soil which co-operate in this process by means of roots, but also to transport them into the assimilating leaves This takes place, however, by means of a current of water ascending from the roots through the stem and branches into the leaves, and this is maintained by means of the continuous evaporation from the leaves. This ascending current of water now requires a special organ in which to move, and that is the woody body; it also requires a richly-developed system of roots to collect the small quantities of moisture of the soil, which contains but little water, and so forth These arrangements, as is at once obvious, are superfluous in a submerged water-plant, and, therefore, proper wood is wanting to it, and its roots are insignificant in comparison with those of a land-plant. It scarcely needs special mention that the most various intermediate forms exist in the connection referred to; and these are still more various because nature generally can attain her object by very different means. Under conditions, for example, where the transpiration of leaves is too copious, forms appear without leaves, as the majority of the species of *Cactus*, and similarly formed Euphorbiaceæ and Stapelias; or forms with thick succulent leaves like the Crassulaceæ, in which transpiration is likewise only very feeble, or, finally, woody shrubs with few and small leaves. But just the most interesting and instructive arrangements which would here present themselves must be passed over for the time being, since they require too lengthy a description.

Just as plants react towards cosmical and inorganic influences generally, so also they exist in a relation of dependence towards various other plants and animals. In this, again, they react in such a manner that the external shape of their bodies and their internal organisation become modified in the most various ways. This is evident in a very conspicuous manner in the life of parasitic plants. When they absorb the whole of their food from other plants, or occasionally even from animals they themselves do not require leaves containing chlorophyll· they are, therefore, devoid of leaves, and accordingly, agreeing with what has already been said, the development of wood also is suppressed. The majority of parasites are massive bodies of tissue, abounding in parenchyma, and with little development of surface, the strange aspect of which usually strikes even the non-botanical observer, not to speak of the further abnormalities, particularly of the sexual organs, which arise from parasitism. On the other hand, however, even plants which contain chlorophyll and are self-supporting may not only be enfeebled in vigour by parasitic plants, but also altered in form Of this, the *Euphorbia* infested with Fungi, as well as the so-called Witches'-brooms (branches of a Fir altered by Fungi) offer well-known examples

Gall-formations are also to be added here. By means of the stimulus exerted by insects during their development in the interior of the plant the growing parts of the plant may develop in monstrous forms, or bodies of very peculiar sharply defined form grow forth from them. In this connection the fact is of special interest that the quality of these galls on the same plant depends chiefly upon the specific peculiarity of the animal which produces the gall by its irritation. On our Oaks alone, more than a dozen different forms of galls are produced by different insects. Nevertheless, although very common, these phenomena are more isolated and incidental. The most remarkable and beautiful dependence of the highly-organised flowering plants upon insects makes itself evident in the mechanisms of flowers, discovered by Conrad Sprengel in 1794. Sprengel showed even then that all beautifully formed and coloured and odorous flowers, in all their relations of configuration, are adapted for being visited by insects of a certain form and size for the sake of their nectar; at the same time these animals transport the fertilising pollen from the anthers on to the stigmas of other flowers of the same kind. Since the development of seeds is only complete in these cases, the reproduction of these plants depends upon the visits of insects; as, again, on the other hand, the entire existence of the insects referred to is conditioned by the flowers of these plants.

Even this small selection of examples will suffice to show how the whole life of a plant—not only with respect to its origin, but also to its maintenance in the widest sense of the word—depends upon external influences of the most various kind. It would be incorrect to suppose, however, that the vegetable world as such, or any individual plant-form, can be called into life at any time whatever by these external causes. All that we have here considered are simply and solely reactions of vegetable substance already existing, towards external influences on the same. The mode in which these reactions are manifested depends, however, upon the nature of the given plant, and a further problem of physiology—and, indeed, the most difficult one of all—lies in the investigation of this innermost nature of the plant, by means of which it is rendered capable of these reactions.

LECTURE XIII.

THE MOLECULAR STRUCTURE OF PLANTS, AND ITS PHYSIOLOGICAL IMPORTANCE.

THE coarser structure of plants as perceived with the unaided eye in their external form, as well as the structure visible with the microscope, have been treated of in previous lectures; and, as occasion offered, reference has also been made to the fact that the explanation of the phenomena of life (that is physiological investigation) cannot be satisfied with the knowledge of this visible structure, but that we are obliged to form more definite conceptions of that structure which is no longer visible, and no longer perceivable even with the strongest powers of the microscope. The attempt may now be made, preparatory to what is to be said later, to bring forward here some of the most important and most general results of investigation in the latter direction. The problem is to draw conclusions from the phenomena evident to the senses, which give us definite information as to the structural relations no longer perceivable by the senses. In such cases it is always advisable not to build conclusions on conclusions, and hypotheses on hypotheses; but to draw, from safely established facts only, the conclusions which immediately follow. At the same time it will be well, for the better guidance of those who are not quite at home in scientific matters, to go back somewhat further than may appear necessary.

Not only physiological, but physical and chemical investigation also, were long ago driven to form certain conceptions with respect to the minute invisible structure of bodies, in order to obtain a more definite insight into natural processes. In chemistry this is done by the assumption of the existence of atoms—exceedingly small, indivisible masses of matter with which the chemical forces are associated It is imagined that the chemical properties of an elementary substance such as Hydrogen, Oxygen, Potassium, Phosphorus, etc, are still existent even in atoms of these substances. Certain chemical phenomena, however, necessitate the assumption that two or more atoms of an element may come together into a closer combination, which is distinguished as a molecule. Chemical combinations of different elements must always necessarily be composed of two or more atoms, and therefore always form molecules. A molecule is, therefore, according to the view of the chemist, the smallest conceivable mass of a chemical compound, since, if the molecule were split up still further, the chemical nature of the object would necessarily be altered, because the combination of the atoms of different kinds would be loosened   Thus carbon dioxide consists of molecules, each of which is composed of one atom of Carbon and two atoms of Oxygen   In like manner water consists of molecules, each of which consists of two atoms of Hydrogen and one atom of Oxygen. The molecules of most other inorganic compounds are more complicated · the molecule of potassium nitrate, for example, consists of one atom of Potassium, one atom of Nitrogen, and three atoms of Oxygen. The composition of the organic chemical compounds produced by plants, however, are to be conceived as being much more complex. They all contain Carbon and Hydrogen, and generally Oxygen also, and the most important of all organic combinations—the proteid substances—contain Nitrogen and Sulphur in addition ; and this in such a manner that in one molecule dozens, or even hundreds of atoms of the elements named are combined with one another. The body of the plant, then, consists chiefly of such polyatomic chemical combinations. The cellulose of the solid frame-work of the plant, and the protoplasm and nuclear substance consist of molecules, each of which contains very numerous atoms of three, four, or five elements.   Even in the province of pure chemistry, however, it is necessary for the explanation of certain phenomena to assume that polyatomic molecules may come together among themselves into closer molecular unions; and that in this manner new chemical properties arise which do not belong to the individual molecules.

With chemical processes in the narrower sense of the word are connected other natural phenomena, in which it is no longer merely a matter of chemical changes, but of movements in space of quite another kind. Here belong, on the one hand, those movements of molecules which a dissolved or melted body exhibits on its solidification as a crystal of definite form, as well as those movements by which a crystal becomes again dissolved into its individual molecules, by a soluble medium or by melting , and, on the other hand, the entrance of water into organised bodies, and the changes in volume effected thereby, as well as numerous other phenomena. We are here particularly concerned with these latter processes, belonging to the domain of molecular physics. For it appears that for the explanation of most processes of life, the assumption of atoms and chemical molecules no longer suffices, but that we are rather obliged to assume combinations of molecules which form very large numbers of small particles, or Micellæ (Nægeli), which are never visible with the microscope however, and the arrangement of which gives rise to certain very peculiar properties of organised bodies[1]

---

[1] It is not necessary to go more closely here into the theory of the internal structure of organised bodies founded by Nægeli   Only the following need be noticed   According to Nægeli a series of the most highly characteristic properties of organised bodies—i e. of starch grains, cell-walls, and crystalloids—may be explained by the assumption that the molecules in the sense of the chemist are united into larger unions, up to many thousands, and so constitute molecules of a higher order, or, as Nægeli more recently terms them, Micellæ (particles)   'Organised substances,' says Nægeli ('Bot Mittheilungen' in den Sitzungsberichten der kgl. bayr Akademie der Wissenschaften, 1862, Marz, p 203), 'consist of crystalline, doubly-refracting molecules (Micellæ), which lie near one another loosely, but arranged in a certain regular manner   In the moist state each of these (Micellæ) is surrounded with an envelope of water in consequence of its powerful attraction in the dry state they are in mutual contact' In my 'Experimental-Physiologie,' 1865, p 443, I first

Crystals are either soluble in water or not. In the latter case the water which is in contact with the crystal, in spite of the force of attraction which exists between both, is unable to tear off any molecules; and the construction of the insoluble crystal also prevents the entrance of water molecules into its interior. If the crystal is soluble in water, however (as a cube of common salt for instance), the attraction between the two substances results in molecules being torn off from the surfaces of the crystal, and intercalated between the molecules of the water

By this means molecules of the salt lying deeper come into contact with the water, and suffer the same fate in it, until the whole crystal is dissolved into its molecules, which now move about within the mass of water, and this movement continues until a completely uniform distribution of the salt molecules in the mass of water results With the attainment of this condition of equilibrium, where every salt molecule is surrounded by exactly as many molecules of water as every other in the same solution, relative rest now occurs If, instead of the common salt, a small portion of Iodine had been placed at the bottom of a large vessel filled with water, a watery solution of Iodine would have been formed in the same way; and the uniform distribution of the Iodine molecules in the water would be recognisable at once in its uniform colouration This condition of equilibrium, however, we could at once bring into a condition of movement if we suspended in the upper part of the solution a bag filled with starch. The Iodine molecules coming immediately in contact with the starch, would then penetrate into the starch grains, affording opportunity to the more distant Iodine molecules also to move towards the starch; and this process would continue until all the Iodine molecules, even the most distant ones, had travelled from the bottom of the vessel up to the bag of starch, and therefore in opposition to gravitation

Organised bodies—to which, so far as the plant is concerned, we may consider the cell-wall, the protoplasm and nucleus, starch-grains, and the so-called crystalloids to belong—behave towards water quite differently from insoluble and soluble crystals. If a dry body of this kind is laid in water, its volume is increased more or less according to circumstances, and by this the consistence of the body is altered Previously hard and brittle, it now becomes soft and flexible. A closer examination at once shows that the increase in volume which the body has undergone by swelling up in water, is almost equal to the volume of the water which it has absorbed. If this so-called imbibed water is again withdrawn from the swollen body, by evaporation or by means of some medium which abstracts water, e g absolute alcohol, its volume again shrinks until it has reached the original size Between the organised body capable of swelling and the water, there exists a mutual attraction, just as between water and a soluble crystal The great difference between the two, however, lies in that the molecules of the latter become separated from one another and distributed between the molecules of the water, in the swelling of an organised body, on the other hand, the water penetrates between its micellæ without these completely losing their connection. They only separate further from

suggested that protoplasm also is an organised substance in Nægeli's sense it had previously been regarded as a structureless slime or even as a fluid This view established by me, that protoplasm is an organised body, is now generally accepted.

one another, or rather they become forcibly driven apart by the penetrating water. This process of swelling is thus something quite other than the entrance of water into a porous unorganised body, e.g. dry gypsum[1], or into a heap of sand, etc. In

---

[1] Although the view of the structure of organised bodies and those capable of swelling cited in the previous note had been established and accepted by Nægeli, the view was nevertheless held tenaciously for a long time, that the imbibition of water by such bodies could be referred to the laws of capillarity in narrow, hollow tubules. That the capillary theory is in no way capable of explaining particularly the movements of fluids in wood follows from Nægeli and Schwendener's considerations ('*Das Mikroskop*,' II Aufl § 371), and indeed the more forcibly since these investigators proceeded from the view that it was self-evident that capillarity was concerned in the matter. I have in my work, ' *Ueber die Porosität des Holzes*,' ('Arbeiten des bot Inst in Wurz- burg,' II. Bd, p 305, 1879), and previously in a preliminary notice, expressed myself on the matter in question as follows 'This view, that imbibition is only a special case of capillarity, was first expressed by De Luc, and in fact because hygroscopic bodies after being completely saturated with water on being brought into alcohol apparently maintain their condition of imbibition. The fact is however incorrectly apprehended. If bodies capable of swelling and free from water, such as animal glue, coagulated dry proteid, dry stems of *Laminaria*, &c, are placed in alcohol almost free from water (98 %) they never swell up in it at all, and never increase in weight, or only very slightly. If they are placed dry in water they absorb very much of it, as is shown by weighing, and their volume increases to nearly the volume of the absorbed water. This increase in volume proves that the water does not penetrate into pre-formed cavities (capillaries), but that it drives asunder the mole- cules of the substance, and that to the extent of its own volume. If such a saturated body is again allowed to dry up it again assumes the previous volume, and the cavities which the water had produced and filled disappear, the molecules again applying themselves to one another. Alcohol and thick glycerine are not able to drive asunder the molecules of dry bodies capable of swelling, and therefore do not penetrate into them. Since, therefore, cavities in which water or glycerine or alcohol could penetrate forthwith do not exist in dry bodies of this kind, a comparison of these processes with the capillary entrance of fluids in large bodies can of course scarcely be spoken of.

'When water, alcohol, or other fluids penetrate into bodies such as cast gypsum, chalk, or burnt clay, which in the dry state possess actual capillary cavities, they drive before them the air contained in the cavities, and this can be exhausted and measured, when water, on the other hand, penetrates into a dry body capable of swelling, no air is driven out, simply because it penetrates into spaces which it first opens itself.'

If dry bodies capable of swelling, which do not absorb alcohol or glycerine, are first placed in water until they are completely swollen, and then brought into very strong alcohol or glycerine, the effect may be very different according to the nature of the body. Glue contracts energetically, since the imbibed water is withdrawn from it without an equal volume of alcohol or glycerine passing in. *Laminaria* behaves quite otherwise it contracts but little in 98 % alcohol, and, as is shown by weighing and determining the volume, alcohol passes into the spaces left by the water. Here, however, the internal condition of the *Laminaria* is altered in the watery state it was flexible and soft, in the alcohol it becomes hard and brittle. Even if the alcohol which has replaced the water is driven out by heat, the *Laminaria* no longer contracts to its previous volume in the dry state it now contains evident capillary cavities filled with air, since it swims on water, while the dry *Laminaria* sinks at once. The alcohol is thus unable to drive asunder the molecules of the cell-walls when dry, if the water however has driven these apart, the alcohol penetrates into the cavities occupied by the water, because as it advances it makes the molecules of the cell- walls immovable and prevents contraction. These experiments explain also why alcohol is so extremely serviceable as a medium for preserving and maintaining the form of plants it takes the place of the water of the cell-walls, while it prevents the contraction of the molecules of the latter. If plants are laid in alcohol quite fresh they preserve their fresh appearance, if drooping portions are placed in it they maintain their drooping aspect. The protoplasm lying within the cell walls so stiffened contracts on the other hand, since it becomes rigid in alcohol.

The imbibition of the cell-wall may be better compared with the process of solution of a salt, than with the capillarity of porous bodies. Just as the water seizes upon the molecules of a crystal, and takes them between its own molecules in solution, so the dry body capable of imbibition seizes upon the water molecules, and forces them between its own. Both processes require time. When

these cases the water penetrates into cavities—into small visible and invisible pores, previously filled with air which now becomes forcibly expelled by the water passing in : no pushing asunder of the solid parts occurs here, as is obvious from the fact that the volume of the porous body is not perceptibly enlarged by the penetrating water.

The chief point in connection with the swelling of an organised body, and upon which stress is to be especially laid, is, as follows from the preceding remarks, that the water of imbibition by no means passes in through pre-formed cavities or pores ; but that it penetrates by forcing asunder the minute particles (*micellæ*) of the swelling body, as is evident at once by the increase in volume. Organised bodies are therefore not porous in the ordinary sense of the word, and the penetration of water into them does not occur by capillarity, so-called. A second point of the greatest importance in the phenomena of the swelling of organised bodies, is with respect to the extraordinary force with which the water penetrates and drives asunder the solid particles. This may be recognised, for instance, in that dry wedges of wood driven into blocks of granite, and then moistened, expand with a force so great that the stone may be split. The impossibility of completely squeezing the water out of swollen vegetable cell-walls by pressure, however great, also shows with what immense force the molecules of water are held between those of the cell-wall, and gives a measure of the force with which they have penetrated into the dry membrane. We shall make use of these facts in the theory of the movement of water, and they will remove for us all those difficulties which have previously been felt The further fact that bodies capable of imbibing, such as dry cell-walls and starch-grains, condense the aqueous vapour from the surrounding air to such an extent that they become entirely or almost entirely saturated with water, or swollen, may also be taken as evidence of the magnitude of the attractive forces between molecules of water and these organised bodies. These however are only incidental

---

however the water molecules are at length distributed equally between those of the swelling body, they are there held as fast as the salt molecules distributed in the water of the solution.

The water-molecules contained in a cell-wall in a state of imbibition evidently exert mutual pressure just as little as the salt-molecules in a solution . the imbibed water-molecules form a coherent mass of fluid just as little as the dissolved salt-molecules of a crystal do. Of course the case is otherwise in a porous capillary body. In such a body provided with pre-formed capillaries the height of the capillary column depends upon the weight of the continuous column of water, and this exerts a pressure on the walls according to its height. In an imbibing body the weight of the water does not come into consideration It is therefore immaterial whether the imbibed water in the cell-walls of a tree is 20 or 100 metres high

The comparison of the imbibed water in a cell-wall or any other body capable of swelling and imbibing with the condition of the water of crystallisation is perhaps still more apparent no one would assume that this is contained in capillary cavities of the crystal The water of crystallisation is also present between the molecules of the salt in a form in which it can no longer be designated a fluid . it exists in a form which prevents the water molecules from exerting pressure on one another and obeying the laws of hydrostatics applicable to a capillary water column, however fine Like the water of imbibition, the water of crystallisation also may be driven off by heat, at least in some cases, but of course the crystalline form is then destroyed. Fundamentally, however, something of the same kind seems to take place in the conducting cell-walls of the wood , for their desiccation even at lower temperatures produces essential alterations in the imbibing properties, since air-dry wood loses the specific property of rapidly conducting the water of imbibition, it may therefore be assumed that ∗ permanent alteration in the molecular structure of the cell-walls is effected by a certain degree of desiccation

[3]   P

phenomena. We obtain an idea of the enormous magnitude of the forces here coming into consideration only through knowledge of the fact that during the penetration of water into dry starch-grains [1] a rise of temperature of several degrees centigrade takes place; for this fact can scarcely be otherwise explained than by assuming that the penetrating water is condensed, and a corresponding heating effect follows. Since, however, a condensation of water by which a rise of temperature of only *one* degree is brought about requires a pressure of several hundred atmospheres, we arrive at the conclusion that the condensation of the water as it forces asunder the particles of the imbibing body must be equivalent to a pressure of many hundred atmospheres.

But organic bodies capable of swelling are able to absorb not merely pure water, but also aqueous solutions: here however peculiar phenomena make themselves apparent   It depends entirely upon the nature of the atoms distributed in the water of the solution, on the one hand, and that of the swelling body on the other hand, how much of the former enters simultaneously with the water between the particles of the latter. In many cases a swelling cell-wall absorbs a larger quantity of water, but a smaller quantity of dissolved matter, from a somewhat concentrated salt solution, than corresponds with the concentration of the solution. It follows from certain phenomena which we will examine more closely later on, that living protoplasm absorbs only pure water from certain solutions, leaving the dissolved substances behind. In other cases, again, the swelling body absorbs a far larger quantity of the dissolved substances than accords with the percentage composition of the solution. This is particularly conspicuous with many colouring-matters, which may be so strongly absorbed, especially by bodies consisting of proteids, such as dead protoplasm and crystalloids, that these bodies become intensely and darkly coloured, even when the solution itself contains but little colouring matter and is very light-coloured.

According to circumstances, the various phenomena of swelling shortly indicated here play a part in the vital phenomena of plants. The changes in volume which cell-membranes especially undergo by imbibition and desiccation, may cause various movements of dead masses of tissue or of individual cells. The dehiscence of dry capsular fruits, for the purpose of distributing their seeds, is in general brought about by the fact that, on the drying up of the pericarps, either their outer or inner sides lose relatively more of the water of imbibition, by which curvatures and even ruptures of particular parts of the pericarp are produced. In some cases these curvatures produced by unequal contraction and dilatation are, according to the structure of the organ, combined with spiral windings or with the rolling up and extension of band-like

---

[1] That heat is set free when water enters into organised, and to a smaller extent also when it passes into unorganised bodies, was, according to Pfeffer, first established by Pouillet. Jungk and I observed the increase of temperature during imbibition by starch in 1865 (cp. '*Lehrbuch der Botanik,*' 1868, p. 500). Naegeli ('*Theorie der Gahrung,*' 1879, p. 133) found that the increase of temperature when perfectly dry starch absorbed water, amounted to 11.6° C., both bodies before the combination being at the temperature of 22° C. Since now, according to Joule, water is heated 0.03° C. by a pressure of 34.3 atmospheres, it follows that a rise of temperature of 11° must correspond to a pressure of enormous magnitude   The water penetrating first into the starch grains undergoes the most considerable rise of temperature, and therefore the greatest compression.

parts. The pentamerous fruit of *Erodium gruinum*, for example, separates into five single parts, each enclosing a seed, and each of which is provided with a long awn which, on the drying up of the fruit, becomes twisted into a spiral at its lower end; if this organ is moistened the awn is extended quite straight, and the very energetic movements produced by alternate drying and wetting, together with various additional adaptations, lead finally to the result that the fruit bores into the earth, to germinate there in the following spring The awns of many grasses behave similarly The so-called warping of wood on drying is also caused by the unequal changes of volume during the drying—i e. the loss of the water of imbibition of the wood, and in the same way many movements of the branches of trees during intense cold are to be referred to the same principle, since the solidification to ice of the imbibed water acts in the same way as desiccation, and, if it occurs unequally on different sides of a branch, must produce curvatures.

The great force with which water penetrates into cells capable of swelling will, as already mentioned, subsequently enable us to understand how the highest trees are enabled to raise the large quantities of water transpired from their foliage, from the roots through the stem into the leaves. A third fact also comes into consideration here: the fluid moving in the substance of the cell-walls as water of imbibition is not pure water, but a very dilute solution of those materials which the roots absorb from the soil, and on account of which (since they are necessary for assimilation) the entire water-current towards the leaves is set in motion. The conveyance of substances produced in any cell whatever towards neighbouring cells can also only take place by the cell-walls, as well as the protoplasmic linings of the cells being able to absorb not merely pure water but also aqueous solutions. This process of the movement of substances from cell to cell requires, however, the consideration of a far more complicated phenomenon, depending upon the processes of solution and swelling hitherto described, and termed *Diosmosis* (Osmose)

If a wide glass tube is closed at the lower end with an organic membrane, and a quantity of salt solution is poured into the tube, which is then immersed in pure water, the latter penetrates the closing membrane as water of imbibition, is taken up by the molecules of salt of the solution in the tube, and serves for the dilution of this solution If this process continues sufficiently long, a remarkable increase in the volume of the liquid in the interior of the glass tube takes place, and the fluid ascends in it, under certain circumstances, to a very considerable height: the cause of this movement lies in the attraction of the particles of salt for the water which permeates the closing membrane from below This process, here described so simply, is designated *Endosmosis* (Endosmose). Under certain circumstances *Exosmosis* (Exosmose) also may occur If the membrane closing the tube is capable of absorbing or imbibing the salt solution in the tube, the attraction of the external water causes a portion of the dissolved salt molecules which have penetrated into the membrane to diffuse out into the water, while at the same time a larger quantity of water molecules ascend through the membrane into the salt solution. It depends however entirely upon the nature of the membrane and the dissolved salt, whether the latter can exude at all by exosmose. In the process of osmose therefore, there are two points of prominent interest—in the first place, the question whether a substance dissolved in water is able to pass through a given membrane; and, secondly, the force with which the water on the one side and the dissolved substance on the other side of the membrane attract one another. It depends upon this, whether a given substance can pass from one cell into another in the living plant, and with what force cells are enabled to take up water into themselves. If, for example, there arises by chemical decompositions, in any cell whatever, a combination of atoms which cannot diffuse out through the protoplasm and the cell-wall into the neighbouring cells, this solution must accumulate in the cell in question, and even attain a high degree of concentration, without passing into the neighbouring cells; on the other hand, chemical compounds which are contained in a cell-tissue may become accumulated to a large extent in any given cell, if they suffer a change of their condition of aggregation in the latter. If, for example, the sugar penetrating into a cell is used for the formation of starch-grains, fresh sugar is enabled to penetrate continually into this cell so long as this change takes place; and, as we shall see later, the plant makes the most abundant use of this and similar processes The distribution of the various chemical compounds in the tissues of plants, their travelling over wide distances, and their accumulation in definite organs, depend upon such processes, a point to which we shall return more in detail subsequently in the theory of nutrition

The use made of the force with which water penetrates by endosmose into the cell is no less varied and general. The first phenomenon produced by this is the so-called turgescence of the cell[1]; which however can take place only in living cells still provided with protoplasm. We have to picture such a cell as a double-walled vesicle, closed on all sides . the external wall consists of cellulose, the internal or second wall, closely applied to it, consists of protoplasm, and the enclosed cavity is filled with solutions of salts (the cell-sap). Let us suppose the simplest case, and that such a cell lies in water The water of imbibition contained in the walls is taken up by the salt-molecules contained in the cell-sap, and an equal quantity penetrates into the two peripheral layers from the exterior. If this process continues for a long time, a large quantity of water gradually penetrates into the interior of the cell; and this is rendered possible only by the double wall becoming distended to a corresponding extent When this distension finally ceases, the wall opposing it, no further flow of water inwards can take place. The cell is now in the state of turgescence—i. e. the walls are distended by the water which has forcibly penetrated into the cell, and since they strive to contract elastically, they exert a pressure on the internal fluid. The main point to be noticed here, is that the force by which the wall is pressed outwards arises from the attracting force of the salts dissolved in the cell-sap towards the water surrounding the cell; and the opposite pressure, which prevents the further penetration of water, is afforded by the elasticity and cohesion of the cell-wall. In this, moreover, another fact is to be especially observed. The cellulose wall, as is known from numerous observations, is, it is true, but slightly extensible

---

[1] Further particulars as to the turgescence of cells and its significance in growth as well as in irritable movements will be given later.

and very elastic, and is thus in so far suited to withstand the endosmotic pressure acting from within, but this property of the cellulose wall would not by itself allow turgescence of the cell to be set up, since the cellulose permits filtration to a very great extent—i.e. the cell-sap pressing from within would be again forced out through the cellulose wall, even with very feeble pressure, and consequently no observable turgescence could arise in this way. As a matter of fact, also, it is shown that all cells merely enveloped with a cellulose wall (e.g. wood cells) are incapable of becoming turgescent. Only those cells in which a protoplasmic utricle is deposited all around the inner surface of the cellulose wall are capable of becoming turgescent. The protoplasmic membrane in fact permits the entrance of the water absorbed by endosmose into the sap-cavity, but it is in a high degree resistent against the pressure of filtration which arises from the increase of the volume of the sap[1]. To this pressure the protoplasmic membrane of the cell is impermeable, and thus completes the necessary properties of the cell-wall, in such a manner that the water which has penetrated by endosmose cannot be again pressed out. Or, in other words, the cellulose wall as well as the protoplasmic membrane permit the entrance of the water absorbed by endosmose into the sap-cavity of the cell, which in consequence of this tends to enlarge; the protoplasmic membrane prevents the water filtering out again in consequence of this pressure, while the external cellulose membrane forms a solid, elastic support, to which the protoplasmic membrane becomes appressed by the endosmotic pressure. It depends upon the extensibility and elasticity of the cellulose membrane how far the volume of the cell-sap can be increased, for the protoplasmic membrane itself is in a very high degree extensible and but slightly elastic, and if the sap-cavity were surrounded only by it the vesicle would extend without resistance, in consequence of the increase in volume by endosmose. The properties of the protoplasmic membrane and the cellulose membrane thus supplement one another in offering resistance to the endosmotic pressure of the cell-sap. That this is actually the case is proved by the behaviour of a turgescent cell when, by evaporation or by exosmose, a portion of the water of its cell-sap is withdrawn[2]. If, for instance, turgescent cells are placed in a highly concentrated but otherwise uninjurious salt solution—e.g. potassium nitrate—a considerable quantity of the water of its cell-sap is withdrawn from the cell by the attraction of the salt; in consequence of this the protoplasmic membrane becomes very strongly contracted, in proportion to the decrease in volume of the cell-sap. The cellulose membrane on the other hand is only slightly contracted, because it was only slightly extended. Both membranes thus become separated from one another; and the protoplasmic membrane lies as a closed utricle free in the cavity of the slightly contracted cellulose membrane. If such a cell is again placed in pure water, the latter is attracted by the salts of the cell-sap and penetrates both membranes, the proto-

---

[1] With respect to the co-operation of the protoplasm in the turgescence of cells, cp my '*Lehrbuch der Botanik*,' IV Aufl 1874, p. 866

[2] The relations between turgescence, the protoplasm, and the cell-wall, established by Naegeli, Pfeffer, and myself, were first clearly explained by Hugo de Vries in his '*Untersuchungen uber die mechanischen Ursachen der Zellstreckung*' (Leipsic, 1877), a publication which may be recommended in the highest terms to those commencing the study of vegetable physiology.

plasmic utricle becomes extended, applies itself in the first place close to the cellulose wall, and as the endosmose proceeds further the latter also becomes distended again to a certain extent, until its elasticity opposes further extension, and the cell is now again turgescent. The cellulose wall may in this sense be compared with a very firm but large meshed wire net, the protoplasmic membrane on the contrary with a very extensible but exceedingly fine, and therefore scarcely permeable, net.

The turgescence of a vegetable cell may be imitated in its most general features by an artificial apparatus. If a pig's bladder is fastened on to one end of a short wide glass tube, and the tube is then completely filled with a solution of salt or sugar, and the second opening also closed with bladder, a sort of

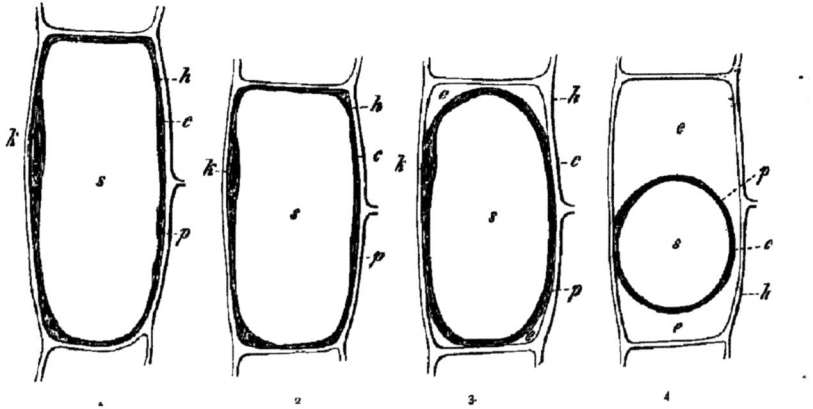

FIG. 189.—1. Young, half-grown cell from the cortical parenchyma of the peduncle of *Cephalaria leucantha* 2. The same cell in a 4°/₀ solution of potassium nitrate 3. The same cell in a 6°/₀ solution 4. The same cell in a 10°/₀ solution 1 and 4 after nature, 2 and 3 diagrammatic All in optical longitudinal section *h* cell wall, *p* protoplasmic lining of the wall, *k* cell nucleus, *c* chlorophyll grains, *s* cell sap, *e* penetrated salt solution (De Vries)

artificial cell results. If this is placed in a quantity of pure water, the latter penetrates by endosmose into the cell, and the increase in volume causes the two distended membranes to project externally like hemispheres, and at the same time strongly resists pressure with the finger, like a solid body. If a prick is made with a fine needle in one of the two membranes, the liquid spurts up to a considerable height, the membranes at the same time collapsing elastically. Here also it is evidently the attraction of the dissolved substance for the water of imbibition of the membrane, which supplies the force by which the two membranes are so forcibly distended, and the turgescent condition produced. The difference consists only in that here, there are not two different membranes which oppose the pressure of the penetrated water, as in the vegetable cell, but that one and the same membrane—i e. the pig's bladder—allows the entrance of the endosmotic current on the one hand, and, on the other, is at the same time elastic and resistent to filtration; while in the living vegetable cell the two latter properties are distributed between the cellulose membrane and the protoplasmic sac. The so-called precipitation membranes also behave similarly, though their resemblance to living vegetable cells has been to a great extent exaggerated[1]. If, for instance, a drop of concentrated solution of chloride of copper is placed in a vessel filled with yellow prussiate of potash, a closed precipitation membrane of ferrocyanide of copper is instantaneously produced on the contact of the two fluids: there thus arises a cell-like structure, and, since the precipitation membrane is permeable to the water of the surrounding solution, this penetrates into the cell, attracted by the chloride of copper in the interior. The increase in volume effects a corresponding pressure on the very thin precipitation membrane, which, since it is not extensible, bursts after a time; it is, however, at once completed again to a closed membrane, since the two salts come in contact for a moment at the gaping fissure, and at once produce a new precipitation membrane. In this way such a cell may gradually grow considerably. Somewhat greater is the similarity of the growth of a precipitation membrane of gelatine tannate, formed when a drop of non-gelatinising solution of glue is placed in a solution of tannin. Such a cell grows more uniformly and without the violent eruptions referred to above. How far this growth may be compared with that of a living vegetable cell, even with reference to the molecular processes in the membrane, depends, however, upon our knowledge of the growth of true vegetable cells. Here we have only to do with turgescence, and it is obvious from what has been said that in these artificial cells the turgescence depends upon properties of the membrane other than in the natural ones.

The capability of becoming turgescent is one of the most important properties of the vegetable cell, since a long series of vital phenomena depend entirely or in part upon it. In the first place, the fact is to be insisted upon, that growth and the increase in circumference generally of living vegetable cells only take place when they are turgescent, a point to which I shall return later in the theory of growth. The opposite of the turgescent condition of a vegetable organ is that of drooping. Every one knows that cut-off leaves or branches, if not placed with the cut surface in water, soon become flaccid, the shoot-axes, previously stiff and brittle, become highly flexible, and are no longer able to support the weight of the leaves, which have likewise become flaccid—the parts sink down: they droop. If the whole was previously weighed in the fresh state, it may be easily demonstrated that the drooping shoot has become lighter: it has given off water by evaporation, and it is simply this loss of water, by which the turgescence of the cells has become diminished, which causes the drooping, since if the shoot is allowed to take up water (which of course does not always succeed to a sufficient extent), the drooping condition disappears, and the young shoot-axes and leaves again become tense and rigid, because the cells again become turgescent With the consideration of this phenomenon we come to the important question, upon what does the stiffness and elastic rigidity of the succulent parts of plants depend? a question which here requires still closer consideration

[1] Traube, the discoverer of the so-called precipitation membranes and the artificial cells consisting of them, studied the properties of the latter, and thereby added to our knowledge of the processes of diffusion, upon which I wrote critically in detail and on the basis of my own researches in my '*Lehrbuch der Botanik*,' III Aufl., 1873. Traube's unfounded claims to priority as the founder of the theory of growth by intussusception, and the astonishing confusion of his artificial precipitation cells with actual vegetable cells, I replied to in 1878 in the 'Bot Zeitung,' p 308 ('*Zur Geschichte der mechanischen Theorie des Wachsthums der organischen Zellen*')

If a large leaf-stalk from a Rhubarb plant, for instance, or a *Heracleum*, &c ,
or even a portion of the growing flowering stem of these plants, is cut off, an
excellent object is to hand for making clear the question here brought forward. Let
us suppose the object cut off square above and below, and its length to be about
50 cm If now a strip of the epidermal tissue together with the collenchyma layers
which strengthen it are removed completely, and the attempt is then carefully made
to lay this collection of tissues again in its place, it is observed that the epidermal
strip is too short · it has become elastically contracted during the separation, and
thus, in the natural condition of the object, had been passively extended. If the whole
epidermis is now removed all round, and the length of the very succulent cylinder
(which consists chiefly of parenchyma and very extensible vascular bundles which
scarcely come into consideration here) is measured, it is found to have increased
very considerably in length during the manipulation[1]. Not rarely, such a cylinder
becomes extended from 50 cm. to 53 or 55 cm., or even more. In the natural
condition, where the epidermis enveloped the succulent cylinder of tissue, the latter
was thus passively contracted, and had a tendency to become extended ; it was
prevented from so doing, however, by the elasticity of the epidermis and collenchyma.   There existed, therefore, in the natural condition of the whole, a mutual
tension between the epidermal tissue and the succulent fundamental tissue; the
latter behaved to a certain extent like the contents of a turgescent cell, which
distend the membrane.   But of course it is not to be supposed that in the passive
compression of the tissue, it depended upon the compression of the water contained in it, since this is, as regards forces coming into consideration here, simply to
be regarded as not compressible.   The lengthening of the peeled cylinder of tissue
depends rather, as we shall see later, on a sudden alteration in the form of its cells—
they become longer and narrower.   Nevertheless, the comparison is apt in other
respects, since it can be shown that in the natural objects also a transverse tension
exists, of such a kind that the inner tissue exerts a pressure on the surrounding
epidermal tissue in the transverse direction also.   Moreover, this condition of
so-called tissue-tensions is only found when the objects named are abundantly
supplied with water : if they had previously been allowed to droop through loss of
water, the separation of the masses of tissue would only give inconsiderable differences in length between the epidermis and the internal body of tissue, or even
none at all.

We must now, however, regard yet another point in our simple experiment.
The leaf-stalk or portion of stem in the fresh state, or at any rate after having
been previously submerged for some hours in water, was tense and stiff: it
possessed considerable elasticity and rigidity.   The removed strips of epidermis,

---

[1] The alterations in dimension taking place on the separation of tissues from one another were
first scientifically established by Brucke in 1848 in his ' *Untersuchung uber die Bewegung der
Mimosen*' on the motile organs of the latter   In my investigation, ' *Über das Bewegungsorgan und
die periodischen Bewegungen der Blatter von Phaseolus und Oxalis*' (Bot. Zeitung, 1857), I treated
of the same phenomenon.   The views on the tensions of tissues were later, however, led in a wrong
direction by various publications of Hofmeister, since he chiefly observed the cell-walls only, and
did not pay sufficient attention to the pressure between the cell-sap and the wall. I then (in my
' *Lehrbuch der Botanik*,' especially in the III and IV editions) again brought the theory of the
tensions of tissues, as a consequence of the turgescence of cells, into the direction previously pursued,

however, are limp as damp paper. the uncovered inner succulent body of tissue is now likewise highly flexible; it is quite impossible, for example, to hold it suspended horizontally, since it at once bends limp downwards. We have here then the case of an elastic, solid, stiff body consisting of two parts, each in a high degree flexible and by no means stiff. only in their natural connection do the epidermal and internal tissues together form an elastic and rigid body, and in fact it is the mutual tension, and the circumstance that the inner tissue is strictly too large for the extensible epidermis (or, conversely, the epidermis too small for the former), which brings about the rigidity of the whole. The same is also the case, however, with a turgescent cell. Its membrane taken by itself is flaccid, and of course we cannot speak of solidity in connection with the fluid contents; nevertheless a turgescent cell is as elastic as a billiard ball. We have the same condition of affairs also in a thin-walled caoutchouc balloon, which, when empty, is a limp wrinkled sac, but which may be converted into a firm elastic sphere by being strongly inflated with air : the solidity of this again depends simply upon the mutual pressure of contents and skin. If we suppose some hundreds of thousands of small caoutchouc balloons thus inflated with air, and all contained together in an extensible caoutchouc vesicle, the latter, together with its contents, would also form a rigid bar like the stem of a plant. If we suppose the small caoutchouc balloons not inflated with air, but filled tense with water, the same effect results ; and it is somewhat in this manner that we have to imagine the rigidity of a petiole or stem produced by the turgescence of the cells. It is at once clear that if the small balloons in the supposed system lose a part of their turgescence by the withdrawal of water, and each thence becomes somewhat smaller, that the tension of these cellular contents towards the enveloping caoutchouc vesicle also diminishes, the latter would then become shorter, and the rigid system must at the same time relax We must picture somewhat in this way the drooping of a cut-off shoot when it loses water by evaporation

The rigidity of succulent shoot-axes and leaves, especially those which are still growing in length, depends essentially upon this condition of the layers of tissue, brought about by turgescence and tissue-tensions, the same is true of the peculiar firmness of succulent fruits, tubers, bulbs, and roots, which all become limp and soft, or as one generally expresses it, shrivel, by the loss of water. The upright position of the young flowering stalks which numerous plants put forth in the spring, and the rigidity of young shoot-axes and the leaves of trees in the spring, are due simply and entirely to the state of things described.

If we further suppose that in a stem, petiole or root so conditioned, a loss of water takes place by evaporation from the turgescent cells only on one side of the longitudinal axis, the object must become shortened a little on this side, and the necessary consequence is that it becomes bent or curved, since the shortened side becomes concave. In like manner the increase of turgescence and extension of the cells on one side of the longitudinal axis would cause this side to become convex. The latter fact may be elegantly demonstrated on the roots, 10—15 cm. long, of the seedling of the Bean, Maize, Gourd, &c. If these are allowed to dry up for a few minutes in the air, they become shortened a little through slight drooping, and if the roots are then dexterously laid on the surface of water, so that only the under side of the root is moistened, the cells of this side at once absorb water, and become larger and longer; the consequence is that since a long stretch of the root becomes curved and convex on the under side[1], the free apex of the root rises high above the level of the water. This movement takes place so rapidly that it can be conveniently followed with the eye.

A long series of induced movements, with which we shall become familiar more in detail subsequently and among which those of the leaves of *Mimosa* are best known, are similarly effected by alterations in the turgescence of one side; only these alterations are not caused by evaporation of the water of the cell-sap. These sensitive phenomena depend upon the remarkable fact that, by simple contact or shaking, the protoplasm of the irritable cells suddenly loses the resistance to filtration which is necessary for turgescence, so that a portion of the cell-sap is driven through the cell-walls of the sensitive organ into neighbouring parts, while the walls, which were previously distended elastically, contract, and thus bring about a shortening of the one side of the sensitive organ, in consequence of which the latter becomes curved concave on this side.

We have already seen that the rigidity of succulent stems and petioles during growth in length, and often also for some time after its conclusion, is caused by the tension of the tissues, depending on the turgescence of the parenchymatous tissue and the opposite pressure of the epidermis often strengthened by collenchyma The rigidity of the older portions of plants which are traversed by woody sclerenchyma strands, and which no longer grow in length, are produced in another way, however That a tree stem, or a woody branch, or even an older lignified flowering stalk of a shrub, or the haulm of a grass, is rigid and elastic, depends on quite other causes. In these cases, where lignified masses of tissue are always present in the organ, it is these alone, or with the co-operation of tissue tensions also, which determine the rigidity of the organ. As is well known, a thin, woody Willow twig stripped of its cortex is firm and elastic, and thin rods cut out of the wood of the stem are likewise extremely rigid; and even very thin slips of wood possess this property in a high degree. Here the rigidity by no means depends upon the mutual tensions of layers which are themselves limp, but upon the fact that the woody tissue is itself rigid, hard, and elastic, much as a metallic rod or a crystal In addition to the remarkable power of rapidly conducting the water absorbed by imbibition in the substance of the cell-wall, the lignified cells have the office in the vegetable world of enhancing the rigidity of the organs, without the intervention of tissue tensions; and the enormous density of the shell of a Cocoa-nut, or of a Cherry-stone, shows how great may be the solidity of lignified cells under certain circumstances. In these examples, however, it is rather the bulky accumulation of the solid materials which brings about the solidity of the body in question. In the construction of their flower stems and leaf stalks, on the other hand, only a relatively small quantity of lignified masses of tissue comes into use in the form of very thin strands or layers; these, however, are so distributed according to mechanical principles in the organs, that they nevertheless produce a high

---

[1] The upward curvature of partially drooping radicles laid horizontally on a surface of water here referred to was first observed by Ciesielski, but was regarded as a phenomenon of growth. I gave the correct explanation in the 'Arbeiten des bot. Inst. in Würzburg,' B. I, pp 395-401.

degree of rigidity. We find particularly exquisite examples of this in the haulms of Grasses, and in the extraordinarily long scapes of many Rushes and Sedges, &c. (*Juncus, Scirpus, Cyperus*). These organs form columns, which, though one, two, or even three metres high, only possess a diameter of a few millimetres. In spite of their exceedingly slender form, they are very rigid under the pressure of the wind they may be bent down into a semicircle, and in spite of being weighted at the apex with fruits and leaves, nevertheless spring up again like elastic steel wire. Examination shows, however, that these slender columns are either hollow, as the haulms of the Grasses, where the wall of the hollow cylinder is often only of the thickness of ordinary paper; or the interior of the columnar organ consists principally of very loose pith. At the circumference of the cylinder, however, either quite close beneath the epidermis, or on the outer and inner sides of the slender vascular bundles, which are arranged in a circle on the transverse section, run thin

cords of strongly lignified elastic fibres, upon which alone the rigidity of such organs depends. These lignified strands of fibre are scarcely at all extensible, and their elasticity may be not inaptly compared to that of wrought iron. As in the artificial construction of a thin hollow column, so Nature distributes these firm layers and strands chiefly at the circumference of the organs, because there their essential properties are at the greatest advantage. If the haulm of a Grass or the scape of a Rush, or any other similarly constructed cylindrical organ is bent, the elastic layers and strands on the convex side must be thereby slightly elongated, and those of the concave side slightly

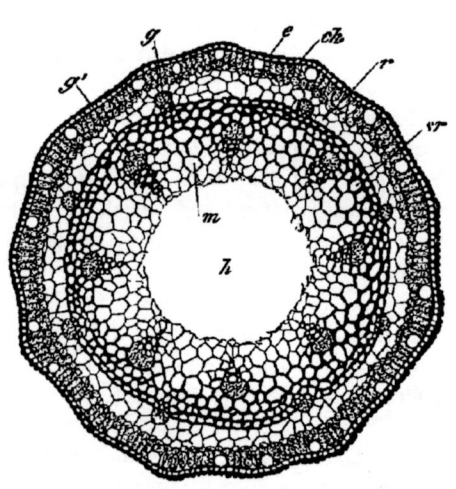

FIG. 190.—Transverse section of the flowering scape of *Allium Schoenoprasum* *sr* the cylinder of supporting tissue consisting of lignified fundamental tissue

compressed; since they possess a high degree of elasticity, however, they forcibly assume their natural length again when the external pressure ceases, and straighten the cylindrical organ. Schwendener[1], who has closely investigated the relations

[1] The significance of the strings and layers of lignified sclerenchymatous cells which accompany the vascular bundles or which run without these beneath the epidermis or in the parenchymatous tissue, as conducing to the rigidity of stems and leaves, especially in the Monocotyledons, was first correctly recognised and established by Schwendener in his book '*Das mechanische Princip in anatomischen Bau der Monocotylen*' (Leipsic, 1874). That Schwendener sought to introduce these forms of tissue into science as 'bast' was however a mistake The supporting ring in the flowering scape of the species of *Allium* for instance consists of parenchymatous fundamental tissue, the cells of which are only narrower, thicker-walled, and strongly lignified I also find that Schwendener laid too little stress upon the fact that the rigidity of stems actively growing in length must depend on quite another principle, since in these the strings and layers in question are not yet lignified and consequently are very extensible Schwendener's researches essentially account only for the rigidity of fully developed internodes and leaves

of construction of shoot-axes and leaves here referred to, showed how the distribution of the elastic strands and layers strictly accords with the principles of theoretical mechanics.   That the mechanical elements effective in the construction of thin stems also find their use in the construction of leaves, is easily intelligible; in this, however, it is a matter not merely of the elasticity and rigidity which determine their free suspension in the air, but also of that kind of solidity which prevents the tearing from the margin inwards.   It has already been explained in a previous lecture (IV), with a series of examples, how foliage leaves are protected against such injury by the mode of distribution of the ribs and veins.

After what has been said, it scarcely requires special mention that the kind of rigidity last described, since it depends on the subsequent lignification of the elastic fibres, only comes into play in the older stems and in leaves which are already fully grown; whereas the kind of rigidity previously described, and effected by the turgescence and tensions of the tissue, serves the organs which are still elongating, or which at any rate are not provided with lignified parts   For the sake of completeness I may add at the same time that young shoot-axes and leaf-stalks in an earlier stage of their growth in length, exhibit yet a third kind of rigidity: this depends also, it is true, on turgescence, but is characteristic in that the walls of the turgescent cells are more extensible and less elastic than in later stages of growth.   The portions of the shoot-axes, some 10–20 cm. long, under the terminal buds of *Clematis* and *Aristolochia*, and under the young flowering spike of *Plantago major*, &c., are in this condition highly extensible.   A longitudinal pull acts on these organs as on a thin thread of caoutchouc, and they are so flexible, like such

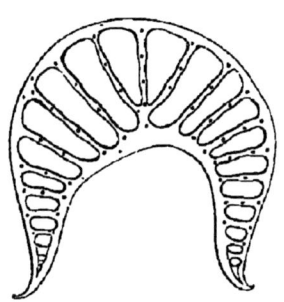

FIG. 191—Transverse section of a petiole of *Musa Ensete*
The lamellæ of tissue at the periphery together form an elastic system ; between these are stretched soft parenchymatous plates, in which run thin vascular bundles

a thread, that they can literally be wound round the finger.   Stretching, and strong bending at the same time, however, make them limp, and effect a diminution of the rigidity: this is brought about by the fact that the limits of elasticity of the still very thin cell walls are easily exceeded by the stretching.   On this peculiarity, by which the young filiform structures obtain the consistence of a leaden wire, or perhaps of a wax thread, depends an easily observed phenomenon, which Hofmeister erroneously explained as a phenomenon of sensitiveness[1].   If shoots with long, slender, still growing apical portions are shaken, it is remarked that after the shaking they hang down limp, to become upright again, in consequence of further growth, only after some time   I showed several years ago that the apparently irritable curvature of young shoot-axes is nothing more than an effect of their great extensibility, in combination with very small elasticity, and that one cannot here speak of sensitive effects.   That such

[1] The bending down of the growing apices of shoots, caused by shakings or blows, was first closely investigated by Hofmeister, but erroneously regarded as a phenomenon of irritability. I gave the true explanation of this phenomenon from the great flexibility and feeble elasticity of growing shoot-axes in the third edition of my 'Text-book,' 1873.

young shoot-axes, and likewise younger portions of root-fibres do, as a matter of fact, so behave, is most easily observed thus: it is possible to give to them with the finger almost any chosen curvature, which they then maintain for a long time, until further changes take place through growth. The shaking of the objects, employed by Hofmeister, may be better replaced by several blows given with a rod, applied on one side of the older lower portions of the shoot. The free apex is thus made to vibrate violently, and the apex in part maintains the strong curvature, so that on coming to rest it hangs down. It is obvious that the powerful vibrations given to slender flower stems by the wind in spring must call forth similar phenomena, and upon this depends, at least in part, the unpleasant aspect of a garden in a strong wind.

PART III

NUTRITION.

LECTURE XIV.

THE ASCENT OF WATER IN TRANSPIRING LAND-PLANTS.

PLANTS require water for the growth of the younger organs, the cells of which must be rendered turgid by endosmose. At the same time the water taken up serves for the production of chemical compounds in nutrition; and if the surfaces of the shoot are in contact with the atmosphere, a part of the absorbed water is exhaled in the form of vapour—a loss which must be again made good by a fresh supply of water, if complete drying up is to be avoided. It depends essentially upon the nature of a plant and its mode of life how the taking up and giving off of the water are accomplished. It is in the first place obvious that these matters will be otherwise in plants submerged in water, or in subterranean plants, than in those which expose large evaporating surfaces in the air; and in these again it is important whether they are small and can endure an occasional desiccation, as most Mosses and Lichens, or whether we have to do with larger and more highly organised plants, the root-system of which extends in the moist earth, and the assimilating foliage of which unfolds in the open air, and cannot endure severe drying up. In the latter circumstances are found especially the erect or climbing Ferns, Conifers, and Flowering plants. ·On account of the great variety of facts which here present themselves, it is advantageous to commence our considerations on a typical case which allows us to recognise the important points clearly on all sides Let us picture to ourselves for this purpose a tree, or even an annual plant, the stem of which stands erect and unfolds its crown of foliage to the air, i.e. plants of the common form, as met with in the Tobacco, Sun-flower, ordinary Palms, Firs and Pines, Poplars, Oaks, or other forest trees.

When in such plants the buds at the apex are to put forth shoots and unfold, they require for the purpose a quantity of water which is nearly as large as the organs themselves which are to be developed , since the latter, in the fresh, fully grown condition, consist of water to the extent of about nine-tenths or more of their volume This water, however, is absorbed far below, by the roots in the earth, and must thus be conveyed to the growing shoots through the stem. As soon as the leaves of the latter are unfolded, moreover, they constantly give off aqueous vapour to the atmosphere; and, as may easily be observed on cut-off shoots, they would completely dry up in a few days if water were not constantly conveyed to them through the stem from the roots. Experience shows now that in land-plants with large and thin leaves, the volume of water made use of for the purpose last named, in one period of vegetation, may be many times larger than the volume of the whole plant itself. We have thus to do here with an exceedingly energetic function; and, disregarding for the time being all other movements of water in the plant, we will concern ourselves in the first place exclusively with the phenomenon last indicated, which is called into play by the evaporation of water at the surfaces of the leaves, and which we may best distinguish as the ascent of water in transpiring land-plants. When the phenomena which here take place and co-operate have been made clear, it will be easy to understand deductively the movements of water in other plants also.

In the first place it will be advantageous to point out the purpose for which the flow of water is brought about by the transpiration of the leaves. The green leaves containing chlorophyll are, as has been already mentioned several times, the organs of assimilation of the plant, and it is in their cells that the carbon dioxide of the air is decomposed, and employed for the production of carbonaceous vegetable substance. Water also is necessary for the formation of this substance; and it is known, and will be shown in detail later on, that a series of salts which the roots take up from the earth are absolutely necessary in addition, if the process of assimilation in the cells containing chlorophyll is to take place. These salts (especially sulphates and phosphates of calcium and magnesium, potassium nitrate, and salts of iron) must therefore be conveyed to the green leaves for the purpose of producing organic substance. This is accomplished as follows an exceedingly dilute solution of these salts, which may be compared at once to ordinary drinking water, flows from the roots through the stem into the leaves. Considering the small amount of salts contained in the ascending water, however, only an extremely small quantity of the nutritive substances would be conveyed into the assimilating cells if the matter ended with the mere flowing in. The assimilating leaves, however, are induced by the warmth of the surrounding air, and especially by the rays of light, to let the water which has streamed into them escape in the form of vapour, this enables a fresh quantity of water charged with nutritive matter to flow up to them from the roots. Thus, by means of evaporation or transpiration, a continuous flow into the organs of assimilation is rendered possible as the water evaporates from these organs, the salts brought by it from the soil remain behind in the assimilating leaf-cells, and take part in the chemical processes of nutrition. This obvious explanation of the ascent of the water, so far as it is caused by transpiration, has hitherto been almost entirely misunderstood in a remarkable manner; and short-sighted people have even maintained that the transpiration of land-plants is a faulty arrangement, which has to be compensated by means of the currents of water. As a matter of fact, however, the whole organisation of a land-plant is only intelligible if one keeps in view the purpose of the water current indicated. The envelopment of the stem with an epidermis which possesses few stomata and hinders evaporation, or, in woody plants, even with a thick periderm, and in large trees with bark, has essentially the object of protecting the nutritive water ascending in the stem against evaporation. The small thickness and large area of the leaves, combined with the existence of the stomata which pierce the epidermis in millions, and which may be closed or open according to circumstances, are likewise only intelligible when it is known that they facilitate and regulate the formation of vapour, in order to render possible the inflow of fresh nutritive water to the organs of assimilation according to requirement. Where this is not necessary, as in submerged water-plants, the arrangements mentioned are also wanting; and in land-plants which possess a large transpiring surface, and are therefore devoid of a large assimilating surface, as in species of *Cactus* and Crassulaceæ, nutrition and accordingly growth also are relatively feeble When it has been sought, very thoughtlessly, to lay stress upon the fact that land-plants assimilate and grow even in an atmosphere saturated with vapour, where transpiration from the assimilating surfaces is not possible, it has been overlooked that in such cases it is a matter of an extremely feeble assimilation only, and accordingly also of a very small supply of nutritive water to the leaves,—a supply so small that, as can be demonstrated, it is maintained without transpiration-currents. Moreover, there is the fundamental error of assuming it as at all possible to maintain a land-plant even but 50 c.m high in a space constantly saturated with aqueous vapour . the fact being that even in this case (since saturation with vapour is effected with extreme difficulty) opportunity occurs for transpiring and maintaining a feeble flow of water Let it but be attempted to bring any tree, or even only a Sunflower or a plant of *Ricinus*, to normal vigorous development with actual prevention of all transpiration, and it will then be seen what comes of it . every horticulturist knows that land-plants grown in very moist air, and therefore with feeble ascending currents of water, are much too poor in substance and too watery to pass as healthy plants

Considering the great importance of the movement of water called forth by transpiration, for the whole well-being of land plants, the chief relations of organisation of which are subjected to this function, it is worth while to consider the phenomena in question more closely, and above all to examine those organic arrangements which specially serve to produce the movements of water, as well as to become acquainted with the mechanics of the remarkable movement itself.

In the first place, it is necessary to convince ourselves that the leaves continually exhale considerable quantities of aqueous vapour. It is only necessary to lay a leaf on the scale of a balance, to notice that it becomes continually lighter, and finally dries up entirely; this simply takes place by the escape of aqueous vapour. In the same way a plant eventually withers and dries up when rooted in a flower-pot and not watered If a plant is allowed to grow in a glass or metal vessel filled with nutritious soil, so that a large number of green leaves become developed, and the upper surface of the vessel is then closed by a lid consisting of two halves, which only allows the stem to pass through the centre; and if the whole is then put on a scale, first placed in equilibrium, it is noticed that the scale-pan loaded with the plant becomes lighter, and rises, although no water can evaporate from the vessel enclosing the roots. Evaporation takes place, however, through the leaves , and if a Tobacco plant, for instance, has been used for this investigation, the total leaf-surface of which amounts even to only a few square millimetres, and the experiment is arranged in ordinary daylight, or in sunshine, the balance shows a loss by transpiration of one or several cubic centimetres of water per hour, and it is easy to calculate that in the course of a few days the same plant evaporates from its leaves several hundred cubic centimetres of water, amounting to more than its own volume. This result is obtained much more readily if Maize, Tobacco, Beans, Cabbage, or other plants are allowed to develop their roots, not in earth, but in aqueous solutions of nutritive matters. If the glass vessel containing the nutritive solution and the roots of the plant is closed by a halved cork, which allows the stem to pass through and fit tight, the level of the nutritive solution is seen to sink from day to day; and in the course of several days the whole of the fluid within reach of the roots disappears from the vessel. The whole of this water has ascended through the stem into the green leaves, there to be evaporated. If the student wishes to convince himself of this, which of course is scarcely necessary on a little reflection, it suffices to cover a plant arranged as described with a bell-glass previously cooled: the aqueous vapour escaping from the leaves soon becomes condensed on the glass wall, and runs down in the form of drops. Of course no measure of the evaporation in the open air would be obtained by this means, because the space under the bell-glass becomes nearly saturated with aqueous vapour, and then almost entirely prevents further transpiration from the leaves. A substance which absorbs water (e g sulphuric acid or calcium chloride) could be brought under the bell glass, however, and the vapour exhaled by the plant would then be absorbed by this substance, and the saturation with vapour of the air surrounding the leaves prevented: the increase in weight of the substance named would then indicate the quantity of water exhaled in a given time. If plants with large leaves stand in spring-time or autumn behind a closed window, it is noticed in the morning that at those parts of the glass near the upper surfaces of the leaves, there is a deposit of water, which has evaporated from the leaves and been condensed on the cold window panes.

It would be quite in vain, however, to attempt to give from researches of the kind above described, an exact account of how much water a plant exhales in the form of aqueous vapour, and takes up through the roots, in a day or in a week. Transpiration depends upon the environment, quite as much as upon the organisation of the plant; experience shows that the formation of vapour from the leaves is increased as the warmth and dryness of the air, and especially the intensity of the light, increase. In moist air, or when fog, dew or rain cover the surfaces of the leaves with water, it is obvious that but little aqueous vapour, or even none at all, can escape from these organs. the transpiration, and accordingly the amount of the water moving in the plant, thus depend upon the alteration of external circumstances; and so far as experience teaches, the well-being of the plant is not interfered with within a wide range of play of these circumstances. However, the extremes must be avoided, since just as the long continued prevention of transpiration is injurious to a land-plant, so a too energetic formation of vapour in the leaves during hot sunshine may lead to the result that the roots do not at the same time absorb as much water as is given off at the leaves; hence the latter droop or wither—a phenomenon observed often enough during dry weather on very hot July days, but which passes away without injury when the temperature sinks at night, and the relative moisture of the atmosphere rises, and the transpiration diminishes so far that the supply of water from the roots suffices to make the leaves again turgid and fresh—i e , to fill them with water.

Although it is not possible to give an exact idea of the quantity of water sent upwards in a given plant during a period of vegetation, it is nevertheless of some interest to know how high the possible maximum of the water carried up by the current may rise. That a tolerably vigorous Tobacco plant at the time of flowering, or a Sunflower of the height of a man, or a Gourd-plant with fifteen or twenty large leaves, takes up and transpires 800–1000 cubic centimetres of water during a warm July day, is certainly no rarity; and so far as may be judged from the quantities made use of by branches placed with the cut surface in the water, it may be believed that large fruit-trees, or Oaks, Poplars, &c., absorb, transport through the stem, and transpire from the leaves 50–100 and more litres of water daily [1]. Now, these large masses of water are carried up, in tall trees, to a height of 50–100 metres in a direction opposed to that of gravity; and it is clear that in these cases the plant performs a work, the magnitude of which is evident most simply by supposing the same mass of water to be drawn up to the height stated by means of a windlass, for instance, worked by a man. The plant of course accomplishes this work in quite another way, and we will now see how it does it.

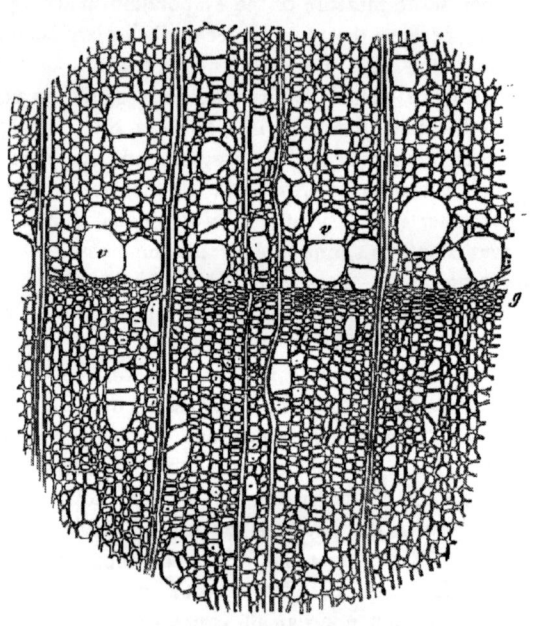

In the first place it is important to establish in what part, i. e. in which tissue of the root, stem, and leaves the water moves. The answer, as already known for nearly 200 years, may shortly be given thus: in the proper woody plants (i. e. the Conifers and Dicotyledons) the ascending stream of water passes through the wood. In the case of the plants mentioned the proof of this assertion is easily furnished; it is simply necessary to separate and remove a ring of cortex, by means of a double

FIG. 192.—Transverse section of the wood of *Rhamnus Frangula*. *g* autumn-wood of the older, *vv* vessels of the spring-wood of the younger, annual ring (after Rossmann).

annular cut on a stem, to completely interrupt all the layers of tissue lying outside the mass of wood. It is advisable to wrap tinfoil, or some other body which prevents drying up, closely round the exposed wood. If the ascending current of

---

[1] Although it is not possible to state for a particular plant any definite quantity of water which it must transpire in order to flourish vigorously (and it is certain that every land-plant has wide limits in this respect), it is nevertheless of value for general guidance to know approximately, on the base of experimental determinations, how large the quantity of water transpired by a plant during its whole vegetative period may be under certain circumstances. According to Haberlandt (cited by Pfeffer, '*Pflanzen-physiologie*,' B. I. p. 153) the water transpired by the Maize in the course of a vegetative period of 173 days = 14 litres; by the Hemp = 27 litres in 140 days; by a Sunflower = 66 litres in 140 days. According to Höhnel, a hectare of beech forest, 115 years old, evaporates 2·3 to 3·5 millions of litres of water between June 1 and December 1.

water were conducted entirely, or even only to a small extent through the various tissues of the cortex, the fact would soon be recognised, since the leaves of the tree would droop, and finally dry up. This, however, does not happen : on the contrary, they remain quite fresh, thus proving that in spite of the interruption of the cortex exactly as much water flows to them as they require for their transpiration. The pith in the middle of the stem does not come into consideration at all, since it is dry or already destroyed ; and in the cases of thicker stems its mass is much too small to be taken into account here. But even the usually darker coloured and harder heart-wood of the stem and older branches is not concerned with the conduction of water , since if a ring of younger wood or alburnum is removed at the same time with the ring of cortex, so that only the 'heart' remains uninjured, the withering of the crown of leaves betrays the fact that the water-supply has ceased. It is thus, put shortly, in the alburnum that the water of trees ascends. But even within the alburnum a difference prevails, in so far that the dense autumnal wood of any one annual ring is less capable of conveying water than the large-celled spring wood of the same ring ; and it appears, indeed, that in this way the spring wood of any individual annual ring represents an isolated conducting layer, not in immediate communication with the homonymous layer of an older or younger annual ring [1].

It is demonstrated by means of the above experiments, chiefly for the compact woody body of the Conifers and Dicotyledons, that the ascending current of water moves in the wood only ; but no such simple proof is possible, on the other hand, in the case of Monocotyledons and Tree ferns. These, as is known, form no proper woody body. Lignified cells are found, it is true, in the xylem of the individual isolated vascular bundles; but the quantity of this wood of the vascular bundles is so small, that it seems scarcely conceivable how the water necessary for evaporation could be conveyed through the thin lignified strands to the huge leaf-crown of a Date palm, for instance. In addition to this, the connection of the vascular bundles in the palm stem does not favour the assumption that only the xylem of the individual bundle can undertake the conveyance of water. The vascular bundles of the stem of a palm commence below as strands of hair-like fineness, which apply themselves where their diameter is extremely small to the older bundles bending out into the leaves. The difficulty disappears, however, if the sclerenchymatous, thick, lignified vascular bundle-sheaths are claimed at the same time as the principal water-conducting organs of the Palms, Dracænas, and other Monocotyledons In their anatomical and histological structure, moreover, as well as in their lignification, these sclerenchymatous strands resemble the more solid parts of true wood , and in view of their considerable diameter, it seems far more probable that the large quantity of water evaporating in the leaf crown ascends in them. If this assumption, which I hold as more than probable, becomes established, the sclerenchymatous vascular bundle-sheaths in the stem and leaf-stalks of large Ferns must also be regarded in the same manner.

---

[1] The proof that the autumnal wood of each annual ring offers great resistance to filtration, as well as the heart-wood, and that the former has probably as little to do with the transpiration-current as the heart-wood, is found in my treatise, ' *Uber die Porosität des Holzes* ' (Arb des bot Inst in Wzbg 1879, B II, § 3)

The necessity of the assumption that in the vascular bundles of the Monocotyledons it is not, or is only in a very subordinate degree, the lignified xylem itself which conveys the ascending current of water, but that rather the lignified sclerenchymatous sheaths play the main part in the process, is very evident on regarding the transverse section of the vascular bundle of a gramineous plant (as Fig 195). Here the area of the lignified xylem is only a fraction of that of the sclerenchymatous sheath. Besides, the fibrous elements of the latter in such cases agree in all essential points with the proper wood fibres of the secondary dicotyledonous wood. In other cases, as in the scapes of species

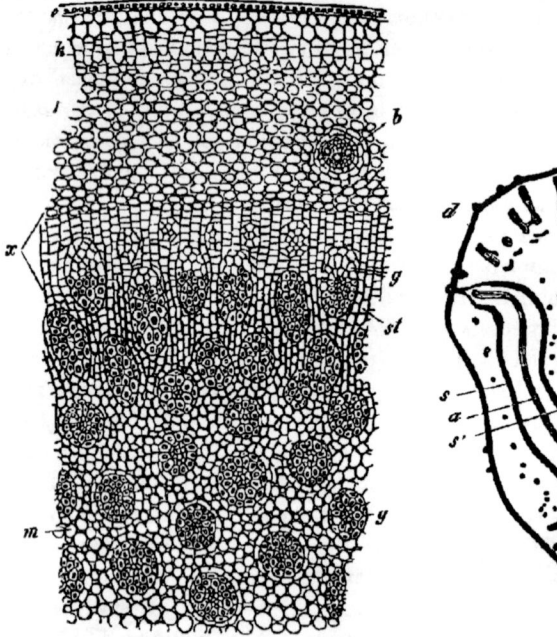

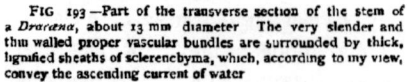

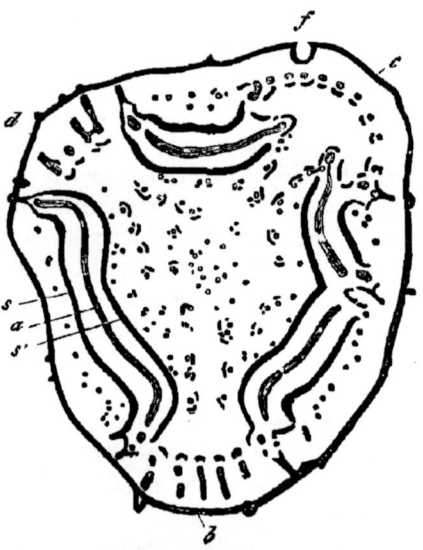

FIG. 193 —Part of the transverse section of the stem of a *Dracæna*, about 13 mm diameter. The very slender and thin walled proper vascular bundles are surrounded by thick, lignified sheaths of sclerenchyma, which, according to my view, convey the ascending current of water

FIG. 194 —Transverse section of the stem of *Cyathea Insrayana* (nat size) All the black streaks (*s s′*) indicate lignified sclerenchyma, the grey streaks and dots vascular bundles (*a*) (De Bary)

of *Allium*, the hollow cylinder of sclerenchyma is practically only lignified parenchyma; but here, as likewise in the *Piperaceæ*, it is not clear in which forms of tissue the current of water ascends, if not in the layers of sclerenchyma. Even in Dicotyledons it often happens that lignified strands or layers of sclerenchyma run through the shoot-axes, in addition to feeble vascular bundles deficient in wood

Hitherto all these sclerenchymatous structures have been considered only as means for promoting elasticity and rigidity, as they and the true wood in fact are. I conclude, on the other hand, that all layers of lignified tissue which may be followed continuously from the root through the stem into the transpiring organs serve as conducting organs for the transpiration-current, though they are at the same time of use as elastic and rigid masses.

The wood and lignified sclerenchyma are certainly not the only tissues which can conduct water within the plant; for simple reflection shows that large fruits, as those of the Gourd, absorb enormous masses of water into their parenchymatous tissues, though no corresponding lignified strands pass through them from the stem. The absorption of water in all young buds, as well as in soft non-lignified napiform roots and tubers, shows that a movement of water is likewise possible in

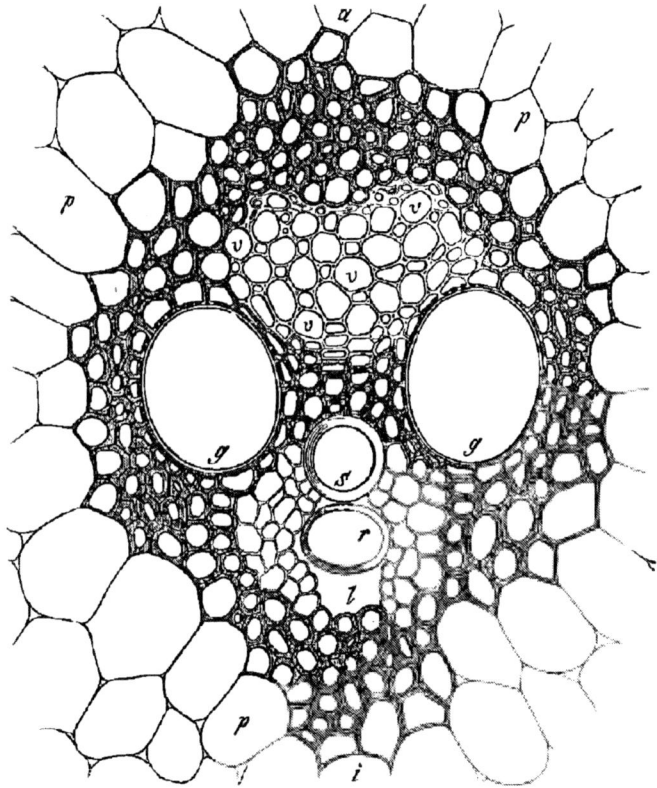

FIG. 195.—Transverse section of a vascular bundle in the stem of *Zea Mays*. It consists of the parts *v, g, s r, l p p* thin-walled parenchyma of the fundamental tissue Apart from the lignified cells between *g* and *g*, only the dark shaded sclerenchymatous sheath which surrounds the vascular bundle constitutes a woody layer worth mentioning and apparently suitable for the conveyance of the ascending current of water.

parenchymatous tissue, even without the presence of lignified cell walls. The distinguishing feature of the wood, however, is the great rapidity with which the particles of water can move in it; and just this rapidity is necessary where the transpiration-current of land-plants here considered is concerned. Hence we see that even very highly organised plants, when they do not transpire, or do so but little, possess no woody bundles, or only very thin ones—as, for instance, submerged and floating phanerogamous water plants, and those root parasites which develop chiefly under ground, as the Balanophoreæ, &c. The lignified layers and strands in the roots, stems, and leaf-stalks of the land-plants thus serve for the rapid movements of water, caused by transpiration [1]; this does not preclude, however, that slow movements of water of the most various kind may also take place in all the other forms of tissue of these plants. In the first place, it is quite certain that the water in the younger absorbing roots must pass through the external parenchymatous layers of tissue, in order to reach the axial woody bundles, and it is easily intelligible, again, that the thin fibro-vascular bundles of the petiole, which spread out and branch within the lamina as the venation, transfer their water to the parenchymatous chlorophyll-cells of the leaf, to which end, in fact, the whole mechanism of the water currents is set in motion. In the same way the cortical parenchyma of the shoot-axes, and even their epidermis, require certain quantities of water in order to make good the feeble evaporation at their surfaces, and there is no doubt that they draw this laterally to themselves from the stream ascending in the wood. Finally, the drooping and renewed turgescence of shoot-axes and thick leaf-stalks abounding in parenchyma, teach us that the water ascending in the woody bundles also passes over into the parenchymatous layers, because otherwise the restoration of the turgescent condition would not be possible. The distinguishing feature about all these movements of water in the non-lignified tissues, however, is the slowness and difficulty with which they occur, and this is clearly indicated in the whole organisation of the land-plants. The course of the woody bundles conducting the water in the leaves is so regulated, and the ramifications of the venation so constituted, that the water conveyed in the latter need only traverse an exceedingly short distance in order to enter into all the parenchyma cells of the leaf. We see also, at the same time, why the venation, especially of the strongly transpiring thin leaves of Dicotyledons, divides up the entire area of the leaf into so many exceedingly small areolæ; because by this means the paths of the water particles in the badly conducting parenchyma are rendered the shortest possible. In like manner the path taken by the water from the woody portions of the stem across into the cortex is never more than a few millimetres long, although a rapid supply is not at all necessary here. In the cases where large gourds, apples and pears, tuberous roots and tubers gradually absorb large masses of water into their parenchymatous tissue, which is not traversed by strong woody bundles, it simply depends not upon a rapid transpiration-current, but, on the contrary, upon an exceedingly slow movement of water, just sufficiently copious to bring about growth—the increase in volume of the cells. In contrast to this we find the woody body, or the strands of tissue equivalent to it, always the more strongly developed the more it is a matter of conveying large quantities of water in a short time to widely distant and large transpiring surfaces; and, remarkably enough, these considerations also confirm the fact that the same distribution of the lignified layers and strands, by which the elasticity and rigidity are obtained in the

---

[1] That the wood cell-walls differ essentially and entirely from other cell-walls as regards their conductibility for water, and the minute quantities of substances dissolved in it, and that, while imbibing less, they hold the water in a very mobile condition, I have also made evident in the treatise mentioned in note 1, p 230. This is opposed to the assumption previously current, and especially contrasts with the views put forth by Nägeli and Schwendener. In note 1, p 208, all that is necessary has been mentioned concerning the fact that imbibition is essentially different from capillarity, although the two have hitherto been always confounded.

stem and in the venation of the leaves, serves at the same time to deliver the water in a proper manner to the badly conducting masses of parenchyma. The lignified supporting tissues in slender upright stems are therefore brought close to the periphery, not only because they thus best promote elasticity, &c., but also because the loss of water at the surface of the epidermis can thus be most easily made good.

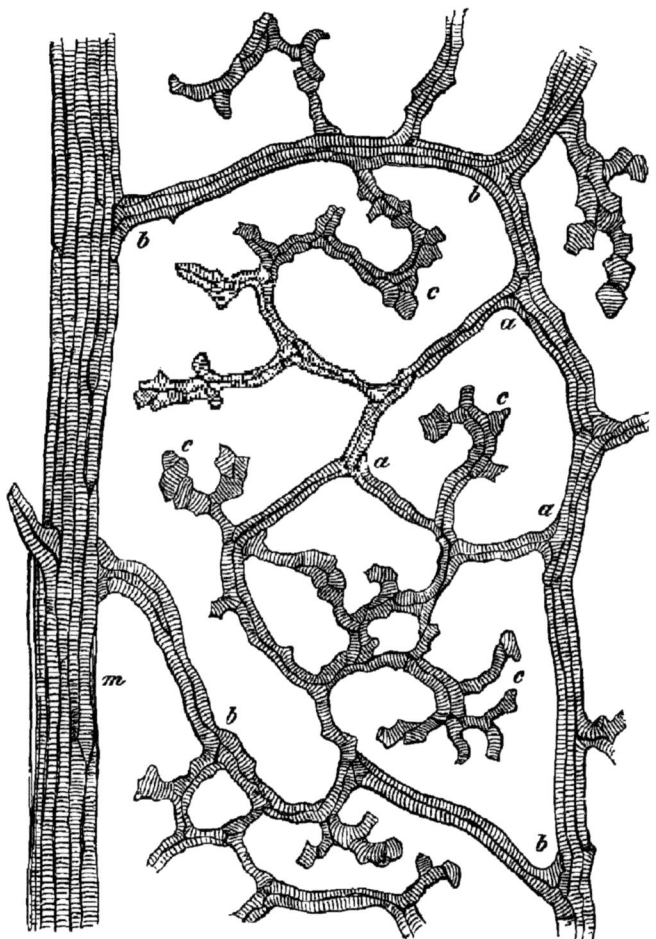

FIG. 196.—Lignified, water conducting spiral cells and fibres in the venation of the leaf of *Anthyllis vulneraria*
The enclosed interspaces or areolæ are filled up with transpiratory assimilating tissue

The same consideration shows that the venation of the leaves serves at the same time their elasticity and rigidity, and the appropriate supply of water

The wood is thus endowed with the specific property of allowing rapid movements of water to take place in it . it is therefore of interest to know how rapidly a particle of water moves in the wood of the stem under particularly favourable circumstances —that is, during very active transpiration from the leaves. Numerous researches which I have made in this direction with various kinds of plants, show that a distance of 50 to 80 or 100, occasionally even of 200 centimetres, is frequently traversed within an hour by a particle of water in the wood. It is obvious that when the transpiration at the leaves is feeble, and the quantity of water consumed small, the rapidity of the flow in the wood also diminishes; and that with the complete stand-still of transpiration, the movement in the wood likewise ceases, or at any rate sinks to a minimum in the event of a small supply of water being necessary for the purposes of growth of parts situated higher. Formerly it was sought in various ways to obtain an idea of the velocity of the ascending current of water, but all the different methods employed for this purpose have been shown to be faulty in the highest degree. I have shown that researches with cut-off branches are for our purpose to be rejected once for all; and that likewise the experiments made for centuries, in which coloured solutions were allowed to ascend in the wood, must ne-cessarily give velocities which are too small This is easily seen on reflecting that the colouring of the wood cell-walls simply consists in their seizing upon and holding fast the colouring matter, while the water of solution thus freed from the colouring matter speeds on in advance. This may be very clearly illustrated by means of the apparatus here represented. A strip of filter paper hangs with its lower end in a solution of colour-ing matter (*a*), e g of aniline violet or indigo. Even a few minutes after the immersion a disassocia-tion of the fluid is noticed : the upper limit of the coloured part (*d*) only ascends slowly in the paper strip, while the medium of

solution (*b c*), freed from the colouring matter, ascends much more rapidly The like must also happen when a cut-off branch is placed with the cut surface in a solu-tion of colouring matter, only in this case it is not observed how quickly the water speeds on in advance of the colouring matter Moreover in this mode of experimenting still further errors are introduced through the rarefaction of the air in the wood, to which I shall refer later Really useful observations on the velocity of the ascend-ing water current are obtained, however, when weak solutions of lithium nitrate are allowed to be absorbed by the uninjured roots of a transpiring plant For this purpose the plants must have been previously grown for some time in earth in a flower-pot, or have developed all their roots in a nutritive solution, according to the method to be described later, since it is impossible to obtain uninjured roots by digging them up and washing them. The lithium solution possesses, as I convinced myself with the aid of the paper strips previously mentioned, the advantageous property of ascending without becoming decomposed; and the lithium is taken up by the cell walls not more energetically than the water. It thus becomes a matter of ascertaining how high the lithium has ascended in one hour in the stem, and thence into the leaves, when a weak lithium solution of say 1–2% has previously been offered to the roots for absorption. The lithium has, moreover, the advantageous property of being recognisable in the interior of the plant, even in the minutest quantities, in an exceedingly simple manner, by means of the well-known intense red line perceived in the spectrum of incandescent lithium vapour by means of a spectroscope. It thus suffices to burn in a Bunsen's flame small chips of wood from the stem of the plant investigated, after this has been cut into small portions, to recognise by means of the spectroscope the presence of lithium; or the same observation may be made with portions of the leaves of the plant investigated. We owe the excellent idea of allowing lithium salts, on account of their easy detection, to be absorbed by plants, to Professor Mac-Nab, his researches however were so uncritically conducted that it required a protracted investigation on my part to put to actual use for our purpose the excellent properties of this substance [1].

With all that has been said hitherto, however, we have still obtained no idea as to the form in which, and as to the forces by means of which, the water ascends in

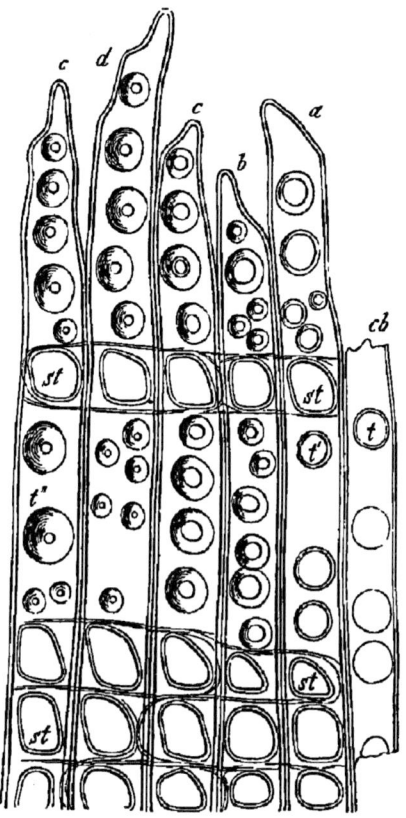

FIG 198.—*Pinus sylvestris* radial longitudinal section through the wood of a vigorously growing branch. *cb* cambium wood cells, *a—c* older wood cells, *b, b', b''* bordered pits of wood cells, in order of age, *st* large pits where the cells of the medullary rays lie in contact with the wood cells (× 550)

---

[1] In my treatise, ‘*Ein Beitrag zur Kenntniss des aufsteigenden Wasserstromes in transpirirenden Pflanzen*’ (Arb des bot. Inst in Wzbg , 1878, II p 148), I subjected to criticism the investigations made by MacNab and Pfitzer with solutions of lithium, and showed that only plants with uninjured roots can give satisfactory results. To quote some numbers here, for example; in a branch of *Salix fragilis*, with abundance of roots which absorbed the lithium solution direct, and not from the earth, the lithium ascended 85 cm. high in 1 hour. in two plants of *Zea Mays* under similar circumstances it ascended 30 and 42 cm respectively. With plants rooted in the soil and watered with the lithium solution, and placed favourably as regards transpiration, the lithium ascended, in 1 hour, 118 cm in *Nicotiana tabacum*, 206 cm in *Albizzia lophantha*, 107 cm in *Musa sapientum* 70 cm in *Helianthus annuus*, and 98 cm. in *Vitis vinifera*. That experiments with coloured solutions give no certain results, I have insisted upon in my ‘*Experimental-physiologie*,’ 1865, p 217.

the wood. To this end we must enter somewhat more in detail into the structure and the physical properties of wood In order to avoid unnecessary complications we will confine our consideration in the meantime to the wood of Conifers, such as the Pine, Yew, and Fir, because these woods possess no vessels, but consist only of tracheïdes, and are therefore relatively simple and homogeneous in structure. We must state, in the first place, the very important fact (shown by Theodore Hartig 20–30 years ago, but denied later by all phytotomists) that the histological elements of the wood are not in open communication one with another, and that the bordered pits of the wood-cells (and vessels of foliage-trees) are not actually perforated, but closed by fine membranes. Thence follows that the woody body by no means represents a system of continuous capillary tubes, but is formed of chambers distinctly shut off on all sides from one another. The purely micro-scopical and anatomical confirmation of this fact would, for our purpose, still leave room for much doubt, if the closure of the bordered pits in the wood were not established with absolute certainty in other ways. This is done most simply by means of the apparatus here figured. A piece of the stem of a Fir, or other Conifer, several centimetres long, and some 2–3 centimetres thick, and still provided with the cortex, is cut smooth at both sec-tions, and the one end fastened by means of caoutchouc to a long glass tube which is connected above with a wide vessel · the tube and vessel are now filled with an emulsion of cinnabar which has previously passed through several layers of filter-paper and therefore contains only cinnabar particles of the most extreme minuteness, which even with the strongest magnifica-tion appear merely as dots, and exhibit the so-called Brownian motion. By means of

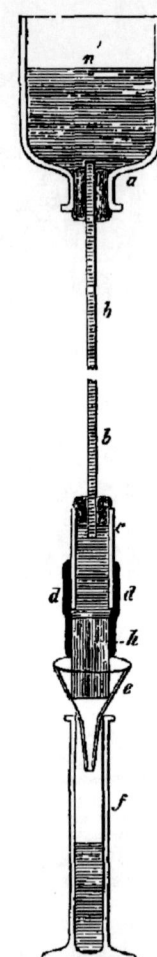

FIG. 199.—Apparatus for the filtration of water or emulsion of cinnabar through pine wood. The fresh piece of wood *h* is fastened by means of india rubber tubing *d* to the wide glass tube *c c* is connected with the narrow glass tube *b* (about 60 cm. long) by means of a cork. This tube is fastened above to the vessel *a* which contains water or emulsion of cinnabar *n* The water filtered through the wood passes through the funnel *e*, and is collected in the graduated vessel *f*

the hydrostatic pressure in the apparatus figured the fluid now filters through the wood: the water running off below appears quite clear and free from cinnabar, for the latter remains in the uppermost portion of the wood, not penetrating deeper than some 1·5 to 2 millimetres. The microscopic examination of this piece after several days' filtration now shows that the long wood-cells, which were opened by the section, are completely filled with the fine cinnabar particles; and that these have penetrated even into the cavities of the bordered pits and completely filled them It may here be definitely observed that the very minute cinnabar particles have penetrated even through the narrow pore of the pit into its cavity, but are there held fast, since a thin membrane prevents their passage over into the neighbouring cells of the wood. Only the cut cells of the upper end of the piece of wood have taken up particles of cinnabar, not the uninjured ones. A similar result is obtained if, instead of cinnabar emulsion, mercury is poured into the apparatus described, and left in it for some time The mercury does not pass through the wood of Conifers; but it fills the cells opened at the upper transverse section and the cavities of their bordered pits, without passing over into the neighbouring cells.

After thus establishing that the wood-cells of the Coniferæ are not in open communication (which is likewise true of the wood-cells and vessels of ordinary foliage trees), the theory which has existed for two hundred years, according to which the water ascending in the wood is considered to move as in capillary tubes, falls to the ground of its own accord. The hypothesis established by Quincke[1], that the ascending water may be drawn up as an extremely thin molecular layer on the surfaces of the walls of these capillaries, is likewise definitely refuted by means of our discovery. Both theories, however, would be wrecked without that, on the fact that even if continuous capillaries were present in the wood, they are closed in the roots below and in the leaves above; and that, further, the transverse section of these capillaries—i e. the wood-cells and vessels respectively—is far too large to explain, according to the known laws of capillary tubes, an ascent of the water in the wood to a height of more than a few metres.

Now, however, there comes in another quite decisive fact, by which the capillary theory of the ascent of the sap is likewise put aside: the fact, namely, that at the time when transpiration is going on in the leaves—that is, at the time when a rapid current of water is ascending in the wood—the cavities of the wood-cells and vessels of foliage-trees are not filled with water, as should be the case according to the capillary theory; rather, the wood-cells and vessels are only to a small extent filled with water, the vessels, however, being quite empty. This highly important fact is already to be concluded from the simple observation that fresh wood, cut out of the stem or branch of a transpiring tree in summer, and then thrown into water, floats; and since the cell-walls of the wood are without doubt specifically heavier than water, if their cavities were at the same time filled with water, such a piece of wood must sink like a stone. Instead of this, however, it floats, i e. it is lighter than water, and this fact is not otherwise explicable than by the assumption that cavities exist in the wood which are not filled with water.

---

[1] The possibility that the ascending water may pass up to the leaves as an extremely thin layer on the inner side of the wood cell-walls, was not suggested by me, but by the physicist Quincke, though it is true it was made public by me in my text-book This view was of course only tenable so long as the bordered pits of the wood were supposed to be open, according to the older statements of Schacht Since the proof that the pits of the wood are closed was afforded, however, by Sanio's and De Bary's anatomical investigations, and by my repetition of the elder Hartig's filtration experiments, Quincke's theory can, of course, no longer be spoken of

This supposition, moreover, is proved to be correct by two further facts. If a piece of fresh wood is placed in the fire, bubbles of gas are seen to be emitted with violence, evidently because the air contained in the wood is expanded by the heat and forced out at the transverse section, at the same time driving out with it a portion of the water contained in the wood. Again, we find that a piece of wood cut from a living tree, when laid upon water, gradually becomes heavier and sinks deeper and deeper, because it absorbs water: this would be

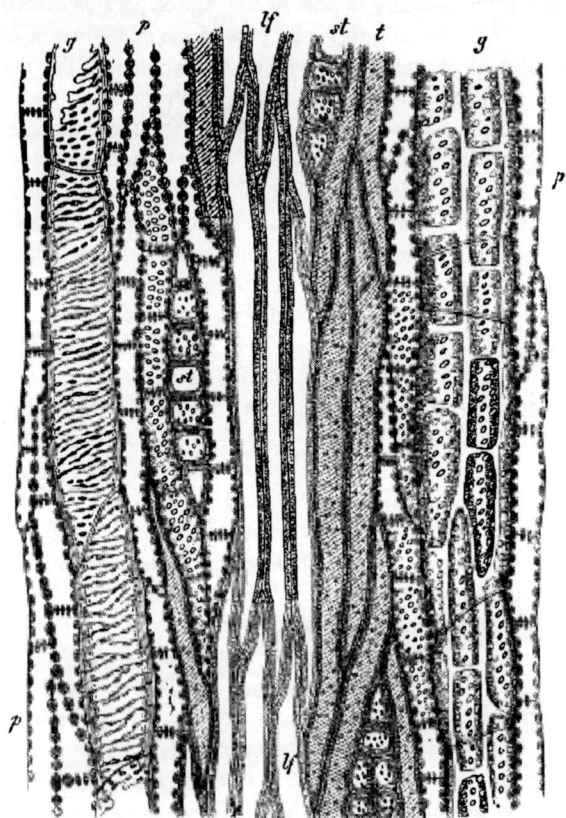

FIG. 200.—Tangential longitudinal section through the secondary wood of *Ailanthus glandulosa*. *g g* vessels; *st* medullary rays cut across; *p* wood parenchyma; *t* tracheides; *lf* libriform cells.

quite impossible if the cavities of the wood were actually already completely filled with water.

These observations prove then most decisively that just at the time of the most rapid ascent of water in the wood, the cavities in the wood-cells cannot be filled with water; that, rather, cavities containing air and vapour must exist in them. By means of more exact considerations and experimental researches, I have succeeded in finding a method by which we are able to determine in any given piece of wood, by a simple calculation, how large the empty space in the wood-cells is. For this purpose the specific gravity of the wood cell-walls must first be exactly determined. Among

other methods, I succeeded in doing this in the following manner:—Since it is
impossible to fill all the cavities in a large piece of wood with water, cross slices
0·1–0·2 millimetre thick were taken of the wood of Firs and ordinary foliage trees.
since now the wood cells are several millimetres long, all the elements in these cross
slices must be opened and cut through transversely. They were then boiled for a long
time in salt solutions, to remove any bubbles of air   These solutions were of calcic
nitrate and zinc nitrate.   The result was that the cross slices mentioned sank in such
solutions, though extremely slowly, when the areometer indicated a specific gravity of
1 56. This number thus expresses almost exactly the specific gravity of the wood cell-
walls; or, in other words, if one had a cubic centimetre consisting entirely of the substance
of the wood cell-walls, it would weigh 1·56 gramme, whence results immediately that
one gramme of wood cell-wall occupies a space of 0·641 cubic centimetre. Furnished
with this number, it is easy now to calculate in any piece of wood cut from a living
tree how large the spaces occupied by the lignified walls, by the water, and by the
cavities filled with air must be   First is determined the volume and the weight of
the fresh wood; it is then dried at 100°, and the weight of the dry wood determined.
The difference in weight obviously gives the weight of the evaporated water, from
which its volume follows immediately, since one cubic centimetre of water is exactly
one gramme. The specific gravity of the wood found above now allows us to
calculate from its absolute dry weight the volume of the cell-walls, since we divide
that weight by the specific gravity, and all else follows. To illustrate this by an
example—a cylindrical piece of wood, consisting of five annual rings, was taken from
the stem of a living Fir on the 2nd of January: the piece was 105 millimetres long
and 33 millimetres thick. From these dimensions the calculated volume is 89·8
cubic centimetres, and it was found, by immersion in mercury, to be 90 cubic centimetres. That the wood, though containing much water, still contained air, was clear
at once from the fact that it floated in water.

Weight of the fresh wood .	.	87 60 grammes
Weight of the dry wood	.	. 34·83 grammes.
Water in the fresh wood		. 52 77 grammes

From the dry weight of the wood we get $\dfrac{34\ 83}{1\cdot56} = 22\cdot33$ cubic centimetres as
the cubic contents of the cell-walls.

From these data it is calculated that 100 cubic centimetres of fresh wood
consist of—

24·81 cubic centimetres = mass of wall (calculated dry).
58·63   ,,   = water (in the cavities, and imbibed).
16 56   ,,   = air cavities.

Since intercellular spaces and vessels do not exist in the wood of the Fir, the
16·56% air cavities were thus contained in the wood-cells themselves, and since the
wood-walls, as we shall see, absorb by imbibition only about half their volume of water,
they thus contained only 12·4 cubic centimetres of water, the remaining water (viz.
46 23 cubic centimetres) must have been contained in the cell-cavities.

Consequently the volume of the cell-cavities is calculated as—

16·56 cubic centimetres containing air.

+ 46·23   ,,   containing water.

= 62 79 cubic centimetres of cavity altogether.

The volume of the saturated cell-walls as—

24·81 cubic centimetres dry mass of wall.

+ 12·4   ,,   water of imbibition

= 37 21 cubic centimetres saturated wood walls.

The space occupied by the saturated walls, therefore, in this case stands in the proportion to the space occupied by the water and air, as 1 . 1 68; or, the space occupied by the saturated walls is greater than a third of the total volume of the wood

It is to be noticed that in this particular case the piece of wood examined contained much water. Had less water been present the calculated space containing air would have turned out to be greater, since we may assume that so long as water is still present in the cavity of the cells, the cell-walls themselves are completely saturated with it[1].

The calculation given depends in part on the assumption that cell-walls, taken as dry, only imbibe water to the extent of the half of their volume. I was led to this assumption by the following considerations and results if a thin cross slice of fresh wood is suspended in dry air, there is generally formed during the drying of the wood a radial fissure, which forces its way from the exterior to the centre. Hereupon the cross slice is dried at 100° C, and the weight of the wood cell-walls determined; from which its volume is reckoned by means of the specific gravity The dry slice of wood is now again suspended in a space saturated with aqueous vapour, where it gradually condenses so much water, and at the same time becomes so distended by swelling, that the fissure produced during the drying again closes up, and this so completely that it is finally no longer to be recognised at all. In this condition the cell-walls must necessarily be completely saturated with water; and there is no fear of water being contained in the cell-cavities also. Weighing once more, gives the result that the water thus absorbed until the cell-walls are saturated constitutes about half their volume.

This last discovered fact is now, however, of particular interest, since it shows that the wood cell-walls have a strikingly small power of swelling, compared with other cell membranes which are capable of swelling, and especially with those which become mucilaginous in water, and take up enormous quantities of that liquid.

Here, then, we are face to face with the proper and specific physiological significance of the wood cell-walls. This consists in that they absorb relatively but little water, but that this small quantity of water of imbibition is strikingly mobile in them.

According to all that has been said hitherto, the ascending current of water in transpiration (in the wood generally) thus moves in the *substance of the cell-walls*

---

[1] The knowledge of the specific gravity of the wood cell-walls gives us also the power of calculating the extent of surface of all the cell-walls in a given piece of wood For a piece of fresh Fir-wood in winter I found, for example, that 100 c cm contained 25 c cm. of solid wall. Since now the thickness of a saturated wall may be assumed to average about 0 0025 mm, by dividing the volume of wall named by this thickness it results that the superficial extent of the walls in a piece of Fir wood 1 m long and 1 sq cm. in diameter = 10 sq. m

[3]   R

themselves   We have thus to imagine the water of imbibition of the latter as being in motion; and this is the main result of our considerations hitherto[1].   Any one may easily supply a striking proof of this, moreover   If the delicate stem of the Hop, Flax, etc be sharply bent beneath a few transpiring leaves, the cells at the sharply bent place must all be so compressed together that cavities containing water no longer exist   Thence follows, however, that the water ascending into the transpiring leaves can only go through the walls of the wood-cells, and that this actually occurs, follows from the fact that the shoots remain fresh above the sharply bent place—they remain thus fresh for weeks and months, even in the sunshine in the open.

The great mobility of the imbibed water of the wood cell-walls already established above, and on which the whole phenomenon of the water-flow thus depends, is a specific property of the lignified cell-walls, a fact which appears the more striking when it is known that other cell-walls capable of swelling to a great extent, though it is true they absorb water in large quantities, hold it immovably fast.   This is very conspicuous, for example, in the case of the stalks of *Laminaria*, the main mass of which consist of cell-walls capable of swelling; if a fresh stalk of this Alga is so placed in water that some centimetres project above, the immersed part remains swollen, but the part projecting above dries and shrivels up—a proof that the water ascends in it not at all or only exceedingly slowly.   Ordinary parenchyma cells appear to behave similarly.

As further characteristic of the wood cell-walls, in so far as they are the conducting organs for the ascending water, it is a remarkable but easily confirmed fact that they lose for ever their main property of conveying water when they have once become air dry.   It would be utterly in vain to look for an ascent of water at all rapid in an old dried up rod of wood placed in water.   The wood once dried has, it is true, the capacity of still becoming saturated with water of imbibition; but the mobility of the latter no longer exists.

It is evident that by the drying of the wood cell-walls, an essential alteration of their molecular structure has taken place, which, however, is not to be detected with the microscope.   Nevertheless this fact is established, and it is of the greatest importance for the life of plants.   The so-called freezing of woody plants in the long-continued cold of winter may serve as proof of this; for this phenomenon is something quite other than the freezing of succulent shoots and living leaves in the late autumn or in the spring time.   The dying of trees in long-continued winter cold depends to a great extent on the drying up of their wood, as we may convince

---

[1] For the guidance of readers not sufficiently acquainted with phytotomy, it may not be superfluous to quote the following from my treatise, '*Über die Porosität des Holzes*,' p. 292.   'The wood consists of a framework of lignified lamellæ, which enclose cavities (cell-cavities)   According to circumstances the cavities may contain water, or air (with aqueous vapour), or both   The walls themselves may be dry, or contain water (imbibed); and their volume or condition of swelling alters with the amount of water contained   The cell cavities of the wood are capillary spaces, the cell-walls, on the contrary, contain no capillaries into which liquid or air could directly penetrate.   In order to be able to judge of the movement of water in the wood produced by transpiration and other causes, it is necessary to sharply distinguish between the capillarity of the cavities and the imbibition of the cell-walls.'   That the ascending transpiration-current moves in the substance of the wood cell-walls I assumed (though with a certain reserve) in my '*Pflanzen-physiologie*,' p 216. it was first expressed definitely, however, in my 'Text-book.'

ourselves directly by cutting off single pieces. This wood, when once dried up, is no longer in a condition to convey water from the roots to the buds, and so the plants perish

We thus see that the wood owes its significance as the organ for conducting water to a series of most remarkable properties, which are found in no other natural body; and after what has been said, it would be simply childish still to attempt, as has been done previously, to derive the properties of the wood and the mechanics of the ascending water current from observations on capillary and porous bodies, such as gypsum, or from the endosmotic processes in an apparatus made with animal bladder, or even from the properties of parenchymatous tissues. The wood is a body *sui generis*, and especially adapted by nature for the purpose of conveying water (and even water laden with nutritive substances) from the roots up into the transpiring organs of assimilating plants The utterly incorrect views of the mechanics of the ascending water-current which were held previously to my re-searches '*On the porosity of wood*,' 1879, were especially characterised by the difficulties arising from the fact that water ascends in the wood up to heights of more than 100 m. into the leaves of tall trees, because it was always assumed here that it was a matter of capillary tubes. It is true water can also ascend in capillary tubes, but to a considerable height only when they are extremely narrow

Here, however, appears the difficulty perceived, but not overcome, by Nägeli and Schwendener, that the capillary movement in very narrow cavities is so exceedingly slow that it no longer suffices for the requirements of transpiration It was simply an entirely false principle from which observers formerly proceeded; since it depends not upon a phenomenon of capillarity, but upon imbibition and swelling, where, as I have shown in the preceding lecture, quite other molecular relations and forces are put in requisition. The force with which water is held fast in bodies which imbibe it is so enormously great, that it is quite immaterial whether the mass of wood saturated with water extends 10 m or 100 m. into the air above the absorbing roots, just as in the case of the salt solution of sea-water it is immaterial whether the dissolved salt molecules are suspended 100 m. or 1000 m above the sea-bottom The one point of special importance to be considered here is the facile mobility of the water thus held fast by the cell-walls This, however, is to be understood on observing that the wood cell-walls are saturated with water from their origin, and that every displacement of a molecule of water in them causes a movement of other molecules of water; whence it will be immaterial to the forces of imbibition whether the water molecule A or B enters into the sphere of attraction of a given molecule of wood.

The main result of all these considerations is this, that the ascending current of water depends upon the motion of the relatively small number of water molecules which are contained between the molecules, or 'micellæ,' of the wood cell-walls This much is established, that this movement can only occur when the wood cell-walls at the upper end of this system lose a portion of their water molecules. By this loss its state of saturation with water becomes disturbed, and the equilibrium altered: the parts of the wood cell-walls which have become poorer in water will tend to restore the equilibrium by attracting water from the nearest wood-cells, which, in their turn and for the same reason, take it up again from parts of the wood situated lower, until finally this movement, extending backwards, proceeds from the foliage of a land-plant down through the stem, into the young roots which absorb the water out of the earth.

That this motion of the water molecules depends upon the activity of their evaporation from the leaves is obvious at once, and has already been stated as a fact. On the other hand, however, it is also evident that the rapidity of the flow of the water must depend upon certain properties of the wood walls, which we designate by the word conductivity; if this becomes lessened by any means whatever, the evaporation at the leaves need not on that account be diminished to a like extent. If the latter now continue to transpire vigorously, while the supply is smaller than the loss of water, a deficiency of water must finally result in the leaves, and then even in the younger shoot-axes, and they will

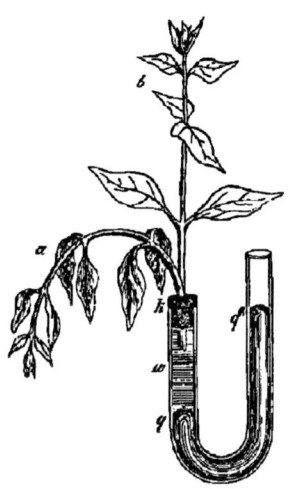

FIG 201 —The U tube is first filled with water, then the bored india-rubber stopper *k*, in which the stem of the plant is fitted, is inserted The shoot droops, as in *a* On pouring mercury into the other limb, so that *q'* stands some 8 10 cm, above *q* the shoot becomes turgid, as in *b*, and remains so, even when the level *q* subsequently stands higher than *q'*

droop, and since further arrangements (to be considered later) are met with, by means of which, with a want of water in the organs of transpiration, the transpiration itself becomes lessened, it follows that under certain circumstances a diminished conductivity can be inferred from diminished transpiration. The behaviour of cut-off shoots placed with the lower cut surface in water, gives occasion for these reflections. It might evidently be supposed that the cut surface of such a shoot would absorb the water in this form, more easily than when the cut surface is still in connection with the wood of the lower part containing water. This is not the case, however, since various experiments show that cut-off shoots placed in water gradually transpire less and less, and droop, which is evidently caused only by the imperfect conduction of water. If the shoot has been cut through far from the apex, at a part already strongly lignified, or if the lignification reaches right up into the apex when the winter buds are already formed and all the upper leaves are completely developed, then the phenomenon mentioned appears in a small degree only, and the drooping takes place only after some days; it occurs after a few hours, however, when a young shoot-axis is cut through, which is not yet, or is but little lignified, and in which the lignification does not yet extend into the apical part—e. g. in the case of the apex of a shoot of the Sun-flower 20–30 centimetres long, or one of *Aristolochia sipho* 40–50 centimetres long. On fixing such drooping shoots into a U-tube, as in the accompanying figure, and pressing the water (*w*) by means of a column of mercury (*q'*) into the cut end, I found that the shoot after some time again became turgescent and tense: the diminished absorption of water was again increased by the pressure, and the power of conduction, even when transpiration was energetic, restored to such an extent that after the pressure of the column of mercury ($q\,q'$) had become equalised, the shoot nevertheless continued to absorb water, and indeed with such force that the level q of the mercury was raised many centimetres high above q'. De Vries, who investigated this phenomenon further, found now that the withering of cut-off shoots only occurs very late, or does not occur at all, if the shoot-axis, before being cut, is bent down into a bowl of water, and the portion under water then cut through. This proves that the contact of the cut surface with air is one of the essential causes of the diminished conductivity at the transverse section; and that the alteration concerns not exclusively the section, but also parts of the conducting tissue higher up, may be concluded from the fact that the conductivity is again increased when a shoot, which has been cut off in the air and then placed in water, is cut through under the level of the water, but several centimetres above the first section. It is still questionable on what this injurious influence of the air, even on only momentary contact with the section, depends, and perhaps the sudden entrance of the air into the cavities of the wood filled with very rarefied gases plays a part in the matter[1] That the absorption of water at a cut surface of wood gradually diminishes, even apart from these circumstances, is shown by the fact that, by cutting off daily a small piece from the lower end, shoots standing in water may be maintained fresh for a much longer time. Evidently the absorbing section becomes altered and diseased by slimy substances and colonisations of Bacteria, and even when this is not the case, since the cut surfaces of the wood cell-walls gradually absorb large masses of water, the fine dust particles always contained in the latter must collect and cover the section with an impenetrable layer. This circumstance also brings it about that, when apparently pure water is filtered through fresh wood, it goes through at first with great ease, after which the filtration becomes slower and slower, if an extremely thin cross lamella is then cut off from the wood, the filtration again proceeds more rapidly for a short time.

---

[1] With respect to the drooping of the apices of cut-off shoots, cp. Hugo de Vries (Arb des bot. Inst in Wzbg I, p. 287)

LECTURE XV.

CONDITIONS OF TRANSPIRATION—ABSORPTION OF WATER AND
NUTRITIVE MATTERS BY THE ROOTS OF LAND-PLANTS.

THE main purpose attained by means of transpiration is, as already mentioned, that large masses of water, containing very small quantities of dissolved nutritive substances, are gradually carried to the organs of assimilation; these nutritive substances in their turn take part in the process of assimilation, while the greater portion of the water in which they were dissolved evaporates. The flow of water described in the preceding lecture thus subserves nutrition in this sense It now concerns us to become acquainted more in detail with the conditions under which transpiration itself takes place, and which accelerate or diminish the rapidity of the flow of water, and therefore that of the supply of nutritive matters also. Upon this depends, again, the rapidity with which the water enters into the absorbing roots; since in a land-plant growing under normal conditions, the quantity of water exhaled as vapour at the leaves is always nearly equal to that taken up by the roots, except in so far as possible additional circumstances, which I shall treat of in the following lecture, cause differences in this relation.

It is very easy to establish the fact that leaves or succulent shoot-axes, from which the epidermis has been taken off, as well as tubers and turnips after the peeling off of their periderm, dry up very quickly That this happens much more slowly in the natural condition, is evidently due to the epidermis or cork-tissue of the periderm respectively. These are permeable with difficulty, not only by water itself, but also by aqueous vapour; and this is certainly true in a still higher degree of the thick bark of old tree stems. Plants produce well-developed periderm and bark, moreover, only at those parts where transpiration is not to be permitted to take place.

We are thus concerned properly with the epidermis only; this, on the one hand, affords protection against the excessive evaporation of the water from the leaves and young shoot-axes, and, on the other hand, is specially organised for the purpose of rendering transpiration possible, and yet more, of limiting or accelerating it according to circumstances. The epidermis accomplishes the first object by means of the cuticle, and the waxy coatings, which, it is true, do not absolutely prevent the evaporation of water from the epidermis cells, but still render it exceedingly slow. The second object—the regulation of the evaporation of water—is accomplished by

means of the stomata, in so far that they can be opened and closed   The stomata
are, as was mentioned before, the external openings of the intercellular spaces of the
parenchyma, and, according as these openings are closed or open, the exit of the
aqueous vapour exhaled from the surfaces of the moist cell-walls in the intercellular
spaces is permitted to a greater or less extent.   The stomata and their movements

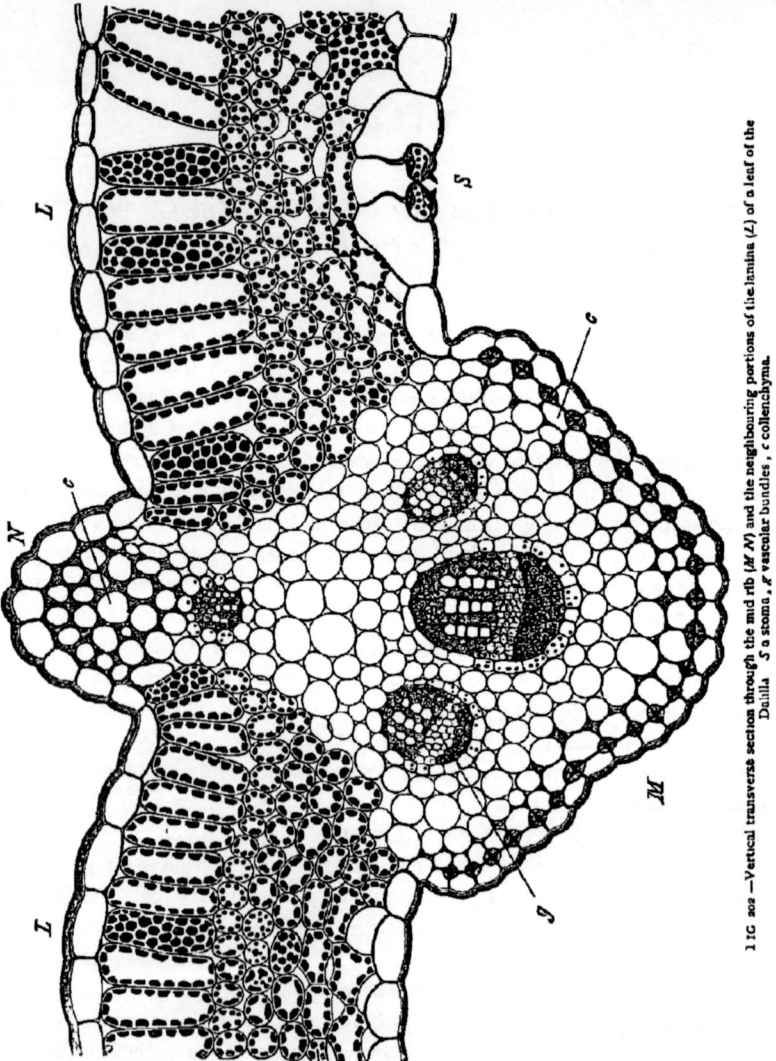

FIG 202 —Vertical transverse section through the mid rib (*M N*) and the neighbouring portions of the lamina (*L*) of a leaf of the *Dahlia*   *S* a stoma, *r* vascular bundles, *c* collenchyma.

which depend on irritability, have, as we see, a meaning only in so far as the epidermis
lying between them, and provided with cuticle and wax, prevents transpiration
in the narrower sense   The aqueous vapour is evidently to be given off not at any
haphazard spot of the epidermis, but by the walls of the intercellular spaces;
and these are particularly large and numerous in the assimilating parenchyma.

As the moist walls of the assimilating cells transpire their water into these spaces, they are enabled to attract a fresh supply of water from the wood bundles, the nutritive materials of which are absorbed in the interior of the assimilating cells. It is easy to see that in this way—that is, by the formation of vapour in the intercellular spaces—a more uniform supply of food to each cell is rendered possible, than if the water evaporated at the surfaces of the leaves themselves. Since, now, this aqueous vapour, arising at the proper places, can only escape through the stomata, the possibility is afforded of concentrating the supply of nutritive matters brought by means of the transpiration at those times when, under the influence of intense light, assimilation is actually taking place in the cells containing chlorophyll: for at this time the stomata are open, while they become narrowed in the shade, and closed in darkness. The mechanism of the opening and closing of the stomata is thus adapted to ensure a flow of nutritive materials from the soil to the assimilating cells, at those times when, through the open stomata, the entrance and exit respectively of the carbon dioxide of the atmosphere and the oxygen set free by its decomposition are much facilitated.

It would be extremely rash to suppose that, because submerged water-plants possess no stomata and do not transpire, the considerations here put forward are unimportant. The mode of life and organisation of water-plants are both essentially different from those of the land-plants. The transpiration and corresponding flow of material which they lack, are simply replaced by their being able, by means of their feebly cuticularised epidermis, to take up water and substances dissolved in it from outside at all parts; accordingly all those arrangements are absent which we are here studying simply as conditions of the life of land-plants. The importance of our considerations is not altered by the fact that small quantities of aqueous vapour can escape from the epidermis even without the aid of stomata. The question as to what extent this happens and whether it is of any use at all for the plant may, in fact, be altogether neglected. It may indeed be said that in no region of vegetable physiology has the concern for insignificant minutiæ led people so far astray from the insight into the great significance of the really important matters of organisation, as in connection with this matter of transpiration and all the concomitant phenomena. All possible minutiæ have been studied; but the principal fact, that it is a matter of the supply of nutritive matters to the organs of assimilation has been scarcely noticed. Since, however, as is clear from the preceding considerations, it is just the opening and closing of the stomata which regulate the transpiration, and with it the ascending current of water, and finally the absorption of nutritive matters from the soil, we will briefly enter a little more in detail upon the mechanics of these movements.

The opening and closing of the stomata are brought about by alterations in the form of the guard-cells, the nature of which is to be perceived most clearly from the figure here given [1] (Fig. 203). The thick lines mark the contours of the guard-cells in transverse section, at right angles to the surface of the leaf when the aperture is open.

---

[1] The statements in our text on the structure of the stomata, so far as the mechanics are concerned, are taken freely from Schwendener's treatise, '*Ueber Bau und Mechanik der Spaltöffnungen,*' Monatsbericht d. Kgl Akad. der Wiss zu Berlin, July, 1881.

The thin lines give the contours of the same cells when the aperture is closed. The figure shows at once that it is not simply a matter of the projection of the inner thin lamella, indicated by *d*; but that the whole guard-cell changes its form in the process of opening and closing. On account of their firm connection with the neighbouring epidermis cells, this has for its consequence at the same time a displacement of both the guard-cells in space also. The other figure (203 *b*) shows the form of the two guard-cells as seen from the surface; the guard-cell *A* is drawn in the condition in which it is when the aperture is closed, while the cell *B* represents the form when the aperture is open. Here, however, it is to be noted that the dark part *a a'*, by no means corresponds to the parts marked *d* in the above figure, but to the ledge there marked *a*. It is to be noticed in this figure that with the opening of the aperture, the curvature of the outline of the guard-cell *B* increases; and that this behaves like a bent tube, which on swelling presses with its two ends against the corresponding parts of the other guard-cell, while the back portion recedes, and the aperture opens. Stomata are found in various plants, it is true, in which the form and position of the guard-cells deviate from those here

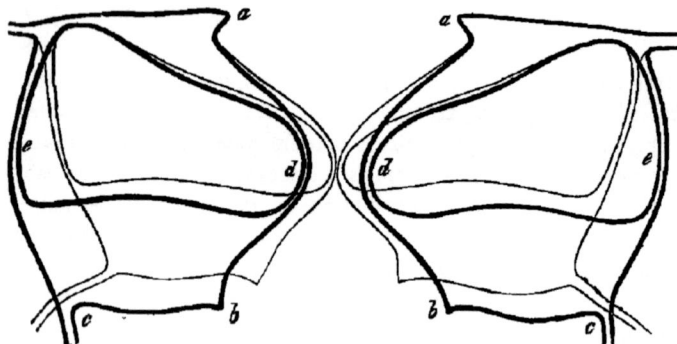

FIG 203 —Transverse section of a stoma at right angles to the surface of the leaf. The thick contours show the form of the guard-cells in the open condition, the thin ones the form when closed.

described: in principle, however, the mechanical relations to be considered are always the same In the first place, the guard-cells are always thick and strongly cuticularised at their outer and inner walls (Fig 203 *a* and *b*), and the cuticle generally forms more or less strongly projecting cushions or ridges at the places indicated, which surround the outer and inner entrances to the aperture On the other hand, two thin walls exist in every guard-cell one, usually the larger, where the guard-cell joins the next neighbouring epidermis cell (*e* in Fig 203), while a thin lamella, generally lower down, bounds the proper aperture of the stoma at *d*. In the relaxed condition, with slight turgescence, the thick places *a* and *b* tend to become straight, and parallel with the slit-like aperture; hence they compress the relaxed cell in such a manner that the thin part at *d* becomes pushed outwards. If, however, the guard-cell absorbs more water, which is facilitated by the thin wall at *e*, the thin portion *d* tends to expand in the vertical direction: now, however, it necessarily becomes itself drawn back, since it assumes a more vertical position, as shown by the thick contours in Fig. 203. It is easily seen that the thick ridges *a* and *b*, which are fastened at the two ends of the guard-cells (cf. Fig. 203, *b*), must become curved by this, and by means of their elasticity they bring it about, that, as soon as the turgescence is diminished, the guard-cell becomes compressed and straight, and that the walls are driven outwards as in Fig 203. These are only the most important and obvious points in the mechanics of the opening and closing of the stomata. So far as concerns the transverse section of a guard-cell, the matter may be briefly put thus: the guard-cell, as turgescence increases, tends to assume a more symmetrical form, and, as the turgescence diminishes and the aperture closes, a less symmetrical form, as is shown at once by Fig. 203[1].

Although the desired certainty does not yet exist with respect to the external conditions under which the stomata open and close, so much is at any rate certain, that the apertures open in sunshine, and under strong illumination generally, when the guard-cells increase in turgescence, and that they close in shade and darkness, when the turgescence of the guard-cells diminishes. In the first place, it is clear that the alterations in turgescence must result from the entrance and exit of water; and that in this process it is the epidermal cells bordering upon the guard-cells which give up or again

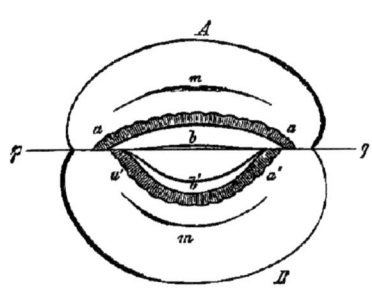

FIG 203 *b* —Stoma seen from above (externally) The upper half of the figure shows the form of a guard cell when the stoma is closed, the lower half that when open.

absorb the water. In this connection the thin lamella *e, e* (Fig. 203) is important, in so far that it facilitates the passage of the water. The question is now, how does the light bring about an increase of the turgescence of the guard-cells; and why does this diminish with declining illumination? With regard to these points, Schwendener, from whom the preceding description is in the main borrowed, has expressed no opinion It appears to me, however, that the fact which I have repeatedly brought forward during the last twenty years —that the guard-cells of all foliage leaves contain chlorophyll-grains and the products of their assimilation, which are usually wanting in the surrounding epidermal cells— can now be explained. The chlorophyll-grains in the guard-cells will, as the illumination increases, produce carbo-hydrates by assimilation; these are at least partly soluble, and act endosmotically, and thus bring about an inflow of water from the neighbouring epidermal cells through the thin boundary wall. Or at least so much may be assumed with certainty, that by the presence of the chlorophyll in the guard-cells generally, a supply of organic substance is ensured in them, which according to circumstances may cause a diffusion current. It will require further researches to decide whether this is really sufficient. Besides this, however, a direct influence of light upon the molecular condition of the protoplasm may come into consideration; so, indeed, that we may here have to do with a phenomenon of irritability in the narrower sense of the word. We may imagine that, as the intensity of the light increases, the protoplasmic utricle clothing the cell-wall becomes more resistant, opposes the hydrostatic pressure of the cell-sap more strongly,

---

[1] See note 1, p. 248

and prevents the filtration of the water from the guard-cells into the epidermis, without, however, interfering with the filling of the cells by endosmose; in the dark, on the contrary, or even as the intensity of the light diminishes, the protoplasmic utricle would, according to my assumption, become more permeable and less resistant to filtration, and in consequence of this a portion of its water might be pressed out from the guard-cells, previously forcibly distended, through the wall *e.* That such an irritability is not opposed to the phenomena of irritability elsewhere existing in the vegetable world will be sufficiently demonstrated by subsequent lectures on the irritability of plants.

To any one ignorant of the facts, the theme here treated of may appear somewhat small and insignificant, on considering how extremely minute the stomata are, and that the diameter even in the open condition amounts to only a few hundredths of a millimetre. Through such extremely fine openings (of which we may obtain an idea by drawing out glass tubes to hair-like fineness) only extremely little water can evaporate or other gas pass even in a long time. But the fact is altered when we reflect how extremely numerous the stomata may be on the assimilating green foliage-leaves—one hundred to two hundred on a square millimetre of the epidermis are common, and they are not rarely much more numerous; so that a leaf say the size of the hand possesses many millions of such fine openings, which simultaneously open when the sun shines on the leaf, and simultaneously close when it becomes shaded. The alteration in the discharge of the aqueous vapour developed in the intercellular spaces, effected by the opening and closing under varying conditions of illumination, is enhanced by the warming of the tissues of the leaf, which usually accompanies intense illumination, so that an increased formation of vapour then takes place Consequently the tension of the vapour is raised, and it is forcibly expelled from the open apertures. In the shade and in darkness, on the other hand, the formation of vapour in the interior diminishes as the temperature falls, and the stomata being closed, the vapour at low tension is retained; whence complete saturation of the intercellular spaces with vapour must soon occur, preventing the further formation of vapour, especially during the sinking of the temperature at night. It scarcely needs mention that all these considerations can only refer to the stomata on the organs of transpiration; and that, self-evidently, those occurring on subterranean shoots and on parasites containing chlorophyll, only come into consideration in so far as they present, since they exist, open paths of communication for an extremely slow exchange of gases, and that we have here to do with organs of modified or even entirely suppressed function

Besides the varying illumination, and the consequent opening and closing of the stomata, account has to be taken of many other factors, by means of which transpiration may be accelerated or diminished In the first place, so much is clear, that even when the stomata are open, the escape of aqueous vapour from them must be less rapid in proportion as the surrounding air is already laden with vapour. In other words, transpiration must be diminished by the moisture of the surrounding air; it is entirely prevented, however, only when the air is completely saturated, and the temperature of the leaves is not higher than that of the surrounding air. Were the latter the case, the aqueous vapour, expanded even more by the higher temperature, could still escape. Since, further, the formation of vapour from moist surfaces, and thus from the cell-walls which bound the intercellular spaces of a leaf, is accelerated by a rise of temperature, transpiration must increase with a rising temperature, always provided the stomata be open. According to some observations made several years ago in my laboratory, it is not improbable that the mere shaking of shoots facilitates the exit of water from the leaves; this is in so far worthy of closer investigation that the significance of the wind, and the vigorous shaking of foliage-shoots effected by it, might be explained more in detail. That motion of the air acts favourably on the transpiration of leaves, as it does on evaporation from any moist body, is obvious on a little reflection; but the shaking of shoots may, in addition, favourably affect the mere expulsion of the vapour from the intercellular spaces.

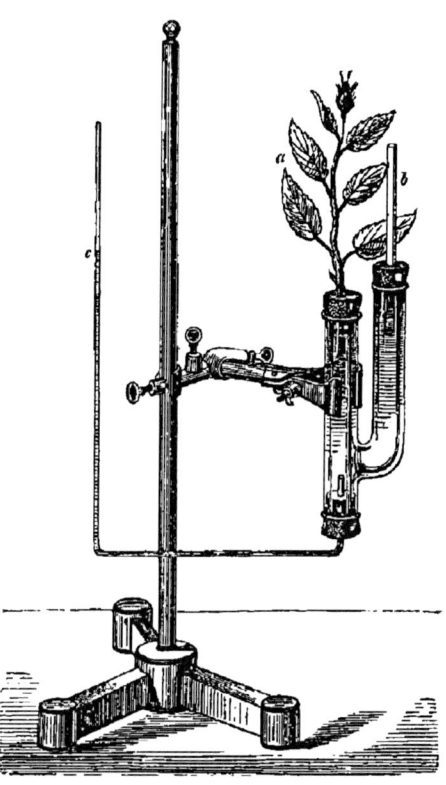

FIG. 204 —Apparatus for demonstrating the suction and transpiration of a shoot under various external conditions. The shoot *a* is fastened water tight into the middle glass tube at *b* a thermometer is inserted in the same way, which, by being pushed in, serves at the same time to bring the level (*c*) of the water in the narrow tube at any time to its original height again, when it has sunk by the suction of the shoot during 1—5 minutes. If the shoot is large enough, and the apparatus not too heavy, it may be placed on a scale and the loss in weight by transpiration be determined at the same time

More than twenty years ago I further confirmed the remarkable fact, already in part noticed by Senebier, that the transpiration from leaves may also be altered by the presence of materials dissolved in the water which the roots take up[1]. Weak solutions of those salts which plants employ as nutritive materials,—e. g. potassium nitrate, gypsum, &c.,— poured on the soil in which the roots are, bring about a noticeable retarding of the transpiration. The same takes place when uninjured roots, developed in solutions of nutritive materials, take up solutions of nutritive salts instead of pure water Cultivated plants in a strongly manured soil will therefore in general transpire more feebly, and make use of less water, than those in a soil poor in food-matters It is at present hardly possible to give an entirely satisfactory explanation of this fact; since, although it is known that aqueous vapour is given off less easily from a salt solution than from pure water, still the pheno-

---

[1] On the changes in transpiration by the influence of salt solutions at the roots, cp. my treatise in the paper, '*Die Landwirthschaftl. Versuchsstationen,*' 1858, I, p. 203, and '*Bot. Zeitung,*' 1860, No 14. More recent facts are quoted in Pfeffer's '*Pflanzen-physiologie,*' Bd. 1, p. 151.

menon in question is far from being explained by that. However, here again we recognise the significance of transpiration for the nutrition of the plant, since it is clear that water strongly charged with nutritive salts requires to be supplied to the green organs of assimilation in less quantity than if it contained but little of these substances.

In concluding the preceding remarks, and as an introduction to what follows, I may now briefly advert to the question whether the water ascending in the wood cell-walls, which evaporates in the leaves, does really carry with it the nutritive matters—the sulphates and phosphates of the alkalis and alkaline earths—dissolved in it, and transport them into the assimilating cells of the leaves. This question is justified, because for a long time the transport of these materials was supposed to take place in another manner. It was assumed that the living cells of the root-cortex, abounding in sap and containing protoplasm, take up these substances from the water of the soil surrounding the roots, according to the laws of endosmosis; and that likewise, proceeding from cell to cell, from the roots right up into the leaves, endosmotic processes transport the salts into the organs of assimilation, without the co-operation of a continuous current of water What is here considered is a movement of the molecules of salt dissolved in the water, independent of a current of the water itself. If we suppose an isolated cell, lying in water which contains saltpetre, for example, while none is present in the cell, then a certain quantity of the molecules of this salt will, in spite of the cell-membrane and protoplasm, pass into the cell, and if this stands in connection with a series of other cells, these also will gradually take up the molecules of salt. This would take place to an extent so much the greater if the salt-molecules were decomposed in the interior of the distant cells, and by this means an endosmotic equilibrium prevented from re-establishing itself. This form of the movement of material certainly occurs in submerged water-plants, in root-parasites growing underground, and here and there also in the tissues of the land-plants, but considerations of the most various kinds led me years ago to the view that in transpiring land-plants, and especially in shrubs and trees, the vital conditions of the plants could not be correlated in this manner. The endosmotic movements of the salt-molecules referred to, are so slow that they could not possibly supply the foliage of a tree with the large quantities of nutritive salts which there co-operate in assimilation, and are actually shown to be present in the leaves by analysis When I had fully substantiated the ideas, already pointed out incidentally by Unger, that the transpiration current of land-plants moves not in the cavities but in the substance of the cell-walls of the wood, the question arose whether the water ascending in the wood cell-walls is not perhaps pure water, or whether it carries with it the soluble salts contained in the soil, and conveys them into the leaves. The probability of the latter assumption was increased by the consideration that we have to deal with only extremely dilute solutions—water in which the dissolved molecules of the salts concerned are contained only in extremely small quantity; perhaps 1 2000 or even less Further, it was to be observed that even in the ordinary endosmotic movement salt molecules go through the substance of cell-walls and protoplasm. I was thus able to conclude, further, that also the few molecules contained in the ascending current are carried forward in the substance of the wood walls, simultaneously with the water. These considerations receive full experimental confirmation by the fact that even a salt (lithium nitrate) not belonging to the ordinary nutritive materials answers the condition required by me, and ascends in the wood walls with the transpiration current.   If, as already mentioned, a weak solution of lithium is poured on the roots of a land-plant, the latter continues to transpire, and after one or two hours the lithium is already found in the leaves situated fifty to two hundred centimetres above the roots.   If the leaves be cut off and immersed, with the exclusion of the stalk, in pure water, lithium may be recognised in the water after a few hours, having come out of the epidermis by diffusion.   It is by no means to be supposed that this rapid movement of the lithium in the plant has taken place by endosmose from cell to cell: it has evidently ascended with the transpiration current in the wood cell-walls, and in the same manner the nutritive salts mentioned are likewise sent into the leaves.   What has been said, however, does not exclude the fact that endosmotic movements of salt-molecules take place where necessary even in woody plants: when the cells of the living cortex, or the assimilating cells of the transpiring leaves decompose phosphate of lime or sulphate of magnesia and the like, in their interior, molecules of these salts, ascending with the water in the wood walls, will be able to enter by endosmose into the interior of the cells named   We shall obtain a correct idea on the whole if we suppose that the water ascending in the wood extends in the first place into all the cell-walls, even of the parenchymatous tissues of the cortex and leaves, and takes with it the salt particles dissolved in it; thus the cell-contents become surrounded on all sides by a layer of water, which is between the molecules (micellæ) of the cell-membrane. The cell-wall framework of the entire plant contains at the same time the store of water and salts for all the cells.   If one of the latter requires water, it finds it in the first place in its wall; if, on the other hand, it requires a number of salt molecules, these also are contained in the water of the cell-wall, and can enter at once into the interior.   Everything is of course far more simple in submerged water-plants, which can take up water and the salts dissolved in it at every point of their surface; with the slender structure and the numerous large intercellular spaces of the water-plants, the path which the materials in the cell-walls have to describe is rarely greater than 1 mm., and even the slowest movement suffices to satisfy the requirement.

The question has for a long time been ventilated whether the leaves are not able, at least under certain circumstances—e. g. during continuous rain, or when they are covered with dew—to absorb water and substances dissolved in it.   Numerous researches directed to this end have yielded no satisfactory result whatever, but it is by no means difficult to apprehend the essential points without that.   If the whole plant is filled and turgid with water, and particularly the leaves, it is not clear how the latter are to take up more water from without; if, on the other hand, they are drooping, and not quite filled with water, it depends upon the constitution of the cuticle whether and how rapidly they are able to absorb water. The fact is, that drooping shoots, especially of wood-plants, when inverted and plunged in water, so that the cut end of the stem projects, often remain drooping for days in spite of the surrounding water, and thus absorb none; and it is obvious that this is the case in general so long as a layer of air clings to the surface and prevents the wetting of the leaves.   If the leaves become actually wetted, however, small quantities of water can also penetrate into the tissue, according to circumstances, and even any particles of salt contained in the water may enter. This must be concluded with certainty from the fact that leaves permeated by lithium nitrate give up the lithium to the surrounding water The same follows also from the fact that drops of water which are allowed to cling to the surfaces of leaves show an alkaline reaction after some time, because small quantities of alkaline salts have diffused out from the tissue [1]; and that substances of the most various kind penetrate from outside into the leaves, is shown by the extraordinary sensitiveness of the latter to vapours of ammonia, chlorine, nitric and sulphuric acids, for example, which injure fields and gardens in the proximity of factories to a large extent But all this does not prove that any considerable quantities of water, and salts dissolved in it, are conveyed by means of the leaves to the land-plants, and that the activity of the roots and of transpiration is supplemented by this means. When leaves and shoot-axes droop after a hot day, and again become fresh as the sun goes down, this happens in no case by the absorption of aqueous vapour from the air which has again become moist, but simply depends upon the fact that with diminution of the transpiration the turgescence of the organs becomes restored by the continued supply of water from below.

It appears from what has just been said, that the normal supplying of land-plants with water and nutritive matters dissolved in it, is the function of the roots distributed in the earth The peculiarities and difficulties, to be spoken of afterwards, with which the absorption of these matters from the soil is connected, as well as the very large quantities of water which must be absorbed, evidently constitute one of the causes which bring it about that transpiring land-plants containing chlorophyll, in contrast to the water-plants and parasites, produce such copiously branched root-systems, consisting mostly of hundreds and thousands of individual root-fibres I have expressed myself more in detail concerning this in a previous lecture The copiousness of the root-system corresponds simply to the extent in surface and function of the organs of transpiration Where, as in submerged water-plants, transpiration is completely wanting, only very few roots or none at all exist; and in the former case these serve in the lower plants (Algæ), as has been shown previously, only as anchoring organs. The floating plants provided with an evaporating surface (e g. *Stratiotes, Hydrocharis, Lemna*) have, it is true, more or less developed roots, the function of which, however, is but little in demand, because the leaves only transpire feebly in the moist atmosphere, and, on the other hand, the roots surrounded by liquid water can absorb it without hindrance. Bog-plants are also in a similar position with regard to the activity of their roots: the crown of leaves, it is true, transpires considerable quantities of water, but their roots are in a soil completely saturated with water, and are able to absorb it unhindered. They are in fact much more abundantly rooted than the floating and submerged water-plants, but still are

---

[1] With regard to the alkaline reaction of drops of water placed on living leaves, and the fact, already discovered by Théodore de Saussure, 1804, that alkalies can be washed out of living leaves, more is to be found in my treatise, '*Ueber alkalische und saure Reaktionen der Safte lebender Pflanzenzellen*' Bot. Zeitung, 1862, p 257.

provided with root-fibres, not so numerous by far or so densely filling up the soil as in the case of the proper land-plants. It is characteristic of the mode of life of the latter that they only flourish, as a rule, when their roots are distributed in a soil which is relatively dry, and only incidentally saturated with water. Thus, just those plants which exhale the largest quantities of aqueous vapour by means of their assimilating leaves are adapted by their roots to a soil in which relatively little water is contained ordinarily, and especially at the time when most water is made use of In order to understand this completely, it is to be noted that it is in the months of May, June, July, August, and September that the transpiration and nutrition of our cultivated plants, field plants, and forest trees are particularly active, that is, at a time when the earth is completely saturated with water by the rain only now and again, while weeks and months often pass, during which these plants are necessitated to take up by vigorous transpiration large quantities of water from a soil which, as the most superficial inspection shows, contains relatively only small quantities of that liquid. And this apparently unfavourable circumstance is really quite necessary for the well-being of the truly terrestrial plants; since, as is well known, fields of which the soil is too damp are made in a high degree favourable to vegetation by drainage, and the like is true of gardens and forests The cultivation of plants in greenhouses and rooms also teaches that land-plants which are rooted in flower-pots very easily perish from rotting of the roots if they are watered too often, and it is one of the most elementary rules of the cultivation of plants in pots, to let the earth in the latter become very dry each time before fresh water is poured on The roots of land-plants thus properly carry on their functions continuously only when the soil surrounding them is as a rule relatively poor in water, although a complete saturation of the soil for a short time does not at once act injuriously The condition normally favourable for the roots of transpiring land-plants is therefore this; that they are distributed in a soil which, in addition to small quantities of water, contains at the same time spaces filled with air, by means of which the respiration of the roots is maintained. Very often, however, during long continued drought, the quantity of water contained in the soil sinks so low that the latter appears almost air-dry; and it seems scarcely intelligible how the roots are able to extract from it the large quantities of water transpired through the leaves. It thus concerns us to obtain an accurate notion as to how the roots of land-plants accomplish the absorption of such large quantities of water, from a soil relatively poor in water. I made this problem the subject of deep reflections and experiments so long ago as 1859 [1], and presented the results in a connected form in my *Handbook of the Experimental Physiology of Plants*, 1865. The figure already employed there to illustrate the behaviour of the roots in the soil, may here again serve for further explanation. For the absorption of water, it is only the younger portions of the individual root-fibres, distant some centimetres from the root-cap, which essentially come into consideration—parts which, not yet covered with periderm, are provided with thousands of root-hairs. It is these root-hairs which bring about the immediate connection of land-plants with the soil which nourishes them We may therefore confine our considerations to the behaviour of

---

[1] For the behaviour of capillary water in the soil, I refer to my treatise in the paper, '*Landwirthschaftl. Versuchsstationen*,' 1859 Heft. IV, p 1.

a single root-hair, which has been protruded from a young root into the surrounding soil.

In Fig 205, *e* is the epidermis of a root which has grown perpendicularly downwards; the root-hair *h h* has been developed as a protuberance of an epidermal cell, and at *g* and *s* it is closely applied to single particles of soil, as seen below. The bodies *T*, shaded dark, are microscopically small particles of earth, between which are cavities containing air—left completely white. Each particle of soil is enveloped by a thin layer of water, which is held fast by surface-attraction: where the attraction of neighbouring particles of earth co-operates at the re-entering angles, these otherwise thin layers of water form thicker masses. These aqueous spheres are indicated in the drawing by waved lines (as at β and γ). The surface of the root-hair is also (as at *a*) clothed with a thin layer of water, and its walls are saturated with that fluid, the spaces left white are filled

FIG 205

with air Let us now regard the root-hair for a moment as inactive, and suppose no disturbance at all to be taking place in the soil Then all the aqueous spheres of the particles of earth are not only in contact with one another, but also in equilibrium. If we were to take away the layer of water at γ, for example, the equilibrium would be disturbed throughout the entire system, and water would flow from δ and β and other places, towards γ, until the forces were in equilibrium If we now assume the root-hair *h h* to absorb the water *a* or *τ*, this penetrates through the membrane into the interior of the hair, or it moves along *τ*, *a*, *S*, in the substance of the wall itself: the surface of this wall at *a* or *τ* thus possesses less water than corresponds to its power of attraction. It attracts it, therefore, at the spot *τ* this then absorbs water from β, and the movement proceeds towards γ and δ, &c, until the molecular equilibrium of all the aqueous spheres is again established. By this means they all become thinner and thinner, and the soil as a whole drier. This desiccation, however, may make itself

[3]   s

evident not merely in the immediate neighbourhood of the root-hair, but at the same time affect the more distant parts, since by the absorption through the root-hair at a or τ, a continuous flow of the adherent water of δ takes place towards γ, β, and a. This assumption is supported by the observation that the earth of large glass vessels in which plants are grown, dries up not merely in the immediate neighbourhood of the absorbing roots, but, so far as the colour of the earth allows us to recognise it, the desiccation increases equally in all parts even far from the roots   This movement of water on the surfaces of the particles of soil, easily deduced from molecular forces, is confined therefore not simply to microscopic distances.' Every root-hair is itself the centre of a current directed from all sides towards it, and at the surface of a small piece of root covered with thousands of root-hairs there results a similar movement, which carries the aqueous particles in the soil from all sides, but especially radially, towards the axis of the root.

If we suppose the aqueous envelope of a particle of soil to consist of several very thin layers, $a, b, c \ldots n$, according to its thickness, so that n is the outermost, and a the one immediately in contact with the particle of soil, then the water molecules of the elementary layer a will be attracted with a maximum force, and in the layers b c, &c., further removed, this attraction diminishes progressively, and if n represents the outermost layer, when the soil is just saturated with water, the molecular attraction in it is only just great enough to prevent the water from dropping off.   In the case last assumed, when an absorption of water takes place at a or τ, the outermost layer of the aqueous spheres moves first, in order to restore the disturbed equilibrium of the whole system, and flows towards a and τ; because this outermost elementary layer is most loosely held, and is therefore most easily put in motion.   The more water the root-hair has already taken up, the thinner are the aqueous spheres of the entire system, and the greater the force with which the elementary layer now outermost (c, for instance) is held fast; and the greater must the forces be which draw the water into the wall of the root-hair, and the more difficult and slow the transmission of a disturbance from a to $β$, $γ$, and $δ$.   A condition of the aqueous envelopes may finally ensue, where the elementary layers still remaining are held so fast by the particles of soil that no more water enters the wall of the root-hair.   In this case, their surfaces may possibly be still clothed with a very thin layer of fluid, which indeed is wanting to no saturated body.   If now the root is in connection with a leafy stem above ground, transpiration from this organ will go on removing water from the plant; this loss, however, under the circumstances given, can no longer be compensated by absorption on the part of the root, and the interior of the plant becomes deficient in water, the cells, no longer sufficiently turgid, become flaccid, and the leaves droop   Conversely, it is also possible under certain circumstances to conclude from the drooping of the leaves, and from the quantity of water known to be contained in the soil, as to the condition which denotes equilibrium between the suction of the root and the forces of adhesion in the soil.

I have in a few cases sought to determine the percentage of water contained in the soil when Tobacco plants rooted in it were no longer in a condition to withdraw the minimum of water from it   This takes place when the leaves droop in a moist atmosphere, even at night, and therefore when the loss by transpiration is very small and the compensation afforded by means of the roots is at a minimum; when this is no longer afforded by the roots, equilibrium has nearly set in between the absorbing forces at the surface of the root and the absorptive power of the soil for water. The carrying out of such determinations cannot from their very nature be quite exact, and thus the following numbers are only intended to afford a definite idea of the matters described. Under certain circumstances a young Tobacco plant began to droop when the soil, a mixture of sand and black beech humus (in a room), still contained 12·3% of its dry weight of water, determined at 100°C. This soil, dried at 100°C., was able, however, to retain 46% of its weight of water by adhesion. Consequently, of the possible amount of water in this soil, only 46—12·3 (i e. 33 7%) was at the disposal of the Tobacco plant; the 12·3% of the imbibed water still present was held so fast, that the roots were no longer able to take it up.

Another almost similar Tobacco plant, standing near this, drooped during a rainy night, when the loamy soil surrounding its roots still contained 8% of water, 100 grammes of this loam, however, were able to retain 52 1 grammes of water by adhesion or absorption; accordingly this soil, saturated with water, gives up to the plant only 52·1—8 (i e. 44 1%) of its water.

Under like conditions a third Tobacco plant drooped when its roots were in coarse-grained quartz sand, which, in 100 parts of its weight, still contained 1 5% water. This sand, dried at 100° C, was able, however, to retain 20·8% water, consequently 20·8—1·5 (i e 19·3%) of water altogether were at the disposal of the plant, after saturation of the soil had taken place.

The more the last remnant of water adheres to the particles of soil, the greater also will be the amount of water contained in the soil at the time when the root is no longer able to extract water from it; the humus soil still contained at this time 12 3%, the loam 8%, the sand only 1 5%. Since the drooping only took place when the soil showed this poverty in water, these examples demonstrate that the Tobacco roots still withdraw at least small quantities of water from the soil up to the time when the soil is air-dry, since the proportions of water named correspond approximately to the air-dry condition of such soils; and these researches show at the same time that plants still withdraw water from the soil even when it is no longer possible to squeeze any out of it by pressure.

From these facts, now, it is to be seen that it is by the intimate contact or attachment of the root-hairs with the particles of soil that they succeed in sucking up into the plant the extremely thin layers of water of the latter. This union of root-hairs and particles of soil has, however, still another very important significance. Only by this means are they enabled to take from the soil the nutritive materials necessary in addition to the water In fact, certain materials indispensable for the plant, such as sulphates of lime and magnesia, as well as extremely small traces of other nutritive salts, are without doubt dissolved in the thin layers of water which surround the particles of soil: this follows from the fact that the water running off from the drain pipes of tillage soil contains these substances. But a number of the most valuable nutritive materials are held so fast in vegetable soil, that it is impossible to wash them out with such quantities of water as are conveyed to them by the rain. These materials (chiefly potash, ammonia, phosphoric acid, and the less important silica) are found in the soil in a peculiar combined condition: they are, as we are accustomed to say, absorbed. An

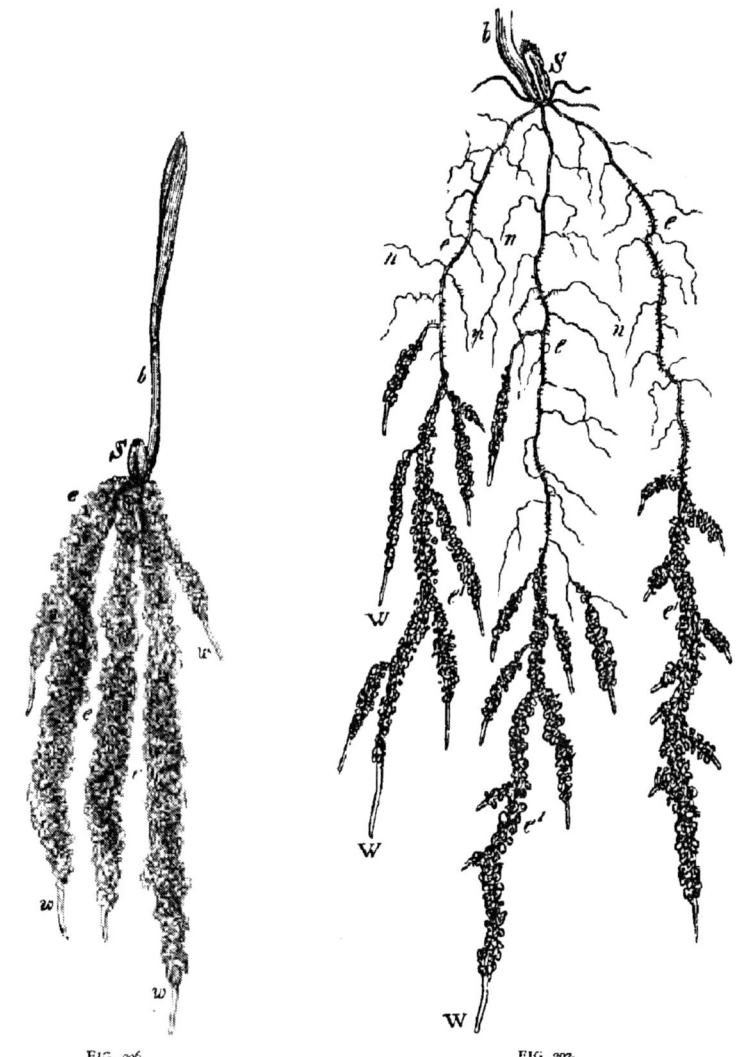

FIG. 206.   FIG. 207.

Fig. 206. Seedling of Wheat plant. Fig. 207. The same four weeks older. *S* the seed coats, &c ; *w* the apices of roots not yet furnished with hairs; *e* parts attached to the soil (in Fig. 206). In Fig. 207 the hairs are already perished on these parts. *e'* younger parts of roots attached to soil.

illustration of this fact[1] is obtained most easily by filling an ordinary funnel

---

[1] On the absorption and taking up of absorbed matters, a very thorough account is found in my '*Handbuch der Experimental-physiologie*,' 1865, p. 178. The corresponding section in Pfeffer's '*Pflanzen-physiologie*' (1881) shows that essentially nothing new is to be added concerning the subjects mentioned in the previous and following notes.

with about a kilogramme of damp soil from a field or garden, and then pouring over it a weak solution of potash salts, phosphates, or ammonia compounds. If the fluid running off below be then examined, only slight traces of the materials named are found in it, or even none at all, though lime and magnesium sulphate are generally present in large quantities. It is therefore necessary to pour on very considerable quantities of pure water, in order to gradually wash out again part of the materials previously held fast in the earth, the soil of vegetation thus acts on these nutritive materials of plants, as animal charcoal on colouring matters and other chemical compounds.

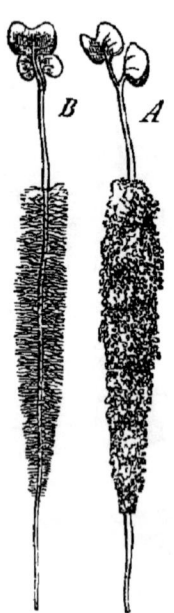

FIG. 208.—Seedling of White Mustard. *A* is taken out of the soil and shows the particles of soil clinging to the root hairs in *B* these have been removed by washing in water

FIG 209 — Root hair of a seedling of Wheat closely attached to particles of soil (highly magnified, cf. Fig. 206).

Meanwhile it is of little interest for us to know in how far purely chemical or even molecular forces come into consideration in the absorption of the materials in the soil So much is at any rate established, that chemical compounds of potash, ammonia, and phosphoric acid, are retained with great force on the surfaces of the small particles of soil, forming extremely fine coats on them. But it is these substances which must be taken up by the root-hairs, and it is obvious that this is only possible by the root-hairs coming into the closest and most extensive contact with the particles of soil. Since the nutritive materials clinging to the particles of soil are not soluble—or but very slightly so—in the layers of water, the root-hairs, as they apply themselves fast to the surfaces of the particles, must themselves effect the solution of the absorbed materials. This they accomplish by means of the extremely thin membrane of the root-hair being permeated with an acid fluid, which, coming in contact with the surfaces of the particles of soil, renders soluble the molecules of absorbed materials adhering there. it thus becomes possible for these substances to penetrate into the root-hairs according to the laws of diffusion, and thence to pass over into the stream of sap, to be carried finally to the organs of assimilation. That the root-hairs are, as a matter of fact, able to bring the whole of the potash salts and phosphates necessary to vigorous vegetation from the absorbed condition into the plant, may be easily demonstrated by repeating an experiment first proposed by Naegeli in 1861. I am accustomed to make the experiment in the following way: bits of peat which, according to chemical analysis, contain practically no potash salts and phosphates, are laid for some days in a 1–2 per cent. solution of any potassium salt (e g. potassium phosphate), or even in a solution of a complete nutritive mixture such as we shall learn more about later on, until they are completely soaked. The bits of peat are now lixiviated for some days in pure water, frequently renewed, until the latter no longer contains any traces of potassium and phosphoric acid: they are then broken up into small pieces, and a large flower pot filled with them. Seeds of Maize, Wheat, Tobacco, Hemp, Gourd, Beans, or other plants are now sown in this medium. It suffices to water in the usual manner with ordinary spring water, which is always rich in sulphates of lime and magnesia, or with a very dilute solution of gypsum, magnesium sulphate, and calcium nitrate in distilled water. On the completion of germination the plants then go on growing as in good garden soil, and attain to complete development and vigorous production of seeds; while plants of the same species cultivated in a similar manner, except that the peat soil had not previously absorbed any phosphoric acid and potassium salts, remain exceedingly feeble, and languish. Such experiments prove that the quantities of phosphoric acid and potash necessary to vigorous development are taken up by the root-hairs from the surfaces of the pieces of peat.

By means of the acid fluid which permeates the walls of the root-hairs, the latter are able to dissolve even solid and crystallised minerals. In the year 1859 I showed[1] that roots which become closely applied to the polished surfaces of marble plates, corrode them, so that after some time a corrosion figure of the roots is obtained on the marble surface. Of course it is not to be supposed that these corrosions penetrate to any considerable depth, they are evident rather only as extremely fine rugosities on the polished surface. I subsequently showed that

---

[1] I first drew attention to the corrosion of polished stone plates, '*Bot Zeitung*,' 1860, p 118, &c. More details in my '*Experimental-physiologie*,' p. 188

similar corrosion figures are to be obtained also on polished surfaces of Dolomite (a mixture of calcium carbonate and magnesium carbonate), of Magnesite (crystalline magnesium carbonate), and of Osteolite (earthy apatite, chiefly tribasic calcium phosphate) when the roots of Beans, Maize, Wheat, Gourd, *Tropæolum*, Peas, and others are caused to apply themselves closely, and grow over the polished surfaces of these stones The experiments were made by laying the plate of stone, with the polished surface turned upwards, at the bottom of a vessel 10–15 c.m. deep; this was then filled with clean washed sand, and several seeds placed in the latter. With sufficient moisture the radicles grow vertically downwards until they abut upon the polished surface, there they bend to one side, grow on horizontally, clinging to the polished surface, and form lateral roots which likewise become closely attached. When after 8–10 days, in summer, the vessel is upturned, and the stone plate carefully washed and dried, the corrosion figure of the roots is seen on the polished surface The experiment succeeds with such certainty that it may be used for demonstration in lectures.

It follows from these facts that the root-hairs, when they meet in the soil with small pieces of stone which contain carbonate of lime, compounds of phosphoric acid, magnesite and dolomite, dissolve small quantities of these salts at their surfaces, and carry them into the plant. Since now the soil of vegetation is a very various mixture of small particles of stone with organic remains, so-called humus, different hairs of the same root, and likewise the hairs of different roots of a plant, find opportunity here and there of taking up sometimes chiefly phosphates, at others potassium compounds, &c., and conveying them into the sap of the plant. In this, each individual root-hair of course accomplishes but very little, the quantity which it is able to take up will perhaps only amount to the millionth part of a milligram. As we know already from previous study, each root-hair remains capable of action but a few days, however, on a plant even of inconsiderable size there are millions of active root-hairs, and as the older of these die, millions of new ones appear in their place, to use up portions of the soil not yet laid under contribution We must here remember what was said in the organography of the roots, that behind each root-apex as it grows forward in the soil, new root-hairs are continually arising, while the older ones further behind on the root perish (Fig. 207). Since now, at the same time, new root-fibres spring in various directions from those already existing, and extend in the soil, new portions of the latter are continually being placed in requisition by the root-hairs, and thus the whole of the soil, permeated by the thousands and hundreds of thousands of fine root-fibres of a plant, is gradually used up.

The roots thus evidently contribute to the chemical decomposition of the solid particles of stone in the soil of vegetation,—a process which proceeds at the same time slowly by means of the carbonic acid contained in the soil, and of the nitric acid contained in the rain water, and if the rotting remains of vegetation are again incorporated in the soil, the vegetable mould must in this way continually become richer in soluble and absorbed nutritive matters. This influence of plants on their mineral substratum is clearly evident where Lichens

and Mosses attach themselves to the free surfaces of rocks, e.g. on high mountains   The solid crystalline surface of the stone becomes gradually converted, by
the activity of the roots of these plants, into a friable crumbling loose substance,
which continually penetrates deeper into the stone, and so presents a substratum
in which even the stronger roots of larger plants can then obtain a hold.
In a certain sense, the roots thus behave towards the mineral constituents of
the soil much as the roots of parasites behave towards the tissues of their host
plants; we shall return to this subject later, however.

If we now throw another glance on the matters treated of in the present
lecture, the fact is clearly demonstrated that the plant undertakes the absorption of its nutritive matters by means of its own activity, and is by no means
simply passive. In the first place the root-hairs, after they have become closely
applied to the particles of soil, have to take up the water clinging fast to
the latter, as well as the equally closely attached nutritive substances   The
next step is to convey these substances to the assimilating organs, the
green leaves   The wonderful properties of the wood cell-walls, which are
comparable with nothing else, permit the ascent of the water and the small
quantities of salt dissolved in it through the stem up to the leaves, but only
in so far as these latter themselves regulate this movement according to their
needs: when strong light promotes turgescence in the sensitive guard-cells of
the stomata, causing them to open, the aqueous vapour escapes from the intercellular spaces of the leaf simultaneously with the oxygen of the decomposed
carbon dioxide, and as assimilation thus commences, the ascending water current is set in motion by this continued open condition of the stomata, and,
starting from the apex of the root-hairs, conveys the constituents of the soil
which are indispensable in assimilation into the tissues of the leaves containing
chlorophyll.

That the roots are not merely passively concerned in the absorption of water
from the soil, but are independently and actively engaged in it in consequence
of certain irritabilities, I convinced myself first in the autumn of 1859, on observing[1] that the leaves of plants of Tobacco and Gourd rooted in flower-pots
drooped when the earth was cooled down to a few degrees above zero, and
thus absorbed less water than was requisite to cover the feeble transpiration.
The warming of the flower-pot sufficed to increase the absorption of water so
far that the drooping leaves again became turgid. This phenomenon can also
be brought about in summer, if the pots in which sensitive plants are rooted
are cooled by surrounding them with pieces of ice. It is not all plants however
which are provided with roots so sensitive to temperature, but only those, as it
appears, which come from warm climates. Cabbages, for instance, and other native
plants did not droop when I cooled their roots. On the other hand, again,
it is certain that in all plants the absorbing activity of the roots is invigorated
by an increase of temperature up to $25°—30° C$; as is apparent, for instance,

---

[1] I have described the drooping of leaves when the roots are in earth too cold for them in the
paper, ' *Landwirthschaftliche Versuchsstationen*,' 1859, I, p 238.

from my success in causing a great number of very different plants to excrete water at the edges of the leaves in the form of drops, by warming the roots—the consequence being a vigorous absorption and forcing up of the water into the leaves.

The excretion of drops here mentioned I shall consider more in detail in the next lecture.

LECTURE XVI.

EXCRETION OF WATER IN THE LIQUID STATE.

ALTHOUGH the phenomena to be treated of here are far less important for the life and maintenance of the plant than transpiration—i. e. the excretion of aqueous vapour by land-plants—it is nevertheless worth while to examine more closely the excretion of liquid water which takes place in plants under very various circumstances; especially since it affords us a deeper insight into relations of structure and of mechanical arrangements in the plant. From this point of view the excretions of water termed 'bleeding' and 'weeping' particularly excited the interest of the older vegetable physiologists at the end of the seventeenth and beginning of the eighteenth centuries

By the terms Bleeding and Weeping are designated those excretions of water which occur under certain circumstances in consequence of injuries, generally such that water is exuded in greater or less quantity fiom fresh transverse sections of the wood. Two essentially different cases have to be distinguished, however, viz, first, the case in which water is exuded from the wood-body in consequence of a rise of temperature, and in which, above all, the activity of the roots does not take any part; and secondly, the case where, from wounds in the wood, relatively large quantities of water are exuded during long periods, which did not previously exist in the wood, but must first have been absorbed by the roots. The first phenomenon, which I shall name the bleeding of wood in winter, can be produced just as well with isolated cut-off pieces of wood as with rooted woody plants; while the other phenomenon, which I distinguish as the weeping of the root-stock, only occurs in vigorous, rooted, living plants, although similar exudations of water, but very much less in quantity, may also occur under certain circumstances with separate portions.

The bleeding of wood in winter[1] is observed in its most typical form if, on a cold but frostless winter day, a portion of a branch of a tree (*Rhamnus,* Hazel, Pine, Walnut, Birch, &c.), about 25-50 centimetres long and 2-5 centimetres thick, is cut off, and the two cut ends smoothed with a sharp knife Outside in the cold air the smooth sections appear relatively dry, and no liquid water is to be seen, even at the lower section, when the piece of branch

---

[1] Cp my treatise, '*Quellungserscheinungen an Hölzern*' (Bot. Zeit 1860, p. 253), where the older literature is collected also. The explanation of the phenomena there described by me is found in my treatise, '*Über die Porosität des Holzes*' (Arb. des bot. Inst. in Wzbg B II, p. 291).

is held vertically. When the object is brought into a warm room, however, or, still better, wrapped in a warm cloth, clear water gradually oozes out from the wood at the lower cut end; and if the latter is then held for some few minutes through the opened window out in the cold air, the exuded water is plainly seen to be slowly sucked in again, until the surface of the section appears distinctly dry. If the cold piece of branch is placed in a cylinder of warm water at 25—30° C., so that only the upper section protrudes, water again oozes forth: this occurs first at the most external layer of the wood and then progressively oozes from the inner and older rings of the alburnum, in accordance with the progressive warming from without inwards. Small bubbles of air come out of the vessels with the water, and are forcibly ejected. If the object is lifted out and at once brought in the same position into a cylinder of cold water, the layer of water on the cut end then sinks again into the wood, again also progressively from without inwards as the cooling effect penetrates, until the section appears dry

From this simple experiment several things are to be learnt. In the first place, it is by the warming of the wood that water is expelled at the cut end, and in fact the water is driven from the warm to the cold place. In accordance with this, cooling brings about the re-absorbtion into the wood of the expelled water   Secondly, detailed studies in the winter of 1859 showed me that the quantity of water expelled always represents only a relatively small proportion of the total quantity of water contained in the wood. It is obvious, and is demonstrated by observation, that the phenomenon only appears at all when the wood contains relatively large quantities of water. The poorer in water it is, the more it must be warmed to bring about the emission of water   As Hofmeister first recognised, basing his opinion on my observations, the whole phenomenon depends chiefly upon the expansion of the air contained in the wood   We saw in the lecture before last, that the wood-cells, even of wood very rich in water, are never entirely filled with water, but that a portion of their cavity is occupied by air-bubbles   It is the expansion of this air, saturated with aqueous vapour, which forces out the water from the wood-cells; and the cooling of these air-bubbles, on the other hand, effects the suction by which the water is again drawn in. That the change of volume of the water itself is far from sufficient to explain the quantity driven out, I had already established by my investigation. Since, however, the wood-cells are closed on all sides, and the vessels may here be neglected for the time being, and since the phenomenon appears also in the wood of Conifers, which has no vessels, the water driven out by the expansion of the air-bubbles in the wood must obviously be forced through the cell-walls themselves; this, of course, will take place most easily and rapidly through the thin portions of wall which close the pits   With a slight rise of temperature, now, the force with which the air-bubbles drive out the water is relatively feeble; and from the fact that the water filters with facility through the wood cell-walls, we draw the conclusion that wood, even when it contains no vessels, must be in a very high degree permeable. In how high a degree this is the case I convinced myself[1] some

---

[1] With respect to the extraordinary facility with which the filtration of pure water takes place through fresh wood, further facts are also to be found in the treatise last cited

years ago, with fresh, vigorous pieces of living Pine. When a film of water was placed with a brush on the upper transverse section of a piece of the stem even 1 — 3 m. long, it sank in a few seconds into the wood, while an equal quantity of water appeared at the lower section,—a proof that the smallest pressure can be equalised by means of filtration through the wood   By this and other experiments I convinced myself, also, that the spring wood of the annual rings is more permeable by far than the autumnal and heart wood.

I may take this opportunity also of mentioning the very remarkable fact that the air in the wood-cells, as well as in the vessels of living plants, is in a high degree rarefied—a fact which I had already stated hypothetically in 1865, but which is now better known, and can be easily demonstrated. The simplest proof that the air in the wood-cells exerts a feebler pressure than the atmosphere, lies in the fact that a freshly cut piece of wood, when laid in water of like temperature, absorbs it eagerly, as may be easily proved from the increasing weight of the wood. This absorption, however, is simply nothing further than the forcing in of the water by the pressure of the external air, which, in its turn, can only exert this influence when and so long as the tension of the air contained in the wood, together with its aqueous vapour, is feebler than the pressure of the atmosphere, or in other words, if the air-bubbles saturated with vapour in the wood had the same tension as the atmospheric air, it is by no means obvious how fresh wood, the cell-walls of which are saturated with water, and the cavities, at least in part, filled with it, could still take up water; and this is, of course, still much less the case if the cavities of the wood were already quite full of water In 1874 Hohnel made known the remarkable fact that when a branch of a living plant is bent down into a bowl of mercury, and there cut through, the mercury penetrates far into the vessels. In a few seconds the mercury penetrates several centimetres into the vessels of both parts of the shoot, and so much the further the wider the vessels are. If the capillary repulsion between the vascular walls and the mercury is also regarded, one is led to the conclusion that the latter must be forced into the vessels by a considerable pressure, or, if one will, suction. The pressing force, however, is no other than the pressure of the atmosphere on the mercury; and this is only in so far effective as the pressure of the air in the vessels is smaller, or, in other words, because the air in these is rarefied. The rarefaction may be very considerable, and Hohnel calculated from his experiments that the pressure of the air in the vessels may sink to $\frac{1}{2}$ or even $\frac{1}{3}$ of the atmospheric pressure, and I have sought to make it probable that, under certain circumstances, younger vessels and wood-cells may even be completely empty of air and only contain aqueous vapour[1]   In fact,

---

[1] I have already propounded my view that wood-cells and vessels may be devoid of air under certain circumstances in '*Arbeiten des bot Inst in Wzbg.*' (II, 1879, p 324) I may simply add one remark here. When, on the death and disappearance of the protoplasm from wood-cells and vessels, the watery sap contained in their cavities comes into immediate contact with the lignified walls, it is imbibed under the influence of the neighbouring wood cell-walls The water contained in the recently developed wood-cells and vessels enters into the ascending transpiration current and is carried forward by this. The imbibing force of the wood cell-walls here effective, however, is, as we know already, enormous, and may be able to withdraw the water from the fresh wood-cells

air from without can only penetrate into the cavities of young vessels and wood-cells with difficulty, when the latter lose the protoplasm and sap with which they were previously filled. Meanwhile, without entering more into detail respecting this point, it is obvious that the air in the wood-cells, which is always rarefied, must become still further expanded and rarefied if a great portion of the water contained in them is quickly conveyed through the wood cell-walls to the transpiring leaves. Hohnel's experiment, moreover, as I have shown, may be made more evident so far as the vessels are concerned, with dark solutions of colouring matter; and again, I have, by cutting off the branches of living Conifers under a solution of lithium, also been able to convince myself that this solution quickly penetrates to a considerable distance into the wood-tissue This is to be recognised by the spectroscope, in the manner previously indicated; and demonstrates anew that the air in the wood-cells as well as in the vessels is rarefied

It is clear that these facts may be employed to explain several still obscure phenomena concerning the water contained in the wood of living trees. The obscure facts to which I here refer consist, not in that the water ascends in the wood cell-walls up into the crown of the highest trees, since this, as we saw before, is quite intelligible from the imbibing force of the wood cell-walls. it has been hitherto unintelligible, however, how the liquid water comes into the cavities of the wood-cells. If only woody plants of a few metres high were concerned, or the lower portions of a tall tree stem, one might believe that the rarefaction of the air in the wood-cells acts as a sucking apparatus But every such suction is simply nothing more than the difference of pressure between the atmosphere and the rarefied internal air. Thus, if the cavity of the wood-cells were entirely empty of air, and devoid of aqueous vapour, the suction, or, what is the same thing in this case, the whole external pressure of the air could only force the water about ten metres high in the wood of the stem, even if the cell-walls opposed no resistance.

It still remains unexplained, moreover, how the action of the atmospheric pressure on the surfaces of the root is to be imagined Moreover, the wood-cells situated much higher in a tree contain liquid water, in addition to air, and this at any rate cannot be explained so simply by differences of atmospheric pressure.

Meanwhile, I only bring these doubts forward here because they render clear the question with which we are concerned Sooner or later it will yet be shown that the rarefaction of the air in the wood, in combination with peculiar arrangements not understood hitherto, brings it about that liquid water gets into the wood-cells, even at considerable heights Concerning this, also, I may mention that the rarefaction of the air is easily observed even in the vessels of small herbaceous plants; and that a fact so general can certainly not be accidental and without significance for the life of the plant. Whether it may be regarded

---

and vessels with such force that the latter become completely empty Vapour under a pressure corresponding to the temperature alone remains in their cavities. When observations show that air (though very much rarified) is contained in the cavities of wood, this must have penetrated by slow diffusion from the exterior.

as promoting the movement of the imbibed water in the lignified cell-walls may well be conjectured, but cannot be proved.

If we bear in mind the phenomena observed on warming and cooling a piece of wood cut off in winter, it is clear that within the stem of a living tree, movements of water will also occur in the interior of the wood, through the unequal warming at different heights which must necessarily occur with sudden changes of temperature. When, for example, the sun shines on a tree after a cold night, the thinner branches are more rapidly warmed than the thick stem, and the water is driven from them into the latter, and conversely, with the increasing cold of night the branches become more rapidly cooled than the thick stem, and take up water from the latter. With a rise of temperature in winter, tension in the wood generally must occur, since the air-bubbles in the wood-cells on becoming warmed tend to force the water through the walls, which is prevented by the cortex. If, however, a hole penetrating as far as the alburnum is made with an auger, and an exit-tube, bent downwards and opening at the bottom of a flask, is placed in it, these effects of changes of temperature may be made visible. As the temperature rises, water flows out of the hole into the flask, this has simply been expelled by the expanding air-bubbles of the wood. On the recurrence of cold weather, however, the air-bubbles contract; and the consequence of this is that the water which had flowed out into the flask is again sucked up through the tube into the wood. Although, as was shown above, the water expelled by the rise of temperature is always only a small portion of that present in the wood, nevertheless several litres of water may be driven out from a large tree in an experiment of this kind, if the increase of temperature is sufficient, since the water contained in the wood of a large tree may certainly amount to hundreds of litres. Moreover, the phenomenon need not be confined to the winter; it may continue also in the spring, and even in summer (e g. with the Birch), since it only depends upon how much water is contained in the wood, and upon the corresponding changes of temperature. The characteristic fact of this kind of bleeding, however, simply lies in that it takes place even in winter, and independent of the period of vegetation.

The second kind of bleeding, or the weeping of the root-stock, is distinguished from that hitherto considered, in that it only takes place during the period of proper vegetative activity, when the roots have already commenced to absorb water from the warm soil. This phenomenon has been observed in the Vine from of old. In spring, when the soil is to a certain extent warmed and the roots incited to activity, if a Vine is cut through close to the earth, or even higher, a quantity of clear water instantly exudes from the wood; and this outflow of water may continue for many days, and, as I know by personal experience, may yield several litres of water. The same happens with many trees in the spring time. Birch-stems, for example, sawn across a little above the soil, send forth streams of water, coming from the alburnum, which exude from the root-stock for weeks. This bleeding is, moreover, by no means confined to woody plants in the narrower sense of the word, as is proved by the old custom of the Mexicans of obtaining enormous quantities of their national drink, *pulque*, from the huge plants of *Agave americana* (the so-called 'hundred-years Aloe'), by cutting out the so-called 'heart' or leaf-bud, within the rosette of leaves, upon which water, driven up from the roots, is excreted into the hollow of the stem This contains sugar and albuminous substances, and therefore passes over into alcoholic fermentation, and, according to the statement of Alexander von Humboldt, hundreds of litres of sap may be gradually obtained in this manner from a single plant It was formerly believed to be a special peculiarity of some few plants thus to expel the water absorbed by the roots at the transverse section of the stem, until Hofmeister showed (about 1850) that the same phenomenon may be observed in any given plant, even small annuals which form little wood; it is only necessary to cut off the stems of *Ricinus*, Tobacco, *Digitalis*, Nettle, Sunflower, Maize, and such like well-known cultivated plants above the roots, when they are already actively vegetating, and to connect a glass tube at the section of the stem, to observe most of the phenomena referred to; and this may be done the more conveniently since even plants cultivated in flower-pots are suitable for the purpose. Such an experiment proceeds best and simplest if the plant is allowed to grow, not in soil, but in an aqueous solution of nutritive substances (Fig 210), until it has developed a vigorous root-system; the stem is then cut off, and the root-stock connected with an exit-tube, and as the roots absorb water from the nutritive fluid, an equal quantity exudes above at the transverse section of the stock.

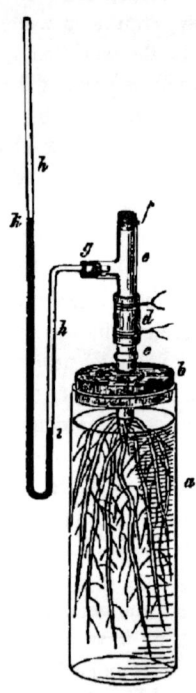

FIG 210.—A Maize plant developed in a nutritive solution in the vessel *a*, is cut off above the cork (*b*) at *c*, and here connected with the glass tube *efg* by means of caoutchouc (*d*) The narrow glass tube *h* passes through the cork *g* *egh* is filled with water, and mercury is then poured in *h* This mercury is driven up by the water expelled from *c*, as shown at *i* and *k*

The weeping of the root-stock has, since the time of Hales (1721), been investigated a thousand times by the most various observers, and it would require many hours to refer to all the results in detail. Instead of this, however, we will commence our further considerations on the phenomenon in question with a definite example. In August, 1881, a very vigorous specimen of the Sun-flower (*Helianthus annuus*), about 3 metres high and with a stem 4–5 centimetres in diameter, which was growing in the open land in my experimental garden, and was thus quite normal, was cut off transversely about twenty-five centimetres above the surface of the earth, and an appropriate exit-tube at once placed on the stump of the stem, the descending curved limb of the latter allowed the water expelled from the root-stock to pass into a graduated cylinder. Since the experiment was commenced on a hot day, the following phenomenon, to which I shall return below, presented itself. the root-stock, instead of expelling water at once, on the contrary absorbed a not inconsiderable quantity of water through the transverse section of the stem during the first few hours. The outflow from the section of the stem only began afterwards, and then continued for fourteen days. During the first few days the expulsion of water was copious: later on it gradually diminished. On the whole, however, 1061 cubic centimetres of water were expelled in thirteen days—a quantity which was at least three times as large as the volume of the whole root-stock; whence follows without further remark that the escaped water could not possibly have been previously contained in the root-stock, but must have been taken up only during the outflow—one of the most fundamental facts connected with this subject.

The circumstances under which the outflow of water takes place, will best be made evident if I here put together in the form of a table the observations made, at least for the first six days. It is only to be noticed that the letters *n, e, m, a* signify noon, evening, morning, and afternoon respectively; the numbers in the fifth column are obtained by division of the quantity of water discharged in the given period of time by the corresponding number of hours

HELIANTHUS ANNUUS.   AUGUST, 1881.

Date.	Hours, from — to	Weather	Temperature-degrees R in the earth	Water discharged per hour— cubic c m.	Remarks.
25 Aug.	12½ n — 7 e	Sunny		8 5	
—	7 e. — 8 m	—	14	2 46	Night
26 Aug	8 m — 9½ m.	—	13	14	MAXIMUM.
—	9½ m. — 12 n.	Clear	16·5	12 8	.
—	12 n. — 4 e	—	19	2 5	
—	4 e — 6 e	—	17	2·5	{ Transverse section of wood washed, at once set in progress again
27 Aug.	6 e — 5½ m.	Rain		1 6	Night
—	5½ m — 8 m	—	13	7·2	
—	8 m. — 9 m.	—	13·2	14	Maximum.
—	9 m — 11 m	—	13 2	13	
—	11 m — 3 a	—	13 5	12	
—	3 a. — 7 e	—	13 5	8	
28 Aug	7 e — 5½ m	—	12	3·6	Night.
—	5½ m. — 8 m	—	12	8	
—	8 m — 10½ m	Cloudy	12 3	10·4	
—	10½ m — 12 n.	—	12 8	10·8	Maximum.
—	12 n — 4 e.	—	13 1	8 5	
—	4 e — 5 e	—	13	6	
—	5 e — 7 e	Rain	13	7	
29 Aug	7 e. — 5½ m.	Clear	9·5	2 6	Night
—	5½ m — 8 m	—	10	5 6	
—	8 m. — 9 m	—	11	8	
—	9 m — 11 m.	—	13	9	Maximum.
—	11 m — 3 a.	—	15	8·2	
—	3 a. — 5 e.	—	14·5	5	
—	5 e — 7 e	—	13	4 5	
30 Aug	7 e — 5½ m.	Cloudy	10	2 5	Night
—	5½ m. — 8 m.	—	10 5	5·2	
—	8 m — 10 m	—	12·5	13·5	Maximum.
—	10 m — 12 n	—	1 5	5·5	
—	12 n — 3 a	Rain	16	5 7	
—	3 a — 5 e.	—	1 5	3·5	

What is conspicuous at once in our table, and has been known for a long time, are the continual fluctuations in the quantity of water hourly discharged. These take place in such a manner that at a certain hour daily—in the present case between 8 and 11 o'clock—a maximum of the discharge occurs; from thence onwards the quantities hourly discharged decrease into the night, to increase again towards morning. It appears, however, that even with the same species of plant the hour of the maximum may be considerably retarded, since another observer, who likewise investigated *Helianthus annuus*, but grown in a flower-pot, gives the time of maximum discharge as between 12 and 2 o'clock, and in general the statements of various observers differ considerably on this point. Even in the same specimen, the hour of the maximum discharge may alter on successive days, as our table in part shows; still for myself I always hold it to be important that a series of observations made in 1860, under peculiarly favourable conditions, on a plant of the common Potato [1], likewise rooted in the open land, gave results which agree with our table in all essential points, especially in that the maximum discharge always occurred in the forenoon. The most remarkable fact in this periodicity lies, however, in that it is independent of small fluctuations of temperature, and even of considerable fluctuations of the moisture of the soil, to such an extent that in spite of these it is still perceptible. Thus our table shows, on August 26, a maximum discharge of fourteen centimetres between 8 and 9 o'clock in the morning, the temperature being only 13° R., while in the afternoon, between 12 and 4 o'clock, at 19° R., only 2·5 cubic centimetres were excreted, and similar relations occur repeatedly in the table. In like manner the quantity of water contained in the earth is not strictly proportional, since even when the soil contains less water a larger outflow may take place; however, numerous experiments in this direction teach that a drying up of the soil to any great extent, as well as cooling of the roots, influences the quantity of outflow. It has been attempted to represent this periodicity in the activity of a root-stock as a consequence of the preceding daily periodicity of illumination, so long as the plant was still intact—an assumption which is hardly supported by the existing series of observations, and from general grounds possesses little probability in itself. Meanwhile the cause of the daily periods is simply unknown.

The inspection of our table yields the further result that the quantity of discharge at the time of the maxima is greater during the first two days than in those which follow; although on the 30th of August, that is on the fifth day, it rises again nearly up to the original height. On the other hand, the minimum hourly discharges in the later days are rather greater than at first. In other words, as the experiment continues, the difference between the daily maximum and minimum diminishes; as is also to be gathered from my old observations of 1860, on the

---

[1] The older literature on the weeping of the root-stock, as well as the facts from which our more recent view as to the mechanism of this process has been gradually developed, are found in the following works. Hofmeister—'*Uber Spannung, Ausflussmenge und Ausflussgeschwindigkeit von Saften lebender Pflanzen*' (Flora, 1862, pp 97, &c.) Sachs' '*Experimental Physiologie*,' 1865, VII. I established the foundation for an understanding of the transpiration-current as well as of the excretion of water in the liquid state in my oft-cited treatise, '*Uber die Porositat des Holzes*' the obscurity prevailing in Pfeffer's '*Pflanzen-physiologie*' (1881), in the section on the movements of water in the plant, might have been avoided if the author had sufficiently regarded this treatise. With respect to my observations on the Potato plant mentioned above, they are tabulated in my '*Experimental Physiologie*' (p 210)

Potato plant mentioned above   All these relations come out clearly, moreóver, if the observations are graphically represented on a system of co-ordinates, in such a manner that the days and hours of the observation are expressed on an abscissa line, while the quantities discharged per hour appear as ordinates. The curve so constructed facilitates a survey of the periodic fluctuations more than is the case with a tabl .

The liquid flowing out from the transverse section of the wood is by no means pure water, but always contains small quantities of those salts which the roots absorb from - the soil   With appropriate reagents, it is easy to detect potassium, phosphoric acid, sulphuric acid, and lime in the discharged water; and small quantities of organic matters, such as sugar and traces of proteids, may also be found —substances which have evidently been washed to a certain extent out of the wood of the root-stock.

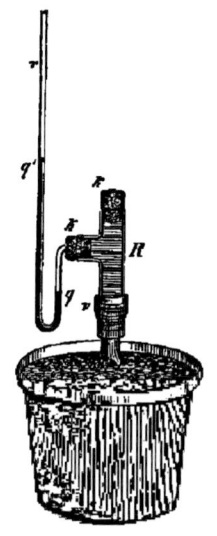

FIG. 212 —Apparatus for observing the force with which water is extruded from the root stock at the cut surface of the stem *r* The glass tube *R* is first tightly connected with the root stock, and the manometer tube *r* then fixed firmly, by means of the cork *k* *R* is then completely filled with water, and closed by the upper cork *k* Finally, mercury is poured into *r*, so that *q'* stands higher than *q* from the first. The level *q'* ascends above *q* according to the magnitude of the root-pressure in each case This apparatus is much more convenient than those formerly employed.

The water flowing out at the transverse section of the root-stock moves from below upwards, and must therefore be set in motion by pressure acting in opposition to gravitation. This pressure, or, as I have previously termed it, root-pressure, may, however, be far more considerable than is necessary for forcing the water out of the short stump of a stem. Even with smaller woody summer plants, as Sunflower, Potato, Tobacco, Nettle, &c, we may convince ourselves, with the aid of the simple apparatus represented in the accompanying figure, that the water exudes from the transverse section of the wood with a force capable of overcoming the pressure of a column of mercury of 20–30 centimetres in height. The root-pressure in old well-rooted stocks of the Vine is much greater; Hales found, for instance, that the water is discharged from the transverse section of the wood with a force which holds in equilibrium a column of mercury more than 100 centimetres high, and some more recent observations show still greater energy on the part of the root-pressure.

If we now attempt to obtain an idea of the nature of this pressure, it is to be noticed above all that the water at the transverse section of the wood wells forth from the vessels and wood-cells, as may be directly observed. This water, however, is evidently taken up from the soil by the root-hairs, or by the outer cells of the absorbing roots generally. Hence the problem to be answered may be stated in this form: how, by means of absorption by the external cells of the root, can the water obtain admittance to the cavities of the wood, and be pressed upwards in these with great force? I attempted, in my 'Handbook of Experimental Physiology,' 1865 (p. 204), to make this problem clear, and partly to solve it, with the aid of the diagram here reproduced.

Fig. 212 is intended to represent, diagrammatically and simply, a piece of a young absorbing root. *A, A* are so many cortical cells of the root, on which we may suppose protuberances to arise as root-hairs; these immediately surround a vessel, *B.* By means of the dissolved substances contained in the cells *A*, the water of the surrounding soil is absorbed by endosmose, this causes the cells, since they possess a protoplasmic lining to the walls on the inside, to become highly turgescent Now, as I have already shown, turgescence in general depends upon the absorption of water by endosmose taking place through cell-walls which resist filtration to so great an extent that a strong hydrostatic pressure becomes established in the cells. Now we may imagine hypothetically that the outer walls *a*, while favourable to the inflow of the water by endosmose, offer much resistance to its filtration, whereas the portions of wall *b*, which bound the vessel, may allow filtration to a greater extent. It is then obvious that

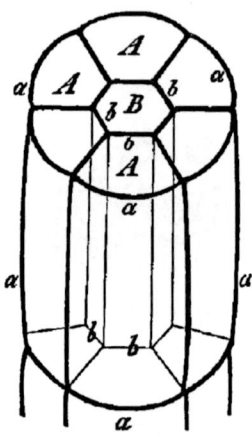

when a cell *A* is highly turgescent, the water taken up through *a* may be filtered out with force through the wall *b*; in consequence of this, the vessel *B* must become filled with water, and this will escape above at the transverse section of the root-stock, since the vessel is closed at the root-tip below. Since we know now that the turgescence of a cell may be equal to a pressure of several atmospheres, it is intelligible that the water enters from the cells *A* into the vessel *B* with a pressure which is able to drive it up to a height of 10–15 metres. To a certain extent, this argument may be demonstrated by an artificial apparatus. In the accompanying figure (Fig. 213), *z* indicates an artificial cell composed of a wide glass tube *g, g*, which is closed at *a* with a double bladder, and at *b* with a single one. After filling *z* with a solution which acts endosmotically, the glass tube *r* is fastened over *b* by means of a caoutchouc cap *K, K*. If this apparatus is now laid in a vessel full of water, the cell *z* absorbs the water by endosmose through the double membrane *a*, and when the turgescence has reached a sufficiently high degree the fluid absorbed through *a* again filters out through the single membrane *b*, which offers a smaller resistance to filtration: it then collects and ascends in *r*. Incomplete though this apparatus may be, it at any rate illustrates the fundamental ideas on which our conception of the essence of root-pressure depends, and in the sixteen years which have elapsed since my publication quoted above, nothing better has been put in its place. I then neglected to mention the various functions which devolve on the one hand upon the cellulose membrane, and on the other hand upon the protoplasmic utricle of the cell, in turgescence and filtration. After I had demonstrated the extraordinary capacity for filtration of the cell-wall, however, the resistance to filtration had to be chiefly ascribed to the protoplasmic utricle. This, supported by Naegeli's old observations on the properties of the latter. has subsequently been done by Pfeffer.

Although as a rule the forcing up of water into the stem only takes place to any considerable extent in copiously branched root-stocks, it is conceivable according to my explanation that here and there similar effects may also occur in parts of shoots without roots. All that is necessary is that vigorously absorbing and turgescent parenchyma cells force out their water into neighbouring vessels, whence it can be extruded. As a matter of fact I found that cut-off portions of the young haulms of various Grasses, when stuck with the basal ends in damp sand and protected from evaporation, allowed drops of water to well forth at the upper cut ends. According to Pitra's very extensive publications, leafy branches of wood plants with the leaves immersed in water, so that the cut end of the shoot-axis projects, allow water under pressure to exude from the latter; this, according to the principle given, appears quite credible, although I will not deny that my own researches in this direction have remained without result.

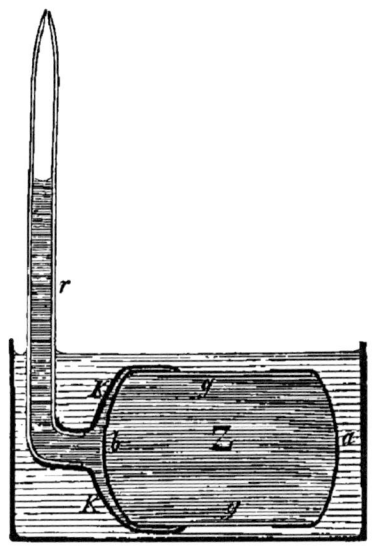

FIG 213.

The forcing up of the water out of the roots into the stem was formerly considered to be probably one of the causes by which, in the transpiration of plants, the water absorbed from the soil is despatched into the leaves. Since we know, however, that the root-pressure is able to lift the water 30–50 feet at most, the ascent of water in trees 200–300 feet high cannot be explained in this manner, recourse can only be had to the root-pressure for the explanation of the transpiration-current in plants of a few metres high. Since I have proved, however, that the transpiration-current ascends in the walls of the wood-cells as imbibed water, and that any pressure whatever from beneath is superfluous, and taking into full consideration the fact that the water ascending by means of the root-pressure moves in the cavities of the wood, the view mentioned above must be regarded as untenable; and the fact that the suction brought about by transpiration requires far more water than is supplied by the root-pressure, shows that it is completely unfounded, as indeed was already to be deduced from the older observations of Hofmeister [1] If the leafy top of a plant of the Gourd, Tobacco, or Sunflower, is cut off above the earth and placed in water, while the

---

[1] That far more water is disposed of in transpiration than the root pressure is able to supply in an equal time, is shown more in detail by my statements, as well as the older observations of others, published by Hugo de Vries in 'Arb. des bot Inst' (B I p. 288).

root-stock is connected with an exit tube, the water disposed of by the leafy top, as well as the outflow from the root-stock, may be directly observed. This proves now that the quantity of water required in suction or transpiration at the top is far larger than that driven into the stem by the root-pressure; the transpiring leafy top of a Tobacco-plant, for instance, took up 200 cubic centimetres of water in the same time that the root-stock discharged only fifteen cubic centimetres. It follows even from this fact that the transpiration-current cannot be explained by the root-pressure. Yet more definitely, however, is this conclusion to be drawn from the fact that, as a rule, no root-pressure at all exists in a plant in which vigorous transpiration is going on. If the leafy top of a Tobacco-plant, Sunflower, Potato, or Gourd-plant, &c., is cut off in sunshine, that is while vigorous transpiration

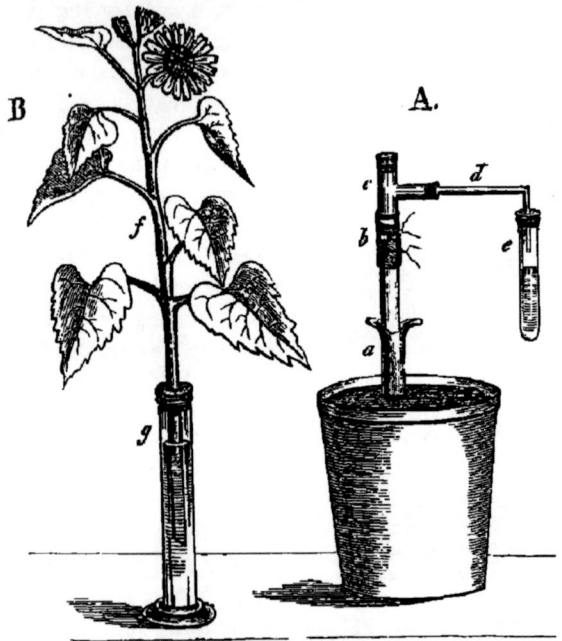

FIG 214.—*A* a stem of *Helianthus annuus* (*a*) rooted in a flower pot and furnished with an exit tube *b*, *c*, *d*, the water forced out at *c* by the root-pressure is measured in *c*. *B* the top of the same plant (*f*) placed in a graduated cylinder (*g*).

and ascent of water are proceeding, and a glass tube is at once placed on the stump projecting out of the earth, and if a quantity of water is then poured into this, it is observed that the latter is sucked into the wood of the root-stock. This proves that at the time of transpiration the cavities of the root-stock are not filled with water, but that they must contain rarefied air, which enables water to penetrate into the cavities. This fact, again, completely excludes the assumption that the forcing up of the water by the root can in any way co-operate in the transpiration-current; it shows, on the contrary, that the phenomenon of the weeping of the root-stock only comes into existence when the transpiration-current has been made ineffectual by cutting off the top, or when, as in the case of the Vine in spring, the transpiring leaf-surfaces are not yet present.

However, even in the case of plants in full leaf, when the transpiration of the leaves is diminished at a low temperature and in moist air—the roots remaining in a moist warm soil—water may be taken up with great energy, and be pressed forcibly into the leaves, to well out in the form of drops, if the necessary mechanisms exist. Thus we have the exudation of liquid water from the living and uninjured plant. The phenomenon is very easily observed when young plants of Cabbage, Maize or other Grasses, species of Alchemilla and many other plants have been cultivated in flower-pots, the pots warmed up to 20°–25°, and the leaves protected

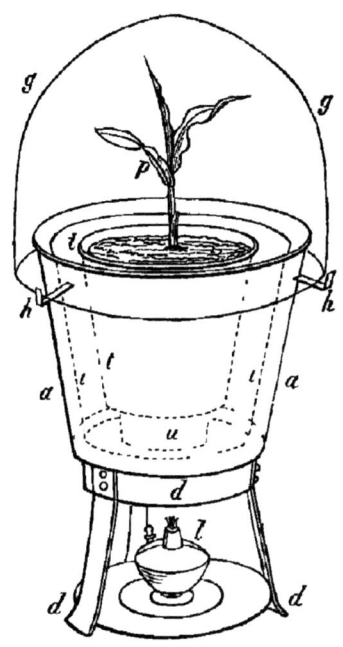

FIG. 215.—The double walled vessel *t, a* stands on the tripod *d, d* which is furnished with the lamp *l* water is contained between the two zinc walls of the vessel. The flower-pot *t*, with the plant *p*, stands on a support, *s, s,* and is covered by the bell glass *g, g,* which rests upon the hooks *h, h*

from too vigorous transpiration by being covered with a large bell-glass[1] After a few hours, occasionally even after 15–20 minutes, drops of water appear at certain places at the apices and margins of the leaves, especially on their teeth; these gradually increase in size, and finally fall off, whereupon new drops become formed. Such drops of water occur particularly copiously at the apices of the leaves of many Aroids, e. g. *Colocasia antiquorum* and *Calla Æthiopica.* In the natural course of events in the open air, the excretion of drops on the leaves is easy to observe when, after a hot day, the air becomes cooler and moister as the sun goes down, while the earth still retains its diurnal warmth, and incites the roots to absorb vigorously. It may then be directly seen that drops of water are extruded at the margins of the leaves of Potatoes, Grasses, species of *Alchemilla,* and many other plants. Much of the water which we find early in the morning on the margins of the leaves of many field and garden plants in the form of large drops, and which are generally taken for drops of dew, is really water excreted by the plants themselves.

That as a matter of fact it is the root-pressure which drives the water forcibly into the leaves, and expels it in the form of drops at appropriate places, may be proved by fastening cut-off branches on the shorter limb of a wide glass tube, as in Fig. 216, so that the cut surface dips into water, which is then forced into the shoot by means of mercury poured into the other limb of the tube. If the leaves are

---

[1] All essential points respecting the extrusion of drops from leaves known up to that time were collected in my '*pflanzen-Physiologie*' (p 237), and the excretion of nectar was discussed at the same time.

protected from active evaporation, a pressure of 10–20 centimetres of mercury generally suffices to render drops of water visible on them after ten minutes, or an hour. or longer, at any time of the day ; and with branches of *Alchemilla alpina*, the common Vine, and others, the excretion of drops in this manner continues for eight or ten days, so that several hundred cubic centimetres of water drop away. That the water forced in reaches the leaves through the wood can be made evident by removing a ring of cortex

It is generally at specially organised places on the leaves that the drops appear. These are often the so-called water-stomata (cf. Lecture VIII p 119); in other cases, however, they are ordinary stomata, and occasionally, in Grasses for instance, mere fissures in the epidermis, or, finally, as Moll has shown[1], the drops occur even at places on the margins or on the surfaces of the leaves where no special openings are to be perceived In Aroideæ, *Fuchsia*, *Tropæolum*, *Helleborus niger*, *Primula sinensis*, and others, the drops exude through water-stomata; and here the water-stomata are usually at the margins of the leaf, and especially at

the upper side of the apex of the teeth, several or many existing together. But in some plants, such as *Platanus*, *Ulmus*, and *Vitis*, according to Moll, the excretion of drops may take place on the under side of the teeth, although they possess water-stomata on the upper side. In *Cestrum roseum*, *Datura*, &c, indeed, he found drops excreted at places where no stomata at all exist. In general, according to Moll, younger leaves are more apt to exude drops than older ones, where the organs of exit not rarely become impassable. If in such cases water is forced into the shoot-axes, it penetrates into and fills the inter-cellular spaces of the mesophyll, and the leaf becomes injected; this does not directly injure the leaves, however, and they remain living when the injected water has

FIG. 216.—This apparatus, already described above (p. 244). may be employed to demonstrate the extrusion of drops from leaves by forcing in water at the cut surface of the shoot.

disappeared from the intercellular spaces by evaporation. A peculiar adaptation to these processes is found in the leaves of the Aroideæ mentioned. Following the margins, in company with the vascular bundles, are certain wide canals, which conduct the water up to the extraordinarily large water-stomata at the apex of the leaf From these as many as eighty-five drops per minute are said to be excreted at night; and one observer even collected 22·6 grammes

---

[1] I have demonstrated the phenomenon of the excretion of drops on the leaves of cut shoots by pressing water into them from below, in my lectures since 1869, and occasionally given instruction in my laboratory on the same subject. Moll has published more detailed researches on this subject in '*Bot Zeitg*' (1880, p. 49) and in '*Mittheilungen der Kgl Akad. der Wiss in Holland*' (Amsterdam, R II Tb 15).

of water dropped in *one* night from the leaves of *Colocasia antiquorum* According to a statement by Musset, the drops of water forced out may even be projected to a distance of several centimetres. Whether the excretion of drops has any favourable significance for the plant, and what, is still unknown; though, considering the generality of the phenomenon, it seems scarcely possible to deny that it must be of advantage in the economy of the plant. Moreover this water is, of course, not pure water on the contrary, it contains traces of the salts taken up by the plant, and occasionally also organic substances as well. On rapid evaporation of the excreted drops, these matters may remain behind as solid masses; and in this way are explained the calcareous scales on the margins of the leaves of many Saxifrages. This shows, however, that special relations of organisation co-operate here, since they do not occur in the majority of other plants[1].

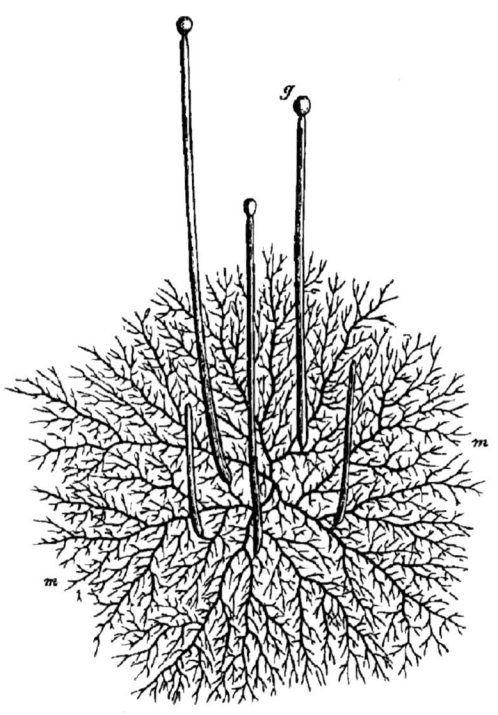

FIG 217 —*Phycomyces nitens*

I have already repeatedly mentioned in preceding lectures that the relations of organisation and vital phenomena of highly organised plants consisting of differentiated masses of tissue, are again usually to be met with also in such very simply organised plants as in the *Cœloblastæ*, which never undergo cell-division in the course of their growth. So also the excretion of drops is observed among the Fungi, on the sporangia of species of *Mucor*. These plants consist, as was shown at p. 5, of copiously branched tubes, their root-portion or mycelium (Fig. 217 *m*) being extended in the nourishing substratum, while thicker tubes grow perpendicularly from these into the air, and form the sporangia at their ends On these sporangia, when they have attained a height of several centimetres, numerous small drops of water now appear, which are evidently being forced out through the closed membrane, the pressure necessary for this, however, is evidently afforded by the endosmotic absorption of the roots in the substratum, and we have here at once the simplest conceivable case of root-pressure, since the entire plant consists of a single tube, never divided off by transverse walls. Thus it is the parts of the tube

---

[1] With respect to the calcareous scales on the leaves referred to, cf De Bary's '*Vergl. Anat. der Vegetations-organe*' (1877, p. 57).

extended in the substratum which absorb the water, and this is forced out again in the form of drops on those parts which protrude above the substratum. Hence, however, it follows that the absorbing root-hyphæ must offer more resistance to filtration than the walls of the sporangium, and we have here at once a case which supports my theory, adduced above, of the causes producing root-pressure. Moreover other Fungi, which consist of ordinary segmented hyphæ, can also excrete water on their fructification above the substratum, this happens, for example, with the commonest of all mould-fungi, *Penicillium glaucum*. When it fruits, after forming a dense membrane on the surface of a nutritive fluid, numerous drops of fluid collect on the upper side of the fungus membrane. The Fungus *Merulius lachrymans*, which is found in cellars and is so exceedingly destructive, has evidently obtained its name from a similar excretion of water.

The drops of so-called nectar are also to be referred to the excretion of liquid water. At the bottom of many flowers, at the base of the petals or stamens, or more particularly on the cushion at the base of the flower, juices containing sugar are excreted at the time of pollination, which are collected by bees and serve for the formation of honey. These juices are distinguished in Botany as nectar. Similar organs—i. e nectaries—also occur however on other parts of plants, as on the under side near the base of the lamina of *Prunus lauro-cerasus*, and right and left on the petiole of *Prunus avium*, &c, also on the stipules of the common field bean (*Vicia faba*). These nectaries excrete juices containing sugar when the parts of the plant concerned are highly turgescent. The arrangements referred to are especially conspicuous in the common Crown imperial (*Fritillaria imperialis*), where large, clear drops of nectar are excreted from rounded somewhat depressed spots at the base of the petals; when these drops are shaken off, they become replaced by others, and this even when the flower-shoot is cut off and placed in water, whence it follows that in this case root-pressure is not needed, but rather that masses of tissue exist in the neighbourhood of the nectary, from which the water and its saccharine contents are excreted—a fact which is also to be observed in other flowers. According to Wilson's researches, the renewal of the drops is suppressed when the external surfaces of the nectary are washed with water; they re-appear, however, if a very small particle of sugar is laid on the surface of the washed nectary. The attraction of the sugar evidently then acts by exosmose on the water contained in the tissue of the nectary; and we may well assume with Wilson that even in the normal condition of the nectary, the solution of the sugar already excreted affects the cell-sap of the nectary osmotically, especially when the sap already excreted becomes by evaporation more concentrated than the solution in the tissue of the nectary. The excretion of the nectar in the first instance, however, must depend upon other causes: either, as has been supposed[1], the outer wall of the nectar-cells becomes transformed into a soluble product, as in the colleters of leaf-buds, or, in so far as this is not the case, a pressure similar to the root-pressure forces out the sap.

---

[1] Respecting the mechanics of the secretion of nectar, cf. '*The Cause of the Excretion of Water on the Surface of Nectaries,*' by Dr. W. P. Wilson (Cambr Mass., U. S A) The matter, however, needs further investigation.

LECTURE XVII.

THE NUTRITIVE MATERIALS OF PLANTS.

In my 'History of Botany' I have shown[1] how, resuming the teaching of Aristotle, Cæsalpinus, so early as the sixteenth century and before any clear idea of chemical science was possessed, attempted to obtain an insight into the mechanism of the nutrition of plants; and how in the seventeenth century van Helmont undertook the first scientific botanical experiment calculated to give information as to the sources of the food of plants. Malpighi, the founder of vegetable anatomy, as early as 1671 made the statement that the proper nutritive organs of the plant are the green leaves, and that these take up food from the air with the co-operation of light. Hales, the founder of the mechanics of the movements of the sap (1727), was much occupied with the view that a large portion of the vegetable substance is obtained from the gaseous condition by condensation, and much useful knowledge of various kinds was collected later, especially by Du Hamel (1758). With the foundation of modern scientific chemistry by Lavoisier, at the end of the last century, the theory of the nutrition of plants also at once assumed a more definite form. Ingenhouss proved (1779) that the most abundant constituent of every vegetable body, carbon, originates from the carbon dioxide of the atmosphere, and a short time afterwards Theodore de Saussure not only established this fact for all time, but it was he also who first clearly perceived the true significance for the production of vegetable substance of the mineral matters taken up from the earth by the roots. From the appearance of his classical work in 1804, up to the beginning of 1840 or so, when Justus von Liebig and Boussingault made renewed and zealous studies of the nutrition of plants, there lies a barren period, but, stimulated by these men, the study of the nutrition of plants has been pursued during the last forty years with great zeal and excellent results. We may in fact say that few departments of science have been cultivated more patiently and with better results than this. The complete revolution which rational agriculture and forestry have experienced through the establishing of the theory of the nutrition of plants, proves how much has been accomplished in this department. It would extend far beyond the scope of this lecture to reproduce even briefly the substance of the literature of the subject. The most significant result of the development of

---

[1] Cf. my '*Geschichte der Botanik*,' Munchen, 1875.

the nutrition theory mentioned is met with, however, in the fact that we are now able to rear plants artificially—that we are in a position, with chemically pure water to which we add some few chemically pure salts, to rear artificially highly developed plants as well as the simplest Algæ (and. *mutatis mutandis,* also Fungi)—that from inconspicuous and often scarcely ponderable quantities of vegetable substance, quantities of it as large as we choose may be produced in this way.

Such being the favourable position of affairs, I regard it as the simplest and most instructive method to connect the main points of the theory of the nutrition of plants, so far as they concern the food materials, with the description of an experiment in artificial nutrition made with a highly organised plant. I think that in this manner the essential and important points come into view more clearly than with any other mode of exposition. In the year 1860, I published the results of experiments which demonstrated that land-plants are capable of absorbing their nutritive matters out of watery solutions, without the aid of soil, and that it is possible in this way not only to maintain plants alive and growing for a long time, as had long been known, but also to bring about a vigorous increase of their organic substance, and even the production of seeds capable of germination[1]. Much disputed at first, this method of artificial plant-culture has been more and more developed and perfected by various experimenters during the last twenty years, so that it now affords one of the most important aids to the study of the various questions of nutrition The description of the ways and means by which such an experiment is arranged and runs its course, in itself gives a clear illustration of the most important processes of nutrition in a highly organised plant.

We will assume that we have to do with the Garden Bean (*Phaseolus*) or the Field Bean (*Vicia Faba*), or Maize (*Zea Mays*), or Buckwheat (*Polygonum fagopyrum*), plants with which the greatest number of experiments of this kind have hitherto been conducted, although others, e. g. the Cabbage (*Brassica*) and Horse-chestnut, &c., are also suitable for the purpose.

It is best to allow the seeds of these plants to germinate in a box filled with well-washed damp saw-dust, until the radicle is several centimetres long After the seedling has been carefully taken out and washed, it is fastened into a perforated cork, *K*, as in Fig. 218, so that only the root dips into the water, *N*, of the vessel in which the culture is being made. It is then only necessary to be careful that the portion of the seed filled with reserve materials, *S*—the endosperm or the thick cotyledons according to circumstances—remains sufficiently moist, without however being submerged in the water. The apparatus, thus arranged, is placed in a sunny window or in a suitable green-house, care being taken however that the root immersed in the water is sufficiently darkened. This is best accomplished by placing the glass vessel in a hollow cylinder of cardboard. This precaution is necessary, not so much because the roots might be injured by the light, as to prevent green Algæ from growing in the water and settling on the surfaces of the root.

---

[1] Cf ' *Die landwirthschaftl Versuchsstationen,*' Dresden, H VI 1860, p 219, and Bot Zeitg 1860, p 113; and, further, Pfeffer's '*Pflanzenphysiologie,*' 1881, I. p. 253.

I assume the vessel in which the culture is made to have been first filled
with pure distilled water. In this case the seedling would nevertheless at first
grow vigorous and healthy, and, if we are dealing with large seeds of Beans or
Maize, produce three or four normal large leaves in the air, and several dozens
of lateral rootlets in the water. These organs arise and grow at the expense of
the materials—the so-called reserve materials—which were already present in the
seed Soon, however, the moment arrives when these materials have disappeared
from their reservoirs, and are completely used up: there is then found in the
endosperm of the Maize seed, or in the thick cotyledons of the Bean, nothing
more of the starch and proteid matters previously abounding, and which in
these cases chiefly represent the nutritive materials reserved for the first stages

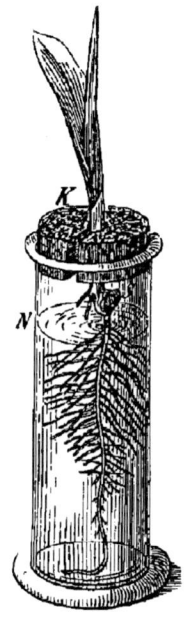

FIG. 218.—Arrangement for cultivation in nutritive solution

of germination. Microscopic examination would show
also that, in the roots, shoot-axes and leaves, the
stores of organic plastic materials are exhausted.
So far, therefore, the mere taking up of water by the
roots has sufficed for the construction of a number of
new plant organs, at the cost of the organic substance
stored up in the seed The seed also contains a quantity of mineral matters—compounds of potassium, magnesium, calcium, iron, phosphorus, and sulphur. If
now the plants remain with their roots immersed in
distilled water, they hold out, it is true, for a long time,
but without growing at all considerably, and at last
they perish.

If now several seedling plants of the same kind, e. g
Maize or Bean, have been allowed to grow up to this
point, we may employ one or several of these individuals for the decisive experiment. We replace (which
of course is better done previously) the distilled water
by a solution of various salts, known to us from a long
series of earlier experiments. The simplest plan will
be to give here at once in a tabular form the salt
solution offered to the plants. I mention the quantities I am accustomed to use generally in water cultures,
with the remark, however, that a somewhat wide margin may be permitted
with respect to the quantities of the individual salts and the concentration of
the whole solution; it does not matter if a little more or less of the one or
the other salt is taken, if only the nutritive mixture is kept within certain limits
as to quality and quantity, which are established by experience. Thus the following
would be a useful solution:—

Water . . .	1,000 cc m.
Potassium nitrate . . .	1 gramme.
Sodic chloride (common salt)	0·5 ,,
Calcium sulphate (Gypsum)	0 5 ,,
Magnesium sulphate .	0 5 ,,
Common calcic phosphate (finely pulverised) . .	0·5 ,,

The calcium phosphate, last mentioned, is but sparingly soluble in the solution and forms a sediment during the course of the experiment

The result of this proceeding becomes evident after a few days, in that the plants appear more vigorous as contrasted with those the roots of which have remained in pure water, and in that new lateral roots grow from their roots, and new leaves from their buds. After some time, however, when the third or fourth leaf of our experimental plant is unfolding, a diseased condition appears. The new leaves which develope henceforth remain completely white, that is, they produce no chlorophyll; and microscopical investigation shows, as Gris first observed in similar cases, that no chlorophyll grains are present in the protoplasm of such colourless leaves. This then is a proof that our mixture of nutritive materials still lacks something, and from the older observations of Gris, we know that the disease of our plants—so-called Chlorosis—is due to a want of iron[1]. Our experiment has thus taught us at the same time how this disease (which occurs not rarely also under ordinary conditions of growth, e. g. in Robinias, Horse-chestnuts, and other plants) may be produced artificially. However, the curing of this disease may also be effected at once · it suffices to add an extremely small quantity of a soluble salt of iron, e. g. a few drops of solution of iron chloride or ferrous sulphate, to the water which the roots take up, in order even after forty-eight hours (or, according to circumstances, after three or four days) to see the white leaves of the Bean or Maize becoming green · after several days they are quite normally green. The action of the iron on the formation of chlorophyll may be demonstrated even more simply; if a very dilute solution of a salt of iron is painted with a camel-hair pencil on the surface of a chlorotic leaf, the formation of chlorophyll in the leaf begins at this place after one or two days, and gradually extends thence. It may here be mentioned that I made auger-holes in the stem of an Acacia, the foliage of which was completely chlorotic, and placed funnels, filled with solutions of iron, in the holes; the solution of iron carried up from the auger-hole through the wood into the leaves of the next branch, in a few days caused the leaves of this branch to become completely green, while the others remained chlorotic. These experiments evidently prove that iron is necessary for the formation of chlorophyll, but they do not show whether the iron forms a constituent of the green colouring matter itself · it is possible, according to recent statements, that the latter is actually the case. It must be mentioned further that only an extremely small quantity of iron is necessary: several milligrammes of a soluble iron salt per litre of nutritive fluid are quite sufficient to remove the chlorosis of the plant under experiment, and larger quantities of iron act as a poison on the roots as well as on the leaves. At the same time, however, the course of our experiment shows how important these small quantities of iron are for the total life of the plant: since if they are withheld the white chlorotic leaves perish after a time. The feeble nutrition by means of the first two or three green leaves of the plant does not suffice to bring about any considerable growth;

---

[1] The literature of these and other facts appertaining here is quoted in my '*Experimental-physiologie*,' 1865, p 141, &c.

and the plant which is supplied with a nutritive solution devoid of iron perishes at length, simply because it is not able to form the proper organs of assimilation, the chlorophyll-grains in the cells of the leaf, and when these are wanting the plant is also unable to produce organic substances.

It is quite unnecessary, and in no way advantageous, to leave the roots of the experimental plants continually in the nutritive solution to which the iron has been added; experience shows rather that the plants flourish excellently if their roots are placed now and again for a few days in pure water, or still better in an almost saturated solution of gypsum. The roots, usually not perfectly healthy in the nutritive solution, then grow again vigorously, and numerous new lateral roots are formed; and when this has happened the plant may again be placed in a new nutritive solution. We may also proceed so that not all the salts given in the above table are simultaneously presented to the roots; the salts may be distributed in two or three fractionated solutions, and the plant allowed to absorb alternately the one or the other of them. In this case also vigorous vegetation is maintained, and indeed I made the first successful experiments on nutrition in this manner

The plants, then, being treated in the way described, new leaves and roots are continually developed, flowers appear after six or eight weeks, and it is only necessary to provide for the pollination of the female reproductive organ to produce fruit As a rule it suffices to let the plants stand at the open window or outside during the time of flowering; insects then provide for the transference of the pollen from the anthers to the stigmas in the usual manner. The ovary then swells, and after a few weeks a greater or less number of fruits are formed containing seeds capable of germination. With the Maize, I have frequently obtained in this manner heads of fruit with more than 100 grains capable of germinating, and with Beans 6-10 pods with 12–20 ripe seeds If to the weight of these seeds that of the organic substance of the shoots, leaves, and roots produced in our water-culture is reckoned, it is shown that the organic substance, in comparison with that of the seed from which the experimental plant was developed, may amount to three-hundredfold and more

We have thus by artificial nutrition raised a plant which has gone through the whole course of its development, and we may employ its seeds for a second experiment of the same kind.

From this experiment it follows that the materials which we have placed at the disposal of the plant completely suffice for the whole process of nutrition, and any other addition of material is entirely superfluous. It should be mentioned here, indeed, that the common salt specified in our table, or any other chlorine compound, may be omitted, since numerous culture experiments have shown that sodium and chlorine are, strictly speaking, superfluous in nutrition. On the other hand, the presence of common salt or some other chloride is of use, in so far that the nutritive solution can thereby be prevented from becoming alkaline[1]; since by the absorption at the roots the chemical composition of the nutritive solution becomes altered more and more in time. Of course this can also be avoided by completely renewing the entire nutritive solution every three or four days

---

[1] Cf. Pfeffer, '*Pflanzenphysiologie*,' I p 254.

This opportunity may be taken of remarking that the roots possess a sort of selective power, as it has been called, as to quantity at any rate, even if not as to quality. That is to say, the roots absorb dissolved matters of the most various kind, it is true, even those which are injurious, and thus are not able to reject any; but on the other hand it was shown by De Saussure, and has been confirmed by more recent investigations, that the roots absorb the nutritive salts at their disposal by no means in the same quantitative proportions as those in which they are met with in the mixed solution. If, for instance, the solution contains more calcium than potassium, the subsequent analysis of the plant-ash may yield more potassium than calcium, and so forth. This fact, depending upon a power of quantitative selection on the part of the plant, is evident in the thousands of ash analyses which have been made of the most various plants [1] developed in the open. Plants of different species which have grown close together on the same soil, or in the same water, exhibit totally different combinations in their ash,—the one having much, the other little, of calcium compounds; in the one magnesium and calcium predominate, in the other potassium, compared with the quantity in which these substances are contained in the soil or (in the case of water-plants) in the water. The latter is particularly conspicuous in marine plants. While sea-water contains $3°/_0$ of common salt, and only very small quantities of salts of potassium, magnesium, and calcium, the salts last named nevertheless predominate in the ash of these plants, and it contains relatively but little of the common salt of the sea-water. Plants thus take what they require from a mixture of salts, without particular reference to the composition of the nutritive mixture. But, again, even this does not exactly occur in the sense that they only and exclusively take up just so much of each material as is necessary for nutrition; since in the ash of plants of the same species are found more or less potassium, calcium, magnesium, phosphoric or sulphuric acids according as they have grown on this or that soil. The composition of the ash of a species of plant is thus not specifically constant, but is dependent, at least in part, upon the composition of the soil or the water. Least variable in this respect are, of course, the fruits and seeds . in these are collected only the materials specifically necessary for the seedling, while in the shoots and roots superfluous matters also may be lodged.

The question still remains, however, whether all the salts which we have added to our nutritive solution are actually necessary for the plant. These salts were, potassium nitrate, calcium sulphate, and magnesium and calcium phosphates; we have already learnt that the iron salt is indispensable, and recognised the incidental significance of the sodium chloride. The question raised may be in the first place simplified by regarding as the essentials, not the salts named as such, but the elements contained in them. As numerous investigations in this direction show, it is simply necessary that the nutritive mixture should contain the elements potassium, calcium, magnesium, iron, phosphorus, and sulphur, in suitable neutral combinations containing oxygen. For reasons the explanation of which would here carry us too far, however, it is best to choose the salts given in our table; and it is at the same time certain that land-plants, as well as water-plants, as a rule, find and take up just these very salts in their environment, since potassium nitrate, gypsum, magnesium sulphate, calcium phosphate,

---

[1] Emil Wolff, '*Aschenanalysen von landwirthschaftlichen Producten,*' Berlin, 1871.

and some compound of iron, are found in every soil in which plants grow, and in the water of rivers, wells, and seas, and are undoubtedly used by the plants.

Mere chemical analysis, by which the presence of the materials in plants is proved, would by no means alone suffice to show whether all the substances detected by the analysis are really indispensable for the nourishment of the plant. As a matter of fact, numerous other elements in addition to those mentioned have been discovered now and then in plants, occasionally indeed in considerable quantity. I need only mention iodine in marine plants, manganese in many land-plants, and the very considerable quantities of zinc in plants which grow on calamine soils, but which in other places flourish just as well without zinc. One of the commonest phenomena of this kind, however, is the accumulation of silica in the tissues of very many plants, although we may regard it as certain that this substance is superfluous for the chemical processes of nutrition, as well as for the molecular movements connected with growth. Among the plants in the epidermis of which particularly large quantities of silica are deposited, we find, besides the Equisetaceæ and some others, the Grasses, and among these the Maize. Although in such plants half of the total ash often consists of silica, I (and subsequently other observers also) nevertheless succeeded in bringing Maize plants to vigorous and complete development with the help of nutritive solutions to which not even a trace of silica was added[1]; the small traces of silica detected with difficulty in these experimental plants could only have been derived from the glass walls of the vessels, or from the dust. Although it is thus shown that this substance, widely distributed in plants, is superfluous for the purposes of nutrition and growth, it would be going too far to regard it as superfluous also in every other connection   The silica is generally deposited in the outer walls of the cells of the epidermis of the leaves and stems, i e. of the transpiring organs: it is conveyed there with the water of nutrition, and, on the evaporation of this, remains behind in the outer cell-wall   By burning the latter on platinum foil, especially with the addition of sulphuric acid, the silica is obtained in the form of so-called skeletons, that is, thin plates which still possess with great exactness all the finer structure of the epidermis cell-walls, and especially of the hairs   The form of these skeletons shows that the molecules of silica have been regularly deposited in the cell-walls, between the molecules or micellæ of cellulose, the walls of vessels, wood-cells, and parenchyma cells in old leaves (e g. of Oaks and Beeches in the autumn), moreover, afford exquisite siliceous skeletons. Among the most remarkable phenomena of this kind is the deposition of silica in the cell-walls of the unicellular Algæ of the subdivision of the Diatomaceæ, of the siliceous skeletons of which the well-known silica deposit of Bilin in Bohemia, for example, consists. It is scarcely probable that these Algæ could flourish in a medium devoid of silica, and whether the Equisetums and Grasses which abound in silica would maintain themselves permanently if the supply of silica were cut off is more than questionable, although it is established that this substance is superfluous for the processes of nutrition and growth, and quite certain that the exceedingly fine masses of silica in the epidermis of these plants scarcely at all affects the elasticity and rigidity

---

[1] Cf my treatise in '*Annalen der Landwirthschaft in den kgl. preuss Staaten,*' Wochenblatt, 1862, p. 184

of the haulms and leaves The somewhat thoughtless assumption that the rigidity of the haulms of cereals is essentially promoted by the silica which they contain, impelled agriculturists, thirty years ago, to manure their wheat fields with costly preparations of silica, hoping thereby to prevent the laying of the wheat—by laying is understood the giving way of the lower joints of the haulms, especially in continuous rainy weather, so that whole wheat fields have their haulms laid flat on the earth before the ripening of the grain. In my *Experimental Physiologie* (1865), and still earlier in my lectures, I demonstrated the incorrectness of this view, and showed that the laying of the wheat has nothing whatever to do with the silica, but is due to deficient lignification of the supporting tissues in the haulms, which stand too closely together, shade one another, and so assume the diseased condition of etiolation, to be described later; and just those wheat-fields best supplied with food, and the plants of which shade one another to the greatest extent, are most exposed to laying It would not now occur to any agriculturist to dig his gold into his wheat-fields in the form of silica[1]. The physiological significance of the silicification of cell-walls is best illustrated by the observation that in numerous plants the deposition of silica begins in the hairs, and especially in the prickles, and extends centrifugally from the base of these to the surrounding epidermis cells. This is particularly well seen in the Hop, Hemp, Gourd, etc.; and takes place on stems and leaves already fully grown, or nearly so.

We now know, therefore, that the silica so common in plants, although it may occasionally be of some advantage, is nevertheless not a nutritive material in the narrower sense of the word—i e it takes no part in the chemical processes of assimilation and metabolism. We know further, that the small traces of iron salts are of the greatest importance in the process of nutrition of ordinary green plants, since without iron the proper instrument of nutrition, chlorophyll, is not formed With this, however, our definite knowledge of the physiological significance of the nutritive substances mentioned is practically exhausted: we know, to put it shortly, nothing certain as to the parts played by potassium, calcium, magnesium, and phosphorus in assimilation and metabolism With respect to sulphur, we know at least that it forms an indispensable constituent in the chemical composition of proteids, and is therefore necessary for the building up of protoplasm With respect to the others, however, only so much is established, that they are absolutely indispensable for assimilation—i. e. for the production of organic plant-substance; for researches on vegetation show that when even only one of these elements (potassium, calcium, magnesium, and phosphorus) is excluded from the nutritive mixture, assimilation soon ceases, and the production of organic plant-substance proceeds no further. The salts of these elements, therefore, certainly take part in the chemical processes which occur during the formation of organic plant-substance from inorganic material, though we do not know what part they play in it.

Moreover, it is also not to be forgotten that the elements mentioned, or their compounds, take part not only in assimilation itself, but also in the meta-

---

[1] With respect to silica in plants, and the fact that the so-called laying of wheat is caused by shading and etiolation, and not by want of silica, as hitherto supposed, what is necessary is stated in my '*Experimental-physiologie*,' 1865, p. 150.

bolism which occurs during growth, etc. In this connection, for example, lime often plays a similar part to silica . just as numerous plants have their cell-walls silicified, others may be calcified by the deposition of large quantities of carbonate of lime, and thus become stone-hard, as the Melobesiaceæ and Corallineæ among the Algæ; and there is scarcely room for doubt that all, or at any rate very many older cell-walls leave behind on combustion an ash containing lime, and occasionally, as in the vessels of the Gourd, it is even possible to obtain chalk skeletons by combustion.

Without wishing to enter more in detail into the thousand-fold investigated ashes of plants, it will still be well to bring forward two facts concerning them. In the first place, every part of a plant, every cell-wall, even the youngest, and likewise the protoplasm, and even starch-grains, leave an ash behind after combustion , and from their general occurrence it may be concluded that certain constituents of the ash at least are indispensable for the chemical composition or for the molecular structure of the cell-walls and protoplasm. A second fact worth noting is the abundance of ash-constituents in the green assimilating leaves: this is at once explained when we know that these constituents are continually being carried by the transpiration-current to the leaves, and are retained in them on the evaporation of the water, and when we observe that no assimilation occurs in their absence, as experiments on vegetation demonstrate.

The quantity of ash, however, as a rule, amounts only to a small proportion of the plant-substance, reckoned without water. It usually varies between 1% and 10%; the wood and seeds belonging to the parts poorest in ash—the former evidently because the ash constituents do not need to be accumulated in it for the purposes of metabolism, but are conveyed to the organs of assimilation. The poverty of seeds in ash-constituents, on the other hand, is explained on reflecting that the seeds take up water laden with mineral matters when they germinate. Finally, ash analyses show that the quantitative composition—i. e. the relative richness in potassium, calcium, magnesium, and phosphorus—changes according to the nature and the age of the organ of a plant. Ripe seeds, for example, usually contain relatively much potassium, magnesium, and phosphorus. Since, however, it is not possible to bring the facts so far known as to the composition of the ash into immediate connection with definite physiological functions, we will now leave this subject for the present.

Turning once more to our water-cultures, we have now to take into consideration another most important question. Our plants, as we have already seen, consist only to a very small extent of the substances which were dissolved in the water, and which have been absorbed by them. In the main, the substance of our experimental plant consists, like that of any other plant, of cellulose, proteid substances, small quantities of fat, and a few other organic matters. Besides nitrogen and sulphur, which are contained in the proteid substances of the protoplasm, the latter, as well as the cellulose and all organic substances employed for the normal construction of the plant, contain hydrogen, oxygen, and carbon. The source of these elements of the organic substance, so far as the hydrogen and oxygen are concerned, presents no difficulties whatever: these are in fact the elements of water, which the plant absorbs in such enormous quantities, and which permeates all parts of it, however small. The sulphur in the proteid substances, where of course it only occurs in very small quantity, also presents no difficulty with respect to its origin · we added it in fact to the nutritive solution in the form of calcium and magnesium sulphates, and if we now find it also in the proteid substances of the protoplasm of our plants, no longer in the form of sulphuric acid but as an elementary constituent in the formula of proteid substance, there is little to be surprised at, since we know how easily sulphur compounds may be decomposed. We also find in the micro-chemical investigation of our plants, as a residuum of this decomposition, crystals of oxalate of lime, the calcium of which passed into the plant in the form of calcium sulphate

Of the elements of which protoplasm, cellulose, and the other organic compounds produced by the plant consist, the nitrogen and carbon still remain to be considered. Our table (p 284) shows that in the water of the nutritive mixture, a salt containing nitrogen, viz. potassium nitrate, is contained, and indeed predominates. The nitrogen in the proteid substances of the plant is, as we may thus assume, the same nitrogen which we presented to the roots in the form of saltpetre. On the decomposition of this salt, its nitrogen must have become a constituent of the proteid substances newly produced in the plant. At any rate the active vegetation of our experimental plants, and the very significant increase of substances of a proteid nature which had been especially stored up in the gathered seeds, show that plants are able to take up from nitrates as much nitrogen as is necessary for the formation of the proteid substances of a vigorous plant

Theodore de Saussure had already proposed the question whether the nitrogen of the atmosphere (which, as is well known, consists of about $\frac{4}{5}$ nitrogen and $\frac{1}{5}$ oxygen) is not used by plants to produce their nitrogenous compounds. Thirty or forty years ago Boussingault endeavoured to decide this question by a long series of exceedingly careful experiments on vegetation, and came to the conclusion that the atmospheric nitrogen is not employed in the process of the assimilation of plants. His experimental plants in each case grew vigorously and produced proteid compounds when he presented to their roots, in addition to the other nutritive substances, various kinds of nitrogenous compounds. They grew, on the other hand, very badly, and their proteid substances did not increase, when such a supply of nitrogen compounds was wanting ; although the nitrogen of the atmosphere was at the disposal of the plants so treated By means of the now much further developed art of nourishing plants artificially, and especially by means of water-cultures, we are in a position at any time to afford ocular demonstration of the important result obtained by Boussingault, by means of simple experiments. Whenever a sufficient quantity of saltpetre is added to the nutritive solution, the experimental plants grow vigorously, produce numerous ripe seeds capable of germination, and give on analysis a corresponding increase of the nitrogenous substance. If on the other hand the nitrate is withheld from the nutritive mixture, the experimental plant continues to grow for a time, it is true, making use of the proteid substances already contained in the seed for the formation of the protoplasm of its organs , and this stunted growth may even continue for some time, since the protoplasm of the first leaves is again dissolved and absorbed from them, to be employed for the formation of a few new leaves , but even in this case analysis gives no increase of the proteid substances.

The view was once held that it was ammonia salts particularly which, being absorbed by the roots of plants, or perhaps indeed by their leaves in the dew and rain water, yielded the nitrogen for the proteid compounds of the plant. But the result of our water-culture proves, in the first place, that plants are able at any rate to absorb the whole of their nitrogen in the form of compounds of nitric acid, but if, on the other hand, the attempt is made to replace the latter by ammonia salts, experimental difficulties make their appearance which we will not here discuss in detail. If, further, it is remembered that the ammonia produced in nature by the rotting and decomposition of organic remains, especially in vegetable soil, is easily transformed in the presence of potassium salts into compounds of nitric acid, which may be detected everywhere in vegetable soils and waters, and that nitric acid is contained in rain water, although in very small quantities, one comes to the conclusion that (apart perhaps from certain special cases, and particularly apart from parasites and Fungi) ordinary green plants obtain the nitrogen for the formation of their proteid substances, and therefore of their protoplasm, from salts of nitric acid. It may here be remarked in addition that the soil of gardens, wheat-fields, vineyards, orchards, and so forth, is usually somewhat deficient in compounds of nitric acid, and that on this account the production of vegetable substance, although all other nutritive matters are present in the soil, proves to be relatively small, a suitable addition of saltpetre is in such cases always calculated to increase the vegetation to its utmost luxuriance, and if other nitrogenous manures act similarly, we may assume that they give rise in the soil, sooner or later, to salts of nitric acid, which are absorbed by the roots.

Finally, the question remains as to the source of the carbon in our experimental plants. If we suppose the plant, after driving off the water, to be dried at 100–120° C., about half of the total dry substance consists of carbon. This element in fact is contained in every organic compound, as well as in the cellulose, protoplasm, and fatty bodies which play the most prominent part in plants. Our plants, nourished with aqueous solutions of salts, could not absorb any carbon compound, however, from this nutritive solution. Investigation shows, on the contrary, that they continually excrete small quantities of a carbon compound, viz. carbon dioxide; and I shall subsequently show that it is entirely erroneous to suppose that the carbon dioxide which usually abounds in the soil is absorbed by the roots and conveyed to the leaves. The question for us now, however, is whence comes this great mass of carbon which is gradually accumulated in the organic compounds of our experimental plants? It is, at any rate, not derived from the nutritive solution. There remains, therefore, only one source, the atmosphere—half of the dry weight of the organic substance of plants must be derived from the atmosphere. This fact now, after two hundred years of scientific progress, follows with absolute certainty from every experiment on nutrition with green-leaved plants. But the founders of the theory of the nutrition of plants, Ingenhouss and De Saussure, discovered this fact—one might almost say the most important fact of biological science—by very different methods; and in my 'History of Botany' I have attempted to show how this important natural process was gradually discovered by these men, and to what misconceptions and foolish objections by incompetent minds, even this now indisputable fact, like every other great discovery, has been exposed, to such an extent, indeed, that some forty years ago the weighty word of Justus von Liebig was needed, before the fact that the carbon of plants is derived solely and simply from the atmosphere was again completely established. We shall not be concerned more in detail with how plants obtain the carbon from the carbon dioxide of the atmosphere until the following lecture meanwhile the source only of this substance interests us here, quite apart from the physiological work of the plant. Many so-called investigators were prevented, for more than forty years after the discoveries of Ingenhouss and De Saussure, from believing in the atmosphere as the exclusive source of the carbon, by the fact, known even then, that the relative quantity of carbon dioxide contained in the air is extremely small. Innumerable analyses of air have shown, in fact, that in 10,000 litres (that is in 10 cubic metres) there are contained on an average but 4–6 litres of carbon dioxide, and since 1 litre of carbon dioxide weighs about 2 grams, 10 cubic metres of air contain 8–12 grams of carbon dioxide. This quantity certainly appears very small, the more so since only $\frac{3}{11}$ of it consist of carbon, and, as we shall see later, the whole of the oxygen of the carbon dioxide (that is $\frac{8}{11}$) are given off by the plant Nevertheless so much is clear, that 10 cubic metres of air contain somewhat more than 2 grams of carbon, from which, by combination with hydrogen. oxygen, nitrogen, and sulphur, according to circumstances in each case, 4–5 grams of vegetable substance may be formed. A plant, however, which in the living state contains 4–5 grams of organic substance, weighs, together with the water contained in it, about 20–25 grams on the average, and this would certainly be a rather small specimen However, not only a plant growing in the open, but even one in a room, has at its disposal much more than 10 cubic metres of air, for, on account of the continual movement of the atmosphere, new air containing carbon dioxide is always being conveyed to the leaves ; and on closer consideration it is seen to depend essentially only upon whether the green leaves are able to snatch these relatively small quantities of carbon dioxide from the atmosphere with sufficient rapidity. That they actually do this is shown by the result—the fact that very considerable quantities of carbon are accumulated in a plant in a relatively short time. I found, for instance, that a very vigorous Tobacco plant in the course of 100 days during its development in the garden absorbed more than 400 grams of carbon from the air, and a Sunflower fixed more than 800 grams in the same time ; quantities which were contained in several thousand cubic metres of air. Moreover, the further fact that a Gourd plant, with a leaf-surface measuring one square metre, is able in the course of ten hours of daylight to produce as much as 8 grams of starch, in which nearly 4 grams of carbon are contained, shows that the carbon dioxide of 20 cubic metres of air has been made use of by this area of leaf-surface in one day[1].

These reflections on the source of the carbon enable us at the same time to perceive that it would be exceedingly unreasonable to make such experiments on nutrition as have been described, in a completely closed space to which the air has

---

[1] [See further Sachs, in *Arbeiten des bot. Institut zu Wurzburg*, B. III, 1884, where the quantities of starch produced are shown to be considerably greater]

not free access. In this way the necessary supply of carbon would be cut off from the experimental plant; and without this no formation of vegetable substance whatever can take place, since all organic compounds contain considerable quantities of carbon. After these considerations, some readers might be in doubt as to whether the great masses of carbon accumulated year by year over the whole surface of the globe in the form of plant-substance are really contained in the atmosphere. Nevertheless, one may be satisfied of this: the carbon dioxide in the whole terrestrial atmosphere is to be reckoned, not by litres, but by thousands of cubic miles, and, as has long been calculated, would provide the total vegetation of the earth with carbon for many years, even if new supplies of carbon dioxide were not continually being formed. It is, it is true, an optimistic fable to suppose that the world is so perfectly arranged that all the carbon dioxide produced by the respiration of animals and men exactly suffices to equalise the consumption of carbon dioxide of the whole vegetation of the earth. Nevertheless, an enormous quantity of carbon dioxide is continually being supplied to the atmosphere by this very respiration of animals, as well as by the processes of decomposition, especially of dead plants themselves, which are taking place everywhere, and by means of innumerable springs charged with carbon dioxide, and by hundreds of smoking volcanoes, and in our time also by hundreds and thousands of smoking chimneys, through which the carbon of coal escapes as carbon dioxide, so that a lack of it need scarcely be expected for thousands of years. An approximate idea of how enormously large the condensation of the carbon of the atmosphere by the assimilation of plants must have been hitherto, is obtained on reflecting that the deposits of coal, lignite, and turf, spread over the whole earth, and the bituminous substances as great or even greater in quantity which permeate mountain formations, besides asphalt, petroleum, &c., are products of the decomposition of earlier vegetations, which in the course of millions of years have taken from the atmosphere the carbon contained in these substances and transformed it into organic substance.

We have not yet done, however, with the consideration of our experimental plant. Any one conducting such an experiment, and not prepared with a knowledge of vegetable physiology, might possibly for convenience, or for some other reason, place the experimental plants with their nutritive solution at the back of a chamber, or in the middle of an ordinary dwelling-room or laboratory. He would then find, after a few weeks, that the plants had grown it is true to some extent, and even that a few fresh leaves had been formed after germination. These plants would, however, look unhealthy, shrivel up, and die, and after drying them and weighing their organic substance, it would be found that the latter, according to circumstances, is scarcely so large as the weight of the seeds employed, and may be considerably smaller. That plants cannot flourish under such circumstances is self-evident, however, on learning from the researches of Ingenhouss and De Saussure, as well as from our own experiments, that the decomposition of the atmospheric carbon dioxide in the green parts, and the consequent production of new plant-substance, only occurs when the organs containing chlorophyll meet with light of sufficient intensity. By this is to be understood in general, so far as vigorous vegetation is concerned, all the daylight reflected from the sky, or, in the case of plants growing entirely in the open, direct sunlight. The whole nature of the plant is adapted to just this intensity of light, and but few species can flourish in the deep shade of woods   In a word, the experimental plants, to which we have hitherto confined our attention, can only yield a satisfactory result when artificially nourished, if they are enabled, by being strongly illuminated, actually to make use of the carbon dioxide present in the atmosphere. Without the co-operation of light of sufficient intensity, the carbon dioxide of the atmosphere is as good as non-existent, so far as the nutrition of the plant is concerned. The light, so to speak, affords to the cells containing chlorophyll the forces necessary for separating the carbon of the carbon dioxide from the oxygen, and uniting it at the same time to other elements, and transforming it into organic plant-substance. Hence it has been said, and correctly, that it is the sun which maintains vegetable life on the surface of the earth; and since the entire animal world derives its food from plants, it may be said that it is the energy contained in the sun's rays which developes itself in the vital movements of all terrestrial organisms—animals as well as plants   The mechanical force contained in the solar rays acts in the chlorophyll-containing cells of the plant like the movements of a watch-key, by which the spring of the clockwork is wound up, and the vital processes of animals and plants resemble the slow running down of the clockwork; for by these vital processes the organic substance produced in the chlorophyll-containing cells by means of the light is gradually destroyed again, and finally re-transformed into carbon dioxide and water, until, on the commencement of a new period of vegetation, the clockwork is wound up anew.

Referring once more to our experiment on vegetation, after these comprehensive considerations suggested by the results, from another side, we have still to consider whether the experimental plants, nourished in an aqueous solution, grow as normally and vigorously as if we had brought them up in good vegetable soil.   The experiment is easily arranged. it suffices to cause several seeds, of the same species as those employed for the water-culture, to germinate and develope in vessels containing an equal volume of good vegetable soil, and to expose these near our experimental plants, and to the same light. It is found by this that the vegetation is in both cases approximately equal, but in neither case so vigorous as when the plants are cultivated in the ordinary manner in the garden.   They there meet not only with more direct light, and other advantages which growth in the open affords, but also, and above all, the roots are able to develope to more advantage in the open soil, becoming much longer and much more copiously branched than in our water-culture, moreover they are in contact partly with air, which they respire, and only partly with fluid, and their root-hairs attach themselves, as we already know, to the particles of soil, from which they take up absorbed food-materials. This is simply the normal condition of true land-plants; and their stay in a nutritive solution must necessarily affect their function abnormally. Nevertheless, the results of our water-culture are scientifically of value; since they show that although the roots are compelled to take up the food materials under abnormal conditions, nevertheless with their help much vegetable substance is formed, which behaves normally so far that with its aid the whole process of development of a plant may be completed, including the formation of seeds capable of germination.

LECTURE XVIII.

THE PRODUCTION OF THE ORGANIC SUBSTANCE OF PLANTS—ASSIMILATION.

HAVING learnt in the last lecture what are the materials which a normal green plant must absorb from without, in order to build up its substance from them, we will now examine the question how and under what conditions the organic substance is manufactured. Since we know almost nothing as to the ways and means by which the constituents of the ash co-operate in these processes, we may limit our considerations to four points. In the first place, the decomposition of carbon dioxide may be treated of. This furnishes, as we know already, the whole of the carbon necessary for the manufacture of the substance of normal plants with green leaves. In the second place, proof is to be given that the cells containing chloro-phyll—or, more properly speaking, the chlorophyll-corpuscles only—are the organs by means of which organic substance is manufactured from carbon dioxide. Thirdly, it is to be observed that the chlorophyll is only effective as an instrument of assimila-tion when the vibrations of the ether which are perceptible to our eyes as light penetrate into its substance, and impart to it the forces necessary to produce organic substance from carbon dioxide and water. Finally, we wish to know what is the immediate result of the decomposition of the carbon dioxide in the chlorophyll under the influence of light.

Concerning ourselves first with the decomposition of carbon dioxide, we may again confine our remarks, for the sake of clearness, to the artificially nourished plant referred to in the previous lecture. The substance of this plant is combustible, and after combustion it leaves behind a small quantity of ash, consisting of the salts taken up by the roots, and which we know to be indispensable for the production of organic substance. The fact that the organic substance of the plant is combustible, however, essentially implies that it consists of chemical compounds poor in oxygen, which are in a condition to become oxidised on the entrance of atmospheric oxygen at a red heat, and hence to be transformed for the most part into carbon dioxide and water. Just as organic plant-substance is produced from compounds rich in oxygen—carbon dioxide and water (with the co-operation of other compounds rich in oxygen)—so also they may be brought back again into the form of the same compounds by oxidation. The fact that plant-substance is combustible, itself implies that in its production from non-combustible compounds containing much oxygen a considerable quantity of oxygen must have been liberated, since otherwise the organic substance could not be combustible.

It is seen from this simple consideration that somewhere and in some manner oxygen must be separated in nutrition, and long before these reflections were established this evolution of oxygen had been, as a matter of fact, observed. Towards the end of the last century, Priestly, Senebier, Ingenhouss, and later, with classical completeness, De Saussure, established the fact that the green organs of plants evolve oxygen under the influence of light, if they are at the same time in a position to take up carbon dioxide from without. It is of importance to the history of botany to make clear how this important fact was gradually established and explained by the men referred to, and how, for forty years subsequently, almost inconceivable misapprehensions again obscured the clearly established fact, until more recently it came to be counted among the indisputable acquisitions of science.

As an essential point, it is at the same time to be insisted upon here that the volume of oxygen evolved is equal to the volume of the carbon dioxide taken in, as De Saussure and, later and more exactly, Boussingault, have already established. This signifies, in other words, that the chemical processes in the cells containing chlorophyll run their course as if all the oxygen of the carbon dioxide taken up was evolved. This fact is of the utmost importance, because further consequences respecting the processes in the assimilating cells can be concluded from it.

Since we are here treating of those chemical processes by means of which the production of organic substance from inorganic materials (carbon dioxide and water) originally takes place in the natural course of events, and since this organic substance affords the constructive material not only for plants but for the whole animal kingdom as well, it must interest the student of vegetable physiology to observe the process for himself. This can, of course, only be effected indirectly, and this most simply by placing water-plants such as *Ceratophyllum, Myriophyllum, Udora (Elodea), Potamogeton*, etc., in water containing carbon dioxide, and taking care that a smooth cross-cut is made at the lower part of the leafy shoot-axis. If the vessel filled with water containing carbon dioxide, in which the shoot is submerged, is placed at a window on which the sun is shining, a stream of small bubbles of gas is at once seen to spring from the cut end of the shoot-axis, and to escape upwards. If a glass tube previously filled with water is inverted over the surface of the water in the vessel, the gas evolved by the water-plant may be collected, and it is then shown that this gas, if the experiment has been properly made, is very rich in oxygen, but contains also carbon dioxide and nitrogen. These two latter gases, however, really owe their presence to a fallacious arrangement of our experiment: for the bubbles of oxygen evolved by the plant ascend into the collecting vessel through water laden with nitrogen and carbon dioxide, and, according to the general laws of diffusion of gases, they must take up carbon dioxide and nitrogen from the water during the ascent. Although this experiment with the above water-plants is particularly suitable for ocular demonstration of the work of plants, a more circumstantial and less obvious mode of procedure is more convenient for rendering clear the true process of the decomposition of carbon dioxide. For this purpose, it is better to employ leaves, or portions of the leaves, of land-plants, pushing them into a glass tube which is cylindrical and graduated below, and dilated above. Into this tube, closed below with mercury, an accurately measured quantity of carbon dioxide gas is placed, together with atmospheric air, and the whole apparatus is then placed in the sunlight. After some time, perhaps an hour, the leaf is withdrawn, and the carbon dioxide and oxygen contents of the air in the glass tube examined, according to known gasometric methods. It now turns out that the quantity of carbon dioxide has diminished, while the proportion of oxygen has increased; and, moreover, it is shown that for each cubic centimetre of carbon dioxide which has disappeared, a cubic centimetre of oxygen has become free. Such an experiment, it is true, is little suitable for demonstration in the lecture room, since it demands at least three or four hours of work, besides corrections and calculations: it supplies, however, incontestable proof that carbon dioxide is decomposed by means of a green leaf, under the influence of light, and that an equal volume of oxygen is evolved in its place. What we here observe, however, in the case of a single small leaf, or portion of a leaf, is proceeding more or less energetically during the whole day in all green leaves of plants in the open, even when the sun is overshadowed by clouds; and what appears in our experiment as the decomposition of a few cubic centimetres of carbon dioxide, is represented in the case of a meadow, a corn-field, or a forest, by hundreds or thousands of litres of this gas.

That it is by means of the chlorophyll of the plant that the absorbed carbon dioxide is decomposed and its oxygen evolved, follows with certainty from the fact that it is only and exclusively those parts of plants which contain chlorophyll that are able to effect this decomposition [1] No organs devoid of chlorophyll, such as roots, subterranean tubers, floral leaves and stamens; no chlorotic white leaves, or yellow etiolated leaves grown in the dark; and again, no non-green parasites or Fungi, yield oxygen in the experiment just described. on the contrary, they continually evolve carbon dioxide from their interior, though in relatively small quantities. In such organs devoid of chlorophyll, therefore, no reconstruction of combustible organic substance poor in oxygen can take place; and thence follows at once that in all plants containing chlorophyll, the organs which are not green consist of organic compounds which have been produced in the organs containing chlorophyll, and in like manner that plants generally which contain no chlorophyll, such as true root-parasites and all Fungi, are necessitated to absorb organic substance poor in oxygen from without, because they lack the organs for decomposing carbon dioxide and producing organic substance. Since, however, all animals are likewise devoid of these organs, and are thus unable to form organic substance from carbon dioxide and water, although they build up their bodies from such substance, it follows obviously that the substance of the bodies of all animals is originally produced in the chlorophyll-cells of plants. The few lower animals which apparently contain chlorophyll—certain *Infusoria, Sponges,* and *Planariæ*—contain

---

[1] That the green-coloured protoplasm, the chlorophyll, is the organ of assimilation, was first expressed definitely by me in my *'Experimental-Physiologie'* (1865, p 319), in opposition to the utterly indefinite statements of earlier physiologists, according to which green plants possess a daily respiration with the evolution of oxygen, and a nocturnal respiration with the formation of carbon dioxide, and after the doubts which even the distinguished Theodore de Saussure entertained as to the signification of chlorophyll. I expressly insisted upon the point that 'it is a striking phenomenon in the history of vegetable physiology that the chlorophyll has not long ago been distinguished definitely as the instrument for the separation of oxygen'

chlorophyll as a matter of fact, not as a proper constituent of the body, but, as Brandt has recently shown, have vegetable cells (Algæ) containing chlorophyll in their bodies: by means of the assimilation of these green bodies, such animals may be nourished under certain circumstances [1]

It matters little in what form the chlorophyll is contained in the cells. whether, as is usual, in the form of soft granules, or, as in the Conjugateæ (a group of Algæ), in the form of green bands or plates, or even simply as masses of protoplasm tinged with green, as in the *Palmellaceæ* and some other Algæ It also makes no essential difference whether or no other colouring matters besides the chlorophyll are present in the cells, as in the red Algæ (*Florideæ*) or the yellow-brown Fucaceæ. It was a fatal mistake of De Saussure's to argue from the red colour of many leaves, such as the red garden Orache (*Atriplex hortensis*), that chlorophyll is unnecessary for the decomposition of carbon dioxide: Cloez, in 1863, first insisted upon the presence of chlorophyll even in such cases. The whole literature on the nutrition of plants, even of twenty or thirty years ago, shows how ill established was the knowledge of the fact that it is the chlorophyll only which effects the decomposition of carbon dioxide: it was always the custom to say cautiously that green plants decompose carbonic acid, without more exactly indicating which organ effects this decomposition. In general, definite recognition of the fact that it is the chlorophyll which is the agent for the decomposition of carbon dioxide has only made way since the appearance of my 'Handbook of Experimental Physiology' in 1865; and when a more recent author finds that, properly speaking, it is not the chlorophyll but the cell containing chlorophyll which is the organ of assimilation, because the one is contained in the other, it is somewhat equivalent to saying that the eye is not properly the organ of sight, since, when taken out of the head, it is no longer capable of seeing. Since no cell assimilates so long as it possesses no green chlorophyll, but does so as soon as it is provided with it, we are justified in distinguishing the chlorophyll-body itself as the organ which decomposes carbon dioxide, and consequently assimilates the organic substance. The most definite proof, however, is afforded by the fact, to be stated more exactly further on, that the first recognisable product of assimilation appears not in any haphazard place in the cell containing chlorophyll, but in the chlorophyll-body itself.

I have repeatedly taken the opportunity of referring in these lectures to the essential co-operation of light in assimilation in the chlorophyll. We are here in fact concerned with the dependence of plant-life upon the external world, and in reviewing the different phenomena of vegetation this must never be lost sight of, if the most mischievous errors are to be avoided. The great importance of the fact that a plant containing chlorophyll, so long as it does not meet with light of sufficient intensity is not able to decompose carbon dioxide, and, therefore, is not capable of producing organic substance of any kind whatsoever, must always be kept in view. For those not familiar with vegetable physiology a misleading difficulty arises in that plants, in spite of being in dark or feebly illuminated situations, are able, according to circumstances, to continue living and even to grow vigorously for some time, particularly when they are well provided with assimilated reserve-materials.

---

[1] K. Brandt, ' *Ueber das Zusammenleben von Thieren und Algen* ' (Verhandl der physiol. Gesellsch. zu Berlin), Dec. 2, 1881.

The uninitiated student easily draws thence the erroneous conclusion that the growing plants must also be nourishing themselves. In the following lecture I shall show more in detail that growth of the organs and assimilation in the chlorophyll are two processes mutually independent in a high degree. In order that a plant, or certain of its parts, may grow, it suffices that organic matters assimilated by the previous activity of chlorophyll are present; and, conversely, a plant may be assimilating vigorously without growing at the same time. When, therefore, plants grow in the dark, or with insufficient illumination in general, this takes place at the cost of such assimilated substances as have previously been stored up in the tissues of the seeds, tubers, bulbs, root-stocks, or in the cortex of the branches of trees, etc, and which are now utilised in growth. Moreover, growth with insufficient illumination destroys considerable quantities of organic plant-substance, in consequence of the respiration connected with it, as I shall demonstrate in detail in a later lecture. Hence it comes about that the dry weight of plants growing in the dark is diminished, and this growth in the dark can therefore only continue until the existing reserve-materials have been used up

For the sake of completeness, this opportunity may be taken of incidentally touching upon another point. As the instrument of assimilation can only have its assimilating activity set at work under the influence of light of sufficient intensity, so also it is in most plants only brought to complete development by the light. The leaves of flowering plants, especially when they are formed by growth in the dark, produce chlorophyll-grains in their cells, it is true, but these are not green; they remain yellow[1], tinged with a colouring matter which is but little different from the green colouring matter, but which is unable to communicate to the chlorophyll-grain the power of decomposing carbon dioxide. Such yellow etiolated leaves do not assimilate, as experiment shows; exposed for some time to light, however, even though feeble, they become green, and are then able to decompose carbon dioxide. Nevertheless, as I established twenty-three years ago, the development of green chlorophyll is not in every case connected with the influence of light the primary leaves of the seedlings of Conifers develope their normal chlorophyll even in profound darkness, and the leaves of Ferns behave similarly. This dependence of the formation of chlorophyll upon light (not, as we see, without exception) often led formerly to the erroneous assumption that the greening of leaves is itself a process of assimilation, and connected with the evolution of oxygen. A direct refutation of this view, however, lies in the observation that very feeble light enables the yellow leaves produced in the dark to become green, although this feeble light is far from sufficient to cause the green chlorophyll-grains to assimilate. This important fact, much too little noticed, may be very easily confirmed by allowing seedlings of Beans, Maize, *Tropæolum*, etc., to germinate in pots situated at the back of an ordinary dwelling-room. Their first leaves become green: that no assimilation follows, however, is shown by weighing the dried plants, which yield a smaller weight of organic substance than was contained

---

[1] On the behaviour of chlorophyll in the dark, cf my '*Experimental-Physiologie*,' p 317, and Pfeffer, '*Pflanzen-Physiologie*,' p. 221 —On the dependence of the formation of chlorophyll upon temperature, see Sachs, *Flora*, 1864, p 497, and 1862, p 129

in the seed. That the greening is for and by itself no assimilation process, however, and that it takes place without the decomposition of carbon dioxide, may be demonstrated further with the aid of the apparatus here figured. The yellow leaves, previously grown in the dark, are placed under the bell-glass, and, when the apparatus stands in the light, become green, even if the plate is filled with a strong solution of potash which completely absorbs the carbon dioxide under the bell-jar.

Finally is to be mentioned the fact that the organ of assimilation, even when it has been previously normally developed in the light, can dispense with the light for a time (in the normal course of things it does so every night) without taking any harm thereby, but more permanent darkness, or even only deep shading (i. e. for several days or weeks), brings about a disease of the previously green cells, their chlorophyll-grains become destroyed, and the leaves turn yellow and finally perish. This even occurs in the feeble illumination in which, as mentioned above, the same leaves previously became green. Nevertheless there are plants, the green organs of which can dispense with light, even for months together, without dying. I found this to be the case for instance with some species of *Cactus* and *Selaginella*. In the main, the dependence upon light here referred to is particularly true for quickly growing summer-plants.

All the relations between the organs of assimilation and light here mentioned, as well as the independence of growth with regard to the latter, must be carefully observed, if the important fact that the decomposition of carbon dioxide and assimilation in the chlorophyll are a function of light is to be properly understood. It follows from what has been said, that not light of any haphazard intensity will do what is

FIG. 219

necessary. Unfortunately we lack photometric methods to enable us to distinguish those intensities of light which come into consideration in assimilation with the same precision, and generally intelligible exactness, as is possible with the thermometer with respect to temperature. The most exact photometric methods, and especially the method proposed by Bunsen, for instance, only give us information as to the intensity of the strongly refractive rays of light, the so-called chemical rays; but these, as I shall show subsequently, only come incidentally into consideration. We must therefore adopt entirely different methods with respect to statements concerning the intensity of light necessary for assimilation, and which will not be here given in detail. Only so much is obvious, that, for the decision of certain questions, use may be made of the law that with double the distance of a surface from a luminous point, the intensity of illumination of the latter sinks to $\frac{1}{4}$; at three times the distance to $\frac{1}{9}$, &c; and that the intensity of illumination of a leaf-surface at the same time depends upon the sine of the angle of incidence. It would cost us too much time, and would moreover lead to no satisfactory result in the end, to enter more in detail into these matters. It must therefore suffice, that assimilation by means of the decomposition of carbon dioxide, in most plants, and especially in the case of meadow-and cultivated plants, trees, and garden-plants of the most various kinds, only takes place with normal vigour and productiveness when the ordinary strong daylight of summer is at the disposal of the plants The much feebler light in greenhouses, or even in ordinary dwelling-rooms, suffices, it is true, with most plants to bring about a less productive assimilation in the green leaves; but the sickliness of the plant shows how feeble is the nutrition under such circumstances. It is also to be observed that a pot plant standing close to a window, under the best of circumstances only receives the light radiating from half the sky, and only meets with the direct rays of the sun occasionally. If the plant stands somewhat further removed from the window, it is only necessary to imagine straight lines running from the plant or a leaf to the edges of the window, and thence direct to the sky, to find the extent of that part of the latter the rays of which fall directly on the leaves: it is then perceived that a plant removed but a few metres from the window, only receives a very small proportion of light from the sky, and as a rule meets with no direct sunlight at all. Accordingly, the nutrition of plants in the middle of a room is extremely poor, and sooner or later they inevitably perish. On the other hand, however, it is also to be observed that while there are many plants which only flourish well in places which receive the full light from the sky, and the direct rays of the sun, others exist which prefer the shade of woods, or even the feeble illumination in the interior of deep caverns. Here belong, for example, besides some species of *Pyrola,* many Mosses, and especially Liverworts; those Algæ which grow exclusively in the depths of large seas, and are thus feebly illuminated, also show that they find the conditions of their existence in less intense light. Just as for each manifestation of life in plants there is an upper limit of temperature, which cannot be passed over without injury, so also there is certainly an upper limit of intensity of the light, at which the chlorophyll-grain can no longer accomplish assimilation. Of course this limit of the intensity of light cannot be exactly given, in the absence of suitable photometric methods; and when Pringsheim makes circumstantial statements concerning the behaviour of cells containing chlorophyll in the focus of a lens, or in the sun's image, as he terms it, these purely pathological processes have about as much physiological value as if, for any reason whatever, a so-called sun's image were allowed to act on the retina of the eye through a burning-glass Much better are the statements of several observers who, employing direct light, allowed the evolution of oxygen of one and the same plant to take place under various degrees of shading, and so established that a maximum effect at a light-optimum exists for this function also. In the absence of photometric measurements of general value however, I pass over these statements also.

We have much more information as to the various effects of the individual constituents of sunlight, than with respect to the cardinal points of the intensity of the light concerned in assimilation. As is well known, the light of the sun, like that of most incandescent bodies, is a mixture of very different luminous rays, which are distinguished by their refrangibility, i.e. by the amount of divergence which they undergo on entering another medium, as well as by their chemical effects; and obviously the question must force itself upon the investigator whether, and in what manner these different rays of light, of which daylight is made up, influence assimilation in the chlorophyll. For the preliminary guidance of those not quite familiar with the physical knowledge appertaining here, the following remarks may be made. If the sun's rays are allowed to fall through a narrow slit in the shutter of a room, they proceed through space in the form of a straight band, which can easily be seen as luminous striæ in the dusty air: if these luminous striæ or bundles of rays are allowed to pass through a triangular glass prism, the edges of which we suppose vertical, two results follow. First, the ray of light is diverted from its straight path—it falls on quite another spot on the hind wall of the chamber than was the case in the absence of the prism; and secondly, instead of the one bright stripe which the solar rays originally formed on the hind wall, there now appears a horizontal coloured band, the so-called solar spectrum, in which the colours of the rainbow, red, orange, yellow, green, blue, and violet, follow one another in such a way that the red portion is least, and the violet most strongly diverted from the rectilinear path of the beam of light. In this spectrum, by proper management, a number of black lines appear, running perpendicularly in the horizontal band of colours, these are the so-called Fraunhofer's lines, which, as Kirchoff and Bunsen have shown, are produced by the absorption of certain rays of light by the incandescent vapours of certain metals in the solar atmosphere. From these fixed lines in the solar spectrum, the most evident of which are distinguished by the letters A, B, C,—H, it is possible to determine exactly the place where definite effects occur. The refrangibility and colour of the different parts of the spectrum are a consequence, as the science of optics teaches, of the different wave-lengths in the vibrations of the luminous æther, of which the light consists.

If now the solar rays, passing through the slit, are allowed to traverse a glass vessel with parallel walls containing a dark blue solution of ammoniacal oxide of copper, the whole of the red and yellow, and part of the green bands in the spectrum disappear; the blue solution has absorbed, kept back, or destroyed these constituents of the sun-light. If a vessel with a concentrated solution of bi-chromate of potash, which appears to our eyes of a deep orange colour, is placed at the same spot, just those parts of the spectrum are cancelled which previously passed through the blue solution—i e. we now see in the spectrum the red-orange, yellow, and a part of the green, while the blue and violet have disappeared. We have thus in these two fluids excellent means for cutting out the one or the other half of the solar light; and we can therefore, with the aid of these two solutions, experimentally answer the question, what effect does the red-yellow or the blue-violet half of the spectrum respectively exert in the decomposition of carbon dioxide? After the preliminary and less instructive researches of Daubeny (1836), I made in 1864 a detailed investigation with regard to this question[1]. In a glass cylinder filled with water containing carbon dioxide a water-plant was placed; at the cut surface of the stem of this the oxygen evolved under the influence of light escaped regularly in the form of bubbles. This cylinder

---

[1] Sachs, '*Wirkungen farbigen Lichtes auf Pflanzen*,' Bot Zeit 1864, p. 353, where the older literature also is collected.

was placed in a second, wider cylinder, and the space between both filled with one or other of the solutions previously mentioned, or with pure water. After careful consideration and preparation, I employed as a measure of the decomposition of carbon dioxide in the plant, the number of bubbles which escaped from the cut surface of the stem in one minute[1] It was now possible to conduct the investigations in such a manner that the plant could be observed alternately for one minute respectively in white complete light, in red-yellow, or in blue-violet light, one immediately after the other, and the gas-bubbles counted. It turned out that in the blue-violet light only very little carbon dioxide was decomposed, while (having regard to accessory circumstances) the effect in red-yellow light was nearly as strong as in the full light which passed through pure water. This result, as well as the observations previously made by Daubeny, Draper (1844), Cloez and Gratiolet (1851), contradicted the prevailing view of the physicists and chemists, that it is the blue-violet part of the spectrum which almost alone brings about photochemical effects. The decomposition of carbon dioxide in the plant evidently depends upon a photo-chemical effect; and yet we here see that that portion of the spectrum which is distinguished by physicists as the one chemically effective, is relatively inactive, while the other half of the spectrum is here the effective one. I directly confirmed this apparent contradiction, again, by placing in the upper part of the glass cylinder containing the plant a small apparatus which enabled me, while observing the separation of oxygen, simultaneously to observe the effect of the coloured light on photographic paper. When the light passed through the blue-violet solution, the evolution of oxygen in the plant was extremely small, while the photographic paper became deep brown; when, on the other hand, the red-yellow solution was interposed, the plant evolved large quantities of oxygen, while the photographic paper reacted but little and feebly

It may here simply be remarked that it was an inaccurate generalisation on the part of physics and chemistry to designate the blue-violet portion of the spectrum as the part chemically active, simply because the corresponding rays of light cause silver salts to decompose and a mixture of chlorine and hydrogen to form

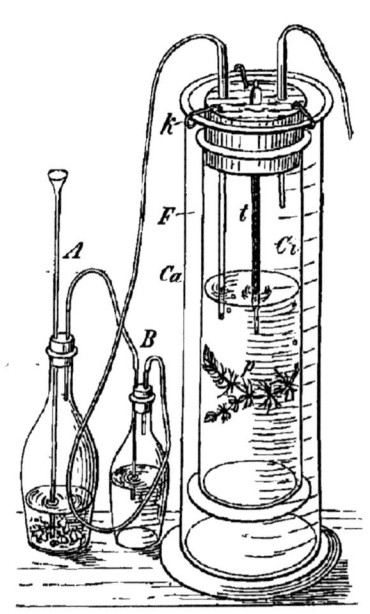

FIG. 220.—The glass cylinder C_2 contains the plant p in water, in which the thermometer t is immersed. The cylinder C_2 is then placed in the larger cylinder Ca, and the interspace f filled with the coloured liquid. k supporting hooks A disengages carbon dioxide, which is washed in water in the flask B

---

[1] With respect to the method of counting the bubbles employed by me, and much discussed later, cf Pfeffer, '*Pflanzen-Physiologie*,' p. 215

hydrochloric acid. The action of the red-yellow light on the decomposition of carbon dioxide which we have established contradicts no fact, but only a false generalisation; since it shows that other chemical processes which take place in the chlorophyll are brought about by other rays of light, namely the red-yellow. As regards the method of experimenting, I subsequently devised a more convenient arrangement. Glass vessels with parallel walls, and as large as possible (so-called *Cuvettes*), were filled with the solutions, and fixed somewhat like windows into opaque boxes; in these, by means of a door at the back, the plant to be observed is placed in water containing carbon dioxide.

So long ago as 1844 Draper had observed the evolution of oxygen from green leaves, by placing them, enclosed in small glass vessels, in various regions of the solar spectrum, and determining the quantities of oxygen given off, and thus learning the effects of the different coloured parts of the solar light. He found

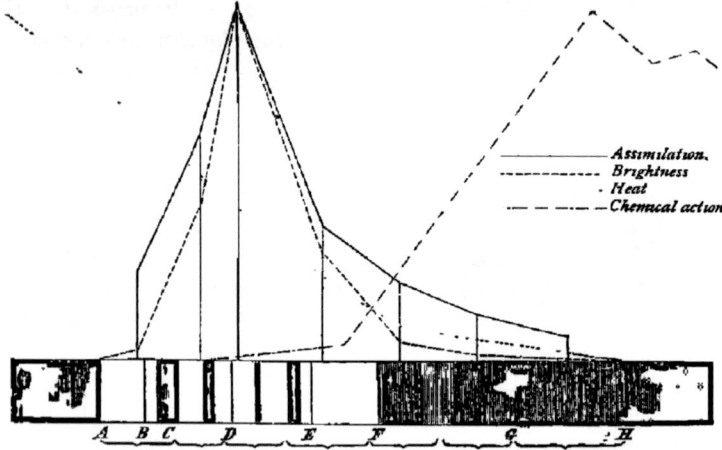

FIG 221 —The curves of assimilation, temperature, brightness, and chemical action of the various regions of the spectrum are represented on the spectrum of chlorophyll (*A H*) as an abscissa

that the effect in the red portion is extremely feeble, rising quickly in the red-orange, and reaching a maximum in the yellow-green, it falls again in the blue of the spectrum to an extremely small quantity. This obviously agrees with the researches described above, where the light passed through coloured solutions. If we suppose the solar spectrum to be an abscissa line, on which the effects discovered by Draper are erected as ordinates, the relative quantities of oxygen evolved in equal times in the various regions of the spectrum appear in the form of a curve, which begins in the red, reaches its maximum in the yellow-green, and then quickly sinks again towards the blue. This Draper's curve, as we may term the law of the dependence of assimilation upon the colour of the light, was tested more exactly by Pfeffer in 1870 by means of the eudio-meter, and then, in 1872, by counting the bubbles, a method employed by me previously[1]. The result of his observations may be understood most simply from

---

[1] Investigations on assimilation in coloured light are collected in Pfeffer's ' *Pflanzen-Physiologie*,' 1881, p 211.

[3]   x

the accompanying figure, in which are represented the effects of the different parts of the spectrum, not only on assimilation in the chlorophyll, but also on the heating of a thermometer as well as on the decomposition of silver salts, and, finally, on the eye. It is seen at once that the evolution of oxygen, or Draper's curve, cannot possibly be due to heating, or to the ordinary chemical effect of the spectrum; since the former reaches its maximum beyond the red end, and the latter in the violet. However, the remarkable fact that the curve of brightness in the spectrum nearly coincides with Draper's curve, has led some to the erroneous assumption that Draper's curve itself is an effect of brightness; such an idea is simply without meaning, since by the word brightness we mean in this case nothing more than the action of light on the human eye, an effect which may possibly be quite different on the eyes of different animals. It is obvious that the action of light upon our eye cannot possibly be the cause of the action of light on cells containing chlorophyll. The entire assumption depends therefore upon want of thought. I expressed the matter of Draper's curve correctly in the third edition of my 'Text-book' in the following words: the evolution of oxygen brought about by the chlorophyll is a function of the wave-length of light, so that only light of wave-lengths which are not larger than $\frac{60}{100000}$ mm and not smaller than $\frac{40}{100000}$ mm. bring about the evolution of oxygen. Proceeding from both extremes, the effect of light on the evolution of oxygen ascends when its wave-lengths approach $\frac{59}{100000}$ mm. where the maximum effect lies. Or, if we start with the medium wave-lengths of the coloured regions of the spectrum, measured in hundred-thousandths of millimetres, the evolution of oxygen is effected by light-waves the minimum length of which begins at about 40; it increases as this ascends to about 59, and decreases again as the wave-length increases, becoming almost nil at a wave-length of about 69. We have thus a phenomenon resembling the case of the curve of temperature, first established by me: as in that case the functions of the plant which depend upon temperature only begin with a certain intensity of the heat-vibrations, and ascend as the intensity increases, until at an optimum temperature the maximum effect occurs, falling again to zero with a further increase of temperature; so also in the case of Draper's curve, we see that the evolution of oxygen in plants begins at a certain small wave-length, and that a wave-length of $\frac{59}{100000}$ mm. represents about the optimum, where the maximum effect occurs, and that with a further increase of the wave-length the physiological effect falls to zero.

Although these results have apparently only a purely theoretical interest, it is nevertheless not to be forgotten that they may be of practical value in the criticism of certain vital phenomena of plants. Plants for example which grow in the deep shade of woods, meet with light which has to a great extent passed through the translucent leaves of trees, and which has lost a great part of its yellow, blue, violet, and ultra-violet rays in the chlorophyll of the latter; and in like manner plants growing in the depths of large seas receive light of totally different composition from that received by terrestrial plants, and to which the highly refrangible rays especially are wanting. Again, it is futile to attempt to improve greenhouses with blue glass, proceeding from the erroneous assumption that the plants will thus have chiefly blue light conveyed to them, and from the further erroneous assumption that this blue light must be useful to the plant because it belongs to the so-called chemical part of the spectrum. It has been shown above that the latter is not the case; and moreover blue glass at most transmits as much blue light as colourless. That it appears blue is simply because it destroys a large proportion of the yellow light; and we have learnt that it is just this yellow light which is the effective constituent of daylight in the nutrition of the plant. The effect of glazing greenhouses with blue glass is therefore directly injurious: it depends on false conclusions from inaccurately established facts

Finally, the question as to the action of different coloured light on the nutrition of plants comes into consideration when artificial terrestrial sources of light are employed for the illumination of plants instead of ordinary sunlight. This has hitherto taken place, of course, only in the interest of scientific research It is theoretically certain, and has been established by experiment that the electric light —i. e. the light from incandescent electrodes—as well as lamplight, &c., when sufficiently intense, can effect the evolution of oxygen from organs containing chlorophyll. Here, however, it is not to be forgotten that every such source of light possesses a different mixture of rays of different refrangibility, or, in other words, a different spectrum; and, from what has been said previously, each source of light particularly rich in yellow rays will cause more vigorous assimilation.

We pass, finally, to the fourth question mentioned in the introduction, which may be shortly answered thus: the first definitely established product of assimilation in the chlorophyll-corpuscles is starch (Amylum), or some other substance equivalent to it. Very indefinite ideas were formerly entertained in this connection It was supposed, as resulted from the statements of the older physiologists and chemists, that an indefinite primordial slime, perhaps composed of various substances and impossible to characterise in detail, arises in the green organs of plants. it was believed that this substance was again recognised on its way in the living cortex of trees, and it was assumed that it penetrated into the various organs and tissues, there to break up into the numerous and various chemical compounds which are found in different parts of the plant In a long series of micro-chemical and experimental researches on the distribution of starch and sugar, of proteid substances and of fats, and their use in growth, I came to the conclusion in 1862[1] that the enclosed starch, which had already been observed in the chlorophyll-corpuscles by Naegeli and Mohl, is to be regarded as the first evident product of assimilation formed by the decomposition of carbon dioxide. I said to myself, if this view is right, the formation of starch in the chlorophyll-corpuscles must cease on the exclusion of light, since the decomposition of carbon dioxide can then no longer take place; and that in like manner renewed access of light to the chlorophyll-corpuscles must also bring about a renewal of the formation of starch in them. These and similar deductions were confirmed by appropriate investigations; and yet more—I had already concluded from my previous micro-chemical analyses

---

[1] The foundations of my theory, that the starch in the chlorophyll is the first evident product of assimilation, were first laid in the following of my works·—‘*Flora,*’ 1862, Nos 11 and 21, and 1863, p 33, ‘*Bot Zeit*’ 1862, p 366; ‘*Jahrb. fur wiss Bot*’ 1863, III, p 199, ‘*Exp.-Phys*’ 1865, p. 320

of entire plants, in the most various stages, that the starch and sugar etc. which pass from place to place and are used up in the petioles, stems, growing buds, etc., were derived from the green assimilating leaves ; and, consequently, when assimilation ceases in these, the starch must also disappear from the chlorophyll-corpuscles themselves. This conclusion also proved correct. This is not the place to repeat in detail the numerous proofs, in part direct, in part indirect, which I brought forward during the years 1862–1865, to establish the fact that the starch-grains observed in the chlorophyll-corpuscles of normally vegetating plants are products of assimilation, and that, after their origin under the influence of light, they are dissolved and conveyed from the leaves, through their petioles, into the shoot-axes, and thence into the buds and apices of the roots, to provide the material for the growth of the organs; and that a portion of this original product of assimilation is made use of in metabolism for the formation of proteid substances, while, on the other hand, fats may arise by relatively slight changes from the carbohydrates, and therefore, ultimately, from the assimilated starch. The thought arose that, in the nutrition of plants, it is only necessary in the first place to decompose carbon dioxide under the influence of light in the cells containing chlorophyll, with the co-operation of certain mineral matters absorbed by the roots, and to produce at the cost of its carbon an organic substance—starch—which then represents the starting-point, so to speak, from which all the other organic substances of the plant proceed by progressive chemical changes. This conclusion has in the course of twenty years become more and more established as the correct one.

LECTURE XIX.

ORIGIN OF STARCH IN THE CHLOROPHYLL, AND IN THE STARCH-FORMING CORPUSCLES· FURTHER BEHAVIOUR AND FATE OF THE CHLOROPHYLL.

IT was stated at the end of the foregoing lecture that the starch arises in the chlorophyll by means of the process of assimilation—i. e. by the decomposition of carbon dioxide under the influence of light—and that it represents the first product of assimilation hitherto known with certainty. The attempt may now be made to establish these facts more definitely.

If seedlings of the Gourd, Sunflower, Maize, or Garden-beans, or the sprouts of Dahlias or *Helianthus tuberosus* are allowed to grow in the dark at a sufficiently high temperature ($15° - 25° C$), until development finally ceases, the tissues of these etiolated shoots, as well as those of the roots, are at length entirely emptied of assimilated substances. The plants in these cases consist almost solely of cell-walls, protoplasm, and water. The most important fact, however, is that the small yellow chlorophyll-corpuscles in the leaves contain no trace of starch, either in the chlorophyll or in the other organs and tissues. If these plants, already green, or even those taken immediately from the dark, be placed at a light window, starch arises in the chlorophyll-corpuscles (which have previously become green) at first in exceedingly small quantity, which rapidly increases in strong light. In the course of several days, $6 - 20$ according to the temperature, abundance of starch is found in the chlorophyll, and subsequently also in certain layers of tissue in the petioles and shoot-axes; this may be followed into the buds, the young leaves of which now begin also to grow anew, since the starch produced in the chlorophyll again supplies material from which the tissues of new organs may be formed. By means of such investigations I first succeeded, in 1862, in experimentally proving that the starch formed in the chlorophyll under the influence of light, is the first visible product of assimilation[1]. In 1863 and 1864 I convinced myself[2] that the starch contained in the chlorophyll of normally developed leaves may disappear again in long-continued darkness; and that it is possible to bring about

---

[1] Sachs, '*Ueber den Einfluss des Lichtes auf die Bildung des Amylum in den Chlorophyllkornern.*' Bot Zeit 1862, p 365.

[2] Sachs, '*Ueber die Auflosung und Wiederbildung des Amylum in den Chlorophyllkornern bei wechselnder Beleuchtung*' Bot Zeit 1864, pp. 289 and 322

the renewed formation of starch by a second illumination   I made these experiments with *Begonia*, Tobacco, and *Geranium peltatum*, placing the entire plants in the dark until the starch had disappeared from the chlorophyll of the leaves, then, the plants being again exposed to the light, a renewed formation of starch resulted.   In the first experiments with *Begonia*, certain portions of the leaves were covered with black paper on both sides, with the result that the starch disappeared from the chlorophyll of the leaves only at these places.   I now employ this form of experiment in my lectures on vegetable physiology, in order to demonstrate the influence of light on the formation of starch; or, better, of darkness on the disappearance of starch.   It suffices for instance to fasten a broad band of tinfoil or lead in summer on plants with conveniently large leaves and growing in pots —e. g Tobacco, Maize, *Canna*, etc., without depriving the plants of light.   After a few days, the leaves so treated are cut off, and thrown for a few minutes into boiling water in order to kill them, and to cause the starch in the chlorophyll to swell   They are then placed for some hours in strong alcohol, which removes the chlorophyll colouring-matter, and the now colourless leaves are finally placed in a vessel containing a weak, pale brown, alcoholic solution of iodine.   After a short time, the parts of the leaf which were not shaded from the light appear blue-black, owing to the formation of iodide of starch: the place shaded by the band of tinfoil, on the other hand, remains colourless, simply because the chlorophyll-corpuscles there contain no more starch.

This experiment demonstrates yet another fact, viz., that the action of light is strictly local, and is not transferred to neighbouring shaded places.   Moreover the action of carbon dioxide is also strictly local, as Moll showed in 1878[1]. The leaves produce starch only at the places directly in contact with air containing carbon dioxide.   If, for example, one half of a leaf is placed in a space the air of which is deprived of carbon dioxide, while the other half remains in the ordinary atmosphere, both halves being equally illuminated, starch arises in the chlorophyll only in the last-named half, the other producing none. Again, if the leaves of a plant rooted in garden soil are placed in a space which contains no carbon dioxide, no starch is produced in the chlorophyll, even with favourable illumination   These experiments prove that the view entertained until quite recently by the older physiologists, that carbon dioxide may be conveyed from the roots into the leaves, and there assimilated, is absolutely wrong

In some cases it is impossible directly to observe starch as the product of assimilation in the chlorophyll-grains.   I found this to be the case in the leaves of our common Onion (*Allium Cepa*), where, however, large quantities of glucose (sugar) are to be recognised as the result of assimilation.   As a rule this plant does not form starch, and the reserve-material in its bulbs also consists of glucose.   It was observed later, that in the leaves of *Strelitzia* and *Musa* also fatty oils are found as a rule in the chlorophyll instead of starch   The assumption that the first product of assimilation of the chlorophyll is in these

---

[1] Moll, ' *Ueber die Herkunft des Kohlenstoffs in der Pflanze* ' Arbeiten des bot. Inst in Wurzburg, II, 1878, p. 105.   See also Vines, *ibid.*, p. 121.

cases not starch, but fat, was refuted however by Holle and Godlewski[1], who showed that, even in these plants, the decomposition of carbon dioxide yields a volume of oxygen equal to that of the carbon dioxide employed, which could not possibly be the case if fat were immediately formed; and that under particularly favourable conditions of assimilation—viz., on supplying larger quantities of carbon dioxide to the surrounding air, and using a stronger light—starch can actually be detected in the chlorophyll. It thus appears that in many plants the starch produced in the chlorophyll may be at once transformed into fat, as may also be the case with some species of *Vaucheria*. this process presents nothing at all surprising, since I showed so long ago as 1859 and later, by numerous examples[2], that the transformation of fat into carbo-hydrates and of carbo-hydrates into fat, is a very common phenomenon in plants; and with respect to the glucose in *Allium*, it is simply to be noticed that it matters little for the plant whether the chemical processes produce starch or sugar, as we shall see again in the following lecture

The formation of starch in the chlorophyll may be more easily observed in the simply organised Algæ than in the leaves of the higher plants Kraus found, in 1867, that in *Spirogyra*, previously kept in the dark and thus deprived of starch, the formation of starch was to be recognised, on illuminating it under the microscope. even after five minutes in direct sunlight, and in the course of two hours in diffused daylight, and similar results were obtained with the leaves of a Moss (*Funaria*), and the water-plant *Elodea*. It being, further, established that assimilation is much more energetic in yellow than in blue light, Famintzin also succeeded in demonstrating, in 1867, that starch is formed more rapidly under the influence of yellow than of blue light.

Although my above-cited researches (collected in my *Experimental-physiologie*) admit of no doubt that starch, or a substance equivalent to it, is to be regarded as the first visible product of assimilation, it was nevertheless a welcome confirmation of my theory when Godlewski, in 1873, demonstrated, by experiments as ingenious as they were simple[3], that in an atmosphere devoid of carbon dioxide no starch is produced in the chlorophyll-corpuscles, even in the light. He also found that the starch produced in the chlorophyll disappears, not only in the dark but even in intense light, when the surrounding air contains no carbon dioxide. Of particular importance is the fact, established by Godlewski, that on increasing the amount of carbon dioxide contained in the air to 8%, the formation of starch is four or five times more energetic in a strong light, while in diffused light the action is much feebler Very large quantities of carbon dioxide in the air, however, prevent the formation of starch, and the more so the feebler the light[4] These statements are the more valuable since Godlewski had previously established,

---

[1] Emil Godlewski, in Flora, p. 215, and Holle, *ibid*, p. 113

[2] Sachs, '*Ueber das Auftreten der Stärke bei Keimung ölhaltiger Samen*' Bot Zeit 1859, p 177

[3] Godlewski, '*Abhangigkeit der Starkebildung in den Chlorophyllkornern von dem Kohlensauregehalt der Luft*' Flora, 1873, p 378.

[4] Godlewski, '*Abhangigkeit der Sauerstoffabscheidung der Blatter von dem Kohlensauregehalt der Luft*' Arbeiten des bot. Inst. in Wurzburg, 1873, Bd. I, p. 343.

by a detailed investigation in my laboratory, that on increasing the carbon dioxide of the air to 5—10% leaves (of *Glyceria spectabilis*, *Typha latifolia*, and *Oleander*) evolve the maximum amount of oxygen in intense light.

On the basis of all these facts, there cannot be the slightest doubt that the starch in the chlorophyll-corpuscles is to be regarded as the first evident product of assimilation; and that it continually undergoes solution in the light as well as in darkness, and becomes distributed in some form from the assimilating organs into the tissues of the plant. There it is either used up immediately for the growth of new organs, or is stored up as reserve-materials in seeds, tubers, bulbs, root-stocks, and the cortex and wood of trees, or it provides the material for the formation of other organic compounds, and especially for the synthesis of the proteid substances.

Since, according to my theory, the basis for the whole of the organic substance of a normal plant is provided by the formation of starch in the chlorophyll of the organs of assimilation, and, above all, the whole of the carbon, in whatever organic combination it may be found later, occurs originally in the form of starch, it is particularly interesting to enquire how great the work of the assimilating chlorophyll may be under definite, and especially under normal conditions of illumination. The question, however, can so far only be approximately answered, since we cannot employ individual chlorophyll-corpuscles for such observations—nor even individual cells, the unicellular Algæ not being suitable for quantitative determinations. Moreover, it is not impossible that the quantitative activity of chlorophyll-corpuscles similar in size and colour may be peculiar for each species of plant; and some observations make such an assumption almost probable. Since in the course of about 100 summer days a huge plant, the dry-weight of which may attain two or three kilograms, is developed from the tiny embryo of a Tobacco seed, while from the much larger seed of a Fir, for instance, there arises in the same time a small plantlet, the dry-weight of which only amounts to a few grams, it may be supposed that, among the very numerous causes which may effect this difference, the activity of the chlorophyll-substance itself is possibly much more energetic in the first example than in the latter. This, however, is not the place to enter more deeply into so difficult a question. But it is desirable to know, even if only approximately, how much starch may be assimilated in the chlorophyll under favourable circumstances. Such considerations impelled me in 1878 to persuade Dr. Weber, then my assistant, to undertake an experimental investigation, in the first place to decide only the question how great is the quantity of starch assimilated in a given time (e. g ten hours of daylight) in the summer and with favourable illumination, by a certain amount of leaf-surface (e. g. a square metre[1]). Even in this very simple form the answer to the question presents great experimental difficulties. This is particularly the case because the starch at first assimilated by the few leaves of the experimental plants is at once used up again for the production of new organs of assimilation; the area of the leaves enlarges from hour to hour, and from day to day; and older leaves cease to assimilate, and younger ones begin to perform

---

[1] Weber, '*Ueber specifische Assimilationsenergie*' Arbeiten des bot. Inst in Würzburg, II, p. 346.

that function. Hence repeated measurements of the leaves must accompany the growth of the plant—an exceedingly troublesome task. We may of course also proceed by preventing a plant, already provided with a large assimilating surface, from increasing the latter and using up its products of assimilation in the shoots, which develope in the dark and thus take no part in assimilation. But even here many difficulties arise. According to the first method, Weber found that in four species of plants distinguished by their thin and relatively large leaves, and by their rapid growth and considerable increase in weight in a short time, a square metre of leaf-surface produces the following quantities of starch in ten hours of daylight .—

Tropæolum majus	4 446 grams.
Phaseolus multiflorus . . .	3˙215 ,,
Ricinus communis	5˙292 ,
Helianthus annuus	5˙559 ,,

It is to be remarked, however, that the ash contained in the dry substance should be deducted from the calculation, and the loss of organic substance by respiration added to it; since the increase in weight of a plant in organic substance is, as a matter of fact, only the difference between the quantities gained by assimilation and the quantities, of course much smaller, lost in respiration. This opportunity may be taken for making the additional remark that the quantities of starch present for the time being, which may be detected incidentally in the chlorophyll-corpuscles, is only transitory, since the starch arising in the chlorophyll by assimilation is continually being dissolved in the light, as well as in the dark, and conveyed into other portions of the plant. During vigorous assimilation its accumulation in the chlorophyll predominates: in continuous darkness, or feeble illumination, on the other hand, the solution and translocation of the starch prevail, and it is this which renders it possible to deprive the chlorophyll-corpuscles of starch for experimental purposes.

Weber's experiments were made, however, not in the open air but in a greenhouse, the illumination of which was very strong, it is true, but still not normal, as in the open We may therefore assume that in the latter case the assimilation would have been more energetic, and the more so since plants in the open can also develope their roots more normally than in Weber's experiments, where they were confined in pots This supposition is to a certain extent confirmed by Kreussler's measurements, which, to be sure, were made by very different and less exact methods. Maize plants, according to these experiments, yielded as much as seven grams of starch per square metre in ten hours, under the above conditions , and observations made later in my laboratory on Gourd plants, rooted in the open, yielded a probable number of eight grams of starch per square metre of leaf-surface per day, which nevertheless would give in 100 days only 800 grams of dry substance, while in a sunflower (*Helianthus annuus*) I obtained in 100 days more than 1400 grams of dry substance, although the foliage during the first fifty days was certainly less than half a square metre, and even later did not amount to a whole square metre. It is thus to be expected that the energy of assimilation may, under certain circumstances, be considerably greater than eight grams per day per square metre[1]. At any rate, the numbers mentioned give an approximate idea of the enormous amount of work which the crown of foliage of a tree, such as a Horse-chestnut, Walnut, etc., must do in the course of a summer In these cases the main mass of the products of assimilation is deposited in the form of wood, whereas in Peas, Beans, and cereals, a great portion of it passes into the fruits and seeds, while we find the products of assimilation of the Potato-plant

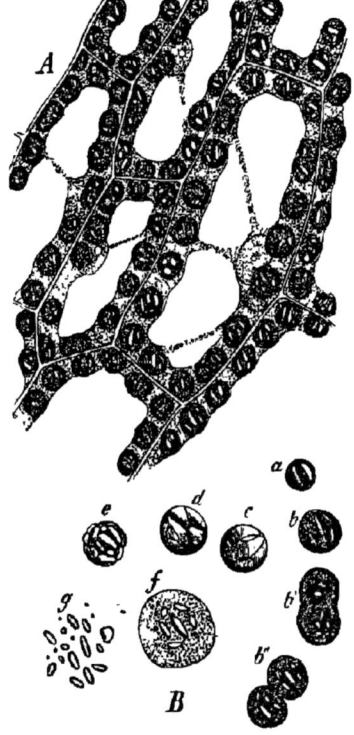

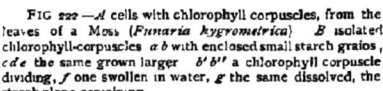

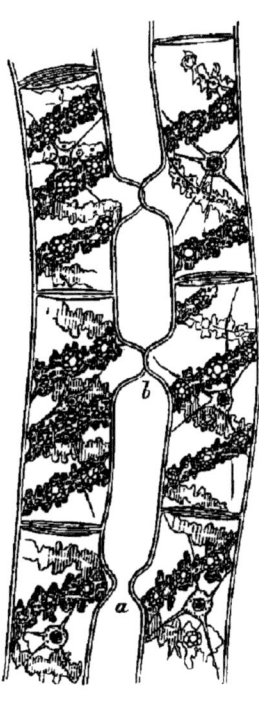

FIG 222 —*A* cells with chlorophyll corpuscles, from the leaves of a Moss (*Funaria hygrometrica*) *B* isolated chlorophyll-corpuscles *a b* with enclosed small starch grains, *c d e* the same grown larger *b' b''* a chlorophyll corpuscle dividing, *f* one swollen in water, *g* the same dissolved, the starch alone remaining

FIG 223.—Two filaments of *Spirogyra* in conjugation, the band of chlorophyll containing groups of starch grains

to a large extent stored up in the tubers, and those of the Beet in the huge root abounding in sugar

Having thus learned to understand the amount of work performed by chlorophyll, first with reference to the external circumstances and then to the quantity, we may now submit the question, what takes place in the chlorophyll-corpuscle itself in these processes? Here a distinction is to be made between the changes immediately perceptible with the aid of the microscope and micro-chemical reactions, and the chemical processes which take place in the substance of the chlorophyll-

---

[1] [Sachs has since proved this to be the case   See *Arbeiten des bot Inst in Wurzburg*, B. III, where experiments show that as much as 20–25 grams of starch per day may be formed by 1 square metre of leaf-surface   An abstract of this paper appeared in 'Nature' for April 10, 1884]

corpuscle, and which cannot be seen but can only be inferred from their consequences and conditions. Confining ourselves first to the visible changes, the old observations of Naegeli and myself show that in the primitively quite homogeneous green substance, starch-grains, at first extremely small, become visible, usually distributed in twos, threes, or more in the mass of chlorophyll of the corpuscle. These enlarge and, as they meet one another during growth, become flattened and applied close to one another with plane surfaces, while their free sides remain rounded and become arranged more or less according to the form of the chlorophyll-corpuscle; occasionally, however, when they arise at the circumference they protrude from the chlorophyll-corpuscle. I also observed, almost twenty years ago, that, under certain circumstances, when leaves (e.g. of Tobacco and Pea) turn

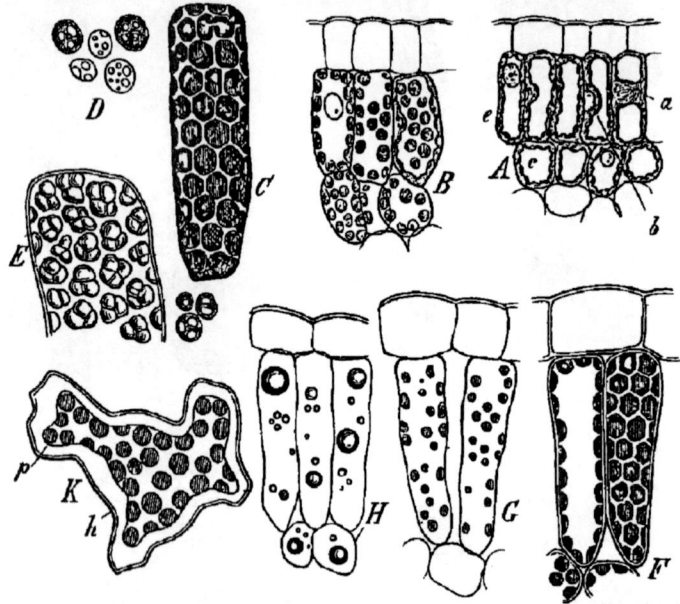

FIG 224 —*A* cells from an etiolated leaf of *Dahlia variabilis* *B* the same but older and with yellow chlorophyll-corpuscles. *C* the yellow chlorophyll-corpuscles turned green and further developed in light. *D* commencement of starch-formation *E* advanced stages in the formation of the starch *F* from the leaf of *Tropaeolum majus* *G* and *H* destruction of the chlorophyll (in *H* yellow oil drops only remain) as the leaves turn yellow in autumn *K* a cell from the leaf of *Vicia Faba* after contraction of the lining protoplasm (primordial utricle). *p k* the cell wall

yellow without being diseased, the starch-grains grow so vigorously in the chlorophyll that the latter becomes, so to speak, entirely displaced by them, and finally, in place of a chlorophyll corpuscle, there lies a starch-grain compounded of several grains (cf. Fig. 224).

Very valuable contributions to the question with which we are here concerned were made by A F W. Schimper in 1880[1] I must refer to these because they throw a new light on the chemical processes presumably taking place in the chlorophyll. In the first place, it follows from Schimper's description that

---

[1] Schimper, '*Untersuchungen uber die Entstehung der Starkekorner*' Bot Zeit 1880, p 881 —Arthur Meyer, Bot. Zeit. 1880, Nos 51 and 52

the chlorophyll-corpuscles in the green parts of the stem behave differently from those in the assimilating lamina of the leaf: this, according to my view, is also demonstrated by the fact that during growth in the dark, the otherwise green parts of the stem and petioles remain white, while the assimilating laminæ appear yellow in the etiolated state. Schimper found that in the stems of many plants the starch-grains do not arise at any haphazard points of the chlorophyll-corpuscle, but exclusively close beneath its surface, so that they soon protrude from its substance. Hence the following distinction results. The grains which remain entirely in the chlorophyll-corpuscle are rounded, and possess a concentrically layered structure, because they are nourished on all sides from the chlorophyll; whereas the starch-grains growing out from the chlorophyll-corpuscls are stratified excentrically, since they grow much more strongly and exhibit more numerous layers on the side connected with the chlorophyll—a proof that they are nourished from this side.

A long series of older inaccurate observations are rectified by Schimper's research, in that the starch-grains so common in organs other than the assimilating organs —petioles, stems, subterranean tubers and roots, and young leaves which do not yet assimilate—are produced by peculiar little bodies which Schimper terms 'starch-forming corpuscles' or Amyloplasts (*Starkebildner*). These starch-forming corpuscles are protoplasmic, usually colourless structures, which become differentiated from the protoplasm just like the chlorophyll-corpuscles themselves, either in the neighbourhood of the cell-nucleus, or also in the rest of the protoplasm. These starch-forming corpuscles now produce starch-grains, either in the interior of their substance (*Colocasia* and endosperm of *Melandryum*), or only at their peripheral portions (*Philodendron, Amomum, Phajus*, and *Canna*), and thus in the same way as the assimilating chlorophyll-corpuscles in the leaves. The peripheral mode of origin appears to predominate however in these non-assimilating starch-forming corpuscles. According to Schimper's statements also the protoplasmic substance of the starch-forming corpuscle is more quickly and essentially altered, or used up, during its functional activity than is the case with the assimilating chlorophyll-corpuscles. The similarity of the starch-forming corpuscles to the assimilating chlorophyll-corpuscles is, however, still further increased, in that the former can in most cases develope into chlorophyll-corpuscles under the influence of light. In this process, they increase considerably in size, and, their starch-grains dissolving, they turn green at the same time—a process long known, for example, in the cortex of potato-tubers allowed to lie in the light for some time, but incorrectly explained

The great difference between the starch-forming corpuscles and the assimilating chlorophyll-corpuscles, however, is established by Schimper himself in the following words—'Etiolated plants which have not yet exhausted their stores of reserve-materials contain, as is well known, no starch in the mesophyll of the leaf, but often have abundance of it in their stems and petioles, and in the vascular bundle-sheaths of their leaves. This starch, which of course can only be a product of metastasis and not a product of assimilation formed there, is produced by starch-forming corpuscles. Good examples of this are afforded by the leaves of *Hyacinthus*, the stems of *Begonia cucullata* and *Oxalis Ortgiesii*, and the cortex of the stem of *Philodendron grandifolium*. These starch-forming corpuscles

(Schimper here somewhat inaccurately terms them Leucophyll) are all only very feebly coloured yellow, or are not coloured at all   In the cases investigated they, like the chlorophyll- corpuscles which the same cells would have contained under normal circumstances, produced the starch-grains at their peripheral portions. Not less important, with respect to the difference between starch-forming corpuscles and chlorophyll-corpuscles, is Schimper's further statement, that in the case of a plant (*Tradescantia rubella*) from the assimilating chlorophyll of which the large starch-grains had been allowed to disappear entirely in the dark, and which was now placed in a feeble light, no starch was produced in the normal chlorophyll-corpuscles of the leaves here developed; but, on the other hand, abundance of starch arose in the starch-forming corpuscles—i. e. in the pseudo-chlorophyll-corpuscles of the vascular bundle-sheaths of the leaves and stem   Schimper draws from these facts the following conclusion.   The fact that the development of starch in the mesophyll of the leaf depends on the same conditions as assimilation, while in other parts of the plant it occurs independently of light, so long as reserve-materials are present, can only be explained by assuming that in the first case it is exclusively a product of the assimilation of the chlorophyll-corpuscle in which it appears, while in the second case it must have in part (I think entirely) a different origin.'

Finally, Schimper expresses himself as follows with respect to the invisible, purely chemical processes —'It is clear that the starch which appears as the first evident product of assimilation (in the true chlorophyll-corpuscles) does not originate directly from carbon dioxide and water, but that more or less numerous intermediate products, still unknown or at any rate known with less certainty, are interposed.   We may assume that the substances conveyed to the chlorophyll-corpuscles are identical with one of these intermediate products, or are at any rate very similar to them; and hence the transformation to starch of the assimilated matters formed there and then, and of those conveyed from other organs, is effected by one and the same process' (probably similar processes is meant).

I cannot here avoid repeating my view on the formation of starch in the assimilating chlorophyll, already expressed in the '*Experimental-physiologie*' (1865); and so much the less, because it has been in the meantime grossly misrepresented, and falsely quoted, by writers unacquainted with vegetable physiology.   I there said (p. 327), 'If, after all, I regard the starch in the chlorophyll as one of the first products of assimilation, it is not therefore to be said that carbon dioxide and water unite forthwith to form molecules of starch within the chlorophyll-substance, oxygen being evolved.   It is not even necessary that any carbo-hydrate whatever should arise immediately; it is possible, and probable, that the process accompanied by the evolution of oxygen is a very complicated one, from which the formation of starch results only by numerous chemical metamorphoses.   It is, indeed, not impossible that certain more immediate constituents of the green plasma itself take part in the process—that decompositions and substitutions, for example, take place in the molecules of the green protoplasm.   This possibility obtains some probability from the observation that in many (not all) cases the chlorophyll-substance gradually decreases in quantity and at length disappears entirely, while the starch-grains are growing in it,' etc.   With reference to Schimper's results, I am now strongly inclined to assume that both in the assimilating chlorophyll-corpuscles and in the non-assimilating starch-corpuscles, the material for the formation of starch consists of sugar. This latter is conveyed to the starch-forming corpuscles of the organs which do not assimilate · it is formed, on the other hand, in the assimilating chlorophyll-corpuscles by assimilation. The question now remains, therefore, how does the sugar itself arise by assimilation? I hold it as probable, even now, that in this process the proteid substance of the assimilating chlorophyll itself co-operates, and undergoes a change. Whether it is right to claim, with Berthelot and Kekulé (1861), formic acid or some other member of the formyl group as the first product of assimilation, on account of its simple constitution, I hold as at least very questionable; and it has hitherto been proved by nothing. I lay still less value on Pringsheim's so-called Hypochlorin; a substance, the chemical nature of which is not established, the genetic relation of which to the starch in the chlorophyll is not known, and the significance of which for the processes of growth has not been investigated. Hypochlorin appears to me, rather, to belong to the same category as the Myelin of the animal physiologists, with which the latter likewise do not know what to do[1].

At any rate, even after all the recent researches, the fact, which I established twenty years ago, that the starch in the assimilating chlorophyll is to be regarded as the first distinctly recognisable product of assimilation, remains unaltered. Even then I left the way open for further knowledge, since I laid stress on the fact that it was a matter of the first *distinctly visible* product, and that probably other products, hitherto not distinctly recognisable however, precede the formation of starch Hence, even if as a matter of fact formyl aldehyde or vegetable myelin (I mean Pringsheim's hypochlorin) were actually an earlier product of assimilation, from which the starch is developed in the chlorophyll, which is not the case, there would still not be the smallest item to alter in the statements which I have made since 1862

Having learnt to understand the most important function of chlorophyll, I will now complete the natural history of this remarkable body by a few passing statements as to the rest of its behaviour in different phases of life of the organs of the plant. It has already been mentioned that leaves which develope from the buds in the absence of light, with a few exceptions, produce the first rudiments of chlorophyll-corpuscles, it is true, but these remain small and usually yellow, and likewise that the green chlorophyll-corpuscles can increase in number by division when the cells grow.

I convinced myself, in 1863, by a detailed investigation of the changes which take place in the assimilating parenchyma of leaves in Autumn, before their fall[2], of the fact that a structure so valuable with reference to the life of the plant as the chlorophyll-substance, is not destroyed and chemically decomposed at once,

---

[1] With respect to Pringsheim's Hypochlorin, Pfeffer expresses himself in his '*Pflanzen-Physiologie*' (B. I, pp 194, 195, and 209) in very measured terms, it is true, but still protesting and dissentient Pringsheim's treatise '*Ueber Lichtwirkung und Chlorophyllfunktion in der Pflanze*' (Jahrb. f. wiss Bot., Bd. XII, p. 288) is thoroughly examined in Hansen's paper on the '*Geschichte der Assimilationstheorie*' (Arbeiten des bot Inst. zu Würzburg, B II, p 606)

[2] Cf Sachs, '*Entleerung der Blätter im Herbst*' (Flora, 1863, p. 200).

at the end of a period of vegetation; but that it is conveyed into the persistent reservoirs of reserve-materials, which put forth shoots again at a later period of vegetation. The process does not always run the same course in trees of different species. In the Horse-chestnut, for example, as well as in *Dioscorea batatas*, the form of the chlorophyll-corpuscles is destroyed at the same time as their green colour, and the chlorophyll disappears simultaneously with the starch contained in it In the Vine, I found that the form of the chlorophyll-corpuscles is first destroyed, while the starch disappears, the green colour of the amorphous chlorophyll being maintained however for some time. In *Sambucus Populus*, and *Robinia*, on the other hand, the starch first disappears from the chlorophyll-corpuscles, while the form and green colour persist for some time longer. In the Mulberry (*Morus alba*), the form of the chlorophyll-corpuscles is first destroyed, then the green colour disappears, and finally the matrix together with the starch contained in it. These observations do not preclude that in the same species of plant the processes in the cells containing chlorophyll may take their course sometimes in the one, sometimes in the other way. It is not always possible to see from the outside whether the autumnal emptying of the leaves has already commenced. When the leaves become pale, however, the destruction of the chlorophyll has already begun, and when they have turned yellow it is completed On the other hand, in leaves which are still green in September and October the form of the chlorophyll-corpuscles may be already destroyed, as in the Vine, Poplar, *Robinia*, and *Sambucus*. With the general disappearance of the cell-contents, the dissolution of the cell-nucleus and protoplasm, the peripheral chlorophyll-corpuslces lose their normal outlines, assume irregular forms, the contained starch disappears, and their colouring matter undergoes changes. they become pale green Oil-drops often appear in the cells, the quantity of chlorophyll perceptibly diminishes, the deformed corpuscles become smaller, and, when they have finally disappeared entirely, a large number of very small granules remain behind in the cell-sap. these refract light strongly and are coloured bright yellow, but they are to be in no way compared with the immature yellow chlorophyll-corpuscles of leaves grown in the dark. They often flow together into large oily drops, and evidently form a residuum of no further use in the economy of the plant. It is these yellow granules which cause the autumnal yellow colouring of so many leaves, and which also remain behind in the emptied cells of leaves which turn red in the Autumn; in this case, however, they lie in a homogeneous red cell-sap

The cell-contents of the leaves of plants placed subsequently in the dark undergo very similar changes, which are particularly rapid at high temperatures. And various other circumstances which disturb nutrition, such as persistent drought, or lack of nutritive matters generally, bring about the same processes even in bright light. In all these cases the process described commences in the oldest leaves, and advances to the younger ones; the leaf-cells remain distended with sap but their volume appears notably to diminish The emptied cell-skeletons are finally cast off for the most part, since, as Mohl showed in detail, a new layer of cells is formed cutting across the base of the petiole, and preparing the petiole for the fall Then, with the advent of the first frosty nights at the end of October or the beginning of November, a plate of ice is formed in this separating layer, which melts in the rays of the morning sun, whereupon the leaves suddenly fall in numbers from the trees.

There can be no doubt that the contents of the assimilating parenchyma of the leaves before the fall are taken up during the changes described into the persistent parts of the plants—into the cortex or young wood of the branches. I was able by micro-chemical methods to follow distinctly the travelling of the materials, especially of the starch, out through the tissues of the petiole into the shoot-axes; and moreover the ash-analyses of assimilating green leaves, compared with those of fallen ones, show that the most valuable mineral constituents of the leaves, specially the potash and phosphoric acid, also pass out through the leaf-stalks simultaneously with the organic substances, and back into the parts of the shoot which survive the winter, evidently to serve, like these, as nutritive matters for the newly sprouting shoots in the next period of vegetation.

While this process repeats itself each Autumn in perennial plants, it only takes place once in the annual summer plants, and, generally, in those plants which only fruit once. In our cereals, for example, and other cultivated plants, all the still useful materials which were contained in the leaves and shoot-axes are collected finally, when the fruit is maturing, in the ripening seeds, either in the endosperm or in the large cotyledons of the embryo, to be employed later, on the germination of the latter, as materials for the construction of the growing parts of the seedling. Hence the vegetative organs of such plants after the ripening of the fruit (generally named straw, etc) contain only exceedingly small quantities of material capable of being employed for further growth: they consist of emptied net-works of cell-walls, with slight remnants of other matters. Of ash constituents, the whole of the silica, as well as the greater part of the lime in the form of calcium oxalate, remains behind, as a rule, in the emptied organs of assimilation.

The processes are somewhat different in the chlorophyll-corpuscles of those organs which are not to be regarded like the leaves as assimilating organs in the proper sense, and the chlorophyll-corpuscles of which are probably only green starch-forming corpuscles in the sense of Schimper. I found, for example, that the chlorophyll-corpuscles in the antheridia of *Nitella* and *Chara*, as well as those of some Mosses, which enclose starch in the unripe state, assume a red colour when the antherozoids are mature, but maintain their form, and the enclosed starch does not disappear: profound chemical alterations of the plastic substances do not, however, take place here. Much more thorough is the destruction of the corpuscles, at first green, in the pericarp of those berry-like fruits which appear red or deep yellow in the ripe state, e. g. *Lycium* and various species of *Solanum*. The chlorophyll-corpuscles of these pericarps, as they turn yellow and red, change their form also . they become angular, two and three pointed, and finally break up into small granules. In conclusion, the remark may be made here that the bearers of the yellow colouring matter to which many floral leaves owe their yellow colour (e. g. the corolla of *Cucurbita*), resemble chlorophyll-corpuscles, or better, Schimper's starch-forming corpuscles.

When organs of assimilation become dormant at the conclusion of a period of vegetation, to renew their activity in the following year, alterations take place in the contained chlorophyll also : under certain circumstances these however are less profound   The green spores of many Algæ, for instance, become deep red, without any essential changes of the plastic material occurring at the same time: with the commencement of the new period of vegetation, the red colouring matter disappears, the chlorophyll again begins to assimilate, and the cells to grow.   In some Phanerogams, the leaves which persist through the winter behave similarly in many respects. here, however, the intense cooling in winter, particularly by radiation, co-operates. After Mohl had remarked these processes in 1845, they were more closely studied by Kraus in 1871 and 1872   These winter-leaves either become simply discoloured and brownish, yellow, or red-brown, as in *Taxus, Pinus, Abies, Juniperus,* and *Buxus,* or of a decided red on the upper side, as in *Sedum, Sempervivum, Mahonia,* and *Vaccinium.*   The discolouration of the first group depends, according to Kraus, on an alteration of the chlorophyll : the chlorophyll-grains lose their shape and distinctness, and form an ill-defined cloudy mass of protoplasm of a red-brown or brown-yellow colour, while the nucleus of the cell remains colourless.   The winter-leaves which are coloured red or purple-brown on the upper side owe this colour, according to Kraus, to a rounded, hyaline, strongly refractive mass, in which tannin predominates, situated in the upper part of the palisade-cells   the chlorophyll-grains themselves are intact, and of a fine green, and are all crowded at the inner ends of these cells. In the spongy parenchyma of the mesophyll, a red or colourless globule of tannin is found in the centre of each cell, and the chlorophyll-grains, likewise intact, are collected into lumps on the sides, sometimes at one, sometimes at several places. In all winter-leaves, as well as in the green parts of the cortex, Kraus found that the chlorophyll-grains had passed from the walls to the interior of the cells, and were there aggregated in clumps.   In the spring, in sufficiently warm weather, the normal condition is restored   the red colouring matter disappears, and the chlorophyll-grains again assume their normal distribution on the cell-walls   If branches of the first-named group of plants are cut off in the cold of winter and brought into a warm chamber, they assume their normal green colour after a few days, even in the dark.

It has already been mentioned that the green colouring matter of the chlorophyll-grains can be extracted by strong alcohol, æther, chloroform, and also by fat oils, the colourless protoplasmic matrix remaining behind.   Chemists have taken much trouble to investigate the chemical nature of this extracted colouring matter, without having obtained so far any satisfactory result   It is not even established whether the chlorophyll colouring matter, for the production of which small quantities of iron are necessary, as I have shown, itself contains iron.   The view proposed by the French chemist Frémy, that the green colouring matter is a mixture of a yellow and a blue, has not been confirmed, since it is scarcely doubtful that the apparent breaking up of the colouring matter into two others is simply a chemical decomposition[1].   It is not necessary, however, to go further into this discussion; since the views so far proposed as to the chemical nature of the chlorophyll colouring matter have no reference to the physiological functions of chlorophyll   The same is true of the

---

[1] See my '*Lehrbuch der Bot*' IV Aufl 1874, p. 731.

spectrum of the chlorophyll colouring matter, so very remarkable in itself. If a parallel-walled vessel filled with an alcoholic solution of chlorophyll is placed in the path of a beam of light (p 303) which affords a spectrum band by means of a prism, the whole of the violet and blue disappears from the spectrum, as do also those ultra-violet rays which become luminous when falling upon a solution of quinine. At the same time, a broad, black stripe becomes visible in the red part of the spectrum, and in the yellow region also a feeble absorption of light occurs. The green colouring matter is also strikingly fluorescent: if the focus of a burning-glass is allowed to fall in a solution of chlorophyll, the white sunlight appears blood-red. As Stokes showed long ago, this phenomenon is caused by the fact that the highly refrangible light-rays become changed into lowly refrangible red ones. By an erroneous inversion of the correct state of affairs—that the light-rays effective in the assimilating chlorophyll must be destroyed as such—Lommel arrived at the fallacy that the rays destroyed in the chlorophyll spectrum are those active in assimilation. In this he left out of account that the rays absorbed in a solution of chlorophyll are the same as those absorbed in a living green leaf. In a solution of chlorophyll, however, no separation of oxygen from carbon dioxide takes place according to Lommel, also, it must be the most strongly absorbed red rays which bring about assimilation, whereas all direct observations show that the maximum evolution of oxygen takes place in yellow light [1].

On the whole, investigations on the spectrum of chlorophyll have hitherto yielded no facts of any physiological value—i. e. we should know quite as much of the physiological function of chlorophyll if its spectrum were absolutely unknown to us.

---

[1] Cf Sachs' '*Lehrbuch,*' p 732

LECTURE XX.

CHEMICAL METAMORPHOSES OF THE PRODUCTS OF ASSIMILATION. PHYSIOLOGICAL CLASSIFICATION OF THE PRODUCTS OF METABOLISM.

STARCH being the sole first visible product of assimilation, it follows obviously that all the other organic compounds of the plant must be produced from it by chemical changes. This statement offers in fact no difficulties even from the chemical side, so far as the majority of the constituents of the plant are concerned, i.e. the carbo-hydrates, of which cellulose, sugars, and inulin especially come into consideration here. These substances are chemically so nearly allied to each other, that not only starch and inulin, but even cellulose may be transformed by the simplest chemical reactions into sugars, and from the physiological processes it may be demonstrated with certainty that starch and cellulose are produced from sugar and inulin within the living plant.

Besides these carbo-hydrates, however, the fats also play a prominent part in the economy of the plant. Perhaps there is no living protoplasm which contains no fat, but its physiological significance becomes much more evident in that the great majority of ripe seeds contain large quantities of fat together with starch, or very great quantities of fat without the latter. They may contain as much as 60% and more of their weight of fat, and even the spores of very many Cryptogams abound in it. That sugar and starch are formed during germination at the cost of the fat which is accumulated in the seeds and then used up, I demonstrated in detail in 1859 on a series of oily seeds[1], and it was already known that, before maturity, such seeds contain no fat, but only starch and sugar. Such unripe seeds (e. g. of *Pæonia*) may be detached from the mother-plant, and allowed to lie in moist air, with the result that the starch disappears and is replaced by fatty oil. From such observations it follows with certainty that the fats of the plant may be produced from carbo-hydrates, and that the latter are formed at their expense. It is practically immaterial for us how far chemical formulas are able to afford information as to the processes here taking place; in any case we arrive at the result that the carbo-hydrates, as well as the fats of the plant, derive their origin from the starch assimilated in the chlorophyll-grains.

The derivation of the third most important group of the materials of the plant, viz. the proteid substances, from the original product of assimilation, does not appear

---

[1] On the formation of starch during the germination of oily seeds, cp Sachs' *Bot Zeitung*, 1859, p 178

quite so simple. It depends here no longer merely upon various transpositions of the atoms of carbon, hydrogen, and oxygen in the molecules, as in the case of the carbo-hydrates and fats : the proteid substances from which protoplasm is formed contain, besides these elements, also a considerable quantity (about 15%) of nitrogen, and a small quantity (about 1%) of sulphur.   It is obvious that if proteid substances are to be derived from the first product of assimilation, starch, this can only take place in so far as, in the course of metabolism, carbo-hydrates, or perhaps also fats, afford the one constituent of proteid matters, while the nitrogen and sulphur are derived from other compounds which the plant has taken up through the roots.   It is certain from what has been said concerning the nutritive materials of plants, that the nitro-gen of the proteid substances is entirely derived from salts of nitric acid, in the more highly organised plants at least ; while the sulphur is provided by salts of sulphuric acid.   It is essential, therefore, in order that proteid substances may arise in the plant, that, on the one hand, starch is produced in the chlorophyll, and that, on the other, salts of nitric and sulphuric acid are taken up by the roots.   These ingredients must somewhere and in some manner come together in the plant : chemical decomposi-tions must take place in which, above all, the salts mentioned yield up their bases, so that the nitrogen and sulphur, after certain unknown processes, may finally come into combination with the elements of a carbo-hydrate or fat in order to produce a proteid. Unfortunately, organic chemistry here leaves us unaided, so far as regards the question of the chemical processes in the formation of proteids from the ingredients mentioned above   The accuracy of our deduction is by no means enfeebled by this, however, and we will now see how far we can proceed by purely physiological methods

It is, in the first place, a very important question whether the whole of the proteid substances of an ordinary plant is or is not produced during the process of assimila-tion in the cells containing chlorophyll . at any rate, sulphates and nitrates can penetrate as far as the green leaves, and there is scarcely anything absurd *a priori* in the idea that the formation of proteids perhaps begins with their aid, even during the process of assimilation in the chlorophyll.   But we have certain facts which show that, although in general only certain non-nitrogenous organic compounds, and espe-cially sugar, exist in them, even cells devoid of chlorophyll, and which therefore do not assimilate, are in a position to produce proteid substances on the addition of nitrates and sulphates.   This proof Pasteur afforded by nourishing yeast-cells with sugar and the salts named ; an experiment which may be easily repeated, and which yields the result that by this means a few yeast-cells give rise to millions of new ones, each of which is filled with living protoplasm.   This is simply possible from the fact that the yeast-cells are able to produce proteid substances from the materials—sugar and salts of nitric and sulphuric acids—offered to them.   If Yeast and other Fungi are able to do this, however, there is no ground for assuming that cells devoid of chlorophyll in the highly organised plants are not also able to produce proteid sub-stances, taking the ingredients for this from their own carbo-hydrates, and from the salts above mentioned which are absorbed by the roots.   On the other hand, again, this does not prove that in special cases proteid compounds may not also arise in cells containing chlorophyll   The so-called unicellular Algæ, the Palmellaceæ, Conjugateæ, etc., consist indeed only of cells containing chlorophyll, and these, so long as they vegetate, increase the quantity of their protoplasm (that is, their proteids) in proportion as their cells divide. Whether this occurs simultaneously with assimilation in the light, or subsequently during the following night, is of course not known. At any rate, the facts brought forward teach that proteid-like compounds from which protoplasm arises can be formed independently of assimilation, provided only that the necessary constituents are conveyed to the cells concerned. Among these constituents an organic carbon compound is essential; and this, in its turn, is of course to be finally derived—though it may be by the most various and round-about ways—from the starch assimilated in the chlorophyll.

In the case of highly organised plants I have already sought to render it probable that the formation of proteid substances takes place in the sieve-tubes of the vascular bundles The sieve-tubes in the younger shoot-axes and leaves contain an amorphous proteinaceous slime, which is by no means to be confounded with protoplasm. It consists, to use a modern expression, not of organised or living, but of circulating proteids, evidently being conveyed through the sieve-tubes to the younger growing organs. We have many indications, however, that it is probably also formed in these sieve-tubes. in the first place we find in the neighbourhood of the sieve-tubes of the organs in question, regular layers of cells which contain fine-grained transitory starch and sugar, and extremely fine-grained starch is frequently found in the slime of the sieve-tubes themselves. I regard this starch as one of the constituents from which the proteinaceous slime of the sieve-tubes is to be formed. Holzner long ago gave expression to the idea that the formation of oxalic acid in the plant is for the purpose of decomposing the calcium sulphate taken up by the roots, and thus setting free the sulphuric acid for the formation of proteid substances which contain sulphur, and it is certainly an observation favourable to this supposition that, very generally, layers of cells in which calcium oxalate crystallises out run in the neighbourhood of the bundles of sieve-tubes, from which indeed it may well be concluded that the sulphuric acid in the calcium salt may be employed here or in the neighbourhood, or even in the sieve-tubes themselves, for the formation of proteid substances With respect to the third ingredient, a salt of nitric acid, we know that saltpetre is distributed in the tissues of a normal plant. The constituents are thus given, and the result, the proteinaceous slime in the sieve-tubes also. The reply to these suggestions, that the quantity of calcium oxalate does not accord with the amount of sulphur contained in the proteid substances in question, appears to me of little weight, since, on the one hand, a decomposition of calcium sulphate by means of oxalic acid may take place also for other purposes in the plant, and thus under certain circumstances (e. g. in some species of *Cactus* and Aroideæ) an enormous quantity of calcium oxalate be accumulated, while in other cases, on the other hand, the decomposition of salts of sulphuric acid may occur without the formation of calcium oxalate.

However, the formation of proteid substances in the plant may also take place in another way, and perhaps in any parenchyma cell whatever, since it may be that another body abounding in nitrogen, one of the group of amides, is first produced, namely, asparagin, a crystallisable substance soluble in the cell-sap, but which contains no sulphur. Asparagin, as recent researches, especially those of Borodin [1]

---

[1] Borodin, *Bot Zeitung*, 1878, p 801, '*Ueber die Verbreitung des Asparagins.*'

have shown, is widely spread in the vegetable kingdom, especially in growing shoots and perennial root-stocks and tubers It is of course still questionable whether the asparagin arises in these organs by synthesis, to be converted by further synthesis and the assumption of sulphur into proteid substances. That something of the sort actually occurs under certain circumstances Pfeffer has demonstrated with seedlings of Lupins, etc. In these cases, however, the asparagin itself had previously arisen by a splitting up of the proteid substances of the seed[1] At any rate the possibility exists that in many cases asparagin may be formed in the first place from carbo-hydrates and nitrates, to be converted later, with the assumption of sulphur from the decomposition of a sulphate, into proteid substances. That, conversely, asparagin arises from the proteid substances of many germinating seeds (e g. *Lupinus*), root-stocks, and tubers (e. g Potato), to be subsequently reconverted into proteid, when the green organs begin to assimilate, cannot be doubted from the researches of Pfeffer, Schultze, and others.

It is now decided that all the various carbo-hydrates, fats, and proteid substances of the plant are derived from the starch assimilated in the chlorophyll. This is practically equivalent to saying that all the organic substances necessary for the construction of the cells and organs of the plant, are to be referred to the activity of the assimilating chlorophyll, since the plant requires for the construction of cells and organs generally only these three groups of materials. I have consequently classified them as the constructive materials of the organs, in contrast to all other organic substances of the plant. Seeds or tubers, bulbs, rhizomes, buds of trees and even spores—the unicellular reproductive organs of Cryptogams—may be made to develope new roots and shoots, and occasionally even flowers, by growth, though no other materials are placed at their disposal than pure water and the oxygen of the atmosphere: the latter however is only necessary for respiration, by which means a considerable portion of the organic substances is completely destroyed. Since now all the parts of plants above named—which we term reservoirs of reserve-materials, because the materials for germination in the widest sense are stored up in them —contain essentially only proteid substances, carbo-hydrates, and fats, or it may be only proteids and fats, as in many seeds (*Ricinus, Brassica, Cucurbita*, Almond, etc.), it is obvious that the new roots and buds are able to develope as the substances mentioned are used up in growth This is still more obvious when the development of seedlings is allowed to take place in profound darkness, where assimilation cannot come into consideration at all , or when the developing seedlings are left in an atmosphere from which every trace of carbon dioxide has been withdrawn At the conclusion of such a process of germination, the reservoirs of reserve-materials are emptied, and when the growth finally ceases, no nutritive matters being admitted from without and no assimilation taking place, we have before us a new plant which consists of cellulose walls and relatively small quantities of protoplasm, cell-nuclei, and chlorophyll-grains (etiolated or not) These constituents of our young plant have been produced from the reserve-materials, proteids, carbo-hydrates, and fats, with the aid of the water and oxygen taken up. Of the two groups last named, how-ever, a considerable quantity has been completely destroyed during the growth, by

---

[1] Cp. Sachs' *'Lehrbuch der Botanik,'* IV. Aufl , p. 690.

respiration, so that the dry organic substance of the young plant weighs less than that of the reservoirs of reserve-material.

These observations, easily made with a little experimental adroitness, show moreover not merely that the three groups of substances mentioned completely suffice for the construction of the organs of the plant; but we obtain from them another important piece of information. In order to render this quite clear, we may suppose

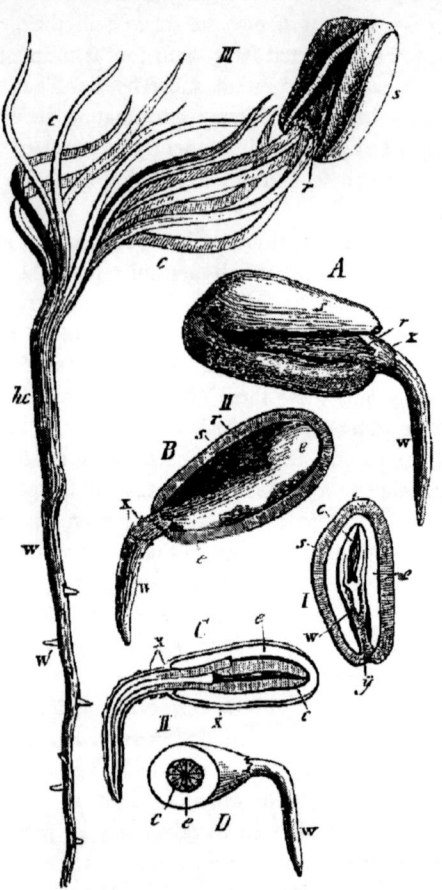

FIG. 225.—*Pinus Pinea.* *I* Median longitudinal section of the seed, the micropyle end being at *y*; *II* commencement of germination, the radicle extruded; *III* end of germination after the endosperm has been absorbed (the seed lay too near the surface of the soil and has therefore been carried up by the cotyledons as the stem elongated). *A* shows the ruptured seed-coat *s*; *B* shows the endosperm *e* after the removal of one half of the seed-coat; *C* longitudinal section of the endosperm and embryo; *D* transverse section of the same at the commencement of germination—*c* cotyledons, *w* primary root, *x* the embryo-sac pushed aside by the primary root (ruptured at *x* in *B*), *h c* hypocotyl, *w'* lateral rootlets, *r* red membrane within the hard testa.

seeds of the Pine, which contain only proteid substances and fat, or those of the common garden Bean, in which only very small quantities of fat but large masses of starch are deposited in addition to the proteid substances, to be allowed to germinate, until all the reserve-materials are consumed. In the seedling of the Pine we then find resin-passages filled with balsam, and tannin may be detected in various cells; in that of the Bean are found numerous longitudinal rows of cells, densely filled with mixed solutions of tannin and red colouring matter. Chemical analysis would in both cases detect small quantities of various other chemical compounds. It is clear that the substances mentioned, resin and tannin, as well as the vegetable acids which are never wanting in growing organs, must also have arisen from the reserve-materials; and since it is known that the quantity of proteid substances is not lessened in germination, it follows that the tannin and resin, vegetable acids, and other non-nitrogenous constituents also of the seedling must have arisen in the Pine from the fat, and in the Bean from the grains of starch. Among these materials, however, the resin and tannin present yet further the remarkable peculiarity that they do not subsequently disappear from the reservoirs in which they are collected during germination; they, as well as the calcium oxalate, remain lying unemployed where they have once arisen. What has here been said of the Pine and Bean, for the sake of example, obtains moreover generally. The resins, ethereal oils, most tannins, as well as various (probably not all) gum-like contents of the reservoirs of secretions described previously, are substances which are withdrawn from metabolism, and find no further use in the nutrition and in the growth of the organs; and they are thereby essentially distinguished from the three groups of constructive materials. It is probable that the vegetable alkaloids are also to be counted among these useless secretions, and the colouring matters so frequently appearing in the vegetating organs certainly are. How and why all these substances, which are very different in different plants, originate is not known, for us, however, the important point remains that they simply find no further use in metabolism.

Finally, it is to be mentioned here that some organic substances do not arise in the metabolism which accompanies growth, but are formed by the later metamorphoses of previously organised parts of cells, and then likewise find no further use in metabolism. To these belong, chiefly, bassorin, gum-tragacanth, gum-arabic, linseed-mucilage, and similar bodies, all of which arise by means of subsequent chemical metamorphosis of the cellulose of certain cell-walls: like the secretions, they may, under certain circumstances, be of use for the plant, but they take no further part in metabolism itself. That protoplasmic structures also suffer subsequent degradation, and either wholly or in part find no further use in metabolism, follows from what has been said in the last lecture on the destruction of chlorophyll, and it appears also that old cell-nuclei, as well as the thin protoplasmic utricles of old parenchyma cells, often remain as inert masses until the destruction of the organ. The share in metabolism taken by some other organic compounds, such as pectinaceous substances, the so-called glucosides, and some still dubious tannins, is still very doubtful. The same is also true of the vegetable acids, malic acid, citric acid, tartaric acid, formic acid, acetic acid, etc.; the wide distribution of which is no doubt usually the cause of the acid reaction of the cell-sap in the parenchyma. According to a view recently expressed by Hugo de Vries[1], the significance of these acids in growth is chiefly mechanical, in so far that they increase the turgescence of the growing cells, and so contribute to the extension of the growing cell-walls. It has already been mentioned above that the oxalic acid (which

---

[1] On the significance of acids in turgescence and in the growth of vegetable cells, cp De Vries, *Bot Zeitung*, 1879, p 847

likewise belongs here) is, as a rule, of no further use in metabolism, especially when it crystallises out as calcium oxalate; nevertheless, under certain circumstances, calcium oxalate becomes again dissolved, and occasionally the acid is found combined with alkalies, as in the Sorrel and the Wood-sorrel. In these cases it is possible that it is not yet entirely withdrawn from metabolism. That the vegetable alkaloids when once formed do not again enter into metabolism, as a rule at any rate, appears probable from what is known as to their occurrence.

The main point in determining the physiological significance of a vegetable substance is always whether, when it has made its appearance anywhere in the tissues, it then again disappears from its receptacle during further growth and progressive metabolism, or remains lying inert in it, in which case a further share in metabolism is obviously excluded. The latter is the case with nearly all the substances contained in the so-called receptacles for secretions. Of course substances which find no more use in metabolism may be incidentally of the most varied significance for the maintenance of the individual, as well as for reproduction. Thus, for example, the lignin which permeates the cell-walls of vessels, wood-cells, and sclerenchymatous fibres, is of considerable importance for the solidity of such cell-walls and the conduction of water in them; and likewise the wax in the epidermis and on the cuticle affords a means of protection against evaporation, and at the same time against the entrance of water; and acids at the surfaces of the roots, as was shown above, aid in the taking up of absorbed nutritive matters. The colouring matters of flowers are assumed to play a great part in pollination, in so far that insects are allured by them to the organs of fertilisation; the large quantities of sugar and organic acids which accumulate in the flesh of fruits,—e. g. Grapes, Oranges, etc.,—are also of course lost to metabolism, but they may be of use to wild plants in so far that birds and other animals devour such fruits, and subsequently rid themselves of the undigested seeds. That the formation of any substance in the plant may also be essentially influenced by culture and the artificial selection of varieties is shown by the ever-increasing number of the various colours of garden flowers, and the great number of different flavoured varieties of orchard fruits and Grapes, all of which have been produced by cultivation.

Meanwhile, however, these are for us but matters by the way, since we are now concerned only with establishing that all the different substances of the plant are derived, directly or indirectly, from the starch arising in the assimilating chlorophyll, and that, in the first place, only a very limited number of products of metabolism—namely the carbo-hydrates, fats, and proteid substances—come into consideration as the constructive materials of the growing organs of the plant. All other substances, occurring as secretions or as products of degradation, are derivatives of these.

When now starch arises in the leaves under the influence of light, it, as well as the other plastic substances produced at its expense, is conveyed through the petioles to the shoot-axes, to proceed in the interior of these organs partly downwards to the growing apices of the roots, partly upwards to the developing buds, and to supply at both places material for the growth of the organs. Hence, as occurs particularly in annual summer plants, assimilation and the employment of the products of assimilation for growth may proceed simultaneously, without any considerable storage of unemployed plastic substances taking place. In most cases, however, and particularly towards the conclusion of the period of vegetation, the quantities of such materials used up for the purposes of growth are smaller than those produced by assimilation The superfluous products of metabolism thus arising are then stored up in the tissues of the plant, to be preserved until the beginning of the next period of vegetation. In this condition they are termed reserve-materials, a name which was introduced by Theodore Hartig some years ago.   The reserve-materials may be accumulated in the parenchyma and phloém of all ordinary perennial organs, particularly in trees and other woody plants, the twigs, branches, roots and stems of which have their cortex and the parenchymatous cells of the alburnum filled during the summer and

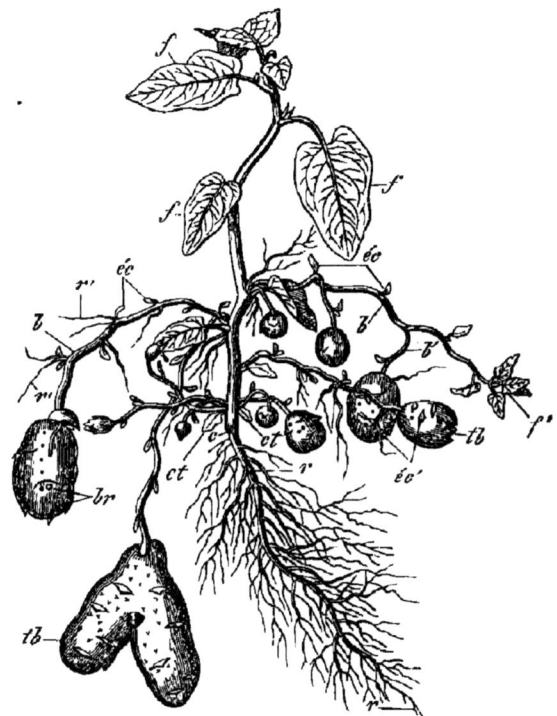

FIG 226.—A Potato plant developed from seed   *r r* the roots, *c* cotyledons, *f f* leaves, *b b* subterranean shoots which produce the tubers *tb* (after Duchartre)

autumn with reserve-materials, which are used up when the buds put forth shoots in the spring.   If the formation of seeds takes place at the end of the period of vege-tation, large quantities of reserve-materials are accumulated to a remarkable degree in these, all non-plastic compounds being excluded, and in annual plants the seeds are in fact the only reservoirs of reserve-materials.   In all perennial plants, however, it is chiefly the subterranean root-stocks, rhizomes, bulbs, and tubers, etc., which especially fulfil the function of storing the substances assimilated during the period of vegetation; and on the formation of the germinal shoots and roots at the beginning of the next period of vegetation, they yield them up to these growing parts. In general, organs of the most various kind may be employed as reservoirs of reserve-materials. In the so-called evergreen plants, even the green leaves serve during the winter as accessory organs for the storage of the products of assimilation; and in the Algæ it is a very common phenomenon that cells abounding in chlorophyll become densely filled with reserve-materials at the conclusion of the period of vegetation. What has here been shortly said is only to serve generally as indicating the most important points, since the vegetable world is simply inexhaustible in the variety of phenomena of organisation connected with the storage of reserve-materials, and their

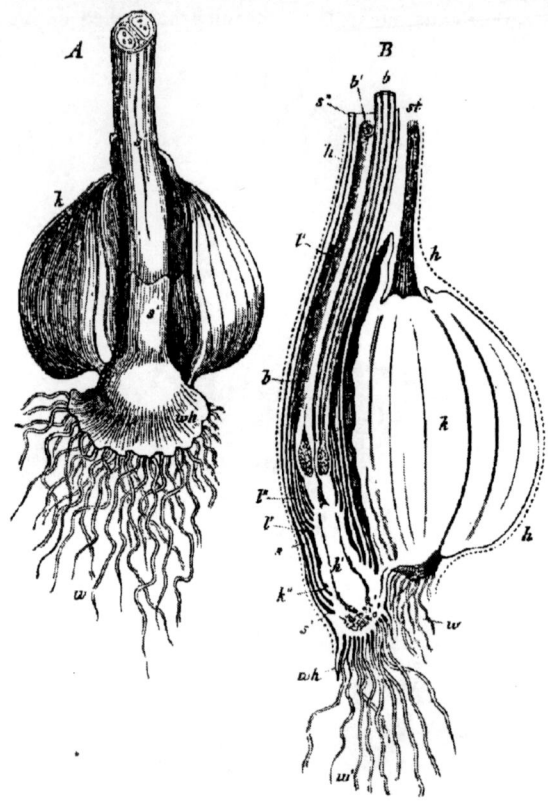

FIG. 227.—Subterranean parts of a flowering plant of *Colchicum autumnale.* *A* external view from the front, *k* the corm; *s'* and *s''* scale leaves enveloping the flower-stalk; *wh* base, from which the roots (*w*) spring. *B* longitudinal section of the preceding (plane of section perpendicular to the paper). *hh* a brown membrane enveloping all the subterranean parts of the plant; *st* the stalk which bore flowers and foliage during the previous year—it is dead, and only its basal portion, *k*, swollen into a corm still exists as a reservoir of reserve-materials for the new plant now in process of flowering. This flowering plant is a lateral shoot from the base of the corm *k*; it consists of the axis, from the base of which spring the roots *w'* and the middle portion of which *k'* swells into the corm for next year, the old corm *k* disappearing in the meanwhile. The axis supports the sheathing leaves *s s' s''*, and the foliage-leaves *l' l''*; in the axils of the uppermost foliage-leaves are the flowers *b b''*, between which appears the free apex of the axis itself. The foliage-leaves are still small at the time of flowering; they, together with the fruits, protrude above the surface of the earth during the following spring. The portion of the axis *k'* then swells up into a new corm, on which the axillary bud *k''* developes into a new flowering axis, while the sheath of the lowermost foliage leaf becomes converted into the enveloping brown membrane.

subsequent employment. Even Fungi, the nutrition of which we shall take more closely into consideration later on, occasionally form reservoirs of reserve-materials— so-called sclerotia. The entire mode of life of a plant is connected most intimately with the ways and means of employing the persistent organs as reservoirs of reserve-materials. Very frequently, at the end of the period of vegetation, nothing more remains of the entire richly-leaved and rooted plant developed in summer, than simply a reservoir of reserve-materials, in connection with one or more buds. This is the case for example in species of *Ophrys*, in *Aconitum napellus*, and in most plants with bulbs and tubers (e. g. *Colchicum* : Fig. 227). The main mass of such a perennial body consists of parenchymatous tissue filled with plastic reserve-materials ; while the germinal shoots to be developed later persist through the winter in the form of small buds   On the whole, the principle is the same in seeds also , the parts of the embryo properly capable of development (i. e the plumule and radicle) which they contain are extremely small, even in very large seeds, while the mass of the reserve-materials is incomparably larger. These reserve-materials are either deposited in the endosperm, from which the young plant subsequently absorbs its nutritive matters on germination ; or the first two leaves of the seedling, the so-called cotyledons, themselves grow to an enormous size, and become filled with the reserve-materials, which are then conveyed on germination forthwith into the tissues of the growing organs. For the elucidation of the matters of organisation which, though closely connected with nutrition, are only slightly touched upon here, I must refer to the figures and explanations distributed throughout the text of this lecture

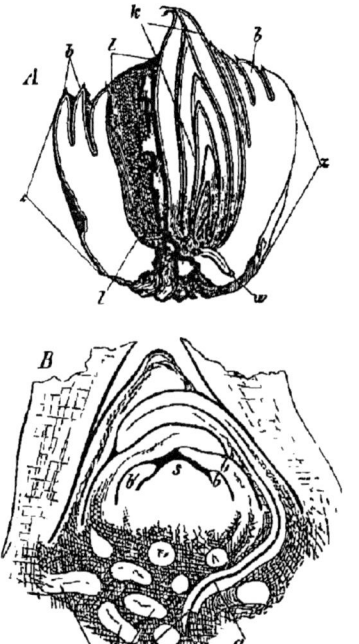

FIG. 228.—Bulbs of *Fritillaria imperialis* in November *A* longitudinal section of the entire bulb (reduced) , *z z* the united lower portions of the bulb-scales, *b b* their free upper portions—they surround a cavity *l* which contains the remains of the decomposed flower-stalk   In the axil of the innermost leaf of the bulb is the bud *k* which will develope in the following year   Its first leaves will form the new bulb, while its stem develops as the flowering-stalk—the root *w* springs from the axis of this bud   *B* longitudinal section of the apical region of the next year's bud , *s* apex of the stem, *b b' bb''* youngest leaves.

The form in which the plastic materials are preserved in the reservoirs of reserve-materials may be very various ; the main point always being that, in addition to proteid substances, non-nitrogenous compounds also are present, the mass of which usually far preponderates. These latter, so far as root-stocks, bulbs, tubers, and other succulent reservoirs of reserve-materials are concerned, are usually carbo-hydrates, with a more or less considerable percentage of fat.   In seeds, on the other hand, it is more frequently the case that the starch entirely disappears on ripening, and, together with the proteid matters, large quantities of fat only remain over as reserve-materials.

The form in which the proteid substances come to rest in the reservoirs of reserve-materials may be that of protoplasm itself, at any rate in succulent organs, such as bulbs, tubers, and rhizomes , at least in many such cases considerable quantities of living protoplasm are found in the reservoirs of reserve-materials, which, when the reserve-materials are consumed, are likewise made use of. This is very distinctly the case, for instance, in the scales of the common kitchen onion and the tuber of the potato. In such cases, however, albumin or a soluble proteid substance appears to be present in the cell sap; in rarer cases a portion, always relatively small, of the non-organised proteid substance may exist in the form of crystalloids. This is best known in the tuber of the common potato, where, especially close beneath the skin but occasionally also in the whole parenchyma, magnificently developed colourless cubes or even tetrahedra are found lying in the protoplasm in autumn and winter. The

FIG. 229.—A crystalloid of the potato tuber, altered by alcoholic solution of iodine and gly-cerine: in the fresh condition it is a perfect cube. A spherical layer enclosing a small cube has become separated in the interior.

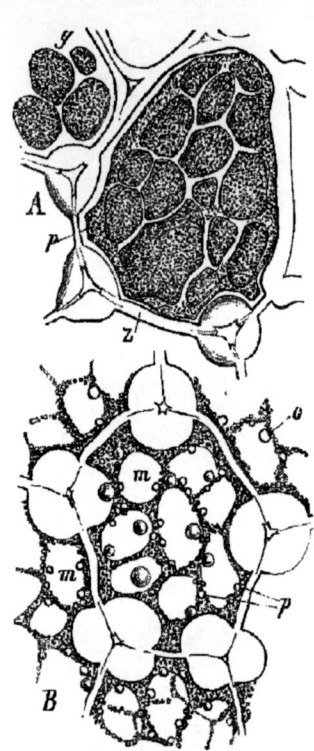

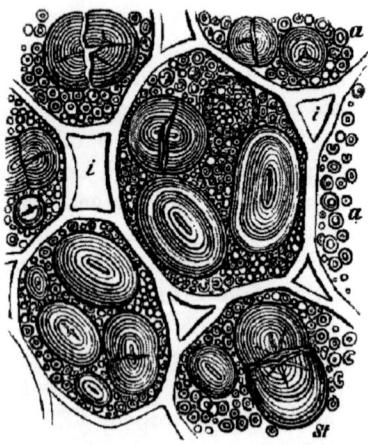

FIG. 230.—A few cells from a very thin section through the cotyledon of *Pisum sativum* still in the ripe seed. The large grains *St* with concentric layers are starch-grains (cut through); the small granules *a* are aleurone-grains consisting chiefly of legumin, with a little oily matter; *i* intercellular spaces.

FIG. 231.—Cells from the cotyledon in a ripe seed of *Lupinus varius*. *A* in alcoholic solution of iodine; *B* after the destruction of the grains by sulphuric acid, *Z* cell-wall; *b* protoplasmic matrix with little oily matter; *y* aleurone grains; *o* drops of oil separated from the matrix under the influence of the sulphuric acid; *m* cavities from which the aleurone grains have been dissolved (800).

careful studies which have been devoted to these crystalloids, and others to be mentioned later, leave not the slightest doubt, on the one hand, that they consist of proteid substances, and, on the other, that they resemble true crystals in all points, but with the single difference that they are capable of swelling by imbibition [1]. The proteid

---

[1] The crystalloids were discovered by Theodore Hartig (*Bot. Zeit.*, 1856), and further investigated by Radlkofer in his book '*Über Krystalle proteïnartiger Körper*' (Leipzig, 1859). Bailey discovered the crystalloids in the potato tuber (*Flora*, 1874, p. 415). Our present views on the nature of crystalloids were founded by Naegeli, '*Bot. Mittheilungen*,' I. p. 217, 1862 (Sitzungsber.

substances of ripe seeds behave differently, according as the other reserve-material is starch or fat. In starchy seeds (e g. Beans, Peas, the cereals, Chestnuts, etc) the cavity of the cell is for the most part filled with starch-grains, the interspaces between these containing proteid substances in the form of small, spheroidal granules, which in the Leguminoseæ consist of vitellin, in the cereals of a mixture of various proteid matters, and in the Wheat particularly of gluten. In fatty seeds (as those of the Coniferæ, Palmeæ, Cucurbitaceæ, Umbelliferæ, Solaneæ, Euphorbiaceæ, etc.) matters are quite different Here, in thin sections through the tissue of the reservoir of reserve-materials (endosperm or cotyledons) the cell-cavities are seen to be filled for the most part with rounded brilliant granules, the so-called aleurone-grains, which always consist of proteid substances. The interspaces between these are chiefly filled with amorphous fat, after the careful removal of which a scanty net-work, poor in substance and of protoplasmic nature, is found, as shown in Fig. 232. The aleurone-grains are soluble either in pure water or in very weak alkaline solutions, or also in a 10% solution of common salt. They, in their turn, contain so-called globoids—i e sphe-roidal, brilliant, minute bodies, said to consist of phosphates of lime and magnesia, and which at any rate probably always contain a magnesium salt [1]. In some cases, but by no means very frequently, a crystalloid of proteid substance is contained in each aleurone-grain: these crystalloids are particularly fine in *Ricinus* and other Euphorbiaceæ, and also in the cotyledons of the Brazil nut (*Bertholetia excelsa*), one of the Myrtaceæ, and in the endosperm of *Musa Hillii*, and many other seeds. These crystalloids remain behind when the amorphous proteid substance surrounding them has been dissolved by

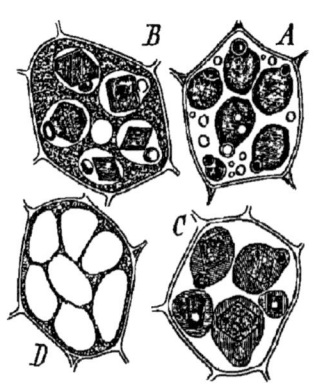

Fig 232 —Cells from the endosperm of *Ricinus communis* (800) *A* fresh, in undiluted glycerine, *B* in diluted glycerine, *C* warmed in glycerine, *D* after treatment with alcoholic solution of iodine, the aleurone grains have been destroyed by sulphuric acid, the proteid substance of the matrix remains behind as a network The globoid and (in *B* and *C*) the crystalloid are seen in the aleurone grains

water: they are thus less soluble than the latter. According to Schimper's very careful researches, all the crystalloids of proteinaceous substance hitherto known belong either to the regular system, as the cubes in the Potato and the octahedra in the aleurone-grains of Ricinus, or to the hexagonal system, as the large rhombohedral crystals of the Brazil nut, and those of *Musa Hillii* and *Sparganium ramosum* This is not the place to enter more in detail into the crystallography of these remarkable structures: it appears more important for the moment to note that in no case does the whole of the proteid substance of a

der k bayer Akademie) On the distribution of crystalloids, see Klein in *Jahrb fur wiss Bot.* (B XIII p 60) What is said in the text is founded particularly on Schimper's works, '*Über die Krystalle der eiweissartigen Substanzen*' in Zeitschrift für Krystallographie (Leipzig, 1880), and, further, '*Untersuchungen uber die Proteinkrystalle der Pflanzen*' (Strassburg, 1878) Cp. also Pfeffer in *Jahrb fur wiss Bot*, B VIII (1872)

[1] Cp. Pfeffer's statements in my '*Lehrbuch*,' IV Aufl, p 55

seed or other reservoir of reserve-materials pass into the crystalline form, but that amorphous substance is always present in addition; and that, as it appears, no crystalloids are met with in the majority of seeds, and certainly not in the large majority of succulent reservoirs of reserve-materials. Where they occur, they become dissolved during germination, and, like the amorphous reserve-substance as well as that existing as protoplasm, are conveyed into the growing parts, there to serve for the formation of protoplasm. Like starch-grains and other reserve-materials, crystalloids of proteinaceous substance occur also in organs which cannot be regarded as reservoirs of reserve-materials in the narrower sense here they are met with rather as temporary deposits of plastic substance for special purposes of metabolism. Here belong above all the crystalloids discovered by Radlkofer (1858) in the nuclei of cells in almost all the parts of *Lathræa Squamaria*, as well as those found by Julius Klein in the nuclei of the cells of *Pinguicula* and *Utricularia* Klein found crystalloids, not in the nuclei, but in the living cell-contents of numerous marine Algæ, especially the Siphoneæ (*Acetabularia, Bryopsis, Codium*, etc) and many Florideæ (*Bornetia, Ceramium, Polysiphonia*, etc) Finally, the Rhodospermin crystals discovered by Cramer, which arise from the cell-contents of the Florideæ under the influence of salt solution, alcohol, or glycerine, may be referred here Klein also found crystalloids in the fructification of *Pilobolus*, a fungus closely allied to *Mucor*.

The various carbo-hydrates are better known chemically than the different kinds of proteid materials From a physiological point of view, however, it may be shown that even the most different members of this group—starch, the sugars, inulin, and cellulose—are in so far of completely equal value that they can replace one another as reserve-materials While in most tubers and other succulent reservoirs of reserve-materials, in the cortex and wood of trees, and in many seeds, starch is usually stored up as the reserve-material, we find exactly the same purpose served in the perennial organs of Compositæ, in the tubers of *Dahlia* and *Helianthus tuberosus*, and in the roots of *Inula Helenium, Taraxacum officinale*, etc, by a concentrated solution of inulin, on the formation of new germinal shoots this is made use of in exactly the same manner as starch is elsewhere. In the beet-root, again, cane-sugar is accumulated in the parenchymatous tissues towards the end of the first period of vegetation, and in the bulb-scales of the kitchen onion a mixture of grape-sugar and other kinds of glucose occur, and here play the same part as does the starch in the bulbs of the tulip and crown imperial But even cellulose itself, which generally occurs only as one of the final products of metabolism, may play the part of a reserve-material. The endosperm of the Date and of some other palms, as well as the large endosperm of the seed of *Phytelephas* (vegetable ivory), consists of exceedingly thick-walled tissue, the laminated and pitted cell-walls of which are formed of pure cellulose: this is dissolved on germination, and passes over into the seedling in the form of sugar, thus playing exactly the same part as starch, inulin, and sugar do elsewhere

A more detailed description of the species of sugars would here lead us too far into the province of chemistry In plants they always occur dissolved; and when obtained in the solid form it is either as true crystals, as in the case of cane-sugar, or as crystalline, crumbling aggregates, as in the case of the glucoses The latter are chemically distinguished particularly by the fact that they easily reduce copper salts in an alkaline solution; whereas cane-sugar only gives a blue fluid with this reagent. Inulin is still more characteristic. It is dissolved in the fluids of living cells: if expressed from these, however, it is precipitated in the form of minute white granules which possess a crystalline structure[1]. The crystalline nature of inulin becomes much more evident, however, when tubers containing inulin are allowed to lie for a long time in alcohol: there are then formed in the tissues so-called sphere-crystals—i.e. crystalline aggregates of knobby, rounded form, which in their turn consist of radially disposed elements proceeding from a common centre. Such aggregates not rarely embrace a considerable extent of tissue. The sphere-crystals in the dark field of the polarising microscope exhibit a bright cross, corresponding to the crystalline structure. On heating up to 50–60° C. the sphere crystals are again dissolved; they are also formed under the influence of frost in the cells containing inulin. The cellulose which occurs as a reserve-material shows no essential differences from that seen elsewhere in strongly thickened cell-walls, except that it never becomes lignified. It is here to be added, however, that the middle lamellæ of such tissues persist on the dissolution of the thickening layers, and are not dissolved with them.

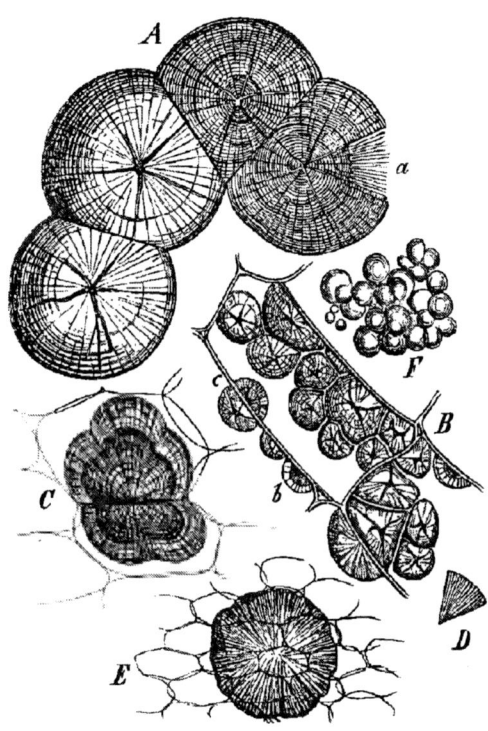

FIG 233.—Sphere-crystals of inulin. *A* from an aqueous solution laid aside for 2½ months. At *a* the action of nitric acid is commencing. *B* cells of the root-tuber of *Dahlia variabilis*—a thin section after lying 24 hours in 90 % alcohol was then immersed in water. *C* two cells with half sphere-crystals which have their common centre in the middle of the intervening cell-wall; from an internode 8 mm. thick at the apex of an older plant of *Helianthus tuberosus* which had lain for some time in alcohol. *D* fragment of a sphere-crystal. *E* a large sphere-crystal embracing several cells (from a large piece of the tuber of *Helianthus tuberosus* after lying some time in alcohol). *F* inulin after evaporation of the water from a thin section of the tuber of *Helianthus tuberosus* (× 550; *E* not so much magnified).

We must devote somewhat more time to the consideration of the starch[2]. This always occurs in the plant in the form of rounded, solid, hard granules, which split on the application of sufficient pressure, and which may grow from a size scarcely visible even with the highest powers of the microscope to grains 0.2 mm. in diameter: generally, however, the grains possess a diameter of only a few

[1] With respect to inulin cp. Sachs' *Bot. Zeitung*, 1864 (p. 77), and Dragendorff, '*Materialen zu einer Monographie des Inulins,*' (Petersburg, 1870).

[2] The chief work on starch-grains is Naegeli's extensive description in the '*Pflanzen-physiologische Untersuchungen*' of Naegeli and Cramer, 1858.

thousandths or hundredths of a mm., and an average specific weight of 1·56. In consequence of these properties, and since they are insoluble in cold water, it is easy to obtain the starch-grains in quantity from starchy tubers, seeds, and other organs: it suffices to rub or otherwise crush such parts of the plant, just as ordinary wheaten flour is obtained by grinding grains of wheat, and then to remove the crushed masses of tissue with abundance of water, to obtain pure starch-meal as a sediment. On observation with the microscope the somewhat larger starch-grains in the cells are conspicuous by their strong refractive power and corresponding lustre. On the addition of solutions of iodine they become coloured, according to the quantity of iodine in each case, of various shades from bright blue to blue-black. The structure of the starch-grain has been investigated very thoroughly, especially by Naegeli (1859), from whose researches a deeper insight into the innermost structure of organised bodies was first obtained. It is not necessary, however, to go further into these matters here In the meantime it suffices to bring forward the fact that starch-grains may possess the most various shapes, and indeed that every plant produces them of characteristic form These characteristic forms, however, only appear in the large, completely developed grains; granules which are still young and very small being mostly spherical, or having the form of segments of spheres, and only developing the characteristic shapes on subsequent growth.

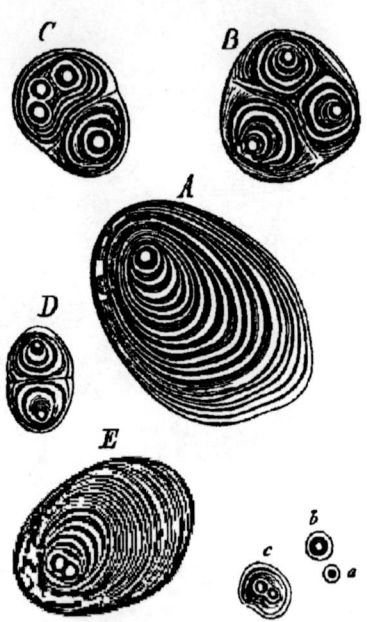

FIG 234.—Starch grains from the tuber of a Potato (800) *A* an older simple grain, *B* a semi compound grain, *C, D* compound grains *E* an older grain the hilum of which is divided, *a* a very young grain, *b* an older one *c* one still older and with divided hilum

To illustrate a few of these only, I may refer in the first place to Fig. 234, which shows various forms of starch from the tubers of the Potato. The large and simple grains are here approximately ovoid, with an eccentric hilum. The starch-grains of the Bean, Pea, and other Leguminoseæ, on the other hand, are ellipsoidal, with a fissure running in the middle of the substance of the grain in the dry state The starch-grains of the Rye and Wheat have the form of bi-convex lenses (Fig. 235 *b*); those of the tubers of *Curcuma* are elliptical tablets, which possess a sort of peg or handle at one end, in which the so-called hilum lies Where the starch-grains are aggregated in large numbers and predominate in the cells of dry seeds, as in the Maize and Rice, they may be polyhedral, and so densely crowded that only very thin spaces filled with proteinaceous substance are left between them (Fig. 235 *a*). These are all simple grains.

Compound grains consist of several or many, or even thousands of individual starch-grains, which, however, are so closely connected that they form together a roundish grain, which with sufficient pressure breaks up into the individual granules;

this is the case, for example, in the endosperm of the Oat, of *Mirabilis Jalappa,* and other seeds. Naegeli terms such forms as those in Fig. 234 *B, C,* and *D* semi-compound: in these cases two or three starch-grains lie not only with their surfaces closely appressed to one another, but they are also embraced by common enveloping layers.

According to Schimper's more recent observations, compound starch-grains arise as follows. In the interior of a starch-forming corpuscle are formed starch-

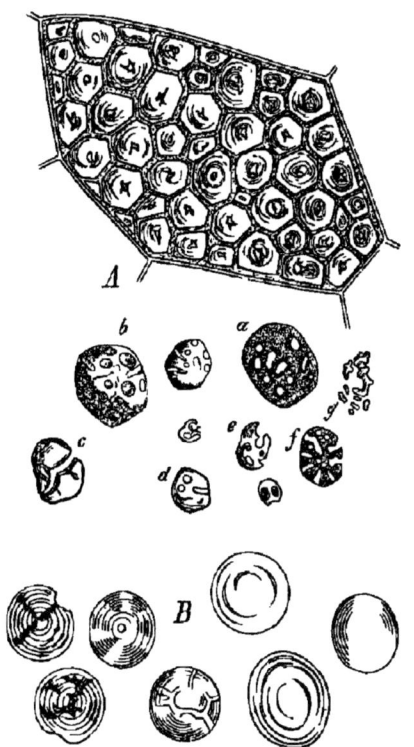

grains, at first like mere dots, then increasing in size: these finally come into contact with one another, and flatten, the surface of the whole mass, corresponding to the circumference of the protoplasmic starch-forming corpuscle, remaining rounded—a process which also takes place in the formation of starch in chlorophyll-corpuscles (cf. Fig. 222). As regards the semi-compound starch-grains, it results from Schimper's description that the grains are produced at two, three, or more points of the surface of a starch-forming corpuscle, and grow most vigorously at those surfaces which are in contact with the starch-forming corpuscle, whence the hilum of each comes to lie eccentrically and towards the outside; and when the substance of the starch-forming corpuscle itself is at length completely consumed, the partial grains are mutually in contact at their surfaces of growth All simple starch-grains with a central hilum and concentric structure originate, according to Schimper, entirely in the interior of a starch-forming corpuscle; and are therefore enveloped by its substance, from which they are nourished. The eccentrically constructed grains, on the other hand, arise beneath the surface of a starch-forming corpuscle, and break through this as they become larger; they then grow at the side connected with the starch-forming corpuscle, so that the hilum is pushed outwards eccentrically.

FIG. 235 —*A* a cell from the endosperm of *Zea Mais,* filled with closely packed and therefore polyhedral starch grains, between the grains are thin plates of dry fine-grained protoplasm. Small cavities and fissures have arisen in the grains owing to the drying *A—g* starch-grains from the endosperm of a germinating seed of Maize *B* lenticular starch grains from the endosperm of a germinating seed of *Triticum vulgare*. the commencing action of the ferment makes itself evident in the first place by the stratification becoming more distinct (800)

To the best known peculiarities of starch-grains belongs their stratification. Around the hilum already mentioned the substance of a starch-grain is not homogeneous, but consists of alternating layers of different density, surrounding the hilum concentrically from within outwards: in grains with eccentric structure, only a certain number of such closed layers envelope the hilum, while more or less numerous layers lie on the growing side and thin off towards the hilum, as seen in Fig. 234. Naegeli first showed that the whole of the visible internal structure of the starch-grain depends upon an unequal distribution of water and starch-substance. The hilum always consists of a watery portion poor in substance: the layers of the grain are formed of starch-substance containing much and little water alternately, and this in such a manner that the outermost layer of a grain is always one poor in water and rich in substance, and dense. Moreover, the proportion of water of all the layers increases from the circumference towards the hilum, whence is to be explained the fact that, on the desiccation of the starch-grain, fissures arise in the hilum, and radiate from this towards the periphery

The chemical substance of a starch-grain, however, apart from this varying difference in the proportion of water, is composed of two substances, chiefly distinguished by their solubility: these are termed granulose and starch-cellulose The first predominates by far in quantity, and is at the same time the one which effects the blue colouration of the starch-grain with iodine. Being the more easily soluble, it may be removed by various solvents from the starch-grain, the starch-cellulose alone at length remaining behind, in such a manner, however, that it still forms a skeleton exhibiting the essential structure of the starch-grain. If large starch-grains are macerated in fresh saliva at $35-55°$ C., or, according to Franz Schulze, digested at $60°$ in a saturated solution of common salt containing 1% of hydrochloric acid, the whole of the granulose is removed sooner or later · i e. it is chemically altered and converted into sugar, while the starch-cellulose remains behind in the form of a laminated skeleton. This latter is coloured copper-red with iodine, or not at all, and represents only a small proportion of the mass of the entire starch-grain. The different solubility of the two substances is also made evident on germination by the behaviour of the starch-grains in the reservoirs of reserve-materials The starch-grains in the living cell, however, may be dissolved in a very different way. In some cases the solution begins with the removal of the granulose, while the cellulose remains behind. This however often takes place only here and there: the extraction proceeds at isolated spots from without inwards. The extracted places are coloured copper-red with aqueous solutions of iodine, the rest of the mass blue. This I found to be the case in the endosperm of germinating Wheat (Fig. 235 *B*) In other cases the solution begins likewise at single spots on the circumference, but the entire substance is progressively dissolved · cavities are produced, and the grain here also finally breaks up into pieces, as seen in Fig. 235 *a–f* In the cotyledons of the germinating Bean, the solution of the ellipsoidal grains begins from within; before they break up into pieces, the granulose is often so completely extracted that the grains assume a copper-red colour with iodine, bluish here and there. Subsequently all is dissolved. In the germinating Potato, and in the root-stock of *Canna*, on the other hand, the solution of the grain proceeds from without inwards, layer after layer being removed. It evidently depends here, as with the action of saliva, upon whether the solvent acts slowly and first extracts the granulose only, or energetically attacks and dissolves the substance as a whole.

When the solution of starch or granulose is here spoken of, a chemical conversion into sugar at the same time is always to be supposed. Starch-grains as such are not soluble simply in water. If they are crushed in cold water, however, a small portion of the granulose appears to pass into solution, and is precipitated by iodine as fine-grained blue pellicles.   Starch-grains ground up with fine sand likewise appear to yield an actual solution of granulose in cold water

To the very characteristic properties of starch belongs the formation of paste. Water of at least 55° C. causes large, watery starch-grains to swell up vigorously: in the case of small denser grains this only results, according to Naegeli, at 65° C. If sufficient water is present at this temperature the watery inner portion of a grain swells first, and then the outer : the outermost layer scarcely swells at all, it is rather blown up and remains behind in the paste produced by the swelling, in the form of pellicular shreds.   A dilute solution of potash or soda produces a similar effect in the cold. The volume of a starch-grain may in this manner increase a hundred-and-twenty-five fold, and so much liquid may be taken up that the swollen pasty grain only contains from 2 to 0 5% of substance. With a sufficiently large quantity of hot water the paste is so distributed that it looks like a homogeneous mass, and this on cooling congeals to a translucent jelly.   After long boiling the starch paste loses the property of gelatinising after cooling : the starch is then converted into a modification soluble even in cold water.

Large, completely-formed, and especially simple starch-grains are found only in the ripe quiescent reservoirs of reserve-materials, in growing or vigorously vegetating shoots and roots, and other organs in general where they are evidently being continually formed and dissolved, they are found only in small and often exceedingly minute granules.   In such cases however even the smallest quantities of starch may easily be detected under the microscope, if thin sections of the portion of the plant in question are either warmed in potash solution or left for some time lying in it in the cold, then carefully washed out with water neutralised with acetic acid, and very dilute iodine solution finally added   The swollen-up minute starch-granules now appear as voluminous blue grains.   I have employed this method thousands of times, particularly in investigations upon the origin of the starch in the chlorophyll as well as its translocation during the growth of the organs, and much information as to the processes which occur during germination and the passage of material from place to place, to be described in the following lecture, has been obtained in this way.

LECTURE XXI.

RENEWAL OF ACTIVITY OF RESERVE-MATERIALS. FERMENTS. DORMANT PERIODS.

THE constructive materials of the organs in the reservoirs of reserve-materials, as well as those within other organs in their temporary conditions of rest, exist in forms not suited for their immediate co-operation in growth. This is in part because they are not soluble in the watery cell-sap, and are therefore incapable of being transported —e. g. starch-grains, many aleurone grains, crystalloids, and slimy proteid substances. It is above all necessary that these materials should diffuse from cell to cell and travel from the places where they are deposited to those where they are used: this is not possible in these conditions.

Another point also comes into consideration here. Even cane-sugar, and similarly inulin, though always dissolved in the cell-sap, only occur as reserve-materials, and are not in a fit condition for direct employment in growth, since when it is necessary to make use of these matters in the growing germinal shoots, they are previously converted into another chemical form, namely into a sugar which reduces cuprous oxide in an alkaline solution, and which, neglecting further differences, we shall term generally glucose.

Since now cane-sugar, inulin, and to a certain extent even dissolved proteids, occur in a transportable condition, and more or less capable of diffusion, it must in this case be not simply a matter of making them capable of diffusion, but we may assume that the chemical alteration also serves to render them in a condition in which they are suited for direct employment in growth. In these changes of the reserve-materials, therefore, it is not simply a matter of making them soluble and transportable, but evidently of also converting them into a form directly serviceable for growth

We may perhaps shortly formulate the matter thus. The plastic substances present two conditions: in the one condition they appear passive, inactive, dormant, whether in the solid or in the dissolved form; in the other they are not only always dissolved and movable, but are also in such a condition that they can directly take part in the nutrition of growing cells. In this state they appear active, in contrast to their passive condition in the reservoirs of reserve-materials.

In both animal and vegetable organisms, organic compounds of peculiar kind are produced, under the influence of which plastic materials are converted from the passive into the active and movable condition; these are the Ferments[1]. They appear to originate from proteinaceous substances, always however in extremely small quantities only, so that their existence in most cases can only be inferred from their conspicuous action; this action consists in their being able to convert very large, perhaps indeed unlimited quantities of reserve-materials into the active state. The ferments affect the latter in a certain sense as stimuli do irritable organs. In what way this action takes place however is still questionable, though it differs from ordinary chemical actions in that the ferment itself is not essentially altered during the process, and does not even enter into a chemical combination. It must be added here, however, that similar alterations are produced on carbo-hydrates, proteid matters, and some other peculiar organic compounds (especially the so-called glucosides) by acids, alkalies, and even by water at higher temperatures. Hence it is not always certain in the present state of our knowledge whether, in a given case not more exactly investigated, the changes of the reserve-materials and glucosides in question are produced by actual ferments, or by certain vegetable acids or alkalies. In this province of vegetable physiology, which has only been opened up during the last few years, there is still much that is problematical and uncertain, so that we are necessitated to depend to a large extent on the experience of animal physiology. Nevertheless the facts already known concerning vegetable ferments quite suffice to show that in this connection also, as in so many others, important agreements exist between the vital processes of animals and plants, especially where fundamental phenomena are concerned.

With regard to the results of their action, two main categories of ferments may be distinguished. In the one case the ferment effects only an insignificant chemical change, as when starch, cane-sugar, or inulin are converted into glucose, or proteids into peptones. In other cases, on the contrary, the ferment action consists in a very profound chemical alteration, of such a nature that from one complicated organic compound two or three simpler compounds very different in kind are produced. The first category may be distinguished as merely alterative ferments, the second as splitting ferments. To the latter belongs, for example, the Emulsin of the Almond, by means of which its amygdalin becomes decomposed into glucose, prussic acid, and oil of bitter almonds, and which is also able to break up numerous other glucosides into glucose and other products. The case is similar with Myrosin, which splits potassium myronate into glucose, oil of mustard, and potassium sulphate. Nevertheless these ferments, as well as the matters upon which they act, are of subordinate importance, since both occur only in individual families or species of plants, and because their significance for metabolism, for the purposes of growth itself, is in these cases very questionable.

The fact is quite otherwise with the first category of ferments, which I have distinguished as merely alterative. These re-invigorate the plastic reserve-materials distributed throughout the vegetable world, and although we have as yet by no

---

[1] More details respecting the ferments are to be found in Schutzenberger's book, '*Die Gahrungserscheinungen*,' (Leipzig, 1876); and also in Pfeffer's *Pflanzen-physiologie*, §§ 47, 56, 59. Both, however, are wanting in criticism of the phenomena. In this connection the best is undoubtedly Naegeli's '*Theorie der Gahrung*' (Munchen, 1879).

means sufficient information concerning them as to whether these changes are always effected by ferments, or do not occasionally occur by other means, the great importance of this category of ferments nevertheless lies in that they are known in very many cases to re-invigorate the plastic substances

In this category, alone to be considered here, two chief kinds of ferments are to be distinguished, namely, the diastatic ferments and the peptonising ferments. The former convert various carbo-hydrates into glucoses, while the different proteid substances are transformed by the latter into peptones. As a third subdivision may be added the emulsifying ferments which act upon fats, and which will be spoken of subsequently.

The longest and best known diastatic ferment in plants is Diastase, produced on the germination of the seeds of barley and other grasses it may be extracted from the seedling by water or glycerine, and is capable of transforming enormous quantities of starch into glucose, especially at higher temperatures below 70° C. A few drops of an extract obtained in this way added to a considerable quantity of boiled solution of starch, transforms it completely into sugar in a few hours; and fresh starch-grains at the ordinary temperature (15-25° C) are in a short time corroded and finally dissolved entirely, as previously described. Since, now, in the germination of all starchy seeds, tubers, bulbs, and other reservoirs of reserve-materials, exactly the same alterations of the starch-grains take place, and the starch disappears with the formation of sugar, it may be supposed *à priori* that in all these numerous cases, diastase, or at any rate similar diastatic ferments, produce the effect mentioned. And, as a matter of fact, Baranetzky has shown that in all cases where he looked for the diastatic ferment in starchy seeds, tubers, stems, and even leaves, it was to be found; and even in organs which contain no starch but abound in sugar, as in the Carrot (*Daucus carota*) and Turnip (*Brassica Rapa*), the same observer found a diastatic ferment. In seeds containing starch, the ferment may appear before the commencement of germination, generally, however, it only appears when growth begins

It was formerly the custom to distinguish, as Invertin, a substance produced by the Yeast-plant, Bacteria, and Mould-fungi, which splits cane-sugar into dextrose and levulose (two species of glucose which reduce cuprous oxide), which then undergo further decompositions under the influence of these Fungi. That a similar ferment occurs also in the wintering Beet-root, may be concluded from the fact that the cane-sugar collected as a reserve-material in its tissues is transformed into glucose in the following spring, when the flowering shoots are developed, and a similar phenomenon occurs on the development of the fruiting spikes of Indian corn, the parenchyma of the stem of which previously contained large quantities of cane-sugar. The inulin in the tubers and perennial root-stocks of the Compositæ, moreover, as I showed twenty years ago, is transformed into glucose when the shoots begin to grow, whence we may conclude that here also a diastatic ferment resembling invertin co-operates.

The ferments appear to be always produced by the growing parts of the seedlings and buds themselves, and to penetrate from these into the reservoirs of reserve-materials, there to dissolve or make active the constructive materials. This is particularly evident in the case of seeds containing endosperm. If the young seedling (embryo) is removed from the seed of the Indian corn (Maize), Barley or other plant, and the endosperm alone laid in moist warm earth, its starch is not dissolved and transformed into sugar. Still more evident than in such cases appears the action of the growing seedling on the reservoir of reserve-materials, in the germination of the stone of the Date, for here the non-nitrogenous reserve-material consists of hard cellulose, which is deposited in the endosperm in the form of thickened cell-walls, and which constitutes the great mass of the date-stone. The embryo, at first very minute, protrudes its root and plumule at the beginning of germination (as seen in Fig. 236), and only the uppermost portion of the primary seed-leaf, which now gradually develops into a cup-shaped absorbing organ, becoming larger and larger, remains within the endosperm. This organ, consists of very delicate parenchyma, and excretes ferments which dissolve the hard endosperm in its immediate neighbourhood. The products of solution are absorbed by the organ, and then conveyed into the growing parts of the seedling; until finally the whole of the hard date-stone is dissolved, and its cavity occupied by the developed absorbing organ The seed of *Phytelephas* (known under the name of Vegetable Ivory), which is at least a hundred times larger than the date-stone, and the endosperm of which consists of much harder cellulose, behaves similarly

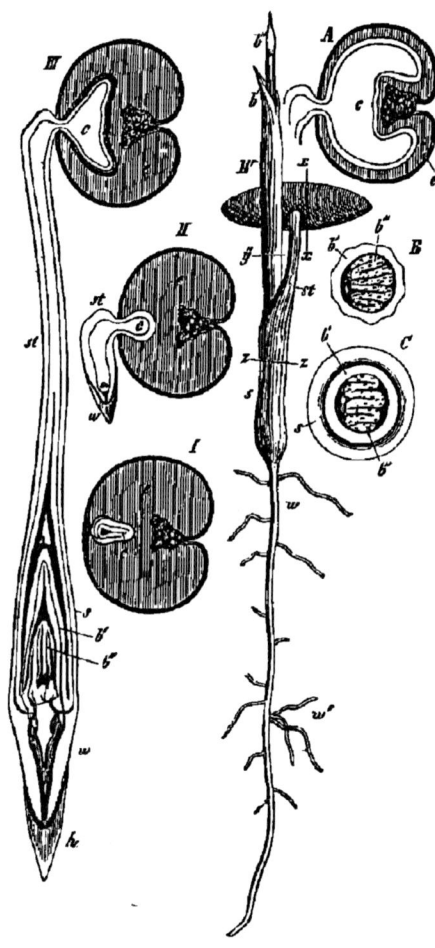

FIG. 236.—Germination of *Phœnix dactylifera* *I* transverse section of the resting seed, *II*, *III*, *IV* stages in the germination (*IV* nat size), *A* transverse section of the seed *IV* at *xx*, *B* transverse section of *IV* at *xy*, *C* ditto at *zz*, *e* the horny endosperm, *s* sheath of cotyledon, *st* its petiole, *g* its apex, developed into an absorbing organ which gradually exhausts the endosperm, and at length replaces it, *w* the primary root, *w'* lateral roots, *b'b''* the leaves which succeed the cotyledon, *b''* becomes the first foliage leaf, in *B* and *C* its folded lamina is seen in transverse section.

The action of those Fungi which destroy wood and kill trees may be compared directly with the action of such seedlings on their endosperm, the thin mycelial threads of these Fungi, as has been shown by Robert Hartig in his magnificent work, penetrate into the alburnum and heart-wood of trees, evidently because they excrete ferments at their growing apices, which dissolve the hard cell-walls of the wood.

Attention was first drawn to the occurrence of peptonising ferments in the

vegetable kingdom by the remarkable phenomena observed in the so-called insectivorous plants, of which I shall speak more in detail shortly. My earlier studies
on the germination of various seeds left no doubt that seedlings dissolve and make
active their proteinaceous reserve-materials by means of peptonising ferments. Gorup-
Besanez was, however, the first to detect peptonising ferments in seeds. This he
did in the seeds of the Vetch, Hemp, Flax, and Barley; and Krukenberg found an
energetic peptonising ferment soon afterwards in the protoplasm of a Myxomycete,
namely, in the yellow plasmodium of the 'flowers of tan' (*Æthalium septicum*). More
recently, a very energetic peptonising ferment in the latex of *Carica Papaya* has
attracted particular attention, and a similar ferment has been detected in the latex
of the common Fig (*Ficus Carica*)[1]. As we come to know the proteinaceous reserve-
materials of plants better, and if we follow their behaviour in the animal body also,
it can scarcely be doubtful that, in spite of incomplete knowledge, the assumption
is nevertheless warranted that peptonising ferments are perhaps universally distributed in plants; moreover, peptones, the result of their activity, have actually been
detected by Schulze in the seedlings of the Lupine. The peptonising ferments in
the animal body, where they occur particularly in the mucous membrane of the
stomach, are much better and more generally known than in plants. Exceedingly
small quantities of them are able to lignify and dissolve coagulated egg-albumen,
blood-fibrin, or muscle, in the presence of an acid, especially hydrochloric acid, with
great energy, and so convert them into a condition in which the proteid matters,
while retaining their essential chemical properties, will diffuse through closed tissue
cells, to be reconstructed into organised proteid substances at suitable spots in the
organism, and to serve for the construction of tissues.

In the peptonising of proteid substances, as in the action of diastatic ferments,
it is a matter of a relatively slight chemical change. A much more profound
decomposition of the proteid bodies takes place, on the contrary, when they are converted into Asparagin[2] and other split products. Among the latter, in any case, a
sulphur compound, probably sulphuric acid, must occur. But, besides asparagin,
Tyrosin, which arises in the artificial splitting of proteid bodies, has also been
observed by Borodin in many cases. It is not yet known whether or how far any
ferment action occurs in this case. In any case, however, the formation of asparagin
has a similar significance for the transport of nitrogenous substance that the formation
of sugar from starch-grains has; since by means of the conversion of proteid bodies
(which are only slowly and with difficulty diffusible even in the dissolved state) into
asparagin, which is a crystallisable substance forming solutions which readily diffuse, a
means is obtained for transporting the nitrogenous substance in the closed parenchyma
to the places where it is made use of. Consequently asparagin is formed on the
germination of seeds, tubers, root-stocks, and when the winter-buds of woody plants
put forth their shoots, this penetrates from the reservoirs of reserve-materials into
the young growing parts, and is there employed for the formation of protoplasm,

---

[1] On the ferment in the latex of *Ficus Carica* cf Hansen, 'Sitzungsber. der physical med Soc
zu Erlangen' (Nov 8, 1880)

[2] The literature on Asparagin is cited in Pfeffer's '*Pflanzen-physiologie*' (§ 59). Borodin's
treatise, the one chiefly made use of in the text, is in Bot. Zeitg. 1878 (Nos. 51, 52)

a restitution into proteid having previously taken place, and non-nitrogenous substance (in the first place probably glucose) being made use of in the process.

This significance of asparagin was clearly perceived by Theodore Hartig,
so long ago as 1858, as is seen from his statement as follows : ' This apparently
general occurrence of this crystallisable substance in all the young cell-tissues,
indicates that its solution is the form in which the nitrogenous nutritive substance
of plants, formed from the reserve-materials, is moved from cell to cell.' The fact
that Hartig's important discovery remained so long in abeyance, is to be ascribed
to the circumstance that this able investigator here, as in many other cases, employed
a very peculiar and often unintelligible nomenclature, and termed asparagin ' *Gleis* '
Our knowledge of this body was only carried further in 1872, by an investigation of
Pfeffer's : he proved that the accumulation of asparagin during germination in the
dark, is due to the fact that in this case there are not sufficient carbo-hydrates present
to afford the material for the construction of proteids out of asparagin. If seedling
shoots grown in the dark and abounding in asparagin are exposed to strong light,
and a fresh supply of carbo-hydrates produced by assimilation, the asparagin disappears, and proteid substances are formed at the same time.

Moreover, in the formation of asparagin, the end appears to be not simply the
rendering the nitrogenous substance transportable. The fact, discovered and insisted
upon by Borodin, that asparagin arises even in cut-off buds and older shoots
which are allowed to grow, and therefore in the cells which are then beginning
to grow, proves that in the formation of asparagin it is not simply a matter of
conveying proteid-forming substance into the young organs, but that here, as in the
formation of peptone and in the inversion of cane-sugar and inulin, we may assume
that it is a matter of giving the plastic substance a form in which it is directly suited
for the nutrition of growing protoplasm; or, as I expressed it in the beginning, to
convert the passive form of the reserve-material into an active one.

The universal occurrence of asparagin asserted by Hartig, but disputed later
by Pfeffer, was again established by Borodin in 1878 in a detailed treatise, going
more exactly into the conditions under which asparagin is to be detected.
Under normal conditions of vegetation during vigorous growth, and especially
under the influence of intense light, the asparagin is usually employed, according to
Borodin, for the formation of proteid, and for growth, as quickly as it is itself produced—an amount sufficiently large for detection only rarely occurs during normal
vegetation. Hence, to demonstrate the presence of asparagin in growing parts, abnormal conditions must be induced ; either by allowing the plants to grow in the dark
or in a feeble light, or, better, by placing branches in water, and employing the same
methods as before. The surest method, according to Borodin, is to make single
buds or the young apices of shoots grow in the dark, or in a feeble light, for by
this means, in part, the addition of carbo-hydrates from older parts, or even from
reservoirs of reserve-materials, is prevented, and in part the new formation of carbo-
hydrates by assimilation is excluded, and thus the reconstruction of asparagin into
proteid made impossible. Asparagin is therefore accumulated under the conditions
named, and can be demonstrated in sections under the microscope by the addition
of alcohol, in which it crystallises in a characteristic manner. In this way Borodin
succeeded in effecting the accumulation of asparagin, and in demonstrating its

presence in numerous cases where none at all was to be detected under normal conditions of vegetation. It is still to be mentioned that the formation of asparagin takes place also in young flower-stalks and buds, young fruits, and growing seeds; on the ripening of the seed, however, it disappears in the reservoirs of reserve-materials.

It is worthy of remark that Borodin succeeded in demonstrating the formation of asparagin in all cases where he investigated the growing parts of plants for that purpose. Unfortunately, there is only a single observation on a Moss: the question still remains to be answered also how the matter stands with respect to Algæ and Fungi.

Finally are to be mentioned the fats I showed, so long ago as 1858, that in the germination of seeds containing fat a transference of the fatty oils from the cotyledons, or from the endosperm into the growing parts of the seedling, appears to take place; and a few years later this was confirmed by chemical analyses by Peters[1] When the roots and shoot-axes of the seedlings of *Ricinus*, Gourd, and Almond have already grown to a considerable size, we find in their parenchyma for some time longer considerable quantities of fat, which have passed in from the cotyledons, or the endosperm, and only disappear later in metabolism. It thus appears that the fats can pass through the closed tissue-cells as such; though of course the greater part of them is transformed into starch and sugar for transport and use Similar phenomena with respect to fats occur moreover in the animal body, where the fats entering into the stomach are in the first place emulsified by the secretion from the pancreas, that is, they become converted into exceedingly fine drops and then saponified This again is brought about by a special ferment According to Schutzenberger, a similar ferment actually exists also in fatty seeds: if such seeds are ground up in water, an emulsion is produced in which, as he says, glycerine and free fatty acids appear forthwith. According to this, however, the presence of fats in the seedling can only be explained by assuming that glycerine and fatty acids travel from cell to cell, and are continually becoming re-united for the formation of fat, a process moreover which presents a certain similarity with the movements of transitory starch. For starch also is found at places in the tissue where it has neither been originally produced nor is employed, and thus in a condition of translocation towards the places where it is made use of; in petioles and the older internodes of growing plants, this fine-grained transitory starch is to be found very generally. It is obvious that it does not pass as such through the closed cell-walls, and its translocation is only intelligible if we assume that the small starch-granules in one cell become dissolved and the solution penetrates into the next cell, there to become separated again as granules by the starch-forming corpuscles of Schimper, the process being repeated from cell to cell

As a rule, the remarkable decompositions of organic compounds brought about by the Ferment-fungi (organised ferments) have also been regarded hitherto as ferment-actions, it being assumed that in these Fungi—Yeast, Bacteria, Mould-fungi, etc —peculiar substances belonging to the category of ferments are produced, which act upon the saccharine or proteinaceous media as do the above-named splitting ferments. Thus, for example, grape-sugar is broken up by the Yeast-fungus into

---

[1] On the translocation of fats, cf. my '*Handbuch der Exp -phys*' (1865, p 304)

alcohol, carbon dioxide, glycerine, and succinic acid, and proteid matters are split up by Bacteria into a long series of chemical compounds. But Naegeli, in his 'Theory of Fermentation' (1879), has given sufficiently strong reasons for believing that the fermentation and putrefaction due to the action of organised ferments are processes

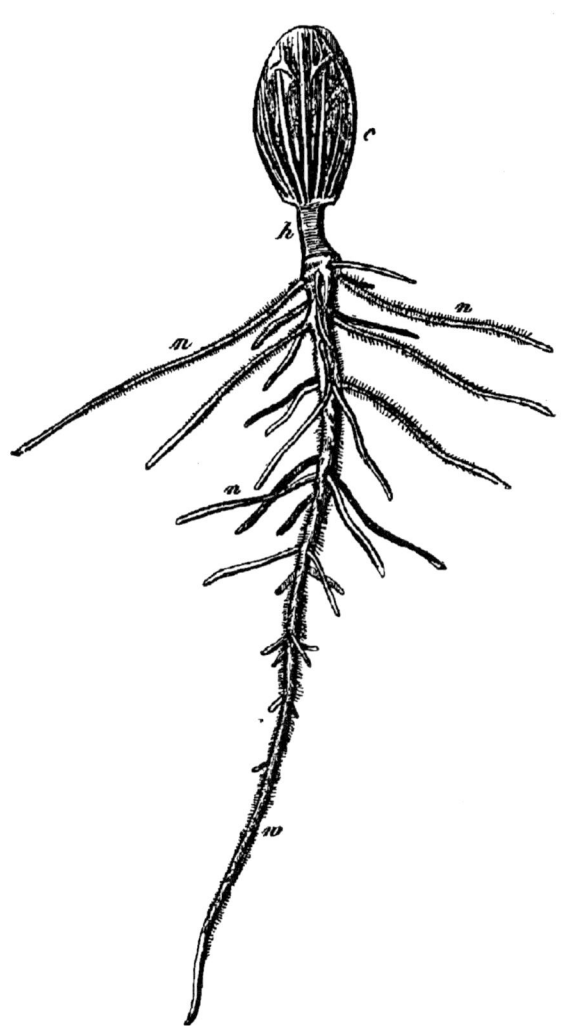

essentially different from ordinary ferment actions. Above all, Naegeli insists, and rightly, that the hypothetical ferment which the ferment-fungi and putrefactive fungi are supposed to excrete has not yet been extracted from the cells and described. On the contrary, the cause which effects the fermentation is inseparably connected with the substance, and indeed with the protoplasm of the living cells of the Fungus.

'Fermentation by means of Fungi,' says Naegeli, 'only takes place in immediate contact with the protoplasm, and so far as its molecular action extends. If the organism needs to affect chemical processes in areas and at distances where it is able to exert no power by means of the molecular forces of the living substance, it excretes ferments. The latter are particularly effective in the cavities of the animal body, in the water in which Fungi live, and in vegetable cells poor in protoplasm. It is even very questionable whether the organism ever forms ferments which shall be active within the protoplasm; since here it does not require them, much more energetic means for chemical action being at its disposal in the molecular forces of the living substance itself.'

FIG 237 —Seedling of the Gourd   *w* primary root , *n n* lateral roots , *b* hypocotyl , *c* cotyledons   At this time the cotyledons contain starch and sugar in addition to much fat   the same is also the case in the hypocotyl, less so in the root. The hypocotyl and root also contain fatty oil derived from the cotyledons.

I find with Naegeli a further particularly striking point of difference in the fact that (apart from split-ferments such as Emulsin and Myrosin) the plastic matters are transferred by the action of unorganised ferments from the passive into the active condition. Fermentation by means of Fungi has, as Naegeli insists, just the opposite character, its products are, without exception, less nutritious compounds, and it destroys especially the most nutritious substances.

'The contrast,' says Naegeli, 'appears most striking in the case of carbo-hydrates and proteid substances. While the action of unorganised ferments produces from them glucoses and peptones, fermentation by means of Fungi breaks up these compounds into alcohol, mannite, lactic-acid, and into Leucin, Tyrosin, &c.,—in some cases several fermentations follow one another; their products then become less nutritious step by step. We may say, generally, that the Yeast-fungi render the medium in which they occur chemically less suitable for nutrition by every process of fermentation which they effect '

In fermentation by means of unorganised ferments the chemical transformation proceeds smoothly and completely: dextrin is entirely transformed into grape-sugar, cane-sugar entirely into inverted sugar, and albuminates entirely into peptones. In the alcoholic fermentation, on the other hand, the products of which alone have hitherto been quantitatively determined, only the greater part of the sugar is broken up into alcohol and carbon dioxide, while, according to Pasteur, about 5% of the sugar is decomposed by the way into glycerine, succinic acid, and carbon-dioxide. It is likewise certain that in the lactic acid fermentation, not all the sugar is decomposed into lactic acid. Carbon dioxide especially appears to be a by-product of all fermentations, due to the action of Fungi and of all putrefactive processes.

The alleged difference between fermentation by means of unorganised ferments and that due to the action of Fungi would be unintelligible if both processes were due to the same cause. Every difficulty vanishes, on the other hand, if fermentation by means of Fungi is caused, not by a contact substance (ferment), but by living protoplasm. We then apprehend that while the ferment as a simple chemical compound alters another chemical compound in a simple and equable manner so that all molecules suffer the same kind of decomposition, an organised substance with its various molecular movements and molecular forces produces more complicated decompositions

In this connection, Naegeli brings forward the fact that, as already remarked above, the effects of proper ferment actions are also produced by acids, alkalies, and even by water, especially at higher temperatures: the fact is quite otherwise with the fermentations which are due exclusively to living Fungi. Naegeli puts his view of fermentation due to organisms as opposed to that produced by unorganised ferments in the following statement.—

'Fermentation is therefore the transference of the movements of the molecules, atomic groups, and atoms of various compounds composing living protoplasm (which remain chemically unaltered in the process) to the fermentable material, by which means the equilibrium between its molecules is destroyed, and it is broken up.'

The older theory of fermentation, which classes it with the action of unorganised ferments, has to assume that the various fermentations are effected by just as many ferments in the Fungi producing them; whereas Naegeli's theory seeks to explain the difference between the fermentations as due to the different internal organisation of the protoplasm of the Fungi which produce them. So much for general guidance as to the unorganised ferments and their differences from the exciting agents in alcoholic and similar fermentations.

Coming now to speak of the hitherto entirely unexplained dormant periods of plants, in connection with what has been said with respect to ferments, it may appear at first sight that no conceivable connection exists I also by no means wish to maintain that the view which I propose here is sufficiently proved, though I do maintain that it opens up for us in the meantime a way to further investigation of one of the most general phenomena of plant life.

Even under the most favourable conditions of vegetation, dormant periods occur in the course of the life of the plant. Under circumstances when the plant would be in a condition to grow most vigorously, because it is provided with reserve-materials, and water and oxygen are at its disposal, and a sufficiently high temperature might be expected to call forth the internal movements, every externally perceptible vital motion nevertheless ceases, and it is only after some months of rest that the growth commences anew, and this frequently under circumstances which appear far less favourable—especially at a conspicuously lower temperature. This periodic alternation of vegetative activity and rest, is in general so regulated that for a given species of plant both occur at definite times of the year, leading to the inference that the periodicity only depends upon the alternation of the seasons, and therefore chiefly upon that of temperature and moisture. Without wishing to deny the co-operation of these factors, a closer consideration shows however that this matter must depend chiefly upon changes which take place in the resting plant, independently of external influences, or only indirectly affected by them. To render the facts in question intelligible to the reader, however, I will in the first place select from the enormous mass of material a few well-known examples.

The leaf-shoot and flowers contained in the bulb of the Crown Imperial commence to grow vigorously in the spring time with us, even at the beginning or middle of March, when the soil in which the bulb has passed the winter possesses a temperature of $6-10°C$; the leaf-shoots protrude forcibly from the cold earth to grow vigorously in the but slightly warmer air. There would be but little to surprise us in this if we did not at the same time notice the fact that a new leaf-shoot is already formed in embryo in the subterranean bulb in April and May. this shoot, however, does not grow to any extent in the warm soil during the summer and autumn. On the contrary, this favourable period of vegetation passes by, until at the end of the winter an inconsiderable rise of temperature above the freezing-point suffices to induce vigorous growth, and, as is well known, the same is the case with most bulbous and tuberous plants, many of which, as the Meadow Saffron, possess two active periods, the flowers developing in the late autumn and the foliage-leaves belonging to them only in the next spring. The best known examples, however, are afforded by the common potato and the kitchen onion. I have many times attempted to induce the tubers and bulbs ripened in the autumn to put forth their germinal shoots during November, December, and January, by laying them in moist, warm, loose soil; but in the case of the potato as well as in that of the kitchen onion, no trace of germination appeared. If, on the other hand, the attempt is repeated in February, or still better in March, the germinal buds begin to grow vigorously even in a few days. At this time of the year, indeed, it does not even require a favourably high temperature and an external supply of water: the shoots begin to develope at much lower temperatures, and this, even when the potatoes and bulbs do not receive the addition of water from without. Not only so, they will put forth germinal shoots when suspended in dry air and shrivelled up by the loss of water. It is evident that some internal change must have taken place in the tubers and bulbs during the winter months when it is impossible to bring them into activity from their state of rest, since no such change is perceptible externally, and the behaviour described appears inexplicable otherwise.

The behaviour of the Water-nut, the fruit of *Trapa natans*, is perhaps still more striking. If at the end of August, or in September, when they are ripe, one of these is placed in a glass full of water, no germination occurs either during the autumn or winter, even in a chamber where the water is constantly at 15–20° C.; but in March or April germination begins although the water is at a temperature of only 8–10° C. The most striking examples of periodic rest and activity are probably afforded however by the majority of woody plants, especially those which produce winter-buds clothed with scales, such as the Horse-chestnut, ordinary fruit-trees, and species of *Pinus* and *Abies*. As soon as this year's foliage and flower-shoots have become unfolded in the spring from the winter-buds of the previous year, the winter-buds for the next year are formed in embryo; the future shoots or even flowers develope slowly within the bud envelopes, but remain in an embryonic condition, and it is impossible by any means to cause these embryonic shoots to develope in the autumn or the beginning of winter. On the other hand, they develope in January, or better in February, if branches furnished with buds are cut off and allowed to stand in water in an ordinary warm dwelling-room—i. e. at a temperature of about 15–20° C. The winter-buds of trees thus behave just like subterranean bulbs and tubers.

It is by no means to be denied that in many of these cases, especially in those of the winter-buds of trees, some bulbs (*Hyacinthus, Crocus*), etc., a considerable time is necessary in order that the embryonic rudiments of the leaf-shoots and flowers within their envelopes may be first so far prepared by slow growth that they are suited for rapid development subsequently. The decisive point certainly does not lie in this, however, as may be seen in the behaviour of the Water-nut. We find the most evident and instructive cases with reference to the question here alone concerned, however, in the spores of many Cryptogams. The majority of the spores of Algæ and Fungi, especially those produced by sexual fertilisation, are distinguished as 'resting spores,' because after their formation in the spring or summer they remain dormant for 8–10 months, either in water or dry, without germinating, whereupon they then put forth their germinal shoots at a lower temperature in the following spring. This peculiarity of resting spores is so much the more striking since many of these plants produce simultaneously or previously other forms of spores, which are capable of germination immediately after their origin. As examples may be mentioned the zygospores of the Mucorini, which require rest, and the conidia of the same fungus which can germinate at any time.

It appears certain that the internal changes which take place in the resting tubers, bulbs, buds, and spores, during the long pause, are promoted, in many cases at least, by a not too excessive drying-up. Numerous experiments with Algæ and Fungi show that by means of desiccation (which must not be carried too far however) the dormant period can be shortened in many cases, and some observations not yet sufficiently confirmed allow of the conclusion that even in the winter-buds of trees something of the same kind occurs. But in all cases where the resting spores, or in Phanerogams the seeds, as those of *Trapa*, go through their dormant period at the bottom of deep water, we cannot speak of the co-operation of desiccation. All this appears to indicate rather that in every case it depends upon chemical changes in the dormant parts of the plant; changes which proceed only extremely slowly, and generally require months for their completion. These chemical changes do not affect the proper reserve-materials as such, however, or at least not throughout their mass, as follows from the fact that in potato tubers, which have been so very frequently investigated, no striking difference has ever yet been found in the chemical composition in the autumn, before the dormant period, and in the spring following it. In the same way the numerous observers have perceived no changes which immediately affect the reserve-materials in the Algæ and Fungi.

On the contrary, all vigorous chemical changes only appear at the commencement of germination, and we know already that these changes of the reserve-materials are in great part effected by means of ferments. From these considerations I come to the conclusion that, in the case of dormant periods, it may be a matter of a very slow production of ferments, which are formed in the buds capable of growth; and that the possibility of putting the existing reserve-materials into the active state in which they are directly suitable for the requirements of growth, only appears when they have been produced in sufficient quantity. That this production of ferments may be in its turn favoured by various external circumstances during the dormant periods—e. g. in many cases by desiccation or the cold of winter—is not to be denied. On the other hand, in cases where spores, buds, tubers, and seeds are capable of germination immediately after their production, it may be assumed that they take up the necessary quantity of ferments or similarly effective matters at the time of their origin, from the mother-plant.

Since at the present time the attention of vegetable physiologists is being directed towards ferments, it is to be hoped that researches will not be wanting to confirm or contradict the hypothesis here put forth. In any case the periodic alternation of rest and vegetative activity, as one of the most general phenomena in the life of the plant, is worthy of greater attention than has hitherto been accorded to it [1].

---

[1] Pfeffer has collected the literature on the annual periods of vegetation in his '*Pflanzen-physiologie*,' pp 106, &c

LECTURE XXII.

PASSAGE OF THE PLASTIC MATERIALS THROUGH THE TISSUES.

THAT the materials serving for the construction of the organs must travel in the growing and assimilating plant over distances more or less extensive, results as a necessary consequence from all the facts hitherto stated. Growth takes place at the apices of the roots on the one hand, and in and beneath the buds on the other, and plastic substances are of course employed there. at the time of germination they are contained in the reservoirs of reserve-materials, and must travel from thence to the places mentioned. In fully-grown plants with assimilating foliage leaves, the latter behave like reservoirs of reserve-materials, the plastic substances necessary for the growth of the buds and of the distant roots pass out from them. That the path which individual molecules of starch and sugar and the substances forming protoplasm pass over may, under certain circumstances, be very long, is obvious on reflecting that the materials of which the subterranean roots of a tree (e g. a Palm) 20 metres high are formed, have been originally produced in the crown of leaves, 20 metres or more distant from the roots

But it is also easy to convince ourselves of this fact experimentally. If, for instance, the bud at the end of a well-developed Gourd plant is directed through a narrow hole into the dark cavity of a wooden box, as in Fig. 238, it is obvious that all those materials which are now employed in the growth of the parts in the dark must necessarily have been derived from the leaves which assimilate under the influence of light outside the box. The figure represents a definite, observed case The Gourd plant made use of in the experiment already possessed thirteen large leaves on its main stem, the total assimilating area of which amounted to about 1·5 square metres when, on the 25th of July, 1881, the terminal bud of the stem was directed at d into the box K. All the buds and leaf-shoots in the axils of the leaves had been previously cut away, in order that all the products of assimilation of the thirteen leaves should pass into the bud which was now in the dark Inside the box, which was about two metres high, one metre broad, and one metre long, there developed, in the course of the next four or five weeks, an extremely vigorous system of etiolated shoots, with white stems and leaf-stalks, and yellow leaves. On the 1st of September, that is, after five weeks, the terminal bud of the etiolated main stem was conducted to the exterior through a hole e in the roof of the box; and the shoot which had grown in the dark inside the box, and which possessed structural peculiarities

[3]   A a

accordingly, now developed further in the light. The whole of the part *C*, up to the 7th of October, was about 95 cm. long, and possessed eight fine green leaves, all the organs, flowers, tendrils, etc being normal in structure. In the meantime, however, from a small flower-bud which had been conducted into the box with the

FIG 238.—A Gourd plant, the main shoot of which was first developed in the dark space, and subsequently again led to the exterior above (cf the text)

rest on the 25th of July, a Gourd fruit had been formed by the artificial impregnation of the flower subsequently developed: on the 8th of October this fruit possessed a circumference of 59 cm, and weighed about 3 kilograms, and contained 195 seeds, a third of which were shown to be capable of germination. It is evident that all the substances which had served for the construction of the organs in the dark had been conveyed from the organs outside the box to the etiolated shoot inside. the necessary water and ash ingredients coming from the roots, and the organic substance from the green leaves. The fruit alone contained about 250 grams of organic substance, and if we assign to the other etiolated organs in the box—the shoot-axes, leaves and tendrils—the very slight value of 50 grams of organic substance, we have about 300 grams of organic substance, conveyed in the course of seventy-four days from the green leaves into the parts growing in the dark Up to the 1st of September the substance was provided exclusively by the thirteen leaves situated outside the box, and they possessed an assimilating surface of 1·5 sq metres The shoots which subsequently grew out, beyond the roof of the box, were able to build up their constructive matters themselves: only the water and mineral matters had to be conveyed to them from the roots through a distance of 4–5 metres. If we had made our experiment with the difference that, after conducting the bud into the box, all the leaves outside were cut away, or themselves placed in darkness in the same way, the bud would then have grown in the box for a few days longer, and then all the parts in the dark would have perished. The incidental abnormalities of the organs developed in the dark come no further into consideration here. If during the period of vegetation, however, we had investigated the etiolated organs in the box micro-chemically, we should have found sugar and starch-grains in the parenchyma of the shoot-axes and petioles, proteinaceous matters in the sieve-tubes of the vascular bundles, protoplasm in all the cells, and etiolated yellow chlorophyll-grains in the yellow leaves [1].

If we now enquire as to the forms of tissue [2] in which the plastic substances from the reservoirs of reserve-materials are conveyed to the growing parts, the answer may be given generally that the albuminous matters move in the phloem of the vascular bundles, while starch, sugar and fats, and the nitrogenous substance asparagin, belonging to the protoplasm-formers. are conveyed in the parenchymatous tissues of the shoot-axes, petioles, roots, etc. The materials mentioned may be recognised at all times on these routes, so long as the conditions for so doing exist—i e if it is observed whence the matters in question come, and where they are made use of. Apart from a few special cases, it is shown that every portion of an organ about to begin to grow vigorously, becomes in the first place filled with proteid matters (or asparagin), and with fine-grained starch and sugar, which are conveyed to it from the reservoirs of reserve-materials, or from the assimilating leaves Then, when any particular part of a root, shoot-axis, or leaf, etc is fully developed, the materials become used up and disappear.

It is not to be forgotten here, however, that by means of growth itself, the organs already developed come to lie between those parts which supply the materials

---

[1] With respect to the behaviour of plants in the dark, cf my treatises '*Über den Einfluss des Tageslichtes auf Neubildung und Entfaltung verschiedener Pflanzenorgane*' (Bot Zeitg 1863), and '*Die Wirkung des Lichtes auf die Bluthenbildung unter Vermittlung der Laubblatter*' (Bot Zeitg. 1865, No 15, &c.)

[2] My first publications directed against the old theory of the descending sap are, '*Über die Leitung plastischer Stoffe durch verschiedene Gewebeformen*,' Flora, 1863 (p 33), and the chapter on the translocation of plastic substances in my '*Experimental-physiologie*' (1865, p 374), where the older literature is also cited

and those where they are made use of; so that with the progressive growth of the shoot-axes and roots, the distance through parts already fully grown which the formative substances must traverse on their way to the parts which are growing and which

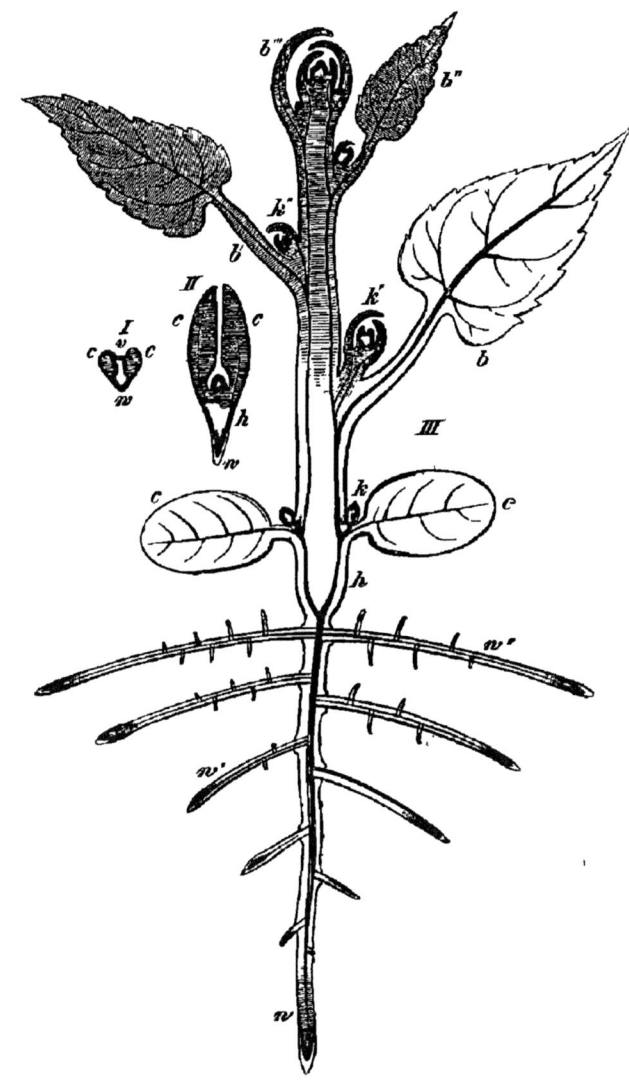

FIG. 239.—Diagram of a dicotyledonous plant. *I* young embryo in the seed, *II* the same somewhat older, *III* the plant after the conclusion of germination when commencing to assimilate independently. The black portions indicate the growing points containing chiefly proteid materials, the grey ones are the parts which are elongating, where the proteid matters are less abundant, but into which starch and sugar have passed to be employed in growth. The parts left white are fully grown, and *c* and *b* are carrying on the function of assimilation.

make use of them becomes greater and greater. Figure 239 may serve to illustrate this, since it represents diagrammatically the distribution of the states of growth of a young Dicotyledon. All the organs already fully developed, and

therefore no longer growing, are simply in outline and not shaded; those which
are actively growing are shaded; and the very slowly developing growing points
are represented black. Let us now assume that this diagrammatic plant has
completed its germination, and is already nourishing itself by means of assimilation. The fully developed cotyledons *c*, which we suppose to contain chlorophyll,
and the fully developed leaf *b*, do duty as organs of assimilation. From these
the products of assimilation and metabolism have to travel on the one hand down
to the roots *w w' w''*, and also, and to a still greater extent, up to the young
parts of the shoot which are shaded dark. It is at once seen that between the
places where the consumption of material occurs, and the organs of assimilation,
parts are intercalated which are no longer growing, and thus do not use up the
materials. Nevertheless the plastic substances must travel through these fully developed parts to the (darkly shaded) growing portions. This takes place, so far
as the albuminous matters are concerned, in the phloem of the vascular bundles
which are indicated in the figure: starch, sugar, and asparagin, on the contrary,
travel in the layers of parenchyma, and, as micro-chemical investigations show,
chiefly in those layers which immediately surround the vascular bundles. This refers
especially to the transitory starch, as to the movement of which a few words more
may be added here Where a young organ commences to grow, its small parenchyma-cells become filled with fine-grained starch, and then sugar appears in addition. As the part goes on growing, the starch and sugar increase; they being
supplied in quantities greater than those consumed. Subsequently, the relation is reversed, and more is consumed than is supplied, and when the organ in question is
fully developed, the starch and sugar have disappeared. This takes place not
only when the supply of food is derived from the starch-forming organs of assimilation, or from reservoirs of reserve-materials abounding in starch, but also when the
reservoirs of reserve-materials previously contained no starch at all, but cane-sugar
as in the root of the Beet, inulin as in the tubers of the Dahlia, or even fat as in
most germinating seeds, or, finally, cellulose as in the Date In a word, apart
from rarer cases of plants in which the formation of starch is almost entirely
suppressed, as in the common Onion, the various kinds of substances which
form cell-walls, before they are directly made use of in growth, are at least in part
transformed into starch, which is then only used up directly as the cell-walls develope. We have as yet no satisfactory explanation of this remarkable fact. Although
no doubt whatever now exists that the starch which enters the young parts of the
growing shoot (in a germinating Oak for instance, or the bulb of a Tulip just putting
forth shoots), and which at first increases but then always disappears at the conclusion
of the growth of the part, is derived from the starch contained in the reservoirs of
reserve-materials—the cotyledons or bulb-scales, nevertheless it is likewise certain,
on the other hand, that these small starch-granules are for and by themselves immovable, and that no single starch-granule is itself in the act of travelling This
follows, on the one hand, from the fact that the transitory starch which has passed
into the growing parts consists of very small granules, whereas that in the reservoirs
of reserve-materials is large-grained and different in shape; moreover it would
be quite impossible for solid starch-grains to pass through the closed cell-walls of the
parenchyma, while the necessary moving forces would also be wanting When in

spite of this we speak of a translocation of the starch, an assumption is necessary in the first place to complete the direct observation. This is in general to the effect that the wandering starch undergoes continual solution and re-formation progressively from cell to cell. In this the activity of Schimper's starch-forming corpuscles co-operates in the cells in question, or, in the younger portions, the change

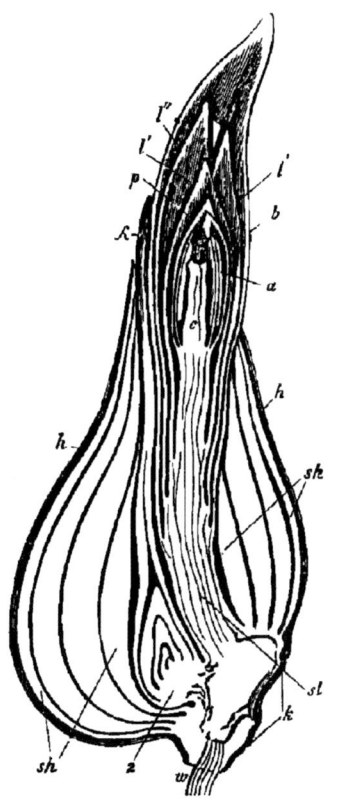

is effected by the protoplasm itself. It is not necessary to enter more into detail respecting this problem, however, it being only intended to do away with a possible error which might arise from the use of the expression 'transitory starch.' Perhaps a similar assumption is also to be made respecting the translocation of fat in the closed parenchyma. Within the parts of the shoot-axes, petioles, and leaf-veins which are already fully developed, the starch, then, passes from the reservoirs of reserve-materials or organs of assimilation to the growing parts, chiefly or exclusively in that layer of parenchyma which immediately surrounds the vascular bundle, or, in many Dicotyledons, separates all the leaf-traces in the shoot-axis from the cortex as a closed layer. This is the layer which we have previously learnt to know as the endodermis, and which, on account of this very function, I introduced into physiology long ago as the starch-bearing layer. If a more extensive movement of starch occurs, it takes place also in the external layers of the pith, internal to the vascular bundles; and, in the case of a very vigorous transport of starch, as when the leaves of trees are being emptied in the autumn, even the phloem of the vascular bundles may take part in it.

FIG 240.—Longitudinal section of a germinating bulb of *Tulipa præcox* *h* brown membrane enveloping the bulb, *k* the discoid portion of the stem of the bulb, which supports the bulb scales *sh*, *sh*, *sl* the elongated portion of the stem bearing the foliage leaves *l' l'*, and passing above into the terminal flower, *c* ovary, *a* anthers, *p* perianth, *s* a lateral bud (young bulb) in the axil of the youngest bulb scale, *λ* the apex of the first leaf of this lateral bud This bud becomes the bulb of next year *w* the roots which arise on the fibro vascular strands of the discoid stem

In the growing points themselves, i. e. in the extremely small-celled tissue of the apices of the roots and shoot-axes, I have never succeeded in detecting transitory starch or sugar. Both appear in these cells only when they pass over from the embryonal stage into that of extension—of more rapid growth—and as soon as intercellular spaces arise in the young parenchyma. The extremely small quantity of cell-wall forming substance which is made use of in the embryonal tissue of the growing point is in accordance with this. In the growing point itself growth is exceedingly slow, the developing cell-walls immeasurably thin, and the embryonal tissue itself densely filled with proteid substances, in which the extremely small quantity of cell-wall forming substance eludes direct recognition.

So far as we are informed with respect to the corresponding matters in trees and other woody plants, the movements referred to take place here also practically along the paths indicated, though with some slight modifications   Here, however, the additional fact comes into consideration that the parenchymatous tissue system extends also into the wood; from the cortex the horizontal medullary rays lead directly into the interior of the compact mass of wood, and the wood parenchyma distributed between the proper wood-fibres and vessels is proved to be in continuity with them, so that medullary rays and wood-parenchyma may be regarded to a certain extent as fine ramifications of the cortical parenchyma, by means of which it extends into the compact mass of wood. Accordingly, during the vegetative period this parenchymatous part of the wood also becomes filled with reserve-materials; chiefly, and usually in our trees, with starch, in some cases also with other cell-wall forming substances—in the North American Sugar-maple for example with cane-sugar   That these reserve-materials stored up in the wood are dissolved when the buds are put forth in spring, and carried away and used up in growth, follows from their disappearance at that time, this proceeds from the thinner bud-bearing twigs to the older branches, and then into the stem, as stated some time ago by Theodore Hartig. This distinguished observer found also that when in the spring a ring of cortical tissue is taken from the stem, and the whole of the ordinary conducting organs thus interrupted, the tree nevertheless puts forth shoots, and makes use of the starch deposited in the wood parenchyma beneath the annular

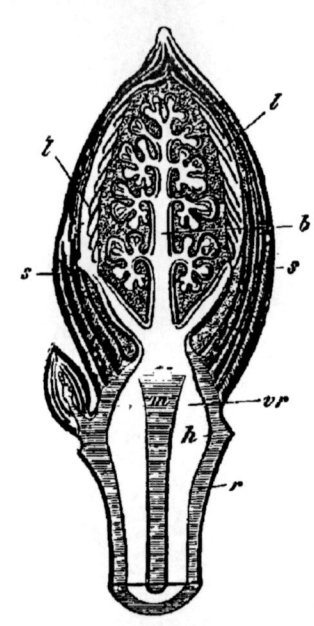

FIG 241.—Winter bud of the Horse-chestnut in longitudinal section   *r* cortex, *k* wood *m* pith of the previous year's shoot-axis *vr*   *s* scales. *l* foliage leaves of the bud which contains the inflorescence *b*

wound in the process, whence it follows that this starch can be conveyed through the wood parenchyma itself. It is easy to demonstrate by micro-chemical investigations as well as by simple experiments[1] that the buds of trees behave exactly like the germinal shoots of tubers, bulbs, and seeds, with respect to the phenomena here spoken of.

I have hitherto taken into consideration only the vegetative organs—roots and shoots. That exactly the same principles hold good for the nutrition of flowers and fruits, so far as the employment and the travelling of plastic substances in growth are concerned, is a fact of which I afforded a series of detailed proofs in my researches

---

[1] See note 2, p. 355.

cited at the beginning[1]; and the very configuration of the parts of the fruit and seed allows in many cases the relations between plastic matters and growth to be perceived particularly clearly. I must here omit the detailed enumeration of these matters, only finding space for the remark that the materials for growth conveyed to the flowers and young fruits are obviously carried, in green plants which possess foliage at the same time, from the assimilating leaves through the flower-stalks. Nevertheless, the shooting of Tulip and Hyacinth bulbs in spring shows that even in the reservoirs of reserve-materials substances serving for the formation of flowers may be stored up; and the same is true of ordinary fruit-trees, Horse-chestnuts, etc, the flowers of which unfold in the spring before or simultaneously with the appearance of the green leaves, employing for that purpose the plastic materials reserved in the wood and cortex

We now come to the further question, by means of what mechanical arrangements are the materials put in motion at the time of growth? It is simply a matter of the transport of particles the inertia of which has to be overcome, and which must be set in motion by particular forces. Here again, however, the facts are not so simple that they can be rendered clear in a few words. At any rate two essentially different mechanical processes have to be distinguished from one another, inasmuch as under certain circumstances pressure is able to effect the normal movements of material, though of course as a rule it is the forces of diffusion which are in play.

Regarding in the first place those phenomena where pressure comes into consideration as the cause of movement, the sieve-tubes and laticiferous vessels may first be mentioned

The albuminous substances contained in the sieve-tubes are but little suited for movements of diffusion, hence the transverse and longitudinal walls of the sieve-tubes are provided with fine perforations, and there is no doubt whatever that though these pores are so extremely fine, very considerable quantities of these substances can be forced through them by pressure. If a fresh stem of the Gourd plant, or other very succulent shrub, is cut across, the alkaline contents of the phloëm-bundles exude in the form of drops which slowly increase in size, it may be till they become as large as a pea, and then (at least in the Cucurbitaceae) coagulate. Now it is clear that these relatively large masses of albuminous substance could not possibly be contained in the segments of the sieve-tubes which have been incidentally cut across, but that the contents of sieve-tubes far distant from the section must here come into view. Taking into account the anatomical constitution of the sieve-tubes, this exudation of the contents is only possible by means of some relatively strong pressure, which must be exerted on their walls. Such a pressure actually exists, moreover, it is brought about by the turgescence of the succulent parenchyma, which strives to extend in all directions. In exactly the same manner as the epidermis in a living shoot is passively distended by the succulent parenchyma (as described in Lecture XII), so also must the soft-walled sieve-tubes be compressed by the parenchyma. Of course so long as they are filled with fluid, in the intact plant, this supports the pressure of the parenchyma,

---

[1] Details as to the behaviour of the matters forming the cell-wall in fruits are found in my treatise, ' *Über die Stoffe, welche das Material zur Bildung der Zellhäute liefern,*' in Jahrb für wiss Bot (1863, pp 270, &c)

since there is no passage for it to escape. In the neighbourhood of the growing buds, however, the tension of the tissue is much smaller, and the pressure of the parenchyma on the young sieve-tubes there situated feebler, whence it follows that even in the intact plant the contents of the sieve-tubes are forced towards the buds by the pressure of the parenchyma of older parts of the shoot, and this, in accordance with growth, need only take place slowly. It is not impossible that yet more special relations of organisation co-operate here ; and the emptying of the sieve-tubes, or, better, the dilution of their contents by water in older shoot-axes, and perhaps also the formation of the Callus (in trees, especially in the autumn), indicates something of the kind. Nevertheless, scarcely anything definite can at present be said in this connection.

With respect to the pressure of the surrounding parenchymatous tissues, the laticiferous vessels[1], where they exist, are in the same position as the sieve-tubes. The simple fact that every wounding of a fresh turgescent plant which contains latex causes the immediate production of a thick drop of latex, and that in old, large specimens of succulent Euphorbias even streams of latex exude, and in a few seconds yield several cubic centimetres of liquid, alone suffices to demonstrate that the latex is extruded from wounds with great force. That this is not in any way a mere outflow, follows at once from the fact that after cutting across a milky stem, not only the lower cut surface of the apical portion but the upper one of the root-stock also extrudes the latex. Besides, the laticiferous vessels are extremely narrow capillary tubes, the normal terminations of which in the buds, leaves, and root-apices are closed : how could fluid flow out at all on cutting such capillaries closed at the ends? It would scarcely have been worth while to introduce these self-evident reflections, were it not for the fact that even celebrated botanists have doubted the action of the pressure which I rendered evident so long ago as 1865 (*Experimental-physiologie*, p. 386). The laticiferous vessels as well as the sieve-tubes behave in this connection exactly like the blood-vessels in the human body : when we wound ourselves the blood does not simply flow out, it is driven out.

On now enquiring what significance this pressure, exerted from all sides on the laticiferous vessels, may possibly have in the economy of the plant, it is to be noticed that the pressure of the tissues diminishes in the neighbourhood of the growing buds and other young organs, and that therefore the stronger pressure of the parenchyma in the older succulent parts must drive the latex towards the younger growing parts ; though this, of course, cannot be regarded as exhausting the mechanics of the subject Nevertheless, we know at present no more than what has been said. However, that a continuous movement of latex from the older and especially the assimilating organs to the young growing parts also comes into consideration for the supply of plastic substances, follows from the fact, confirmed by numerous observers, that larger or smaller quantities of proteid substances, fats, and carbo-hydrates (in the

---

[1] After Schultz-Schultzenstein had previously ascribed to the latex an unduly high significance for the life of the plant, and had at the same time connected with it the most confused errors, in a prize essay rewarded by the Parisian Academy, the importance of the latex was again far under-estimated by Hugo von Mohl in a critical reply. I led the way for the correct appreciation of the significance of latex and its receptacles for the nutrition of the plant in my '*Experimental-physiologie*' (1865, p. 386)

Euphorbiaceæ particularly starch-grains) are as a rule contained in the latex
Knowing how economical the plant is with these—its constructive materials—it will
scarcely be assumed that these substances are contained in the laticiferous vessels for
any other purpose than to be conveyed to the growing organs.   Of course it is not
to be forgotten that the laticiferous vessels contain at the same time considerable
quantities of secretions—caoutchouc, resins, ethereal oils, alkaloids, etc.; that is,
substances not employed in growth but produced as bye-products.   The presence of
these substances in the laticiferous vessels by no means proves that the constructive
materials likewise present are useless, however, any more than the presence of
carbon dioxide and various products of the decomposition of the tissues in the veins
of animals warrants us in regarding the useful constituents of their blood as useless
With this view, which I put forth in 1865, a series of experimental researches by
Faivre [1] on *Ficus elastica, Morus alba,* and *Tragopogon* agree.   Nevertheless, here
again a rich field still lies open for experimental and microscopical investigation, and
its fruitfulness is perhaps enhanced by the fact that very active peptonising ferments
have already been discovered in the latex of some plants, e. g. *Carica Papaya* and
Ficus Carica.

The pressure of the tissues, as evinced by the outflow of fluids from wounds, is
observable, however, not only in the case of sieve-tubes and laticiferous vessels: even
the succulent turgid parenchyma itself exhibits an exactly similar phenomenon.   Any
transverse section made with a sharp knife through a succulent stem, or petiole, shows
that far more sap exudes from the cut surface of the parenchyma than could have
been contained in the few cells incidentally opened by the section: the greater part
of this exuding sap is evidently pressed out from parenchyma cells some distance
removed from the section.   Here, however, the fact is not so simple as in the case
of the sieve-tubes, since it depends upon the exudation of sap from closed living
parenchyma cells, where the expressed fluid must filter, not only through the cell-
walls, but, what is more, through their protoplasmic linings, the pressure evidently
being afforded by the strong turgescence of the parenchyma cells themselves.
However profitable it might be to enter more in detail into this remarkable phenomenon and its consequences, the mere mention of them must suffice here.

We have to seek the most general cause of the movements of the materials in
plants, however, in diosmotic processes.   These consist in the attraction between
water and soluble substances, which in the case before us undergo important modifications from the fact that the processes in question must take place through cellulose
walls which are clothed with living protoplasm.   The most essential facts on this
subject have already been mentioned (Lecture XII)   Since space does not allow of
our entering specially upon the mechanics of the diosmotic processes coming into
consideration here, I must content myself with a few general remarks [2].

Every process of diffusion or of diosmosis between a living cell and its environment must, sooner or later, if undisturbed, pass over into a certain condition of

---

[1] Cf Faivre on Latex, '*Ann des Sc Nat*' 1866, vol vi (p 33), and 1869, vol x (p 97),
'*Comptes rendus,*' 1879 (p 369), and Pfeffer, '*Pflanzen-physiologie*' (p 325), Hansen, *Sitzungsber.
d ph. med. Ges*, Erlangen, 8 Nov. 1880.

[2] With regard to the theory of diosmosis I refer to the detailed account in Pfeffer's '*Pflanzen-
physiologie,*' chap ii, and Sachs' '*Experimental-physiologie,*' 1865 (pp 157, &c)

equilibrium, in accordance with the diosmotic conditions just given, and then all further movements of diffusion cease. If, for example, a cell is able to take up sugar by endosmose from its environment, the absorption ceases so soon as an equal concentration occurs within and outside the cell, or even earlier. If, however, the sugar which enters into the cell is made use of, to form starch for example, then so long as the formation of starch continues more sugar will be able continually to pass into the same cell, and it is obvious that the chemical metamorphosis of the diosmotic body here prevents the establishment of an equilibrium of diffusion, and contributes to the continual transport of larger quantities into the cell, which thus behaves towards its saccharine environment as a centre of attraction. Something very similar will happen if proteid-forming substances diffuse into a cell, and are there employed in the formation of crystalloids. In like manner it is obvious that when starch-grains are transformed into sugar in a cell, and neighbouring cells take up the sugar by diosmosis, equilibrium can only be established when the formation of sugar ceases in the cell containing starch, or, in other words, a cell in which a soluble substance arises behaves in diffusion as a centre of repulsion.

This view may be also extended to whole aggregates of tissues and organs, and at the same time we obtain from it the reason why chemical metamorphoses of the plastic matters are so generally connected with their transport To give a few examples only.—Starch is assimilated in the leaves of the Beet in the petioles it is found again in the form of glucose (i. e a sugar which reduces cuprous oxide). This glucose now enters the growing and swelling root, and is transformed into cane-sugar in its parenchyma As each particle of glucose, which evidently passes from the petioles and enters the root, is transformed into cane-sugar, it acts, according to the laws of diffusion, as if it had been annihilated, and so long as the transformation of glucose into cane-sugar takes place in the root, fresh glucose can continually flow in. In this manner, in spite of the influx, the root goes on behaving like a body destitute of glucose, and acts on the product of assimilation of the leaves as a centre of attraction. The formation of starch in the growing tubers of the potato plant is another case in point, here also the product of assimilation of the leaves is carried through the stem into the tubers in the form of glucose, in these, however, it disappears as such, being employed for the formation of starch. An equilibrium of diffusion does not take place, therefore, so far as the glucose is concerned; it streams continually into the tubers, because it is there continually being converted into starch. Chemical metamorphosis acts in the same way in the using up of reserve-materials in growing seedlings. If the reservoirs of reserve-materials contain cane-sugar, inulin, or fat, glucose arises in the seedlings at the commencement of growth, at the expense of these materials, and from this starch-grains, which are then finally again dissolved and employed for the growth of cell-walls. To mention one other example only, the genetic relation between proteid substances and asparagin: in the reservoirs of reserve-materials proteid substances only are generally present; at the commencement of the growth of the seedling, however, a part at least of these is transformed into the easily soluble and diffusible asparagin, which now passes into the younger buds, and is again transformed into proteid substance.

We may thus say, to put the matter simply, every growing part of the plant acts on the existing constructive materials as a centre of attraction; every reservoir of reserve-materials, and every organ of assimilation, on the contrary, is passive towards a growing portion, or, it may be, behaves as a centre of repulsion. The stimulus to the movements of material, however, is always given by the growth of the young organs   The buds of a tree put forth shoots in the spring by no means because the nutritive sap enters into them, as people are in the habit of saying; but exactly the reverse—the nutritive matters are set in motion because the buds begin to grow.

All the considerations in this and the last lectures have chiefly had reference to the highly organised so-called vascular plants.   But in a few words I will show that the essential points are true also for the simply organised Mosses and

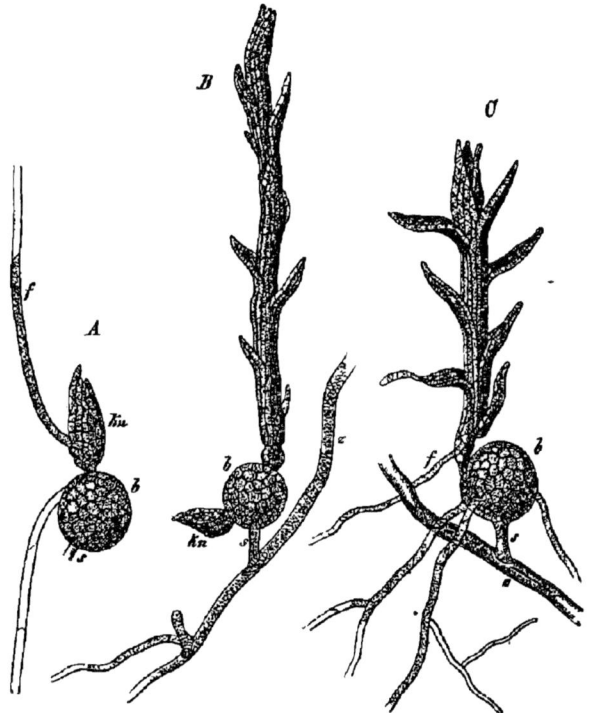

FIG. 242 —Germinating tubers of a Moss (after Muller)

Algæ, down to the most simple unicellular forms.   We meet everywhere, even in these lower regions, with the same relations between the metabolism which occurs during growth, and assimilation. the storing-up of reserve-materials in perennial parts, e.g. in the tubers so common in true Mosses, and quite generally in the spores, which, although they consist only of single cells, behave in the main like seeds   Indeed, the germinating spore of a Moss or of an Alga affords us the simplest . possible scheme for the process of germination described previously. under the eye of the observer the reserve-materials disappear in proportion as they are used up for the growth of the germinal tubes, just as the reserve-materials in the plumules of the higher plants travel towards the growing ends of the organs, etc.

In the lectures on physiological organography, I frequently mentioned the remarkable fact that non-cellular plants, such as the Siphoneæ among the Algæ, behave, so far as their external organisation and all biological matters connected therewith are concerned, like ordinary cellular plants, and that the continually progressive cell-formation of the latter implies no essential difference whatever as opposed to the processes of configuration of the non-cellular plants This is confirmed anew on seeing how, in *Caulerpa* for instance, the part of the non-cellular vesicle which corresponds to the stem produces assimilating leaves containing chlorophyll, on the one hand, and rhizoids on the under side, on the other; and, so far as we are informed concerning the assimilation and metabolism, and the movements and metamorphoses of material, and the relations between these and growth, essentially the same processes take place in this non-cellular vesicle (which is nevertheless externally and internally so sharply differentiated) as were found to occur in the most highly developed plants with their microscopic cellular structure. Everything, of course, becomes more and more simple the simpler the growth and mode of life generally assumed by the Alga.

LECTURE XXIII.

THE ABSORPTION OF ORGANIC NUTRITIVE MATERIAL. PARA-SITES. COPROPHYTES (SAPROPHYTES) INSECTIVOROUS PLANTS.

ALL that has hitherto been said on the nutrition of plants has been with reference immediately only to those which are provided with abundance of chlorophyll, and the land-plants provided with large transpiration surfaces were placed especially in the foreground as the typical chlorophyll-plants, in which all the chemical and mechanical processes of nutrition are called into play. As to the nutrition of these normal plants, two chief points were noticed · first, the formation of new organs takes place at the expense of the reserve-materials which have been produced by the mother-plant and stored up in the reservoirs of reserve-material, after these materials have been consumed, or, as we may also say, at the conclusion of germination, the second period of nutrition begins, the assimilation of organic plant-substance by the decomposition of the atmospheric carbon dioxide in the organs containing chlorophyll, under the influence of light.

There are, however, numerous plants which are entirely devoid of chlorophyll, or which possess so little of it that it is scarcely of any importance in nutrition. Since now the decomposition of carbon dioxide; and the resulting formation of organic plant-substance are effected exclusively by means of the chlorophyll, it follows at once that all the plants of this second section are incapable of exercising the nutritive activity which is characterised by assimilation. Plants devoid of chlorophyll exist during their whole life in a condition which corresponds to the germination of normal plants · like the seedlings of seeds which contain endosperm, like the germinal shoots of tubers, bulbs and root-stocks, and like the unfolding winter-buds of trees, plants devoid of chlorophyll take up the whole of their food for the purpose of growth directly, in the form of organic compounds of already-formed vegetable substance. They do not produce organic compounds containing carbon, but they absorb them, and change them in accordance with the purposes of their own growth.

On the whole, it is practically the same whether the plants devoid of chlorophyll absorb their organic nutritive matters from other living plants or living animals, or whether they make use of the dead bodies of plants and animals or their dissolved constituents for their nutrition. In the first case they are distinguished as Parasites, in

the second as Coprophytes or Saprophytes   The comparative insignificance of this
distinction, if the aim of nutrition is exclusively kept in view, is seen at once from the
fact that some Fungi which are usually parasitic can grow in artificially prepared
nutritive solutions—e. g. *Agaricus melleus*   Several species of *Mucor* again are able
to obtain nutriment for their mycelium from the tissues of fresh Apples, although they
also flourish in saccharine nutritive solutions or in gelatine.   The main fact is simply
that plants devoid of chlorophyll are necessitated and are able to absorb their carbonaceous substance from without in the form of organic compounds   This however by no means excludes the fact that in general each individual species is met
with in the natural course of things only as a parasite or only as a saprophyte, and
that very often the most capricious choice of nourishing substratum is exerted in the
matter.   Most parasites flourish only on perfectly definite species of other plants or
animals , nay, many of them, particularly parasitic Fungi, can only enter into
perfectly definite parts of their host-plant.   Even saprophytes hit upon a careful
choice of their substratum   It also happens, it is true, that certain parasites settle on
the most various host-plants and some saprophytes inhabit any substratum whatever
It is evident that biological points here come into effect which are connected not
directly and exclusively with nutrition, but with other physiological properties of the
plant in addition.

. Although plants which contain very little or no chlorophyll are necessarily parasites or saprophytes, it by no means follows that all parasites must be devoid of
chlorophyll   I have already had occasion in Lecture III to mention the Loranthaceæ,
which abound in chlorophyll and are nevertheless parasitic , particularly the Miseltoe
In such cases the parasite really needs to absorb from the host-plant only water and
mineral substances dissolved in it though it is not excluded that certain organic
compounds of the host-plant may possibly be indispensable to the parasite in very
small quantities   Plants which contain chlorophyll also occur among the saprophytes, as *Neottia Nidus-avis, Corallorrhiza*, etc in the family of Orchideæ [1], where at
least the flowering-stems which project above the surface of the soil contain chlorophyll, of course in quantities so small, and appearing so late in the life of the
plant, that it comes into consideration for the total process of nutrition just as little
as does the chlorophyll developed under the peel of a potato lying in the light for
the development of the tuber.

I have also already spoken in Lecture III of the parasitism of *Thesium* and
Rhinanthus.   These green-leafed plants develope a somewhat richly branched system
of roots in the earth, single threads of which become united by means of small
haustoria with the roots of neighbouring plants containing abundance of chlorophyll
It is not yet known, however, how far this partial parasitism is of importance for the
life of these plants.

. The most remarkable case of supplementary nutrition in plants containing
chlorophyll, by the absorption of organic substance, is offered, finally, by the
so-called insectivorous or carnivorous plants, to which I shall return in detail
further on.

. We will, first, once more regard the processes in parasites and saprophytes

---

[1] Drude, '*Die Biologie der Monotropa Hypopitys und Neottia* (Gottingen, 1873), pp 32, 33

devoid of chlorophyll, as presenting the typical case of the absorption of organic substance.   It is at once conspicuous that in the life of these plants it is by no means simply a matter of the want of chlorophyll, and the compensation of the chlorophyll-function by the absorption of organic substances : on the contrary, the internal causal interdependence of all vital phenomena involves that the whole internal and external organisation of plants devoid of chlorophyll should deviate essentially from the normal.   I have already, in Lectures III and V, referred in this sense to the organographical peculiarities of parasites and sapro-phytes, and laid special stress on the fact that with the absence of chlorophyll the presence of large transpiration surfaces would be superfluous, or even injurious, and that therefore plants devoid of chlorophyll possess no large leaves, and for the same reason they form no true wood.   Where plants devoid of chlorophyll tend to the formation of more vigorous vegetative and reproductive organs, these are never conspicuous for their superficial development, but, on the contrary, for their small superficies and relatively large mass.   Nutrition by the absorption of organic substance thus reacts on the whole organisation of the plant.   No single plant devoid of or containing but little chlorophyll possesses the ordinary habit, and least of all the large leaves and surface development and slender growth generally, of normal plants.   This is so far the case that every one, even those unfamiliar with botanical matters, recognises in the parasites and saprophytes devoid of chlorophyll organisms of peculiar structure.   No other biological condition effects a change in plants so deeply affecting the whole organisation as does the want of chlorophyll and the ab-sorption of organic substance.   This goes so far that even the reproductive organs are influenced by it and degraded to a great extent : all plants devoid of chlorophyll, even when they are descended from highly organised types of Phanerogams, are remarkable for their exceedingly small, often almost microscopic seeds, and the embryos in these seeds often consist of only a few cells, and are not segmented externally.   In the Rafflesiaceæ, Balanophoreæ, Orobanchaceæ, and *Monotropa*, the embryos have no trace of radicle and plumule, and in the Cuscuteæ there is only a feeble indication of such.

Parasitism, moreover, works not only to the degradation and alteration generally of the organisation of the parasite itself, but the living plants attacked by the parasite are altered by it.   In the first place, it is clear that the withdrawal of a certain quantity of plant-substance, which the parasite puts in requisition for itself, must enfeeble the host-plant, and in many cases this goes so far that the latter is prevented by feebleness from concluding its life in the normal manner.   This is the case, for example, when numerous specimens of *Orobanche speciosa* attach themselves to the roots of *Vicia Fabia*.   In other cases, however, the effect on the host-plant goes further.   The parasite induces phenomena of irritability on the part of the host-plant, bringing about vigorous local growth—for example, the active wood-formation and production of tuberous swellings in woody plants attacked by *Viscum* or *Loran-thus Europæus*, and many Fungi inhabiting wood, cause the formation of resin in Conifers, and injure the latter in consequence (Robert Hartig).   But even the normal processes of configuration of the host-plant may be rendered abnormal by parasites. For example, the ligneous bundles of the roots of the host on which *Balanophora* is parasitic grow into the tuberous vegetative body of the latter, and serve to a certain extent as vascular bundles for the parasite   Still more striking is the morphological change suffered by the branches of Pine-trees infested by the fungus *Æcidium Elatinum*, these are known under the name of Witches Brooms, and are distinguished by a form of branching otherwise foreign to the lateral shoots of the Pine, and their needle-like leaves fall off like those of summer plants, to be renewed annually.   Such a branch of the Pine attacked by the Fungus exists on the mother-branch in the form of a small deciduous Fir-tree, which may become ten years or more old (De Bary[1]).   *Euphorbia cyparissias*, so very common in Germany, also has its whole habit altered by a Fungus (*Æcidium*) dwelling in its tissues.

No less remarkable is the chemical influence of many Fungi on their nutritive substratum, in so far that they not only extract from it the material necessary for their nourishment, but, in addition, cause the destruction of organic substances quite unnecessarily, so to speak, and even to their own injury.   The Fungus (*Phytophthora infestans*) which causes the potato disease, for instance, vegetates in the tissues of the Potato-shoot, in the first place in order to nourish itself when its fructification protrudes through the stomata of the shoot, however, a decomposition of the organic matters in the tissues of the latter is set up, which kills the Potato-shoot itself, and makes the further nutrition of the parasite impossible. In the same way, by the mycelium of *Mucor Mucedo* developing in a fresh Apple, the tissue of the fruit is not merely extracted for the nourishment of the Fungus, but is at the same time converted into a soft smeary mass, alcohol and ethereal oils being formed.   The most striking of such cases are the decompositions of the media not directly serving for nutrition, by the ferment fungi (Yeast) and *Bacteria*; while these Fungi take up from their substratum only exceeding small quantities of sugar and proteids for their own nourishment, they destroy enormous quantities of these substances by profound decompositions.   Many fungi which kill trees by destroying the wood behave similarly.

Regarding still further the ways and means by which these plants are connected with their substratum, we find conspicuous differences even in the case of parasites   In the first place, the parasite may, on the whole, exist and grow entirely external to the host-plant, only being placed in connection with its tissues by means of peculiar, relatively small organs, the so-called haustoria, as is to be seen particularly clearly in the Cuscuteæ and in *Thesium* and *Rhinanthus* : these haustoria are, as has already been shown in the organographical introduction, metamorphosed roots which penetrate into the tissues of the host-plant.   According to circumstances, this metamorphosis is only inconsiderable, as in the Miselto, which abounds in chlorophyll, and the whole root-system of which is contained in the host-plant ; or the roots are converted into haustoria and lose their typical character entirely, as has already been described in the case of *Cuscuta*, where the tissue of the haustorium breaks up within the host-plant into single filaments of cells.   In saprophytes also, especially the Orchideæ containing little or no chlorophyll, a degradation of the root-system makes itself evident, in that the roots remain short, are very thick, branch but little, and form either no root-cap at all or but a very feeble one.

---

[1] De Bary, ' *Die Erscheinung der Symbiose*,' p 27 (Strasburg, 1879).

An unusually simple and clear example of the penetration of the haustoria of the parasite into the host-plant is found in the case of the mould fungus *Piptocephalis Freseniana* (Fig 243). Both the parasite and the *Mucor* attacked by it are non-cellular plants, consisting of simple tubular hyphæ, various ramifications of which represent the organs. The figure shows the mycelial tubes *m* of the *Piptocephalis* having become closely attached to the *Mucor*, *M*, and put forth root-like haustoria

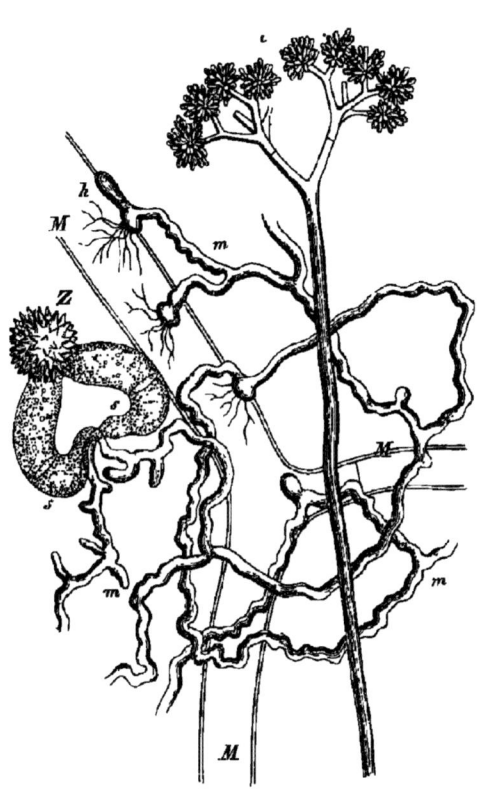

into the interior of the latter, by means of which they absorb the protoplasm of the *Mucor* and transfer it to the parasite.

In the form of haustoria the parasite only penetrates the host-plant by means of a small part of its body. In the lectures on organography, however, I have already mentioned that under certain circumstances the whole of the vegetative body of a parasite may be developed inside the host-plant In Fungi, e g the Peronosporeæ, Æcidiomycetes, etc., this is a very common occurrence : only the mature reproductive organs—and even these not always—protrude outside the tissues of the host-plant. Similar cases also occur, moreover, in Phanerogams which, as follows from the structure of their flowers, belong to highly-organised types. According to the remarkable investigations of Graf zu Solms-Laubach, this is the case especially in the Rafflesiaceæ, where the whole of the vegetative body is developed in the interior of the cortex and wood

FIG. 243 —*Piptocephalis Freseniana* (after Brefeld) *M* a portion of the mycelium of *Mucor Mucedo* from which the mycelium *m m* of the *Piptocephalis* obtains its nourishment, *h* haustoria which have penetrated the *Mucor* filaments, *c* conidiophore, *ss* the two conjugating mycelial branches which form the zygospore *Z*

of its host-plant In these plants (*Rafflesia, Brugmansia, Pilostyles* [1]) parasitism has had a degrading influence to so great an extent, that not only is the whole vegetative body of the parasite enclosed in the tissues of the host-plant, and there dispenses with any differentiation whatever into root and shoot, only consisting in fact of growths of tissue between the tissues of the host-plant, but even the flower-buds are formed in the interior of the host, only bursting through its cortex and appearing in the open at the very last. In the case of *Pilostyles*, investigated with particular care by Graf Solms-Laubach, and which dwells in the foliage shoots

---

[1] Graf zu Solms-Laubach, *Bot Zeitg.*, 1874 (Nos 4 and 5) and 1876 (p 449).

of species of *Astragalus* (Papilionaceæ of Asia Minor), the entire vegetative body consists indeed of single, jointed cell-filaments, which this investigator terms simply mycelium. He follows this up into the growing-point of the host-plant, and shows how, out of this vegetative body, in the tissue of the leaf-base of the host, cushion-like swellings arise, from which the flower-buds of the parasite develop, and which finally protrude right and left out of the base of the leaf

It has been mentioned above that many Fungi complete their vegetative development entirely in the interior of their host-plants (and animals), finally putting forth only their fructifications to the exterior. In this class of plants, so remarkable also in other respects, we meet however with exactly the opposite

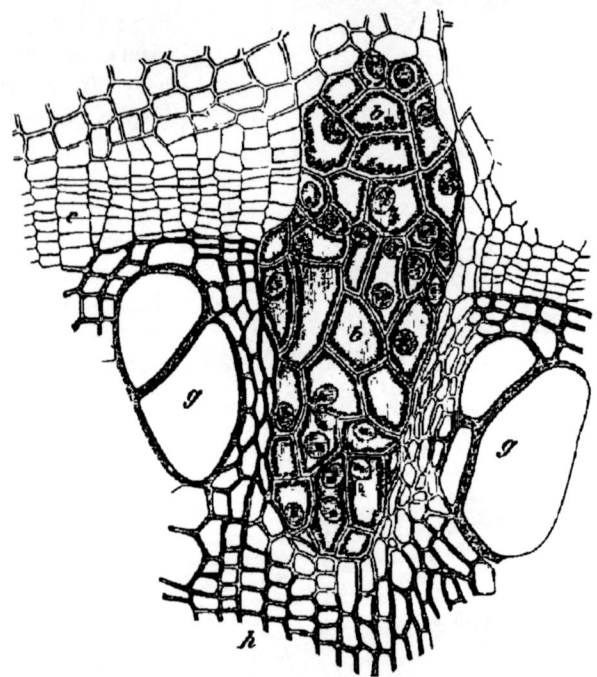

FIG. 244.—*hcg* Tissues of the root of a *Cissus* in which the vegetative body *bb* of a *Brugmansia* has penetrated. Transverse section—highly magnified (after Graf Solms-Laubach)

extreme, namely, that the host-plant is entirely enclosed within the parasite—that the parasitic Fungus grows around the Alga which nourishes it on all sides, so that Fungus and Alga together constitute in a certain sense a single mass consisting of two forms of tissue, of colourless fungal tissue and of green algal cells. This is the case in the Lichens.

If we now cast a short glance at the saprophytes, we find the ordinary case among the Phanerogamic species to be that the plant, after germination, developes within the nourishing substratum (mostly loose humus), while its vegetative body dissolves and absorbs the vegetable remains enveloping it. Only after prolonged nourishment and invigoration of the plant does the saprophyte send up flowering shoots above the surface. This is the case with *Neottia*, *Epipogon*, *Corallorrhiza*, and *Monotropa*; and it is still to be remarked that in the case of *Corallorrhiza* the vegetative body lying in the humus is a rootless, branched shoot, while in *Monotropa*, on the other hand, it is, according to Kamiensky, at first a shootless, branched root-system, out of which the flowering shoots spring later, like the fructification from a mycelium.

With respect to the nutritive processes in question here, only very little is known, however, in the case of parasitic Phanerogams In the first place, so much is at any rate established, that they are not able to produce starch by the decomposition of carbon dioxide; for this, not only is the chlorophyll wanting, but light also, during the greater part of the period of vegetative activity in the majority of parasites and humus plants, for these plants, apart from *Cuscuta*, only allow their flowering shoots to protrude free from the substratum at the very last, when the entire mass of organic substance is already wholly or for the most part collected. Where then, as usual, we find considerable quantities of starch and other carbo-hydrates in parasites and humus plants containing very little or no chlorophyll, this is owing in no case to the activity of the chlorophyll in the plants in question; on the contrary, the starch and other carbo-hydrates are here derivatives of those chemical compounds which have been dissolved and taken up from the host-plants, or, in the case of the humus plants, from the remains of dead plants. With respect to the proteid substances of these plants which contain little or no chlorophyll, these may according to circumstances likewise be derived from the host-plant, or, as may be supposed, are first formed in the tissues of the parasite. When, for example, the entire vegetative body, up to the development of the flowers, developes within the host-plant, as in the Rafflesiaceæ, it may be assumed that here not only the non-nitrogenous but also the nitrogenous vegetable substance of the parasite is absorbed from the host-plant, and the same may be the case in *Cuscuta*, since this parasite, slung around the host-plant, possesses no roots at all in the soil, and therefore extracts the whole of its food from the host It *may* at least be otherwise in the Orobancheæ. These parasites are firmly fixed by a haustorium to their host-plant, and without doubt extract the whole of the carbonaceous substance which they require from the host, but they also produce several roots besides; these roots are short, it is true, but they penetrate into the earth, and the surface of the shoot is, like that of the Balanophoreæ, for a long time in contact with the surrounding soil: they may thus take up ash constituents and probably saltpetre also from the earth, the nitrogen of which is possibly employed for the formation of proteid substances in the tissue of the parasite.

One of the most important questions is, how does the parasitic Phanerogam commence to absorb from its host-plant the substance assimilated by the latter? It is to be observed in the first place that the union of the parasite and host is usually very complete, so much so indeed that it requires the most careful examination to discover the limit between the tissues of the parasite and those of the host-plant The Rafflesiaceæ, completely enclosed in the tissues of the host-plant, behave, in fact, as if their vegetative body were simply another form of tissue in its interior: the sharp distinction between parasite and host only begins on the development of the flowers. The fact is here of the utmost interest that the nutritive substances which the parasite takes up from the tissues of the host-plant nevertheless serve for the production of an organism of an entirely different kind, whence it is perceived that, in nutrition, it depends by no means simply upon the chemical nature of the food-materials, but far more upon the inherited nature of the species of plant

The majority of phanerogamous parasites are connected with their host-plant only by means of small haustoria the rest of the body lies outside the host All the organic substance from the host-plant must now pass over to the parasite through this relatively small surface of the haustoria, as is conspicuously the case in the Orobancheæ and Cuscuteæ But it is just in this apparently most difficult point of parasitism that the plants in question agree with the seedlings of normal plants · the embryos of seeds provided with an endosperm also take up the whole of their nourishment from the endosperm by means of special haustoria, which in this case are always parts of leaves An uncommonly clear example illustrating what has been said has already been given in the case of the Date seedling (p 344) The same may be said of the Grasses, the haustorium of which is usually termed the scutellum by botanists I have referred to this on p 38 (Fig. 28, cf Fig 35) Moreover, most Monocotyledons afford similar examples of the absorption of the endosperm by a haustorium of the seedling[1] Probably the most striking case is that of the germinating Cocoa-nut, the tiny embryo of which, when it begins to grow, developes at the apex of its first leaf a haustorium resembling that of the Date seedling this subsequently attains the size and form of a turnip, in order to absorb the nutritive materials contained in the huge seed. In these cases it is peculiarly organised haustoria on the leaves of the seedling which absorb the substances of the endosperm at their surfaces, and transfer them to the seedling . in many other cases, especially in the Coniferæ and some Dicotyledons (*Ricinus* e. g), the cotyledons themselves, which developes subsequently into normal green leaves, accomplish this. In all such cases, however, the seedling acts like a parasite, which by means of peculiar organs absorbs its nourishment from a vegetable body (the endosperm) filled with reserve-materials. The most conspicuous difference, in contrast to the haustoria of parasites, consists in that the absorbing organs of seedlings are only slightly in contact with the endosperm, and by no means organically connected with it; whereas, as already stated, the haustoria of parasites become so intimately connected with their host-plants, that it is often difficult to decide where the boundary between the two lies Parasites have therefore in this respect an advantage over normal seedlings; they behave towards their host-plants rather like the buds of a germinating tuber or bulb. Just as the assimilated nutritive substances pass over from the endosperm, or from the tissue of a tuber or rhizome, into the seedling shoots, etc , the assimilated materials of the host-plant also can pass over into the haustorium of the parasite; and just as it is from the seedling of a seed, or the sprout of a tuber, that the force for transferring the reserve-materials into its tissues proceeds, so the parasite possesses the forces for extracting and storing up in itself the assimilated materials from the tissues of the host-plant If this takes place in the case of seedlings by the excretion of ferments, however, we can scarcely doubt that ferments are also formed in the haustoria of parasites, and transferred into the tissues of the host-plant. In *Cuscuta* I have had the opportunity of convincing myself that the starch stored up in the tissues

---

[1] Cf my treatise, ' *Ueber die Keimung des Samens von Allium Cepa,*' Bot Zeitg , 1863 (p. 57)

of the stem of a *Linum* attacked by it disappears when a haustorium penetrates into the cortex[1].

In the case of phanerogamic humus plants which contain little or no chlorophyll, (*Neottia, Corallorrhiza, Epipogon, Monotropa, Lathræa*, etc.), the relations referred to are not so clear as in the case of the parasites. Although there can be no doubt that these plants take up the whole of their organic substance, or at any rate the greater part of it, from the humus remains of the soil surrounding them, special haustoria are nevertheless not known at all in these plants. Even in *Neottia*, the relatively small length and number of the roots is noticeable, and in *Corallorrhiza* they are entirely wanting. In these cases the root-hairs which spring from the roots or subterranean shoot-axes appear to serve as haustoria, which are connected with the still unrotted remains of fallen leaves or other humous substances; and which excrete ferments to dissolve them and absorb the products of solution. The generally very slow increase in mass and vigour of such plants accords with this incomplete arrangement.

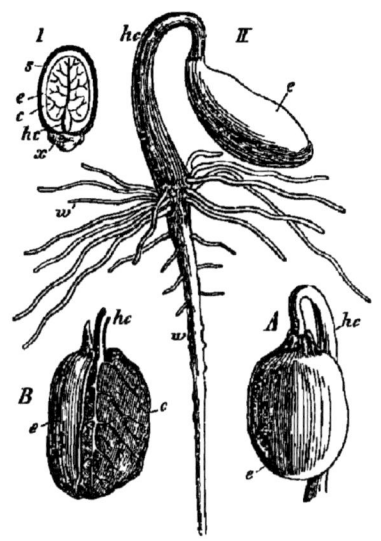

FIG 245.—*Ricinus communis* I ripe seed in longitudinal section, II seedling the cotyledons of which are still in the endosperm—compare A and B, s testa, e endosperm, c cotyledon, hc hypocotyl, w primary root, w' its lateral roots, x an appendage of the seed peculiar to Euphorbiaceæ The endosperm increases during germination in proportion as the seedling leaves which it envelopes it is at length absorbed entirely by them and the remains cast off

With respect to the absorption of organic nutritive materials, the so-called 'Insectivorous Plants' are better known than the true parasites and humus-plants. The striking adaptations which promote the absorption of organic substance in them have for many years astonished a large number of observers and led them to active investigation. It appears to me that in the case of the insectivorous plants we meet with a remarkable case where nature has contrived complicated mechanisms for the attainment of an extremely unimportant effect, for although it cannot be doubted that the small quantities of proteinaceous substance which the insectivorous plants absorb from animal bodies are useful for their welfare, the contrast between the complicated adaptations to this end and the evidently very small amount of biological work which they perform is nevertheless, on the other hand, very striking. Moreover, it is certainly not doubtful that just the most pronounced insectivorous plants, as *Nepenthes* and *Dionæa*, can also thrive continuously without this occasional supply of organic substance. With respect to the absorption of nutritive matters by true parasites

---

[1] I established exactly the same line of thought as that in the text, in my '*Handbuch der Experimental-physiologie*,' 1865 (§ 55, p 192) This statement, depending on careful investigations, appears however to have been completely overlooked by more recent writers who have been concerned with the absorption of organic substance by plants, as Pfeffer, Darwin, Drude, and others

it is a matter of life or death, and yet matters are so simple in them; in the insectivorous plants it is simply a matter of more or less vigorous flourishing, since, being possessed of chlorophyll and true roots, they are able to supply themselves with nutriment, and nevertheless expensive and remarkable mechanisms exist in order to add a small quantity of proteid substances. Only on knowing that the minute embryo of a Date-stone or of a Cocoa-nut or of a *Ricinus* seed absorbs the endosperm, a hundred or a thousand times larger than itself, is it clearly apparent how extremely insignificant is the work done by insectivorous plants when they absorb the contents of small gnats and flies. Again, there is nothing peculiar, as many observers have believed, in the fact that the insectivorous plants absorb nutritive substances through their leaves, since the seedlings of all Conifers, Monocotyledons, and those Dicotyledons which are provided with endosperm, do exactly the same. The marvel of the insectivorous plants thus lies by no means in this point, but exclusively in the fact that leaves which contain chlorophyll, and are moreover capable of assimilation, are enabled, by means of very peculiar relations of organisation and irritabilities, to seize small animals, and exhaust their proteid substance. In this again, however, the important point is the seizing arrangement, and not the fact of the absorption of organic substance; since numerous Fungi (*Saprolegniæ, Sphæriæ,* etc.) nestle on and

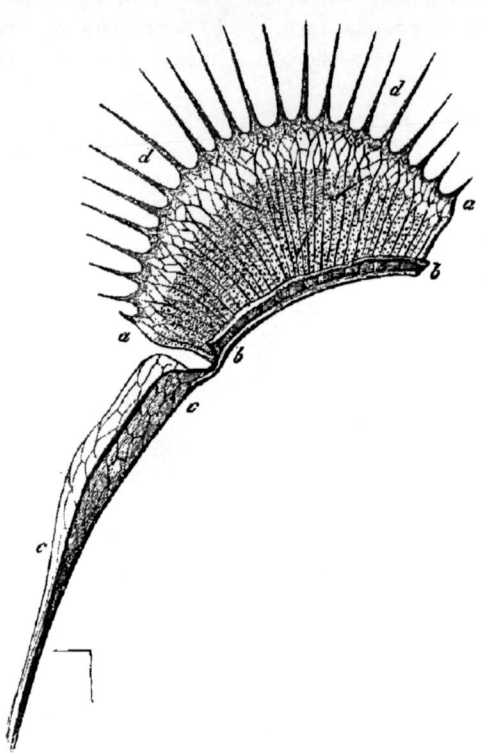

FIG. 245—Leaf of *Dionæa muscipula* after the removal of the anterior half of the lamina *bb*; the posterior half presents its internal (upper) side with the three sensitive hairs; *c* the winged petiole (slightly enlarged).

in living animals, kill them, and convert the substance of their bodies into fungus-substance.

Referring to the works mentioned in the notes [1] as regards the general biology,

---

[1] Charles Darwin, '*Insectivorous Plants*' (London, 1875). Oscar Drude, '*Die insectenfressenden Pflanzen*,' in Schenk's 'Handbuch der Bot.' 1881 (p. 113), where the further literature is introduced. The first experimental researches on the digestion of animal substance were carried out, according to Drude, by the American Kanhy (1866) on *Dionæa*, and by Mrs. Treat (1871) on *Drosera*. The first comprehensive description was given by Hooker in an address to the British Association at Belfast (1874). Darwin's very thorough work, cited above, appeared in 1875.

I will select as examples a few only of the nevertheless considerable number (fifteen genera) so far proved to be insectivorous.

The 'Venus' Fly-trap' (*Dionæa muscipula*) is a small member of the Droseraceæ, inhabiting the moors of North and South Carolina. The main shoot is a creeping rhizome, from which only a few long and thin roots arise, and at the anterior end of which five or six leaves form a rosette, from the centre of which a vertical flowering stem shoots up subsequently. The leaves may attain a length of six to eight cm. and have the form represented in Fig. 246, *c c* is the petiole, provided with two green wings, on which the lamina (*a b d*), consisting of two sharply segmented halves, is situated. In the figure, the half on the side towards the observer has been removed. In the non-irritated condition the two halves of the leaf stand so inclined to one another, that they form almost a right angle at the mid-rib (*b b*). The lamina contains chlorophyll, and its venation is visible in the figure. Three long, fine, easily overlooked bristles stand on the inner face of each half of the leaf; and any ungentle touch of one of these bristles effects an instantaneous closure of the two halves of the leaf when the plant is sufficiently irritable, which only occurs at high temperatures and during the most vigorous vegetation. The two halves then lie closed like the cover of a thin book. The movement is chiefly effected by the tissues of the mid-rib and neighbouring parts, and is rapid as lightning in the cases mentioned: in feeble plants, however, it takes place slowly. By means of this mechanism small animals in green-houses, such as wood-lice, often a centimetre long, are seized as they creep over the leaf, and the closure of the two halves of the lamina is so firm that even so strong an animal does not succeed in breaking out. Immediately after this closure a second mechanism co-operates in addition—the very stiff outgrowths (*d d*) at the margins of the leaf. At the instant of closure, these organs interlock somewhat as when the fingers of both hands are pushed between one another, and in this way form a firm closure at the upper convex border of the coincident halves of the leaf. After the closure described the sensitiveness still goes on acting, and the two halves of the leaf now adapt themselves pliantly around the form of the imprisoned animal, so that its outlines are seen from the exterior. If the bristles have been irritated with some solid body, or if a non-digestible mass has been placed between the halves of the leaf, the closure follows in this case also, but after some time the two halves of the leaves again diverge from one another. If, however, a thin lamella of hard-boiled proteid, or a small piece of muscle or similar substance is inserted, or if a suitable animal has been seized by the leaf, the closure becomes more and more complete and tight, and the third and most remarkable mechanism now comes into activity. Hundreds of glandular hairs bearing peltate capitula on very short stalks, and which in the quiescent state were quite dry like the rest of the leaf-surface, now begin to excrete a fluid in relatively very large quantities: I have occasionally seen it exude in dense drops at the anterior fissure between the closed halves of the leaf. This vigorous secretion is evidently a consequence of the stimulus which the animal substance exerts on contact with the glands. The secretion contains an acid, and, in addition, a peptonising ferment. The whole process thus reminds one most vividly of the processes in an animal stomach after a supply of nutritive substance. The ferment, like other peptonising ferments, may be dissolved out by glycerine, and then acts in a test tube in the same manner, converting bodies of the kind mentioned into peptones. This digesting secretion permeates then the body of the imprisoned animal and completely dissolves it, so that at last, since the leaf again completely absorbs the secretion together with the products of solution into itself, only the extremely fine chitinous envelope of the animal remains behind. This I found to be the case with several vigorous leaves which spontaneously opened again in from four to six days after the seizure of large wood-lice, and then continued living and healthy. The quantity of proteinaceous substance which the leaves obtain in such cases is relatively very considerable, and in my earlier researches I showed that just those plants which had occasionally digested two or three wood-lice developed very vigorously, while the majority which were prevented from seizing animals remained small and did not flower If, on the other hand, pieces of coagulated proteid scarcely as large as a wood-louse are allowed to be digested by the leaves, the latter effect the process, it is true, but they subsequently become discoloured and perish : only very small pieces of coagulated proteid are digested without injury The culture of these plants for years has convinced me that they are able to develope into quite healthy, though small specimens, without animal food, but that the digestion of animals invigorates them considerably.   Evidently it is here a matter of an addition of nitrogenous substance, since the leaves are able to produce starch independently by means of their chlorophyll contents, while the roots, few in number, evidently obtain but very little nitrogenous substance from the cushions of *Sphagnum* in which they live; and the same appears to be the case with all insectivorous plants The digestion of small animals appears to be not exactly an absolute necessity for their existence, but an aid to vigorous thriving.

Our native species of *Drosera*, especially *D. rotundifolia*, found everywhere in *Sphagnum* bogs, and occasionally in other places also, and which may be very easily cultivated in windows if placed with the substratum in a flower-pot and watered with pure water, belong to the same family as *Dionea*, but exhibit quite different adaptations for the seizure of animals.   The plant is small, and consists of a rosette of 8–10 leaves, from the midst of which a copiously flowering stem at length shoots up, while only very few roots penetrate into the moss or turf The leaves support, on a petiole 2–5 cm. long, an almost circular lamina containing chlorophyll, the whole area of which but rarely attains 1 sq cm   At the margin of the lamina, as well as on the whole of its upper surface, numerous so-called tentacles are situated ; these are stalk-like outgrowths, each of which bears at its apex a gland of complicated structure   The tentacles at the margin are the longest, those in the middle of the lamina the shortest. In the non-irritated condition the tentacles are extended straight outwards, and each glandular head is enveloped with a slimy secretion, forming a brilliant drop. If a small gnat, or fly, or other minute insect now comes in contact with the slime of the tentacles, it remains hanging to it, and finally, after ineffectual struggles to free itself, perishes.   Here again the resulting phenomena can be called forth by laying on the lamina a very small piece of hard proteid, flesh, or bread, some 1–2 mgr. in weight; and here also the stimulus produces two effects—movements and chemical action.   The movement consists in that the stalks of the tentacles in the course of a few hours so curve at their basal portions that the glandular heads come to lie exactly over the body of the insect, whether the insect lies at the margin or in the middle of the lamina of the leaf, the tentacles always curve in such a manner that they all become applied to the prey with their heads, and completely envelope it in the fluid secretion. After some time (10–20 hours) the lamina itself also becomes curved, and all the movements of the leaf called forth by the stimulus may be approximately imitated by laying a small body on the palm of the hand while the five fingers are outspread, and then curving the fingers in such a way that they all touch the body with their tips, while the palm itself becomes at the same time curved round the body The chemical action in the case of *Drosera* consists in that the secretion of the glands (which is already present and contains a peptonising ferment, but was hitherto neutral in reaction) now becomes acid in consequence of the stimulus The digestive fluid is thus rendered complete, since it, like pepsin, only acts as a peptonising agent in an acid liquid.   Rees and Will [1] were the first to extract the peptonising ferment out of the leaves of *Drosera* by means of glycerine, and to establish its digestive action on blood-fibrin—a fact which is the more deserving of mention, since this was the first demonstration of the existence of a peptonising ferment in plants.   After complete digestion and absorption of the products of solution, the tentacles of the *Drosera* leaf again return to their original position, and the lamina becomes extended and flat.   On the leaves of *Drosera* in the open the empty remains of numerous small insects are to be found at any time.   Nevertheless the plants may easily be cultivated in a room under a bell-glass until the ripening of the seeds, without their catching insects: this, however, does not prove that the latter does not act favourably for nutrition, and the researches of Francis Darwin and Rees make it at least very probable that *Drosera* plants fed artificially flourish more vigorously than those not so fed.

The course of affairs in our native species of *Pinguicula* (Utricularieæ), which inhabit moist shady spots, is unusually simple.   Here also there is a rosette formed of a few tongue-shaped leaves, from the midst of which the flowering stalk subsequently arises.   These plants also may be easily cultivated and observed in pots The surface of the leaves, which contain abundance of chlorophyll, presents a velvety appearance, owing to very numerous epidermal glands, which possess approximately the form of a mushroom, some with long and others with short stalks.   The capitula of the glands are moistened by the secretion which they exude, and hold fast any very small insect, or bread-crumb, or piece of proteid laid on.   After one or a few hours the small body is noticed to be enveloped in a drop of fluid of considerable size, and with an acid reaction, at the same time the margin of the leaf begins to curve upwards, and in the course of several hours the digestible body is completely covered by the leaf margin arched in over it After a few days, when the products of digestion have been completely absorbed, the leaf again opens out flat.

Finally, we may shortly describe another of the most complex and remarkable mechanisms for the purpose of digesting insects.   The so-called 'Pitcher-plants' of the genus *Nepenthes*, which are extended over Madagascar, Ceylon, and elsewhere in South-Eastern Asia, are thin-stemmed climbing plants, provided with large simple leaves abounding in chlorophyll.   From the apex of a leaf, a filiform tendril slowly develops, which, like other tendrils, is able to wind round the branches of neighbouring

---

[1] Rees and Will, *'Einige Bemerkungen uber fleischfressende Pflanzen'* (Bot. Zeitg 1875, p. 713).

plants, and so to serve as a climbing organ. At the end of this tendril a peculiar appendage is noticeable very early; this developes later into the pitcher, so remarkable in every respect, and the common form of which is shown in Fig. 247. In the majority of species the pitcher is only 4–10 cm. high, and 1–3 cm. broad; but there are species with pitchers 30 cm. high and of corresponding breadth. The pitcher is provided with a lid, which, however, in the developed condition never closes the opening The whole organisation of this wonderful organ is calculated to allure small animals, especially ants, &c, in such a manner that they are guided by two wings running outside the pitcher to the margin *d d*, where an exudation of honey invites them further. Immediately beneath this margin, and on the interior, the pitcher is bright and smooth, so that even the foot of an insect finds no hold the animals fall down to the bottom of the pitcher, and are there received into a copious fluid secretion This secretion, which may easily be poured out of large pitchers in quantities amounting to several or many cubic centimetres, is excreted by some thousands of small epidermal glands (at *b* in the figure) In the non-irritated condition the liquid has a neutral reaction, but even then contains a peptonising ferment, as Gorup-Besanez and Vines have demonstrated, since on adding an acid the secretion is able to digest fibrin[1]. Just as in *Drosera*, the acid necessary for digestion is only excreted after an insect has

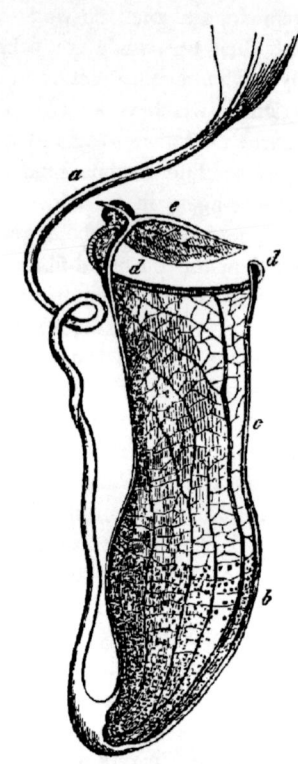

FIG 247 —Leaf-tendril *a* of *Nepenthes lævis* with the pitcher bisected longitudinally (the interior of the posterior half of the pitcher is shown), *b* basal region with digestive glands, *c* upper smooth portion, *d* margin of pitcher, *e* lid (nat size)

fallen into the abundant secretion. The great difficulties attending the culture of *Nepenthes* in our hot-houses may depend chiefly upon the fact that this addition of proteid substance in nutrition is mostly deficient

---

[1] S H Vines, '*On the Digestive Ferment of Nepenthes* (Linn. Soc. vol xv p 427). E v Gorup and H Will, '*Fortgesetzte Beobachtungen uber peptonbildende Fermente im Pflanzenreiche*' (3 Mitth) in Berichten der deutsch chem Gesellschaft (Berlin, 1876) I mixed the secretion of two pitchers of *Nepenthes Sedeni* (amounting to about 12 c c) with three drops of hydrochloric acid and, later, an equal volume of water This fluid gradually digested enormous quantities of swollen blood-fibrin, which I estimated at about 8 c cm

LECTURE XXIV.

LECTURE XXIII CONTINUED. NUTRITION OF FUNGI. LICHENS

THOSE parasites and saprophytes devoid of chlorophyll which have been considered so far, all belong to the highly organised subdivisions of the vegetable kingdom, in spite of their not inconsiderable numbers in species, they are, nevertheless, in contrast to the enormous mass of normal green plants, to be regarded as rarities, which only come before the eyes of the non-botanical observer exceptionally, and play a very subordinate part in the economy of Nature; they belong, however, to the most various families of flowering plants, and in each small group of these colourless plants we meet with peculiar biological deviations from other nearly allied but typical forms.

Matters are quite otherwise in the case of the Fungi. We here meet with a class of plants enormously rich in species, all the members of which are devoid of chlorophyll, and are thus adapted to nourish themselves by parasitism, or at least by making use of organic remains. The Fungi[1], in their sharply-expressed individuality, so to speak, form an organic kingdom by themselves, to such an extent indeed that up to the time of Linnæus, and indeed even in the present century, doubts have been entertained as to their vegetable nature.

The variety of the forms of Fungi is simply enormous. From the simplest Bacteria and their allies, distinctly visible only with the strongest powers of the microscope, finely graduated transitions occur to the highly organised forms with massive bodies, often more than a kilogram in weight and with well-marked differentiation of tissues, the latter being offered us particularly by the Gasteromyces in extremely remarkable forms Nevertheless, apart from a few of the very simplest genera, the body of the Fungus is always constituted of the hyphæ already described —thin colourless threads, usually segmented by transverse septa, these either live singly for themselves, as in the Mould-fungi, or are united in large numbers and

---

[1] Since I have been compelled several times in the text to refer to mycological facts which may not be known to the reader, I here cite the most important works for consultation. 1. De Bary, '*Morphologie und Physiologie der Pilze, Flechten und Myxomyceten*' (Leipzig, 1864). 2 De Bary and Woronin, '*Beitrage zur Morphologie und Physiologie der Pilze*,' R I–IV. 3 Luerssen, '*Medicinisch-pharmaceutische Botanik oder Handbuch der system. Bot.*' B I (Leipzig, 1874). 4. Goebel's new edition of the systematic portion of my '*Lehrb der Bot.*' (Leipzig, 1882). 5 Frank, '*Die Krankheiten der Pflanzen*' (Breslau, 1880).

form a massive body, as every one has seen in the case of the well-known Mushroom But even in these large Fungi the mycelium, the root-like vegetative and feeding organ, consists very commonly of single branched hyphæ creeping in the substratum The non-botanical observer usually sees only the massive fructification of the fungus, which protrudes above the substratum, because the mycelium remains hidden in the substratum, or at any rate only grows out from this into the moist air under certain circumstances, and is moreover only clearly visible with the microscope. So far as the question of nutrition is concerned, however, it is just the knowledge of the mycelium and its mode of life which is of special importance ; and what is to be said here with respect to the Fungi, refers essentially only to the mycelium.

Many Fungi are satisfied with dissolving and absorbing from their substratum only so much substance as is necessary for their nutrition, either as parasites or saprophytes. Hence they usually act destructively on their substratum only to a slight extent ; and even when they inhabit living plants or animals, the injury caused by them is insignificant—e. g. the majority of Rust-fungi (Æcidiomycetes). Others grow and nourish themselves harmlessly in the tissues of higher plants, finally, how-ever, when themselves producing fructification, to effect malignant destruction, as *Phytophthora infestans*, which causes the Potato disease, and the Smut of Wheat, which at last completely fills up the interior of the grains with its masses of black spores. To the worst enemies of the higher plants, however, belong the tree-killing Fungi, the mycelia of which nestle in the wood even of older huge trees, and not only take from it the nourishment necessary for their nutrition, but decompose the masses of wood until they are converted into soft spongy or powdery humous substances. Even wood which has already been employed for various kinds of building, &c, is destroyed by Fungi. *Merulius lachrymans* destroys the timber-work of houses, converting it into a mass of dirt, &c. Even living animals are attacked and killed by Fungi. Our house-flies are destroyed annually in autumn, with the exception of a few specimens which live through the winter, by a fungus (*Empusa Muscæ*) which infests them, and innumerable caterpillars are killed by *Sphæriæ*. In these cases the whole living substance of the body of the animal is finally con-verted into a mass of Fungus; the aquatic *Saprolegniæ* in this way consume dead insects which have fallen into the water, until only the hard chitinous covering is left.

Nevertheless, these are all only individual phenomena, in contrast to the universal distribution of other Fungi wherever organic life in general is possible. One may well say that if there were no Fungi, the entire surface of the earth would be covered with dense layers of the bodies of plants and animals which had accumulated for thousands of years , since it is essentially the Fungi, and particularly the minute forms of very simple structure, which have year by year in the course of geological time decomposed the dead plants and animals and again resolved them into carbon dioxide, water, and ammonia. Only where perished organisms have been protected from the access of the air, which Fungi require, by being enveloped on all sides by mud, or sunk in turf, etc , have their remains been preserved, or at least a great part of their carbon, which could not be oxidised during intramolecular spontaneous de-composition by the small quantity of oxygen contained in the organic compounds themselves. This has happened in the formation of coal, and is still taking place in the formation of lignite and turf This enormous labour, however, is chiefly performed by universally distributed Fungi, which not only absorb the materials necessary for their nutrition, which would result in effects only extremely insignificant, but destroy in addition the substances which they do not take up. We find this peculiar destructive action taking place to the greatest extent by means of the Fungi of fermentation and putrefaction in the narrower sense. That others also effect similar work has already been mentioned above, in connection with the Fungi which destroy wood, and the mouldering and final disappearance of the masses of fallen autumn leaves in woods must be ascribed to similar destructive actions of Fungi, the quantity of Fungus produced itself remaining extremely insignificant.

So far as the Fungi simply derive nutriment from their substratum, their nutrition resembles in the main that of phanerogamic parasites and saprophytes; what particularly distinguishes very numerous Fungi, however, is the decomposition of the organic substratum as already mentioned, the products of the decomposition not being taken up by the Fungus Only in this way is it possible for Fungi to prevent the continual accumulation of organic substances on the surface of the earth, since if they were to make use of their organic substratum only for the purposes of their own nutrition, there would simply result an enormous accumulation of these plants

If we now attempt to obtain a more exact insight on the one hand into the nutrition of the Fungi, and, on the other, into the destruction of their substratum effected in addition by many of them—and thus into the nature of fermentation and putrefaction—we shall find that the shortest way here, as in the case of the nutrition of normal plants, is at once to make clear the results derived from the artificial nutrition of Fungi, and the experimental study of the phenomena of fermentation.

The first experimental investigations into the nutrition of Fungi were undertaken by Pasteur about thirty years ago I here pass over the methods of cultivating Fungi, especially the highly organised forms, in decoctions of fruit and dung, and in various mixtures of gelatine and sugar, etc, which have meanwhile been much further developed, because in these methods of culture, highly important as they are for the biology of the Fungi, it has only been sought to bring various kinds of Fungi to normal development, in order to make clear their growth and reproduction and the configuration of their relations of organisation, the proper—i.e the chemical—questions of nutrition not coming further into consideration. Naegeli[1] (with the co-operation of Dr. Loew) has, however, recently made some very detailed investigations and theoretical considerations on the matter. Hence we shall obtain the desired glimpse into the processes of nutrition and ferment action of the Fungi most quickly, if I shortly present the most important results of Naegeli's work in this province

The Fungi, like other plants, require in addition to those compounds which afford them the elements of the proteid substances, fats and carbo-hydrates—viz, Carbon, Hydrogen, Oxygen, Nitrogen and Sulphur—also certain mineral matters, the presence of which is necessary in the chemistry of nutrition and for the mole-

---

[1] The works of Naegeli (and Loew) referred to are to be found in the Sitzungsber der kgl. bayr. Akad under the title '*Ernahrung der niederen Pilze*' (1879), and '*Über die Fettbildung der niederen Pilze*' (1878)

cular structure of their organised parts. But the Fungi, according to Naegeli, make smaller demands than plants containing chlorophyll with respect to their choice of mineral matters They can exist provided three elements—viz, phosphorus, one element of the series potassium, rubidium, and cæsium, and, finally, one of the series calcium, magnesium, barium or strontium—are supplied to them. Since, now, the other elements here mentioned—viz., rubidium, cæsium, barium and strontium—certainly do not occur at all places where Fungi grow, we may say they require phosphorus, potassium, and, in addition, calcium or magnesium The difference between them and normal plants lies in the latter needing calcium and magnesium at the same time. Iron appears to be necessary only for the formation of the chlorophyll of normal green plants, and is thus wanting in the Fungi; and with respect to chlorine and silica, which Naegeli reckons among the requirements for the nutrition of the higher plants, the necessary facts have been already stated in Lecture XIV. The essential difference between Fungi and the normal green plants, so far as the mineral matters are concerned, would thus lie, according to Naegeli's researches, only in that the Fungi do not need to take up magnesium and calcium at the same time, but only require one of the two ; and that instead of this they can also make use of barium and strontium, and, instead of potassium, of rubidium and cæsium These are Naegeli's results concerning the elements necessary for the nutrition of Fungi.

Since the Fungi are not able to decompose carbon dioxide and thus to produce carbonaceous organic substance, because they lack chlorophyll, a carbonaceous organic compound must be presented in the artificial nutrition of Fungi, in addition to the compounds of the elements named above According to all experience hitherto, it appears that organic carbon compounds of the most various kinds can be taken up by the Fungi, and then be employed for the formation of cellulose and protoplasm by means of internal metabolism. Of special interest, however, for scientific insight into the matter is the knowledge of those nutritive substances which are distinguished by their peculiarly simple composition, and the other chemical properties of which are so exactly known that definite conclusions may be drawn from them respecting the chemical processes probably occurring in the nutrition of the Fungus. In this sense Pasteur employed, so long ago as 1858, ammonium tartrate for the artificial nourishment of the Mould-fungi, Yeast and *Bacteria.* For the nourishment of Yeast-fungi, Naegeli distinguishes as well chosen a nutritive solution employed by Adolf Mayer in 1869 I here subjoin the composition of this, in order to give the reader a clear idea, but it is not therefore to be supposed that every nutritive solution in which Yeast is to grow must have exactly this composition—it is simply an example for illustration. The solution in question was as follows :—

Water . .	100	Cu cm
Sugar	15	grams.
Ammonium Nitrate	1	,,
Acid Potassium Phosphate	0·5	,
Tribasic Calcium Phosphate	0·05	,,
Magnesium Sulphate	0 25	,,

If then this nutritive mixture is a suitable one, a considerable multiplication of Yeast-cells must be obtained in a short time, if a few of them have previously been placed in the fluid by means of a needle point, etc., exactly in the same way as we expect, in the artificial nourishment of a plant containing chlorophyll, that a plant of normal size with numerous ripe seeds will develope from a seed. This the solution mentioned accomplishes; though there still remain several things to be considered Naegeli says, that, theoretically considered, from a quantity of Yeast which cannot be weighed 3–4 grams of new Yeast should be produced in the fluid described, whereas in reality only 1 gram is produced. Nevertheless the result must not be underestimated, since a single Yeast-cell weighs only about $\frac{1}{2000000}$th of a milligram, and thus in our solution there would arise from one or a few such cells some 2000 millions of new cells, and a corresponding increment of protoplasm and cellulose also takes place. However, as already explained, I only introduce these numbers in order to give a general idea of the matter to those unacquainted with such things. As a matter of fact, Yeast-fungi, *Bacteria* and various Mould-fungi can flourish in very different nutritive mixtures, if only a suitable carbon compound is present in addition to the mineral matters mentioned

The most suitable carbonaceous food is always found by these Fungi in sugar (glucose), and the best nitrogenous food in proteids and peptones. According to Naegeli the nitrogen may be taken up simultaneously with the carbon also from Acetamide, Methylamine, Æthylamine, Prophylamine, Asparagin and Leucin; whereas Oxamide and Urea can supply merely the nitrogen, but not the carbon. As sources of nitrogen the Fungi can also make use of all ammonia-salts, and the Mould-fungi and *Bacteria* even of nitrates. Free nitrogen, on the contrary, cannot be used for the formation of protoplasm by the Fungi exactly as is the case with the green plants. In the same way Cyanogen compounds are unfitted for this purpose. According to Naegeli, almost all carbon compounds are suitable for nutrition as carbonaceous material, if they are soluble in water and not too poisonous; but Cyanogen, Urea, Formic and Oxalic acids, and Oxamide are unsuitable for this purpose. The best nutritive material in all cases is afforded by a mixture of peptone and sugar.

With regard to the production of plastic matters from the nutritive materials taken up in the interior of the Fungus-cells, Naegeli has studied chiefly the formation of fat (starch is as a rule not produced in the Fungi). There is not the slightest doubt, after what I have stated previously, that fat is formed in ripening seeds from carbo-hydrates, particularly starch, since this transformation takes place in the nearly ripe seed even when taken out of the fruit, where no other material is available under the circumstances for the formation of fat. It results now, from Naegeli's investigation, that in the lower Fungi also fat is formed from carbo-hydrates, but also from albuminates and other nitrogenous carbon compounds. If Fungus-cells are placed in pure water, fat is formed in them at the expense of their proteid substance, since the protoplasm diminishes in quantity. This is very easily demonstrated in the case of the Mould-fungi and Yeast. That albuminates and other nitrogenous carbon compounds can yield material for the formation of fat may be proved, according to Naegeli, when these substances (with the addition of the necessary mineral matters) are exclusively employed for the nutrition. The *Bacteria* (Schizomycetes) flourish in a solution of proteids, or still better of peptones formed from proteids; and the Mould-fungi grow in it when the solution contains a little phosphoric acid. Now if merely a trace of spores or of Fungus is sown in the solution, an increase of the Fungus, and thus of fat, to the extent of more than a millionfold is obtained. The proteid may be replaced by Asparagin or Leucin with a like result. Moreover, sugar and ammonia or ammonic tartrate, with the addition of ash-constituents, suffice for nutrition Instead of sugar, mannite or glycerine, and instead of tartaric acid, acetic or salicylic acid or some other organic acid may be used. In most cases, again, ammonia may be replaced by nitric acid as the source of nitrogen. 'If, instead of ammonia or nitric acid, albumin or peptones are employed as nutriment, the production of fats and cellulose from sugar or tartaric acid etc is demonstrated, when only a little of the former, but a large quantity of the non-nitrogenous compound is present in the solution. The analysis of the crop in this case shows that only the albuminate can be derived from the proteid of the nutritive solution, and that the whole, or at least a great part of the fat and cellulose must be derived from the constituents of the sugar or tartaric acid The facts alleged undoubtedly prove that the Fungus cells can take the material for the formation of fats from the most various nitrogenous and non-nitrogenous compounds' Moreover, the theoretical chemical explanation of these processes is rendered more difficult by the fact that the chemical constitution of the nutritive solution appears to be, as Naegeli says, almost without significance for the formation of fat in the Fungi.

Concerning the relation of the formation of fat to respiration, Naegeli remarks · 'The Mould-fungi only grow when they have access of free oxygen, and abound in fat : Beer-yeast requires very little oxygen for its development and is deficient in fat, and the same is true of the Schizomycetes (*Bacteria*). The Mould-fungi living on the surface of the nutritive fluid contain more fat than their own submerged budding forms. Free access of air is necessary for the formation of spores which contain much fat. The Saccharomycetes (Yeast-fungi), as is well known, only develope spores when they are spread out on a substratum and lie in a half dry condition : the Schizomycetes likewise, as it seems, never produce their spores in the liquid, but only in the covering at the surface. Mould-fungi living in liquids only form resting spores abounding in fat on the hyphæ which rise up into the air Why the Fungi thus require oxygen for the production of fat, however, remains in the meantime an open question.'

These details as to the formation of fat in the Fungi, which may probably be extended in essential points to more highly developed forms also, are the more interesting since the Fungi collectively and individually produce no starch, and even form true sugars only in small quantity or not at all, though mannite, on the other hand, often occurs in them. Even the cellulose of the Fungi is in some respects different from that of other plants, not giving the usual blue coloration with iodine and sulphuric acid.

It has already been remarked that Yeast and the *Bacteria*, besides many other Fungi, not only use up the surrounding substratum to extract from it the constituents of their own nourishment, but that they cause fermentation and putrefaction at the same time, i.e. decompose the complex molecules of the carbo-hydrates and proteid substances, and this in far greater quantity than is in any way necessary for the purposes of their own nourishment. This ferment-action is peculiarly energetic in

[3]

the case of Yeast, which decomposes sugar into alcohol and carbonic acid, glycerine, and succinic acid. Naegeli found[1] that 1 gram of bottom-Yeast (dry weight) in a 10 per cent. solution of cane-sugar containing tartrate of ammonia, as food material, and through which air was continuously passed, fermented about 70 gr. of sugar in twenty-four hours at 30° C., the weight of the Yeast itself increasing to more than 2·5 gr. during the twenty-four hours. On the average, therefore, 1·7 gr. of Yeast were effective during twenty-four hours, and decomposed forty times that weight of cane-sugar. For further criticism of this process, into which however we cannot here enter in detail, the additional remark may be made that the volume of a cell of Beer-yeast amounts to something like $\frac{5}{10,000,000}$ths of a cubic millimetre, which corresponds to a weight of about $\frac{5}{10,000,000}$ths of a milligram. Naegeli calculates further that in the fermentation of 1 kilogr. of cane-sugar (or, after its inversion, of 1·0526 kilogr. of grape-sugar), whereby 0·51 kilogr. of alcohol are produced, 146·6 thermal units of heat appear. The temperature of a fermenting sugar solution may, if no loss of heat occurs, be raised more than 14° C.

The greater part of the sugar is broken up in fermentation into alcohol and carbon dioxide. Pasteur showed, however, that about 5 per cent. of the sugar breaks up into succinic acid, glycerine, and carbon dioxide. Although, according to Naegeli, the ferment-action of Yeast is more energetic on the access of oxygen, it nevertheless takes place when oxygen is completely excluded from the fermenting liquid. In the arts this is in fact the common experience: the vats containing the wine-must are provided with special valves at the bung-hole, which allow of the exit of the enormous quantities of carbon dioxide, but of no entrance of oxygen, and in experiments on a small scale it is also easy to convince ourselves that fermentation proceeds energetically in a sugar solution utterly deprived of oxygen.

Of the species of *Mucor*, the mycelium of *M. racemosus* especially breaks up in a saccharine liquid into spheroidal cells, which multiply by budding like Yeast, and which, though to a much smaller extent, effect alcoholic fermentation. If a few spores of *Mucor* are placed on a perfectly sound apple from a small part of which the skin has been removed, the mycelium of this Fungus grows through the whole of the parenchyma of the apple in a few days; the latter is thereby converted into a soft and subsequently deliquescent mass, the odour and taste of which demonstrate the formation of alcohol and ethereal oils.

A peculiar form of fermentation is produced by the putrefactive Fungi (Schizomycetes—*Bacteria*). These are much smaller than the cells of Yeast, and are spheroidal or rod-shaped, and remarkable chiefly in that they also decompose saccharine solutions, in the presence of proteid matters, in a manner which differs according to the species of Fungus. They convert grape-sugar into lactic acid, and the lactic acid into butyric acid, with the formation of carbon dioxide and hydrogen; and if some grape-sugar still remains over in this fermentation, it is converted into mannite. These decompositions also may run their course without direct co-operation of the oxygen of the atmosphere. In the formation of acetic acid from dilute alcohol, by means of

---

[1] Naegeli's comprehensive treatise ('*Theorie der Gährung*') appeared in Abhandl. der kgl bayr. Akad d Wiss, B XII Abth. 2 (München, 1879), and is indispensable to any one interested in Fermentation

another *Bacterium* ('mother of vinegar'), the access of oxygen in abundance is necessary.

Putrefaction in the narrower sense properly affects only the proteid substances which are decomposed by colourless, yellow, red and blue Bacteria. Moist bread, meal, boiled white of egg, etc. exposed to the air for some time show in the first place colonies of Bacteria at certain spots, which become extended more and more, and which, in the case of the pigment Bacteria especially, are very conspicuous. It is only necessary to touch these spots with a needle point, and then to touch with the needle an egg boiled hard and deprived of its shell, and lying in damp air, to observe at the infected spot within a few days a colony of Bacteria extending itself with all the effects of putrefaction. The profound decomposition which the proteid substances undergo under the influence of the Bacteria is most easily recognised by the escape of evil-smelling gases—ammonia, sulphuretted hydrogen, and ammonium sulphide. Finally, the proteid substances are completely destroyed.

It is now scarcely doubtful that common Yeast, as well as Bacteria, are only special vegetative forms of Fungi which consist of hyphæ, just as the Mucor-yeast is only a peculiar vegetative form of *Mucor racemosus.* Zopf has lately shown, especially with respect to Bacteria, that they arise by segmentation from exceeding fine filamentous Fungi (*Beggiatoa, Cladothrix*), and that these forms of Fungi again proceed from them. The bacteria-form of these Fungi reproduces itself, under conditions favourable to nutrition, by continually repeated transverse divisions. Similar vegetative forms also occur indeed in many Algæ, and even in the protonema of Mosses The remarkable and conspicuous facts in the

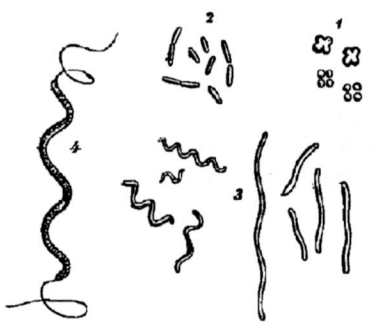

FIG 248.—Schizomycetes. 1 *Sarcina,* 2. *Bacterium* 3. *Vibrio* 4. *Spirillum* (after Cohn)

Yeast-fungi and Bacteria, however, lie chiefly in their power of decomposing such exceedingly large masses of carbo-hydrates and proteid substances by means of fermentation, while they themselves make use of only small quantities for their growth.

In the Yeast-fungi and Bacteria we have thus found the ferment-action accompanying nutrition proper, increased to a maximum. That a similar thing takes place in other Fungi also, however, though to a smaller extent, is shown by the behaviour of the common forms of *Mucor,* the mycelium of which, penetrating into sound apples and completely permeating their parenchyma, is by no means satisfied with extracting the material necessary for its nutrition: on the contrary, the substance of the apple is decomposed into a soft mass smelling of alcohol and ethereal oils. Apart however from what has been stated with respect to the ferment-fungi, a closer insight into the chemical changes effected by Fungi on their substrata is so far wanting. The best we possess in this connection are Robert Hartig's statements as to the destruction of wood by tree-killing Fungi. Before I quote his statements on this subject, however, it will be well to make a few preliminary remarks with regard to these Fungi.

It has been established by the memorable labours of Robert Hartig[1] that the stalked Fungi growing out from diseased tree-trunks, such as *Agaricus melleus* and very many species the fructification of which tends to grow out from tree-trunks in the form of a sessile fan-shaped structure, such as *Trametes pini, Polyporus fulvus, P. vaporarius, P. mollis,* and *P. borealis,* all of which occur on Conifers, as well as *Hydnum diversidens, Telephora perdrix, Polyporus sulphureus, P. ignarius, P. dryadeus,* and *Stereum hirsutum,* all of which infest Oaks, and others, are by no means the harmless parasites they were formerly considered to be, he shows, on the contrary, that the delicate filamentous mycelium of these Fungi penetrates into the roots (*Trametes radiciperda* and *Agaricus melleus*—the latter creeps in the soil and constitutes the subterranean '*Rhizomorpha*), or often directly into the stems and branches, usually through wounds previously produced, and vegetates for years in the wood and destroys it. In consequence of this, even large trees may be killed by the mycelium dwelling in them, or at least their wood be made useless From the mycelium vegetating in the interior of the wood, in all the species named, the fructifications already referred to at length appear: these are often very large, and in many cases themselves go on growing further for years (e. g *Polyporus ignarius*).

Referring to Hartig's works[1] for the mode of life of these plants, I will here, where we are concerned with questions of nutrition, subjoin only some of his results with respect to the changes which the wood of Conifers undergoes by the action of the mycelium. The changes of the cell-walls of the wood, says Hartig, which are produced by the Fungus, are of great interest. In the first place, it is an important fact that the hyphæ of the Fungus always vegetate in the interior of the wood-cells, and only bore through the septa, whereby however it is not precluded that they occasionally grow forward also laterally or upwards or downwards in the walls, and become branched in them. The mycelium of *Agaricus melleus* lives in fact in the latter form, chiefly in the hard substance of the cell-walls of the wood. The holes bored in the walls (which either have from the first the same diameter as the fungus-filament or are often distinctly smaller, because the hyphæ inside the wall penetrated by them thin off) eventually become widened, as a rule considerably, since the solution of the substance of the cell-wall appears to take place more rapidly outwards, starting from the perforation. The activity of the fungus-hyphæ in the interior of the woody tissue varies. Sometimes they absorb directly and unaltered the organic substances met with on the way, and produce fungus-protoplasm and cellulose from them, with the separation of carbon dioxide on the other hand, they extract from the organic compounds at a greater distance certain substances which they require for their nourishment, and thereby, according to Hartig, cause a chemical alteration of the cell-contents or cell-walls. The fungus-hyphæ penetrating into the sound wood of the Oak absorb the tannin unaltered, and it can be detected in them by means of salts of iron. The numerous lateral hyphæ, which bore through the walls like haustoria, entirely absorb the dissolved substance of the cell-walls of the wood, through their apices; they exert in addition a very profound decomposing influence on the contents and walls of the

---

[1] Robert Hartig, ' *Wichtige Krankheiten der Waldbaume*' (Berlin, 1874), and ' *Die Zersetzungserscheinungen des Holzes der Nadelbaume und der Eiche*' (Berlin, 1878).

cells far beyond their immediate neighbourhood, extracting from them certain matters which serve for the nourishment of the fungus-hyphæ, whereby the most extraordinary differences, characteristic for each species of plant, appear. In many cases the wall of the wood-cells again assumes completely the character of cellulose: it becomes colourless, flexible, capable of swelling, and is coloured a beautiful violet by chlor-zinc iodine. In other cases, on the other hand, the wood cell-wall becomes brown and very brittle, its substance largely soluble in ammonia, and yielding a brown fluid with solution of potash. This, in other words, evidently means that some of these Fungi take up chiefly wood-substance (xylogen) from the cell-wall and leave their cellulose behind, while others take up the cellulose itself, and leave behind the wood-substance impregnating it. The former is the case for example with *Trametes pini*, and the latter with *Polyporus mollis*. Hartig is of opinion that the greater part of the organic substance of the wood finally breaks up into carbon dioxide and water, without being previously taken up into the hyphæ. In very much decomposed wood of Conifers the turpentine appears no longer fluid but hardened, filling the cavities of the wood-cells in amorphous pieces. In the wood of Pines much decomposed by *Trametes radiciperda*, the tracheides, previously permeated with turpentine, become filled with crystals, the solubility of which in turpentine admits of the conclusion that they are hydrate of terpin. Obviously the mycelia of the tree-killing Fungi take up their ash-constituents also from the wood, and these pass into the fruit bodies situated on the exterior. As in the case of most other Fungi, crystals of calcium oxalate are here also excreted during nutrition, both in the nourishing wood and in the organs which bear fructification.

If we now cast another glance backwards on what has been said concerning the nutrition of Fungi, we find forms which are satisfied with taking up from their living or dead substrata simply and only so much of what is needed for the construction of their bodies as is necessary; as well as those which, in addition to absorbing their nourishment, produce copious decompositions in the substratum and destroy it. This latter effect, which, as it seems, occurs in the most various degrees down to those which are scarcely noticeable, we may comprehend in general—even in cases where the decomposition of wood is concerned—under the extended idea of fermentation. With respect to the true nature of fermentation, and especially with respect to its essential difference from ferment-actions, I have already said what is necessary (Lecture XXI) Here it may be still further insisted upon that neither action need exclude the other. In the first place, we must assume that every Fungus exerts a ferment-action on its substratum, simply in order to obtain its nutritive material from it. When a fungus-filament grows through a hard cell-wall, we must assume that a ferment exists at its surface, by means of which not only is cellulose dissolved, but also lignine, and, under certain circumstances, cuticular substance also. In the same way the germinal hyphæ of various parasitic Fungi bore through the coverings of the bodies of insects, for which purpose (in the same way, and probably necessarily) a ferment must exist at the surface of the germinal hypha, which in this case, where the solution of proteid substances and perhaps even of chitin is concerned, may be regarded as a peptonising ferment In general it will suffice that the fungus-filament which penetrates into a substratum contains an exceedingly small quantity of ferment, since even in the seedlings and buds of Phanerogams only extremely small

quantities are produced.   Moreover, the action of this ferment at any time need only
be exercised close to the surface of the growing end of the fungus-filament, so that
at distances measurably removed no further decomposition of the substratum follows.
This at least explains how it is possible for the fungus-filaments to bore smooth
holes (which they completely fill up) through the cuticularised epidermis of living
plants, and through lignified cell-walls, and even through starch-grains.   Evidently
this fermenting action of a fungus-filament is to be compared with those which I
have already described (p. 344, Fig. 236) in the germinating Date.   As the delicate
soft haustorium of the first leaf of the seedling there grows into the hard mass of
endosperm, because it dissolves and absorbs the hard cellulose as well as the proteïd
substances and fat of the endosperm close to its surface, by means of its ferment action,
so, too, we may suppose the fungus-filaments penetrate into their solid substratum,
which is insoluble in mere water.

      That the ferment-fungi also exert ferment-actions on their substratum is shown
in the first place by the invertive action of Yeast, since it converts cane-sugar into
glucose, and we may certainly assume that in the nutrition proper of all Fungi which
have a destructive action on their substratum, ferment-actions first take place by
means of which a portion of the substratum is brought into a form capable of
nourishing the Fungus, besides this ferment action, fermentation proper then comes
into play, by means of which the substratum (occasionally to the injury of the Fungus
itself) is destroyed.   The peculiar behaviour of *Peronospora* (*Phytophthora*) *infestans*,
which nourishes itself for months in the tubers and green shoots of the Potato without
causing injury, and finally, as the fruit-bearing organs develope, rapidly extends and
kills and destroys the nourishing tissue, demonstrates that in this case the same
Fungus in different periods of life sometimes exerts ferment-actions and sometimes
promotes fermentation on its substratum.   In contrast to the destructive action which
the Fungi of fermentation and putrefaction in the widest sense exert on their substratum, we find, however, a large group of Fungi abounding in species, which, on the
contrary, influence their living substratum favourably, even promoting their activity
in order the better to make use of them.   This is the case with the Lichens[1].   It

---

      [1] With respect to the history of the discovery of the true nature of Lichens, De Bary expresses
himself as follows in his lecture, ' *Über die Erscheinung der Symbiose* ' (Strasburg, 1879), p 17:—
' From their (the gonidia) constant occurrence in every Lichen there has long been not the slightest
doubt that they are organs of these otherwise Fungus-like plants. their resemblance to Algæ was
also obvious, and the Lichens were therefore regarded as a group standing between Algæ and Fungi.
These views obtained a particularly firm basis by Schwendener's thorough studies into the structure of
the Lichen-thallus, from which it seemed to result that the gonidia arise as small branches or as the ends
of branches of the filaments devoid of chlorophyll   However, several matters still remained obscure.
In particular, the first origin of the gonidia-bearing thallus from the typical reproductive organs, the
spores ; since when these were sown, and the sowing kept under rigorous control, there always arose on
germination only those temporary Fungus plantlets referred to in the text, and no gonidia-bearing
Lichen-thallus, and in rare cases where such were obtained on sowing it was not clear whence the
gonidia had come   On the ground of these and similar considerations I first expressed in 1866 for
certain Lichens the hypothesis (based on extensive unpublished investigations) that they might
possibly result from the union of a certain definite Fungus with an Alga.   The extension of this
hypothesis to all Lichens was not admissible by the then existing researches, particularly Schwendener's   Afterwards, when, by the works of Famintzin and Baranetzki especially, the probability
became more and more prominent that the so-called gonidia are identical with Algæ which occur
independently, Schwendener was enabled by his later investigations to establish the theory summed

will be necessary, however, in order to make clear to the reader the true state of affairs in connection with these remarkable plants, to refer very briefly to their anatomical structure. It has long been known that the body of the Lichen consists of two entirely different forms of tissue : of typical fungus tissue, which also produces the organs of fructification, and of cells containing chlorophyll, mostly spheroidal or of some other shape, which present an unmistakeable similarity to simpler forms of Algæ. In the year 1864 De Bary first pointed out that these gonidia, in a certain group of Lichens at least (the gelatinous Lichens), may be true Algæ, which, interweaved by the hyphæ of true Fungi, serve to nourish the latter. This idea, suggested by De Bary, was generalised later by Schwendener, and by means of a series of experimental works by Baranetzky, Reess, and Stahl, complete certainty was attained that all Lichens are, as a matter of fact, nothing other than Fungi belonging to the subdivision

of the Ascomycetes, which are accustomed to weave themselves around Algæ, usually microscopically small, and entirely to envelope them, so that an organism compounded of a Fungus and an Alga arises. Figure 250 shows, according to Bornet, a few examples of the ways and means by which the germinal filaments of the corresponding Lichen-fungus lay hold of and weave themselves around Algæ. The Fungi also germinate, it is true, in the absence of the Algæ, but they then perish ; and a Lichen-body only comes into existence when the germinating Fungi are able sufficiently early to become united with the Algæ with which they are adapted to form a Lichen, since each Lichen-fungus, according to its specific nature, is confined to certain forms of Algæ

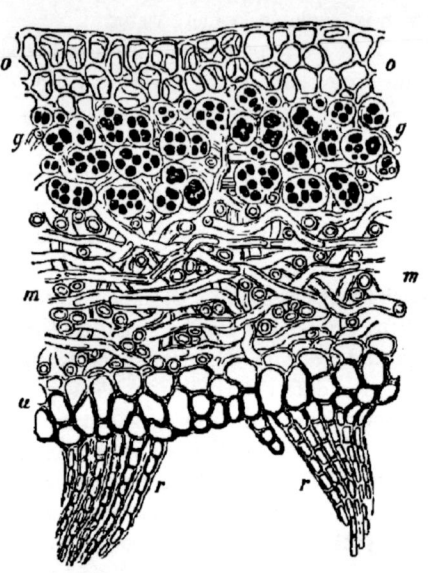

FIG 249.—*Sticta fuliginosa*, transverse section through the foliaceous thallus. *o* upper, *u* lower epidermal layer *m m* tissue of matted fungus hyphæ, *r r* roots, *g g* cells of the Alga dividing and increasing (highly magnified).

It has been demonstrated, particularly by Bornet and Stahl, that in consequence of the union of Fungus and Alga the vigour of both is promoted. Without going further into detail, it is only necessary to mention that the Algæ imprisoned by the

---

up in the text. He put aside all at once the matters referred to above as hitherto obscure and doubtful. Moreover, direct proof was forthcoming by the method of synthesis: i. e. by the union of definite autonomous Algæ with suitable Fungi a designed Lichen-thallus was produced. Reess and Stahl have now shown that this may be accomplished with comparative ease by observing certain precautions '

More details on the Lichens are found in my '*Lehrbuch*,' Aufl IV, pp. 319-330 An interesting general description also by Reess, '*Uberdie Natur der Flechten*' (Berlin, Hahel). The highly interesting work of Stahl's referred to is '*Beiträge zur Entwickelungsgeschichte der Flechten*,' Heft 2 (Leipzig, 1877, Felix) Among the finest and most instructive works is that of Ed Bornet, '*Recherches sur les Gonidies des Lichens*,' Ann des sc nat. 5⁰ sér Tome XVII, 1ᵉʳ cahier

fungus-tissue, in accordance with the growth of the whole, continually increase
in number by division, and, according to the nature of each Lichen, constitute with
the fungus-tissue a more or less homogeneous mixture (homoiomerous Lichens), or
form a layer within the tissue of the Fungus, beneath the surface of the latter
(heteromerous Lichens).

It is obvious that the green Algæ in the body of the Lichen act as organs of
assimilation, exactly as the chlorophyll-cells in the cortex of a green stem or in a
leaf. Their products of assimilation serve as nutritive material for the Lichen-fungus;
while, on the other hand, the ash constituents necessary for assimilation are conveyed
to them by means of the Fungus. By means of this commensalism, however, the

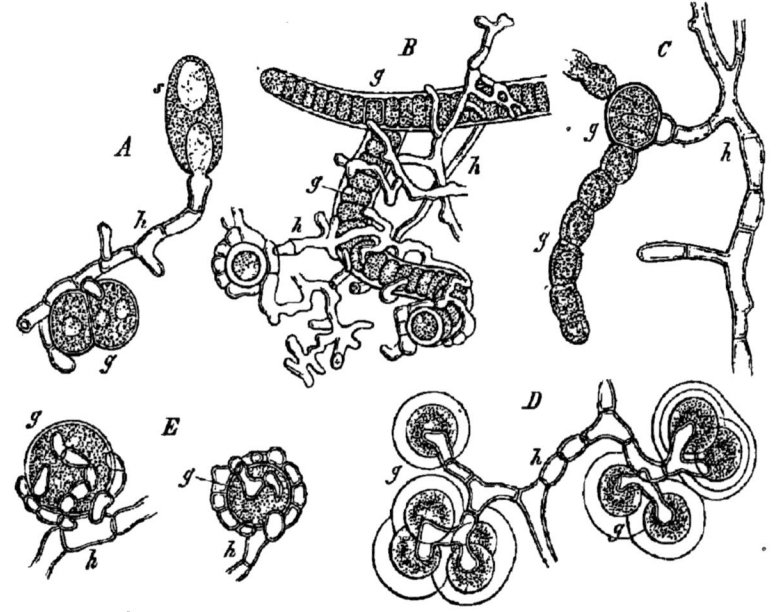

FIG. 250.—Various Algæ attacked by Lichen fungi, the Fungus hyphæ are everywhere denoted by *h*, the Alga cells
(gonidia) by *g*   *A* germinating spore of *Physcia parietina* the germinal tube *h* having fixed itself upon *Protococcus viridis*
B a filament of *Scytonema* invested by the hyphæ of the Fungus *Stereocaulon ramulosum*, *C* from the tissue of the
Lichen *Physma chalazanum*, the end of a hypha is penetrating into a cell of the *Nostoc*   *D* from the tissue of the Lichen
Synalyssa symphorea   the Alga *g* is a *Glœocapra*   *E* from the tissue of the Lichen *Cladonia furcata*, the host Alga *g*
belonging to the genus *Protococcus* (highly magnified—after Bornet).

Lichens are now independent of an organic substratum ; while all other Fungi are parasites or humus plants, Lichens are able to establish themselves on purely mineral substrata, or even on the surface of crystalline rocks, since the enclosed Alga makes them
independent, and when Lichens exhibit a predilection for the bark of trees, this
certainly does not happen in order to extract their organic nutritive material from
the bark, but for other reasons. While other Fungi decompose organic substrata, we
find numerous Lichens capable of decomposing the inorganic substance of stones,
e g granite, in order, like the roots of the higher plants, to obtain those mineral
matters which their chlorophyll-cells (the Algæ in their tissue) require for assimilation. Inasmuch as these Fungi thus come into connection with certain Algæ, in

order to be nourished by them, they obtain a freedom in the choice of their dwelling-place which is enjoyed by no other Fungus.

There is however yet another remarkable consequence which results from the commensalism of Fungus and Alga, in that the external form of the body of the Lichen generally no longer remains that of the ordinary Fungus, but behaves rather like that of non-parasitic plants which contain chlorophyll. It is true there are many so-called crustaceous Lichens which grow closely attached to the substratum. But where larger growths more separated from the substratum are formed among the Lichens, the restrictive significance of the chlorophyll for the whole configuration of the vegetable world at once makes itself prominent again. The thallus of the Lichen then becomes developed either in the form of a flat leaf-like extended plate, as in the so-called foliaceous Lichens, or in

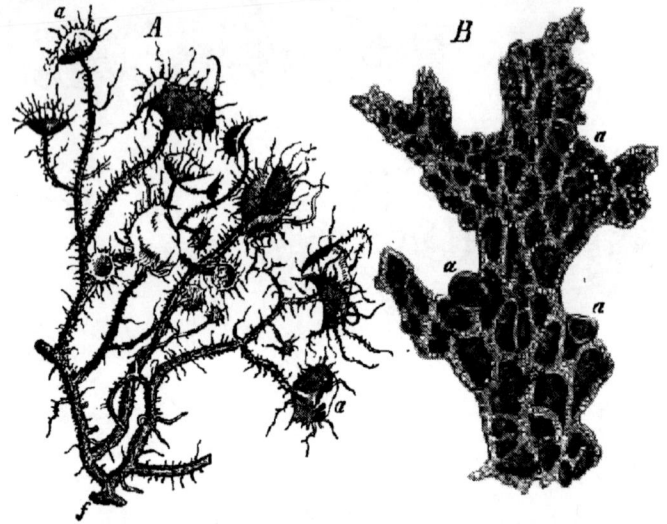

FIG. 251.—*A. Usnea barbata*, a fruticose Lichen (natural size). *B. Sticta pulmonacea*, a foliaceous Lichen (natural size) seen from below. *a* fructification; *f* the disc by means of which *A* is attached to the bark of a tree.

the form of a much branched shrubby plant. In both cases the purpose is attained of presenting the chlorophyll elements of the Lichen body to the light in thin laminæ, in order to accomplish the function of assimilation; for, as was shown in the first lectures, it is this principle which dominates the relations of configuration of all shoots containing chlorophyll, and as among the higher plants there are massive and succulent as well as graceful forms, so also among the Lichens succulent forms, the so-called gelatinous Lichens, are found, the translucent bodies of which allow the light to penetrate deeper, whereby a looser but more homogeneous distribution of the cells containing chlorophyll is possible in them. Thus as we have repeatedly found already in Phanerogams as well as Cryptogams, that in correlation with the disappearance of the chlorophyll, on the one hand dependence upon organic substrata, and, on the other, massive forms of body are produced; so, conversely, we find here in the Lichens that typical Fungi devoid of chlorophyll, in correlation with their commensalism with green Algæ, assume forms otherwise propei only to typical chlorophyll-containing plants. It was certainly this totally different facies of the Lichens as contrasted with other Fungi which chiefly contributed to make the new theory of the nature of the Lichens so unacceptable to the older Lichenologists

Another highly important lesson may be drawn from the nature of the Lichens as now understood, namely, that the external foim of a plant is not at all dependent upon its histological natuie. Evidently it does not lie in the nature of the fungus-hyphæ that the fruticose and foliaceous Lichens assume such characteristic forms as shrub-like bodies and flat extended surfaces, and still less do the Algæ concerned themselves—i e. when living independently—tend to the formation of bodies which assume the forms represented in Fig 251. These forms however may well result from the union of the two, and this chiefly according to the principle that in the case of a plant containing chlorophyll it is important to present the green cells in a suitable manner to the light and air. Finally, again to mention the fact, the commensalism of Fungus and Alga brings about that the former no longer becomes differentiated into a mycelium and fruit-bearing organs as is usually the case. In other Fungi the mycelium is endowed with the properties of true roots, and penetrates into the substratum in order to take up nourishment: the necessity for this disappears in the Lichens. The Algæ contained in the tissue constitute the nourishing substratum for the hyphæ, and they must be exposed to the light and air, and thus, instead of a mycelium, a body is developed which is attached to some solid support by organs of attachment only at one or a few places, somewhat as in the case of many large Algæ. These organs of attachment in the foliaceous Lichens may assume the most essential properties of roots.

According to recent investigations, a commensalism similar to that between Alga and Fungus in the Lichens appears to occur also between certain Algæ and various simply organised animals. It has long been known that some Rhizopods, Paramæcia, Stentors, Voiticellas, the fresh-water Sponge (*Spongilla*), oui small fresh-water Polyp (*Hydra*), and various Rotifera (*Vortex*) contain in the transparent substance of their bodies green graius which have been supposed to be chlorophyll-corpuscles. According to a recent investigation of Brandt[1], it appears now that these apparent chlorophyll-corpuscles are small spheroidal algal cells provided with a nucleus, and further that the animals concerned, when they contain such 'vegetable cells which are capable of assimilation, can dispense with the further absorption of food. These animals are thus nourished like the Lichen-fungi by means of the Algæ imprisoned in them. If on the contrary they contain no Algæ, they are necessitated to feed as animals in the ordinary manner—i. e. to take up nutritive substances through their mouths.

----

[1] Brandt, '*Über das Zusammenleben von Thieren und Algen*,' Verhandl der physiol. Ges. zu Berlin (Dec 2, 1881).

LECTURE XXV.

THE RESPIRATION OF PLANTS. SPONTANEOUS EVOLUTION OF HEAT. PHOSPHORESCENCE.

PLANTS, like animals, must be continually making exchanges with the atmosphere, and be able to absorb its oxygen in order to maintain life. The chemical changes and molecular movements of which the life of plants as well as that of animals consists, are accomplished only so long as the free oxygen of the atmosphere is able to enter into them. If the supply of this gas is cut off from them, the internal movements which effect growth cease, and the streaming of the protoplasm in which we find the most direct expression of life is brought to an end; the periodic movements of foliage leaves and the parts of the flowers cease, and the organs which respond to stimuli lose their irritability. If, when the conditions of vegetation are otherwise favourable, the supply of oxygen is interrupted for a short time only, the plants still retain their vitality, and the internal and external movements brought temporarily to a standstill may return as soon as the access of the oxygen is again permitted. If, on the other hand, the interruption of the vital movements through lack of oxygen continues for a long time, destructive processes take place in the cells in consequence of the so-called intra-molecular respiration, to which I shall return subsequently; the capacity for living is destroyed sooner or later, and a too late access of oxygen no longer recalls those peculiar movements which are termed vital[1]

---

[1] The most essential facts respecting the respiration of plants and its resemblance to that of animals had already been clearly recognised by Ingenhouss and Theodore de Saussure before the beginning of this century. The theory was further developed later by Dutrochet, Grischow, Meyen, and others. But in consequence of a quite unwarranted dictum of Liebig's, which struck out the respiration of plants from vegetable physiology, the matter simply passed into oblivion, at least in Germany, from about 1840, and accordingly the universality of an evolution of heat in living plants also was apparently put aside. An extreme confusion of ideas was at the same time, in spite of De Saussure's clever work, brought about by the fact that, by a scarcely conceivable thoughtlessness and obtuseness, people had accustomed themselves to speaking of a double respiration of plants—of a so-called diurnal respiration, meaning assimilation, and a so-called nocturnal respiration, by which was understood the evolution of carbon dioxide which occurs in true respiration. In spite of Boussingault's splendid work, and Garreau's repeated and accurate putting of the difference between assimilation and respiration, this confusion nevertheless persisted. By means of the very detailed collection of the whole of the literature which had appeared up to 1865, and the putting forward of the radical difference between assimilation and respiration which I accomplished in my ' Handbuch

These statements are now to be supported more in detail by adducing the most important facts [1].

That the chemical processes and molecular movements which constitute the growth of plants only take place when the atmospheric oxygen envelopes them and is distributed throughout the organs, was first proved by the investigations of Theodore de Saussure in 1804, with the caution and accuracy peculiar to this highly-gifted experimenter Dutrochet first showed, however, that air containing oxygen diffused in the tissues of the periodically motile and irritable organs is a condition of their motility. On the sensitive leaves of a *Mimosa* standing beneath the receiver of the air-pump, exhaustion at first acted like a mechanical shock: in the vacuum, however, they assume a permanent but rigid position. The periodic oscillations are suppressed—they are not sensitive to shocks. The irritability and periodic movements of the leaves return, however, when the plants are subsequently exposed to the air again. In the same way, the periodically motile flowers of *Leontodon taraxacum* and *Sonchus oleraceus* became fixed in Dutrochet's vacuum According to later researches by Kabsch, the stamens of *Mahonia* and *Berberis*, which are sensitive to contact, are rendered rigid and cease to be irritable when the air under the air-pump is much rarefied: the same is the case with the stamens of *Helianthemum vulgare*. On renewed access of air—i.e. of its oxygen—the motility of these organs again returns. Kabsch showed that this is due merely to the oxygen, by allowing the organs mentioned to remain for some time in pure nitrogen. On again exposing them to the atmosphere after 10–15 minutes, they regained their irritability; while they lost it for ever on remaining for a longer time in nitrogen. A stay in pure hydrogen acted similarly. With respect to the indispensability of an atmosphere containing oxygen for the maintenance of the streaming of the protoplasm in cells, as well as in the naked protoplasm of the Myxomycetes, Kuhne published detailed observations so long ago as 1864. This phenomenon also, according to his observations, disappears on the exclusion of atmospheric air, but returns, if it had not continued too long, after a few minutes on the access of ordinary air.

I have given prominence to these facts, because they demonstrate directly and without any need of comment the importance of oxygen respiration. As animals are suffocated by withdrawal of atmospheric oxygen, so with plants also: their functions come to a standstill, and if the respiration is not restored at the right time, the standstill in permanent, and death results. It is true, as we shall see later, the respiration of plants is far less energetic than that of warm-blooded animals, but probably it can be compared in all respects with that of cold-blooded animals

---

der Exp. Phys ,' the path to a correct understanding of the respiration of plants, lost for twenty-five years, was first recovered Numerous more special investigations have since appeared, without, however, essentially altering the matter itself; only the so-called intra-molecular respiration, occurring in plants just as in animals, can be regarded as an important addition to the facts long known.

[1] What here follows in the text is essentially a short extract from the chapter '*Die Athmung der Pflanzen, Warmebildung und Phosphorescence* in my 'Exp Phys ' (1865, pp. 263–304) The more recent literature is collected in Pfeffer's '*Pflanzenphysiologie*' Of the newer works, Borodin, '*Sur la Respiration des Plants*' (Florence, 1873), and '*Untersuchungen uber die Pflanzenathmung*' in Mém. de l'acad imp. des sc de St. Pétersbourg, VIIe Sér. t XXVII, No. 4, 1881, are to be mentioned

Like the respiration of animals, that of plants also consists in chemical exchanges between the oxygen taken up and the organic compounds of the living body, so that finally carbon dioxide and water are produced at the expense of these compounds. The formation of water at the expense of the organic substance can only be demonstrated indirectly by chemical analysis, as we shall see . on the other hand, it is one of the easiest experiments in the province of vegetable physiology to demonstrate the exhalation of carbon dioxide. In general, the evolution of carbon dioxide is the more energetic the more vigorous the vital activity generally of the organ observed; and since the latter increases as a rule as the temperature ascends to a certain optimum (say 25°-30° C.), so also the respiration and formation of carbon dioxide increase in a like manner It is particularly in the processes connected with energetic utilisation of material in the growth of seedlings, unfolding buds, and especially in flowers, that the evolution of carbon dioxide takes place most vigorously and can be observed most certainly. The observer only meets with difficulties in determining the changes in the composition of the air surrounding the plant which are produced by the respiratory process when he is concerned with organs abounding in chlorophyll, which are at the same time exposed to the influence of the light, because in this case carbon dioxide is taken up and oxygen evolved in the process of assimilation, and thus an exchange of gases takes place which affects the surrounding air in a manner exactly opposite to that due to respiration. Nevertheless there is no doubt, either theoretically or with reference to Garreau's experimental results, that even green organs occupied in assimilation continually respire in the ordinary manner like all other living organs. That green leaves, when not assimilating— e.g. in a feeble light, or in the dark—respire somewhat energetically is established with as much ease as in the case of organs containing no chlorophyll.

If it is required to show that plants or entire organs convert a definite quantity of the oxygen of the surrounding atmosphere into carbon dioxide, the simplest experimental methods suffice. It is only necessary, for instance, to shut off with wetted mercury an ordinary graduated absorption-tube, into which a Bean, Pea, Acorn, etc which is commencing to germinate has been placed, to convince oneself, by the absorption with potash of the carbon dioxide found in the tube after a few days, of the fact that the whole of the oxygen has been converted into carbon dioxide. It is at the same time observed in this simple experiment that the seedling saturated with water, at first, so long as oxygen is still present in the absorption-tube, goes on growing, but that after the oxygen is completely used up growth ceases

An optical demonstration of the formation of carbon dioxide by respiration may be provided still more easily in the following manner. A glass cylinder of about 2-3 litres capacity and furnished with a well-fitting stopper is filled with about 400-500 germinating peas in layers alternating with damp filter paper; or in the same way several hundreds of unfolding flower-buds of *Camellia* or of some fruit-tree, or the unfolding leaf-buds of any plant, may be employed. After carefully closing the cylinder, it is allowed to stand for 10-20 hours On then carefully and slowly raising the stopper, and slowly lowering a burning taper fastened to a wire into the cylinder, the flame and the incandescent wick are extinguished, exactly as if the vessel had been filled with pure carbon dioxide. Carbon dioxide is, as is well known, a very heavy gas which does not immediately pass out of the opened cylinder: hence the result of the experiment. In exactly the same manner we may convince ourselves by the same means of the respiration of large developing Fungi, as well as of mould growing on bread or on a liquid. The enormous energy with which growing plants absorb the oxygen in their neighbourhood, and give it back as carbon dioxide, is particularly conspicuous in that the whole of the oxygen in an absorption-tube is made use of for respiration, as follows at once from the fact that the carbon dioxide absorbed by potash after the experiment corresponds exactly to the volume of the oxygen originally present, unless, indeed, it happens that by means of intra-molecular respiration, to be described later, an excess of carbon dioxide is found.

For the purpose of more exact studies as to the carbon dioxide formed by respiration, the apparatus here figured may be employed. The two bottles *f* and *g*

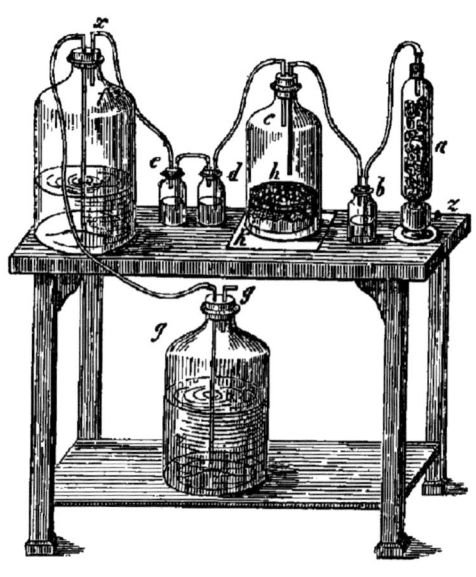

FIG 252

serve as an aspirator, since the water flows out from *f* down to *g*, whence of course the air which enters at *z* (on the right) must pass through the various vessels of the apparatus. It is first freed from any small quantities of carbon dioxide in the vessel *a*, which contains pumice-stone saturated with potash: if the lime-water in the flask *b* remains clear, it proves that this is accomplished. The air thus comes into the receiver *c* quite free from carbon dioxide. In this receiver is a trough *h* covered with wide-meshed gauze, which touches the surface of the water contained in the trough. On the gauze lie 20–30 germinating seeds of Peas, Wheat, &c., or unfolding buds or flowers or suitable vitally active parts of plants generally, from which carbon dioxide is evolved by respiration. The receiver *c* is fixed air-tight on to the glass-plate *k*. The air, now laden exclusively with respired carbon dioxide, streams through the two flasks *d* and *e* containing lime-water. The carbon dioxide is nearly all absorbed in *d*—i.e. a white precipitate of calcium carbonate is formed—and usually, when the air only streams slowly through the apparatus, scarcely any further precipitate of calcium carbonate results in the second flask *e*. Should this be the case, however, a third flask must be interposed. The calcium carbonate is now collected on a filter, and from its weight the quantity of carbon dioxide developed in the plants is calculated. Another form may also be given to the apparatus by replacing the two vessels *a b* as well as the flasks *d e* with Liebig's bulbs filled with potash solution. The chief point is that in this apparatus new air containing oxygen is continually supplied to the plants, and the carbon dioxide formed is removed, so that the plants can respire in a normal atmosphere, and we are at the same time able to determine the amount of carbon dioxide respired from time to time, without the plants themselves being thereby destroyed

In the course of very numerous investigations on the respiration of plants, various observers have made use of several different kinds of apparatus, which however mostly do not offer the advantages mentioned, and do not allow of a long-continued normal growth of the plants in the apparatus.

It would carry us much too far for my purpose to quote even abstracts of the experiments, but the general results obtained from the numerous experiments may well be referred to.

With respect to the absolute magnitude of the respiration—i. e the quantity of carbon dioxide which is expired by a definite weight or volume of plant-substance —Garreau found for example that twelve buds of *Syringa vulgaris*, which when dried at 110° C weighed two grams, exhaled 70 c cm. of carbon dioxide in twenty-four hours, the leaves having unfolded during the experiment. In the same way five buds of *Æsculus macrostachya*, the dry weight of which amounted to 0 85 gram, produced 45 c.cm. in twenty-four hours, the leaves having unfolded in this case also. Garreau further sowed seeds in fine sand, moistened with rain-water, and then brought the seedlings, deprived of the seed-coats, under the receiver, where the carbon dioxide exhaled at 16° C. was determined. Seedlings of *Papaver somniferum*, which weighed 0·45 gram when dried subsequently, evolved 55 c.cm. of carbon dioxide in twenty-four hours, and in the same way seedlings of *Sinapis nigra*, the dry weight of which was 0 55 gram, evolved 32 c.cm. of carbon dioxide in twenty-four hours

Charles Lory investigated phanerogamous parasites—*Orobanche*, *Lathræa*, and the humus plant *Neottia*, which contains small quantities of chlorophyll, and found that they are always taking up oxygen and exhaling carbon dioxide At 18° C *Orobanche Teucrii* in full bloom used up its own volume of oxygen in thirty-six hours —i. e 42 c.cm. per one gram of substance, corresponding to a loss of 2·26 mgr. of carbon.

The activity of the respiration—i e the carbon dioxide exhaled in a given time by a certain weight or volume of living plant-substance—varies according to the state of development, the activity of growth, and according to the vitality generally of the part of the plant concerned. At the commencement of the germination of seeds and buds, therefore, but little carbon dioxide is at first disengaged its quantity increases with progressive development, to diminish again later, when the material for respiration in the interior of the organ begins to fail. The activity of respiration, in fact, does not depend upon the total mass of substance which may happen to be present in the plant, but upon how large a quantity of it is being immediately employed in growth and other vital processes. When such material begins to fail, the energy of respiration diminishes also.

Since not only growth but also all other functions which depend upon respiration become more energetic as the temperature rises up to the optimum, so also the carbon dioxide exhaled increases, other relations being the same, as the temperature rises, reaching its maximum at the optimum temperature.

The energy of respiration of an organ also varies according to its physiological nature. Even De Saussure found that the respiration of flowers is more energetic than the green leaves of the same plant, weight and volume being equal. The respiration of leaves, however (in the dark), again transcends that of shoot-axes and fruits. To mention a few examples only, he found that the flowers of *Lilium candidum* consumed five times their volume of oxygen in twenty-four hours, while the leaves, on the other hand, only consumed 2 5 times their volume. In *Passiflora serratifolia* the relation of flowers to leaves was 18·5 to 5 25, and so on. Even the individual parts of flowers respire with different energy; thus, De Saussure found as follows:—

Cucurbita Melo-Pepo.

In 10 hours.	Volume of oxygen consumed compared with that of the organ = 1
Male flowers	7 6
Female flowers . . . . '	3·5
Anthers (separated from their bases)	11 7
Stigma (separated from ovary)	4 7

In general, with normal conditions of respiration and sufficient access of oxygen, the volume of carbon dioxide exhaled is equal to that of the oxygen taken in, as De Saussure had already found. The same investigator also showed, however, as long ago as 1804, that in the germination of fatty seeds this equivalence of volume no longer exists the volume of exhaled carbon dioxide is in this case smaller than the volume of oxygen taken up A portion of the latter, in fact, is not used for respiration in the narrower sense of the word, but for the formation of carbo-hydrates at the expense of the fats present, remaining meanwhile as a constituent of the sugar in the plant.

It is clear that the carbon contained in the exhaled carbon dioxide can only be derived from the substance of the plant itself, and that a diminution of the carbon contents of the plant must thus be effected by respiration. Now this carbon exists in the plant in the form of carbo-hydrates, fats, and proteid substances. Thus if a part of the carbon escapes from these chemical compounds in the form of carbon dioxide, they must suffer a profound decomposition which we may in general term combustion; and according to Boussingault's investigations, no doubt remains that in this combustion, as is to be expected, water also is formed from the organic substance. The loss in organic substance by means of respiration may, under certain circumstances (e. g. during advancing germination in the dark, when no replacement by assimilation takes place), even go so far that more than half the organic substance is destroyed by respiration. In other words, the organic substance of a seedling grown in the dark until it is completely exhausted, at last weighs only half as much as the organic substance of the seed employed for germination, or even less, and there is no doubt whatever that matters are exactly the same in the shooting of buds and in growth without assimilation generally.

From the investigation of Boussingault, however, results further the highly important fact that this combustion effected by respiration concerns only the non-nitrogenous constituents of the assimilated substance; and since the fats are converted into carbo-hydrates in metabolism, one may say only these latter are burnt to carbon dioxide and water in respiration. This conclusion is fully warranted by the fact that even in prolonged respiration accompanied by great loss of substance, no loss in nitrogenous assimilated material—i. e. of proteid substances—is to be detected. And this result is so much the more remarkable since we have every reason to assume that it is strictly in the nitrogenous substance of the protoplasm that respiration directly occurs. Like all the vital phenomena of plants, respiration also is brought about by means of the protoplasm · however, the protoplasm only initiates the process, and is not itself injured in constitution by it.

Some light is thrown upon this remarkable behaviour of the protoplasm in respiration by the recent researches on so-called intra-molecular respiration[1]. Grischow noticed so long ago as 1819 that in the respiration of Fungi, more carbon dioxide is occasionally evolved than accords with the oxygen absorbed. In my laboratory, also, other researches showed that occasionally portions of plants of various kinds go on evolving carbon dioxide even when they are unable to take up oxygen. These facts first gained in general interest however when Pfluger observed in 1875 that frogs not only go on living for some time when they remain in an atmosphere devoid of oxygen, but they also exhale carbon dioxide. Pflüger concluded from this that both constituents of this gas must be derived from the organic substance of the frog itself, in other words, that the molecules of the organic substance undergo a decomposition, even without the access of oxygen, of such a kind that atoms of carbon and of oxygen come together within these molecules themselves to form carbon dioxide, which is then exhaled This process is termed by Pfluger intra-molecular respiration. There can be no doubt that the evolution of carbon dioxide by plants in a space devoid of oxygen, which has long been observed by us, depends on the same process of intra-molecular respiration , since from all the facts known to us the respiration of plants agrees with that of animals point for point. After having convinced myself that seedlings which remained for days in an atmosphere devoid of oxygen evolved carbon dioxide and ceased to grow, but on being planted in the earth again lived and grew vigorously, I requested Dr. Wortmann in 1878 to undertake a thorough investigation of this question in my laboratory. This was done with skill and judgment. His experiments with seedlings, flowers, and growing stems were made for the most part in the Torricellian vacuum, and yielded the following important results . 1 the intra-molecular respiration during the first few hours yields just as much carbon dioxide as does respiration under the influence of the atmosphere containing oxygen: 2 the energy of the intra-molecular respiration sinks considerably, even after a few hours, thus showing an abnormal condition of the plant as contrasted with normal respiration. This fact is, I believe, decidedly opposed to the view established by Pfeffer, to the effect that respiration is identical with alcoholic fermentation. This view is, of course, supported by the fact that the most various parts of plants on being excluded from oxygen, produce small quantities of alcohol, besides disengaging carbon dioxide. But, apart from the fact that this production

---

[1] On intra-molecular respiration cf Pfeffer, ' *Das Wesen und die Bedeutung der Athmung in der Pflanze,*' in 'Landw. Jahrb' (Berlin, 1878). Julius Wortmann, ' *Über die Beziehung der intramoleculare zur normalen Athmung der Pflanzen,*' in 'Arb d bot Inst zu Wurzburg' (1879), II B, p 500 Eriksson, ' *Über Warmebildung durch intramoleculare Athmung,*' in ' Untersuchungen aus dem bot Inst zu Tubingen' (Leipzig, 1881)

of alcohol under the circumstances named in the higher plants has never yet been quantitively determined, emphasis must be laid on the fact that wherever alcoholic fermentation has been observed in the absence of oxygen (of course apart from the Ferment-fungi) objects have been exposed which have not merely undergone intra-molecular respiration for 1–2 hours, but have been cut off from the access of atmospheric oxygen for days or weeks. Now Wortmann shows (though he himself inclines to Pfeffer's view), that after the first few hours the intra-molecular respiration already indicates an abnormal condition of the plant, whence I draw the conclusion (to which Naegeli and Borodin had already arrived in another way), that the formation of alcohol in the absence of oxygen is an abnormal process throughout, and has nothing to do with ordinary respiration

The most important fact, however, and one which must never be lost sight of in comparing intra-molecular and normal respiration, lies in that intra-molecular respiration cannot provide the forces necessary for growth and the motility of irritable organs So long as the access of external oxygen is excluded, the plants are immovable, rigid, and growth comes to a standstill: a point to which Wortmann has already referred at the conclusion of his excellent work.

The true meaning of respiration, however, still remains unexplained. Nevertheless, so much is established, that it is a function of active living protoplasm. Since although it results from Boussingault's investigations that carbo-hydrates only are consumed in normal respiration, this takes place on the other hand only when they are exposed to the influence of living protoplasm. And that it is not in any way the proteid substances, regarded as chemical compounds, which maintain the respiratory process, results directly from the fact that in non-organised proteid substances neither normal nor intra-molecular respiration is to be observed. Dormant protoplasm never respires. It is, on the contrary, a property of active and living protoplasm to respire; or, perhaps better, the respiratory process is the first and most fundamental expression of the vital processes in protoplasm The substance of what intra-molecular respiration teaches, according to the facts established by Wortmann, is that it is not the oxygen penetrating from without which gives the first impulse to the chemical changes of respiration; but that primarily, and in the protoplasm in the first place, a decomposition of the molecules of the proteids occurs, which terminates with the formation of carbon dioxide; that, however, by means of the entrance of oxygen from without a *restitutio in integrum* takes place, when a carbo-hydrate, and especially sugar, is consumed.

These are, moreover, only preliminary attempts to obtain an insight into the process of respiration It is certain that numerous patient and laborious investigations will yet be necessary ere we attain complete clearness as to these matters.

While hitherto the evolution of carbon dioxide, and (as we are warranted in assuming from Boussingault's researches) the formation of water from the organic substance, have been placed in the foreground as expressing the activity of respiration, only the terminal result of the process is intended to be thus characterised. That a long series of chemical processes in addition are first induced in the plant by respiration, on which the whole vital process finally depends, there can be no doubt whatever. We may perhaps regard the formation of those acids which abound in oxygen at the commencement of germination, and likewise in shooting buds, as the most obvious indication of the processes of oxidation connected with normal respiration, and that these oxy-acids, which evidently arise at the expense of the carbohydrates and fats, in their turn constitute important points in the complex of vital processes, may be concluded from the universality of their occurrence Moreover, Hugo de Vries' idea that the vegetable acids play an important part in the turgescence of the cells, and therefore in growth also, is scarcely to be put aside. On the one hand it is a direct or indirect consequence of the process of respiration that in germination and in the growth of buds also, compounds containing very little or no oxygen arise from the splitting of carbo-hydrates and fats, since it is only during normal respiration and the growth depending upon it that resins and ethereal oils are formed. There is nothing extraordinary in the view that by means of a process of oxidation (and respiration is a very intense process of oxidation) compounds poor in oxygen as well as those abounding in it arise, but of course further investigations will first have to render clear the details in these processes.

It may appear absurd that plants which decompose carbon dioxide by means of their organs containing chlorophyll, in order to produce carbonaceous vegetable substance, on the other hand destroy such carbonaceous substance again during their whole life by means of respiration, and thus effect a loss of the capital gathered together by themselves. It may have been this reflection which drove so keen a mind as that of Justus von Liebig to the quite unwarranted decision that no respiration at all takes place in plants But what was said at the beginning of this lecture leads us to the right conclusion, in opposition to Liebig's, which depended upon mere perplexity. It is in fact not simply a matter of accumulating a quantity of organic vegetable substance by assimilation, but rather, this gain in substance is only to serve the purpose of promoting the vital processes Starch, fats, and proteid substances are of course products of assimilation, but by and for themselves they are inert material, just as bricks and mortar constitute merely the material for the construction of a house For these to be set in motion, and for the structure actually to come into existence, moving forces are necessary, and it is respiration which provides these in the organism The loss of substance which results in addition from respiration, serves to develope mechanical forces by means of which the atoms and molecules of the remaining substance are set in those movements from which growth and the other functions of the living plant result In a word, respiration is the source of the energy from which all the phenomena of life derive their vital forces; while assimilation in the organs which contain chlorophyll supplies the materials which are subsequently to be set in motion for the purposes of life. This, expressed quite generally, is the physiological significance and object of respiration, and it is certainly not too dearly bought by a relatively small loss of substance.

In respiration, as we have seen, carbon dioxide and water are produced at the expense of organic substance. This process, according to a general law of nature, is connected with the development of heat. As in every other process of combustion of carbon and hydrogen to carbon dioxide and water, so also in respiration a definite quantity of heat must be produced, though not exactly the same quantity as when carbon and hydrogen in the elementary state burn with oxygen, since a portion of the heat-producing force is destroyed in the former case, because

the carbon and hydrogen must first be torn asunder from their molecular combinations   In any case, so much is certain, that heat is produced by respiration in
the plant, just as the heat of the animal body is produced by respiration.   While
this remark depends on general natural laws, it may appear somewhat paradoxical
that respiring plants possess either only the temperature of their environment,
or, if living in the open air, may even be cooler than it is.   On closer consideration, however, this result is seen to be quite natural, since the temperature
of a body depends not only upon the heat developed in it, but quite as much upon
the causes which carry away this heat, and thus effect cooling.   Apart from special
cases, it is the cooling influences which are particularly energetic in plants, because
the very large surfaces and relatively small mass facilitate the exchange of heat
with the environment.   In submerged aquatic plants and subterranean organs
every increase of temperature produced by respiration is very easily equalised
by means of the bulky surrounding medium, so that such parts of the plant
exhibit simply the temperature of the environment.   Leaves and their shoot-axes
in the open air, however, are more exposed to cooling than these.   They lose such
considerable quantities of heat, not only by radiation, but also by the absorption
of heat in the formation of aqueous vapour, that they are usually colder than the
surrounding air.   During clear nights the temperature of the leaves may fall by
radiation several degrees below that of the air; and when the latter is some 2 or 3°
above zero, for instance, the former may cool down 3 or 4° below zero, and the
aqueous vapour of the surrounding air be precipitated in the form of ice crystals
(hoar frost) on the plants.   On the other hand, the leaves may be even warmer than
the surrounding air in strong sunshine; and this of course does not depend upon
respiration.   In observing the temperature of the wood of trees earlier observers
allowed themselves to fall into much confusion.   They found, for instance, that the
temperature of the wood at night is higher than that of the surrounding air, and
many held this to be an indication of spontaneous heating, although, as later and
more exact observations showed, this phenomenon, as well as the opposite difference
of temperature in the day, depends simply upon the slow conduction of heat by
wood   As a matter of fact, also, the wood of a tree is the least suitable of all
materials for the observation of the spontaneous heating of plants; since in the
wood, apart from the relatively small quantity of parenchyma, respiration (and consequently also spontaneous heating) does not occur.

However, if cooling—i.e. the removal of the heat of respiration—is prevented,
it is easy to demonstrate rises of temperature in the most various parts of plants by
means of suitable thermometric observations.   The fact longest known in this
connection is the rise of temperature, often very high, of germinating barley in the
preparation of malt: here the respiring seedlings are accumulated in large quantities,
and protected from cooling to any great extent.   Goppert's experiments made in
1832 with various seeds, bulbs and tubers, depend on the same principle the
seeds etc. were accumulated in large quantities, and rose in temperature several
degrees, though great sources of error were overlooked.   Evidently it is not sufficient
simply to accumulate large quantities of germinating seeds, bulbs and tubers in
the neighbourhood of a thermometer; it is also necessary to afford access to the
atmospheric air in the process, in order that respiration may proceed.   This may

be accomplished by means of the simple apparatus here figured. The bottle *f* contains a strong solution of potash or soda *l*, which absorbs the carbon dioxide liberated in respiration. In the opening of the bottle a funnel *r* is inserted, in which a large number of germinating seeds or flower-buds are contained. The bell-jar *g* is for the purpose of preventing the radiation of the heat, without however excluding the access of the atmospheric air, which can enter at the lower margin of the bell-jar, as well as through the pad of cotton-wool *w*. A thermometer *t* is pushed through the latter, so that its bulb is immersed among the respiring plants. For observation two such pieces of apparatus should be arranged close together in a chamber, the thermometers being previously compared. In the second apparatus, the funnel *r* is loosely filled with moist filter-paper instead of with portions of plants, etc., in order to establish

similar conditions of evaporation and radiation In order still more to regulate the evaporation, a divided glass lid, through the central hole of which the thermometer passes, is laid on the funnel *r*. The apparatus, as well as the parts of plants experimented with, should have been already exposed to the temperature of the space in which the observation is made for several hours before the commencement of the experiment.

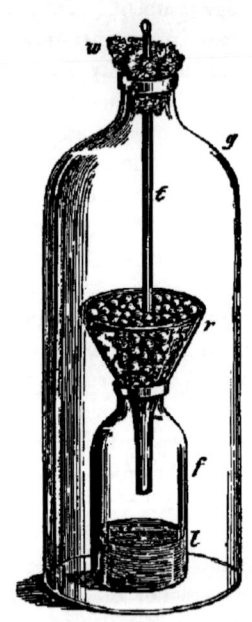

FIG. 253 —Apparatus for observing the spontaneous heating of germinating seeds and flowers.

By these means, with temperatures favourable for vegetation, I succeeded in observing a spontaneous heating of 1·5°C. in the case of 100–200 germinating Peas as their roots developed The anthers of a *Gourd* caused the mercury of a somewhat large thermometer, the bulb of which touched them on one side only, to rise through 0·8°C. A single flower-head of *Onopordon acanthium* showed a spontaneous heating equal to 0·72°C., and the stamens of a single flower of *Nymphæa stellata* showed a rise of temperature of 0·6°C. Numerous flower-buds of *Anthemis chrysoloica*, heaped round the bulb of the thermometer, were heated through 1·6°C. during the unfolding. In large, vigorously developing Fungi, it sufficed to push a thermometer into their substance to observe the rise of temperature.

The apparatus for observing respiration figured above (Fig. 252) may also be employed for these experiments, if a thermometer is inserted in the bell-jar *c*, so that its bulb is immersed among the respiring plants.

The idea that the spontaneous heating of plants is a consequence of respiration was expressed by Theodore de Saussure so long ago as 1822; although his own thermometric observations on flowers afforded no very satisfactory results, because they were made in the open air

The spontaneous evolution of heat is very easily observed in a most instructive manner in the inflorescence of the Aroideæ. Nature has here brought together in a confined space a large number of very actively respiring flowers. The rise of temperature of such inflorescences, especially when large, amounts to 4 or 5 to 10 or 12 or even 15 and more degrees Centigrade, and therefore may be perceived by the senses even without the thermometer Older observers had already made close observations on these exceptionally favourable objects as to the relation between the respiration of oxygen and the evolution of heat. we owe the most exact of these to Garreau, who has done much for the theory of respiration. He found in the inflorescence of *Arum Italicum*, for example, a spontaneous heating of $3 \cdot 2°C.$; $11 \cdot 1$ c.cm of oxygen being respired by 1 gram of substance in one hour. The same spike showed a spontaneous heating of $8 \cdot 3°C$, 1 gram of the spike consuming $28 \cdot 5$ c.cm. of oxygen (i.e. converting it into carbon dioxide) in one hour. These examples at any rate show that the respiration of plants may under certain circumstances reach an intensity which may be compared with that of warm-blooded animals.

In large single flowers like that of *Victoria regia*, as well as in the flowering spikes of Aroideæ, we find during the period of spontaneous evolution of heat, first a rise of temperature up to a maximum, and then a decrease in the spontaneous evolution of heat, evidently in consequence of the advancing development. Observers give in addition also periodic oscillations of the spontaneous evolution of heat, the true nature of which, however, has not yet been explained.

Since respiration, like every other vital process, obtains in intensity as the temperature increases, until an optimum of the latter is attained, it follows that the spontaneous evolution of heat at higher but favourable temperatures of the surrounding air must be more intense than at lower temperatures of the latter, and when the temperature of the environment is so low that growth and respiration do not occur at all, it is obvious that no spontaneous evolution of heat is to be expected. These theoretical results find their confirmation in the observations before us.

The observation of the rise of temperature in the respiration of green shoots is more difficult than in the cases hitherto referred to Dutrochet in 1840 employed for this purpose a thermo-electric pile of great delicacy, by means of which he succeeded in demonstrating in the interior of individual growing shoots rises of temperature of $\frac{1}{10}$th and $\frac{1}{100}$th of a degree. He found the greatest rise always in the case of unfolding buds, which of course was to be expected.

From the point of view of purely scientific discovery, however, all these observations have relatively little value, and I have only introduced them in confirmation of the theoretical results. Much more important would be the determination of the quantities of heat, expressed in thermal units, produced by the consumption of a known quantity of oxygen in respiration.

As already said, the production of heat is a universal and necessary consequence of respiration. In rare cases, however, the production of light, or phosphorescence, also occurs. Avoiding here many extremely doubtful statements, I confine myself to mentioning several cases of luminous Fungi established by good observers, where it is essentially a matter of showing that phosphorescence may be a consequence of the respiration of living plants In this connection, the illumination of the 'Rhizomorphs,' the mycelium of a tree-killing Agaric (*Agaricus melleus*) has been longest known   Tulasne mentions, as examples of spontaneously luminous Fungi, *Agaricus igneus* from Amboyna, *A. noctilucens* from Manilla, and *A. Gardneri* from Brazil   The best investigation of the spontaneous luminosity of such Fungi was supplied in 1855 by Fabre in the case of *Agaricus olearius*.   This golden yellow Fungus grows throughout Provence at the foot of olive trees in October and November.   According to Delile and Fabre only its hymenium is luminous, and not the white spores   According to Tulasne the stem also, at least here and there, is in many cases luminous; and even the interior of the Fungus is said to develope light, according to him.   Fabre, who made his observations at a lower temperature of the air, could not detect this.   The observers mentioned, however, agree that the Fungus is only luminous during its period of vegetation, and that the phenomenon ceases at death.   Even very young specimens are actively luminous, and they retain this property so long as they live.   Fabre describes the light as steady, white and homogeneous, resembling that of phosphorus dissolved in oil.   His observations were made in November, at 10°–12° C , and he first established that the Fungus is luminous during the day as well as at night, as had already been shown by Schmitz to be the case in the Rhizomorphæ   A previous exposure to sunlight has no noticeable influence on the subsequent luminosity in the dark, and the degree of moisture of the air likewise seems to have no perceptible effect   The Fungus is luminous in rainy weather and in dry, and is just as luminous in air saturated with vapour.   If it is dried to such an extent that death ensues, however, the luminosity ceases.   In the case of the Rhizomorphs, according to Tulasne, this takes place sooner   At temperatures lower than $+4°$ or $+3° C$ the phosphorescence is very quickly lost, but returns again when the temperature of the air rises.   The maximum of luminosity is reached at 8°–10° C., and is not increased by further heating   If plunged into warm water, the Fungus retains its luminosity; but as soon as the temperature rises to 50° C , the luminosity disappears for ever, the Fungus being then killed.

In water containing air the phosphorescence is as pronounced as in the air; but if a luminous Fungus is plunged into boiled water, the luminosity ceases almost instantaneously, returning, however, when the Fungus is withdrawn and brought into the air.   The phosphorescence is immediately and completely extinguished in a vacuum, in hydrogen gas, and in carbon dioxide.   After remaining for several hours in a vacuum or in these gases, the Fungus at once regains its light on being again brought into the air . a longer stay in carbon dioxide injures it however.   In pure oxygen the light does not become more pronounced . on the contrary, it is enfeebled after thirty-six hours in this gas   The most important fact discovered by Fabre is that *Agaricus olearius* in its phosphorescent condition forms much more carbon dioxide than when it is not luminous.   The pileus with its lamellæ in pure oxygen at 12° C. yielded, in thirty-six hours, 4 41 c cm of carbon dioxide for each gram of its weight : a gram of non-luminous substance only yielded 2 88 c.cm. of carbon dioxide.   On the other hand, on treating a luminous piece of Fungus in the same way at a lower temperature, where the luminosity ceased, this yielded in forty-four hours for each gram of its substance, only 2 64 c cm. of carbon dioxide; and another piece, not luminous at all, 2 57 c.cm.   Hence the substance capable of luminosity, when prevented from emitting the light, exhaled only as much carbon dioxide as the substance which is not luminous at all.

Fabre concludes his work with the remark that phosphorescence is the effect of the respiratory activity of the Fungus, and depends upon the same causes as the spontaneous evolution of heat at the time of flowering in certain parts of Phanerogams, particularly the Aroideæ. Nevertheless, it must be allowed that very peculiar arrangements must exist for light to be a consequence of respiration in the Fungi, since the flowers of the Aroideæ, and even those of *Cucurbita*, form relatively far larger quantities of carbon dioxide, and develope heat without being luminous. The taking up of oxygen is evidently only one of the various causes the co-operation of which produce luminosity.

PART IV.

GROWTH.

LECTURE XXVI.

THE DISTRIBUTION OF THE PHASES OF GROWTH IN SPACE AND TIME

AT the beginning of any new period of vegetation the buds of trees, sub-terranean rhizomes, bulbs, and tubers put forth new foliage-shoots and often flowering stems also. in a relatively short time the previously naked trees are covered with green foliage, and the meadows, gardens, and fields with flowering plants   The plant-substance, which together with large quantities of water affords the constructive material for this rapid growth, has been produced in the previous period of vegetation by means of assimilation, and stored up in the wintering organs of the plant in the form of reserve-materials, now to be made use of for growth.

But even the organs themselves, the foliage and flower-shoots which make their appearance during the first warm days of the spring, had already been produced in the previous summer and autumn ; but, small and in part even microscopic in size, had passed into a condition of rest before further development.   With the beginning of the new period of vegetation they renewed their activity, in a word, the organs themselves, as well as the materials necessary for their further growth, passed the winter in an undeveloped, embryonic condition   It is the same also in the case of seeds, which contain in addition to the young developing organs of the embryo the nutritive materials for their first growth also.

The new germinal and foliage-shoots and flower-stems having been formed then in the spring at the cost of the reserve-materials preserved through the winter, and a widely-spread root system having been developed in the soil, assimilation—i. e. the formation of new plant-substance—is renewed, and according to the nature of the plant, this is soon again employed for the formation of new organs, or deposited in the reservoirs of reserve-materials for the next year, or both processes are combined in very various ways.

It is easy to conclude from these remarks, which lend themselves directly to the inference, that nutrition and growth need not coincide either in time or in space.   Nutrition—i e. the production of vegetable substance—is usually carried on most energetically at a time when the growth of the organs in the main has already taken place ; and we find the most vigorous growth taking place at the beginning of a new period of vegetation, without nutrition occurring at the same time. This fact may perhaps be demonstrated still more plainly by simply allowing seeds, tubers, and bulbs, thoroughly saturated with water, to lie or hang in moist air, where the germinal shoots and roots make their appearance, and grow up to a certain point, without taking up nutritive substances from without, but only with the aid of the respired oxygen and the heat supplied by the environment.

Growth and nutrition thus by no means coincide: but it is self-evident that growth can only occur if constructive materials—plant-substance capable of organisation—are already present. It follows from this fact, that we can never infer simply from the occurrence of growth a simultaneous occurrence of nutrition; and in the same way it is by no means to be concluded from the fact that nutrition is proceeding, that the organs of the plant are at the same time growing. This appears most evidently in the organs of assimilation—the green leaves themselves—the nutritive activity of which only predominates when they are themselves completely developed. If, now, the growth of a single leaf, a shoot, a flower, or of any other organ is observed from its origin up to the moment when it is completely developed—the developmental history, as it is usually termed—two points are noticed, viz. on the one hand the volume becomes larger and larger, until it finally attains a definitive size and increases no more; and, on the other hand, the form of the organ, at first sketched out only in its coarsest outlines, so to speak, becomes further developed and more finely elaborated during the increase in volume, until finally its definitive form is perfected.

Growth is thus an increase in volume, closely combined with a change in form.

It may perhaps contribute to the elucidation of the idea if we compare the growth of a plant thus defined with that of a crystal, on the one hand, and with that of an animal on the other.

In the case of the crystal, two points are also to be distinguished in the growth: the increase in volume, and the formative forces. From the material in a dissolved, or fused, or even gaseous state, minute and scarcely visible crystals are formed, which then increase in size. But in their growth the geometrical form given from the first remains unaltered, and the increase in volume is not, as in the case of plants and animals, a specifically limited one. Under favourable circumstances a crystal may go on growing further and further; it is never, like an organ, 'fully grown.' Moreover, the mode of growth is essentially different; for in the first place a crystal takes its origin from amorphous fluid matter, and then grows by means of the deposition of new, minute, invisible particles on its surfaces. A vegetable body, on the other hand, never originates directly from a fluid, but always as part of an existing and already formed plant-organ; or, if one will so express it, all crystals arise by 'spontaneous generation,' which is never the case with organisms. Crystallisable substances may completely give up their form on solution, fusion, or evaporation, and assume it again under suitable external conditions: organisms, on the other hand, exhibit an uninterrupted continuity of their existence. The substance of a plant or of an animal dissolved and in an amorphous condition never resumes the organised form: this only proceeds from an organised substance already present.

With reference to the increase in volume, also, a fundamental difference exists between organs and crystals, in that the enlargement of a crystal takes place by the deposition of new substance at its surfaces; whereas the plastic substance serving for the growth of the organ is present in its interior, and is conveyed to it internally from other organs. Organs grow not by apposition, like crystals, but by intussusception: their growth is an extension acting from within.

Nevertheless we have cause to assume that, apart from all external matters, even the growth of the organs of the plant—namely, their elementary structures, cell-walls, protoplasm, and nucleus—depends fundamentally on forces which correspond essentially with the forces of crystallisation, only that here, since the supply of substance capable of being organised takes place from within, complications which are not easily intelligible present themselves. If the comparison here pointed out meets the case, it must be mentioned that only the smallest particles of a cell-wall, protoplasm, or nucleus (the *Micellæ* of Naegeli) grow after the manner of crystals; and thus, not the external form of an entire plant-organ, but the invisible structure of its elementary constituents might be immediately referred to the forces of crystallisation. Naegeli has undertaken, in a long series of important researches, to follow up and explain further these (his own) ideas. His theory of growth by intussusception is concerned in the first place with the question how the smallest invisible elements of the organised parts of plants grow. It is clear, however, that only one who is familiar with all the details of the internal and external structure of vegetable organs can be in a position to enter into the questions here raised. Moreover, the theory of intussusception has by no means as yet attained to that degree of clearness which renders it possible to explain in detail from it the growth of vegetable organs—leaves, roots, &c. I renounce, therefore, in the interest of the reader, even an attempt in this direction, in the conviction that the mere mention of this problem suffices to indicate the difficulty of the task with which the theory of growth has to do; meanwhile we will keep more to the surface of the matter, and attempt to make clear those processes of the growth of the organs which are immediately perceptible to the senses.

The growth of the plant has been so far compared with that of the crystal. In the essential points of comparison animals agree with plants. Comparisons between the two kingdoms of organised beings, however, again yield some important differences. Apart from a few of the most simply organised forms, animals attain by means of their growth a definitive condition, of such a kind that in a fully grown animal all the organs are fully developed, each contributing by its physiological labour to the maintenance of the entire body; the completely developed animal consists of completely developed organs, each performing its functions to the utmost. The case is quite otherwise with plants. They are never completely developed. It is true we find on every living plant completely developed parts, but besides these there are always present in addition the rudiments or beginnings of new organs, capable of further development.

A plant without those growing-points which effect further development is no longer a normal plant. Moreover, even the cut-off parts of living plants are very often able to originate new growing-points of like kind.

The continuity of animal life (apart from some plant-like lower forms) is brought about by means of continually repeated reproduction, the single individuals having normally only a limited and often very short period of life. Something similar occurs, it is true, in the case of certain plants also, the so-called annuals; but the vast majority of plants owe the continuity of their existence chiefly to the circumstance that, besides organs already fully developed, new growing-points capable of development are continually being originated, by means of which the life and growth of the same plant-specimen is continued from year to year, or even from century to century. It is owing to this fact, also, that the idea of the 'individual' —i. e. that which is only capable of indivisible existence—can find no rational application whatever in the case of the great majority of plants; since it is mere trifling with empty terms either to distinguish with Schleiden each individual cell, or, with Alexander Braun, each shoot-bud emphatically as an individual. At any rate, no deeper insight into the nature of plants can be obtained in that way.

Plants, therefore, in the condition in which they are usually observed (i.e apart from the microscopically minute primary embryonic state), always consist partly of mature, fully-developed portions which no longer grow, and partly of immature portions; these latter, as in the case of winter-buds, may be dormant, but subsequently develope further, or they may be portions which are developing—i. e. increasing in volume and changing in form. In order to guide himself aright even in the most elementary doctrines of vegetable physiology, it is absolutely necessary for the student to acquire the clearest possible idea of these relations: the theory of growth, especially, has no sense or meaning whatever for him who is not sufficiently familiar with these matters. I shall therefore attempt to make clear by a few examples the distribution of the phases of growth in space, as well as their changes in time. It may be remarked at the outset that I distinguish three phases of growth, which are continually passing over into one another, but which are nevertheless sharply characterised.

Organs are first met with in an embryonic condition: growing further, they enter upon a second phase, that of elongation, by means of which they attain their definitive volume and their definitive external configuration. Only in a third stage of growth is the internal structure also of the already elongated organs completed. I distinguish this last phase of growth as that of internal development, upon which the condition of being fully grown—the mature state—at last follows.

As an example serving for the illustration of these matters, let us consider Fig. 254, which represents in the form of a simple diagram the phases of growth of a young, erect, dicotyledonous plant. In the unripe seed of this plant, at the proper time, an embryo would be found in the form represented at *I*. On this are observed the growing-point (*v*) of the future shoot (plumule), and that of the radicle (*w*): the two protuberances *c c* are the two primary leaves (cotyledons) of the seedling in a rudimentary state. The nearly black shading of *v* and *w* is intended to indicate that these parts still consist entirely of embryonal tissue; while the lighter shading of *c c* indicates the second phase of growth, the cell tissue already beginning to pass over into the stage of elongation. This condition of development of the embryo has resulted, however, from one still earlier, where the embryo had almost the form of a sphere, and where no differentiation whatever, either into various organs or into various forms of tissue, was as yet to be recognised: the entire embryo then consisted of homogeneous, embryonal cell-tissue, the commencing differentiation of which is already indicated in *I*.

In the ripe seed of the same plant we should find the embryo in the form *II*. Between *v* and *w* is now intercalated a mass of tissue, which is elongating, and which subsequently forms the hypocotyledonary segment (*h*) of the shoot. The first leaves, or cotyledons, *c c*, have grown considerably. Of the embryonal tissue, of

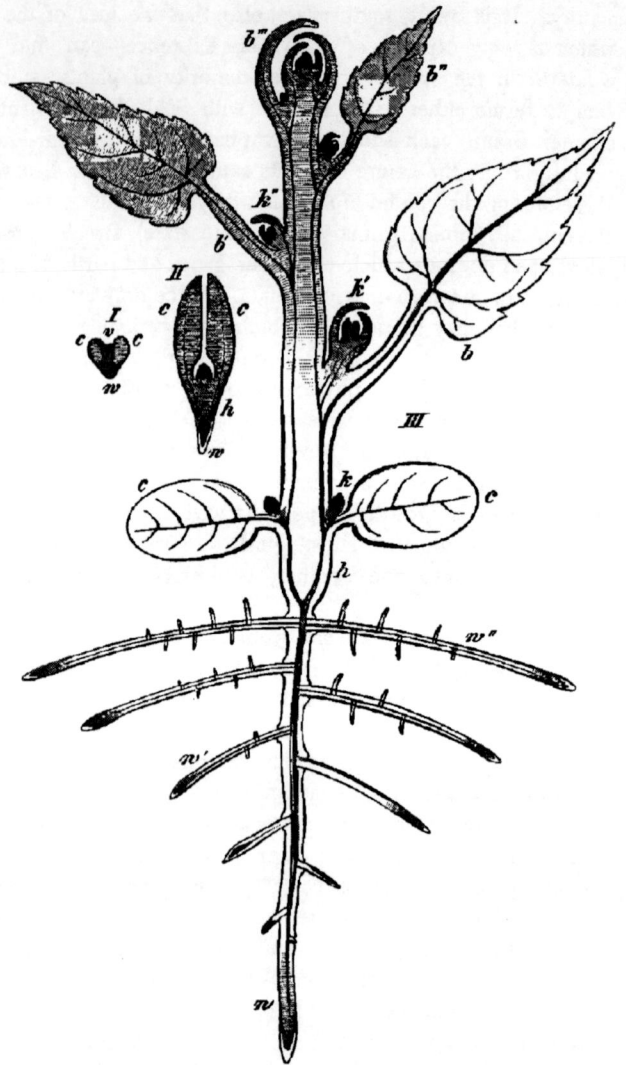

FIG. 254.—Diagram of the distribution of the various phases of growth in a dicotyledonous plant.

which the entire embryo formerly consisted, there now remain only two portions, separated from one another; the upper one of these constitutes the growing-portion of the future plumule, and the lower that of the radicle (*w*).

In *III* we have represented the same plant as in *II*, after the conclusion of germination. At the uppermost end of the germinal stem, shaded black, is still to be recognised the growing-point marked *v* in *I*; also the growing-point *w* of the primary root. New growing-points have now arisen in addition at *k k' k''*, &c., and have already in part proceeded to the formation of new lateral shoots. Each of these new growing-points has originated, during progressive growth, out of the primary growing-point, *v* in *I*. The lateral growing-points *k* were first protruded in the axils of the two cotyledons, *c*, *II*: the primary growing-point then grew further, and produced the leaves *b*, *b'*, *b''*, *b'''*, &c, a new growing-point arising each time from the axil of the leaf, as it was put forth from the growing-point (*k' k''*, &c.). In the course of the growth leaf-buds have already been put forth from these new growing-points. The leaves and portions of stem also produced from the primary growing-point *v*, have in the meantime however grown much more rapidly, and have already entered into the second and third stages of growth · the leaves, *b'*, *b''*, *b'''*, as well as the parts of the shoot-axis belonging to them, are still found in the elongating condition, as indicated by the light shading. The cotyledons *c*, and the leaf *b*, as well as the parts of the shoot-axis belonging to them, which are not shaded at all, are on the other hand already fully developed externally—i. e. they have attained their definitive volume, and their permanent external form. These parts, however, are now in the third phase of growth—i. e. their internal development is now being completed; the lignification of the vascular bundles, the development of sieve-tubes, the thickening of the walls of the parenchyma cells, formation of stomata and development of cuticle on the epidermis are being completed in these portions. All these histological differentiations have already commenced in the parts of the plants indicated by the shading; but it is only after they have attained their definitive volume and permanent form that the histological development also is completed

Let us now take into consideration in the same way the subterranean root-system of our plant (Fig 254, *III*). It is to be noted that the lateral roots *w' w''* were produced originally close behind the growing-point (*w*) of the primary root. Each of these lateral roots was originally itself only a new growing-point, by the further growth of which the filiform lateral roots have been produced; and the same relation exists between the lateral roots of the second order and their mother-roots. Meanwhile, it need only here be mentioned by the way that the growing-points of the new roots originate in the interior of the tissue of their mother-roots; while the new growing-points of the shoots are superficial outgrowths of the primary growing-point.

In the roots also the growing-points are represented black in our figure, but, it will be seen, they are surrounded by an additional light zone, the root-cap, which originates simultaneously with the first rudiment of the growing-point of a root. Behind each of the growing-points of the root, which are shaded black, is a short piece marked by lighter shading: this is the elongating portion of the root-fibre, and, as is seen at once, it is strikingly short in comparison with the elongating region of the shoot-axis.

A very important point, which will already have been noticed by the way in the above description, must now be made quite clear. All the growing-points of the plant *III*, shaded black, originated in the first place from the two growing-points *v* and *w* of the embryo *I*; and these themselves are both, as already said, simply remnants of the perfectly homogeneous cell-tissue of which the embryo at first consisted. All the growing-points, therefore, are directly derived from the primary embryonic tissue; in such a manner, however, that we have to suppose the substance of the latter as being nourished and continually increasing in quantity. If the growth of the plant were entirely confined to that of the growing-points, it would consist in an exceedingly slow increase in volume of the original embryonic tissue. We might imagine all these small growing-points, so to speak, cut off and then united into one whole: we should then have a very small structure, consisting of nothing but embryonic tissue, from which the individual growing-points would stand out as protuberances. Having clearly apprehended this, it is now obvious that in reality the various growing-points in the developing plant described above have been pushed asunder and removed to a distance from one another; between each two of them a longer or shorter piece of shoot-axis (or in the roots a piece of mature root-tissue) has been intercalated. This mutual separation of the growing-points, or intercalation of new masses of tissue between them, is moreover, as is easily observed, effected in the second phase of growth; and this always consists fundamentally simply in the elongation of those portions of tissue which are situated at the base of each growing-point.

On reviewing these processes according to all that has been said so far, it must be allowed that the growth of a plant, even wholly apart from the processes taking place in the individual cells, is a very remarkable and extremely complicated phenomenon, which the student must try to apprehend perfectly if he wishes to obtain any clear ideas at all of the life and being of plants.

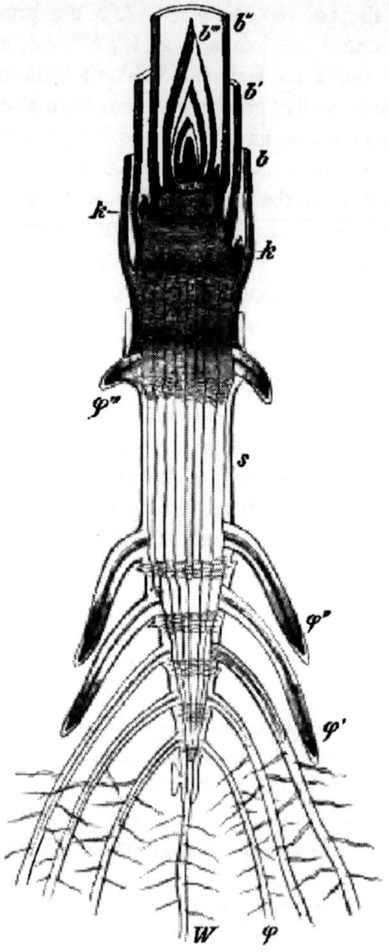

FIG. 255.—Diagram showing the distribution of the phases of growth in a Monocotyledon.

Considering the difficulty which the right understanding of these processes must necessarily present to the beginner, it will not be superfluous to take into consideration yet a few other examples.

Fig. 255 illustrates, also diagrammatically, the processes in question in the case of an erect monocotyledonous plant. The figure represents a plant of the Maize (Indian Corn); but would hold good, with but few alterations, for a Palm, and numerous other

Monocotyledons. It is advisable, in the first place, once more to regard closely the germinating stages of the Maize-plant represented in Fig. 28 (p. 38), looking upon the present figure, to a certain extent, as a continuation of that one. Here again W is the primary root, from which several thin lateral roots have originated. While, however, in the dicotyledonous plant of the previous diagram the entire root-system arises from the primary root, we find in this monocotyledonous plant that the primary root, with its ramifications, remains small and plays an extremely subordinate part. Of course as growth proceeds the entire root-system enlarges here also, but this is accomplished by new roots ϕ', ϕ'', ϕ''', springing from the lower part of the stem (s) itself, the process taking place from below upwards: these roots penetrate into the earth and there branch. The higher up the stem the root arises the more vigorous it is. Although these secondary roots (ϕ'—ϕ''') appear at a great distance from the two primary growing-points of the radicle and plumule respectively, it is nevertheless not improbable that the rudiments of their growing-points were already formed long before; and that on close investigation, which of course entails great difficulties, it would be possible to detect these growing-points of the roots as direct derivatives of the growing-point of the shoot of the plant. However, a question is raised here which will have to be taken more closely into consideration in the next lecture. The point in view now is rather to distinguish the three phases of growth, and here again the growing-points are shaded quite black, the elongating parts grey, and those which are completing their internal development and are fully grown are left without shading. The leaves b—b''' of the monocotyledonous plant in question, in each case envelope the whole circumference of the shoot-axis with their sheath-like base; and each younger leaf is, like the younger part of the shoot-axis, completely enveloped by the sheath of every older leaf. The apex of such a shoot, therefore, consists mainly of a convolution of leaf-sheaths closely wrapped around one another, and we have only to imagine these becoming thick and stout to have the whole presenting the form of a bulb. It will scarcely be necessary to repeat that the buds $k k$ proceed from secondary growing-points, which in their turn originated in the primary growing-point of the main shoot of the seedling.

Immediately above the base of each leaf, the figure (Fig. 255) shows, within the lightly shaded parts, certain darker transverse zones, by means of which a peculiarity of the growth of this and many other plants is to be explained:' for at these zones the tissue maintains a more or less embryonic character, and its cells situated further above (in the acropetal direction) gradually pass into the stage of elongation and definitively complete their development. Such transverse zones at the base of the internodes may be termed zones of intercalary growth, the tissue of which they are composed, however, is directly derived from the embryonic tissue of the growing-point. The presence of such intercalary zones brings it about that in the plants concerned the individual segments of the shoot-axis are pushed up from below out of the older leaf-sheaths, hence the youngest—i. e. the least developed—portions of the internodes are situated, not next the growing-point, but next the basal end. This remarkable state of affairs, by which the processes of growth in a shoot become still more complicated, occurs not only in many Monocotyledons, particularly in all Grasses and in the flowering scapes of bulbous plants, but is extremely clear also in the Horsetails (Equisetaceæ), among which *Equisetum hyemale* is particularly distinguished in that the internodes are each year slightly pushed up from below out of the older leaf-sheaths. Similar peculiarities occur moreover in some Dicotyledons—e. g. the Polygoneæ, Umbelliferæ, &c.

In the Grasses and Liliaceæ (and in a less degree also elsewhere) there occurs combined with this intercalary growth of the internodes a very similar process in the leaves. These also go on growing at their basal parts, which are in the phase of elongation when the apex of the leaf has long been completely developed: they become, so to speak, pushed up from below out of the body of the plant, as may very easily be observed in Hyacinths in the spring.

It will not be difficult for the reader to discover the points common to the two diagrams described. These points in common, moreover, we may regard as the type of growth prevailing in the vegetable kingdom. It exists almost without exception in the Mosses and Vascular plants, and we find it in its simplest features in many Algæ and even in some Fungi. Nevertheless, as follows from what has been said on p 84, and may be illustrated by further examples (*e g Macrocystis*, &c.), entirely different distributions of the phases of growth may occur among the Algæ and Fungi; these, however, remain confined to a few small groups and will therefore be passed over here.

After this preliminary sketch, I now proceed to a more exact description of the three phases of growth.

(1) The condition of embryonic growth in the growing-points is distinguished chiefly by the following characters :—

The development of new organs takes place exclusively in the growing-points.

The growth of the young organs at the growing-point, both with respect to the increase in volume and the changes in form, is exceedingly slow.

The mass of a growing-point, from which the very large volume of tissue of an entire shoot or root-system proceeds finally, is for and by itself extremely small, and but very rarely amounts to $\frac{1}{100}$th of a milligram.

This small quantity of matter is continually being regenerated by the addition of suitable nutritive substances, while the basal portions of the growing-point gradually pass over into the condition of elongation, and then into permanent tissue.

The growing-points, as well as their outgrowths—i. e. the young organs in an embryonic condition—consist of a cell-tissue which is usually termed primary meristem, but is better distinguished as embryonic tissue.

The embryonic tissue of the growing-point and very young organs forms a solid, somewhat hard, and occasionally even brittle mass, which consists essentially only of protoplasm and the substance of the cell nuclei; the cell-walls being extremely thin. These substances are, it is true, permeated with water; but fluid cell-sap in the form of so-called vacuoles is not present, or only in very small quantity.

The cells of the embryonic tissue are very small, the nuclei, on the contrary, being relatively very large, and their rounded form adapted to the shape of the cells. If the latter are tabular, the nucleus is flattened like a cake, if cubical, the nucleus is spherical; if cylindrical or prismatic, the nucleus is elongated also. The nucleus, however, always forms a very considerable portion of the mass of the cell; and thus the embryonic tissue is chiefly characterised by the predominance of the substance of the nuclei, in which, again, nuclein plays a chief part.

The growing-points, as well as the young organs which are still in an embryonic state, constitute a mass which is homogeneous in itself; the cells appearing as mere chambers, the growth of which depends upon the growth of the growing-point as a whole.

It is not quite correct to say, as is often done, that the cells in the growing-points and in the young organs—in embryonic tissue generally—are perfectly homogeneous among themselves. On the contrary, differences in form make themselves evident even close to the apex of the growing-point, as well as in its very young outgrowths; and in the growing-points of roots especially, it is possible to detect with certainty, even close behind the apex, those cells which will subsequently become developed as segments of vessels, or as endodermis, &c. (Fig. 257). In the same manner, the external layer of the growing-point and every embryonic organ is easily recognised as what will be the future epidermis. According to the various form of plant in each case, however, this commencing differentiation of the tissues in the growing-point is very different. The doctrine of the three so-called histogenic layers, according to which, besides the future epidermis, a so-called

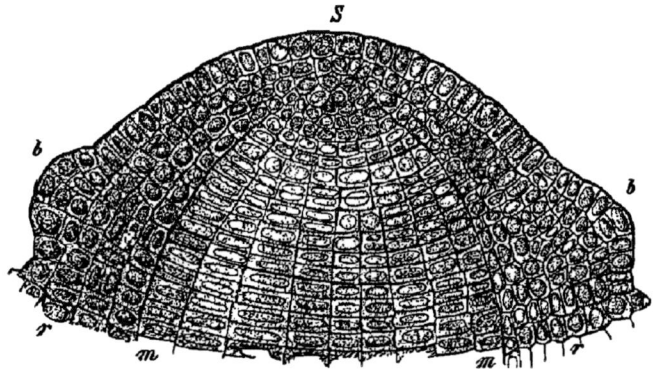

FIG. 256 —The growing point of a shoot (winter bud) of the Pine. *S* apex of the growing point, *b b* youngest leaf-rudiments, *r r* young cortex, and *m m* pith of the future shoot axis (highly magnified) The whole consists of embryonic tissue, of very small cells with relatively large nuclei.

periblem (young cortex) and a plerome are sketched out in the growing-point itself, cannot therefore be applied universally; although the tissue differentiations referred to often do occur, particularly in the growing-points of roots.

(2) The second phase of growth, the so-called condition of elongation, is introduced by the cells at the base of the growing-point beginning to grow more rapidly, and to approach their definitive development. The following are the chief points to be noted here:—

By means of the elongation, the segments of the shoot-axis, as well as the leaves and the corresponding parts of the roots, attain their definitive size and their permanent external form.

This process may continue for a longer or shorter time, and, accordingly, the elongating piece of shoot-axis or root-fibre is longer or shorter, and attains during the elongation a more or less considerable breadth and thickness. The length of the elongating portion in a root-fibre is about 3–10 millimetres behind the growing-point, in long flower-stalks 10–20, or even 50–80 centimetres. It often happens, however, that the growth in length generally, by elongation, is very insignificant, particularly in shoot-axes; so that the fully developed leaf-bases completely cover the shoot-axes, as in the Fern *Aspidium filix-mas*, and in all cases where so-called radical rosettes

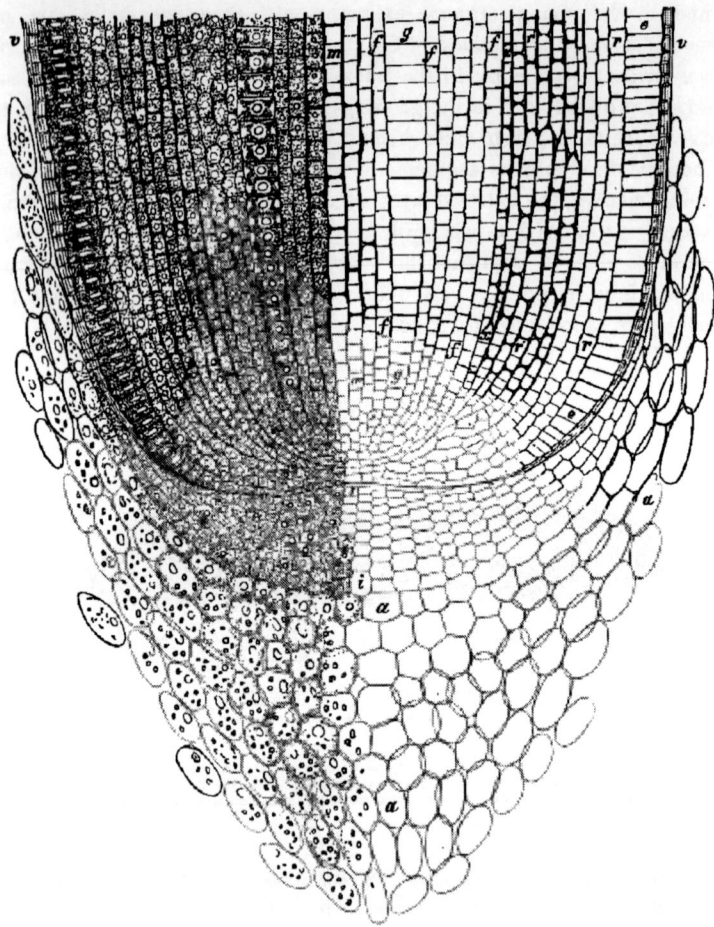

FIG. 257.—Growing-point of a root of Maize (*Zea Mays*). *a a* older portion of root-cap; *i* younger part of same; *s* apex of growing-point; *e e* external layer of tissue of root—the cell-walls are thickened (*v v*); *r r* young cortex; *ff* cells of axial vascular bundle; *g* flattened cells of a large vessel, which will subsequently form long cylindrical segments with bordered pits; *m* parenchyma of the pith in the axial strand (highly magnified).

are formed by the leaves. If the points of insertion of the leaves are pushed apart, the shoot-axis forms internodes or interfoliar parts between them.

By the mode of growth of shoot-axes during the phase of elongation, therefore, a very material influence is exerted on the definitive form of the entire shoot; in so far that it depends upon this, for example, whether the leaves are situated close above one another and form a rosette, or are removed some distance apart, and arranged in whorls, or are situated alternately or scattered on the elongated stem.

The leaves which have been developed at the growing-point of a shoot, generally grow much more rapidly than the parts of the latter situated above their insertion on the shoot-axis   In this lies the cause of the formation of buds at the end of the shoot (Fig. 258).

In the leaves also various changes in form are brought about during the process of elongation.   The elongation in the leaves may either begin at the apex and end at the base, or conversely, and in complicated forms of leaves much more complex distributions of growth may occur.

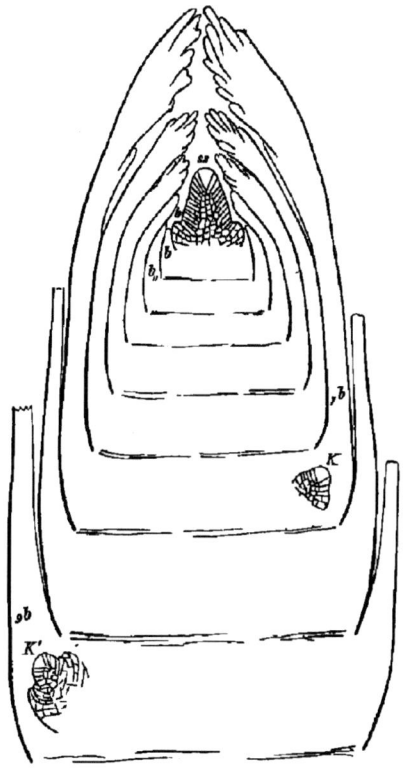

This phase of growth by elongation effects also the most various changes of form during the increase in volume, especially in the case of shoots.   The entire form of a mature shoot depends in general essentially upon the processes of configuration which take place during elongation. Contrasted with the growing-point, however, this phase of growth is distinguished by the fact that no more new organs are developed: only those already present obtain their definitive size and form.

While the extremely slow growth of the embryonic tissue takes place by means of a proportionate addition of proteid substances and nuclein, elongation, on the contrary, consists in an enlargement of the cells which is chiefly effected by the addition of water.   The cells which in the embryonic condition are solid, and consist merely of protoplasm and nucleus, change during elongation into vesicles filled with water, the volume of which may attain a hundred or a thousandfold that of the original embryonic cells : in this, however, no proportional increase of the organic substance

FIG 258.—*Equisetum arvense* Longitudinal section of a subterranean bud in March   *s s* apical cell of stem , *b—g b* the leaves , *K K'* two lateral buds exposed by the section   The subsequently very long internodes of the shoot-axis are not yet formed (slightly magnified)

takes place, but, in the main, the intercalation of water only.   This, however, does not preclude that the still thin cell-walls also have cellulose deposited in them, and that the protoplasm may increase slightly in quantity.   The enormous intercalation of water may, however, go so far that shoot-axes, leaves and root-fibres just fully grown contain more than 90 per cent., or even more than 95 per cent. of their weight and volume of water.

During this active increase in volume of the cells, especially at first, numerous additional cell-divisions take place : subsequently, however, these become rarer, and gradually cease with the cessation of elongation.

The elongation commences with the differentiation of the primitively homogeneous embryonic tissue into the various systems of tissues. Intercellular spaces soon appear between the cells of the parenchyma; the different kinds of cells gradually obtain their characteristic shapes; the cells, at first only parts of the whole in the growing-point, now become more individualised, peculiar processes of growth making themselves evident in each one; the size, external form, and the differentiation of the contents of each cell are apparently independent of those of the others—but of course only apparently. The various forms of tissues become differentiated; the single cells individualised.

At the time when the organs, or parts of organs, have attained their external form and definitive volume by elongation, they are still immature—not yet fully developed internally. It is true that the differentiation of the forms of tissues begins even in the embryonic tissue of the growing-point, and continues during the elongation, so that, at the end of the latter process, the epidermis, vascular bundles, and the various parts of these, as well as the different forms of fundamental tissue, are already to be plainly distinguished; but the development, especially of the cell-walls, is not completed in this state.

(3) The third phase of growth makes its appearance as soon as the organs and their parts have attained their permanent size and external form by means of elongation, while, however, still further changes are taking place in the interior

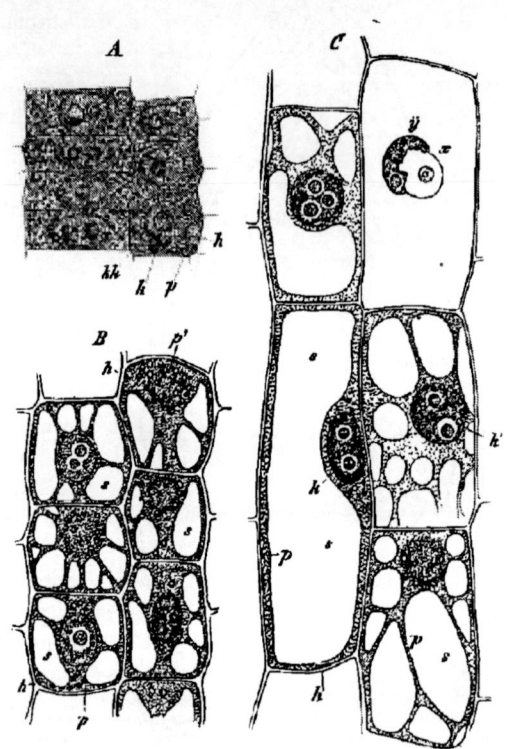

FIG. 259.—Parenchyma cells from the median layer of the cortex of the root of *Fritillaria imperialis* (longitudinal sections × 550). *A* very young cells situated close above the apex of the root, still without cell-sap. *B* the same cells about 2 mm. above the apex; the cell sap *s* forms isolated drops (vacuoles) in the protoplasm *p*, plates of protoplasm lying between them. *C* the same cells about 7—8 mm. above the apex; the two cells to the right below are seen from in front, the large cell to the left below in optical section; the cell to the right above has been opened by the section, and its nucleus is affected by the penetrating water and exhibits a peculiar swollen appearance.

of the tissue. The lignification in the vascular bundles, the thickening of the cell-walls, and the various kinds of pitting connected with it; the development of the sieve-tubes, the lignification of the sclerenchymatous elements; and more particularly the further development of the epidermis, especially the stomata, cuticularisation and perhaps silicification, and the development of hairs, now first attain completion. The internal development of the tissues, which only occurs late and after elongation is accomplished, is particularly striking in the case of the roots.

In those of the Grasses and *Liliaceæ* (e. g. Maize, *Fritillaria*, &c.) elongation is completed about 8–10 mm. behind the growing-point; but even 50–60 mm further back the bordered pits of the large vessels are found to be only just fully developed, and similarly with other tissue-structures. The internal development and strengthening of the tissues, which continue for some time after the completion of elongation, are also plainly to be recognised from the exterior of the organs Leaves and shoot-axes which have just finished elongating are delicate, watery, easily torn, and soon droop; whereas they subsequently become much stronger, richer in substance, and more solid.

It would be superfluous to formulate the characteristics of this third stage of growth, since all that has been said in the lectures on Organography and on the theory of the tissues, with regard to the external form and internal structure of the organs of the plant, concerns this last developmental stage.   Only one point further need be mentioned here. With the exist-

FIG. 260.—Longitudinal section through the apex of an erect shoot of *Hippuris vulgaris* *s* apex of stem, *b b b* the leaves (in whorls), *k k* axillary buds of the latter and which all become flowers, *g—g* the first vessels The dark parts of the tissue indicate the internal cortex with its intercellular spaces

ence of the cambium in the shoot-axes and older roots of the Conifers and woody Dicotyledons, of course a new process of growth is ushered in, and the cambium corresponds in many respects to the embryonic tissue of the growing-point. It is distinguished from this latter, however, in that, normally, it only produces new masses of tissue, but not new organs . nevertheless the latter process also may take place under certain circumstances. In the case of cut-off woody stems, for example, the cambium swells, grows out, and forms a so-called callus—i e a cushion consisting of soft tissue—in which growing-points for the development of new shoots are developed.

The three phases of growth here distinguished usually pass into one another without interruption, so that no definite line can be drawn between the embryonic condition and that of elongation, or between the latter and that in which the internal development is being completed. The relation between them is very simple in the roots; whereas the most various complications may occur in shoots, according to the nature of the plant in each case.

The growing-point of a shoot is only apparently merely the end of the shoot-axis, as it is generally held to be.   The manner in which the leaves and lateral shoots are developed from the growing-point of a shoot shows, on the contrary, that the latter is not merely the termination of the shoot-axis, but is the embryonic beginning of the entire shoot, which, in its turn, consists of shoot-axis and leaves.

Just as new growing-points of shoots can arise from growing-points of shoots, so also on a young leaf, so long as it still consists of embryonic tissue, a large number of secondary growing-points may arise, which may then produce tertiary growing-points, and even those of a higher order, as shown in Fig. 261. Hence the subsequent external form and segmentation of a leaf becomes sketched out, and this then, according to the mode and course of elongation in each case, becomes a branched, divided, pinnate, lobed, or simply a toothed leaf   In the great majority of cases the whole of the embryonic tissue of a leaf is finally transformed by elongation into permanent tissue : the whole leaf is then completely developed.   Nevertheless, cases also occur where the apex of the leaf persists for a long time in the embryonic condition, while its basal portions become elongated and fully developed.   This happens even in the case of some large pinnate leaves of Dicotyledons—e. g *Ailanthus, Robinia,* &c. : after some time, however, the growing-point of the leaf in these cases becomes transformed wholly into permanent tissue.   In some Ferns, on the other hand (*Nephrolepis, Gleichenia, Mertensia, Lygodium*), the ends of the leaves, or of their lateral segments, remain in the embryonic condition for years, so that a continual or periodically repeated lengthening of the organ takes place by elongation just as in perennial shoots.

The growing-points of shoots, however, may also, on the contrary, become wholly transformed into permanent tissue, when they of course cease to be growing-points : this is the case, for example, in the formation of the thorns of *Rhamnus cathartica, Gleditschia,* and others. In the latter instance they are branched shoots, which only produce very small leaflets, and consist at first of very delicate tissue, which subsequently, however, lignifies to masses hard as stone : the points of these thorns are the previous growing-points, which are now likewise lignified.

All that has been said so far refers to the relations of growth in the Vascular plants and the majority of the Muscineæ · as already pointed out above, the same processes of growth may also be recog-

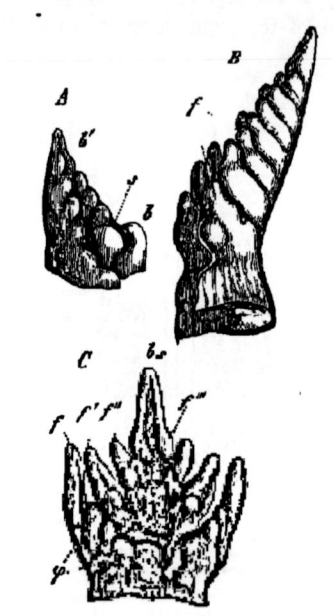

FIG 261 —*A B* young leaves of *Pastinacea sativa C* of *Levisticum officinale, f* pinnæ , φ pinnæ of second order

nised even in the Algæ and Fungi, though often only in a rudimentary form and taking a much simpler course   Besides these, however, as was stated in the lectures on Organography, entirely different types of growth also occur.   These may both be illustrated by a few examples.

One of the most remarkable cases is found in those Algæ the growth of which is not accompanied by cell-divisions, and among which the *Caulerpa* in Fig. 262 may serve as an example   The figure shows at once that we have here to do with a plant the whole vegetative body of which is moulded on, and therefore grows according to, exactly the same plan as that of a creeping vascular plant.   The creeping shoot-axis *v s* produces branched roots on its lower side, and leaves containing chlorophyll on its upper side.   As in the case of a creeping phanerogamous plant, the roots as well as the leaves arise from the advancing apex—the growing-point—which is here projecting, however, so that the youngest leaf and the youngest root are somewhat distant from the apex : hence no proper bud enveloping the growing-point exists at all. What is most important for us, however, is the fact that no cell-formation whatever takes place in the interior of this plant : no cell-walls exist either in the growing-point or in the completely developed organs.   In the cavity of the thick-walled vescicle, however, the ramifications of which constitute the entire plant, numerous bars consisting of cellulose are found, which traverse the lumen of the cell like pillars and rafters, in order to confer greater firmness on the whole structure : in more slender forms of Cœloblasteæ, however, as

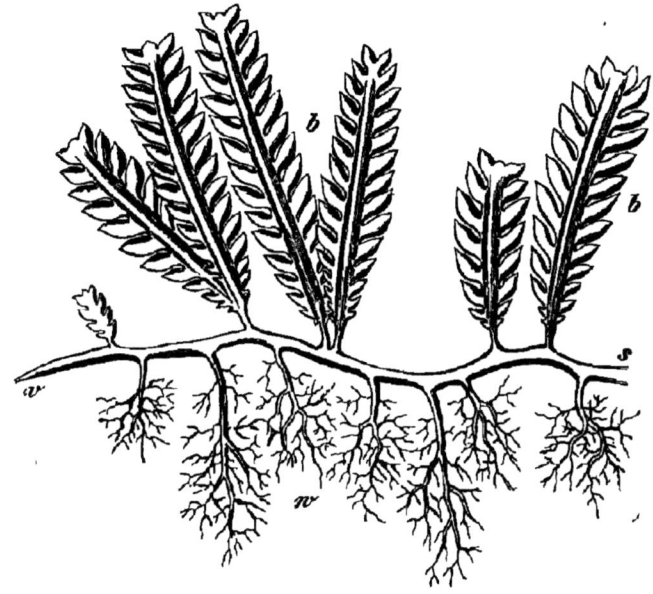

FIG. 262—*Caulerpa crassifolia*   The entire plant consists of a vesicle which is not divided into chambers or cells   *v* the growing point of the creeping dorsi ventral shoot-axis *s*, *b b* leaves, *w* roots (nat size)

in the common *Vaucheria*, even these are wanting   It is now only necessary, therefore, to leave out from what has been said above as to the difference of the three phases of growth all that refers to the cellular structure, which does not exist here, and all the rest applies even to this non-cellular plant.

A second example may be taken to show the corresponding condition of affairs in one of the more highly organised Fungi   The accompanying figure (Fig. 263) shows the development of a Mushroom of the genus *Agaricus*.   At *I* is represented a small piece of the mycelium (*m*), the thicker filaments of which consist of numerous hyphæ running parallel to one another.   The mycelium behaves in all essential points like the branched root-system of a higher plant ; at the end of each filament there is a growing-point from which new growing-points are developed as buds   At certain points of this mycelium, at *a* and *b*, organs of reproduction are formed, one of which is represented somewhat enlarged at *c*, to the right above: the apex of this consists of a growing-point, while the lower portion is already in process of elongation. The somewhat older fructification represented at *II* and *III* is commencing to form the umbrella-like expansion (*pileus*) at its apex, the elongation at the top ceasing meanwhile; hence the mass of tissue becomes extended radially all round the growing-point, as shown still further developed at *IV*. The embryonic character of the fungal tissue now disappears at the apex and on the upper side generally of the developing pileus, but is maintained for some time longer on its lower surface, from which very numerous thin lamellæ now grow out, radiating from the stem to the periphery of the pileus. From these the reproductive organs are developed. It is not difficult to recognise in the processes of growth briefly indicated in *Agaricus*, relations similar in the main to those which we meet with in the more highly organised plants, which is in this case so much the more remarkable since the mycelium and the fructification of the Fungus consists of single filaments or hyphæ, each individual one of which represents as it were an independent growing plant, in which growing-points and the various phases of growth are to be observed, as in the Mould-fungi. In the mycelium and fructification of the present Fungus, however, hundreds and thousands of such hyphæ are combined in such a manner that all their growing-points become united in the growing-point of a branch of the mycelium, or that of an organ of reproduction.

It would not be difficult to find dozens of other cases among the Fungi and Algæ in which the typical processes of growth still make their appearance, it is true, here and there, but in which they yet are replaced more or less by widely different arrangements. As a particularly striking example in this direction, I may mention one

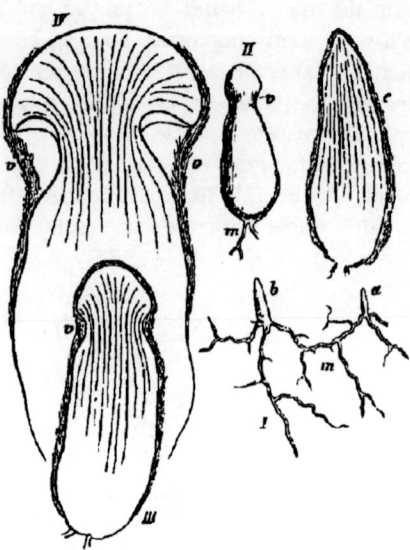

FIG 263.—*Agaricus variecolor* *I* Mycelium (*m*) with young fructification *a* and *b* (nat size), *c* one of the latter in longitudinal section (magn). *II* older fructification, the pileus is beginning to be formed. *III* the same in longitudinal section *IV* the pileus further developed, *v* velum. The lines in the longitudinal sections indicate the course of the hyphæ.

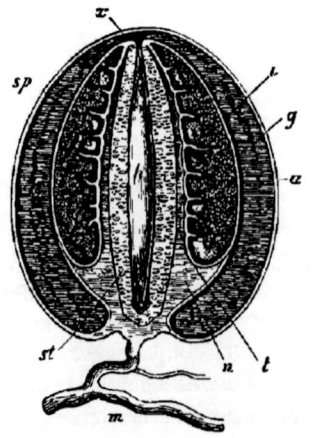

FIG. 264.—Vertical section of a young fructification of *Phallus impudicus* (cf the text—⅓ nat size)

of our most remarkable Gastromycetes, *Phallus impudicus*, the mycelium of which, consisting of thick white threads growing in the soil of forests, presents essentially the same appearance as that of the Agaric considered above. The fructification of the *Phallus* arises as a spheroidal protuberance, composed of interwoven hyphæ, on one of the superficial branches of the mycelium. This protuberance while young may be looked upon as a growing-point, the mass of tissue of which, however, while growing up to the size of a hen's egg, undergoes a differentiation quite other than in the cases hitherto considered, for although here also the polarity existing between the base and apex of the structure is not entirely given up, still that process of growth which may be compared with the elongation of a normal plant affects the fungal tissue, which has passed out of the embryonic stage, in such a way that concentric layers of tissue are differentiated. This occurs chiefly as follows: the most external layer, *a*, and one lying deeper, *i*, attain considerable solidity, while the layer *g* situated between them becomes transformed into a soft deliquescent jelly. The portion of tissue

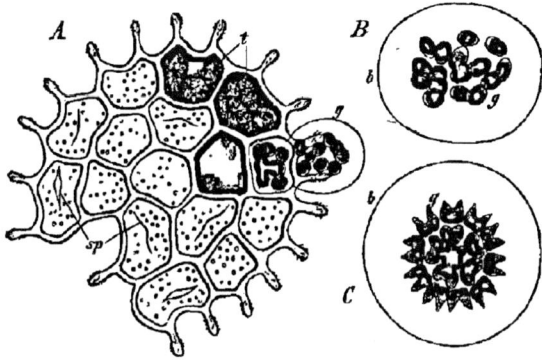

F:G 265.—*Pediastrum granulotum*, after A Braun (400)   *A* a disc consisting of cells which have grown together At *g* the innermost membrane of a cell is just emerging   it contains the daughter cells produced by the division of the green protoplasm, *t* various stages of division of the cells, *sp* slits in the walls of cells already emptied   *B* the entirely emerged inner lamella of the wall of the mother cell (*b*) much swollen and containing the daughter-cells *g*, which are actively swarming   *C* the same cell-family 4½ hours after emission, and 4 hours after the coming to rest of the small cells—these have arranged themselves into a disc which is already beginning to develope into one like *A*

marked *st* forms a hollow cylinder, the apex of which (*x*) is in connection with the firm membrane *t*: in its interior, *h*, is a hollow cavity. The mass marked *sp* consists of the spores or reproductive cells of the Fungus. When this complicated differentiation of tissue (reminding one of the formation of certain berry-like or plum-like fruits of Phanerogams) is completed, a final act of growth suddenly takes place in damp weather. The stalk *st* now becomes extended in a few hours to a length of 20–30 cm., its diameter being 3–4 cm. · by this the membrane *a* is ruptured at the apex, while the membrane *t*, together with the mass of spores *sp*, remain pendent from the top of the elongated stalk, and the base of the latter is surrounded by the ruptured layers *a*, *g* and *n*, much as if by a broken egg-shell. The deviations from the normal type of growth prevailing in the vegetable kingdom go still further in some other Gastromycetes, as in the genera *Clathrus*, *Geaster*, and *Crucibulum* (cf. Fig. 162)

But even in the Algæ, the majority of which follow the type of growth previously described, various families are found with very considerable deviations from it. In the lectures on Organography, I have already referred in detail to the genus *Laminaria*, belonging to the subdivision Phæosporeæ. In *Laminaria*, the intercalary growing-point of the shoot adds to the length of the shoot-axis downwards, producing each year a new frond, on the contrary, upwards, the new frond is thus interposed between the old frond and the intercalary growing-point.

Referring to p. 70 for further details, I may now make a few remarks on the Algæ in the subdivisions Hydrodictyeæ and Volvocineæ, where a totally different arrangement in space of the embryonic and later stages of growth takes place, though even here the sequence with respect to time is still maintained. One of the simplest examples in this connection is afforded by *Pediastrum*, a plant common in our waters and the development of which is illustrated in Fig 265. The mature plant *A* consists of a flat disc, the cells of which are arranged in concentric circles. In the process of reproduction the contents of the cells break up into a large number of small cells, which, enveloped in a vesicle (*B*), escape into the water and there swarm for some time with a trembling movement The young cells, which taken all together have to be regarded as the embryonic condition of a new plant, then arrange themselves spontaneously in the form of a disc, made up of concentric circles, and as soon as this has taken place, as in *C*, they all begin to grow, and the very young plant is now in the stage of elongation Some little time before the end of this phase, however, the third phase of growth—the completion of development of the cell-contents and cell-walls—commences. until the stage *A* is again reached

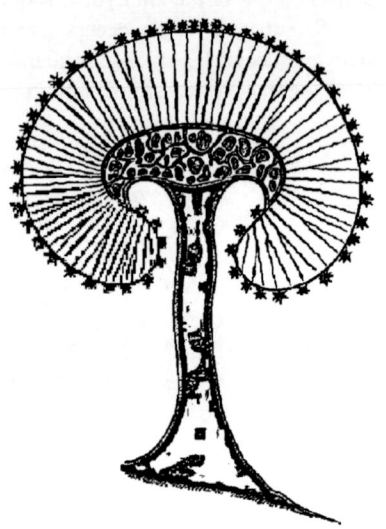

FIG. 266.—*Didymium serpoceum* (a Myxomycete) in fructification only the solid network produced from the plasmodium is represented (after Rostafiaski)

Furthest removed from all other modes of growth is that of the Myxomycetes. These consist, in their first period of life—that in which nutrition occurs—of naked motile masses of protoplasm, creeping forth from the nutritive substratum as a so-called plasmodium Such a plasmodium, according to its specific nature in each case, may assume the most various, and often extraordinarily beautiful forms. Not rarely it developes at last into a stem, situated on the substratum, and passing above into a clavate, spherical, or umbrella-like expansion, as in Fig. 266. So long as this process of construction continues, the entire plant consists of soft protoplasm, and in this condition the Myxomycete may be compared, to a certain extent, with the embryonic condition of a higher plant, although even this comparison fails in some respects. Only when the external form is completed does the outer layer of protoplasm harden to a firm membrane, while its inner portions develope tubular filaments of the most various forms, the so-called capillitium:

the remainder of the protoplasm, that which is capable of true development and which is contained between the capillitium, breaks up into innumerable, minute, rounded portions, which constitute the reproductive cells or spores.   Thus we have here processes of growth where even the last trace of accompanying cell-formation has disappeared.   While in the Cœloblastæ the entire plant, if we wish to extend the comparison to the utmost, may be regarded as a single cell, since it is enveloped by a firm cellulose membrane, this is no longer possible in the case of the Myxomycetes, although, as we have seen, they develope definite forms and grow.   In this case, an extremely simple form of cell development appears only when the growth is concluded ; this, however, has nothing more to do with the growth itself

It is important to refer to this point, since for a long time the utterly mistaken view was held, that the whole configuration and increase in volume of a plant may be explained from the life of its individual cells.   Such is evidently not the case: just as the growth of the whole plant and of one of its entire organs, so also that of its individual cells results from general laws of configuration, which dominate organic quite in the same way as inorganic material.

LECTURE XXVII.

RELATIONS BETWEEN GROWTH AND CELL-DIVISION IN THE ·EMBRYONIC TISSUES

GROWTH—i.e the increase in volume and change of form—may take place in plants even without accompanying cell-divisions. In this connection, I have already repeatedly referred to the non-cellular plants, such as *Botrydium, Caulerpa, Vaucheria*, etc., and particularly to the Myxomycetes. It is important to bear this fact in mind ; because it proves that the formation of cells is a phenomenon subordinate to, and independent of, growth The excessive importance for organic life hitherto ascribed to cell-formation found expression in this direction also, in that it was believed that growth depended upon the formation of cells. This is, however, not the case. On the other hand, however, the fact is of course important, that while a few hundred simple forms of plants exist in which growth is not accompanied by cell-division, in all other plants growth and cell-division are intimately connected with one another. In attempting, then, to make clear the relations of the two processes—growth and cell-division—it is above all to be insisted upon that growth is the primary, and cell-division the secondary and independent phenomenon.

The following is an epitome of a detailed investigation of the matter which I published in 1878–79[1] The matter here depends upon geometrical, and in part

---

[1] We owe the first investigations which laid the foundations as to the relations between growth and cell-division, as so much of the best of our literature, to Naegeli's ingenious researches ; he started with a series of treatises on this subject in his '*Zeitschrift für wissenschaftliche Botanik*,' published with Schleiden, in 1844–1846, a literature consolidated by numerous observers in still more numerous treatises All Naegeli's successors, however, held exactly to the scheme established by him, according to which also Schwendener, with Naegeli's co-operation, further represented the relations between growth and cell-division in their book '*Das Mikroskop*,' II. Aufl. 1877, pp 544, &c

I established the point of view explained in my lecture, and which has given an entirely different turn to the ideas concerning this subject, in my treatises, '*Über die Anordnung der Zellen in juugsten Pflanzentheilen*' (Arb des bot Inst in Wzbg B II, H. 1, 1878) and '*Über Zellenanordnung und Wachsthum*' (ibid H 2, 1879)

In the first-named treatise I sought to give precision to my view as to the processes of growth in growing-points and other embryonic masses of tissue by stating (p 52), 'If we abstract from the so-called individuality of the cell, and pay attention only to the course of the layers which cross one another in three directions, we obtain a structure which may be compared with the internal structure of a much thickened cell-wall The three systems of layers in the growing-point correspond to the system of concentric layers and the two systems of so-called striation of the cell-wall, as they have been described by Naegeli. Stratification and striation of the cell-wall, as is known, depend on a regular alternation of denser and less dense substance in three directions, which cut one another, as

purely mechanical, considerations, which can only be rendered quite clear by very careful thinking; since, however, I have set myself the task in these lectures of only expounding what is immediately capable of comprehension, I must confine myself to making clear a series of the most elementary and easily intelligible facts.

Above all, it is important to point out that, apart from a few exceptions, the directions in which the new cell-walls of a growing plant-organ appear, depend upon the internal distribution of growth as well as upon the external form of the growing organ the direction of any newly formed division-wall whatever is determined in advance by these factors. Sections through growing, and especially through young parts of the plant, always show arrangements of the cells which are quite definite, and in the highest degree characteristic; the directions of the cell-divisions are by no means accidental, and an observer sufficiently acquainted with geometrical and mechanical science at once recognises in the structures presented by the totality of cell-walls within an organ, cut in the proper manner, that we have here to do with a conformity to law, the true meaning of which, however, is difficult to decipher. It will be well, therefore, in the first place to illustrate the dependence between growth and cell-division by a few examples of the simplest kind.

The simplest case is presented by thin, filamentous organs, which consist of a single row of cells, as in the case of many Algæ and in the hyphæ of Fungi. As a rule, the cell-walls here occur as transverse septa of the filament—i.e. each new division-wall cuts the long axis and the circumference of the filament at right angles. Nevertheless a few exceptions are found even here. In the root-filaments of the true Mosses, as well as of the Characeæ, the transverse septa are oblique to the long axis, for which in the meantime no satisfactory explanation can be given. However, in contrast to the enormously large number of cases in which cell-filaments are divided by transverse walls cutting at right angles, these are but rare exceptions.

When we take into consideration the growth and cell-division of isolated cells the volume of which becomes enlarged in all directions, the problem is a more complicated one. We meet with such, for instance, in a large number of simple Algæ,

---

Naegeli aptly remarks, like the three cleavage planes of a crystal By means of stratification and striation the substance of a cell-wall is cut up into polyhedral areolæ, so that the three systems of densest layers form a network, in the meshes of which the less dense areolæ (containing most water) are enclosed The substance of a thick cell-wall is built up like the primary meristem of a growing-point The cell-walls mutually cutting in three directions correspond to the densest lamellæ of a thick cell-wall, and the protoplasmic bodies of the cells of the primary meristem to the soft areolæ I will not here follow this comparison (which is without constraint) further, but only remark that it becomes the more apt the smaller the cells of the primary meristem are.'

Two years after this statement of mine a treatise by Schwendener appeared, ' *Über die durch Wachsthum bedingte Verschiebung kleinster Theilchen in trajektorischen Curven*' (Monatsber. der kgl Akad d Wiss, zu Berlin, 1880), where he entirely adopts the new points of view which I had opened out, only that (p 426) he believes that he finds an important difference between his own view and mine He says, ' According to my (Schwendener's) view the cell-divisions constitute an independent phenomenon—and the formation of series of trajectories is everywhere ruled by the same mechanical principles which condition the direction of the rows of micellæ in starch-grains and thick cell-walls,' &c

I consider that the quotation from my treatise, which had appeared two years previously, differs from Schwendener's view just cited only in so far that it puts exactly the same ideas more in detail and more clearly, and at the same time directly contradicts Schwendener's older views (1877) on the relation of growth and cell-division

the individual cells of which grow independently after each division ; as in the genera *Chlorococcus, Merismopedia, Tetraspora, Glæocapsa,* and many others.   In more highly developed plants similar processes take place in the mother-cells of spores and pollen grains.   In these cases the fact is particularly clear, that the mode in which the cell-divisions follow one another depends by no means on the physiological or morphological nature of the cells, but upon their mode of growth and external form—especially upon the latter.   Fig. 267, for example, shows six different forms of cell-division in the pollen mother-cells of one and the same plant, the Orchid *Neottia nidus-avis.*   In *A* the pollen mother-cell had approximately the form of a circular disc, which, by means of two divisions at right angles to one another, is cut up into four quadrants.   It is to be noticed, however, that the two vertical division-walls in Fig. *A* do not exactly meet one another, so that a small piece of the horizontal division-wall remains intercalated between the points where they join it . this intercalated piece of the previous division-wall appears like a breaking of it, and we meet with such interruptions of the walls very generally

in the division of tissue-cells, a point on which I lay some stress, because in the more complex cases of tissue-formation they interfere with the otherwise easily recognisable regularity of the network of cell-walls.

   The pollen mother-cell *C* had grown more vigorously in one direction, and had become long and elliptical before its divisions.   Accordingly, in the first place two transverse walls were formed at right angles to the long axis of the cell, so that they divided the latter into three approximately equal parts : the middle one of these cells has again been divided, however, by a longitudinal wall.   Here again, therefore,

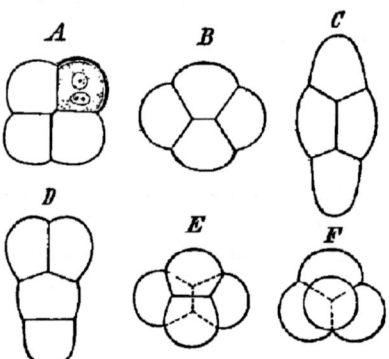

FIG 267 —Differently shaped and therefore differently divided pollen mother-cells from one and the same anther of *Neottia nidus-avis* (after Goebel)

four daughter-cells have been produced by division of the pollen mother-cell, but, as is seen, in an order different from that in *A*, corresponding to the elongated form which the mother-cell had assumed before the division.   Whether the form of division represented in Fig. *B* was developed from the type *A* or *C* cannot well be decided ; but in *B* as well as in *C* we perceive how the primitively straight or slightly curved walls appear broken after the joining on of a younger wall, somewhat like stretched threads strung together by another thread.   The division-walls which meet one another correspond with their three angles to a so-called string-polygon, as also is usually the case in a multicellular tissue.

   The dependence of the directions of division upon the external form of the mother-cell is manifested again in another way in Fig *D*.   Here the mother-cell consisted of a sort of cylindrical stalk with a little spherical head accordingly, two walls have arisen in the stalk-like portion cutting the external wall at right angles ; in the hemispherical head, however, the wall is longitudinal.   In Fig. *E*, the mother-cell was approximately globular before the division : it is bisected into two hemispheres by a division wall. Of these, the one has become elongated in a vertical, and the other in a horizontal direction · each of the two halves, however, is divided by a cross-wall produced at right angles to the long axis of the secondary cell, and thus have arisen two pairs of cells in a crossed position. The mother-cell *F* was probably more completely spherical than the previous one, and, accordingly

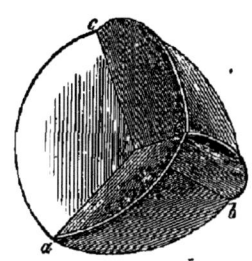

FIG. 268.—The six division walls of a spherical cell divided tetrahedrally

also, the form of division is different. The mother-cell has here become divided in a tetrahedral manner, as we are accustomed to say—i e. six division-walls have been produced *simultaneously*, in such a way that the spherical mother-cell has become cut up into four daughter-cells, each of which would resemble a tetrahedron if the outer wall were plane instead of arched outwards. The position of these division walls is illustrated in Fig. 268, and it may be recognised at once, that in this case

the six walls simultaneously produced do not cut one another at right angles. It may be shown, however, that this case can be brought with that of the ordinary rectangular cutting of the succeeding division-walls under a common general expression

In all these various cases of the division of a mother-cell, the rule, also common elsewhere, makes itself evident, that the daughter-cells which arise simultaneously are equal in volume to one another—i.e. the division consists in a halving of the mass of the mother-cell   This rule also of course suffers various exceptions in

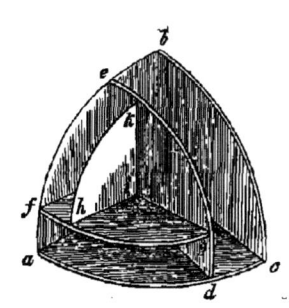

FIG. 269.—Diagram of a tetrahedral apical cell *a b c* as met with in Equisetum and elsewhere, seen from above   *d e f g, h k*, the walls of three successive divisions , *s* the corner where the three walls cut one another like the sides of a cube

particular cases · otherwise, however, it is so comprehensive that it may always be laid down as the ordinary case.

As the general rules of successive cell-division in growing organs, therefore, we can already state (1) that the daughter-cells are usually equal to one another in volume, and (2) that the new cell-walls are situated at right angles to those already present.

· Simple though these two rules may appear, it is nevertheless difficult to prove their validity in many instances, according to the form of the mother-cell in each case. For example, when the dividing-cell has the form illustrated in Fig. 269—i.e. the shape of a tetrahedron with curved surfaces—and if the successive divisions in it halve the volume each time, and in doing so stand at right angles on the preceding walls, a structure is obtained like that shown in the figure, from which the existence of the relations above mentioned can only be determined by careful geometrical considerations.

That the mode of cell-division depends only upon the increase in volume and the configuration of a growing organ, and not upon its morphological or physiological significance, is one of the most general and important facts to which I have referred in my treatises already quoted   It was formerly supposed to be possible to characterise the true morphological or phylogenetic nature of an organ by the way in which its cell-divisions took place, and hundreds of treatises and laboriously drawn plates were devoted to this purpose.   In the exposition which follows, I shall have plenty of opportunities of showing how erroneous this assumption is.   Meanwhile, however, I will refer to a particularly clear case (Fig. 270).   It is at once obvious that Figs. *C* and *D* exhibit essentially the same laws of cell-division. in both cases we have a stalked capitulum, with transverse divisions in the stalk, and in the head itself transverse and longitudinal divisions which cut one another at right angles.   But *C* is a glandular hair of the Gourd plant, and *D* a very common form of the embryo of a Phanerogam.   In Fig. *A* also we at once recognise the type of cell-division represented in *C* and *D*, in accordance with the outline of the simple organ ; but here the stalk remains undivided, having only formed the cell marked *h* (*Hypophysis*)   Above this the capitulum becomes divided into sectors, which, as shown in *B*, grow in breadth, and so give to the whole glandular hair the form of a mushroom.   The comparison of the most various organs of the most different nature would only afford further examples of what has been stated above —that the form of the cell-division depends entirely upon the growth and outward form (especially the latter), and not upon its physiological and morphological significance.

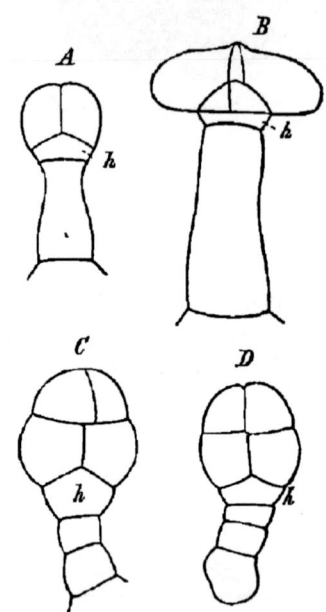

FIG. 270.—*A, B* hairs of different ages from the leaf of *Pinguicula vulgaris C* hair of *Cucurbita*, *D* embryo of *Nicotiana* (tobacco), *h* the so-called Hypophysis.

Among the most instructive relations between cell-division and growth I count also the fact that the cell-division need not take place during growth itself, but may appear only after its conclusion.   In this connection, a particularly clear case has been established by Geyler in the shoots of *Stypocaulon,* one of the Algæ belonging to the Phæosporeæ (Fig. 271).   The whole of the apical region of such a shoot, marked *s* and *z*, as well as the region of the lateral shoots marked *x* and *y*, corresponds not only to the growing-point of an ordinary cellular shoot, but also to the portion which is elongating.   Only the parts which have grown to their full extent, and marked I, II, etc, become gradually converted by division-walls into smaller and smaller cells, as shown in Fig. 271 ; and Geyler has established that in the course of these cell-divisions no more growth takes place.   We have therefore, in this case, at the upper end of the shoot growth without cell-divisions, and in the older portions of the shoot cell-divisions without growth.

On regarding a transverse section of an organ properly taken in accordance with its relations of symmetry, a characteristic pattern is as a rule presented. The individual cells lie by no means without order among themselves, but exhibit definite groupings and arrangements of the most various kinds, and, on a little reflection, certain arrangements are always visible, which are repeated even in the most different organs. It is beyond all doubt that these net-works of cells, as the pattern presented to the observer may most simply be termed, are an immediate expression of the processes of growth prevailing in the parts of the plant concerned;

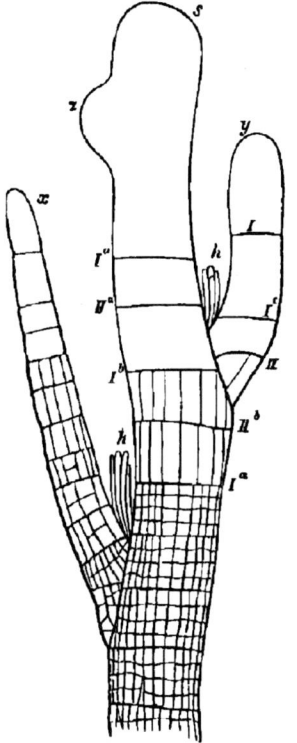

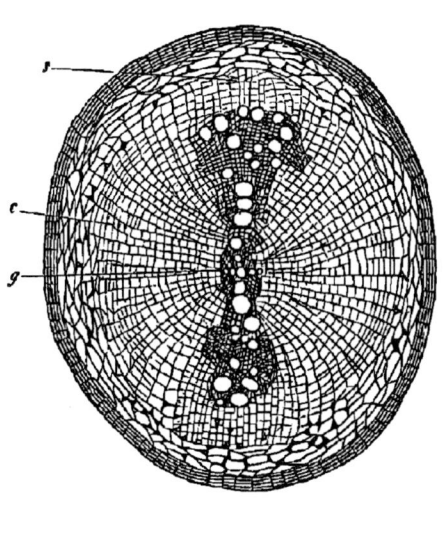

FIG 271 —A branch of *Stypocaulon scoparium* with two smaller branches *x* and *y*, and the rudiment of a third *z* (after Geyler). All the lines indicate cell-walls

FIG 272.—Transverse section of a root of the Nettle (*Urtica*) *g* the group (horizontal in the figure) of five vessels which existed at a very early stage, the other vessels and lignified cells form a double group (vertical in the figure) *c* cambium from which the latter and the radially arranged tissue have arisen Externally is a layer of cork, beneath which lies a layer of irregular tissue displaced by the growth in thickness (after De Bary)

and this in a manner exactly similar to what was explained previously by a few very simple examples, only that in organs which are composed of very numerous cells the relation between growth and the arrangement of the cells may often be not so easy to discover.

For the preliminary guidance of the reader the following three statements may here be made in the first place.

(1) The form of the pattern presented by a network of cells depends chiefly upon whether, after the successive cell-divisions, vigorous growth of single cells or

groups or layers of cells (it may be with subsequent cell-divisions) takes place. In this case individual cells or groups or layers of cells may grow differently, their volume and form altering in a different way from the remainder, and in this case the one must necessarily have a definite effect on the other: mechanical influences of single cells or groups on those surrounding them, must take place; tensions and pressures must make themselves felt, and only an exact investigation and consideration of the prevailing circumstances can give information as to what mechanical processes have co-operated in influencing the arrangement of the cells in the organ. We meet with this case wherever we are concerned with the external and internal development, and therefore the later phases of growth of the organs[1].

(2) The processes are otherwise so long as an organ is still entirely in the embryonic condition. In this case experience teaches that the entire mass of embryonic tissue grows as a whole[2], that definite geometrical and mechanical relations exist between the whole arrangement of cells and the outward form of the growing organ. Only when the tissue passes from the embryonic condition into the second phase of growth, does the grouping and differentiation in the interior of the organ mentioned under (1) begin, and at the same time the pattern of the cell arrangement becomes essentially different.

(3) The fact that organs of like external form may nevertheless present quite different patterns of cell net-works in their interior, causes peculiar difficulties in the understanding of these processes. In other words, the distribution of the processes of growth in the interior of organs which possess like external form may be very different.

In our further considerations we will confine ourselves, in the first place, to the relations presented in the embryonic tissue, and further, to such cases where the arrangement of the cells of the embryonic tissue are no longer essentially altered by subsequent processes of growth, as the latter occurs especially in the development of the woody mass from the cambium, and in the growth of various plants of simple organisation.

Fig. 273 represents the view from above of a flat extended Alga (*Melobesia*), and for the sake of simplicity we may assume that the entire body of the Alga consists of a simple layer of cells only (which, as a matter of fact, however, is not the case). It is easily recognised that the portion of the disc, expanded to a certain extent like a fan, has been produced by a further growth outwards having taken place on the one side of the primitively elliptical germinal disc. The cell-network in this case comes into existence by the flat extended plant-substance having become divided into small areolæ—i.e. cells—by two systems of lines, which correspond to the cell-walls. Of these systems of lines, or directions of cell-walls, the one series radiate in a fan-like manner towards the periphery of the body of the plant, which

---

[1] I shall refer to this point more in detail in Lecture XXXIII

[2] Cf note 1, p 431. With reference to a statement of Pfeffer in his '*Pflanzen-physiologie,*' II pp 97, 98, I need only remark that my quoted treatise '*Über Zellenanordnung und Wachsthum*' was only possible from my regarding the cell-wall network as a necessary consequence of '*Wachsthumsbewegung,*' this had not been done before, apart from Hofmeister, with reference to whose view I have remarked all that is necessary.

they cut more or less exactly at right angles, and as they become further distant from one another in this course towards the margin new lines of cell-walls are continually being intercalated between them. The fan-shaped structure thus produced is shown particularly clearly on the right side of the figure; and it is noticed that the very various curvings of the radiating fan-like walls stand in definite relation to the curving of the line bounding the circumference which is, as a rule, cut by them at right angles.

Besides this, however, the figure shows, especially on the left side, a larger number of lines—i.e. cell-walls—which run parallel with the periphery, or, to put the fact better, conformably with it, and in the main these lines cut the previous system of fan-like walls at right angles. Geometrically expressed, the two systems of lines which divide up the surface of the body of the Alga into areolæ or cells of nearly equal size are orthogonal trajectories. The regular pattern of this cellular structure comes into existence essentially from the fact that only the cells at the

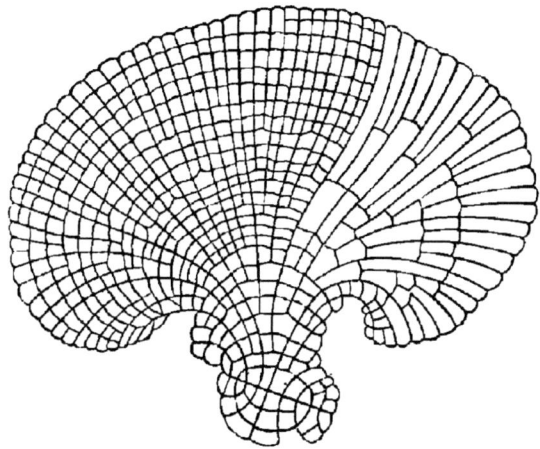

FIG. 273.—*Melobesia Lejolisii* (an Alga of the subdivision Florideæ) seen from the upper surface (after Rosanoff).

external margin of the surface grow radially outwards, and become divided now and then in the tangential direction. Cell-divisions thus take place only at the margin, and the cells further distant from it grow no more, either in the radial or in the tangential direction. Were the latter the case, the cell-network could only maintain its form by a perfectly equal distribution of the growth: in every other case, however, it must be altered.

Attention may here be drawn by the way to the further fact that the fan-like radiating walls have all been drawn, even on the right side of the figure, though in this portion the majority of the walls running tangentially have been omitted. It is seen that in this way there arises a cell-network different from that on the left side; though the difference only depends on a minor point, viz. that the tangential division-walls exist in smaller numbers than on the left side, and we could easily quote examples of other Algæ in which the whole cell-network resembles that represented on the right side of the figure. In such a case, however, the body of the plant gives the impression of having been produced from dichotomously branched cell filaments, whereas this subjective impression is not produced by the left side of the figure—unless by peculiar modes of thinking.

From reasons which will become clear in the further course of the exposition, I distinguish all those cell-walls, or directions of cell-walls, which run conformably with the circumference of the part of the plant under consideration, as *Periclines*, in contrast to the *Anticlines* which are directed towards the circumference, or actually cut it, and these terms are now introduced generally into botanical phraseology. The periclines of our figure are therefore, according to what has been said above, usually orthogonal trajectories of the anticlines.

Without too great theoretical difficulties, now, we may suppose the above figure to be the transverse section of an irregularly grown woody body. In this case the rows of cells lying at the margin, and alone bringing about the growth in surface, would correspond to the wood-cambium. The cells proceeding from the peripheral layer would then be developed as wood-cells As in the case of the Alga, so also the wood-cells exhibit no growth to speak of when they pass over from the cambial or embryonic condition into their definitive form: the arrangement of the cells produced by the growth and cell-division in the cambium likewise undergoes, therefore, essentially no alteration. The processes of cell-formation in the cambium of wood, so far at least as the transverse section is concerned, are made evident, however, not merely in the individual cells, but also in quite the same sense in the annual rings of the wood and in the medullary rays or 'silver grain' which

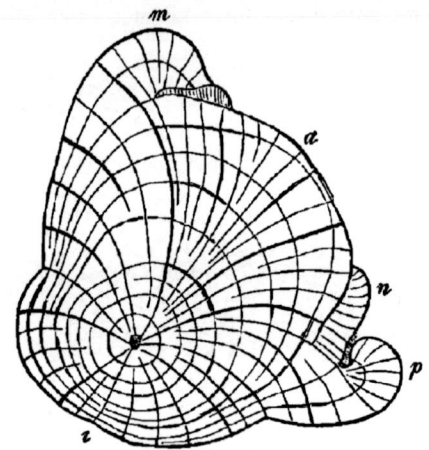

FIG. 274.—Transverse section of the wood of a cherry stem (*Prunus cerasifera*) which had been deprived of its cortex on the side *a* two years previously whence prominences had been produced at *m n p* The thick radial lines are fissures produced by the drying of the wood their course follows the same law as the medullary rays represented by thin lines

traverse them. The annual rings appear here as periclinal layers of the mass of wood, the medullary rays as anticlinal lines of cells representing the orthogonal trajectories of them. If, as is the case with the inner annual rings in Fig. 274, the mass of wood is nearly circular in transverse section, the annual rings, if of equal thickness all round, form concentric circles, and the medullary rays then appear as radial lines, since they cut these circles at right angles The figure shows, however, how the woody body has grown continually more irregular with increasing age: the annual rings (periclines) having grown much more in thickness towards the side *a*, than on the side *i*. Finally, by a wound, the formation of wood had ceased at *a*, while it proceeded only so much the more vigorously at the margins of the wound *m, n, p*. In accordance with the course of the periclinal layers of wood thus produced, the medullary rays directed as anticlines have also now assumed other directions, so that they everywhere cut the annual rings or periclines at right angles. The peculiar and very various curvatures

of the medullary rays are simply nothing further than the expression of the general
rule that the anticlinal cell-walls are the orthogonal trajectories of the periclines.
Supported by this general rule it is also possible in any given transverse section of
wood, the annual rings of which are known, to register at once the course of the
medullary rays; or, when the latter are more distinctly recognisable than the
annual rings, to make out the converse.

In these cases we have had to do with processes of growth where increase
in volume takes place in an easily intelligible manner only at the margin or
circumference, the cells there formed, however, undergoing no further growth worth
mention, although they pass over into the definitive condition of permanent tissue,
in which the second phase of growth—i. e elongation—is suppressed.

We will now, however, turn our attention to those cases, at first of the simpler kind,
where an organ consisting entirely of embryonic tissue grows throughout its entire
mass; where increase in volume
takes place not merely at the circumference but also in the interior,
and accordingly division-walls appear also in the interior. For
the facilitation of the problem
we will even here only concern
ourselves with transverse and longitudinal sections, or structures
naturally flat, because the consideration of proper stereometric
relations would not only cause
great prolixity, but can also be
dispensed with in the meantime
for our purpose. The simplest
case is of course presented by
flat organs which consist of a
single layer of cells only.

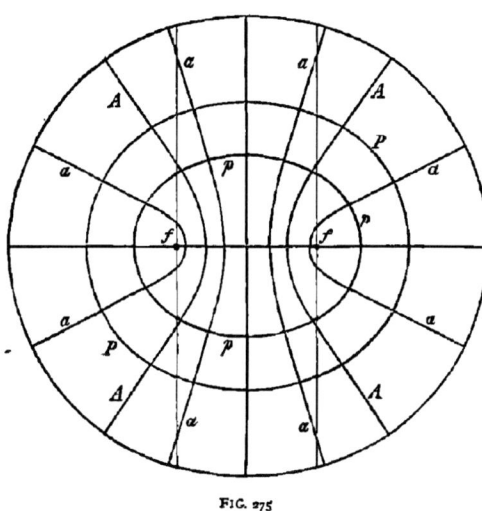

FIG. 275

Our further considerations will gain in clearness, and will be much facilitated
if we construct for ourselves on paper in advance various possible cases. It is
already clear from what has been said so far that the ordinary case consists in the
rectangular intersection of the periclines and anticlines. We may thus, for example,
imagine an elliptical disc (Fig. 275) consisting of embryonic substance, and propose
to ourselves the question, In what direction are the division-walls formed in it,
if the growing surface (which always remains elliptical) is cut up into a large
number of cells by periclinal and anticlinal division-walls intersecting at right
angles? Now the problem is solved according to geometrical principles in the
elliptical figure given. In the first place, the area is divided into four quadrants by the
major and minor axes of the ellipse, and the two foci are marked *f f*. As periclines,
two other ellipses, *P* and *p*, are drawn, possessing the peculiarity that their foci are
likewise situated in *f f*; or, in other words, the three ellipses drawn are confocal.
Instead of three we might draw a large number of confocal ellipses. In order
that the anticlines to be drawn in the figure everywhere cut the periclinal ellipses at

right angles, they must represent hyperbolas, and in such a way that around each of the two foci *ff* a larger or smaller number of hyperbolas run, the axes of which coincide at the same time with the major axis of the confocal ellipses : or, in other words, the anticlines *A* and *a* are confocal hyperbolas In each case, according as we wish to have large or small cells in the disc, the number of confocal ellipses and hyperbolas may be increased. It is noticed—to remark it by the way—that those hyperbolas the apices of which lie nearest to the foci *ff* there make a strong curve : on the contrary, the apical curvature of the hyperbolas is so much the smaller the further they are distant from the foci *ff*, and the nearer they approach the minor axis of the ellipse If we further suppose the whole figure so altered that the two axes become equal to one another, then the two foci *ff* coincide in one focus, the confocal ellipses

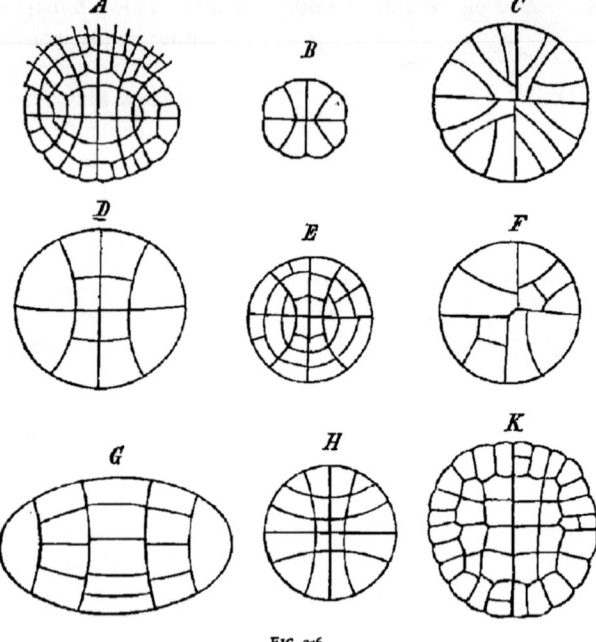

FIG. 276

become converted into concentric circles, and the hyperbolas *A* and *a* then appear as straight lines which run from the centre to the periphery, and are thus radii of the circle.

We have thus, by means of our geometrical construction, obtained a general scheme for the way in which the cells must approximately be arranged in the supposed disc, if we divide it up into cells by periclinal and anticlinal partition-walls cutting one another at right angles . it will scarcely be necessary to say that the quadrangular portions of surface, or areolæ, between the anticlines and periclines represent the cell-cavities.

Having, then, closely impressed on the mind this scheme, the geometrical significance of which is readily understood, we find everywhere in such flat objects the cells arranged in patterns which obviously accord with our scheme. In order to demonstrate the validity of this construction on only a few examples taken quite at random, we may consider Fig. 276. In this case A represents the approximately elliptical germinal disc of the Alga (*Melobesia*) which we have already considered above. We at once recognise the walls corresponding to the major and minor axes of the ellipse, by means of which the originally unicellular embryo-plant is cut up into four quadrants: moreover, in spite of a few disturbing interruptions in the walls, two confocal ellipses are recognised as periclines and two hyperbolas on either side as anticlines. At the circumference of this disc we of course notice cell-walls which are not continued inwards; if, however, they were completed inwards, they too would form hyperbolas. I may take this opportunity of pointing out that in an object which is in other respects constructed according to our scheme, individual portions both of the periclinal and anticlinal lines may nevertheless be wanting, because the corresponding cell-divisions have been suppressed. the scheme only implies that when cell-walls do arise they must lie in the directions given. That the scheme holds good for the most various cases, is at once shown on regarding Fig. 276, D, which represents a transverse section through the slender growing-point of *Salvinia*, and G, which represents the transverse section of the vein of a young leaf of a Fern (*Trichomanes*)

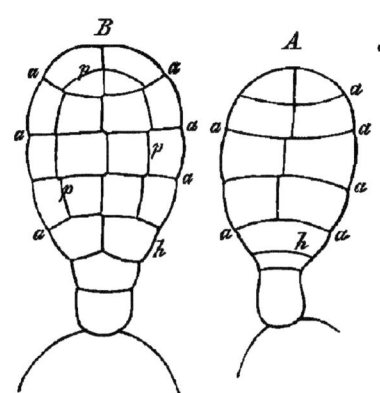

FIG 277 —*A* a young, *B* an older embryo of *Alisma plantago a a* the anticlines, *p p* the periclines

When the elliptical circumference approaches the circular form, or actually becomes a circle, as in the Figures C, E, F, H, K, here also two anticlinal walls (in this case radial walls) are the first to appear, by means of which the disc is divided into equal quadrants. If further cell-divisions now follow inside the quadrants, it would at once contradict the law of rectangular intersection if these new walls were to run from the centre to the periphery; since these anticlines (radii) would then meet in the centre of the disc at very acute angles. This never occurs: on the contrary, all such objects show that the anticlines running inwards from the circumference make a curve in order to abut laterally on one of the preceding walls of the quadrants, though the direction in which these curved anticlines run may be different in each quadrant.

While, in the construction of the foregoing scheme, I started from a geometrical form with perfectly defined outline—i. e. an ellipse—it was thereby implied, if the anticlines and periclines cut at right angles, that the periclines must be confocal ellipses and the anticlines confocal hyperbolas. It would, of course, be impossible to produce with the same exactness geometrical constructions for every kind of outline which an embryonic organ can show; but it is at once clear that even when the outline is not actually an ellipse, but only more or less resembles one, the entire cell-network must nevertheless present a pattern similar to the one which there exists, if the anticlines and periclines cut one another at right angles. For example, in Fig. 277

A B the resemblance to our scheme is again perceived at once, although the outlines can hardly pass as ellipses. Besides, we have here the case that the organ which we are considering as cut up into cells simultaneously with growth is provided on the one side with a stalk. In such cases a hypophysis (*h*) regularly makes its appearance at the boundary between stalk and head. Hanstein formerly held this to be an organ peculiar to the embryos of Phanerogams : it is, however, nothing further than the expression of the general law of cell-division for the case here given.

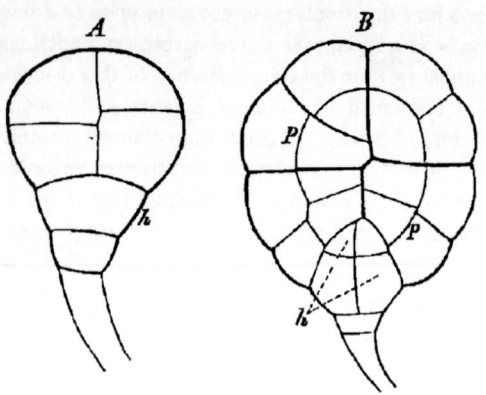

FIG. 278.—*A* a very young, *B* an older embryo of *Orobanche* (after Koch)

In these figures we meet with yet another fact of experience, in that the sequence in time in the origin of the anticline and pericline walls, even in very similar objects, is variable in a high degree. Sometimes, as in Fig. 277 *A*, numerous anticlines are produced, the periclines (*p* in *B*) only following subsequently ; or periclines arise followed at once by the anticlines, as in Fig. 278 *B*. But even this in no way alters the validity of the scheme described above, in the construction of which it is of course immaterial whether the anticlines or the periclines are drawn first.

As a rule, the external form of very young organs which still consist of embryonic substance changes as they gradually develope. Hence the case occurs, not rarely that walls which have already been produced undergo displacements and curvatures during the alteration in form of the entire structure, in such a manner that they now become adapted to the new form of the organ as if they had only been produced after its attainment. Since this case, hitherto little noticed, is of peculiar importance for the theory of growth, because it throws new light on the intercalations and movements taking place in the embryonic

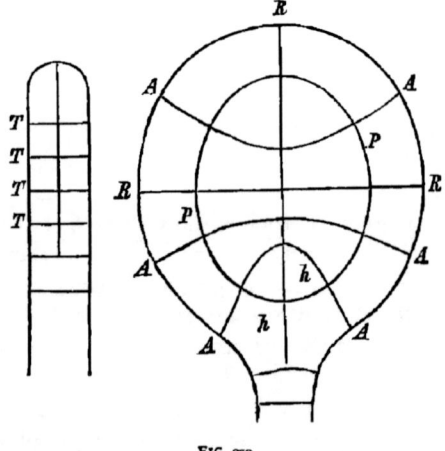

FIG 279

mass of tissue, I may here adduce an illustrative scheme and an example. In Fig. 279 to the left is represented a filamentous structure, which is divided by several transverse walls *TT* and by one series of longitudinal walls. The figure on the right shows us the same structure after the filament has become transformed into a stalked elliptical disc : one of the preceding transverse walls T is still present as a straight transverse wall RR, and the series of longitudinal walls referred to above also still exists as a straight longitudinal wall in the direction of the major axis of the ellipse. In accordance with the mode of growth mentioned, however, the other walls previously marked T have now become converted into hyperbolically curved anticlines A. This figure is only constructed hypothetically, and agrees with the requirement that a filament consisting of two longitudinal rows of cells shall become converted into a stalked ellipse, under such conditions that the walls still cut one another at right angles.

In Fig. 280, which represents the development of a gemma of *Marchantia,* there will be perceived at once, in Figs. *I–IV,* alterations of the cell-network which agree in all essential points with the processes illustrated in the diagram (Fig. 279).

On the other hand, however, it also happens that networks of cell-walls undergo

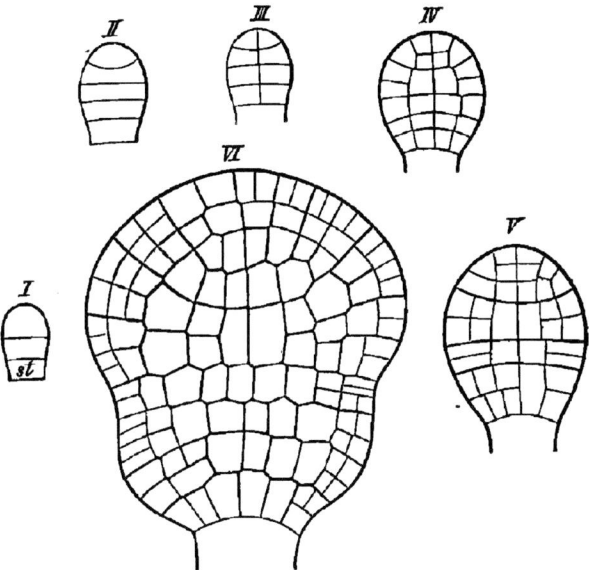

FIG. 280. Development of the gemma of *Marchantia.*

displacements by growth, of such a kind that the usually rectangular cutting of the anticlines and periclines passes over into one more or less oblique. This is occasionally the case in growing-points, the growth of which we shall only consider later on. It is to be recognised more easily and frequently, however, on transverse sections of woody bodies with excentric layers. This process also may be made clear most easily by means of a hypothetical construction. In Fig. 281 I have assumed that a mass of wood which is circular in transverse section possesses a pith situated very excentrically. The first ring of wood, I, is equally thick all round; but all the succeeding annual rings, *II–VII,* have grown much thicker on the north side (N) than on the south side (S). In order to simplify the construction it is assumed that the circumference of each annual ring is nevertheless circular. The scheme may be so imagined that the points 2, 3—7 on the line NS are the centres of the six annual rings following one another   Now if the medullary rays were exact orthogonal trajectories of the annual rings, as is the case where the growth of the wood is regular, they must cut the circumference of the disc of wood at the points *r r*. But all the medullary rays, on the contrary, are curved towards the point *N*, and therefore away from *S*, or, in other words, they are driven over towards the line of strongest growth, which reaches from the pith to *N*. This scheme is intended to illustrate no theory, but only the fact, which is very often to be observed on transverse sections of wood, that the medullary rays are driven towards the side of strongest growth of the wood, and therefore sacrifice their rectangular intersection with the periclines—i.e the annual rings. Fig. 282 represents a particularly clear example in the transverse section of an excentrically grown stem of the Lime. It is easily noticed that the medullary rays *s t* are driven from the right as well as from the left towards *a*, the line of strongest growth.

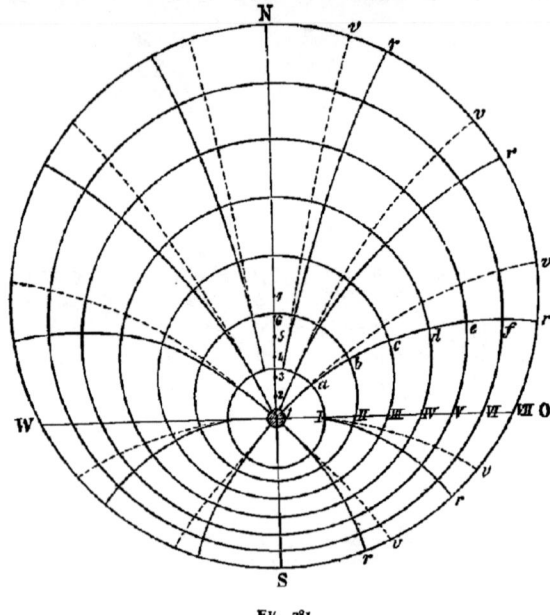

Fig. 281

It is not to be forgotten, however, that we are here concerned with a transverse section of wood, the growth and cell-divisions of which take place exclusively in an outer narrow zone of the periphery, viz. in the cambium, whereas in similar cases in growing-points the entire mass of embryonic tissue with its anticlines and periclines is growing.

We have hitherto regarded the cell-network as a superficies only, and the anticlines and periclines as simple lines. If we give a certain thickness to these flat structures, nothing is essentially altered thereby; what are mere areolæ in the above figures then behave like the stones of a mosaic, and are actual cells. The matter is quite otherwise, however, when we come to look upon the figures hitherto considered as longitudinal or transverse sections of ellipsoidal or spherical bodies, or when the organ possesses any such form as that of a lens, or a compressed ellipsoid, &c.

Our space being limited, however, it must be left to the reader to reflect upon the matters in question. I will only refer to one particular case, since it is common everywhere. When an ellipsoidal, or spherical, or similar body becomes divided, walls

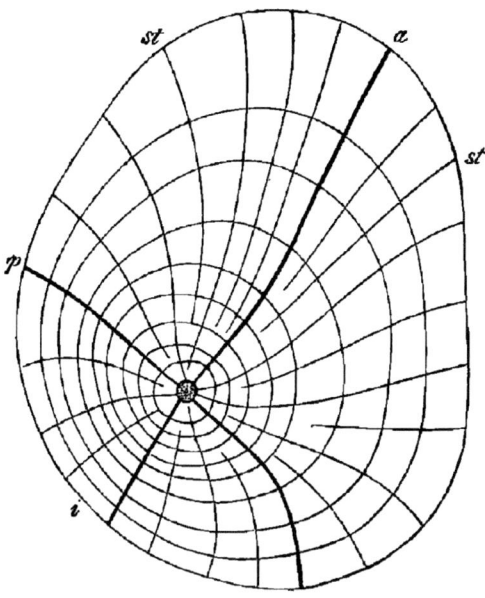

FIG. 282.—Transverse section of the wood of a Lime (*Tilia platyphyllos*) *st* medullary rays, *ap* fissures produced by drying, *i* side of feeblest, *a* that of strongest growth in thickness.

regularly occur in three directions, cutting one another at right angles, in such a manner that the body is first cut by a wall into two usually equal halves, each of which is then bisected by a wall standing at right angles to the first wall, and then a wall at right angles to the first and second cuts the whole into eight octants. In each of these, anticlinal and periclinal cell-walls now appear, so that transverse and longitudinal sections give figures such as we have already considered. Here, as already said, it is of no moment whether we regard the capitulum of a hair, an embryo, an antheridium, or any other organ. For example, Fig. 283 represents a median longitudinal section (of course very diagrammatic) of the embryo of a Fern, produced from the fertilised oosphere. The anticlines and periclines are at once recognised as we constructed them in our scheme for an elliptical disc, particularly in the case of the walls marked *Aa* and *Pp*. In order to obtain an idea of the true state of affairs in this

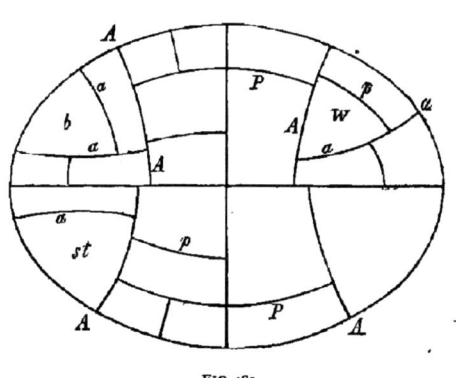

FIG. 283.

case, however, we must suppose the figure to have made a complete revolution round the long axis of the ellipse and thus described an ellipsoid in space. The drawing then represents only a median longitudinal section of this ellipsoid, the entire cellular structure of which would only be perceived when also viewed from above, from below, from behind, and from before. It would then be found, moreover, that the whole ellipsoid is also completely divided by a wall in the plane of the paper, and thus that not merely four quadrants are present, as our figure shows, but eight octants. In each of these octants, again, there has arisen in the first place an anticline, *A*, approximately of the form of a watch-glass, or, since according to our construction the anti-clines A are hyperbolas, each of the walls A would represent a hyperbolic surface in the body of the embryo, and in like manner the periclines P and p would represent portions of ellipsoidal surfaces. The further growth and formation of organs in this embryo then proceeds by means of the cells b, st, and w, which arise in the octants. In the two lower octants to the left, two cells (as st) are formed: these are the so-called apical cells, of which, however, only one is con-cerned with the further growth, and constitutes the apex of the stem of the young Fern. This apical cell of the stem has the form of a tetrahedron (cp. Fig. 269, above) in which, as growth proceeds, new division-walls continually appear parallel to the anticlines. The same happens also in the apical cell of the first root w, where, however, in addition to the anticlinal segmentations parallel with A and a, pericline-walls p are also cut off for the formation of the root-cap. In accordance with the origin there are properly also two such root-rudiments present in the octants situated to the right above, but the actual formation of a root takes place in one of them only. The apical cell b becomes united with the corresponding one of the octant lying next it for the formation of the first leaf of the embryo Fern.

We here become acquainted with a new relation between cell-division and growth. From what has been said it may be observed that certain cells, previously determined by the general law of growth in the embryo, make themselves evident as the points of origin of the new organs of the stem (st), of the root (w), and of the first leaf (b); and with respect to the apical cells st and w which, as stated, possess the form of a tetrahedron, the important fact may here be brought forward that the production of these apical cells is a necessary consequence of the law of cell-division prevailing in the embryo. This observation is of importance, because, until the appearance of my investigation on the arrangement of cells, the causal relation was believed to be an entirely different one. Indeed, people went so far as to regard the fertilised oosphere itself as the first apical cell of the stem, just as, in general, an entirely unwarranted importance had been attributed up to that time to the apical cells which are found in the growing-points of many Cryptogams This will become clearer in the sequel.

The subject of the relation between growth and cell-division in the growing-points of shoots and roots is more difficult than in the cases considered hitherto, but even here I have succeeded in making the facts clear on the principles laid down at the commencement of this lecture, after hundreds of careful investigations on the cellular network of the growing-point had provided material, welcome and valuable, it is true, but by no means intelligible. Just as do the organs hitherto considered, which consist entirely of embryonic substance, so also do the growing-points of roots and shoots show characteristic cell-wall networks or cell-arrangements on properly directed longitudinal and transverse sections, and these everywhere, even in the most different species of plants, agree with the type. This depends essentially upon the fact that the embryonic substance of the growing-points, as it increases in volume on all sides, becomes divided up into compartments, or chambers, by cell-walls which cut one another at right angles. The longitudinal section of a growing-point always shows a system of periclines, cut by anticlines which in their turn constitute the orthogonal trajectories of the former. If we are here concerned with growing-points of flat structures, then only these two systems of cell-walls are present, if, on the other hand, the growing-point is hemispherical, or conical, or of some other similar shape—i.e. not merely flat, but forming a solid body—then there exists still a third system of cell-walls, viz. longitudinal walls running radially outwards from the longitudinal axis of the growing-point.

It will conduce to intelligibility, however, if we here again confine our further considerations to a scheme constructed arbitrarily, but according to definite rules. We may, in the first place, take simply the superficial view of a longitudinal section through a growing-point. Confining our attention to Fig. 284, the outline *EE* of which represents the longitudinal section of a conical growing-point, we may premise that this outline, which is often nearly realised in nature, possesses the form of a parabola, and that the chambering of the space occupied by the embryonic substance of the growing-point again takes place in such a manner that anticlinal and periclinal walls cut one another at right angles. With this premiss we can now construct the network of cells in Fig 284 according to a well-known law of geometry.

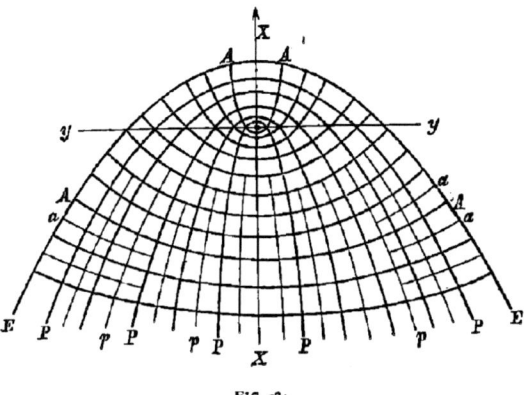

FIG 284.

Given that *xx* represents the axis, and *yy* the direction of the parameter, all the periclines denoted by *Pp* form a group of confocal parabolas. Similarly, all the anticlines *Aa* form a system of confocal parabolas having their focus and axis in common with the preceding, but running in the opposite direction. Two such systems of confocal parabolas cut one another everywhere at right-angles.

We may now see whether a median longitudinal section through a dome-shaped and approximately parabolic growing-point presents a net-work of cells essentially agreeing with our geometrically constructed scheme; and we at once find in the growing-point of the Larch, for example (Fig. 285), the corresponding internal structure, simply noting that in the figure the two protuberances *bb* disturb somewhat the symmetry of the figure. These are young leaf-rudiments budding off from the growing-point. However, we at once recognise the two systems of anticlines and periclines, the curvatures of which it can scarcely be doubted cut one another at right angles as in our scheme above; or the anticlines are the orthogonal trajec- tories of the periclines. As in our scheme, also, only a few periclines under the apex *S* run round the common focus of all the parabolas, the others as they come from below only reach the neighbourhood of the focus. In other words, the corresponding cell-divisions only take place when the periclines beneath the centre of curvature have become sufficiently far removed from one another for new periclines to be intercalated between them; and the same is true of the anticlines *A a*. It is easy to see on the scheme, Fig. 284, that the curvatures of the construction-lines are particularly sharp around the common focus of all the anticlines and periclines.

Many hundreds of median longitudinal sections through growing-points of shoots and roots, drawn by very different observers without even the most distant perception of the fundamental principle, accord with the construction which I have given, and demonstrate its accuracy; and, further, it may be said that all these observations have been made under the influence of two false premisses; first, that growth—i.e. increase in volume—takes place chiefly at the apex of the growing-point, and secondly, that cell-divisions are an essential cause of growth. That the latter is unfounded has already been insisted upon above, and I have shown clearly that it is just the apical region of the growing-point which is that where growth is slowest

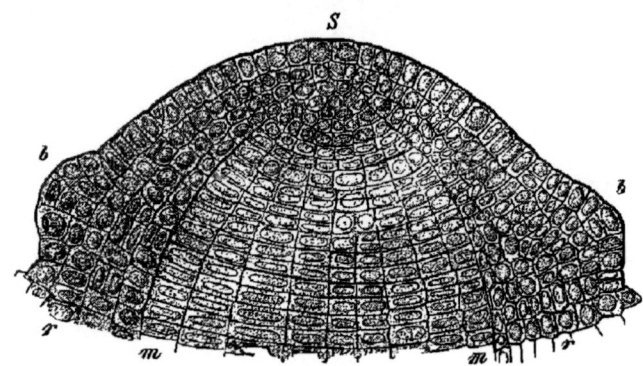

FIG. 285.—Longitudinal section through the growing-point of a winter-bud of *Abies pectinata* (× about 200).
s apex of growing-point; *b b* youngest leaves; *r* cortex; *m* pith.

and increase in volume least. The details of this, however, would here carry us too far. It need only be mentioned that the mere consideration of the cell-network at the growing-point and the course of the anticlines and periclines shows most clearly that growth must be less active at the apex itself than at any point lying further back. It is only necessary to suppose that in the scheme (Fig. 284) growth —i.e. the intercalation of mass—is more active in the neighbourhood of the focus of the anticlines and periclines than further back, to see that, according to the described laws, the cell-network must assume quite another form—i.e. the course of the anticlines and periclines must be essentially different.

Perhaps this important and formerly incorrectly apprehended relation will be rendered sufficiently clear if we here again make use of an arbitrary construction. We may assume that in Fig. 286 the lower figure represents a square surface consisting of 36 cells, and, for the purpose of better guidance, the lines *qq* and *vi* are drawn thicker. Let us now suppose that these 36 cells begin to grow as a whole, and that the upper figure arises therefrom. The line *vi* then represents the longitudinal

[3]

axis or axis of growth which divides the entire figure symmetrically in both cases. The lines *q q*, on the other hand, are intended to show the boundary between two different forms of growth in the given cell-network. In the cells lying beneath *q S q* growth has taken place as in the growing-point considered above; the lines *y y*, *h h* form confocal parabolas. On the other hand, the growth above the line *q S q* has taken place as it was formerly supposed to do—namely, the growth in length has here been most vigorous at the apex. It is at once obvious that in this way an entirely different cell-network arises, and that the periclines and anticlines assume quite other directions than at the apex of an ordinary growing-point. In the case of

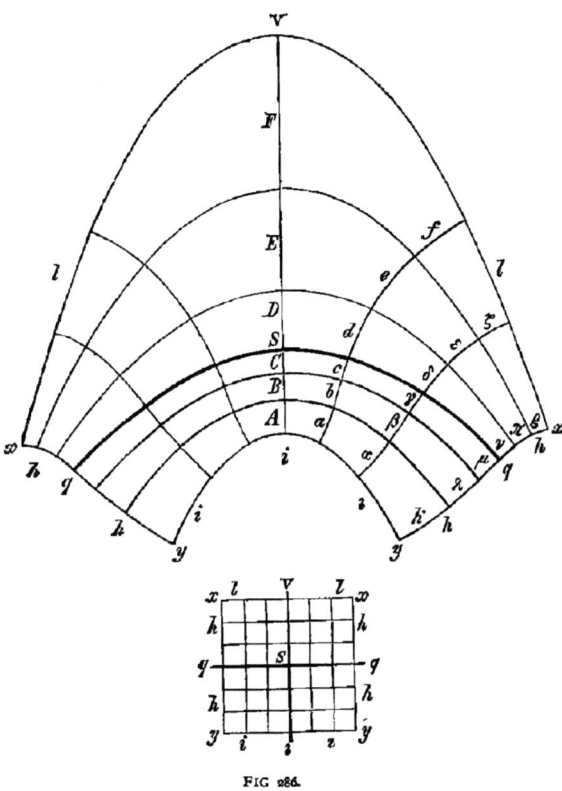

FIG. 286.

the latter, the pieces λ β *b* and *B*, intercalated between the periclines, become shorter in the given direction; above the line *q q*, on the contrary, the pieces π ε *e E*, intercalated between the periclines, increase in length in the order given.

The state of affairs arbitrarily constructed in this scheme, however, is found as a matter of fact in many roots of vascular plants, as shown in Fig. 287. The growing-point of the root, the outline of which is here indicated by the line *K K K*, presents the cell-network as in our scheme Fig. 284, and accordingly as in the portion situated below *q S q* in Fig. 286. On the other hand, the mass of tissue marked by the outline *h h h* is the root-cap, and it is at once perceived that this corresponds with that mode of growth which is represented in Fig. 286 above the line *q S q*.

Moreover, such a separation between the growing-point of the root and its cap does not exist in all true roots; there may occur quite other distributions of growth at the apex of the root, and accordingly also very different net-works of cell-walls.

That distribution of growth by which the intercalation of mass increases from the apex downwards, and at the same time from the longitudinal axis outwards, and by means of which, as we have seen, the anticlines are caused to radiate like a fan, occurs, however, not only in root-caps, but also in many other cases, especially, for example, in the growth of very young ovules Fig 288 may finally give another simple scheme for the cell-wall net-work, and the course of the anticlines and periclines in such a case It must be left for the reader, however, to picture how the structure *B* has arisen from the two cell-series in *A* by means of the corresponding pro-

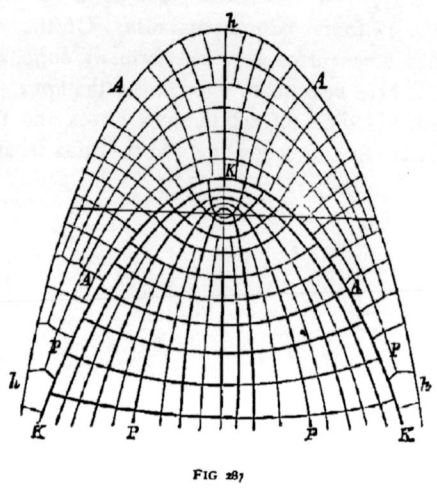

FIG 287

cesses of growth and subsequent cell-divisions, it being simply observed that the walls marked *a* and *b*, as well as those marked 1, 2, 3, 4, are in both figures the same.

Finally, the remark may be added that the first described arrangement of the cells at the growing-point may be termed confocal, while the last one may be regarded as co-axial, or fan-shaped, and that young organs of similar outward form present sometimes the one, sometimes the other structure in other words, the intercalation of mass in the interior of an organ may accord with the one or the other type, though the external form of the organ is the same in both cases.

If we now return once more to the parabolic, dome-like growing-point, from the consideration of which we started, and the median longitudinal section of which is here once more represented, we may now assume further that the figure included by the line

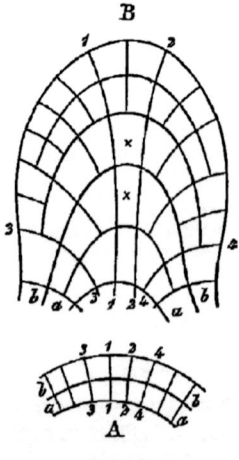

FIG. 288.

E E has made a complete revolution round the longitudinal axis *X X*. It is intelligible that then also each of the periclinal and anticlinal lines must have described a parabolic surface, and if we represent to ourselves the resulting figure,

it consists of a large number of superposed concavo-convex layers, the curvature
of which increases upwards, these are the layers the vertical sections of which
are represented by the antıclınal lines *A a* of our scheme. Since, however, in the
postulated revolution about the longitudinal axis *X X*, each of the perıclınal lines
P p has also descrıbed a parabolıc surface, these concavo-convex layers are dıvided
up ınto correspondıng rıngs whıch run concentrıcally around the longitudinal axıs
X X. Now, ın order that these concentrıc rings may fall into approxımately cubıcal
cells, in agreement with the problem, we must suppose still another system of cell-
walls to be ınterpolated, which radıate out from the longıtudınal axis *X X* in radıal
dırectıons to the surface *E E* of the growıng-poınt. These are the radıal longıtudınal
walls, of whıch, however, only four can cross one another ın the longıtudınal axıs
X X : the others only commence further outwards, and will, according to our
construction, exhibit approxımately the same course as the medullary rays on the
transverse section of a woody body. Or, in other words, the transverse sectıon

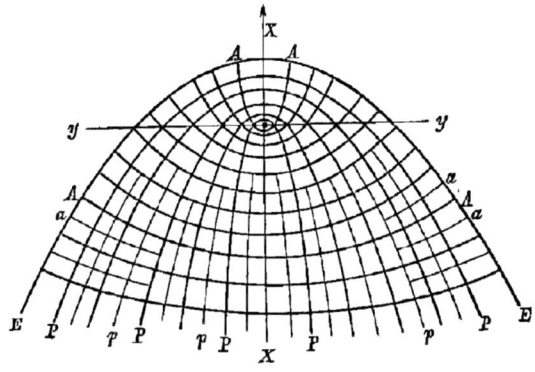

of a paraboloidal growıng-point shows concentrıc layers of cells which at the same
tıme exhıbit radıal rows, splıttıng up more and more as we proceed outwards.

Growing-points of this descrıptıon, as a matter of fact, are very common both
among roots and shoots. They may, however, also be formed quite otherwise, and
especıally so that two successıve longıtudınal sections standing at right angles have
different dıameters or parameters—ı. e. the growing-point appears compressed on
the one side and dılated on the other, and accordıngly the network constıtuted of the
antıclınal and perıclınal walls wıll then also present different forms. However, here
agaın this indıcatıon must suffice.

In a large number of Algæ and most Hepaticæ, all true Mosses, Equisetums,
Ferns, and Selaginellas, there ıs found at the apex of the growıng-point of the shoots
and roots a cell, which is usually characterısed both by ıts sıze and shape, and
which occupies the actual apical region of the growıng-poınt: by the repeated dıvisıons
of thıs cell into two, as it itself goes on growing, daughter-cells become cut off ın
defınıte sequence, from the further growth and repeated cell-dıvisions of which the
whole of the tıssue of the growıng-point in question arıses These daughter-cells cut
off from the apical cell are termed segments, and Naegelı, who first described thıs

important fact in 1845, showed how all the tissue-cells, not only of the growing-point but also all those subsequently produced by their agency, may be comprehended as descendants, with definite sequence in space and time, from the segments of one apical cell. For more than thirty years the most careful investigations have been devoted to this study, and for this reason alone it is necessary for us to concern ourselves here somewhat more closely with it, and especially because serious errors with respect to the relations between growth and cell-division

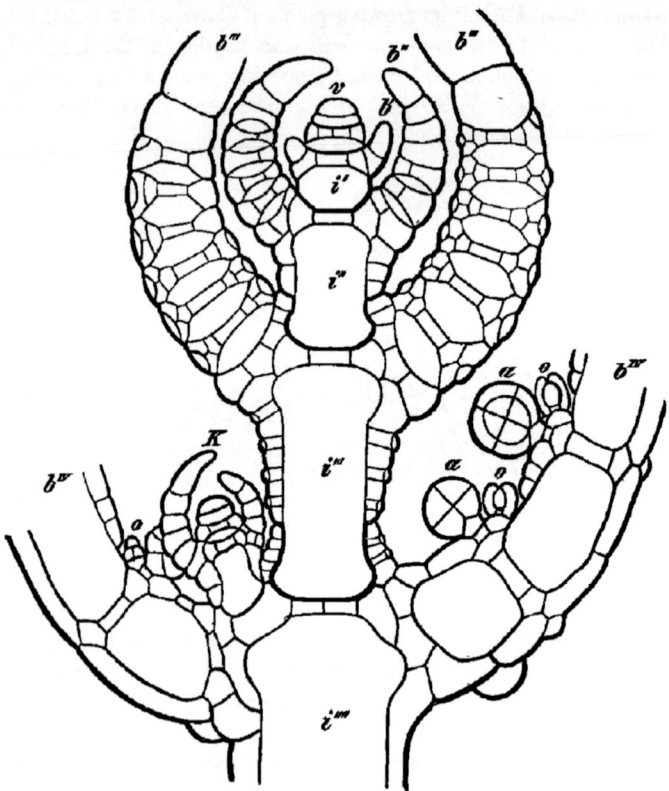

FIG. 290.—Apex of a shoot of *Chara*—longitudinal section

have slipped into the subject—errors which have retarded the development of the whole doctrine of growth. In the first place, however, it is necessary to make the reader acquainted with the facts.

When an algal filament or a fungus-hypha grows in length, this takes place usually, but by no means always (e. g. not in the case of *Spirogyra* and other Conjugatæ), in such a manner that transverse divisions are formed only at the end of the filament which represents the growing-point. The cell at the end, which alone grows forward and divides, may be distinguished as the apical cell . such a cell is also found at the end of the rhizoids of Mosses and Characeæ, where, however, the transverse septa are placed obliquely. The significance of the apical cell comes out more conspicuously and characteristically when the products of division (segments) arising from it not only themselves grow further but also undergo essential changes of form and corresponding cell-divisions, as is the case in many Algæ, and especially in the Characeæ. Fig. 290 may serve as a scheme for the latter. The cell marked v, at the end of the shoot, is in this case the apical cell, from which all the organs and tissue-cells of this plant can be derived by the formation of segments and the growth and further division of the latter. Every time this cell elongates a little in the direction of the longitudinal axis, there appears in it a transverse wall, an anticline, convex downwards. The cell cut off by this is the segment. This now grows also in length and in circumference, and after a short time is divided into two cells by means of a transverse wall convex upwards, viz. into an upper one which possesses the form of a bi-concave lens and into a lower one shaped like a bi-convex lens. The growth and further fate of these two daughter-cells of the segment in this case then differ in important respects. The lower bi-convex cell thenceforward grows vigorously in length, without undergoing further divisions; the figure shows how this cell gradually assumes the forms i', i'', i''', i'''', and how the longitudinal axis of the shoot is produced by numerous such cells. The bi-concave daughter-cell of the system, on the contrary, soon undergoes vertical divisions, and is transformed into a disc, or so-called node, consisting of cells, since it grows chiefly in the transverse direction, and only very little in the longitudinal direction of the shoot. Certain cells situated at the margin of this disc now grow out and project upwards, b', these outgrowths then develope further into the leaves b'', b''', b'''', and subsequently, by the growing out of certain cells at the nodes, lateral shoots K, and from the leaves themselves sexual organs a and o arise. It will best be seen what can be produced from a segment of the apical cell by means of the growth described and the subsequent cell-divisions, on observing that the parts marked in each case alike with i and b and surrounded by a thick contour have always proceeded from one segment. It would occupy too much time for our purpose to show how all the various cells in the tissues of these organs gradually arise from the originally bi-concave nodal cell, in perfectly definite sequence and in accordance with the law of cell-division described above, and how these organs eventually become altered in form by means of elongation and increase considerably in size

On account of its simplicity and intelligibility, Fig. 291 may be examined in addition with respect to the apical cell and its segmentation. This represents the growing-point of an Alga, *Dictyota*, which has just split into two similar growing-points, a and b, by so-called dichotomy. In a we see the apical cell, shaped in accordance with the slightly arched form of the thin ribbon-like shoot, like a bi-convex lens, from which, after having elongated a little in the direction of the axis of the shoot, the segment 1 has been produced, and this has already become divided by a median longitudinal wall into two equal halves. The groups of cells marked 2, 3, 4, and 5, are older segments of the apical cell, in which, as they have grown in length as well as in breadth, more and more numerous anticlinal and periclinal walls have gradually made their appearance; and here also it is easily understood how the whole mass of tissue of the shoot arises from the segments of the apical cell. In b, a longitudinal wall has arisen in the apical cell itself, wherewith is given the commencement of a dichotomous branching of this growing-point which itself proceeded from a dichotomy. As for the rest, how-ever, the same relations as before prevail, and it is at once noticed in the figure how the two growing-points *a* and *b* show by the anti-clines further backwards their origin from a previous dichotomy.

In the two cases examined the segments are cut off from the apical cell by simple transverse walls. Fig. 292 may serve as an example of the case where from an apical cell on a flat organ (leaf of the Fern *Cera-topteris*) the segments are formed by successive division-walls situated obliquely right and left (*S*), whereby two rows of segments arise, from the further growth and corresponding cell-divisions of which the whole of the tissue of the leaf is produced. The thick lines in the figure are the

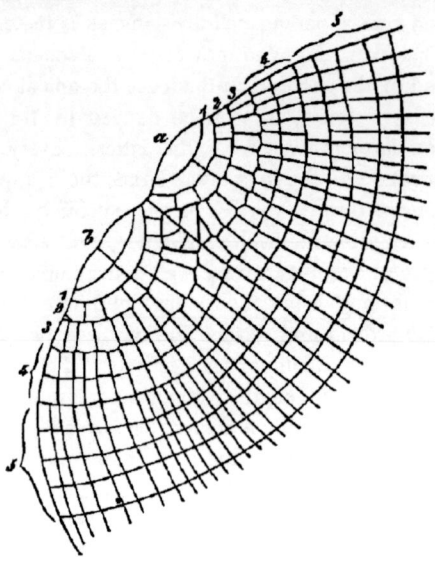

FIG. 291.—End of a ribband shaped flat shoot of the Alga *Dictyota.*

older segment-walls of the apical cell; and it is noticed, proceeding backwards from this, how the superficies of the segments have become larger and divided by anticlinal and periclinal cell-walls in accord-ance with their age. At *L* a lateral lobe of the leaf is protruding; this, as is easily seen, belongs to two dif-ferent segments, and since numerous anticlinal walls already exist in it, which radiate in a fan-like manner into the lobe and participate in its whole growth, no apical cell is formed here.

Such apical cells, segmented in two rows, are common in flat organs, as in the leaves and flat shoot-axes of many Algæ, Liverworts, and in some dorsiventral shoot-axes of Vas-cular plants—e.g. in many Ferns and all Selaginellas. In growing-points the transverse section of which is circular and the growth upright,

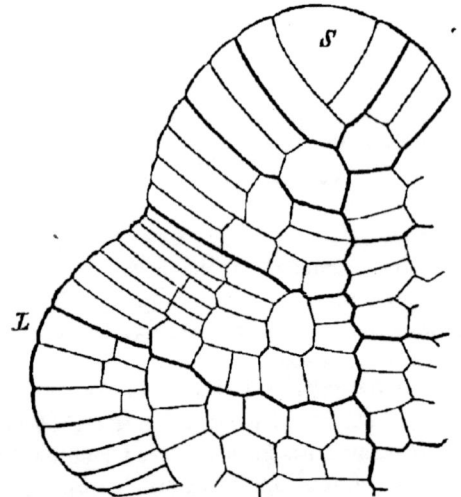

FIG. 292.—Young leaf of *Ceratopteris* (after Kny)

and especially in the true roots of the Vascular Cryptograms, we find, on the contrary, at the tip of the growing-point an apical cell from which segments are cut off on three sides. This can of course only be recognised with certainty when the apical cell is observed from above, or in transverse section; since such a tetrahedral apical cell seen in longitudinal section presents a very similar appearance to the biseriate ones described above. This state of affairs will be clear on regarding Fig. 293, *A* represents the longitudinal section, and *B* the view from above of the apical region

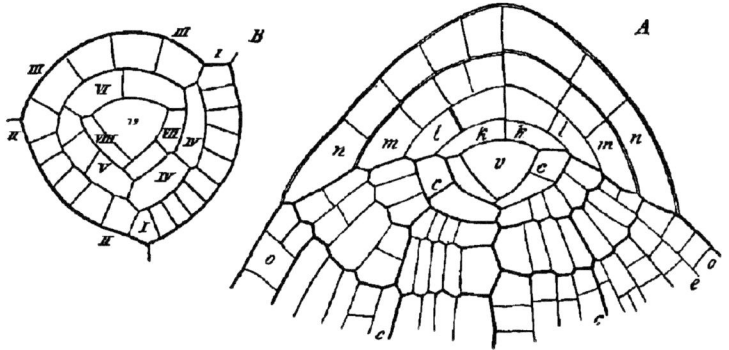

FIG. 293.—Apical region of the roots of Ferns. *A* longitudinal section through the end of the root of *Pteris hastata*. *B* transverse section through the apical cell and the surrounding segments of the root of *Asplenium filix femina* (after Naegeli and Leitgeb)

of the growing-point of the root of a Fern, *v* being the apical cell in each case. In *B* the numerals *I–VIII* mark the transverse sections of the concentric segments of the apical cell *v*: in *A* these are to be recognised in the longitudinal section by their walls being drawn with thicker contours. In this example there is added a further complication, however, since we are concerned with a root, and accordingly also with a root-cap. This root-cap is indicated in Fig. 293 *A* by means of the letters *k l m n*, and its cap-shaped superposed layers are in fact also segments of the apical-cell *v*, which have been produced by successive transverse divisions which have then grown

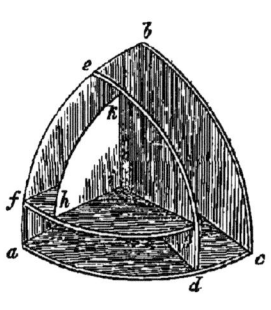

FIG. 294.

further. In the growing-point of a shoot with a tetrahedral apical cell these caps *k l m n* would be absent. It is not quite so easy to see that even such tetrahedral apical cells obey the law of rectangular intersection of the division-walls; and even the most distinguished observers in this difficult province have for years erroneously supposed that the segment-walls of a tetrahedral apical cell cut one another at angles of 60°, because such appears to be the case from the view in transverse section, which represents an equilateral triangle. I have shown, however, that such an apical cell is correctly apprehended by supposing a corner so cut off from a cube that the triangular surfaces which meet in the corner are equal to one another, and, in addition, that the four bounding surfaces are arched outwards, as shown by the lines *a b c* in Fig 294. This represents the upper view of a tetrahedral apical cell, and the walls *d e, f g, h k* are the successive segmentations which appear in it:

i being the corner in which the three youngest segment-walls always cut one another. The preceding figure (Fig. 293) shows now in the main for this case also, how the whole of the tissues of the organ in question arise by successive cell-divisions from the segments of such an apical cell.

The segment-walls of apical cells with two or three sides are in fact simply anticlines, and the subsequent division-walls in the segments are sometimes anticlinal and sometimes periclinal, so that the segments, just as we have seen to be the case before, break up into a network of walls consisting of orthogonal trajectories. A simple alteration of the scheme given in Fig. 289 here comes in only in so far that the anticlines under consideration (Fig 295 *A a*) do not at once cut through across the whole apex, but meet one another from two or three sides: Fig. 295 *B* shows, however, how each of the anticlinal segment-walls is subsequently completed by means of a further piece into a complete anticline *A a*. The difference, which is of importance, will be evident at once on comparing the figures *A* and *B*. Moreover, since tetrahedral apical cells only occur in solid

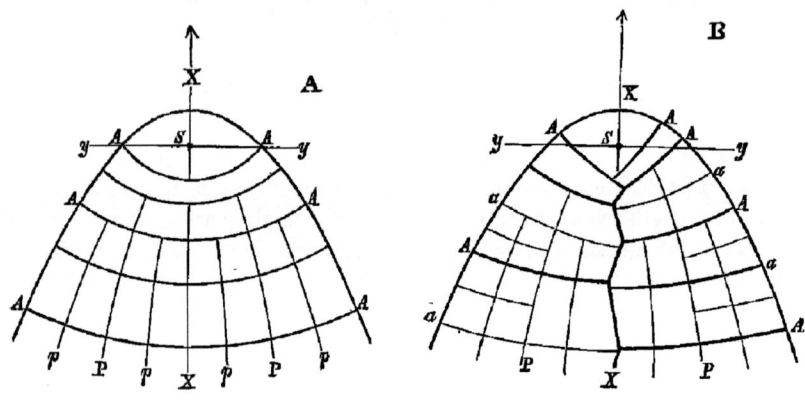

FIG 295.

growing-points which are circular in transverse sections, and not in flat ones, radial longitudinal walls also appear in the segments in addition to the anticlines and periclines, and alternating with them.

Since, as Naegeli showed so long ago as 1845, all the tissues of a root or shoot may be derived progressively and in genetic sequence from the apical cell, wall for wall, the opinion arose gradually that the whole process of growth in the growing point is ruled by the apical cell itself, which, by means of its segments, adds stone upon stone to the structure like a builder. Nay, matters even went so far that the belief arose, without any foundation, that the apical cell is in fact the position of most rapid and vigorous growth in the embryonic tissue of the growing-point. I have already referred in my previously quoted treatises to the erroneous character of both views: the apical cell, as also the apical region corresponding to it in growing-points not provided with such a cell, is, on the contrary, the place of slowest growth, and in no part of the growing-point do cell-divisions occur so rarely as the segmentations in the apical cell This can be concluded with certainty from the increase in volume of the successive segments, and from the number of partition-walls in segments of different ages

So far as regards the importance of the apical cell as the ruler of the whole growth in the growing-point, however, I showed that that cell represents merely a break in the constructive system of the growing-point—i e. the apical cell is that spot in the embryonic tissue in which neither anticlines and periclines nor radial longitudinal walls have as yet been formed. In order to understand this, it is only necessary to compare Fig. 295 with the previous scheme, Fig. 289. There, a few of the periclines run continuously round the focus beneath the apex, and in the same way the uppermost region of the apex is traversed by anticlines, so that the proper apical region of the growing-point is occupied by small areolæ or cells. In Fig. 295 *A*, which possesses an apical cell, the periclines all cease, on the contrary, at some distance from the apex; we need only complete these, however, into confocal parabolas with the focus *S*, and suppose in addition a few sharply curved confocal and parabolic anticlines interpolated above the uppermost anticline *A*, and then the impression of an apical cell disappears altogether, and we have a growing-point such as is found in all Phanerogams and many Cryptogams. Or, conversely, we need only suppose in our scheme, Fig. 289, the anticlines next the apex and the upper curved portions of the periclines to be wanting, and we obtain an apical cell, as in Fig 295 *A*. In apical cells from which segments are cut off on two or three sides, the relation referred to is, it is true, a little more complicated, but it is easily noticed on regarding Fig 295 *B* that here also we are enabled by properly completing the periclines *P*, with the help of a few anticlines, to convert the apical cell into a small-celled mass of tissue   As a matter of fact, corresponding transformations of apical cells actually occur when the growing-points cease to grow further as such, e.g in the prothallia of some Ferns.

By means of this explanation of the apical cell which I have established, the criticism of the constructive processes in the growing-point obtains as a general principle   While growing-points with and without apical cells were previously regarded as essentially different, and the opinion was even entertained that an apical cell must be found even in all phanerogamous growing-points, according to my view of the matter, on the contrary, the presence or absence of an apical cell appears as an interesting but quite secondary point in the growth of the growing-point.   Even the case as it occurs, for example, in the roots of the Marattiaceæ among the Ferns, where a group of large apical cells is present, may be referred without constraint to the principle mentioned.   It is to be mentioned on the other hand that apical cells are only possible, in the sense here employed, when the periclines and anticlines constitute systems of confocal curves, or, shortly, in growing-points with confocal structure.   If, on the contrary, the growing-point is traversed by anticlines which run in a fan-like manner, and the increase in volume is greatest towards the apex, as was shown above in Fig. 288, it is then possible, under certain circumstances, still to assume the existence of apical cells in the wider sense, but in these cases authors have not spoken of apical cells, and so we also may overlook them   In any case, in the older mode of looking at the apical cell, it must remain enigmatical why this varies so extraordinarily in its occurrence and even in its form that, as it was formerly expressed, the growth of one lobe of a leaf takes place by means of an apical cell, and that of another lobe merely by so-called marginal cells, as in Fig. 292. From my way of looking at the relations of dependence of cell-division upon growth, however, such cases appear thoroughly explicable.

Flat structures, such as the shoots of many Algæ and Liverworts, and many leaves, often show on a vertical section through the flat tissue-body an arrangement of the cell-walls which will be intelligible from Fig. 296. A certain similarity of the cell-network with that of a slender growing-point with an apical cell impelled the earlier observers to assume in such cases a special type. They regarded cells lying beside one another at the margin as a series of neighbouring apical cells : this, from a purely formal point of view, is of course possible, but it contributes nothing further to the explanation of the processes of growth.

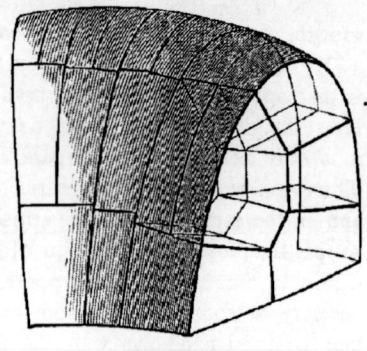

FIG. 296.

It must now suffice to have brought forward the few cases adduced from the copious material obtained by observation : a further extension of these considerations would without doubt presuppose more patience than may be expected from readers who are not Botanists.

LECTURE XXVIII.

FORMATION OF ORGANS AT THE GROWING-POINT: BRANCHING.

THE growing-points already considered to such an extent in the two preceding lectures, scarcely ever come under the notice of those not trained in botanical science, or at any rate they are passed over, not only on account of their minuteness, but also because, as a rule, they are hidden from view; those of most roots because they are in the earth or other substratum, those of leaf-forming shoots because they are completely enveloped by the young leaves. Nevertheless, it will already be clear to the reader (and it is one of the most important facts of the whole of the physiology of plants) that all formative processes are initiated at the growing-points—that all the organs of a plant arise from these tiny masses of embryonic tissue which we have to seek in the form of growing-points at the apices of the roots, or at the ends of shoots inside the buds.

Here again, also, the profound difference between root and shoot comes out sharply. Roots produce only organs of like kind, namely, new roots, by means of which the branching of the root-system is brought about; whereas the activity of the growing-points of shoots is entirely different and much more various: they produce not only growing-points of new shoots, and thus of course subserve branching, but from them alone also all leaves arise, and together with or on these the true reproductive organs—sporangia, oogonia, and antheridia, since all reproductive organs may be referred to these three forms. Thus, when in botanical investigations it is important to examine organs of any kind whatever in their first stages of development—in their primitive mutual relations—it is always the first object of the observer to investigate the growing-points, and the formation of organs taking place on them. Owing to the extreme minuteness of these objects, this has always to be done with the aid of the microscope.

Here again we shall only concern ourselves with the commonest phenomena, or those which offer features of special interest, and according to the plan of exposition which I have adhered to so far, I again confine myself in the first place to the typical and complete forms. We may first regard the growing-points of leaf-forming shoots as found in all Vascular plants, most Muscineæ, and even in many Algae: the abnormal forms then present no further difficulties. Before entering more closely upon our proper theme, however, it may be advantageous to make a few preliminary remarks as to the form of the growing-point, and its position on the shoot.

In leaf-shoots which are growing vigorously in length, the growing-point has usually the form of a cone arched outwards like a paraboloid, and which appears simply as the end of the shoot-axis; in rarer cases, as for example in the water-plants *Utricularia* and *Azolla*, which are so remarkable also in other respects, this cone is considerably elongated and rolled inwards spirally at its anterior end. When the shoot-axis elongates more slowly, on the contrary, and especially when a flower or an inflorescence is to arise at the apex of the shoot concerned, the growing-point generally assumes the form of a flat and broad elevation, which very often becomes eventually extended horizontally, and forms a disc several milli-metres in diameter This is well seen at the apex of those leaf-shoots of the Compositæ (e.g of the Dahlia and the Sunflower) which are preparing for the formation of flowering capitula : the growing-point, previously conical, is flattened to an almost level disc, on which the embryonic rudiments of young flowers bud forth on all sides from the circumference towards the centre—i.e, the apex of the growing-point. If, on the other hand, a long flowering axis is to be produced, to be covered later with numerous small flowers, as in the Palms, Aroids, and Grasses, the growing-point becomes elongated into a cylinder, often several millimetres long, on which the lateral shoots of the future panicle, or even the flowers themselves, then arise pro-gressively from below upwards. The subsequent form of the whole inflores-ence is thus already marked out in the form of the growing-point; of course the formative processes connected with the elongation also co-operate later to an important extent, in the completion of the form.

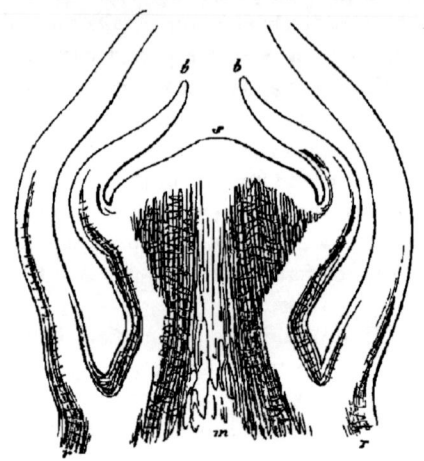

FIG 297 —Longitudinal section of the apex of the primary stem of *Helianthus annuus*, immediately preceding the development of the flowers. *s* apex of the broad growing-point, *b b* youngest leaves , *r* cortex , *m* pith.

Even where individual flowers are to be developed, either as lateral out-growths from a growing-point or at the end of leaf-shoots, the flower assumes in its embryonic condition, long before the organs of the flower themselves bud forth, the form of a hemi-spherical dome or flat disc, or very frequently even that of a hollow cup, whereby the foundation for the subsequent form of the flower is laid : this may then of course again undergo the most various transformations by means of the changes of form connected with elongation.

The category of these modifications and departures from the ordinary type also includes the far more striking cases of depressed growing-points. A very simple example is afforded by the broad flat shoots of many Liverworts (*Metzgeria, Mar-chantieæ*) and particularly clearly by the prothallus of Ferns. As soon as these flat leafless shoots attain a certain breadth, the elongating tissue last produced by the growing-point becomes arched forwards right and left in the form of two lobes, between which a deep depression marks the place where the embryonic tissue of the growing-point lies, Fig 298 *v.* In this behaviour of leafless shoots, where of course the formation of buds does not occur, we may probably recognise chiefly a provision for protecting the substance of the growing-point, which is as delicate as it is important. The same explanation applies to the similar depression of the growing-point in the neighbouring tissue (in this case surrounding it on all sides) on the likewise leafless shoots of species of *Fucus*, where a narrow long slit at the end of each shoot opens into a narrow cavity, the base of which is occupied by the growing-point, which here, as Rostafinski has shown, exhibits a series of curious apical cells. A very similar arrangement also protects the growing-point of the sub-terranean creeping shoot-axis of the Bracken fern (*Pteris aquilina*), because here, in

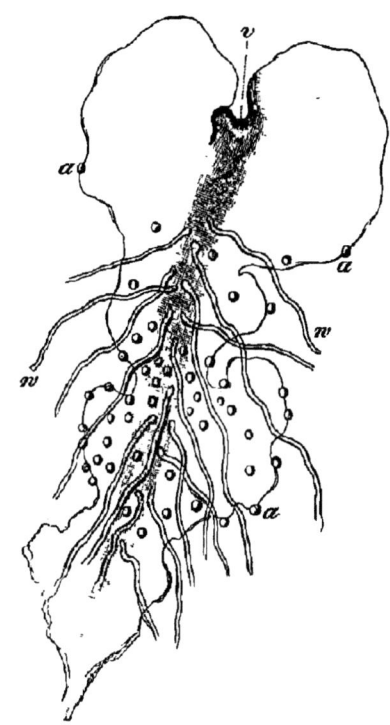

FIG. 298.—Prothallium of a Fern seen from below *v* growing-point, *a* antheridia, *w* roots (slightly magnified).

consequence of the extremely sparse pro-duction of leaves, together with other circumstances, no leaf-bud exists to enve-lope the growing-point, and therefore the leaves cannot protect the growing-point in the soil.

In Phanerogams which persist by means of subterranean tubers or bulbs, it not rarely happens that at the end of a short (or occasionally long) subterranean lateral shoot, a body filled with reserve-materials is formed; and this contains the bud with the growing-point at the bottom of a central cavity. In these cases, how-ever, peculiar displacements of the leaves and of the parts of the axis which support the growing-point usually take place at the same time. The elucidation of these processes, however, would carry us much too far, the chief points will be clear from the consideration of Fig. 299.

In the researches, as numerous as they are brilliant, of Thilo Irmisch, who has done so much good service for our knowledge of the subterranean organs of plants, is to be found abundant material derived from the observation of cases be-longing to this category[1]. Here, again, it is evidently a matter of obtaining the

---

[1] It is the phenomena of growth here treated of which especially comprehend the subject of the very copious morphological literature. A more detailed consideration of the phenomena belonging here would lead to a morphological review of the natural system; from the general point of view which I have attempted to establish in the preceding lecture, however, these phenomena belong also to physiology; in fact, they form in a certain sense one of the foundations of the physiology of growth

This being the case, it would scarcely be to the purpose to quote this or that treatise for proof; however, it may be welcome to those readers who are unacquainted with botanical literature and seek further instruction, to find quoted here a series of the most important works affecting this

necessary protection by the depression of a growing-point in a mass of resistent tissue, which at the same time abounds in nutritive substances , since such arrangements as that in the figure occur chiefly in tuberous and bulbous plants, the entire vegetative body of which perishes annually, leaving behind in the soil only these organs from which new individuals subsequently arise

Depressed growing-points are everywhere common in the development of young flowers, or even young inflorescences, where it is also usually important that a protective hollow structure should be formed, in which the very tender young parts of the flower, and especially the ovules with their contained embryos, are then to be produced. A somewhat more complicated case of this kind is presented in Fig 300, which represents the longitudinal section of a young flower bud of *Geum rivale*, a plant belonging to the Rosaceæ. The growing-point, *x*, here projects in the form of a cone from the bottom of a cup-like hollow structure *yy*, the inner side of which, at least at the basal portions, likewise consists of embry-

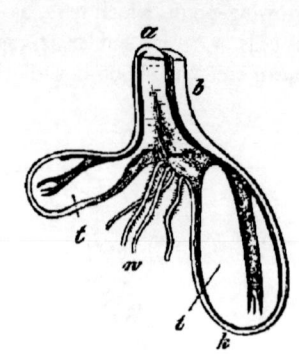

FIG 299.—Development of tubers of *Gagea pratensis* (after Irmisch) *a* shoot axis, *b* leaf sheath, in the axil of which the bud *k* with the tuber *t* has been produced.

onic tissue, from which the young stamens *a* are arising. The elongation which subsequently sets in, in this case results in that the wall *yy* of the hollow structure becomes extended like a flat plate ; in the Rose, however, and in many other cases, the part *yy* also subsequently forms a hollow cavity, open above by means of a narrow mouth only. The depressed growing-point, *x*, of the flower, produces at its outer margin numerous small leaves, which subsequently grow together at their edges and constitute the so-called ovaries, in each of which an ovule arises

subject For this purpose I may mention those from which I have myself derived the best instruction in years gone by—above all the fundamental works of Naegeli, as follows —

'*Zeitschrift fur wiss Bot*,' Schleiden und Naegeli (Zurich, 1844-46), the memoirs on *Caulerpa*, *Delesseria*, laws of growth of Mosses and Liverworts, *Polysiphonia*, and several other treatises

'*Pflanzenphysiol Untersuchungen*,' Naegeli und Cramer, Heft I, 1855, growth of *Pterothamnium*, *Hypoglossum*, the leaf of *Sphagnum*, leaf of *Aralia* , also Heft III, on *Lycopodium* and *Equisetum* (by Cramer)

Further, '*Beitrage zur wiss. Bot*.,' Naegeli, Heft I (Leipzig, 1858), '*Über das Wachsthum des Stammes und der Wurzeln von Gefässpflanzen*,' and H. 4, '*Enstehung und Wachsthum der Wurzeln*,' by Naegeli and Leitgeb (München, 1867) On roots also, *Recherches sur l'accroissement terminal des racines*,' by E de Janczewski, in Ann des sc nat, Ser 5 (Paris, 1874)

Also '*Uber den Vegetationspunkt der Angiospermenwurzeln*,' H G Holle, *Bot. Zeit*, 1876, No 16

'*Zur Entwicklungsgeschichte des Blattes*' Dissertation by A W Eichler (Marburg, 1861)

'*Die Scheitelzellgruppe im Vegetationspunkt der Phanerogamen*,' J Hanstein, in *Festschrift der niederrhein Ges fur Natur- und Heilkunde*

'*Traité d'organogénie comparée de la fleur*,' by J B Payer (Paris, 1857)

'*Recherches sur la ramification des Phanérogames*,' by M Eug Warming (Copenhagen, 1872)

'*Die Coniferen und die Gnetaceen*,' Strasburger (Jena, 1872)

That many other treatises may be named in addition to these comprehensive works has already been stated.

Similar depressions are occasionally met with in leaf-shoots also: this is particularly clear, for example, in the winter buds of the common Pine, as shown in Fig. 301. At the end of the shoot of the previous year is situated the still quite embryonic rudiment *z* of the next year's shoot, with the growing-point *v*. This embryonic shoot, however, is protected by means of an annular wall for the purpose of passing the winter. This wall arises from the tissue of the shoot of the previous year, and produces numerous bud-scales, *s*, which completely envelope the embryonic shoot of the next year. These bud-scales, moreover, as Goebel has shown, are simply abortive foliage-leaves, which may be transformed by means of vigorous nutrition into the ordinary green acicular foliage-leaves of the Pine.

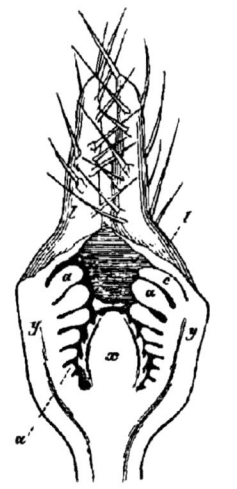

FIG 300.—Longitudinal section of a young flower of *Geum rivale* (slightly magnified).

I may, in conclusion, refer briefly to the formation of the Fig, as a particularly remarkable case of the depression of a growing-point, and of a further departure from the typical state of affairs dependent thereupon. The Fig, which in popular language passes for the fruit of the Fig-tree, is as a matter of fact a structure of quite a different nature from the ordinary fruits of Angiosperms. It is a so-called pseudo-fruit. The Fig is a hollow structure provided with fleshy walls, which abound with sugar These walls are constituted by a hollowed-out shoot-axis, on the inside of which hundreds of small flowers (subsequently fruits) are situated: these latter constitute the hard granules found in the pulpy mass of a ripe Fig. Fig. 302, which represents the development of a Fig (*I-III*), shows that it is originally an ordinary shoot, the growing-point of which, however, after giving rise to several leaves *I a*, assumes the form of a flat disc. In the centre of this disc is situated the proper apex of the shoot, which takes no part in further growth however: on the contrary, it is the margin of the disc which retains the embryonic character, and therefore

FIG 301.

constitutes an annular growing-point. By means of the tissue formed by this there now arises a hollow cylinder, *III a*, at the upper margin of which the leaves previously developed are situated, while further below arise new ones in addition, closing the opening of the cavity of the Fig above.

The cases of depression of the growing-point here mentioned constitute a few examples only, which might easily be increased by hundreds of others.

We may now return once more to the normal forms of the growing-point, and to the theme which we are immediately concerned with, the formation of organs upon it. Two extreme cases occur at the outset. The one consists in that the entire growing-point, including its apex, is transformed into an organ—into a mass of permanent tissue—where of course the growing-point as such completely gives up its existence, and at the same time growth in length ceases as soon as the elongation of the younger portions is concluded: such a shoot is said to have a limited (definite) growth in length, in contrast to the other extreme case, where the growing-point of a shoot remains persistently capable of living, and the tissue proceeding from it continues to produce new axial portions and lateral organs by elongation. This may be distinguished as unlimited (indefinite) growth in length. As a few striking examples of this case the growth of the main stem of Tree-ferns, Palms, Cycads, and species of *Abies* and *Pinus* may be adduced; the growing-point of these plants after tens or even hundreds of years is still the direct prolongation of the growing-point of the embryo in the seed.

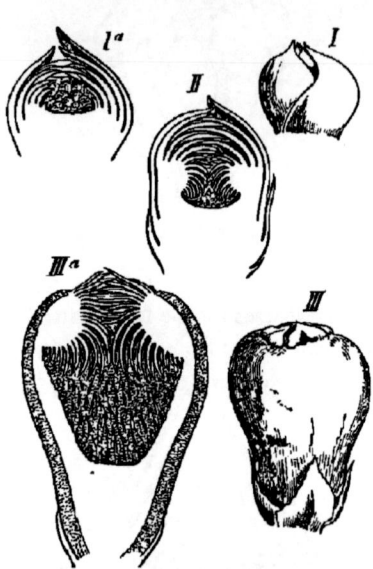

FIG. 302.—Development of the Fig (*Ficus Carica*), after Payer

We meet with proved cases of a transformation of the entire growing-point, including its apex, into an organ of definite physiological function, and consisting of permanent tissue, chiefly in the formation of reproductive organs at the end of the shoot. Although, strictly speaking, not all the foliage-shoots of Phanerogams provided with so-called apical flowers belong here, there are nevertheless numerous cases which are certainly to be so considered; namely, all flowers with central ovaries in which is developed a single central ovule, as in the Polygoneæ, Juglandeæ, Chenopodiaceæ, Piperaceæ, and other families. In Fig. 303 the portion of the young Rhubarb flower marked *k k* is the nucellus of the ovule, in which arises the embryo-sac with the oosphere. This portion together with the two envelopes surrounding it constitute the future seed, and from microscopic investigation there is no doubt that in this and similar cases the nucellus of the ovule has proceeded directly from the growing-point, which had previously given rise to the carpels *f*, the stamens *a*, and the floral envelopes *s p*. Equally without doubt is the fact in question in the formation of the sexual organs of many true Mosses. Leitgeb showed long ago that in the Bog-mosses (*Sphagnum*) at least the first female organ (archegonium) of the 'flower' arises directly from the apical cell of the fertile shoot. Kühn observed later that in the case of another Moss (*Andreæa*) the first archegonium arises similarly from the apical cell, and the following archegonia of the same

[3]   H h

'flower from its last segments. I have myself confirmed this in various other Mosses According to Kühn and Leitgeb, moreover, the male organs or antheridia of *Andreæa* and of the aquatic Moss *Fontinalis* arise in the same way as the archegonia, so that the apex of the growing-point of the Moss may be transformed into a female or into a male reproductive organ We may, in addition, also regard the formation of the sporangium of *Mucor* at the end of the simple utricular branch as a case of the formation of an organ directly from the apex of the growing-point: the end of the hypha, which functions as a growing-point, dilates into a sphere and produces the spores in its interior.

When in these and other cases the growing-point of a shoot is directly transformed into a special organ, its previous growth in length is, as already mentioned, brought to an end. A limitation of the latter may also take place, however, simply by the embryonic tissue becoming entirely transformed into permanent tissue, as in the case of ill-nourished Fern prothallia, which then dispense with their growing-point: with a proper supply of food-materials, however, a new growing-point may arise. The formation of thorns affords an entirely different example of this class The hard point at the end of the small-leafed shoot of *Gleditschia*, and in similar cases, is evidently the growing-point transformed into lignified permanent tissue. In other cases, again, the activity of the growing-point simply comes to an end; it disappears, so to speak, its tissue becoming merged into neighbouring permanent tissue. This is the case, for example, in many flowers with a central ovary but without a central ovule. Finally, the terminal bud of a

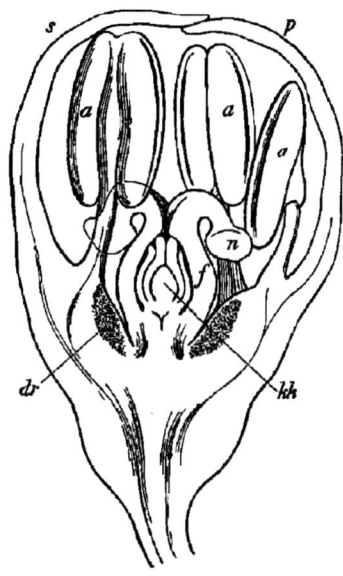

FIG. 303.—*Rheum undulatum* Longitudinal section of the flower-bud *s p* floral envelopes, *a a* anthers, *d r* glands at base of stamens, *f* ovary, *n* stigma, *k l* nucellus of the ovule (slightly magnified)

foliage-shoot, together with its growing-point, may periodically die off, the next lateral bud continuing the growth of the previous axis. in this way are formed sympodia, the stem of the Lime being an example.

The peculiar characteristic of the growing-point becomes clear, however, in the cases of so-called indefinite growth. Here the apex continues to grow undisturbed, while underneath it (or, when the growing-point is flat, in circles around the central apex) organs of like kind are produced in continuous succession; these appear at first as mere protuberances of the embryonic tissue, but become transformed later wholly into permanent tissue. In this continuous repetition of products of like kind from the circumference of the growing-point, we have one of the most universal laws of growth of the whole vegetable kingdom; organs of the most various kind—roots, lateral shoots, sporangia, and sexual organs, may spring in this way in continual repetition from one and the same growing-point. This is most distinctly seen, however, in the formation of leaves.

When organs of like kind arise from a growing-point in continual repetition, this occurs generally, though not without exception, in such a way that the youngest organ always stands nearer to the apex of the growing-point than any older organ of the same kind. It follows from this that when we proceed from the base of a shoot and follow organs of like kind—leaves for example—ascending in series on the shoot-axis, and necessarily running spirally around the latter, or ascending it in a zigzag manner, this sequence in space also represents the sequence in time or age in the production of the organs concerned. Such a sequence in the production of organs of like kind is usually termed acropetal. This is to be observed particularly clearly in the case of ordinary foliage-shoots, where the leaves arise without exception acropetally, as may be demonstrated especially in the case of a young, elongating shoot, even without microscopic investigation. The numerous lateral roots arising from a root, again, usually arise in acropetal order, and the same is the case when numerous roots are produced close beneath the growing-point of a shoot, as is the case, for example, in many Ferns

The importance of the growing-point lies, as has already been mentioned, in that it consists of embryonic tissue and gives rise to new organs. Confining ourselves to this essential character, the growing-point need not always be situated at the end of a root or of a shoot, but, on the contrary, a portion of embryonic tissue may be intercalated between masses of permanent tissue.

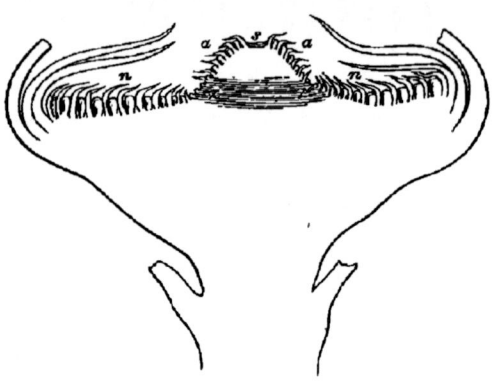

FIG. 304.—Median longitudinal section through a young inflorescence of the Sunflower (*Helianthus annuus*) the growing point *s* of which had been injured

One of these rarer cases has already been noticed on p 70, Fig. 66, and another above in the formation of a Fig, where the true growing-point at the base of the hollow structure loses its function as such, the further growth of the receptacle and the production of leaves and flowers in its interior taking place by means of an annular zone of embryonic tissue. Even in such cases the organs further distant from the zone of embryonic tissue are older than those next it—in fact, a similar relation exists to that found in ordinary terminal growing-points. This similarity, however, cannot well be expressed by the phrase acropetal succession, and Goebel has therefore, in order to bring out the general fact in the various cases, proposed the term progressive series or sequence. Complicated cases of the progressive formation of organs at growing-points which are not terminal are frequent enough, especially in the development of flowers. For the elucidation of this matter, however, I will employ a monstrosity which I discovered accidentally, and where the fact in question comes out particularly clearly. The accompanying figure (Fig. 304) represents the vertical longitudinal section through a young flower head of the Sunflower (*Helianthus annuus*) Its true growing-point was situated in the middle of the disc *n n*, but the central apex of this growing-point had been damaged by some means · the young tissue in its immediate neighbourhood had lost the nature of a growing-point, but had become elevated in the form of a protuberance *a s a*, while at the base of the latter *z z*, a zone of embryonic tissue had been formed.   The rudiments of new flowers and the bracts belonging to them only arise now on this zone.   So long as the central apex of the flowering head was yet living, the flowers and bracts were produced on the disc in acropetal succession *n n*, or, as we may say in this case, in centripetal order: the flowers next the circumference are the oldest, those nearest the centre the youngest.   After the destruction of the central apex, as the protuberance *a s a* was elevated from the zone *z z*, however, the previous centre or apex behaved exactly as if it were the oldest part of the protuberance: the production of flowers proceeded from the point *s* of the protuberance successively towards the zone *z z*, and we perceive that at the circumference of

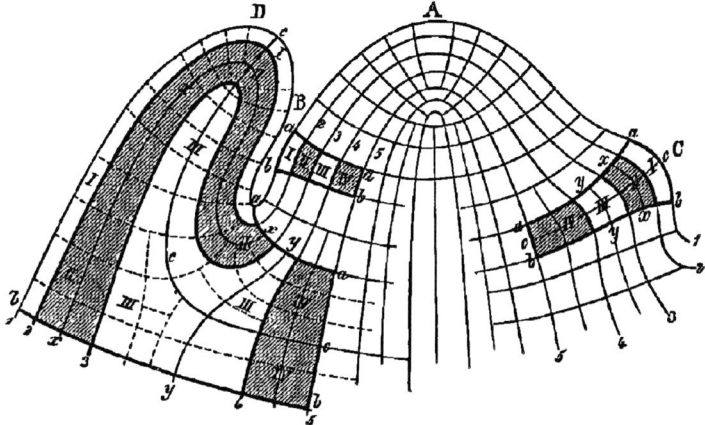

FIG. 305 —Diagram to illustrate the mode in which leaves are developed from the growing point of a Phanerogam

this zone the youngest normally formed flower-rudiments are situated, as well as the youngest abnormally formed ones.   The arrangement in both cases is still more clearly manifested by the relative position of the bracts and the flowers which belong to them   it is noticed that on the normal portion of the inflorescence each bract is situated on the outer side of the flower which belongs to it; on the abnormal portion *a s a*, on the contrary, the bracts are situated nearer to the former apex *s* than the flowers which belong to them.   To come back now to the starting-point of our consideration, we may thus say that the formation of organs before and after the destruction of the central apex has occurred in progressive order; that is, progressive towards the true apex before the injury, and progressive towards the embryonal zone *z z* after the injury · and it is clear that it would not be quite to the point to designate the sequence of the formation of organs on the protuberance *a s a* as acropetal.

The acropetal or progressive order of development is strictly maintained by the leaves on ordinary vegetative shoots, at least no exception in this connection is as yet known.   In the region where flowers are formed, on the contrary, cases occur as a matter of fact where organs of leaf-like nature are interpolated between organs already existing, so that the youngest are no longer next the apex Payer has detected such cases in a large number of flowers where two or more circles of stamens (that is, metamorphosed leaves) are present, as,.for example, in *Dictamnus* and *Geranium*. He shows that the second circle of stamens arises on the receptacle outside the first, and therefore further from the apex or centre of the flower. Of course in these and similar cases the question might be raised whether the true embryonic formative tissue is not always perhaps to be sought only at the place where the youngest organs arise—a place which indeed need not always be situated at the apex. However, further pursuit of this question would involve us in difficulties with which I need not trouble the reader of this book.

The leaves arise at the growing-point of the shoot without exception as super-ficial outgrowths. This does not mean that only the outermost layer of tissue of the

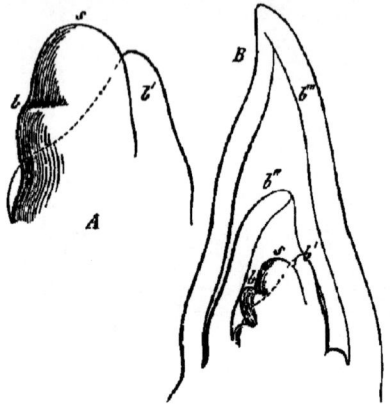

FIG. 306.—Apical region of two main shoots of *Zea Mais* s growing point consisting of very small cells from which the leaves *b' b'' b'''* proceed as multicellular protuberances which soon embrace the stem and envelope it and the young leaves like a hollow cone In the axil of the third-youngest leaf *b'* the youngest branch rudiment is seen as a rounded protuberance

FIG. 307 —Growing point at the end of the leaf-shoot of *Hippuris* (magnified)

growing-point is employed for the formation of the leaf; but the expression signifies that this layer always takes part in the origin and growth of the young leaf As a rule, however, layers of tissue situated deeper also co-operate in the formation of the leaf. It may thus be stated as the characteristic point that, in the origin of a leaf, complete continuity of the homonymous layers of tissue of the leaf and of the shoot-axis exists from the first, as is clear at once from the diagram Fig. 305, where *A* is the apex of the growing-point, which, like all growing-points which produce leaves, possesses the confocal structure described in the preceding lecture. *B*, *C*, and *D*, mark various stages in the origin of a new leaf, and the cells and perichnal walls denoted by Roman and Arabic numerals show how the individual cell-layers of the growing-point take part in the origin of a new leaf. The letters *a*, *b*, *c*, *x*, and *y*, in the figure, show how the existing anticlines and periclines are displaced in these processes of growth. Only when the leaf-rudiment has attained a certain

size does the differentiation of the vascular bundles take place, in the embryonic
tissue of the shoot-axis as well as the young leaf, as mentioned previously, so that the
vascular bundle curving out into the leaf represents the upper end of that which
descends in the shoot-axis.   The differentiations of tissue are similar when a normal
growing-point of a shoot arises from a growing-point already existing, that is, in the
branching of the shoot.   The case is quite otherwise in the origin of new roots,
however, as already pointed out in the lectures on Organography.   Whether the
roots arise from a mother-root or from a shoot they are always produced in the
interior of the tissue, so that the young root, when elongation begins at the base of
its growing-point, has to break through the external layers of tissue (cortex and
epidermis) of the mother-organ.   Of course in this case also a complete continuity of
the homonymous layers of tissue comes to exist subsequently, but only subsequently,

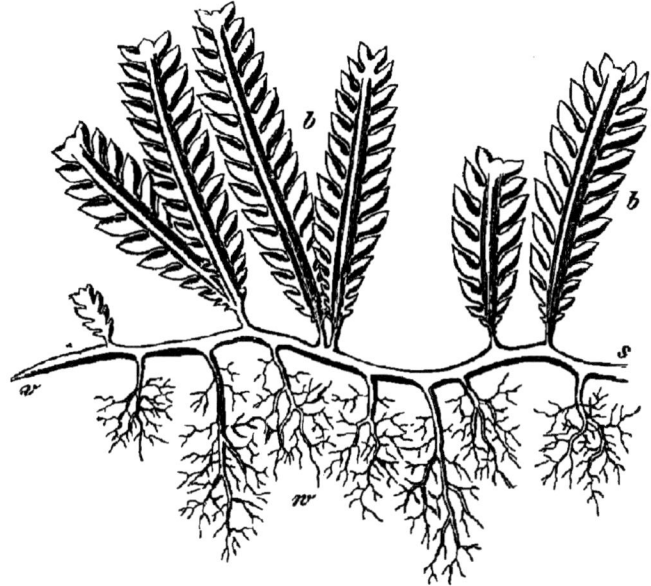

FIG 308.—*Caulerpa crassifolia*   *s* the shoot-axis, *v* its growing-point, *b* leaves, *w* roots

and the microscopic structure gives the impression that it is here so to speak a matter
of patchwork

For the subsequent form of the entire shoot it is important what portion of the
circumference the young leaf-rudiment occupies on the growing-point.   In most
cases it is only a small part of the circumference, and obviously this is always the
case when two, three, or more leaves are put forth at one and the same transverse
zone, that is, when a whorl of leaves springs from the growing-point.   In many
Monocotyledons (Grasses, Sedges, Aroids, Palms, &c.) and even in some families of
Dicotyledons, such as the Umbelliferæ and Polygonaceæ, however, the whole circumference of a transverse zone of the growing-point is occupied by the rudiment of
a leaf   In such cases the base of the leaf appears on further development as a
sheath surrounding the shoot-axis, at the upper edge of which the true leaf, the

so-called upper leaf, buds forth only on one side. If the leaf is subsequently segmented into petiole and lamina, which of course does not always happen, the petiole
is to be regarded as a structure subsequently interposed between the leaf-base and the
lamina, a subject to which we shall return in the next lecture

In the Mosses and Vascular plants the leaf-rudiments generally arise so closely
above and by the side of one another, that none of the free surface of the growing-
point at all is exposed beneath the youngest leaf. Only through the further course
of development in the second period of growth is it then decided whether the leaves
which arise closely one over the other are separated from one another by the
secondary intercalation of interfoliar parts on an elongating shoot-axis, or whether
this does not occur; in the latter case none of the free surface of the shoot-axis at all
appears, even in the fully grown condition, because the
leaves, situated close above and below one another,
occupy the entire surface of the shoot-axis, as for
example in the common Fern *Aspidium* and in the
short twigs of many trees, and the so-called radical
rosettes of many biennial Dicotyledons   Cases where
the leaves at the growing-point are from the first
so far distant from one another that naked interfoliar parts of the shoot-axis exist between them, are
probably extremely rare , as an example may be
mentioned the Bracken Fern (*Pteris Aquilina*), where
the growing-point of the horizontal stem annually produces only one leaf, which requires two years more
for its completion   In the leaf-forming Algæ also the
leaves usually arise quite close above and by the side
of one another on the shoot-axis, even though very long
interfoliar parts separate them subsequently, as is very
clearly the case in the Characeæ (cf Fig 95, p 96).
The genus *Caulerpa*, on the other hand, presents a
good example of the other case (Fig 308), where the
growing-point *v* of the shoot-axis always first elongates to a considerable extent before a new leaf
buds forth from it again.   We meet with similar
conditions of affairs in those Algæ also where the

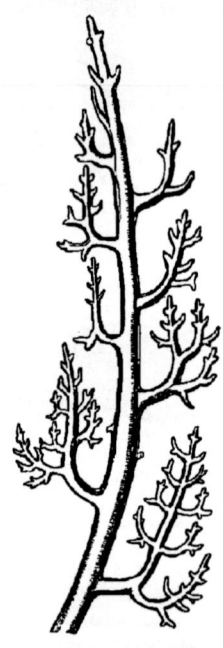

FIG 309.—Branching of a
leafless shoot of the Alga *Gelidium* (one of the Floridéæ)

lateral outgrowths of the growing-point of a shoot do not develope into flat leaves
in the ordinary sense, and where therefore the shoot constitutes a mere branch
system, as in Fig 309, where it may be noticed that the youngest branches appear at
some distance apart from the very first

Shoots, however, produce not only leaves and other organs, but new growing-
points of shoots generally arise again from their growing-points , that is, they
branch.

Only in very few plants does no branching take place—that is, no formation of
growing-points of secondary shoots.   The best known examples of these are found
in some small acrocarpous Mosses, and above all in a few Vascular Cryptogams
The longest known instance of this is the genus *Isoëtes*, the stem of which grows

for years, and nevertheless always remains short, and only produces leaves and roots, but no shoot-buds. The Ophioglossaceæ and Marattiaceæ also behave in exactly the same way, as well as the tall Tree-ferns. In all these cases the single existing growing-point of the shoot of the unbranched plant, even in advanced age, is the very same which was developed directly from the fertilised oosphere. Even the Cycadeæ, so similar to the Ferns, do not as a rule become branched from the growing-point, though this may occur in advanced age after the formation of flowers. It occurs also occasionally as an abnormality in the otherwise so copiously branched Pines that no secondary growing-points are produced from the original one of the seedling, and the tree remains for many years without branching. As an approximation to this, however, we may perhaps consider the case when the primary shoot developed directly from the embryo grows out into a dominant main stem, the lateral branches of which always grow considerably less vigorously than the stem itself,

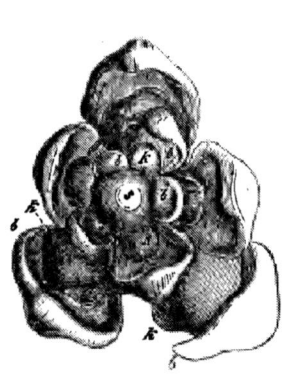

FIG. 310.—Apical region of a primary shoot of *Dictamnus Fraxinella* seen from above. *s* apex of the primary shoot; *b b b* the young leaves; *k k* their axillary buds. The two youngest leaves have as yet no axillary buds.

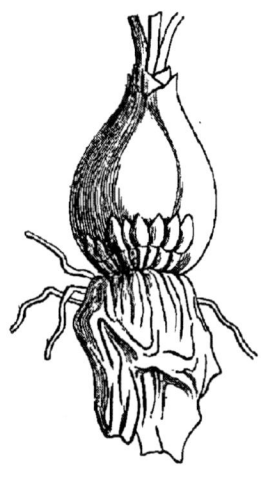

FIG. 311.—Bulb of *Muscari botryoides*. One of the lower bulb-scales (leaf) is turned back in order to show the numerous buds situated one beside the other in its axil.

as is the case in the Conifers and some other trees. In many species of Cactus a similar condition of affairs is found in that the shoot-buds, elsewhere developed so universally in the axils of the leaves of dicotyledonous plants, only rarely attain to further development: here, also, the growing-point of a shoot which has once attained the necessary vigour dominates the entire growth, and a lateral shoot is not easily permitted to make its appearance (*Cereus, Echinocactus, Mamillaria*).

In contrast to these rarer cases of the absence, or paucity of branching, however, the tendency prevails in the great majority of plants to produce new growing-points of shoots from the primary ones, and tertiary ones from the secondary ones; that is to develope branch-systems. In Monocotyledons and Dicotyledons it is an almost universal rule within the vegetative region (that is so long as flowers are not being formed) that a new growing-point of a shoot is formed in the axil of every leaf, and in fact very soon after the origin of the leaf itself; this makes its appearance either exactly in the angle between the leaf-base and the axis, or more on the leaf-base itself, or even on the shoot-axis above it. Not rarely indeed several growing-points of shoots arise in the axil of the leaf, and if the base of the leaf is very broad, as in the Monocotyledons, numerous shoot-buds may arise close to one another, as for example in the case of many bulbs, and the flowers in the broad bracts of species of *Musa* In Dicotyledons with a narrow leaf-insertion, moreover, two, three, four or more growing-points of shoots are often produced one above the other from the interfoliar part which is in process of elongation, as for example in *Gleditschia*, *Aristolochia*, and some other woody plants This regular production of new growing-points of shoots in the axils of the leaves obtains however, even in the Monocotyledons and Dicotyledons, only within the vegetative region: in the inflorescences it is a frequent phenomenon that flowering shoots arise without the previous formation of bracts (*Aroideæ, Cruciferæ*). Conversely, however, no growing-points of shoots make their appearance in the axils of the foliar structures of the flower itself The theory of the older morphology which culminated in the establishment of a so-called principle of axillary branching, therefore, does not generally obtain even in the Phanerogams with which that morphology was almost exclusively concerned, and this is still less the case with the other classes of plants If we confine ourselves in the first place to the Coniferæ, the nearest related to the Phanerogams, the rule certainly obtains here also that within the vegetative region shoot-buds are produced only in the axils of the leaves, but with the difference that although the leaves are exceedingly numerous, but few of them produce growing-points in their axils· in spite of the copious and magnificent branching of the Coniferæ, it is, from the point of view of its development, only sparse in comparison with that of the Monocotyledons and Dicotyledons. In the Vascular Cryptogams, however, and so far as is known in the Muscineæ and Algæ, the formation of secondary growing-points, or the branching of the vegetative shoot, is entirely unconnected with the axils of the leaves, although the tendency always exists for lateral shoots to make their appearance by the side of or under the insertion of individual leaves However it would be superfluous for our purpose to treat in greater detail here of the individual cases which have been more exactly investigated.

We have hitherto confined our attention, with respect to branching, to the ordinary case, where new growing-points of shoots spring laterally from a growing-point, or from a shoot-axis, or from a leaf-base, the parent growing-point itself continuing to grow undisturbed. Much rarer, and confined to a few small subdivisions of the vegetable kingdom only, is the so-called Dichotomy of the growing-point. We may take as the characteristic distinction of this that the embryonic tissue of a given growing-point obtains two apical points, each of which now constitutes the apex of a new growing-point, and thus the embryonic substance of a growing-point becomes, so to speak, split into two growing-points, situated close beside one another and equal in value. This case is particularly clear where an apical cell exists from which two new apical cells arise, each of which then forms its segments as I have already explained in the previous lecture (cf. Fig 291). The accompanying figure (Fig 312) may serve to illustrate the branch-system of the same plant, proceeding from the dichotomy. It will be observed that a depression occurs at the apex of the shoot, and that the prominences which lie right and left of it grow further and constitute branches of the shoot. The behaviour of a dichotomy of course becomes more complicated when leaf-forming shoots are concerned, as in the Lycopodiaceæ, where in all the genera and species not only the shoots but also the roots branch in a dichotomous manner. In contrast to the ordinary lateral, or as it is also termed monopodial branching, there is this characteristic feature, that the formation of the two new growing-points from the older one takes place not only above the youngest leaf (simply because it takes place in the apex itself) but it also stands in no relation whatever to the preceding leaves.

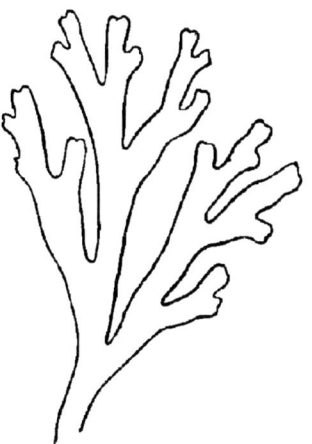

FIG. 312.—Dichotomously branched shoot of *Dictyota dichotoma*, a marine Alga.

A long misunderstood but nevertheless very simple case of dichotomy, and one which is not essentially different from those hitherto mentioned, is found in those Liverworts which possess broad band-like creeping shoots, especially the Marchantieæ and leafless Jungermannieæ. If we put aside the sequence of cell-divisions, which have been studied in every detail, as well as the presence or absence of an apical cell, here also the dichotomy consists in that the group of embryonic tissue at the base of the deep depression previously described becomes slightly extended in breadth, as shown in Fig. 313; the middle portion of this embryonic tissue then

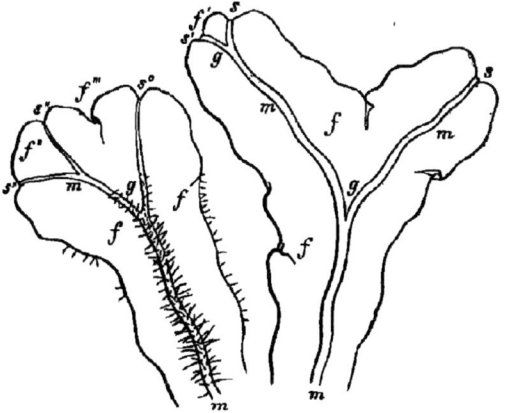

FIG 313.—Flat dichotomously branched shoot of *Metzgeria furcata.* (× about 15), *m m* mid rib of several layers, dichotomising at *g g*, *s s* growing-points, with projecting wing like outgrowths *f' f''*.

grows vigorously, and becomes transformed into permanent tissue, which now projects in the form of a wedge arched in front, while right and left of it the rest of the embryonic tissue remains as such and now constitutes two growing-points developed from one.

The formation of new growing-points of shoots in any of the above-mentioned ways constitutes, however, merely the ground-plan of the branch-system which will be ultimately developed, for it is only in rare cases that all the growing-points of shoots which have gradually arisen from one another, and ultimately form the primary shoot of the seedling, come to complete development. Very frequently this happens only in the case of a few, while the others pass over into a dormant condition, either to attain complete development in the next period of vegetation, or to remain unchanged for an indefinite time as the so-called dormant eyes of many forest trees, until by the removal of vigorous shoots opportunity is afforded to them for further development. The sprouting of numerous twigs from the older branches and stems of forest trees when the apical parts have been removed consists in the sudden invigoration of these dormant buds, which have often been developed many years previously when the corresponding part of the stem itself was yet in the condition of a bud. Such dormant eyes must not be confounded with the adventitious shoots to be described subsequently.

Like the leaves, the new lateral shoots usually arise exogenously, or superficially, so that not only the internal but also the outermost layers of tissue of the growing-point take part in their production, and thus a complete continuity of the systems of tissue is brought about, exactly as in the case of leaves. It was for a long time supposed that the Equisetums formed a peculiar exception to this very general rule. As a matter of fact we find, on cutting longitudinal sections through the buds of the haulms of these plants, the lateral buds situated in the axils of the leaf-sheaths, and completely enveloped by the tissue of the main shoot, much as in the case of roots, but more exact investigations have shown that this is only due to sub-sequent change, and that, even in the Equisetaceæ, the very youngest bud-rudiments, or lateral growing-points, proceed from superficial layers of tissue of the growing-point which gives rise to them. The matter is very similar, though more complicated, in the case of the two trees *Symphoricarpus* and *Gleditschia*, much cultivated in our gardens. We may say a few words with respect to *Gleditschia*: the thorns on the leaf-shoots are the original axillary shoots of the leaves, but by the growth of the mother-axis they become pushed some distance upwards from the axil of the leaf. A series of further buds then arise progressively towards the axil of the leaf, the embryonic tissue at the axil evidently persisting as such for a long time. These later buds remain very small at first, and, as Hansen established, become so enveloped and overgrown by the cortex of the mother-shoot during the current period of vegetation, that when they begin to sprout in the following spring it looks as if they had been produced in the interior of the cortex which they then break through. As the biology of plants everywhere affords thousands of examples of the fact that young buds are preserved for future periods of vegetation, and protected and enveloped in the most various ways, so we find even in some woody plants (e g. *Virgilia lutea*) that the broad base of the leaf encircles its axillary bud so completely that nothing at all is to be seen of it from without, and it only comes into view after the removal of the leaf-stalk

In contrast to all these various cases of an only apparently endogenous origin of shoot-buds, it appears however that flowers and inflorescences may arise in the interior of previously more or less amorphous masses of tissue, particularly in the case of parasitic Phanerogams; so that in the Balanophoreæ, Rafflesiaceæ, and perhaps also in the Orobancheæ, these reproductive shoots must first break through an envelope of tissue when they begin to elongate (cf Fig. 18, p. 28). However, the matter requires further investigation, and the same holds good probably also of certain growing-points of shoots in the Jungermannieæ among the Liverworts, which Leitgeb assumes to originate endogenously.

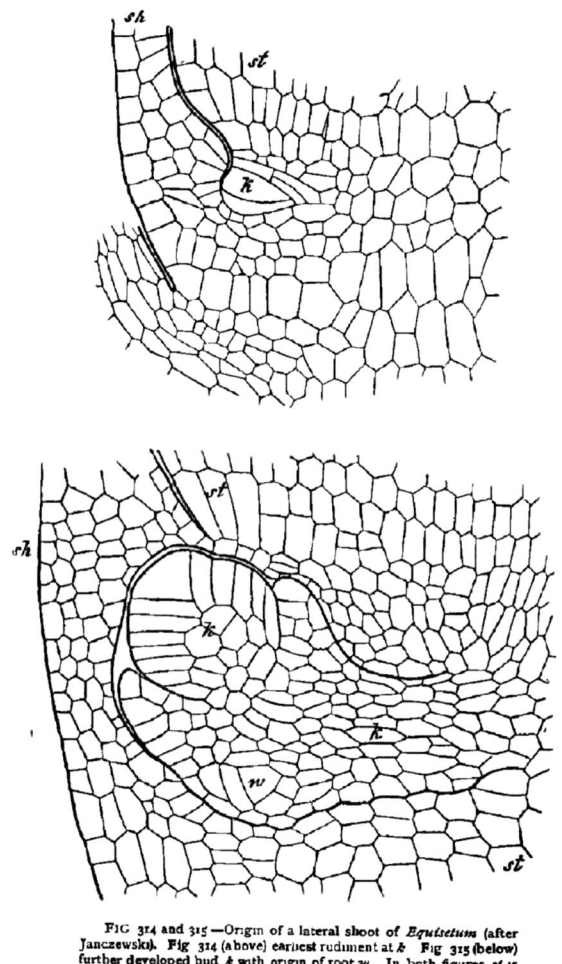

FIG 314 and 315 —Origin of a lateral shoot of *Equisetum* (after Janczewski). Fig 314 (above) earliest rudiment at *k* Fig 315 (below) further developed bud *k* with origin of root *w* In both figures *st* is the internode above the sheathing leaf *sh* (highly magnified)

The endogenous mode of origin is, on the contrary, a general peculiarity of the growing-points of roots; concerning which the most essential facts have already been stated in the introductory lectures on Organography (p 15). It is only necessary now to make the additional remark that the young lateral roots only make their appearance on the mother-root, as a rule, at a considerable distance from its growing-point. This, however, does not prove that they did not already exist in embryo in the neighbourhood of the mother growing-point, or even in it   Unfortunately, in spite of innumerable examinations of the apex of the root, special investigations on this question are wanting : only so much is certain, that in many cases the first visible rudiments of the young growing-points of roots are already to be found a few tenths of a millimetre behind the apex of the parent-root.   It has likewise already been mentioned in the lectures on Organography that the young roots arise progressively from a special simple layer of tissue at the circumference of the axial strand of the mother-root, and this, corresponding to the vascular strands, in two, three, or more longitudinal rows.   Since the first beginnings of these tissue-differentiations are recognisable right up to the apex of the growing-point in the mother-root, the facts given do not prove that the growing-points of the lateral roots did not already exist in embryo in the embryonic tissue at the growing-point of the mother-root.   While they then develope very slowly, the apex of the latter grows rapidly in length, and thus it appears as if they had been produced far distant from the parent growing-point. In the absence of exact investigations on this point (which entail very considerable difficulties moreover), we must not overlook the possibility that the first rudiments of young roots may be formed at a distance from the parent growing-point, here, however, the further assumption would present itself that the layer of tissue surrounding the axial strand, and from which the young roots originate, contains traces of embryonic substance derived from the growing-point.   This layer of tissue would then, with respect to the formation of organs, behave much as the cambium of wood-plants with respect to the formation of tissue, since we may regard the cambium also as a thin layer of embryonic tissue, which, however, only in rare cases produces growing-points of shoots.   This is saying nothing new, since even the tissue of the growing-point was formerly designated Cambium.

We have hitherto concerned ourselves exclusively with the formation of new growing-points from growing-points which already exist, or, to speak more generally, from embryonic tissue already present.   In this way arises the ordinary normal branching of shoots and roots, and the foundation for the complete normal architecture of a plant is laid.   It also happens, however, that new shoots and roots may originate at places where the tissue has already passed over into the permanent condition . in fully developed roots, in the interfoliar parts of shoot-axes, and more particularly in foliage leaves, the tissue of which is already completely differentiated and developed, new growing-points of roots and shoots may appear in somewhat numerous cases.   I distinguish these new formations exclusively with the name adventitious structures—a name which formerly signified many other things also— thus implying that they constitute something merely additional, something superfluous for the normal structure of the plant.   This is not saying that they are superfluous for the whole biology and maintenance of the plants concerned . on the contrary, adventitious roots are often important organs for the support of a plant, while adventitious shoots serve as organs of propagation which sooner or later become separated from the mother-plant as so called bulbils, and, forming adventitious roots, become independent plants.

Adventitious roots may originate, often in large numbers, at the most various places between existing lateral roots from a main root, or on shoot-axes or leaves, or even close beneath the growing-point of shoots, and may be indispensable even for the normal maintenance of the plant: this is the case, for example, with many Ferns, and with the runners and rhizomes of numerous other plants.

The occurrence of adventitious shoot-buds is much rarer. It takes place chiefly on fully developed or on young leaves. As particularly well-known examples may be mentioned those in the indentation of the margin of the leaf of *Bryophyllum calycinum*, and the bulbils regularly formed in the angles on the ramifications of the veins of the leaves of *Cardamine pratensis* and *Nasturtium officinale*. Very striking examples of such buds are found moreover in *Nymphæa micrantha* at the centre of the peltate leaf, and in various Aroideæ—e.g *Atherurus ternatus*, where the adventitious buds have the form of tubers or bulbs, which subsequently become free and form new plants. In a considerable number of other Monocotyledons and Dicotyledons also adventitious buds appear on the foliage leaves in the ordinary

FIG 316.—*Asplenium decussatum* Middle portion of a fully developed leaf the rachis *st* of which supports the pinnules *ll*, at the base of one of these has arisen the bud *k* which has already put forth a root (nat. size)

course of vegetation. these, however, so long as the mother-leaf is actively vegetating, continue in the bud-state, as in the cases mentioned previously.

Adventitious shoots are particularly common on the large foliage leaves of the Ferns, and they appear regularly in the angles of the pinnatifid laminæ of *Ceratopteris thalictroides*, and on the rachis of *Asplenium caudatum, A. decussatum*, and other species of this genus: they occur also on the under side of the mid-rib of *Woodwardia radicans* and others. In these cases, as in *Cardamine*, they grow while still connected with the mother-leaf into vigorous copiously branched plants, which sooner or later become free from the mother-leaf and can at once proceed to active vegetation. Among the most interesting examples of this kind we have moreover the formation of adventitious buds on the back of the living basal portions of the older foliage leaves of *Aspidium filix-mas* (the common Male-Fern), for this plant developes no lateral buds whatever except these adventitious shoots (which are moreover very isolated) and possesses no normal branching. It has already been stated in the introductory lectures on Organography that adventitious shoots are also developed not rarely from the roots of vascular plants, and new independent plants then proceed from these: this is the case, for example, in *Robinia, Ailanthus*, and also in the Fern *Ophioglossum*. To these cases also we may in a certain sense refer the production of shoot-buds from the growing-points of roots, as mentioned on p. 22.

In opposition to the view formerly held by Hofmeister, that all adventitious growing-points arise in the interior of the tissue, and that all so arising are to be designated adventitious, it is to be noticed that in that case almost all roots would have to be regarded as adventitious With respect to adventitious shoots it is demonstrated by recent investigations, and especially those of Hansen on *Cardamine*,

Nasturtium, and *Atherurus,* and is very probable for the remaining cases, that they do not arise endogenously at all, but exogenously; in fact Hansen showed that in the cases mentioned cell-divisions and other changes appear in various directions at the points in question, in the epidermis and cortical tissue of leaves which are already fully developed, thus transforming the permanent tissue into embryonic tissue, which then forthwith forms a conical growing-point whence leaves and, subsequently, roots proceed.

If the definition above given is adhered to, to regard as adventitious all growing-points which proceed from already differentiated permanent tissue, we must also regard the origin of the leafy stems of a true Moss as altogether adven-

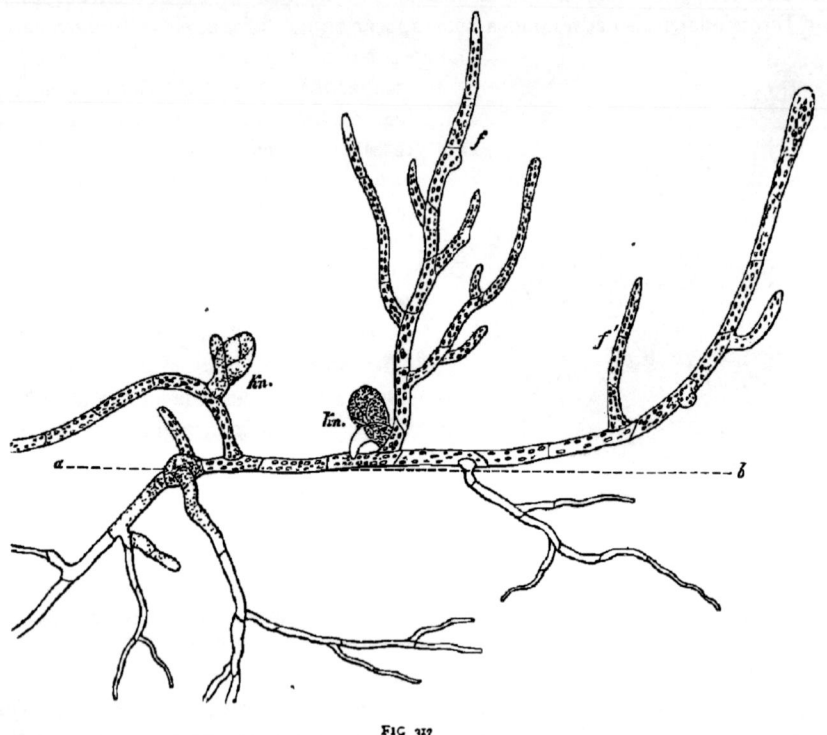

FIG 317

titious, since, as has already been said in the introductory lectures on Organography and as is to be seen from Fig 317, these arise from certain cells of the protonema which have already acquired the character of permanent cells. Here, as in other cases, it simply results that sharp limitations with regard to Nature are always ineffectual; since, though we see in adventitious structures in the higher plants something superfluous for their architecture, this no longer holds good in the case of the Moss.

In a certain sense the formation of so-called gemmæ in the simply organised Liverworts, Algæ, and some Fungi depends upon adventitious budding; the protoplasm of the already fully developed cells of leaves or other organs may become isolated from the remaining tissues, surround themselves with new cell-walls, and after a period of rest develope into new plants.

All these phenomena of adventitious budding apparently stand in contradiction to the previous statement that the formation of organs in the vegetable kingdom proceeds from the embryonic tissue of the growing-point, which we have in its turn regarded as a derivative from the embryonic substance of the fertilised oosphere   But considerations from general points of view, to which I shall return subsequently, render this apparent contradiction irrelevant; as the growing-points which occur so universally are subordinated to the still more general conception of embryonic tissue, so also this latter again may be looked upon simply as a collection of embryonic substance formed during the process of nutrition in the plant, and collected at definite spots according to circumstances in each case.

In the cases of the adventitious formation of shoots and roots hitherto considered, it occurs in the particular species of plant at certain definite points, and belongs moreover to the normal phenomena of life.   At another opportunity, however, and proceeding from other points of view, I shall have to show that adventitious growing-points may arise at almost any given spot on the older parts of plants, when these are cut off or injured, and that in this manner a new shoot provided with roots may arise from the separated portions of shoots and roots of many plants.   It is better to reserve these phenomena for subsequent consideration, however, since they serve to demonstrate particularly clearly the influence of external forces on the production of new organs.

LECTURE XXIX.

AXIS OF GROWTH; POLARITY; LATERALITY, RELATIONS OF POSITION.

THE terms at the head of this chapter denote a series of relations in space within the plant, the consideration of which we cannot here entirely pass over, because they afford us clear ideas on certain general processes of growth; and it is shown at the same time that a series of the most important relations between growth and external influences—i.e. phenomena of irritability—are only intelligible if we abstract from the relations of form evident to the senses, and keep in view these relations which are only accessible to abstraction.

On every organ it is easy to distinguish two opposite ends, which we may designate base and apex[1] The base is the place where the organ arises from its parent-organ, and is fixed to it; the other end, the apex, on the contrary, is free and movable As the organ elongates, it is the apex which is pushed forwards in space by means of the growth taking place between it and the base. When the bud at the end of a shoot, or the growing-point of a root, gradually traverses a path of several centimetres, or even of several metres, in a perpendicular, horizontal, or oblique direction, this is accomplished by means of the growth between apex and base, by the intercalation of new substance, and, simply because the base is fixed while the bud with the apex is free, it is the latter which is moved forwards in space.

A line which is supposed to run in the interior of the organ from the base to the apex gives the longitudinal direction, or the direction of growth in length; and a plane which takes in this line is a longitudinal section. Every surface standing at right angles to this plane is a transverse section.

---

[1] In my '*Lehrbuch der Botanik*' (Aufl II 1870, § 26) I have already referred sufficiently in detail to the significance, not only morphological but also physiological, of the distinction between apex and base of the organs of plants; and I pointed out in my treatise '*Über Stoff und Form der Pflanzenorgane*' (Arb des bot Inst in Wzbg, B. II, pp 452 and 689) that Voechting had subsequently, in his book '*Über Organbildung im Pflanzenreich*' (1878), given another inaccurate meaning to the polarity designated by base and apex. In my text-book, as well as in my later treatise, '*Über die Anordnung der Zellen in jüngsten Pflanzentheilen*' (Arb des bot. Inst in Wzbg, B. II, p. 101), the previous entirely inaccurate definition of the axis of growth by Hofmeister was also corrected

If the growing-point is situated at the free end or apex of the organ, then the base of the latter is its oldest part, and every transverse section meets a part so much the younger the nearer it lies to the apical growing-point. If, however, the embryonic tissue which represents the growing-point is situated at the base of the organ, as is the case in many leaves, internodes, etc., then the relative age is in the reverse direction.

The longitudinal direction does not suffice to fix the position of the axis of growth in an organ. To define this more exactly the transverse section of the organ in question must be taken into consideration · in the transverse section of any organ there is a point which, with respect to the outline and the anatomical structure, constitutes the organic centre. Every small portion of the surface of the transverse section exhibits in its structure a side turned towards the periphery, and one turned towards this organic centre, and is bounded laterally by lines which we may term the

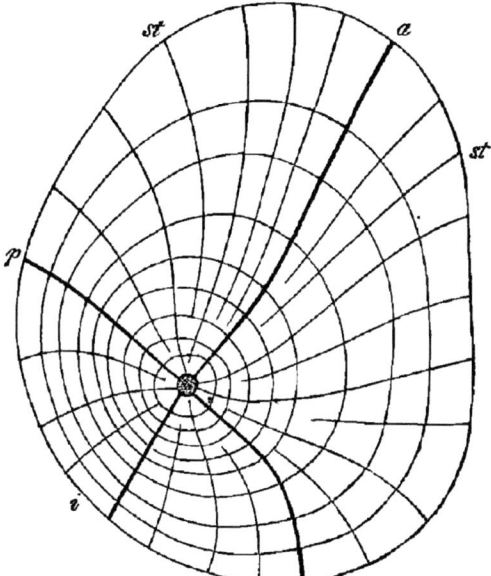

FIG 318.—Transverse section of the woody body of the stem of a *Lime*

radii of the transverse section. Just as the organic centre by no means necessarily coincides with the geometric centre of the transverse section, so also the radii are not always straight, but often curved lines, as is clear at once from the consideration of Fig. 318. Very generally the internal structure of the organ exhibits peripheral layers and radial arrangement at the same time, as is distinctly perceived on any transverse section of wood ; but every hair also, and even petioles and leaves, as well as the transverse section of single cells, may be thus regarded.

If we now suppose the organic centres of all the transverse sections of an organ (a shoot-axis, the mid-rib of a leaf, or a root, etc.) to be connected together by a line, this is the longitudinal axis, and also the axis of growth of the organ ; and, according to circumstances in each case, it may be a straight or a curved line, or if at first straight it may subsequently become curved, and conversely. A plane which contains the axis of growth is an axial longitudinal section. If the axis is curved in one plane there is of course only one axial longitudinal section; if, however, the organ is itself spiral, the axis of growth also describes a spiral line which cannot be contained in one plane.

As a rule the growth in the direction of the longitudinal axis is more vigorous—i e is more rapid, or continues longer, or both together—than is the case in directions across the axis, as is at once seen in the case of most shoot-axes, roots, leaves, and hairs. This character, however, cannot be employed for the general definition of the axis of growth there are cases where the growth takes place more energetically transversely to the longitudinal axis than parallel with it, as, for example, in the stem of *Isoetes,* in the short and broad fruits of some varieties of the Gourd, and in many leaves which are broader than they are long   However, no doubt can ever arise with respect to the axis of growth in such cases, since it is always possible to determine with certainty whether the transverse or the longitudinal section of an organ is under observation, and with a little practice even a very small portion of a transverse or longitudinal section suffices for the recognition of its true nature.

If the growth in the direction of the axis is unlimited in the sense given above, the formation of external organs as well as the internal structural relations repeat themselves in the same direction; the organ becomes segmented into a series of parts which may be distinguished as Metameres—an expression already employed in Zoology.   The individual internodes of a shoot, with the leaves or whorls of

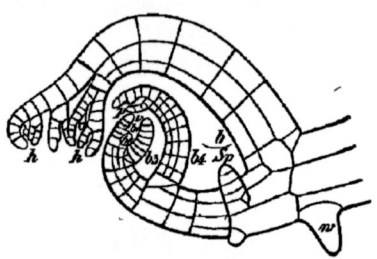

FIC 319.—Anterior portion of a shoot of *Herposiphonia repens* (one of the Florideæ) From the shoot axis, which is curved forwards and upwards, and the growing point of which is at *v* the leaves *b'—b*[?] arise , these are likewise curved *sp* lateral shoot , *w* root (after Goebel)

leaves, lateral buds and other organs belonging to them, represent these metameres. If, however, the free growing-point of a shoot or leaf normally concludes with the formation of some special organ, metameres may still be present, but they are not similar to one another; on the contrary, they undergo metamorphosis from the base towards the apex, as is particularly evident, for example, in the different forms of the foliage leaves on upright shoot-axes which conclude with a terminal flower (*Ranunculus acer, Papaver somniferum*).   The shoots of many horizontal creeping or climbing plants, on the other hand, consist of metameres which resemble one another, e.g *Lysimachia nummularia, Cucurbita, Glechoma, Marsilia,* etc.

The presence of an axis of growth does not necessarily imply a distinction of base and apex also, although other cases may occur only among the very lower Algæ.   For instance, the filaments of the Algæ *Spirogyra* and *Sphæroplea,* as well as the filamentous cell-families of the Desmidieæ and Diatomeæ, have always a longitudinal axis, though the two ends of the filament exhibit no distinction of apex and base   With this state of affairs is connected the fact that such plants are not fixed by the end to a substratum.   In the globular cell-families of the Volvocineæ we find no distinct axis of growth at all, but only a middle point around which the whole organisation is more or less symmetrically arranged on all sides , and some flat discoid

Algæ, as *Pediastrum* and *Coleochæte scutata*, may be looked upon, so far as their relations of growth are concerned, as representing a thin transverse disc cut out of a radially constructed shoot-axis.

The ordinary case, however, is that of polar structure—i. e. the external and internal organisation exhibit a peculiar arrangement along an axis of growth, in such a way that all the relations of organisation are directed from the base towards the apex. This is very evident, for example, in almost all shoots, where it is possible to see with the greatest clearness even on small pieces which is the anterior and which the posterior end, or which is the base and which the apex   Doubt could only exist on this sub-

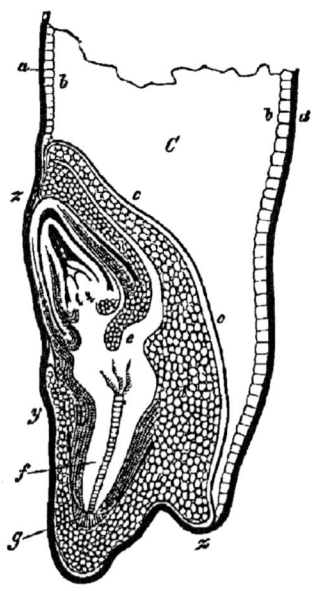

ject, in the absence of exact investigation, in the case of roots deprived of the apex. The polarity to which I here refer thus indicates a progressive differentiation in the direction of the longitudinal axis, which may be compared to a certain extent, at least so far as it concerns the innermost nature—the capacity for reaction—to that of a magnet.

The polarity appears more sharply ex-pressed, however, in the development of a new individual from a spore or from an oospore, where a distinct con-trast is at once observable between the root-end and the shoot-end. This is the case in the simplest and most elegant form with the ovoid swarm-spores of many Algæ. The narrower colourless end, which is anterior and provided with cilia during the swimming movement, already indicates the root-pole even before germination, while the other end, green and thick, may be distinguished as the shoot-pole. The swarm-spore subsequently clings by means of the root-pole to a solid body,

FIG. 320.—Longitudinal section through the grain and embryo of the Wheat, only the lower part *a x a* being shown *C* lower part of endosperm, *f* primary root, *g* its root-cap, *e e* the so-called *scutellum* or ab-sorbing organ of the embryo

and the root-like organ of attachment is developed there, while the free shoot-pole developes into a simple or branched shoot. This is not the place to go into many other cases, and I may therefore at once refer to the behaviour of the young embryos of the Vascular plants.   Here also, as in the case of a swarm-spore, the con-trast between root-pole and shoot-pole makes itself evident at an early period, and when the embryo is to a certain extent further developed, especially in the ripe seed in the case of the Phanerogams, it already actually consists of a root at the one end and of the first shoot at the other.   That these two poles, which make their appearance even in the fertilised oosphere, subsequently come to act as root and shoot, and have an importance which is not merely something external and formal, but which dominates the whole being of the plant, follows not only from the different relations of growth of root and shoot, but equally from the reactions of both parts towards external influences, or, what is the same thing, from their irritability, and the phenomena of irritability which appear in all parts of the plant without exception, will only become clear and comprehensible in all respects when the polarity of the organ is taken into account also. That a tree developes its crown in the air and its root in the earth is ultimately to be referred to the polarity of the root-end and shoot-end already present in the fertilised oosphere, by means of which the capacity to re-act towards light, gravitation, &c. is so distributed that the upright position of the tree finally results from it. Of course this can only become intelligible when the phenomena of geotropism and heliotropism are more closely studied What has just been stated is only for the purpose of pointing out that it is no mere play-ing with empty terms when we speak of polarity in the plant, on the con-trary, polarity denominates its whole life and growth.

Those plants which creep on the surface of the earth, or float horizontally on water, usually under-go a change of their polarity on further development. This may take place to such an extent that the original root perishes, while roots make their appearance on the under or shaded side of the forward-growing shoot, the upper side of the same shoot producing leaves and other organs. In this way arise dorsi-ventral plants, the shoot-axes of which possess a ven-

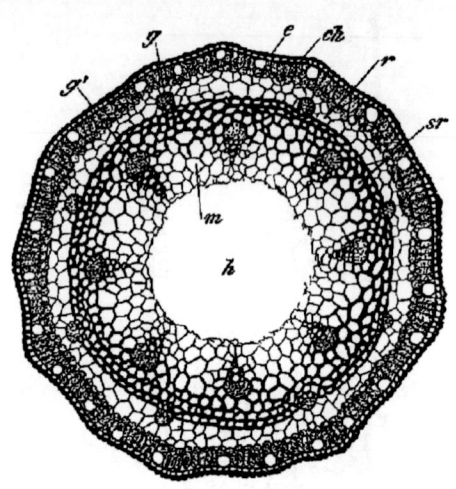

FIG 321 —Transverse section of the flower-scape of *Allium schœno prasum* (× about 30) *e* epidermis, *ch* chlorophyll cells, *r* colourless parenchyma of the cortex, *m* parenchyma of pith, *gg'* vascular bundles, *sr* ring of sclerenchyma

tral side whence the roots spring, and a true shoot-side (as one may best term it) or upper, light side There thus appears a polarity transverse to the axis of growth—a polarity which elsewhere exists in the direction of the shoot-axis itself. However, I shall return to this important point, apart from which the life of very many plants remains a puzzle.

As a preliminary, it is necessary to make ourselves acquainted somewhat more in detail with respect to the distribution of the relations of organisation on the transverse section, or rather around the axis of growth. Unfortunately there is no satisfactory word to designate what is here referred to, for lack of a better the term Laterality may be employed[1] It includes the two cases of radial

---

[1] The mutual relations of the parts of a plant, designated Laterality in the text, correspond in the main to what was formerly termed the symmetry of plants After a very valuable treatise of Mohl's (*Vermischte Schriften*, 1845, p 12) botanists for more than twenty years did not concern themselves with these very important matters, until I again took up the subject in the second edition of my 'Text-book,' 1870, p 26, though proceeding from other points of view. In my treatise *Über orthotrope und plagiotrope Pflanzentheile* (Arb. des bot Inst B II, p 226) I then brought into notice the intimate connection between radial structure and orthotropic growth, and between dorsi-ventral structure and plagiotropic growth

and dorsi-ventral growth. These apparently purely geometrical relations determine, like polarity, in every respect the external form and internal capacity for reaction of the organ towards external influences   The entire mode of life of a plant or of a single organ is essentially dependent upon whether it belongs to the radial, bilateral, or dorsi-ventral type.   Above all it depends upon these properties in which direction an organ attains its normal position.

The radial structure is most distinctly shown on transverse sections of roots and perfectly upright shoot-axes.   In the transverse section of such an organ the various masses of tissue appear arranged in three, four, or more directions in such a way that if we suppose the transverse section cut in half, the one half is, so to speak, the reflected image of the other, and three, four, or more such divisions may be imagined.   If a radially constructed organ branches, the branches which resemble one another appear on it in three, four, or more directions.   Particularly clear examples are afforded by shoots with the leaves in whorls, but those with spirally arranged scattered leaves also belong here   The radial structure of an organ is evinced in general as much in its anatomical structure as in its capacity for producing outgrowths (roots, leaves, lateral shoots); but perhaps the fact is still more important, and at any rate it stands in the closest connection with the above, that radially constructed organs are also sensitive in an equal degree on all sides of the axis of growth to external influences or stimuli, or, as I have designated it shortly, such organs are orthotropic—i.e. when they are submitted to a directive force acting from without, as gravitation or a ray of light, they become curved until the axis of growth of the organ has acquired exactly the direction of the acting force.   Meanwhile the object here is only to indicate preliminarily the importance of this property.   For the moment it will be well to render the reader somewhat better acquainted, by means of a few easily intelligible examples, with the meaning of the word Radial.

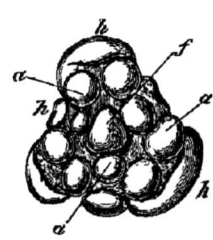

FIG. 322 —Very young flower of *Rheum Rhubarb)* seen from above   it still consists entirely of embryonal tissue   *h* three of the six perianth leaves, *a a* the anthers arranged in two whorls, *f* the ovary (highly magnified)

Since the expression radial (and the same is true of bilateral and dorsi-ventral) refers to the arrangement of the relations of organisation around the longitudinal axis of an organ or of an entire plant, the relations in question are observed most conveniently on a transverse section.   With respect to the out-shoots from a common axis, the mere view from above, as in Fig. 322, often suffices for obtaining a satisfactory picture of the arrangement.   That this flower, still in an early stage of development and composed essentially of embryonic tissue, is radially constructed is obvious at once if three straight lines are drawn from the central point of the ovary *f* to the three outer floral envelopes *h*, and then produced backwards.   The whole flower is divided by each of these three lines into two practically symmetrical halves in each case, and it is unimportant which of these three bisections is taken into consideration; the halves produced in each case are alike in nature.   The radial structure with respect to out-growths also appears very clear on transverse sections of the buds of shoots, as in Fig. 323   If we suppose straight lines to be drawn from its centre, where the shoot-axis is situated, to the points marked 1, 2, 3, 4, 5, in the midribs of the leaves, and produced to the other sides, five divisions of the entire system are obtained, in which the transverse sections of the subsequent leaves 6, 7, 8, 9, 10 are also arranged; only care must be taken lest error be made on account of a few minor irregularities, which depend in part upon the mutual pressure of the organs closely packed together in the bud-scales I–V, but which are in part artificially produced in the cutting. It is noticed further that the leaves numbered 1–9 in order of age, in spite of the radial arrangement, are nevertheless not arranged in circles as in the preceding examples; on the contrary, an inspection of the same shoot after its unfolding, when the interfoliar parts have elongated, would demonstrate that the leaf 2 is situated higher than 1, 3 higher than 2, and so forth. The leaves are, as is usually said, arranged spirally around the

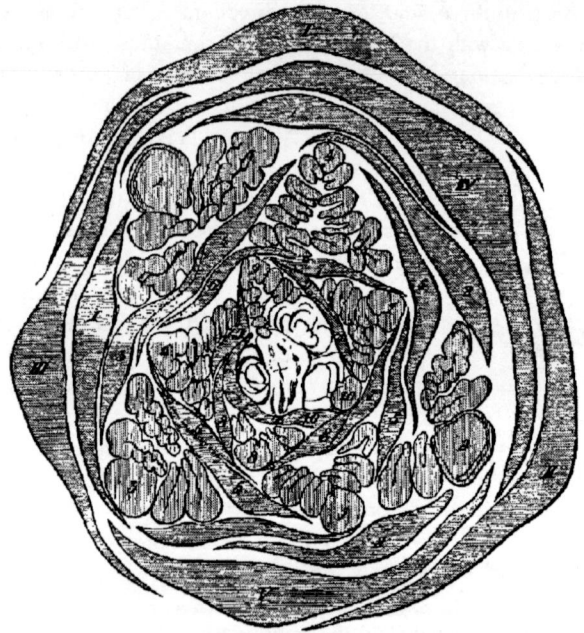

FIG. 323.—Transverse section through a winter bud of *Spiræa sorbifolia*. *I—IV* bud-scales; 1—9 the pinnate leaves, with their stipules (numbered similarly).

axis, that is, if a line is supposed to run round the shoot-axis so that it takes in the points 1, 2, 3–9, it forms a spiral. By means of longitudinal sections such a shoot with spirally arranged out-growths would never be divided into actual or even approximately symmetrical halves, as the young flower considered above; nevertheless it is advantageous on physiological grounds to regard this very common case also as belonging to the radial type. The off-shoots radiate in five directions, not from the same but from different levels on the shoot-axis, a fact which is of subordinate importance for physiological conclusions. Instead of a transverse section then a so-called diagram serves to represent the arrangement not only on an individual shoot but even on an entire shoot-system. The whole is supposed to be looked at from above, and a sufficient number of concentric circles are drawn on the paper;

these circles represent as it were successive transverse sections, and this so that the outermost circle represents the lowest transverse section, and the following ones sections at higher and higher levels. On these circles the organs which arise at the different transverse sections are transferred in the order established by careful study. In this way is produced in Fig. 324 a diagram of an entire plant of *Euphorbia helioscopia* in flower, with the exception of the root. It is only necessary to observe that the leaves *cc* and 1–10, and the central figure *B* which represents the first terminal flower, belong to the same shoot-axis. The five figures arranged around the centre, on the other hand, represent the diagram of five lateral shoots which have been developed from the axils of the leaves 6–10; each of these five shoots has produced only three leaves and a terminal flower *B*, and in the axils of the three leaves appear

FIG 324.—Diagram of a small plant of *Euphorbia helioscopia*   *c c* cotyledons, *II* the first, 1—10 the subsequent foliage leaves, 6, 7, 8, 9 and 10 form a whorl, *B I* (in the centre) the terminal flower of the primary shoot, *B II* the terminal flower of one of the five axillary shoots, *III* in each case leaves of axillary shoot of second order

again three shoots, each with three leaves. Without going more deeply into the varied relations of symmetry of this entire system, I may simply remark that the shoot commences with two opposite leaves *cc* (the cotyledons) upon which follow two foliage-leaves (*I*) decussate with them. Further upwards, however (i.e. further inwards in the diagram), the leaves 1–10 are situated, no longer in pairs but singly, at various heights on the axis; at the same time appear lateral displacements, so to speak, the leaf 3 stands above 1, but the leaf 5 stands not exactly over 2, as would correspond to the original order with which the arrangement of the leaves began, and finally we find the five leaves 6–10 arranged in a circle, and forming a whorl, whence the shoot-axis which lower down puts forth leaves radiating in four directions is now surrounded by leaves equally disposed in five directions. The central flower *B* also has five more such enveloping leaves, which alternate however with the preceding leaves 6–10, i.e. fall in the interspaces between their five radii. finally, the tripartite figure in the centre of the flower *B* is the ovary composed of three leaves. It is thus seen that the arrangements of the leaves on one and the same axis changes in this as in most other cases; moreover, the arrangement of the leaves on the five lateral shoots, as the diagram shows at once, is again different from that on the main shoot. In spite of all these irregularities, however, the radial type is nevertheless maintained, at least on the main shoot of the plant; the outgrowths radiate in four or five directions, and there would be no essential difference if they radiated in eight or thirteen directions. These very few examples will probably suffice to show the reader what is implied by the term radial

Radial structure stands in direct contrast to bilateral structure, and here we have at once to distinguish two different cases, namely, ordinary bilaterality[1], and the bilaterality which is combined with dorsi-ventral organisation If, for example, we have an upright shoot furnished with two opposite rows of leaves, and we suppose this so bisected longitudinally that all the leaves are at the same time also bisected, the two halves of the shoot appear nearly symmetrically alike If, on the contrary, we make the plane of division at right angles to the previous one, so that the leaves are not divided, we again obtain in the same way two similar halves, which are now however conditioned differently from the halves of the first division. In the first case each half of the shoot has two rows of half leaves; in the second case each has one row of whole leaves Such a structure might just as well be named quadrilateral as bilateral, or even doubly bilateral In any case, a symmetrically similar second half exactly corresponds to each half, and when gravitation, light, and other directive forces act equally from all sides on such a shoot it places itself vertically—it is orthotropic, like a radially constructed shoot, and it is physiologically to be relegated to the radial type

Much more frequent and essentially different from the latter, however, is the dorsi-ventral bilaterality met with in very many creeping and climbing shoots, in all leaves, and even in very many lateral shoots which spring from orthotropic and radial main shoots. The dorsi-ventral organisation has always as a consequence that the organs concerned are plagiotropic towards external influences, i e the effect of gravitation, light, and other directive forces induces such organs (which are usually moreover extended flat) to place themselves across the direction of gravitation and of the ray of light. We have to regard as the commonest examples of dorsi-ventral bilaterality the ordinary flat foliage-leaves Their bilaterality is at once clear on observing how two halves of the lamina exist right and left of the mid-rib; these are usually nearly symmetrical in leaves on upright shoots, in those on horizontal or oblique shoots they are generally more or less unsymmetrical. The leaves of the Elm and the so-called oblique leaves (e g. *Begonia*) afford well-known examples of

---

[1] The doubly bilateral but not dorsi-ventral organs are closely connected with radial organs, both as respects geometric considerations and their reactions towards external influences, in particular they are, like those, orthotropic, as is easily perceived in the case of the very excellent example of the gemmæ of *Marchantia* Hence, although from a purely formal and geometrical point of view, the chief contrast appears to lie between radial and bilateral organs, nevertheless, so far as physiology is concerned, the contrast between radial and dorsi-ventral organs is much more important

this. If the leaf is divided or branched, then in like manner the halves of the entire leaf situated right and left of the mid-rib are symmetrical or unsymmetrical nevertheless they are always equally and oppositely constructed, as our right and left hand Fig 325 shows several foliage-leaves of an Aroid, the orthotropic and radially constructed stalk of which grows vertically out of the earth, while its bilateral, symmetrically branched lamina is at the same time dorsi-ventral, and thus situated oblique or horizontal.

Flat foliage-leaves, as every one knows, are differently constituted on the under and upper sides—they are dorsi-ventral. The lower side is frequently hairy while the upper is smooth. the veins project as ribs below, while on the upper side there are generally corresponding depressions : the under side is dull, the upper side shining and dark green, and so forth The difference between the upper and lower sides appears still more conspicuous on regarding the transverse section of a leaf under the microscope, as represented in Fig. 326. If we suppose the mid-rib MN bisected by a vertical line, this corresponds to the principal section of the leaf, and divides the whole bilateral lamina into a right and a left half We can imagine no plane of division situated in any way at right angles to this, however, by which the transverse section of the leaf would be so divided into equivalent upper and lower halves. As the figure shows, the whole organisation of the leaf is differently constituted in the upper and lower halves, though no very definite boundary line

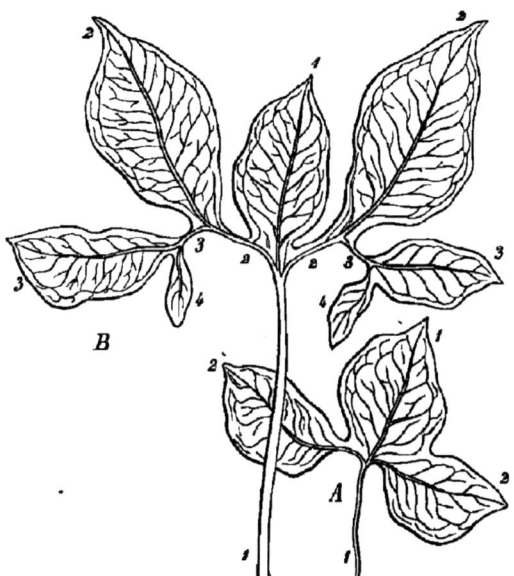

FIG 325.—Leaves of *Amorphophallus bulbosus* *A* is branched once, *B* three times.

exists between the two; and it is just in this that the character of the dorsi-ventrality lies. It must be noticed, however, that the visible anatomical structure which we here take into consideration, is itself again simply the expression of a dorsi-ventral constitution situated still more deeply in the invisible organisation. It can be shown that in every individual cell of the leaf the half turned upwards is differently constituted and re-acts differently towards stimuli from the lower one. This remarkable fact comes out still more clearly in the case of those plants which consist not of cell-tissue but of simple vesicles : in such cases the dorsi-ventrality is often not to be established by means of the microscope, but by the reactions towards gravitation and light, which compel us to the assumption that in such simple utricles the molecular structure presents corresponding relations of direction across the axis of growth.

The flat shoots of the Liverworts exhibit a dorsi-ventrality like that of the foliage-leaves, which they resemble in other respects also, and the same is the case with many Algæ and the prothallus of the Fern. In all these cases the contrast between the upper and lower (or dorsal and ventral) side is still more peculiarly characterised by the nature of their off-shoots: the roots always arise from the

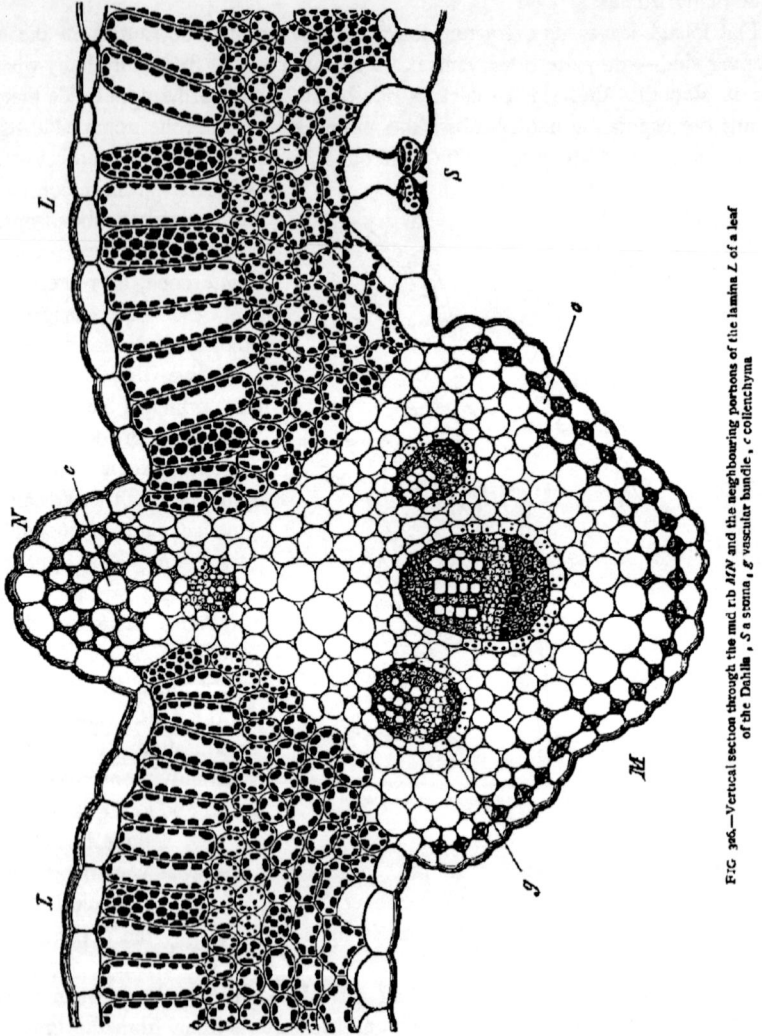

FIG. 306.—Vertical section through the mid. r.b *MN* and the neighbouring portions of the lamina *L* of a leaf of the Dahlia, *S* a stoma; *s* vascular bundle; *c* collenchyma

lower or ventral side, which is turned away from the light, while the sexual organs of the dorsi-ventral Liverworts arise from the upper side; those of the prothallus of the Fern from the lower side, which is turned from the light.

The relations are more complicated when a shoot possesses dorsi-ventral organisation, and at the same time a sharp segmentation into axis and leaves;

and this case is very common. The genus of non-cellular Algæ *Caulerpa*, so often referred to already, presents a clear example of this As shown in Fig. 327, the shoot-axis *s v* is sharply segmented off from the roots *w* and leaves *b*. The shoot-axis creeps horizontally, and its dorsi-ventrality comes out far less in its anatomical structure than in its producing exclusively roots on the under side and exclusively leaves on the upper side; and when lateral shoots originate from the shoot-axis (which rarely happens however) these come forth alternately on the right and left flanks. It may here also be mentioned in anticipation that the roots and leaves which spring from the dorsi-ventral, and therefore plagiotropic shoot-axis, are, in their turn, orthotropic. the roots grow vertically downwards and branch radially, the leaves grow vertically upwards and branch bilaterally. Just as in this unusually clear case, the dorsi-ventral character of the branching occurs in other Algæ which undergo cell-divisions

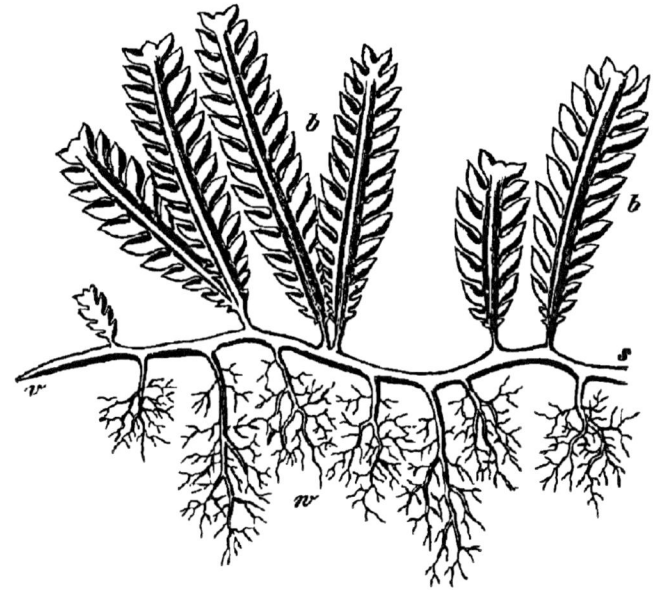

FIG 327.—*Caulerpa crassifolia.*

as they grow, and even in many highly organised Cryptogams and Phanerogams. The entire group of Rhizocarpeæ behave like *Caulerpa*, and among the Phanerogams *Utricularia* especially is to be mentioned, because in it the lateral shoots sprout from the dorsal side and the leaves from the flanks of the dorsi-ventral axis, among the Ferns again the genus *Lygodium* is especially remarkable, because in it the leaves arise in *one* series from the dorsal side of the dorsi-ventral creeping stem

In these and other cases it is the plumule which, gathering strength as the main shoot, assumes the dorsi-ventral structure, so that the entire plant is dominated by the dorsi-ventrality in its organisation. It happens much more frequently, however, particularly in Phanerogams, that the plumule possesses a radial structure from the beginning, with its off-shoots on three or more sides, and grows upwards, and then not only all leaves, but also the lateral shoots springing from the orthotropic main shoot, are dorsi-ventral in structure. This is unusually clear in some Conifers, especially in the genus *Abies* all the lateral branches springing from the radially constructed stem, which grows perpendicularly upwards, are here bilateral and dorsi-ventral in structure, and grow out in a horizontal direction Even in many Dicotyledons the same occurs, e. g. in the edible Chestnut, the Red Beech and others, where the vertical main shoot exhibits radial phyllotaxis and branching, but the lateral shoots bilateral and dorsi-ventral structure—bilateral branching combined with a tendency to horizontal or oblique direction.

As follows from what has been stated hitherto, the capacity of the organs of a plant to react towards gravitation, light and other directive forces, so that they grow in a definite position of equilibrium with respect to the horizon, co-operates causally with their radial or dorsi-ventral structure, or, as we may also say, the Anisotropy[1] of the organs is determined at once by their radial or dorsi-ventral structure. A more detailed consideration of this matter is better relegated, however, to the chapter on the phenomena of irritability, though on account of the close interdependence between growth and anisotropy the subject could not be entirely passed over here.

For the elucidation of the most essential difference between radial and dorsi-ventral structure of an organ, however, the following considerations may serve in addition. Let us imagine an ordinary foliage-leaf, in which the upper and lower

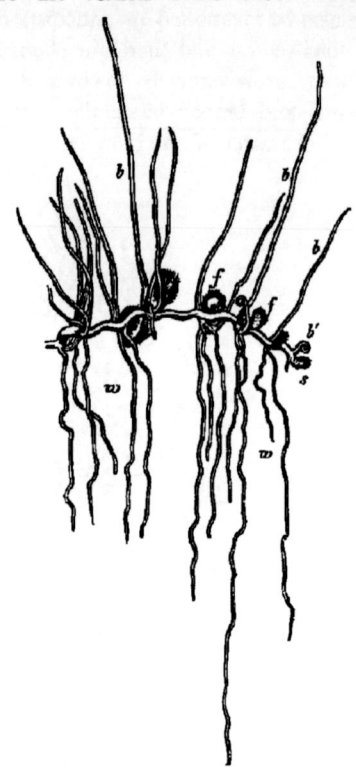

FIG. 328.—*Pilularia globulifera* (nat size).
s terminal bud of the stem, *b b'* leaves, *w* roots,
f sporocarps

sides are sharply characterised, and which is therefore a distinctly dorsi-ventral organ, so rolled together parallel to the longitudinal axis that its lower side appears as the convex outer side. As Fig 329 (*C* and *A*) shows, a radially constructed organ is thus produced from the dorsi-ventral one, since it is clear that a transverse section of the rolled-up leaf must exhibit equal distributions of the organisation in all directions. If, conversely, we suppose any hollow stem whatever slit up in the direction of its length, and then spread out flat, there arises from the previously radial organ a dorsi-

---

[1] I first pointed out generally that Anisotropy, i e the different capacity of the organs of the plant to react towards similar external directive forces (gravitation and light), is a necessary result of the radial or dorsi-ventral structure, in various editions of my Text-book, and then made it quite clear in my treatise ' *Über orthotrope und plagiotrope Organe*' (Art des bot Inst, B II, pp 274, &c)

ventral one, one side of which is differently organised from the other. Finally, we may suppose yet a third construction· assuming some hundreds or thousands of seedlings, each of which possesses a radicle and a plumule, to be placed beside one another and parallel in the ordinary direction, and closely connected together, then these seedlings form a whole in the direction of a line or in a surface, all the roots being on the one side, all the shoots on the other   We have then a dorsi-ventral structure, one side of which is composed of roots and the other of shoots.   And conversely, many dorsi-ventral organs may also be so broken up into individual elements that each of the latter possesses a root-end and a shoot-end; if, for example, a piece is supposed to be cut out of the horizontal flat shoot of a Marchantia, perpendicular to the surface, by means of a narrow cork-borer for instance, this portion bears on the under side one or several rhizoids, and on the upper side cells containing chlorophyll, and it behaves like a small upright plant.   Similarly we may isolate from a *Marsilia* or *Pilularia*, by means of two transverse sections of the shoot-axis, a so-called node, on which a leaf is situated above, a root below.   That such a mode of looking

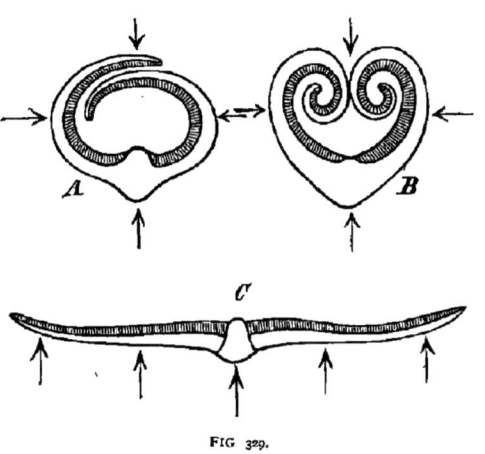

at dorsi-ventral structure is not an arbitrary playing with words, but, on the contrary, accords with the true being of such a plant, follows, as I have definitely shown previously, from the behaviour which dorsi-ventral organs exhibit towards the influence of gravitation and light   from every dorsi-ventral organ which places itself across the direction of gravity and of the rays of light, and is thus plagiotropic, a radial organ can be produced simply by rolling it together, and this, under the influence of gravitation and

FIG 329.

light, behaves as a radial orthotropic organ.   Nature herself makes this experiment in cases where young foliage leaves are rolled round one another in the bud and constitute a radial orthotropic structure, when the older leaves become freed from the bud and unroll, they then appear as dorsi-ventral organs which place themselves across the directions of light and gravitation.

From what has been hitherto said it obviously follows that the radial or the bilateral dorsi-ventral organisation of a plant-organ constitutes a fundamentally primary property of it, upon which depends not only the reaction towards external directive forces, but also the ways and means by which new formations—secondary offshoots— proceed from a given organ.   The arrangement of the leaves and lateral shoots on a shoot-axis is above all determined by whether the latter itself possesses radial bilateral or dorsi-ventral structure [1].   In this simple point lies at once the complete refutation

---

[1] The statements of fact here referred to are borrowed from Goebel's work, ' *Über die Verzweigung dorsiventraler Sprosse*' (Arb des bot Inst., B. II, pp 353, &c)   I need only remark that

of the so-called doctrine of phyllotaxis founded by Schimper and Alexander Braun, and the spiral theory lying at the foundation of it, and which has dominated Botany for more than forty years. This theory was derived from the consideration of the upright radially-constructed shoots of the vascular plants, in which the above-named spiral arrangement of the leaves commonly occurs. On imagining the leaves of such a shoot-axis connected together by a line in the order of their age, this line took the form of a spiral line continually winding round the shoot-axis, and this was designated the genetic spiral; in it the fundamental law of growth of the vegetable kingdom was supposed to be perceived. It was therefore sought, even in cases where the leaves stand in two straight rows on the shoot-axis, and further, where they are distributed in decussate pairs or in alternating whorls (Fig. 331), and even in such cases where they appear on one side only of the shoot-axis, to carry out the spiral arrangement as the fundamental law of growth, whereby it was necessary to employ the aid of a series of the most arbitrary assumptions.

An unprejudiced observation of the processes at the growing-point, taking into

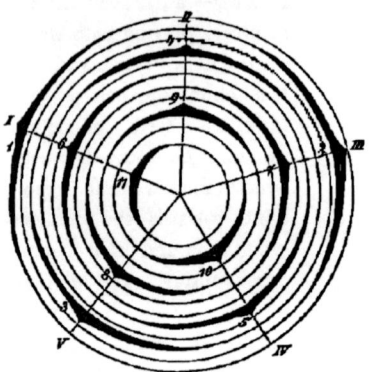

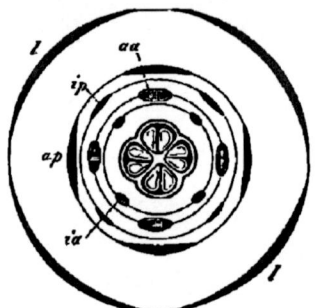

FIG 330.—Diagram of a shoot, the leaves of which are scattered with a divergence of 2 5ths

FIG. 331.—Diagram of the flowering stem of *Paris quadrifolia* *l l* whorl of large foliage leaves beneath the flower, *a p* outer, *i p* inner perianth, *a a* outer, *i a* inner stamens In the centre is the young fruit consisting of four carpels

account at the same time the physiological relations of growth, demonstrates, however, as Goebel has already expressly shown, that the spiral theory is not transferable to dorsi-ventral shoots, because it directly contradicts the facts; the above-mentioned relations of growth of *Caulerpa, Lygodium,* the Rhizocarpeæ, Liverworts, etc., show that not only the places of origin of the leaves but also those of the lateral shoots, roots, and sexual organs, are to a certain extent determined by the dorsi-ventral or radial structure of the mother-shoot. There is not the smallest ground for regarding the single rectilinear series of leaves on the dorsal line of the stem of *Lygodium* in any way as an expression of spiral arrangement, and just as little is this possible with the phyllotaxis and branching of the Rhizocarps, and even the very numerous cases of two-rowed phyllotaxis, especially for example in the Grasses, and likewise the

---

I, for my part, in the establishment of the idea of dorsi-ventrality by no means had in view exclusively the anatomical structure, but just as much, on the one hand, the molecular structure, and, on the other hand, the capacity to produce different organs in different directions Only there was no necessity for me to go more in detail into the latter point, Goebel having done it so well

numerous cases of decussate pairs of leaves, as in the Labiatæ, contradict in every
way even the merely formal arrangement in a so-called genetic spiral running round
the shoot-axis   This latter, moreover, even where it can be carried out, viz. in the
case of radial shoots with scattered leaves, is only subjective and imagined as
belonging to the plant by the observer, and has no significance whatever for the
knowledge of the processes of growth themselves.   Innumerable cases may be
adduced from which it results definitely that the arrangement of the leaves and
lateral shoots on a shoot-axis essentially depends upon whether the latter is already

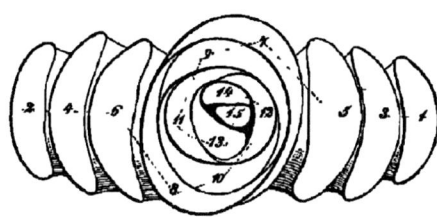

FIG. 332.—Transverse section of a shoot of *Aloe serra*

radially or dorsi-ventrally constructed
at its growing-point.   A few examples only will serve to illustrate this
Fig. 332 represents a transverse section through the lateral shoot of an
Aloe.   It grew out from the mother-
shoot at first horizontally, and produced its leaves right and left in two
alternating rows, as may be seen by
the numbers 1–6.   eventually the
growing-point of this shoot took an upward direction, and it became orthotropic
and radial   This change found its expression in the fact that the primitively straight
rows of leaves now pass over into two spirally-wound ones, as is to be seen from the
two dotted lines 7, 9, 11, 13, 15, and 8, 10, 12, 14.   The completely erect shoot
bears a rosette of leaves radiating on all sides.

    Among the inflorescences of Phanerogams are to be found very many, especially
in the families of the Boragineæ, Papilionaceæ, and Urticaceæ, which are termed
unilateral in descriptive botany, that is to say, the shoot-axis from which the more or

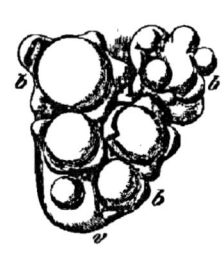

FIG. 333.—Young inflorescence
of *Symphytum.* *v* growing point,
b b the young flowers

less numerous flowers arise as lateral shoots is itself
dorsi-ventral, and therefore produces flower-shoots only
on its dorsal or only on its ventral side   The spiral
theory was compelled, in order to vindicate itself
in such cases, to put forward the most extraordinary
and improbable accessory hypotheses.   By means of
careful investigation of the processes at the growing-
point, Goebel showed, however, that it is altogether
impossible to entertain the spiral theory in such cases,
simply because the leaves on the dorsi-ventral parent
axis bud forth, as a matter of fact, only on one side, in
one, two, or more rows. Fig. 333 shows this behaviour
at the growing-point of an inflorescence of *Symphytum,*
and the case is exactly the same in the common Forget-me-not (*Myosotis*).   In the
latter plant especially, any one may easily perceive how the axis of the inflorescence,
which is rolled spirally inwards and downwards, bears flowers arranged in two rows
on its convex upper side only: the mature state observed with the unaided eye,
as well as the processes at the growing-point, forbid every attempt to speak here of
a spiral arrangement

    But even in individual flowers the case occurs that the different phylloid organs, which spring from the growing-point, appear in a sequence and order which excludes the employment of the spiral. Payer, who has done such excellent service with respect to the developmental history of flowers, showed that the flower of the common Mignonette (Fig. 334) is a strictly bilateral structure. From its growing-point the sepals, petals, stamens, and carpels are put forth in such a manner that their development begins at one point of the circumference, and then proceeds right and left on both sides of the young flower towards the opposite point.

Closely connected with the spiral theory, was also the view that lateral shoots from a main shoot can only arise in the axils of the leaves. But even this so-called principle of axillary branching presents itself on unprejudiced observation only as a special case, occurring chiefly among the Phanerogams, and even there only when lateral shoots arise on erect and radially constructed shoots. Where the dorsi-ventrality of the mother-shoot is sharply expressed, however, as in the cases mentioned above, the lateral shoots may arise on the flanks of the mother-axis while the leaves are situated dorsally, or vice versa. In Ferns and Mosses, the most careful investigations into the development have shown that normal lateral shoots may arise on the back or on the flank of the base of the leaf, or even quite independently of any relation to the leaf. Even in the Phanerogams, from which the older theory of phyllotaxis started, it is not always possible to apply the so-called principle of axillary branching: the floral region especially affords numerous examples of this Not rarely, as in the Cruciferæ, many Papilionaceæ and Boragineæ, in Aroideæ, and others, the flowers arise on the

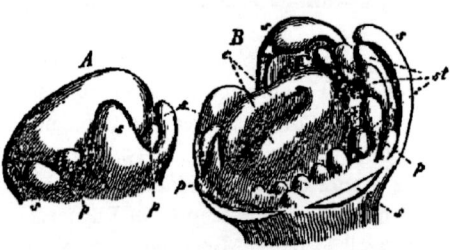

FIG. 334.—Development of the flower of *Reseda odorata* (after Payer) To the left a young, to the right an older bud, the anterior sepals *s* are cut away from the latter the posterior ones remain *p p* petals, *st* stamens, the posterior ones already advanced in size, the anterior ones not yet developed, *c* carpel—rudimentary fruit.

mother-axis without being preceded by leaves, in the axils of which they might arise They are leafless branch-systems; and in some Boragineæ and Crassulaceæ, where it is true leaves are formed on the dorsi-ventral axis of the inflorescence, these are situated with no obvious relation to the flowers, and even the number of these leaves does not always correspond to the number of the flowers.

The theory of phyllotaxis, with its assumption of the spiral as a fundamental law of growth, has, to the great injury of all deeper insight into the growth of the plant, established itself so firmly that even now it is not superfluous to show up its errors point by point. Thus, among the errors of this theory is the one that the spiral arrangement of all organs on a common axis must necessarily follow from its so-called parastichies. By the term parastichy is understood the serial arrangement of lateral organs in two or more directions which cross one another; this appears very clearly in cases where numerous organs are situated close beside one another on a common axis. If in such a case the organs have approximately the same form, they involuntarily present rows to the eye, which it can follow from right to left or from left to right. The two dotted lines *a* and *b* in Fig. 335 will at once show what is meant Now it is of course possible, with certain premisses which the founders of the spiral

theory arbitrarily made, to construct the so-called genetic spiral out of these parastichies by certain geometrical artifices. But, on the one hand, direct observation
shows that these premises by no means always fit the case, and that nevertheless
very fine parastichies arise; and very often it may be said, on the other hand, that
when numerous figures or bodies similar
to one another are placed close beside one
another on a common foundation in any
sequence whatever in time, they must
necessarily present to the eye viewing
them series crossing right and left. Even
ordinary wall-papers show such parastichies, and in the same way the arrangement of the scales on the bodies of fishes,
of the hairs on the skin of mammals, and of
the tiles on a roof exhibits such parastichies
clearly enough. They are particularly well
seen in the case of the scales of pine
cones, and in the numerous flowers of the

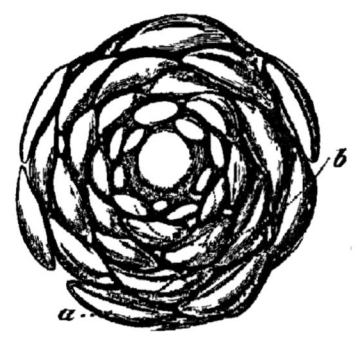

FIG 335.—The growing point of a bud of the Larch,
seen from above

capitulum of the Compositæ, especially that of *Helianthus annuus*, or the flowering
head of *Dipsacus* and of the Aroideæ, and it was these objects particularly which the
supporters of the spiral theory employed by preference, for the purpose of constructing
the genetic spiral from the parastichies. Nevertheless it is very easy to show in
these very cases how uncertain were the facts on which the spiral theory was often
supported. Fig. 336 may serve for the illustration of this. The figure represents

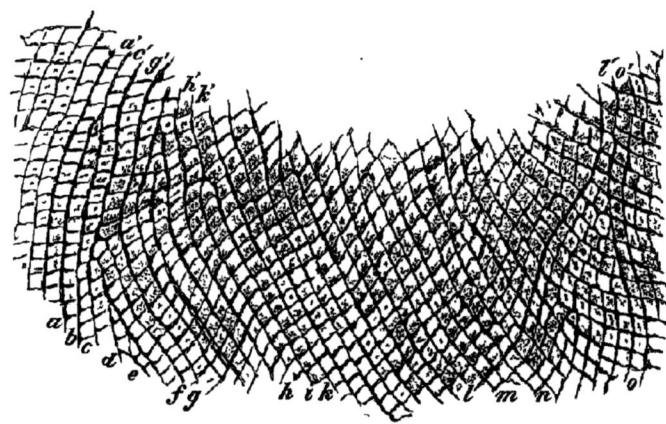

FIG 336.—Arrangement of the young fruits on the conical axis of a flower-head of
Dipsacus fullonum (Fuller's Teazle).

the arrangement of the unripe fruits of *Dipsacus fullonum* closely crowded on the
conical floral receptacle, but transferred from the natural curved surface to the plane
of the paper : this was attained by blackening the conical flower-head with printer's
ink, and subsequently rolling it on the paper   The figure is thus in all essential
points quite true to nature. We perceive at once two mutually crossing systems of

parastichies ascending right and left: these however exhibit irregularities which are inexplicable by the spiral theory, but otherwise easily intelligible. The irregularities simply depend upon the fact that the rhomboidal quadrangular fruits are everywhere nearly equal in size, but the receptacle on which they are situated becomes smaller above, since it is conical where youngest. Hence the number of the fruits occurring side by side at the same height decreases upwards; also the number of parastichies must be diminished by certain of them simply ceasing at different heights. Thus the series b in the figure ceases between $a\,a'$ and $c\,c'$, and in the same way several others besides m and n terminate on the right of the figure between $l\,l'$ and $o\,o'$.

The doctrine of phyllotaxis based on the spiral theory, which according to the so-called principle of axillary branching was regarded as dominating the position of the lateral shoots, laid, further, great stress on the fact that on shoot-axes richly provided with leaves or off-shoots generally, certain 'divergences' repeat themselves more frequently than others. By divergence is understood that portion of the circumference of the shoot-axis which lies between two consecutive leaves, thus, in two-rowed phyllotaxis it amounts to $\frac{1}{2}$, in three-rowed to $\frac{1}{3}$, in five-rowed to $\frac{2}{5}$, in eight-rowed to $\frac{3}{8}$ of the circumference, and so on In the case of some axes abundantly provided with outgrowths (Pine cones, shoots with crowded leaves, &c) it is shown now that the divergences on the so-called genetic spiral remain constant for more or fewer of the segments of the chain, and (a point on which particular stress was laid) that the very divergences named—viz. $\frac{1}{2}$, $\frac{1}{3}$, $\frac{2}{5}$, $\frac{3}{8}$, $\frac{5}{13}$, &c.—recur somewhat frequently. These fractions (parts of a continued fraction) appeared to constitute the expression of a mysterious law which was assumed to dominate growth in a supposed spiral manner But it was nevertheless seen to be necessary, in addition to the relations of phyllotaxis represented by that fraction, to add yet others, which of course led to any continued fraction whatever, whereby however the point lost in significance. The numerous cases of dorsi-ventral shoots however remained entirely outside the system: in these, homologous off-shoots arise only on one side of the axis or on two opposed flanks, and these could in no case be placed on a spiral running round the axis. Further, it was fatal to the theory that the mysterious divergences by no means remain constant even on one and the same shoot-axis, but mostly begin with simple fractions, such as $\frac{1}{2}$ or $\frac{1}{3}$, or quite irregularly, and then pass over into $\frac{2}{5}$, $\frac{3}{8}$, and so on, probably to be continually returning again to simpler ones, or yet others. In addition to this it turned out that even in very closely allied plants the relations of position are often importantly different, and, which I would lay more stress upon than on anything else, the whole spiral theory, with its divergences and continued fractions, found no application whatever to the branching of roots—the roots had no existence, so to speak, for the spiral theory

Nevertheless the frequent occurrence of the divergences $\frac{1}{3}$, $\frac{2}{5}$, $\frac{3}{8}$, $\frac{5}{13}$, &c. is a fact of observation. The secret of this occurrence and the frequent absence of other divergences is explained, according to Schwendener's investigations[1], by

---

mechanical and geometrical considerations, among which the mutual pressure of the young organs on a common axis plays an important part. It would require far too much space here, however, to go more in detail into Schwendener's somewhat prolix account: it suffices that, as he shows, it is possible to demonstrate by means of simple models (figures in a displaceable frame) how from purely mechanical causes arrangements corresponding to the divergence $\frac{2}{5}$, for example, must pass over into such as correspond to $\frac{3}{8}$ and $\frac{5}{13}$, the transition from one divergence into the other being accomplished somewhat suddenly   Schwendener's description is based on the circumstance, previously made evident by Hofmeister and myself, that the laws of phyllotaxis assumed by the spiral theory only appear at all where the young organs (leaves or shoots) arise on the growing-point of a mother-shoot in large numbers, and quite close beside one another, so that at first no free surface whatever of the axis is presented. By means of this very close position, the place of origin of the outgrowths newly added acropetally is in part determined, and at the same time, in consequence of the close packing, pressures and torsions must make their appearance during growth, by which the relations of position assume their definitive condition.

Where the offshoots of an axis appear at some distance from one another from the commencement, none of the relations spoken of occur.   Apart from some Algæ which we might adduce here, I may refer the reader to the known case of the whorls of branches of the Pines.   The leaves of these trees arise close above and beside one another on the main shoot, and since they are from the first numerous and small in relation to the growing-point, they present complicated and somewhat constant divergences: the position of every new leaf which makes its appearance at the growing-point is simply determined by these conditions   The whorl of branches developed in any one year on a Pine, on the contrary, only arises after the growing-point of the main shoot which produces it has grown far beyond the whorl of branches of the previous year; the consequence is that the consecutive whorls do not alternate regularly as elsewhere, but are situated one above another in any direction on the stem.

Since the older morphology as expressed in the genetic spiral with its parastichies and constant divergences which were supposed to stand in mysterious connection with one another, and further with its principle of axillary branching, cannot exist in the face of an unbiassed criticism of the facts, simply because it sets up a few relations of position, which only occur on radial orthotropic shoots, as the fundamental law of all vegetable growth, we must now rather acknowledge that there is no general law which can be formulated for the arrangement of the organs on a parent-

---

read clearly enough in the four editions of my text-book   That the whole doctrine of Schimper and Braun depends, not, as it were, merely upon the inaccurate interpretation of single facts, but that it rather stands in direct opposition to scientific investigation, and was based on the foundation of the idealistic direction of the '*Naturphilosophie*,' was clearly expressed by me in my '*Geschichte der Botanik*' (1875)   The fundamental ideas of this criticism were also subsequently placed by Schwendener, in his '*Mechanischen Theorie der Blattstellungen*' (1878), in the foreground of his considerations   A historical description well worthy of note of all the views on leaf-position hitherto held, as well as a theory of his own, is contained in Casimir de Candolle's '*Considérations sur l'étude de la phyllotaxie*' (Genf, 1881)

axis; that on the contrary, according to circumstances in each case, special causes determine whether the relations of position turn out to be this or that. Among these causes the most important is the radial or dorsi-ventral character of the growing-point, which in its turn also may again depend upon whether the growing-point in question has arisen as a lateral offshoot of another grow-ing-point. Further, the more or less close crowding of the young organs at the grow-ing-point causes new organs to emerge at definite places, and during the growth dis-placements, torsions, pressures and strains take place In all this, however, there is still much that remains unexplained— for instance, that the orthotropic radial shoots of the Grasses have their leaves alternating in two rows, while those of the Labiatæ have them in decussate pairs; why the radial shoot bears in one case whorls, and in another spirally-arranged leaves, why vegetative lateral shoots of the Monocotyledons mostly begin with one first leaf turned towards the parent-axis, and lateral shoots of the Dicotyledons (Fig. 337) mostly with two, situated right

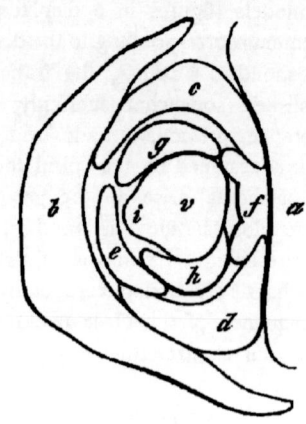

FIG. 337 —A young lateral shoot of *Spiræa sorbifolia.* *a* the axis of the mother-shoot, *b* a leaf developed from this. *v* growing point of the young axillary shoot, from which the very young leaf-rudiment *t* is arising *c d* the first leaves, and *e—i* the succeeding ones of the young shoot (somewhat highly magnified)

and left, why in the true Mosses one leaf proceeds from each segment of the two- or three-sided apical cell, and so forth. But the chief point is that we feel ourselves free from the formalism of the doctrine of phyllotaxis, and that these phenomena of growth have now become transferable to the region of causal investigation—i. e. to the physiology of growth.

LECTURE XXX.

CAUSAL RELATIONS OF GROWTH OF THE DIFFERENT ORGANS OF THE PLANT ONE TO ANOTHER.

(CORRELATIONS)

THE processes of growth described in the last four lectures must for the time being be taken simply as facts, the determination of the causes of which is at present impossible. That the embryonic rudiments of all organs proceed from growing-points, which are themselves remains or continuations of the fertilised oosphere of the embryo, that in these the differentiation of the embryonic tissue takes place, that in post-embryonic development they not only increase in size, but also only attain their permanent outward form during this period of growth, and so forth—all these matters of growth appertaining to the development must in the meantime be taken as facts: that is, we must be satisfied meanwhile to look upon the phenomena in question as purely objective, and free from preconceived ideas, in order to obtain subsequently a glimpse into the causes which bring it about that things go on as they have been described, and as direct observation shows. Vegetable physiology finds itself with respect to these phenomena of growth in the same position as is crystallography, for instance, respecting the question why common salt, the diamond, copper, &c, in spite of their differences in other respects, crystallise in the regular system, whereas graphite, calc-spar, quartz, &c. assume forms belonging to the hexagonal system.

Nevertheless, in our considerations on growth so far, we have already obtained here and there glimpses of causal relations by the way. With respect to cell-formation in the growing-points, the law of the rectangular intersection of cell-walls presented to us a causal element from which we were able to make intelligible the arrangement of the cells in the most different embryonic tissues· in the same way we found in the radial or dorsi-ventral structure of the growing-point the most immediate cause for the fact of the organs being placed vertically, obliquely, or horizontally, and producing their outgrowths on all sides, or only on one side, and so forth. Evidently there lie in these relations, at least the beginnings of a causal understanding of the matter, although we are by no means in a position to follow causes and effects step by step according to current mechanical conceptions

In this and the following lectures we shall be concerned with those phenomena of growth in which the effective causes or the causal principle are more clearly manifested, though even here we must be satisfied with following the causes and effects of growth in their general outlines only. Even here also it must be left for the future to analyse the processes further, and to resolve the causal relations into their several factors.

A better survey of the phenomena lying before us will be obtained if we first distinguish between the internal and external causes of growth We regard it as the effect of internal causes of growth when by means of the growth of one organ the growth of another organ of the same plant is promoted or hindered, thus recognising a mutual causal relation in the growth of different organs of a plant. This mutual causal relation has been termed the correlation of the growth of the organs of a plant. On the other hand, however, experience also shows that the growth of individual organs, or parts of organs, may be promoted or hindered by purely incidental external actions, by light, gravitation, contact, pressure, and other influences of the environment

Here, however, we enter upon a province where it is very difficult to obtain certain information, not only because the connection between causes and effects is in itself extremely complicated in each of the two cases, but still more because experience teaches that the relations of growth of the plant to the external world, as well as the correlations, are variable in the highest degree. Processes of growth which in the one species of plant are established once for all, and appear spontaneously by the internal connection of development, are only called forth in other species by definite external influences, and no sharp line is in this respect to be found anywhere We are in the habit of saying that such phenomena are in the one case hereditary and constant, while in the other case they are caused by irritability; but it must not be forgotten that nothing is explained by such statements, only a logical classification—i e one suited to our preconceived ideas—is obtained.

Here also I regard it as beyond my task to state all that is known with respect to correlations and external conditions of growth, but rather, in this and the following lectures, to make clearer, with a few examples only, the meaning of the questions here raised, and to show with what problems the theory of growth has to concern itself, and at the same time I must refer to the fact that it is exactly in the post-embryonic conditions of growth, with which we have chiefly to do here, that the organs of the plant are in a high degree sensitive to internal as well as to external influences. In spite of all difficulties and indefiniteness, however, profound interest is always attached to such considerations, because the question which here presents itself is as to what causes determine the internal structure and the external form of organisms. Only a short time ago the forms of organic bodies were regarded as something lying beyond the region of causality, and every organism was held to be a more or less successful realisation of an 'idea.' We here stand therefore on the boundary between two different modes of viewing the universe, of which the one, the idealistic—or, to put it in a more concrete form, the platonic—knows and will know nothing whatever of effective causes in the domain of organic form; whereas my view starts from the fundamental notion that organic forms, exactly as the configurations of crystals, and all matters of form whatever—it matters not whether we are concerned with the shape of a drop of water, a planet, a cloud, or any other product of nature—must be called forth by effective causes, which are determined by the nature of matter and its forces under the given circumstances.

From this point of view, even the rudimentary beginnings of a causal explanation of the processes of organic growth appear of importance, even though we are not in a position to explain in any given case the connection of cause and effect link by link and step by step. It suffices that it can be said at all definitely that this or that relation of configuration in the province of organic beings may be referred to definite causes.

As already mentioned, then, we are in this lecture concerned with those causal factors, which by the growth of one organ of a plant are given for the growth of another organ of the same plant, or, to put it shortly, with the correlation of growth of the different organs of a plant.

A very plastic subject for experimental researches in this province is the common Potato. On the subterranean portion of the shoot-axis, which developes above ground as the leaf-shoot, there arise in the axils of small scale-leaves in the normal course of things, thin filiform horizontally spreading subterranean shoots, which likewise only produce small scale-leaves, and which finally give rise to the potato-tuber, by vigorous growth in thickness at the tip of the shoot-axis. If at the period when the formation of tubers has not yet commenced, the portion of the leaf-shoot which is above ground is cut off, the terminal buds of the still young filiform runners become converted into ordinary leafy shoots, which ascend and grow out above the surface of the soil. Thus by removing the young main shoot it is possible to cause its lateral shoots, which would otherwise form tubers, to assume an entirely different form of growth; and we may therefore infer that in the ordinary course of the vegetation of this plant, the growth of the foliage-shoot brings it about that its subterranean lateral shoots become, not foliage-shoots likewise but potato-tubers. It is also possible to cause the production of tubers at will on the sub-äerial leaf-shoot, if the subterranean lateral shoots destined for the formation of tubers are carefully cut away from a vigorously growing potato plant, and the possibility of the formation of tubers below ground prevented. The materials normally adapted for the formation of potato-tubers now pass into the axillary buds of the sub-aerial foliage leaves, and cause their axial portions to remain short and to swell up and thicken, while their leaves develope but feebly. The existence of the subterranean runners, then, brings it about in the normal course of affairs that the materials destined for the formation of tubers do not prevent the development of the sub-äerial buds into leafy shoots.

No less evident and easy to observe is a similar correlation between the apical shoot of many trees and the lateral shoots beneath the apex. If the terminal shoot of the Fir *Abies excelsa* and several species of *Abies* allied to it (e g *A. cephalonica*) is broken off, or destroyed by frost, &c., the horizontal lateral shoots of the uppermost whorl gradually erect themselves, and occasionally a similar effect is observed even on lateral shoots of the next lower whorl. After 1-3 years one of these lateral shoots has usually obtained the upper hand, and has not only become erected vertically, but has also lost its bilateral nature; the originally horizontal shoot has gradually become radial and completely orthotropic, and it produces henceforth four- or five-rayed whorls of branches exactly as the original terminal shoot of the main stem. We may conclude from these facts that in the normal course of growth a causal relation exists between the growth of the young lateral shoots and that of the apical shoot of the main stem; the growth of the latter evidently brings it about that the lateral shoots are dorsi-ventral, grow horizontally, and become branched right and left chiefly in a horizontal direction. A similar relation, however, also exists between the various shoots of a whorl: if these are equally strong among themselves they all rise up after the removal of the apex, but usually the strongest overcomes the others and obtains the mastery which the true apical shoot exerted previously In the Red Pine, however, it happens not seldom that after the removal of the apex of the main stem two or even three lateral shoots develope into complete apical shoots. Much less plastic in this relation is the Fir *Abies pectinata*, and probably also some of its nearest allies. I have often removed the apical shoot from young trees of this species, but only seldom, after two or three years, has one of the uppermost lateral shoots erected itself to develope into a new apex It is more commonly the case with this Fir, that close beneath the place whence the apical shoot has been cut off, or even from the upper side of the base of the nearest lateral shoot, small, previously unnoticed dormant eyes begin to put forth shoots, sometimes not until 1–2 years after the removal of the apex, of which one then usually grows more vigorously than the others, and in the course of years is transformed into a new radially constructed apex.

Very similar mutual relations between main stem and branches also exist in other wood-plants, and especially many forest-trees, and are made use of in various ways in forestry, and especially in the art of felling timber, in order so to interfere artificially with the process of growth as to promote the development of certain buds and to suppress that of others exactly the same occurs, however, also in small herbaceous plants and even in seedlings. If, for example, the common Scarlet Runner (*Phaseolus multiflorus*) is allowed to germinate till the primary root is about 10–12 cm. long, and the young germinal shoot between the two cotyledons, the so-called plumule, is then carefully cut off, then, as the root-system increases in strength and activity, vigorous shoots grow out from the axils of the two cotyledons These shoots do not usually develope in this plant, because as a rule the normal primary shoot attracts to itself the whole of the supply of nutriment from the seed, so far as it is suited for the formation of leaf-shoots In our experiment, on the contrary, the shoot-forming substances of the seed penetrate into the growing-points in the axils of the cotyledons and cause them to sprout vigorously. Not rarely, however, an abnormality makes its appearance here; these vigorously growing axillary shoots of the cotyledons exhibit so-called fasciations—i e. the shoot-axes become broad and band-like, and crooked, and still other abnormalities occur. Since fasciations not rarely occur in plants of the most different kinds— e g. in Willows, Compositæ of the Camomile group, &c —it is at any rate of some interest to know that it is also possible to produce such abnormalities artificially.

Goebel, a few years ago, in his ' *Beiträge zur Morphologie und Physiologie des Blattes* [1],' supplied copious and well considered experimental material respecting correlation of growth; but I must rest satisfied with shortly reproducing here a few only of his results Goebel's researches are chiefly concerned with the correlations

---

[1] Goebel, '*Beitrage zur Morphologie und Physiologie des Blattes*' (Bot Zeitg 1880, p 753, &c).

between the normal green leaves and the scales of winter-buds which envelope the young foliage-leaves until the next period of vegetation (cf. Fig. 301). He shows in the first place, by simple observation, that the bud-scales as well as the small scale-like leaves of the subterranean shoots of many plants are according to their origin and as a matter of fact ordinary foliage leaves, which, however, during further development are arrested in so far that the blade of the leaf (lamina) very soon ceases to grow, often even when it is not yet, or is scarcely, visible ; whereas a lower portion of the leaf, which is but little or not at all developed in normal leaves—the so-called leaf-base—in many cases grows up vigorously and constitutes the body of the scale proper.

In order to examine the matter more closely, it must be noticed in the first place that Eichler established, so long ago as 1861, that two or three stages must be distinguished in the development of a leaf. The body which comes forth immediately from the growing-point of the shoot as the leaf, is termed by Eichler the primordial leaf: it appears as a crescentic or annular cushion of embryonic tissue. This primordial leaf becomes segmented in the first place into two chief portions; a stationary zone, which takes no further part in the formation of the leaf, and a portion which gives rise to the leaf proper. The former is the foliar base, the latter the so-called upper-leaf, from which the blade of the leaf arises in every case : when a petiole is developed it is intercalated, as it were, subsequently, between the foliar base and the young lamina. Goebel shows now that the scales on the winter-buds of *Syringa, Lonicera, Daphne,* and others, come into existence by the rudiments of the foliage-leaves being arrested at a middle stage of their development, the formation of the otherwise normal petiole being altogether suppressed.

A second category of bud-scales is found in the species of Maple, Horse-chestnut, and other trees. In these cases the bud-scale arises by the above-named foliar base of the primordial leaf developing vigorously while the lamina of the leaf, though it exists in a rudimentary state, is soon arrested, and may then be detected at the apex of the scale by means of the microscope. If sprouting winter-buds of the Maple and Horse-chestnut are examined in the spring, intermediate forms between ordinary bud-scales and foliage-leaves may often be found ; the scale-like portion (that is the developed foliar base) is then smaller, but the arrested lamina is so large that it can be recognised at once as a foliage-leaf

In a third category of winter-buds, it is from the so-called stipules—that is, leaf-like structures which protrude laterally right and left from the foliar base at the sides of the leaf proper—that the bud-scales arise In various species of *Alnus* and in the Tulip-tree, the enveloping of the winter-buds is effected simply by the lowermost, tolerably normally developed foliage-leaf having its two stipules modified in the form of bud-scales. In our native Oaks also, and in the White Beech and Red Beech, it is the stipules of arrested foliage-leaves which envelope the winter-buds ; in these cases, however, the laminæ of the leaves in question are completely arrested very early, although their true nature can still be distinctly perceived by means of the microscope. Even the bud-scales of those Coniferæ and Cycadeæ which form resting-buds are, according to Goebel's investigations, simply modified foliage-leaves. Of subterranean scales, those on the rhizomes of *Dentaria, Chrysos-*

plenium, Anemone hepatica, and other species of Anemone, may here be mentioned. In all these cases the subterranean and sometimes succulent scales have arisen by the further development of the foliar base, while the lamina, though still more or less evident, is arrested.

That, so far as these scale-structures are concerned, it is actually a matter of correlation of growth, Goebel has experimentally demonstrated in the case of *Prunus padus,* among others. The growth of this tree proceeds as follows. In the spring the axillary buds of the shoots of the previous year become unfolded and again form axillary buds in their turn : these produce in the first place bud-scales, and pass through the period of rest during the summer and following winter enveloped in these The bud-scales which thus arise in the spring come into existence in *Prunus padus* by the vigorous development of the foliar base, which bears above indications of not only the proper lamina of the leaf but also of two stipules, all, however, very small and only recognisable by means of the microscope

On the 14th of April a number of growing shoots and young plants of *Prunus padus* were partly deprived of leaves, and partly lopped at the apex; that is, the terminal buds were removed. On the 10th of May the result was that the axillary buds which should normally unfold only in the next spring had commenced to put forth shoots, and vigorous normal leaf-shoots were subsequently developed from them. Apart from other results of this experiment, it teaches that the leaves impelled to further growth immediately after their origin did not become developed in the usual manner into bud-scales, but assumed the form of ordinary foliage-leaves. The rudiments of foliage-leaves, which when the shoot is left to itself have their laminæ arrested and develope their foliar base as bud-scales, here developed into normal foliage-leaves; and this because the development of the leaves of the mother-shoot formed in rudiment in the previous year had been prevented early, by taking away or lopping the apex. Thus the nutritive materials necessary to the development of true foliage-leaves were able to reach these young leaf-rudiments, which, as a rule, develope as scales—or in other words, the growth of the foliage-leaves of a shoot of *Prunus padus* which is putting forth leaves prevents the lateral shoots which simultaneously arise in the axils of its leaves from completing the development of their foliage-leaves also This demonstrates the correlation of the two, and the case is similar in many other plants. This was experimentally confirmed by Goebel in the case of the Horse-chestnut, and in Maples, Roses, Syringas, and Oaks. Into Goebel's more involved researches, and those made on plants which may be less known to the reader, we will not here enter.

The complications which make their appearance in the experimental investigation of the correlations of growth are chiefly due to the fact, that with the altered growth of an organ all its reactions towards the environment also become changed · this shows at the same time, as I stated in the first lectures, that the true physiological nature of an organ is to be sought not so much in its outward form and anatomically visible structure, as in its irritability or capability of reaction. Even in the first-named example of the potato, and in the substitution of the removed apex of the stem of trees, it is clear enough how, with the change of growth by means of interference with the correlations, the geotropism also—i. e. the capability of the organ to react towards gravitation—is *eo ipso* modified; and it may be shown in other cases how by such interferences even the reaction to the action of light of the organ which is being modified becomes changed.

From the small number of examples by which I have sought to illustrate the conception of correlation of growth, it is not to be concluded that we are here concerned only with incidental and isolated phenomena : on the contrary, we have every reason to believe that similar relations between the growth of any one organ and that of all the others of a plant, however difficult to detect, are very general.   In animals, and especially the more highly organised species, a mutual correlation, in consequence of the sharply marked individuality, not only exists between all the organs (which, it is true, are all nourished by the same blood), but is also more easily intelligible than in the case of plants ; for from daily but superficial experience, the very common opinion has been formed that in plants every organ is formed and grows quite independently of the others.   The possibility of raising new entire plants from cut-off pieces of leaves, shoot-axes, or roots, by the regeneration of the missing organs, easily leads to the belief that no intimate mutual relation of the vegetable organs at all exists.   But a deeper insight into the whole nature of vegetation leads to the opposite conclusion.   In the plant also, it is true that every growing organ derives its constructive materials from the common store of nutriment which is collected and distributed in the tissues by the assimilation of the leaves, or has been deposited in quantities in the reservoirs of reserve-materials from a previous period of vegetation ; and it is obvious that when numerous different organs are simultaneously drawing their materials for growth from the common store, one may take what the other needs, and it may happen, as for example the experiment of *Prunus padus* cited above teaches, that through the growth of a shoot the simultaneous growth of its lateral buds may be prevented.   Above all, from this point of view, equivalent organs must be regarded as competitors at the common store of unsorted nutriment   the growth of a shoot will re-act especially on that of other shoots, the growth of a root chiefly on that of other roots ; since it requires no proof that the mixtures of materials which the shoots draw from the common store of nutriment of the plant differ in nature from those which afford the constructive materials of the roots   In the same way experience teaches that in the nutritive substances produced by assimilation and altered further by metabolism, peculiar mixtures of materials become differentiated from which the sexual organs and (in the Phanerogams) the flowers arise.   If the first young flower-buds are removed from a plant, the usual result is that other much younger flower-buds, which would probably not have developed at all, begin to grow so much the more vigorously ; or that flower-buds, the rudiments of which are not yet formed, arise at places where they would not have arisen at all without the interference—a fact upon which the old knowledge of fruit-culture in part depends.   If the flowers, foliage, shoots, and roots were constructed from the same mixtures of substances, it would not be obvious why the removal of young flower-buds should not also call forth an invigorated growth of leaves and roots.   The latter indeed occurs under certain circumstances, but only in consequence of further interdependencies which we cannot here follow further.   Here also we are not further interested in the question how we are to imagine the production chemically, as it were, of these various organ-forming mixtures of substances. Considerations on this point[1] are found in my treatises '*On the Substance and Form of the Organs of Plants,*' and later, when we are concerned with reproduction, I shall probably find opportunity of taking up the subject again Here my intention is to mention only one of the most essential and important factors which co-operate in the correlation of growth, but by no means to assert that still other causes do not interfere and affect the matter. Above all there is one point to be insisted upon—that the various organs growing from the common nutritive material of the plant, and as competitors for that material, stand opposed to one another in a certain sense as enemies; though, on the other hand, it is to be noticed that the various organs, especially shoots and roots, afford support to one another by their functions, and are so far indispensable to one another. This latter is the case, however, as a rule, only when they are fully grown and completely developed for their specific function · a mature, fully grown foliage-leaf promotes the production of new foliage-shoots, because by means of its assimilation it affords new material for growth, and so forth. Considerations of this kind, however, would carry us into matters of which I have already treated in detail in the theory of nutrition.

Again, it cannot be expected that all correlations of growth are so easy to demonstrate by experimental interference on the part of the observer, as in the cases considered above on the contrary, causes may exist in the plant which lead the result of such experiments into paths quite different from those desired However, even without experimental interference we may, supported by what I have so far stated, obtain a deeper insight into very extensive correlations of the whole organisation of a plant As one example I might especially quote the relations, repeatedly indicated in previous lectures, which exist between the properties of the chlorophyll and the whole external and internal organisation ; this is of such a kind that one may regard, without exaggeration, the whole relations of form in the vegetable kingdom, and particularly the very different aspect of plants in comparison with that of animals as depending on the properties and activities of chlorophyll In this of course we enter upon a province which extends far beyond that of the correlations of growth shown above, but still, since the whole organisation of a plant is the result of its growth, we may nevertheless take into our present sphere of thought what follows.

It is my intention to show somewhat more in detail, that, as a matter of fact, the most essential relations of organisation of the plant are causally determined by the properties of chlorophyll

We may start from the fact that the cells which contain chlorophyll are the only assimilatory organs of the plant, and that they alone are able to produce, from carbon dioxide and water, organic and organisable substance suitable for the growth of new organs, and that for this purpose they require those materials which can only be absorbed from the soil by means of the roots, the so-called ash-constituents, with which a nitrogenous compound, nitric acid, is associated for the purpose of forming proteids

---

[1] Sach's '*Stoff und Form der Pflanzenorgane*' (Arb des bot Inst in Wzbg B. II, H 3, 1880, p 452, and H 4, 1882, p 689)

Experience teaches that even a very thin layer of tissue containing chlorophyll completely uses up all those rays of light which effect assimilation   A thick layer of chlorophyll-tissue has therefore no meaning whatever: in fact it would be a waste of material in the plant.   Accordingly, we find that everywhere in the vegetable kingdom only very thin layers of green assimilatory tissue come to be employed— layers of one or a few tenths of a millimeter thick—even when, as in the case of succulent plants, the leaves or soft shoot-axes are very thick and massive, in which cases the thin layer of green tissue lies as near as possible to the surface of the organ, in order the better to make use of the incident light.

It is, on the contrary, of the greatest importance for energetic assimilation, or the production of substances capable of promoting growth, that the thin layers of green tissue should form surfaces as extensive as possible, if the construction of a vigorous growing plant is to be at all accomplished.

These reflections then show why, as the organisation of the plant gradually approaches perfection from its first beginnings, it is above all necessary to produce organs which are very thin, and possess the largest possible surface of tissue containing chlorophyll.   In the lower Algæ this is attained by their assuming the form of thin and long hair-like filaments, or else that of thin flat lamellæ, so that in both cases the volume of the body remains very small, as compared with its surface.   These two forms, where the entire plant is thin and filamentous and usually much branched, or else flat and leaf-like, is found again not merely among the highly-organised Algæ, but also among the Mosses, and even in some Vascular plants—such as the leafless shrubs *Psilotum, Spartium*, and others.   Here the principle is ever maintained that only a very thin peripheral layer of assimilatory tissue, accessible to the light, exists.   But the purpose mentioned is attained much more completely when the shoots become differentiated into leaves and axial portions, as is the tendency frequently enough even among the Algæ, and almost universally among the Mosses and Vascular plants.   By this means it is possible for the shoot-system to present to the light (and thus to the nutritive process) a large number of thin lamellæ containing chlorophyll and at suitable distances from one another; and only with such a differentiation into a support (shoot-axis) and lamellæ containing chlorophyll (leaves) springing from it, does vegetation in general attain to its higher stages of organisation, and especially to the massive forms inhabiting the dry land, as known to us in the large Ferns, Palms, Conifers, Forest trees and dicotyledonous shrubs.   How otherwise could the problem be solved so to construct and support a sheet of assimilatory tissue scarcely o·2—o·3 mm. thick and often many square meters in area, such as is met with in the crown of a Beech or an Oak with its thousands of leaves, or in the few but large leaves of a Banana or Palm?   If we imagine a plant, for instance, of such a kind as *Marchantia*, where the green shoot itself bears the thin sheet of assimilatory tissue, as large and heavy as a huge Palm or Oak, then it is obvious what a monstrous organisation we should have, and how contradictory it would be to the higher types of the vegetable kingdom.   Of course leaves are wanting to plants like the *Cacti* also · they are satisfied with a thin layer of chlorophyll at the periphery of the thick shoot, and hence their increase in organic mass is relatively very slow; and, what is perhaps more remarkable, their leafless green shoot-axes assume, even frequently, forms similar to those of leaves—e. g.

Phyllocactus, many species of *Opuntia*, &c. This occurs in a still higher degree in shrubby plants furnished with Cladodes, as *Ruscus*, *Phyllanthus*, &c.

The vegetable kingdom, so far as it is self-nourished by means of green tissue, is solely and entirely, so far as form is concerned, ruled by the principle of developing on relatively thin supports, or shoot-axes, the greatest possible number of green organs with the thinnest and largest surface possible. The exceedingly graceful growth of plants which contain chlorophyll, so familiar to all, is thus due simply to their containing chlorophyll, because the activity of the assimilating parenchyma only comes into full effect in this case. The contrast presents itself to us at once in the case of plants devoid of chlorophyll, the fructifications of Fungi, and parasitic and saprophytic Phanerogams. It is simply the want of chlorophyll which here makes altogether superfluous the extension of the surface in the form of large leaves; the body of the plant is therefore developed chiefly as shoot-axes and appears naked, stout, massive, and ungraceful. To them also, as to all and even highly organised water-plants, the formation of true wood is wanting, because they do not need it: since in plants devoid of chlorophyll (which moreover never attain to the size and massiveness of a tree, or even of a large shrub, but usually remain small and inconspicuous) the want of large leaf-surfaces also entails that of organs of transpiration, and thus the current of water flowing in woody plants from the root to the leaf-crown is dispensed with—they do not require wood because they possess no leaves containing chlorophyll. Moreover, true water-plants are devoid of wood for physiological reasons; it is true they often possess very large leaf-surfaces, but these are submerged, or they float on the surface of the water, and can themselves take up from the environment the water which they require, and thus do not need an active current of water coming from the roots. We may thus say simply that the formation of wood and (as must be added from what has been previously stated) the formation of numerous thick strands of sclerenchyma is due to the fact that the shoot-axes of terrestrial plants are elevated above the soil, extend their leaf-surfaces to the air and to the light, and find in the lignified tissues of the stems and branches not only elastic and rigid supports, but at the same time the organs which convey to them from the roots water provided with nutritive materials. I have already attempted to make clear by what arrangements the current of water ascending in the wood is conveyed directly into the transpiring green leaves, and how, by means of the venation or distribution of the vascular bundles in these, this water flows into thousands of fine canals, from which the chlorophyll-cells of the leaves take up their nutrient water. I have already shown, moreover (p. 50), how as the size of the leaf-area increases, and thus the extent of the chlorophyll-tissue, the additional and important function falls to the venation of keeping the exceedingly thin lamella of the leaf extended flat, and at the same time of protecting it from lateral rupture.

This consideration, which it is true only brings out the more obvious features of the organisation of plants, is always traversed by the thought—a guiding thread as it were—that all these arrangements are intelligible and full of purpose only because the plants concerned are nourished by the chlorophyll under the influence of light.

If however we turn again to the current of water ascending in the wood and distributing itself in the veins of the leaves, we know already that it has fundamentally only the one purpose of conveying the nutritive substances of the soil to the assimilating tissue. But these substances are dissolved in very large quantities of water taken up by the roots in the soil, and I have previously shown in detail what difficulties the roots of terrestrial plants have to struggle with in order to obtain these large quantities of water from a soil which is scarcely moist, and that they are even compelled first to dissolve a portion of the nutritive materials by means of their innumerable root-hairs, in order to transfer it to the current of sap. The roots, however, are only adapted for this function when they in their turn obtain not only the necessary surface, but also a sufficient number of points of contact with the particles of the soil. The former is attained in the first place by the great length which the totality of all the root-fibres and their ramifications reach in the soil, by means of this development in length, and the usually very small diameter of the absorbing roots, a relatively large surface extension is already attained, but this is supplemented in an exceedingly advantageous manner by the production of the multitudinous root-hairs, and their continual new formation behind the forward-growing apex of the root. All these properties of the roots, which have already been referred to in the lectures on Organography, are developed only in terrestrial plants which contain chlorophyll these alone need a root-system so extensive and so organised. We must again perceive that it is to the properties of the chlorophyll and its nutritive activity that the organisation of the roots of terrestrial plants is due. Land-plants devoid of chlorophyll, since they need no transpiration-current, also possess but few roots, and these are short and for the most part thick: water-plants on the contrary are again, for another reason, spared the trouble of developing an extensive root-system, since they are in a position to take up water and nutritive materials at the whole of their surface, or, if the leaves float, at least at their lower surface, no root-system whatever is needed, or at any rate only an accessory one, to maintain the nutritive activity of the chlorophyll. In Algæ, and even in some aquatic Phanerogams, the roots are chiefly or it may be exclusively organs of attachment to fix the plant in its position, thus again contributing to keep those parts of the plant which contain chlorophyll in such a position that they can assimilate under the influence of the light.

Evidently the relations of organisation which are merely sketched here, have arisen by correlations in the progressive development of the vegetable kingdom, and in fact we can see up to a certain point how this has come to pass, so that the better the chlorophyll-tissue was able to extend itself to the light in thin broad sheets, the more capable it would be of producing large quantities of vegetable substance, which would provide the material for the formation of the huge masses of wood; and on the other hand we know that the more complete aeration of the soil as the roots of the land-plants need it, directly and essentially contributes to promote the lengthening and branching of the roots. In proportion as this occurs, the roots in the earth are also able to transmit larger quantities of nutritive water to the chlorophyll, which in its turn produces the material not only for the conducting wood-body but also for the growth of the root.

We can, however, adduce numerous other relations of organisation as necessary correlates of the activity of chlorophyll. The Geotropism of the roots as well as that of the shoot-axes serves (as does also the heliotropic sensitiveness of the latter and of the leaves) above all to bring those parts of the shoot which contain chlorophyll into a position favourable for their illumination, and the root-fibres into one suitable for their activity. In many cases, as with twining plants and those which climb by means of tendrils, peculiar relations of organisation are developed in order to bring the assimilating leaves into the light in spite of the fact that the shoot-axes are thin and feeble in the same way, the numerous leaves endowed with so-called sleep-movements are always so organised and so react towards the light, that they present their surfaces to it at the beginning of the day, and when the light becomes too strong turn themselves so that the rays meet them at small angles, and are thus rendered harmless It is obvious that these irritabilities also have meaning and purpose only in so far as it is important to bring the assimilating organs containing chlorophyll into the most favourable position possible for illumination.

Even these correlations, which, as already mentioned, must have made their appearance in the course of the progressive development of the vegetable kingdom, may be at least in part subjected to experimental control, and indeed every-day experiences in the cultivation of plants confirm the above conclusions. Here is one example only If a Tobacco-plant, or a *Ricinus,* or a Sunflower, &c., is allowed to develope in the open and in good soil, there is formed in the course of 100–120 days a powerful stem, occasionally as thick as the arm, with numerous very large leaves and an enormous root-system If, on the other hand, we cultivate such a plant in a flower-pot filled with three litres or so of the best garden soil, the plant in its pot standing in the open and being even watered two or three times daily with proper solutions of nutritive substances, we obtain in 100–120 days a stem of the thickness of a finger, and a total leaf-area which amounts to scarcely a fifth or a sixth of that in the previous case, and, shortly, a small insignificant plant, in spite of all the artificial supply of nutriment at the roots, and in spite of the bright illumination of the leaves. But the cause exists in the limitation of the space for the roots in the flower-pot it is true any one unacquainted with the matter is astounded at the apparently very large quantity of roots in the ball of earth lifted out of the pot, but as a matter of fact this is extremely small in comparison with the rooting of a similar plant in the open land. Moreover the roots are unfavourably situated they are all crowded together, with their growing ends and the parts specially adapted for the absorption of food materials close to the inside of the pot, and there forming a dense felt work all round, which not only hinders further growth and branching, but also completely excludes most of the roots from the soil in the pot, and even makes impossible the proper employment of the nutritive solutions with which they have been watered. The result of this inefficient growth of the roots is a diminished supply of nutritive materials in the assimilating leaves, in consequence of which their activity remains insignificant, and this again affects the formation of wood in the stem.

In this case the pernicious correlation proceeded from the roots; but it may start from the leaves also (even though the roots are fully developed in the earth), when they are so feebly illuminated that assimilation, although not entirely prevented, is reduced to a minimum. Together with a somewhat abnormal aspect of the plant in other respects also, it is then especially found that the stem remains thin, forms but little wood, and that this wood is soft. The stem of such a shaded plant may be easily cut through with a pocket-knife, though this is not the case with a normally grown plant of the kind mentioned above, on account of the hardness of the wood. I have already mentioned in a previous lecture and. in another connection that the so-called laying of wheat when it grows too rank is due to the shading of the lower joints of the haulm, and its deficiency in sclerenchyma.

We have already become acquainted with a particularly fine and instructive example of the influence of chlorophyll on the whole mode of growth of a plant, in our previous considerations on the nutrition of the Lichens. We found that the Lichens are true Fungi (Ascomycetes) and nevertheless their bodies have in general forms quite different from those of all other Fungi. All that appears above the substratum in the case of ordinary Fungi is usually a fructification, the Lichens on the contrary are developed entirely outside the substratum, or they send their root-hairs only into it The body of the Lichen, instead of showing a tendency to the formation of thick fleshy or even woody masses, as other Fungi, assumes either the form of thin leaf-like expansions, or bands, or thin much-branched shrubby structures. In other words, the tendency prevails among the Lichens to assume the form of ordinary plants with flat extensions or branched filiform structures, and this, as I have already said, is solely in consequence of the fact that the tissue of the Lichen-fungus encloses Algæ, which contain chlorophyll and look as if they constituted a normal anatomical constituent of its tissue This, however, is equivalent to saying that since these chlorophyll-cells are simply for the purpose of assimilating they must be presented to the light in thin but relatively extensive surfaces, and this is accomplished in the case of the foliaceous Lichens just as in ordinary foliage-leaves, and in the fruticose Lichens just as with leafless shrubs, where the assimilating tissue is situated in the external cortex If the correlation between chlorophyll and the whole growth of a plant comes out clearly at all, it is certainly in the comparison of the forms of Lichens with those of the bodies of other Fungi Here we have to a certain extent the test for what I have said concerning the correlation between chlorophyll and the configuration of the plant generally.

LECTURE XXXI.

INFLUENCES OF THE ENVIRONMENT ON THE PROCESSES OF CONFIGURATION IN THE PLANT.

WE are now acquainted with a considerable number of cases where, by means of external influences, and particularly those of Gravitation, Light, Pressure, and by stimuli due to animals or plants, processes of growth are modified or are even induced; this however not simply in the sense of accelerating or retarding the increase in volume—on the contrary, I have here in view the processes of configuration itself, the production of new growing points and their embryonic outgrowths, and further extensive qualitative alterations of organs already existing in a young state, by means of external influences.

The processes to be described have to be regarded as phenomena of irritability in the growing parts of plants, since, as has already been incidentally mentioned, phenomena of irritability in general are fundamentally nothing but specifically peculiar reactions of the organism towards external stimuli, and it is just the cases which are to be considered here which belong to this category. The province of the phenomena of irritability, however, is so extensive that, properly put, the whole of physiology is everywhere and always concerned with it, so that in fact physiology might simply be designated the science of the phenomena of irritability But it is exactly on this account that I wish to bring forward the facts to be described here particularly and by themselves, apart from the endless number of phenomena of irritability, and not to put them off to the subsequent and more detailed consideration of the induced movements, because they contribute in an important manner to render our insight into the nature of the growth of plants more profound.

Until quite recently the opinion has been retained, dating from times immemorial in the period of the development of human thought, that organic forms are something fixed and unalterable from all eternity, and thus removed from the region of causality; and with reference to this mode of viewing the matter it is probably worth while to convince ourselves, by taking a few well marked cases more closely into consideration, of the fact that incidental external stimuli are able to aid in determining the processes of configuration in organisms in very definite ways. This old mode of representing matters is of course now opposed by the theory of descent, according to which, organic forms are by no means fixed from the beginning and simply copies of purely ideal types (Platonic ideas): on the contrary, the theory of descent states that every organic form is the result of a historical process, in which the co-operation of two factors—the transmission of peculiarities already acquired, and frequent small deviations from these, or variation—appear as causes of organic form. Of course there lies in this view the recognition of a creation in time of organic forms, but it leaves the forces therein concerned still in the main undetermined. The theory of descent demands in the first place only the recognition of the fact that in the course of time organic forms have been produced by some concatenation of causes; it leaves to us, however, the responsibility of the answer to the question what forces have been effective in determining the production of organic forms in any given case. Some, to be sure, imagine that heredity and variation are such forces; but they forget that these terms are simply words for facts which are not understood, and that heredity and variation are not forces in the sense of Science in general—i e. they are not causes of motion.

I premise these general considerations however, only with a view of throwing light upon the apparently insignificant and trivial matters with which we are here to be concerned, and to make their significance clear from a general point of view. So much is it at any rate obvious, that the processes of configuration in the vegetable kingdom which are connected with growth, result from the co-operation of two factors, the one of which lies in the quality of the organic material itself which is capable of configuration, while the other factor exists in the continuous influence of universally co-operating cosmic forces, or in occasional accidental stimuli. To employ an illustrative example taken from inorganic nature, I may remind the reader how it depends on the physical nature of water that it becomes solidified in hexagonal columns at low temperatures. In this capability the original nature of the water is expressed; but it then depends upon accidental external circumstances whether these hexagonal columns arrange themselves into a solid lump of ice, apparently without any internal structure, or whether we have innumerable minute hexagonal ice-crystals joined together on a window pane in the most various forms, as so called ice-flowers, the growth of which depends upon differences in the external conditions. As in this case, the organisable substance of the plant also seems to be subject to certain unalterable formative forces, which however, under the influence of accidental external causes, may experience the most different combinations and variations.

Proceeding now to a somewhat detailed description of some of the most interesting observations appertaining here, it will be advisable to divide them into two groups, of which the first comprises those cases where it is a matter of the origin of growing-points, or of the influence of external forces on the formation of organs on these, whereas a second group presents phenomena which are called forth by the influence of external forces on post-embryonic growth.

1. *External influences on embryonic configuration.* I may here in the first instance describe a case where, by the influence of an external force, gravitation, the place at which the growing-points of new shoots are formed, is determined.

Thladiantha dubia belongs to the Cucumber family, and produces on its very long and thin root-fibres subterranean tubers of a size varying between that of a Hazel-nut and that of a medium-sized Potato. These tubers are swellings of the thin root-fibres, and the growth in length of the latter is not interrupted by their formation. Consequently we find in the middle of a root-fibre 1–2 metres long, one to three tuberous swellings, the transverse section of each being approximately quadrangular, with rounded corners; the tubers are thus four-sided prisms, and usually lie in the soil in such a manner that one of the flat sides is uppermost, and the other turned downwards. In Autumn, the plant together with its root-fibres perishes, and only the tuberous swellings of the latter persist in the soil through the Winter. In April we find on these, numerous thin root-fibres proceeding from all sides, as well as young shoots 1–2 cm in length: it is with the latter we are here concerned. If the tuber lies horizontally in the earth, all the shoot-buds arise on the upper side if, on the contrary, the acroscopic end of the tuber (i.e. the end directed towards the apex of the root) is directed upwards they are all situated on this, around the point whence the root-fibre continued its growth. To me this fact leaves no doubt that we are here concerned with an effect of gravitation on the production of the growing points of the shoots, since light was excluded, the object remaining underground. It should also be mentioned, however, that in all cases the shoot-buds arising from the tuber are more crowded towards its acroscopic end A large number of experiments[1] which I made with the tubers of *Thladiantha dubia*, yielded distinctly the result that the shoot-buds are formed exclusively on that side of the tuber which lies uppermost (towards the zenith) during their development, and that, moreover, in virtue of an internal disposition the acroscopic end of the tuber is preferred in the formation of buds. Here, therefore, are two different causes working together, and determining the place of origin of the adventitious growing-points of shoots—internal causes bring it about that the end of the tuber situated towards the apex of the root is especially qualified for the formation of buds, while at the same time the influence of gravitation determines that the buds arise on the side of the tuber which is turned away from the centre of the earth

Not less instructive are my observations on the genus *Opuntia*, one of the best known forms of Cactus. In *Opuntia ficus Indica* and *O. crassa*, with which I experimented, the sub-aerial vegetative body consists of elongated flattened segments of the shoot-axis, on which the positions of the suppressed leaves are indicated only by tufts of prickles. Under normal conditions of vegetation, new flattened segments arise chiefly from the apex of the segments which then happen to be uppermost, and especially from their margins or angles, the angles directed upwards being always preferred in the process. It is easy to see that an impulse exists in the plant which leads to the appearance of new shoots above, and at the same time preferably at the narrow angles of the flat segments: it is only extremely rarely that a new shoot makes its appearance on the flat broad side of an old segment. The tendency for new shoots to appear chiefly at the apical portions of the older ones, is in fact very common in plants generally, but

---

[1] More details as to the behaviour here described of the root-tubers of *Thladiantha dubia* and of the shoot segments of *Opuntia* are found in my treatise '*Uber Stoff und Form der Pflanzenorgane*,' Arb des bot Inst in Wzbg. B. II, 1882, p 698.

in this case experiment teaches that it is an effect of gravitation.   In the first place, we
have sometimes an opportunity of observing in gardens where Opuntias are cultivated
the case represented in Fig. 337 a.   This figure shows a very large shoot-segment of
the plant, *I*, which has given rise in the usual manner on the right and left angles to
the lateral segments marked *II*.   After the production of the latter, the segment *I*
had accidentally bent over at its apex, so that one of its flat sides was turned downwards and the other almost horizontal and facing upwards.   When new segments
began to shoot forth in the next spring, they appeared not exactly at the angles of *I*,
but rather more on the uppermost surface of the segment, but nevertheless not far

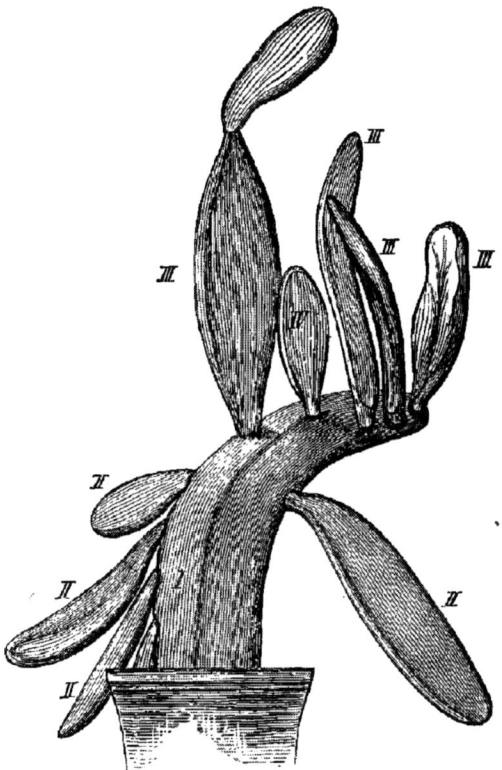

FIG. 337 a.—*Opuntia Ficus indica.*

from its two margins, as shown at *III* in the figure.   Only in the following year did
a further shoot *IV* arise, quite independent of the two lateral angles, on the up-turned
surface of the mother-segment.   It thus required two years to overcome the tendency
to form shoots at the angles, through the influence of gravity, and perhaps with
the co-operation of light, so that the shoot *IV* could arise at the middle of the
upper side of the shoot *I*.   To see how far the relations of configuration of this plant
are subject to external influences, however, it is first necessary to know that the two-
edged flat form of the shoot-segments is in its turn due to illumination, since the
segments of *Opuntia* assume this flat two-edged form only under the influence of light,

whereas they become more or less cylindrical or prismatic when grown in the dark. That the normal offshoots thus arise from the margins is an indirect consequence of light, that they arise chiefly from the upper surface of the existing segments is a direct effect of gravitation, which can in its turn conquer the preceding influence of the light if the segment which produces the new shoots assumes the proper position We may easily convince ourselves also by means of an experiment, that the places of origin of new growing-points are actually dependent on the influence of gravitation, as illustrated in Fig. 338. A plant which already consisted of the segments *I, II, III*, and growing in the pot *c*, was placed in an inverted position on an iron support *a*, in such a manner that the plant was directed downwards and the pot *c* upwards, the falling out of the soil being prevented by the interposition of the divided cover *b*   The experiment began immediately after the formation of a new growing-point at the apex of the plant, and this growing-point was cut off   In the next few weeks were then produced five new growing-points, from which the shoots marked 1–5 in the figure developed. The origin of the shoots 1, 2, and 3 from the segments *II* and *III* simply present nothing surprising, since they arise at the apical portion of the plant.   That the segments 4 and 5 however have arisen also from the old basal segment *I*, proves that here, in consequence of the inversion, an effect of gravitation has made itself evident: the shoot-forming substances which previously streamed towards the apex have now gone back, in part at least, upwards into the segments *II* and *I*, to produce the shoots 4 and 5, which in the normal position of the plant

FIG. 338 —*Opuntia Ficus indica*

would certainly not have happened   But the places of origin not merely of the shoots but also those of the roots are determined in *Opuntia* by external forces, and probably chiefly by gravitation.   In experiments to elucidate this, however, difficulties are met with arising from the fact that the plant was previously growing in its ordinary normal position, and a strong predisposition thus induced On cutting off vigorous *Opuntia* segments and then placing them with their basal ends in the soil of a pot, and leaving them in the same position as in Fig 338, there appear, within a few weeks, from the basal ends (now turned upward) of the segments, vigorous and much-branched roots which fill the soil of the pot.   In this is expressed the tendency of the root-forming substance to be driven to the basal end even when this is turned upwards; though here the moisture and darkness surrounding the basal end co-operate as favourable factors.

If however cut-off segments of *Opuntia* are set with the apical end (a piece of which
has been cut off transversely) in the soil, in such a manner that the basal end is again
turned upwards but projects into the air, two to five months pass by before any
roots make their appearance from the apical end of the shoot segment, thus
directed downwards   We may explain the result of this experiment by the assumption
that root-forming substance exists in the shoot-segments of the *Opuntia*, but that in
the normal position of the plant it always seeks to move in the direction of the base,
in order to strengthen the subterranean root-system of the plant.   By this is produced
a predisposition in the tissue of the shoot-segments which facilitates the movement
of the root-building substance towards the base, whence is explained that also in
inverted shoot-segments—but with the base planted in the soil—new roots are produced rapidly and vigorously at the basal end.   If on the contrary the apical end of
the shoot-segment is planted in the soil, and at the same time turned downwards, it
requires a long time before the root-forming substance is able, in opposition to the
previous predisposition and in obedience to gravitation, to make its appearance at
the apical end in the form of roots.   That this happens at all in the present
case is essentially aided by the additional influence of darkness and moisture, which
promote the formation of roots at the planted apical end.

In the experiments last quoted we have to do in the main with the reproduction
of organs on separated portions of plants, concerning which numerous experiments
have for a long time been to hand, and which have been recently investigated by
Voechting [1], but in part incorrectly explained   Practical gardening has known from of
old the fact that it is possible to obtain new plants from even small portions of older
ones, roots and shoot-buds being formed on them: For this purpose it is usual to lay
the cut-off pieces in moist sand or soil ; for scientific purposes, however, it is often
better, as Voechting did, to suspend the separated portions in moist air, in order to
attain an equable environment favourable to growth.   If these cut-off pieces of the
shoot-axes of woody or herbaceous plants are suspended in a horizontal or vertical
position, the usual result is that roots arise from their basal ends, and shoot-buds
from their acroscopic or apical ends—from which however the true apex has been
cut off.   As a rule the behaviour is the reverse in the regeneration of cut-off pieces
of root; here the tendency prevails to produce shoot-buds at the basal end, and
roots at the acropetal end—i.e. the end turned towards the growing-point.
Finally, if the same experiments are made with cut-off leaves, buds and roots arise
at the base of the cut-off petiole, the buds usually being turned upwards, the roots
downwards.   Voechting has attempted to bring the results of numerous experiments
in this direction which he has made under a general expression, intended to mark
everywhere a distinction between what he terms the apex and the base of the regenerating organ.   It is obvious, however, that in this sense the facts shortly referred
to above cannot be collated at all.   According to my view, on the contrary, it is easy
to get at the heart of the matter if we proceed from certain allowable assumptions, and
keep in view the immediate effective causes which determine that roots and shoots must
arise at definite spots on cut-off parts of plants.   In fact, as I have clearly shown in

---

[1] Voechting, '*Über Organbildung im Pflanzenreich*,' Bonn, 1878   Compare my reply in the
treatise quoted in note 1 (p 517).

detail in my treatises on '*Stoff und Form der Pflanzentheile*[1],' two causes, which usually co-operate, come into consideration here: on the one hand it is to be noticed that the substances for the formation of organs (apart from germinal stages where they proceed from the reservoirs of reserve-material) are produced in the foliage leaves by assimilation, and pass out thence into other parts of the plant.   So long as a vigorous main bud of the shoot is present, mixtures of substances suited chiefly for the formation of shoots pass into it from the leaves, whereas the substances fitted for the formation of roots flow in the opposite direction, into the roots which already exist. If then a portion of the shoot-axis is cut off and kept in a moist warm environment, the substances suitable for the formation of shoots which are already present in it will, as heretofore, move in the acropetal direction, and those which form roots, on the contrary, in the basipetal one—i e the shoot-buds will make their appearance on a cut-off piece of stem at the apical end, the young roots at the basal end.   Exactly the reverse must take place, however, in the regeneration occurring in a cut-off piece of an old root: since here the root-forming substance is in continual movement towards the apex, the roots produced by regeneration will arise at the acropetal end, and if any bud-forming substance at all has reached the roots it may come forth at the basal end of the piece of root, if the second external cause to be mentioned hereafter co-operates.   That roots as well as shoot-buds appear at the basal end of a cut-off leaf is explained, according to this view of the matter, simply by supposing that during the assimilatory activity of the leaf, and in accordance with its normal function, shoot-forming as well as root-forming substances are continually passing from the leaf through the petiole into the shoot-axis.   If then the petiole is cut off, this customary movement proceeds no further, being, as in the case of cut-off pieces in general, to a certain extent checked at the section, and buds as well as roots will grow out from the petiole near the section.   These considerations then show that effective causes are given in the organisation and vital activity of the plant itself by which the places of origin of new roots and shoots are determined.

A second cause, however, has already become known to us in the examples quoted above; this is the influence of gravitation, which, so far as we are as yet informed, affects different plants in very different degrees, in that new shoot-buds arise more easily in cut-off portions on the ends directed upwards, new roots on those directed downwards.   If we suspend a cut-off piece of a shoot-axis in moist air, with its basal end downwards, two influences are working together to induce roots to arise at the latter, and at the same time to cause shoots to spring from the acropetal end.   If, however, we give the cut-off piece the reverse position, with the acropetal end downwards, the two causes mentioned must work in the opposite way · the internal disposition in this case induces the formation of buds at the acropetal, lower end, while the influence of gravitation strives, so to speak, to draw the root-forming substance downwards, and to push up the shoot-forming substance to a corresponding extent, and thus bring about the opposed position of the new organs.   It depends now entirely and simply upon the reactive capacity of the plant concerned, whether

---

[1] That in regeneration occurring in cut-off parts of plants an internal disposition depending on the organisation of the plant co-operates with a direct effect of gravitation and other forces, I have shown in detail in Arb des bot. Inst B II, pp 691, &c

and to what extent the influence of gravitation succeeds in affecting the position in relation to it of the new organs.

Since, then, as Voechting had in part found, and as results definitely from my experiments on *Thladiantha* and *Opuntia*, gravitation acts in such a way as to move the root-forming substances downwards and the shoot-forming substances upwards, we must assume that this is the case not merely with cut-off pieces, but also with entire plants living and rooted in the soil; in this case, however, the internal disposition and the influence of gravitation work to the same end, at least in so far as plants with erect stems and down-turned roots are concerned. In accordance with this it is also the rule that in horizontal creeping or climbing shoots the formation of roots takes place on the axis progressively behind the terminal bud, on the underside of the shoot, and in such cases the illumination of the dorsal side of the shoot also evidently has for its effect that the roots make their appearance exclusively on the ventral or shaded side.

Instructive examples to illustrate the fact that the light in many cases prevents the formation of the growing-points of roots upon the directly illuminated side of the shoot-axis, so that they only appear on the shaded side, may be afforded in the first place by the leaf-shoots of the Ivy[1] When these climb up on a wall, or on the stem of a tree, the clinging roots necessary for climbing arise exclusively on the side turned towards the solid substratum. in this case, however, the active cause lies, not simply in the contact or pressure suffered by this side of the shoot-axis, but in the fact that it is turned from the light. The horizontal pendent shoots of the Ivy teach this directly: the anchoring roots here are always formed only on the side turned away from the light. But still more: it is possible experimentally to cause shoots of Ivy to form aerial roots on what was hitherto the lighted or dorsal side, by illuminating them for some time on the side which was previously the ventral or shaded side Fig. 339 illustrates this in the case of an Ivy-shoot, the lower end of which was rooted in a flower-pot, and fastened upright to a rod. The arrows give the direction of the rays of light. At *A* we have the upper part of the shoot with what was hitherto its dorsal side turned towards the light, and bearing roots only on the side turned from the light, at the same time the shoot-axis exhibits a negatively heliotropic curvature towards the shaded side. A shoot, together with its pot, was now placed at the window so that the side which bore roots hitherto was turned towards the light. The shoot now made in the first place the heliotropic curvature represented at *C*, opposed to the previous one, and then grew on horizontally: meanwhile new groups of aerial roots arose on the now horizontal and at the same time shaded side—the previously illuminated dorsal side. With many other dorsi-ventral shoots of course this reversal of ventral and dorsal side is not so easy as in the case of the Ivy, since all the influences of external forces here treated of are dependent upon the specific capacity for reaction of the particular plant.

Another object resembling the Ivy in this connection was found by Voechting in the broad, two-winged, leafless shoot-axes of a cactus-like plant, *Lepismium radicans*, in which likewise each of the two flat sides is able to produce roots, but only when it is turned away from the source of light[2]

---

[1] The properties of the Ivy shoot here referred to are described in detail in my treatise '*Über orthotrope und plagiotrope Pflanzentheile*' (Arb des bot Inst. Wzbg B II, p 257)

[2] That the formation of roots is promoted by the absence of light I have already insisted upon

So long ago as 1863 I described various examples showing that the formation of roots upon shoot-axes by darkening them, may be induced at spots where otherwise no roots arise: here however I need only mention *Tropæolum majus* (Indian Cress). If one of the long thin leafy shoots is bent down as it were into a depression of the surrounding garden soil, so as not to break it off and so that an apical portion of the shoot, some 10–12 cm. long, remains upright, and can be surrounded with damp soil, new roots arise after a few days all around the vertical piece of shoot-axis, while the older piece of the same shoot-axis, lying horizontally and likewise covered with earth, developes roots exclusively on its lower side. This experiment shows not only that the exclusion of light generally induces the development of roots on the shoot-axis, but the simultaneous influence of gravitation is here very clearly apparent also: the horizontally placed shoot-axis forms roots only on the lower side, the vertically upright one on all sides. Of course in this experiment the growth of the new roots is promoted by the moisture of the surrounding soil. The cause of their first production, however, by no means resides in that, since the same result is obtained if a leaf-shoot of *Tropæolum* is directed into the dark cavity of an opaque box without separating it from its parent plant, only in this case the new roots remain very short unless the air in the box is in some way kept moist artificially.

These examples refer to the origin of new growing-points of roots on shoot-axes, but, in many cases, roots may arise in the translucent tissue of sub-aërial shoot-axes,

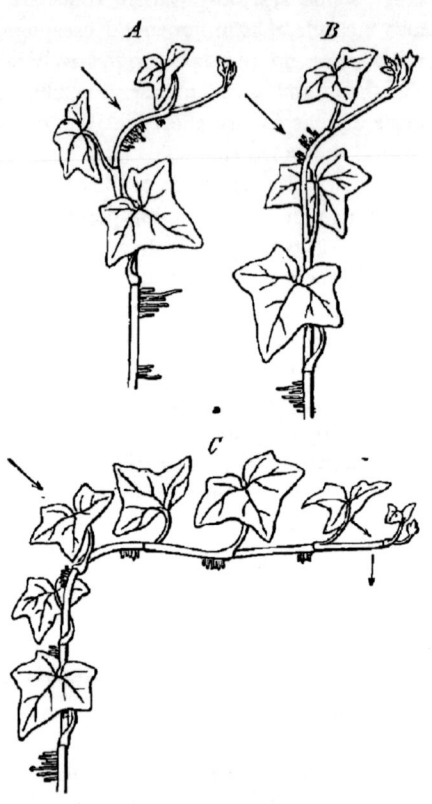

FIG. 339.—Ivy shoot (*Hedera Helix*) *A* has been illuminated on the dorsal side for several days, *B* has undergone similar treatment on the ventral side   *C* a later stage of *B*

that is under the influence of light, although it may be feeble   Thus, in the creeping or climbing shoots of the Gourd-plant we find a rudimentary root to the right and left of each leaf, and similarly on those parts of the erect stem of the Maize plant which are about 10–12 cm. above the surface of the soil: here the roots come forth in large numbers in a crown above the insertion of the leaf.

several times in my researches, '*Über den Einfluss des Tageslichtes auf Neubildung und Entfaltung verschiedener Pflanzenorgane*' (Bot Zeigt. 1863, supplement , and the same, 1865, pp 117, &c)

In both cases however they remain short; but it suffices to darken the parts mentioned to make them elongate. Of course this takes place much more energetically if the surrounding air is moist; or best if the parts of the stem concerned are surrounded with soil, by which means they are darkened and kept damp at the same time.

Much more energetic than in the case of the highly organised vascular plants is the influence of gravitation, and still more so of light, on the formation of organs in the Muscineæ and other plants of simple structure. Since it is here possible to submit plants in the very earliest stages of development, as they proceed from the spores or gemmæ, to a definite influence of external forces, the effect begins before the plant has yet had time to become organised in a manner unknown to the observer. It is thus possible to allow plants of this category to grow so that one can determine

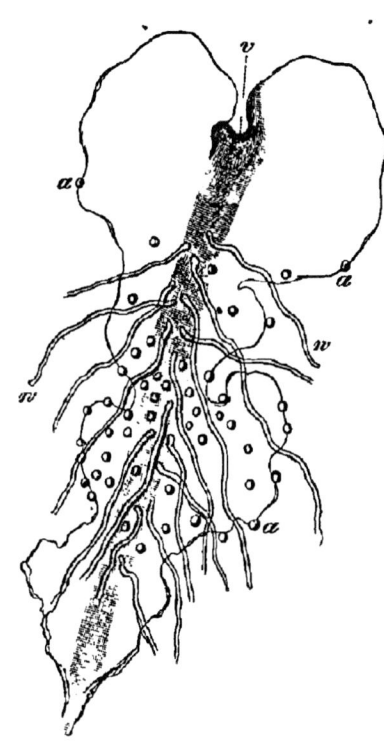

FIG 340.—Prothallus of a Fern (*Osmunda regalis*) seen from below   *a* antheridia, *w* root hairs, *v* growing point (magnified)

beforehand and arbitrarily the disposition of the organs one to another and towards external influences. One of the most interesting cases in this connection was first described by Leitgeb[1] in the prothallia of Ferns. As is already known to the reader (p 31) the germinating spore of a Fern does not give rise forthwith to a Fern again, but first to a plantlet of quite another form—the prothallium. The germinating spore first forms a germinal filament segmented by transverse walls, which subsequently spreads out anteriorly, and at length grows into a very thin leaf-like flat lamella, which is deeply indented in front and consists of only one layer of cells containing chlorophyll later, however, it produces in the centre, behind the growing-point, a cushion, several cells in thickness, from which the female organs of reproduction or archegonia arise in large numbers, while on the posterior portion of the lamella, or at its margins, the male fertilising organs or antheridia arise. Previously to this, numerous cells at the hinder part of the prothallus have grown out into long root-hairs. The whole of this structure now is most distinctly dorsi-ventral: root-hairs, antheridia, and archegonia arise exclusively on the under side, if the prothallus grows on a horizontal substratum and is lighted from above in the usual way. Leitgeb has shown, now, that the dorsi-ventrality, as such, is in this case an effect of light, and in the growing parts of the prothallus may be reversed at will if what was hitherto the shaded side is illuminated, the sexual organs always being formed

---

[1] Leitgeb, '*Über Bilateralität der Prothallien,*' in Flora, 1879, p 317.

on the shaded side. Leitgeb demonstrated this highly important fact very elegantly by sowing the spores of a Fern, *Ceratopteris thalictroides* (which, moreover, grows in very wet places) on the surface of a clear nutritive solution, where they produce floating prothallia If the sowing is illuminated from above, the archegonia and root-hairs arise on the under side—the latter also from the margins—and both grow down into the liquid, if the illumination takes place from below, however, the prothallia grow downward into the liquid, but become curved, as soon as they begin to develope the flattened surface, so that the latter is directed at right angles to the incident light. Here both the surfaces of the plate of tissue are in the water, and nevertheless the archegonia and roots are developed only on the side turned away from the light. Prantl has extended this experiment with the prothallia of other species, and varied it in many ways, with reference to which, however, I cannot here go more into details. I will only lay stress on one point, that not only the dorsi-ventrality but also the extension into a bilateral thin plate of tissue is determined by the light, and that such a plant rendered bilateral and dorsi-ventral by the light also places itself with its surfaces at right angles to the incident light.

Those Liverworts which consist of flat shoots behave also exactly like the prothallia, in them also, as Mirbel partly demonstrated with Marchantia about fifty years ago[1], the dorsi-ventral organisation and bilateral extension are induced by the light. The germination of the spores of Marchantia runs its course very much as in the case of the Ferns described above, and if they are sown on the surface of soil or damp turf, and care is taken that they are lighted from one side only, it is found that the young, approximately heart-shaped plantlets extend their surfaces all at right angles to the direction of the incident light, although their axes of growth may assume the most various positions The root-hairs appear exclusively on the shaded side, the stomata only on the upper side. It is still easier to make use of the gemmæ of Marchantia for experiments of this kind, for example by letting them float on an aqueous solution of nutritive substances in a transparent glass vessel, if the water is illuminated from below by means of a large mirror (for which however very intense light must be employed) while the upper side of the vessel is covered with an opaque lid, the gemmæ grow in the usual manner, and produce broad ribbon-like shoots floating on the surface of the water, which develope their root-hairs chiefly upwards and away from the light, and their stomata on the under side which is turned towards the light. The whole significance of this action of light is only apprehended however on noticing (see Fig. 341, which represents a piece of a transverse section at the margin of a shoot) that the structure here concerned consists of several layers of cells, the relations of growth of which are very complicated, and that the whole of the organisation, represented in the figure in outline only, can be brought by the influence of the light into a completely inverted position. If the Fig 341 for example is supposed to be illuminated from below, the picture

---

[1] Mirbel's statements occur in his celebrated work, '*Recherches anatomiques et physiologiques sur le Marchantia polymorpha*' (Mem de l'acad d scienc de l'institut de France, 1835) These important statements of Mirbel's remained unnoticed till I induced Pfeffer in 1870 to test them, and where possible to study the phenomena more closely The latter published his results in the '*Arb des bot Inst in Wúrbg.*' B I, p 77.

itself must be completely reversed, i e. the side marked *o* would become the lower side. It is to be mentioned moreover that the Marchantia shoot produces on the under or shaded side two series of membranous leaves near its middle line, and very numerous root-hairs. That it is possible to shape this shoot at will during continuous illumination from one side so that its organic light-side is turned downwards or upwards, forwards or backwards, is greatly owing to

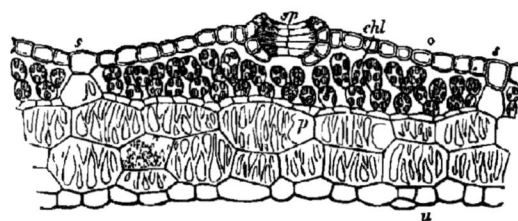

FIG 341 —Vertical section through the lateral portion of a flat shoot of *Marchantia polymorpha* *o* epidermis of upper, *u* of lower side , *p* colourless parenchyma of lower side , *chl* assimilatory cells containing chlorophyll , *sp* stoma , *s s* boundary between two areolæ

the circumstance that neither the spores nor the gemmæ from which the shoots arise are differentiated dorsi-ventrally. Thus with the beginning of the growth of the new shoot the influence of the light upon it can come into effect at once, without being modified by previous influences In this connection the gemmæ of Marchantia have already been investigated. They arise from papillæ in small cup-shaped receptacles on the light side of older shoots, and constitute later approximately lenticular bodies, the two convex sides of which are organised quite alike and are sensitive to external influences in exactly similar degree. As shown on the transverse section (Fig 342) through such a gemma, certain cells *a* exist

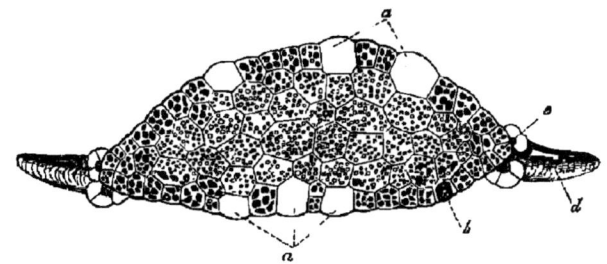

FIG 342 —Vertical section of a ripe gemma of *Marchantia*, carried through the two growing points *a* hyaline cells which develop into root hairs , *b* cell filled with peculiar contents , *d* wing of recess in which the growing-points *e* are situated (× 165)

on both the convex sides, which are destined, according to circumstances in each case, to grow out into root-hairs , if both the surfaces of the gemma are equally illuminated those grow out which are able to follow directly the influence of gravitation, i. e. those of the lower side, whereas those of the upper side are prevented from developing The influence of the light however is stronger than that of gravitation, since, as Zimmermann has shown[1], if the lower surface is illuminated it is chiefly the roots of the shaded upper side which develope

---

[1] On this point cf Zimmermann, '*Über die Einwirkung des Lichtes auf den Marchantien-thallus*' (Arb des bot Inst in Wzbg B II, p. 665)

Moreover, a branch-system consisting of simple cell-filaments can also behave towards the light like the flat shoot of Marchantia, which consists of continuous tissue. If the spores of one of our commonest Mosses, *Funaria hygrometrica*, are sown on a brick-shaped piece of damp turf which is artificially saturated with nutritive substances, and care is taken that the light for weeks and months always falls only on the same side, there is developed from the spores the protonema, Fig. 343, already described above (p 30), the filaments of the primary shoot of this creep on the turf like rhizomes, putting forth roots below and producing on their upper side erect branched filaments containing chlorophyll, from which again secondary and tertiary lateral shoots arise It is shown now that these upright branch-systems become extended in a plane at right angles to the incident light, and I have carefully convinced myself of the fact that this is due not simply to heliotropic curvatures and torsions, but that the bi-serially arranged offshoots come forth from their parent axes strictly right and left.   In other

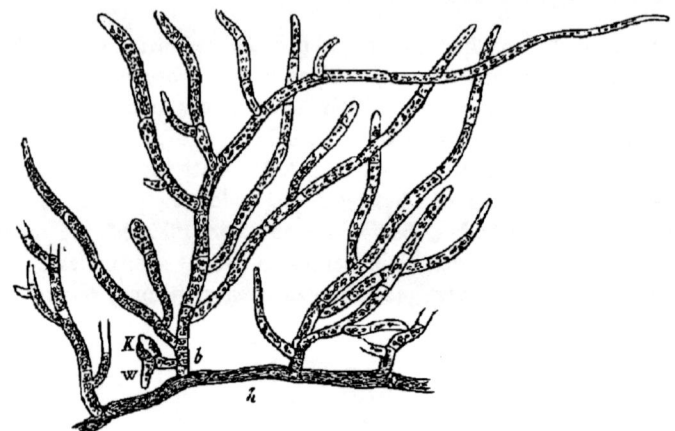

FIG. 343—Protonema of *Funaria hygrometrica*   *h* a creeping main shoot, from which arise the lateral shoots, containing chlorophyll and branched in two series *K* a bud which will develope into a Moss plant , *w* its first root.

words, the light in this case causes the growing points of the lateral shoots to arise only on the flanks of the mother-shoots, if these are always illuminated from one side[1].

Supposing now that the lateral shoots which arise from the filament *b* in the figure, stand so close together as to be everywhere in contact, we should then obtain a leaf-like surface of tissue developed at right angles to the incident light. So it is however as a matter of fact with the flat shoots of Marchantia, and with those of the Opuntia , they become narrow and filamentous in the dark, but in intense light falling from one side develope their normal flat form, in such a manner that the surfaces stand at right angles to the incident rays.

So far it is gravitation and light which have produced the described effects

---

[1] The relation here described between the protonema of *Funaria hygrometrica* and light was first cited in my treatise ' *Über orthotrope und plagiotrope Pflanzentheile* ' (Arb des bot Inst. in Wzbg B II, p. 256) I have completely set aside the doubt I there expressed, by means of later investigations, and thus established the result expressed in the text

on growth, and at the same time we have had to consider the relations of direction and position under which the embryonic rudiments of new organs arise, and of the external and internal symmetry of their organisation. These relations are possible simply because gravitation and light, according to their nature, act on the plastic substance of the plant in definite directions; and we shall have opportunities subsequently, when considering geotropism and heliotropism, of becoming acquainted with other effects of these two natural forces, where it is also a matter of effects appearing in definite directions, but of effects on organisations already more or less fully developed, whereas we are here concerned exclusively with the effects of external forces on the developing organisation itself.

Having thus become acquainted with the influence of gravitation and light on the embryonic rudiments of the organs, by means of a few examples, I now proceed to show how the same forces co-operate during the further growth of organs already established, or, as we may say generally, how they affect post-embryonic growth.

2. *Post-embryonic relations of configuration.* In this case also, as will be shown further on, the influence on growing organs in a definite direction may still come into consideration; but, in the majority of the known cases, the effects of gravitation and light here present themselves in far more complicated forms, indeed so that the whole physiological quality of an organ may be determined by them.

In this sense the behaviour of the subterranean shoots of *Dracæna* and *Yucca* will at once illustrate what is meant [1]. These well-known large Liliaceæ develope from the base of their upright stems root-like shoots of a thickness varying between that of the thumb and that of the arm, which grow down vertically into the earth, and in their turn produce numerous long roots which feed the whole of the large plant, but remain thin and filiform. These subterranean shoots produce, it is true, numerous leaves at their broad growing-points, but these leaves remain rudimentary and form annular thin membranes. So long as the plant remains undisturbed, proper foliage leaves never arise from the growing-points of these subterranean shoots. Their development can be effected, however, simply by completely inverting such a plant placed on a support, as in Fig. 344 *h g*, and directing the root-system *f* contained in the flower-pot upwards. The growth of the now down-turned bud is injured if it has no opportunity of curving upwards; the development of the growing-points on the thick rhizome shoot *a d*, however, is promoted The leaves produced here develope henceforward no longer as annular membranes, but in the form of foliage-leaves, finally coming above the soil, and thus leaf-shoots arise directly from the up-turned rhizomes It is evident that in the experiment nothing whatever has been altered except the direction in which gravitation acts on the plant. The rhizomes in the opaque soil are inaccessible to the light both before and after, the relations of moisture in the surrounding soil are the same as before, and nevertheless the post-embryonic development of the leaves arising at the growing-point are forthwith altered: instead of so-called cataphyllary leaves or scales, vigorous foliage-leaves are produced, which, however, of course only become green and flat when they grow forth above the soil. Moreover, it is possible to make the experiment

---

[1] What is said in the text as to *Yucca* and *Dracæna* (sub-genus *Cordyline*) is described more in detail in my treatise ' *Über Stoff und Form* ' (Arb. des bot Inst. in Wzbg B II, pp 475, &c).

still more easily by taking an entire plant of *Yucca* or *Dracæna* out of the earth and submerging the apex in a glass vessel full of water, so that the thick rhizomes are directed upwards. Even in this case, and under the influence of light, the changes described take place, and after all that has been said, they cannot well be ascribed to

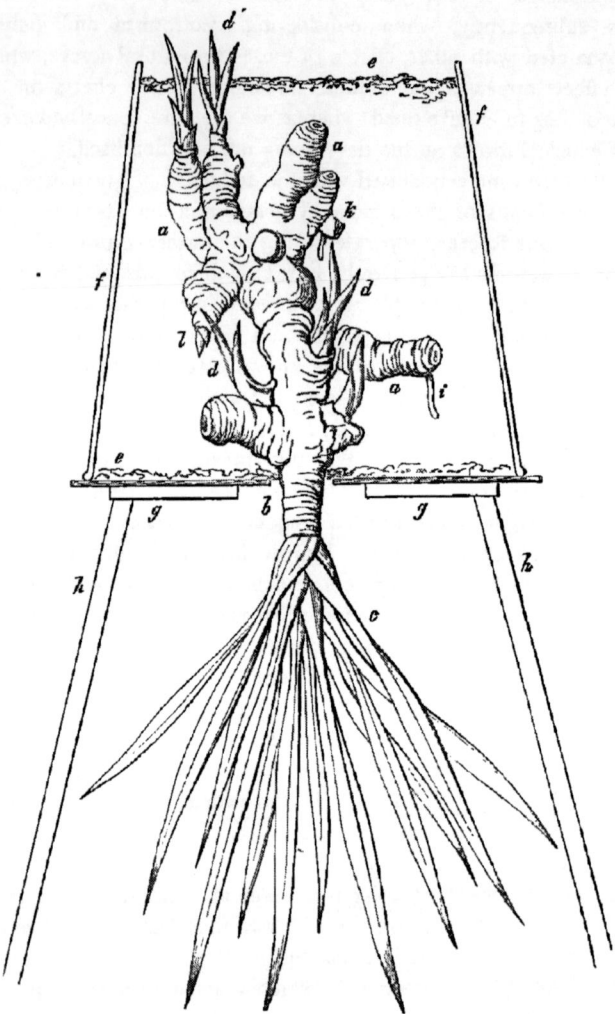

FIG. 344.—*Yucca gloriosa.* *a a* rhizome; *b* stem; *c* leaves at apex; *d* subterranean leaf-shoots from the basal part of the rhizome; *d'* leaf-shoots from the terminal buds of two shoots of the rhizome; *e e* soil of pot *f f*; *g g, h h* the wooden support for the inverted plant; *i* a new root; *k* and *l* new buds of the rhizome. The roots are omitted in the figure.

any other influence than that of gravitation, although it is at present quite impossible to form any clear idea whatever as to the way in which this influence leads to the final result described. We are here simply in the same position as with almost all the effects of light and gravitation, pressure, injury, and other external influences:

[3]   M m

we simply perceive the cause and the last effect, while the probably very long series
of intermediate causes and effects remain for the time being unknown. The
same is the case, indeed, with all the phenomena of irritability, among which even
the best-known, both in animal and vegetable organisms, always present ultimately
something entirely inexplicable and unintelligible according to ordinary ideas of
mechanics.

Here again our information as to the influence of light on the development of
organs, the rudiments of which are already formed, is much more abundant, although
here also, as in the whole of this province, we have as yet gained only the first dim
glimpses into very involved processes of Nature. We may in the first place keep
apart two cases; on the one hand we ask the question, what happens when organs
which normally complete their post-embryonic growth under the influence of light are
necessitated to complete their development in constant darkness? We have in this
case to do with the so-called Etiolation of plants. In the second place, the case is
to be noticed where organs, especially leaf-forming shoots, which, as a rule, pass
through their whole course of development underground, and therefore in profound
darkness, are compelled to do this under the influence of light.

In spite of the very numerous researches on Etiolation, as it is called—i. e the
alteration induced by want of light in organs which normally grow in strong light—
it must nevertheless unfortunately be confessed that we here enter upon a province
which until quite recently has been closely bestrewn with gross errors. However,
this is not the place to discuss that matter, and I must be satisfied with acquainting
the reader with those facts which can easily be observed[1].

If the seeds of Phanerogams are sown in soil and allowed to develope their
seedlings in the dark, there appear after a short time abnormalities, in general of
such a kind that the shoot-axes are longer by far than is the case when the
illumination is normal, whereas the first leaves of the seedling usually remain much
smaller, and do not complete their extension in one plane, and at the same time
(except in the Coniferæ[2]) the formation of chlorophyll is suppressed: the leaves

---

[1] What is here said concerning etiolation is based on my two treatises, '*Über den Einfluss des Tageslichtes auf Neubildung und Entfaltung verschiedener Pflanzenorgane*,' Bot. Zeitg 1863, supplement; and 1865, *Wirkung des Lichtes auf die Bluthenbildung unter Vermittlung der Laubblatter*, pp 117, &c. I have of late years carried on in Wurzburg similar investigations with the aid of better methods than were to hand at that time. the results of these have not yet been published in detail. Gregor Kraus ('*Über die Ursachen der Formanderungen etiolirter Pflanzen*,' Jahrb fur Wiss. Bot. VII, p 209) and Godlewski ('*Zur Kenntniss der Ursachen der Formanderungen etiolirter Pflanzen*,' Bot. Zeitg. 1879, pp 81, &c) have both dealt with the excessive lengthening of the internodes and the dwarfing of the leaves of seedlings in the dark, but without taking into consideration my much older statements on the etiolation of shoots nourished by foliage-leaves exposed to light. Moreover, the text above is chiefly concerned not with the mechanical causes, but only with the facts themselves, wherefore I need not here go further into the statements of these observers. Kraus' assumption, in particular, that etiolated leaves remain small because leaves in general are only able to grow from their own products of assimilation, is strikingly contradicted by the experiments described and illustrated in the text. That the dwarfing of leaves in the dark is a phenomenon of disease, and cannot be compared with the growth of leaves under normal conditions, has been shown by Prantl's investigations in my laboratory, '*Über den Einfluss des Lichtes auf das Wachsthum der Blätter*' (Arb des bot Inst in Wzbg, B I, p 371).

[2] That the seedlings of Conifers produce leaves which contain chlorophyll even in profound darkness I first stated in the publication '*Lotos*' (Prague, Jan. 1859); and I showed later that

developed in the dark become yellow, it is true, whereby of course a step towards the formation of chlorophyll is accomplished, but the greening of this yellow imperfect chlorophyll is only completed when such etiolated leaves are subsequently exposed to light   Moreover, the size of a plant thus developed in the dark, as well as the number of roots and leaves formed, are proportional chiefly to the volume and mass of the seed or, better, to the quantity of the reserve-materials accumulated in it.   From the minute seed of the Tobacco plant there developes in the dark a correspondingly tiny seedling with two cotyledons, from the large seed of a Bean or of a Horse Chestnut, on the contrary, there may be produced in the dark a plant of considerable size with copiously branched roots, and several, though small and yellow, leaves   At length, however, after a few days, or in the case of very large seeds after a few weeks, the growth in the dark always ceases, and the whole plant becomes diseased and perishes, in many cases, as with *Phaseolus*, &c., not until all the reserve-materials of the seed have been completely used up for the formation of organs ; in other cases, however, as in the Gourd, growth and the development of organs cease while the cotyledons still contain considerable quantities of unused formative substance.   The malformation of such etiolated seedlings, as well as their final perishing, show that they are in a sickly condition, and this at length affects the processes of growth proper, which alone interest us here. Although the fact that the shoot-axes become elongated more rapidly in the dark agrees with the observation that their growth under normal conditions of illumination takes place more rapidly during the night, or during occasional short periods of darkness, than under the influence of light—a point to which I shall return in the next lecture ; yet the dwarfing of the etiolated leaves of seedlings might lead to the conclusion that their growth is directly retarded or inhibited by deficient light, and thus might be accelerated by illumination.   That is a mistake, however, since, as we shall see later, healthy green foliage-leaves which have previously been exposed for some time to the action of light, grow more rapidly during the night or during other periods of darkness which last for a few hours only.   From this it evidently follows that the dwarfing of etiolated leaves of seedlings must have other causes, which we simply imply by terming the etiolated leaves (and the same is true of the excessively long shoot-axes) diseased   Of course this appears to be contradicted by the fact that young etiolated leaves when brought into the light grow vigorously after a few days ; but this growth is not a direct result of the action of light, but rather a consequence of the fact that, by means of the illumination, in the first place a normal healthy condition is created in the tissue, and this in its turn makes further growth possible.

That seedlings which have grown up in the dark soon fall victims to an actual disease of their tissues, and that their abnormal relations of growth depend essentially on morbid changes in their tissues, due to want of light, and that consequently points come under consideration which have hitherto scarcely been noticed, and that, above all, the supply of suitable constructive materials plays a great part, it is easy to convince ourselves by a modification of the experiment

Instead of allowing seedlings to grow up from seed in the dark, I directed

---

leaves developing in the dark from the older stem of various Ferns form chlorophyll, which, on the contrary, is not the case with *Equisetum*

in my experiments in 1863) the buds of plants provided with numerous leaves
into a dark box, in such a way that the shoots which proceeded thence must
develope inside it, while from numerous leaves, which were as large as possible
and exposed to the most intense light available, the products of assimilation outside

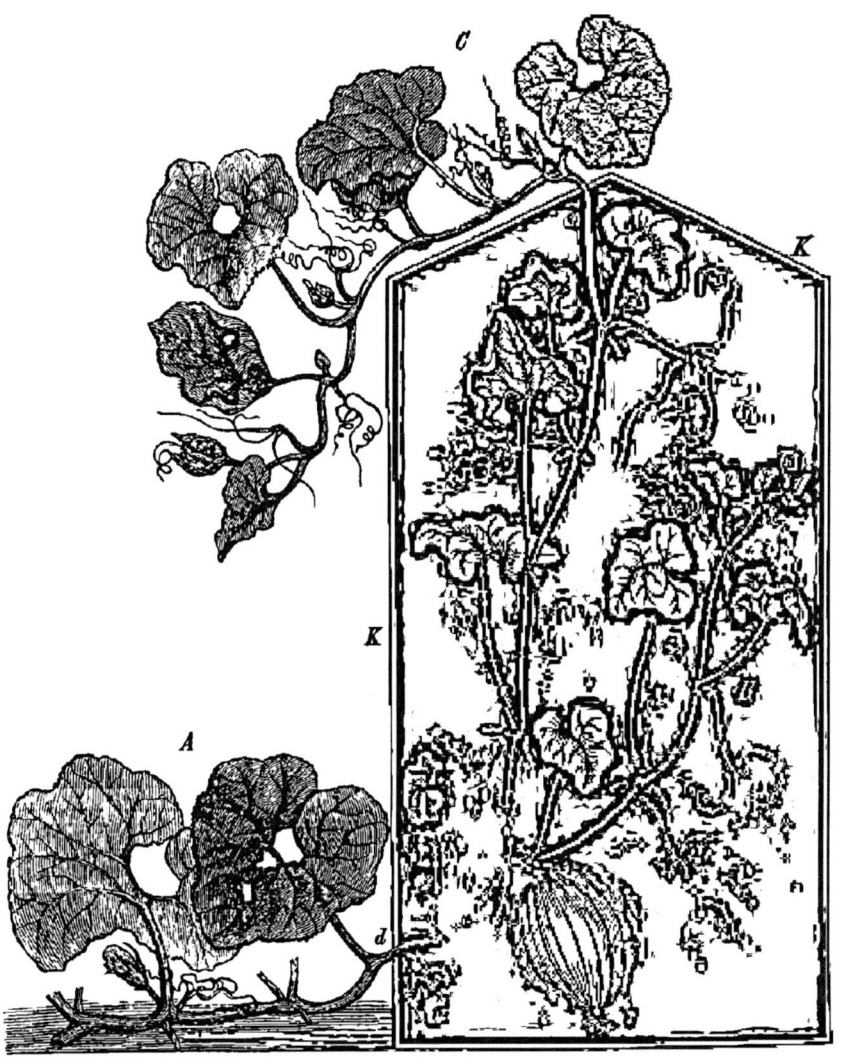

FIG. 345.—*A B C* a Gourd-plant, *K K* a large wooden box, in which the part *B* of the plant is
etiolated in the dark (cf. text on p 555)

were transmitted to them; thus in proportion as the growth in the dark progressed,
substances available for growth were also formed by the assimilation of the illuminated leaves, and carried to the places where they were used. Fig. 345 illustrates an
experiment of this kind, as I am in the habit of arranging it for the purposes of
demonstration. After all the axillary shoots have been cut away from an already

very strong and well-grown Gourd-plant, furnished with about ten to twelve large green leaves, the apical portion of the main stem is directed through a hole d, as small as possible, into a large thick-walled wooden box K, and gently secured; the box is provided with a large well-fitting door. The figure shows how from the apical bud directed through d, not only numerous leaves, tendrils, new shoots, and flowers (at B) have been formed, but also a large fruit f, only these parts were considerably more numerous than is shown in the figure. When the space became too small for the shoots growing in the dark, I pushed the active terminal bud through a hole (e) in the roof of the box out into the open air, and then made the necessary closure   The figure shows how this shoot-bud which, originally directed into the box at d, had then developed further in this for several weeks (B), on now being again exposed to the light, has become quite normally developed again above the roof of the box at C. The sojourn of this shoot-bud in the dark box was, so to speak, only an episode in its life, during which it by no means ceased to produce leaves, leaf-shoots, tendrils, roots and flowers in the usual manner. The foliage-leaves, which were of a clear bright yellow colour, attained a considerable size, as seen   One of the largest had a lamina 625 sq. cm. in area, while an average-sized leaf of the same plant previously produced in the light, and dark green in colour, measured 825 sq. cm. The leaves in the box attained on the average $\frac{2}{3}-\frac{3}{4}$ the normal area, although they were only illuminated once every three or four days for a few minutes for the purpose of observation, and produced no trace of chlorophyll. Still less was the effect on the growth of the shoot-axes: the magnificent large tendrils were as sensitive as it is possible for tendrils to be, the male and female flowers completely normal in form, size, and colour, and, finally, the fruit f when ripe weighed 4 kgr., and possessed 195 seeds, a third of which were capable of germination; and, in a word, apart from the chemical process of greening and a few insignificant disturbances in the growth of the foliage-leaves, as may be seen in the figure, the growth in the dark, both in its embryonic and in its later stages, was essentially normal, and that of the reproductive organs in particular quite normal   On now noticing further that Gourd-seedlings in the dark exhibit the disease of etiolation in the highest degree, and that their first leaves especially remain very small, the above experiment teaches us that in this case it must be a matter not so much of a direct influence of light on growth, as rather of the production of substances which bring about growth subsequently. This follows also from the fact that the growth of the organs enclosed in the dark cavity is so much the more vigorous and normal the larger the assimilating leaf-area exposed to the light is, and the more intense the light itself is outside the box.

So long as nineteen years ago I obtained results similar to those with the Gourd, with *Phaseolus*, *Tropæolum* (Indian Cress), and *Ipomæa purpurea* (Red Bindweed). Of especial interest in all these cases is the unusually vigorous and normal production of flowers and fruit, so long as the assimilation of the leaves exposed to the light proceeds energetically.

Since the products of assimilation of the leaves up to a certain extent accumulate in the latter and in the shoot-axes, before they are made use of for further growth, it is often possible to obtain vigorous shoots and flowers even in the dark by simply placing entire strong plants (e. g. Tobacco, Wall-flower, &c), which are already beginning to form flowers, in the dark : the production, however, is always more restricted, and the development of normal flowers particularly is insignificant, or conspicuous abnormalities in the growth of the flowers appear, simply because the flower-forming substance has not been previously accumulated in sufficient quantity

These experiments as to the dependence of the formation of flowers on the preceding or simultaneous activity of the foliage-leaves in the light, now explain to us also one of the most universal relations of growth in plants. The flowers appear either singly or several together in the axils of foliage-leaves, evidently because the formative substance produced in the latter can thus be most easily transferred to them   In very many other Phanerogams there are formed single or many flowers (Inflorescences) on long shafts, so that the completely developed flowers are far distant from the assimilating leaves: this is the case with almost all Grasses, and many Liliaceæ (*Allium*, *Aloe*, *Dracæna*, &c.).   But it must not be overlooked that in such cases the flower-buds are already fully developed in all essential points while the eventually very long floral support or shaft is still extremely short, and the entire inflorescence is thus situated either in the axil of a foliage-leaf or in the midst of a rosette of numerous leaves, so that in such cases also the formative substances are conveyed by the shortest route to the young flowers   When then the stalks of the flowers or inflorescences become elongated, and the flowers removed further away from the leaves which supply them with nutriment, it is a matter simply of their unfolding, and this depends essentially upon the necessary supply of water. We may probably go a step further, and assert that the proper reproductive organs in the narrowest sense of the word (the spores, male fertilising cells, and oospheres) take up their formative substance from the assimilating organs, and since only shoots can be assimilating organs at all, an explanation is offered of the fact that all true organs of reproduction are produced exclusively by shoots, and are usually formed on leaves or in the axils of leaves, or at any rate in some close connection with them.   It may be objected that in the case of plants which contain no chlorophyll, the reproductive organs are also connected with the shoots.   We can however reply that such plants are phylogenetically derived from plants which contain chlorophyll, and that it is also advantageous for the reproductive organs in general if they arise on the shoots protruding above the substratum.

These considerations may at first sight appear scarcely to harmonise with the fact that bulbs of Hyacinths, Tulips, &c , when germinating in profound darkness, nevertheless produce magnificent normal flowers, while the leaves at the same time become etiolated, though not strongly   But this favourable result of growth in the dark depends essentially on the fact that in the preceding period of vegetation the foliage-leaves of the bulbous plant were able to assimilate in intense light, and that flower-forming substance was thus already collected in the interior of the bulb, and then, during the apparently dormant period in summer and winter, nourished the flower-buds deep in the interior of the bulb, so that when such a plant is eventually allowed to put forth its shoots in the dark, it is only a matter of the last stages of development, which here also are accomplished chiefly by the addition of water.   This opportunity may be taken of mentioning the fact that many plants provided with bulbs, tubers, or large rhizomes, and especially phanerogamous root-parasites and humus-plants, pass through all their essential processes of development, and especially all their processes of embryonic growth, in profound subterranean darkness, so that the foliage-leaves only come forth annually and for a short time into the light, in order to assimilate and to fill the subterranean parts with nutritive substances; and the flowers come forth beyond the surface of the earth not because they require light for their growth, but in order to ensure pollination by the aid of insects.

I have so far, for the sake of simplicity, in considering the subject of etiolation, always regarded only the contrast between full daylight and profound darkness; it must be added, however, that etiolation also occurs in feeble light, and is the more marked in proportion to the diminution in intensity of the light Here, however, it is a matter of one important point chiefly, that is whether the intensity of the light is at all sufficient to effect assimilation in the chlorophyll; if this is not the case, as for example often happens in the interior of a dwelling-room, then though green leaves may be formed, it is true, so long as the store of nutriment lasts, still, since no new assimilation takes place, this store is gradually exhausted, and the plants grow themselves to death—a very common case when they are left on flower-stands in rooms

In contrast to the unusually energetic growth which takes place even in profound darkness when there is a considerable store of assimilated substance accumulated, either in reservoirs of reserve-materials (seeds, bulbs, tubers), or when it is produced at the time by assimilating green leaves, are now to be mentioned the spores and gemmæ of the Cryptogams, which so far as is known do not germinate at all in the dark, although in most cases a feeble light is sufficient to induce their growth.

I must content myself with these few remarks with reference to the questions connected with etiolation, although much more might be added.

I will now quote a few more cases belonging to the above-named second category, concerning the fact that organs which normally develope in the dark may be abnormally compelled to grow in daylight. Here again the common Potato, as in so many other cases, forms an unusually favourable object for physiological observations. It may be premised in the first place that potato-tubers lying in a dark damp place develope, as is well known, numerous etiolated shoots, which are often very long, and which are furnished with extremely small leaves : in this, after what has already been said, there is simply nothing peculiar. However, if potato-tubers are laid on damp sand, for instance, and covered with a transparent bell-jar in the spring and summer and kept at a bright window, there grow out it is true numerous thin roots from the so-called ' eyes ' (buds) but the shoots themselves remain for 2–3 months of continued cultivation extremely short, and none of their leaves are developed—in other words, they are extremely sensitive to the action of light, which retards their growth to a striking extent. So far as I understand this phenomenon (which still needs careful investigation), it chiefly depends simply upon the fact that the potato-tuber in the normal course of life is covered with several centimetres of soil, and must therefore also be darkened when the sprouting shoots develope from the eyes. It is chiefly the growth of the 2–3 lowermost internodes of the shoot which are concerned here, and it is from these that the roots and stolons arise. These lowermost segments of the shoot are adapted to darkness and can scarcely grow in the light; whereas the later segments and rudiments of leaves, on the contrary, require the light in a high degree in order to grow normally. This fact is so much the more remarkable since very many roots and subterranean shoots exhibit no signs of such sensitiveness [1].

While the lower segments of the potato-shoot afford us an example of the fact that under some conditions the growth of parts of the plant is almost entirely prevented by the light, an example of the contrary is afforded, according to Goebel's observations, by the scale-leaves of some rhizomes, which normally grow in subterranean darkness. These if exposed artificially to the light have their growth and all the processes of configuration promoted, and become transformed into true foliage-leaves. Goebel [2] cultivated plants of species of *Circæa* so that the otherwise subterranean stolons were forced to develope further in the light · their otherwise scale-like leaves now became transformed into normal green foliage leaves.

The fact established by Stahl that the assimilating parenchyma of the foliage-leaves undergoes conspicuous changes in the form of its cells according to the intensity of the light, definite relations between the directions of growth and the direction of the ray of light being apparent at the same time, also belongs to the effects of light on post-embryonic growth. As is shown in Fig 202 (p. 247) the assimilating tissue of the usually thin flat leaves forms two layers; an upper one turned towards the light consists of palisade-like upright cells elongated in the direction of the incident rays of light, the lower half of the assimilatory parenchyma is composed of cells which are rounded or often transversely elongated in a plane parallel to the surface of the leaf, and between which there are usually large intercellular spaces. These layers are distinguished as the palisade layer and the spongy layer of the mesophyll. In leaves with vertical surfaces, as the Iris, and in stems like those of *Equisetum*, the palisade cells on the other hand lie horizontally, in the former on both sides of the leaf, in the latter radially directed on the whole towards the periphery. According to Stahl the palisade cells, however, constitute that form of assimilating tissue which is especially produced by intense light striking the surface of the leaf directly, since he shows that in the same species of plant the formation of palisade tissue diminishes in proportion as the intensity of light decreases. Leaves grown in the shade possess chiefly or only spongy parenchyma, those grown in strong light chiefly palisade tissue. As an example the Beech may be mentioned, as well as other trees. We have here in view, in the first place, only the fact that light is the cause of these relations of organisation; but it must be added that the histological differences thus produced are in their turn again of use for the process of assimilation, a matter however into which we cannot here proceed further.

Our considerations so far have been concerned with the action of Gravitation and of Light on growth. The former is always acting continuously on each of the minutest parts of the plant light, however, only acts on those parts which are above ground,

---

[1] The action of light on young Potato-shoots described above is the more remarkable when the nights are taken into consideration it might be supposed that although the growth is completely arrested in the day-time, it could nevertheless proceed in the night, and perhaps the extremely slight growth actually takes place only during the nights. But the growth is so slight that even on this assumption it seems probable that an after-effect of daylight persists even during the night.

[2] Goebel on *Circæa*, in his '*Beitrage zur Morphologie und Physiologie des Blattes*' (Bot Zeitg 1880)

and it undergoes periodic alterations each day   Evidently, however, in both cases the effects on growth, so far as they occur at all, must be cumulative; though perhaps in the course of a few hours or of a day unnoticeable, these actions after months and years may produce very considerable effects, which however up to the present are but little known.   Since however we already know a large series of such effects, though notice has only quite recently been directed towards them, it may be expected that many more will be discovered, and if it is remembered that while the vegetable world from its origin onwards has been gradually evolving from its lowest forms the highly organised ones—that during this time all processes of growth have been continually affected by gravitation, and at least periodically and partially acted on by light, it may be presumed that almost all relations of organisation must gradually have been modified to a very large extent by gravitation and light. In other words, the forms and modes of life presented by plants, and which the botanist studies, must have been to a large extent induced by the continued action of gravitation and light.   We can now artificially induce or prevent some of these actions, but others are perfectly hereditary and have become constant.   Evidently there here lies before us one of the most fruitful provinces for botanical investigation.

Finally, it remains to mention still a few other cases of the action of external forces on the growth connected with configuration; but this must be done quite shortly, in order not to spin out this lecture too long.   I have already referred to cases where by the growth of parasitic Fungi the tissue of the host-plant is not destroyed, but is even enormously promoted in its growth.   One of the finest examples is presented by the formation of the so-called "Witchs' brooms" on Firs; —on the horizontal branches permeated by *Æcidium elatinum* are produced abnormally orthotropic shoots, growing like small primary stems   Another category of growths abnormal for the plant itself occur in the numerous gall-formations, so common everywhere,—insects, especially Gall-flies, lay their minute eggs in the tissues of young growing parts of plants, and while the small larva is developing from the egg the vegetable tissue surrounding it becomes hypertrophied, and thus forms the Gall. The common "gall-apple" of the Oak, and the galls of the Rose-bush furnished with their moss-like appendages, and others are known to all   Two points in the formation of galls are especially worthy of note.   First, every species of gall possesses a definite anatomical structure and external form, as if the gall were an organism *sui generis*, and secondly, this complex organisation is induced simply and only by the development of a specifically distinct insect larva, so in fact that entirely different galls are produced on the same plant by different insects.   It may here be mentioned by the way that certain aphides produce gall-like structures, among which the large hollow Chinese galls, and the galls resembling pine-cones produced by *Chermes viridis* on our Red Firs, are especially noteworthy.   It has lately been established by Peyritsch, moreover, that some monstrous floral developments, so-called green flowers (*Chloranthy*), especially of species of *Arabis*, can be artificially induced by placing certain species of *Aphis* on the still young inflorescences.

In these cases it is abnormal external stimuli which induce abnormal growth   It is of very common occurrence, however, not only in the vegetable but also in the animal kingdom, that new growth results in a perfectly normal manner from fertilisation. Here again the important matter is that a material influence acts on the female organ from without, by means of which the oosphere is transformed into the embryo, and the latter into a new organism. It will be the object of my last series of lectures, however, to go into this matter in detail : only the one point need now be noticed, that not only in the Phanerogams but frequently in the Cryptogams also, the result of the fertilisation of the oosphere is not merely its development into the embryo, but also that other parts of the mother plant are thereby incited to further growth. In the Phanerogams the formation of endosperm in the seed, the swelling of the ovary and its development into the ripe fruit, are due to the action of the pollen : the infinitesimal quantities of fertilising substance which are transferred by means of the pollen-grains, e g. of a Gourd-plant, to the female flower, are the cause of the development from the ovary, by growth, of a fruit which is occasionally a hundred pounds in weight. A still more remarkable case however in this connection, as Hildebrand[1] has shown, is presented by the Orchideæ : at the time when the pollen reaches the stigma, the ovules in the ovary, and which are to be fertilised, are either still incomplete or have even not yet commenced to be developed at all, and if no pollen is transferred to the stigma these essentially female organs of reproduction develope no further. The growth of the pollen-tubes into the stigma acts as a stimulus on the ovary, and the latter now begins to grow vigorously, and in it the ovules only now develope, or even begin to be developed.

In the case of the action of gravitation and of light we had to acknowledge that the connection between cause and effect is entirely unknown to us, and in the case of all the phenomena just mentioned we are no less compelled to say that all explanation as to how the effects perceived result from the causes perceived is wanting.

---

[1] Hildebrand, ' *Die Fruchtbildung der Orchideen ein Beweis für die doppelte Wirkung des Pollens* ' (Bot Zeitg. 1863, pp 329, &c).

LECTURE XXXII.

THE COURSE OF GROWTH DURING ELONGATION.
PERIODIC VARIATIONS

We have hitherto treated of growth only in so far as it is concerned with the production of configuration—of the external and internal form of the organs, and through this of the whole plant. In the present lecture we are to be concerned with growth from an entirely different aspect. We place before ourselves the question, in what manner does the growth of any small portion of a plant run its course when it passes over from the embryonic condition into that of elongation, in order subsequently to reach the stage where its external growth ceases?

Here again, in order at once to keep in view a concrete case, and to avoid the tedious enumeration of the manifold combinations in the distribution of growth in different plants, we may first confine our remarks to the typical shoots and roots which have a terminal growing-point; and, in order to limit the problem still more, we may first concern ourselves exclusively with the increase in length of such organs— i. e. with growth parallel to the axis of growth[1].

As the most important result, it is first to be insisted upon that every part of a plant, and in fact every transverse disc of it, however short, elongates slowly at first, then, with increasing rapidity, attains a maximum velocity of growth, and then again grows slowly and still more slowly, until the growth finally ceases altogether. In order to illustrate this in as simple a case as possible, we may take the young long primary root, about 2-4 cm long, of a seedling of *Vicia Faba* (the common Broad Bean). Two transverse lines of Indian ink are drawn immediately above the growing-point, by means of a small sharp camel-hair pencil, so that they are exactly 1 mm apart; this then denotes the length of a transverse disc of the root. The seedling being now left in a place where it can at the same time absorb water and respire energetically, and therefore where growth takes its normal course at the expense of the assimilated reserve-materials, it is only necessary to measure the length of the transverse disc (originally 1 mm) at certain intervals of time, in order to

---

[1] The modern fundamental work on growth in length, is my treatise, '*Über den Einfluss der Lufttemperatur und des Tageslichts auf die stündlichen und täglichen Änderungen des Längenwachsthums der Internodien*,' in Arb. des bot Inst in Wzbg, B I, pp 99, &c, where also all the then existing literature is thoroughly and critically incorporated. On the growth in length of roots, detailed statements and quotations are found in my treatise '*Über das Wachsthum der Haupt- und Nebenwurzeln*,' op. cit p 385 (1873 and 1874) The periodic variations of growth first brought into notice in my first-named treatise were subsequently investigated in detail by Oscar Drude (*Leopoldina*, B XXXXVIII, No 3, Halle, 1881) in the leaves of *Victoria regia* he obtained no better information as to the cause of them, however

ascertain the elongation or growth which has taken place in the same intervals, subtracting each time the preceding length from the one subsequently measured, and denoting the remainder as growth   It is necessary to take care, however, that the temperature remains constant during the periods of observation, or, since this is very difficult to attain, that it varies within equal limits, and it is also well to exclude the light from the object under observation, because this also influences the rapidity of growth; since the point is to observe the process of growth under constant external conditions   Thus, I found in the case of a transverse disc, originally 1 mm long, above the growing-point of the primary root of a seedling of *Vicia Faba* growing in moist air, with a daily recurring variation of temperature of 18°–21.5°C, the following alterations in a period of 24 hours :—

	Growth
1st day .	1.8 mm.
2nd „	3 7 „
3rd „	17 5 „
4th „	16.5 „
5th „	17.0 „
6th „	14.5 „
7th „	7 0 „
8th „	0 0 „
Total .	78 0 mm.

A similar transverse zone of the internode of a shoot-axis, marked off by transverse lines on the youngest part that can be manipulated, behaves also much in the same way as that on a root. Thus, for example, a transverse zone, 3.5 mm long, of the first internode of a seedling of *Phaseolus multiflorus*, was marked by lines, and the following elongations or growths observed in each period of 24 hours—the daily variation of temperature being from 10 2°—11° R.

	Growth.
1st day .	1.2 mm.
2nd „	1.5 „
3rd „	2.5 „
4th „	5 5 „
5th „	7 0 „
6th „	9.0 „
7th „	14 0 „
8th „	10 0 „
9th „	7 0 „
10th „	2.0 „
Total .	59.7 mm.

Numerous other measurements leave no doubt that the growth in length of transverse discs of leaves and other organs also runs its course in the same way, and from observations of another kind we may conclude that in organs which consist only of simple vesicles not divided up by cell-walls, the behaviour is the same.

Every small transverse zone of a growing organ thus exhibits a periodic variation of its growth, which is independent of temperature, light, and other forces which influence growth. Since, however, with the periodical variation of these latter, still other periodic fluctuations in the growth in length of such a part may make their appearance in addition, I have, in order to distinguish it more exactly, designated the phenomenon characterised above as *the grand period of growth.*

If we now take such a transverse zone as the above, limited by two lines as before (but further distant from the growing-point), and then measure its lengths after certain intervals of time, it is obvious beforehand that this transverse zone, since it is older and further distant from the growing-point, must be from the start already in a further advanced stage of growth. The case may occur, for instance (if we have hit upon exactly the right distance from the growing-point), that the first measured elongation forthwith coincides with the stage of maximum growth, so that every further measurement must present decreasing elongations, or the zone marked by the transverse lines, if still further from the growing-point may be found already from the beginning in a condition of decreasing growth, so that the first measurement yields a small and each succeeding measurement an ever smaller amount of growth. And if we have taken the marked zone still further removed from the growing-point, it may happen that it has already ceased to elongate—that therefore every succeeding measurement gives the same length.

Thus if we had drawn a large number of transverse lines on a root, beginning from the growing-point, or on a shoot-axis, beginning beneath the bud, in such a way that the lines are at first equally distant from one another—say 1 mm or so—then on measuring the lengths of these portions after equal intervals of time, we should find that the portions nearer the growing-point at first show an increasing rapidity of growth, and that some one of these portions reveals a maximum rapidity, whereas the transverse zones further distant from the growing-point exhibit in the same period growths or elongations which are so much the less the more distant they lie from the growing-point in each case

In order to illustrate this also by a definite example, the following observation may be quoted. I had the primary root of a seedling of *Vicia Faba* subdivided into transverse discs, each 1 mm. long, by means of lines of Indian ink, beginning from the growing-point. After 24 hours (at 20 5° C), the root having grown in moist air, the marked zones showed the following increments :—

Number of transverse disc	Increase
(Upper) X .	0 1 mm
IX .	0 2 ,,
VIII	0 3 .,
VII	0·5 ,,
VI .	1·3 ,,
V	1 6 ,,
IV	3 5 ,,
III	8 2 ,,
II	5 8 ,,
(Root-apex) I	1 5 ,,

Total growth in length   23 0 mm.

Here, then, that transverse disc in which the maximum growth took place was situated above the second zone from the apex of the root; or, in other words, it was

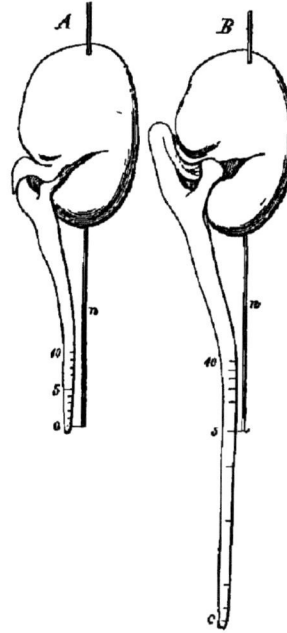

FIG 346.—A seedling of *Vicia Faba* (Broad Bean) *A* at the beginning of the observation The plant is fastened to a cork by means of a needle *n*, its root being in water the growing region is divided by means of painted lines into transverse zones (0—10) *B* the same plant after 22 hours, at 21° C., the lines, removed some distance apart, show the distribution of the growth

the third of the marked zones in which an increment of 8·2 mm. resulted in the 24 hours—the original length being 1 mm. Nearer to the apex, as well as further from it, the amounts of growth were smaller. We may thus say, shortly, that at a distance of 2–3 mm. from the growing-point of this root the growth had attained its maximum rapidity, whereas it was very slow immediately behind the growing-point, and much further distant from it (10 mm. in the present example) only amounted to 0 1 mm. In transverse zones still further distant, no further growth at all was to be detected.

The same is the case also with shoot-axes. Since in these, however, the growth is distributed over longer stretches, it is well to take longer transverse zones at once from the commencement. Thus, beginning from the upper end of the first internode of a seedling of *Phaseolus multiflorus*, a number of equidistant transverse lines were drawn, marking off pieces or zones each 3·5 mm. long. After 40 hours the lengths of these portions were measured, and the following growths found to have occurred :—

	Number of zone		Increase
(Beneath the bud)	I	. . . .	2·0 mm
	II	. . . .	2·5 ,,
	III	. . . . .	4·5 ,,
	IV	. . . .	6·5 ,,
	V	. . .	5 5 ,,
	VI	. . .	3 0 ,,
	VII	. . . . .	1 8 ,,
	VIII	. . . . . .	1·0 ,,
	IX	. . . .	1·0 ,,
	X	. . .	0 5 ,,
	XI	. . . . .	0·5 ,,
(Lower part of plant)	XII	. . . .	0·5 ,,
		Total growth in length	29 3 mm.

After what has been said above, it is now obvious that the transverse segment No. IV, if we had observed it 40 hours previously, would have shown an increment of only 4·5 mm , and if we had observed it 40 hours subsequently, an increment of only 5·5 mm. The segment IV simply happened to be in its stage of maximum growth during the period we observed it ; or, in other words, the segment No. III would have behaved during the next 40 hours exactly like IV, whereas the segment V had been, during the preceding 40 hours, in the same stage that IV was during our observation. That is to say, in other words again, the whole growing region of a root, or of an internode, or of any organ whatever arising from a growing-point, consists of transverse zones, which, according to the age in each case (i e. according to the distance from the growing-point), are in different stages of development each of these transverse zones begins to grow slowly, then grows more and more rapidly and attains a maximum growth, and then decreases and finally ceases to grow altogether. Although it has been impossible hitherto to draw transverse lines in a similar manner on the non-cellular utricles of such plants as *Vaucheria*, *Mucor* and similar Cœloblastæ, we have nevertheless every reason to believe that even in them the state of affairs is exactly similar

This method of observation affords us at the same time an opportunity of learning how long is the piece of a root, shoot-axis or other organ which is actually growing. Having drawn equidistant transverse lines, starting from the growing-point of a root, or from the bud of a shoot, and finding at a certain distance from the growing-point, after some time—say one or two days—that certain transverse lines have not separated further from one another at all, but have retained their original distance apart, this signifies that at these places no more growth in length whatever is taking place, and the distance between the first line which has not moved and the growing-point gives us the length of the growing region of the particular organ. Even a glance at the small tables above at once shows that this length is strikingly different in roots and in internodes; in the primary root of the seedling of *Vicia Faba* growth has already ceased at a distance of 10–11 mm. from the growing-point; in the first internode of the seedling shoot of *Phaseolus*, on the contrary, it only ceases at a distance of 12 × 3 5 mm. (i. e about 4 cm.) behind the growing-point. The differences. however, may be much greater still, according to circumstances in each case . in thin lateral roots the growing portion behind the apex may be 2–4 mm. in length, while it may attain a length of even 50 cm in the long flowering scapes of some Phanerogams [1]. I found, for example, as follows .—

In—	Length of growing region beneath the bud	
Fritillaria imperialis	. 7–9 cm	
Allium Porrum	. about 40 „	within one internode
Allium Cepa .	. 30 „	(of the scape).
Allium atropurpureum . .	50 „	
Cephalaria procera	35 „	(3 internodes).
Polygonum Sieboldi	15 „	(4–5 internodes).
Asparagus asper .	20 „	(numerous internodes)
Valeriana Phu .	25 „	(4 internodes)
Dipsacus Fullonum .	40 „	(3–4 internodes).

[1] With respect to the distribution of growth and the lengths of the growing portions in erect flowering shoots, cf my treatise ' *Über Wachsthum und Geotropismus aufrechter Stengel*,' in Flora, 1873, p. 322.

It is seen from this table that the growing region of a shoot-axis may embrace one or several internodes. In the latter case, especially when the individual internodes are sharply marked off from one another by large leaves which clasp the stem, there may be present within any one of them again a transverse zone situated at the base, or even beneath the node, which behaves just like a growing-point, and in relation to which the increments of growth increase or decrease in a similar manner.

It will also not be superfluous to point out that measurements of this kind, especially on shoot-axes, only give a clear idea when the latter have already attained a certain length: for at first, when the entire shoot-axis is still short and young, all the parts of it are growing in length; only when a certain length (i. e. a certain age) of the oldest portions is attained, does growth cease at certain places, and it is then for the first time that we have, at a definite distance from the growing-point, a region which is no longer growing, as was assumed in our last table. In addition, however, the case may also occur that the growth as a whole first disappears beneath the bud of a long flower-scape, while at its base it continues for some time longer, proceeding from an intercalary zone of embryonic tissue. In this case then the sequence of the partial growths is reversed, the shoot-axis being pushed up as it were from its base. The same may take place in very different ways, even in closely allied plants; for instance, I found the usual form of distribution of growth in the flower scapes of *Allium atropurpureum*, whereas in those of *A. Porrum* and *A. Cepa* in the later stages of growth there is a basal vegetative zone with the properties indicated.

What has here been said of the roots and shoot-axes holds good generally (*mutatis mutandis*) of all organs, so long as they possess a growing-point at their apex or base, since the matter depends simply upon the passing over of the smallest transverse zones from the embryonic into the definitive condition, and it is to be remarked especially with respect to leaves, that the processes in question take place not only in the longitudinal direction, but also in the direction of the lateral veins, much as in the case of the lateral shoots of a main shoot.

The fact that the maximum elongation in roots, as well as in shoot-axes, occurs only at a certain and often considerable distance from the growing-point, together with other observations, warrants the assertion that in the growing-point itself only an extremely slow growth in length takes place, and that, consequently, no growth in length occurs at all at the apical protuberance of the growing-point: it results on careful consideration also that no growth in length can take place at the apical protuberance, but, on the contrary, always occurs first beneath the apex, and reaches its maximum at a greater distance from it. This remark is not superfluous, since for a long time past, with incomprehensible thoughtlessness, the growing-point, and particularly its apex, was held to be the place of most energetic growth in length.

If it is observed now how the apex of a shoot, as it grows upwards in the course of a day, elevates itself several centimetres, or in very rapidly and actively growing plants some decimetres, or moves forwards in space generally, this movement must not be ascribed in any way to this so-called apical growth of the shoot: on the contrary, the bud behaves in the main passively in the process, since it is pushed forwards by the transverse zones which are beneath it on the shoot-axis. The movement of the shoot-bud in space is the sum of the elongations which the transverse sections of the shoot-axis beneath the bud are simultaneously undergoing. This is more especially of interest in the case of the roots: in their case also the so-called apical growth is a meaningless expression, for the growing-point covered with the root-cap is driven forwards passively, by the elongation of the older transverse zones of the root which lie behind it. In this case, however, the length of the growing portion is remarkably short, only 2–10 mm.: this, however, appears really to be of advantage when the object is to drive the root-apex forward in the soil. The root behaves in this respect like a nail being driven into solid wood by the strokes of a hammer. Where this regard for the mechanical conditions of the forward movement of the apex of the root is not necessary, we find that the relations of growth are different even in roots. In the long aërial roots of Aroids, and of a species of *Cissus*, I found[1] by measurements that the elongating region situated behind the growing-point is of considerable length, amounting to several centimeters, as in the case of shoot-axes; this is evidently because it would here be superfluous to concentrate the force which drives the growing-point forward a few millimeters behind the latter, as is necessary in the case of roots growing in the resisting earth.

Instead of the transverse lines mentioned so often, it is also possible in some cases to make use of certain natural marks for observing the distribution of growth, provided of course that there is sufficient ground for the assumption that these natural marks are equidistant at first, and also stop at equal distances finally. Thus, Askenasy[2] employed the leaf-whorls of the Characeæ, or, what amounts to the same thing, the lengths of the internodes, in order to gain information as to the alterations in space and time of the growth, from the growing-point to the parts fully developed. In the same way it is possible in the case of any other chosen stems with numerous internodes (which, however, must finally attain equal lengths) to find the stages of growth of the individual internode to a certain extent severally represented in the then existing stages of growth of all the internodes which are still elongating. It is obvious that such an experiment will not be possible if the plant is of such a nature that the various internodes attain different lengths, or differ in any other way as to their relations of growth.

In the case of organs the growing-point of which terminates in an apical cell which forms either one series of segments by transverse walls, or two or three series of segments by oblique divisions, the length of the surface lying between each two segment-walls may be similarly employed, like the space lying between two artificially made transverse lines. Provided (and this is actually realised in most cases,) that the successive segments have equal lengths originally, the process of growth may be judged from the relative lengths of the segments lying one over the other. Under certain circumstances, in the case of very simple organs which consist of one cell

---

[1] I described the abnormal behaviour of aerial roots respecting the length of the growing region in Arb. des bot. Inst. in Wzbg., B. I, p. 593 (1874).

[2] The ingenious treatise of E. Askenasy, depending on careful reflection, '*Über eine neue Methode, um die Vertheilung der Wachsthumsintensität in wachsenden Theilen zu bestimmen,*' is in the Verhandlungen des naturhistor.-med. Vereins zu Heidelberg, N. S. II, 2 H. (Winter). Unfortunately I have not space to go further into the contents of this treatise

only, it is likewise possible to employ certain equably distributed sculpture markings on the cell-wall for the criticism of the ways and means by which the growth between them advances   Nevertheless these natural aids have only been used now and again so far.

Assuming that in the entire length of the growing region of a shoot-axis or root, or even in any one portion of this length, at any time whatever, the growth takes place a little more rapidly on the one side than on the opposite side, it is obvious that a curvature must thereby be produced, and that this is the more pronounced the greater the difference in the elongation of the two opposite sides.   Such phenomena now are as a matter of fact to be observed very commonly during the process of growth in length: they are distinguished as Nutations, and are perceived the more easily the longer the growing portion and the more energetic the elongation itself is.   Hence nutations are particularly evident in the case of rapidly growing erect flower - stalks.   The leafless flower - scapes of species of *Allium*—e g. the common kitchen onion—are found, so long as they are still growing in length, to be always bent over towards one side, often to such an extent that they describe more than a semicircle, and the thin flowering scapes of *Allium rotundum* and other species even make loops in this manner of more than a whole circle.   Finally, however, when the growth is ceasing they straighten themselves completely, and stand quite erect.   On observing such nutating flower-stalks from hour to hour, now, and if possible in the dark in order to exclude the heliotropic curvatures due to light, it is soon noticed that the curvature does not always remain the same, but alters in such a manner that the side which was previously concave becomes convex after several or many hours, and therefore, of course, the pendent apex bends over towards the opposite side.   In the intervals also, sometimes one, sometimes another side of the stem becomes convex, so that the apex is gradually turned towards all parts of the horizon; and in particularly exquisite cases the change proceeds so that the apex is gradually carried round in a circle, or to put it better and more accurately, it moves in the form of an ascending spiral line, because during this rotating nutation a continuous elongation, and therefore an ascent of the apex in space, takes place.

After what has been said above, the phenomenon finds its explanation in the fact that first one and then another side of the organ elongates more rapidly than the rest. If this takes place alternately on two opposite sides, the apex therefore bends over at one time to the left, at another to the right , but if at the circumference of the organ different sides in succession gradually take their turns in the process, then the pendent apex must rotate in space.   The latter case, however, is regularly observed to any considerable extent only in strictly radially constructed shoot-axes. I found such to be the case, for example, in the scapes of *Allium*, in the flower stem of *Brassica napus* (Rape), and in the stem of *Linum usitatissimum* (Flax), as mentioned in my ' *Handbuch der Experimental-Physiologie* ' (1865), p. 514[1].

---

[1] The first communication, so far as I know, made on the phenomenon which I subsequently mentioned in my ' Text-book ' as revolving nutation, and which has been lately extended by Darwin to excessive importance as circumnutation, is found expressed in my ' *Experimental-Physiologie,*' 1865, p. 514, among the movements due to the process of growth itself, in the words — ' Here also belongs the hanging over of rapidly growing leaf and flower shoots, which, without exhibiting torsion, become

The phenomenon in question, as later observations have shown, occurs very commonly indeed in orthotropic organs, and those which grow rapidly in length, but it is certainly an unwarranted exaggeration on the part of Darwin, who designates it circumnutation, to consider this as a universal property appertaining to all growing organs; above all, it is certainly not true of normal and vigorously growing roots That Darwin ascribes circumnutation to the latter depends on imperfect observation, since it may easily be demonstrated that his roots were improperly cultivated and diseased. I had, long before Darwin's observations, shown that the roots of terrestrial plants growing in moist air soon become diseased, assume abnormal conditions, and may then exhibit pronounced nutations which, however, are not to be observed in normal primary roots of seedlings growing in damp earth or in water.

The nutations which take place during the unfolding of most foliage leaves are very conspicuous. so long as these belong to the bud at the apex of the shoot, their posterior side (outer, and subsequently under side) grows more strongly, a fact upon which the formation of buds depends. When now the oldest external leaves of a bud are about to unfold, the growth in length commences—and to this we may in this case consider the growth in surface of the lamina as due—to become stronger on the inner side (the subsequent upper side) than that of the dorsal side, and this continues till the leaf has assumed a horizontal or oblique position, in which it then becomes fixed In most simple leaves the process presents little that is remarkable, in the large complex leaves of the Ferns and Cycads, on the contrary, the young leaves are rolled inwards at the growing-point like a helix, the lateral parts of the lamina each for itself showing lateral involution at the same time. With increasing growth the leaf-stalk and midrib, and likewise the lateral parts of the leaf, now become extended straight, beginning from below and proceeding upwards, so that in the middle stages of unfolding the upper younger part of the leaf is still coiled up like a helix, whereas the lower is already unfolded and extended flat. At last the uppermost part of the leaf also becomes completely unrolled and extended ; however, in some Ferns the upper end of the leaf continually retains this involution, because a growing-point exists at its apex by means of which such a leaf is capable of a so-called unlimited growth in length.

The long, filiform, and even branched tendrils of the cucurbitaceous plants behave, with respect to their nutation, quite like the leaves of Ferns. Concealed in the young state between the leaves of the bud, they are coiled up into a helix with numerous turns, subsequently, proceeding from below upwards, they become completely unrolled and extended straight The matter does not end here, however, but during the growth in length which still continues for several days nutations make their appearance, causing the tendril to bend over in all directions

---

bent in turns towards the east, west, north, and south, quite independently of the position of the sun, and altogether independent of the light (e g *Allium Porrum, A. Cepa, Brassica napus, Linum usitatissimum*), since it occurs even in profound and constant darkness.' These short statements of mine were based on very detailed investigations, which, however, have not been published cf. note 4, *loc cit* also Dutrochet, moreover, had already observed nutations in *Pisum* ('Comptes rend' T. xvii, 1843, p 989) Darwin subsequently made evident the significance of the nutation of twining and tendril-bearing plants, but did not recognise as such the spiral and spontaneous nutation of twining plants, whence arose his entirely false theory of twining.

successively like the flower-stems described above. The advantage which not only these but also all other tendrils derive from this nutation we shall consider more closely later, when considering their phenomena of irritability. There I shall also show more in detail that the still in part obscure movements of twining shoot-axes, such as those of the Hop, Bindweed, *Aristolochia, Akebia, Menispermum* and many others depend in part at least simply on nutations, or are introduced by such; if tips of shoots, 20–30 cm long, of twining plants which have not as yet coiled round a support are cut off, and placed singly in tall glass cylinders with a little water, they grow on actively for some days, becoming coiled in the form of a spiral which not rarely exhibits 3–4 or more turns. However, I shall return to the details, merely mentioning this phenomenon now as a particular case of nutation[1].

As tendrils and twining plants derive advantage from nutation (which is indeed indispensable for the life of these plants), so also numerous plants derive other advantages from the often active nutations

FIG 347.—Nutation of the stamens of *Dictamnus fraxinella* those the anthers of which have not yet opened are curved downwards, those with opened anthers upwards.

of their stamens. It is a very common phenomenon, especially in large flowers with long stamens, that the stamens, when the anthers are about to empty their pollen, undergo various curvatures as they grow, as is perceived unusually clearly for example in the Indian Cress (*Tropæolum*), and still more in *Dictamnus* (Fig. 347). These nutations of the stamens are frequently accompanied by corresponding movements of the style, and usually serve the purpose of giving the anthers that position in the flower which is necessary in the transference of the pollen by insects from one flower to the stigma of another.

The nutations thus present us with instructive examples of how a capacity of the plant conditioned by growth, and for and by itself useless, is found to be very common, and how certain plants then develope this movement further and make it useful for themselves, sometimes in order to live as climbing plants, sometimes in order to ensure their fertilisation.

The majority of twining shoot-axes exhibit torsions—i.e. where angles or grooves project on the segments of the stem and at first run parallel with the axis of growth, they are subsequently found on the fully grown internodes in the form of spiral lines running round the shoot-axis. It is easy to see on internodes which are growing how the torsion gradually arises and proceeds; but it would be very difficult without geometrical discursions to show the processes of growth through which the

---

[1] Concerning the spiral nutation of twining stems, statements in some detail are found in my '*Notiz uber Schlingpflanzen*' (Arb des bot. Inst. in Wzbg. B II, 1882, p 719)· further on, however, in the fifth series of the present lectures, I shall make these more complete on the basis of my most recent observations.

torsions come into existence   A sufficiently clear idea of the matter may be obtained by taking a straight piece of caoutchouc tubing or a leaden tube, and fastening one end of it in some manner, while the other end is seized with the fingers or a pair of tweezers and then twisted. By this means the superficial layers of the body will be subjected to elongation, while its axis, or middle line, undergoes no elongation at all, or if it is at the same time pulled in this direction, only a slight one   It is obvious that something similar must occur by means of the processes of growth during the torsion of the stem.

Since then the internodes of a twining stem which are some distance from the bud are made to undergo torsion by growth, the bud and the youngest internodes which have not yet suffered torsion must be passively twisted or rotated around their own axis—a movement which may easily be demonstrated by observing one of the younger leaves from hour to hour   it is then seen that it is found first on the upper side, then for example on the left flank, subsequently on the underside, and finally on the right flank of the oblique or horizontal freely suspended tip of the shoot. The torsions of twining plants must in some way be causally connected with their very strong and long-continued growth in length , since even in shoot-axes which do not climb, and which in the normal condition are absolutely without torsion, it is possible to produce torsions by intensifying the growth in length[1]   I pointed out twenty years ago in this connection that the seedling stems of the Gourd, Buckwheat, and other plants, when allowed to grow in profound darkness, where they attain an enormous length, exhibit very evident torsions, and in consequence of the movements connected with this occasionally become wound around neighbouring objects of like kind, much as two twisted packthreads lying parallel and close together spontaneously wrap themselves round one another

The question has often been raised whether any difference in the growth of the plant by day and by night exists, and what it is. The question is in itself more of practical than of theoretical interest. Its experimental treatment, which I accomplished in the years 1870–71, gave me an opportunity, however, of going more deeply into the difficult problem of growth, since it was soon shown that this apparently so simple question is only to be answered when all the external and internal factors of growth are known and carefully balanced against one another , and since my treatise concerning the matter (*'Uber den Einfluss der Lufttemperatur und des Tageslichtes auf die stundlichen und täglichen Anderungen des Längenwachsthums der Internodien'*) first provided a firm basis for investigations in this direction, and has become the starting-point of various investigations during the last ten years, it may be well to go somewhat more in detail into the contents of this treatise[2].

'The influence,' I wrote, 'which the varying temperature of the air and the periodic alternation of daylight and nocturnal darkness exert on the growth in length of internodes and leaves after they have passed out of the bud-condition, has often

---

[1] I first described the torsions of the stems of etiolated seedlings mentioned in the text in my treatise *'Über den Einfluss des Tageslichts auf Neubildung und Entfaltung'* (Bot Zeit , 1863, 2te Beilage, p 16—on p 17, to the left, however, the words *'von Cucurbita'* should be added after *'das hypocotyle Glied etiolirter Keimpflanzen'*)

[2] The general considerations on growth here given in abstract are contained in my treatise first cited (cf note 1, p 539)

been the subject of investigation. Christopher Jacob Trew, even so long ago as 1727, published long-continued daily measurements on the flower-scape of *Agave americana*, combined with observations on the temperature and weather; but it was not till a hundred years afterwards that Ernest Meyer (1827) and Mulder (1829) gave a new impulse to investigation in this direction, and they were then followed by Van der Hopp, De Vriese (1847–48), and others. The important questions, however, were gone into more thoroughly by Harting (1842), Caspary (1856), and Rauwenhoff (1867)

'These observations, industriously and perseveringly carried on, led to no definite answer, nor even to the establishment of an actually useful method, and a careful survey of them shows that scarcely any two observers came to the same conclusion, and that the discovery of any causal relation of growth in length to temperature and light was in fact impossible, since on the one hand the questions to be answered were not put with sufficient clearness and definiteness, and on the other, the probable sources of error, and, accordingly, the difficulties of accurate observation, were left more or less unnoticed. Meanwhile there appeared another series of publications simply of repeated measurements of lengths, no regard at all, or not sufficient, being paid to the external conditions, whence although some idea was obtained of the continual want of uniformity of growth during different days and at different times of the day, the causes of these were not registered: some observers, in fact, confined themselves to merely demonstrating the difference between diurnal and nocturnal growth, not reflecting that 'day' and 'night' signify to the plant different and very variable complications of conditions of growth, and that such a mode of stating the question cannot possibly lead to the discovery of causal connections, so long as the individual factors which are contained in the ideas day and night (so far as the plant is concerned) are not known. In this sense the contributions of Seitz, Meyen, Martins, and Duchatre, for example, are useless for our purpose.

'I have, though with considerable interruptions, been engaged since 1869 with the completion of more exact methods of observation, and have attempted to classify and render clear the questions to be answered.'

This was done by means of the following considerations. 'With few exceptions the majority of observers of growth in length have selected parts of plants which are remarkable for a very considerable growth in a short time. The huge flowering stems of the Agaves especially afforded repeatedly, on account of their rapid growth, the inducement to the making of such observations: such objects were selected because observers were satisfied simply to measure the growth in length with a rule laid directly on the part of the plant observed. But even granted that in the case of quickly growing plants sufficiently exact measurements are to be made in this manner in intervals of time of from one to several hours, still, other evils make their appearance of which I will particularise two only. In the first place, plants which grow so rapidly that even only four to six sufficiently exact measurements daily can be made, are rarely to be obtained: one is at the mercy of chance, and a methodical and connected series of observations can scarcely ever be completed. In the second place such plants (e g. Agaves, Musaceæ, *Victoria regia*) are usually so large that it is necessary to undertake the observations in greenhouses or in the open air, and therefore under conditions where they are exposed to very large and irregular changes of temperature and light, and of the moisture of the air and soil, which it is quite impossible for the observer to regulate and to overcome. The comparison of the earlier observations shows that these circumstances have contributed in an important degree to make the results not only of different observers, but even of the same observer, conspicuously different and mutually contradictory.

'On these grounds I regarded it as the first problem to discover a method of observation which allows of the measurement of any chosen and even slowly growing small plant with sufficient accuracy, and where possible hourly. Suitable objects, completely adapted for the purpose, are even in this case sufficiently difficult to obtain, but still may be prepared by careful cultivation in pots: once obtained, however, they may be submitted to observation in the laboratory under conditions which can be varied as may be desired.

'The mode of putting the question here arises, as in all experimental investigations, from the consideration of pertinent phenomena already known, whence may be drawn the conclusions which may possibly be expected.

'If the object is to gain information as to the process of growth in length of a part of a plant, in such a way that one obtains not only a connected idea of it from the beginning to the end, but is also able to criticise the effects which definite variations of temperature, illumination, and moisture induce, it is absolutely necessary to measure the growths during short intervals of time—i. e. in one, two, or three hours—and at the same time to know how the process of growth would have proceeded if these external causes had remained constant.

'That in the plant itself causes are active which, quite independently of the variation in external conditions, sometimes accelerate the growth in length, sometimes retard it, was moreover to be expected, and might be in part concluded from what was hitherto known. Harting had already found that the stems of Hops grow at first slowly and then more and more quickly, attain a maximum of rapidity, and then again grow more and more slowly till growth at length ceases. Munter also, although his numerous observations were made at very varying temperatures, recognised this fact, and expressed it in these words:—"In addition to the daily rhythm, composed of exacerbation and remission, an increase, climax and diminution (*incrementum, acme, decrementum*) of the intensity of growth take place   The lengths produced rhythmically at first increase, ascend to a certain height, and then diminish down to complete cessation." Rauwenhoff, so far, has most definitely expressed the fact that in the course of a period of vegetation the growth of the stem first increases, attains a maximum, and then slowly ceases.'

I then pointed out, from the statements of Harting, Münster and Rauwenhoff, the existence of a grand period of growth, and demonstrated it for individual transverse zones of stems and roots—a fact with which we have indeed already become acquainted above. The irregular variations of growth, subsequently mentioned over and over again, although without satisfactory result, by different observers, and apparently effected chiefly by internal changes, were likewise first formally expressed by me in this treatise:—'If then the grand curve of growth affords an example of how the rapidity of growth of a part of a plant becomes equably changed independently of external influences, or even in spite of them, it is to be insisted upon, on the other hand, that the powerful fluctuations in the growth in length perceived in half-hourly or hourly observations indicate the existence of other internal causes which, likewise independently of external influences, aid in determining the rapidity of growth. I have designated this phenomenon as " discontinuous variations of growth."

' I have no doubt that the knowledge of the grand period, as well as that of the discontinuous variations of growth, will at some subsequent date be of considerable use for a theory of the mechanics of growth. Here however I have only brought forward both phenomena because a knowledge of them is absolutely necessary to the study of the effects of external influences on growth in length, and because the experimental establishment of causal relations is rendered extremely difficult by them. Given for example the case where a growing internode is observed in constant moisture and darkness but with variable temperature, then the differences of growth obtained in considerable periods (several days for example) are not to be taken forthwith as functions of the different temperatures, since the phase of the grand period is altering at the same time; it may happen that the higher temperature (beneath the optimum) coincides with a smaller hourly or daily growth, because the internode at this time is in a condition where it is less capable of growth generally. It is easy to suppose, in order to avoid this difficulty, the plant exposed to different temperatures quickly one after another, and the phase-difference of the grand period thus reduced to a minimum; but the discontinuous variations of growth which make their appearance quite irregularly might sometimes increase, sometimes diminish, the effect of the temperature on the growth, without our being in a position to decide how much is to be placed to the account of one or of the other. Very much the same difficulties would repeat themselves when the temperature is constant, with regard to the action of variable illumination or moisture in short periods of time.

'This complication with internal disturbances, in cases where the object is to become acquainted with the effects of external agents on growth, makes it not only necessary to multiply the number of observations enormously, but it also entails our being but seldom in a position to derive from the numbers expressing hourly growth any causal connection at all; in order to ascertain this it is necessary to draw these numerical values as co-ordinates, and the curves, properly constructed, then generally reveal the causal relations.' I then showed further in what manner the moisture of the environment may co-operate in influencing the rapidity of growth, by means of its influence on the turgescence of the cells, and how in considerations of this kind this fact has to be borne in mind. In the second place the influence of temperature on growth required quite special and closer consideration, which I gave in the following words:—' That growth only begins when a certain lower temperature (the specific zero point) is passed, that it is accelerated so much the more the higher the temperature is, and that at a certain higher temperature, the optimum temperature (between 20° and 30° C.), a maximum rapidity of growth occurs, and that, moreover, as the temperature rises still further the growths again decrease, I have already shown to be true for seedlings, and Koppen has confirmed it in his work quoted. Moreover Harting (1842) had already inferred from his observations a similar behaviour on the part of the shoots of the Hop, but without contributing convincing proofs of it.

' These facts are to be realised, so far as the problem lying before us is concerned, only in so far that it must be noticed in the first place that temperatures below the specific zero-point exert no influence on growth whatever, or, put better, do not allow it to take place, and that temperatures beyond the optimum act injuriously Since, however, in the natural course of things temperatures above the optimum only seldom occur, and in experiments can be avoided, I shall in what follows pass over that entirely, and understand by higher temperatures only such as are below the optimum, and therefore favourable.   That even within these limits no simple relation between temperature and the rapidity of growth exists, follows already from Harting's investigations, and I have demonstrated it in detail elsewhere in the case of seedlings, and it is even obvious, because in view of the existence of the grand period and the discontinuous variations of growth, a simple proportionality between growth and temperature is inconceivable, when one and the same part of the plant is concerned at different times.   In the present state of our knowledge only so much can be said, that, starting from the specific zero up to the optimum, the rapidity of growth is the greater the higher the temperature.

'When one speaks of the action of temperature on growth, it is tacitly assumed that the temperature indicated by the thermometer also actually exists in the growing part of the plant.   Where roots are concerned, which are growing in soil and round a thermometer stuck between them in the soil, the assumption is certainly warranted, such is not the case, however, when the temperature of the air, according to a thermometer suspended in it, is compared with the growth of a part of a plant in the air.   Since the bulb of the thermometer as well as the part of the plant concerned owe their temperature to the conduction and radiation of heat, and these are certainly materially different in the two cases, for this reason alone it will occur but rarely that the temperature of the growing tissue is exactly given by the thermometer suspended near it.   To this is to be added that in an atmosphere not completely saturated with aqueous vapour the plant transpires, and thereby becomes cooled, and this does not take place in the case of the dry thermometer ; on the other hand, however, it is certain that a wet thermometer will be much more cooled by evaporation from its surface than the plant, the evaporation from which is much smaller in relation to the surface and mass. Unless the opportunity occurs therefore to plunge the thermometer into the observed internode itself (and that has never been done so far, and is impossible in the case of small plants), the thermometer near the plant gives the temperature of the latter only in a very unsatisfactory manner. If the observation is made in the open air, in draughts and rapid variations of temperature, or under circumstances where the plant observed receives the direct rays of the sun, the temperature of the plant will often be very different from that of the thermometer , but even this source of error is reduced to a minimum when the observation is made in a room with still air, slow and small variations of temperature, and in diffuse light. I shall indicate subsequently the means which I employed to render this error of observation as slight as possible.

'Quite apart from the fact that under certain circumstances the temperature of a growing sub-aerial part of a plant may be altered also by the temperature of the water taken up by the roots, and by the exchange of heat with the soil, the influence of the soil is of importance in yet another connection. If the air, and with it the part of the plant above ground, undergoes rapid and large variations of temperature, these make themselves felt only slowly and to a less extent in the soil and roots , by this means, however, the turgescence of the plant may be altered; for instance, if the soil is very warm the roots take up much water and the turgescence is increased, if the temperature of the air does not suffice to cause active transpiration (such is the case for example in the evening after a warm day); on the contrary, the turgescence is diminished if, the temperature of the soil being low, the roots take up water slowly, while a warm wind or sunshine incites the leaves to transpire strongly (as, for example, after sunrise after a cold night). By the alterations of turgescence thus brought about, however, the recorded rapidity of growth will be affected at the same time. During observations in the open, also, these conditions may distort the result as to the effect of temperature, which is being investigated, until it is unrecognisable, and thus observation in the laboratory again recommends itself, where the air is quiescent, and very slow and slight variations of temperature take place, to which the earth in the flower-pot can adapt itself: although under such conditions the temperature of the latter is usually several degrees lower than that of the air, the difference is nevertheless small and almost constant—i. e. the temperature of the air and of the soil (in the pot) if represented as curves almost coincide.'

A third category of influences affecting the daily course of growth occurs in the alternation of light and darkness—in the decrease and increase in the intensity of the light. 'Unfortunately,' I said, 'we have as yet no convenient method of so measuring the varying intensities of light that the measurements are directly applicable to the observation of plants: measurements of the brightness perceptible by the eye, even if they could be conveniently determined, would present something other than the required measurement of those rays of light which influence growth in length; for these, as direct observation and the heliotropism occurring in coloured light show, are the blue, violet, and ultra-violet, that is, the inappropriately so-called chemical rays for which Bunsen and Roscoe have devised a method of measurement, the manipulation of which, however, for our purposes would entail great difficulties. Since it results from the determinations made by the observers mentioned, that the " chemical intensity" of daylight, in general rapidly increases from sunrise to mid-day, to decrease thence till sunset again with similar rapidity, and since this suffices in the meantime for the purpose pursued by me, I have not undertaken any photometric measurements.'

From these considerations, now, we may preliminarily, at least presumably, put together what course the rapidity of growth under the influence of varying moisture, temperature and illumination may possibly assume. On this subject I expressed myself as follows: 'If we now attempt, on the basis of the observations made, to form for ourselves an idea of the course of growth (or of its graphic representation, the curve of growth) of an internode, which is exposed to the varying and different causes of growth, especially in the open, it is at once clear that the curve of growth may assume the most various forms, according as the different causes work in unison or in opposition, and according as the growing member is in this or that phase of its grand period. In order forthwith to dispose of the often raised question whether growth is stronger or feebler during the night than during the day, and to render its meaning clear, we may attempt an analysis of the combinations of causes of growth and their effects denoted by the words day and night. As a rule the average temperature during the day is higher than the average temperature during the night, accordingly growth in the daytime must be more energetic than during the night. Day light, however, works in the opposite way, and the question will therefore arise whether the intensity of the effective rays suffices to nullify the effect of the temperature. The result also appears to adapt itself according to the specific nature of the plant, since it is conceivable that some plants are more sensitive to light than others In the daytime, also, the difference of tension of the aqueous vapour in the atmosphere is usually greater than during the night, and transpiration is thus increased, and it may easily happen that turgescence during the day is less than at night, and growth likewise may be retarded thereby. The case might occur, therefore, that the growth during the day, in spite of the higher temperature, was smaller than at night, and this will certainly be the case if the temperature during the day is the same as that at night, or lower than that. If, on the contrary, the excess of temperature of the day as contrasted with the night is very considerable, it is probable that the effects of light and transpiration will be overcome, and that the diurnal growth will remain more energetic than the nocturnal, although the latter is promoted by the darkness and, as a rule, higher turgescence.

'We may further notice yet a few more extreme cases which are here possible It might happen that the temperature at night was higher than that of the following day, and that at the same time rain falling during the night increased the turgescence to a maximum, while on the following day (the brightness being considerable) for example a cold wind prevailed; in this case the nocturnal growth would be the more intense. In the Spring-time or in Autumn it may happen that the air sinks during the night below the specific zero-point of the plant, so that the moisture and darkness are unable to promote the growth; cessation then occurs, and growth takes place only during the day when the temperature is raised sufficiently above the specific zero-point.

'If we further suppose the external causes of growth so distributed that they . would not of themselves effect a too considerable difference of growth by day and by night, then the difference may be exactly compensated or even reversed by the different capacity for growth of the plant at different times, e g. by the influence of the phase of the grand period. For instance, if an observed internode at night, when the conditions are otherwise unfavourable, has attained its maximum growth (the apex of the grand curve), the growth on the following day may still be smaller, though otherwise the conditions are more favourable.

' These and numerous other combinations are possible, then, when we compare only the average values of day and night. The number of possible cases is still larger when the attempt is made to form an idea of the events from hourly observations. If we suppose the grand curve of growth of an internode to be drawn, the hourly alterations of temperature and the hourly alterations in the intensity of the light, and of the psychrometric difference, will alter the course of the curve sometimes in one way, sometimes in another· the curve, which during constant external conditions ascends and descends in the form of a simple arc, will become transformed into a much and variously zigzagged line, in the steps of which the daily and nightly up-and-down oscillations of the growth are more or less clearly recognised, the size, form and position of these steps results for the time being from the co-operation of temperature, moisture and light.

' These indications will suffice to show of how little use it is for observers to simply establish in what relation the nightly and daily growth stand to one another without exact investigation of the causes of growth. They show, more-over, how difficult and indeed impossible it is to infer the influence of any single co-operating factor (temperature, light, moisture, grand-period, periodic variations) from observations made in the open air or in green-houses, where all the causes of growth are at the same time subject to continual and violent variations.

'The object of earnest research in this direction must on the contrary be simply this—to study the effect of each individual cause of growth in detail by itself· from this the common and natural course of the phenomena may then be analysed, combined, and predicted more exactly than was previously possible.'

Since 1869 I had been much occupied with preliminary investigations for the measurement within short periods of the growth even of ordinary rather slowly growing-plants, by means of a new apparatus Of those described in the treatise quoted I will here however only shortly describe the one represented in Fig. 348, which I have designated the self-registering Auxanometer, since soon after my publication this instrument became the model for numerous other instruments for the measurement of growth, of which I consider only the one constructed by Baranetzky as an actual improvement.

The apparatus is especially for the purpose of observing the growth in length of a sufficiently vigorous stem, in such a way that (1) the actual elongations are magnified for the purposes of observation, (2) a writing or registering of the growth in each hour is accomplished by the apparatus itself. Of course it is only possible after considerable practice, and with trained hands, so to use such an apparatus that it yields scien-tifically useful results

On a firm table stands a solid iron support *A*, on which by means of a movable cross-bar the pulley *r* is movable : an indicator *z*, consisting of a straw, is fastened to the pulley The plant *f*, grown in a pot, is in this case surrounded by a suitable receptacle *B*, which can be opened in two halves and has a hole at the top for the thread: this receptacle is for the purpose of keeping the growing plant in the dark. Beneath the bud of the plant a pliant silk thread is attached by means of a loop, and this is hooked on to a piece of thin wire, which is again connected with a pliant silk fibre above this thread passes over the groove in the pulley *r*. The small weight *g* hanging on the pulley serves to give the coupling an equal tension.

It is now clear that if the plant *f* becomes slightly elongated the pulley *r* will revolve a little towards the left, and the apex of the indicator *z* therefore describes a proportionately larger path : for example, if the indicator is twelve times as long as the radius of the pulley, as was usually the case in my apparatus, then if the plant becomes elongated 1 mm., the indicator must describe a path of 12 mm., and thus the growth is proportionately magnified for the observer. The apex of the indicator might of course be allowed to play on an arc of a circle of equal radius, and the successive growths be observed on the graduations of this arc To spare the observation hour by hour, and for other advantages, however, I employed the hollow cylinder *C*, made of stout sheet metal, and so fixed on the upright axis *a* of the pendulum clockwork *D* that it can be easily taken off. *w* is the weight and *l* the pendulum of this clockwork, which is for convenience so arranged that the cylinder *C* makes one complete revolution in exactly one hour, and that the clock-work needs to be wound up only once a day Previous to the observation a piece of paper *pp* is so affixed to the cylinder *C* that it shows no creases of any kind: this paper must be as smooth as possible on its outer surface, so as not to hinder the movement of the apex of the indicator which is to mark on it.

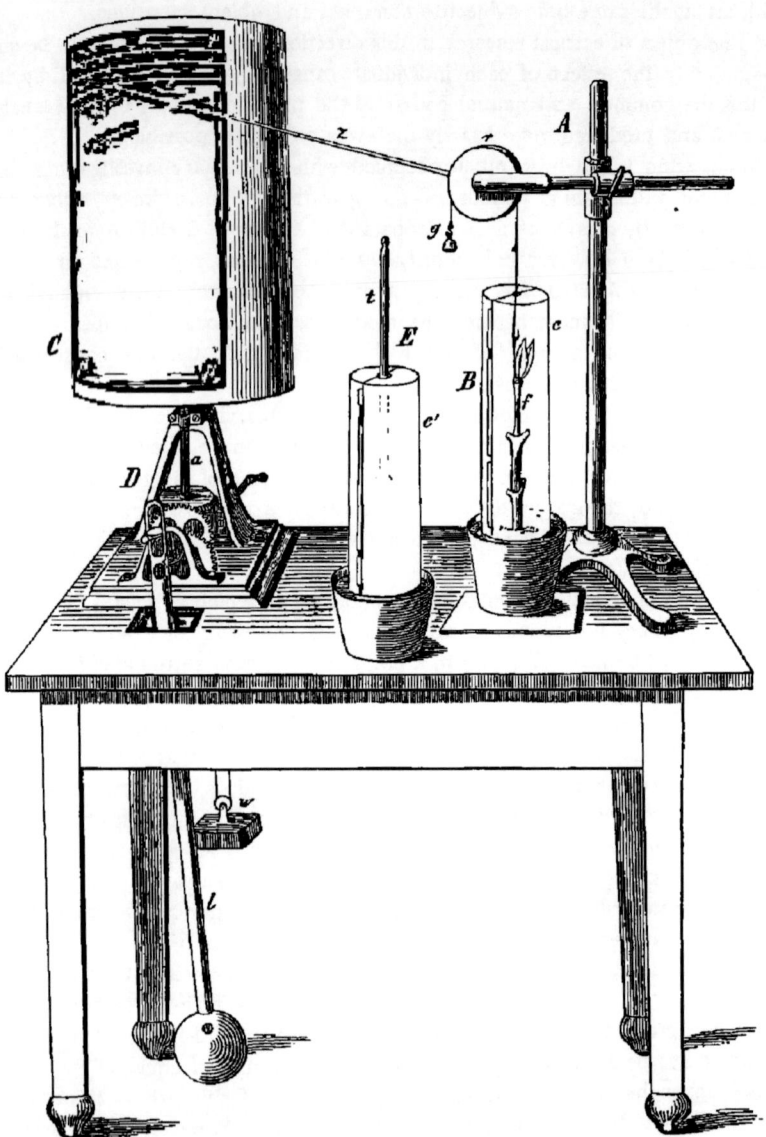

FIG. 348.—The self recording Auxanometer in its original form

Before the cylinder is fixed on to the clockwork, the attached paper is moved to and fro over the smoky flame of an oil lamp, until the smooth surface of the paper is completely covered with soot. After fixing the cylinder, the indicator *z*, the apex of which is provided with a laterally directed style, is so arranged that the style rests lightly just beneath the upper margin of the paper, and the clockwork is then set in motion. As the cylinder revolves, the apex of the indicator describes a line *s* on the blackened paper; when the second revolution of the cylinder begins the plant has grown somewhat during the hour, and the apex of the indicator has therefore fallen, and thus the second line which is now described on the paper lies at a certain distance below the first. In this manner, hour by hour, a new line is described, and it is clear that the distances between these lines can be used for obtaining, by the aid of certain geometric considerations, an exact determination as to the successive hourly elongations of the plant. In order to attain this, the clockwork is finally stopped, and the paper cut off from the cylinder, the observer having first seized the apex of the depressed indicator and carried it upwards, across the paper on the cylinder, in order to mark the path on which the measurements of the distances between the lines are to be taken. Immediately on its removal the blackened paper is drawn through a bath of a solution of colophony in alcohol, and then dried, when the necessary measurements can be taken. If the diameter of the cylinder is sufficiently large, however, and the indicator long enough, the errors of measurement in my apparatus are so small (as may easily be calculated), that they do not come into consideration at all if the experiment is properly conducted in other respects. Moreover, in my treatise, I explained in detail all imaginable sources of error, which are to be sought far more in the nature of the plant than in the apparatus, so that subsequent observers who have given my apparatus a modified form have had the means of knowing in advance what were the important points.

With the Auxanometer described, and other apparatus, I have for years past made hundreds of experiments, and thousands of measurements, the results of which, in spite of a few insignificant differences of opinion, have received confirmation also from the careful observations undertaken by Baranetzky in 1879, with (as already mentioned) an actually improved apparatus [1].

We started above from the question as to how growth proceeds by day and by night, and Fig. 349 will afford the shortest answer to this question. Since the essential points are mentioned in the explanation to the figure, I may confine myself simply to remarking that the rapidity of growth of a normal healthy stem attains a daily maximum in the morning soon after sunrise, that then the hourly elongation during the course of the day diminishes until evening, again to increase in rapidity as the darkness comes on, often even before sunset; and this increase of growth continues until after sunrise, when the maximum is again reached. In this connection the fact indicated in the figure by the dotted line 3 *s* is especially interesting; it shows that while the temperature gradually falls during the course of the night, the rapidity of growth on the contrary may simultaneously increase. The contrary may also be observed, that while the temperature is slightly rising, a diminution

---

[1] J. Baranetzky, '*Die tägliche Periodicität im Langenwachsthum der Stengel*' (Mém de l'acad imp des sc. de St Pétersbourg, VIIe série, 1879). There also is described and figured the improved Auxanometer referred to. With respect to the view proposed by Baranetzky that the periodicity in the dark is an after-effect of the preceding illumination, it is absolutely necessary to read carefully the treatise itself, and particularly pp. 16–18, since his preliminary publication (Bot. Zeit., 1877, p. 639) omits just the most decisive facts.

of growth occurs; or, in other words, the daily period indicated, the increase of growth during the night, and the progressive diminution during the day, cannot be regarded as a result of the daily variation in temperature. This fact, however, comes out sharp and clear only when the hourly variations of temperature are by tenths of degrees, and only amount to a few whole degrees in the course of the day: where the variations in temperature are large, the movement of the curve of growth follows in the main the ups and downs of the curve of temperature, and this is the chief reason why the daily period, which is independent of temperature, was either not

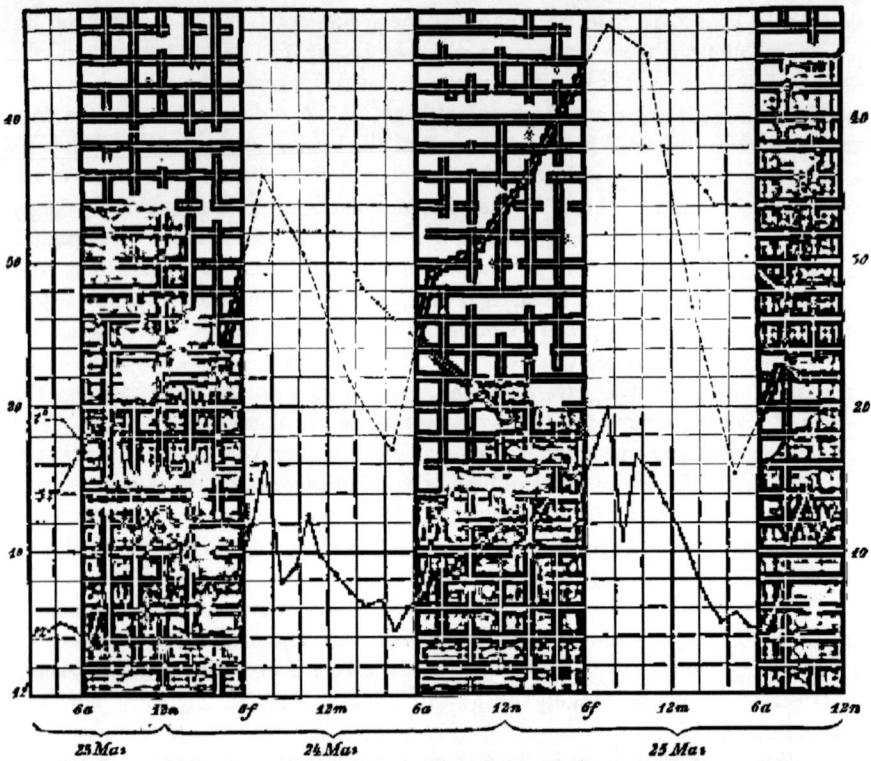

FIG 349.—The curve *x x* represents the hourly growth, and the curve *3 x* the growth every three hours of a shoot-axis of *Dahlia*. The curve *t* indicates the temperature On the abscissa, *6 a* denotes *6 p m.*, *12 n* = midnight, *6 f* = *6 a m.*, and *12 m* = noon. The dark areas correspond to the night, the light ones to the day

recognised at all or only indistinctly by the earlier observers, because their plants were exposed in the open to variations of temperature which were for the most part very large

On the other hand, however, the assumption suggests itself that the daily period of growth, so far as it is independent of variations of temperature, may be chiefly induced by the daily alternation of illumination, for that the light causes a retardation of the growth of stems and green leaves may be proved in various ways, and since the plant remains exposed to light from sunrise till evening, its retarding effects would assert their influence more and more in the course of several days, i. e. the hourly growths would become smaller and smaller. When, however, the intensity of the light decreases in the evening, and the darkness of night follows, the retarding action of the light does not disappear instantaneously, but the forces of growth, now set free as it were, obtain more and more the upper hand in the plant, and the growth is accelerated until the morning, attaining a maximum until the moment when the increasing intensity of the light is again in a position to exert its retarding influence. A series of observations made by Prantl on normal green foliage-leaves yielded exactly similar results for these also.

But however satisfactory this explanation appears to be (and it is certain that the alternations of light and darkness co-operate in the way referred to), further observations show that even quite independent of the daily variation in illumination, a daily increase and decrease of growth nevertheless takes place, e g. in continuous darkness. I had ascribed this fact, which I was the first to observe, hypothetically to the circumstance that my observing-chamber did not admit of complete darkening, but the very detailed observations of Baranetzky allow of no doubt with respect to this very point, that a periodic up-and-down variation of the hourly growth in length takes place entirely independent both of temperature and of light. Baranetzky, however, is inclined to regard this periodic variation, which still exists even in constant darkness, as an after-effect of the previously existing daily light-period, for which, moreover, he adduces various apparently plausible reasons; but, apart from other objections, Baranetzky himself has brought forward the fact that in the case of completely etiolated shoots, which had been developed in the dark from the beginning, from tuberous roots of *Brassica rapa*, the periodicity came out if possible still more sharply than with normal shoots of the same plant. .This single fact suffices completely to set aside the theory of after-effects, since no one, probably, would be inclined to believe that we have here an after-effect which has been for a long time latent, so to speak, in the bud. That would be much as if a pendulum commenced to swing spontaneously after it had been standing still for some time. Moreover, Baranetzky himself adduces the fact that in different plants of the same species the appearance of the maxima in the dark is observed at very different times of the day, although in normal daily illumination this does not occur.

I, on the contrary, am of opinion that in the plant, or at any rate in its growing parts, periodic variations occur in some way quite independent of variations of temperature and of light; and these, as I conclude from Baranetzky's observations, may continue for periods of very different lengths. If now the plant is subjected to the regular alternation of day and night, and the variations of temperature are very small, the above-mentioned influences on growth make their appearance, by which its maximum is transferred to the morning hours, and its minimum to the evening, the above-mentioned periodicity arising from purely internal causes being concerned as the weaker factor in a definite daily period of time. So long ago as 1863 I gave a very similar explanation of the spontaneous periodic movements of foliage-leaves. There also a periodic up-and-down variation takes place in constant darkness, but this, through the alternation of day and night, is modified to a daily period. However, I shall return to this point later on.

Of special interest is the fact demonstrated by Dr. Vines[1] in my laboratory,

---

[1] Sydney H. Vines, 'The Influence of Light upon the Growth of Unicellular Organs' (Arb. des bot. Inst. in Wzbg. B. II, pp. 133, &c).

that in the case of *Phycomyces nitens* (Fig. 3, p. 5) one of the Mucors already so often mentioned, and a plant not only devoid of chlorophyll but also a non-cellular one, a direct action of light on the rapidity of growth occurs of such a kind that even light of feeble intensity causes a retardation of the growth in the course of a single hour, while a similarly short period of darkness accelerates it. Here also, just as in the case of the highly organised plants, it is the more refrangible rays of the light, the blue and violet, which retard the growth—a point to which I have already expressly referred—while it is chiefly the less refrangible rays, the yellow, which cause assimilation in the chlorophyll Since this is a very important point in vegetable physiology, I may take this opportunity of describing the apparatus which I have constructed for the purpose of such measurements of growth on small and simple plants, and with which Vines made his observations The apparatus here figured (Fig. 350), although constructed on exactly the same principle, is still more convenient. On a very strong, firm, wooden tripod, a thick slab is arranged by means of the triangular prismatic foot *A*, so that it can be moved vertically and fixed. On the slab stands a very firm cathetometer *E*, the horizontal telescope of which affords an enlargement of about fifteen diameters, at 12–20 centimeters focal distance. The apparatus *B* is a very strong and carefully constructed clockwork, which is for the purpose of allowing a vertical axis which supports a horizontal brass plate to make exactly one revolution in an hour. On this plate is placed the plant to be observed, in our case, for instance, a *Phycomyces* bearing sporangia, *D*, which

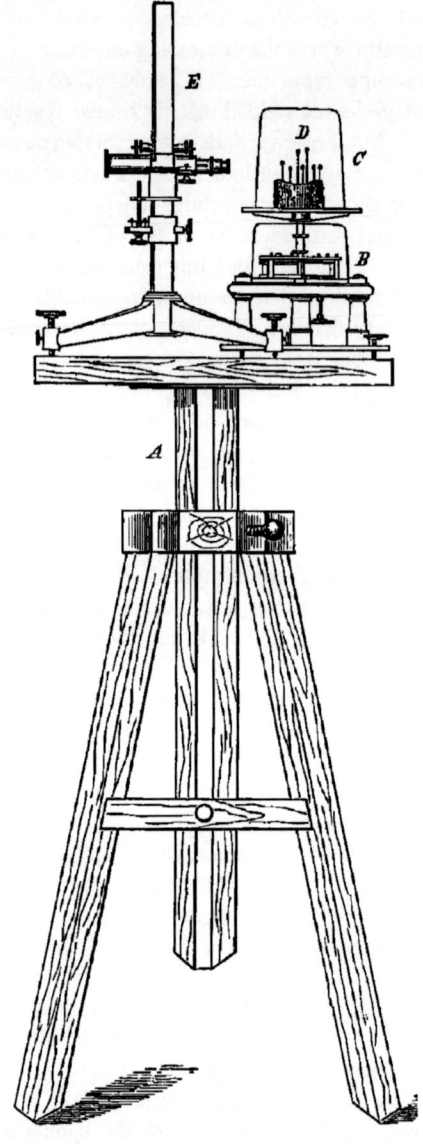

FIG 350 —Apparatus for measuring the growth in length of small plants (*D*) by means of the cathetometer (*E*)

grows on a piece of bread, and is covered with a glass bell-jar *C*. The telescope of the cathetometer, which contains a micrometer scale on which o·1 mm. can be read off, is now so fixed that the observer sees distinctly one of the erect hyphæ with its sporangium, and that its apex apparently touches one of the division lines in the telescope. The clock-work is now set in motion: the plant on the plate revolves once in exactly one hour, and then comes again into the field of view of the telescope, and the growth which has taken place during one hour is now marked by the displacement of the sporangium on the scale; and so with each successive revolution. The measurements made hourly on this species then give an idea of the course of growth in the thin hyphæ of this Fungus, each consisting of a single vesicle only. Since these objects not rarely elongate 2–3 mm. in an hour, while it is possible to measure less than 0·1 mm., we obtain an exactitude of measurement quite sufficient for our purpose. It may now be asked, for what purpose the revolution of the plant by means of the clock-work is necessary, this is simply in order that the plants shall grow quite vertically upwards; for they would not do this if they were exposed to illumination on one side from a window, but would bend over towards the window, and make any measurement of their growth impossible. By means of the slow revolution, however, the observed part of the plant is successively illuminated on all sides during the course of the hour, and this acts exactly as if it received equal light from all sides. Hence no heliotropic curvature takes place. I regarded it as an important advance when, in the year 1873, I first hit upon the idea of entirely doing away with the heliotropic curvatures, so exceedingly disturbing in observations on growth, by means of such revolutions on a horizontal disc.

It is of course obvious that the glass bell-jar *C* may be replaced by an opaque vessel, or, what is better, on account of the susceptibility of the object towards the atmospheric moisture, the glass vessel may be retained and an opaque receptacle (of cardboard for instance) placed over it   In this way the small plant may be exposed alternately for one or two hours to the influence of light or of profound darkness, or different coloured glasses may be interposed to demonstrate the effect of lights of various colours, and so forth.

Hour of the day	Growth per hour.	Temperature
8–9 morn	2·70	22 9° C
10 ,,	2 70	24 3
11 ,,	2 30	26 0
12 ,,	2 90	25 0
1 aftern	2 70	25·8
2 ,,	3·20	25 8
3 ,,	3 50	25 2
4 ,,	2·90	25 0
5 ,,	3 20	25 1
6 ,,	2 80	25 3

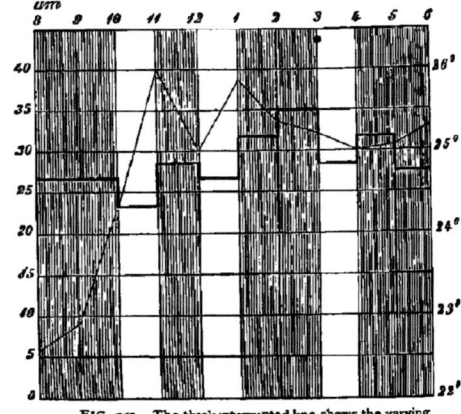

FIG. 351.—The thick interrupted line shows the varying rapidity of growth of a hypha of *Mucor* in alternate light and darkness. The thin line marks the temperature

As an example of the course of such a series of observations I subjoin a table and the corresponding curves drawn from observations made by Vines (Fig. 351).

LECTURE XXXIII.

MECHANICAL CAUSES AND EFFECTS OF THE GROWTH
OF CELLS AND ORGANS

WHEN vegetable cells pass over from their young condition into that of more rapid growth, or we may also say when organs pass out of the embryonic state into that of elongation, the taking up of water into the interior of the cells plays a particularly important part. A longitudinal section through a root or a shoot, which takes in at the same time the growing-point and the older parts of the organ, shows at once that with the increasing volume of the growing cells the water in their interior also increases, and exactly the same is observed in isolated living cells of Algæ and Fungi[1]. The increase in volume of the vegetable cells corresponds almost exactly with the quantity of water passing into their interior. It has already been mentioned that the very young cells of embryos and growing-points, as well as the youngest organs, are entirely filled with protoplasm and cell-nucleus; in proportion as they increase in length, breadth, and volume generally, the water of the cell-sap increases, and the mass of protoplasm becomes more and more insignificant: the at first solid protoplasmic body becomes changed into a sac filled with water and which is closely applied to the cell-wall, as shown in Fig. 352. The cell-wall at first, where the increase in volume of the individual cell or of a multicellular organ is concerned, continually increases in extent only, without obtaining essentially in thickness. Only when the increase in volume of the cells has ceased does the subsequent growth in thickness of the cell-wall begin: a fact of the highest significance for the theory of growth generally, and of fundamental importance, since it implies essentially that growth in surface of the cellulose walls takes place only so long as the latter are still exceedingly thin and accordingly extensible: strongly thickened cell-walls are no longer capable of increasing in extent. These facts may be directly established by microscopic observation, and there can be no doubt as to their mechanical significance; moreover Gregor Kraus has also demonstrated the fact mentioned

---

[1] The contents of this lecture have in the main, but much more in detail than here, been already published in the third and fourth Editions of my 'Text-book' under the title 'The Mechanics of Growth,' and in cases where the special literature is not quoted here, I refer once for all to that chapter. There, for the first time, the growth of the cells and tissues in combination was considered from the mechanical point of view. With respect to tissue-tension, the last part of my 'Handbuch der Exp Phys.' (1865) may be consulted.

experimentally, by determining the dry weight of growing parts of various ages[1]. By this means he obtained the following results, agreeing with what has just been said.

'In a growing shoot or internode, the percentage amount of the contained water continually increases from the youngest internodes to those which are older, up to a maximum, and then gradually diminishes again;' this decrease occurs

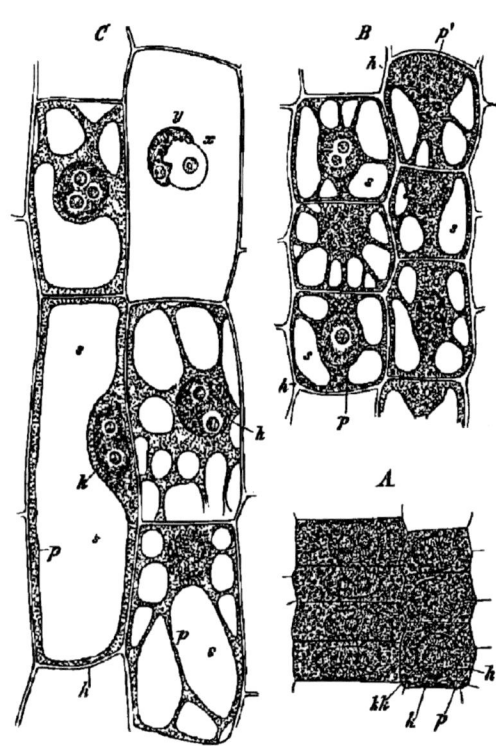

'only when the growth in length ceases, and the organ at the end of this growth contains most water;' i.e. the decrease of the water per cent. at the conclusion of growth in length coincides with the thickening of the cell-walls which now makes its appearance, and in part also with the deposition of dissolved or solid matters in the cell-contents. It need only be added that all this is true not merely of the internodes of the shoot, but in exactly the same way of the leaves, and of the transverse zones lying one behind the other in a root-fibre. The quantity of water which young organs may have gained at the end of their growth in length and surface is shown particularly clearly by weighing seedlings, in the fresh and dry states, at the time when all the reserve-materials have been consumed by growth; it is then found that such young plants of the Beet, Bean, Maize, and other species sometimes contain only 4—5 % dry weight, and

FIG 752.—Parenchyma cells from the median layer of the cortex of the root of *Fritillaria imperialis* (longitudinal sections × 550). *A* very young cells situated close above the apex of the root, still without cell-sap *B* the same cells about 2 mm above the apex , the cell sap *s* forms isolated drops (vacuoles) in the protoplasm *p*, plates of protoplasm lying between them. *C* the same cells about 7—8 mm above the apex , the two cells to the right below are seen from in front, the large cell to the left below in optical section , the cell to the right above has been opened by the section, and its nucleus is affected by the penetrating water and exhibits a peculiar swollen appearance.

similarly, completely developed Mushrooms and submerged water-plants are also found to be extraordinarily rich in water in the later stages of growth. I have found further that pith (parenchymatous tissue) from the interior of various plants, e. g. *Senecio umbrosus*, which at first contained 4·23 % of solid substance, when

---

[1] Gregor Kraus, '*Über die Wasservertheilung in der Pflanze,*' in Festschr. der naturforsch Ges. in Halle, 1879.

laid in water, became very considerably elongated by growth, and at last possessed only 1·97 % of solid substance.

The facts here mentioned allow us to explain in the first place why active growth in plants is only possible when the supply of water is abundant. When, in the Spring for instance, the buds of trees, rhizomes, and bulbs unfold, and in the course of a few days numerous shoots cover the gardens, woods, and fields with their leaves, this process consists chiefly in an extension by means of water of the small organs already existing in the winter-buds. Just as a small soap-bubble grows as the air is driven in, and its volume increases a hundredfold or more, so the cells of these organs become distended by the water taken up; but of course even this comparison falls short of the truth, like others, since the cell-walls distended by water do not become proportionally thinner as they increase in extent, as does the wall of a soap-bubble, but grow with the increase in extent in such a manner that they rather perhaps increase a little in thickness.

A second fact of fundamental importance for the growth of the cells and tissues is this, that they grow only when turgescent. Turgescence is, if not the only cause, at any rate one of the most important causes of the growth in surface of the cell-walls; or in other words cell-walls only grow in surface—i e. the organs elongate and become broader—only in proportion as the water contained in the interior of the cells strives to press the cell-walls outwards, or to stretch them. We have already (Lecture XIII) learnt to know this condition of the cells as turgescence, and, to repeat, we understand by this term the hydrostatic pressure which the cell-sap exerts on the cell-wall, so that the extensible but at the same time elastic cell-wall becomes distended. It is obvious that by means of the elasticity of the distended cell-wall a contrary pressure is exerted on the cell-sap which stretches it, or mutual tension occurs, it is this condition which we designate turgescence, and since experience teaches that cells only grow in extent if they are turgescent, we thence conclude that turgescence is one of the most essential causes of growth : the cell-wall grows in the direction of its circumference only so long as it is stretched by the watery cell-sap The turgescence will cease at once if the growing cell-wall, by the deposition of new particles of substance in it, actually assumes the form which has become forced upon it by distension; but as the cell-wall grows in extent new water is continually being taken up into the cavity of the cell, and thus the already larger wall becomes again distended, and thus the tension due to turgescence is maintained even in the growing cell, until finally another condition comes in where the cell though turgescent grows no more, or where, through the growth of the cell-wall, its passive extension is compensated without further distension being produced by the entrance of fresh water. In these two cases the cell, or the growing organ, is fully grown, i.e it increases no more in surface, though the thickening of the cell-walls may now begin, and the relations of rigidity especially become altered as described in Lecture XIII.

It was further stated there that the turgescence of vegetable cells depends upon three things :—(1) By means of the endosmotic action of substances dissolved in the cell-sap, water is continually being absorbed into the cell from without; this is the moving cause of the whole process; (2) The water forcibly absorbed into the cell, in spite of the strong pressure which it exerts, must not filter out again, and this is prevented by the peculiar properties of the protoplasmic sac lining the cell-wall, (3) Although the sac of protoplasm itself prevents filtration, it is true, it would be more and more distended by the water forcibly entering by endosmose, were this not prevented by the firm elastic cellulose wall which surrounds it. The protoplasmic vesicle does not allow filtration, but it is exceedingly extensible; a limit is imposed to its actual extension, however, by the slight extensibility and great elasticity of the cellulose wall, which however on its part permits filtration to a large extent[1].

It is now important to make out by means of what forces the water is absorbed from without through the cellulose wall and the protoplasmic vesicle. We know so far of no other cause for this than the attraction which the substances dissolved in the water of the cell, and in part contained in the wall itself, exert on the surrounding water: by means of this attraction the molecules of water are drawn through the cellulose wall and the protoplasmic sac into the interior of the cell, and increase the volume of the sap, which therefore presses the walls outwards. Since, however, the cellulose walls in virtue of their elasticity oppose considerable resistance to this pressure, the entrance of the water must take place with still more considerable force; or, in other words, the endosmotic attraction must be greater than the elasticity of the cellulose walls. It has been found that this endosmotic attraction may attain considerable magnitude, so much in fact that the absorbed water may exert a pressure of 6-7 atmospheres on the surrounding wall—i. e. the cell-wall under these circumstances must behave as if a column of mercury 6-7 times as high as the barometer column were pressing on it from within[2]. It was formerly believed that such powerful endosmotic effects could only arise if the cell contained large quantities of dissolved substances; and it was also assumed that it is chiefly substances of the nature of gums, sugars, or proteids which bring about the endosmotic action. But the investigations of Pfeffer have shown that crystallisable salts under the circumstances here given exhibit far greater endosmotic force than the organic substances mentioned; that, for example, saltpetre acts much more vigorously, and that even very dilute solutions of this and other salts exert vigorous endosmotic action. Subsequently De Vries pointed out good reasons for believing that in the turgescence of the growing parts of plants the vegetable acids or their salts are especially important; in fact, as I had already shown in 1862, all parts of plants which are actively growing in length have an acid reaction; and Graham had pointed out that the organic acids common in the plant, and their potassium salts, are remarkable for their attraction for water, and according to De Vries sensitive phenomena in motile organs of plants are accompanied by an increase in the acid reaction, when an increase of turgescence is taking place at the same time[3].

---

[1] The difference in the significance of the protoplasm and the cellulose wall for the processes of diffusion in living cells was first recognised and thoroughly worked out by Naegeli, in his treatise on the '*Primordial Utricle*' (Pflanzen-physiol unters von Naegeli und Cramer, H I, 1855, p. 1). The principal subsequent workers on this subject have been De Vries ('*Sur la perméabilité du protoplasma des betteraves rouges*,' Arch. Néerlandaises, VI, 1871, p. 117), and Pfeffer ('*Osmotische Untersuchungen*,' 1877)

[2] Very detailed statements on the magnitudes of endosmotic force and the resulting turgescence of the cells are found in Pfeffer's '*Osmot Unters*,' Leipzig, 1877.

[3] Hugo de Vries, '*Über die Bedeutung der Pflanzensauren für den Turgor der Zellen*,' Bot Zeit, 1879, p 847.

These statements of Pfeffer and De Vries harmonise completely with my experiments, according to which the strongest turgescence is to be observed in just such parts of plants, the dry weight of which amounts to only a small percentage, which in the main are to be put to the account of the cellulose walls and the protoplasm, so that only a very small proportion can come from the substances dissolved in the cell-sap.

If from our theoretical considerations it results that within a growing cell or a growing mass of tissue such a tension exists between the sap and the cell-wall, we must also suppose that on the cessation of this tension the cell-wall must contract, and the part of the plant concerned diminish in size, and if the extension due to turgescence has taken place chiefly in the longitudinal direction, a corresponding shortening must take place on the cessation of turgescence. There is, however, a very simple means of stopping turgescence: it is simply necessary to prevent the addition of water to growing parts of plants, and to promote the evaporation of water from the cells; in this case, as already explained, parts of plants which are filled with sap droop and become flaccid, and measurement shows that internodes and roots in this condition are considerably shortened. The cells which become contracted by the evaporation of the water of their cell-sap behave like a soap-bubble, which, hanging from the blow-pipe, contracts and drives back a portion of the inflating air and thus becomes smaller. This shortening on the cessation of turgescence, then, is effected by the elastic contraction of the cell-walls which had been previously extended by the water which had penetrated by endosmose. At the same time, the diminution of turgescence must cause cells and tissue-bodies to become more extensible, just as a strongly inflated caoutchouc balloon when it loses air again becomes extensible and flaccid (cf. what was said in Lecture XIII). It must also be admitted as a further consequence of our theoretical considerations, that a non-turgescent and drooping part of a plant cannot grow, since otherwise our theory would be false; but it has already been stated above that, as a matter of fact, only turgescent organs grow, and it is easy to convince ourselves by measurements that roots and leaves which have become flaccid and droop do not grow. Indeed a marked flagging is not necessary to arrest growth, but only a certain diminution of turgescence: for example, if plants are cultivated at a window, and the soil in the flower-pots kept continually nearly air-dry for weeks and months, then although the leaves remain fresh to a certain extent, the young shoots do not grow; and something similar is observed in the open in the Spring when the air and the soil are for some time persistently dry.

We have to thank De Vries for exact and very careful investigations on the significance of turgescence for growth in length. From his ‘ *Untersuchungen uber die mechanischen Ursachen der Zellstreckung* ’[1] I may quote the following. If growing parts of plants are laid in certain salt-solutions, they lose their turgescence completely in two or three hours, contracting at the same time. Young shoot-axes may thus lose 4 or 5 °/o of their length. As solutions particularly suitable for this purpose De Vries mentions those of saltpetre and of common salt. The shortening mentioned, accompanied no doubt with a thinning of the part, that is the total diminution

---

[1] Hugo de Vries, ‘ *Unters uber die mechanischen Ursachen der Zellstreckung,*’ Leipzig, 1877, a treatise which must be studied by any one desirous of making himself acquainted in detail with the mechanics of growth

of volume, indicates how much the cell-walls were extended by the turgescence. As I have already shown in Lecture XIII, and as is to be observed in the accompanying figure (Fig. 353), the protoplasm becomes withdrawn from the cellulose wall through the action of the solution (containing from 5–10 °/₀ of salt), at first here and there, and then on all sides, since the cell-sap gives up a great part of its water to the salt-solution; this latter penetrates through the cell-wall, but cannot enter into the protoplasmic sac, but draws the water of the cell-sap from this: the sac thus contracts, closely surrounding the cell-sap, which has now become more concentrated. The pressure which the sap enclosed in the protoplasm previously exerted on the cellulose wall herewith ceases, and the cell-wall left to itself then contracts back to its natural size; its elastic contraction is here certainly less than that of the protoplasm, relations which become clear at once on careful consideration of the accompanying figure, borrowed from De Vries. It is also obvious that by means of feebler action of a salt solution, or by feeble evaporation which acts in a strictly similar

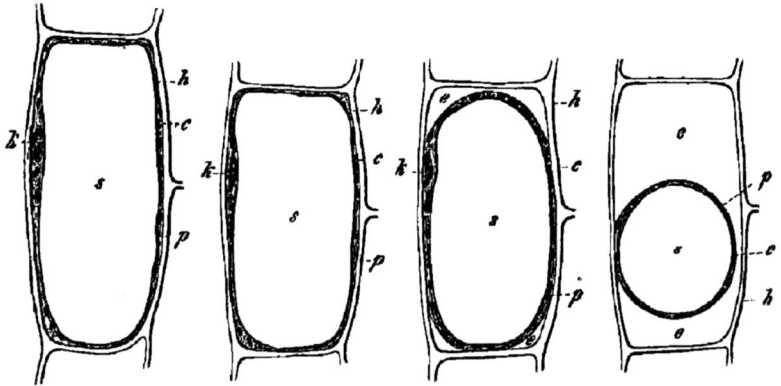

FIG. 353 —1 Young, half grown cell from the cortical parenchyma of the peduncle of *Cephalaria leucantha.* 2 The same cell in a 4 °/₀ solution of potassium nitrate 3 The same cell in a 6 °/₀ solution 4. The same cell in a 10 °/₀ solution 1 and 4 after nature, 2 and 3 diagrammatic All in optical longitudinal section *h* cell wall, *p* protoplasmic lining of the wall, *k* cell nucleus, *c* chlorophyll grains, *s* cell sap, *e* salt-solution which has passed through the cell wall (De Vries)

manner, only a partial stoppage of turgescence will take place, no withdrawal of the protoplasm from the cell-wall necessarily occurring at first; as soon, however, as this does occur, even if only here and there, turgescence ceases.

According to De Vries, if any part of the plant, young stem, or root, rendered flaccid by plasmolysis, is again brought into pure water, the penetrated salt-solution gradually soaks out, the protoplasmic sac again takes up pure water into its interior, becomes distended, and applies itself on all sides to the interior of the cellulose membrane, and as this assumption of water and absorption proceed further, the cellulose membrane also becomes again extended, the condition of turgescence begins anew, and the part concerned obtains practically the same volume, and above all the same length, which it possessed before the investigation. That no injury to the organ takes place here the investigator named has sufficiently demonstrated, and it is unquestionable that the object again becomes turgescent, and then begins to grow anew, and that this growth may even be considerable.

The importance of turgescence for growth—in other words, the importance of the passive extension of the cell-wall for its proper growth—as I had previously concluded on other grounds, was demonstrated by De Vries particularly by the establishment of the proposition, that 'the rapidity of the growth in length in the partial zones of growing organs rises and falls with the magnitude of the extension caused by turgescence.' That is to say, the extension due to turgescence first increases in passing backwards from the apex of a shoot or of a root, attains its maximum in the region of most active growth, and diminishes thence towards the base, just as does the partial growth; at the boundary between the fully-grown and the growing region lies also the limit of extension due to turgescence. In order to comprehend this matter quite clearly, it is necessary to refer to what I said in the preceding lecture concerning the distribution of growth—the partial growths. Finally it need only be mentioned that the contraction of a growing organ in the salt-solution, and its subsequent re-extension in pure water, is to be regarded in the first place only as the measure of the existing extension of the growing cell-walls, but not as a measure of the magnitude of the force of turgescence. This is at once clear on again referring to a non-cellular plant—e g. the *Phycomyces* already mentioned so often evidently the turgescence in the much branched utricle of which this plant consists is everywhere equal in magnitude, though extension of the membrane is only actually taking place at the growing ends of the utricle.

So much at any rate follows definitely from the considerations and facts so far, that vegetable cells only grow when their cellulose walls are passively extended by the pressure of the cell-sap, and therefore that this extension is an essential mechanical cause of the growth itself.

It appears, however, that in certain layers of tissue in the more highly organised plants, the passive extension which is necessary for growth may also be produced in another way, as we might conclude from the fact of the tension of the tissues, which has also already been described. From the phenomena which result on separating the various layers of tissue of a growing shoot-axis, it follows that the epidermis, as well as the vascular bundles and the as yet non-lignified strands of sclerenchyma, are subjected to continual passive extension, due to the much more rapid growth of the soft parenchyma, especially the pith. Although some points still remain doubtful, we may nevertheless assume that this passive extension of the epidermis, vascular bundles, and strands of young sclerenchyma by the growing parenchyma, is to be looked upon as an important factor in the growth of these passively extended portions of tissue.

We previously noticed the tensions of tissues only in so far as they affect the rigidity and elasticity of the young growing shoot-axes and leaves, and it has only to be added to this that the rigidity even of many fully-grown parts, particularly of petioles and the ribs of leaves of the Dicotyledons, depends even in the fully-grown condition on these tissue-tensions.

Now, however, we have to regard the tissue-tensions as a mechanical property of the growing organs of multicellular plants, and to see in what relation they stand to growth itself. In the first place, so much is certain, that the parts of plants concerned only grow at all so long as tissue-tensions exist in them: if these are destroyed by doing away with the turgescence in the parenchymatous tissue, the growth ceases also, and the more pronounced the turgescence of that tissue, the more energetic the growth tends to be. On the other hand, however, it is of importance to note that the tissue-tension itself is called into being by differences in growth, especially differences in the lengthening of the various layers of tissue. It begins with their histological differentiation behind the growing-point, and the further this differentiation of epidermis, vascular bundles, strands of sclerenchyma, and parenchyma proceeds, the more pronounced also, up to a certain point, is the of tension, or, put better, the differences in length of the layers of tissue which make their appearance when the layers are separated. But when the vascular bundles and layers of sclerenchyma have become lignified, and the growth in length of the whole organ at this place therewith concluded, the tissue-tension may still persist, though on the separation of the layers the difference in length is not so great; for it is obvious that a very strong tension may be existing in the tissues when only very small or even unmeasurable elongations and shortenings occur on the separation of the layers, for this only demonstrates that the extensibility of the tissues in a state of tension towards one another has diminished. We must not therefore regard the changes in dimension on the separation of the layers of tissue forthwith and generally as the immediate expression of the force of tension; that would only be possible if the extensibility remained the same at different ages, which is not the case. In spite of this objection, very important for the specialist, it is nevertheless necessary for the understanding of the mechanical properties of the growing parts of plants to return once more to the most important phenomena of the tension of tissues [1], even if only to afford the reader a general idea. For this purpose I may take the following statements from my '*Handbuch der Experimental Physiologie*' (1865). In the first place a portion of the shoot-axis under consideration was measured, then the tissue-layers mentioned were cut out, and these also measured. In the following tables the original length of the part is regarded as 100, the shortenings being denoted as negative and the lengthenings as positive numbers per cent.

Plant.	Number of internode, proceeding from youngest to oldest	Alteration in length of the isolated tissues in percentages of the parts measured		
		Cortex	Wood	Pith
Nicotiana Tabacum	I—IV	— 5·9	— 1·5	+ 2·9
	V—VII	— 3 1	— 1 1	+ 3 5
	VIII—IX	— 3 5	— 1 5	+ 0·9
	X—XI	— 0·5	— 0·5	+ 2·4
Sambucus nigra . . .	I	— 2·6	— 2·6	+ 4·0
	II	— 2·0	— 2·8	+ 5·5
	III	— 1·5	— 0 0	+ 1·5

Similar shortenings of the external layers of tissue, and lengthenings of the

---

[1] A more detailed discussion of the idea of the intensity of the strain in tissue-tension, and above all as to the fact that the mere changes of length of the separated strips of tissue only present a measure for the prevailing forces if the extensibility of the compared tissues remains unaltered, as well as on other considerations appertaining here, are to be found in my '*Lehrbuch*,' Aufl IV, 1874, p 763. There also are to be found numerous examples of the behaviour of the separated strips of tissue of growing parts of shoots.

parenchyma, may easily be demonstrated in growing petioles, especially those of considerable length and thickness, such as those of the Beet, Rhubarb, *Philo-dendron*, &c.

If a growing internode or leaf-stalk is split by means of a longitudinal section, or by two sections at right angles, the parts curve concave outwards, because the pith side is extended and the epidermis contracts, a state of affairs which must necessarily lead to such curvature. The phenomenon appears most clearly if a lamella is taken from the middle of the whole organ by means of two parallel longitudinal sections, and this lamella laid flat on the table and the pith halved lengthwise; then, in proportion as the knife travels forward, the two halves also curve concave outwards. If now, instead of halving it, thin strips of tissue are separated from this median lamella of the organ, progressively from without inwards—first one which contains the epidermis, then one which contains the cortical tissue, and then a further one containing the young as yet unlignified woody layer—they all curve concavely out-wards; because the layers which abut on one another are all extended negatively on the outer side and positively on the inner side, so that on separating them as above the outer side of each strip must shorten and the inner side lengthen. Here also I may adduce a few examples from my very numerous measurements.

Name of the Plant.	Length of the whole inter-node	Radius of curvature of the sector	Shortening of the concave epidermal side	Lengthening of the concave pith side	Half thick-ness of the internode.
Sylphium perfoliatum—					
Left half .	69 5 mm	4 cm	2 8 %	9 3 %	3 0 mm
Right half .	69·5 ,,	4 ,,	2 4 %	9 3 %	3 0 ,,
Older internode of same—					
Left half .	190 0 ,,	3-4 ,,	2 8 %	9 5 %	3 5 ,,
Right half . .	190 0 ,,	3-4 ,,	2 6 %	10 8 %	4 5 ,,
Macleya cordata—					
(hollow) .	134 5 ,,	5-6 ,,	0·74 %	7 1 %	3 3 ,,

A considerable rapidity of growth in length, with a simultaneous progressive differentiation of tissue-layers, as met with in upright leaf-shoots, strong petioles, and tendrils, seems necessary to promote this tissue-tension; since it is not observed in very slowly growing shoot-axes, and in these cases the tissue-differentiation also proceeds but slowly, e. g. in the downward growing thick rhizomes of *Yucca* and *Dracœna*. Finally, no morphological differentiation of tissues at all is necessary to produce such tension of tissues · this is proved by the stalks of growing Agarics, which consist entirely of homogeneous hyphal tissue, and nevertheless exhibit powerful tensions between the outer and inner tissue-layers.

When, on isolation, the previously passively extended tissues become suddenly shortened, and the previously positively distended pith as suddenly lengthens, both can only be effected by means of a corresponding change in form of the cells; for even a merely relatively large alteration in volume is not to be thought of, because neither the water of the contents nor the membranes saturated with water can change their volume by pressure and traction by means of the forces which are here acting. Hence we must assume that the strips of tissue which shorten increase in diameter, and that the elongating pith becomes correspondingly thinner. · These alterations in transverse dimensions are, however, not directly capable of measurement.

At any rate it follows from what has been said that the passive extension in length makes the cells of the epidermis, the vascular bundles, and the not yet lignified sclerenchyma strands narrower, and that the epidermis especially, since it is properly too short for the growing parenchyma, must also be too narrow for it. In like manner the pith, prevented by the epidermis from extending, must tend to be distended transversely : since the pith (and soft parenchyma generally) is too long for the passively extended tissues, it must also at the same time be too thick for them, and tend to extend them (particularly the epidermis) tangentially. In other words, it follows at once from the easily measurable tissue-tension in the longitudinal direction of a growing shoot-axis, that transverse tensions also must exist; or, since the passively extended tissues are too short for the soft parenchyma, they are also too narrow for it, and this conclusion may be directly proved. If thin transverse discs are cut from the organs in question, and split open by means of a radial longitudinal section, they gape, because the epidermis contracts peripherally, since it was previously properly too short for the internal tissue—i e it was passively stretched. However, we will not here go further into detail as to the changes in form of split transverse discs of growing organs, because it would be impossible to avoid difficult mechanical considerations of various kinds. I will refer only to the one obvious fact, that the increase in circumference of many internodes and leaf-stalks which are subsequently hollow is effected by this extension of the external layers of tissue, while the internal pith is no longer able to grow transversely in proportion; the latter therefore becomes ruptured, its outer layers remaining in connection with the external tissues which are growing in circumference, while a cavity arises in the interior. This may be easily observed in the flower-stems of the Teazel (*Dipsacus*), the scapes of the common Onion and Dandelion (*Taraxacum officinale*), in many Umbelliferæ and true Grasses, &c.

The cylinder of pith of a dicotyledonous shoot when freed from its enveloping layers of tissue is very limp, extensible and pliant, but if laid in water it soon becomes turgid, stiff, and elastic : it is then longer and apparently also thicker. The elongation in water may in a few hours amount to 40 per cent. or even more of the original length. This proves that the cells of the pith absorb with great force the water surrounding it, and that their cell-walls are still in a high degree extensible, and thus that they did not possess that degree of turgescence, while yet in the interior of the uninjured organ, of which they are capable. Further observations on such isolated cylinders of pith, particularly of Compositæ and Solaneæ (where they often attain a very considerable thickness and are peculiarly suited for experiments of this kind), may be employed for further instructive investigations, of which I will only describe one more in detail here. The isolated pith of a piece of the shoot of *Senecio umbrosus* 235·5 mm. long increased in length 5·7 per cent at the moment of isolation, and weighed 5·3 gr It was divided into three parts by marks of indian ink : of these I was the oldest and III the youngest. The lengths were I = 100 mm., II = 100 mm., III = 49·9 mm.

The prism of pith was placed in a wide glass tube, which was then corked at both ends. In the course of fourteen hours the following elongations had occurred :—

The part I had elongated 4·5 mm.
    „   II   „   „   6·5 „
    „   III „   „   2·0 „   (i. e. 4·1 °/₀).

The pith had however meanwhile lost 0·15 gr. water.

After another twenty-six hours stay in the glass tube the following fresh changes had made their appearance :—

The part I was still longer by 2 5 mm.
    „   II   „   „   0 5 „
    „   III was shorter by   0 5 „

During this interval no further loss in weight had occurred, because the air in the glass tube was now saturated with aqueous vapour, and thus no more evaporation could take place.

The pith was then laid in water, and in six hours the following changes had occurred .—

The part I was longer by 18 mm.
    „   II   „   „   23 „
    „   III „   „   11 „

The pith had at the same time become considerably thicker, and had absorbed 6 gr water; though at first, as said, it had only weighed 5·3 gr.

The determination of the dry weight showed that there was in this state only 0 22 gr. of solid substance , this substance after the isolation of the pith was combined with 5·08 gr. water, and then lost 0·15 gr.   At the end of the experiment, however, it took up 6 gr more ; or, at first the pith contained 4 23 °/₀, at the end only 1 97 °/₀ of solid substance.

It is seen from these statements, as I have already pointed out, that in the cells of the pith at any rate only an extremely dilute solution capable of causing endosmose can be present, and that this nevertheless causes a very pronounced absorption of water, turgescence, and growth.   There is one other point in our experiment to be explained, however, namely, the original elongation of the pith in spite of a loss (though small) of water. The explanation lies, however, in the very pronounced drying up of the surface, which could not well be due only to the small loss of water by evaporation; it is on the contrary probable that the inner cells of the pith took the water from the outer ones and thus elongated, the external desiccated ones being passively extended just as the epidermis is elsewhere   That this was actually the case is shown by the stiffness of the pith in other experiments of this kind; if the prism of pith which has become dry on its outside is bisected longitudinally, the parts gape outwards, as when a living shoot-axis is split longitudinally.   I drew from these facts the following conclusion. If the inner pith cells are able to abstract water from the outer ones, it may be assumed that the external cells of the pith also are able to abstract water from the tissues surrounding them, and therefore retard their turgescence, whence their growth is retarded, and the further consequence is that they become passively extended by the pith, which robs them of water.

It is evident from these observations why longitudinal halves or quarters of growing shoots laid in water curve outwards to such an extraordinary extent— a phenomenon which is exhibited particularly well by the flower-scapes of the Dandelion (*Taraxacum officinale*) where longitudinal strips lying in water form numerous coils of a helix.

The passive extension of the epidermis, and of the hypodermal strands of collenchyma and sclerenchyma which behave similarly, is thus due chiefly to the vigorous growth in length of the parenchymatous tissues. From this extension in the longitudinal direction, however, a simultaneous transverse tension must necessarily arise. If we suppose a caoutchouc tube extended longitudinally, it is at once noticed that it tends to become smaller in diameter at the same time, and the epidermis with its strengthening layers must behave in the same way when it is passively extended longitudinally. If, on the other hand, a solid cylinder of caoutchouc is supposed to be compressed from above downwards, it becomes at the same time thicker transversely, and the growing pith or parenchyma generally of a young stem must behave in just the same manner. These considerations at once demonstrate that when the epidermis of a growing internode is extended by the pith, and the pith, on the contrary, compressed transversely by the epidermis, transverse tension must necessarily occur, and it is at the same time clear that this latter must be a necessary consequence of the longitudinal tension. It has already been mentioned that this transverse tension may be actually recognised.

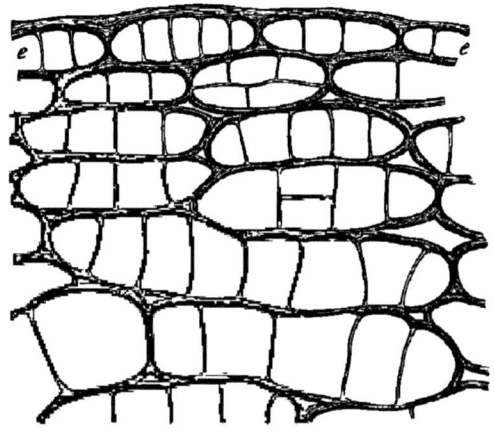

FIG 354.—Transverse section of epidermis and cortex of a Sun-flower, rapidly growing in thickness, the cells have elongated peripherally and then become divided by radial walls

If, however, at the conclusion of growth in length of an internode, subsequent growth in thickness is ushered in by a cambium zone, a further intensification of this transverse tension results. Since the wood arises on the inner side of the cambium, the whole of the cortex surrounding the wood must necessarily be distended outwards. This tangential extension is perceived with the greatest clearness by means of the microscope, in the form of the cortical cells in transverse sections through the cortex of stems of *Ricinus, Helianthus*, &c, which are rapidly growing in thickness. Since, however, the cortex and subsequently even the periderm and bark of woody stems are very slightly extensible and highly elastic, it results that a strong opposite pressure of all the cortical layers lying outside the cambium must respond to the outward pressure due to the growth of the wood; strong tension takes place between cortex and wood, and the cambium itself lies in the position of greatest pressure. We shall learn subsequently how this affects the formation of the wood itself; here it need only be remarked that Gregor Kraus has demonstrated this transverse tension between cortex and wood by means of detailed investigations[1]. To convince ourselves of its existence, it suffices to mark out a ring of cortex from a stem which is growing rapidly in thickness, by means of two superposed annular cuts, and then to make a longitudinal cut in this ring, and separate the cortex from the wood. On now attempting to replace this ring of cortex in its normal position around the wood, it is found to be too narrow, and gapes; it would require a very powerful force so to extend it that the gaping margins again touch one another, and thus exactly surround the wood. This, however, signifies simply that the cortex was previously compressed radially, and forcibly distended in the tangential direction by the growing wood.

Gregor Kraus, moreover, recognised 14–15 years ago[2] that a daily periodicity occurs both in the longitudinal and tangential tissue-tension, such that a decrease of the tensions is noticeable from early morning to mid-day or afternoon, and an increase thence till early morning again. Millardet found and confirmed this periodicity in an entirely different way, which can only be more exactly shown when we come to the consideration of the sensitive organs. It is scarcely possible to doubt that these periodic alterations of tissue-tension depend on the same causes as the similarly periodic variations of growth, the weeping of the root-stock, the daily movements of leaves, &c.

All these considerations hold good strictly of shoot-axes, petioles, and the midribs of leaves only. The radical contrast between root and shoot again comes out here; for in the first place it is important to notice that the conspicuously short growing portion—3–10 mm. long—of normal terrestrial roots exhibits a phenomenon of tissue-tension which differs at least superficially. If the growing portion of a vigorous root is split by means of a longitudinal section, or by two sections at right angles, in the direction of the axis, the parts do not gape concave outwards, and, at first, no separation at all takes place. If roots so treated, however, are left to go on growing in water, the longitudinal halves become curved convex outwards, that is in exactly the opposite manner to those of shoot-axes and leaf-stalks. The phenomenon is explained simply by the fact that the parenchymatous cortex of the root grows more vigorously in length than the axial strand, and that the latter is still highly extensible within the growing region. The tension between the cortex and the axial strand is therefore so small, that the effect in question only makes its appearance on growth occurring subsequently to the splitting.

The contrast between roots and shoot-axes, however, is much more conspicuous in parts of the root which are already fully grown. We are here concerned with the fact already mentioned in the lectures on Organography (Lecture II) that the part of a root-fibre which is no longer growing in length may shorten itself very considerably during a long period, so that seedlings may have their stems eventually drawn down into the soil. Referring to what I said in the lecture quoted, we are here only concerned with the causes of this phenomenon itself: this was investigated by

---

[1] The transverse tension between cortex and wood was first investigated in detail by Gregor Kraus, *Bot. Zeit.*, 1867, p. 113

[2] Kraus (*loc. cit.*, p 121) first described the periodic variation of tissue-tension.

De Vries. The shortening of the root, discovered by Fittmann as long ago as 1819[1] and then forgotten, and at length again observed by Irmisch and myself, is manifested in the first place by the production of transverse folds on the surface of those parts of the root which have for some time ceased to grow in length; the roots of many marsh-plants, those which grow in water especially, as well as those of Hyacinths, various species of *Iris*, &c., easily permit the observation. De Vries made marks at determined distances on the primary roots of young plants of Red Clover and Beet, and then allowed them to go on growing in soil or nutritive solution, and found that after 3–6 weeks the regions marked had become shortened by 10–15 $\%$ and in some cases even 20–25 $\%$ of their length. On letting the main roots of actively vegetating plants of the Caraway, Teazle, and Artichoke, taken out of the soil and separated from the tuft of leaves, lie for 3–4 days in water, they shortened about 4–8$\%$, increasing in thickness the while (sometimes even 4–8$\%$), and accordingly an increase in volume and simultaneous stiffening took place. Isolated parts of the tissue in water showed the same changes : the axial strand as well as the parenchymatous cortex became shortened in the longitudinal direction and extended transversely. According to De Vries it is in both the parenchymatous tissue alone which initiates this change, which in fact was directly measured microscopically by him the cork envelope as well as the vessels and bast-like fibres become passively bent, and cause in part the formation of the transverse folds referred to. De Vries sums up the most important points of his observations as follows —'The contraction (shortening) on taking up water is a phenomenon of turgescence, and is reversed by all agents which stop turgescence. This is shown most simply by the fact that the contractile roots do not shorten on flagging, as growing root-apices or stems tend to do, but become elongated. In the same way they lengthen if the protoplasm is in any way killed, or if it is forced to separate itself from the cell-wall by the action of salt-solutions. On the cessation of turgescence the tissues become drawn together in the transverse direction.'

The shortening effected by the absorption of water is rendered permanent by subsequent growth, just as the turgescent elongation of stems and leaves becomes fixed by subsequent growth. It at once results from this, as De Vries remarked, that just those roots which have the best marked transverse folds exhibit the most distinct shortening in water. Thus as we explain the longitudinal extension by turgescence of parenchyma-cells in shoots, chiefly by the fact that the cellulose walls are more extensible in the direction of their length than transversely, we must, on the contrary, assume as regards the root-parenchyma that the cellulose walls are more extensible transversely than longitudinally, since it is always to be maintained that the hydrostatic pressure which causes the turgescence is equal in magnitude on all sides.

It may be concluded, from a long series of various phenomena in the life of plants, that the form and size of the individual cells within the tissue depend to an important extent upon how they are connected with neighbouring cells. In other words, we may assume that the shape and size of each tissue-cell is determined

---

[1] Hugo de Vries, '*Über Verkürzung pflanzlicher Zellen durch Aufnahme von Wasser,*' Bot Zeit., 1879, p. 650

chiefly by two factors : on the one hand by the causes of growth which are given in the chemical and molecular structure of the individual cell itself, while on the other hand this individual formative effort can only make itself effective in proportion as the mechanical obstructions permit it.   These obstructions, again, are generally of two kinds ; the individual growing cell is prevented from extending equally on all sides by the pressure of neighbouring cells, or it suffers, since it is closely connected with its neighbours, passive strains in the longitudinal and transverse direction.   How the relative position of an individual cell or cell-layer will determine the effects produced by pressure and strain, may be in general determined beforehand geometrically, with certain premisses; and if it is at the same time borne in mind how growth in any one direction is usually followed by cell-divisions at right angles to it, a deeper insight is thus obtained into the causes which determine the fact that we find the cells on the transverse section of a wood-body arranged in regular radial and tangential rows, and that the forms of the cells and their groupings in the cortex of a woody stem which is growing in thickness must be situated and layered otherwise than before the beginning of growth in thickness, and so forth.   Put shortly, ' the plans of transverse sections of stems and roots in particular may be understood geometrically, so far as their histological construction goes, with the aid of the above principles'   This was first done, as regards the structure of wood, by Naegeli [1], and was then treated generally by Detlefsen [2], in his treatise ' *Uber das Dickenwachsthum cylindrischer Organe.*' Unfortunately I must here pass over the contents of these two unusually instructive treatises, since they could not be presented without digressions, and especially without geometrical figures and mathematical formulæ which might not be welcome to the reader of this book.

Several other facts however may be without difficulty set forth clearly in words. It is certainly not uninteresting to learn that a matter of structure so conspicuous and well known as the formation of the annual rings in wood depends, in the main at least, on alterations of pressure between wood and cortex   I had expressed this hypothetically in 1868, since it struck me that the cortical crevices of the older stems and branches of trees are deepest during the winter and spring, evidently pointing to an increase of pressure between wood and cortex.   In the spring, after these crevices have been formed, the tension must thus be diminished ; and at the same time the amount of water used in the unfolding of the leaves may also cause a slight shrinking of the alburnum   With increasing thickening of the wood, however, during the vegetative period, and with more pronounced drying up of the external layers of cortex, the tension between wood and cortex must increase . the layer of wood formed in the spring is therefore produced under diminished pressure, and consists of cells which are larger in the radial direction, while with increasing cortical pressure the extension of the wood-cells and vessels in the radial direction is interfered with,

---

[1] The first geometrical and mechanical treatment of the arrangement of cells on the transverse section of the wood is that of Naegeli, in his treatise ' *Uber das Dickenwachsthum des Stengels und Anordnung der Gefass-strange bei den Sapindaceen,*' Munchen, 1864

[2] Emil Detlefsen, ' *Uber Dickenwachsthum cylindrischer Organe*' (1878), in Arb d bot Inst zu Wzbg , B II p. 18   The investigations of Detlefsen referred to further on in the text ('*Versuch einer mechanischen Erklarung des excentrischen Dickenwachsthums verholzter Axen und Wurzeln,*' Wismar, 1881) is also found reprinted in Arb d bot Inst zu Wzbg., B II p 670.

and the denser autumn wood thus formed.   It is not improbable that other causes also co-operate here [1], of which, however, we know very little at present; but in any case the very extensive investigations of De Vries (1872–76) have shown [2] that my supposition was in the main correct.   He intensified the cortical pressure in spring by binding cords tightly round certain spots on two- to three-year old branches; the result was that the thickness of the annual ring beneath the ligature was less than the average thickness of the corresponding ring at some distance above and below that place.   In some branches the difference was so marked, that the place experimented on was visibly thinner—an impression which was strengthened by the formation of woody cushions at the upper and lower margins of the ligature, the latter evidently because at these places cortical tension must have been lessened by the pressure of the ligature.   Moreover, the thickness of the layer of autumn-wood, which (as usual) ceased to grow in August, was greater beneath the ligature than in the normal case.   The autumn-wood at this place, in very different species (e.g. Maple, Willow, Poplar, Horse-chestnut, &c.) investigated by De Vries, was formed of wood-fibres with the transverse section compressed radially, and the number of vessels was smaller than in the normal wood.   These observations show then, that under increased pressure the formation of autumn-wood begins at a time when, during normal growth, wood-tissue with wide cells and many vessels would still be formed.   A diminution of cortical pressure is obtained by splitting the cortex into several parts by means of radial longitudinal sections.   The strips of cortex thus produced contract somewhat in the tangential direction, because they were previously extended in this direction; necessarily, the pressure which the cortex exerts on the cambium and young wood is thus diminished, and this most in the immediate neighbourhood of the margins of the cuts; the new wood-tissue now arising close to these deviates considerably from the ordinary structure of wood.   Incisions were made in June and July, after the formation of the normal autumn wood had already commenced, by the middle of August it was seen that the two- to three-year branches experimented upon had grown considerably more in thickness at the places where longitudinal incisions had been made, than above and below.   On transverse sections the thickness of the wood-growths was greatest in the neighbourhood of the incisions, and thence diminished constantly up to the middle line between two incisions. De Vries found in all cases that the newly-formed wood was outside the layer of autumn-wood which had already been formed before the experiment; therefore everything produced after the diminution of the pressure was composed of wood-fibres not at all compressed in the radial direction, and at the same time the vessels in this wood were more numerous—i.e. a layer of wood had been formed under diminished pressure, which resembled the spring-wood more than the autumn-wood.

By means of these experiments also Knight's old experiments (1801) find their explanation.   He fixed young apple-trees, with stems about an inch in diameter, in

---

[1] E Russow, in his fundamental investigation, '*Über die Entwicklung des Hoftüpfels, der Membranen der Holzzellen und des Jahresringes bei den Abietineen, in erster Linie von Pinus silvestris*' (134 Sitzung der Dorpater Naturforscher-Ges, Dec. 24, 1881), expresses himself differently from the view given in the text as to the causes of the difference between spring and autumn wood

[2] Hugo de Vries, '*Über den Einfluss des Rindendruckes auf den anatomischen Bau des Holzes,*' Flora, 1875, No VII, and, further, '*Über Wundholz,*' Flora, 1876.

such a manner that their lower part (three feet) was rendered immovable, while the upper part of the stem with the crown could bend under the pressure of the wind. During the period of vegetation the upper movable part of the stem increased considerably in thickness, the lower immovable part much less so, this is easily explained by the fact that the bending to and fro of the upper part of the stem, under the influence of the wind, causes the cortex to be extended on the convex side each time and so loosened, and the pressure thus diminished. The growth of wood in a young tree which was free to move under the pressure of the wind exclusively north and south, behaved in a corresponding manner: in this north and south direction the growth of wood was stronger, and stood as regards that formed east and west as 13:11. Knight himself, however, gave an incorrect explanation of the phenomena observed by him.

The promotion of the growth of wood by means of longitudinal incisions in the cortex of the stems of young trees, continued from the crown to the root, has also been employed for a long time practically, and as I have convinced myself for some years past, with the best results: the stems grow more rapidly in thickness, the thicker alburnum can convey more water containing nutritive materials from the roots to the crown of the tree, and thus promote assimilation, and this in its turn again promotes the formation of wood in the stem.

We owe a new contribution to our knowledge in this direction to an investigation by Emil Detlefsen (1881), who first pointed out the fact that in stems and branches with excentric layers (e g. of the Pine, Maple, Walnut, Vine), and therefore where, as in Fig. 318 above, the annual rings are thicker on the one side than on the other, the formation of cortex is also more energetic on the side of the stronger growth of wood, and the thickness of the cortex more considerable. The necessity of this is at once obvious, since the pressure which the cortex exerts on the wood re-acts also conversely from the wood on the cortex Detlefsen's remarks on the very commonly occurring causes which must effect a diminution or increase of cortical pressure are particularly valuable however Wherever a branch arises on a stem, and at the places of origin of the roots, an increased growth in thickness is found From the places of origin of the thicker branches descend buttresses of the stem, it may be metres long; and in like manner we find at the lower end of the stem the places of origin of the large laterally spreading roots made recognisable by thick buttresses running upwards On the branches, strongly thickened places are found always and only running in the direction towards the roots, and on the roots, on the contrary, in the direction towards the stem. Above the places of origin of the branches moreover, and laterally from these, increased growth in thickness occurs, and conversely in the roots. The explanation of this universally observable fact is, according to Detlefsen, a very simple one 'By means of a branch growing in thickness, and by means of a lateral root behaving in the same way, the cortex of the organ whence they spring is pushed apart and the cortical tension thus diminished, and this naturally induces an increased growth in thickness. The extension of the thickening buttress also is very easy to understand if the anatomical constitution of the cortex is borne in mind It is clear that a pull acting on the cortex must make itself noticeable over much greater stretches in the direction of the course of the bast-fibres than in the direction at right angles to this. The same is of course true also of the diminution of the cortical tension, and this explains the extension of the thickening buttresses which appear at the places of origin of lateral organs.

'From the changes in dimensions of the cortex during growth in thickness we get the following results :—

'(1) The tension of a convex piece of cortex is increased by the growth in thickness, that of a concave piece of cortex, on the contrary, is diminished by it.

'(2) The alteration of cortex-tension produced by the growth in thickness is *cæteris paribus* the more considerable the more strongly the cortex is curved.

'For a convex surface of cortex must become enlarged during growth in thickness, a concave one, on the contrary, must diminish, and the changes in size of the surface produced by equal growth are the more considerable the more considerable the curvature of the surface is.'

Further, the changes, hitherto unexplained, in the direction of the branches on a tree-trunk are referred by Detlefsen to this principle ; here, however, it is the weighing down of the branch which depresses it more and more as it increases in length from year to year. 'Since the weight of the branch forces it downwards, it becomes, like any bent rod, stretched on its upper side but compressed below ; the cortical tension of the upper side is thus (and this most evidently at the base of the branch) increased, that of the lower side diminished. The inequality of cortical tension at the insertion of the branch, produced by the weighing down, is often much more considerable than that due to the form of the cortical surface at this place. In the first case the buttresses which run down from the places of origin of the branches spring from their under side, whereas otherwise they run down from above over the two sides of the place of insertion.' For the proper appreciation of these considerations, what has already been said above must of course be borne in mind, namely, that every longitudinal tissue-tension must necessarily induce transverse tensions also, and conversely, every transverse tension must call forth longitudinal tensions.

Straight branches directed nearly horizontally always show, according to Detlefsen, a promotion of the growth in thickness of their under side, and this is in fact usually most evident at the base of the branch, and gradually diminishes thence towards the apex—branches or stems which stand nearly upright and have their leaves on one side, and which are situated at the margin of a wood, or which by prevalent winds in a certain direction have had the development of their crowns prevented on one side, always show a predominant growth in thickness on the side where most leaves exist. It is often shown externally by the transverse folds of the cortex that it is compressed on the side towards which the unilateral weight of the crown presses down the stem, while the increased tension on the convex side of such objects is betrayed by the smooth surface of the cortex. 'Here,' says Detlefsen, 'where the inequality of the cortical tension is obvious, the usual explanation, that the excentric growth in thickness is a result of one-sided nutrition, is quite untenable.'

'If the foliage is abundant,' he continues, 'a marked alteration of the form of the bent branch is produced by it. Thus the older branches of orchard trees are seen to be bent by the weight of the leaves and fruit, and to sink more and more the older they become. While the young branches of the Lime tend upwards, the older branches of the same tree fall in curves towards the earth. The same is seen in the older branches of the Pines The youngest lignified branches at the apex of the Fir *Picea excelsa* ascend obliquely into the air, further down the branches are horizontal, and the lowermost even curve downwards.' This phenomenon is still more evident in vigorous specimens of *Pinus austriaca*: the tender annual shoot at the end of each horizontal branch stands erect, then becomes curved a little obliquely outwards, and in the course of the year becomes more and more oblique, and then when the new shoot is developed next year—again vertical—the last year's piece of branch sinks till nearly horizontal, to become completely so in subsequent years. Thus it is that a horizontally extended branch of this tree is composed of distinct annual shoots, each of which at first stood perpendicularly erect.

In these processes occurring in woody branches and stems we have been chiefly concerned with a greater or less obstruction of growth, by means of the mutual pressure of layers of tissue. I may now add a few examples showing how vitally active cells begin to grow anew on being relieved from pressure.

One of the finest examples in this connection is presented by the formation of so-called Tyloses[1] in the vessels of the wood of Dicotyledons. If the vessels, especially the wide ones, of *Robinia*, the Oak, Vine, and many other woods are examined microscopically, when they have attained a certain age, they are found to be entirely filled with a parenchymatous tissue, which was observed and figured even by the first vegetable anatomist, Malpighi, though of course he had no idea of its origin. Not before recent researches, especially the careful labours of Reess (1868), were accomplished, was the remarkable origin of the tyloses rendered clear. They arise in fact by the very thin closing membranes of the bordered pits, at the spots where the vessels abut on soft parenchyma cells, becoming forced into the cavity of the vessel under the turgescence of the latter, and then beginning to grow vigorously. A club-shaped vesicle is thus formed, which, as it grows, undergoes cell-divisions, and when such structures protrude from numerous pits, they fill up the cavity of the vessel and compress one another, and thus produce a parenchyma-like tissue.

The whole process would be quite impossible if the tube of the vessel itself was filled with sap and turgescent; but, as it is, the vessel loses its sap, and the air contained in it is even rarefied, and thus the turgescence of the neighbouring parenchyma cells must drive forwards the fine closing membranes of the pits into the cavity of the vessel. I observed something of the same kind, but on a larger scale, in 1854, in the internodes of Bean seedlings which had become hollow: the pith cells which surrounded the cavity had grown into it in the form of club-shaped or spheroidal papillæ, and had even undergone division several times. The same cells, however, had the pith not been ruptured by the stronger tension of the external layers of tissue,' would have remained as polyhedral parenchyma cells compressing one another on all sides in the usual manner.

---

[1] Max Reess. '*Zur Kritik der Bohm'schen Ansicht über die Entwicklungsgeschichte und Funktion der Tullen*,' Bot Zeit. 1868, p. 1.

The pressure to which the tissue-cells are normally subjected, and which prevents their free growth, may easily be relieved artificially on one side by cutting across a soft stem or leaf-rib, or even a root, and then surrounding the cut surface with water or damp earth; in this case there is formed, in many species of plants at any rate, if not always, the so-called callus, which consists essentially in that all the cells of the epidermis, cortical parenchyma, cambium, &c., which are still vitally active, now grow forth from the cut surface and divide, and so form a cushion of soft tissue which at length covers the surface of the section: this cushion is the callus These callus-cushions have moreover the highly remarkable property of giving origin to new growing-points of shoots and roots, from which new plant-individuals become developed.   The callus-cushions can be obtained with the greatest ease if large pieces of branches, as thick as the arm, of Poplars and many other trees, are cut off and cut smooth above and below, and kept during the winter in a moist warm chamber: a thick swollen callus arises at the boundary between the cortex and wood. The same thing happens if fresh living foliage-trees are cut across above the soil In such cases dozens or even hundreds of young leaf-shoots are often seen to sprout forth from the callus formed on the cut surface of the rooted portion.

Hansen[1] has investigated in detail the formation of the callus on the cut-off leaves and flower-stalks of *Achimenes grandis*, leaves of *Begonia rex* and shoots of *Peperomia* These organs planted with the cut surface in water, or moist sand or soil, develope the callus there.   The section by which the ' cutting ' is separated from the parent plant is the external stimulus to the commencement of processes of growth on the surface of the wound.   In the first place the layer of cells bounding the cut surface perishes ∙ this dead tissue is frequently separated from the living tissue still further by the formation of several layers of cork, a process also common elsewhere, and which may be produced by wounding masses of tissue which are still living.   Beneath this protection there now begins an active growth of all the tissue-elements still provided with protoplasm : i. e. the cells of the epidermis, collenchyma, and cortical tissue The epidermal cells here perform in addition a peculiar function, growing out into long root-hairs which supply the young callus with water and nutritive salts.   The callus grows not merely from the cut surface, but also extends laterally, so that the stem of a leaf-cutting often swells up to double its original diameter, and the callus as a thick cushion includes the cut end of the petiole.   This mass of tissue at first consists of nothing but similar parenchyma cells, but after some time numerous vascular bundles are differentiated in it, and extend in all directions towards the surface of the callus At various spots on the tissue of the callus superficial cells now become rich in protoplasm, divide actively, and produce a small-celled embryonic tissue, which is conspicuously marked off from the surrounding tissue of the callus.   These embryonic masses of tissue or growing-points soon become elevated, produce leaves, and thus emerge as young shoots.   At the same time embryo roots develope in the interior of the callus, these break through the tissues, penetrate the soil, and contribute to the nutrition of the new shoots.

Begonia leaves cut off and laid flat on damp sand exhibit still other curious

---

[1] Hansen's researches on the formation of callus are found in his paper, ' *Vergl Unters uber Adventivbildungen*,' in Abh der Senkenbergischen naturf. Ges , B XII, 1881.

phenomena. In the first place, the section which separates the leaf-stalk not only induces the formation of callus, shoots and roots at the wound, but also at a place some distance from it, namely where the petiole passes over into the lamina, and where at the same time the primary ribs of the leaf arise. If the nerves in a leaf so treated are cut through here and there, callus-cushions, shoots and roots are likewise formed at those places. Moreover isolated cells in the epidermis of the leaf-nerves, situated at a distance from the sections, are stimulated in a remarkable way to renewed life. They grow vigorously, division-walls are formed in them in various directions, and finally the small-celled growing-point of a new shoot is developed in them.

These and many other observations show that a cut made in an organ of a plant, when the vegetative conditions are otherwise favourable, is to be looked upon as a stimulus to growth—as an impulse to extensive and complex activities. In the first case of course the tissue adjoining the section is simply freed from certain hindrances to its growth; and the beginning of the formation of callus depends on this. When

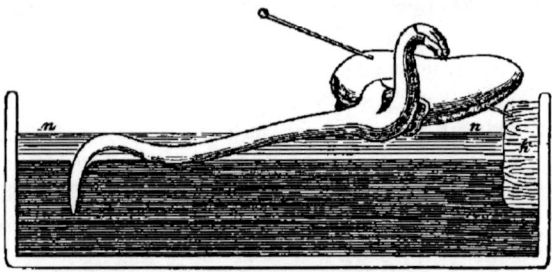

FIG. 355.—A seedling of *Vicia Faba*, the root and plumule of which were straight, was so placed that the root apex lay almost horizontal on the surface of the mercury (black in the figure), and fixed in that portion to the cork *k* by means of a pin *n n*. layer of water on the mercury. The figure shows the seedling about 24 hours later. The growing part of the root has curved sharply downwards, so that the apex enters the mercury perpendicularly. the resistance which it meets with is expressed by the form of the root behind the downward curved portion. The stem has become sharply erected at its basal portion. the nodding position of the bud is a phenomenon of nutation, independent of gravity.

this has proceeded to a certain extent, however, growing-points arise in the tissue of the callus, which of course are to be regarded, not as for and by themselves immediate effects of the section, but as consequences indirectly due to it.

While the preceding considerations and facts show that the tissue-cells undergo passive strains and pressures during their growth, on the one hand, and on the other hand are compelled to act in this way mechanically on their environment, it is implied at the same time that by means of the processes of growth work is done (in the mechanical and physical sense of the word) in the interior of the tissues. The store of energy of the growing cells is not entirely exhausted by this work, however, as follows at once from the fact that growing plant-organs can also exert powerful pressures externally, on bodies which come in contact with them. This takes place very generally when the apices of growing roots are necessitated to drive their way into the resisting soil, they not only have to glide between the small particles of soil, but to push them asunder. The elongating region immediately behind the growing-point of any root pushes forwards the apex, clothed with its root-cap, and thus drives it between the closely packed particles of soil much as a nail is hammered into a board. A very clear idea of this external work which, together with the internal work, is performed during growth, is obtained by allowing the thick primary roots of active seedlings to grow so that the apices are compelled to penetrate into mercury. This fluid, which is nearly fourteen times as heavy as water, and therefore about fourteen times as heavy as the growing-point itself, of course affords a very powerful resistance to the entry of the latter; nevertheless, the apex of the root penetrates to a depth of 1–3 cm., and would certainly penetrate still deeper if the mercury lying in close contact did not prevent respiration and poison it.

The external effects in the case of growing tree-trunks with a hard bark are much more powerful, however. I have myself had opportunity of seeing how in still weather a solidly built stone-wall was overthrown simply by the growth in thickness of an old tree. To the more frequently observed phenomena in this direction belongs the slow elevation of huge, powerful, heavy trees by their superficial roots, which are endowed with vigorous growth in thickness. It is a very common occurrence that old Poplars, Pines, and Larches have their upper horizontal roots subsequently protruding above the surface of the earth; the under side of these roots, which were at first entirely concealed in the soil, bears up against the substratum, which is continually becoming more resistant, and as growth goes on not only are the roots themselves forced to project from the soil, in consequence of this resistance, but also to carry up at the same time the stem, which often weighs many thousands of kilograms. W. S. Clark, who has investigated this phenomenon, reminds us especially of the well-known fact that the delicate seedlings of Beans, Oaks, &c. often push up clods of earth of large size, and states that in England a boundary stone weighing eighty pounds was pushed aside by three large Fungi growing up beneath it; and the case is known of a Hazel in England which had accidentally grown through the central hole of a mill-stone, completely filled it up, and then being lifted up by the growth in thickness of its roots also carried the mill-stone up with it. In order to study more closely this external work of growth, Clark placed a sort of iron waist-coat (which need not here be described in detail) on a young Gourd fruit, and so arranged matters that a weight of more than 4000 pounds could be brought to bear on the surface of the fruit, even this did not entirely prevent the growth. Unfortunately the experiment is not described with sufficient exactness to admit of a very clear judgment, but a calculation based on probable data yields the result that a pressure of only eighteen pounds to the square inch was here obtained—little more than the pressure of one atmosphere.

PART V.

IRRITABILITY.

LECTURE XXXIV.

GENERAL CONSIDERATIONS ON IRRITABILITY.

With the word irritability I designate the mode of reaction to stimuli, which is peculiar to living organisms. This is of course in the first place a mere arbitrary definition of a word; but such definitions of terms are necessary for mutual intelligibility, although they are unfortunately often neglected in the province of natural science. That such a bare definition of the term—which moreover I have come to regard as right only after many years of thought—has its uses, is illustrated directly by the following remarks I say the mode in which *living* organisms only react to stimuli, is irritability· by this I imply at the same time that all irritability in the tissues is due to the protoplasm. For there is no difference of opinion as to this one point, that all the processes of life depend upon protoplasm, and that where no protoplasm is present no vital processes can occur It follows thence, however, that the essential cause of all phenomena of irritability must be situated in the protoplasm, because we regard irritability as a property of living organisms only. And as a matter of fact, in all cases where the phenomena of irritability have been successfully and sufficiently analysed, the investigations have led to the result that living protoplasm plays a chief part in the matter; though this is not intended to imply that a phenomenon of irritability is conditioned entirely and solely by the properties of protoplasm On the contrary, mechanisms which are influenced in a secondary manner only by the stimulated protoplasm determine to a large extent the final external character of a phenomenon of irritability, especially in a complex organ. At the same time it follows from what has been said, that all living cells, cell-tissues, and living organs of the plant must be irritable, according to our definition ; for they all contain protoplasm, and there is no doubt that all protoplasm is irritable, at least in certain conditions—i. e. it reacts to external stimuli in a way which lifeless bodies do not as a rule do ; although, as we shall see later, reactions occur even in crystals which present a very striking similarity to certain phenomena of irritability.

On the other hand, our definition of irritability excludes the assumption that every reaction of organised bodies whatever may be regarded as irritability For, in the first place, organised bodies, quite apart from their specific peculiarities, are also at the same time physical objects, and must react to external influences according to the laws of physics: for example, when the growing haulms of cereals, and other shoot-axes, bend beneath the pressure of the wind and then again become erect, this is simply in consequence of their elasticity, and thus of a physical property; and in like manner when the cell-membrane of a turgescent cell becomes extended, or contracts on the cessation of turgescence, that also is an action of a physical nature. If a long-stemmed plant is laid horizontally and left free to move, the stem at first bends more or less downwards, because it is flexible and elastic—that is one of its physical properties; but if we allow it to stay quietly in this position, we find after several or many hours that the still growing apical portion of the stem now ascends until it stands perfectly erect—and this is not a physical but a physiological phenomenon, which only occurs in a living plant, and only there when the part of the stem referred to is still growing   If possible, the accuracy of the proposition expressed above comes out still more distinctly in the case of some movements of the parts of plants, which in fact present great external similarity with some phenomena of irritability, but are nevertheless purely physical and mechanical actions, since they occur in dead though organised bodies.   The upper leaves of the common involucre of *Carlina acaulis*, a kind of Thistle, radiate outwards and downwards when the plant has long been dead, and remain in this position as long as it is dry; but on plunging such a dead flower-head in water, or letting it remain in very damp air, the leaf structures referred to become directed upwards and inwards, and the whole of the dried flower-head closes up; and if desiccation again follows later, it reopens—i. e. the involucral leaves again project outwards and downwards.   These changes ensue still more rapidly in the upper leaves of the involucre of another composite, *Myriocephalus*.   In both cases the movements mentioned are effected by short transverse zones on the lower part of the dried involucral leaves ; the cell-walls on the lower side at these places swell up more strongly when they imbibe water than those on the upper side, and when they dry they contract more strongly than those, thus causing the movements described.

The various movements of dry fruits and their parts, which, as has already been pointed out on pp. 210–211, may sometimes be very complicated, depend on similar phenomena due to the change in volume of cell-walls on the absorption and rejection of water.   In many other cases also something similar occurs I will mention only the so-called Rose of Jericho, a plant which belongs to the family Cruciferæ, and which grows wild in Egypt, though it may be easily cultivated in Europe.   Its radiating branches, on which are situated the ripe fruits, spread themselves out on the ground, and when the whole plant is dried and dead throw themselves inwards, very much as the five extended fingers of the hand are laid together in forming a closed fist   If the dried plant is moistened, the branches thus rolled together into a ball open out again.   This process is found to occur in some other plants also, e. g. an American species of *Lycopodium*; and again, the hygroscopic movements of the peristome of the Moss capsule (p. 150) depends on similar processes, and so with many other phenomena in the vegetable kingdom.   In all such cases, however, it is not phenomena of irritability but purely physical actions which come into play, such as the imbibition of water and the alteration in volume of the cell-walls concerned.

We now come to another very characteristic point, which distinguishes all phenomena of irritability, viz. *the disproportionality existing between the external stimulus and the ultimate action.* In the cases of movements of parts of plants due to imbibition and desiccation as just considered, there is an easily intelligible proportionality between cause and effect: when a certain quantity of water penetrates into the walls of cells, the latter become distended according to the volume of water, and upon this the movement depends. In like manner the bending of a flexible haulm of straw, or of a woody branch, corresponds to the pressure which acts from without and gives rise to the curvature, and we have the simplest case of such purely mechanical effects, for example, when an elastic ball is driven against another one of equal size and elasticity, as is well known, the former comes to rest because it has given up the whole of its momentum to the latter. All this has no resemblance to phenomena of irritability; on the contrary, a very characteristic point of the latter lies in the fact that neither the quantity nor the quality of a phenomenon of irritability need have any kind of similarity or proportionality to the stimulus, and it is simply on this that the peculiarly wonderful and even startling effects of irritability depend, and here probably we have the reason why until quite recently the phenomena of irritability, which are at bottom identical with those of life, were set off against those of the rest of nature as something entirely different, and regarded as the effects of a special force—vital force. A calm criticism of the prevailing circumstances, however, leads to an entirely different conclusion. The conspicuous inequality in kind and in degree between the cause and the effect arises rather from the fact that in the living irritable organ a series of causes are already in existence, which taken together with the external stimulus give rise to the effect. The disproportionality between cause and effect in irritability is simply and only apparent, not real, as will be brought forward still more clearly from subsequent considerations. In the first place, however, the main fact with which we are concerned may be illustrated by a few other examples

If growing stems or petioles are illuminated from one side for some time, they generally become curved in such a manner that the apex bends over towards the source of light There is no doubt that it is the rays of light which effect this curvature, and it is just as little doubtful that the mechanical energy of these light-rays would be far too insignificant to cause such a curvature of the parts of the plant; on the contrary, very peculiar mechanisms must exist in the latter which, on being stimulated by the rays of light, bring about this curvature Still more striking in this connection are the geotropic curvatures. If an upward-growing stem is laid horizontally, it curves upwards; if the same is done with a primary root, its apex curves downwards. The simple change of position of the axis of growth of these organs with regard to the radius of the earth and the direction of gravitation effects changes in the growth in length, which stand in no comprehensible mechanical relation whatever to the other effects of gravitation. That it is here, however, entirely and simply a matter of adjustment conditioned by the organisation of the plant, follows at once from the above-named circumstance, that the one part of the plant becomes curved upwards and the other downwards when its position with respect to the radius of the earth has been altered.

Similarly we meet with the disproportionality between cause and effect in cases where, by means of a slight touch on the under side of the motile organ, a leaf of

Mimosa suddenly falls down limp, and its parts become folded together, or when a similar effect is produced simply by sudden darkness. And matters are similar in all phenomena of irritability, not only in plants but also in animals, and in our own bodies. What qualitative similarity or quantitative proportionality exists, for example, between the vibrations of the luminiferous ether and our sensation of sight, the vibrations of the air and our sense of hearing? What I am here insisting on is still more evident in the innumerable reflex actions of the human body

It will lead to clearness if we again try to render intelligible the meaning of certain words, because by an inaccurate use of them at this stage the greatest confusion may be introduced into the matter, against which we must guard ourselves so much the more since the difficulties in the subject itself are sufficiently great, and should not be rendered still greater by indefinite language. It will be well to keep sharply apart from one another the three ideas, 'Stimulus,' 'Stimulation,' and 'Irritability' or 'irritable structure.'

Stimulus is the name which I give to any alteration in the environment of the irritable organs by means of which stimulation is caused. Experience shows that changes in the intensity of the light, variations of temperature, alterations of electrical conditions, instantaneous shocks, sudden pressure, etc may act as stimuli. Constant illumination, or constant temperature, etc, on the contrary, is not to be regarded as a stimulus However, it is conceivable that even with constant external conditions of life, the internal states of the irritable organs undergo change, and that thus their capacity for reacting towards unaltered external influences undergoes differences, and this must then have the same effect as if the influence of the external circumstances had been altered The main point is, that any change whatever, whether it originates from within or from without, is to be regarded as a stimulus; since if both the external and the internal conditions remain constant, no stimulus whatever appears to occur In most cases where phenomena of irritability are concerned, the accuracy of these reflections is at once clear, but there is a series of vital phenomena very frequently occurring, which can scarcely be grouped elsewhere than among the stimulations, but which nevertheless make their appearance with especial clearness just where the external circumstances are constant. These are the movements which I have previously designated autonomous or spontaneously periodic, and to which we shall return later still more in detail.

It has already been said that a conspicuous feature of the phenomena of irritability lies in that they correspond with the stimuli neither qualitatively nor quantitatively, and it is in this very fact that the essential distinction between phenomena of irritability and simply mechanical, physical, and chemical actions lies. It has moreover already been shown above in what the explanation of this remarkable circumstance essentially lies, viz. in the irritable structure of the organ.

It will perhaps contribute to the intelligibility of this statement if we here again figure to ourselves a few examples from inorganic nature. Something similar to a phenomenon of irritability occurs, for example, in the case of a heated steam-engine the valve of which is suddenly opened. Previously at rest, the mere opening of the valve puts the engine in motion and accomplishes a definite amount of work The possibility of this was already given in the tension of the steam and in the internal structure of the engine, there was wanting simply the external impulse, by means of which the valve was opened, to call forth the working of the engine, the movement of which however essentially depends on the construction and putting together of its parts. It is obvious that neither the mere movement of the hand in opening the valve, nor the mere tension of the steam thereby set in action, constitutes the cause of the working of a steam engine, but that this is rather to be sought to a great extent in the internal structure of the latter; and in this sense we have also to regard the internal structure of the plant, which is set in motion by opportune external changes, as the essential cause of phenomena of irritability.

Perhaps we obtain the clearest expression for the internal condition of an irritable organ by saying, that *its parts are in a condition of unstable equilibrium,* with the addition, however, that every disturbance of this unstable equilibrium will become sooner or later again compensated, whereby the irritable condition again reappears, since the peculiar characteristic of irritable organs consists in that, in consequence of a stimulus, a stimulation is in fact called forth—i. e a new condition, in which the same stimulus can no longer be effective—but that after some time the stimulation ceases, and the organ again returns into its original state, whence it can then again be driven to the same stimulation by the same stimulus. The peculiarity of irritable organs lies less in the fact that their parts can be set in motion in virtue of the unstable equilibrium, than in the fact that they subsequently again resume their irritable condition—their unstable equilibrium—spontaneously.

Let us dwell a little longer upon these matters We may look upon a house of cards, as built by a child, as a very well-known example of unstable equilibrium a slight push suffices to make the whole of the artificial structure tumble down. Here also we have a strikingly large effect consequent on a small cause, as is usually the case with phenomena of irritability; but the fallen card-house does not rebuild itself again on its own account, and is thereby distinguished from an irritable organ Something very similar occurs with crystals The same chemical compound, the same salt may often crystallise in two different forms, but so that the one crystalline form arises only under very definite and narrowly circumscribed external conditions, and corresponds to an unstable equilibrium of the molecules; while the other crystalline form of the same salt is stable. The one unstable arrangement of the molecules can therefore be transformed by insignificant external alterations into this second stable form, and this occurs in a manner which calls to mind very strikingly the phenomena of irritability of organisms Among the numerous examples known I will only dwell upon one, because I have myself had the opportunity of becoming more closely acquainted with it. It was first, however, described in Gmelin's *'Handbuch der Chemie,'* B I, 1843, p. 95 'Potassium nitrate (saltpetre) usually crystallises in prisms of the arragonite-form If, however, a drop of the potassium nitrate dissolved in water is allowed to evaporate on a glass plate, and the crystals observed under the microscope as they form, it is noticed that in addition to crystals of the arragonite form, obtuse rhombohedrons of the calcspar form also are formed at the edges of the drop On further growth, as the two kinds of crystals come into proximity, the rhombohedra become rounded off and dissolve, because they are more easily soluble, while the prisms of the arragonite-form go on growing. If the two kinds of crystals come into direct contact, the rhombohedral ones instantly become cloudy, the surface uneven, and prisms soon grow out from many points of their margins. On contact with other solid bodies also, the rhombohedra are transformed if still moist. If the liquid is in very thin films and dries up around the rhombohedra before they are destroyed, the crystals retain their form for weeks without efflorescing, and endure moderate pressure of foreign bodies without change; but with stronger pressure or scratching, as well as on mere contact with a prismatic crystal of saltpetre, they become transformed into the prismatic form—a delicate cloud spreads over the surface, starting from the point of contact, and they now behave to solid bodies like a heap of fine dust, remaining at the same time transparent however.'

I myself observed in a group of rhombohedra of potassium nitrate, in mutual contact in a drop under the microscope, that when a prismatic crystal of the same salt was pushed into the drop and came in contact with one of the rhombohedra, the latter not only at once became cloudy, but the rhombohedra which were in contact with one another were also progressively rendered cloudy. This clouding, moreover, indicated the breaking up of the rhombohedron into innumerable small prisms of the arragonite form. The most remarkable point in the matter is, that it is only contact with saltpetre crystals of the arragonite form which is able to call forth this alteration in the rhombohedric saltpetre crystals, for the quadratic tablets of potassium ferrocyanide and the triclinic prisms of potassium chromate may be in contact with the rhombohedral saltpetre crystals in a common mother-liquor, without any change whatever occurring

These processes have one point in common with the phenomena of irritability in organisms; viz. that an entirely specific and at the same time mechanically insignificant external influence produces an effect which corresponds to it neither quantitatively nor qualitatively And similarly also in many other cases. Thus Gmelin says (loc. cit.), 'Mercuric iodide (HgI_2) crystallises at ordinary temperatures in red quadratic tables; on sublimation at a high temperature, on the contrary, in yellow rhombic tables. The red crystals whenever they are heated become yellow, and again turn red on cooling. The yellow crystals obtained by sublimation remain unaltered on cooling, but on rubbing or contact the point touched turns red, and this colour extends itself through the entire group of crystals, with a movement as if the mass were animated. The external form of the yellow crystals is here maintained, while the molecules take up the position of the other crystalline system. Each time these are heated they become yellow, and again turn red on cooling.'

Among numerous other examples I will only quote the behaviour of sulphur, mentioned by Roscoe and Schorlemmer. If a hot solution of sulphur in alcohol, oil of turpentine, or carbon disulphide is quickly cooled, there separate out first a few monoclinic and then rhombic crystals. The rhombic ones correspond to the stable equilibrium at ordinary temperatures, since Mitscherlich found that monoclinic sulphur (which is formed on quickly cooling from a high temperature) slowly passes over at ordinary temperatures into rhombic, the monoclinic crystal being transformed into a group of rhombic crystals This transformation proceeds more rapidly if the monoclinic crystals are shaken or scraped, or exposed to the sun, and a definite quantity of heat is set free in the process. ·

I have quoted these remarkable processes occurring in crystals in illustration of the fact that the same chemical substance is able, according to circumstances, to have its molecules arranged either in unstable or stable equilibrium, and that by means of certain external impulses the unstable arrangement may pass over into the stable one. The majority of the phenomena of irritability, however, give the impression that in their case also conditions of unstable equilibrium are transformed into conditions of stable equilibrium by means of small external influences. This comes out with especial clearness in such cases as the irritable leaves of the Mimosæ, where a light touch or other mechanically insignificant influence suffices to transform the state of unstable equilibrium of the organ suddenly into a new state, which we might regard as the stable one; only of course with the difference already mentioned, that in this case, when the stimulus has ceased to act, the new condition returns again to the previous one—the stable condition returns to the unstable one. There is, however, yet another series of facts which support this view. Just as the unstable crystalline form of certain salts continues only within narrow limits of external conditions, passing over into the stable form when they are transgressed, so also the irritable condition of an organ exists only within certain limits of external influences, during specially favourable circumstances; if these are transgressed the irritable—i.e. the unstable—condition ceases to be, and the organ loses its irritability, i.e. it assumes a condition of stable equilibrium. It is of special interest for an insight into the phenomena of irritability to take these facts somewhat closely into consideration. this I did in the year 1863 in a treatise entitled ' *Vorubergehende Starrezustände periodisch beweglicher und reizbarer Pflanzenorgane.*'

From among the details in the work just mentioned I may take the following statements as examples :—

(1) Temporary cold-rigor occurs in the motile organs of *Mimosa pudica*, the conditions being otherwise favourable, when the temperature of the surrounding air remains for some hours below 15° C. The lower the temperature falls below 15° C. the more rapidly the rigor sets in; the first to disappear is the irritability for contact and shaking, later that for the influence of light, and finally even the spontaneous periodic movement. When the temperature of the air is below 22° C. the lateral leaflets of *Hedysarum gyrans* are rigid, according to Kabsch.

(2) Temporary heat-rigor occurs in *Mimosa*, in moist air at 40° C. within 1 hour; in air at 45° C. within 30 minutes; in air at 49–50° C. within a few minutes. The irritability returns after a few hours in air at a favourable temperature. In water the cold-rigor of *Mimosa* occurs even at a higher temperature (viz. within 15 minutes at 16–17° C.) and the heat-rigor even at a lower temperature (viz. at 36–40° in 15 minutes) than in the air. During the heat-rigor, in air as well as in water, the leaflets are closed, as after stimulation; but the stalks are directed steeply upwards, whereas in the stimulated condition they point downwards.

(3) Temporary dark-rigor. If plants with periodically motile leaves, which are also irritable for light or shaking, such as *Mimosa, Acacia, Trifolium, Phaseolus, Oxalis*, are placed in darkness, the spontaneously periodic movements occur, apart from the changes in position effected by the light stimulus, only so much the more distinctly, and also the irritability for contact remains at first undisturbed. But this motile condition disappears completely when the darkness continues for one or several

[3] Q q

days, rigor due to darkness sets in.   If then a plant which has passed into the state of rigor due to darkness is again placed in the light, the motile condition reappears after several hours, or, according to circumstances, only after several days' exposure to the light.

Very profound darkness is by no means necessary for inducing this condition of rigor, however; on the contrary, it sets in when a plant which requires much light, as *Mimosa*, remains exposed for several days to deficient illumination, such as prevails at a distance from the windows in the interior of an ordinary dwelling-room.

In contrast to the rigor due to darkness I have designated the normal condition of motility caused by the alternation of day and night as Phototonus.   From what has been said, then, such a plant after it has been placed in the dark is found for some time longer (several hours or even days) in the condition of phototonus, which then gradually disappears; in the same way the plant under normal vital conditions is in the condition of phototonus during the night   A plant which has passed into the state of rigor due to darkness, on the other hand, retains this rigor for some time (hours or even days) after being placed in the light.   Both conditions of the plant therefore pass over into one another only slowly

Even on the setting-in of rigor due to darkness, in the case of *Mimosa* the irritability for shaking disappears first, then the periodically spontaneous movement. In like manner a *Mimosa* which has passed quite into the state of darkness-rigor regains first its periodic movements, and then the irritability.

The position of the various parts of the leaves of *Mimosa* in rigor due to darkness is different from that produced by darkness on phototonic plants, and even different from that in heat-rigor. in rigor due to darkness the leaves are fully expanded, the secondary petioles directed downwards, and the primary stalk almost horizontal.

Alterations in the intensity of the light act as stimuli to movement only on healthy plants which are in a state of phototonus. leaves in a state of rigor due to darkness do not react to variations in the intensity of the light, until owing to long-continued illumination they have regained the phototonus, when they then become stimulated to movements by changes in the intensity of the light.   I convinced myself of this in the case of *Acacia lophantha*.   A specimen had been left for five days in the dark, where for forty-eight hours it had given up nearly every trace of its spontaneous periodic movements.   It was then placed in a window where, the sky being cloudy, it placed its leaflets decidedly downwards within two hours, and then small changes of position took place in the secondary petioles also, in this condition, however, the plant was nevertheless in a state of darkness-rigor, for when it was placed in the dark about 12 o'clock (noon) with another plant of the same kind which was in phototonus, its leaves did not change their position, and its leaflets remained open, whereas the other one within an hour assumed the most pronounced nocturnal position and its leaflets closed.   Both were then placed in the window, where the plant in a state of dark-rigor opened its leaves in one hour, the sky being cloudy. In the evening of this day the lower six leaves remained still rigid and open, but the upper eight or nine leaves were closed: next morning, however, all the leaves again expanded to the normal diurnal position.   *Trifolium incarnatum* behaves in a similar manner, although differing in details.

It is to be noticed that in the case of the plants which I have observed, the positions of the leaves in rigor due to darkness resemble the diurnal position much more than the nocturnal position of those of phototonic plants.

(4) Temporary drought-rigor.   I have only observed this in plants of *Mimosa pudica*.   If the soil in the pots in which they are growing is left for some time without watering, the irritability of the motile organs visibly diminishes as the drought increases, and an almost complete rigor then sets in, the primary petioles stand horizontally, and the leaflets are expanded.   In this case the leaves which have become non-irritable to stimuli are neither withered nor drooping; but watering the soil causes a return of irritability within two or three hours.

(5) Temporary rigor due to chemical influences.   In this category I include particularly the condition termed by Dutrochet *Asphyxia*, which occurs in Mimosæ when they remain for a time in the vacuum of the air-pump.   During the exhaustion the leaves become folded together, probably in consequence of the shaking; then the leaflets expand, the petioles become erect, and while the leaves assume a position similar to that in rigor due to darkness, they remain rigid, and are neither periodically motile nor irritable to shaking   When brought into the air the plant again becomes motile.   It can scarcely be doubted that the vacuum causes the rigor essentially by withdrawing the oxygen of the air and therefore suspending respiration

Kabsch confirmed these statements, and showed that the stamens of *Berberis*, *Mahonia*, and *Helianthemum* also lose their irritability in a vacuum, regaining it in the air.

The disappearance of irritability of the stamens mentioned, in nitrogen and hydrogen, is according to Kabsch probably also to be referred to the mere suspension of respiration· the irritability returns on the access of air   It must, on the contrary, be regarded as a positively injurious chemical effect— poisoning—when the irritability of the stamens of *Berberis* disappears in pure carbon dioxide, or in air containing more than 40 $\%$ of that gas, as the same observer states to be the case.   If they remain for three or four hours in carbon dioxide the irritability returns only after several hours in the air   Carbonic oxide gas mixed with air to the extent of 20–25 $\%$ 'annihilates' the irritability; whereas nitrous oxide gas behaves indifferently.   The stamens placed in nitric oxide, on the contrary, become bent after $1\frac{1}{2}$ to 2 minutes towards the pistil, and lose their irritability.   Ammonia gas appears to produce a transitory condition of rigor after a few minutes.

Even in pure oxygen, according to Kabsch, a condition of rigor sets in after $\frac{1}{2}$–1 hour, from which the stamens recover subsequently in the air.

The vapours of chloroform and ether suspend the irritability of the motile organs (for variations of light also?) without destroying the life, if the effect does not continue too long.   If entire plants or separated branches of Mimosa are placed in an atmosphere highly charged with these vapours, the irritability may disappear even in a few minutes.   If the organs have been previously stimulated, they nevertheless now rise up (without being irritable), at the same time becoming more rigid.   The action of the vapours of chloroform or ether is a purely local one, only the organs directly exposed to them losing their irritability.

(6) By means of frequent stimulations (vibrations) repeated at short intervals

the pulvini of Mimosæ are put into a condition in which they do not respond to stimuli, although they rise during the continued stimulation, and assume a position of rest as if they had been left alone after the first shock. The irritability for new shocks—i.e. descent under their influence—does not begin to be restored until 5–10 minutes after the cessation of the shocks.

(7) Temporary rigor due to electric influence was found by Kabsch to occur in the gynostemium of *Stylidium*. A feeble current acted as a stimulus like vibrations, a stronger one caused a loss of irritability, which returned again, however, after half-an-hour. In *Hedysarum gyrans*, on the other hand, the leaflets which had become immovable in cold-rigor (at 22° C.) were set in movement by the action of induction currents.

There are two other observations regarding stimulation which have led to particular remark, and even astonishment; these are the propagation of a stimulus, and the after-effects of it. Careful consideration, especially based on the phenomena described at the beginning of the present lecture, shows, however, that both the propagation and the after-effect of a stimulus can be by no means accidental peculiarities, but that both must be necessary characters of all phenomena of irritability.

The propagation of a stimulus, regarded in the first place merely as matter of fact, is particularly well seen in the Mimosæ and in tendrils. If, for example, any one of the small leaflets of a leaf, on a shoot of *Mimosa* with five or six leaves, is stimulated by means of the hot focus of a burning glass, all the other leaflets of the same leaf gradually fold together, and after a short time the large motile organ at the base of the main petiole also becomes bent, and again after a few seconds the stimulation extends to the nearest neighbouring leaf, then to the succeeding one, and so on, till at last all the leaves of the shoot have made the movement. this of course only happens if the *Mimosa* is in a condition of the highest irritability. In the case of long tendrils the propagation of the stimulus is effected in such a way that a curvature results first at that point of the tendril which is immediately in contact with a solid body; the curving action proceeds from this point, however, both upwards and downwards in the tendril. The latter then forms, in the course of a few minutes or hours, a wide loop which narrows more and more, and closes on the thin support: then follows the free end of the tendril, which winds itself fast round the support, and finally, after several hours, the stimulation makes itself evident also in that part of the tendril which lies between the clasped support and the base of the tendril. This portion becomes rolled up spirally like a corkscrew.

These examples illustrate particularly clearly both the propagation in space and the after-effect in time of a stimulus. As another example, especially concerning the after-effect, I may refer in anticipation to the heliotropic and geotropic curvatures. If, for instance, an erect shoot-axis growing vigorously in length (e. g. seedling stems of Buckwheat, Indian Cress, Mustard, the flowering scape of the Crown Imperial, &c.) is illuminated from one side, even for only one or two hours, when there is at first no very noticeable curvature, and if the plants are then left for a time in profound darkness, the curvature towards the previous source of light already introduced continues for some hours, and may become very considerable.

The case is very similar with geotropic effects: if an erect growing stem (e. g of *Dipsacus*) is allowed to remain for one or two hours in a horizontal position, here also the curvature is as yet scarcely noticeable. If the shoot is now placed erect, and thus brought into a position where the stimulation due to gravitation ceases, the stimulation already introduced during the horizontal position nevertheless goes on acting; the stem continues to curve for several hours, the concavity becoming more and more pronounced on that side which was turned upwards in the previous horizontal position And no doubt in the case of every phenomenon of irritability there is not only a propagation in space of the stimulus, but also an after-effect in time, although not always so evident as in these cases.

As regards the explanation of these phenomena, it may be said quite generally, first, respecting the after-effect in time, that every effect whatever in Nature occupies a certain time — in fact Time itself is nothing more than the course of natural phenomena. When a cannon is fired off at 1000 meters distance, the flash of light is seen almost simultaneously, because the movements of light travel so exceedingly rapidly; the report however is not perceived until several seconds later, because the waves of sound travel much more slowly. The interval of time lying between cause and effect depends on the properties of the medium in which the effect is propagated. And the same is the case with the phenomena of irritability; it depends on the irritable structure of an organ whether the external stimulus or shock sets it in motion suddenly—i. e. in a very short time—or whether the given shock requires a longer time for its action. If the leaf of a *Mimosa* is irritable in a high degree, a vibration acts almost instantaneously, and the same is the case with a leaf of *Dionæa*, but if these organs are feebly—i. e less—irritable, then the movement caused by the shock is slow. Or, as we may also say, the more unstable the equilibrium in the molecular structure of the irritable organ is, the more rapidly will any shock acting as a stimulus set the organ in motion. Nevertheless it may also depend upon other circumstances how much time intervenes between the external influence and the subsequent visible stimulation: the more complicated the mutually acting causes and effects are which finally bring about the visible stimulation movement the longer will be the time consumed in the matter. Since then the effects of stimulation in general usually depend upon very complicated chains of causes, they also as a rule make their appearance slowly, and this is especially true of most of the stimulations occurring in plants. It was this very slowness which caused the general fact of the irritability of plants to be so long overlooked, and subsequently under-estimated.

If the effects induced by contact, vibration, alterations of light and temperature, &c. occurred with the same rapidity in plants as do the corresponding stimulations in animals, plants would appear no less irritable than animals; and if we imagine the stimulations which are continually occurring in plants to take place a hundred times as rapidly as they really do, our gardens, fields, and meadows would present very strange and uncanny movements

The rapidity with which stimuli call forth their corresponding effects is in animals, as a rule, much greater. Between the opening of the closed eye and the perception of light scarcely any time at all seems to pass, and in like manner a sudden wounding of the finger seems to call forth its reflex motion instantaneously. But no physiologist doubts that in both cases a small interval of time elapses, and compared with the enormous velocities with which cause and effect may follow one another in the domain of pure physics and chemistry, even the perceptions of our senses are but very slow processes

Respecting the propagation in space of stimuli in plants, then, we may here refer to quite similar relations among purely physical processes. A physical effect is scarcely ever confined exactly to the spot where the effective cause acts, and this is to be explained simply from the fact that the material parts of the body in which the action takes place are mutually held together and arranged by means of forces. If a stretched string is jerked at one point, the whole string vibrates; if one end of a long train of gun-powder is set on fire, the whole train explodes progressively, and so on. And we have to conceive of the propagation of a stimulus in an organ in a similar manner. If, for example, a single place of an irritable tendril is stimulated by contact with a solid body, this means that at this spot the unstable equilibrium in the molecular structure of the organ is disturbed, but the neighbouring parts are also connected with those immediately disturbed, and stand in a certain equilibrium with these, so that if this equilibrium is disturbed at one point, the disturbance is propagated to the neighbouring points also, and the propagated disturbance acts again and again on neighbouring points, so that at last parts of the organ far distant from the points originally stimulated are set in motion; and it is just in these things that the previously mentioned disproportionality between stimulus and stimulation comes out particularly clearly. But in this respect also the effects of stimulation in animals usually surpass those in plants. In tendrils, irritable Mimosæ, and in many other cases, the propagation of the stimulus proceeds only exceedingly slowly: several seconds, minutes, or even hours pass before the local stimulation has traversed a path of 10 to 20 or 30 cm. This takes place much more rapidly in the case of animals, where, moreover, special organs exist—viz the nerves—for the rapid propagation of the stimulations: these are wanting in plants. But even in the nerves of man himself the stimulus advances only about 30 meters per second, and this must be termed an exceedingly slow movement, compared with the inconceivable velocity of an electric current or of a ray of light, or even compared only with the velocity of sound in air.

We may, as already mentioned, regard the numerous periodic movements in the vegetable kingdom as a special category of phenomena of irritability. In cases where the external conditions are quite constant, where the temperature, light or darkness, or the degree of moisture is perfectly constant, where no vibration occurs, and so forth, periodically motile organs, as found particularly often among leaves, perform movements of such a kind as to bend sometimes to one, sometimes to the other side, either with considerable velocity or very slowly. Thus we find continual vibrations to and fro in the case of the small lateral leaflets of the compound leaf of *Hedysarum gyrans* (an Indian papilionaceous plant allied to our Sainfoin) when the temperature and illumination are high and constant; and in the same way the leaves of *Mimosa, Oxalis, Trifolium, Acacia*, and other plants go on moving in constant darkness—i. e. their motile organs slowly bend upwards and downwards by turns.

The most astonishing point in such cases, to those unacquainted with science, lies in the fact that effects are here taking place for which no apparent causes are present. When a movement is induced by a mechanical shock, however slight, or by a mere alteration in the intensity of the light or of the temperature, &c., this obviously accords with our requirements of causality; but in the processes mentioned that is simply not the case, and it is just this which must impel us to seek for the causes or shocks which produce the movements named. At present, however, we can only offer suggestions in this connection. We may, if need be, imagine that by means of the continually recurring chemical processes in the living parts of plants, changes are produced in the state of the protoplasm, and by this again in the turgescence of the cells, and if the latter are more pronounced sometimes on the one, sometimes on the other side, the parts of the organ concerned must bend alternately to and fro. Now this is of course simply a hypothesis, because we are seeking a cause which renders these phenomena explicable. We have it is true already met with the fact that the excretion of water in decapitated root-stocks exhibits a periodically varying course, which is apparently independent of external impulses, and in the same way we found a periodicity in growth in length; and this presents very great similarity with the periodic movements referred to, i.e. the periodically varying nutations of growing stems, tendrils, and so forth, for which likewise external impulses are wanting, or at least appear to be wanting. We thus find ourselves here on the boundary of a still very obscure domain of science, and in such cases it is often an advantage even to be able to avoid the grosser errors. But such an error would decidedly exist in the assumption that periodic phenomena must necessarily be due to periodically varying causes—an error which, as it almost seems, prevails in the whole literature of this province, although there is by no means a lack of examples showing that, in the domain of mechanical and physical science, periodic movements are produced by constant causes which do not vary periodically. The periodic vibrations up and down of the haulms in a field of corn are due to the pressure of a constant current of wind and the constant elasticity of the haulms, and thus we have the interesting phenomenon of wave-motion in a field of corn In the same way the periodically varying action of a hydraulic ram is effected by the constant flowing of water into the machine itself, other circumstances also being constant. Nay, even the periodic alternations of day and night and of winter and summer arise from the constant revolution of the earth, and its constant course round the sun.

It would lead us into very tedious and difficult developments of ideas if I were to attempt to show how periodically varying phenomena must proceed from causes which act constantly; it suffices here to make the fact evident as such, because it protects us from the error of regarding it as necessary to refer the periodic movements of many organs of plants to a periodic variation of their causes. There are, however, also many other likewise periodic changes in the vegetable kingdom, which can be easily referred to definite periodically varying causes · for instance, the so-called sleep-movements of leaves, and the periodic opening and closing of many flowers. In the case of the phenomena here under consideration it is not so, however.

Nevertheless, we are warranted in regarding the so-called spontaneous or independent periodic movements as phenomena of irritability, just as animal physiologists place the periodic pulsations of the heart in the series of phenomena of animal irritability. While it is in other cases the first object of research to understand the course of a manifestation of irritability from a known external impulse, in the present case on the contrary the first problem is to seek for the impulse, because we premise on the basis of the principle of causality that such an impulse must actually exist. The preceding considerations will at least have made it clear that the constant course of molecular and atomistic processes which constitute life in general may give rise to periodic alterations in the interior of the cells, and we may regard these latter again simply as stimuli, from which the visible periodic movements arise as effects.

I have repeatedly had cause to refer to certain resemblances between the phenomena of irritability in the vegetable kingdom and those of the animal body, thus touching a province of investigation which has hitherto been far too little cultivated. In the last instance, indeed, I might say animal and vegetable life must of necessity agree in all essential points, including the phenomena of irritability also, since it is established that the animal organism is constructed entirely and simply from the organic substances produced by plants, and ultimately it is simply from the properties of these substances that all vital movements both of plants and animals are to be explained. Since it is possible for not only other animals but even man to be nourished by seeds and tubers of plants, and the substance of the human body produced by this nutriment is able to carry out all sensitive perceptions, all the periodic motions of the heart, and finally also the functions of the entire nervous system, including those of the brain, we must refer it to the properties of those substances which have been produced by plants from mineral matters, water, and carbon dioxide under the influence of sunlight.

Returning from these general considerations to definite comparisons between the animal and the plant, I would make special mention of that exceedingly remarkable phenomenon in animal life, termed by its great discoverer, Johannes Muller, the specific energies of the sensory nerves. As is well known, we understand by this the fact that for instance the optic nerve responds to any given excitation whatever with the sensation of light: true, this sensation is as a rule called forth by the vibrations of the luminiferous ether, but even electric currents or mere concussion or diseased conditions impel the optic nerve to the sensation of light. In the same way the auditory nerve is impelled to the perception of sound not merely by waves of sound, but by every change which affects it, and similarly with the remaining organs of sense.

Now I pointed out several years ago that even the organs of plants are provided with similar specific energies. Irritable organs in plants are indeed, like the sense-organs of animals, sensitive to a definite category of stimuli, but they can very often be affected by other stimuli also, and in this case the stimulation is always the same. This appears most distinctly, for example, in the case of growing internodes and leaves. If they are illuminated from one side they become curved, and if brought out of their normal position they are caused to make exactly similar curvatures; the one mode possible for responding to any stimulus whatever is simply this curving. The matter only obtains its full significance by means of the fact, which I rendered clear, that every individual plant-organ responds to the influence of light as well as to that of gravitation in a manner specifically peculiar to it, and it is upon this that the previously mentioned anisotropy of the parts of plants depends. No less clear is the specific energy of tendrils: as a rule their irritable movement results from gentle contact with a solid body, but vibration as well as cutting off or burning the apex of the tendril causes its upper side to curve, since it grows more rapidly than the lower side, and these curvatures only differ in the different cases because external mechanical conditions influence the course of curvature. The identity of the effect of stimulation in cases where totally different stimuli act on the growing root-tips is particularly striking: illumination from one side, geotropic action, pressure on a solid body, the influence of adjacent moist surfaces, and, as it appears from Elfving's recent researches, even constant electric currents produce exactly the same kinds of curvatures. The organ possesses only this one mode of responding to stimuli of the most various kinds In our subsequent consideration of the phenomena of irritability in Mimosæ, when the details are more closely examined, we shall moreover be permitted to obtain a deeper insight into the specific energy, since we shall there be in a position to understand the mechanism of stimulation generally, and therefore also to comprehend why entirely different stimuli must call forth the same effect in the organ.

In concluding these considerations there are still a few remarks to be made on the significance of irritability for the life of the plant generally. Clothed in words somewhat different from those employed at the beginning of the present lecture, we may define irritability as the mode in which a given organism, or a definite organ belonging to it, reacts to the external world. On this continuous reaction between the external world and organic structure depends generally the life not only of plants, but of animals also, as was described in detail in Lecture XII The organism itself is only the machine, consisting of various parts, and which must be set in motion by the action of external forces: it depends upon its structure what effects these external forces produce in it. It would betray a very low level of scientific culture to see in this comparison a degradation of the organism, since in a machine, although only constructed by human hands, there lies the result of the most profound and careful thought and high intelligence, so far as its structure is concerned, and in it there subsequently become effective the same forces of Nature which in other combinations constitute the vital forces of an organ. The comparison of organic life with inorganic processes can thus only be held as a debasement of the former, if one has become so foolish as to look upon the latter as something low and common, whereas the incomprehensible magnitude and all-pervading power of Nature is equally evident in both cases

If then irritability is, as said, fundamentally nothing other than the reaction of the organs towards the outside world, determined by means of their structure, which in fact argues by itself a similarity in kind of both, it follows thence directly that the phenomena of irritability both in the vegetable and animal kingdom must in the main be full of purpose. What I understand by this has already been stated at the conclusion of Lecture I: all those adaptations in the organism are purposeful, which contribute to its maintenance, and insure its existence. This is not to say that every individual irritability is at once or absolutely decisive for the life of an organism, since organisms are fortunately not so perfectly adapted to external conditions; but we may probably say that, on the whole, the possibility of life depends on the co-operation of the irritabilities of the various organs. To emphasise one point only; how could an ordinary terrestrial plant live if its roots were not impelled by various kinds of irritabilities—heliotropism, geotropism, sensitiveness to contact, damp surfaces, &c.—to penetrate into the soil in order to collect nutritive substances and to obtain a hold-fast, while the assimilating shoots and organs of reproduction are impelled by irritabilities of other kinds to grow forth above the substratum and receive the vivifying influence of light, in order to assimilate and bear fruit?

By this example we are led on to yet another point of great importance, namely, the fact that by means of the same external influences reactions exactly opposite in kind, though otherwise similar in nature, may be called forth, so that we may in fact speak of a positive and a negative heliotropism for instance; and a similar contrast is noticeable in the case of other reactions also. Of course the facts here coming into consideration can only be rendered clear in succeeding lectures, but so much may be said even here, in anticipation of more exact knowledge of them, that if the same external cause induces exactly opposite effects in the organs, the explanation of this must simply be sought in the different structure of the organs. If one organ when illuminated from one side becomes curved so as to be concave on the side turned towards the source of light, while another becomes convex on that side, the cause can only lie in the internal structure of the organ. But it is just on such differences of structure that the great variety of reactions which the most different plant-organs exhibit towards the same external influences depends; and, fundamentally, all that we term Biology—the modes of life of organisms—depends upon the fact that different organs react differently towards the same external influences, and these reactions differ not only qualitatively but also quantitatively, the finest gradations existing in both cases.

LECTURE XXXV.

IRRITABILITY AND MOBILITY OF PROTOPLASMIC STRUCTURES.

THE phenomena to be described here have already been in part superficially examined in Lecture VI, but only a few of the chief points were there touched upon ; this was necessary in order to give those still unacquainted with the nature of the vegetable cell an approximate idea of the nature of protoplasm What has there been said may therefore serve as an introduction to the present subject, and I may at once pass on without preliminary explanations to the subject itself. Here also there is no lack of bewildering variety in the phenomena, and this affects the treatment of the subject the more, since we are as yet by no means in a position to refer the irritabilities and movements of protoplasm to any general principle whatever. At present it is scarcely possible to speak of a comprehension of the processes from the point of view of mechanics, indeed in many cases the merely sensible apprehension of the processes, which are for the most part microscopical in range, presents great difficulties even to a trained eye. Since in these lectures I avoid on principle entering into difficult questions with discursive and technical discussions, and while with respect to this point I refer to the notes at the end of the lecture, I shall select from the variety of phenomena only a series of such as we may regard as different types. This will perhaps best conduce to the reader obtaining a clear idea of the matter

The protoplasmic structures of which the movements and irritability are particularly conspicuous to the observer are the swarm-spores of many Algæ and some Fungi already occasionally referred to, and the antherozoids (also in other respects similar) of the Mosses and Vascular Cryptogams. Swarm-spores are naked, sharply-defined protoplasmic bodies, usually of the shape of a fowl's egg the larger thicker half, in the case of those Algæ which contain chlorophyll, being green, the anterior narrower moiety colourless. Deviations from this common form, however, appear in various degrees : the size also differs extremely, the swarm-spores of some Vaucherias, for example, being visible in a good light even to the unaided eye of a sharp observer, while the smallest forms can only be seen with high powers of the microscope. Between these extremes are found all possible degrees of bulk. It may be noted by the way, though it need concern us no further here, that many swarm-spores are true sexual organs, while others are not. Some of the minute organisms belonging here are during their whole period of life in oscillatory motion, in others this motile stage is very soon over, they become fixed to some body by the end which swims forwards, and which now developes into an anchoring root, and then begin to grow. This question also has no interest for us just now—we are concerned only with the mobility and irritability. That this can in no way be due to the contained chlorophyll, follows at once from the fact that there are also swarm-spores—those of the Fungi—which contain no chlorophyll, and in like manner the antherozoids or spermatozoids, like them so far as motility and irritability are concerned though usually very different in shape, are devoid of chlorophyll. Here also I exclude those structures which in other respects resemble swarm-spores in origin and function, in which the movements of translation are produced partly or wholly by alterations in the form of the body, and where we have thus to do with creeping movements, the typical form of which, moreover, we shall subsequently consider in the case of plasmodia. Still more definitely to be excluded here are the movements of the Oscillatoriæ, Bacteria, Bacillariæ or Diatomaceæ, and similar cases, since we are still utterly in the dark even as to the preliminaries with respect to the nature of their movement.

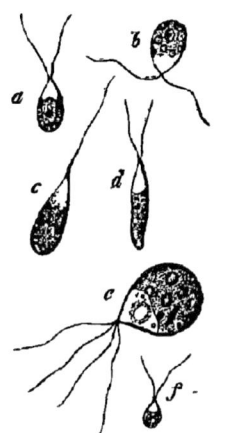

FIG 356 —Swarm-spores (Zoospores) *a b* of *Acetabularia mediterranea*, *c d* of *Botrydium granulatum* (see Fig *a*, p 4), *e f* of *Ulothrix zonata a b d f* are sexual zoospores, or so called gametes

The true swarm-spores and spermatozoa thus do not change their form and size during the movement. They owe their locomotion to certain very minute organs which even at the best and with very high powers are visible only with difficulty. these are the so-called Cilia, which may be compared as to form and mode of motion to an oscillating whip-lash, and that is about all that we perceive in them. As a rule, the cilia are situated at the narrower anterior end, singly, or more often in pairs, or fours; in *Œdogonium* (p. 82, Fig. 79) a circlet of numerous cilia exists at the boundary between the hyaline and green portions. The large swarmers of *Vaucheria* (p. 108) are covered with innumerable very short cilia, as with a dense pile of velvet. Some spermatozoids also, especially those of *Equisetum* and the Marsiliaceæ, possess very-numerous cilia, which are also very long. In some small swarmers, e g. the spermatozoa of the Vaucheriæ, one cilium is situated at the side, the other on the pointed anterior apex, and in the case of the Euglenæ so common in foul ponds, and others, there is only a single very long active cilium at the pointed anterior end: in *Chytridium*, on the other hand, the single cilium is at the posterior end, like a rudder. As an especially interesting case again, mention may be made of the Volvocineæ, a subdivision of the Algæ: since here entire cell-families, consisting of 4, 8, 16, 32 or more individuals formed exactly like swarm-spores, make their movements in common because they are held together by a common exceedingly watery delicate cellulose envelope, so that the family constitutes a quadrangular tablet, or a sphere, or an ellipsoid, from the surface of which the long whip-like cilia of the individual elements project in pairs into the water.

The various arrangements of these minute motile organs, which however always produce essentially the same kind of movement, shows already that a complicated problem of mechanics is here concerned, since we know almost nothing further of the movements of cilia than that they make serpentine or lashing movements in the water, from which the motion of the entire body then results. Where numerous cilia move simultaneously in this way, it is even questionable whether their oscillations are always simultaneous and alike in character; in fact it is not necessary to assume this in the case of the production of the ordinary rotating movement of swarmers, since we know from Thuret's investigations that the relatively large oospheres of the Fucaceæ are set in rotating motion by the convulsive movements of the numerous spermatozoa clinging to its periphery—this rotation evidently results from the very irregular strokes of these extremely minute (in comparison with the oosphere itself) bodies.

Among the most significant mechanical points is the always considerable size of the swarm-spores in comparison with the extreme minuteness of the motile organs,

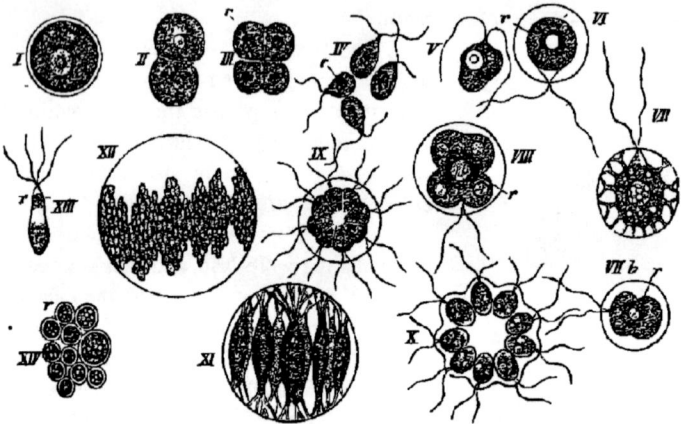

FIG. 357.—*Stephanosphaera pluvialis* (after Cohn and Wichura) *I* resting spore, *II—VIII* swarm-spores produced by the division of *I*   *VIII—X* the family produced by division of one swarm spore, *XI* a mature family rotating, *XII—XIV* microspores produced by division of the cells of *XI*

the cilia. Of course their work is essentially facilitated by the fact that the swarm-spore possesses nearly the same specific gravity as the water; but it is obvious that it must always be a little heavier, owing to the specifically heavier proteid substance of the protoplasm. Dead swarm-spores therefore always sink to the bottom The swimming itself, so far as it only concerns suspension in the water, is thus work done by the cilia, but the friction which must necessarily take place during the rotation and progressive motion at the surfaces of the swarm-spore is perhaps greater even than this. From all that is known so far we must probably ascribe to the cilia also the irritability of which we shall consider the different manifestations later on.

The form of movement which all the objects here under consideration exhibit consists in that in the first place they rotate on their own longitudinal axes, usually swimming forwards at the same time, the movement is thus approximately that of a planet with its diurnal rotation and simultaneous flight away into space, or that of a shot which is discharged through the air from a rifled barrel.   Naegeli seems to have been the first not only to exactly study the motion of swarm-spores, but also to criticise them from the physical and mechanical point of view.   It may therefore be of service to the reader to be made acquainted with his exact expressions as to the apparent and true velocity in the progressive movement of swarm-spores.

'The movement of swarm-cells,' says Naegeli[1], 'is usually described as very active, and the rapidity with which they bustle about is no trivial reason for their having been designated animals.   In this it has often been forgotten that one is looking through the lenses of the microscope, and that the swarm-cells are in reality much less active than they appear to be.   When we observe them with a power of 300 diameters, it is not only that the cells appear to us 300 times larger, but the motion also appears 300 times more rapid, since the space traversed in a given time is in fact also increased under the microscope 300 fold.   In a watch laid under the microscope, with a power of 100 diameters we see the apex of the long hand engaged in fairly rapid trembling and jerking movements, while the apex of the short hand proceeds extremely slowly, the movement scarcely perceptible.   I observed the slowest continuous movement of the cell contents in *Chara* when the temperature of the water was 1°C, the most rapid in the same plant when the temperature of the water was 37°C.   The length of one foot, if the motion is calculated to that measure, would be passed over in the first case in fifty hours, in the second case in thirty minutes.   Diatomaceæ at the ordinary temperature of the laboratory traverse one foot in 14–21 hours, they thus move about six times more slowly than the apex of the long hand of a watch.   Swarm-cells take mostly about one hour, the most rapid only a quarter of an hour to pass over a distance of one foot.   The most nimble equal in their movements the apex of the long hand of a clock, the face of which has a diameter of one foot and a-quarter, and would be left far behind by the laziest of snails[2].   Without magnification, even if the little plants were quite visible, their movement would not be seen, on account of its slowness —The Infusoria move but little faster than the vegetable cells.   Instead of the active animal movement of the latter, it would be more correct to speak of the slow plant-like movement of the former.

'Whether the movement of a body appears to us rapid or slow, however, depends also on the relation between its size and the space passed over in a definite time.   If an elephant and a mouse traverse an equal distance in the same time, we call the first slow, the second quick.   A man in walking passes over somewhat more than half his length in one second.   The most rapid swarm-cell traverses in the same time a distance which is two and a half times as great as its diameter; the Diatomaceæ only the one-tenth part of their length, and short filaments of *Oscillatoria* merely the one-hundredth part of their length, longer ones much less.'

According to Naegeli, swarm-cells have three forms of movement; in many

---

[1] Naegeli, '*Die Bewegung im Pflanzenreich*,' in his '*Beitr zur wissensch Bot.*,' Heft 2, 1860, p 13

[2] The movement of swarm-spores is thus slower than that of a particle of combined water and lithium which ascends in the wood during active transpiration.

of them the anterior end (hyaline and provided with vibrating cilia) as well as the posterior green end of the axis of the body remains exactly in the path of progressive motion, be this straight or curved—they swim forwards rigid, and without deviations. Others describe a direct or more or less curved spiral line, a rotation on the axis of the body always corresponding to a spiral revolution, so that the same side of the cell is always turned outwards while the axis of the body runs parallel with the axis of the spiral path. Thirdly, there are swarmers the anterior end of which describes a spiral line, while the posterior end describes a straight one, or a spiral with a smaller diameter. These forms of motion are only to be detected when the rotation and progression are slow. The motions of spermatozoids essentially agree with these, according to Naegeli, and he is convinced that if the form were regular and the mass distributed symmetrically, the cells would swim in a direct line in a homogeneous medium, and that all deviations from this and the simple rotation round the proper axis of the body depend upon the fact that the moving bodies are not symmetrically constructed, that their centres of gravity are not in the centre, and that they do not experience equal friction all round. The direction of the rotation is usually constant for each species, genus, or family; nevertheless there are exceptions, as in the tablets of *Gonium*. It is often impossible, however, to convince one's-self of the direction of rotation in the case of unicellular swarmers; and this, as Naegeli shows, depends on a peculiar optical illusion not yet understood (*Tetraspora lubrica*). The end which carries the cilia usually goes forwards, but it may also go backwards, and it then rotates in the contrary direction (*Ulothrix speciosa*) This reversion occurs when the swarmers rebound · they then rotate for a time at one spot, stand still, and go back (without turning round the body). The reversal of the rotation only takes place, however, in so far that the end bearing the cilia is always regarded as the anterior one, if, on the contrary, the end which is in front during the progressive movement (even when reversed) is termed anterior, then the direction of rotation is always the same, the backward movement always continues for a short time only, and is soon exchanged again for the usual one.

The progressive and rotating movements stand also with respect to their velocity in a relation not exactly determined, and both are, according to Naegeli, apparently due to the same cause. As a rule the one increases or decreases with the other; but if a swarm-cell strikes anything it remains at the spot, but continues to rotate, and occasionally one may be seen to move forwards without revolving. In the absence of all obstructions, however, both movements appear to be always combined. On the other hand, cells are also seen which, with an equal number of revolutions in the unit of time, swim forwards with unequal rapidity, or with equally rapid progress revolve with unequal rapidity.—In these matters there are evidently individual differences (depending upon the organisation). Swarm-cells occurring in the field of view at the same time, and thus exposed to the same external conditions, move with unequal velocities · the cells of *Tetraspora lubrica*, for instance, traverse at 14°C a space of one-fifth of a mm in 1 2–2 4 seconds, and revolve, striking against the upper or lower glass plate, once in o 3–1 8 seconds —Heat also accelerates these movements of protoplasmic structures. According to Unger, the swarm-spores of *Vaucheria* traversed a distance of one inch in 63–65 seconds.

The fact must not be overlooked that swarm-spores and spermatozoids commence their movements before they are yet free. In dividing Palmellaceæ I have seen the movements begin in the early morning long before the division was finished; the daughter-cells still hanging together in the middle trembled actively and began to swarm inside the mother - cell. The swarming is no doubt on the whole the same movement as that of the free swimming cells, only restricted by the continual impact of the cells one on the other within the confined space of the mother cell-wall. A similar phenomenon exists in the movement of the spermatozoids within their cell-wall, before they break through it. Thuret says of those of the Characeæ, ' The anthero-zoids are seen to be agitated and to twist in all directions within the segments (cell-segments of the an-theridia) which enclose them; after several more or less prolonged efforts, they escape to the exterior by a sudden movement, like the elastic rebound of a spring.' In the case of *Pellia*, the Ferns, and *Pilularia*, according to Hofmeister, the spermatozoid also revolves before it escapes from its cell-membrane.

Fig. 358.—Warm-chamber for the examination with the microscope of the movements of protoplasmic structures at different and constant temperatures. The chamber is constructed of zinc, and possesses double walls below and at the four sides, the space between being filled with water; it is open above to facilitate the insertion of the microscope *m*, the fine adjustment-screw of which appears at *s*; *d d* lid; *f* window which takes coloured or colourless glass; *t* thermometer.

The movements of swarm-spores, since they are true vital pheno-mena, only take place between cer-tain limits of temperature, and that an optimum temperature must exist for them at which the maximum of motility occurs, is only a special case of what was stated generally in Lecture XII: I shall therefore not go further into that matter. The irritability of swarm-spores for light, however, belongs not only to the most remarkable phenomena of irritability in the vegetable king-dom, but also, from the most recent investigations of Stahl and Strasburger, to those best known.

Before giving the most important results, however, I have still to mention a fact which comes of necessity into consideration here, and which was established by me about six years ago: this concerns the purely passive movements which the swarm-spores undergo under certain circumstances, simply from currents in the water, and the result of which was formerly also ascribed to their active movements[1].

In stagnant pools, ponds, hollows in stones, &c., the water is often found, especially in the spring time, to be coloured of a more or less intense green by innumerable swarm-spores. If such green water is poured into an ordinary plate or other shallow vessel, and placed in the neighbourhood of a window, it is observed after some time that almost all the swarm-spores are collected at the margin of the vessel turned towards the window; occasionally, as shown in Fig. 359 A, there appears at the same time, floating in the middle of the liquid, a green figure, the apex of which is turned towards the window. If the fluid contains at the same time large and small swarm-spores (macro- and micro-zoospores), e. g. of *Hæmatococcus pluvialis*, &c., all the micro-zoospores are found after a little time at the margin of the water turned towards the window, and also at the surface; while the macro-zoospores are collected at the margin of the vessel which is turned away from the window, and also at the bottom of the water. If, on the contrary, the vessel referred to is allowed to stand in the middle of a room where the temperature is equable, or even outside the building where the temperature is everywhere alike, cloud-like aggregations of swarm-spores are formed in the centre of the liquid, and these may present the most various shapes, differing, however, from the preceding in that neither the outer nor the inner margin of the vessel seems to be preferred. On the contrary, the swarm-spores form cloud-like collections, as rounded groups extending from the surface to the bottom of the liquid, or as concentric circular clouds coexistent with radiating and rounded groups, as in Fig. 359 B, or even as reticulate figures extended over the whole vessel.

I found now that both kinds of aggregation of swarm-spores may occur in the fluid in the most varied manner, and that they appear also when the vessel is covered with a glass bell-jar or with an opaque card-board receptacle. Light, as such, exerts no influence on the formation of these figures; on the other hand, it is the currents formed in the water by the warming and cooling which produce the aggregations of swarm-spores referred to. If the vessel in question stands at a window, and especially when it is cool or cold outside while the chamber is heated by a fire, then a continual streaming of the water goes on in the plate or vessel, so that the cooled water at the margin of the vessel next the window sinks to the bottom, flows thence to the opposite margin, and then ascends and streams on the surface as warmer water to the margin of the vessel next the window again. This continually circulating current of water carries the swimming swarm-spores with it, and causes, in combination with their active movement, their collection in the manner described, either at the surface at the colder margin next the window, or at the bottom of the vessel at the warmer margin turned towards the chamber. That it is here actually and simply a matter of a difference in temperature between the two margins of the vessel, and not of illumination, follows not only from the above-mentioned fact that the phenomenon occurs even under an opaque receptacle, but

---

[1] Sachs' *'Über Emulsionsfiguren und Gruppirung der Schwarmsporen im Wasser,'* Flora, 1876, p 241.

[3]   R r

also from the fact that the aggregations of swarm-spores at the margins, just mentioned, can be induced by placing the vessel with the one edge on a cold body and the opposite one on a warm body: it matters not whether the light here cooperates at all or falls in any given direction, or not, the superficial collection of swarm-spores at the margin is always formed where the water sinks in the vessel at the colder place. In like manner the rounded groups mentioned above, networks, concentric clouds, &c. (Fig. 359 *B*), are produced quite independently of the light, when the temperature of the vessel is the same on all sides, by the bottom of the vessel having a different temperature from its surface, and particularly if the latter is uncovered and evaporation takes place; vertical currents are thus produced, ascending and descending in the liquid, and the contained swarm-spores collect at the relatively still places. I was able to produce all these phenomena in exactly the same way by employing, instead of water containing swarm-spores, a mixture of water and alcohol in which coloured olive-oil was distributed in the form of very small drops, simply taking care that these fine drops of oil were a little lighter or a little heavier than the mixture of alcohol and water

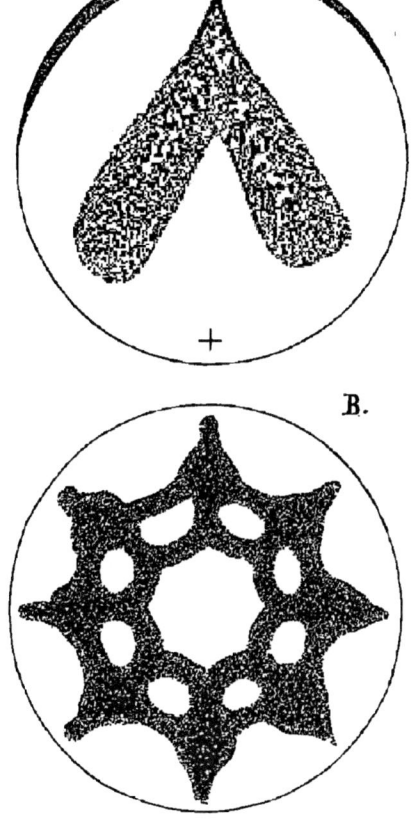

A.

B.

FIG. 359.—Emulsion-figures. Oil coloured with alkanet was thoroughly shaken up with a mixture of water and alcohol of nearly equal (somewhat greater) specific gravity, so that a fine emulsion was produced, and this was poured into a plate *A* arrangement of the oil drops after a short time when one edge of the plate (the upper in the figure) is cooler than the other *B* when the plate is equally warm on all sides, but the bottom of the liquid warmer than the upper surface.

Quite apart from these currents produced by differences of temperature in the liquid, and by which the swarm-spores are passively carried and caused to form the above-named cloud-like aggregations in the vessel, the swarm-spores themselves possess a peculiar irritability for light, which consists in that in their swimming movements, which moreover occur also in the absence of light, they pursue a definite course, and this so that they either move away from the source of light, or in the contrary direction, and in the line of the rays of light. If a large number of similar swarm-spores are contained in a drop of water under the microscope, and if they are suddenly illuminated from one side, they all swim towards the source of light or away from it   This is the phenomenon which has been studied in detail by Stahl and Strasburger, and I may take yet another series of special facts from the statements of the latter[1]. He investigated chiefly the swarm-spores of *Hæmatococcus lacustris, Ulothrix zonata, Chætomorpha ærea,* and of *Ulva, Botrydium granulatum, Bryopsis,* and other Algæ, and especially those of *Chytridium,* an Alga devoid of chlorophyll. Walz had already discovered in 1868, and Cornu had confirmed the discovery, that the final formation and expulsion of the swarm-spores and antherozoids from their mother-cells is dependent not only upon a proper temperature, but also upon a sufficient quantity of oxygen dissolved in the water; but light also promotes the birth of these small organs, as Thuret had already discovered, so that, in fact, by keeping the Algæ concerned in the dark and then suddenly illuminating them, the moment of swarming can be artificially induced. In the natural course of events, the dependence upon light referred to causes the swarm-spores to escape from their receptacles and commence to swarm in the early morning, as a rule at definite hours—i.e. when the light has attained a certain intensity.

Strasburger describes the action of the light as follows. if particularly striking phenomena are desired, it is well to begin the experiments with the swarm-spores of *Botrydium granulatum,* the Alga figured on page 4 (Fig 2). A preparation made one day before-hand by sowing the spores, when brought from the dark into the light, shows that at the moment of observation, all the swarm-spores are equally distributed in the drop; nevertheless they instantly become directed with their anterior ends towards the source of light, and now rush towards it in straight but otherwise fairly parallel paths. After a few—usually $1\frac{1}{2}$ to 2—minutes, almost all the swarm-spores have arrived at the illuminated side of the drop, and here swarm together in and out. If the preparation is turned round so that its illuminated side is now away from the source of light, all the swarm-spores which are still in motion instantly leave the margin of the drop, now turned away from the source of light, and rush to what is now its illuminated margin.

For the sake of brevity the margin of the liquid which is turned towards the source of light may be termed positive, and the opposite one negative.

'If the swarm-spores of *Ulothrix* are selected for observation, the phenomenon becomes in a certain sense still more striking. These also rush rapidly and in almost straight paths to the positive margin of the drop, but it is only seldom that all do this, in most preparations, on the contrary, a larger or smaller portion of them are seen to move equally rapidly in the opposite direction, and therefore towards the negative margin. It is possible then to see a curious spectacle—the swarm-spores thus rushing in opposite directions, and therefore with apparently double velocity, past one another. If the preparation is turned round through 180°, the swarm-spores collected at what was previously the positive side are seen to rush at once to the negative side, and those previously collected at the negative side to rush to the positive side. Arrived here, the swarm-spores move about in and out, keeping more or less close to the margin, according to the preparation. One continually notices also, both at the positive and at the negative side, individual swarm-spores suddenly abandon the margin and rush directly through the drop to the opposite margin. Such an interchange continually goes on between the two margins. nay, it not rarely occurs that single swarm-spores just arrived from the opposite margin again return thence. Yet others

---

[1] Strasburger, '*Wirkung des Lichtes und der Warme auf Schwarmsporen,*' Jena, 1878. Stahl in '*Verhandl der med-phys Ges. Wzbg,*' 1879.

remain stationary in the middle of their course, and then rush back to the point they started from, eventually repeating the play to and fro for some time, like a pendulum.'

The phenomena are usually less striking in the case of *Hæmatococcus.* In this form, as well as in *Ulothrix,* however, Strasburger noticed that the smallest swarm-spores exhibit the most rapid movement, and the colourless ones of *Chytridium vorax* behaved exactly like those of *Hæmatococcus,* whereas other colourless swarm-spores, such as those of the Saprolegniæ, were not affected by light.

One of the most important results of Strasburger's and Stahl's investigations is the discovery that there are swarm-spores which constantly rush towards the source of light only, as well as such which move towards or from it, the ciliated end moving forwards in the one or the other direction. In this matter the intensity of the light, again, plays a very important part, usually so that when the intensity of the light is less the swarm-spores move towards the source of light, when stronger away from it. This may be confirmed either by the observer moving his preparation further and further from the window, or by remaining there and interpolating translucent shades. If the light is strong, and the swarm-spores are collected at the negative margin of the drop, a point at which the light is less intense is thus attained, at which they begin to swim towards the positive margin. Another property of swarm-spores here comes into action, which Strasburger designates their Phototonus—a property which even with swarm-spores of the same species may vary with the time, and which consists in that the reactions mentioned come into play only when the light reaches a higher or lower intensity. If I understand Strasburger's statements correctly, however, this phototonus is fundamentally nothing other than a lower or higher degree of irrita-bility, of such a kind that swarmers which are adapted to low degrees of light are sensitive to light of low intensity.

The rapidity of the movement of swarm-spores, as Naegeli had already stated, appears not to be influenced by light; but Strasburger asserts that the swarmers move in lines the more direct the more intense the ray of light which directs them is.

Although the mechanics of the movement in all these cases, just as in the case of the heliotropism of unicellular and multicellular plants, remains unknown to us, it is nevertheless to be insisted upon that even in the latter, exactly similar degrees of sensitiveness to light appear, and especially I have long ago established that shoot-axes of the same plant—e. g. *Tropæolum majus*—may be negatively heliotropic in intense light, and positively heliotropic in feeble light.

It should not be omitted that, according to Strasburger, the influence of light in directing the movements of swarm-spores is the less the larger they are. To the largest known swarm-spores in particular, he denies all irritability to light whatever, as Thuret had already done also. Nevertheless there are exceptions: the small yellow swarm-spores of *Bryopsis* appear not to be sensitive to light, whereas the large green ones are very sensitive.

With respect to the refrangibility, colour, or wave-lengths of the effective rays of light, Strasburger here also confirmed the law which I had already established, that the mechanical actions of light on plants are due chiefly or exclusively to the highly refrangible, blue portion of the spectrum. When he allowed the light acting on the swarm-spores to pass through a dark solution of ammoniacal copper oxide, which transmits the blue and violet light, the swarm-spores reacted exactly as in ordinary white daylight. When, on the contrary, the light passed through a concentrated solution of potassium bichromate, which transmits green, yellow, and red rays, the swarm-spores did not react at all, and the same was the case when the light was allowed to act through a ruby glass, which transmits essentially only dark-red and green light, or when he allowed the nearly pure yellow light of incandescent sodium vapour (of a sodium flame) to act.

Finally, as regards the intensity of the light, it is to be remarked in the first place that the swarm-spores in the dark move in all directions, in curved and often sinuous paths, and only come to rest when they perish, or in any way become fixed. The particular intensity of the light which influences the direction of their movements at all differs, according to Strasburger, in different species. *Chilomonas curvata* on cloudy days did not collect at all at any particular margin, but remained distributed throughout the entire drop, when the sky brightened, however, they travelled to the light side of the drop. The swarm-spores of *Hæmatococcus*, on the contrary, became aggregated at the illuminated margin of the drop, when the light was scarcely bright enough to read printed matter by

Amœboid movement is the name given to the locomotion of small free-living protoplasmic bodies, which, according to their nature otherwise, might also be fitly designated swarm-spores, and in fact some of them proceed from such as later stages of development, as shown in Fig. 360. Here are to be mentioned particularly, the so-called Myxamœbæ—i e. the early developmental stages of the Myxomycetes. In contrast to the true swarm-spores, the relatively rigid bodies of which,

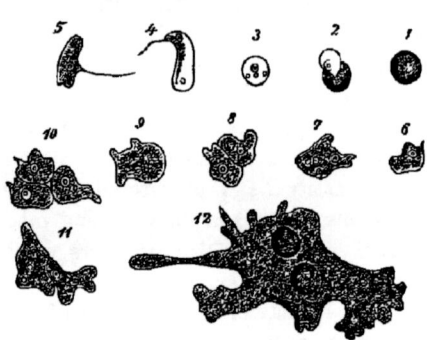

FIG. 360.—*Physarum album* (after Cienkowski). 1, spore, 2, emission of its contents, 3, the free contents, 4, 5, the same as swarm-spore with one flagellum, 6, 7, the same after losing their flagella, 9, 10 11, fusion of amœbæ, 12, a small plasmodium.

as it appears, are made to move forward passively, by means of the vibrations of the cilia, the amœboid movement consists in the protoplasmic body (which is sharply defined, however) adhering to a solid substratum, altering its external form and creeping along the substratum, the peripheral portions of protoplasm being put forth at some parts of the margin, and withdrawn at others; and so the mass slowly moves from place to place. This form of movement will perhaps be best illustrated by comparing figures 9–12 in Fig. 360. As to the mechanics of such movements there is practically nothing known, although for twenty years repeated attempts have been made to explain them [1]

---

[1] That an explanation of the amœboid movement of protoplasm and its circulation in the cells is not obtained by ascribing 'contractility' to the substance was insisted on by Hofmeister ('Flora,' 1865, p 8) I attempted at the same time in my '*Handb der Exp -phys*' (1865, p 454) to replace the indefinite idea connected with the word contractility by more definite assumptions, which of course did not reach beyond the region of mere hypothesis, though they have so far not been replaced in their turn by better I therefore quote the most important ones 'I imagine that living protoplasm consists of molecules of definite form (not round), but not capable of imbibition, these have a

The movements of Plasmodia are directly connected with these amœboid movements[1]. Plasmodia arise by the fusion of numerous myxamœbæ, whereby a large, and sometimes even immense protoplasmic mass is formed, as to the nature and movements of which I have already stated what is necessary (p. 83, Fig. 80). The creeping amœboid movement is altered in the case of plasmodia, according to their size, into a more flowing one, looking in the main very like the flowing of a thick tenacious slime. Of course this is only an external appearance, since, while in the case last mentioned the slimy mass passively obeys external forces, particularly gravitation, we are in the case of plasmodia concerned with vital movements, and the mutual displacements of their smallest particles which are effected by internal forces. Inside a coherent matrix, sharply defined externally, but with its outlines continually changing, there are formed more fluid portions containing numerous granules, which are in active streaming movements, the direction and intensity of which vary (see Fig. 80 *A*, p. 83), though no external stimuli produce these changes in any way. I demonstrated the irritability of the plasmodia to the influence of light fifteen years ago. If large heaps of tan, in which numerous small yellow plasmodia of the so-called 'flowers of tan' (*Æthalinum septicum*) are contained, are placed on a plate and kept in the dark, all the plasmodia creep forth in a few hours on to the surface of the tan, and there fuse into large yellow masses. If the preparation is placed at the right time in a light chamber, the

---

powerful attraction for water, and hence surround themselves with relatively thick watery envelopes, so that the mutual attraction of neighbouring molecules, which diminishes with the distance more slowly than their attraction for water, can effect only a feeble holding together of them (a slight cohesion). Under the influence of these two forces an unstable equilibrium of all the molecules of a mass of protoplasm will be set up, and these will at the same time be displaceable by slight external shocks, and the whole exhibit many of the properties of a fluid; it is also to be seen why different and feeble influences so easily deprive the protoplasm of a part of its water and strengthen its cohesion. It may then be further supposed that the molecules, in virtue of their mutual attraction, strive to lay themselves next one another in such a way that they turn their smallest diameters towards one another, because this position ensures the closest approximation of their centres of gravity. In this attempt, however, they will be in part prevented by the aqueous envelopes, and, on the other hand, it may be assumed that the molecules are endowed with directive forces, so that, for example, they seek in virtue of these latter to turn their longest diameters towards one another. One may here indeed suppose an electric polarity to exist in the molecules. Evidently, through the play of three attractions which are independent of one another in value, it would be possible for a position of equilibrium to be set up in which relatively considerable quantities of energy are present in the form of tension; the most insignificant shock might here disturb the equilibrium, and a disturbance occurring at one point must at once be propagated to the neighbouring molecules, and the movement must gradually affect places further and further distant from the starting-point. If the question is now raised as to the shocks which are able to set free the forces in tension in this molecular system (when it is itself left in equilibrium) very different ones may be supposed. Within the living protoplasm chemical processes are continually going on: these may at individual places alter the molecules chemically, or increase or diminish their attraction for water, their mass, or their polarity. Independently of the chemistry, moreover, small thermal, electric variations, imperceptible vibrations, &c., will affect sometimes one, sometimes another part of the protoplasm and disturb its unstable equilibrium.'

[1] The path to our knowledge of plasmodia, so exceedingly important for the theory of protoplasm, was first opened by De Bary, in his celebrated treatise, '*Über die Mycetozoen*,' in the '*Zeitschr. f wissench. Zoologie*' (1857, B 10), and a second edition, reprinted separately (1864). Cf further, Cienkowski in '*Jahrb f wiss Bot*' B III. pp 525 and 500. Also Strasburger, '*Studien über Protoplasma*,' Jena (1876), Sachs, '*Lehrbuch*,' IV Aufl, p 265.

plasmodia again disappear from the surface, creeping into the interior of the tan, to come forth once more on the renewal of darkness: this may be repeated several times during the course of the day   According to the statements of Baranetzky[1], it appears also that plasmodia which have crept up glass plates, and there become extended in the form of elegant networks, withdraw themselves from those places which are intentionally illuminated, and become collected at the shaded ones.   This irritability to light, however, only exists during a certain condition of life of the plasmodia; when their internal development is so far completed that they are proceeding to the formation of sporangia, &c., they make their appearance on the surface of the tan even when the light is strong   I have also already noticed the remarkable creeping of the plasmodia up the stems of plants, up flower-pots, and other objects, sometimes very high   They may be impelled to do this very easily, by placing moistened glass plates vertically in the tan, which contains young plasmodia just about to creep on to the surface; in the course of a few hours the reticulated masses ascend the glass plates up to the highest points, and they may now be removed and placed directly under the microscope, in order to observe their internal movements more in detail.   There is probably little doubt that this impulse to creep upwards is to be regarded as a geotropic stimulation—i. c. that a still unknown action of gravitation on the molecular structure of the protoplasm so affects the displacements of the molecules that the result mentioned follows.   It is, however, scarcely necessary to say that the individual mechanical processes in the matter are entirely unknown.

In all essential points the so-called Circulation of the protoplasm[2] in the interior of living cells agrees with the movement of plasmodia, only in this case the extent of the space within which the motions of the protoplasmic body can occur is once for all determined by the resistant cell-wall.   It has already been described and illustrated by figures on pp. 80—82 how this comes about, when the cells at first entirely filled with protoplasm grow by absorbing water, whereby in the first place small water cavities or vacuoles appear in the interior, and how the water or cell-sap then increases more and more, so that in the subsequently much enlarged cell the protoplasm constitutes a more or less thick sac, everywhere closely applied to the inside of the cell-wall and enveloping the cell-sap, traversing which are strand-like or plate-like filaments of protoplasm, and how all is in movement.   The accompanying figure, reproduced from my Handbook, will contribute still more to give the reader an idea of the protoplasm thus in circulation.   The latter is represented in the figure as a finely punctated mass in which lie larger bodies also, especially chlorophyll granules which contain starch; in one place also is to be seen a small crystal of calcium oxalate.   It is practically the movements of these small granules or microsomes and the larger bodies which betray the streaming movement of all parts of the protoplasm, only an outermost layer,

---

[1] Baranetzky, '*Influence de la lumière sur les Plasmodia des Myxomycètes,*' Mém. de la soc. nat des scienc. nat de Cherbourg (T. XIX. 1876).

[2] Dr Klebs has carefully collected the literature on circulation and rotation as well as on all the movements of the protoplasm here referred to in the '*Biologisch Centralblatt,*' ed by Rosenthal, 1881 (Nos 16, 17, and 19).

closely applied to the cell-wall, remains as it appears relatively at rest   Having already (*loc. cit.*) characterised in the main the form of movement, and since a detailed description would not give the reader any notion of the motile forces, I may here confine myself to mentioning briefly the few facts which we know concerning the irritability of the circulating protoplasm, and fundamentally this will apply also to the rarer form of movement, the Rotation of the protoplasm, which is also mentioned in the same place. Whether and how far gravitation may in any way influence the movements is not known. That rotation and circulation take place even in profound and continued darkness, and likewise in coloured light, and that by illumination under the microscope at least no striking change is undergone, is well known[1], although this does not exclude the possibility that more exact studies in this direction may demonstrate an irritability to variations in the light. Considering the great sensitiveness of swarm-spores and plasmodia for light, it is hardly credible that the protoplasm within the cells should be indifferent towards it; moreover all heliotropic organs, which are thus sensitive to light, of course contain protoplasm in their cells, and we have every reason to believe that the light-stimulus in heliotropic organs affects principally their protoplasm, and that the corresponding alterations in the cell-walls are initiated by this. It is thus obvious (and the reasoning applies to geotropic organs also) that all protoplasm enclosed in cells is irritable to gravitation and light, only of course in a manner not

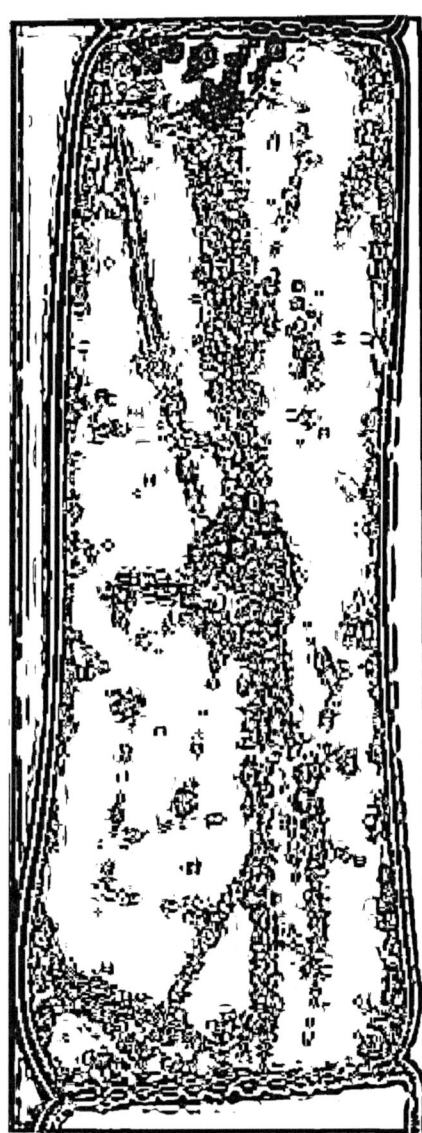

FIG 361 —Optical longitudinal section of the middle cell of hair of the Gourd (from the calyx of a young flower-bud) Cell-wall simply in outline—the fine granules in the protoplasm drawn too coarse The central vacuolated clump encloses the nucleus of the cell The streaming filaments, everywhere in active movement, carry chlorophyll-corpuscles (containing starch) in their substance, at one place (to the left) a crystal is also carried along

---

[1] In the *Bot. Zeitg.* 1863 (Supplement, p 3) I stated that the protoplasm circulates even in the cells of etiolated organs, e. g. hairs of *Cucurbita*: in fact, I prefer to employ wholly or partially etiolated plants for the demonstration of protoplasmic movements, on account of several advantages.

directly perceptible by means of the microscope: moreover it need not be simply in an alteration in the circulation and rotation that the irritability of the protoplasm to gravitation and light has to express itself; and in the subsequent consideration of the movements of the chlorophyll-corpuscles we shall see that these are probably to be referred to the stimulation of colourless protoplasm by light.

Heat acts very energetically as a stimulus, and this so that the streaming movement is accelerated as the temperature increases up to an optimum. Temperatures beyond this optimum, again, retard the movement, and finally (at about 45° C) the filamentous network of circulating protoplasm contracts into a clump; however, if this action has not continued too long, the normal configuration of the protoplasm may be restored after a short time at a lower and more favourable temperature[1]. Strong electric shocks act similarly, and it is here to be especially insisted upon that pressure on the cell-wall occasionally induces similar effects, and in some cases at least a complete arrest of the movement: subsequently it returns. Hence it happens that in recently made preparations of hairs or internal cells abounding in protoplasm, the circulation and rotation are not observable at all during the first few minutes, or it may be for some time, whereas the same preparations often exhibit vigorous movement a few hours later   According to Dehnecke's recent observations, moreover, lying in water for some time, and therefore probably a certain diseased state of the protoplasm, acts so as to accelerate the movements, so that they are often much more vigorous a long time after the preparation was made than in the normal condition[2]. It should be mentioned here that the rotating and circulating protoplasm continues its movements even when the water of the cell-sap is affected exosmotically by the action of sugar-solution, the protoplasm separating from the cell-wall on all sides and contracting; in fact in the case of the root-hairs of *Hydrocharis* it is sometimes even possible to break in pieces the contracted protoplasm within the cell-wall, and each of the pieces forms a thick-walled vesicle of protoplasm, the substance of which continues to rotate actively for some time longer.

So long ago as 1861 I had called attention to the remarkable fact that the leaves of the most various plants appear bright green in very intense sun-light, and dark green in the shade, and that it is possible accordingly to obtain a sort of light-picture by laying a strip of black paper on a leaf on which the sun is shining · on removing the paper the shaded part appears dark green, the parts exposed to the light bright green. I did not at that time succeed in obtaining the right explanation of this fact, but now, from later researches by Famintzin, Frank, Borodin, and especially by Stahl, it has been discovered : they showed that the chlorophyll-corpuscles under the influence of the light assume different positions within the cells, and this necessarily gives to the whole leaf the appearance described above   Since these phenomena pave the way to still more general points of view and accurate ideas as to heliotropism proper, it is worth while to enter into

---

[1] Details on these matters are found in my treatise, '*Uber die obere Temperatur-grenze der Vegetation*,' Flora, 1864 (p. 37). Velten, '*Einwirkung der Temperatur auf Protoplasma-bewegung*,' Flora, 1876 (Nos. 12-14)

[2] Dehnecke, in '*Flora*,' 1881 (Nos 1 and 2)

them more in detail, and in doing so I shall make use of Stahl's very thorough work[1]. He studied particularly the filamentous Alga *Mesocarpus*, in which the phenomena in question are particularly clearly shown. 'The elongated cylindrical cells of this Alga are connected into long filaments, and contain an axial band of chlorophyll running the whole length of the cell, and the margins of which now and then extend all round to the protoplasm lining the cell-wall; in this case the whole cell is divided by it into two approximately equal halves. The band of chlorophyll is usually extended in one plane : on observing it from the surface the whole cell thus appears uniformly green ; if the Alga is turned round through 90° so that the band of chlorophyll is seen no longer from the surface, but in profile, the otherwise transparent cell is traversed along its whole length by a dark-green thin longitudinal strip' If various filaments of this Alga are placed beneath the microscope the observer sees these plates of chlorophyll from the surface, or in profile, or in positions midway between these. 'Left to itself and undisturbed, such a preparation presents after some time a different aspect—for it is found that in the straight filaments all the bands are arranged in one plane. The orientation of the plates is the same in all those which lie parallel to one another, but differs in those which cross one another.' For the sake of simplicity we may here take into account only those filaments which lie horizontally, and receive the daylight (from a window) at right angles to their long axes. In this case it is easy to demonstrate that the plates of chlorophyll all turn their broad surfaces to the light, so that they receive its rays perpendicularly. If the direction of the incident rays is altered, the plates of chlorophyll slowly turn, so that they always present their surfaces at right angles to the rays of light ; in warm weather actively vegetating plants complete these movements in a few minutes. Direct sunlight, on the contrary, effects after a short time an entirely different disposition of the plates of chlorophyll : they turn one edge towards the sun, or in other words place their flat surfaces parallel to the incident rays. 'Light thus exerts a directive influence on the chlorophyll apparatus of *Mesocarpus*. In feebler light it is disposed perpendicularly to the path of the light (this is termed by Stahl the plane position), in more intense light its plane coincides with the direction of the rays (he terms this the profile position)'

In the vesicles of *Vaucheria* (p. 108) there are rounded chlorophyll-corpuscles embedded in the protoplasmic lining to the wall. According to the intensity of the light these also are arranged in a manner which is understood most simply by regarding the chlorophyll-corpuscles themselves as parts of the plate of chlorophyll described in *Mesocarpus*. If the intense light persists for some time, the chlorophyll-corpuscles become collected into distinct heaps—a process which De Bary saw occurring with great energy in the vesicles of *Acetabularia* (a marine Alga), and described as follows —'If actively growing vesicles a few mm long receive the rays of the sun directly, the protoplasm which carries the chlorophyll instantly rounds off and contracts into irregular clumps. The individual grains are seen to leave their place rapidly, and as it were tumble up against one another, becoming collected

---

[1] Stahl, '*Uber den Einfluss von Richtung und Starke der Beleuchtung,*' in Bot Zeit, 1880 (p 297), where the literature of this subject is also given in detail.

into balls at certain points; these aggregates thicken as new corpuscles are continually being added, and obstruct the vesicle as they swell up into clumps filling up the whole diameter, all the chlorophyll disappearing from the intervening portions After a few minutes, therefore, the previously uniformly green tube appears to the unaided eye, or under a lens, divided into unequally large and irregularly arranged dark green zones alternating with colourless transverse ones.'

We may now turn to the behaviour of the chlorophyll-corpuscles in ordinary cells united into tissues, and first consider an example where these cells form a single layer only, as in the case of the leaves of the Moss In ordinary diffuse daylight the chlorophyll-corpuscles in the leaves of the Moss, as well as in the similarly constructed prothallia of Ferns, lie only on the outer surfaces of the cells, the walls which separate any two cells from one another, and which are situated at right angles to these not being furnished with chlorophyll-corpuscles. In *Funaria* (p. 85, Fig. 82), according to Borodin, even a short exposure to darkness suffices to alter this disposition; the chlorophyll-corpuscles abandon the free outer walls of the cells, and travel over on to the side walls, so that after a time the upper and lower surfaces of such a leaf, and of any one of its cells, are completely deprived of chlorophyll If the leaves are exposed to the light the previous arrangement very soon re-appears. In the similarly one layered parenchyma of

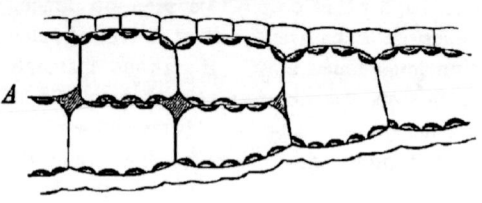

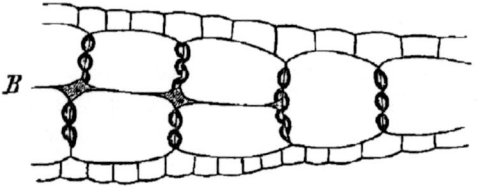

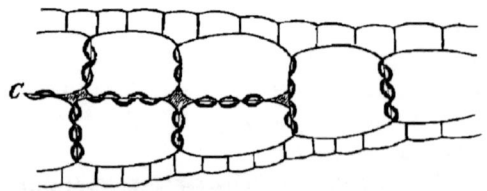

FIG 362 —Transverse section of the leaf of *Lemna trisulca* (after Stahl) *A* plane position (in daylight), *B* arrangement of the chlorophyll-corpuscles in intense light, *C* position in the dark

Lemna trisulca (one of the Duckweeds) the free superficial walls of the cells are likewise found to be furnished with chlorophyll-corpuscles in ordinary daylight; but if such a plant is exposed to the action of direct sunlight there takes place, as Borodin. found, a rapid alteration in the distribution of the chlorophyll-corpuscles. After 10–15 minutes they cover the side walls evenly, as shown in Fig. 362 *B*; seen in plan the chlorophyll-corpuscles form in this condition a regular network, the meshes of which correspond to the individual cells. After exposure to continuous sunshine for some time this is no longer the case; the corpuscles now form irregular groups, which occupy the angles where several cells are contiguous. Continuance of the illumination results in no further change; but if the plant is removed from the sunlight and exposed merely to diffused daylight, the chlorophyll-corpuscles abandon the above position and spread themselves on the outer walls of the cells. The changes in position described can be called forth at will, and often by alternately intense and feeble illumination.

Of Stahl's numerous observations on the chlorophyll-tissue in the leaves of Phanerogams we may here refer further to his statements with respect to *Oxalis Acetosella* (Wood-sorrel) 'The cells of the uppermost layer next the epidermis are developed into more or less obtuse cones, the bases of which are situated on the epidermis. The two lower layers of the mesophyll consist of flat stellate cells as in Fig. 363. Healthy leaves of this plant were laid flat on a plate and exposed to the rays of the sun falling perpendicularly on them. By pouring fresh water over them the leaves were prevented from becoming too warm Individual leaflets were protected from the direct rays of the sun by means of paper shades. After an hour the marked leaflets were placed in alcohol, in order to fix the cell-contents in their position. The decolorised leaflets were so transparent that mere observation with transmitted light was sufficient to demonstrate the different distribution of the chlorophyll-corpuscles in the shaded

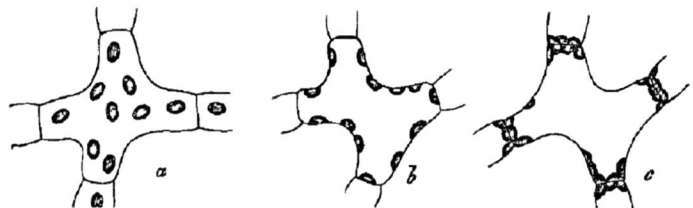

FIG 363—Cells of the lowermost layer of spongy parenchyma from the leaf of *Oxalis acetosella*, seen in a direction at right angles to the surface of the leaf. *a* plane position of the chlorophyll corpuscles in diffuse light, *b* profile position after a short exposure to the sun, *c* after longer insolation (after Stahl)

leaflets and those exposed to the sun. Fig 363 *a* shows the surface view of a stellate cell in a shaded leaf, the chlorophyll-corpuscles are distributed approximately uniformly on the walls parallel to the surface of the leaf. In Fig. 363 *b* the grains have passed over on to the walls which are perpendicular to the surface of the leaf, this distribution is found after insolation which has not been continued too long. If the leaves have had the sun shining on them for a longer time—an hour or more—the arrangement of the chlorophyll represented at *c* is met with; the corpuscles are collected into clumps, lying on the walls common to two neighbouring cells.

I may here interpolate, with reference to what has been said above as to the alteration in colour of the leaves in intense and in feebler light, that it is now easily intelligible from the examples given, how the different positions of the chlorophyll-corpuscles must effect alterations in the intensity to the unaided eye of the green colour of the leaves, it is obvious that a leaf, the chlorophyll-corpuscles of which all lie on the side walls of the cells, must appear to the eye of a brighter green than one where they lie on those walls which are parallel to the surface of the leaf

With respect to the mechanics of these phenomena, I have already expressed the opinion, based on Frank's observations, that the chlorophyll-corpuscles are passive in the matter, and that the movements referred to belong to the protoplasm itself in which they are embedded. Frank and Stahl agree with this view · if it is right, however, as is hardly to be doubted, then all the statements so far made as to the chlorophyll-corpuscles apply properly to the protoplasm itself, thus confirming and more exactly characterising its sensitiveness to light.

Again, the change in form of chlorophyll-corpuscles in varying illumination, already demonstrated by Micheli in a piece of work done with me in 1866, was confirmed and more exactly described by Stahl. In the Moss *Funaria* he found that in diffuse daylight the chlorophyll-corpuscles are disposed on the outer surfaces of the cells nearly touching one another, and separated only by narrow strips of colourless protoplasm. The grains are in this condition flat and polygonal On exposure to direct sunlight they withdraw their projecting angles and become rounded and smaller in circumference, and thus further apart. Similar phenomena were also observed by Stahl in the so-called palisade parenchyma of the leaves of Phanerogams, and it is only necessary to add here that in sunshine, as in shade, the chlorophyll-corpuscles of these cells have the so-called profile position—i. e. are situated on the walls parallel to the rays of light ; in the shade the chlorophyll-corpuscles are in this case approximately hemispherical, in the sun more flattened and discoid. Stahl demonstrated similar changes also ·in the assimilatory paren-chyma of those Liverworts which have flat extended shoots, and was able to detect the phenomenon generally wherever he sought for it. At the same time it should be remarked that in some leaves, clump-like aggregations of the chlorophyll-corpuscles are formed in the palisade cells by continued insolation.

From all his numerous observations Stahl concludes then as follows. ' In feeble illumination the largest surface of the chlorophyll-corpuscle is turned towards the source of light , the light is absorbed as much as possible. An opposite behaviour is noticed in very strong illumination a smaller surface is presented to the light. One and the same end is attained in utterly different ways , the chlorophyll-bodies sometimes protect themselves from too intense illumination by turning round (*Mesocarpus*), and sometimes by travelling, or by alterations in shape. These phenomena in the chlorophyll-apparatus proceed, again, hand in hand with the position assumed by entire leaves in very strong or feeble illumin-ation, this also was investigated in detail by Stahl. As we shall see later on, many leaves have the power of placing themselves in feeble light by means of peculiar mechanisms, in such a position that the rays of light fall upon their surfaces perpendicularly, whereas intense light induces them to assume the profile position—i. e. to turn one edge to the sun, and thus place their surfaces parallel with the sun's rays, thereby avoiding a too strong influence of the latter. Arrange-ments of the most various kind combined with corresponding irritabilities for light thus exist in plants in order to bring, not only the assimilatory apparatus, such as a whole multicellular organ, but also its individual chlorophyll-bodies into particular positions, which we must in any case regard as favourable for the employment of the light.

With reference to the heliotropic phenomena to be described later, and parti-cularly with reference to my theory of heliotropism, I must notice two other important facts already contained in what has preceded. In the first place that in all the phenomena here described it can only be a matter of the direction of the rays of light. No one will assume that a swarm-spore swimming towards the light does this because its anterior end is more strongly illuminated than its posterior. Still less will it be supposed in the case of the chlorophyll-plate of *Mesocarpus*, when assuming its position in plan or in profile, or in the corresponding movements of chlorophyll-corpuscles, that the movements of the protoplasm referred to can in any way be produced by the one side being more strongly illuminated than the other; on the contrary, it can only be a matter of the direction in which the ray of light falls upon the irritable protoplasm.

In the second place I would lay stress on the fact that both in the case of swarm-spores and in that of the movements of protoplasm containing chlorophyll, entirely different, or even opposite effects occur, according as the incident light is feeble or very intense. This phenomenon also we shall again meet with later in the heliotropism of shoot-axes and leaves. We shall see that many such organs become curved concave on the illuminated side in a feeble light, and in a strong light convex.

I shall return again to these facts when treating of heliotropism

LECTURE XXXVI.

THE PERIODIC MOVEMENTS OF LEAVES AND FLORAL
ENVELOPES (SLEEP-MOVEMENTS).

On glancing at the general aspect of the plants in a garden or a meadow shortly after sun-down in the summer, it is obvious that the leaves of many of the plants have assumed attitudes and positions different from those assumed in the daytime. This is very striking, for example, in the case of plants like the Clovers, and in all trees and shrubs (*Robinia, Colutea*, &c) with similarly organised compound leaves, especially where three or more leaflets are attached to a common leaf-stalk. It is then found that the leaf-stalks are more erect or more pendent at night than during the day, and the leaflets which they bear are drawn closely together, whereas during the day they are usually extended horizontally. Similarly also with other compound leaves, particularly those of the Clovers, &c., and, generally, all those (of Cryptogams as well as Phanerogams) in which the laminæ of the leaves are connected with the shoot-axis or leaf-stalk by means of a special cylindrical peculiarly organised portion. It scarcely needs mention that such plants cultivated in pots and standing at the window or in a green-house, also exhibit the same phenomena.

In these cases, then, in all Leguminosæ and Oxalideæ, and many less well-known plants, it is always by means of peculiar organs at the base of the petiole, or at the place where each lamina is connected with the stalk, that the changes in position of the leaves are effected. Besides these organs, which put in motion the parts situated on them by means of their up and down curvatures, all other parts of the leaves, the laminæ as well as the proper petioles, are non-motile— i. e. they are only passively directed upwards and downwards by the motile organs mentioned.

As a rule the change consists in the leaves which are extended flat during the day, and which present their chlorophyll-surfaces perpendicularly to the incident light where possible, becoming folded together at night. With the commencing light of morning the motile organs become curved, so that the laminæ of the leaves situated on them again assume the above-named extended diurnal position, while in the evening an opposite curvature of these organs produces the nocturnal position. This phenomenon has been termed the waking and sleeping of leaves [1].

---

[1] The older literature as to the periodic movements of leaves and flowers may be here passed over, inasmuch as it is treated in detail and criticised fully in Pfeffer's works I shall therefore

But the foliage-leaves of very many other plants also, in which no special motile organs are observable, make daily movements resulting in the production of diurnal and nocturnal positions. the growing petioles undergo curvatures by which

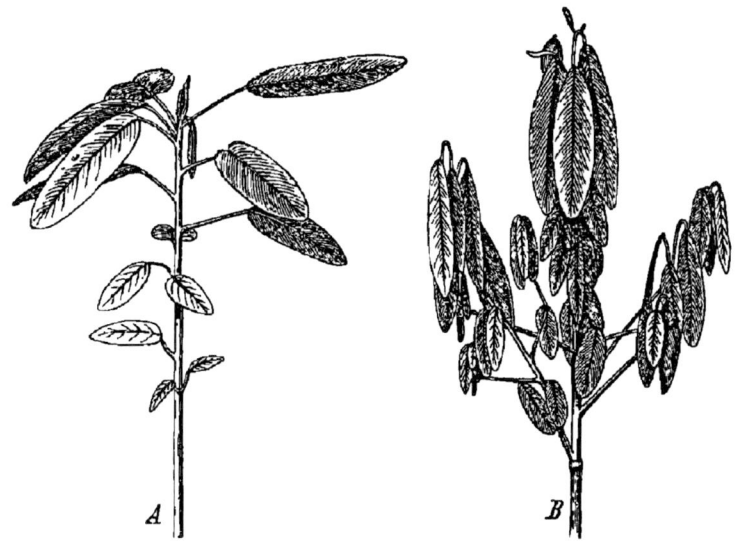

FIG 364.—*Desmodium gyrans* *A* shoot during the day, *B* shoot with leaves asleep.
From reduced photographs (Darwin)

the laminæ situated on them are presented to the light during the day, and at night are directed upwards or downwards.

---

mention only a few more recent works which will at once place the beginner on the right path in this province

Sachs, '*Über das Bewegungsorgan und die periodische Bewegungen der Blätter von Phaseolus und Oxalis*,' Bot. Zeit. 1857 (p 793)

Sachs, '*Die vorübergehenden Starrezustande periodisch beweglicher und reizbarer Pflanzenorgane*,' Flora, 1863 (Nos 29, &c.)

Paul Bert, '*Mémoir d l soc. d scienc phys et naturell d. Bordeaux*' (1866)

Millardet, '*Nouv recherches sur la périodicité d l tension*,' 1869 (Mém de la soc natur de Strasbourg)

Batalin, '*Über die Ursachen der periodischen Bewegungen der Blumen und Laubblätter*,' Flora, 1873 (p 433)

Pfeffer, '*Physiologische Untersuchungen*,' Leipzig (1873 and 1875).

Sachs, '*Lehrbuch der Botanik*,' IV Aufl, 1874 (pp 844–869)

I cannot agree with the nomenclature introduced into this subject by Pfeffer His '*Receptionsbewegungen*' are simply '*Reiz-bewegungen*,' the peculiarity of which, that they take place only while the organ is in a condition of phototonus, I characterised in 1865 by the expression '*paratonic stimulation*,' an expression moreover which Pfeffer accepts, though it makes the term '*Receptions-bewegung*,' which in fact can only hold for this case, superfluous Again, I can by no means agree with Pfeffer's designation of the periodic movements of non-articulated foliage-leaves as movements of nutation, although he himself as well as Batalin demonstrated their dependence on variations of light, for the term 'nutations,' previously introduced by me, applies simply to inequalities of growth on different sides of an organ, which are not induced by external influences It would be much to be deplored if in this difficult province, where Nature herself presents plenty of confusion, still further difficulties should be produced by an indefinite nomenclature

Similarly with many flowers, the corollas of which open in the morning, rarely in the evening, while they close again in the evening or morning respectively, definite hours not being followed as a rule.

These are the phenomena with which we shall now be concerned more in detail. One of their characteristics is that they vary with the alternations of day and night, and thus constitute daily periods. Now since in the morning, when the leaves and flowers open, the temperature and dryness of the air usually increase, and in the evening when they close the temperature falls, and the moisture of the air therefore increases, it might be supposed at first that these points must be of special importance for the movements of sleeping and waking of leaves and flowers. As a matter of fact, the opening and closing of many flowers, as the Tulip and Crocus, are directly dependent on changes of temperature; and it cannot be denied that in other cases also changes in temperature and moisture affect the phenomena to a more or less subordinate extent. Nevertheless, so much is certain, that the daily periodic movements are called forth chiefly and almost exclusively by alterations in the brightness of the light, particularly in the morning and in the evening. the nocturnal position of the leaves and flowers is due to the darkness which supervenes as the sun goes down, and the diurnal position is equally a consequence of the morning brightness. That temperature and moisture are entirely subordinate and unimportant in the matter is conclusively shown by means of a very simple experiment. A small plant of the common Garden Bean (*Phaseolus*) or of the Wood Sorrel (*Oxalis*), rooted in a flower-pot, and with the leaves extended in the diurnal position in the forenoon, may be completely submerged in a large glass vessel filled with water. If the illumination remains approximately as before, the leaves maintain their diurnal position, although the water in which they are submerged is many degrees colder than the air which previously surrounded them, whence it follows that neither change of temperature nor of moisture produces an observable alteration in the diurnal position. If, however, such experimental plants, when they have assumed their diurnal position—it matters not whether they are in the open air or under water—should be suddenly darkened, e.g. by covering them with an opaque box, or with a cylinder of wood or card-board, the leaves assume the nocturnal position after a short time, say half an hour to an hour; and on again letting in the light during the day, the leaves would again take up their ordinary diurnal position. By means of such simple experiments therefore we can convince ourselves conclusively of the fact that the matter is one of stimulations due to variations in the light—illuminating and darkening.

With the establishment of this fact, however, we have for the first time obtained a foundation on which a deeper insight into these phenomena may be based by means of further research. Dwelling for the moment on the most general relations, it is above all to be insisted upon that, with respect to organisation, it is always organs with dorsi-ventral structure which are here concerned, as is clear from the fact that we have to do in all these cases with true leaves, or at least with metamorphosed foliar organs, which always possess dorsi-ventral structure—i e. the parts capable of curving and of receiving the light-stimulus are organised on the lower side more or less differently than on the upper side. Since then all these organs, simply because they are leaves, are situated on a shoot-axis, and since the

[3]   s s

upper and lower sides of the leaves always stand in definite relation to this, it results that the upward and downward curvatures of the motile parts take place in a plane which may at the same time be regarded as a longitudinal plane of the shoot-axis—i. e. the motile foliar organs approach the part of the shoot-axis situated either above or below their origin, or, regarding the apex of the shoot as the centre, we may say the movements take place in a centripetal or centrifugal direction. This is particularly well shown in the case of flowers, which are in fact metamorphosed shoots with very short axes while in the case of ordinary foliage-leaves we distinguish an up and down movement, we have in flowers to do with an in and out movement. This rule, however, only applies to entire leaves; in compound leaves the individual leaflets move upwards and downwards with reference to the common rachis, or they make at the same time twists directed forwards or backwards.

Although broad, thin, flat parts of leaves are not entirely exempt from sleep-movements, it is nevertheless found that in the more exquisite cases, where the alternation of diurnal and nocturnal positions is very marked, and the light-stimulus thus acts with great energy, the organs or parts in question assume a more or less cylindrical shape, as is particularly conspicuous in the motile organs of the Legumimosæ and Oxalideæ, and true compound leaves generally. As a rule, a motile organ of this kind is a more or less elongated cylinder consisting of succulent parenchyma, in the axis of which runs a non-lignified and very flexible strand of vascular bundles. Since the movements of these organs consist in up and down curvatures, it is obvious that sometimes the upper, sometimes the lower side of the succulent envelope of tissue must be lengthened, though the axial strand need not undergo either elongation or shortening, because it lies in what may be called the neutral axis of the motile organ. It is sufficient if this strand is flexible and not rigid; its length need not alter during the movement. Where the up and down curvatures of foliage-leaves are effected by means of ordinary petioles, or parts of the laminæ, of course vascular bundles traverse these parts as usual; but they also abound in succulent parenchyma, and the movement continues only so long as no lignification has as yet occurred in the vascular bundles. These points are especially to be borne in mind with respect to the mechanics of such movements, to be described more in detail subsequently. However, before we go into the mechanics of the movements, it is necessary for us to become somewhat better acquainted with the movements of the leaves themselves.

Our present theme is the so-called sleep-movements, caused by the daily variation of the light at sunrise and sunset. Now we shall at once see that even these movements for and by themselves are combined of two kinds of actions, namely of a direct stimulation, and of after-effects induced by the stimulus itself. It was, however, by no means easy to establish this apparently simple fact, since other movements are combined in the most various ways with the proper daily periodicity, though they have absolutely nothing to do with it. This is very evident when such a plant as a Mimosa, Bean, Oxalis, &c. is suddenly excluded from the light there then occurs at once, in fact, a sleep-movement; in from half an hour to an hour the leaves assume the nocturnal position. On again looking at it the next morning, however, the leaves, although they have not received any light at all, are found to be in their diurnal position, with their laminæ extended: next evening they fold up in the nocturnal position again. This suggests the question whether there is any light-stimulus at all in the matter. We have here, however, to do simply with an after-effect of the previous light-stimulus, which after a few days ceases in constant darkness just as it does also in constant light.

If, on the other hand, the Field Clover (*Trifolium pratense*) is used in the above experiment, or *T. incarnatum, Oxalis acetosella* and some other plants, they would be found to be in continual movement, so that at any time after the course of a few hours an apparent nocturnal position alternating with an apparent diurnal position occurs. In this case, however, we have to do with a movement independent of the variation of light, and therefore not to be regarded as an after-effect of it. From internal changes, as yet not understood, the leaves make up and down movements in periods of time of a few hours. Since these leaves also are sensitive to light, however, and have true sleep-movements, this independent so-called spontaneous or autonomous periodicity is hardly noticed under ordinary circumstances, simply because the influence of the light is stronger than the spontaneous movement. Nevertheless the converse occurs also; this in a very striking degree, for example, in the case of another clover-like plant (*Hedysarum gyrans*), the leaf of which is here figured. The two small lateral leaflets of this make in the course of a few minutes periodic oscillations, it matters not whether they are in light or darkness, if only the temperature is rather high—at least 22° C.

These spontaneous movements, not called forth by external changes, must therefore be sharply distinguished in the first place from the sleep-movements, with which they are more or less combined, since the point to be established is that the daily periodicity of sleep-movements

FIG. 365. A leaf of *Hedysarum gyrans* (nat. size)

is due to variations in the light, and is thus causally essentially different from the spontaneous movements.

But we have to do with yet other complications, not less calculated to lead to error in the study of daily periodicities and their causes. The leaves in question, or rather their motile organs, are also heliotropic, i.e. dependent on light in quite another way: in the case of that stimulation of light which produces waking and sleeping, the stimulus lies in the *variations* of the intensity of the light—it is not the light as a constant force which effects these movements, but the varying intensity; the increasing intensity in the morning induces the waking and extension of the leaves, the decrease of the light in the evening the nocturnal position or closing. In the heliotropic curving of the motile organs, on the contrary, it is the constant influence of the light which effects the curving, just as in the case of heliotropic stems and roots. If one of the above-named plants stands for some time undisturbed at a window, all the laminæ become turned towards the light; if the plant is turned round, the motile organs make other curvatures until the laminæ again turn their upper sides to the light. The movements of waking and sleeping go on undisturbed in such heliotropically curved organs. A further great difference between these heliotropic curvatures and those which bring about the sleep-movements, lies in the fact that the organs can make heliotropic curvatures in all directions, e.g. left and right, so that the one flank of the motile organ becomes convex and the other concave, according to which side the light falls on. The movement of waking and sleeping, on the contrary, only takes place as already mentioned in one plane, which divides the leaf and the motile organ symmetrically; and it is thus unimportant here in what direction the rays of light fall upon the motile organ, but only important that light is present at all and increases or decreases in intensity.

The above will suffice for the distinction of the movements of waking and sleeping from the heliotropic curvatures. In order to obtain a shorter expression for the former, however, I have since 1865 proposed to term those effects of light which cause the opening of the leaves as the intensity increases, and their closure as darkness comes on, *Paratonic effects*, because they only take place if the leaves are in the normal vital condition which I term *Phototonus*. If such leaves are entirely excluded from the light for several days, they pass into a condition of rigidity due to the darkness—i.e. they are no longer capable of being set in movement by variations in the light, though this recurs after long exposure to light, by which means the phototonus is restored. We may thus say shortly, the movements of waking and sleeping are called forth by paratonic light-stimuli, whereas the spontaneous movements of the same leaves are independent of any light-stimuli, but probably depend on phototonus; heliotropic curvatures, on the contrary, have nothing to do with phototonus.

If we now wish finally to distinguish the daily periodic movements induced by paratonic light-stimulus, from the various other movements of the same leaves, often combined with them, I must, in conclusion, notice a phenomenon which is perhaps the most confusing one of all in this province. I have so far assumed that the waking leaves, in the diurnal position, only receive ordinary bright daylight, or if the direct rays of the sun only temporarily and not too strong. However, if they are exposed to very intense insolation, especially about noon, the leaves close up and assume what looks like the nocturnal position. We have here, in fact, again to do with the profile position characterised by Stahl, which I have already described in detail in the previous lecture as regards the chlorophyll-grains, and have referred to as regards the leaves. Not only leaves which are paratonic and irritable, but others also have this peculiarity, that under very strong illumination they undergo curvatures or torsions, by means of which the lamina is so placed that the fierce rays of the sun are parallel to it, or at any rate fall upon it at a very acute angle; by this means a too intense action of the light is avoided.

It will readily be admitted that it is no easy task to detect the differences between all these various influences which cause alterations in the positions and disposition of the leaves, and to keep them apart and refer each to its causes, and eventually to recognise in its undisguised form the true daily periodicity which may be combined with all these variations. I first succeeded in 1863 in separating the spontaneous periodic movements from the paratonic ones, and in distinguishing between phototonus and rigidity due to darkness; and Pfeffer in 1875 first recognised the true daily periodicity as a phenomenon made up of a direct paratonic action and its after-effect, previous observers having already established the fact that the leaves endowed with daily periodicity are sensitive to mere darkening and illumination.

We have now only to do with the true movements of sleeping and waking, which are thus induced by paratonic light-stimuli and their after-effects, and in the first place we shall consider those leaves which we may look upon as the most completely organised in this direction, namely, the compound leaves of the Leguminosæ, Oxalideæ, and others of that type. It will then be relatively easy to make intelligible the phenomena in question in the case of other leaves where special motile organs are not developed, and in the case of flowers.

It is in the first place important to obtain a clear idea of the motile organs themselves, and this is probably to be obtained in no way better than by examining the common Garden Bean (*Phaseolus multiflorus* and *P. vulgaris*), a single leaf of which is represented in Fig. 366 in the nocturnal position. At *a* is the motile organ of the leaf-stalk proper, by means of which it is connected with the stem; at *b* and *c*

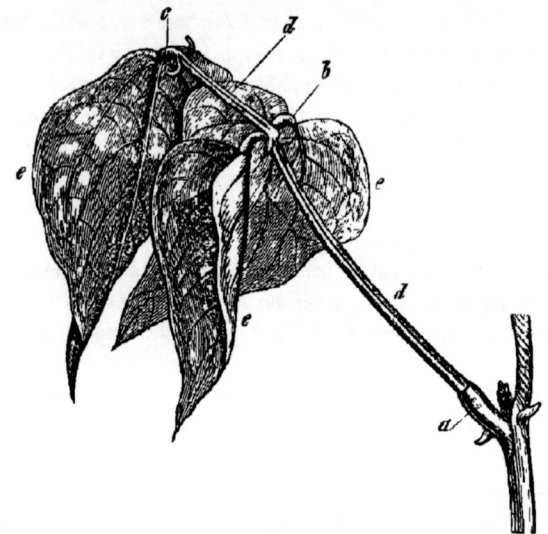

FIG 366.—Leaf of the Scarlet Runner (*Phaseolus multiflorus*) in the nocturnal position, *a* the large motile organ at the base of the leaf-stalk *d d*, *b c* the small motile organs of the three leaflets *e e e*

are the motile organs of the individual parts of the leaf, the so-called leaflets. The portions *d d* of the leaf-stalk are stiff, and immovable on their own account, as are also the laminæ of the leaflets *e e*. It is clear that if the motile organ *a*, which is now in the nocturnal position, elongates a little on its upper side, it must necessarily curve downwards, and the stalk *d d* naturally falls, if at the same time the motile organs *b* and *c* undergo a slight elongation on their lower sides, and accordingly an upward curvature, the individual leaflets *e e* become raised, and we will assume this to occur so that they all come to lie in one and the same plane. In this case, then, the leaf attains the diurnal position, and it may be incidentally mentioned that the change here described is induced by the increasing light in the morning, the opposite change, which carries the leaf back to the sleeping position again, results from the decrease in the brightness of the light in the evening. Although to superficial observation it is the movement of the petiole and of the lamina which is most striking, this is

nevertheless only passive, and is due to the curvature of the motile organs. Fig.
367 may serve to illustrate the true process more exactly; after the removal of the
laminæ there remain only the three motile organs of the leaflets on the common
leaf-stalk, as represented. In *A* these are very decidedly in the diurnal position:
the leaflets are no longer all extended in one plane, but are more upright; at *B*
these motile organs have assumed their nocturnal position. It is hardly necessary to
add that as the light varies, and from its after-effects, these organs may assume all
possible positions and curvatures between those of *A* and *B*.

The coarser anatomical structure is illustrated in Fig 368. *C* is a transverse
section through the rigid portion of the leaf-stalk itself; as in most other stiff petioles
which are channelled above, there are several vascular bundles *G* arranged
approximately in a circle, in addition to two more slender ones (*g*) running in the
edges of the channel; the remaining tissues are green cortex *c*, and soft pith *m*. The
appearance is quite otherwise in the transverse section *D* of the motile organ,

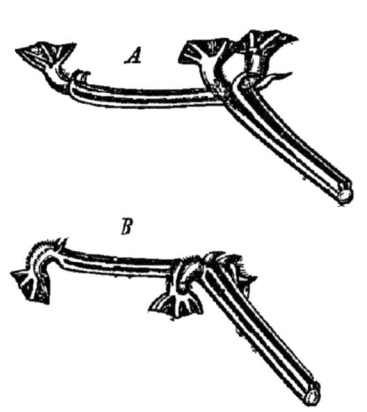

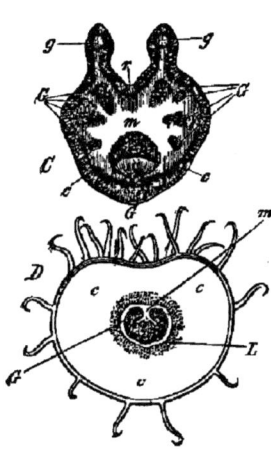

FIG 367.—Upper portion of the leaf stalk of the
Scarlet Runner, with the three motile organs of
the leaflets. *A* diurnal position, *B* nocturnal
position

FIG 368.—*C* transverse section through
the rigid portion of the leaf-stalk of the Scarlet
Runner *D* transverse section of a motile
organ (slightly magnified).

although it is fundamentally nothing more than a modified portion of the leaf-stalk
itself. The cortex *c* is here much more strongly developed, and consists of very succulent, strongly turgescent, parenchyma, a little thicker on the lower side than on the
upper, though otherwise there is no important difference on the two sides. It is important to mention this point, since in this tissue we have the active motile substance
of the organ, and we shall afterwards see that the movements and curvatures of the
latter depend essentially only upon a different reaction of the upper and lower parenchyma *c c* towards variations in the light. Here again, therefore, the matter depends
not on visible relations of organisation, by means of which irritability is to be explained,
but on invisible molecular structure; however it must by no means be forgotten that in
discussing the mechanics of the movements themselves, the coarser structural relations
are also to be kept in mind. In the middle of this mass of active parenchymatous
tissue runs a strand *G*, which, on being highly magnified, is at once seen to be composed of a large number of fused vascular bundles; it has to be supposed that the

strands marked *G* and *g*, in Fig. *C*, here come close together, leaving a channel above which is filled up with the pith *m*. As regards the finer anatomical structure of the motile organ, reference may be made to Fig. 371 below, which represents the transverse section of the motile organ of *Oxalis*, the relations in both cases agreeing in all essential points. The epidermis of the motile organ is relatively insignificant and not strongly cuticularised, but furnished with hairs which, however, do not interest us further.

A property of the motile organ of the Bean which is important for our purpose, and which also is again met with in all other similar motile organs, consists in the tension of the tissues; for the movements are practically nothing but alterations in the tissue-tension as a whole, and their relative sizes on the upper and lower side of the organ. In this is conspicuous above all the extraordinary magnitude of this tension, which depends on the one hand on the strong turgescence of the irritable parenchyma, and on the other hand on the toughness and elasticity of the non-lignified strand. By means of the one the thick parenchymatous envelope tends to be forcibly extended, and this is prevented by means of the other. The obvious consequence is, as explained in Lecture XIII, that the entire motile organ, although consisting of eminently succulent tissue, nevertheless possesses a very high degree of rigidity, which is also absolutely necessary in order that it may support the

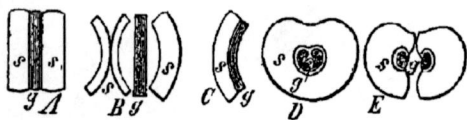

FIG 369.—Transverse and longitudinal plates from the motile organs of the leaf of the Bean, lying in water in order to show the changes in turgescence.

weight of the leaf-stalk and leaves, the centre of motion of which lies just in this organ. If, by the decrease of turgescence in the parenchyma, the organ became limp, the partial loss of rigidity would result in the attached leaf being depressed by its own weight: with the changes produced in the parenchyma by variations in the light, alterations in the turgescence are, as a matter of fact, connected.

Since it is absolutely impossible to obtain a clear idea of the facts here under consideration unless this point is kept in view, I may attempt to illustrate the above-mentioned properties of the motile organ still further, by means of Fig. 369. *A* represents a longitudinal section (or better, a longitudinal plate) of the organ, cut off transversely above and below. It is noticed how the two halves *s s* of the parenchyma swell and project above and below, because the axial strand *g* is too short for them. In *B* the right half of the swelling parenchyma *s* has been separated from the axial strand by a longitudinal section, and it at once becomes curved in the manner shown at *s* on the right. By means of a second section, the left half of the swelling tissue has been first bisected, and then the inner part separated from the strand; this became curved concave towards the strand, while the external half became curved concave outwards. From *B* then, it is clear that in the parenchymatous envelope of the organ the external layers are likewise in a state of tension towards the internal layers, but so that the entire mass of tissue tends to become convex on the outside. This kind of tension is still more clearly shown in *C*, where only the one side of the swelling tissue is separated from the strand, and the latter now becomes itself curved by the extension of *s*; had the right side

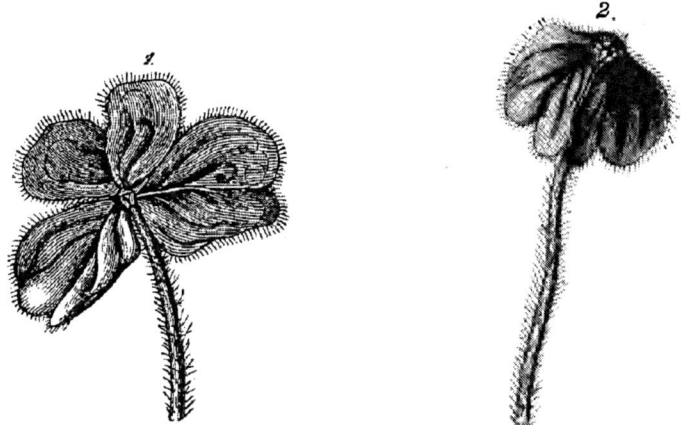

FIG. 370.—Leaf of *Oxalis carnea.* 1 diurnal, 2 nocturnal position.

of the parenchyma not been cut away from *C*, but had it instead lost only a part of its turgescence, then also the organ would have been compelled to make a similar curvature to that in *C*. With the longitudinal tension thus shown, the

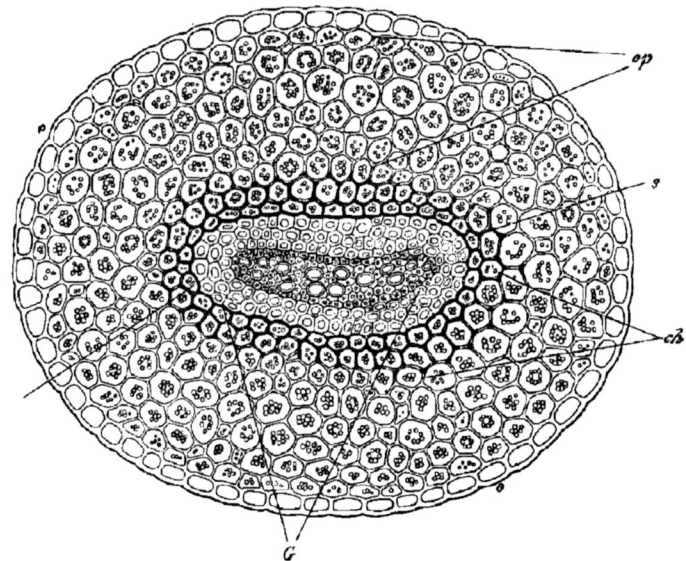

FIG. 371.—Transverse section of the motile organ of a leaflet of *Oxalis carnea.*

corresponding transverse tension also is connected, as is obvious at once from *D* and *E*. *D* is a transverse plate of the organ, and in *E* it has been divided into two halves by a longitudinal section: it is noticed in *F* how the tissue *s* projects in both halves beyond the strand. If the observations are carried out in the way here described, the parts cut out of the organ must be laid in water on a glass plate, in order to avoid drying up, since that would destroy the turgescence and tissue-tension. That the relations described exist in the living organ in exactly the same way, however, is at once perceived on making proper sections through such an organ still attached to the stem.

It will certainly not be superfluous to illustrate the relations of organisation again in the case of *Oxalis*. Fig. 370 shows a leaf, at *1* with its three leaflets in the diurnal position, at *2* in the nocturnal position. Further description of these is unnecessary. It is noticed, however, that the motile organs which connect the three leaflets to the top of the petiole are in this case very small, and in

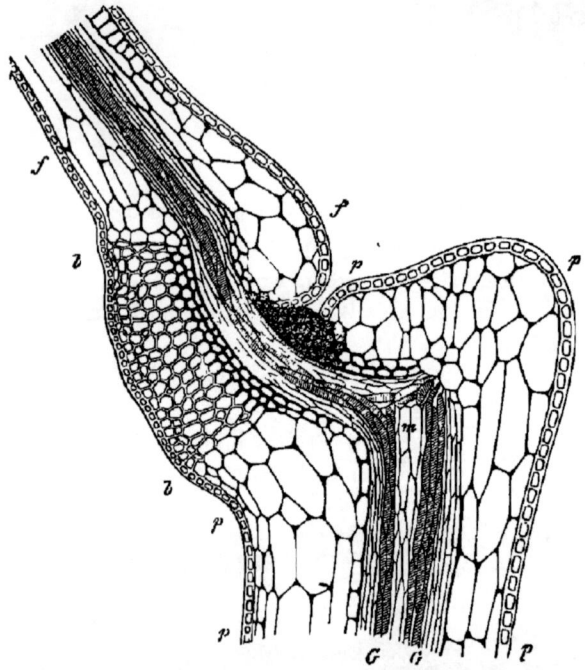

FIG. 372.—Longitudinal section of the motile organ *b b b* of a leaflet of *Oxalis carnea*.

fact broader than they are long. The transverse section of such an organ is represented in Fig. 371, somewhat highly magnified: beneath the epidermis *o* there is here again a relatively thick mass of parenchymatous tissue, which has distinct intercellular spaces only between the cells of its innermost layers *ch*: its cells contain chlorophyll-corpuscles as in the swelling tissue of the Bean, and in other such cases. Within the vascular bundle-sheath *s* lies the axial strand *G*, which here also is to be regarded as a union of numerous vascular bundles running together in the petiole and separated in the laminæ. Here, also, this strand consists of thick-walled, very firm, but by no means lignified tissue; since it is important that while it is very elastic, it shall yet be exceedingly flexible, for it has to undergo very strong curvatures, both towards the upper and towards the lower side, according to the degree of illumination, when either the lower or the upper side of the swelling parenchyma is much expanded.

Fig. 372 may afford an approximate, though not an exact idea of the changes in dimensions of this parenchyma in the alternating diurnal and nocturnal positions. It represents a longitudinal section through the uppermost portion of the common leaf-stalk, on which, to the left, is situated one of the three motile organs, with the mid-rib *ff* of the corresponding leaflet. Beneath the epidermis *p* the parenchyma of the petiole as well as of the mid-rib consists of large thin-walled cells; in the centre the vascular bundles *G G* ascend in the petiole, with the pith *m* between them; but as soon as they enter the motile organ, they close together and form an axial strand devoid of pith, which eventually enters the lamina of the leaflet to form the mid-rib with its lateral ribs. In making this preparation, care was taken to make the section somewhat thicker on the lower side of the motile organ (at *b b*) than on the upper side, where the plate is very thin: hence the turgescence of the lower side and its tendency to expand were increased (the preparation lying in water), and those of the lower side lessened. The organ has, therefore, become curved upwards, just as if it were in the diurnal position, and the thicker lower side *b b* presses the axial strand, by means of its tendency to expand, concavely upwards; and this pressure is at the same time so strong, that the swelling tissue of the upper side is very strongly compressed, as seen. If the section is made so that the swelling tissue of the upper side remains thicker than that of the lower side, a preparation is obtained which represents approximately the nocturnal position: the swelling tissue of the upper side, when the preparation lies in water, is then expanded, that of the lower side compressed.

I think these somewhat prolix descriptions will sufficiently prepare the reader to understand what now follows. I shall here rely partly on my own older observations, but chiefly on a detailed investigation by Pfeffer.

Proceeding first then from the easily demonstrated fact that by darkening an entire plant or even one leaf only, the nocturnal position results after from half an hour to an hour, and when this has occurred the diurnal position is restored on the subsequent access of light; the next question is naturally, What changes in the swelling tissue call forth these two antagonistic movements? Of course it is at once clear that in a downward curvature the upper side must become longer than the lower, and that in an upward curvature the contrary must take place. Provided that a fully developed motile organ is under consideration, it may be established by observation and calculation that even after numerous up and down curvatures no permanent elongation of the entire organ, or, what amounts to the same thing, of the axial strand, results. From this, then, it is to be concluded that when one side of the organ has become convex, i.e. longer than the other, or again relatively shorter when the curvature is in the opposite direction, a corresponding increase or decrease of the water in the half of the organ concerned must have taken place, because no other change whatever is conceivable. For the present we may leave out of account the question how this is accomplished, and use this conclusion simply to obtain an expression for the mechanics of the movement itself, for we may now say, as darkness comes on, that side of the organ which is to become convex in the first place obtains more water—i. e. its turgescence and its volume increase and become greater than on the opposite side. This is induced by the change in the intensity of the light. There is still, however, a very important point to be observed here, namely that in darkness an increase of rigidity of the whole organ and therefore an increase in the amount of water which it contains occurs, while on illumination a diminution of the expansive tendency of the parenchyma and thus a decrease in the quantity of the water and rigidity of the whole organ takes place ; in the nocturnal position, the entire organ is more rigid than in the diurnal position, as Brucke, and subsequently Pfeffer, proved. Moreover, Millardet showed, and Pfeffer confirmed, that in darkness an increase of turgescence appears simultaneously in the upper and lower half of the organ, and in like manner, on illumination, diminution of rigidity occurs in both simultaneously, but although these changes occur simultaneously they do not occur with equal rapidity on both sides of the organ. That side in which the increase of turgescence results more rapidly thus first becomes convex, and the other side is passively compressed by its extension, meanwhile, however, the same change takes place, though slowly, in the now concave other half, and this begins to extend and then presses the organ over towards the other side. This process requires from a few to as many as twelve hours. Then, according to Pfeffer's description, the reverse change begins spontaneously. the side of the organ which has at last become concave, again becomes convex, and this process also is then reversed, and this goes on, the movements becoming less and less marked, till after a few days the organ comes to a stand-still.

This result, i. e. this long-continued after-effect, only occurs in an undisguised form, however, when the plant remains for several days in the dark, after having been exposed to the normal alternation of day and night, and has assumed its nocturnal position ; or when, normally vegetating, it has assumed its diurnal position and is then constantly illuminated for some days. In both cases the after-effect, swinging to and fro like a pendulum, dies away, but with a different final effect in each case ; for if the plant remains in constant darkness until the after-effect ceases, it is then in a state of darkness-rigor, and is no longer sensitive even to sudden strong illumination, though if continuously illuminated it may again return to the condition of phototonus ; if, on the contrary, the movement ceases during constant illumination, the motile organs are at once irritable for a subsequent darkening, and assume the nocturnal position.

From the behaviour here described, as was first shown by Pfeffer, the ordinary daily periodicity now arises, the sleeping and waking, the daily recurrent variations of light combining with the after-effects—i. e. when the leaves have assumed their nocturnal position in the evening, there still follows during the darkness of the night, as an opposite effect, a tendency to assume the diurnal position. If then in the morning the light falls on such a leaf, this also induces a tendency to the diurnal position: after-effect and the influence of direct light thus combine, and since these changes in the organs, which have produced the diurnal position, are now followed in their turn again by the tendency to attain the nocturnal position coming in spontaneously, the latter is aided by the darkness which comes on in the evening It is clear that the periodic variations caused by the after-effect need not always exactly coincide with the daily variations in brightness, and that therefore several kinds of differences in the combined actions must result.

The above, then, embraces in the main the theory of the sleeping and waking of periodically motile leaves which possess special motile organs. I may still add that Pfeffer, by means of ingenious researches, has also measured the magnitude of the forces at work in the motile organs: in the case of the common Garden Bean, for instance, the increase of the expansive force in the upper half of the organ in the evening may equal a pressure of five atmospheres, so that the total expansive force then amounts to a pressure of more than seven atmospheres—i. e. if we suppose the transverse section of the motile organ to measure 1 sq. cm., a pressure of more than seven kilograms would be acting on it. Of course the transverse section of such an organ is usually only about 1 sq mm., for which the pressure would amount to only the hundredth part of the above.

The reader will no doubt be desirous of having the theoretical statements made above in the abstract, illustrated clearly by means of a few examples. I will therefore next quote a series of observations which I made with *Acacia lophantha*. 'On the 20th April, 1863, a young plant of *Acacia lophantha* furnished with new, fine, very healthy looking leaves, was placed in a wooden case, in which was also a thermometer hanging close beside the plant

'The observations were here made hourly, but I will include in the table only those observations where some change is shown, in order not to make it inconveniently long; wherever 4–10 hours are passed over in the table, it signifies that there was no noteworthy alteration in that time.

April, 1863.	Hours.	C°.	*Acacia lophantha* in the dark
20	9 p m	17 5	Nocturnal position
21	6 a.m.	17·5	Leaflets opened 90°.
	8 „	17·5	Opened further.
	12 noon	18·0	Leaflets opened 180°
	6 p m.	17 5	Leaflets opened about 60–70°.
	9 „	17 0	The older half-opened, the younger quite closed
22	6 a m.	17 0	Leaflets opened about 130°, lateral stalks irregularly downwards.
	8 „	17 8	Leaflets opened about 180°, secondary stalks irregular.
	12 noon	18 0	The same
	4 p m	18·7	Leaflets beginning to close
	9 „	18 0	Lower leaves open, upper half-open.
23	7 a m.	17 7	All leaves regularly expanded flat.
	12 noon	16·2	The same.
	10 p m.	16 2	The same.
24	6 a m.	15·6	The same—inner ones not quite flat
	12 noon	16 2	All leaves quite open (180°).
	10 p.m.	15 6	The same—upper leaves irregular
25	6 a.m	15 0	All open and expanded flat.

'The plant had thus for 48 hours discontinued its periodic movements all but mere traces. After the last observation it was placed in the window, where, the sky being cloudy, its leaflets placed themselves decidedly downwards (the angle of opening being far beyond 180°) within two hours, and then appeared slight changes in position in the secondary stalks. About 12 o'clock (noon) this *Acacia* suffering from rigor due to darkness together with one in the normal condition were placed in the dark: the leaflets of the former did not alter their position but remained open, while those of the latter, on the contrary, assumed a pronounced nocturnal position within an hour.

Both were then placed at the window, where the leaves of the rigid plant again maintained their position unchanged, whereas the previously closed leaves of the normal plant opened again in an hour, the sky being cloudy. In the evening of this day (about 5 o'clock) the lower six leaves still remained stiffly open, the upper ones (8 and 9) closed. next day the periodic movement was completely reinstated. The plant had taken no harm, and is now vegetating actively.'

In the year 1870 Paul Bert, as Pyrame de Candolle had already done at the beginning of this century, exposed Mimosas to continuous illumination with lamps during the night and ordinary daylight during the day, and found that the extent of the movement of the principal leaf-stalk gradually diminished, but subsequently, under the influence of the daily variation of light, was again restored The effect of continuous illumination was also investigated in detail by Pfeffer, who employed for this purpose two Argand gas-lamps, which, however, were likewise employed only for illumination during the night, the plants being exposed to diffused bright daylight during the day. Pfeffer expresses himself as follows respecting an investigation made in this way with *Acacia lophantha*.—

'In continuous illumination the amplitude of the daily periodic movements gradually decreases, and if no autonomous movements affect the experimental objects, the leaves at length become motionless, but are at the same time perfectly sensitive paratonically In an experiment made with *Acacia lophantha*, a small pot plant bearing four leaves was kept in diffused light on 13th June, 1873, and illuminated in the evening. On this day the leaflets closed completely ; on the next almost completely ; on June 15th the amplitude of the movement of each leaflet was about 70°, on the 16th June 15–35° ; on the 17th June 5–20° ; and then on June 19th, variations in the brightness being avoided as much as possible, the amplitude was at any rate less than 5°. The periodic movements had thus practically ceased, the leaflets on the older leaves being expanded nearly flat, those on young leaves being inclined towards one another as much as 130°'

Plants which have become motionless in the light are just as sensitive to darkness as are plants which have been submitted in the usual way to the daily variation of illumination

'In the leaves of the above-named plants,' he continues, ' no autonomous movements can be demonstrated with certainty, but where such exist they continue even when the illumination is constant, and apparently do not lose in amplitude. The autonomous movements of the leaflets of *Trifolium pratense* are very considerable, the terminal leaflet may accomplish a movement of 30–120 degrees in the course of $1\frac{1}{2}$–4 hours. If such a plant, previously exposed to daily variation of light, is illuminated in the evening and thenceforth kept continuously in the light, no further closing movement corresponding to the daily period was to be observed even on the following evening, apparently because it was obscured by the autonomous movements, which went on with an amplitude of as much as 100 degrees, and with a rhythm of about two hours. These autonomous movements continued also unchanged while the plant was kept constantly illuminated for two days longer. Autonomous movements of less amplitude and shorter persistence occur in the primary leaf of *Hedysarum gyrans*, in which occasionally an amplitude of vibration of only 8 degrees in a period of ten to thirty seconds is observed. If this plant

is submitted to artificial illumination, in the manner just described for *Trifolium*,
it is possible on the evening of the following day still to perceive clearly the
sinking corresponding to the after-effect of the daily period, the autonomous
movements going on all the time. The independence of this from the daily
periodic movements here comes sharply into view, and the same is the case when
the plant is kept in the dark, where it behaves much as in continuous light. This is
true also for *Trifolium pratense*—i. e. even on the first day of its being kept in the
dark the daily period is no longer perceptible, on account of the great amplitude of
the autonomous movements.'

In agreement with the fact which I had previously established, that movements
in the vegetable kingdom which are induced by light depend upon the strongly
refrangible or so-called chemical rays, it is also found that the paratonic stimulation
of periodically motile leaves is caused by the light of the blue half of the spectrum.
I demonstrated so long ago as 1857 that in the case of the leaves of the Bean and Wood
Sorrel, when in their diurnal position, covering them with a dark blue glass bell-jar which
excludes all the yellow, green and orange light, produces no change whatever in the
position of the leaves, although to our sense of sight a strong darkening is connected
with it; to the plant, however, it reacts not like darkness but like complete light. If
the plant, or a single leaf of it, is covered with a bell-jar of ruby coloured glass
which transmits only red and a trace of green light, then the effect is exactly as
if an opaque receptacle had been employed: the leaf in a short time assumes its
nocturnal position, and thus reacts to the red light as towards darkness. It
would be a mistake to suppose from what has been said above, however, that only
the plant covered with the blue cobalt glass would awake again next morning; for
the one under the ruby-coloured glass does so also, and we know indeed that
it would do so even if it remained in profound darkness.

Attacking at last the question as to what the first effect of the stimulus
properly consists in, which an alteration of the intensity of the light produces, we
must adhere to the conclusion already arrived at and drawn directly from
the facts (p. 634) that it concerns changes in the turgescence in the two halves
of the tissue of a motile organ, and that these under the prevailing circumstances
can only depend upon the addition and abstraction of water. Darkening thus
causes an increased flow of water into the whole motile organ, but more rapidly
into the one half than into the other; increased brightness of the light, on the
other hand, must cause an abstraction of water from the entire organ, because
it becomes more flaccid, and this again in the one half more quickly than in
the other. This water, however, is inside the cells, surrounded by protoplasm
and cell-walls, and in part is also present in the protoplasm or in the cell-walls
themselves. Two possibilities thus present themselves. Either the light acts on
the imbibition-forces of the cell-wall, increasing them by darkening and diminishing them by brightening; or the variation of light influences directly the properties
of the protoplasm itself, and induces in this changes by which the turgescence
may be increased or diminished. For the first of these assumptions no certain
analogy is known, and on closer reflection it only leads to new difficulties.
On the contrary I shall show in the next lecture that we can analyse certain
phenomena of irritability of the organs of Mimoseæ and others, so far as to say

that the stimulus first produces a change in the molecular structure of the protoplasm, which thereby becomes more capable of filtration, i. e. allows water to escape, whence it penetrates also through the cell-wall, and consequently the cell becomes smaller. In this manner curvatures, exactly like those here considered, are produced in the similarly motile organs of the leaves of *Mimosa* and other plants by means of mere vibration. Supported by this analogy then it is probable that we may decide in favour of the second of the two alternatives mentioned above We may assume as probable that an increase in the intensity of the light makes the protoplasm in the cells of the periodically motile organs a little more capable of filtration, so that the already very high pressure of the cell-sap on the wall causes a small quantity of water to filter out and enter the neighbouring parts of the stem or petiole; whereas on darkening, the capacity for filtration of the protoplasm is increased, making possible a greater turgescence and extension of the cells.

This is of course, in the meantime, only a conclusion based on analogies, but it appears to be supported by all that we know otherwise of irritability in the vegetable kingdom, and as to turgescence and the properties of protoplasm. However, I must refer to the next lecture for more particulars

In conclusion, before dismissing the subject of daily waking and sleeping, and the paratonic irritable movements of the leaves due to light, so far considered, I may make a few short remarks on a point concerning the mechanism of these movements, which Pfeffer first insisted upon and investigated in detail. When, in the case of a compound leaf, like that of the Bean, the motile organ is situated at the base of the petiole, the size of the angle between the petiole and the shoot-axis is altered with its movements; the entire leaf rises and falls—in the Bean, for example, it rises in the evening and sinks in the morning—in the evening the apex of the angle is smaller, in the morning larger. Simultaneously with these changes, however, the position of the three leaflets at the other end of the leaf-stalk is also changed; in the evening they all curve downwards, and especially the most anterior leaflet By this, however, the moment of rotation which the weight of the leaflet on the petiole exerts as a lever on the lower motile organ becomes smaller. This favours the erection of the whole leaf-stalk, or the diminution of the angle between it and the shoot-axis, and the reverse must occur on the access of the light in the morning; by the direct stimulus of the light the chief organ of the leaf-stalk not only becomes curved downwards, but also a little more flaccid, and the weight of the three leaflets causes a further depression, and in addition the leaflets now become expanded and thereby exert a greater moment of rotation on the motile organ, and this also acts again in the same sense that the leaf-stalk falls somewhat more than would have happened simply by the stimulus of its motile organ by light. In this case, then, the changes of position of the leaflets in connection with their sleep-movements, acting on the petiole as a lever, produce a similar effect to that of the paratonic stimulations on the lower motile organs of the leaf-stalk itself. In the Mimosa, on the contrary, Pfeffer showed that the sleep-movements of the two or four secondary petioles at the end of the main stalk produce lever-actions on the latter which influence the paratonic movements of the large motile organ at the base of the leaf-stalk in the opposite sense; since, on darkening, the secondary petioles and leaflets lay themselves together, the lever on which their centre of gravity acts becomes longer, and thereby the moment of rotation of the leaf-stalk so increased, that it sinks in the evening, and its motile organ curves downwards, although it strives, in consequence of the action of the light in itself, to erect itself as in the case of the Bean. I give these remarks on Pfeffer's authority, not having yet had an opportunity of making decisive observations for myself.

There are perhaps not many opportunities where it is possible to make so clear to the non-physiologist the extraordinary difficulties which are often connected with the investigation of the phenomena of life as here, in the case of the sleep-movements of compound leaves, and it is chiefly on this account that I have dwelt on them at so great a length.

As already stated, there are also numerous foliage-leaves, at the base of which no specially developed motile organ exists, and where also the individual parts of the leaf are not sharply separated, and not connected with the stalk or mid-rib by means of special motile organs, but in which, nevertheless, very evident or slightly perceptible sleep-movements as well of the whole leaf as also of its parts take place, and this again in such a way that the entire leaf rises and falls, approaching or retiring from the upper part of the shoot-axis, while in many cases the lateral ribs of the lamina curve at the same time upwards or downwards, leaving the lamina flat or curved. However, only the movements of whole leaves produced by upward and downward curvatures of the petioles, or the lower parts of the laminæ, have been investigated in detail; and the following statements refer to these only. According to Batalin and Pfeffer the movements in question are very evident in the following well-known plants. Several Balsamineæ (*Impatiens noli-me-tangere*), Chenopodieæ, Atripliceæ, Solaneæ, *Mimulus, Mirabilis Jalappa,* species of *Silene* and *Alsine,* some Compositæ, *Malva rotundifolia, Œnothera, Portulacca, Linum grandiflorum,* species of *Polygonum, Senecio vulgaris, Ipomæa purpurea* (Blue Bindweed), *Brassica oleracea* (Cabbage); I may also add the leaves of *Helianthus annuus* (Sunflower), and particularly the leaf-like cotyledons of many dicotyledonous seedlings

From the investigations of the observers mentioned, the movements of such leaves agree with those of the group described in detail above, in all essential points except one; these leaves are not furnished with special motile organs, and are found to be in periodic movement only so long, and are only so long paratonically sensitive for variations of light, as they are still growing, and in fact the irritability begins to make its appearance when the young leaves come forth from the bud; the irritability increases, and the magnitude of the daily movements likewise, in proportion as the growth is accelerated, in accordance with the grand period of growth; when the growth becomes slower again, the irritability and motility also decrease more and more, until at length, on the cessation of growth, the sleep-movements also disappear. Here, also, the motile part, capable of curvature, need not remain the same; if the zone of strongest growth advances along the petiole, or forwards from the base of the lamina, the curvatures also occur at corresponding places.

With regard then especially to the mechanism of this movement, practically all that has been said of the proper motile organs, applies to these cases also, at least according to Pfeffer's account, only with the difference that the important matter here is not, as there, a periodic lengthening and shortening of the upper or lower side of the organ, but each elongation with its consequent curvature is permanent, when the other side becomes elongated, with a corresponding curvature in the opposite direction, this elongation is also permanent, and so on—i. e. the upward and downward curvatures are here caused by first the one and then the other side growing more vigorously.

Fundamentally, however, there is no difference whatever in principle, as is evident from the fact that even in the case of the leaves of the group first considered the periodic movements commence before the motile organs are fully grown. Still more important, however, is the following consideration; it has already been shown in previous lectures that growth in general depends upon the turgescence of the cells, and that as the turgescence of the tissue increases its growth is accelerated, and as it diminishes, it is retarded. If now changes in turgescence are caused by illumination and darkening, just as in the motile organs of the first group, so also changes in the rapidity of growth must occur in growing organs. In this case, for upward and downward curvatures to result, the alterations in turgescence here also must take place more quickly on the one side of the organ in question than on the other.

From Pfeffer's descriptions it is particularly clear in the case of the young leaves of *Impatiens noli-me-tangere*, which are very sensitive to variations of light, that they agree in every respect, apart from the difference just explained, with the leaves of the group first considered above.

Pfeffer established in 1873 that those corollas which exhibit so-called sleep-movements—i e. which open and close at certain hours of the day—likewise owe this periodic movement to periodic alterations in the growth in length of the outer and inner sides of the petals. Since, therefore, we are here no longer concerned with a new principle, but only with peculiarities of floral structure, and specific differences, I shall desist from descriptions in detail, and only dwell on one point.

While in the case of the foliage-leaves of the first group, the effect of changes of temperature is of entirely subordinate importance, compared with the paratonic action of variations of light, in the case of the foliage-leaves of the second group, where growth is the prominent feature, the variations of temperature exert great influence. But it is in periodically motile flowers that sudden variations of temperature induce the most active movements, and of such a kind that an elevation of temperature causes the flowers to open, and thus produces an outward curvature of the petals, while sudden cooling effects their closure, that is an inward curvature, by the more active growth of the outer side. In addition to the flowers of the Crocus and Tulip, Pfeffer mentions as very sensitive to changes in temperature the corollas of *Adonis vernalis, Ornithogalum umbellatum, Colchicum autumnale*—i e. particularly flowers which are apt to open in the Spring or late Autumn, when the temperature of the air is low, and which are only occasionally warmed by the sun. Less sensitive are those of *Ficaria ranunculoides, Anemone nemorosa*, and *Malope trifida*, all of which execute

movements at all times of the day under the influence of changes of temperature, but the more energetic the longer the interval since the last movement was
accomplished. This is still more conspicuous in the case of *Nymphæa alba, Oxalis
rosea* and *O. valdiviensis, Mesembryanthemum,* and the motile flowers of Compositæ.
These close in the evening, and then even increments of temperature to the extent of
10–28° C. scarcely effect their opening; in the morning, on the contrary, a
rise of temperature causes these flowers to open even when it is dark.

The reader may easily see for himself these effects of variations of temperature by taking Crocuses and Tulips cultivated in flower-pots, in the Spring
when the weather is cool and the flowers outside are closed, and placing
them simply in a warm room, where they will often open after a few minutes.
The observation may be made even more simply: if a closed Tulip-flower
is placed with its stalk in warm water at 20–25° it opens visibly, and this in
fact was the experiment by which Hofmeister first detected the influence of
variations of temperature on the opening and closing of flowers. In the case
of the Tulip and Crocus, Pfeffer was able by warming and cooling the flowers
to make them open and close eight times in one day; but even in these cases
the opening was more energetic if the flowers had been closed for some time,
and conversely. Particularly sensitive Crocus flowers may be made to open and close
completely by a variation of 5° C. in eight minutes; with variations of 12–20° C. this
resulted in as little as three minutes. Pfeffer found, moreover, that Crocus flowers
are sensitive to even $\frac{1}{2}$° C., and those of the Tulip to variations of 2° C.

Those flowers which are sensitive to variations of temperature are moreover sensitive to variations of light. Nevertheless the sensitiveness is greater
for the one or the other according to the species of plant: the flowers of
the Crocus and Tulip which are so very sensitive to variations of temperature,
become closed when suddenly placed in darkness, and opened on being illuminated,
and this indeed with an energy which is capable of overcoming the effect of opposite
though feebler stimuli due to temperature. On the other hand greater variations in
temperature are again able to reverse the opening or closure effected by light
and darkness. In *Oxalis, Nymphæa alba, Taraxacum,* &c., on the contrary, the
closure in the evening cannot be arrested by raising the temperature, and just
as little can lowering the temperature in the morning prevent the opening. If
however these flowers are kept closed during the day, they can be opened in
the evening by raising the temperature, and so on.

From this different susceptibility for variations of light on the one hand, and
for variations of temperature on the other, we obtain the simplest explanation of
the fact that some flowers in the open exhibit a marked daily periodicity, while others
close and open at any time of the day on sudden changes in the weather; evidently
the former are sensitive for the daily variation of light more than for variations of
temperature, the latter, on the contrary, are very susceptible to sudden warming and
cooling.

Finally it has yet to be mentioned that some flowers close when the light is
too strong, as well as when the temperature is too high, thus resembling periodically
motile foliage-leaves—with which, however, this only happens when the light is too
intense. Pfeffer observed this in the flowers of *Oxalis valdiviensis, Calendula,*

&c., when in the direct rays of the sun. Still it is of course doubtful whether in such cases the effect is to be ascribed to the light or to the heat.

If in conclusion we raise the question as to the purpose and uses for the plants concerned of all the periodic movements and changes directly resulting from stimuli here described, of course only a special consideration of the mode of life of each individual species could afford the answer in detail; still their utility can be recognised in a general sense even without that. That flowers with rare exceptions open in the morning, as the brightness and warmth increase, and close in the evening, is evidently connected with the function of pollination—i.e. with the transference of the pollen from one flower to the female organ of another flower of the same species. For this transference is effected by insects, which as a rule only visit the flowers in bright and warm weather: at night, when the conditions are different, the sexual organs of the flower are protected by the closure of the corolla against excessive cooling by radiation and wetting with dew, and probably from several other dangers. The opening and closing of foliage-leaves may in some cases enhance the above described protection of the sexual organs, though as a rule it may be assumed that by pronounced erection or depression of the laminæ of foliage-leaves in the evening, the excessive cooling of the highly important chlorophyll-tissue during the night is avoided; on knowing that these thin tissue-lamellæ may be cooled by mere radiation at night, particularly when the sky is clear and serene, to 5–8° C. below the temperature of the surrounding air, it is obvious that even during nights when the air is at 5°–6° C. such a cooling may fall below the zero point and lead to the danger of freezing. The extended diurnal position of the foliage-leaves is simply and only adapted for temperatures and lights favourable to vegetation, and only useful for assimilation within these limits; wherever the conditions are unfavourable in this respect, particularly in the case of thin delicate foliage-leaves, they become closed or assume the profile position, as well in excessive sun-light as in the darkness and cold of the night.

LECTURE XXXVII.

THE IRRITABILITY OF MIMOSA AND OTHER PLANTS.

Like several other Mimosæ and Oxalidæ, the Sensitive-plant (*Mimosa pudica*) is noted for the fact that the motile organs of its leaves are irritable not only in response to the various stimuli mentioned in the previous lecture, but also to small vibrations and other disturbances. These are the most easily perceived and therefore the longest known phenomena of irritability, and indeed up to the present century they were regarded as the only ones in the vegetable kingdom. The effects of stimulation and the mode in which those effects are produced in this case have now been studied so often, so thoroughly, and with such good results, that we may regard them as affording so far the most solid foundation in the whole province of the phenomena of irritability, so that not only a series of organs which behave similarly, but in fact almost all other phenomena of irritability, become more or less intelligible by means of them.

Mimosa pudica, a Leguminous plant belonging to the widely spread tropical family Mimoseæ, is a native of Brazil, and is now commonly met with in the East Indies and other tropical countries; even with us it produces abundance of seeds capable of germination, and this not only in pots and cultivated in the window, but even in the open, so that anyone may grow this remarkable plant, and with little trouble observe the phenomena of irritability now to be described. Growing in the open, especially in bright sunshine, it forms several vigorous foliage-shoots, often 60–80 cm. long, which lie prostrate on the soil, in a chamber, on the contrary, i.e in a feebler light, the principal shoot grows erect, and only a few lateral shoots come out obliquely from below On each shoot-axis there are 6–10 doubly compound foliage-leaves; on a petiole 4–8 cm. long, we find two, or a couple of pairs of secondary petioles each 4–5 cm. in length, and each of which bears 15–25 pairs of small leaflets. Each leaflet is about 5–10 mm long and 1·5–2 mm broad (see Fig. 373 *A*). All these parts are mutually connected by well developed motile organs. Each leaflet is situated directly upon a motile organ, 0 4–0 6 mm. in length, joined to the secondary petiole; the four secondary petioles in their turn are connected to the end of the primary leaf-stalk by a somewhat larger organ which is 2–3 mm. long and about 1 mm. thick The base of the primary leaf-stalk itself is transformed into a motile organ 4–5 mm. long and 2–2·5 mm. thick.

The structure of these motile organs in general agrees with that of those of the Bean and Wood Sorrel which have been described in the preceding lecture : each motile organ consists of a thick covering of parenchyma enveloped by a feebly developed epidermis devoid of stomata, and which surrounds an axial, flexible, but only slightly extensible strand of vascular bundles; the individual bundles of this strand arise from the vascular bundles of the shoot-axis, and at the other end of the organ where they enter into the leaf-stalk they become again isolated, as has been described in the case of the Bean. The parenchyma consists of rounded cells which in the neighbourhood of the vascular strand enclose rather large intercellular spaces containing air; these spaces are much smaller, however, in the 10–20 outer layers of the parenchyma, and are altogether absent in the neighbourhood of the epidermis. These air-cavities between the cells communicate with one another from the strand to the middle layers of tissue; the very small intercellular spaces of the outer layers of cells, on the contrary, appear as separate three-cornered lacunæ, and, in specimens under the microscope, are filled with water. The cells of the lower side of the organ are thin-walled, those of the upper side have walls about three times as thick, which like the former are traversed by numerous pore-canals. In addition to abundance of

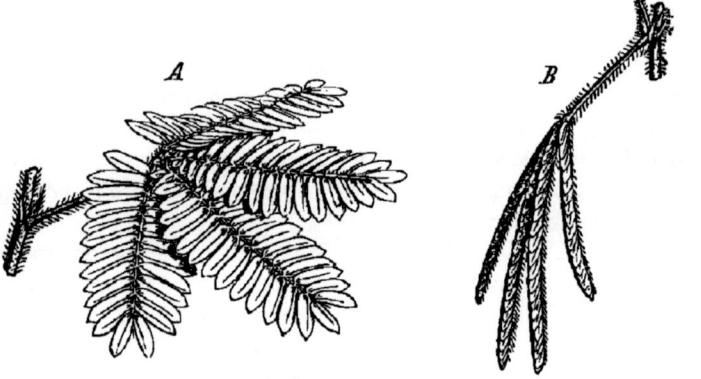

FIG. 373.—Leaf of *Mimosa pudica*, half natural size. *A* the diurnal non irritated condition. *B* the nocturnal position, or after irritation by a shock (after Duchartre)

protoplasm, nucleus, and small chlorophyll-corpuscles and starch-grains, the cells contain each one large spherical drop suspended in the sap-cavity, and which consists of a solution of tannin surrounded by a delicate pellicle. Unger also found similar structures in the motile organs of *Desmodium gyrans* and *Glycyrrhiza*, which, however, are not sensitive to contact and vibration. Again, the organs of *Mimosa* are irritable even in the young state, when the cell-walls in the upper half of the sheath of parenchyma are not yet thicker than those of the lower, and the spheres referred to are still wanting. Too great importance therefore is not to be attributed to these anatomical matters, in respect to the specific phenomena of irritability; and this so much the less, because the corresponding anatomical characters of the irritable tissue in other organs to be considered later, differ in several respects, although the phenomena of irritability are the same in all essential points.

When a Sensitive-plant is left to itself during the day, its petioles are directed obliquely upwards, the secondary petioles with their leaflets being extended almost exactly in one plane, as in Fig. 373 *A*. Any vibration (unless very gentle) affects the whole plant, so that the motile organs of all the primary petioles curve downwards, those of the secondary petioles forwards, and those of the leaflets forwards and upwards, as shown in Fig. 373 *B*. This condition resembles outwardly that of a leaf in the nocturnal position, or the one induced by sudden darkness; internally, however, it differs from it, because vibration still induces stimulation in leaves which are already in the nocturnal position, as is particularly evident by the relaxing of the lower large motile organ. Mention may here be made of the very important fact, that the nocturnal position induced by darkness is connected with an increase of turgescence and rigidity of the organ, whereas it suffers a very marked relaxation under the influence of vibration, so indeed, that a Mimosa leaf stimulated by contact or vibration, may swing loosely to and fro until it again assumes the irritable condition. In the day-time this follows after a few minutes, the leaves assuming the position represented in Fig. 373 *A*, whereupon they are again sensitive to vibration.

In the case of the motile organs of the primary petiole and secondary petioles, in very irritable Mimosæ, a slight touch of the hairs on the lower side suffices to induce the movement; and the lightest touch of the glabrous upper side causes the movement of those of the leaflets.

The sensitiveness of the Mimosæ depends to a large extent on the elevation of the temperature, and upon the moisture of the air: as these increase, the water contained in the whole plant increases, and particularly the turgescence of the motile organs. With the air at 25–30° C, and sufficient moisture, the irritability of the *Mimosa* is so great that the mere shaking as one passes by the plant acts as a shock sufficient to irritate it, and its leaves fall and close up; it is thus almost impossible to lift up and replace a plant in a flower-pot, even with great care, without inducing the effects of stimulation.

Of peculiar theoretical interest also is the unusually clear propagation of the stimulus in the Mimosæ, which is effective over distances 50 or more centimeters in length. If, for example, one of the terminal leaflets is snipped off, or its motile organ touched, or the sun's rays concentrated to a focus on one of these leaflets, a movement is at once produced, and the opposite leaflet rises almost simultaneously, the neighbouring leaflets then following in pairs, and so on with leaflets further and further away, down to the base of the secondary petiole: after a short pause the lowermost leaflets of a neighbouring secondary petiole then begin to fold together, and this proceeds from below upwards, and is repeated by the leaflets of the other secondary petioles, and finally (often only after a long time) the primary petiole of the leaf also falls downwards. If the plant is only irritable to a moderate extent this is all that happens, and the stimulated leaf resumes its normal position after a few minutes; but in very irritable and quite healthy plants, the irritable movement of the first leaf is followed after a few seconds by the sudden falling down of one of the nearest leaves situated higher or lower on the shoot, and thence onwards, proceeding in series, the irritable movement of all the leaves of the same shoot following as if the plant had been shaken. Thus, in the course of a few minutes all the leaves of a shoot of a vigorous Mimosa may be set in movement, although only a single leaflet had been stimulated originally; occasionally it happens that individual motile organs are passed over, only to be put in motion later. If the plant is left to itself, the leaflets and secondary petioles again expand after a few minutes, the primary stalks become erect, and all the motile organs are then again irritable.

Just as a motile organ can be stimulated by cutting into a small leaflet, or by burning it, so too it is possible, especially in the case of very turgescent, and therefore highly irritable Mimosæ, to stimulate the leaves from the internodes of the shoot-axis. Taking care that the shoot-axis is firmly fixed, and then placing the edge of a very sharp razor carefully and without shaking on the epidermis of the shoot-axis, and cutting gently into the succulent cortex until the resistance shows that the razor is penetrating the wood, a drop of water at once oozes out, especially if the razor is at once removed, and very soon one of the neighbouring leaves (or even several of them) is set in motion and relaxes. This experiment was known to the older vegetable physiologists, Dutrochet and Meyen, and is exceedingly instructive: it shows that the mere movement of water within the tissue induces the position of the leaves produced by irritation. This conclusion is the more certain, since the incision as far as the wood only induces the effect described, when a drop of water wells out from the wound. if the tissue is not sufficiently turgescent to exude water after the wounding, no movement of the leaves in the neighbourhood is induced. Evidently the incision of a leaflet with a pair of scissors, or burning it in the focus of a lens, produces nothing more than a sudden movement of the water in the tissues, which is propagated into the irritable organ, and induces the actions yet to be described. In 1865, in my '*Handbook*,' I drew from these facts the conclusion, that in the irritability of the Mimosæ the only essential factor must be the movement of water in the tissues, and corresponding changes in turgescence in the motile organs[1]. Further proofs of this, and a more exact insight into the processes occurring on stimulation were obtained by Pfeffer in 1872[2]. By means of linear measurements on the organ, at first not stimulated and then stimulated, he established in the first place that the volume of the lower parenchymatous half, which becomes concave in the curvature due to irritation, diminishes, and that of the upper, as it elongates, increases, but the increase in volume of the upper half is much less than the decrease in volume of the lower one, whence it follows that the whole motile organ becomes smaller—decreases in volume—as it curves down in consequence of stimulation. From all the facts, it follows that the decrease in volume of the lower parenchyma can only be due to the escape of water from the tissue, and Pfeffer demonstrates this in the following manner;

---

[1] I gave a comprehensive description of the irritable movements of the leaves of *Mimosa* on the basis of my own extended investigations and with reference to what was then known in my '*Experimental-physiologie*,' 1865 (p 479), and there first laid stress on the fact that displacement of water in the tissues is of importance in the matter.

[2] Very thorough investigations not only into the leaves of *Mimosa* and *Oxalis*, but also into the stamens of the *Cynareæ* and *Berberis* were given by Pfeffer in his '*Physiologischen Untersuchungen*,' Leipzig (1873) With respect to his results mentioned in the text, I then gave a renewed description of the phenomena of irritability generally in my '*Lehrbuch*,' IV Aufl, 1874 (pp 850–869), and the preceding lecture contains essentially only an extract from that work, to which I may refer the reader as regards several points which can only be briefly touched on here

and I have myself repeated the experiment several times. After cutting across the motile organ at the boundary of the petiole, where the axial strand is still undivided, the organ is at first in the highest degree stimulated, and thus curves downwards. If the plant is now left in an atmosphere saturated with moisture, under a large glass bell-jar for instance, the motile organ thus freed from its leaf-stalk erects itself again, and after a short time becomes again irritable: on now attentively regarding the cut surface, and irritating the lower side of the organ by means of a somewhat rough touch with a blunt needle, the organ curves downwards, and a drop of water escapes immediately from the section This water, as Pfeffer showed, comes from the parenchyma itself, and almost exclusively out of that which surrounds the axial strand and contains large intercellular spaces; occasionally, however, I have seen the transverse section of the strand itself become moist. If the parenchyma of the upper side is removed from a motile organ, and the rest of the organ makes a vigorous movement of irritation, it is occasionally possible, according to the above observer, to see water escape from the horizontal longitudinally cut surface of the motile organ.

It is thus certainly established that in the movement of irritation water escapes from the lower parenchyma. The small increment of volume of the upper parenchymatous half during the curvature above mentioned, shows moreover, that part of the water enters into this tissue; the decrease in volume of the whole organ, as well as its becoming flaccid during the movement, as already mentioned, show just as definitely that a portion of the water expelled from the lower parenchyma must flow somewhere else, probably at the same time into the rigid tissue of the petiole and into that of the shoot-axis; probably a very small quantity also passes into the axial strand of the organ.

The importance of the subject may justify further reference to Fig 369, and to the changes in turgescence in the motile organs, especially the large ones at the base of the petiole in the Mimosæ.

On cutting away the parenchyma of the upper side of the large motile organ, as far as the axial strand, the petiole not only erects itself again subsequently, but it becomes in fact more erect than usual, and the organ operated upon retains a certain degree of irritability. If, on the contrary, the parenchyma of the lower side is removed, the petiole falls sharply downwards, and the organ operated upon exhibits no further irritability. Thus it is the lower side only which is irritable, the parenchyma of the upper side being only accessory in the movement

If one of the large motile organs is cut away close to the shoot-axis, without being separated from its petiole, it becomes curved as usual, a drop of water escaping from it at the same time. If it is then split by a longitudinal section which divides the axial strand into an upper and a lower half, the former curves still more strongly downwards, but the lower one becomes almost straight or only a little bent downwards. If, further, the upper and lower parenchyma are separated from the axial strand by means of two longitudinal sections, the former becomes curved strongly downwards and the latter a little upwards, both elongating at the same time, so that they project considerably beyond the axial strand.

These and other experiments show that considerable tension exists between the parenchyma and the axial vascular strand, even in the stimulated organ which has lost water, and that the tension in this condition is greater between the parenchyma of the upper side and the strand, than between that of the lower side and the strand.

If an organ prepared as above and still attached to the petiole is laid in water, in order to replace the loss of water consequent on the operation, and thus to produce a condition which approaches the normal one, the downward curvature of the upper half becomes still more pronounced; but now the lower half curves strongly upwards, and its tissue, previously flaccid, becomes very tense and almost as hard as cartilage, as in the other half. This shows that the turgescence of the parenchyma of the lower side was more diminished in the operation causing the loss of water than that of the upper side, and that by the re-absorption of water it increases in a higher degree than that does. In other words, the irritable lower side gives up its water more easily than the upper side, and takes it up again with greater energy; the upper parenchyma is always tending to press down the axial strand, while the lower only tends to curve it strongly upwards when it is very full of water. The latter is the case with the parenchyma, however, only when it is not irritated; the stimulation consists simply in the strongly turgescent parenchyma of the lower side expelling water.

Lindsay noticed a long time ago that the irritated side of a motile organ becomes darker in colour; Pfeffer fastened the non-irritated petiole so that the organ could not become curved on stimulation: on then touching a spot on the irritable side he saw a darker colour extend with lightning-like rapidity from that spot. He concludes from this that the air is driven from the intercellular spaces, and replaced by water expelled from the stimulated parenchyma-cells, since the darkening only appears to be thus explicable.

Putting together all that has been mentioned, Pfeffer also eventually comes to the conclusion already arrived at by Dutrochet and myself, that the propagation of the stimulation in *Mimosa* is effected by means of the vascular bundles So long ago as 1865 I supposed the manner of this to be somewhat as follows. The water contained in the irritable parenchyma as well as in the vascular strand and in the wood of the shoot-axis, is to be regarded as a continuous mass, which, in the non-irritated condition of the plant is in a state of relative rest; every disturbance of this equilibrium, every movement of a portion of this water, brings about an expulsion of water, chiefly from the lower half of the motile organ, and it is obvious that the movement of a leaf must necessarily effect a disturbance of the equilibrium mentioned, and even over wide distances, and each organ entering into the irritable condition must in its turn at once cause a new disturbance of this unstable equilibrium

Most of the other leaves which are irritable to shocks and vibrations are far less sensitive than those of *Mimosa pudica* In the case of the leaves of the False Acacia (*Robinia*) and of the Wood Sorrel (*Oxalis acetosella*) really powerful vibrations are needed to produce movements. However, so far as the mechanics have been investigated in these cases, they depend in all essential points on exactly the same processes as in *Mimosa*. Among the organs most irritable to contact or shocks are the leaves of *Dionæa muscipula*, already described in Lecture XXIV : as there stated, the laminæ clap their two halves together with lightning-like rapidity when one of the six hairs of the upper side is roughly touched   From -Batalin's detailed researches[1] it may be concluded that in the case of *Dionæa* also it depends essentially upon similar changes in the tissue of the mid-rib, and in part of the lamina, as in *Mimosa* ; but several new points with respect to the relative arrangement of the active parts necessarily come in, and a lengthy description would be necessary to give the reader a really clear idea of the mechanism of the leaves of *Dionæa*. It suffices for the purpose of this book to have shown in one example what is most important concerning the phenomena of irritability produced by contact and vibration.

I will here refer to one point only by the way.   Burdon-Sanderson, by employing the well-known very sensitive electrical apparatus used by animal physiologists for the detection of electrical changes in nerves and muscles, found that, on stimulation, electric currents arise in the leaves of *Dionæa*, and considering the general ignorance which prevails as to botanical matters it can scarcely be wondered at if the conclusion was drawn from these observations that something of the nature of animal nerves exists in the leaves of *Dionæa*, as appeared moreover to accord excellently with the insectivorous propensities of these plants.   Our ideas of the irritability of plants, explained with so much trouble and labour, will one day be applied to the utterly obscure views as to the so-called negative variation in animal nerves.   Without entering more in detail into the criticism of the matter, it may simply be mentioned that at my suggestion, and in my laboratory, Dr Kunkel[2], well versed in the technicalities of electrical investigations, established the fact that each movement of the water in the tissues of a plant induces feeble electrical currents in it.   In the case of a slight bending of a shoot-axis or of a leaf-stalk, which must entail movement of the water in the tissues, electrical disturbances can at once be detected with delicate instruments.   Since now, as has been shown above, every movement of irritation of the leaves is connected with what amounts to a very considerable displacement of water in the tissues, this also must produce electrical disturbances, and conversely, it is also obvious that electric disturbances acting from without must act as stimuli to movement.   These have been longest known in *Mimosa*.   In any case, then, we have no necessity to refer to the physiology of nerves in order to obtain greater clearness as to the phenomena of irritability in plants ; it will, perhaps, on the contrary eventually result that we shall obtain from the processes of irritability in plants data for the explanation of the physiology of nerves, and this, although it is as yet a very distant hope, gives a special attraction to the study of the irritable phenomena of plants.   I shall therefore invite the reader to consider with me, somewhat in detail, the more important phenomena of irritability in the stamens of the Cynareæ.

The Cynareæ are a subdivision of the great family of Compositæ, in which

---

[1] Batalin, '*Mechanik der Bewegungen der insektenfressenden Pflanzen,*' *Flora*, 1877 (pp. 33, &c), where *Drosera* and *Dionæa* are treated with especial care.

[2] Kunkel, ' *Über elektromotorische Wirkungen an unverletzten lebenden Pflanzentheilen,*' in Arb des bot. Inst. Würzbg ,' 1878, B II (p 1) ; and further, ' *Über einige Eigenthümlichkeiten des elektrischen Leitungsvermogens lebender Pflanzentheiles,*' 1879 (ibid., p. 333).

more or less numerous small flowers are situated on a common broad floral receptacle, surrounded by an involucre of many small leaves. the whole impresses the non-botanical observer as a single flower. Those not skilled in botanical matters will easily see their way when I add that the common blue Corn Flower and its allies (*Centaurea*), the common Thistle (*Carduus*) and the well-known Artichoke (*Cynara*), together with many other genera, belong to the Cynareæ Each individual floret contained in the flower-head of these plants consists of an inferior ovary, from which rises a long narrow flower-tube which suddenly opens out above, assuming the form of a bell, the margin of which has five spreading teeth. At the place where this widening of the corolla occurs five stamens arise, the anthers or pollen-sacs of which are in all Compositæ so coherent laterally that they form a tube, through which the upper part of the style projects, arising from the inferior ovary at the base of the corolla-tube.

Now the five stamens referred to are the objects with which we have to do here[1]. These are fixed by their lower ends to the corolla-tube, as shown in Fig. 374, and at the upper end to the tube formed by the anthers Left to themselves, and before the emptying of the pollen from the anthers, the five stamens are strongly curved convexly outwards. If one of them is touched, as with the point of a blunt needle, it extends itself straight, i e it becomes proportionally shorter, it may then happen that, in consequence of the curvature experienced by the style passing between the stamens, the other stamens also become dragged or pressed on to the corolla-tube, and this acts on them as a stimulus, whence they also contract, and the anther-tube with the style going through it becomes curved towards the other side again. The whole sexual apparatus of such a tubular flower may thus be put into a condition of pendulous movement to and fro

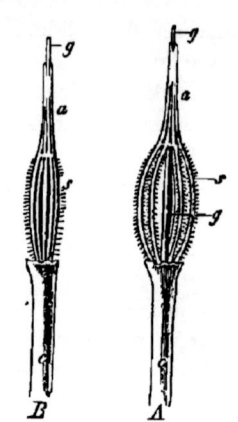

FIG 374.—Stamens of *Centaurea jacea* freed by removal of the corolla *A* in the non irritated *B* in the contracted state (magnified). *C* corolla-tube, *s* filaments, *a* anthers coherent into a tube, *g* style.

For the purpose of more exact studies it is well to take single florets out of the capitulum, and to cut away the corolla down to the origin of the filaments, or to cut across the corolla-tube, stamens and style, above the insertion of the filaments, and fix the freed sexual apparatus in damp air by means of a needle. When the filaments have recovered from the stimulation due to the operation, they stand sufficiently convex outwards—concave towards the style—for free movement. The filaments are not round: the radial diameter (with reference to the flower) is considerably smaller than the tangential one Each consists of an envelope of 3-4 layers of long, cylindrical parenchyma cells, separated by thin straight transverse walls, and surrounded by a layer of similarly shaped epidermis-cells (with a strong cuticle), which in many places grow out into hairs, each of which is

---

[1] As to the stamens of the Cynareæ, the reader may compare, in addition to Pfeffer's work already quoted, Franz Unger, '*Über die Struktur einiger reizbaren Pflanzentheile*,' Bot Zeit., 1872 (p. 113)

divided by a longitudinal wall. Between the parenchyma-cells lie spacious inter-cellular passages; the centre of the parenchyma is traversed by a delicate fibro-vascular strand, which, like the epidermis, is strongly extended by the turgescent parenchyma.

If in the first-named preparation one of the filaments, curved convexly outwards and fastened to the corolla below and to the anther-tube above, is touched, it becomes straight and thus shorter, and applied to the style; if this happens with all the filaments, their shortening is rendered noticeable by the downward withdrawal of the anther-tube After a few minutes the filaments again elongate, becoming arched convexly outwards, and are then again irritable. If the second kind of preparation is employed, where the filaments are cut off and freely movable below, it is easy to convince one's self that every time they are touched a rapid movement follows: if the outside is touched this becomes first concave and then convex, if the inside is touched this becomes concave and then occasionally likewise convex. The shorten-ing of the irritated filament begins at the moment of contact, and soon reaches its maximum, whereupon the elongation begins again at once, and this proceeds rapidly at first and then more slowly.

As to the mechanics of these movements, we have an investigation of Pfeffer's in which the filaments of *Cynara Scolymus* and *Centaurea jacea* were chiefly employed. The following embraces the more important results

The filaments of the species mentioned are 4–6 mm. long : the tangential diameter of those of the Artichoke (*Cynara*) is about 0 42 mm , the radial diameter 0 2 mm ; in *Centaurea* about 0 24 and 0·14 mm. The axial vascular bundle is thin and delicate, the irritable parenchyma-cells in *Cynara* 2–3 times, in *Centaurea* 4–6 times as long as broad. Their transverse walls are at right-angles to the longitudinal axis: all the cell-walls, even those of the strand, are thin, only the outer walls of the epidermis being thickened to any considerable extent. The very abundant cell-sap of the parenchyma-cells is surrounded by peripheral protoplasm, which is relatively abundant, and in which lies a nucleus; the protoplasm exhibits rotation In the cell-sap a little tannin and a good deal of glucose are dissolved.

The filaments are irritable along their whole length, i. e. they can shorten them-selves in consequence of contact anywhere. By means of special apparatus Pfeffer succeeded in measuring the shortening under powers of 100 or 200 diameters. The shortening may amount to 8–22 $\%$ of the length in the non-irritated condition, a thickening of the filament occurring at the same time, which is, however, far too slight to correlate the shortening with mere change of form , it points rather to a very considerable diminution in volume. This decrease in volume is due to the escape of water from the cells into the intercellular spaces, it wells forth from these spaces on transverse sections of the filament just as in the organs of the Mimosæ, as Pfeffer directly observed. If the intercellular spaces are filled with water by injec-tion, the filaments are still irritable, and the expulsion of water at the transverse section in consequence of a stimulus is then still more evident.

The filaments are very extensible and at the same time perfectly elastic ; they may be stretched to double their length, and yet they will contract again to their original dimensions

In the irritable condition the axial strand and the epidermis are strongly extended by the turgescent parenchyma, and even in the irritated state after the contraction there still exists a similar though much feebler tension.

Having now made ourselves acquainted with the facts of the movements due to irritation so far as is accessible to direct observation, the question arises, in what does the effect of stimulation essentially consist? As in the previous lecture, where we were concerned with the stimulus of light, so also here we must again keep in view as the chief point, that the irritable organ, or we may say each of its irritable cells, is turgescent in a high degree, and that in consequence of a touch or shake this turgescence is suddenly diminished, producing a sudden escape of water from the interior of the cells. The question thus resolves itself into the following.—How is the sudden expulsion of water from the cells produced in consequence of a stimulus?

According to all that we know as to the condition of turgescent cells, from De Vries' researches on plasmolysis, Pfeffer's descriptions, and my own considerations and experiments, it can scarcely be doubted that the cellulose walls themselves are always in a high degree permeable to water, and that the condition of turgescence of the cells depends upon the protoplasmic utricle opposing the expulsion of the endosmotically absorbed water even under high pressure A sudden escape of water from turgescent cells can thus be rendered possible only by this property of the protoplasmic utricle undergoing some change, or, in other words, by the hitherto non-permeable protoplasm becoming permeable in consequence of the stimulus, and thus letting water escape.

It must at the same time be added that we can at present form no idea why this change in the protoplasm occurs in consequence of a stimulus, and with what molecular changes it is connected; it must suffice for us meanwhile to know that the externally perceptible effects of stimulations so far described are caused by the change referred to in the protoplasm itself, and the question now is how the mechanics of movements due to irritation are to be understood from this.

It is to be observed, in the first place, that the escape of the water from the tissues is connected with a proportional diminution of their volume It follows thence that the cellulose walls themselves must contract in the movement in proportion as the water at a high pressure in the cells filters out through the irritated and therefore permeable protoplasmic utricle, it penetrates to the exterior also through the cellulose walls, and these then contract elastically, whence follow directly the movements described above.

It will be noticed that in this mechanism the extensibility of the cellulose walls plays an important part: true, neither the extensibility nor the elasticity of the cellulose walls is altered directly by the influence of the stimulus, though both properties are probably put in action. In order that a movement of the organ may come to pass in consequence of the movement of the protoplasm, the cells concerned must in the resting condition be strongly distended by turgescence, so that, when the protoplasm suddenly becomes permeable, they can contract to a corresponding extent, since only by this means is the movement itself called forth in consequence of the stimulus.

We might even suppose that the protoplasm forming a closed sac on the interior of the cellulose wall, allows water to filter out in consequence of a stimulation, and that, at the same time, it undergoes contraction, as occurs in the plasmolysis of ordinary non-irritable cells, where the previously slightly extended cellulose wall contracts, but not to the same degree, so that between it and the contracted protoplasmic utricle there arises an interspace filled with water, as in Fig. 189. If we now suppose that the alteration of the protoplasmic utricle just mentioned actually occurs, in consequence of a touch, shake, sudden illumination, electrical disturbance, or any other stimulus, but that the corresponding contraction of the rigid cell-walls does not occur, then no movement of the organ would be perceived externally, although the protoplasmic utricles had been irritated and had, in fact, reacted to the stimulus   We see thence that in the case of the irritable organs of plants two essentially distinct points come into consideration ; on the one hand the action of the stimulus on the protoplasm, and on the other the extensibility and elasticity of the cellulose wall.   Nature herself presents us with examples of the case here only assumed for purposes of illustration   In *Spirogyra* (Fig. 223, p. 314) the protoplasmic utricle which was hitherto closely applied to the cell-wall contracts, for the purpose of subsequent conjugation, into a rounded vesicle, and this is evidently only possible by the water of the cell-sap escaping out through its substance.   The protoplasm, however, separates from the cell-wall in the process, as in a plasmolysed parenchyma-cell (Fig. 189), because the cell-wall itself was only slightly extended previously, and accordingly only suffered a slight contraction.   If the cellulose wall of such a *Spirogyra* cell had been previously much distended, and if then the protoplasmic utricle became contracted, water being expelled, the cellulose wall would also contract and the entire cell would act like an irritable organ.   Evidently we might suppose the tissue of an irritable organ of *Mimosa,* or of a stamen of *Cynara,* composed of cells resembling those in *Spirogyra,* and then the consequence of a stimulus would be that their protoplasmic utricles would contract, but the cellulose walls would remain unaltered, and we should perceive no external movement.   Indeed it is not at all improbable, that such processes actually occur in the ordinary apparently non-irritable parenchyma of plants, since we know, as a matter of fact, that in many Algæ, hairs, &c., the protoplasm becomes contracted by mere pressure from without, the cell-wall not contracting to the same extent.

In conclusion I will mention, simply in passing, the irritable stamens of the genus *Berberis.*   These, six in number, stand in a circle around the central ovary, and in the opened flowers are thrown radially outwards   A slight touch on the inner side causes the filament to dart suddenly inwards, so that the anther comes to lie on the stigma.   If an electric current, generated by numerous small elements, is conducted through the flower in such a way that it runs longitudinally through the pedicel and ovary to the stigma, or takes the reverse direction, the following remarkable phenomenon is observed. each time the current runs from the stigma to the pedicel a stimulation of all the stamens follows, while a current in the reverse direction causes no stimulation.   I discovered this fact so long ago as 1878, but have not had an opportunity since of pursuing it further; it would certainly be not uninteresting to know, whether a similar phenomenon occurs in other irritable organs also.

The irritable stamens of *Berberis* differ as to their mechanism from those of the Cynareæ considerably, above all in that they are irritable only on the inside and not on the outside. It appears more important, however, that the irritable parenchyma contains no intercellular spaces; the cells, which are moreover thin-walled, have abundance of so-called intercellular substance between them, which has the property of swelling up. A touch on the inside of the filament causes it to curve along its whole length, and Pfeffer succeeded in showing here also that if the filament is cut across, stimulation causes an expulsion of water to take place at the cut surface.

The point around which physiological interest centres in the phenomena of irritability so far described, exists of course in the recognition of the internal processes causing them, and which we have been able to trace back to the protoplasm, so that, in fact, we perceived that it is the protoplasm which is properly irritable, whereas the external effect, the irritable movement itself, depends chiefly upon the extensibility and elasticity of the cellulose walls   But the question as to the uses which the plants referred to derive from these remarkable adaptations, leads us in an entirely different direction of physiological investigation   With respect to *Dionæa muscipula*, and the obviously very different adaptations in *Drosera*, the statements in Lecture XXIV may be referred to; it was there pointed out that the very complicated effects of stimulation in these plants seem nevertheless to exercise only a somewhat insignificant effect on their total nutrition   It is probably otherwise in the case of irritable stamens, the movements of which are evidently calculated to be started by insects visiting the flowers for the sake of the honey, whence, in accordance with the other mechanisms of the flower in each case, the pollen from the anthers has a chance of sticking to the body of the insect, to be rubbed off subsequently on the stigma of another flower.   Irritability here therefore occurs in the service of reproduction, while in other flowers other adaptations serve the same purpose.

So far as I am aware, no one has as yet attempted an explanation of the use of the irritability of the leaves of *Mimosa*, but I believe that I am able to afford one. For I have often had opportunities of observing that after a severe hail-storm, when plants of the most various kinds, and even robust plants, close to my Mimosas before the window or in the open, have been dashed and broken by the hail-stones, the Mimosas, in spite of their delicate structure, have come out quite uninjured; a few minutes after the rough weather they expanded their leaves again entirely unhurt.   The matter is easily explained.   The blows of the first drops of rain or of a single hail-stone cause all the leaves of the *Mimosa* to pass into the irritated condition, the primary stalks to hang down limp, and the double rows of leaflets to close together like clasp-knives ; the now limp and pendent leaves may be struck even by large hail-stones without taking harm, because they yield to the blows like pendent threads, whereas stiff leaves are pierced or their turgescent stalks bruised simply because they resist.   This action is, so far as the laminæ are concerned, promoted to the utmost by the fact that the folded secondary petioles and leaflets can only be struck by a hail-stone in a particularly unfortunate case.   Just as against hail, this behaviour (reminding us of the contraction of many animals when danger threatens) may also probably be of use on other occasions. as, for instance, when large animals invade the place where Mimosæ grow, where at the same time the very strong prickles to the right and left of each leaf-base are of service; both arrangements must also render it difficult and distasteful for phytophagous animals to eat the foliage of the Mimosæ.   A more exact insight into the matter is of course only to be obtained in the original home of these plants by careful observation of their relations with the external world.   Of course the irritability of the foliage leaves in the cases indicated can only be of use if they are sensitive in a high degree; it would be very difficult to detect any such use in the slightly irritable foliage leaves of our Wood Sorrel, *Robinia*, and several other plants, which only fold up slowly when sharply struck or shaken.

LECTURE XXXVIII.

THE REVOLVING OF TENDRILS AND TWINING PLANTS

THE great majority of sub-aërial leafy shoots are enabled, by means of their rigidity and geotropism, to maintain themselves erect so as to spread their organs of assimilation to the light, to render their flowers visible to the insects which pollinate them, and to mature their fruits and seeds in the air so that they can be easily detached from the parent plant and disseminated by the wind or by animals.

In very many other plants, on the contrary, the long shoot-axes are too slender and too flexible to be able to maintain themselves in this upright position beneath the weight of the organs which they support, although as a rule the above advantages accrue to them in proportion to the elevation they attain. They ascend, however, by quite other means—not by simply growing erect, but by climbing.

The climbing plants, again, differ in their habit of life, and in their modes of climbing. The Blackberry, for example, and the Rattan- or Cane-palms (*Calamus*) (with stems about as thick as the finger and sometimes 100 m long), fling, so to speak, their long shoots on the jungle and on the branches of trees, and hang there by means of their hooks. Much more completely organised, as climbing plants, are the Ivy and others. The long thin shoot-axes of the Ivy apply themselves closely to a wall, the stem of a tree, or a rock, &c , and then grow perfectly erect, or, in the case of lateral shoots, obliquely, on the surface of these supports, and fix themselves by means of numerous small attaching roots to the vertical surfaces on which they are climbing.

Twining plants are adapted for climbing in an entirely different manner. In these, e. g. the common Hop, species of Bindweed (*Convolvulus*), &c , the axis of the leaf-shoot, which is at least at first thin and flexible, twines itself around a body which stands vertical or obliquely upright, and is usually thin, such as the trunk of one of the more slender trees, a branch of a shrub, or, in the case of smaller twining plants, such as the common Corn-bind, around the haulms of ordinary grasses, the erect flower-stalks of meadow plants, &c. But it is the tendril-plants which are to be looked upon as the most perfect of all climbing plants, having special organs exclusively adapted for climbing. Moreover, their peculiarities are better known than those of any other climbing plants, and they may therefore be first taken into consideration.

[3]   L u

Departing from the every-day terminology which often designates as tendrils long shoots like that of the Ivy, botanists understand by this term thin, long filiform organs, which when typically developed are distinguished by being in a high degree irritable, especially to continued contact with a solid body. By means of this property tendrils are enabled to twine closely round a thin rod, the stem or haulm of another plant, or the branch of a woody shrub, &c., much as a cord or thin wire may be wound round a pencil, and thus bind themselves fast, and, since numerous tendrils on any shoot act in the same way, they fasten the latter to foreign bodies and enable it to climb upwards   The shoot-axis is entirely passive in this process : a tendril-plant climbs somewhat in the same way as a gymnast who, without using his feet, hangs by means of his hands and climbs up the steps of a ladder or the branches of a tree, only of course with the great difference, that each tendril when it has once established a hold-fast remains where it is, new grasping organs being continually developed at the apical portion of the climbing shoot, to seize hold of steps situated higher and higher (Fig. 375).

We may regard as the most perfectly organised of all tendril-plants the common Vine and the whole of the family to which it belongs, as well as the Gourd and its allies the Cucurbitaceæ, and the Passifloraceæ.

On examining a Vine there are found opposite many but not all the leaves, and springing from the shoot-axis, the dichotomously branched tendrils, which are often 20–30 cm. long and 2–3 mm. thick; these twine and make themselves fast round any body with which they come in contact, even the foliage-leaves of their own shoot.   The tendrils of the Grape Vine are, like those of the Wild Vine (*Ampelopsis hederacea*), practically metamorphosed shoots, for they possess a minute leaflet at the base of each of their branches.   They are, moreover, also remarkable in that they arise not from the axils of the leaves, but from the side of the shoot-axis exactly opposite the leaf, a fact which German morphologists have created unnecessary trouble about because it does not accord with the so-called principle of axillary branching   But it is a physiologically remarkable fact that between the tendrils and the inflorescences of the Grape Vine and its allies, every stage of transitional structure occurs.   It is only necessary to investigate a few dozen Vines to find tendrils which, while maintaining the tendril character completely in other respects, bear one or two flowers on individual branches; in others a portion of the tendril is converted into a small bunch of grapes, near which one or two filamentous tendrils still remain ; in other specimens, again, all degrees of metamorphosis to completely developed bunches of grapes are to be detected.   It may thus be said that the tendrils of the Vine and its allies are inflorescences which have remained more or less, or it may be entirely barren, and have assumed the properties of climbing organs; and the same may be said of the Passifloræ and several less well-known plants (*Cardiospermum*). The tendrils of plants of the Gourd family spring from the shoot-axis to the right or left close to the petioles, and are distinguished in the Gourd itself, the Bottle Gourd (*Lagenaria*), and in *Sicyos* and *Bryonia* (the White Briony), and others by their enormous length—occasionally 30 or even 40 cm.—and tenuity   Both peculiarities render them extremely effective climbing organs.   They differ from the tendrils of other plants still more by the fact that when they are young and first project from the leaf-bud of the shoot, they are closely rolled together in the form of a helix, and this in such a way that their outer side is convex; only on further development does the helix uncoil itself, progressively upwards from the lower part of the tendril, until it is approximately straight along its whole length. The tendrils of other plants are more or less straight from the beginning—i. e. they are not coiled up.

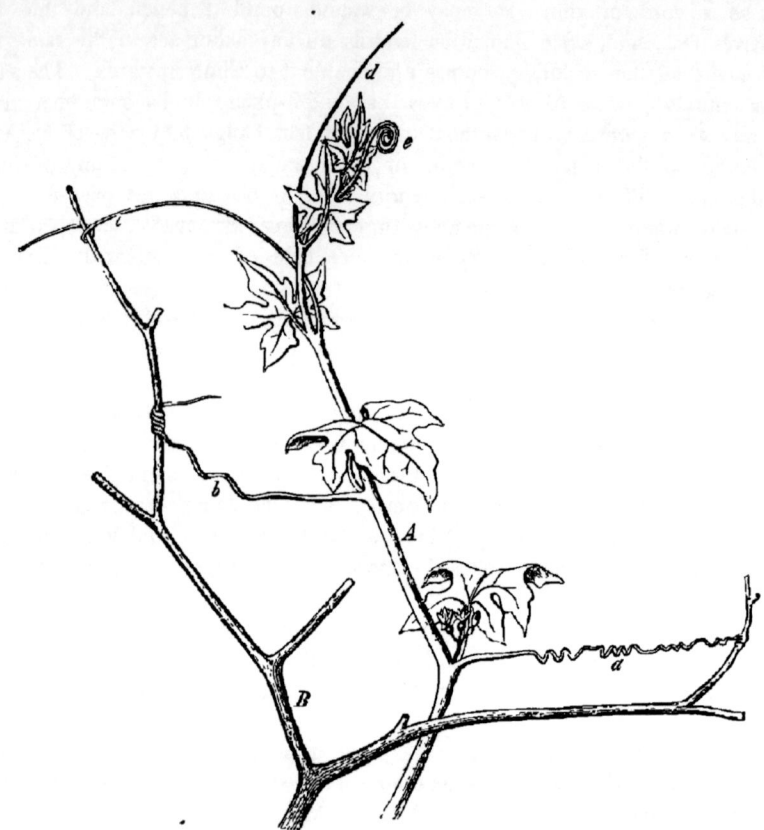

FIG. 375.—A shoot *A* of the White Bryony (*Bryonia dioica*) climbing by means of tendrils *a b c d*
B a dry twig serving as a support.

In the examples quoted we have true typical tendrils. In other cases, however, it is peculiarly developed parts of leaves, specially endowed with irritability and more or less filiform and sensitive to contact, which assume the chief properties of tendrils. In many species of *Clematis*, in the Indian Cress (*Tropæolum*), *Maurandia*, *Lophospermum*, *Solanum jasminoides*, &c., the petiole itself acts as a tendril, as shown in Fig. 376; in the common Fumitory (*Fumaria officinalis*) and the allied *Corydalis claviculata*, the whole of a leaf is branched into fine slender filaments, and is irritable to contact and able to twine its separate parts round thin bodies. In the case of *Gloriosa Blandii* and *Flagellaria Indica* the midrib projects beyond the apex of the broad simple lamina and serves as a tendril, and similarly with the Pitcher-plants

(*Nepenthes*), where, however, the ' pitcher ' already described (Fig. 247, p. 379) only arises at the tip of the tendril after the latter has wound itself round a support. In many Bignonias, *Cobæa scandens*, the common Pea, and its allies the Vetches, &c., the anterior portion of the pinnate leaf becomes transformed into very thin, filiform, and (in the first-mentioned plants) much-branched tendrils; and in *Lathyrus aphaca* indeed the whole leaf is replaced by a tendril.

These tendril-plants, of which Hugo von Mohl (1827) already knew 465 species, but the number of which is certainly far larger, occur for the most part among Monocotyledons and Dicotyledons, although several Cryptogams are possessed of similar organs. They are met with, however, in most abundance among the Dicotyledons, where in fact the distribution of physiological labour in general attains the highest development. The formation of tendrils is, as a rule, by no means to be found in all the members of a group in which it occurs. In the Cucurbitaceæ, Ampelideæ (the

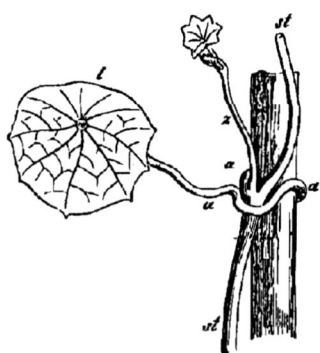

Vine and its allies), and the Passifloræ this is of course the case; but elsewhere it is usually only individual genera of a family, or individual species of a genus, which form tendrils And this, moreover, is true of all climbing plants Among the allies of the Ivy, it is this plant only which climbs in its peculiar way, and that the same is the case with twining plants is shown by the very close relationship between the Hop and the Hemp — the former being a typical twining plant, the latter a stiff, upright, and anything but a climbing species Just as in the case of the climbing species, also, the other physiological properties are independent of the systematic relationship; in the genus *Ranunculus*, for example, we find submerged or floating

FIG. 375.—*Tropæolum minus* The long petiole *a a a* of the leaf *l* is sensitive to continued contact, and has coiled itself round the support and round its own stem *st* so that the latter is fixed firmly to the former   *x* is the axillary bud of the leaf

aquatic plants, as well as marsh and terrestrial plants; among the Orchideæ ordinary land-plants with or without chlorophyll, and in the tropics epiphytes living on trees, and the aèrial roots of which serve as organs of attachment These may suffice to show the reader by the way how independent the systematic or phylogenetic relationship of the physiological adaptations may be, and conversely. We may now return to the exclusively physiological consideration of the tendril-plants.

The distinctive properties of tendrils are the more pronounced the more exclusively they serve the one purpose of organs of attachment for climbing, and therefore the less they partake of the nature of leaves or parts of stems in other respects—in a word, the more completely the metamorphosis is accomplished. Among these are especially to be noticed the simple or branched filiform tendrils of the Cucurbitaceæ, Ampelideæ and Passifloræ. One of these typically developed tendrils is shown at Fig. 375 *a* in the mature state, after it has embraced a support with its apical part and then become rolled up. What is here stated applies particularly to such true tendrils.

The characteristic properties of tendrils become developed when they have completely emerged from the bud state, and have reached about three-fourths of their definitive size; in this condition they are extended straight, and the apex of the shoot which bears them usually makes revolving nutations. The tendril itself also exhibits the same phenomenon, becoming curved along its whole length (usually with the exception of the rigid basal portion and the hooked apex), in such a manner that the upper side, the right, the lower, and the left side become convex in turn; no torsions make their appearance. During this revolving nutation the tendril is rapidly growing in length and is irritable to contact; i. e. every more or less pronounced touch on the irritable side effects a concave curvature at the spot touched, and this curvature then extends further up and down. If the contact is transitory, the tendril subsequently straightens out again. The degree of irritability[1] is very different according to the species: in *Passiflora gracilis* a pressure of one milligram suffices to effect the curvature in a short time (25 seconds); with others a pressure of 3 or 4 milligrams is necessary, and the curvature occupies a longer time (after 30 seconds with *Sicyos*). The tendrils of other species become curved within a few minutes after being rubbed slightly at one spot; in *Dicentra thalictrifolia* after half an hour, in *Smilax* not till after more than an hour; in *Ampelopsis* still more slowly. The curvature on the touched side increases for some time, then stops, and then after some time (often several hours) the tendril again becomes straightened, in which condition it is again irritable. Tendrils the apices of which are slightly incurved are only irritable on the concave lower side,

---

[1] The following publications treat of both tendril-plants and twining-plants —

Hugo Mohl. '*Über den Bau und das Winden der Ranken und Schlingpflanzen*,' Tubingen, 1827.

Charles Darwin: '*The Movements and Habits of Climbing Plants*,' London, 1875.

On the irritability and movements of tendrils the following may be consulted.—

Hugo de Vries: '*Langenwachsthum der Ober- und Unterseite sich krummender Ranken*,' Arb. d bot Inst. in Wzbg., B I, p 302.

'*Über die inneren Vorgange bei den Wachsthumskrummungen mehrzellige Organe*,' Bot Zeitg , 1879, p. 830.

Casimir de Candolle: '*Observations sur l'enroulement des Vrilles*,' Bibliothèque universelle de Genève, Jan., 1877, T LVIII.

Treub describes (*Ann. du Jardin botanique de Buitenzorg*, vol iii, pp 1–87, Leiden, 1882) a new class of climbing plants, the climbing organs of which are in effect very short, curved, hook-like tendrils, which on contact with a support grow in thickness to an unusual extent.

On twining plants the following may be consulted —

Hugo de Vries. '*Zur Mechanik der Bewegung von Schlingpflanzen*,' Arb d bot Inst zu Wurzbg , B. I, 1874, p. 317.

Schwendener '*Über das Winden der Pflanzen*,' Monatsber der Berliner Akad , Dec , 1881

In opposition to the latter treatise, which depends on very scanty observations, I wrote a note ('*Notiz uber Schlingpflanzen*') in Arb d bot Inst zu Wzbg , B II, p. 719.

Schwendener's reply to this note (Jahrb f wiss Bot , B XIII, H 2) leaves no doubt that he was entirely unacquainted with the most important phenomena described in the present lecture, and in my note referred to, whence his reply is completely without object. I believe that in this lecture that, without setting up any theory, I have indicated the path along which the true cause of twining is to be found; in the case of phenomena so involved it is above all important to test the scientific weight of the individual observations, and little is won by making a few observations on one or several plants and seeking to give to these a particularly important look by means of mathematical formulæ

others, as those of *Cobæa* and *Cissus discolor* are so on all sides; in *Mutisia clematis* the lower side and flanks are irritable, the upper side not so.

While in the condition of revolving nutation and irritability, the tendrils attain their complete length in a few days; the revolutions cease, the irritability disappears, and, according to the species in each case, further changes now take place. In some, the fully developed tendrils become immovable, remain straight, decay, and fall off—e. g. the Bignonias, *Vitis*, *Ampelopsis*. More frequently it happens that the tendril on the cessation of growth in length becomes slowly rolled up with the lower side concave, commencing at the tip and proceeding to the base, so that it at length forms a helix (*Cardiospermum*, *Mutisia*), commonly a spiral narrowed upwards into a cone (like a cork-screw), in which condition it then dries up (Cucurbitaceæ, Passifloræ, &c).

These processes, however, are to be regarded as abnormal, in as far as the tendrils have in these cases failed to attain their object, which consists in their coming into contact with a support by means of their revolving nutation during the irritable stage and while they are still growing; if this happens on the irritable side curvature results at the point of contact, and this extends also to the neighbouring untouched parts of the tendril, so that after a short time—a few minutes or hours according to circumstances in each case, a coil is produced. This coil, however, is by no means closely applied to the support if it is very thin, but touches it only at one point of the concavity. The continued contact at this point, however, increases the irritable action more and more, and the coil becomes closer, until it has adapted itself to the support along a complete turn. By this means of course the contact-irritation is simply increased still more, and the free end of the tendril becomes curved still more and goes on closing gradually in new coils around the support, until even the extreme tip applies itself closely to it. The nearer the place first touched lies to the base of the tendril, the more numerous the coils around the support and the firmer the holdfast; nevertheless even a few coils around the support with the end of the tendril suffice to fix this latter very firmly.

Those parts of the tendril which are between its base and the point where it is fixed are obviously not able to coil themselves around the support, although the stimulus which causes the curvature is propagated to this region ; the effect of the stimulus is simply that the portion of the tendril lying between the fixed point and the rigid base becomes coiled in the form of a cork-screw, often with very numerous coils. This coiling is essentially the same as that which occurs in most of the tendrils which have matured without meeting with a support; but it differs in two respects from that spontaneous coiling. In the first place it always occurs, simply in consequence of the stimulus in all the tendrils which have become attached to a support, and not only in some ; further, in that it takes place after a short time (several hours or a day after the seizure of the support), during a period when the tendril is still perfectly irritable, and rapidly growing in length, whereas the spontaneous coiling up takes place when growth and irritability have ceased. Moreover, the spiral coiling consequent on the stimulus of contact follows much more rapidly than the spontaneous one. Both are easily seen on the same shoot, where it is possible to find older tendrils which are not fixed and still straight, and younger ones fixed and already coiled up. This coiling up of tendrils fixed to supports is thus, in the same sense as the twining round the support itself, an effect of irritability, and it is only the mechanical impossibility of its twining round the support which impels the part of the tendril between the support and the base to coil up in this peculiar way. Like the curvature of a long piece of tendril in consequence of contact at a single point, this spiral incoiling also is a proof that the local stimulus is propagated along the tendril for a considerable distance, down to the rigid basal portion. The after-effect of the stimulus is not ended even with these processes, however, for tendrils fixed to a support subsequently grow in thickness, often even very strongly, they lignify, become solid, and are endowed with longer vitality than those tendrils which have failed in their purpose. This long continued after-effect is very striking in the case of the petioles which act as tendrils in *Solanum jasminoides*; the petiole, when it has twined round the support, swells up to 3–4 times its former thickness. This effect is less marked in the case of the tendrils of the Vine, though it happens not seldom that some weeks after the fixing of the tendrils the part closely applied to the support becomes considerably thicker than the parts not in contact. The most conspicuous example of such cases, however, is afforded by the tendrils of the so-called Wild Vine (Virginian Creeper); if these fail to attain their object they dry up completely and fall off, whereas the fixed tendrils become thicker, lignify, and after they have perished serve for years to fix the shoots to their supports. In many other tendrils, it is true, there is very little of this after-effect to note, but it must be added that the activity of the tendrils promotes the growth and well-being, and therefore affects the whole of the plant. On cultivating tendril-plants in the open for many years one cannot fail to perceive that those specimens which are afforded the opportunity of fixing themselves to bushes, cords, wires, &c, by many tendrils, grow and thrive much more vigorously than such as have to clamber up unsuitable supports and are fixed by few tendrils only

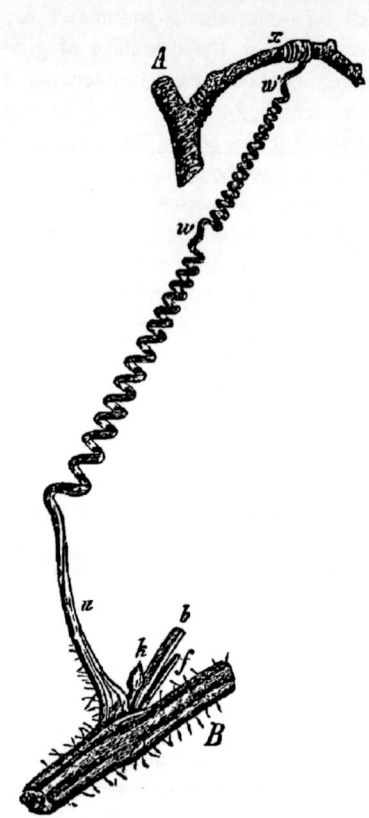

FIG. 377.—White Bryony (*Bryonia dioica*) *B* a portion of the shoot-axis from which, close to the petiole *b* and the bud *h*, the tendril *u w* arises. The lower piece of the tendril *u* is rigid (not tendril-like), its upper portion *x* has become coiled round a branch The long middle portion of the tendril between the rigid base *u* and the fixed point *x* has become coiled up into a spiral, thus raising the stem *B*   *w* and *w'* points where the direction of the coils is reversed

The coiling up of the fixed tendrils differs again by another peculiarity from that of those which are coiled up spontaneously; for in the latter all the coils of the spiral run evenly in one direction, whereas in the turns of the spiral of a tendril fixed to a support there are points where the direction is reversed (Fig. 337 *w, w'*), between each two of which there always lie a number of turns in the same direction, which is opposite to that of those between the next such points. In long closely-wound tendrils there are often five or six such points of reversal. Darwin has already pointed out that this is not a peculiarity confined to tendrils, and still less a specific consequence of the stimulus; on the contrary, the occurrence of points of reversal is a mechanical necessity. If a body which tends to coil up is fixed at both ends so that neither end can twist round, coils in opposite directions must of necessity occur, in order to compensate for the torsion inseparable from the coiling up. This behaviour of fixed tendrils can be imitated by cementing a narrow stretched strip of caoutchouc on to one which is not stretched; on releasing the former, it contracts and forms the inner side of a spiral, the outer side of which is constituted by the strip which was not stretched. On now seizing both ends and extending the double strip straight out, and then again bringing the two ends closer together, spiral turns will be produced to the right and to the left, as in a tendril which is fixed. If one end is set free, the strip will twist up and become coiled into a spiral.

Since all the movements of tendrils here mentioned result from growth, they only take place when the external conditions are favourable for growth, and the more energetically the more favourable the conditions are—that is when nutrition is active, the temperature high, and the plant abundantly provided with sap, caused by an abundant supply of water when the loss by transpiration is small. Given these conditions, tendrils can, as I have shown, carry on their nutation and irritable movements, wind around supports and become coiled up, even in the dark (e g. plants of *Cucurbita Pepo*, growing with the apical portions in a dark vessel, and nourished by green leaves exposed to the light).

As regards the mechanism of the irritable curvatures induced by contact (the twining and coiling up of attached tendrils), as well as the coiling up of free tendrils, there can be no doubt that it depends upon the process of growth in length and its modification due to transverse pressure on the side which is growing more feebly. Tendrils are irritable to contact or pressure only so long as they are growing in length, a passing curvature due to irritation may, it is true, be equilibrated again during growth, just as for example the passive curvature of growing shoots caused by vibration. If the stimulus at the support continues for a longer time, however, and the tendril twines round it, the difference in length of the convex and concave sides becomes permanent, and can no more be compensated. The cells of the convex side are proportionally longer than those of the concave side (just as in roots which have curved downwards, and the nodes of Grasses which have curved upwards); in the case of thick tendrils wound round their supports the difference in length is so striking, that it is at once detected by the eye, without measurement, as I have convinced myself in various cases. Recent experiments by De Vries, who marked tendrils which were still straight with cross divisions, and measured them after they had twined or coiled up, have shown that the growth of the convex side is more pronounced and that of the concave side less so, than is the case with regions on the same tendril which remain straight above and below the curved portion. A tendril of *Cucurbita Pepo*, for example, had coiled round a support 1 2 mm. thick; after the completion of the curvature the increment on the curved portion for each mm of the original length amounted to 1·4 mm. on the convex side, but only 0·1 mm. on the concave side. The mean increment on the portion which remained straight on both sides amounted to 0·2 mm. If the growth of the whole tendril at the time of contact with a support is but small, a considerable increase of growth in length is found to occur on the convex side, but on the concave side there is generally no elongation at all, or there may be even a contraction; in the case of a tendril of the Gourd this shortening amounted to almost a third of the original length.

Similar alterations in the length of the convex and concave sides are to be observed in the spontaneous coiling up of tendrils, as well as in the coiled up portions lying between the support and the base of attached tendrils; since in these cases the growth of the whole tendril is usually slight shortly before, the contraction of the concave side is also a very general phenomenon. (De Vries.)

The whole of these phenomena and others not here described lead to the conclusion that the growth in length of the untouched side is increased by the pressure of the support; this forces over the side which is in contact, and in the curvature which now follows the concave side is compressed and retarded in growth, or even shortened. It seems to me probable that at the same time a relaxation of the parenchyma of the touched side (due to its giving off water to the parenchyma of the upper side), and a corresponding elastic contraction of its cell-walls co-operate here; at least, in the case of tendrils which are growing slowly, the shortening of the side which is in contact appears explicable in no other way. But how the slight pressure of a light thread or the pressure of the nutating tendril on a support effects these alterations in the growth, not only at the parts in contact but along the whole tendril, remains for the time being entirely unknown.

The spontaneous coiling up of tendrils which are not fixed to supports is probably only due to the fact that the upper side goes on elongating for some time after the lower side has already ceased to grow; the cells of the growing upper side probably withdraw a portion of their water from those of the lower side (as the inner layers of pith do from the outer layers, cf. p. 573), whence the latter become shorter, while the former elongate.

According to later investigations by De Vries, the first directly perceptible effect of a stimulus consists in the increase of turgescence on the free untouched upper side of the tendril, and it is directly in consequence of this that the growth also of this side is accelerated.

The real problem here again, therefore, as in the case of the motile organs of leaves sensitive to light and contact, is why the conditions of turgescence on opposite sides of the organ are modified by the stimulus, and here again we shall point out that it is evidently the protoplasm which in the first place receives the stimulus, and then, by alteration of its molecular condition causes the turgescence of the cells to change. In principle, we may say, the stimulation in the case of a tendril is the same as in the case of a motile organ of *Mimosa*, only that it is here a matter of a continuous though very slight contact, and the alteration of turgescence leads to a permanent change by means of growth.

Without going further into the numerous questions of a purely mechanical nature connected with the curvatures of tendrils, it need here simply be shown why thick tendrils are unable to twine round very thin supports. On comparing two tendrils, one of which is twined round a slender and the other round a thicker support, it is obvious that in the former the proportional difference in length of the outer and inner sides must be greater than in the latter. If a thick and a thin tendril twined round supports of equal thickness are compared, the proportional difference in length of the outer and inner sides will be greater in the case of the thick one than in that of the thin one. If we now suppose the support to become thinner and thinner, the proportional difference in length increases more rapidly for the thick tendril than for the thin one, and it then becomes a question whether the growth in length of the two sides of the tendril can or can not attain any given value. As a matter of fact, the difference in length attainable by unequal growth of the two sides of the tendril has its limit, as is shown by experiment. The thin tendrils of *Passiflora gracilis* can coil closely round fine threads of silk, whereas the thick tendrils of *Vitis* can only coil themselves round supports which are at least 2–3 mm. thick. The most strongly curved Vine-tendril which I could find had coiled itself tightly round a support 3 5 mm. in thickness, and this only in one almost circular coil, the average thickness of the tendril at this spot was 3 mm. The concave side of one turn was therefore nearly 11 mm., the convex outer side nearly 29 mm long, and thus the relative lengths of both sides nearly as 1 2 6. If however this tendril, 3 mm. in thickness, were supposed to coil itself round a support only 0·5 mm. in thickness, an almost circular coil of it would then have a length of only 1 6 mm. on the concave side, and of 20 4 mm on the convex side ; the two sides would then stand as 1 . 13, and it does not appear that such considerable differences in the length of the two sides of a tendril are possible by growth. If on the contrary the problem were for a tendril which itself is only 0·5 mm. thick to twine itself round a support 0·5 mm. thick, closely and in an almost circular coil, the inside of a coil need only be 1·6 mm. long, and the outer side 4·7 mm , and thus the relative lengths of the inner and outer sides as 1 . 3

In order that a tendril shall cling firmly to its support, it is not sufficient that its coils simply lie on the support, on the contrary they must press themselves closely to it. That this actually takes place is shown by the fact that if tendrils are allowed to coil round smooth supports which are then withdrawn, the coils at once become narrower and their number increases (De Vries) This fact shows at the same time that the tendril irritated by contact with a support strives to make a curvature the radius of which is smaller than that of the support, provided that the support is not too thin and the tendril not too thick.

With regard to the pressure which the coils of a tendril exert on the support, those cases are very instructive where thin leaves are entwined by strong tendrils, and are thereby compressed and folded.

Since the biological object of tendrils is to grasp supports—usually other plants—and thus to enable the thin stems of the tendril-plant to climb, it becomes a matter of primary importance to bring the tendrils into contact with supports; this is usually accomplished in a wonderfully complete manner by the fact that at the time when they are irritable, not only the tendrils themselves but also the apex of the shoot which bears them are endowed with revolving nutation, with the result that every object which can be used as a support, and which is by any means brought within the area swept by the tendrils, almost certainly comes in contact with one. The apex of the shoot bearing the tendrils usually describes elliptical ascending spirals, the course of which is completed in from 1 to 5 hours. As with twining

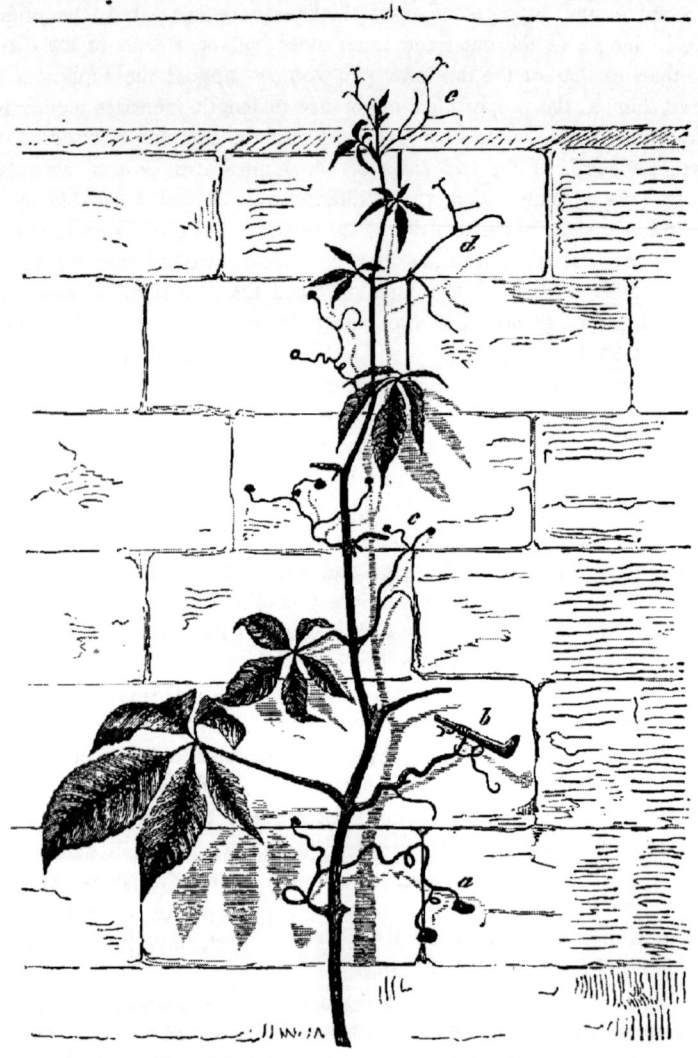

FIG. 378.—Upper portion of the end of a climbing shoot of the Virginian Creeper (*Ampelopsis hederacea*). *b* a tendril which has coiled itself in the ordinary manner round a nail; *a c* tendrils which have become fixed to the wall by means of cushion-like outgrowths or clasping organs; *d* a tendril which is still nutating—its tips are groping about on the wall, but are still devoid of clasping organs; *e* young tendrils.

stems so also with tendrils, a pronounced positive heliotropism would often carry them away from the support, and would therefore be injurious. Some in fact appear to be not heliotropic at all (*Pisum* according to Darwin), in others a feeble positive heliotropism makes itself evident by the fact that the circular nutating movement takes place more quickly towards the light than away from it. Some tendrils, particularly those of *Ampelopsis hederacea* (the Virginian Creeper), and *Bignonia capreolata*, have the remarkable property of developing broad cushions of tissue at the apices of their branches, when they remain for some time in contact with hard bodies: these cushions apply themselves to rough surfaces like suckers, and thus make it possible for the plants mentioned to climb up vertical walls, when they find no thin supports around which to twine. In this case it is evidently important that the tendrils should turn towards the wall serving as a support, in order to fix themselves to it, and this is attained by means of negative heliotropism, which drives the tendrils towards the wall shaded by the foliage, where they then, in virtue of their nutations, make various, one might almost say groping, movements, and glide over the surface, dipping especially into depressions and cracks, and then develope their attaching discs.

I now pass on to the twining plants, which have already been shortly characterised at the commencement of this lecture. In the first place stress is once more to be laid on the fact that we are here concerned not with special climbing organs springing from the shoot-axis, but with the shoot-axis itself which supports the foliage-leaves and flowers, and which is at the same time adapted for climbing up supports. The function of a twining shoot-axis is to twine round an upright support in the direction of a spiral line, and to apply itself so close to it that, by means of the mutual friction it clings sufficiently fast to the support, not to slide off from it again even under the weight of the appendages; the latter event does happen, indeed, even with the best of twining plants, if the surface of their vertical support—a rod for instance—is too smooth to furnish a strong mutual friction. This explains why most twining shoot-axes tend themselves to have very rough surfaces, provided by means of torsion-ridges and furrows, or curved, hook-like, silicified hairs, &c. · nevertheless, there are also twining plants the shoot-axis of which is perfectly smooth, e. g. *Bowiea volubilis.*

One of the chief differences which distinguish twining shoots from tendrils, must be understood from the beginning, and clearly borne in mind; namely, that twining plants only coil themselves round and climb up upright supports. This distinguishes them at once from tendrils, which are able to coil themselves round horizontal as well as upright supports, and downwards as well as upwards. It appears to be best that the upright support of a twining plant should stand quite vertical, though it is not impossible for these plants to twine round obliquely upright supports: it appears that these may be regarded as still not unfavourably situated even when the angle with the horizon is as much as 45°. The majority of twining plants, however, are no longer able to twine actively if their support forms a smaller angle with the horizon, although it cannot be denied that, under peculiar circumstances, some climbing plants are able to make a few turns round even horizontal supports In our further considerations we shall always assume for the sake of simplicity that we have to do with nearly vertical supports.

A further point, conspicuous even on superficially regarding the matter, lies in the fact that twining shoot-axes wind themselves round the support in a definite direction, according to the species of plant in each case. The Hop, the Honeysuckle (*Lonicera caprifolium*), and a few less well known plants such as *Tamus elephantipes, Polygonum scandens*, &c. twine to the right, as we are in the habit of saying—i. e. from the right below to the left above as one looks at the support; but the majority of twining plants twine to the left—i. e. from the left below to the right above when the plant and its support are looked at from the exterior. The latter is the case, for example, with the Bindweeds (*Convolvulus and Ipomœa*), *Aristolochia*, the Kidney Bean (*Phaseolus*), and a few less known plants such as *Thunbergia, Jasminium, Asclepias carnosa, Menispermum canadense*, &c.   Nevertheless, not all species are constant as to the direction in which they twine; in the case of *Blumenbachia lateritia*, one of the Loasaceæ, it is easy to observe that not only different shoots of the same stock twine to the right or left, but it happens here, even commonly, that the same shoot after having twined to the right for some time, grows straight upwards for a bit and then twines to the left, and vice versa. According to Charles Darwin, something of the same kind takes place in the case of *Scyphantus elegans* and *Hibbertia dentata*, though these are rare exceptions.

The first internodes of twining shoots, whether arising directly from the seed as in the Kidney Bean, or as lateral shoots from root-stocks as in the Bindweed (*Convolvulus*), or from sub-aërial perennial parts as in *Aristolochia*, are not as yet capable of twining, but grow erect without supports   It is not until the following internodes of the same shoot are developed that it is able to twine round a support; these internodes first elongate considerably, the foliage-leaves meanwhile growing out very slowly, and even 30—50 cm from the tip the leaves, separated by long internodes, are still in the bud-state.

In consequence of its own weight the elongated apex of the shoot inclines to one side, and in this position its revolving nutation begins—a rotatory movement which is produced, without the co-operation of external stimuli, by growth in length taking place progressively along various longitudinal lines on the surface more rapidly than along corresponding lines on the sides opposite. By these means the freely pendent apex describes a curve, commonly in the form of a drawn out S, but which is properly a portion of a very elongated open spiral   This freely hanging portion is in constant movement, whence the apex is carried round in a circle or ellipse. If a plant which twines to the right, such as the Hop, is taken, and a longitudinal black line painted on this portion of the shoot-axis, so that it lies on the convex side when the bud is pointing to the South, the painted mark is found subsequently, when the bud inclines to the West, to lie laterally on the north flank; as the bud then proceeds round to the North, the mark comes to lie on the concave side; and, later still, when the bud points to the East, it again lies laterally on the north flank of the shoot-axis   These revolving nutations are completed in quickly and vigorously growing plants in from 1 to 2 hours, or sometimes even in half an hour, so that in long pendent shoot-apices, the circular movement on a hot summer's day can be directly seen. in other cases, however, it requires many hours to complete a revolution. As a rule two or three of the younger internodes exhibit revolving nutation at the same time, and since these are all in different phases of growth, the curvature of nutation of the older usually does not coincide with that of the younger one. As new internodes develope from the bud they also begin to nutate, the older ones ceasing the movement; a new form of movement then takes place in the latter, viz. Torsion—i. e. the angles of the older internodes obtain a spiral twist round the true axis of growth, very much as the individual fibres of a cord are twisted round its long axis. I may here mention at

the same time that, in the explanation of twining, too much importance has been attributed to these torsions, as follows from the fact that some twining plants (e. g. *Bowiea*
volubilis and species of *Cuscuta*) exhibit no such phenomenon at all; moreover the torsions referred to only make their appearance as a rule after the shoot-axis has already become closely wound round a support, though in other cases it is true they extend close up to the bud, as in the Hop and the Bindweed (*Convolvulus*). It must be admitted that the study of the mechanics of the twining of twining plants is rendered difficult in the highest degree by these torsions, but on the other hand it is established that they are to be regarded as a bye-phenomenon only, as an adaptation the better to fix the stem to the support around which it has already become twined, and I shall subsequently refer to yet another useful effect of the torsions in shoots which have not yet twined round a support, as well as to the fact that another torsion, which is usually scarcely noticed, is necessarily and obviously combined with twining itself. It will certainly facilitate the understanding of the matter, however, if I take no further notice of all these torsions for the time being, simply adding that the direction of the revolving nutation always coincides with that of the torsions and with the spiral lines described round the support.

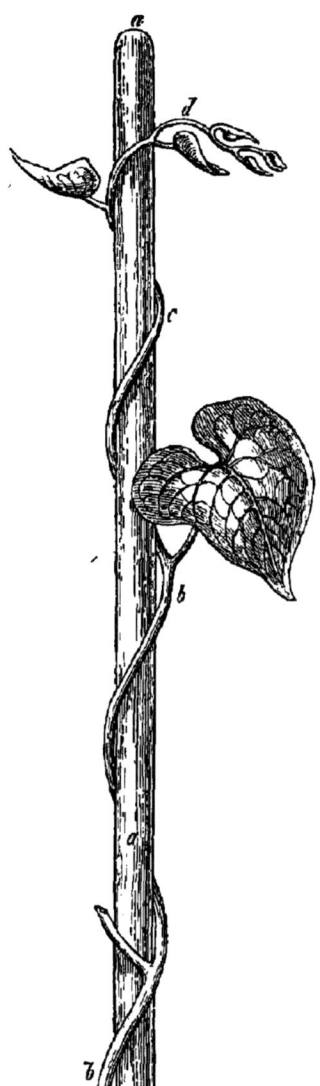

Let us now return to the revolving nutation of the free pendent apex. It is obvious that this, which is usually very long—not rarely 50–80 cm.—must during its sweeping circular movement occasionally come in contact with a support, a thin stem or a stick, &c.; like a tendril which is still nutating in a similar manner, the free sweeping apex of the twining plant behaves much as a man whose arm is extended horizontally and groping towards all points of the compass in order to fasten on a support. In fact, the twining plant seeks in this manner to reach a support, and when it meets with such with the anterior portion

FIG 379.—Shoot apex *b c d* of the Blue Bindweed (*Ipomæa purpurea*) winding—*i. e* twining round the rod *a a* Flowers, lateral buds and hairs omitted.

of the sweeping apex, the part of the apex lying towards the bud curves round it, and grows spirally up it. The uppermost coils of the spiral which the apex of the shoot throws round the supports are usually nearly horizontal, but as the apex goes on creeping further up the stem in this form, the internodes situated further behind undergo still further elongation. On the one hand the uppermost coils of the shoot are passively driven up the support by these lower internodes, since they only lie loosely on it; on the other hand the older coils thus become steeper and more erect. Hence it is commonly found, especially with thin smooth supports, that the lower already completely developed parts of the shoot-axis, run round the support in steep long-drawn coils, whereas the uppermost coils lie nearly horizontally, or obliquely with a slight gradient. Subsequently, as they become older, they also ascend more steeply. This is particularly clear in the case of thick shoot-axes, such as those of the Hop or the Blue Bindweed (*Ipomœa*) when twining round a cord or a wire: where the support is thick, it is due to purely mechanical causes that even the fully developed older turns are not very steep

The terminal bud of the twining shoot is often applied continuously close to the support when the latter is sufficiently thick; but where the support is thinner it often happens that the uppermost coil of the stem is twined quite loosely round the support, or presses on it only at one point In other cases again the bud may be curved sharply downwards close to the support, or even outwards and away from it, or upwards, evidently in consequence of nutations and torsions occurring in the uppermost parts of the twining stem.

As regards the true cause of twining and its mechanism, no completely clear insight into the matter has as yet been obtained. The twining of twining plants is not so well understood as the coiling of tendrils, and the views on the matter do not agree as to whether irritability is in twining plants likewise the important factor Where the circumstances are so involved it is perhaps better to put together the most important results of observation, without adopting any theory.

I lay especial stress in the first place on the fact that in the twining of twining plants some form of geotropism—i e an influence due to gravitation—very evidently plays a conspicuous part. this results from the following observations. On growing a twining plant—e. g a Kidney Bean, Bindweed, or Hop—in a pot until it has climbed up a rod, and then inverting the whole plant together with its pot so that the pot is uppermost and the twining apex of the plant lowermost, the youngest two or three coils of the shoot loosen themselves from the rod, and the terminal bud, first becoming free, turns sideways, and then erects itself and again grows upwards close to the rod. Mere up-turning thus reverses the twining round the support which has already been accomplished so far as concerns parts of the shoot which are still growing, though the parts which are fully developed and wound round the support are not further affected.

If a twining plant grown in a pot and provided with a support, is laid horizontally, the terminal bud in like manner loosens itself from the support and directs itself at once vertically upwards, and if the pot and support are rotated for several hours in a direction opposite to that of the coils of the support, those parts of the shoot which are still capable of growth gradually uncoil themselves. To remark it by the way, it obviously follows from these observations that twining plants (apart from special circumstances) are unable to twine round a support either in a horizontal or in an inverted position, and there is certainly no doubt that this behaviour depends upon an influence of gravitation which cannot be immediately identified with the ordinary geotropism of orthotropic shoot-axes.

There is a second series of facts of, if possible, still greater significance, since they show that twining plants are able to make spiral curves, even without a support, very similar to those they make when twining round a support; only it is necessary in this case that they are by some means maintained in an upright position   Hugo de Vries (1873) fastened a fine thread to the terminal buds of the freely sweeping shoot-apices of Kidney Beans and various other twining plants (*Pharbitis hederacea* and *Quamoclit luteola*), and, by means of a small weight of 2–3 grams, carried the thread over a pulley so that the apex of the shoot was drawn vertically upwards.   In the course of a few days spiral turns were developed, and after the portion of the apex here under consideration was fully grown, he observed torsions on it at the same time (though the number of both was such that no causal connection between them could be established), just as if the shoot had twined round a rod.   De Vries also fixed a revolving shoot-apex by gumming to a rod the side which was posterior during the revolution, and obtained a half to a whole spiral turn.

FIG 380.—Three coils, which have been developed independently of the support, of a very vigorous shoot of *Menispermum canadense* which had been cut off and placed in a glass cylinder. The coils are represented exactly, but the leaves, flowers, and hairs are omitted   the line *ff* is simply to render the direction of the coils evident.

The experiment with the thread is particularly instructive, and I have also obtained excellent results with it : it suffices to employ a weight just sufficient to pull the thin shoot-apex upright   With *Polygonum dumetorum* and *Apios tuberosa* I obtained in this manner in 15–16 hours 1–2 complete spiral turns, as well as torsions.   In these experiments, as De Vries noticed, the essential point is only the prevention of nutations —i e of the circular sweeping movement of the apex.   There are, however, various other causes which promote the development of free turns in the absence of a support—above all, the continued upright position of the growing shoot.   This may be elegantly demonstrated by cutting off the apical portions 20–30 cm long of shoots of the Hop, the Red Bindweed (*Ipomœa purpurea*), *Menispermum canadense, Dioscorea batatus*, &c, which have been grown in the open, and as yet have not attached themselves to supports, but are nearly straight, or curved into the form of a long S, and placing them in a glass cylinder 30–40 cm high and 5–8 cm. in diameter, at the bottom of which are a few cubic centimetres of water. Under these circumstances the shoots grow actively and elongate 5–10 cm., and in the course of 2–3 days there are developed 2–4 complete spiral turns, which present exactly the same appearance as if the shoot had wound itself round a rod of 1 5–3 cm. diameter.   Here also the upper parts of the coiled shoot (cf. Fig. 380) are almost or quite horizontal.   The further down the coiled parts of the shoot lie, and the older they are, the steeper and narrower they are, exactly as if the shoot had twined round a thin support.   No essential difference whatever is to be found.   If the glass cylinder containing such a shoot is now simply laid horizontally on the table, and rotated through 90° about every hour, so that every side of the spiral shoot-apex is in turn directed downwards, the spiral turns uncoil themselves again, and the whole shoot becomes perfectly straight. It is even possible to produce spiral turns in the shoot a second time by again placing the cylinder upright.

But even when the plants are left to themselves in the open there are frequently formed, as previous observers had already found, free turns which embrace no support. This occurs very often in the manner shown in Fig. 381, when the twining apex grows out beyond the rod up which it had climbed, if at the same time the now free shoot-apex is sufficiently light and rigid to maintain its erect position. If, on the contrary, it is very flexible and grows rapidly in length, it falls into a horizontal or oblique position, and begins to describe circular movements which lead to the formation not of close spiral coils but only of open S-shaped curves.

We now come to the question why the free, horizontally sweeping shoots make no spiral turns. In the first place we have already seen that the apex of a twining plant coiled round a rod, spontaneously uncoils itself from the rod if the plant is laid in a horizontal position and slowly rotated, and, as I have said above, even the spiral coils produced in a glass cylinder again become straight if the whole is laid in a horizontal position and slowly rotated. But a long thin sweeping shoot-apex finds itself in the same position, as its posterior parts make torsions the anterior pliant apical portion is thereby passively rotated, as if it had been fastened to a horizontal rotating axis—a movement which I shall, for reasons which will appear later, designate klinostat-movement. By this means the pendent, freely sweeping and nutating shoot-apex, is placed in the same position as a pot-plant twining round

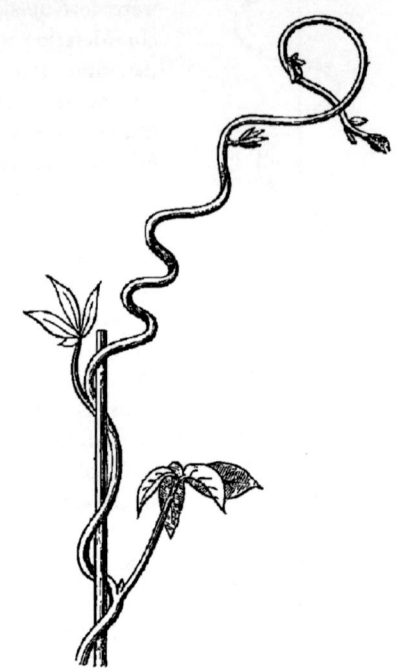

FIG. 381.—Apex of a shoot of *Akebia quinata* which has grown out beyond the support and formed free coils

a rod, which when placed horizontally and slowly rotated, again uncoils itself from the rod.

I am indeed convinced that the prevention of the formation of spiral turns in free-growing shoots, simply in consequence of this klinostat-movement, is of great use for the plant, for if every free sweeping shoot were to make spiral turns, it would be impossible for it to seize a support, whereas if this is prevented by means of the klinostat-movement the apex of the shoot maintains a form which enables it to coil round a support immediately it comes in contact with it. Darwin and De Vries had already mentioned the easily demonstrated fact that feebly growing shoots of twining plants make free coils which often have the greatest resemblance to old, free, coiled-up tendrils, and I am of opinion that the

[3]   x x

cause in both cases may be essentially the same; as in the case of a tendril which is still straight but actively growing in length, so also in the case of the shoots of twining plants, so long as they are still elongating, the tendency to make spiral coils exists, but the tendency is not exhibited, or only to an insignificant extent, simply in consequence of the rapid growth. If the growth is enfeebled, however, and approaches complete extinction, the side which will be concave on coiling first ceases to grow entirely, while the opposite one continues to elongate for some time longer as the growing side. It thus happens, and not very seldom, that even long pendent shoots, which have found no support and therefore have their growth interfered with, finally make several corkscrew-like turns, and then die off altogether, as I have often observed in the case of *Dioscorea batatus* and *D Japonica*. But it happens much more frequently that feeble shoots before they cease to grow altogether, first give up their circular nutation, suddenly erect themselves, and then, in the course of several days, make 2–5 corkscrew-like, and usually very narrow flat coils, and then cease growing altogether. In this case there are evidently two factors working together to the same end, on the one hand, the tendency already referred to, resembling that of tendrils, to roll themselves up spirally, and, on the other, the vertical position due to geotropic erection, and which even in vigorously growing shoots induces the formation of free coils.

It will, however, certainly need further and very careful researches to derive the mechanical theory of twining from the statements just made, and which I put forward simply as facts

It is a question as yet undecided whether twining shoot-axes are irritable. The question was answered in the affirmative on insufficient grounds by Mohl (1827) to whom we owe the first useful investigation of twining plants; but subsequently denied on still less sufficient grounds by Darwin. From De Vries' researches the question also appeared to me to be decided in the negative; but a more careful apprehension of the term irritability gives the matter another aspect. When Darwin denies irritability to twining plants because they make no twining movements when slightly pressed or rubbed, it is much as if sensitiveness to light were denied to the retina of the eye because mere rubbing of the eye-lid does not produce vision. The better reasons which De Vries adduces against the irritability cannot be so quickly disposed of, though in my opinion they cannot be maintained.

It is above all important what is meant by the word irritability. I understand by this term, as already said, that kind of reaction which the living organism exclusively, as such and in consequence of its vital capacity, exhibits towards external influences. When it is found then that an inverted twining plant spontaneously uncoils itself again from the support, when the apex coiled round a support and artificially uncoiled spontaneously straightens itself and nutates, when merely placing the shoot erect causes it to make spiral turns as if it had a support—I find in all this the essential characteristics of irritability in the above sense, though of course it affords no explanation of the true mechanism of twining

The irritability of twining shoot-axes, however, comes in not merely as one of the causes of twining. I have for many years observed thousands of twining plants throughout their lives, and found that vigorous shoots when they grow out beyond the support or meet with none at all, become moribund; it is easy to observe that a shoot which has been growing for some time without a support, on being afforded opportunity to twine round a support obtains after a few days a new lease of life, so to speak, and grows much more actively. Here, then, we have an effect similar to that met with in the case of tendril-plants, where likewise the whole plant attains greater vigour when it can employ its tendrils

With regard to the question as to the irritability of twining plants being a cause of twining itself, the fact must moreover be mentioned that by no means all twining plants agree in this respect It was long ago made known by Mohl that the Dodder (*Cuscuta*) is impelled by mere continued contact with a support to twine closely around it, exactly like a tendril; these plants, however, are at the same time slightly geotropic, and as they twine they thus tend to ascend in which they resemble twining plants. A few more words, again, as to the leaf-stalks of *Lygodium*; these, as is usually said, behave exactly like twining shoot-axes, and in fact exhibit the greatest possible similarity to them, yet Mohl with equal right designates them as tendrils. According to my observations, in fact, the leaf-stalks of *Lygodium* act at the same time both as tendrils and twining plants · tendrils in so far as they are induced to twine round a support, exactly like true tendrils, only by continued contact; while they resemble twining plants in that they run round the stem only upwards, though in doing this they can, like *Blumenbachia*, alter the direction of the spirals.

The opposite extreme is afforded by the peduncles of the female inflorescence of the water-plant *Vallisneria*, which are often more than a metre long and about as thick as sewing-thread At the period when fertilization takes place these long filaments are extended in order that the female flowers may float on the surface of the water; after fertilization, however, the filament contracts in close spirals like a cork-screw, evidently because the one side shortens or the other lengthens, just as in the case of the coiling up of tendrils or erect twining shoots which have met with no support.

Unfortunately there is not space here to render clearer the question as to the true nature of twining shoot-axes, though I must still mention one or two of the more important facts

It has already been stated that the upper end of a spirally wound twining stem makes flat and nearly horizontal turns, whereas the older turns, further removed from the bud, are steeper; and the same is the case when no support is present. In other words, the turns are at first flat and become higher and steeper with increasing age, especially when the support is thin It is scarcely to be questioned that this change is due to the influence of gravitation, in any case it is of use to the plant, since when the coils which at first lie only loosely on the support raise themselves and tend to become straighter, they must at the same time go on clasping the support more closely To make this clear, it is only necessary to wind a flexible caoutchouc tube round a rod in loose low coils, and then extend the two ends of the tube with the hands; the coils will then become steeper and apply themselves more closely to the rod. But even young coils begin to exert pressure on the support, if the latter is smooth and is then withdrawn from the coils, they become closer, exactly as in the case of coiling tendrils.

I stated above that the numerous torsions observed on many twining shoots, and which sometimes in the case of the Hop and of the common Bindweed extend close up to the bud, have nothing to do with the problem of twining proper, although they are probably of use for fixing the shoots to the support eventually. On the other hand a torsion is necessarily connected with the actual twining itself, even in the case of twining plants in which the above-mentioned torsions never occur, simply because the laws of mechanics demand it. Since this unavoidable torsion is usually not visible at all, it will be well for the student to convince himself of its necessary existence. Suppose a long caoutchouc tube laid on the table in the form of a helix : hold the outer end of the tube fast with one hand, and seize the inner end with the other, and raise the arm till the whole tube stands vertical on the table : supposing a black or white straight line to have been previously drawn on the tube so that, when the tube lies on the table the line runs, for instance, on the convex side of the turns of the helix, it is then noticed that, after the tube has been stretched in the manner described, that the line runs round the tube in the form of a spiral, and this so that one turn of this torsion line comes on each turn of the original helix, but in the opposite direction to the original coils of the helix.

Finally, the additional remark that the numbers of twining plants known are greater than those of tendril-plants, and, like the latter, they occur in all parts of the world, but especially in America. Mohl, even in 1827, gave the numbers of twining plants known to him as 866, and it is certain that more than a thousand could now be enumerated.

The preceding considerations have always reference to the young shoot-apex only, and its movement on or without a support. Further considerations might now have to be extended to the other biological relations of these plants, and in this connection those twining plants, especially tropical ones, &c., in which the shoot-axis after having wound round a support then developes wood and secondary cortex by subsequent growth in thickness, would be of peculiar interest. However, we must here leave these matters and the conclusions to be drawn from them.

LECTURE XXXIX.

GEOTROPISM AND HELIOTROPISM[1].

It appears to naïve unprejudiced mankind a self-evident fact that a tree, e g. a Fir-tree, grows with its stem upright (in this case exactly vertical) and that its apex always tends upwards again in the same direction; whereas the primary root in like manner penetrates the soil vertically downwards. The main branches of the stem, however, stand horizontally, and put forth horizontally lateral branches, and even the needle-like leaves of the Fir lay themselves horizontally in the plane in which the main branches subdivide; the lateral rootlets springing from the main root, again, have their proper directions with respect to the horizon, they grow horizontally or obliquely downwards, but produce in their turn lateral rootlets of second and third order which are able to grow out in all directions. Exactly as in the case of the Fir-tree, so with many thousands of other plants, although with some subordinate

---

[1] The older literature on Geotropism as well as on Heliotropism, up to the year 1865, is collected and criticised in my 'Handbuch der Experimental-Physiologie,' pp 38, &c, and pp 88–112

Of the more recent works on Geotropism the following will be most serviceable to the beginner,—

Sachs 'Langenwachsthum der Ober- und Unterseite horizontal gelegter, sich aufwärts krummender Sprosse' (Arb d bot Inst zu Wzbg B I, p 193)

Sachs . 'Über das Wachsthum der Haupt- und Nebenwurzeln' (ibid. B I, pp 385 and 584).

Sachs 'Über Wachsthum und Geotropismus aufrechter Stengeln' (Flora, 1873, pp 321, &c).

Sachs: 'Über Ausschliessung der geotropischen und heliotropischen Krümmungen während des Wachsens' (Arb. d bot Inst zu Wzbg B II, p 209), where I described the Klinostat (the idea of which had already been indicated in my 'Handbuch,' 1865), and the horizontal revolution as means for eliminating heliotropic curvatures

Detlefsen's work referred to in the text, 'Über die von Darwin behauptete Gehirnfunktion der Wurzelspitzen,' is also found in Arb d bot Inst. zu Wzbg (B II, p 627).

I refer the reader, finally, to the detailed description of geotropic curvatures in my 'Lehrbuch' (IV Aufl 1874, pp 811, &c.)

Of recent works on Heliotropism I quote only the following —

Hermann Muller (Thurgau) 'Über Heliotropismus' (Flora, 1876, Nos 5 and 6). I have here to remark that my new theory of heliotropism was first published in the introduction to this treatise, and that Muller expressly mentions this, I may indeed add that the introduction in question consists of my own words It is therefore not right that certain more recent authors should speak of my theory as Muller's In sharp contrast to my theory of heliotropism stands that of Julius Wiesner in his very extensive treatise, 'Die heliotropischen Erscheinungen im Pflanzenreich' (Denkschr der kaiserl. Akad. der Wiss in Wien, B 39, 1878, and B 43, 1880) I can with confidence leave it to the future to decide the matter, and entertain not the slightest doubt that my theory, as soon as it is but generally understood, will be accepted on all sides.

differences as regards the lateral shoots and roots; the petioles especially of most plants tend to direct themselves obliquely upwards, and the laminæ to place themselves so that the rays of light fall perpendicularly on their surface.

There are, however, many other plants the shoots of which do not become erect, and which have no primary root penetrating vertically into the earth; plants which creep horizontally on the soil, or cling close to the oblique or vertical surfaces of rocks, walls, trees, &c., and extend themselves upwards or laterally. There are also numerous leaf-forming shoots which, like primary roots, penetrate vertically downwards into the soil, or permeate it obliquely or even horizontally, and in general we find that the various organs of one and the same plant assume the most various directions with regard to the horizon of the situation they may happen to occupy. Frequently it also happens that an organ grows when young in a different direction from that followed subsequently; this is very conspicuous with the branches of most species of *Pinus*, the spring-shoots of which stand erect and subsequently assume slowly the horizontal position.

It is clear that the whole aspect of a plant depends essentially upon these different directions of growth of its different organs, as is at once intelligible if one supposes all the roots and lateral shoots of a Fir to grow vertically upwards like the main stem, we should then have, instead of the beautiful tree-form, an ugly shapeless conglomerate of organs, and the whole would be entirely incapable of maintaining its existence, because none of the various organs would then be in a position to discharge their proper functions.

This very simple reflection shows at once that peculiar causes must exist to compel the different organs of one and the same plant to assume different and fixed directions for each organ, with respect to the horizon. One of these causes, as with all vital phenomena, lies in the nature, i e. in the internal structure of the organ itself; another cause is the influence of some external force on this structure of the organ, and it is in fact, as has already been pointed out, gravitation—the gravitating force of the earth, or the general attraction of mass between the earth and the minutest particles of the plant-organs—which acts on the latter in such a way that they are compelled to grow in definite directions with respect to the horizon, or, what amounts to the same thing, under definite angles with respect to the vertical at their position. This latter is indeed only the direction of the resultant of all the attractive forces of the whole earth on a definite point in the organ of a plant. If it is, however, as we now know definitely, the gravitation of the earth which causes the organs of a plant to assume their specifically peculiar directions with respect to the horizon, it follows directly that the specific differences in their directions of growth can only be due to the differences in their internal organization: the gravitation of the earth acts on every cell of the plant in the same direction and with the same force, and if the organs are nevertheless caused to react differently thereby, the cause can only be sought in a difference of the internal structure of the organ itself. But as in almost all cases of irritability in the animal and vegetable kingdoms, it is this very peculiarity of structure conditioning the reaction, which is not perceptible to the senses, even the highest powers of the microscope teach us nothing as to why the apex of a Fir-stem grows upwards, and the tip of a lateral shoot horizontally, under the influence of gravitation, and perhaps nothing brings out the point here at issue so much as the fact that the non-cellular plants behave, with reference to geotropism, exactly like those with cellular structure, whence also every explanation of these phenomena which is based on differences of cellular structure must be at once put aside as false.

The fact here treated of generally may be expressed as follows. If the parts of a plant are displaced by any cause whatever out of their original customary position into a different one, they become curved until they again assume the same inclination towards the horizon as before. This curvature, however, is caused exclusively by growth, and hence only those organs which are still capable of growth can regain their normal and original position with respect to the horizon. If a plant grown in a flower-pot, for instance, is laid with its pot horizontally, all those parts which are already completely developed retain the new position, and only those which are still capable of growth commence after some time to curve · the still growing shoot-axes, if they previously stood upright, become curved until they again stand upright, and the short growing portion of the primary root curves until its apex is again directed vertically downwards. Parts which originally grew horizontally do not rest until they have again become horizontal, those usually oblique become curved until they have resumed the same oblique position.

In order to simplify the description, I will first regard in what follows those organs which originally grow vertically upwards or downwards, and assume that such organs have been placed in a horizontal position Fig. 383 will serve to illustrate what then happens. *A* is a diagram of any seed-

FIG 382 —Growing flowering shoot of Crown Imperial (*Fritillaria imperialis*), the upper part of the bulb *s* being cut away all round, in order to expose the lower part of the scape *d*. The plant was then laid horizontally, and after about twenty hours the shoot at first straight (*a*) erected itself through *b* into the position *c*

ling whose plumule *S* originally grew vertically upwards, and its main root vertically downwards; this plant is now laid horizontally, care being taken that it can go on growing After a short time it is seen that the plumule has become curved upwards as in *S'*, until its apex is directed vertically upwards, and in like manner the primary root has curved, at the short part which is growing in length, until it can again grow vertically downwards. It is the custom to designate organs which behave like this plumule as negatively geotropic, and those which behave like this primary root as positively geotropic The lines *o u* in *S* mark a portion of the shoot-axis which is still growing, and the negatively geotropic curvature may be especially observed here; the posterior transverse section *o u* which lies at the limit of the fully developed basal portion has not altered its position to any marked extent, the anterior transverse section *o u*, on the contrary, has become displaced by the upward curvature into the position *o'u'*, and it is noticed that the under side of this portion of the shoot *u u'* has elongated considerably, whereas the upper side *o o'* has not elongated, or has even become somewhat shorter. A similar state of affairs is shown by the lines on the root, *W*, only here the upper and lower sides behave in a manner exactly the opposite from the above

The portion of the plumule *S* here considered is again represented in another manner at *B*, the case here selected being, it is true, not the most usual, though it is the most instructive : the upper side *o o* shortens to *o'o'*, while the under side elongates much more considerably, as shown by *u'u'*. The curvature which necessarily results from the shortening and lengthening is, however, not indicated in this diagram, so that the relative lengths may come out better on the straight lines. It is easily intelligible that it would also suffice for the purpose of curvature if the upper side *o o* retained its original length, while *u u* elongated, and in fact the line *o o* might elongate if only *u' u'* showed a greater elongation : in this case also such a curvature would result that the upper side *o o* becomes concave, and the lower side *u u* convex. All these three cases may actually be observed in the upward curvature. Exactly the same applies to the diagram *C*,

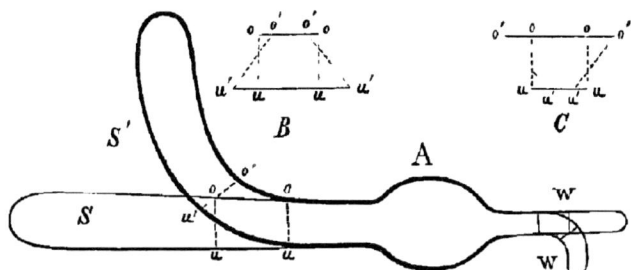

FIG 383.—Diagram to illustrate the upward and downward curvatures due to geotropism (see the text)

which represents that part of a root in which curvature is chiefly taking place, only that all the matters relating to the upper and lower sides are converse to those in *B*, bringing out sharply the meaning of the expressions positively geotropic and negatively geotropic . *B* represents the process of growth in a negatively geotropic organ, *C* that in a positively geotropic one.

We might now suppose Fig. *A* to represent a germinating non-cellular plant, such as *Vaucheria* : in this case the whole structure is a continuous utricle, the cellulose-wall of which is indicated by the outlines. Our observations here simply refer to two equally long portions *o o* and *u u* of the upper and lower sides of the utricle. We might, however, also assume this utricle to be subdivided by more or less numerous transverse septa into a series of cells, and that the portion *o o, u u,* represents one of these cells, and it is intelligible that the above considerations would not be essentially affected thereby. Finally, we may also assume that within the outline of Fig. *A* not only transverse walls but also longitudinal walls were present, and that thus the whole of the space included by the outline consisted of more or less numerous layers of cell-chambers. Even in this case the diagrams *B* and *C* would again serve to represent two individual cell-chambers, and we might suppose the cell *B* just as well situated on the lower side of the shoot *S* as on its upper side, and exactly the same would hold good of the diagram *C* with respect to the root *W*.

I may remark here that the reader can only hope to understand the phenomena of geotropism if he reflects most carefully on the considerations connected with Fig. 383, and makes them perfectly clear to himself.

Nevertheless the preceding simply shows how we have to figure the geotropic up and down curvatures in space, though nothing has there been said as to the cause of the change. We may now attempt to make this latter clearer.

It is sufficient then, as said, to place parts capable of growth out of their usual position, the erect one for instance, into another, e g the horizontal, this suffices as an external impulse or stimulus, which alters the processes of growth as shown in Fig. 383 By thus placing the perpendicularly (upwards or downwards) growing parts horizontally or obliquely, however, no more has happened than a change of their position with respect to the radius of the earth, and the next question is as to how far this can act as a stimulus on the growing parts. There is nothing for it here but to suppose the vertical line representing the radius of the earth as the direction in which a force of some kind is acting, which influences the growth of the plant-organ, and that the main point is what angle this force makes with the axis of growth of the organ Every change of this angle acts as a stimulus by which the growth is so influenced that the above described differences between the upper and lower sides appear, until the younger still growing portions again stand in the same direction to the radius of the earth as before

Now there is but *one* known force which acts everywhere at the surface of the earth, where plants grow, in the direction of the radius of the earth; and that is gravitation—the attraction of the mass of the earth The mere reflection that the relative directions of the organs of plants of like kind with respect to the earth's radius at different points of the earth's surface are the same in every place, shows at once that gravitation alone can be concerned here; if at our antipodes, or in South America, or in Japan, and therefore at the most different points on the globe, the stem of a Fir grows vertically upwards and its primary root vertically downwards, that means in other words that at each of these places the apical bud of the stem grows away from the centre of gravity of the earth, while the tip of the primary root, on the contrary, behaves as if it were attracted by the centre of gravity of the earth, or, both organs behave as if affected by a force supposed to be radiating in all directions from the centre of gravity of the earth There is, however, only one such force, and that is gravitation—the attraction of the mass of the earth—the force which causes a pendulum to hang downwards, and an air-balloon to ascend vertically upwards It is this force, therefore, which affects the growth of the plant-organ, as is shown particularly clearly when the longitudinal axis of a plant-organ is placed in a different direction, with reference to gravitation, than that in which it had hitherto been growing, and it is well to notice that this stimulus continues until every organ of the plant has resumed that direction which accords with its internal nature; or, we may also say, every plant-organ has its peculiar proper angle, i.e. the property of growing at a definite angle with respect to the direction of gravitation, and if this is accidentally altered, of curving until its axis of growth again forms the same angle with the vertical.

These reflections, with the necessary clearness of thought, should suffice to

recognise in gravitation the cause which influences growth in the geotropic
curvatures; but this recognition was, as a matter of fact, obtained in quite another
manner. It is usually by round-about paths that truth is detected, because the
direct path to it in most cases requires greater clearness of thought. so it was here.
The fact that it is gravitation which influences the growth of the plant was demonstrated in 1806 by an Englishman named Knight, as follows. He exposed seedlings
to the continued action of centrifugal force, by submitting them to rapid rotation

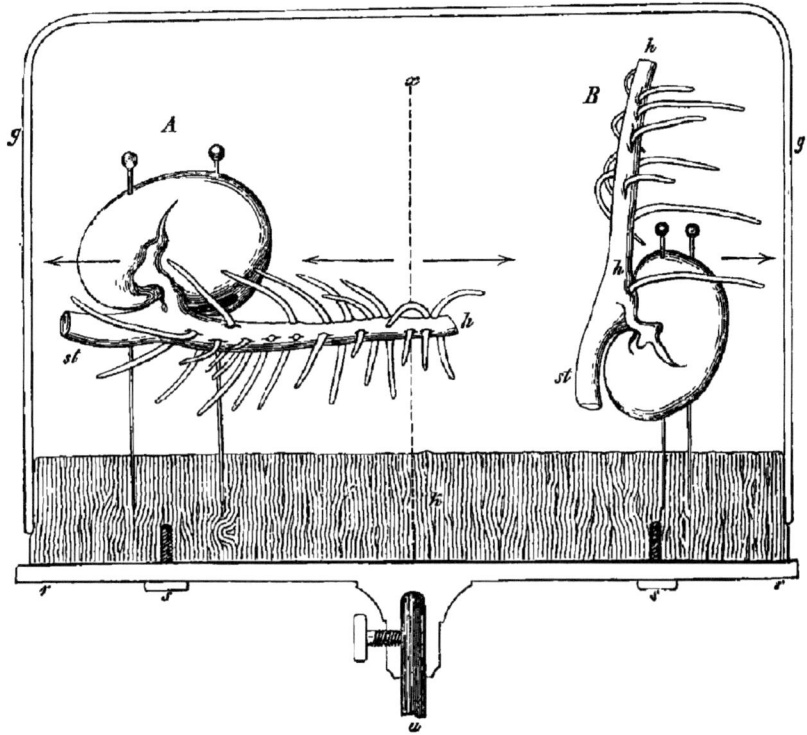

FIG 384.—The axis *a* is kept in continual rapid rotation   To it is fixed the circular
disc *r r* supporting the circular plate of cork *k*   On this, by means of two needles in each
case, the seedlings *A* and *B* are fixed   *st* the plumule   *h* the primary root   The lateral
roots are all curved outwards in consequence of the rapid rotation   *g g* a glass cover   *x* axis
of rotation

either in the vertical or the horizontal plane   It was shown that the growing
root-apices behaved in this case exactly as if they were simply projected from
the centre of rotation like the weight of a pendulum made with a thread and swung
rapidly round in the hand; while the shoot of the seedling behaved in exactly the
contrary manner, and grew towards the centre of rotation.

In the case of centrifugal force, as in that of gravitation, it is also an effect of
mass which comes into play, and it was in this fact that Knight perceived the
proof that the geotropic directions of plant-organs generally are produced simply
by the action of the mass of matter, and such an action could only be referred to
the centre of gravity of the earth   It is clear, however, that this kind of proof

necessitates much more complicated intellectual exercise than the reflections given above, which lead to the same conclusions much more simply.

It will probably be not undesirable for the reader to learn, at least as an example, how the action of centrifugal force on the direction of growth of the organs of plants can be demonstrated, and this more conveniently than Knight did it. I refer therefore to Fig. 384 and its explanation

If, then, it is gravitation, which we suppose to be situated in the centre of gravity of the earth, so to speak, and the action of which takes place in the direction of the earth's radius, or, what is the same thing, in the vertical line, it must be possible to nullify this action by compelling growing plants to continually alter their direction with respect to the vertical, in such a manner that the gravitation acts on the symmetrically opposite sides of a growing part of a plant for equal periods in opposite directions Starting from this reflection I constructed an apparatus which I called the Klinostat. This apparatus, which may be constructed in very different ways, has essentially the one object of slowly rotating, by means of clock-work or other motive power, a solid rod of wood or metal which must be exactly horizontal, and this so that a rotation is completed in 15–20 minutes. On this rod (*b* in Fig. 385) growing plants, e. g. seedlings, may be so fixed that they participate in the rotation of the rod without hindrance to their further growth. It matters not in what direction the growing organs are fastened on the rotating axis as long as the rotation is equable, so that every growing part of the plant turns the same side up-wards as well as downwards during equal periods of time, so that the influence pro-ceeding from the centre of gravity of the earth must act on the growing portions of the plant during equal periods in exactly contrary directions. If this occurs, no action of gravitation whatever can make itself effective on the direction of growth, since a longer or shorter time is necessary for this, and before the part of the plant has had time to make a curvature downwards or upwards, it finds itself already, in conse-quence of the rotation, again in a position which would necessitate its making the exactly contrary curvature, and thus no curvature at all is accomplished: it goes on growing in exactly the direction arbitrarily given to it when it was fastened to the axis.

After these preliminary remarks, I may now attempt to describe more exactly the processes which take place during the geotropic curvatures upwards or down-wards. Here I find myself in the agreeable position of being able to depend, step by step, on my own very detailed investigations.

We may first consider the upward curvature of shoot-axes which normally grow erect.

My observations have been made chiefly with the thick, rigid, long internodes of such flower-stalks as attain considerable heights in short periods, and the smooth surfaces of which admit of being marked with Indian ink, and of exact measurement of the marked portions The measurements on the straight shoots, as well as on the concave and convex sides of curved ones, were accomplished by means of•flexible rules stamped on stiff paper.

In order to be able to criticise the processes during the up-curving of shoot-axes it is necessary to be previously acquainted with the distribution of growth in them. this has already been described in Lecture XXXII. At first the whole internode, as well as the shoot consisting of several internodes, is elongating; subsequently the growth ceases at the base of the segmented stem, and only a certain portion of it beneath the apical bud forms the growing region—the region capable of geotropic curvature. In the case of individual internodes of sharply segmented shoot-axes, the

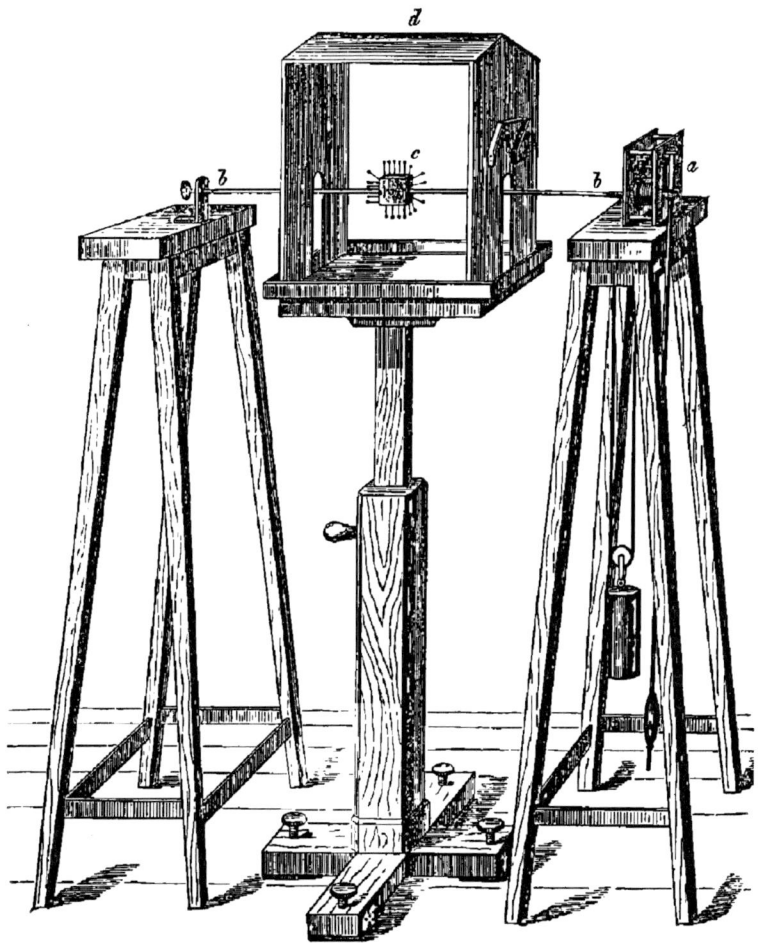

FIG. 385.—A klinostat. *a* the clockwork, with weight and pendulum, which slowly rotates the axis *b b* on this axis is fixed a cube of bread at *c* on which a fungus (*Phycomyces*) is growing The middle portion of the axis is surrounded by a glass box *d*, which stands on a dish filled with water, in order to keep the air around the plant moist (about $\frac{1}{14}$ nat size)

subsequent growing region may be situated near either the apex or the base: apical growth is the usual, basal growth the rarer case.

The length of the growing region, if parts which are already fully developed are present, is at a certain time at a maximum and then decreases, to fall to zero finally when the whole stem is fully developed In that middle period I found, in cases where the growing region was very long, the lengths quoted on page 543.

Within this growing region then, as has already been mentioned, the rapidity of growth is so distributed that it increases from the bud up to a certain distance from it, reaches a maximum, and then declines further back from the bud, and finally passes over into the region of fully grown parts. In this connection stems with many joints which do not form pronounced nodes (e. g. Asparagus) behave like individual long internodes, such as the scapes of the Leek. If, on the contrary, the shoot-axis is sharply segmented into separate internodes, as in the case of *Polygonum Sieboldi*, each internode exhibits its own curve of partial growths which increase upwards from the node next below, attain a maximum at some one place, and again decrease up to the node next above. The form of the geotropic curve in this case suffers interruptions at the nodes. Apart from these matters, however, all that has been said of single long internodes or that is to be said of shoot-axes with many leaves and no joints, applies in general and in detail to a jointed stem.

To understand the form of the geotropic curvature, however, a few other points have still to be mentioned. In the first place, every transverse zone of a growing stem first begins to grow slowly, then grows more rapidly and reaches a maximum, and then slackens in growth till it finally ceases. The more rapid the growth is at one place, the more pronounced the curvature it experiences through geotropism The rapidity, however, with which the geotropic curvature occurs, depends in addition essentially upon the thickness and elasticity of the part capable of curvature, since it is obvious that a thick shoot in order to make the same curvature as a thinner one, must suffer a greater difference in the length of the convex and concave sides, for which a relatively longer time is necessary, and that this also needs a greater expenditure of force where the elasticity is greater. Moreover the curvature which actually takes place at any place on the shoot-axis depends upon how long this has been submitted to the influence of gravity transverse to its longitudinal axis, and, further, the after-effect which makes itself especially marked in the case of geotropic curvature comes into consideration Shoots or single internodes which have been lying horizontally for one or two hours without curving perceptibly, may, when subsequently placed erect or fixed on a klinostat, become curved eventually in consequence of the geotropic influence to which they were previously subjected.

Finally, in criticising the form of curvature exhibited after some time by an orthotropic shoot laid horizontally, in consequence of geotropism, the circumstance has to be considered at what angle the vertical cuts the longitudinal axis of the shoot. Experiment teaches that a shoot which is at first vertical and then placed obliquely, is less strongly affected geotropically than if it had been laid horizontally: the geotropic stimulation is the greater the nearer the inclination of the shoot-axis to the vertical approaches a right-angle. If a shoot with a long growing region is laid horizontally, and geotropic curvature then begins, the anterior portions situated nearer to the bud will soon become erect, not only on account of their own geotropism, but also passively on account of the curving of the older portions, and by this means they come into a position in which gravitation is acting only at an acute angle, and thus exerts a more feeble geotropic action.

The co-operation of these very different factors brings it about that the form of the curvature, so long as the geotropic movement is taking place at all, is continually changing, even in the same shoot, and that it is different in different shoots. Only the final effect is the same, i e. the whole growing region finally erects itself vertically, and then goes on growing in that direction.

In order to avoid unnecessary details, and still to give an idea of how geotropic erection of a shoot laid horizontally is finally accomplished, we may suppose that *a b c d*, in Fig. 386, is a shoot which grows at the apex, the bud of which is indicated by the arrow-head. A few hours after it was laid horizontally, it had assumed the form *e f c d*; it is noticed that the fully developed portion *c d* now, as also subsequently, undergoes no alteration, whereas the still growing portion *e f c* has undergone a curvature which is nearly the arc of a circle. Some hours later, again, this portion of the shoot-axis has assumed the form *g h c*; in consequence of the geotropic after-effect, the region *h*, which is here that of strongest growth, has curved so much that the part *h g* has been carried passively back beyond the vertical. This phenomenon, however, comes forth clearly only in the case of very vigorously growing, long, and especially thin shoots; in those of the Corn-flower (*Agro-*

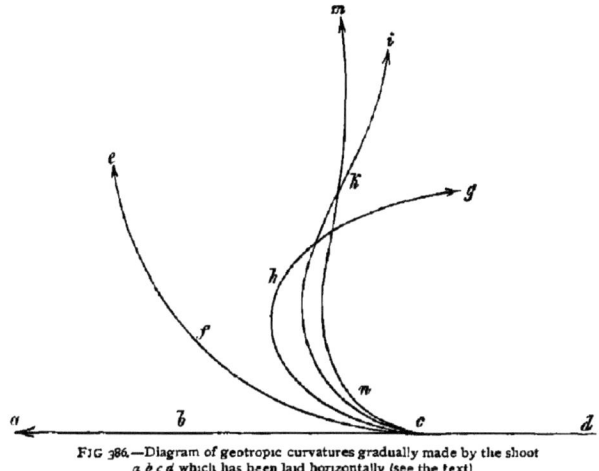

FIG. 386.—Diagram of geotropic curvatures gradually made by the shoot *a b c d* which has been laid horizontally (see the text)

stemma Githago), for instance, the part *g h* may after 6–8 hours be directed not only horizontally but obliquely downwards and backwards. Fig. 386, however, represents the curvatures of a horizontally laid flower-scape of a bulbous-plant, *Allium atro-purpureum*. When the apical portion *g h*, then, has assumed the position indicated, it is once more submitted to geotropic influence, which, however, must induce a curvature in a direction opposed to the preceding one, while at the same time the part *h c* goes on further erecting itself in the same way as before; hence the whole growing portion now obtains the form *i k c*, and this subsequently passes over into the still more erect and elongated form *m n c*, which finally extends itself perfectly straight. It is to be noticed that at last the persistent curvature of the geotropically erected shoot lies in the region *n c*, i. e. in that region where, during the whole process, the growth in length was at first slow and then ceased altogether. This region is, by its connection with the fully developed portion *c d*, in the most favourable position to remain nearly at right-angles to the direction of gravity for a long time, and thus to be submitted to strong geotropic influence during the whole process, although all other factors in the process are not favourable to the curvature of just this part.

It may thus be said, in a completely erect shoot the strongest and finally permanent curvature is at that place which offers most resistance to the influence of geotropism.

The erection of a shoot-axis by geotropism is, as we see, the result of somewhat complicated movements, which are influenced by numerous accessory causes; nevertheless the final erection in the case of fairly sensitive shoot-axes is mathematically exact, i e. even the feeblest curvatures which arise in the course of the geotropic movement become at last so compensated that the growing parts again become perfectly straight and upright. This is seen with extraordinary clearness, for example, in the case of one of our most remarkable water-plants, *Utricularia vulgaris*, the primary shoot of this plant, with its finely divided leaves, floats horizontal and quite free on the water, only the flower-scape rising perfectly vertically, 15–20 cm. into the air, although the slightest obliquity suffices to turn the horizontally floating main shoot round, so that the flower-scape falls horizontally on the water.

It scarcely needs mention that what has been so far said as·to the upward curving refers to the commonest cases only; there are several others in addition, where the behaviour is different on account of the organisation of the parts concerned. I will only dwell upon two cases, in both of which, however, it is not strictly the geotropic erection of shoot-axes which is concerned, but of peculiarly organised parts of leaves. I here refer to the so-called nodes on the haulms of Grasses, and the motile organs of compound leaves, especially those of the Leguminosæ, already so fully considered. These organs, when their leaves are completely developed, also cease to grow, it is true, but their anatomical and physiological constitution betray the fact that they are, so to speak, in a persistent condition of youth, their parenchyma is highly turgescent, and the lignification of the bundles is suppressed, and, above all, these organs (especially the nodes of Grasses) can be impelled to renew their growth simply by being laid in a horizontal or oblique position.

On the fully developed haulms of the Grasses, to which group our cereals belong —Wheat, Barley, Rye, Oats, Maize, &c —there are to be noticed at considerable distances (5–30 cm. or more) apart certain knot-like swellings, sharply marked off from the thin cylindrical parts, and usually coloured differently. If the haulm is split longitudinally, it is easily seen that the knot in question is nothing further than the annular and strongly thickened basal zone of a leaf-sheath, which envelopes the internode of the shoot-axis above the knot as a very thin but stiff inrolled sheath. In young haulms these internodes are very tender and flexible; the rigidity and elasticity of haulms not yet quite mature depend entirely upon the firmness of these leaf-sheaths

On bending a haulm sharply above the soil, so that the whole of its apical portion, about 1 m. long, comes to lie horizontally, it is noticed after 2–4 days that knee-like curvatures have been formed at its nodes, in consequence of which the apical portion of the haulm has again erected itself vertically; as a rule 2–3 nodes take part in this change. It is sufficient moreover if pieces of the haulm containing one or a few nodes are cut off and placed horizontally with one end, it matters not which, in damp sand, to obtain after a few days the same strong knee-like curvatures. These knee-like formations are produced exclusively by the nodes referred to, the other portions of the haulm exhibiting no geotropic curvatures whatever, the curvature of the node is due to the fact that its under side when placed in the unwonted horizontal position becomes elongated vigorously by means of growth, while the upper side grows feebly or not at all, and in fact often shortens considerably. If the piece of haulm with the curved node is turned so that the convex side comes to lie uppermost, then what was previously the upper side of the node which had become concave begins to grow also, and just as strongly; it therefore becomes straight and is thus at last much elongated, whereas a similar node on a piece of haulm treated in the same way, but which remains erect, shows no elongation of any kind. The convex under side of a strongly curved node appears smooth, translucent, and bright; the concave upper side dark and rough from minute transverse folds. On this side moreover there is often perceived a deep infolding, looking as if the node had been artificially bent till it cracked; this evidently depends upon the fact that the lower side as it vigorously elongates and curves upwards compresses the tissue of the passive upper side, a process which is intensified by the latter in its turn losing water, as can be concluded with certainty from the very considerable shortening. Of my very numerous measurements in this connection, I will only quote one in illustration of what has been said. A node of the Maize, about 12 mm. thick, was 5 mm. long on all sides; after it had lain six days in a horizontal position the upper side had become shortened by 0 5 mm. (i. e. $\frac{1}{10}$th of its original length), while the lower side had become elongated by 7·5 mm., i.e. to 12 5 mm. In other cases, however, the shortening of the upper side was still more considerable, (e. g. from 4 mm. to 3,) while the length of the under side increased from 5 mm to 11. Microscopic examination shows that the cells of the

FIG 387 —A piece of the haulm of the wheat (*Triticum*) laid horizontally, with its nodes curved upwards.

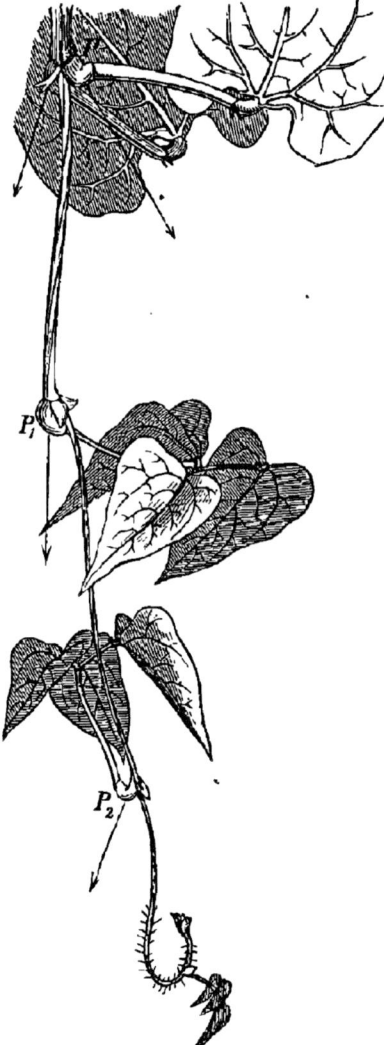

FIG 388 —Portion of a Scarlet Runner which, originally growing erect, has been for some hours turned upside down to show the geotropic curvatures of the motile organs P P_1, P_2.

epidermis and of the parenchyma of the lower half of the node have elongated to an extent corresponding to the above numbers, but without undergoing transverse division. As in all similar cases of curvatures due to growth—e.g. even in the case of tendrils and, as we shall see later, of geotropically curved root-apices—the tissue of the side which has become convex consists of large cells, containing abundance of water and relatively little protoplasm, that of the concave side, like very young tissue, of small cells with little water and much protoplasm.

That the motile organs of periodically motile compound leaves can execute geotropic curvatures I first showed in 1865 in my 'Handbook,' employing the figure here reproduced (Fig 388) · it represents a young Kidney Bean which together with its flower-pot was placed for about 4–6 hours in an inverted position, with the apex downwards and excluded from light. The petioles had the directions indicated by the arrows when the plant was inverted; but in consequence of geotropism the motile organs $P P_1 P_2$ became curved as represented in the figure, and thus the petioles, which are not at all geotropic on their own account, assumed the positions shown Pfeffer showed subsequently that in these geotropic curvatures of the motile organs, it is not a corresponding growth of the down-turned upper sides which occurs, but only a very considerable extension of the cells, combined with the taking up of water, and later, when the plant is once more placed upright this is again completely compensated after about 24 hours It is not until the plant has remained in the inverted position for several days that a permanent elongation by growth takes place on the convex side. The motile organs therefore afford an opportunity of confirming the theory of growth which I had previously established, in so far that, according to this theory, any growth of the cell-walls is preceded by marked extension due to turgescence, and this, as we see, can be again annulled even though it has attained a very considerable value, because the growth which takes place, in consequence of the extension due to turgescence, only follows some time afterwards.

Passing now to a more detailed description of the processes which occur during the downward curvature due to geotropism, I shall again select an object which, in consequence of the geotropic stimulation, finally places its free end quite vertical. This is very generally the case with the primary roots of the seedlings of Dicotyledons, although other organs also, e. g. the first seed-leaf of many Monocotyledons, such as the Kitchen Onion and the Date Palm, behave similarly, and again many lateral roots, especially those springing from stems, enter the earth vertically. The lateral roots which grow obliquely downwards, and other organs which behave similarly, I shall for the time being leave out of consideration; we are only concerned with rendering clear what happens in the case mentioned.

In such experiments with roots not only is great precaution necessary, but also the experience of years and an extensive knowledge of vegetable physiology, to avoid falling into errors, as did Charles Darwin and his son Francis, who, on the basis of experiments which were unskilfully made and improperly explained, came to the conclusion, as wonderful as it was sensational, that the growing-point of the root, like the brain of an animal, dominates the various movements in the root.

It is not necessary here to enter in any way into a refutation of this view, since this has been done by Detlefsen in the most forcible manner It is true that, to demonstrate the geotropic irritability of a root from which the growing-point has

[3] Y Y

been cut off, is a matter of some difficulty. But if Darwin's view were correct it is probable that in the case of geotropic shoots also the growing-point at the end of the shoot-axis plays a similar part, this is, however, by no means the case, as I showed long ago, since pieces of growing shoot-axes from which not merely the growing-point but even the whole apical portion has been removed, are able to make vigorous geotropic curvatures, and even thin lamellæ prepared by means of two longitudinal sections from such decapitated shoots are still geotropically irritable.

For roots also the statement holds good, that only the parts which are growing in length react geotropically, and are therefore capable of curving, and that the curvature is due to alterations in growth. Since now the whole of the growing region, as has already been repeatedly shown, is usually but 8–10 mm. long, even in the case of thick strong primary roots, and the curvature makes itself evident only in the middle transverse zones of this portion—i. e. the zones which are growing most actively—the curvature of roots in general appears to be much more pronounced than in the case of long geotropically curved shoot-axes; or, in other words, the radius of curvature is much smaller.

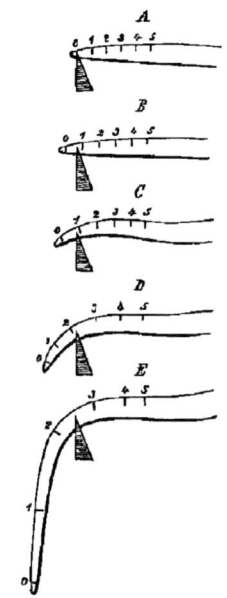

FIG. 389.—The growing end of the radicle of a Bean, curving under the influence of geotropism

The accompanying figure (Fig. 389) affords a sufficiently clear idea of the manner in which a vigorous primary root, previously growing vertically, when laid horizontally in loose damp soil, curves downwards behind a thin plate of talc The six marks indicated were drawn on the root with Indian ink, so that the mark o denoted the growing-point enclosed in its root-cap, while the others were about 2 mm. apart from one another. On the transparent plate of talc, behind which the root was situated, a triangular index of paper was gummed, as shown in the figure, and by the aid of this the movements of the root-apex could be better determined; the figure shows how, in consequence of the growth in length, the marks o, 1, 2, &c. gradually pass beyond the point of the index, because they are driven forward by the elongation of the parts lying behind. The relative displacement of the marks shows at the same time the distribution of growth within this region; at first it is the portion 2–3 which elongates most, then the piece 1–2 grows more strongly, and finally the principal elongation takes place in the youngest portion o–1. The oldest portion 4–5 has grown but little during the observation, because it was already towards the end of its growing phase at the beginning of the experiment, and, during the course of the experiment, soon ceased to grow altogether, similarly with the portion 3–4. In the figure, A denotes the condition of the root at the commencement of the experiment; B after 1 hour; C after 2 hours; D after 7 and E after 23 hours

The curvature is, as observed, after two hours (C) distributed along the whole of the growing region, though still feeble everywhere; after seven hours (D) the curvature is most pronounced in the region 1, 2, 3, where also most elongation has taken place. By means of the curvature, again, the piece 1–2, and still more the piece 0–1, has come into a position where it is directed nearly vertically downwards, and where the active component of the force of gravity can exert but a very feeble geotropic influence; the very feeble curvature obtained at the beginning of the part 1–2 is thus no longer appreciably increased, whereas the part 2–3 in consequence of its more favourable position, in which it is still cut by the direction of gravity at a tolerably large angle, becomes still more curved. From all that has been said, it will be noted that the youngest part 0–1 becomes directed downward chiefly passively, by means of the curvature of the parts lying behind it, and when it has attained this vertical direction it simply goes on growing in it.

The careful observation of numerous roots by this and other methods leaves no doubt that the geotropic processes are here in all essential points the same as in the up-curving of shoot-axes, only they take place in exactly the opposite direction, and on this account it is quite correct to distinguish the two phenomena by means of the terms positive and negative Moreover, as I have demonstrated, the down-curving of roots agrees with the up-curving of shoot-axes in that a re-tardation of the elongation of the axis of growth occurs during the curvature, while the side which will be convex grows more strongly and that which will be concave more feebly than would be the case in the vertical direction.

The proof of the identity of the processes resulting in positive and negative curvature which I brought forward, was important because not only Knight but Hofmeister also had referred the down-curving of roots to essentially other causes than those to which the up-curving of shoot-axes is due. In particular, it was believed that the down-curving of the root must be regarded as the mere sinking of a viscous pasty mass. This view was opposed by Frank, among others, and it is, in fact, utterly erroneous, as can be demonstrated at once by compelling the down-curving root to set in motion a weight much greater than its own For this purpose I have placed vigorous roots horizontally and with their apices sub-merged in a small shallow vessel full of water, from which a thread, suspending a weight of 1–1·5 gr, was carried over a pulley. Should the root-apex curve down-wards it must set the weight in motion, and this actually occurred. The experiment illustrated in Fig. 390 is simpler and more elegant,, but is of course less obvious · the result, however, is the same A seedling of the Broad Bean (*Vicia Faba*), the root and plumule of which were perfectly straight, was fixed into the piece of cork *k* by means of a needle, so that the root-apex lay horizontally on the surface of the mercury, figured black *n n* denotes a thin layer of water on the mercury. After about 24 hours the seedling had taken the form represented in the figure. The plumule with its sharply curved bud had become directed vertically upwards; but the tip of the root had become directed vertically downwards in the usual way, having meanwhile penetrated the mercury (which is about 13 6 times as heavy as the watery substance of the root) to the depth of about 1 cm Thus the part which had penetrated the mercury had displaced a weight 13 6 times as great as its own. It is obvious that the weight of the mercury presents an equivalent resistance to the entrance of the root-apex, and this makes itself evident in the figure by a curvature resembling a drawn out *S* being produced behind the curve due to geotropism. Moreover, the entrance of roots into the earth, and the driving in of the root-apex, in which process the particles of soil must be pushed asunder, show that the movement can by no means be compared to that of a flowing viscous mass; the root-apex, on the contrary, penetrates the earth much as does the point of a nail hammered into a board, or as a worm does. In thus entering a heavy or coherent substance a point of application must of course exist: this is afforded in Fig. 390 by the fixing of the seed with the needle. If such a point of application does not exist the root-apex cannot penetrate into the mercury, but executes sinuous movements on its surface. This is why it is so important that germinating seeds should not simply lie on the surface of the soil, but should be covered with a layer of earth sufficiently thick to enable them to offer sufficient resistance so as to maintain their equilibrium whilst the root is penetrating into the deeper layers. Germinating seeds which are not covered, or are too slightly covered, turn their root-apices downwards, it is true, but they cannot penetrate into the earth, because the small seed does not offer sufficient resistance. It is to be remarked, however, that

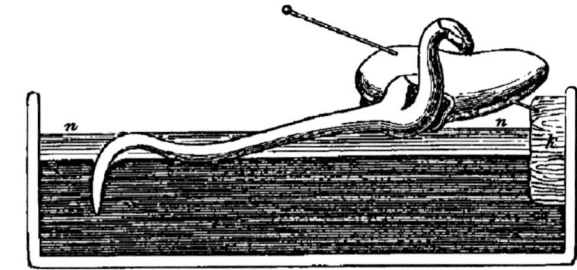

FIG. 390.—A seedling of *Vicia Faba*, the radicle and plumule of which had grown straight in the erect position, the seedling was then laid horizontally on the surface of the mercury

seedlings possess manifold adaptations in order that even when they are not covered, or insufficiently so, they may cling fast to the surface of the soil, so that the root-apex obtains a point of application on entry; this is often accomplished by means of numerous root-hairs being developed very early and fixing themselves into the soil.

With respect to the phenomena of Heliotropism, I may treat of them much more shortly than with respect to those of Geotropism, because, as we shall see immediately, they agree completely in all essential points: the effects of heliotropic stimulation are exactly like those of geotropic, only the stimulus is a different one, namely, Light. However, it is first necessary to describe generally the phenomena to be here spoken of. In the case of plants growing in the open or in a garden there is usually not much to be seen of heliotropic effects, especially if the plants are nearly equally illuminated on all sides, as happens when the light is reflected in all directions from clouds, &c. The direct light from the sun of course produces unilateral illumination, but the source of light revolves, so to speak, around the plant, and thus a similar effect is produced to that which I have already described in connection with the apparatus on page 561. Nevertheless, in very sensitive plants, e.g. young Flax-stems and flower-shoots of the Sunflower (the latter being named

Sunflower, *Tournesol*, on that account), it is possible to notice how its apical parts follow the course of the sun from morn to eve, always inclining towards it

The point is, then, that growing parts of the plant should be illuminated from one side only, or at any rate more strongly there than on the opposite side; hence in most plants cultivated in a room or in a greenhouse very evident heliotropic curvatures of the shoot-axes, petioles, and, in part, the lamina itself may be noticed. Apart from exceptions to be mentioned later, the apical portions of the shoot become directed towards the window and curved convex on the side next the room: petioles behave similarly as a rule, and, in general, by means of the heliotropism of both, the final effect is that the laminæ, especially if freely movable on long stalks, assume such a position that the upper side presents itself approximately at right-angles to the strongest incident rays of light. This betrays at the same time the chief purpose of the heliotropic curvatures: in combination with their geotropic properties, the heliotropism of the shoot-axes and leaves acts in such a way as to place these organs in positions favourable to the well-being of the plant. In this sense it is also to be understood that some organs, in accordance with special relations of life of the plant, turn their free ends away from the source of light towards the darkest side, and thus behave as negatively heliotropic in contrast to the above described positively heliotropic ones: this is the case, for example, with the aerial roots which serve for climbing in Aroids, &c, as well as the climbing shoot-axes of the common Ivy, which, when cultivated in a room, always tend to curve away from the window. It is very remarkable also that roots, which normally grow beneath the soil, when cultivated in transparent water or

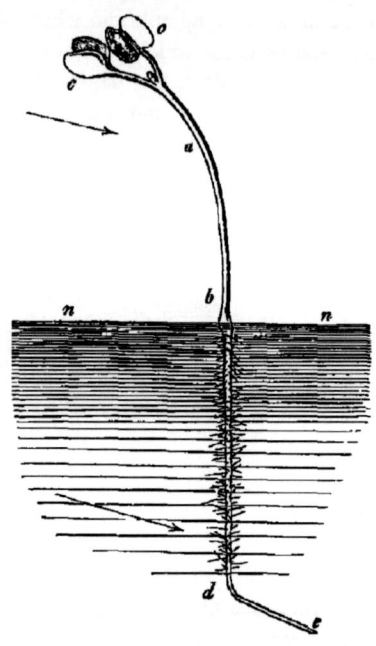

FIG. 391.—Seedling of White Mustard (*Sinapis alba*), showing the heliotropic curvature of the shoot-axis and root.

in moist air, prove to be heliotropic, some of them positively, others negatively; these roots thus possess in their heliotropism a form of irritability from which, under normal conditions of life, they derive no use whatever, and which therefore certainly cannot have been inherited by them according to Darwinian principles.

However, these remarks are merely preliminary. In order to study the phenomena themselves more closely, we may avail ourselves of a very simple experiment. We assume the seedling of the White Mustard (*Sinapis Alba*), shown in the accompanying figure (Fig. 391), to have its root *b de* submerged in clear water *n n*, contained in a transparent glass vessel. We further suppose the plant to be fixed in this position in any convenient manner, and to have been placed hitherto either in the dark or on a horizontal revolving disc in the light, so that it was either not illuminated at all or was equally so on all sides. In both cases the primary root grows downwards perfectly vertically, and the primary stem vertically upwards. We now place the vessel in the middle of a room, so that the plant is lighted from the left, as shown by the arrows, and preferably so that the rays of light meet the root and shoot at right-angles or nearly so. Even after 1–2 hours it will be seen that the growing parts of the plant have made the curvatures shown in the figure, and these after a few hours are considerably more pronounced; the plumule has bent over towards the window whence the light comes, and the illuminated side has become concave, i e it is positively heliotropic, and since at this time the upper two-thirds of the length of the organ are still growing, the whole of this region has become curved: the lower portion, already fully developed, has remained straight.

The root of this plant is negatively heliotropic and has become so curved at *d* (since growth was still proceeding at this part), that the convex side is turned towards the source of light, and the free root-apex *e* accordingly away from it. The part of the root *b d*, which was already fully grown before the experiment began, has remained quite straight.

The positive and negative curvatures of the heliotropic parts lie in the same vertical plane, which may be supposed to extend from the source of light to the dark side of the room.

What has been said sufficiently describes the heliotropic behaviour of most plants; of course there are also other cases, just as with geotropism, where, in consequence of the stimulus of light, the growing parts of plants tend to place themselves transversely or obliquely to the incident ray of light, but I shall take these and other cases into account in the next lecture; meanwhile, we here keep in view only the typical case illustrated by the figure.

In the plant experimented with in Fig. 391, however, neither the positive nor the negative heliotropism can properly exert its full effect, since the organs concerned are at the same time geotropically irritable also. If, then, in consequence of the stimulus of light, the apical part at *a* assumes an oblique or even horizontal position, the geotropic stimulation comes into play, in consequence of which it strives to become erect. The curvature which it actually presents after several hours, therefore, results from two tendencies—the inclination towards the light, and the tendency to erect itself. The plumule is thus in a position of unstable equilibrium between two mutually opposing forces. on shading the plant, the plumule becomes erect because the heliotropic curvature is then feebler; on illuminating it more strongly, the heliotropic curvature prevails over the tendency to geotropic erection, and the same (but with the converse result) would apply to the negative curvature of the root

If, therefore, for the purpose of more exact investigations, the heliotropic curvatures are to be made visible in their pure form, the action of geotropism must be eliminated. This can be accomplished by fixing the plant to the klinostat described above (p. 684), and placing the axis of the instrument so that it stands at right-angles to the window; on then fixing the plant so that it stands at right-angles to the axis of the klinostat, and thus revolves in a plane parallel to the window-panes, the effect of geotropism is eliminated, while the plant is continually illuminated from one side and can therefore show the heliotropic stimulation free from secondary influences. In this way Hermann Muller (of Thurgau), who was then my assistant, made a long series of investigations during the summers of 1874 and 1875, with much skill and with excellent results.

The object of his investigation was suggested by theoretical considerations which I then put forward as to the true nature of heliotropism. It was necessary to refute the antiquated and no longer serviceable, though in its time very plausible view of Pyrame de Candolle. According to this, heliotropic curvature was to be looked upon as the result of one-sided etiolations, since shoot-axes in the dark or in shade elongate more rapidly than when illuminated strongly on all sides, he assumed that in heliotropic curvature the side turned away from the source of light grows more rapidly than the illuminated side. This explanation seemed quite sufficient for ordinary cases of positive heliotropism, but various other observers had already sought in vain to explain negatively heliotropic curvature also on the basis of De Candolle's theory; at all events it was possible among other things to assume that negatively heliotropic organs, the above Mustard root, for example, or the aerial roots of Aroids, grow more slowly in the dark than in the light. But already observations which had been made in my laboratory by Wolkoff, contradicted this assumption, and Hermann Müller proved that as a matter of fact even negatively heliotropic roots, exactly like positively heliotropic ones, grow more rapidly in the dark than in the light, and the same resulted from much older observations by Schmitz on the negatively heliotropic and spontaneously luminous mycelial strands of the Rhizomorphs. All this shows that De Candolle's theory, although it seems to explain positive heliotropism, can by no means be applied to negative heliotropism. But positive and negative organs agree as to their heliotropism completely, exactly as with respect to their geotropism, only that the effects themselves are in each case opposite, positive or negative. After I had previously established this agreement concerning positive and negative geotropism, I could scarcely doubt any longer, from the whole position of affairs (which of course can only be indicated here), that with respect to positive and negative heliotropism, exactly the same would apply. It necessarily followed from this that the standpoint assumed by De Candolle must be abandoned, and that the whole subject of heliotropism must be looked at in an entirely different way—a view which impressed me the more, since according to all the facts then known a striking agreement exists between heliotropic and geotropic effects, and at the same time I had even then come to see that geotropism and heliotropism are to be looked upon as phenomena of irritability. In addition to these reflections, also, I came to the conclusion that in heliotropic curvatures the important point is not at all that the one side of the part of the plant is illuminated more strongly than the other, but that it is rather the direction in which the ray of light passes through the substance of the plant This view became probable to me from the fact that even very thin and in the highest degree transparent organs are able to make heliotropic curvatures —that is, organs in which the side turned towards the source of light is only a little more brightly illuminated than the other. Thus, for example, the root-hairs of the Marchantias are negatively heliotropic, whereas the very thin and translucent sporangiophores of *Mucor* are positively heliotropic. Similar examples are to be found also among highly organised plants. the thin stems of the Balsams are extremely translucent, and yet they are at the same time strongly heliotropic, whereas, according to De Candolle's theory, it must be premised that heliotropism is the more pronounced the less the light falling on one side penetrates into the tissues of the shaded side.

That in geotropic curvatures the important point is only as to the direction in which gravitation acts on the part of the plant, and that it is not in any way a matter of a stronger effect on the lower side and a feebler effect on the upper side, requires no proof; and these considerations led me to the conclusion that in the case of heliotropic curvatures also, it might not depend upon a *difference in the intensity* of the acting force on opposite sides of the organ, but that, on the contrary, the heliotropic influence is due to the fact that the rays of light enter the tissue of the plant, or even only . single cells, in a definite direction.

This view would be rendered highly probable if it were possible to detect the same relations between the rays of light and the heliotropic curvature, as I had established with respect to gravity for the geotropic curvatures. This required demonstration was afforded by Hermann Müller point by point. But unfortunately the space here at disposal does not admit of my going more particularly into the details of his demonstration: I must therefore refer to Müller's excellent treatise mentioned in the notes.

For nearly eight years I have been able to find no fact which contradicts the theory I have proposed, whereas numerous facts only recently established are to be pointed to as in its favour. Even in the case of the influence of light on the movement of swarm-spores, the important point can only be as to the direction of the rays of light, not as to whether the given swarm-spore is illuminated more strongly in front or behind. The same applies to the movements of protoplasm, in consequence of which the chlorophyll-corpuscles travel in the cells. With these and other movements which are produced in plants by light, moreover, the heliotropic curvatures agree also in that they are due chiefly to the highly refrangible rays of light. If seedlings like that in Fig. 358 are placed in a box which only receives such light as has passed through a solution of potassium bichromate, no heliotropic action whatever takes place; now this light contains only the red, orange, yellow and part of the green rays, and appears very bright to the eye. If the plant is placed in an exactly similar box, and receives the light through a dark blue solution of ammoniacal oxide of copper, the heliotropic curvatures occur with the same energy as if the plants had been exposed to full daylight; but this blue light only contains the blue, violet, and ultra-violet rays of the solar light. I obtained exactly the same result when the light fell on the plant through sheets of coloured glass Behind a pane of very dark blue cobalt glass, which transmits red rays as well as the whole of the blue half of the spectrum, the heliotropic curvatures follow as in ordinary daylight. Behind a pane of dark ruby-red glass, which permits the passage of very little besides the red rays, no curvature whatever resulted.

Guillemain examined seedlings in the various parts of the spectrum itself, and came to the conclusion that the heliotropic curvature takes place under the influence of all the rays, with the exception of the least refrangible heat-rays. According to him a maximum effect is produced by the ultra-red and ultra-violet rays. Wiesner, on the contrary, finds that in the objective solar spectrum all kinds of rays, from the ultra-red to the ultra-violet, with the exception of the yellow only, exert heliotropic effects; the greatest stimulating force always resides at the boundary between violet and ultra-violet, proceeding thence the effect sinks gradually until the green, and suddenly disappears in the yellow part of the spectrum, thence onwards it begins again in the orange and ascends up to the ultra-red, where a maximum is reached which is smaller than the one first mentioned. In the yellow portion of the spectrum there is, according to Wiesner, not only no heliotropic effect whatever to be noticed, but it even appears that it diminishes the influence of the orange and yellow rays.

The observations behind coloured screens then, do not quite agree with those in the objective spectrum; but I have already pointed out in my 'Handbook' (1865, p. 42) that there are certain sources of error connected with the latter mode of observation, and we may be sure that more has yet to be done in the matter.

Finally we come to the question in what manner do gravity and the rays of light act on the processes of growth, that they are able to produce geotropic and heliotropic curvatures? In spite of many hypotheses, however, as good as nothing is known about the matter. That when curvature takes place the turgescence of multicellular organs increases on the side which becomes convex is practically obvious, the question is simply why this takes place when gravity or a ray of light meets a geotropic or heliotropic organ transversely or obliquely to its longitudinal axis, and why the effect ceases as soon as that axis has assumed the direction of gravity or of the ray of light The question, however, only obtains a perfectly clear and strict form if the geotropic and heliotropic curvatures of the non-cellular plants also are taken into consideration, where the positive and negative curvatures of simple vesicles are concerned, and where there can be no question of a difference of turgescence on the convex and concave sides of the organ.

It would be a poor makeshift to try to explain the geotropic and heliotropic processes in multicellular plants by themselves, and to seek another explanation in the case of the non-cellular plants, and this for a very simple reason. If we take the case of a single cell in the primary stem or primary root of the Mustard plant considered above, which cell is situated in a curved portion, then this one cell behaves exactly like a curved non-cellular utricle of *Mucor, Vaucheria,* or any other similar structure.

LECTURE XL.

THE ANISOTROPY OF THE ORGANS OF PLANTS[1].

I use the above expression to denote the fact that the different organs of the plant assume very various directions of growth under the influence of the same external forces. It must be remembered in this connection that the direction in

---

[1] The first attempt to describe and classify the vital phenomena of plants here considered, was made by Hugo v Mohl (1836) in his treatise '*Über die Symmetrie der Pflanzen*,' contained in his '*Vermischten Schriften botanischen Inhalts*' (Tubingen, 1845, p. 12). Since that, scarcely any one troubled himself further about these matters till I again brought the subject into notice in 1870 in my '*Lehrbuch*,' in the second and subsequent editions, in the paragraphs on the directions of growth Meanwhile Hofmeister had introduced great confusion into this province by neglecting all the facts depending on the internal symmetry and other correlations of growth, and by ascribing the directions of growth of the organs of plants to the influence of light and of gravitation, and especially in cases where this had nothing to do with the matter, but the worst was that Hofmeister, in the consideration of the relations of direction of the lateral buds of woody plants, made a scarcely conceivable error of observation in describing the buds which stand right and left as arising above and below on the parent-axis, and drew conclusions therefrom.

The description given in this lecture is based chiefly on my treatise, published in 1879, '*Über orthotrope und plagiotrope Pflanzentheile*' (Arb d bot Inst Wzbg, B. II, 1882, p 226), where I first made clear the causal relations between orthotropic growth and radial structure, and between plagiotropic growth and dorsiventral structure.

More detailed statements, especially as to the directions of growth of the lateral shoots of the Coniferæ and Begonias are found in my '*Lehrbuch*' (Aufl III and IV) in the paragraphs on directions of growth

Hydrotropism is treated of in my publication (1872), '*Ablenkung der Wurzel von ihrer normalen Wachsthumsrichtung durch feuchte Körper*' (Arb d. bot. Inst Wzbg, B. I, 1874), and in my treatise '*Über Ausschliessung der geotropischen und heliotropischen Krümmungen während des Wachsthens*' (Arb d bot Inst Wzgb, B II, p 209), I first pointed out that orthotropic shoots and sporangiophores place themselves vertically with respect to the surfaces of a cube rotating on the klinostat, and that this is apparently a consequence of negative hydrotropism This was then confirmed by Wortmann in his treatise, '*Ein Beitrag zur Biologie der Mucorini*' (Bot Zeitg, 1881, p 368)

The reader superficially acquainted with our literature may be somewhat surprised that I have made no further mention in the preceding series of lectures of Darwin's book, 'The Power of Movement in Plants' (London, 1880) I find myself with regard to this book in the most painful position, and can only regret that the name of Charles Darwin appears on it The experiments which he, together with his son, describes, are made without sufficient practical knowledge, and are badly interpreted, and what little good is found in the book concerning general views is not new. The main conclusion to which Darwin comes in his book, that all the movements of irritability in the vegetable kingdom depend upon 'circumnutation,' characterises better than anything else the position which the two authors occupy It is unnecessary to say anything on this subject Detlefsen has said sufficient as regards the brain-function of the growing-point of the root (Arb. d. bot. Inst Wzbg, B. II, 1882, p 627).

which any part of a plant grows is determined by its geotropism and heliotropism, and we shall see further on that other external influences also are effective to the same end.

Before attempting to understand this phenomenon, which prevails throughout the vegetable kingdom, however, it will be well to make the fact itself clear by means of a few examples. In very many land-plants the original plumule grows vertically upwards, and the primary root vertically down-wards, and, as we have seen, both in consequence of their sensitiveness to the influence of gravitation, so long as one-sided illumination of any kind does not deflect the vertical directions of growth into oblique ones by means of heliotropic curvatures. But the lateral roots of such plants—e g Sunflower, *Ricinus*, Fir, &c.—either grow horizontally or descend oblique-ly, and the lateral roots of the second and higher orders which arise from these may grow out in all directions, according to their origin. The case is very similar with the lateral off-shoots of the vertical shoot-axis which is developed from the plumule. its leaves assume an oblique or horizontal position, the upper side being always turned towards the light, while the lateral shoots grow horizontally, or up-wards at an oblique angle.

In other cases, on the contrary, the primary shoot developed from the plumule at once grows in a horizontal direction, and forms on its under side roots which descend vertically, and on its flanks or its upper side leaves, which bear horizontally extended laminæ on vertically erect leaf-stalks, as for example Fig. 392, and the same is true, as has already been stated, of the common Bracken Fern, *Pteris aquilina*, (Fig. 55, p. 60).

FIG. 392.—*Marsilia salvatrix*, anterior portion of stem with leaves (⅓ natural size) *K* terminal bud , *bb* leaves , *ff* sporo-carps, arising from the petioles at *x*

In many tuberous and bulbous plants, and particularly in the case of some Aroids, such as *Sauromatum*, the strong leaf-stalks spring from the subter-ranean central body, and likewise become raised vertically upwards, like the stem of a Fir.

It is otherwise, again, in the case of the Ivy, for instance, the shoots of which, pressed closely to a wall, rock, tree-trunk, &c , grow vertically, obliquely, or hori-zontally, while the petioles are turned away from this substratum in order to present their laminæ at right angles to the incident light, whereas the aerial roots turn away from the light and attach themselves closely to the vertical substratum.

In Agarics which grow up from the soil of woods, the stalk, which is fundamentally nothing other than a shoot-axis, places itself vertically upright, though the umbrella-like pileus is horizontal, and the lamellar, tubular, or conical hymenial projections on which the spores are produced, and situated on the under side, are directed downwards. I showed in 1860 that this depends on geotropic sensitiveness on the part of these Fungi, for if an Agaric which is still growing is placed in a horizontal position, the stalk erects itself vertically, till the pileus is horizontal; whereas if this erection is prevented, or if it does not follow quickly enough, the lamellæ, tubes or conical outgrowths of the hymenium make energetic curvatures downwards like the ends of primary roots

Even stemless Agarics, such as those frequently growing out from the trunks of trees, exhibit a similar anisotropy in their various parts. As shown in Fig. 393, Agarics grow out from a prostrate horizontal tree trunk from the upper side as well as from

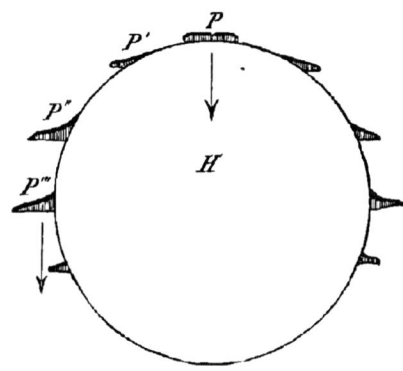

FIG 393.—Transverse section of the trunk of a tree, on which Fungi (of the genus *Thelephora*) are growing, *P—P'''*

the flanks, but always so that the sterile substance of the pileus itself strives to assume a horizontal position, while the spore-forming hymenial outgrowths are directed vertically downwards.

Exactly similar facts of anisotropy are met with in non-cellular plants, e.g. the Mucorini, which are so instructive in other respects also. If the spores of a *Mucor* or *Phycomyces* are sown on a cube of damp bread *B*, which, as in Fig 394, is fixed by means of a needle *N'N* to the lid of a large glass cylinder, the bottom of which is covered with water, the root-like mycelium extends itself in the substance of the bread, and after a few days slender sporangiophores arise on all the surfaces of the cube; those on the horizontal upper surface of the cube of bread at once grow vertically upwards, those on the horizontal lower surface and on the vertical sides, at first stand out at right angles to these surfaces, as will appear later, but subsequently they erect themselves geotropically as shown in the figure at *f'*. The mycelium of the Fungus, however, behaves exactly like a root-system: after it has permeated the nutritive substratum, individual branches of the mycelium also come out from the lateral surfaces of the cube of bread, but more particularly from its horizontal lower surface, and grow thence downwards into the damp air, while their lateral branches assume oblique directions.

Now, whether the parts of plants grow upwards, downwards, horizontally or obliquely, depends by no means upon their so-called morphological nature. Organs which, and with good reason, receive the same names in descriptive botany, may nevertheless assume entirely different directions of growth in different species of plants. Shoot-axes, as has already been stated, may grow vertically upwards, obliquely or horizontally, or even vertically downwards, as happens not rarely with

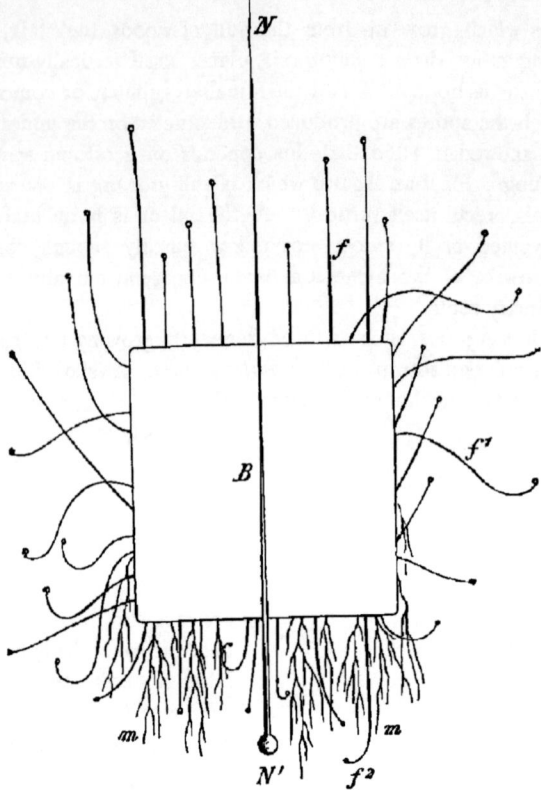

FIG 394 (see the text)

the lateral shoots of perennial shrubs and water-plants. Thus the first lateral shoots of some plants with labiate flowers, as well as those of the Equisetineæ or Horsetails, penetrate vertically into the earth like primary roots, and certain lateral shoots of the rhizome of *Typha, Sparganium*, some species of *Potamogeton*, and many others behave very similarly. It has also been already mentioned that leaves may grow horizontally, obliquely, or even erect; but there exist also not a few foliar structures which grow vertically downwards like primary roots, or, put better, are negatively geotropic. Peculiarly fine examples of these are found in the first seed-leaves or cotyledons of some Monocotyledons, e. g the common Kitchen Onion (Fig. 395): here, as shown in the figure, the primary

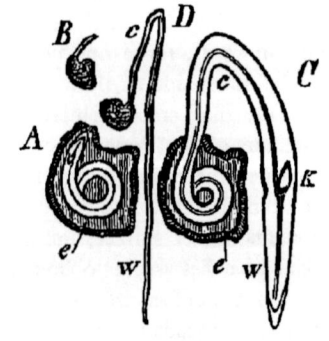

FIG 395.

root together with the plumule is pushed out of the testa by the vigorous elongation of the cotyledon, the filamentous first seed-leaf. If the seed lies on or in the soil, so that the tip of the root is directed upwards by this elongation, as in the figure (*B*), then it is not the root but the cotyledon which curves geotropically downwards, so that the root-apex is compelled to penetrate into the soil (*C* and *D*).

Those as yet unacquainted with such matters may be not a little surprised to see in the germination of the Water-nut (*Trapa natans*), the tip of the root (*w* in Fig. 396) of the seedling direct itself vertically upwards instead of penetrating into the soil, but the anomaly is only apparent, for the part *h* does not belong to the primary root at all, but forms the so-called hypocotyledonary segment of the stem, the rudiment of the root at *w* being completely aborted, and not having grown at all it is thus unable to accomplish any geotropic curvature downwards.

Moreover, there are other seedlings which exhibit a similar phenomenon, when taken from the soil and laid on a damp plate for instance. If a portion of the plumule is already developed, but the cotyledons still remain fixed in the seed, and if the latter is heavy enough, the seed remains quiescent in consequence of its great weight, whereas, in consequence of the geotropic up-curving of the seedling-stem, the root-apex is carried up because it is lighter; in this case of course if the primary root goes on growing its end may curve downwards. Geotropism, exactly like heliotropism, brings about only the curvature of sensitive organs, as already described; which end of the organ is to be directed upwards in the process depends entirely and simply upon the position of the fixed point.

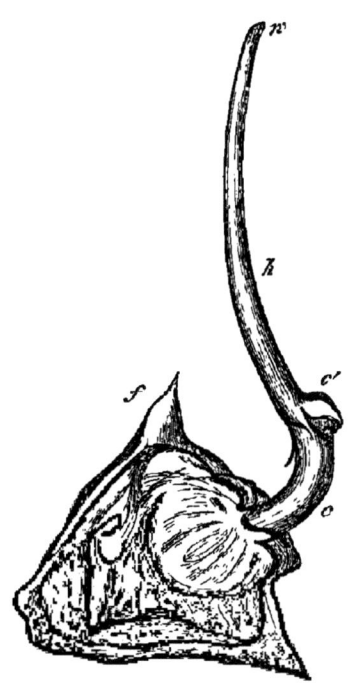

FIG. 396 —Germinating Water nut (*Trapa natans*) *f* coats of the fruit, *w* aborted root, *h* hypocotyl, *c* petiole of the large cotyledon which is buried in the seed, *c'* the small second cotyledon Between the two cotyledons is the bud of the primary shoot

These examples will suffice to show that in anisotropy we are concerned with one of the most general properties of vegetable organization; indeed it is quite impossible for us to have any idea of how plants would look, or could exist, if their various organs were not anisotropous, and since their anisotropy is nothing other than the expression of their different irritability to the influence of gravitation and light, with which are associated, in some cases, a sensitiveness for unequal distribution of moisture in the environment, and probably some other less well-known influences, it is at once obvious that it is the different irritability of the organs from which the external configuration of plants in general arises—a statement from which I started in the lectures on Organography. Even the most important differences in the biology of plants are the expression of the different distribution of anisotropy, of which innumerable examples may be quoted. To mention one only, the stem of Palms generally grows vertically upwards, but there are also Palms (*Sabal*), the primary stem of which, with its bud and the large foliage-leaves which it produces, bores down into the earth, and since it cannot there advance, being a thick mass, it pushes the old, properly lower, part of the stem upwards higher and higher above the soil, similarly the great contrast between the common Ivy and its allies, the majority of the Araliaceæ, lies in their mutual difference in anisotropy· the shoot-axes of the Ivy climb, whereas the others erect their shoot-axes independently without climbing.   The Ivy teaches us, indeed, yet another important fact, viz that the distribution of anisotropy in one and the same plant may alter at different periods of life   It is well known that the leaf-shoots of the Ivy do not always climb, but that when the plant is old enough leaf-shoots are produced which grow out independently, and then form leaves differently shaped and placed, and finally flowers and fruits.   Another case of this kind is very common with plants which form runners or stolons, of which the Strawberry affords probably the best known example.   Its sub-aerial stolons grow horizontally, a meter or so in length, and at last the terminal bud changes its character. it suddenly produces large foliage-leaves in the form of a rosette, and erect flowering shoots.   A very similar state of affairs exists in the case of many subterranean stolons, e. g. the Umbellifer *Ægopodium podagraria*, so common in gardens, and which is on that account regarded as one of the most troublesome of weeds.   To quote a case of quite another kind, the great difference in habit between the pyramidal Poplars, as contrasted with the Black Poplar and other species, depends essentially upon the branching of the crown of the tree. in the pyramidal Poplars all the branches turn sharply upwards, whereas in the other species they stand off from the primary stem at large angles ; and just this difference can be produced in the formation of varieties, and therefore by very small internal changes.   A large number of the most different woody plants, which otherwise form broad spreading crowns, produce varieties of the form of the pyramidal Poplar, among others the common Juniper (*Juniperus communis*), which even forms a third variety, which is shrubby and has the branches spreading along the ground.

However, all these statements are merely intended to show what is properly understood by anisotropy ; and it is now time to examine the facts a little more closely.   In the investigation of natural phenomena which appear under very different aspects, but in which something common to all is felt to be the important and essential feature, it is always well first to introduce method so as to refer the differences to the fewest types possible.   This may best be done in the present case by dividing anisotropic organs into two classes, which I have distinguished as Orthotropic and Plagiotropic   Orthotropic organs are those which under ordinary conditions of life, where the surface of the soil is horizontal and the illumination equal on all sides, grow perfectly vertical upwards or downwards, as for instance the primary stems of most trees, particularly of Firs and Pines, and the leafy stem arising from the plumule of very many annual plants, such as Sunflower, Tobacco, Flax, &c.; and, generally, all organs which are positively or negatively geotropic or heliotropic, in the way described in the preceding lecture   Thus primary roots which grow vertically downwards and shoot-axes which tend vertically upwards are anisotropic, but resemble one another simply in that both place themselves vertically with reference to the place where they grow.   In this they differ from all plagiotropic organs, lateral rootlets, side shoots, and leaves, which under the influence of the same external forces assume directions oblique to the horizon or even horizontal positions, and at the same time strive to present their flat surfaces at right angles to the strongest light.

True to the fundamental principle which we have throughout adopted, that when organs react differently towards the same external influences, this must necessarily be caused by a difference in their organisation, we now inquire in the first place whether all orthotropic organs are distinct in their organisation from all plagiotropic ones. It can be shown that in very many cases the relations of organisation are such as are indicated by the question, for all orthotropic organs are radially constructed, and, on the other hand, all dorsiventral structures are plagiotropic. Nevertheless it must be added that there are also many plagiotropic organs which

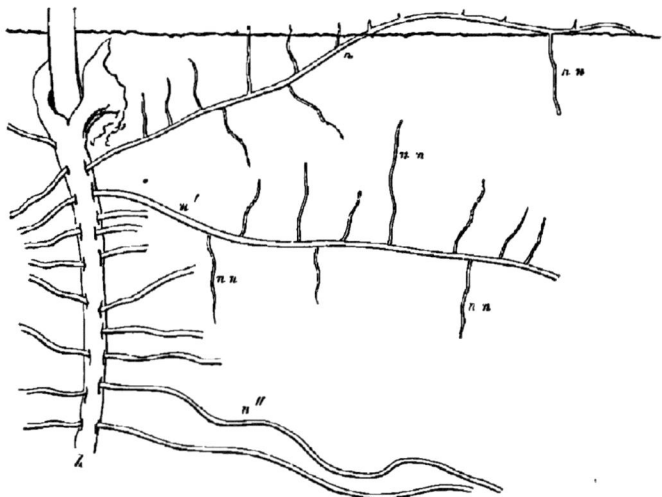

FIG. 397 —*Phaseolus multiflorus*, growing in damp soil behind a sheet of glass *k* primary root, *n* lateral roots of the first order, *n n* lateral roots of the second order   The roughly horizontal line denotes the surface of the soil.

as regards their coarser anatomy appear to possess radial structure, such as obliquely growing lateral roots and side-shoots which arise from orthotropic parent-organs; but we may assume in such cases that certain peculiarities of structure not yet known, and which are not necessarily visible by means of the microscope, determine the plagiotropism, and at the same time correlations of growth very often appear to co-operate also. For example, as has already been shown, the horizontal or oblique growth of the branches of a Fir, depends upon the presence of the orthotropic apex of the primary stem, and it may be added that a similar dependence exists also between the primary and lateral roots of many plants. For example, if the tip of the radicle of a Broad Bean or seedling Oak is cut away, one of the lateral roots situated immediately above the section grows not obliquely but vertically downwards; it becomes orthotropic, and from henceforth replaces the orthotropic primary root. Exactly the same thing occurs in the long aerial roots of tropical Aroideæ.

Between anisotropy and the correlations of growth generally, the closest connection exists. The lateral structures which grow out from a strictly orthotropic radial organ—lateral roots, side-shoots, leaves, &c —are as a rule plagiotropic, and in many cases, particularly leaves, are also distinctly dorsi-ventral in structure; and conversely, orthotropic petioles with radial structure, and, similarly orthotropic radial side-shoots, very commonly arise from plagiotropic shoot-axes. In the case of plagiotropic lateral roots this makes itself evident in that they produce lateral rootlets of the second and third order which are apparently not geotropic at all, as a rule (see Fig 397).

The relations between anisotropy and the correlations of growth come out, if possible, still more clearly, when plants are allowed to grow on the axis of a klinostat, and at the same time the effect of heliotropism is eliminated. Even in this case, where gravitation and light can have no effect on the direction of growth of the organs, they nevertheless grow so that they form certain angles with one another; but the questions here opened up still require investigation.

I now proceed to describe the relations between radial or dorsi-ventral structure on the one hand, and orthotropic or plagiotropic growth on the other, relations which have hitherto been studied chiefly by myself

When an orthotropic shoot-axis or primary root is laid horizontally, there results in the case of the former the upward, and in that of the latter the downward curvature described previously, and it is wholly immaterial which side of the organ lies upwards or downwards; it is just in this that the radial structure of such organs, even with reference to their irritability, makes itself evident—i e. they react in the same way on all sides. Radial orthotropic organs also behave in exactly the same way towards the light when illuminated laterally they curve until the free movable end lies in the direction of the ray of light itself, or, what is the same thing, is illuminated equally on all sides; this part then grows straight forward and in the direction of the ray of light, towards or away from the source of light—I am here, for the time being, excluding certain cases of so-called negative heliotropism.

Dorsi-ventral plagiotropic organs behave quite differently If a still growing leaf of a Gourd, for instance, is laid horizontally with the normally upper side downwards, the whole lamina becomes curved concave upwards; if such a leaf is illuminated from below it likewise becomes concave In this way it is shown that the venation of the leaf possesses the same kind of geotropism and heliotropism as ordinary orthotropic shoot-axes; but a great difference makes itself evident in that this only happens when the lower side of the lamina is turned upwards, or towards the source of light If such a growing leaf is laid horizontally with its upper surface upwards, or if the light is allowed to fall vertically on its upper surface, the latter does not become concave; on the contrary, the lamina extends itself in one plane. It is thus seen that the lamina of a growing leaf reacts differently according as gravitation or a ray of light affects it from below or from above, and it is just in this the dorsi-ventral structure of the lamina with reference to stimulation is made evident.

The dorsi-ventral flat shoot of a Marchantia (pp. 69 and 526) and other similar flat shoots, and, generally, all the organs with strictly dorsi-ventral structure known to me, also behave like a leaf.

If now we suppose a plane thin organ with dorsi-ventral structure, such as the lamina of an ordinary leaf or the flat shoot of a Liverwort, rolled together parallel to the direction of its longitudinal axis, so that either the ventral or the doisal surface of the organ is everywhere turned outwards, the rolled up organ constitutes a radially constructed body, and certainly the most elegant confirmation of the above statements lies in the fact that the dorsi-ventral organ in this rolled up condition, where it has only incidentally become radial, now reacts also towards gravitation and light as an orthotropic organ. Figure 398 will serve to show what is meant. *C* represents the transverse section of a lamina in its extended condition, and the arrows indicate the direction in which the structure changes, proceeding from the lower to the upper side. If we now suppose this rolled together either as in *A* or *B*, it is easy to see, and is indicated by the arrows, that what was previously the lower side now runs round the rolled up organ as an external layer, and that the dorsi-ventral structure has passed over into a radial one, which now confers on the rolled up organ the character of an orthotropic one towards gravitation and light.

It is not practically easy, either in the case of growing leaves or of the flat

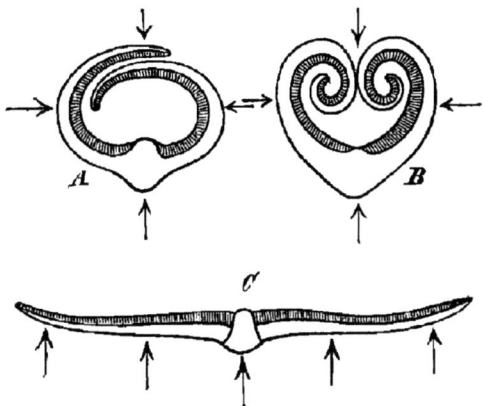

FIG 398.—(See the text.)

shoots of Liverworts, artificially to roll up the already extended organ in the manner indicated, so that it will go on growing undisturbed, but the converse change also demonstrates what I wish to prove. The subsequently flat leaves of very many plants—e. g. of all Grasses, most Liliaceæ and other Monocotyledons, and even those of many Dicotyledons, as the Water-lilies (*Nuphar, Nymphæa*), *Pinguicula*, and many others—are in the bud-state rolled together as in Fig. 398 *A* and *B*, either each individual leaf by itself (*B*), or so that the young leaves envelope one another (*A*), on subsequent growth the rolled-up margins are drawn apart, and the leaves become extended flat, as in *C*. Now so long as the young leaves remain in the rolled-up condition, in the bud-state, as in *A* and *B*, they are orthotropic, because they constitute a radial convolute structure; but as soon as they have extended themselves, they become plagiotropic, and are placed obliquely or horizontally with reference to gravitation, and extended at right-angles with respect to the rays of light.

That this is not simply a special peculiarity of a certain class of plants is shown by reference to Fig. 399, which represents the fertile marginal lobes of the large flat Lichen *Peltigera canina*. The organisation of the vegetative body, which grows on the flat surface of the soil in woods, is sharply dorsi-ventral, it is green and smooth on the upper side, colourless and furnished with roots on the lower (cf. Fig. 249, p. 391), and in consequence of this dorsi-ventral structure it is closely appressed to the horizontal surface. Of the lobes at the margin, those which bear the fructifications or apothecia, *a* (*r r*, Fig 399), rise up vertically, because this part of the otherwise flat vegetative body becomes rolled up, as shown at *r r* in the figure. In this case it is the upper side which comes to be external on the rolling up. in the Lichen called 'Iceland Moss (*Cetraria Islandica*), which consists of branched ribband-like shoots, the inrolling takes place in such a way that the organic under or ventral side comes to be external, and in this case also the flat dorsi-ventral structure gives rise to a radial one, which, for that reason, is orthotropic. Yet another Lichen, *Cladonia pyxidata*, well known from its elegant appearance, may also serve for the demonstration of what has been said above It has two forms of shoots the exclusively vegetative shoots are thin, flat, and dorsi-ventral, and therefore lie closely on a horizontal substratum; from these spring the shoots of the second form, structures shaped like a tall old-fashioned champagne-glass and circular in section · these are strictly orthotropic.

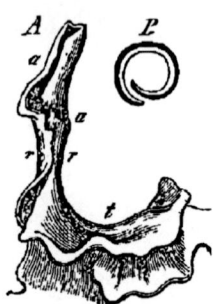

FIG. 399 —*A* a fructification (Apothecium) *a* of the Lichen *Peltigera canina* on the rolled up supporting portion *r r*, which springs from the flat vegetative body *t B* transverse section of *A*

It will be seen from the foregoing that the clear understanding of the relations between radial or dorsiventral structure, on the one hand, and orthotropic or plagiotropic growth on the other, involves ideas which present much that is extraordinary and difficult, and I confess that it was only after many years of thought that I was able correctly to apprehend the matter; it must be added that even now several points still await investigation. This is especially true of the fact that the orthotropic or plagiotropic growth in some cases is due exclusively to gravitation, in others to the co-operation of geotropism and heliotropism, and in others again the so-called hydrotropism co-operates.

I will give one or two examples of each of these cases.

I demonstrated in 1874 that the lateral roots which originate from primary roots assume their oblique direction solely under the influence of geotropism. and this was the first case of geotropism of this kind which was known at all. Suppose Fig. 400 to represent the upper part of the primary root of a seedling of *Vicia Faba*, which has been grown behind a pane of glass in a box filled with loose soil, and has developed numerous lateral roots, which have grown straight out laterally and downwards at oblique angles with respect to the horizon At that time it was doubtful whether the latter happened in consequence of a geotropic effect, the question therefore was, whether lateral roots are geotropic at all. By means of the apparatus represented in Fig 384, p 682, I convinced myself in the first place that the lateral roots are very clearly affected by centrifugal force, curving away from the centre of rotation, which removes all doubt as to their geotropism.

When I reversed the box, in which the seedling just referred to was growing, so that the apex of the primary root was turned upwards, the tip of the root curved vertically downwards; the direction of growth of the lateral rootlets changed also, their apices likewise curving downwards not vertically, but only obliquely, and this so that they grew on at about the same angle with respect to the horizon as before the reversal of the box. Those portions of the lateral rootlets which are quite black in the figure are the portions which were growing during the inverted position. The box was then placed upright again, and the lateral roots once more curved obliquely downwards, again to grow straight out at the same angle with the horizon as before the first inversion of the box. It has not yet been explained hitherto what relations of organisation cause these geotropic organs to grow obliquely to the direction of the earth's radius. Elfving found subsequently, it is true, that runners growing horizontally in the soil—e.g. shoot-axes of *Heleocharis, Sparganium,* and *Scirpus maritimus*—owe this horizontal direction of growth to geotropism; if they are placed obliquely or vertically upwards they curve under the influence of geotropism, until the bud lies horizontally, and it then goes on growing in this direction.

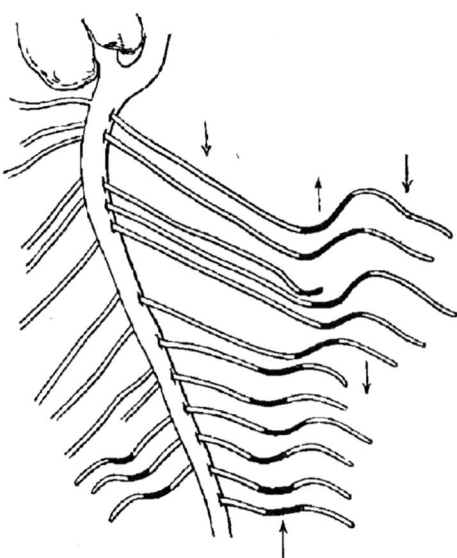

FIG 400—Roots of *Vicia Faba* growing in soil behind a pane of glass, at first in the normal, then in the inverted, and then again in the normal position. The arrows show the direction in which gravitation acted with respect to the lateral roots in the different positions

When sub-aerial shoots with dorsiventral structure are at the same time heliotropic and geotropic, two cases may occur; either the heliotropic influence coincides with the geotropic one, or each strives to give the organ different directions, so that, as a matter of fact, a middle direction results. In order to be correctly understood in what follows, I may premise that in the case of plants growing in the open the heliotropic effect is to be supposed as if a vertical ray of light fell on the plant from a luminous point in the zenith; since just as we must suppose all the influence of the gravity of the earth to proceed in a straight line only from the centre of gravity of the earth to the plant, so we may also imagine the effects of the light reflected from the whole sky as produced by a single resultant ray. We shall now make use of this supposition in what follows.

The well-known Liverwort, *Marchantia polymorpha,* forms broad shoots which are green on the upper side, and on the lower side colorless and provided with numerous root-hairs. these shoots are also seen to be strictly dorsiventral structures as regards their internal organisation. In the open, with unlimited light on all sides, these shoots grow with their lower surfaces close to the soil, into which the long roots penetrate deeply. Subsequently they produce shoots quite different in shape, long stalks as much as 10 cm. in height, each of which supports either a lobed disc with male organs, or a parachute-like structure with female organs. The stalks of these shoots are orthotropic and, when growing in the open, are directed perfectly upright. Transverse sections show however that they are not properly radial in organisation, but have become radial by the rolling together of the two lateral margins of a narrow flat shoot, much as in the case shown at Fig. 398 *B*. It is to this that they owe their orthotropism. In the further consideration of this highly remarkable plant I shall confine myself to the two organs referred to, although there are many other things which might be mentioned. If the *Marchantia* is cultivated—it is very easily reared from spores, or still better from its gemmæ —on the surface of soil in a flower-pot in a room, not too far from a window, the young or-thotropic stalks become curved towards the window, exactly like ordinary seedling stems, and then grow straight on at an angle of about 45°. The flat vegetative shoots on the contrary behave quite differently those which have their anterior depressions turned towards the window remain closely appressed to the surface of the soil; those on the contrary whose depressions (in which the growing-points lie) are directed away from the window towards the room, raise themselves from the substratum until they are directed obliquely

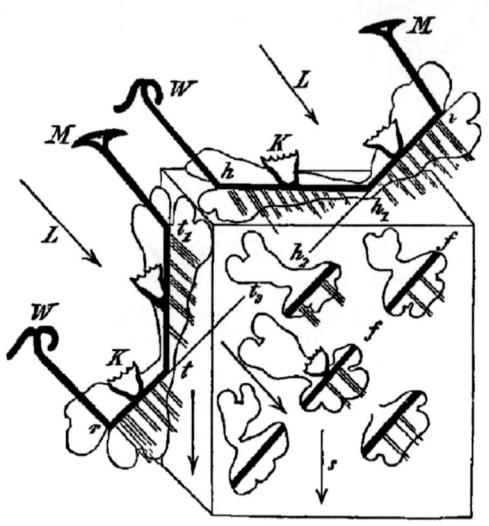

FIG. 401.—(See the text) *K* the orthotropic conceptacles in which the gemmæ are produced

at an angle of about 45°, so that in this case again the anisotropy between the flat shoots and the orthotropic stalks is approximately at right angles.

This behaviour was for a long time quite inexplicable to me, until I pro-posed the question, how would matters be if the *Marchantia* were made to grow on vertical surfaces of the substratum, with the light falling obliquely from the window? For this purpose I employed blocks of turf, carefully cut into the shape of cubical bricks and saturated with nutritive solutions, and covered with opaque boxes provided with a pane of glass only on the side turned towards the open sky. A few gemmæ were laid both on the horizontal surface of the block of turf, and on the vertical sides—on the anterior face turned towards the light as well as on the two flanks. These were easily retained by the damp sub-stratum and at once began to grow on it. After 2—3 months, vigorous and even fructifying plants were produced, and the result of the experiment may be illustrated by the diagram in Fig. 401. It represents one of the turf-blocks seen from the left flank, this presents a square outline, the body of the block being to a certain extent drawn in perspective, so that the anterior surface turned towards the ray of light L is to be supposed foreshortened to the observer.

The conformity to law of the phenomena now comes out clearly. The orthotropic stalks M and W of the supports of the sexual organs have placed themselves tolerably exactly in the direction of the incident ray of light L—a proof that their positive heliotropism must act far more strongly than their geotropism. On the contrary, the flat vegetative shoots to the right above and to the left below in the figure are placed nearly at right angles to the incident rays, and also the flat shoots at h to the left above and t_1 would have exactly the same direction—i.e. the direction h_1, h_2 and likewise t_1, t_2—if they were not prevented by the resistance of the solid turf. If possible these relations come out still more clearly in the case of those flat shoots which are growing on the square flank of the turf-block turned towards the observer, only it must be observed that the shoots provided with the thick black lines stand out from the plane of the paper at approximately a right angle. The root-hairs on the under side of the flat shoots are also seen, indicated by thin parallel lines · they also are orthotropic, like the supports M and W, but turned away from the source of light.

After what has already been said of geotropism and heliotropism, the ortho-tropic organs of this plant need no further description, as regards the plagiotropic flat dorsi-ventral shoots, on the contrary, considerable space would be needed to explain their behaviour. Referring the reader therefore to my detailed treatise published in 1879, I will only remark that the plagiotropic position of these shoots results from the co-operation of their heliotropic and geotropic properties, and perhaps the reader will most readily apprehend what is intended by supposing one of the root-hairs on the underside of the flat shoot to represent the primary root of an ordinary seedling; it is then to be further supposed that there is in connection with this one root-hair a very narrow piece of the tissue of that part of the flat shoot which belongs to it, much as if it had been cut out by means of a cork-borer. This piece of tissue would then correspond to the shoot of a seedling Phanerogam which had placed itself in the direction of the ray of incident light L. Now it is easy to understand that the whole of the flat shoot of a *Marchantia* with its root-hairs might be imagined as consisting of many thousands of minute seedlings, laterally connected with one another; or, in other words, the whole plagiotropic flat shoot consists fundamentally of nothing but orthotropic ele-ments, which however are combined into a flat surface. However I must unfor-tunately avoid pursuing this very fruitful idea to its further consequences.

The common Ivy (*Hedera Helix*) may be adduced as a second example of plagiotropic growth under the simultaneous influence of different directive forces. If a seedling or a rooted cutting of the Ivy grows in the neighbourhood of a wall or a vertical surface of rock, the leaf-shoot applies itself closely to the surface of the wall, &c, so that the leaves are situated to the right and left; the free anterior surface of the shoot-axis bears no leaves, and the surface applied to the wall produces clinging roots which fix the shoot. Closely applied to the wall up to the bud, then, the shoot grows up vertically. The lateral shoots which now arise, however, grow upwards obliquely at an acute angle, but behave otherwise like the parent shoot. There thus results a fan-shaped radiating system of climbing shoots, which sooner or later reach the top of the wall. As soon as this happens the shoot-axes curve over at the angle of the wall, and then go on growing closely appressed to its horizontal surface, till they come to the other angle of the top of the wall · here they do not bend sharply downwards, however, to grow down attached to the hinder surface of the wall, but they go on growing free straight onwards from the hinder angle of the wall, often quite horizontal for 50 cm, and then sink down obliquely under their own weight. When the one vertical side of the wall is thickly covered with such appressed shoots, another phenomenon makes its appearance, there arise numerous shoots which grow out away from the wall freely sweeping in the air, and horizontal, at least at first, until they bend down obliquely under their own weight. The orthotropic fruit-bearing shoots of the Ivy arise usually at the highest point which the plagiotropic climbing shoots have reached; the former are distinguished from the latter by their radial structure, their free upright growth and by their differently shaped leaves, which are here spirally arranged with a divergence of $\frac{2}{5}$, whereas in the plagiotropic shoots they stand in two rows on the right and left flanks.

We need however no longer concern ourselves with the orthotropic shoots, since they behave towards light and gravitation like ordinary seedling stems; only the plagiotropic shoots climbing up the wall or freely sweeping horizontally require further consideration. Such shoots, cut off and placed with their lower ends in soil in flower-pots, where they soon become rooted, and fastened up to near the apex to vertical rods stuck in the soil, form convenient subjects for experiment. If such a plant is now placed at a window so that the aerial roots are turned towards the room, and the upper sides of the leaves towards the light, the apex of the shoot curves away from the window in a few days and then goes on growing horizontally, while the long thin leaf-stalks curve towards the window, because they are orthotropic (cf Fig. 402 *A*). The plagiotropic shoot-axes of the Ivy are thus at any rate in some way negatively heliotropic; only it turns out that they continue to curve away from the source of light only until they become horizontal. If they were negatively heliotropic in the same way as most aerial roots, or the primary root of the White Mustard, they would then curve not merely till they assumed the horizontal, but until they were directed obliquely downwards. That this does not occur is at least in part due to the geotropism of these shoot-axes; in proportion as they approach the horizontal, they come into a more and more favourable position for the action of the geotropic influence under which they tend to become erect We may therefore assume that the horizontal position of plagiotropic shoots results from the co-operation of light and gravitation; how this occurs, however, and particularly in what degree each of the influences is concerned in the realization of the direction of growth cannot be stated in detail even in this case

It is easily intelligible that the power of the climbing shoots of the Ivy to cling closely to a vertical wall or to a horizontal surface is due to the behaviour just described—i. e to their negative heliotropism—while the striving of the primary shoot to climb vertically upwards, and that of its lateral shoots to climb obliquely upwards are to be ascribed to their differing geotropism, in so far as this makes itself evident chiefly at the flanks where the leaves are situated

It has already been shown in a previous lecture that in the case of *Marchantia* and similar structures the dorsi-ventral organisation is itself induced by the direction of the incident light; this once accomplished, however, the side which was hitherto ventral and shaded cannot again be transformed, by being subsequently illuminated, into an organically upper side—the dorsi-ventral structure cannot be reversed

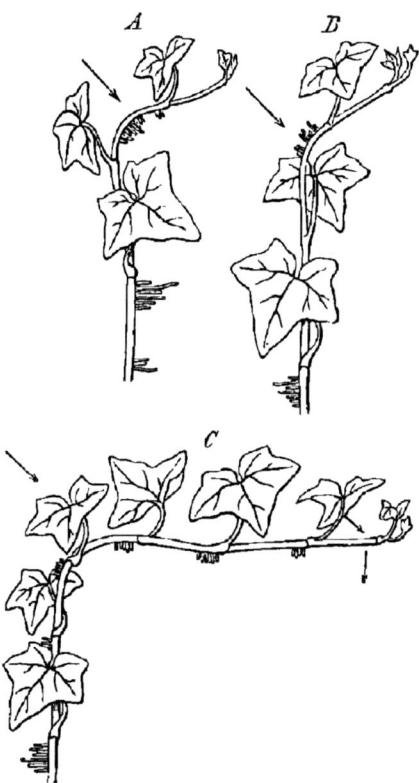

FIG. 402.—Plagiotropic curvatures of the shoots of Ivy (see text)

The Ivy behaves very differently in this respect—i. e. so far as the shoot-axes of the plagiotropic shoots are concerned, if one of these rooted shoots is fastened to a vertical rod up to close beneath the apex, and is placed at a window so that the side which had hitherto borne roots, or, what is the same thing, had hitherto been the shaded side of the shoot-axis is turned towards the light, as in Fig 402 *B*, it is noticed in the first place, that the backward curving of the apex of the shoot takes place much more slowly than in the reverse position, evidently because the sensitive organisation which had been induced by the previous relations is only slowly altered; but it is actually altered, for the growing apex of the shoot becomes not only horizontal, as in Fig. 402 *C*, but even developes roots on the side which was previously illuminated, and which is now converted into the shaded side.

There is still to be mentioned here an interesting peculiarity of the plumule of young seedlings of the Ivy. When seedlings growing at a window have emerged from the soil, the first segment of the shoot (the hypocotyl) is curved concavely towards the window, it is therefore positively heliotropic. On further growth, however, the new internodes of the axis curve away from the window, and the same then takes place with the first one also, its heliotropism, at first positive, thus becoming negative.

A similar behaviour, but in some respects different, is exhibited also by the Indian Cress (*Tropæolum majus*) I mentioned this then unknown case so long ago as 1865 The seedling-stem (here the epicotyledonary segment) is at first decidedly positively heliotropic, but if the plants remain undisturbed at a bright window, in summer, the seedling-stem together with the new developing internodes subsequently become curved convex outwards, the apex of the shoot thus turning away from the light, while the leaf-stalks, as in the Ivy and in all similar cases, are decidedly positively heliotropic, and the laminæ of the leaves are placed at right angles to the incident light   The apices of the shoots turned away from the light never become quite horizontal, however, probably because their geotropism works to the contrary ; but in the open, where the light is more intense, the negative heliotropism overcomes the geotropism, and the shoot-axes lie horizontal and close to the earth.   It is in consequence of this effect of light also that the plant is able to apply itself closely to the vertical surface of a wall, and if provided with a trellis in order to hold it fast, to climb up it   If, on the other hand, the plant developes in the shade, where the light is feeble, the shoots grow erect, and in fact become even positively heliotropic, and it is further to be mentioned that even those shoots which are curved towards the shaded side when the illumination is strong on one side possess no permanent dorsi-ventrality.   If the plant is turned round so that what was hitherto the shaded side is now strongly illuminated, the part of the stem already fully developed maintains its curvature, it is true, but the younger internodes which are still growing become curved backwards, with the apex of the shoot turned away from the window   With *Tropæolum*, however, such experiments must be made in bright summer weather ; in the autumn, when the light is feebler, the shoot-axes are always positively heliotropic

The Gourd plant also behaves in all essential points like the Indian Cress. That its stem, at first orthotropic, subsequently lays itself horizontally and prone on the earth is an effect due to strong light   plants cultivated in the shadow of a room remain erect for a long time, or curve but slightly obliquely away from the window.   For these reasons Gourd plants are able to climb up vertical walls provided with a trellis, the apices of the shoot becoming so to speak pressed to the wall by the light, and are then able to fasten themselves to the lattice by means of their tendrils   In the open, where the light is strong, the long shoot-axes of the Gourd lie horizontally on the earth ; but if the plant grows in the shade of undergrowth, the apex erects itself and, with the aid of the tendrils, climbs between the branches of the underwood into the full light.   In the case of Gourd-shoots lying horizontally on the earth, the apical portion bearing the terminal bud is erected in ordinary daylight so as to assume approximately the form of a horse's neck, the bud, bent sharply downwards, representing the head.   It is now easy to observe that on very bright days this horse's neck lays itself flatter on the earth, while in dull weather it is more erect.   If the apex of the shoot is directed through a hole into the dark cavity of a box, as in Fig. 238 (p 354), it then goes on growing perfectly upright.

It would be very easy to quote numerous other instances of plants which behave towards different intensities of light like the Indian Cress and the Gourd   in addition to the common Vine, I will only name *Glechoma hederacea*, one of the Labiatæ   In connection with the phenomena just mentioned, induced by light in highly organised plants, however, I must return once more to *Marchantia*, to add that the described plagiotropic position of the flat shoots in this plant also is assumed only in a sufficiently strong light, if the light is unilateral and feeble, the *Marchantia* shoots erect themselves, but without losing their typical broad form.   When the light is very feeble, the shoots at length remain narrow and become nearly stalk-like, losing their plagiotropism and curving towards the light in a way which shows that they are positively heliotropic.

In all the cases so far considered the point has always been simply that the organs, under the influence of gravitation and light, make curvatures in a plane which includes the direction of gravity and of the light. Very commonly, however, twistings—torsions of the shoot-axes—come into existence, and these have the effect of so turning or twisting parts of the bud which were originally arranged in a vertical plane, that they finally lie in a horizontal or oblique plane. This occurs quite commonly in the case of woody plants with erect stems from which horizontal or oblique branches arise. The buds of these branches produce their very often biserially arranged leaves in a vertical or at any rate approximately vertical plane, as in Fig. 403. Now if, on the unfolding of such buds, all the parts maintained their mutual positions, the leaves of the shoots of the second order would be situated above and below on the developed axis; the ordinary case, however, as found in the Limes, Elms, Celtidæ and very many other trees and shrubs, is that the lateral shoots arising from such buds extend their two series of leaves in a nearly horizontal plane, which, with reference to the young states (shown in Fig. 403) is only possible by a twisting of the young shoot-axis during elongation. Not rarely indeed it happens that shoot-axes with crossed (decussate) pairs of leaves undergo torsions at their internodes alternately to the right and left, whence the leaves on the developed shoot appear to be arranged in two rows only, instead of in four, and become extended in a horizontal or oblique plane.

FIG. 403.—Vertical section of a lateral bud of a horizontal branch of *Cercis cana densis* in December. *1, 2 ... 7* the consecutive leaves with their (similarly numbered) stipules. The outer bud scales are omitted, the inner ones are numbered 3 3. In the centre is the growing point of the shoot. *b* position of the leaf from the axil of which the bud arises. *a* axis of parent-shoot. *v* direction of gravity.

However inadequate this treatment of the anisotropy of the organs of plants must appear, owing to limited space, it will nevertheless serve to show how extraordinarily various are the phenomena which are induced by the action of gravitation and light; and I may again insist that for the illustration of general ideas, I have selected a few isolated examples only. These phenomena are universal in the vegetable kingdom. For instance, what has been said above as to the influence of light on swarm-spores may be compared with the phenomena occurring in *Tropæolum* and *Cucurbita*, and in spite of the enormous difference in organisation a great similarity in their sensitiveness to light is to be found: we saw how most swarm-spores swim towards the shaded side only when the light is intense, whereas when the light is feeble they turn towards the source of light, and here we find that for example the shoots of *Tropæolum* turn away from a strong light, while they turn their apices towards the source of light when it is feeble.

I here add, in conclusion, a few words on so-called Hydrotropism, simply because the experimental material to hand is not sufficient to devote a special lecture

to it   After the older vegetable physiologists, especially Dutrochet, had suggested
that roots may be caused to curve by the moisture of their environment, but
owing to unsuitable experiments had arrived at no results, I found in 1872 that this
supposition is, as a matter of fact, correct   Fig 404 will make the facts easily intelligible.   *a a* represents the vertical transverse section of a very shallow cylinder or
ring of zinc, which by means of three threads *c c* is suspended obliquely at *d*.   The
zinc frame *a a* had been previously covered with large meshed netting and then filled
with damp saw-dust, the upper surface of which is shown at *f f*.   Peas or any other
seeds saturated with water were then laid in this saw-dust *g g*.   In virtue of their
strong geotropism, the seedling roots at first grow vertically downwards and at
length come forth into the air between the meshes of the netting at the oblique lower

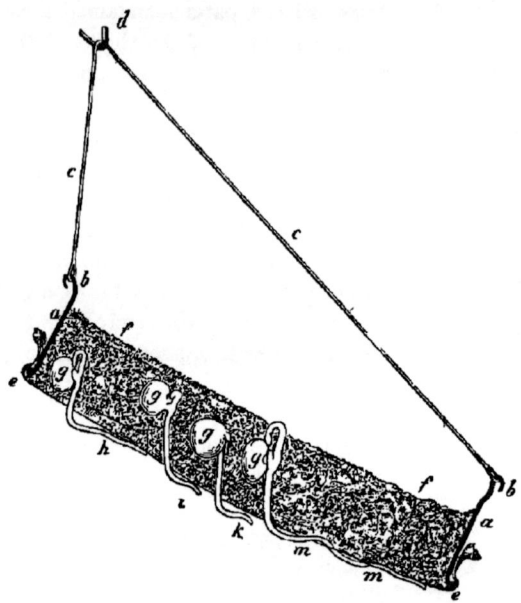

FIG 404.—Apparatus for observing the hydrotropism of the primary roots of seedlings

surface of the apparatus.   If the air is completely or nearly saturated with vapour the
roots grow down vertically into it, if this is not the case, however, and the air is
only to a certain extent moist, but not saturated, the root-apices projecting from the
meshes curve laterally until they again come into contact with the lower side of the
saw-dust, as at *h* and *i*   Very often they grow obliquely downwards closely applied
to this oblique surface ; occasionally the tip of the root again penetrates through the
meshes into the damp saw-dust, at once bending downwards again geotropically,
however, to repeat the same process   In this way a root (*m m*) may fairly sew itself
like a needle and thread passing up and down between the meshes of the netting

It is certainly, as numerous further experiments showed, only the difference
in the moisture of the surrounding air which produces these phenomena ·   aqueous

vapour is continually being evaporated from the damp saw-dust, and the air in its immediate neighbourhood is saturated with it; a little distance from it, however, the air is relatively drier, and the root apices thus become curved, as the experiment shows, so that they are concave on the damper side.

In the experiment described the hydrotropism of the root has to overcome its geotropism; but if the seeds are allowed to germinate on the surfaces of a damp block of peat (*T*, Fig. 405) which is fastened to the axis *A* of a klinostat and slowly

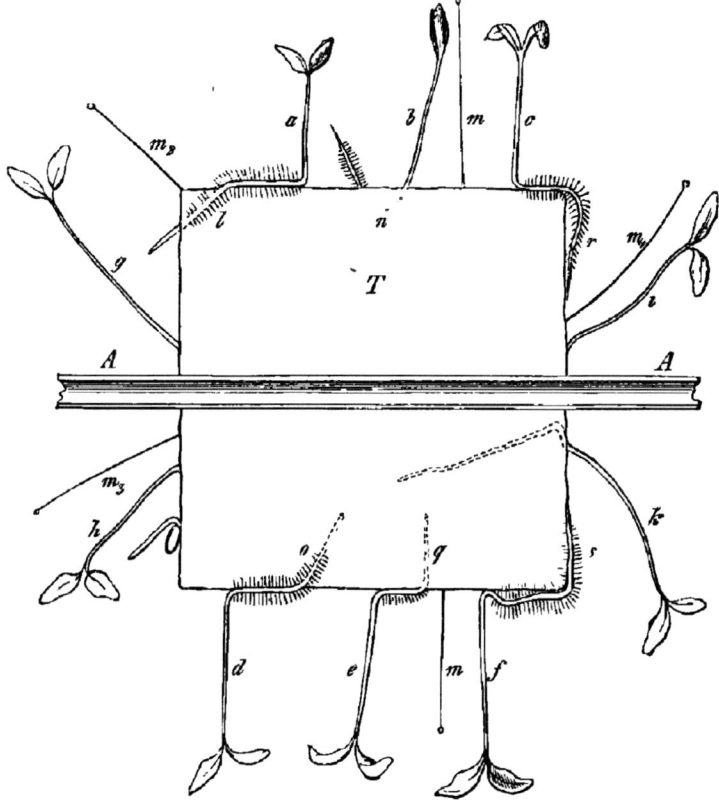

FIG. 405.—Cubical block of peat *T* on the horizontal axis *A* of the klinostat
(see the text)

rotated, geotropism, as we already know, is rendered ineffectual. In this case then the roots also grow closely applied along the damp surfaces, it is true, but if it accidentally happens that the apex penetrates into the turf itself it then goes on growing as in *l, o, q*, continually deeper into the turf, and, according to circumstances, probably even again comes out from it, as at *l, n*.

In this, however, there is yet another cause acting on the roots; for I have found that growing root-apices, when they are pressed on the one side by a solid body, behave like tendrils (only much more tardily) and become curved so as to be concave on the touched side

This is perhaps also the proper place to mention that the power which roots have of penetrating into the soil, and of continuing their progress in it, does not depend exclusively on their geotropism, but that the contact-stimulus and hydrotropism just described are also effective in the matter; however, I cannot here go more in detail into this subject.

The klinostat experiment (Fig. 405) yields, however, yet another result. Apart from disturbing influences, as at *g, h, i, k,* the plumules erect themselves so that they stand out at right-angles on all the surfaces of the rotating cube, as *a, c, d, f,* for which I can discover no other cause than this—that they likewise, but in an opposite way to the roots, are hydrotropic—i e. as the latter are so to speak attracted by a damp surface, so the thin seedling stems are repelled by it. this is of course only to be taken as a metaphorical mode of expression. The result is much more distinct, however, when, instead of a cube of peat, a cube of bread is fastened to the axis of the klinostat and a few spores of *Phycomyces,* the Fungus we already know (p 5, Fig. 3), are sown on all its surfaces The root-like mycelium penetrates into the bread and there becomes copiously branched, since it is not induced to grow downwards by gravitation as in Fig 394 on the contrary, the sporangiophores (cf. Fig. 3, p. 5) grow out from the bread, so that they all stand upright on the various surfaces of the cube, as in Fig. 405 *m m.* If one of them comes out by chance at one of the corners of the cube (as at *m₂*) it makes equal angles with the two neighbouring surfaces.

Wortmann, by means of special investigations with *Phycomyces,* has subsequently confirmed my previous supposition that the sporangiophores are repelled by damp surfaces, and I have no doubt that we may apply this result to the thin seedling stems of Fig 405 also.

In concluding the consideration of the movements of plants induced by irritability, I may again remind the reader of what I stated in the first introductory lecture of this book, and what I have laid at the foundation of all considerations on the vital phenomena of plants, that irritability is universal in the vegetable kingdom, and that vegetable life without irritability is just as inconceivable as is animal life without irritability Irritability is the great distinguishing characteristic of living organisms, the dead organism is dead simply because it has lost its irritability.

PART VI.

REPRODUCTION.

LECTURE XLI.

THE ORGANS OF REPRODUCTION.

GENERAL CONSIDERATIONS ALGÆ, FUNGI, ARCHEGONIATA

It will be convenient to defer to the last of these lectures the general consideration of the nature and physiological significance of the reproductive processes; for to a reader unacquainted with the organography of reproduction they would be at least in part, if not entirely, unintelligible. The present lecture therefore will be devoted exclusively to the description of the reproductive organs themselves. It will suffice for our purpose, moreover, to select from the abundant material which laborious investigators have accumulated in this province, a series of well-known and particularly striking cases, from the description of which it will become sufficiently obvious that notwithstanding all the variety of reproductive organs, there is nevertheless but one essential point, the organographical differences being fundamentally accessory matters and concerning externals only.

All reproductive processes serve the purpose of producing new independent living organisms, and this is always accomplished by a portion of the substance of an already existing organism affording the material from which the new structure is to proceed.

Reproduction in this widest sense of the word may occur, especially in the vegetable kingdom, in extremely various forms. In the first place there is the mere regeneration by means of incidentally separated portions of a plant. It is a fact well known to every one that, in the cultivation of plants, it is possible to produce new plants from cut-off pieces of shoots, leaves, and often even of roots, under favourable conditions of vegetation, and it has already been explained to a certain degree in a previous lecture how this occurs Botanists have also long known that even in the case of very small and in fact microscopic Algæ and Fungi, accidentally isolated pieces are able to acquire through growth organs which were wanting to them, and to develope into new individuals Indeed, cases are even known of small lumps of protoplasm artificially expressed from the cells of Algæ surrounding themselves with a cellulose wall and then continuing their growth, as I have myself had the opportunity of seeing in Stahl's preparations of *Vaucheria*.

With such processes is connected the very common phenomenon that in many plants, as a result of the normal mode of life. the individual shoots which had previously been developed from common growing-points, subsequently separate from one another and go on growing independently. This happens very frequently in the case of species provided with stolons (runners) or rhizomes (creeping root-stocks), the connection of these shoots with their parent shoot is sooner or later destroyed by the dying off and final rotting of their older parts, so that each individual shoot can now grow into a new independent plant. Many Mosses, Ferns, Equisetums, Grasses and Reeds, the Strawberry, and numerous other plants may be mentioned in this connection.

It very often happens, however, that the shoots destined to become separated assume special and characteristic forms, so that they may be distinguished in a

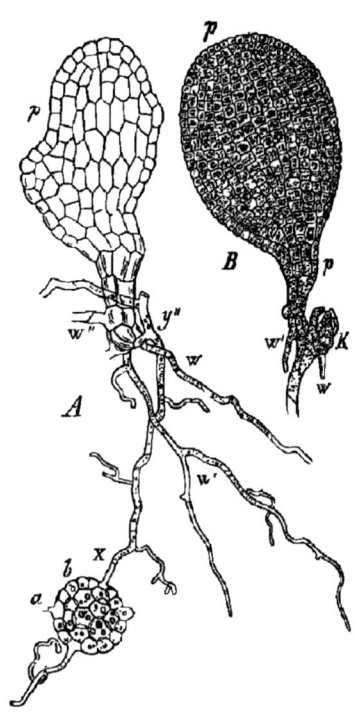

FIG. 406.—*Tetraphis pellucida*, a Moss. *A* a plant bearing gemmæ (natural size). *B* the same magnified; *y* the cup in which the gemmæ collect. *C* longitudinal section through the apex of *B*, *b* the leaves forming the cup. *K* gemmæ in various stages of development; the older ones are torn off from their stalks by the later growth of the younger ones, and forced over the edges of the cup. *D* a mature gemma (× 550) consisting at the margin of one, and in the centre of several layers of cells.

FIG. 407.—Development of *Tetraphis* from gemmæ. *A* shows a gemma (*b*) torn off from its stalk at *a*, the protonema filament *xy* has been formed by the growing out of a marginal cell of the gemma, and the flat structure *p* has been developed as a lateral outgrowth of the protonema; this has also put out root-hairs *w w'* and *w''* (× 100). *B p* a flat protonema, from the base of which a leaf-bud *K* and root-hairs *ww'* have sprung. The base of the flat protonema often puts forth a number of new flat protonemata before a leaf-bud is formed.

certain sense as reproductive organs. In this connection I need only remind the reader of what was said, in the lectures on Organography, concerning bulbs and tubers, adding that some plants are propagated for innumerable generations solely by bulbs or tubers—the potato for instance—so that reproductive organs in the narrower sense of the word appear to be superfluous. In the simply organised Cryptogams (Algæ and Fungi) such phenomena are quite general. Deciduous cells, Conidia, are produced on special supporting organs, usually in great numbers, and sometimes, as in the very common mould, *Penicillium glaucum*, the reproduction takes place only in this way, unless true reproductive organs arise under very special conditions.

In the true Mosses almost any cell of the roots, leaves and shoot-axes, and even of the immature sporogonium, may grow out under favourable conditions, become rooted, form new shoots, and give rise to an independent living plant Besides this, however, there are some species, like the *Tetraphis* illustrated in Figs. 406 and 407, which produce, in addition to true organs of reproduction, peculiarly formed gemmæ in special receptacles, and these contribute essentially to the multiplication of the individuals. The Liverworts behave similarly. in many of them not only are the individual cells of the leaves able to separate and germinate, but here also various species are found which give rise to multicellular complex gemmæ in special receptacles, of which the Marchantia figured on page 69 may serve as the most convenient and best known example.

All these different cases, which could be increased by many others more or less abnormal, are properly left out of account when referring to reproduction in the narrower sense. they may be collated under the name of organs for vegetative propagation, in contrast to the reproductive organs in the stricter sense of the word. All these vegetative organs of propagation are fundamentally nothing more than parts of the vegetative body itself, or at any rate are not essentially distinct from it. their organisation presents, in contrast to the rest of the vegetative body, nothing essentially new or abnormal, and especially it may here be insisted upon that by means of merely vegetative propagation the properties of the parent plant are usually transmitted to the descendants much more strictly than is the case with reproduction in the narrower sense of the word—a point to which I shall return

The proper reproductive organs, on the contrary, differ from the vegetative organs in their whole organisation and development, and particularly in the manner and means by which they fit into the life-history of the plant

The true reproductive organs, again, are distinguished from merely vegetative organs of propagation by the fact that they serve exclusively and only for the purpose of reproduction. They are in no way concerned (apart from a few exceptions such as *Spirogyra* and other Conjugatæ) either before or afterwards in the function of nutrition, or in the simple maintenance of the existing individual : their proper task is that of reproduction. But of course, here, as in the whole kingdom of organic life, no perfectly strict distinction can be maintained. Here again our ideas are best developed in considering the most sharply characterised forms—i e typical forms With these, just as was found to be the case with the vegetative organs, two categories of more or less deviating forms of organs are connected; on the one hand the rudimentary organs, which we may regard as incomplete but archaic, and on the other the degraded organs which have degenerated, so to speak, subsequently from the typical height of organisation

In the case of the vegetative organs, shoots and roots, we had above all to take cognisance of the remarkable fact that organs of like genetic significance may assume different forms in order to fulfil different functions. In the case of the proper organs of reproduction we find exactly the opposite : their function, the origination of new individuals, always remains the same, since this is, as already mentioned, their single object Nevertheless, if we take in review the whole vegetable kingdom, proceeding from the simplest plants, the reproductive organs assume very various forms; so indeed that the reproductive organs of the Flowering-plants give to the uninitiated the impression of having not the remotest similarity to those of the Cryptogams. Nevertheless, my short description will show that from the reproductive organs of the simplest Algæ up to those of the most highly developed Flowering-plants all conceivable transitions exist, leaving no doubt whatever, that (with the exception of a few Algæ and Fungi) all the reproductive organs in the Vegetable Kingdom are to be referred to a single type, the clearest expression of which is found in the Mosses and in the majority of the Ferns and Equisetums. And what may probably be termed the most astonishing result acquired during the last forty years is the fact which will shortly become clear, that the reproductive organs of the Flowering-plants, while in a certain sense the most highly organised it is true, are in another sense again simply reduced and degenerated forms.

Approaching the matter more closely, and starting from the clearest cases, as exemplified in a large number of highly-developed Algæ, some Fungi, all Mosses and in most Vascular Cryptogams, there are always produced in the course of the developmental history of such a plant two kinds of organs of reproduction, viz. sexual organs, and asexual organs (Sporangia).

The sexual organs are male or female: the male organs produce zoosperms (antherozoids), the female organs oospheres. In the present state of science it would therefore be the simplest and most accurate plan to denote all male organs Spermogonia and all female organs Oogonia, in contrast to the Sporangia which produce the asexual reproductive cells—Spores. However it will scarcely be possible to establish this simple nomenclature as yet, since a series of different names for the same organs have become naturalised in different subdivisions of the Vegetable Kingdom

As already stated, there occur in the life-history of a plant of the above-named subdivisions both sexual and asexual reproductive organs, and this in such a way that by the co-operation of the male and female sexual organs, or to put it shortly by means of the fertilisation of an oosphere, a plant-structure of some kind is produced: this in its turn gives rise sooner or later, often as the result of very protracted processes of growth and configuration, to a plant-structure of totally different organisation, on which at last sporangia again make their appearance. The entire process of development of a plant of this kind constitutes an *alternation of generations*, as it is shortly termed. This consists then, according to what has been said, in the whole life-history of a plant being divided into two chief sections. The developmental-history is twice commenced from a reproductive process; once with the germination from asexual spores, the other time with the development of an embryo from the fertilised oosphere, and—a point of extreme importance—the phase of life of the plant in question which proceeds from the germination of the spore results in quite other relations of organisation than the other. As a rule higher organisation is attained in that phase of life which proceeds from the fertilisation of the oosphere.

Such is, briefly, the meaning of the phrase ' alternation of generations.'

If we now consider the mode of reproduction in some other Algæ and Fungi, there is found more or less agreement in the relations of the alternations of generations described, some forms, however, can scarcely be referred at all to these schemes. In the case of a few highly-developed Vascular Cryptogams, to which the Coniferæ and their allies are directly related, on the other hand, we meet with very complicated structural arrangements, which may perhaps be most easily denoted by saying that in them the generation which proceeds from the spore remains included in the spore itself, and no longer enjoys independent life, and in the case of the Flowering-plants this generation at length disappears so far, that it is only recognisable in its last remnants by careful comparative investigation.

After these preliminary explanations, which could not well be avoided, the description of a series of examples may now follow.

Among the Algæ and Fungi there are many forms, the whole development (and especially the reproduction) of which departs from the above type sometimes in one way and sometimes in another. I will select but two examples. Fig. 408 shows at *m* a portion of the mycelium of a Fungus, *Piptocephalis*, parasitic on the *Mucor*, *M*, and which has bored into the latter with its haustorium at *h*. As a rule this mycelium produces conidiophores, as at *c*, from the ramifications of which small conidia are abstricted in large numbers, and by means of which this Fungus, *Piptocephalis*, usually propagates itself. Under particularly favourable circumstances, however, a second kind of reproductive organs is developed, which we may distinguish as sexual, since the chief mark of sexuality lies in that the contents of two cells fuse with one another, in order to produce a product capable of development, whereas each cell by itself would be incapable of this. This is also true of the so-called conjugation of the Fungus in question: two approximating or perhaps mutually touching branches of the mycelium, *s s*, swell up considerably, become densely filled with protoplasm, and, after a transverse division has occurred in each, their apices come in contact and fuse, and the separating walls dissolve, whereupon the fused portion swells up into a relatively large sphere *Z*, which becomes segmented off from the conjugating branches *s s* as a special cell filled with protoplasm, and forms a thick prickly envelope. This so-called zygospore—or, following a new terminology, zygote—requires, like most sexually produced reproductive cells of the Algæ and Fungi, a long resting period, before it germinates and produces asexual conidiophores, whose spores again give origin to mycelia.

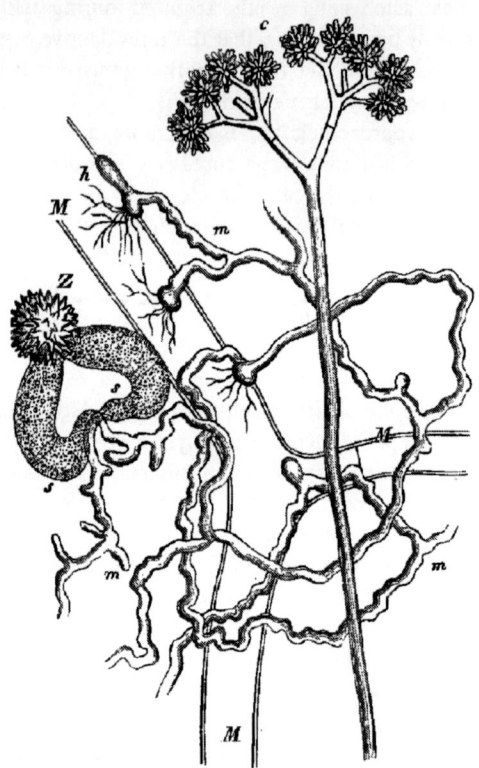

FIG. 408.—*Piptocephalis Freseniana* (after Brefeld). *M* a portion of the mycelium of *Mucor Mucedo* by which the mycelium *m m* of the *Piptocephalis* is nourished; *h* the haustoria of the latter penetrating into the hyphæ of the *Mucor*; *c* a conidiophore; *s s* two conjugating branches of the mycelium, forming the zygospore *Z*.

In *Piptocephalis*, as in all Mucorini or Zygomycetes, the result of the fertilisation is thus a single large cell capable of development (the zygospore or zygote). Matters are strikingly different in the case of *Ascobolus*, an Ascomycetous Fungus studied in detail by Janczewski, as shown diagrammatically in Fig. 409. Here also *m m* are certain of the ramifications of the richly branched mycelium. The end of a branch *c* becomes filled with protoplasm, swells up considerably, and undergoes several transverse divisions; a neighbouring filament then applies itself closely to the anterior cells of the carpogonium *c* by means of its thin branches *l*. This organ has been named the pollinodium. Whether a direct fusion of its protoplasmic contents with those of the carpogonium results, or whether a soluble fertilising substance passes over from it, is not known, but analogy with all other known processes of fertilisation scarcely permits a doubt that one or the other occurs, and that we here have an actual process of fertilisation. Its effect, however, is here quite different from that in the previous case.

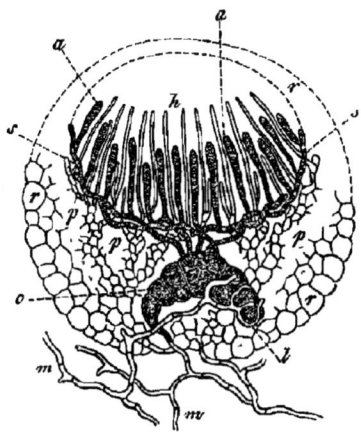

F:G 409—Diagram of a transverse section through the fructification of *Ascobolus furfuraceus*, an Ascomycete (from Janczewski's figures) *m* mycelium, *c* carpogonium, *l* pollinodium, *s* ascogenous hyphæ, *a* asci, *rp* sterile tissue of the fructification, from which the paraphyses *h* are developed

The result is not one resting cell capable of germination, but, stimulated by the fertilisation, a fruit-body or fructification is developed which is very voluminous and highly organised in comparison with the mycelium. This body in its turn consists of two essentially different parts · from one cell of the carpogonium (i. e. from the female cell) a large number of segmented fungus-hyphæ *s s* grow forth, on which the sporogenous asci *a* at length arise in great numbers, as terminal branches. Long before this spore-forma-tion is accomplished, however, the mycelial branches in close proximity to the ferti-lising apparatus have also been stimulated to renewed, vigorous, and entirely altered growth; they envelope the fertilising ap-paratus, together with the ascogenous filaments *s s*, with a parenchymatous investing layer *pp*, *rr*, within which also the spore-forming asci *a* arise. Between the latter are noticed thin barren hyphæ, the so-called paraphyses, which originate from the envelope. Finally, it hardly needs mention that the spores produced in the asci *a*, when they germinate on a proper substratum, again give rise to a new mycelium, on which, so to speak as a second generation in the above sense, the fructification arises in consequence of the sexual act of fertilisation

In *Ascobolus*, as shown in Fig. 409, the cell which is fertilised, i. e. directly touched by the pollinodium, is not the one which eventually gives rise to the asco-genous filaments *s*, and the sporogenous asci on these. The case is exactly similar in that great subdivision of the Algæ, the Florideæ, where the female sexual organ likewise consists of a multicellular body, from which springs a single cell, the trichogyne, in the form of a long filament, which takes up the male fertilising substance, thus in the Florideæ also it is other cells of the carpogonium which by means of their further growth eventually produce the spores, and, usually, also an investment around them Here, however, it is to be mentioned that in the Florideæ the fertilisation is accomplished not by pollinodia, as in the Ascomycetes considered above, but by means of very small cells which are developed in large numbers in special male organs; these cells are set free and passively carried by the water, and then, coming into the neighbourhood of the trichogyne referred to, fix themselves on to it, and empty their contents into it. Stahl has shown that the fructification of many Lichens also is accomplished in a very similar way.

Although their external appearance is extremely different, the Mucorini never-

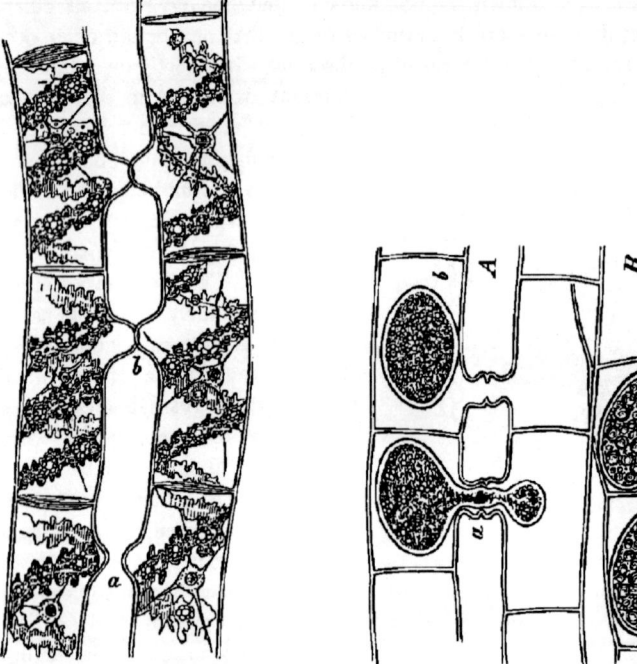

FIG. 410—*Spirogyra longata.* To the left several cells of two filaments which are about to conjugate. They show the spiral chlorophyll bands in which crown-like arrangements of starch grains are lying, as well as small drops of oil The nucleus of each cell is surrounded by protoplasm, from which threads go to the cell wall *b* preparatory to conjugation *A,* to the right, cells engaged in conjugation The protoplasm of the one cell is just passing over into the other at *a*, in *b* the two protoplasmic masses have already united In *B* the young zygotes are clothed with a wall.

theless agree essentially with the Conjugatæ—a subdivision of Algæ—in so far as in the latter also cells externally alike in nature, and especially equal in size, combine with one another and allow their protoplasmic contents to fuse into a single mass, which then forms a resting zygote and only becomes capable of germination in the following year. Of this process, which of course presents numerous modifications again in the various species of Conjugatæ, Fig. 410 will serve to elucidate the most important points. Fig. 410 represents, to the left, short portions of two long filaments of *Spirogyra*, found everywhere in May and June, as matted green masses floating on still water. These two filaments have (within the dense mass of the Alga) become laid parallel to one another for some distance, whereupon, in each case from mutually confronting cells of the two filaments, protuberances have grown out, as at *a* and *b*, which come into contact with one another, at the points of contact their cell-walls then dissolve, and a joint canal is thus formed between the two confronting cells, as seen in Fig. 410 *A* at *a* Meanwhile the thin lining of protoplasm which clothes the cell-wall, and in which the band of chlorophyll lies, contracts so as to form a spherical mass, a process only possible by the expulsion of water. Now, however, comes in a distinction between the two mutually confronting protoplasmic bodies: the one remains stationary, whereas the other, as if attracted by the former, puts out a process into the canal, which comes into contact with the former, and as soon as this contact is accomplished, the whole of the movable protoplasmic body glides over to the other, the process resembling the contact and fusion of two oil-drops floating on water (cf Fig. 410 *A*, *a*). The union is complete. After its accomplishment no trace is perceived of the fact that the body *b* (in Fig 410 *A*) has arisen from two; even the two spiral bands are said to join ends and become one The zygote thus produced now surrounds itself with a membrane composed of several shells, and after the fertilised filaments of the *Spirogyra* have sunk to the bottom of the water the zygotes contained in them remain dormant until the next spring; they then germinate in the manner represented in Fig 24 (p. 33), and, ascending to the surface of the water, again develope into long filaments divided into chambers by means of transverse divisions

In *Spirogyra*, more distinctly than in the examples previously considered, the fact comes forth that fertilisation consists essentially in the fusion of the contents of two cells In contrast to the slow movement, which is here executed by only one of the two sexual cells (which we may designate male) a great number of Algæ are now known whose sexual cells swim actively about in water like ordinary asexual swarm-spores, and then, when they come into mutual proximity, attract each other, come into contact, and then fuse together. To distinguish these from non-sexual swarm-spores, such sexual swarm-spores are called Gametes, and the product of their union, which usually moreover has to undergo a period of rest, the Zygote. I will describe these processes in connection with certain Algæ of the family Volvocineæ, in which this form of fertilisation was first observed in 1869 by Pringsheim.

Pandorina Morum, Fig. 411 *I*, is one of the commonest of the Volvocineæ. The sixteen cells forming an individual or cœnobium are packed closely together and surrounded by a thin gelatinous envelope, from which the long cilia project. The asexual multiplication is accomplished by each of the sixteen cells repeatedly breaking up into sixteen smaller cells, which group themselves into a cœnobium in exactly the same manner as will be described below for *Eudorina*. The sixteen daughter-cœnobia (*II*) become free by the dissolution of the gelatinous envelope of the parent, and each of them, again invested with a gelatinous envelope, grows up to the original size of the parent family. The sexual reproduction also is commenced in exactly the same way. The gelatinous envelopes of the young families deliquesce, and the individual cells are thus set free, and each swarms by itself independently (*III*). These free swarmers differ much in size; they are rounded and green at the posterior end, and pointed, hyaline, and provided with a red corpuscle at the anterior end which also supports the two cilia. During the swarming of these bodies, some are observed to approach one another in pairs, as if seeking each other ; they come in contact at their apices, and fuse into a zygote which is at first biscuit-shaped (*IV*) and which gradually contracts into a sphere (*V*), in which the two red corpuscles and the four cilia at the enlarged hyaline spot are at first still perceptible, though they all disappear soon afterwards. A few minutes after the beginning of the conjugation the zygote is a spherical cell (*VI*), which then remains dormant within its cell-wall for a long time, its green colour passing over into a brick-red one. On placing the

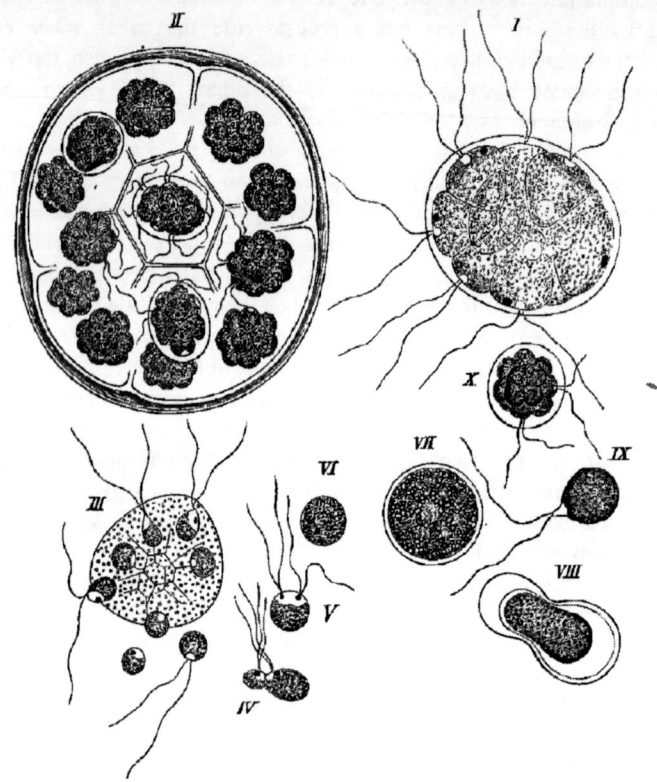

FIG. 411.—Development of *Pandorina Morum* (after Pringsheim). *I* a swarming family ; *II* a similar family divided into sixteen daughter-families ; *III* a sexual family, the individual cells of which are escaping from the gelatinous investment ; *IV, V* conjugation of pairs of swarmers ; *VI* a zygote which has just been completed ; *VII* a fully grown zygote ; *VIII* transformation of the contents of a zygote into a large swarm-cell ; *IX* the same after being set free ; *X* a young family developed from the latter.

dried up, and meanwhile considerably grown, spheres into water, germination begins after about twenty-four hours. The external shell of the cell-wall breaks away, and a layer within it swells up, and now contains one or two, or even three large swarm-spores, which finally escape (*VIII* and *IX*), and after swarming for a short time surround themselves with a gelatinous envelope, and, by means of successive divisions, break up into sixteen primordial cells, which now again form a family as in Fig. *I.*

Particular stress was formerly laid on the fact that both in *Pandorina* and in the Conjugatæ (e. g. *Spirogyra*), the two cells which unite sexually are equal in size

and are apparently also similarly constituted, and such sexual acts were named
Conjugation, in contrast to the ordinary acts of Fertilisation which exclusively occur
in Mosses and Vascular Cryptogams particularly, where the one of the two sexual
cells, relatively large and non-motile, functions as the Oosphere, and is fertilised by
a relatively very minute and actively moving zoosperm (antherozoid). The investigations of late years, however, have brought to light numerous cases from which
it must be concluded that no essential difference exists between conjugation and
ordinary fertilisation by means of antherozoids; this may be concluded from the
fact, among others, that both forms of sexual process occur in very closely allied
species. Goebel found, for instance, in the case of one of the Volvocineæ which is

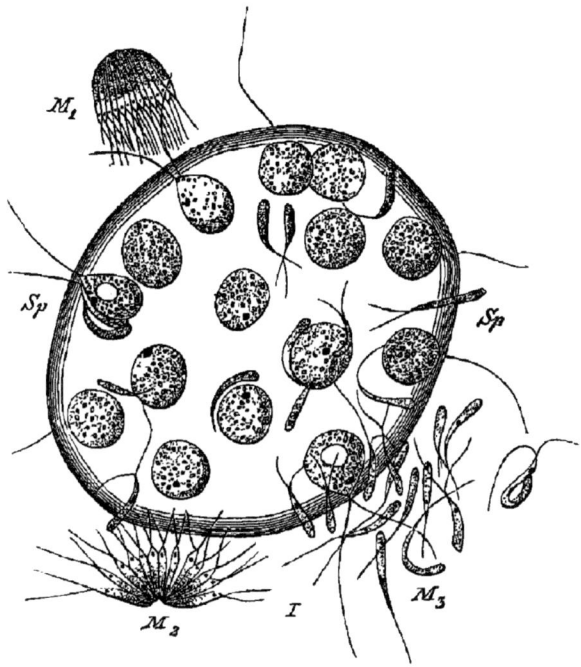

FIG 412.—*Eudorina elegans*, a female colony (cœnobium) around which antherozoids *Sp* are swarming
(after Goebel)

closely allied to the *Pandorina* described above, and, like that, consists of a revolving
cœnobium, that the sexual cells are differentiated into oospheres and relatively minute
antherozoids. The plant in question, *Eudorina elegans*, consists of gelatinous vesicles
of elliptical shape, in which are contained 16 or 32 cells, each of which possesses two
cilia, which project through holes in the envelope far into the surrounding water.
Active multiplication occurs by the asexual method, each individual cell of a family
becoming transformed by appropriate divisions into a family consisting of 16 or
32 cells again: these young families are set free by the disintegration of the parent
envelope. Sooner or later, however, a sexual difference makes its appearance
between different cœnobia · some become male, others female. In the latter, 16 or
32 cells assume the character of oospheres, not conspicuously different from ordinary

vegetative cells. In the male cœnobia, on the other hand, 16–32 antherozoids arise by the division of each individual cell: these antherozoids are minute elongated bodies with two anterior cilia, their colour being at first green but eventually passing into yellow. The antherozoids M_1 aggregated into a bundle begin to move while still enclosed in the cavity in which they have been produced, and then escape and swarm in the open. On meeting with a female cœnobium the cilia on both sides become entangled, and the male cœnobium is thus fixed; it then falls to pieces as in Fig. 412 M_2 and M_3, whereupon the isolated antherozoids, which now elongate considerably, bore through the gelatinous vesicle of the female cœnobium (Sp). Here

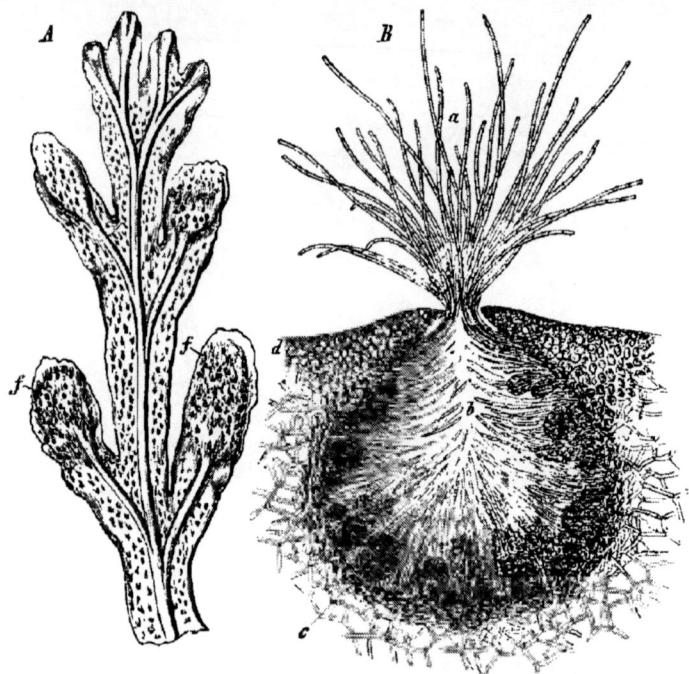

FIG. 413.—*Fucus platycarpus* (after Thuret). *A* the end of a large branch (natural size) ; *ff* fertile branches ; *B* transverse section of a conceptacle ; *d* the epidermal tissue surrounding all ; *a* hairs projecting through the orifice of the conceptacle ; *b* internal hairs ; *c* oogonia ; *e* antheridia.

they penetrate as far as the oospheres, and, after groping and creeping around them, apply themselves (often in some numbers) to these. It may be assumed, as has been actually observed in many other cases, that one of these antherozoids bores into each of the oospheres. Here also fertilisation is followed by the development of two membranes, and the transformation of the green colour into a brick red, in which condition the fertilised oosphere then passes through a period of rest.

Slight though the similarity of the fertilisation last described to that of the Mosses and Vascular Cryptogams may appear to be, there exists nevertheless no real difference as to the main points, since here as there the important fact is the fusion of a small antherozoid with a relatively large resting oosphere ; a great difference exists only in the fact that in the Mosses and Vascular Cryptogams special

organs—archegonia and antheridia—arise on the vegetative body, in which the
oospheres and antherozoids are developed. But even of this the first (of course
simple) cases are found in the Algæ and Fungi. The vegetative body gives rise to
special organs, but of very simple structure, the oogonia, in which oospheres are
produced, and to others, antheridia (which would be better designated as spermogonia) in which numerous antherozoids (zoosperms) are developed. Sexual organs of
this kind occur in a very perfect form in the various species of *Fucus* (Figs. 413, 414),
which are also worthy of mention here, because in some species two or several oospheres
are developed in one oogonium: these become surrounded by the numerous antherozoids
and fertilised only after they have escaped from the oogonia, and are floating free
in the water, though they have no proper movement. In some Phycomycetes also
several oospheres are produced in one mother-cell, that is in one oogonium. The

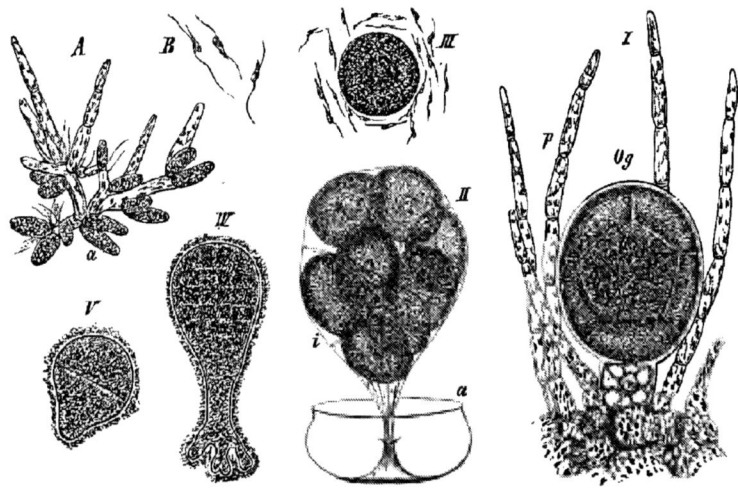

FIG. 414.—Sexual reproduction of *Fucus vesiculosus.* A cell-filaments bearing antheridia ; B antherozoids. I oogonium *Og* with paraphyses *p* ; II the outer membrane *a* of the oogonium has burst, exposing the inner one containing
the oospheres ; III an oosphere which has escaped, and is surrounded by antherozoids : V first division of the fertilised oospore; IV young *Fucus* produced by the growth of the latter. (After Thuret—B × 330, the rest × 160.)

typical cases of the Muscineæ and Vascular Cryptogams, however, are approached
by those Algæ which never produce more than one oosphere in an oogonium, which
remains immovable within the membrane of the oogonium, and is fertilised by the
antherozoids entering through a neck-like aperture in it.

One of the clearest and best observed cases of this kind is met with in the
genus of non-cellular Algæ, *Vaucheria,* common everywhere, figured on p. 108 (Fig.
107). On cultivating this Alga in a vessel of water at the window in the spring, it
reproduces itself at first only asexually. At the ends of the tubular branches,
which are abundantly supplied with chlorophyll, and which constitute the shoot of
this plant, a large portion of the protoplasm collects, and it is then separated off
by means of a transverse septum. This mass of protoplasm, which has previously contracted somewhat, then forces its way through an opening formed at
the tip, and escapes into the water, as shown on p. 108 at *A.* The body *B* thus

set free is an asexually produced swarm-spore, which is provided with a velvet-like pile of minute short cilia over its whole surface; it swims about with a rotatory motion for a short time only after its exit in the early morning, and at length becomes fixed somewhere and then germinates (*D* and *E*, p. 108). In the figure referred to is represented the sexual apparatus also of this *Vaucheria*, at *F* in *og* and *h*, and the Fig. 415 annexed gives a more exact insight into the processes of fertilisation. It is only after prolonged cultivation, when numerous generations of plants have been produced by means of asexual swarm-spores, that sexual organs also appear. These, in accordance with the simple structure of the *Vaucheria*, are formed by the development of protuberances from the utricular shoot, as in Fig. 415 *A* at *og* and *h*. The

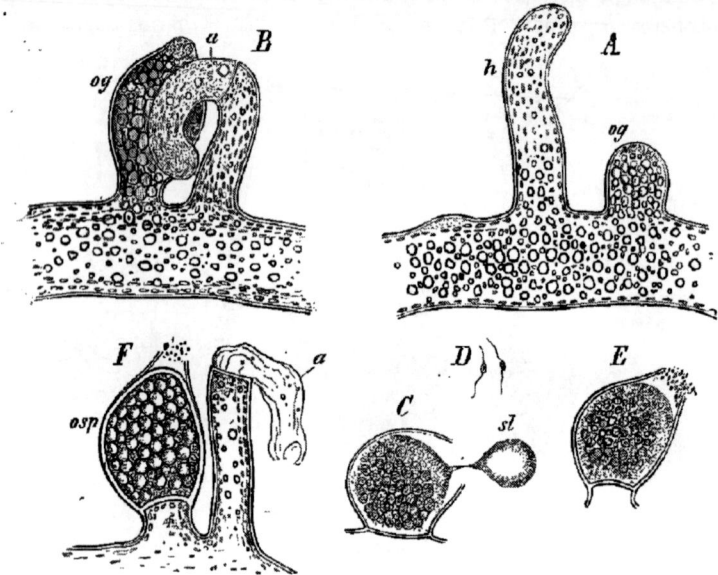

FIG. 415—*Vaucheria sessilis*. *A, B* development of the antheridium *a* on the branch *h*, and of the oogonium *og*. *C* an oogonium which has opened and sent forth a drop of slimy substance. *D* antherozoids. *E* antherozoids collecting at the mouth of an open oogonium. *F, a* an emptied antheridium; *osp* oospore in the oogonium. (*A, B, E, F* from Nature; *C, D* after Pringsheim.)

stouter shorter protuberance, the future oogonium, fills itself with protoplasm containing abundance of chlorophyll, and grows up into a body which has approximately the shape of an oblique lemon (*og* in *B*) joined to the tubular vegetative branch by a very short stalk-like portion. At this place the mass of protoplasm which has collected within the oogonium becomes separated off from the vegetative part of the plant by a transverse wall. At length the apical papilla of the oogonium opens, the protoplasmic body contracts a little, rounds itself off, and expels a drop of slime through the open neck—a process which occurs in many other cases of fertilisation, and is perhaps quite general—(*C* at *sl*). While the oogonium thus prepares for fertilisation, there is developed on the tubular process *h*, which eventually becomes curved like a beak, the antheridium *a* (in *B*). In this also protoplasm collects, and becomes divided off by a transverse wall from the stalk-like portion of the beak, and then breaks up into a very large number of extremely minute corpuscles, each of which is provided with two cilia: these are the antherozoids, *D* in Fig. 415 About the time when the neck of the oogonium opens, the antheridium also bursts at the apex, and allows its numerous antherozoids to escape.   For reasons which will appear later it is not very probable that the fertilisation which now follows takes place between the two sexual organs which, as in the figure, stand close together, on the contrary, it is probable that as a rule the antherozoids of another sexual apparatus effect the fertilisation of the oosphere in the oogonium.   At least one antherozoid enters the oosphere, whereupon the latter becomes clothed by a thick firm membrane, and, after the whole oogonium has become separated from the parent plant, the dormant period sets in, after which the fertilised and encysted oospore is in a con- dition to germinate.

With the reproductive processes last described, although they take place in an Alga so simple as to be even non-cellular, we have, as already stated, made an approach to the typical reproductive processes of the Mosses and higher Cryptogams. In fact the alternation of generations (the first as yet dim beginnings of which, more- over, are to be recognised in many other Algæ and Fungi) here comes more clearly into view.

We may now turn to the reproduction of the Moss, and since it is by no means my object to give a complete review of all the subdivisions of the Vegetable King- dom, I shall take from the whole of this immense group (passing over the Liverworts) only one example from the subdivision of the true Mosses, selecting the most highly- developed forms

Fig. 416 may serve for preliminary guidance in the matter.   It represents one of our commonest Mosses, *Catharinea undulata*, at the height of its development. There are to be noticed numerous erect shoots furnished with leaves, and bearing at their apices the 'Moss-fruits' or Sporogonia; these are curved capsules on long slender stalks, each being provided with an anterior beak, and clothed with a cap, the so-called calyptra.   These apparent 'fruits,' however, are something quite different from the fruits of a Flowering-plant   If it is wished to obtain the latter—e g. the cherries from a Cherry-tree—separately and independent, they must be torn or cut away, for such fruits are part of the plant on which they are situated.   The case is quite otherwise with the Moss, however.   With a little force, the stalk of the 'Moss-fruit' can be easily pulled out from the shoot in which it is situated ; its tissue is not really continuous with that of the shoot, but the stalk is simply stuck, so to speak, into a sheath   The developmental history shows that the so-called Moss-fruit is, as a matter of fact, not a part of the parent plant at all, but an independent body of quite different organisation, which is situated on the green leafy shoot of the Moss-plant like a parasite, and simply for purposes of nutrition.   We see in the figure, in fact, the two chief phases of the life-history—the two alternate generations.   The Moss-plant, con- sisting of roots and leafy shoots, was developed originally from a spore, and was thus produced asexually ; on the leafy shoot were subsequently developed the two kinds of sexual organs, female (archegonia) and male (antheridia).   Each archegonium con- tained an oosphere, and each oosphere, after fertilisation, by means of very slow growth and numerous cell-divisions, developed into a Moss-fruit, and this in its turn finally brings forth asexually developed spores in the capsule ; the capsule opens by the anterior beaked portion falling off like a lid, and the spores fly out like dust.   The Moss-plant proper, however, is not developed forthwith from these germinating spores, but the latter give rise in the first place to a pro-embryo, a preliminary stage of the proper plant, and which is termed the Protonema; all that is most essential respecting this has been stated in Lecture V (p. 68). On this protonema the leafy shoots arise by altered growth and correspondingly altered cell-divisions. I pay no further attention to this structure here, although it forms one of the most effective organs of propa-

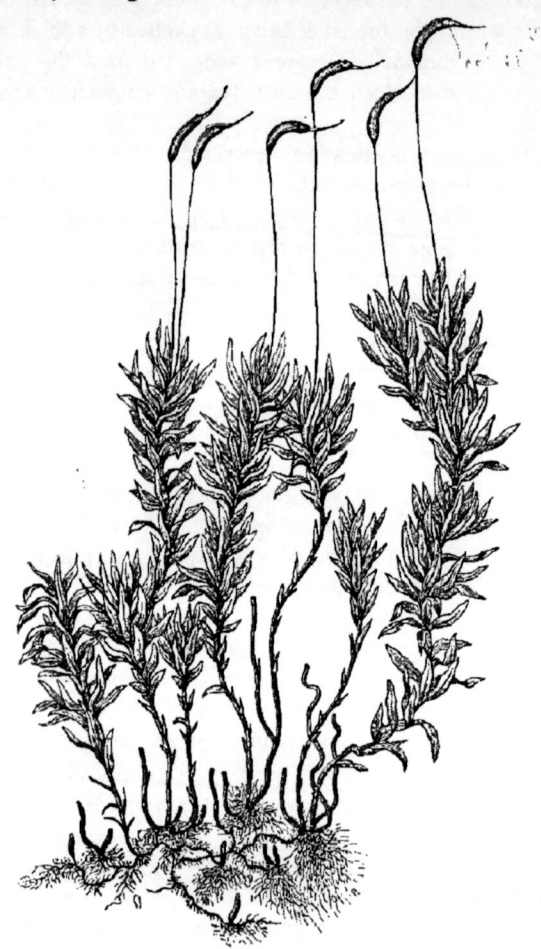

FIG. 416.—*Catharinea undulata*, a Moss (after Schimper).

gation, and in some cases, indeed, goes on living for years, whereas the proper Moss-plants on it only recur annually as temporary structures.

More detailed consideration of the true reproductive organs may be made in connection with another Moss, *Funaria hygrometrica*, already mentioned previously, which occurs very frequently in dense clumps on grass-plots, in woods, &c., and is conspicuous even to the non-botanical observer by means of the very numerous and long-stalked bright orange-red 'fruits.' The plantlets themselves are small, only a few millimeters high, the stems being furnished with only a dozen or so of leaves. The stem bears at its apex groups of sexual organs, and these groups may almost be spoken of as 'flowers.' The smaller specimens are male, and produce exclusively antheridia, which stand crowded together in large numbers within a rosette of leaves surrounding them like a perianth. The female plantlets are larger and bear at the apex of the stem a dozen archegonia, which are surrounded by a more bud-like and closed perigone.

It has already been pointed out that the archegonia of the Moss and also of the Vascular Cryptogams are fundamentally essentially the same as the oogonia of

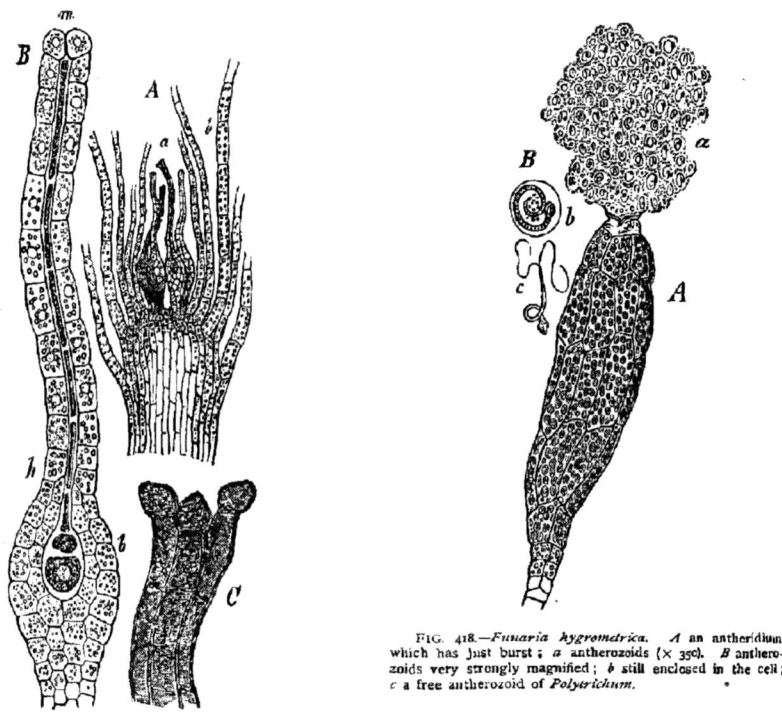

FIG. 418.—*Funaria hygrometrica.* *A* an antheridium which has just burst ; *a* antherozoids (× 350). *B* antherozoids very strongly magnified ; *b* still enclosed in the cell; *c* a free antherozoid of *Polytrichum.*

FIG. 417.—*Funaria hygrometrica* (a Moss). *A* female 'flower'; *a* archegonia ; *b* enveloping leaves. *B* a single archegonium before the opening of the cover *m* and the neck *h* ; *b* the ventral portion with the oosphere. *C* the neck of an old archegonium after fertilisation.

the Algæ, and that in like manner the antheridia are only more complicated in structure than is the case in the latter.

In Fig. 417 are shown, at *A* the female flower in longitudinal section, with a group of archegonia at *a*, and the perigone-leaves in section at *b*. *B* represents the anatomical structure of an archegonium at the time when the oosphere is not yet ready for fertilisation, but will be so in a short time. At *b* is the ventral portion of the archegonium, which is supported on a short and somewhat thick stalk; from *h* to *m* is the neck, which is in most Mosses remarkable for its great length, and which is still closed above, at *m*, by four covering cells. In the ventral portion is seen a long ovoid cavity, from which a canal runs through the entire length of the neck up to the covering cells *m*. Fundamentally, however, both together form one row of cells, occupying the axis of the entire archegonium, the protoplasm of which is contracted in the figure and rendered more visible by the mode of preparation The lowest and largest mass of protoplasm constitutes the still unripe oosphere; in the central cavity above it lies a smaller cell, the so-called ventral canal-cell, and the narrow neck-canal is still filled up by thin long-drawn masses of protoplasm, the neck canal-cells. When the archegonium is quite ripe, and if water gains access suddenly, the now deliquescent canal-cells swell up strongly and exert a pressure which causes the neck to open at *m*, the covering cells parting asunder. the mucilaginous substance contained in the canal then escapes, and an open passage is thus formed, at the base of which, in the belly or venter of the archegonium, the now completely developed and spherical oosphere lies. In this condition fertilisation can take place

The antheridia of the male plant, which have meanwhile become completely developed, are, in the mature condition, sac-like bodies situated on thin pedicles. The wall of the sac consists of a single layer of cells, containing chlorophyll, the colouring matter of which turns red on ripening. The whole of this enclosed cavity is filled with innumerable very minute cells, each of which produces an antherozoid If the antheridia are completely developed, and a drop of water lies on the male flower, the antheridia become ruptured at the apex in consequence of its absorption, and, as shown in Fig 418 *A* (at *a*), a dense mucilaginous mass is extruded from the opening, consisting entirely of the mother-cells of the antherozoids, as shown at *B, b*. By absorption of water these cells swell up, and become isolated, and the antherozoids soon escape from their envelopes and swarm actively in the water The antherozoids of the Moss are spirally wound filiform bodies thicker at the posterior end, and pointed and provided with two long cilia anteriorly (Fig. 418 *B, c*)

As in all Mosses and Vascular Cryptogams, the archegonia as well as the antheridia open after they have become quite ripe, but only if they are immersed in water. The completion of this process in the case of the Mosses is favoured by their tufted habit: the plantlets stand close together, and when it rains the tufts, with their small interspaces between the leaves, act like a sponge, the male and female flowers become thoroughly wetted, and those archegonia and antheridia which have just become ripe open: the antherozoids now swim about in the water which saturates the tuft of Moss, and some of them occasionally come near the mouth of an archegonium Then, as if impelled by an attraction exerted by the oosphere and by the mucilage extruded, they collect together at the aperture of the neck, some penetrate by their own movements into the canal, and finally one antherozoid reaches the oosphere, and certainly penetrates into it and dissolves its substance in it.

Herewith, then, fertilisation is accomplished, and as usual the immediate effects are that the oosphere excretes a cellulose membrane, and then slowly begins to grow; this growth is accompanied by corresponding cell-divisions, and thus is produced a multi-cellular embryo (Fig 419 *A, ff'*) in the venter of the archegonium (*b b*) During the further growth of the embryo, the venter of the archegonium also goes on growing vigorously in company with it, as may be easily seen from Fig. 419

B and *C*. It will be noticed how the neck *h* of the archegonium, which has now turned red, and is decaying, is still situated above. This still growing venter, investing the embryo as a loose sac, is the Calyptra.

Enclosed within the calyptra the embryo of the Moss now grows up into a long approximately spindle-shaped body *f*, the lower end of which bores into the tissue of the Moss-stem, but without coming into true organic connection with it. When this elongated embryo has attained a certain length, the calyptra tears away near its base: the lower part remains attached to the stem as the so-called vaginula, while

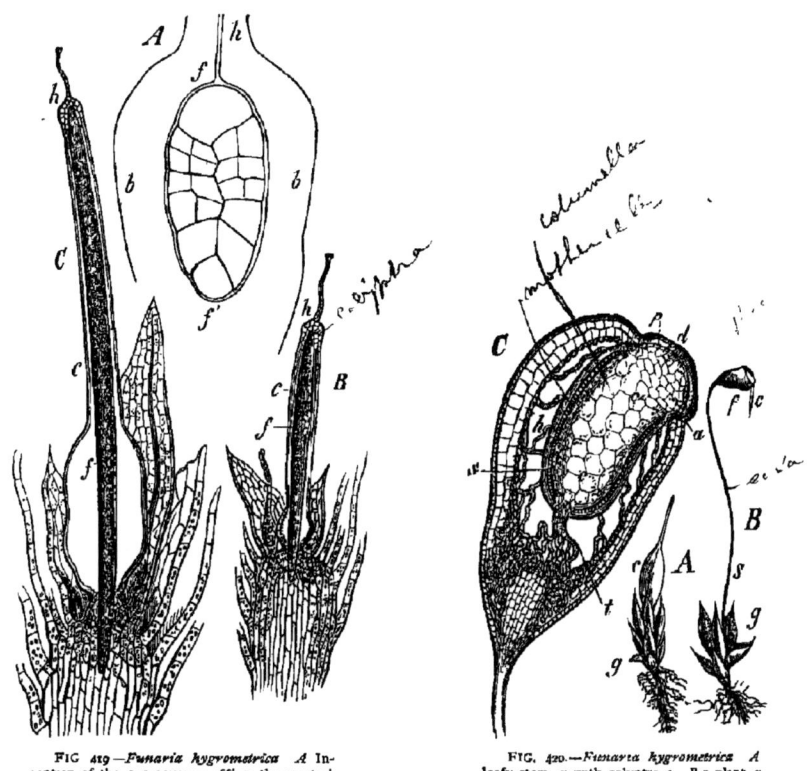

FIG. 419.—*Funaria hygrometrica* *A* Inception of the sporogonium *ff'* in the ventral portion *bb* of the archegonium (optical long sec. × 500) *B, C,* further stages of development of the sporogonium *f* and of the calyptra *c*, *h* neck of archegonium × (about 40)

FIG. 420.—*Funaria hygrometrica* *A* leafy stem *g* with calyptra *c* *B* a plant *g* with sporogonium nearly ripe *s* seta, *f* capsule, *c* calyptra *C* longitudinal median section of the capsule (turn) *d* operculum, *a* annulus, *p* peristome *cd* columella, *h* air space. *S* primary mother cells of the spores The tissue of the columella becomes loose and filamentous below

the whole of the upper part of the calyptra is carried up by the elongating embryo, which it invests closely, and by which it is nourished. The upper portion of the still stalk-like embryo, within the calyptra, now swells out and becomes thicker: this forms the spore-capsule of the Moss-fruit, the calyptra still remaining on it.

It would require too much space to describe in detail the development of the Moss-fruit: all that is necessary may be explained by means of Fig. 420. Here is shown (*c* in *A*) the calyptra still enveloping the whole of the embryo; at *B* the latter has already become developed into the Moss-fruit or Sporogonium, consisting of a long thin stalk *s* (Seta), and the spore-capsule *f* (Theca) on which the calyptra *c* is situated. *C* represents a longitudinal section through the spore-capsule, which consists of various layers of parenchymatous tissue within a very strong and well developed epidermis, and forms anteriorly the lid (Operculum) *d*, already mentioned. A central mass of tissue (*c′*) composed of large cells, is separated by means of large intercellular spaces *h* from the peripheral layers of tissue of the capsule, and is distinguished as the columella A layer close to the periphery of the columella produces the mother-cells, each of which gives rise to four spores by repeated bipartition. It may here be remarked that the spores of the Vascular Cryptogams, just like those of the Mosses, also arise from their mother-cells as tetrads (quarters), and that the pollen-grains of the flowering plants do exactly the same, since they also are in fact nothing other than spores

When the spores of the Moss-capsule are ripe, the operculum *d* (Fig 420 *C*), which consists of epidermis, becomes loosened from the urn-shaped portion of the fruit at *a*, the large-celled parenchyma becoming disorganised and thus the cavity containing the spores opens. In the more highly organised Mosses there remains, after the falling away of the operculum, a simple or double crown of beautifully formed organs, the Peristome, composed of solid portions of the cell-walls of the tissue which fills up the cavity of the operculum, thus contributes to the dissemination of the spores, the 'teeth' of the peristome rolling up and unrolling hygroscopically Fig 421 shows the structure of a double peristome in a particularly excellent example

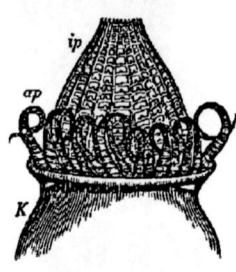

FIG 421 —Mouth of the urn (theca) of *Fontinalis antipyretica* (after Schimper × 50), *op* external peristome, *ip* internal peristome

The spores when emptied out of the capsule germinate and give rise to the protonema from the consideration of which we started above

I will describe the reproductive organs and alternation of generations of the isosporous Vascular Cryptogams so far as is needful for our purpose, in the case of the Equisetaceæ or Horse-tails, taking as an example the largest and handsomest of our native species, *Equisetum Telmateia*, with which moreover the common *Equisetum arvense* of the fields, abundant everywhere in pastures &c , agrees All the species of *Equisetum* live chiefly under ground, where their shoots, which have the form of rhizomes, grow on in part horizontally, in part downwards, and often occupy large areas. On the rhizome are produced buds which are directed upwards from the first, and in the spring grow upwards, often from considerable depths, to expose themselves to the daylight, these shoots, however, are of two kinds Some of them, which do not emerge until later, when the weather is warmer, grow up to the height of a man and produce in the axils of their membranous leaf-sheaths whorls of thin lateral shoots, which then again branch in like manner, these are the foliage shoots of these plants, the tissue containing chlorophyll however being developed not in the inconspicuous leaf-sheaths, but in the cortex of the secondary and tertiary shoot-axes. Their products of assimilation pass into the subterranean rhizomes, and these, under favourable conditions, may probably go on living for hundreds of years.

The other kind of orthotropic shoot, which comes forth into the daylight, makes its appearance early in the spring, produces no chlorophyll, and has only the one object of bringing to maturity the asexual spores produced long previously when the shoot was still under ground, and to scatter them to the wind and so sow them. These sporangiophores, which only attain a height of 20–30 cm., terminate above in an ovoid or cylindrical 'fructification,' if one will so term it; i. e. the apical portion of the shoot-axis bears, in closely superposed whorls, numerous hexagonal shields (metamorphosed leaves), fixed on slender horizontal stalks, and bearing on their

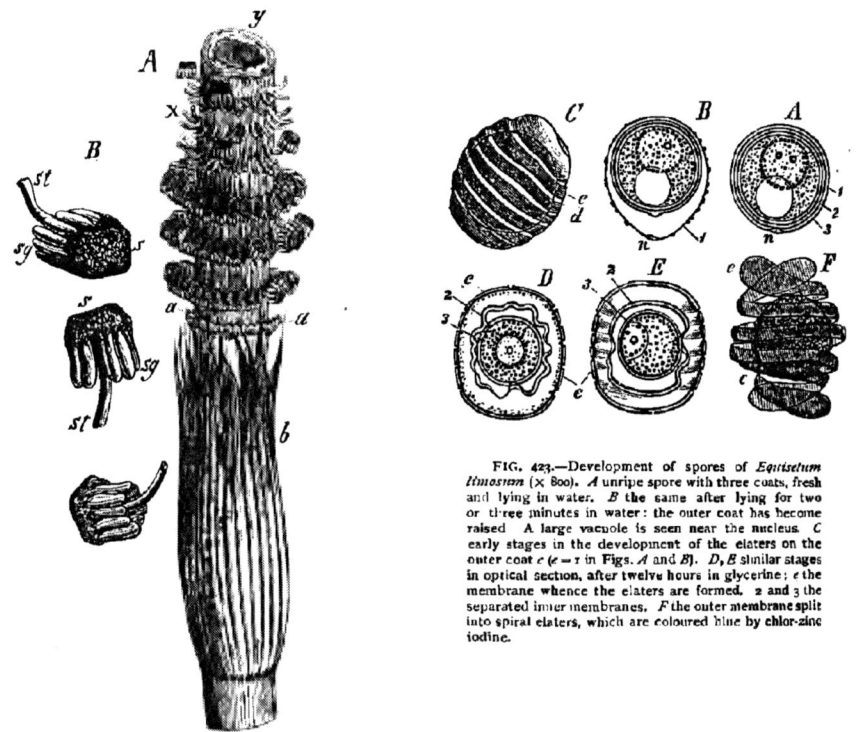

FIG. 423.—Development of spores of *Equisetum limosum* (× 800). *A* unripe spore with three coats, fresh and lying in water. *B* the same after lying for two or three minutes in water: the outer coat has become raised A large vacuole is seen near the nucleus. *C* early stages in the development of the elaters on the outer coat *e* (*e* = 1 in Figs. *A* and *B*). *D*, *E* similar stages in optical section, after twelve hours in glycerine; *e* the membrane whence the elaters are formed. *2* and *3* the separated inner membranes. *F* the outer membrane split into spiral elaters, which are coloured blue by chlor-zinc iodine.

FIG. 422.—*Equisetum Telmateia.* *A* upper part of a fertile shoot with the lower half of the sporiferous spike (nat. size); *b* leaf-sheath; *a* so-called 'annulus' (bracs; *x* the pedicel of sporangial leaves which have been removed; *y* transverse section of the axis. *B* peltate sporangial leaves in various positions (slightly magnified): *st* pedicel; *s* shield; *sg* sporangia.

under-side (the one turned towards the axis) a large number of thin-walled delicate sacs, the sporangia. These points will be rendered sufficiently intelligible, even without detailed descriptions, from Fig. 422. The ripened sporangia dehisce, each by means of a longitudinal fissure, and allow their spores to escape. It is only necessary to tear off one of these sporangiophores in March or April and knock the head on a plate, for instance, to obtain the spores in large quantities in the form of an extremely fine greenish powder. On collecting this on a piece of paper, for instance, and breathing lightly on it, an agitating writhing movement is noticed in it: this is still more obvious when the same experiment is made with a few spores on a glass slip under the microscope, with a low power. It is then observed that each individual spore is a spherical cell provided with a thin tough membrane and with protoplasm containing chlorophyll, and has two mutually crossing long bands attached to it at one point (*n*, Fig. 423 *A*, *B*). When the air is dry these crossed bands are thrown widely apart, but it suffices while looking through the microscope to simply breathe lightly, and thus supply the spores with damp air, to put the bands in motion at once, and they then roll themselves together round the spore with extraordinary rapidity, as in Fig 423 *F*, energetically opening out again at once when the small quantity of moisture hygroscopically absorbed evaporates. These movements of the 'elaters' take place so energetically and rapidly that the spores are put into jumping movements, which will evidently also occur in the open as the moisture of the air changes, and may in some way contribute to bring the spores into suitable places for germination.

The sporangiophores of the above Equisetum disappear after the sowing of the spores; other species, however (e g. *E. limosum*, which sometimes completely fills up large swamps) send up shoots of one kind only above the soil, which contain chlorophyll, and bear the spikes of sporangia at the apex at the same time

The whole of the Equisetum-plant so far described is devoid of sexual organs; the only reproductive organs it produces are the sporangia described The whole plant is thus quite asexual, and this holds good not only of the Horse-tails, but in exactly the same way of the Ferns and Lycopodiaceæ and Selaginellæ, &c. In all these cases the ordinary, long-lived and sometimes (as in the case of Tree-ferns and extinct *Lepidodendra*) huge tree-like plant is asexual, it always produces as reproductive organs sporangia only.

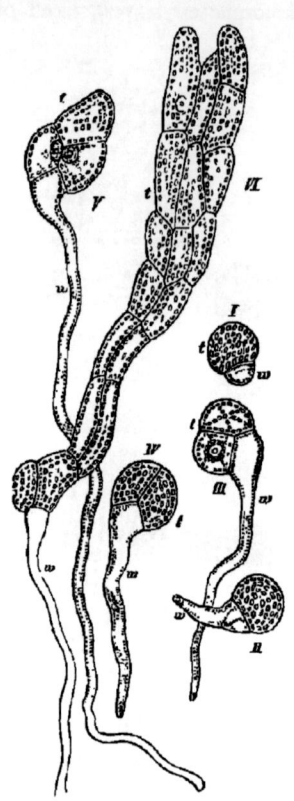

FIG 424.—First stages in the development of the prothallium of *Equisetum Telmateia w* first root hair, *t* incipient shoot. The development is in the order of the numbers *I—VI* (× about 200)

If now the spores of the Horse-tail are sown on the surface of water, for instance, on which they float, an opportunity is easily afforded of observing their early stages of germination These are represented in Fig. 424 In *I* and *II* the germinating spore is seen to be in the first place segmented into root (*w*) and shoot (*t*); the root, a simple utricle, turns geotropically downwards, while the shoot containing chlorophyll (*t*) floats on the water and undergoes numerous successive cell-divisions Germinating on ordinary water, however, the plantlets usually develope no further than in Fig 424 *VI*; they attain their complete development, however, if the spores are sown on loamy soil or on the surface of a block of turf saturated with nutritive substances. The result is that in the course of several weeks tiny plantlets are produced, usually in dense tufts, which on closer investigation are seen to be of two kinds, namely, smaller male plants as in Fig. 425 *A*, and much larger female plants as in Fig 426. Consideration of the figures referred to shows that the plantlets produced from the spores (which moreover are very difficult to cultivate) present not the slightest similarity to an Equisetum plant. The latter is in every respect a highly organised plant, its roots accord entirely with the type of the higher plants, its shoot-axes and leaves are clothed with a very strongly developed epidermis, and the fundamental tissue of the shoot-axes contains strands of sclerenchyma, in addition to colourless and green parenchyma, and the vascular bundles, although thin and delicate, nevertheless possess all the essential elements of such. Matters are quite otherwise with the plantlet produced from the spore, the branched shoot of which possesses assimilating chlorophyll, it is true, but in other respects presents the simplest cellular structure, the roots are simple long utricles

It is already clear that the germination of the spore of a Horse-tail signifies something very different from the germination of a seed of the flowering plants; even the tiniest seed, such as that of Tobacco or of a Campanula, contains a young plant, an embryo, which on its first development at once reproduces the characters of its mother-plant. It would therefore be very inappropriate to name the small plantlets developed from the spores of the Equisetum simply embryos, since they play an entirely different part in the developmental history, they are usually termed prothallia

The small male prothallia of *Equisetum* give rise at their margins to several antheridia which form only a few antherozoids. They consist of a simple layer of cells and a core of tissue each cell of which produces one antherozoid. The appearance of the latter is shown in Fig. 425 *B* and *D*; like those of the Ferns the antherozoids of the Equiseteæ have also numerous cilia for the purpose of executing swimming movements, since as in the case of the Algæ and Mosses, and as in all Vascular Cryptogams, fertilisation by means of antherozoids can only take place with the aid of water, even though the prothallia grow on soil which is only damp, where the sexual organs become so far ripe that on the opportune saturation of the whole tuft with water the antheridia and archegonia open, and the antherozoids can swim from the former to the latter

The archegonia of the female prothallia are represented in Fig 426 at *a* They have in the main the same structure as those of the Moss, only they are more simply organised and their ventral portion is immersed in the tissue of the prothallium, from which only the neck protrudes. Here also the oosphere arises in the venter of the archegonium as a rounded mass of protoplasm lying free in the central cavity. Here also an open canal leads to the exterior from which the deliquescent canal-cells are expelled at the moment of opening. I am not aware that any one has as yet observed the entrance of an antherozoid into the oosphere itself, in Equisetum, but that this occurs there can be no doubt, since in the case of the Ferns and their allies various good observers have repeatedly succeeded in directly observing the act of fertilisation.

After fertilisation the canal, as in all archegonia, becomes closed. The oosphere, now invested with a new cellulose wall, and the embryo produced from it are thus completely enclosed in the tissue of the parent-plant. While the embryo itself slowly grows up, with accompanying cell-divisions, the tissue investing it also increases in volume, and cell-divisions result in it. The manner in which, not only in the case of the Equisetaceæ but also in the Ferns, the growing oospore (or

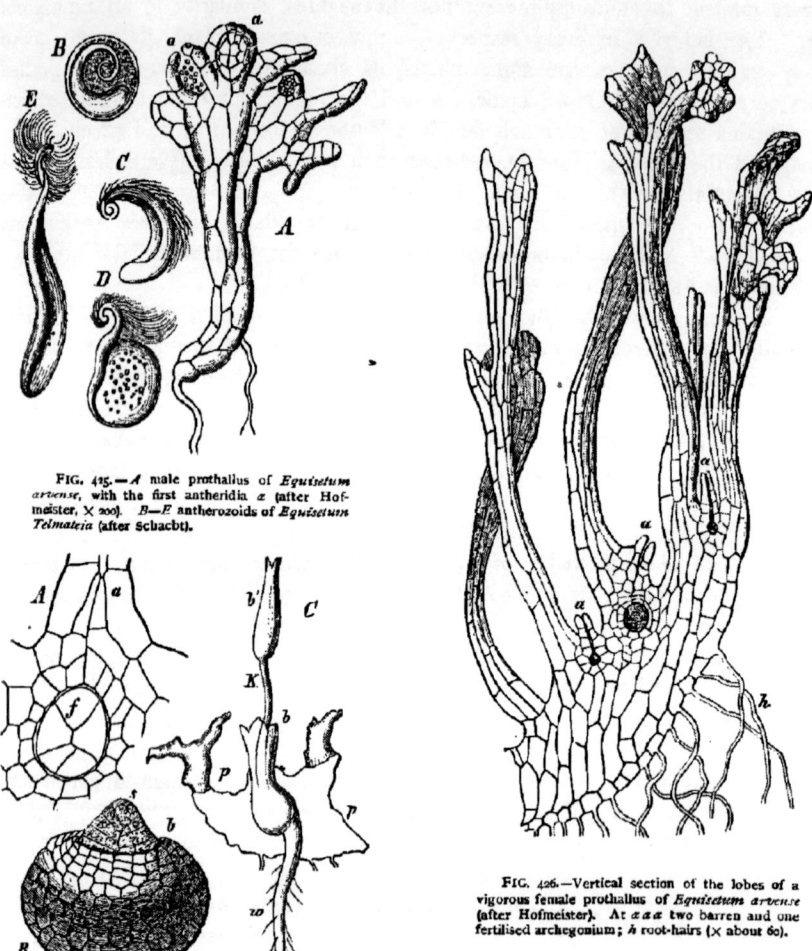

FIG. 425.— *A* male prothallus of *Equisetum arvense*, with the first antheridia *a* (after Hofmeister, × 200). *B—E* antherozoids of *Equisetum Telmateia* (after Schacht).

FIG. 426.—Vertical section of the lobes of a vigorous female prothallus of *Equisetum arvense* (after Hofmeister). At *a a a* two barren and one fertilised archegonium; *h* root-hairs (× about 60).

FIG. 427.—Development of the embryo of *Equisetum arvense* (after Hofmeister). *A* vertical section of archegonium *a* with embryo *f* (× 200). *B* a free embryo further developed : *b* incipient first leaves ; *s* apex of the first shoot (× 200). *C* vertical section of a lobe of a prothallus *p p* with a young *Equisetum* : *w* its first root ; *b b* its leaf-sheaths (× 10).

what is the same thing, the young embryo) first breaks up into so-called octants by means of three walls standing at right angles to one another, which then become further divided up by means of anticlinal and periclinal cell-walls, and how in this way there arises at last a tetrahedral apical cell for the first root and a similar one for the young shoots, and how the first inception of the leaf takes place, have already been indicated at another opportunity (p 446, Fig. 283) and it may be at once pointed out that the development of the embryo of the Vascular Cryptogams generally may be referred to that scheme, although occasional deviations occur However, it lies quite beyond our present purpose to enter more closely into these embryological details. What especially interests us is sufficiently explained by Fig 427 At *A* is seen the neck of the archegonium *a*, and at *f* the young embryo; at *B* is an embryo somewhat further developed, of which however only the shoot-portion can be seen, the growing-point of which is at *s* and its first still very young leaf-sheath at *b*, in the form of an annular wall. In *C* the young Equisetum is already growing up; its shoot *K* already supports two leaf-sheaths *bb'* and the first root *w* is growing downwards. The base of the plantlet (and this is here the true embryo) is still inserted into the tissue of the prothallium *pp*, by which it is still chiefly nourished. When the whole Equisetum itself becomes stronger the prothallium disappears, the embryo remains somewhat feeble during

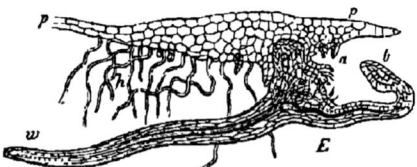

FIG. 428 —*Adiantum Capillus-Veneris* Vertical section through the prothallus *p p* and the young Fern *F h* root hairs, *a* archegonia, *b* first leaf, *w* first root of embryo (× about 10)

FIG. 429.—*Adiantum Capillus Veneris* Prothallium seen from below *p p* with the young Fern attached *b* first leaf, *w'* primary root, *w''* secondary root, *h* root hairs of prothallus (× about 10)

the first year, however, though it produces from its lower leaf-sheaths a few lateral shoots, which penetrate downwards into the soil to continue the growth next year, since the plantlet arising directly from the embryo itself perishes in the autumn.

In the Ferns and Lycopods all the essential points of reproduction repeat themselves as in the case of Equisetum, so that a detailed description would be superfluous To present a few points of resemblance only, I may briefly mention that in our better known native Ferns, and in very many others, the sporangia arise on the lower side of ordinary large foliage leaves, or on metamorphosed portions of them (as in the Royal Fern, *Osmunda regalis*) mostly in enormous numbers, and very small in size; they are stalked capsules, which appear to the unaided eye as minute granules. On sowing the very resistent fern-spores from the spontaneously burst sporangia, they germinate after some time and produce in the normal course of events a prothallium, which possesses approximately the form of a cordate leaf, 0 5—1·5 cm. long and broad, on the lower side of which are developed antheridia, and archegonia, from the fertilised oospheres of which the new Fern-plants arise. The most essential points here coming into consideration are illustrated in Figs. 428 and 429.

LECTURE XLII.

THE ORGANS OF REPRODUCTION (*Continued*)[1].

HETEROSPOROUS VASCULAR CRYPTOGAMS; GYMNOSPERMS, ANGIOSPERMS

THERE existed during previous geological epochs Horsetails with two kinds of spores, but the species are extinct. Nevertheless we have still two small families of Fern-like plants, mutually very distinct, which in spite of their great differences are usually grouped together under the absurd name Rhizocarpeæ: these are the Salvineæ and the Marsilieæ in which are formed two kinds of spores entirely different in nature, and the same peculiarity is again met with in the case of the third great subdivision of the Vascular Cryptogams, namely the Lycopodiaceæ (*Dichotomeæ*). Here also there are two very different families, the Selaginellæ and the Isöeteæ, in which two kinds of spores are produced. I cannot here suppress the remark that it harmonises little with Darwin's views when we see repeated in three very different classes of the vegetable kingdom, with otherwise similar spores, a phenomenon so important as is the production of two kinds of spores with their consequences. Certainly it cannot be explained by natural selection in the struggle for existence. This however simply by the way.

The consideration of a few cases where the development of two kinds of spores takes place is essential to the reader, since a satisfactory insight into the reproduction of the Coniferæ (Gymnosperms) and in fact of the true flowering plants can only be attained by this means. One of the most magnificent results in the province of Embryology was Hofmeister's demonstration in 1851 of the fact that the formation of seed in

---

[1] As in the first eleven lectures, which are to be regarded simply as an organographical introduction to the physiology proper, so also in the two preceding lectures my wish has been only to give a very condensed sketch of the organography of the reproductive apparatus. From the astounding variety of materials to hand only a few examples could be taken into account; those who desire more detailed information concerning the organisation of the reproductive system, and (what can scarcely be avoided here) as to their phylogenetic or systematic connection in the various subdivisions of the vegetable kingdom, will find in my 'Text-book of Botany' a rapid but very thorough survey in this connection. Still further details, especially with respect to the most recent observations on the Algæ and Fungi, and the remarkable developmental relations of the sporangia of the Cryptogams to those of the Phanerogams, are to be found in Goebel's new edition of my text-book, which has just appeared under the title '*Grundzuge der Systematik*.' There is an English edition published by the Clarendon Press, Oxford.

the Phanerogams is essentially nothing different from the processes in the germination of the large spores of those Cryptogams which possess two kinds of spores. Hitherto it really appeared as if a deep and impassable gap existed between the reproductive processes of the Cryptogams and Phanerogams; but Hofmeister showed thirty-one years ago that this gap does not really exist, that it is filled up by those forms of Cryptogams which develope two kinds of spores, or in other words, certain forms of Phanerogams, particularly the Gymnosperms (Cycadeæ, Coniferæ) approximate in their seed-formation so closely to certain heterosporous Cryptogams, that we might now include these plants equally justly with the Cryptogams as with the Phanerogams. This discovery has cast an entirely new light on the interdependence of the whole vegetable kingdom.

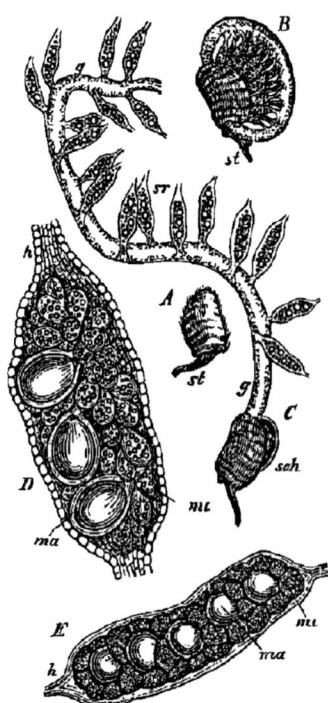

FIG. 430.—*Marsilia salvatrix* A a sporo carp (nat size), *st* upper part of its stalk B a sporocarp burst in water and extruding the gelatinous ring C the gelatinous ring is ruptured and extended *sr* chambers containing sori, *sch* coats of sporocarp. D one of the chambers containing a sorus, from an immature sporocarp E a similar chamber from a ripe sporocarp *mi* microsporangia, *ma* macrosporangia.

In the case of *Marsilia*, already shown in Fig. 392 (p. 699), there arise from the petioles of the foliage leaves stalked sporocarps approximately of the shape of a Bean. In the interior of these a large number of delicate-walled sporangia are formed, which at first are in so far alike that in each of them a large number of mother-cells are developed, which in their turn divide each into four daughter-cells, as occurs generally in the spore-formation of all Muscineæ and Vascular Cryptogams, and in the development of the pollen of Phanerogams. From this point onwards, however, a difference occurs. In a number of the sporangia all the spores produced by division into four attain to complete development; but they remain small and are therefore called *Microspores*. In the other sporangia of the same fruits, on the contrary, only a single one of all the spore-cells already produced attains completion; this one, however, attains such vigour that it fills up the cavity of the sporangium—it is the *Macrospore.*

Lying in water the spore-fruit of the *Marsilia* bursts, and by means of a very remarkable mechanism the macro- and micro-sporangia become expelled from the sporocarp (Fig. 430), whereupon the further development of both kinds of spores begins at once.

The contents of the microspores break up by successive bi-partitions into sixteen or thirty-two small round cells, in each of which arises an antherozoid which possesses the form of a cork-screw with many turns. As soon as the antherozoids are completely developed, the external hard shell of the microspore opens, and an inner thin membrane swells up as a vesicle, and eventually contains the antherozoids, which then by deliquescence of the vesicle emerge free into the water, in which they move forwards, their spirals rotating, as in many other cases a delicate vesicle clinging to their hinder end is carried with them (Fig. 431)

In the narrower end of the very large macrospore, which is filled with starch-grains and invested with a very thick firm membrane, the first rudiment of the prothallus arises under the apex by the collection and rapid division of a mass of protoplasm   Thus the prothallium is incepted in the interior of the spore: it is separated off from the remaining (far larger) cavity of the spore, by means of a transverse wall, the diaphragm. Then the apex of the spore opens, and as the diaphragm protrudes beyond the opening as a vesicle, the young prothallium is forced out of the spore-cavity, and thus comes into the lower part of the so-called 'funnel,' which is formed by a trans-lucent soft gelatinous mass situated at the anterior end of the macrospore, a funnel-shaped canal in this gelatinous mass leads down to the prothallium. The latter is, however, very small in comparison with the very large macrospore, and from its whole cell-structure it may be looked upon as practically a single archegonium

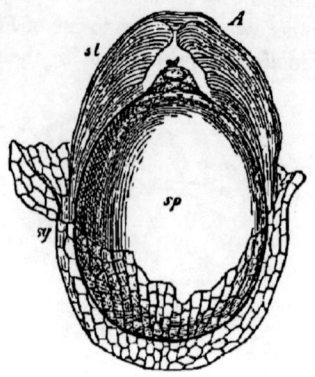

On allowing the sporocarp of a Marsilia to open in a glass of water, the stages of development of the macro- and micro-spores described may be obtained after from ten to fifteen hours, the temperature being suitable   The water swarms with thousands of the rapidly moving antherozoids, hundreds of which now crowd into the funnel-opening of the macrospore, while others bore directly through the soft jelly, some of them reach the naked oosphere lying in the venter of the archegonium, from which in the course of two days an embryo like that in Fig. 432 is then developed, which already possesses the first leaf b, the apical-cell of the shoot-axis s, the primary root w, and the so-called foot f By means of this foot f the embryo is attached to the protruding vesicle of the macrospore c, and is nourished by the latter.   The whole structure at this stage is strikingly suggestive of the develop-

FIG. 431.—*Marsilia salvatrix* Upper figure Macrospore *sp* with gelatinous envelope *sl*, and apical papilla protruding into the funnel In the papilla is a flattened yellow drop, *sg* ruptured wall of macro-sporangium (× about 30) Lower figure, ruptured microspore after the escape of the antherozoids *ex* epispore, *dl* extruded endospore, containing granules, *s z* spiral antherozoids, *y y* their vesicles, containing starchy granules The gelatinous envelope of the microspore has disappeared The protuberances on the exospore are wrongly represented (× 550)

ment of a Fish still bearing the yolk-sac at its ventral surface. As in the Mosses and Ferns, so also here the archegonium goes on growing for some time longer, and appears in the figure as an envelope consisting of two cells and investing the embryo, the neck portion of the archegonium (a) being still quite evident. From the lower part of the archegonium or prothallus ($p\,t$) numerous long root-hairs grow out ($w\,h$) by means of which the whole structure is anchored firmly at the bottom of the water; since it is one of the first objects of every embryo-plant to obtain a fixed position in order that it may maintain a definite direction with respect to the external world. Finally, it should be remarked that in Fig. 432 also the gelatinous mass referred to (*s l*) is still to be seen, enveloping the whole germinating apparatus.

When at length the whole of the store of nutritive material in the macrospore is exhausted, and the young plant has produced several roots and leaves, it becomes free from the prothallus and other parts concerned in its origin, and developes into a perennial plant

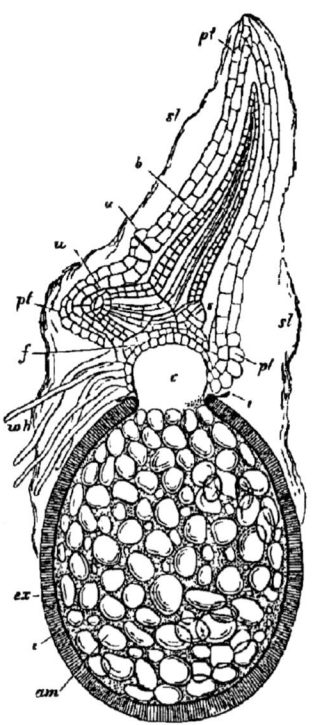

FIG 432.—*Marsilia salvatrix*. Longitudinal section of macrospore, prothallium, and embryo (X about 60) *am* starch grains in spore, *i* inner membrane ruptured above, *ex* epispore, with prismatic structure, *c* cavity beneath the protruded diaphragm on which the basal layer of the prothallium is situated, *pt* prothallium, *wh* its root hairs, *a* archegonium, *f* foot of embryo, *w* its root, *s* its stem apex, *b* its first leaf, which distends the prothallus, *sl* gelatinous envelope of the spore, at first it forms the funnel above the papilla and it still envelopes the prothallium (50 hours after sowing).

We have here a first step in the transition from the germination of a spore to the development of a seed. The two parts prothallium and embryo represent, as we see, the two alternate generations which we found completely separated in Equisetum and the ordinary Ferns, each as an independent living plant. Obviously, we might also suppose the prothallium to be developed in the interior of the macrospore and not protruding, and that it, together with the embryo developed in it, remained enclosed in the thick membrane of the macrospore; in this case the germinated macrospore would constitute the essential part of the seed of a Phanerogam.

The behaviour on germination of those Lycopodiaceæ which possess two kinds of spores, however, actually accords with the idea just put forward. Fig 433 shows at *A* the macrospore of the genus *Isoëtes* and at *B* the prothallus with its archegonium *a*, developed entirely in its interior.

These points come out still more clearly in the germination of the spores of the genus *Selaginella*. The sporangia here arise in the axils of the leaves at the ends of the foliage shoots. Fig 434 *A* shows the fertile shoot of a *Selaginella* looked at from the outside, *B* is the same in longitudinal section. The sporangia situated in the leaf-axils are obvious at once, and it is observed that those on the right side contain only four (only three are visible) large spores, whereas the sporangia on the left side contain numerous microspores. If the macrospores and microspores are sown separately on a suitable damp substratum, both develope, it is true, but no subsequent fertilisation occurs: the unfertilised macrospores give rise to prothallia with archegonia, it is true, but no embryo arises in these. This fact, which can be confirmed in the case of the most different Cryptogams, is in so far of great value as it is not always feasible to observe directly the entrance of antherozoids into the oosphere; the suppression of the fertilisation and development of the embryo when the access of antherozoids is prevented, however, is a certain proof of the necessity of the union for the formation of an embryo.

The processes of reproduction which alone interest us here can be rapidly apprehended from Fig. 435. *I* represents a widely open macrospore; from the aperture through the very thick external spore-membrane, the prothallium *d a* projects, bearing at *a* an unfertilised archegonium; at *II* is seen a young unfertilised still closed archegonium, in which the lower shaded cell represents the as yet unripe oosphere, and the conical portion lying above it is the canal cell, which, when the neck of the

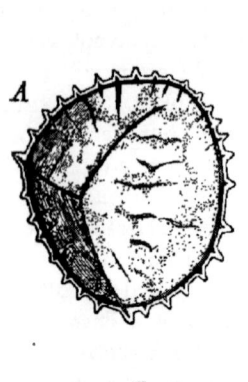

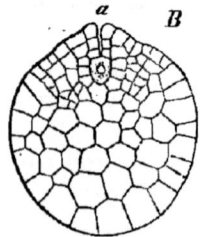

FIG. 433.—*Isoetes lacustris*
(after Hofmeister). *A* macrospore
a fortnight after sowing, rendered
transparent by glycerine (× 60).
B longitudinal section of the prothallus a month after sowing the
spores; *a* archegonium (× 40).

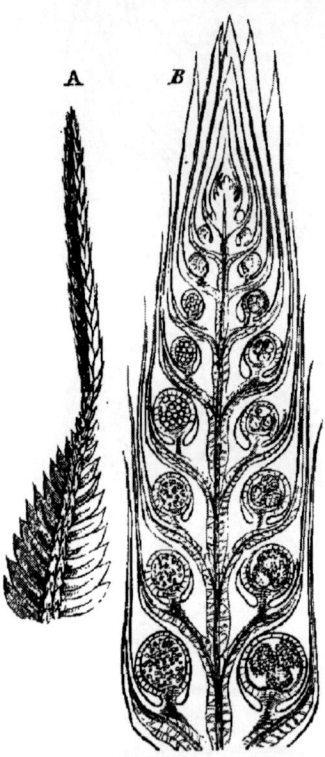

FIG. 434.—*Selaginella inaequalifolia.*
A fertile branch (× 2), *B* longitudinal
section of apex of *A*, bearing microsporangia
to the left and macrosporangia to the right.

archegonium opens, is extruded as mucilage. *III* is the archegonium with a fertilised oosphere already divided by a horizontal wall. While the archegonia are preparing for fertilisation, preparations for the development of the antherozoids are also taking place in the microspores *A–D*; after a small cell (*v* in *D*) which does not take part in the formation of the antherozoids, has been as it were cut off, further cell-divisions occur in the remaining cells which constitute together, so to speak, a reduced antheridium. This is well seen in *D*: each of these small cells gives rise to an antherozoid of very simple form, just as in the Mosses.

Returning to the germinating macrospore again, it is to be noticed that the true prothallus is separated off from the large spore-cavity by the diaphragm $d\,d$: in this cavity there arises a large-celled tissue, such as we shall meet with later in the embryo-sac of flowering plants—the so-called Endosperm. Figure I, then, shows at e' a young embryo, developed from a fertilised oosphere, and at e one already further developed, the shoot portion of which (only roughly indicated) has bored into the endosperm tissue, but which subsequently grows out from it again.

In order to proceed hence to the formation of the seed in the Coniferæ, we need only assume that the macrospore does not open at all, the prothallium and endosperm

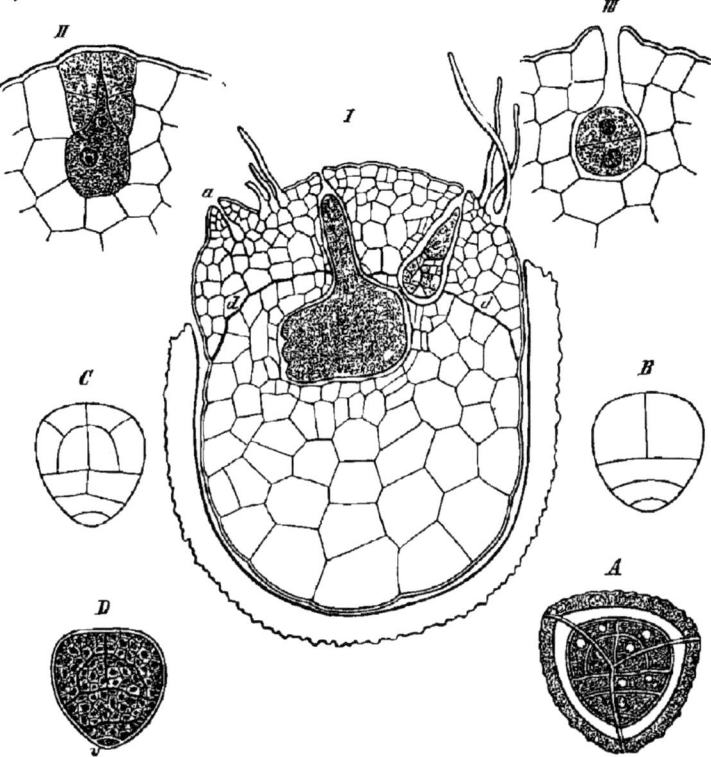

FIG. 435.—Germination of *Selaginella* (after Pfeffer) *I—III S. Martensii, A—D S. caulescens* *I* longitudinal section of a macrospore filled with prothallus and endosperm (*d* diaphragm) in which two embryos *e e'* are developing *II* a young archegonium, not yet opened *III* an archegonium containing a fertilised oospore, which has undergone one division *A* a macrospore, showing the divisions of the contents *B C* different views of these divisions *D* mother cells of antherozoids, in the mature antheridium.

arising in its interior, and one or two embryos becoming developed Of course, in the case of the Coniferæ and all Gymnospermous plants, what actually occurs is not only what has just been mentioned, but moreover the macrospore itself also in which these processes occur remains lying in the very massively developed sporangium, and no opening of any kind exists through which antherozoids for instance could penetrate to the oosphere. Here, in fact, we reach a turning-point in the history of fertilisation; in that not only in the case of the Gymnospermous plants (Coniferæ, Cycadeæ), but even in a still higher degree in the true flowering plants, the oospheres remain completely enclosed in masses of tissue, and thus the possibility of their fertilisation by means of motile antherozoids ceases. The fertilising material—and this is the only essential in the matter—is carried to the oosphere in quite another manner, namely, by the male microspores (which are distinguished in the Phanerogams as pollen-grains) fixing themselves to a portion of the female organ of reproduction, and thence emitting a tubular prolongation, which makes its way through the tissue-masses surrounding the oosphere, and finally penetrates to the oosphere, to which it subsequently transmits the male fertilising substance   This tube is called the *Pollen-tube*

It is unfortunately necessary to add here a few definitions of terminology, since the history of our science has brought it about that organs of like kind in different classes of plants, in spite of their homology, were previously held to be essentially different and have therefore had different names assigned to them   At the present time, when we perceive clearly the true connection of these matters it would be possible, and is demanded in the interest of science, to designate the *pollen-grains* simply microspores, and the *embryo-sac* simply the macrospore, in order to indicate their homologies, never-theless the old nomenclature can now scarcely be entirely put aside, since it is too deeply fixed in the literature, so that to the uninitiated doubts might arise as to the meanings of terms in reading different books.

As already mentioned, the gymnospermous plants (Coniferæ, Cycadeæ, and Gnetaceæ) are directly allied in their reproductive processes to the higher Cryptogams with two kinds of spores: nevertheless this was by no means an easy matter to establish. The investigations of many years were needed to arrive at this conclusion. If I quote a few examples, it will be at once seen that the essential and important points are not directly obvious.

The facts of fertilisation come out particularly clearly in the case of the Yew (*Taxus baccata*)   Each Yew-tree is either entirely male or entirely female, and thus it is only trees of the latter kind which bring forth the seeds, which are found in autumn surrounded by an elegant red thick envelope   The male and female trees flower in the spring.   The male flowers are situated on the under side of the horizontal lateral shoots of the tree: they are small buds (*A* Fig 436) bearing numerous minute scale-leaves at their lower parts, and at the apex eight to ten peculiarly formed structures *a* which remind one forcibly of the sporangiophores of *Equisetum*.   A stalked disc bears on its under surface four or five pollen-sacs, which may be forthwith designated sporangia, when these open, they set free their microspores, which however are generally known as pollen.

On the female Yew trees also minute bud-like shoots are found in the spring on the lower side of horizontal branches (*C*, Fig 436)   Here also numerous scale-leaves *s* are present, anteriorly, however, is a peculiar projecting structure *s k*   This is the *Ovule*, so termed because the seed containing the embryo is developed from it after fertilisation. Fundamentally, however, this ovule is simply a very highly developed macrosporangium, as will be more clearly seen later on.   It will also be well to regard more closely the longitudinal section through the whole female shoot *D*. Here is seen the ovule at the apex of the shoot, and it is observed that it consists of two different structures   The approximately hemispherical body *K K* is the so-called *Nucellus* of the ovule, and it constitutes the essential part: this is the proper *macrosporangium*, in which the so-called embryo-sac or macrospore arises subsequently   The portion *i* surrounds the nucellus of the ovule as a closely investing envelope formed of several layers of tissue, and narrows anteriorly into a canal.   This investment is called the *Integument*, and the canal in it just referred to, which thus leads from the exterior down to the nucellus of the ovule, is the *Micropyle*

It will be of further service for preliminary guidance if Fig. 436 *E* is compared with the preceding   The ovule is here represented in a more advanced stage: *i* is again the integument, now with closed micropyle, much larger, and closely investing the nucellus of the ovule *k k* on all sides.   Within the latter we now find the part *e*: this is the embryo-sac filled with endosperm—or, as we may also say, the macrospore filled with the prothallium.   In this structure the young plant, the embryo, arises in consequence of fertilisation.   To note it by the way, the portion marked *m*, in the form of an annular cushion surrounding the base of the ovule, is that which in the autumn surrounds the whole ovule (or, better, what is then the seed) in the form of a red succulent investment.

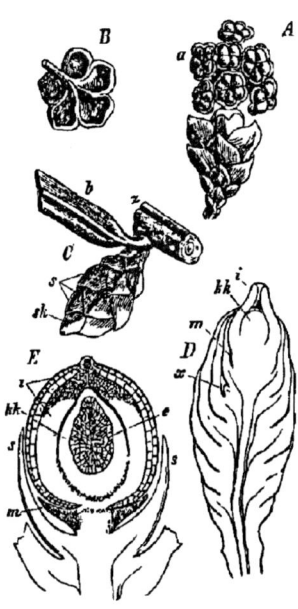

Fig 436 – *Taxus baccata   A* male flower (enlarged)   *a* the pollen-sacs   *B* an anther with the pollen sacs opened, seen from below   *C* portion of a leaf-shoot, with a foliage leaf *b*, from the axil of which springs the female flower, *s* its scales, *sk* its terminal ovule   *D* longitudinal section of the same (magnified) *i* integument , *kk* nucellus of the ovule , *x* a rudimentary axillary ovule.   *D* longitudinal section through an older ovule, before fertilisation   *i* integument , *kk* nucellus   *e* endosperm, *m* arillus , *s* enveloping leaves

In this description, I have for the time being made no reference to fertilisation itself, but have only described the complex of organs which co-operate in that process: in like manner it will, I think, be advantageous if we look at the result of the fertilisation, before describing the processes themselves. This result is the development of the ovule into the seed, capable of germinating, the parts of which must be understood before a proper insight can be obtained into its origin and significance. This can be accomplished with the aid of Fig. 437, which represents the germination of the seed of the Stone Pine, with which the other Coniferæ essentially agree. *I* is the seed in longitudinal section, consisting of three parts; *s* the hard thick testa developed from the integument of the ovule after fertilisation ; *e* is the so-called endosperm, or further developed prothallium—the black line separating the testa and endosperm is to be supposed to represent the membrane of the macrospore, or, what is the same thing, the embryo-sac. Finally, we have lying in the middle of the endosperm the young embryo. *w* is its incipient root, *c* a whorl of leaves which, owing to an extremely unhappy idea of the older botanists, it is still the custom to term cotyledons. This again is an entirely meaningless word, which however unfortunately can now scarcely be expunged from scientific language; it may be translated seed-leaves. It is simply bad taste however to speak of them as seed-lobes.

The rest of the drawings in Fig. 437, concerning which the explanation of the figure gives further information, show how the germ-plant (the embryo) contained in the seed, then developes further; how first the root *w* and then the primary shoot-axis *x* elongates and emerges from the seed: the radicle enters the soil, the cotyledons *c* still remaining enclosed in the endosperm, to absorb the nutritive materials there stored up. It is not until this has been accomplished, and the exhausted endosperm is reduced to a mere membrane that the plumule elongates upwards, and the cotyledons are withdrawn from the coats of the seed.

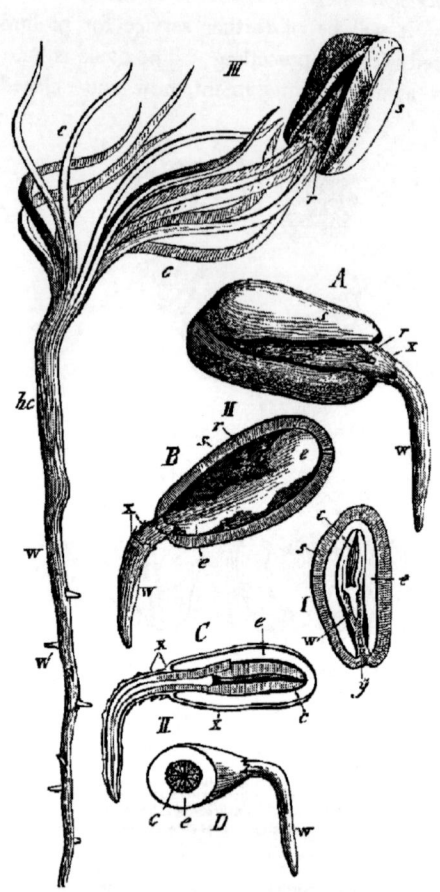

After these preliminary explanations, it is scarcely necessary to point out more particularly how great is the difference between reproduction by means of ordinary spores on the one hand and by means of seeds on the other. In the former case individual cells — i. e. the spores — become separated off from the mother-plant, and the new plant-life begins, so to speak, entirely anew. Here in the case of the seed-plants the seeds also separate from the mother-plant, of course, to carry on a new plant-life, but the young plant is already there, and, in most cases, already consists of the first rudimentary organs, a primary shoot and radicle, and these organs are composed of innumerable minute cells in which the tissue-systems are already differentiated. The young plant which

FIG. 437.—*Pinus Pinea.* *I* median longitudinal section through the seed, *y* being the micropyle end. *II* commencement of germination, the root emerging. *III* conclusion of germination, after the endosperm has been exhausted (the seed was not deep enough in the soil, and was therefore carried up by the cotyledons as the stem elongated). *A* shows the ruptured testa at *s*. *B* shows the endosperm *s* after the removal of one half of the testa. *C* longitudinal section of endosperm and embryo; and *D* transverse section of the same, at the beginning of germination; *c* cotyledons; *w* primary root; *x* the embryo-sac pushed aside by the root (it is ruptured at *B x*); *hc* hypocotyl; *w'* secondary roots; *r* red membrane lining the hard testa.

lies in the seed is already formed while the seed itself is still part of the parent plant, and is so far nourished by this that subsequently, on the germination of the seed, little more than a mere enlargement of the embryo is necessary. Seed-plants may therefore in this sense be compared with viviparous animals. A comparison of the Cryptogams or spore-plants with oviparous animals, however, would be but a very lame one, since spores are not eggs at all, it is only in the lowest regions of the vegetable kingdom, especially in the Fucaceæ and a few other forms, that oospheres are separated from the mother-plant

From these preliminaries we may now proceed to the consideration of the processes of fertilisation itself. Here however there are concerned so many organs boxed one within the other, that it is scarcely possible to make clear all the parts in their mutual relations in any one figure taken directly from Nature. In the interest of the reader, therefore, I prefer to illustrate the essential points by means of a diagram.

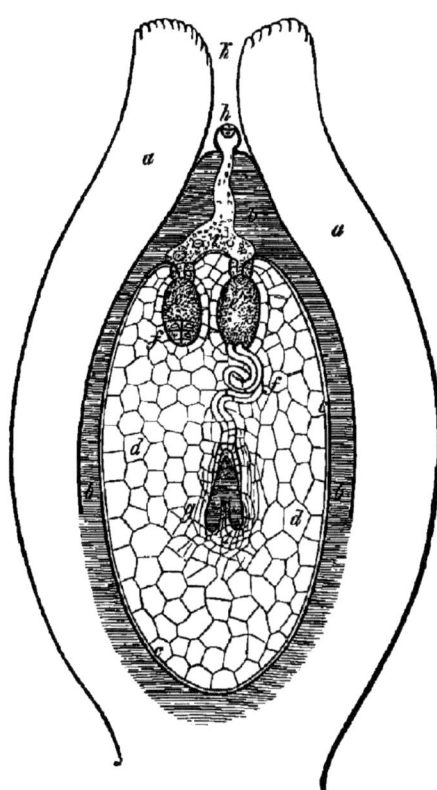

Fig 438 is a diagrammatic longitudinal section through the whole ovule of a gymnospermous plant: *a* is the integument, and *k* the micropyle, which in the case of the Gymnosperms is relatively wide open at the time when the pollen-grains or microspores commence their business of fertilisation. At this time also a drop of fluid is frequently excreted, and exudes from the micropyle, the pollen-grains carried here by the wind stick to this, and when the fluid contracts, the pollen-grains also are drawn in with it and come to lie on the projection of the nucellus of the ovule *b b.* Such a pollen-grain is seen at *h.* This process, namely the conveyance of the pollen-grains to the female organ in the case of the Phanerogams, is termed *pollination,* and it occurs in many Gymnosperms at so early a time that the true reproductive organs within the ovule have not as yet even begun

FIG 438.—Diagram of the ovule of a Gymnosperm in longitudinal section

to develope, and in the case of the Pines a full year may pass before the fertilising tube of the pollen already contained in the closed micropyle reaches the archegonia.

The embryo-sac or macrospore arises in the Gymnosperms deep in the interior of the nucellus of the ovule, and grows slowly up to a considerable size; in the case of the very large-seeded Cycadeæ it may attain a length of 2 cm. or more and a breadth of 1 5 cm. or more It becomes filled with a succulent cell-tissue, the endosperm *d d*, in which (mostly only after a long time, and sometimes not before the seed appears to be already nearly ripe) the archegonia *e e* are formed: these archegonia are of very simple structure, though at the same time relatively large . in the case of the large-seeded Cycadeæ the central cell is often 3–5 mm. long and 2–3 mm. broad. The neck of the archegonium differs much in structure in the different forms of Gymnosperms, but there can be no doubt whatever that these organs are in every respect to be looked upon as archegonia resembling those of the higher Cryptogams and Mosses

When the prothallium (endosperm) with its archegonia is sufficiently developed, usually only after some months, fertilisation can follow. the pollen-tube *i* bores through the tissue of the nucellus of the ovule *b*, and applies itself with its anterior end either as a thin tube, or more frequently as a broad sac, to that part of the embryo-sac where the archegonia are situated : protuberances of the pollen-tube then bore their way into the necks of the archegonia and penetrate as far as the central-cells. It is not yet known in what way the male fertilising material now passes over into the central cell of the archegonium, filled with the oosphere It is not certainly established whether an extremely fine actual opening in the membrane of the pollen-tube facilitates the direct entrance of the fertilising protoplasm, or whether the membrane remains closed and the fertilising substance diffuses over as a true solution.

It is for our purpose practically the same thing whether the whole of the proto-plasm contained in the large central-cell of the archegonium is to be regarded as the oosphere, or whether only a certain part of it answers to this designation. It suffices for us to know that in the lower portion of the central-cell *e*, cell-divisions now take place by means of which two or three tiers are produced, each of four cells placed cross-wise and close together, as in *f*. This is however, strictly speaking, not as yet the inception of the embryo. On the contrary, these cells, at first very short and discoid, grow out to long tubes (*f'*) which bore into the endosperm-tissue and become curved and twisted in the process. The cells *f* situated at the ends of the tubes, hitherto but little grown, and which previously occupied the basal region in the archegonium—i. e. the one turned away from the neck—and which are pushed out from the archegonium by the formation of the tubes, subsequently give origin to the embryo *g* ; this then goes on growing, with continual cell-divisions, and finally displaces the rest of the parts and occupies the middle of the endosperm. Among the many peculiarities in the seed-formation of the Gymnosperms, it is found that in some cases fertilisation takes place, and the seeds even become fully ripened and fall, without the embryo having developed further. I observed this remarkable fact in the autumn of 1868 in the case of the plum-like seeds of the Japanese plant *Gingko biloba.* On opening the ripe fallen seeds in October I found apparently no trace of an embryo in them, and therefore regarded them as unfertilised. On again examining the seeds after they had been laid aside for two or three months, there was found in each of them a large well-developed embryo, and the seeds all proved to be capable of germination. Strasburger has investigated this fact in his great work on the Gymnosperms, and we now know that the Cycadeæ also behave similarly.

The ripened seeds of the Gymnosperms, especially those of the Cycads and of the *Gingko biloba* just referred to, often bear very little resemblance to what is elsewhere termed a seed in the Phanerogams, those of the last-named plants being in the ripe state like small yellow plums or large cherries , for the integument of the ovule has become transformed into a thick pulpy mass which encloses a 'stone' like that of a plum, in which the endosperm is enclosed; and matters are similar in the Cycadeæ In *Cycas revoluta* the seeds attain the volume of a medium-sized apple. In most of the Coniferæ, however, the integument becomes transformed into a hard seed-coat, and the seeds resemble those of other Phanerogams in other respects also.

A remark is still to be added regarding the pollen-grains of the Gymnosperms. That these, from their developmental history and function and also from their origin in receptacles which are obviously sporangia, are to be regarded as micro-spores, has already been mentioned. A further similarity with microspores however exists in the formation, in the interior of each pollen-grain, of a small cellular body which calls to mind the sterile cells in the interior of the microspores of *Isoetes* and *Selaginella*. Fig. 439 shows the structure in question at *y*, though it is not equally well developed in all Gymnosperms.

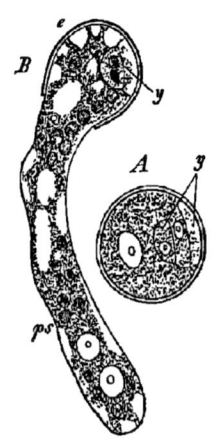

Besides this structure, there still remains a large mass in the pollen-grain or microspore, which alone takes part in the development of the pollen-tube, as may be seen in Fig. 439 *B*. This portion of the pollen-grain, which contains the fertilising substance, corresponds to the antheri-dium of the microspore (as in the case of the Rhizocarp *Salvinia*), while the small cellular body *y* may be looked upon as the last remnant of a reduced prothallium.

With the Monocotyledons and Dicotyledons— among which are found the most highly organised plants in the vegetable kingdom, and which, apart from the Coniferæ, practically constitute what non-botanical people are in the habit of thinking of under the term 'plants,'—the Gymnosperms last con-sidered agree as regards their reproduction in that they give rise to ovules which are rendered fertile

FIG. 439.—*A* a pollen-grain (microspore) of *Ceratozamia longifolia* a Cycad *B* emergence of the pollen tube *ps* from the ruptured outer membrane (exine) of the pollen grain. At *y* are seen the sterile cells (Juranyi)

by means of a pollen-tube, and then develope into a seed containing an embryo. Hence all these plants may be contrasted, as Spermaphytes, with the Cryptogams or Sporophytes

Nevertheless the fertilising apparatus of most Monocotyledons and Dicotyledons appears to be strikingly different externally from that of the Gymnosperms. What is commonly termed a flower is simply the fertilising apparatus of these plants (which may therefore be contrasted as Flowering-plants in the narrower sense of the word with the Gymnosperms), but here again it is of course to be borne in mind that all such distinctions are only admissible when the typical forms in both cases are contrasted with one another. It needs only a somewhat broader con-ception of the idea Flower to justify the application of the term even to a Fir-cone or even to the very unobvious fertilising apparatus of the Yew. Of course the distinction between the flower of a Lily or of a Rose, and that of a Fir or Pine or other Gymnosperm is very great, but between the two, even externally considered, there are numerous stages of flower-development which show us that the difference is not one of principle but only of degree. That which conspicuously distinguishes particularly the large and elegant flowers of true flowering-plants from those of the Gymnosperms is the floral envelope, which is very often a double one and is then termed Calyx and Corolla Even the most magnificent flowers when stripped of these envelopes so that only the essential organs of reproduction remain, show nothing more of the immense contrast indicated above, and we have here to do particularly with these proper reproductive organs only, although I shall show in the next lecture that the floral envelopes are by no means superfluous for starting the process of fertilisation (i. e. pollination), and in many cases are in fact indispensable.

In considering the fertilising apparatus of a flower, as I now have it in mind, it is above all evident that both kinds of reproductive organs, the male and female, are very generally united in one flower, and therefore stand next one another close to its growing-point ; or, in other words, most flowers are hermaphrodite, whereas the floral structures of all Gymnosperms always contain only male or only female organs, both kinds of flowers being distributed on the same tree or on different trees of the same species. These two cases of diclinous flower-development are it is true by no means rare even in flowering-plants, the Monocotyledons and Dicotyledons, plants of the Cucurbitaceæ for example having male and female flowers on the same foliage-shoot, whereas the Hemp or Hop bears always only male or only female flowers on a plant The prevailing rule however is that the flowers are hermaphrodite—a fact which is of importance physiologically, because a long series of the most remarkable mechanisms for pollination are entailed by it, to which I shall have to refer later Also the two kinds of fertilising organs, as such, are very different from those of the Gymnosperms. Whereas the male spores or pollen-grains of the Gymnosperms arise in receptacles which obviously agree with the sporangia of Cryptogams, and particularly in that they are developed on leaves which are often only slightly different from ordinary foliage leaves, we find on the contrary that the male fertilising organs of the true flowering-plants, the stamens, usually have forms which do not easily disclose their true morphological nature. Very generally a stamen consists of a stalk-like support (the filament) which bears above the so-called *Anther*, this again consists chiefly of four sacs joined in two pairs, or occasionally of only two sacs, in which the pollen-grains or microspores arise. These sacs are to be regarded as the same as the sporangia, especially the microsporangia of the Cryptogams and Gymnosperms; but it is shown only after further examinaion and consideration that the filament and the portion (connective) connecting the pollen-sacs of an anther are together to be regarded as a metamorphosed leaf.

Still more important than these peculiarities of the male fertilising organs, is the structure of the female organ Here we meet with a profound difference between the true flowering-plants and the Gymnosperms. In these latter the ovules arise at the margins or on the surfaces of foliar organs, and this so that they are either freely exposed, as in *Cycas revoluta* and *Gingko biloba*, or else so that they are simply concealed between the closely packed leaves at least the micropyle of all Gymnosperms is in open communication with the atmosphere at the time of pollination. Nevertheless in most Coniferæ the pollinated ovules usually become so completely enclosed in enveloping leaves subsequently, that all ommunication with the exterior ceases, as in the case of Fir- and Pine-cones, or so that even capsular fruit-like bodies arise, as in *Thuja* and other *Cupressineæ*.

The case is quite otherwise with the flowering-plants   Here the ovules arise from the beginning in the cavity of a special receptacle, which (with few exceptions) completely excludes them from the atmosphere—a receptacle in which they will even have to be sought out by the pollen-tubes subsequently.   Accordingly the pollen-grains cannot, as in the Gymnosperms, reach the micropyle of the ovule directly, but are conveyed on to a special part of the receptacle, and thence send out their tubes to the ovules. This receptacle bears the name of Ovary (*Germen*). it is this particularly which distinguishes the female reproductive apparatus of the flowering-plants from that of the Gymnosperms Since the Greek word 'Αγγεῖον denotes a receptacle, (in this case the ovary) it is customary to group the flowering-plants—the Monocotyledons and Dicotyledons under the name *Angiosperms*, and thus contrast them with the *Gymnosperms*, or naked-seeded plants.

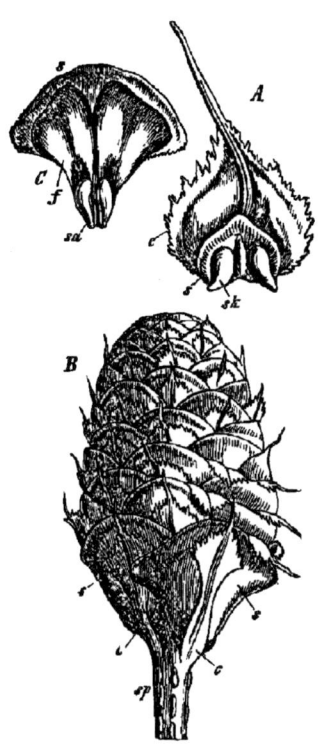

FIG. 440.—Fir-cone of *Abies pectinata* (after Schacht)   *A* a leaf separated from the female floral axis and looked at from above it bears the ovuliferous scale *s* with the ovules *sk* (magnified).   *B* upper part of the female flower (cone) in the mature state. *sp* axis of the cone (floral axis), *c* its leaves, *s* the much-enlarged seminiferous scales   *C* a ripe seminiferous scale *s* with the two seeds *sa* and their wings *f* (reduced)

After these definitions, probably not entirely superfluous for some of my readers, we may now enter more in detail into those points which alone really interest us here; it is unnecessary for our purpose at present to regard the two classes of Angiosperms separately.   I select therefore an example to hand, the flower of one of our handsomest Monocotyledons, the Flowering Rush (*Butomus umbellatus*), for the preliminary description of the reproductive organs.   In Fig. 441 *A* is represented a flower in its natural size; in *B* the floral envelopes and the nine stamens are cut away, and the whole female reproductive apparatus consisting of six single separated carpels is represented slightly magnified.   Each carpel bears above a narrow process, the so-called *Style*, which in its turn bears at the upper end a brush of hairs, the *Stigma n*, this has the function of holding fast the pollen-grains which have been carried to it from the opened anthers, in order that they may germinate there, and put forth their pollen-tubes first in the tissue of the style and then in the cavity of the ovary.

It is easier in the case of *Butomus* than in many other plants to perceive that the carpel together with its style and stigma constitute practically a leaf with the margins folded together longitudinally: this is obvious in Fig. 441 *C*, which represents three carpels in transverse section.   In other cases it is of course not so obvious, though the pods of the Bean, Pea, Bladder-Senna (*Colutea*) and Pæony present easily observed cases of the same kind. The foliar nature of the ovary is somewhat more difficult to decipher when (as is in fact the commonest case) two, three, or more carpels are united to form a simple two or more celled ovary. Suppose the three carpels represented in *C* united inwards with one another and with the three which are absent, by their infolded margins: we should then have a six-celled ovary, consisting of six carpels. Considering the enormous variety of the flowering-plants, the numerous

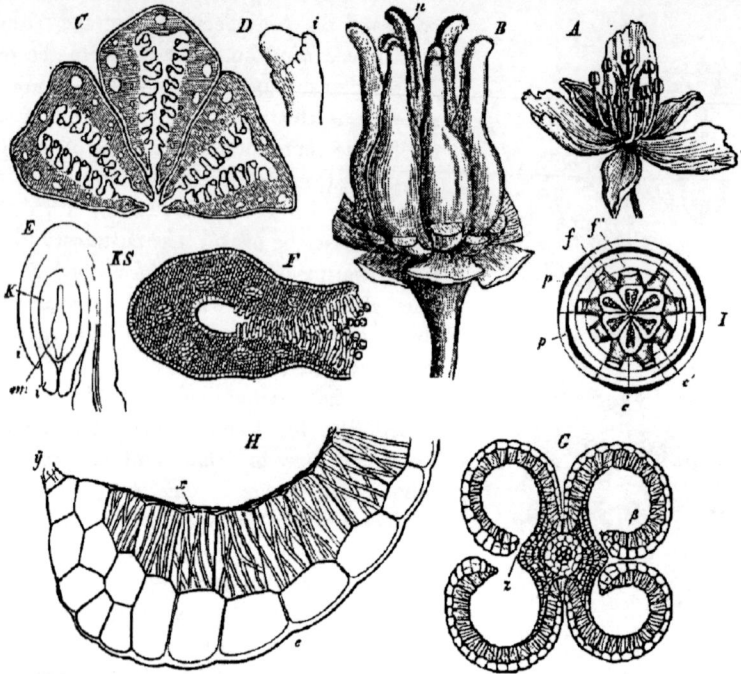

FIG. 441.—*Butomus umbellatus*, *A* flower (nat. size). *B* carpels, after removal of the floral leaves and stamens (magnified); *n* stigmas. *C* transverse section of three of the monomerous carpels, each bearing numerous ovules on the inner side. *D* a young ovule; *E* the same immediately before fertilisation, *i i* integuments, *K* oucellus, *KS* raphe, *em* embryo-sac. *F* transverse section through the stigmatic portion of a carpel (more highly magnified); pollen-grains are attached to the stigmatic hairs. *G* transverse section of an anther; it is quadrilo-cular, but the dehiscence of the lobes *β* at *z* takes place in such a way that it appears bi-locular. *H* part of an anther-lobe (corresponding to *β* in *G*); *y* the place where it separates from the connective, *e* the epidermis, *x* the layer of fibrous cells (endothecium). *I* diagram of the whole flower; the perianth *p p* consists of two alternate trimerous whorls; the androecium likewise, but the stamens of the outer whorl are doubled (*f*), those of the inner *f'* simple and thicker. The gynoecium also consists of two trimerous whorls, an outer one *c'* and an inner one *c'*. There are thus six alternate trimerous whorls, with duplication of the segments of the first staminal whorl.

families of which are characterised and distinguished especially by their ovaries, it scarcely needs mention that what has been said only indicates the most essential points. I may make one more remark for the sake of those who are not botanists, however, so that the word ovary shall not lead to error: the ovary is, put shortly, the young fruit; or, conversely, the subsequent fruit is the ovary which has grown up and become ripe, just as the ovules are nothing further than the young, as yet unfertilised seeds.

The ovules of most flowering-plants arise at the united margins of the carpels, as can be seen with the greatest clearness in the half-ripe fruits of the Bladder-Senna and of the Pæony. It is only in rare cases that, as in *Butomus,* the ovules arise on the whole of the inner surface of the carpel, and occasionally as may be seen in Fig. 303, p. 466, an ovule appears to be the true end of the floral axis.

In the main the ovule of the flowering-plants is not essentially different from that of the Gymnosperms, although it usually differs in several external matters. Fig. 441 *E* represents one of the commonest forms, an 'anatropous' ovule . on a stalk-like funiculus *KS* is situated the nucellus of the ovule *K* invested by two integuments *i* and *i'* and in such a way that the micropyle comes to lie next the base of the stalk. There are, however, other forms also: straight or 'orthotropous' ovules as in Fig 303, p. 466, for instance. Moreover there are not always two integuments, but often (especially in many Dicotyledons) only one. The embryo-sac—and therein lies an important difference in contrast to the Gymnosperms—often grows up as far as the micropyle even before fertilisation (*e m* in *E*), and indeed cases are not rare (*Pedicularis* and other Scrophularineæ, and also *Santalum*) where the anterior end of the embryo-sac grows out beyond the nucellus of the ovule, pushing its way into the micropyle or even projecting out beyond it. However I shall here pay no further attention to such peculiarities.

A very important difference between the angiospermous flowering-plants and the Gymnosperms comes out when the processes in the embryo-sac previous to fertilisation are considered : the Angiosperms form no prothallium with archegonia, unless we consider a sort of rudiment of them to exist in three cells which occur very frequently in the hinder basal-end of the embryo-sac (*u* Fig 442), and which bear the curious name 'antipodal' cells—i. e antipodal with respect to the oosphere. Starting from the consideration of what occurs in the embryo-sac of the Gymnosperms, the proper reproductive apparatus inside the embryo-sac appears to be a mere remnant, as it were, which still retains only what is most essential and indispensable. Thus, in the anterior end of the embryo-sac turned towards the micropyle there arise before fertilisation, with rare exceptions, three naked cells close together. One of these, marked *z* in Fig. 442, is the oosphere, from which the embryo is formed after fertilisation ; the two others, marked *v*, which occupy the proper apex of the embryo-sac, were designated by Strasburger the *Synergidæ* (*Gehülfinnen*) Strasburger, to whom we owe our more exact knowledge of the processes in the embryo-sac, assumes that it is these synergidæ which first take up the fertilising substance from the pollen-tube and then pass it over to the oosphere

While these things are undergoing preparation in the embryo-sac, the pollen-sacs of the anthers dehisce. By means of the wind, and much oftener by means of insects or other animals seeking honey in the flowers. the pollen-grains are conveyed to the now moist and usually papillose surface of the stigma, where they remain attached, and they put forth their pollen-tubes as a rule within a few hours (cf *z* Fig. 443)· If there is only one ovule in the ovary, it is sufficient if one of the pollen-tubes grows down through the style as far as the cavity of the ovary, and finally penetrates the micropyle *m*, applying its end to the embryo-sac where it comes in direct contact with the synergidæ. Since, as is seen, each ovule requires a pollen-tube to fertilise its oosphere, at least as many pollen-grains as there are ovules in the ovary must reach the stigma and perfect the developement of their tubes. Not rarely however an ovary contains hundreds and even thousands of ovules, and accordingly the dusting of the stigma with pollen-grains must be profuse if all the ovules are to be fertilised, and since not every pollen-tube accomplishes its end, even a greater number of pollen-grains are needed.

Also in the pollen-grains of the Angiosperms there is still found a last remnant (one might almost say a feeble and indistinct memento) of the cell-formation which occurs in the microspores of the Cryptogams and Gymnosperms. It is to Stras-

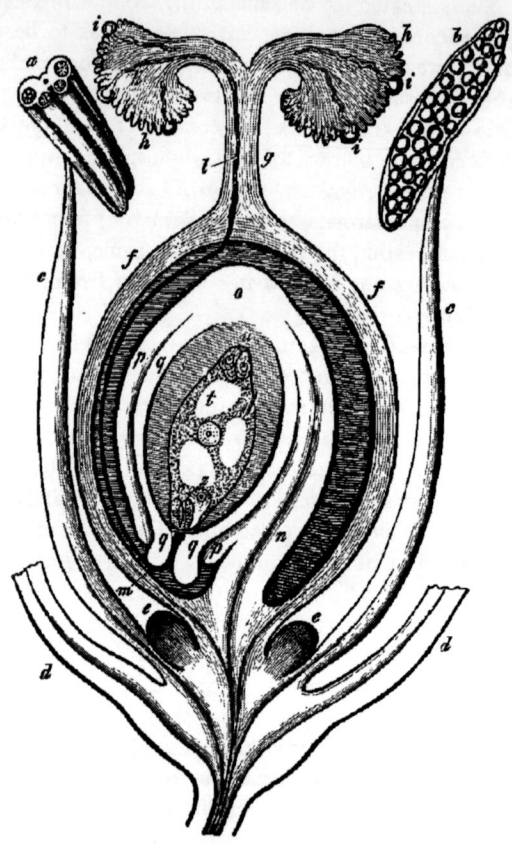

FIG. 442.—Diagram of a very simple flower in longitudinal section. *a* transverse section of an anther before its dehiscence; *b* an anther dehiscing longitudinally, with pollen; *c* filament; *d* base of floral leaves; *e* nectaries; *f* wall of carpels; *g* style; *h* stigma; *i* germinating pollen-grains; *k l m* a pollen-tube which has reached and entered the micropyle of the ovule; *n* funicle of ovule; *o* its base; *p* outer, *q* inner integument; *s* nucellus of ovule; *t* cavity of the embryo-sac; *u* its basal portion with the antipodal cells; *v* synergidæ; *x* oosphere.

burger's investigations, which have been of such immense service to the theory of fertilisation, that we owe the knowledge of the remarkable fact that the ripe pollen-grains of the Angiosperms regularly contain two cell-nuclei, and that sometimes indeed, a division, although transitory, of the contents is indicated.

The pollen-grains of the Angiosperms differ much in form and size. The usually thick cuticularised external membrane, the so-called Extine, very often shows beforehand the spots from which the pollen-tube or tubes are to emerge later. As in the germination of spores generally, it is the second membrane consisting of cellulose (the so-called Intine) of the pollen-grain which grows out and forms the pollen-tubes. The places at which this will take place are, as already stated, indicated beforehand, and sometimes, as in the Cucurbitaceæ, circular excised pieces of the extine are set like lids into the apertures, and are simply pushed aside by the emerging pollen-tubes, as in Fig. 443. The pollen-tubes have now to make their way through the tissue of the stigma and style down into the cavity of the ovary, inside the latter they either enter directly into the micropyle of the ovule, which how-ever occurs but seldom, or, as is more usual, they grow down along the walls

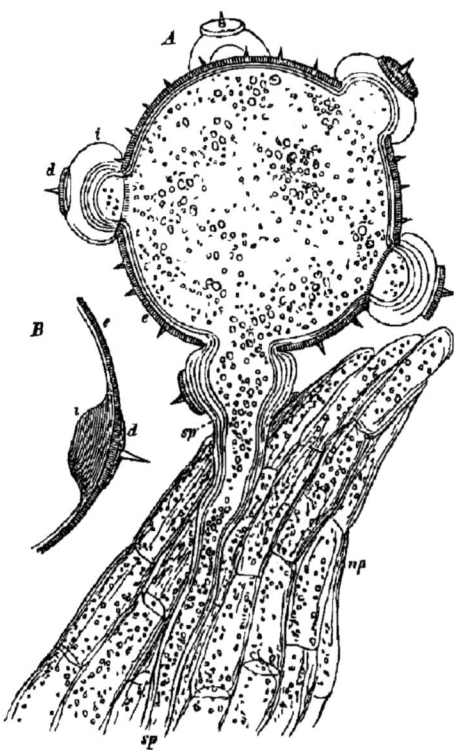

FIG. 443.—*A* a pollen-grain (in section) germinating on the stigmatic lobes   The outer membrane (extine) has a number of circular openings closed by the lids *d* , the inner membrane of the pollen-grain (*i*) is thick-ened beneath the lid—it swells, protrudes through the hole, and thus pushes aside the lid   One of these swollen cushions of the intine is grow-ing into the stigmatic tissue as the pollen tube *sp*   *B* a piece of the pollen membrane ; *i* intine *e* extine, *d* a lid.

of the ovary until they reach the micropyle. To this end the paths to be traversed are often indicated beforehand by special relations of organisation on the wall of the ovary. The pollen-tubes of the Angiosperms are for the most part very delicate, their walls being relatively thick; they may thus be easily passed over in the tissue of the style, and it is always one of the difficult tasks of microscopy to discover their fertilis-ing end penetrating into the micro-pyle. Sometimes the distance which the pollen-tubes have to traverse from the stigma to the micropyle, is very considerable—e g. in the Maize it is 20–40 cm. and in many other long-styled flowers it is from 3–10 cm

The effect of fertilisation makes itself evident chiefly in two points, in the development of the oosphere into the embryo, and in the in-ception of the endosperm .

By means of rapidly repeated bi-partitions of the nucleus of the em-bryo-sac, as Strasburger has shown, there are produced in a short time as a rule very numerous nucleated masses which distribute themselves at regular distances from one another in the protoplasmic lining of the embryo-sac. Around each of these nuclei a portion of the protoplasm collects as around a centre of attraction   At the boundaries of these portions of protoplasm arise thin cellulose walls (cf. Fig. 106, p. 106) and thus is formed a layer of tissue which is at first applied to the wall of the embryo-sac, the ex-ternal layer of endosperm ; as its cells grow in towards the interior of the embryo-sac, and undergo transverse divisions parallel to its wall, the cavity of the embryo-sac is gradually filled up with cell-tissue. If the embryo-sac is very narrow, or even tube-like as often occurs, the endosperm presents the appearance of a number of transverse walls dividing its cavity into chambers; if, on the contrary, the embryo-sac is very large, it may happen that the endosperm commences to form on the wall but never fills up the whole of the cavity. This is conspicuously the case in the Coco-nut, and is not rare to a slighter extent in other large-seeded plants : the hard shell of the Coco-nut is clothed internally by the wall of the embryo-sac, and we have here, therefore, an instance of a cell which attains a volume of 500 c cm or more The development of endosperm in the Coco-nut however proceeds only so far as to form a layer of tissue 4–5 mm thick at the circumference of this enormous embryo-sac, in which the relatively tiny embryo lies: the whole of the remaining cavity is filled with the watery cell-sap of the embryo-sac, known by the name of the milk of the Coco-nut, and employed as a drink In many other cases also the embryo-sacs of- the Angiosperms are distinguished by their large size (as single cells) immediately after fertilisation and subsequently· on cutting a half-ripe Bean it appears as a vesicle filled with water In like manner in the case of the Walnut, before the shell of the nut becomes hardened, the large cavity which it surrounds is found to be filled with watery fluid In these and many other cases the cavity described is the hollow of the embryo-sac, which subsequently becomes wholly or partly filled with endosperm-tissue.

The endosperm of the flowering-plants is distinguished from that of the Gymnosperms, as is clear from what has been said above, from the fact that it only arises after fertilisation It resembles it, however, in that when the ovule ripens into the seed it becomes filled with products of assimilation (proteids and starch or fat) the at first extremely delicate cell-walls of the endosperm often undergoing enormous thickening, so that the endosperm at last forms a very hard thick mass. Such is the case for example in Coffee , the so-called Coffee-bean, as it comes into the market, being the horny hard endosperm. In the same way a Date-stone consists entirely of very thick-walled endosperm-tissue (cf p. 344) One of the most remarkable examples in this connection is afforded by the large seeds of *Phytelephas*, a tropical palmaceous plant, which on account of their enormous hardness and solidity are worked by turners as vegetable ivory . the whole of the hard mass is thick-walled endosperm, in which the small embryo lies at one point of the periphery, and when it germinates it dissolves and absorbs the whole of this hard mass. To remind the reader of but one more example, well-known to all, it may be stated that the flour-yielding substance of our cereals is the endosperm in the embryo-sac of these seeds, in this case consisting of very thin-walled large cells containing proteids and starch.

There are both among the Monocotyledons (Orchidaceæ) and among the Dicotyledons various families in which the formation of endosperm is either extremely scanty or entirely suppressed. Such cases, however, must not be confused with those where no endosperm is to be found in the ripe seed owing to its having been absorbed by the embryo during the development of the seed. This is the case particularly often among Dicotyledons: the kernel of such fruits as Cherries and Almonds, Apples, and the Walnut and Hazel-nut, Acorns and Beech-nuts, the seeds of the Sun-flower and of all Compositæ, the seeds of Gourds and Cucumbers, Peas, Lentils, Beans, etc. contain in the ripe state no endosperm because it has been already absorbed again by the cotyledons of the embryo before and during the ripening of the seed. In consequence of this the cotyledons in such seeds grow so large that they completely fill up the whole of the very considerable space within the seed-coats, whereas the plumule and radicle of the embryo form but minute appendages

In what has been said however I have been anticipating the developmental processes which occur after the fertilisation itself: some points have yet to be mentioned concerning the origin of the embryo from the oosphere. As occurs even in the Selaginellæ, and to a much greater extent in the Gymnosperms, so also in the Angiosperms there is developed from the fertilised oosphere not only the embryo

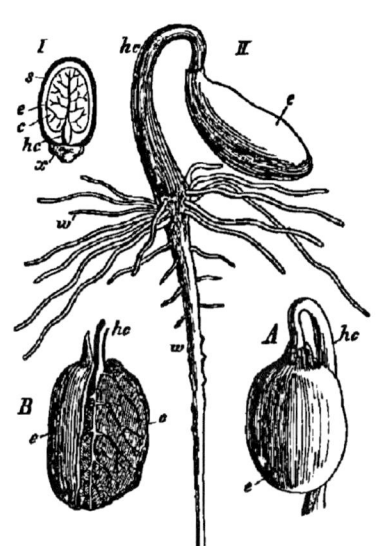

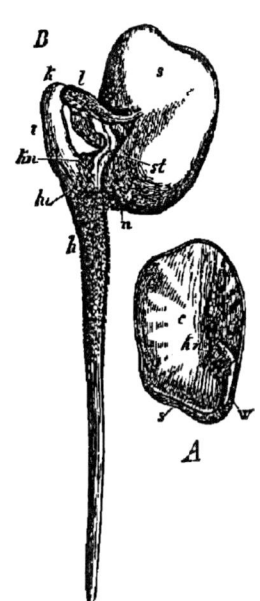

FIG. 444.—*Ricinus communis* I the ripe endosperm seed in longitudinal section. II the seedling of the cotyledons which are still in the endosperm—compare A and B s testa, e endosperm, c cotyledon, hc hypocotyl, w primary root, w' secondary roots x the caruncle, an appendage characteristic of Euphorbiaceæ.

FIG. 445.—Bean (*Vicia Faba*) A the exalbuminous seed after removal of one of the cotyledons, the other is still present c w radicle, kn plumule of the embryo, s testa. B germinating seed, s testa, l its ruptured lobes, n hilum st petiole of one of the cotyledons k curvature of the epicotyl t, hc the very short hypocotyl, h primary root, w s its apex, kn bud in the axil of one of the cotyledons

proper, but a support or pro-embryo, by means of which the embryo is connected with the membrane of the embryo-sac. The young embryo hence appears generally as a sphere on a stalk which may be long or short; for the fertilised oosphere grows in the first place more or less in length, forming a tube which becomes segmented by transverse walls, and finally, the true embryo arises from the most anterior of these cells, which then breaks up by divisions in three directions situated at right angles to one another, into octants, and as it grows up becomes further divided in the pericline and anticline directions. These processes will be sufficiently clear from Fig. 446 *I–IV.* It is not before the spherical body is transformed into a small-celled mass of tissue that the inception of the first leaves and primary root begins All that represents the future shoot-axis is practically only the mass of tissue which connects the parts named.

If, as in Fig. 446 *V* and *VI*, two opposite first leaves or cotyledons arise simultaneously, we have to do with a plant from the class of Dicotyledons; in the Monocotyledons there is developed first a single leaf, which usually grows round the whole circumference of the embryo, and which is subsequently followed (as a rule not before germination begins) by a second likewise sheathing leaf. Usually the growth of the embryo is very slow, as is that of all masses of embryonic tissue, hence it is found at

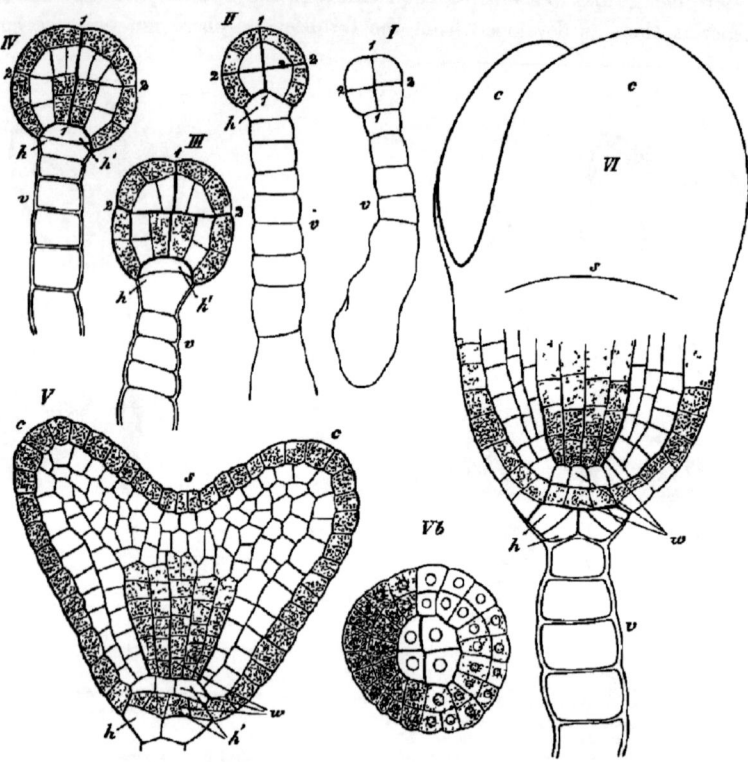

FIG 446.—Development of the embryo of *Capsella bursa pastoris* (after Hanstein) The order of development is from *I—IV* (*Vb* end of root seen from below) *1* 1—2, 2 first divisions of the apical cell of the pro-embryo, *kk'* hypophysis, *v* pro embryo (suspensor), *c* cotyledons, *s* apex of the axis, *w* root. The dermatogen and plerome are shaded.

the time when the seeds have already attained nearly their permanent volume, as a still very small body in the cavity at the apex of the embryo-sac. I may here take the opportunity of pointing out as a remarkable fact, belonging to the category of phenomena previously described under the name of correlations of growth in their dependence upon chlorophyll, that the embryos of plants devoid of chlorophyll generally remain very small. According to Hofmeister, the embryo of *Monotropa* is only two-celled in the ripe seed, and in the Orobancheæ, Balanophoreæ, and Rafflesiaceæ a small mass of cells is formed, it is true, but it exhibits no segmentation into definite organs The embryo in the seed of *Cuscuta* is larger and stronger, but even it is devoid of the radicle, and probably also of the first leaves. It is evidently not parasitism *per se* which induces this phenomenon, but chiefly the want of chlorophyll; since the embryo of the Mistleto and other Loranthaceæ abounding in chlorophyll attains not only a considerable size but is also provided with cotyledons and radicle.

It has already been remarked that in all seed-plants the seed containing the embryo is simply the further developed ovule: the ovule in its turn, however, is as we saw a macrosporangium, and the embryo-sac a macrospore, in which, after fertilisation, the young plant—the embryo—has been developed from the oospore. We might therefore designate the ripe seed still as a macrosporangium, but in most instances this would not quite meet the case, for in the great majority of Angiosperms the growing embryo-sac squashes the tissue of the nucellus of the ovule (i e. of the sporangium) before or after fertilisation, so that it is finally surrounded only by the integuments. From these, or from certain cell-layers of them, is gradually formed the testa, the structure of which may be very different in the various species.

LECTURE XLIII.

THE ACTION OF SEXUAL-CELLS UPON ONE ANOTHER.

(CONTINUITY OF EMBRYONIC SUBSTANCE)

So far as our experience goes it appears that organic life never commences otherwise than by means of small masses of substances separating themselves off from an organism which already exists. These substances however are not fluid in nature—not watery solutions—although saturated with water, they are not crystalline, nor in the ordinary sense of the word solid. Moreover, it is here, as it appears, never a matter of a simple chemical compound, but always of a mixture of substances; or, to put it shortly, the material concerned is a minute mass of protoplasm, which usually, especially in the case of asexual reproduction, contains in addition certain plastic materials for growth, such as starch or fat Nay, many spores take away with them from the mother-plant organs of assimilation also.

We have every reason to believe, moreover, that most of the visible substance in a reproductive cell forms as a matter of fact only materials for growth in the ordinary sense of the word, and that in addition, there is present a perhaps infinitesimally small quantity of a substance which, though not well understood itself, constitutes so to speak the *primum movens* by means of which the other substances of the reproductive cell are sooner or later put in motion, and the processes of growth called forth

This view of the nature of a reproductive cell obtains a certain degree of probability from the whole of the peculiarities of sexual reproduction. The essence of the latter lies in that in the course of the development of a plant (or of an animal) two kinds of cells are produced, each of which is incapable of further development on its own account, but from the union of the materials of which a product results which is capable of development. Only this latter, the fertilised oospore (or in some lower Algæ and Fungi the so-called zygote or zygospore) is a reproductive cell in the strict sense of the word, since without fertilisation it is not in a position to give rise to a new organism. It is true it appears exceptionally that even a non-fertilised oosphere may be capable of forming an embryo; but the as yet little understood cases of so-called parthenogenesis may turn out to be, as will be shown in the course of these considerations, rather a confirmation of what I regard as the essential in fertilisation

An oosphere (or in the case of the Algæ a swarming gamete) is rendered

capable of development by taking up the fertilising substance which is brought to
it by another cell (or another gamete) generally a zoosperm (antherozoid), or in the
case of the phanerogams by a pollen-tube. Now it would be somewhat absurd to
suppose that this fertilising substance is of exactly the same constitution as that of
the oosphere itself; though something of the sort might perhaps be supposed in such
cases as those of the Conjugateæ, Mucorini and some Gamosporeæ, where the two
conjugating cells appear to be externally of like constitution.

On this assumption fertilisation would merely consist in a union of the substance
of the reproductive cells   That this is just not the point, however, is shown by all
those cases where a relatively large oosphere is fertilised by a very minute zoosperm,
the whole substance of which scarcely amounts to the thousandth part of the mass
of the oosphere, and the same conclusion follows naturally from all observations
on the behaviour of the pollen-tube when it fertilises the oosphere of a seed-
forming plant.   Even the different shapes of the two sexual cells—of an antherozoid
or a pollen-grain compared with the oosphere—indicate definitely that both are
constituted differently as to material, since the external form as well as the internal
structure of any body are the necessary expression of its material constitution.
Difference of form always indicates difference of material substance.

We can thus say, then, the fertilisation of an oosphere (or of a gamete)
consists in that *something is added to its substance which was hitherto wanting to
it, but which it needs for further development.*   What this fertilising substance may
be is still in a high degree doubtful; at any rate it is not the whole mass of an
antherozoid, and much less the whole mass of a pollen-grain which can answer
to the title of fertilising substance.   The extremely small quantity of the latter,
however, generally effects conspicuous alterations in the oosphere at once: the
excretion of a cell-wall, growth and cell-division, the formation of the embryo, and
finally all those successive changes which take place in the neighbouring parts of
the mother-plant itself—the completion of the seed and walls of the fruit—and not
rarely the consequences of fertilisation extend over the whole plant, which at length
dies down after the ripening of the seeds

If in the case of so extremely peculiar a natural process as fertilisation it is
permissible to look for an analogy at all, we might be reminded especially of the
action of the ferments, which at least present a similarity in so far that extremely small quantities of them are able to put in motion large masses of
matter, and thereby chemically alter the latter.   There is not much gained
by this however, since the action of ferments is itself as yet not understood.
Fertilisation also presents similarity with many phenomena of irritability, though that
again does not say much for our point of view, since we may say that fertilisation is
the most pronounced of all phenomena of irritability : I understand irritability to be,
as already stated, the mode of action of a living organism towards all external
stimuli, and therefore fertilisation belongs obviously to this category, the oosphere
being the organism which, under the stimulus from without of the fertilising
substance coming into contact with it, reacts in so astonishing a manner that new
processes of configuration and growth arise from it.

In asexually produced spores, however, we find cells capable of reproduction which, without the addition of a fertilising substance nevertheless

begin and accomplish further development, and it might almost appear as if our preceding considerations were completely invalidated by this fact.   However, the logical conclusion seems to be this: since the asexual spores germinate without fertilisation they simply contain all that is necessary.   They do not, as is the case with the oosphere, lack something which must be first transferred to them in order that they may become capable of development; they do not need fertilisation because they have all they require, and exactly the same conclusion may be also employed in the very rare cases of well-established Parthenogenesis and Apogamy, where female reproductive organs arise and are able to form embryos without being fertilised.   Here again we may say, since they are able to do this they contain in themselves all that is necessary for development, and if this is the case such female organs are also only apparently female, since this term should probably be reserved strictly for those cases where a cell is stimulated to further development only by fertilisation   Those cells which do not need fertilisation, such as the spores and gemmæ of Muscineæ, the conidia of Fungi, and the asexual spores of many Algæ, and which give rise to new plants, resemble in this point ordinary vegetative cells, which in fact are also able under favourable circumstances generally to give rise to new plants

The question is thus, how comes it that sooner or later in the course of development certain cells are produced which have lost the capacity for further development, *per se*, 'but which are therefore in a condition to afford by means of the union of their substance a product capable in the highest degree of development.   That this is no incidental occurrence, but must be dependent on something in the deepest being of the organism, I conclude from the elaborate preparations for the attainment of the given purpose, since we may regard the formation of the various sexual organs in which the sexual cells eventually arise as such a preparation,—and the higher the organisation the more comprehensive this preparation for the development of sexual cells appears to be—this segregation of the organic constructive substances into two different substances, male and female, which only yield a vegetative product subsequently by means of their union.

I have already repeatedly taken opportunities of mentioning the hitherto much too little noticed fact, that the continuity of plant-life is expressed essentially in the continuity of the embryonic substance.   I have set forth in detail that in the normal course of the life of a plant, even of a tree which lives hundreds of years, the newly formed growing-points are always the descendants of preceding growing-points, and that finally all the numerous but small growing-points of a much-branched plant are derived from the first growing-point of the seedling   But this is a direct remnant of the substance of the fertilised oosphere, or of what I term embryonic substance.   The question is, then, whether the embryonic substance of the oosphere itself also carries on this continuity, and this question must be answered decidedly in the affirmative: the numerous careful embryological researches of the last forty years leave no doubt that the oospheres as well as zoosperms and pollen-grains arise from mother-cells which are direct descendants of growing-points, from which the more elaborate sexual organs which give rise to them proceed; Goebel's recent investigations especially show emphatically that already in the earliest stages, the cells from which the proper sexual cells are to

[3]   3 D

proceed may be recognised fiom the maternal peculiarity of their contents, at a time when the surrounding tissue still possesses entirely the character of the so-called primary meristem, or embryonic tissue of the growing-point. The differentiation of the two sexual products thus begins in the interior of growing-points, and the product of the sexual union is an embryo whose tissue is identical with that of a growing-point, and from which the first growing-points of the new plant are to be derived as remnants. Thus, strictly speaking, sexual reproduction is no more calculated to produce a new organism than is asexual reproduction; the elements from which the embryo aiises are simply products of the embiyonic substance of a pievious plant, and finally, we may say, that what has since the beginning of organic life on the earth continually maintained itself alive amidst the perpetual change of all forms, in the continuous alteination of life and death, and has continually regenerated itself, is the embryonic substance of the growing-points, which in certain cases becomes differentiated into male and female, and these unite again subsequently. In these extremely minute masses of matter, organic life has continually maintained itself through the slow course of geological epochs; those parts of the plant which present themselves directly to the eye—fully grown roots, shoot-axes, leaves, woody-masses, &c.—all these are products of that embryonic substance which is continually regenerating itself. These, its products, it is true outweigh it in mass a million-fold, but they are not capable of regeneration. It is not in these that the continuity of organic life is 'maintained, but it is these, which by means of their work in common, carry on the processes of assimilation and metabolism, and a very small quantity of the substance which they do not themselves employ for their growth, is made use of for the nutrition of the embryonic substance of the growing-points and sexual cells

After this probably not entirely superfluous digression I now return to my theme, the mutual interaction of the sexual cells, resuming the discussion from another side. The reasons have already been given which impel us to the assumption that in order to make the oosphere fertile, some substance on the part of the male cells must be added to it which it wanted previously. The most recent investigations of Schmitz, Strasburger, Zacharias, and others, lead in the first place to the result that the fertilising substance is to be sought in the nuclear substance, the nuclein of the male cell. It appears, according to the observers mentioned, to be established as regards zoosperms (antherozoids), that their proper body is formed from the nuclein of the mother-cell, while the part which bears the cilia appears to proceed from the protoplasm. The nucleus of the mother-cell of the antheiozoid enlarges until it has taken up into itself the whole of the protoplasm of the cell, or nearly so The peripheral layer then condenses into an annular or spirally inrolled band, while the central portion becomes less dense and constitutes the vesicle which newly escaped antherozoids usually trail at their hinder ends, but which they often soon lose. Zacharias has attempted to establish by microchemical methods that the actual body of the antheiozoid is identical with nuclein, and has pointed out that in this respect animals agree entirely with plants

Thus what is cairied into the oosphere by the antherozoids is nuclein, since we may believe that the only impoitance of the cilia (which do not consist of nuclein) is simply that of motile organs

In agreement with this, Strasburger has for several years past laid particular stress on the fact that in the Phanerogams the two cell-nuclei which were already present in the pollen-grain pass forward into the growing-end of the pollen-tube, and are carried with this into the micropyle and then disappear, thus probably

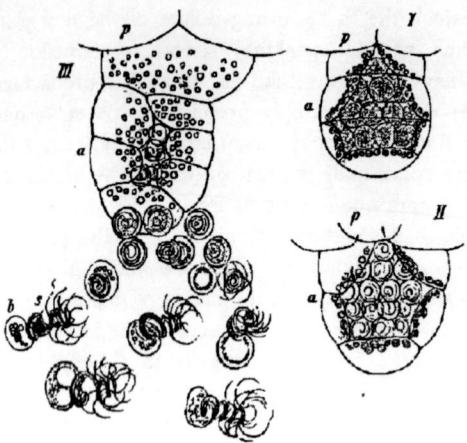

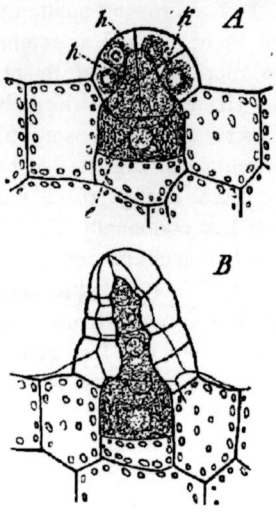

FIG. 447.—Antheridia of *Adiantum Capillus-Veneris* (× 550) in optical longitudinal section. *I* is still immature; in *II* the antherozoids are already formed; *III* has ruptured by the peripheral cells swelling radially, and the antherozoids have nearly all escaped. *p* prothallium; *a* antheridium; *b* its vesicle, containing starch-granules.

FIG. 448.—Young Archegonia of *Pteris serrulata* (after Strasburger). *e* oosphere; *h h* neck; *k'* canal-cells.

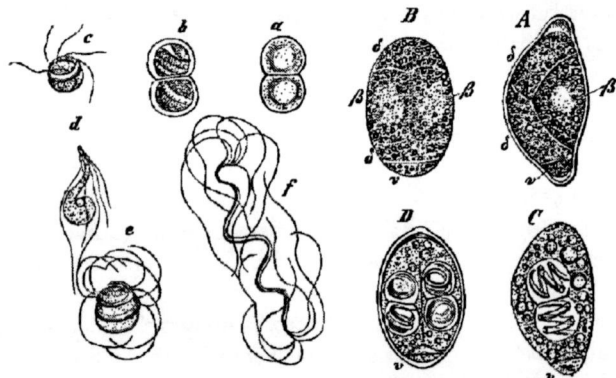

FIG. 449.—Germination of microspores and development of antherozoids of *Isoëtes lacustris* (after Millardet). *A* and *C* microspores from the right side; *B* and *D* from the ventral side. *A* and *B* show the development of the antheridium. *δδ* dorsal cells; *ββ* ventral cells. *C* and *D* show the development of the antherozoids. *δ* and *β* have disappeared. *v* in *A—D* is the vegetative cell (Millardet's prothallium). *a—f* development of the antherozoids. (*A—D, a* and *d* × 580, *e* and *f* × 700.)

becoming dissolved, and, hypothetically at least, we may assume that here also it may be the nuclein which is passed over to the oosphere in a state of solution by the agency of the synergidæ. In cases where numerous pollen-tubes are developed from one pollen-grain, the nuclear substance is, according to Strasburger, previously dissolved in the protoplasm, apparently in order to distribute itself in the various tubes. Only the mere reference can here be made to the complicated processes, combined in fact with cell-divisions, which Strasburger describes in the pollen-tubes of the Gymnosperms.

The inference from these statements, apparently so obvious, may seem to be contradicted again by other facts. In the first place by the fact that the oosphere itself already possesses a cell-nucleus, with nuclein in it, before fertilisation, and in the conjugation of *Spirogyra* it is expressly stated by Schmitz and Strasburger that the nuclei of the two conjugating cells simply fuse with one another, and Strasburger has demonstrated the same in other cases also When therefore it comes to answering the question, what kind of substance is transferred to the oosphere as fertilising material, we must allow that the question is not yet sufficiently answered by the observations named As a hypothesis it may in the meantime be assumed that the nuclein of the two sexual cells is not alike in constitution, and that the nuclein of the male cell thus carries into the oosphere something other than it already possesses. Meanwhile we must leave the problem here shortly treated of in this incomplete form.

One of the most surprising facts connected with the reproductive processes is the action at a distance, or mutual attraction of the two sexual cells towards one another. I select this expression for the facts to be examined because it is short and at least clearly denotes the matter; though the words 'action at a distance' and 'attraction' are not to be understood in exactly the same sense as in physics.

In the numerous descriptions given by observers as to the behaviour of the antherozoids in the neighbourhood of the oosphere, and of swarming gametes and even of antheridia in the neighbourhood of oogonia, we meet almost without exception with most definite expressions of the fact that a certain mutual interaction of the sexual cells at a certain distance exists, and this always of such a kind that the union of the two cells is thereby accomplished or promoted This process is the more remarkable because immediately after fertilisation has been accomplished this mutual attraction has disappeared.

From a large number of such cases I will take a few only, as follows Speaking of the fertilisation of the Ferns, and especially of that of *Ceratopteris thalictroides*, so favourable for observation, Strasburger says ('*Jahrb fur wiss Bot.*' vii., p. 402) —

'If a prothallium with ripe sexual organs is laid in water, the antheridia usually open first, and in favourable cases the archegonia soon after In the case of *Pteris serrulata* one has nevertheless to wait probably about half an hour or more on the average, with *Ceratopteris thalictroides*, however, rarely more than twenty minutes

'The antherozoids, which at first come by chance near the apex of the archegonium, just as near other foreign bodies, here behave very curiously as soon as the neck has opened The instant they meet with the slime in front of the canal their movement becomes slower; it is seen that they are here held back and their movements impeded by a resistent medium Some remain fixed in the slime, some succeed in freeing themselves and hurry away: in most cases however, neither of these events occurs, but the antherozoid is so directed by the slime poured radially out of the canal that it steers, apex forwards, into the mouth of the current. A diffusion current cannot here be assumed, and just as little a vortex suddenly seizing the antherozoids and hurling them towards the opening, since even very minute granules remain completely at rest in front of the opening of the canal The motion of the antherozoid in the slime is decidedly slower, but it does not cease to revolve about its axis The slime, however, leads it into the canal, so that its action here may be compared with the activity of the stigmatic fluid and the conducting tissue, which conduct the pollen-tube of the phanerogams to the ovule At the same time we can here convince ourselves most decidedly how little warranted is E. Roye's assumption that it is the vesicle at the hinder part of the antherozoid which contains the fertilising substance. Most of the antherozoids have already lost this vesicle before they even come at the archegonium, others which still possess it now lose it in the slime, and none take it with them into the interior of the archegonium. I have, among others, exactly recorded a case in *Ceratopteris*, where five antherozoids just escaped from their antheridium, penetrated into the central-cell, and six such vesicles were to be noticed in the slime before the opening of the neck.'

'Arrived at the interior of the canal, the coils of the antherozoid become drawn widely apart and, if no other disturbing influences affect it on the way, it soon reaches the interior of the central cell, where the emptied canal-cells have left a sufficiently large cavity Here the coils again contract, and the movements again become freer. The first antherozoid that penetrates usually does not remain the only one, but others soon follow it. their number inside the central cell may amount to four or even five, so large is the space here afforded by the canal-cells. They then move actively in and out and between one another, somewhat like the antherozoids which remain behind in an antheridium. Antherozoids coming later remain stuck in the canal of the neck. in *Pteris serrulata* their number may increase enormously, each new arrival screwing itself in between those already present so long as its movements are still possible, and at last becoming extended quite straight. It thus happens that in some cases the canal of the archegonium appears as if filled with long threads. New antherozoids now arriving can no longer be taken in, I have however observed a few cases in *Pteris* where they nevertheless screw themselves with their anterior ends between the previous arrivals, and there is thus formed a great struggling crowd of antherozoids, extending radially from the canal.

'In this crowd some of them are seen to revolve about their axes for some time longer, and sometimes even to get loose again and hurry away. In *Pteris serrulata* I have repeatedly counted over a hundred antherozoids in such a crowd, and even half an hour after the entrance of the first antherozoid a few still remain fixed in the slime. Such aggregations, it is true, are exceptional, and the number of the antherozoids which enter into an archegonium is usually limited to a few only, these aggregations moreover only occur in the case of *Pteris*, they are not possible in the case of *Ceratopteris*, not only because the prothallium here developes relatively few antherozoids, but also because the slime expelled from the neck of the archegonium diffuses far more quickly in the surrounding water, and only holds for a short time the antherozoids which are hurrying by.

'After what has been said above there can be little doubt that it is actually this slime which acts specifically on the antherozoids. However I was able to convince myself still more definitely of this action by moving the cover-slip and thus bringing the slime out of its original place, or even removing it entirely by means of the needle. The antherozoids then, held by the slime wherever it came to lie, strove to free themselves from it or perished in it after a longer or shorter swarming, but they were no longer directed towards the opening of the archegonium-neck.

'We will follow yet further the behaviour of the antherozoids inside the central cell. *Pteris* is, as already seen, unfavourable for this observation, so that among the numberless observed cases I was only able to see this process twice here Once on a transverse section which laid bare the archegonium, without injuring it, and antherozoids from a neighbouring antheridium crowded into it; another time on a superficial view of the prothallium, where the archegonium on the declivity of the central cell-cushion came to lie so that I could see its optical transverse section.

'The whole process may be followed comparatively easily however in *Ceratopteris thalictroides*. The prothallium is so translucent that it is very easy on surface views to see both the whole central cell and its contents, the tendency of the archegonia to be placed at the inturned margins of the prothallus being still more favourable for observation The antherozoids are relatively larger than in *Pteris*, and thus can be easily followed.

'The first antherozoid which penetrates into the central cell abuts, generally at once, or it may be after a short swarming, with its anterior end on the pale spot (the receptive spot) seen about the centre of the top of the oosphere, and at once remains fixed at this spot; it then revolves rapidly round its axis and its apex sinks slowly into the oosphere. Its movements become slower, and sometimes cease entirely, it disappears more and more into the oosphere, and its mass fades in it, till after 3–4 minutes (in all cases) nothing more is to be seen of it. This process, as I have just described it, I have succeeded in following quite undisturbed only five times out of the many cases observed, that is when only one antherozoid had penetrated into the central cell, and this occurred mostly only when access to the canal was impeded by means of external disturbing influences, e g. when air-bubbles or other foreign bodies blocked the entrance to it. In most cases several other antherozoids follow the first one, which thus becomes displaced by the new comers, unless it has penetrated already with its apex to a certain depth. The antherozoids now move in and out, and it is very difficult to follow the individuals. Often two or even three antherozoids are found simultaneously hanging by their apices at the receptive spot: they rotate rapidly on their axes, mutually crowding, till one obtains the upper hand, and is so far absorbed that its posterior coils cover the receptive spot. The remaining antherozoids are then never retained longer and swarm in and out for some time. Often their movements cease for a time, to be resumed again after a few moments; this continues for 8–10 minutes, and then all come to rest, and each individual antherozoid remains at the spot where it came to rest and is here visible for some time longer. In one case where only two antherozoids had entered the central cell, the second only came after the first had already laid for one and a half minutes on the central receptive spot, and its anterior coils had been taken into the oosphere. It was not able to displace this, and remained no longer fixed to the central spot after this first antherozoid had been entirely absorbed, but remained, after swarming sideways for some time, lying on the oosphere Of the first antherozoid no further trace was visible after four minutes, the second became invisible only after thirty-five minutes.'

Juranyi describes the processes in the case of a species of *Œdogonium*—a genus of segmented filamentous Algæ—in the following words (Jahrb. für. wiss Bot IX, pp. 7-19) .—

' After the swarmers have swarmed for from half an hour to an hour they come to rest and fix themselves on the oogonia, or at least on the cells in its immediate neighbourhood, and form unicellular dwarf males The swarmers produced by the antheridia-cells of the males are thus true androspores. The dwarf males fix themselves generally 3–6 together round or on an oogonium, though cases are by no means rare where they surround the female sexual organ in larger numbers. Thus I have often seen oogonia surrounded by from twenty to forty or even fifty dwarf males.

' The antherozoids thus escaped behave in a very striking manner. Their movement is not progressive, but a sort of twitching, or convulsive trembling, in consequence of which they can only change their position clumsily and slowly. By this means they describe a zigzag line around the oogonium, travelling in this way until they have found the opening of the fertilising tube, or until they perish —Since these antherozoids are contractile to no small degree they continually change their shape during the swarming, consequently they are seen sometimes as globular, sometimes again as ovoid or as acuminate wedge-shaped corpuscles, which sometimes desist in their peculiar movements—as if they would come to rest—for several seconds. When they remain free their movement may continue for two or three hours

' When the antherozoid has discovered the opening of the fertilising tube it meets with an obstacle which impedes its entrance to the oosphere; for the size of the antherozoid surpasses the width of the opening of the neck of the oogonium so much that it could not freely slip through it without altering its size and shape. To overcome this obstacle the antherozoids are aided by their extreme contractility Hence the antherozoid is seen to suddenly contract before the opening of the neck of the oogonium, its form also changing at the same time so that its anterior portion with the crown of cilia are directed forward towards the opening, and it becomes wedge-shaped The narrowed and pointed anterior portion of the antherozoid is now slowly drawn in through the opening of the neck of the oogonium, and as it enters it becomes more and more elongated at its anterior end, it is at the same time very clear to see how the cilia of the corona move themselves vigorously like whip-lashes. This movement of the cilia continues only until the anterior end of the antherozoid has approached so near to the surface of the oosphere, that the cilia reach it, and, coming in contact with the soft protoplasmic mass of the oosphere, remain attached to it Here the antherozoid is now held fast and cannot go back again : a sort of convulsion then follows, and the antherozoid touches the oosphere with its anterior end. At the moment this contact of the two sexual cells occurs, the oosphere turns pale at the point of contact and there appears a somewhat large rounded colourless and bright spot— the receptive spot—which is however somewhat translucent at the edges, and this indicates the place of fusion of the sexual cells : its appearance and occurrence in this way have not yet been observed in other plants. Immediately after the appearance of the receptive spot, the union of the antherozoid with the substance of the oosphere begins, a vigorous contraction of the latter and the slow gliding in of the former being very clearly observable The contraction of the oosphere is so vigorous that its change of form thus produced induces at the same time a change of form in the oogonium also.

'The slipping in of the antherozoid through the narrow opening of the neck of the oogonium, and its union with the female sexual cell remind the observer involuntarily and in the most forcible manner of those phenomena which have been observed in the conjugation of *Spirogyra,* for instance , since here, as there, we see that the fertilizing sexual cell, in order to be able to unite with the one to be fertilised must make its way through an opening which is disproportionately narrow in relation to its size, and accommodate its form and size to this opening—here as there contraction of the sexual cells takes place before and during their union, and just as clearly also, on account of the striking difference in colour and size of the antherozoids their fusion with the substance of the oosphere may be followed in the clearest manner.'

Finally may be given the description afforded by De Bary and Strasburger (*bot Zeit.* 1877, p 748) of the behaviour of the sexual swarm-spores or gametes of *Acetabularia,* a non-cellular marine Alga :—

'In spite of the fact that the drops used for observation appeared to form a thoroughly efficient medium for the development and movement of the swarmers, I nevertheless saw that at first all the swarmers perished, without one of them having germinated In doing this the swarmers rounded themselves off, formed vacuoles in their interior, their chlorophyll-grains became disorganised and emptied of starch-grains, and soon the whole resembled an amoeba of indefinite outline, which finally resolved itself into a granular spot

'The movement of the swarmers in this case continued for twenty-four hours in the most favourable cases, and I saw swarmers which remained in the interior of unopened spores often still moving even after forty-eight hours. As a rule a tendency to disorganisation began after a few hours, however, in some cases after a few minutes.

'The circumstance that I now also saw two spores, which from the appearance of their vesicles had probably opened simultaneously, suggested to me that the copulation only takes place between swarmers of different origin. Several weeks then passed till the fortunate accident which showed me what is now known. It happened eventually on a very sunny and warm day that numerous spores, favoured by previous warm weather, emitted their contents

'I saw about mid-day two neighbouring spores, utterly indistinguishable from one another, open under my eyes, and the swarmers of both hurry straight to the margin of the drop next the window. Here there soon presented itself a sight quite different from the ordinary one.

'For while I saw the swarmers from one and the same spore evidently evade one another and distribute themselves at about equal distances apart, there were soon formed numerous copulating groups, if I may so say, i. e. collective groups into which the individual swarmers, so to speak, precipitated themselves headlong. I now saw continually new pairs of united swarmers leaving these copulation-centres. Frequently, also more than two were anchored together. The swarmers as a rule abut on one another with their anterior ends, but at once lay themselves together sideways, and then fusion follows It begins at or near the apex, and soon extends over the whole side. The cilia remain free and active meanwhile, so that the copulating swarmers go on swarming with the four cilia, their movement being particularly tumultuous. The swarmers in the previously mentioned cases are directed parallel, but in other and by no means rare cases they are seen to be fused laterally, so that their ciliated ends are turned away from one another. The union may also first take place at the hinder portions of the swarmers, so that they diverge from one another at their anterior ends. Finally, I also saw cases where they were united in a cross-like manner. This however seemed to me to exhaust the variety of cases of pairing.

'As already mentioned, more than two swarmers may exceptionally fuse with one another The simplest case here again was that they laid themselves together parallel to one another They then worked on with six cilia, going forward like simple swarmers. I saw also complexes in which two swarmers took up one direction, and the third the opposite one, and finally also such which owed their origin to a large and often indefinite number of swarmers I could see from an approximately cuboidal mass a large number of colourless spots project, each moving its pair of cilia The whole showed an irregular rotating movement.

'The red streak of the swarmers may assume any position during the copulation.

'After swarming for some time, in all cases longer than in the case of those swarmers which remain free, each copulation-product rounds itself off. At first it is possible still to recognise the colourless spots of the copulated swarmers in the complex, and even the cilia may be still retained on the sphere. The colourless spots and cilia then disappear, however, and we have a sphere coloured green with chlorophyll, in which a corresponding number of red streaks are to be distinguished.'

Still more remarkable and astounding than the above statements, which I have expressly taken *verbatim* from the original memoir, are perhaps De Bary's most recent statements in his ' *Untersuchungen uber die Peronosporeen und Saprolegnieen*' (1881), where he devotes a special chapter to the fact, established by himself, that in these Fungi the oogonia are usually the first to develope, the male fertilising tubes not having been present meanwhile these latter however are developed during a certain stage of development of the oogonium, and exclusively in its neighbourhood, either from a branch which belongs to the same shoot as the oogonium, or else on other tubes which are not at all connected with the oogonium genetically, but lie sufficiently near it to be influenced by it Of course the distance is not great, and De Bary states that it amounts to about the diameter of an oogonium. In other cases again, the young oogonia exert a modifying effect on the growth of such tubes on which male organs (antheridia) may be formed. 'As soon as a vigorously growing lateral branch of this kind,' says De Bary, 'attains a certain distance from a young oogonium, its end is seen to bend over towards it, and then develope into an incipient antheridium.' He then continues, 'the divergence of the lateral branch described cannot be referred to any other cause than special properties of the oogonium.'

To my mind there can scarcely be a doubt that the pollen-tube of the Phanerogams also is specially influenced by something which induces it to grow with its end containing the fertilising substance directly towards the opening of the very narrow micropyle, to penetrate eventually to the oosphere. It is remarkable that this matter has as yet scarcely been thought worthy of investigation. When one reflects how extremely inaccessible the micropyle of the ovule in the cavity of the ovary usually is, how narrow it is, how great the distance often is which the pollen-tube must traverse from the stigma through a long style down to the ovary, and when one further considers that for the fertilisation of any ovary which contains only one ovule, even a very few pollen-grains on the stigma ensure that a pollen-tube reaches the micropyle (e. g. this is conspicuously the case with *Mirabilis longiflora*), further, that on the stigma being sufficiently pollinated, often hundreds and thousands of ovules in an ovary each receives its pollen-tube, and when one further observes how the pollen-tubes of some Orchids grow down free through the cavity of the ovary to the ovules, and so on, it must be obvious that the entrance of the pollen-tubes into the micropyles can by no means be a matter of chance, but that definite arrangements must exist which lead the growing end of the pollen-tube to its destination. It is true the tissue of the stigma and of the style are especially suited to at least offer no hindrance to the pollen-tubes on their way to the cavity of the ovary; moreover, in many cases special relations of organization exist on the inner walls of the ovary, which evidently have the purpose to show the pollen-tube the way, so to speak, which conducts it to a micropyle. But why do the pollen-tubes when they germinate on the surface of the moist stigma, grow directly into its tissue; why do they bend from the stigmatic lobes into the conducting tissue of the style, and why do they follow in the ovary the indicated road-marks where space and opportunity exist for deviations, and so on? It appears to me that in addition to the visible coarser relations of organisation referred to, invisible arrangements and unknown forces exist which chiefly determine that the pollen-tubes find their way from the stigma to the micropyle.

LECTURE XLIV.

TRANSMISSION AND BLENDING OF THE PATERNAL AND MATERNAL PROPERTIES BY FERTILISATION [1].

(HYBRIDS)

As a rule the sexual union takes place between two cells which originate either from the same mother-plant, or from two plants of the same kind (species or variety), each of the two sexual cells thus transmits to the embryo properties of its own kind, and it cannot be forthwith determined which of these properties the male and which the female element carries into the new plant   The case is quite otherwise when the fertilisation takes place between two different species of plants.   In this case the male reproductive cell contributes to the union different properties from the oosphere, and whenever such a union is possible between sexual cells of different species, if an embryo capable of development results therefrom, it must be investigated in what way the various properties derived from the different parents are transmitted to the descendants and combine with one another   It must be investigated whether any and what properties in the descendant are derived from that plant which provided the male fertilising element, and which of them have been transmitted to it through the female cell   Experiments show that plants of different species can be successfully combined sexually,   such a union is termed Hybridisation or Bastard-formation, their product being the Hybrid or Bastard, according as different varieties of a species,

---

[1] The first plant-hybrids were produced and carefully described by Christian Gottlieb Kolreuter. He was engaged for a very long period with this subject, and this so profoundly that subsequent investigators were practically unable to add anything essential   His chief work bears the title ' *Vorlaufige Nachricht von einigen das Geschlecht der Pflanzen betreffenden Versuchen und Beobachtungen* ' (Leipzig, 1761, and continuations, 1763, 1764, and 1766)

The most prominent of the subsequent works are —

William Herbert, ' Amaryllidaceæ, preceded by &c , and followed by a treatise of cross-bred vegetables' (London, 1837)

Gartner, ' *Versuche und Beobachtungen uber die Bastarderzeugung im Pflanzenreich* ' (Stuttgart, 1849)

Wichura, *Die Bastardbefruchtung im Pflanzenreich, erlautert an den Bastarden der Weiden* (2 tables in Nature-print, Breslau, 1865)

Naegeli in ' *Sitzungsber d kgl bay. Ak der Wiss* ' (Munchen, 1865, 15 Dec , and 1866, 13 Jan)

Charles Darwin, ' *Results of Cross- and Self Fertilisation in the Vegetable Kingdom* ' (London, 1879)

different species of a genus, or two species from different genera have united sexually, the resultant hybrid product may be designated as a variety-hybrid, a species-hybrid, or a genus-hybrid.

Of Cryptograms only a few hybrids are known with certainty Thuret (*Ann. des Sc Nat* 1885) obtained hybrid embryos by mixing the oospheres of *Fucus vesiculosus* with the zoosperms of *Fucus serratus*. In a few other groups of Cryptogams forms have been found which from their properties are referred to a hybrid origin Thus A Braun (*Verjungung,* p. 329) mentions hybrids of the Mosses *Physcomitrium pyriforme* with *Funaria hygrometrica,* and *Physcomitrium fasciculare* with *Funaria hygrometrica,* also Fern hybrids of *Gymnogramme chrysophylla* and *Gymnogramme calomelæna, Gymnogramme chrysophylla* with *G. distans,* and of *Aspidium filix-mas* with *A. spinulosum.*

The hybrids of Phanerogams obtained by artificial transference of pollen are however preferably valuable for scientific considerations regarding hybridisation, which at the same time render clearer the meaning of sexuality generally. Naegeli (1) has collected the results of many thousands of hybridisations, made by Kölreuter in the last century, and later by Knight, Gartner, Herbert, Wichura and other observers. From this critical survey of Naegeli's I take the following statements as examples.

(1) Only such plants as are systematically nearly allied can form hybrids with one another. Hybridisation is effected most easily and completely as a rule between different varieties of the same species; the production of hybrids is more difficult, though in many cases possible, between two different species of the same genus. Only a few cases are known of hybrids between species which are placed in different genera, and it is probable that such species, one of which successfully fertilises the other, should be placed together in the same genus. The ability of species to form hybrids exists moreover to very different degrees in different orders, families, and genera of Angiosperms. The following are as a rule favorable to hybridisation: the Liliaceæ Indeæ, Nyctagineæ, Lobeliaceæ, Solanaceæ, Scrophularineæ, Gesneraceæ, Primulaceæ, Ericaceæ, Ranunculaceæ, Passifloreæ, Cactaceæ, Caryophyllaceæ, Malvaceæ, Geraniaceæ, Œnothereæ, Rosaceæ, and Salices. Hybridisation of species succeeds not at all, or only exceptionally, among the Gramineæ, Urticaceæ, Labiatæ, Convolvulaceæ, Polemoniaceæ, Ribesiaceæ, Papaveraceæ, Cruciferæ, Hypericineæ, Papilionaceæ. Moreover the genera of the same order or family behave differently. Among the Caryophyllaceæ the species of *Dianthus* may be easily hybridised, those of *Silene* with difficulty; among the Solanaceæ the species of *Nicotiana* and of *Datura* are prone to hybridise, but not those of *Solanum, Physalis* and *Nycandra*, and among the Scrophularineæ the species of *Verbascum* and *Digitalis,* but not those of *Pentastemon, Linaria,* and *Antirrhinum* ; and among Rosaceæ the species of *Geum,* but not of *Potentilla.*

Hybridisation between different genera has been observed between *Lychnis* and *Silene, Rhododendron* and *Azalea, Rhododendron* and *Rhodora, Azalea* and *Rhodora, Rhododendron* and *Kalmia, Rhododendron* and *Menziesia, Aegilops* and *Triticum, Echinocactus, Cereus,* and *Phyllocactus,* besides a few wild forms which are apparently to be explained as genus-hybrids.

(2) Besides the close systematic relationship, a certain relation of the plants concerned to one another in addition decides as to the possibility of the formation of

hybrids: this expresses itself only in the success of hybridisation, and may be designated, according to Naegeli, sexual affinity. The sexual affinity does not always go parallel with the external similarity of the plants, for instance, no one has yet succeeded in producing hybrids of Apple and Pear, of *Anagallis arvensis* and *A. cærulea*, of *Primula officinalis* and *P elatior*, of *Nigella damascena* and *N sativa*, and other systematically very similar species of the same genus, while in other cases very dissimilar forms unite; for example, *Aegilops ovata* with *Triticum vulgare*, *Lychnis diurna* with *L flos cuculi*, *Cereus speciosissimus* and *Phyllocactus Phyllanthus*, Nectarine and Almond. The difference of sexual affinity and systematic alliance is still more strikingly demonstrated by the fact that sometimes the varieties of the same species are mutually sterile in whole or part, e g *Silene inflata*, var. *alpina* with var. *angustifolia*; var *latifolia* with var *litoralis*; &c

(3) When a sexual union of two species *A* and *B* is possible, it usually happens that *A* can yield hybrids with pollen from *B*, as well as *B* with pollen from *A* (reciprocal hybridisation); there are also cases however where the species *A* can only be the father, and the species *B* only the mother, the pollination of *A* with the pollen of *B* remaining without result   Thus Thuret found that, as already stated, oospheres of *Fucus vesiculosus* yield hybrids with the zoosperms of *F serratus*, whereas the mixture of the oospheres of *F. serratus* with the zoosperms of *F vesiculosus* remains without result.   According to Gartner *Nicotiana paniculata* is very prone to form hybrid seeds with the pollen of *N Langsdorfii*, whereas *N Langsdorfii* forms no seed with the pollen of *N paniculata*   Kolreuter was able to obtain seeds easily from *Mirabilis Jalappa* with the pollen of *M. longiflora*, but more than two hundred pollinations of *M. longiflora* by *M Jalappa* during eight years remained without result.

(4) The sexual affinity presents the most various degrees. The one extreme lies in the complete failure of pollination with the pollen of another variety or species, so that the pollen-tubes do not even enter the stigma, and the pollinated flower behaves as if no pollen had reached it: the other extreme shows itself in the formation of numerous hybrids which not only develope vigorously, but also reproduce themselves sexually.   Between the two extremes the most various gradations and transitions occur.   The lowest stages of the influence of pollen of another kind consist in that various alterations take place only in the floral parts of the mother-plant itself, the ovaries or these and the ovules growing, but without an embryo being developed.   A higher stage of the influence evinces itself in the development of ripe normal fruits with seeds containing embryos, but the embryos are incapable of germinating, a further advance then appears with reference to the number of ripe embryos capable of development in the pollinated ovaries (cf Hildebrand, '*Bastardirungsversuche an Orchideen.*'—Bot Zeit 1865, No 31).

(5) When different kinds of pollen are simultaneously transferred to the same stigma, only one kind effects fertilisation, that to which the greatest sexual affinity may be ascribed   Now since in general pollen acts most favourably on the fertilisation of another flower of the same species—in other words, since the sexual affinity attains a maximum between the flowers or individuals of the same species—when pollination occurs simultaneously with pollen of the same and of another species, only the former is effective in fertilisation ; since on the other hand hybridisation between varieties is sometimes more effectual than the fertilisation of a variety by means of its

own pollen, in this case the pollen of the other kind may exclude that of its own kind from the fertilisation. If various kinds of pollen come on to a stigma at different times, and if the later comer is of greater sexual affinity, it can only then be still effectual in fertilisation if that which first entered has not yet effected fertilisation, or injury; in *Nicotiana* hybridisation can no longer be prevented by its own pollen after two hours, in *Malva* and *Hibiscus* after three hours, and in *Dianthus* after five or six hours.

(6) The hybrid stands, according to its systematic characters, somewhere between the different ancestral forms. For the most part it maintains the medium; more rarely it resembles one of the two parent forms more than the other, this being more conspicuous in the case of hybrids between varieties than with those between species. Hence it follows that in the case of reciprocal hybrids of species *A* and *B*, the hybrid *A B* is in general externally similar to the hybrid *B A*. Nevertheless both may exhibit certain internal differences. Thus, according to Gärtner, the hybrid *Nicotiana paniculato-rustica* is more fertile than the reciprocal hybrid *N. rustico-paniculata.* An internal difference between reciprocal hybrids also expresses itself in that the one is more variable than the other; thus, according to Gärtner, the progeny of *Digitalis purpureo-lutea* are more variable than those of *D. luteo-purpurea*, and those of *Dianthus pulchello-arenarius* more variable than those of *D. arenario-pulchellus.*

When two species *A* and *B* form hybrids, and the one species *A* exerts a greater influence on the form and properties of the hybrid than the other species *B*, the hybrid, when it and its descendants are fertilised by *A*, must be transferred into the parent-form *A* more rapidly than it passes over into the parent-form *B* by fertilisation with *B*. Thus, according to Gärtner, the hybrid of *Dianthus chinensis* and *D caryophyllus* when repeatedly fertilised by the latter, was transferred into *D. caryophyllus* after three or four generations, whereas fertilisation with *D. chinensis* yielded descendants of the form of *D chinensis* only after five or six generations

(7) The characters of the parent-forms are as a rule transmitted to the hybrid in such a way that in each character the influence of both parents is evident a mutual fusion of the various characters occurs. In the case of species-hybrids this is more decidedly expressed than with hybrids between varieties. In the latter certain unessential characters of the ancestors occasionally occur separated next one another; for instance, various kinds of streaks and spots instead of a corresponding mixture of colours. A hybrid which Sageret derived from *Cucumis Chate* (female) with *C. Melo Cantalupus* (which possessed a reticulate peel) produced fruit with yellow flesh, reticulate markings on the peel, and fairly strong ribs like the father, but white seeds and sour taste like the mother; another hybrid of these two species had on the contrary fruit with sweet taste and yellow flesh, like the father, but white seeds and 'smooth peel, like the mother. To this category belongs also the hybrid between *Cytisus Laburnum* and *C purpureus*, the branches of which resemble, wholly or in part, sometimes the one, sometimes the other parent-form. I found what was very probably a hybrid of *Antirrhinum majus*, the inflorescence of which bore on the one side of the axis only uniformly dark red, on the other side yellow flowers, between the two halves of the inflorescence stood one flower which was coloured half red and half yellow.

(8) Besides the inherited peculiarities, the hybrid usually possesses new characters

in addition, which distinguish it from both of its parent-forms. One new property of the hybrid, particularly of the variety-hybrid, for example, is the tendency to vary more than the parent-form does : species-hybrids are usually sexually enfeebled, but those of closely allied species are often more vigorous in their growth than the two parent-forms, whereas the hybrids of more remote species are more feebly developed The luxuriant growth of hybrids between closely-allied species expresses itself in the development of more numerous and larger leaves, higher and stronger stems, richer root-systems, and more numerous shoots (stolons, layers), &c. Hybrids also have a tendency to greater longevity, perennial hybrids arising from annual and biennial parent-forms, but this is probably in consequence of the usually scanty seed-formation. Moreover hybrids are noted for commencing to flower sooner, and for doing this longer and more copiously than the parent-forms ; they sometimes produce extraordinarily large numbers of flowers, which are moreover larger, better scented, more intense in colour, and more persistent. The flowers of hybrids have a tendency to become double, multiplying their carpellary and staminal leaves and developing them as petals. In addition to this luxuriant growth the sexuality is mostly enfeebled, and this in the most various stages. 'The stamens are in some cases completely developed to all appearance, but are wholly or partly barren, since the pollen-grains do not attain the normal perfection ; in other cases all the stamens are aborted and reduced to minute rudiments. The pistil (carpels, ovaries) of hybrids cannot as a rule be distinguished from those of the ancestral species, but their ovules are either incapable of conception, or are only slightly capable of it, no oospheres are formed, or the embryo which begins to be developed from the oosphere perishes sooner or later In the most favourable cases, when seeds capable of germination are developed, they exist in smaller quantities, and evince in their slow germination and in the short period during which they maintain the power of germinating, a certain feebleness' (Naegeli). The enfeeblement of the sexuality is in some variety-hybrids hardly noticeable, in others slight, it increases as a rule in proportion with the remoteness of the systematic relationship and sexual affinity of the ancestors If the species-hybrids are able to form seeds by self-pollination, the fertility usually decreases, on continued self-pollination, from generation to generation, a phenomenon which perhaps depends less on the sexual feebleness of the hybrids than on the circumstance that probably the flowers of the hybrids have often been self-fertilised instead of being crossed with other flowers or with other individuals of the same hybrids. According to Naegeli the rule may in general be applied that the male organs of species-hybrids are enfeebled to a greater extent than the female ; nevertheless there are exceptions

(9) 'Hybrids generally vary in the first generation the less the more remote in relationship the ancestral forms are from one another ; and thus species-hybrids less than variety-hybrids, the former often being distinguished by great uniformity, the latter by great variability If the hybrids are self-fertilised the variability increases in the second and following generations the more, the more completely it was wanting in the first; and three different varieties appear the more certainly, the more remote the parent-forms are from one another—one, which agrees with the original type, and two others which more resemble the parent-forms These varieties have however, at least in the earlier generations, little constancy, and are not trans-

formed into one another; an actual reversion to one of the two parent-forms (the breeding being purely in and in) occurs chiefly when the parent-forms are very nearly related, as in the case of hybrids between varieties and species which resemble the varieties. When it occurs with other species-hybrids it appears to be confined to those cases where one species has exerted a dominant influence in the hybrid fertilisation ' (Naegeli).

(10) If a hybrid is sexually united with one of its parent-forms, or with another parent-form, or with a hybrid of different descent. a *derivative hybrid* arises, which in its turn again can be united with one of the parent-forms or with hybrids of other descent. If the union of a hybrid with one of its parent-forms is accomplished, and if the derivative hybrid thus obtained is again united with the same parent-form, and this continued through several generations, the derived descendants acquire more and more the peculiarities of the one parent-form, and at last completely resemble this, the derivative hybrid reverting to the parent-form employed in the process According as the one or the other of the two parent-forms is used, more or fewer generations are necessary for the derivative hybrid to become like the one parent-form, from this behaviour Naegeli has deduced certain numerical expressions (formulæ of inheritance) which give in figures the amount of the influence of one species with respect to the inheritance of the properties in hybridisation. In proportion as the derivative hybrid approximates to the one parent-form its hybrid nature diminishes more and more, and its fertility especially is increased.

If a hybrid is sexually united with a new parent-form or with a hybrid of another species, there arises a derivative hybrid in which three, four, or more species (or varieties) are fused, Wichura has combined even six different species of Willow into a derivative hybrid. Such hybrids, which may probably be better designated compound hybrids, follow, with respect to their form and other relations, in general the rules given for the simplest hybrids, the compound hybrids are so much the more sterile the more different parent-forms are united in them, and they are also generally very variable. Wichura showed from his own and Gartner's observations that the progeny from the pollen of the hybrids are more variable (more multi-formed) than those from the pollen of true species.

In the preceding, hybridisation has only been regarded from its theoretical side : that it has practical value also is shown by the innumerable hybrids of cultivated flowering-plants which have long adorned our gardens, and which are increased every year by new forms. Perhaps the most important of all hybrid plants practically however are the hybrid forms of the Vine, except the Willows (*Salix*) there is scarcely any other genus of plants whose species are so easily crossed as those of the genus *Vitis*. The Vine cultivated in Europe, *Vitis vinifera*, comes from western Asia. numerous other species grow wild in N. America. Since the time when the Vine-insect (*Phylloxera*) began to devastate the vineyards, especially in France, the American vines and their hybrids, together and with our old cultivated species, have obtained great practical importance, because several of them withstand the attacks of the Vine-insect, and present to the Vine-growers a means for further culture. My friend A Millardet, Professor of Botany in Bordeaux, has been engaged for ten years with the study of the devastation caused by the Vine-insect in the French vineyards, and has especially investigated the question of the resistance of the American species of Vines and their hybrids, and has at my request furnished me with the following remarks on hybridisation within the genus *Vitis*

'The genus *Vitis* is one of those of which the sexual inter-crossing of species is very extensive and clearly established

'In N.America the following species of Vine are found :— *Vitis rupestris*, eastward of the Mississippi, and along the banks of the Missouri as far as Texas : *V riparia* over nearly the whole region of N. America from Canada to Texas, and from the Rocky Mountains to the Atlantic Ocean : *V. cordifolia* in the centre and south of the United States, and in Texas . *V monticola* in Texas and New Mexico : *V cinerea* (*V aestivalis*, var. *cinerea*) from Missouri to Texas *V aestivalis* in the centre and south of the United States : *V. Lincecumii*, in the south of the Union and Texas . *V. labrusca*, in the east of the Union from the Alleghanies to the Atlantic Ocean : *V candicans*, in the south of the United States and Texas : *V. caribœa* in Florida (?) : *V. californica* in California, and *V. arizonica* in Arizona *V. rotundifolia* in the south of United States.

'A careful study of the wild Vines which are annually imported in millions into France from over the whole Union (especially from Missouri and Texas) leads me to the conviction that all these species (except the last four, which I have not hitherto been able to examine with the necessary care) can be crossed (hybridised) with one another, and this in the most capricious manner I have so far become acquainted with the following crosses :— *V riparia* with *V rupestris* (Missouri ?)— *V riparia* with *V candicans* (Iowa)— *V rupestris* with *V. candicans* (Texas)— *V cordifolia* with *V. candicans* (Indian territory)— *V. cordifolia* with *V rupestris* (ditto)— *V cordifolia* with *V aestivalis* (Missouri)— *V. cordifolia* with *V cinerea* (Missouri)— *V aestivalis* and *V. cinerea* (ditto)— *V aestivalis* and *V candicans* (S W of Missouri).

'All these hybrids are binary I have however also recognised the following ternary ones—the variety '*Solonis*' (Arkansas ?) as a hybrid of *V riparia*, *V. rupestris* and *V candicans* ; *V aestivalis* with large berries, which Hermann Jäger found in the wild state in S. W. Missouri and the neighbouring districts. In some of the hybrids of *V. aestivalis* and *V candicans*, there is also a strain of *V Lincecumii*.

'These are the results of my (Millardet's) investigations on the Vines growing wild in the United States The study of the Vines cultivated in the vineyards of the same country has lead to similar results Perhaps no one sort of those I have observed is a pure descendant of a wild species, in spite of all that the growers, ampelographists and botanists may say. all are products of more or less complicated crossings, in which the European Vine (the culture of which has been attempted at various times in the Union) has often co-operated. As examples I will mention only the most important of these spontaneous wild hybrids.

'The so-called 'Clincton' is a hybrid of *V riparia* and *V labrusca*, and 'Taylor,' 'Elvira,' 'Noah,' 'Franklin,' are of the same composition 'York Madeira,' is a hybrid of *V labrusca* and *V. aestivalis* ; and the same is the case with 'Eumelan,' 'Alvey,' 'Morton's Virginia,' 'Cynthiana,' &c. 'Delavare' is a hybrid of *V. labrusca*, *V. vinifera*, and *V aestivalis*. 'Jaquez' is a hybrid of *V. aestivalis*, *V vinifera* and *V. cinerea* (?) 'Cunningham,' 'Rulander,' and 'Herbemont,' are hybrids of *V aestivalis*, *V. cinerea*, and *V vinifera*. Finally, the Vine now called 'Gaston-Bazille' (the American name is lost) presents a still more complex composition ; it is a hybrid of *V labrusca*, *V. aestivalis*, *V. rupestris*, and *V riparia*.

[3] 3 E

'These facts, so interesting scientifically, have at the same time considerable practical importance, as is seen from what follows.—

'Experiments have shown me that (apart from *V. labrusca, V. Lincecumii* and *V candicans*) all the species named above absolutely resist the *Phylloxera*, and that the resistance of the hybrids depends upon their composition: for example, a hybrid of *V. riparia* and *V. rupestris* is capable of absolutely withstanding the insect, whereas a hybrid of *V. riparia* and *V. labrusca* ('Clinton,' 'Taylor'), or of *V. aestivalis* or *V. cinerea* and *V. vinifera* ('Jacquez,' 'Cunningham,' 'Rulander') possesses a diminished, or insufficient, resistance to the insect which no variety of *V. vinifera* withstands.

'Another fact well worth attention is the following ·—All the species of United States Vines (except *V. californica* and *V. arizonica*) are adapted to a climate which is much wetter than the wettest that is to be found in Europe; they are consequently much more resistent against all attacks of Fungi—*Oidium,* 'Anthracose,' Mildew (*Peronospora viticola*)—than our European varieties of *Vitis vinifera.* It is found moreover that those species which are most resistent against these evils are at the same time those which thoroughly withstand the *Phylloxera* (*V. riparia, V. rupestris, V. cordifolia, V cinerea*, &c.).

'Starting from this experience I (Millardet) was the first to make the suggestion to employ the hybridisation of our European Vine (*V. vinifera*) with various American ones, as a protection both against the *Phylloxera* and the fungoid diseases referred to   All these hybrids withstand to a certain extent both the *Phylloxera* and the injurious Fungi   It only becomes a matter of seeking out the best and most resistent ones   Only by this means will the Vine-culture again become possible in districts with a damp summer climate, where the *Peronospora viticola* makes its ravages, as in the valleys of the Garonne, the west coast of Portugal, and in various places in Italy, Algeria, and Switzerland.   The numerous investigations in this direction which I have made for two and a half years establish provisionally that it is possible to confer upon our Vineyards the power of withstanding all the above evils, even *Phylloxera* not excepted.   I now possess more than two hundred new hybrids which afford conclusive evidence of this.

'It yet remains to be seen however what will be the quality of the fruit; but even in this direction I have great hopes of attaining a satisfactory result, thanks to the localisation of the hybrid characters in the case of the Vine   I am convinced, for example, that among a certain number of hybrids of 'Chasselas' and *Vitis riparia* an individual may be found with fruits like that of 'Chasselas,' with leaves like those of *V. riparia* (resistent to Fungi) and with roots resembling those of the latter species (withstanding *Phylloxera*).   Analogous cases into which I cannot here go sufficiently authorise me to make this assumption.

'To sum up, my investigations now warrant me in making two statements ·—

(1) All varieties of the European Vine are capable of hybridisation with all the American species of *Vitis* without exception.   The complexity of these inter-crossings may probably be very great, since it is just as easy to produce quaternary as binary hybrids.

(2) Even from the first generation onwards it is possible to obtain hybrids which are endowed with great power of resisting *Phylloxera* and Fungi' (Millardet).

LECTURE XLV.

INFLUENCE OF THE ORIGIN OF THE SEXUAL CELLS OF THE SAME SPECIES ON THE RESULT OF FERTILISATION [1].

THE male and female cells, or the organs which produce them, arise either close to one another or at a distance on the same plant, or they arise on different individuals of the same species; the sexual cells of the same species of plant may thus, according to their origin, be more or less closely related, behaving towards one another as sister-cells, or as cousins, or as their grand-children and great grand-children, and so on   The question now arises as to what influence this relationship in the origin of the male and female cells exerts on the result of fertilisation.   At present it is true no general law can be formulated in this connection, but by far the majority of the phenomena point to the view *that the sexual union of very closely related sexual cells is generally avoided, and this the more the more advanced the morphological and sexual differentiation*   It is only in the case of a few of the lower plants that it happens that the sexual cells which unite with fertility are sister-cells, e. g. in *Rhynchonema* among the Conjugatæ, even in most of the other Algæ and Fungi the sexual cells of the same plant are more distantly related (*Spirogyra, Œdogonium, Fucus*

---

[1] The remarkable relations of insects to the fertilisation of flowers treated in this lecture were first described at length by Christian Conrad Sprengel in his extremely remarkable and inspired work, '*Das neu entdeckte Geheimniss der Natur im Bau und in der Befruchtung der Blumen*' (with 25 copper plates, Berlin, 1793), after Jos Gottlieb Koelreuter (1761) had already pointed out in his '*Vorlaufigen Nachrichten, das Geschlecht der Pflanzen oetreffend*,' the necessity of the aid of insects in the pollination of many flowers   Sprengel indeed expressed the fruitful idea, ' since very many flowers have separate sexes, and probably at least as many hermaphrodite flowers are dichogamous, Nature appears to be unwilling that any flower shall be fertilised by means of its own pollen ' Sprengel's work remained unnoticed until about twenty years ago , it was rescued from obscurity by Charles Darwin, and the doctrine extended by new observations of the latter and incorporated with the theory of descent.   Stimulated by Darwin's work on the fertilisation of the Orchids (1862) and by other works of the same author, an extensive literature on this subject has been developed, of which I will only quote one or two titles

Friedrich Hildebrand, '*Die Geschlechtsvertheilung bei den Pflanzen und das Gesetz der vermiedenen und unvortheilhaften stetigen Selbstbefruchtung*' (Leipzig, 1867)

The most exhaustive and fundamental work on the facts of this subject is Hermann Muller's comprehensive work, '*Die Befruchtung der Blumen durch Insekten und die gegenseitigen Anpassungen beider*' (Leipzig, 1873)   Translated into English by D'Arcy W. Thompson.

platycarpus, &c), and in all cases in which fertilisation is accomplished by means of active or passive motile zoosperms, at least the possibility is given of their meeting with oospheres of more distant origin. Even in the case of *Vaucheria*, where the antheridium is the sister-cell of the oogonium, the curvature of the former and the direction in which the zoosperms are emitted, points to the fact that fertilisation generally takes place not between the organs which stand next one another, but between those more remote, or even between those of different individuals.

The tendency to allow only sexual cells of the most different origin possible to fertilise one another within the limits of the same species, is evinced by very various arrangements. The simplest way is by only male or only female organs being produced on each individual of the plant; thus the whole development of the two plants concerned lies between the two sexual cells which come into union, if they originate from the same parent-plant, and a still longer series of developmental processes if the plants in question themselves originate from different parent-plants. Now this distribution of the sexes, which we may designate generally as *diœcious*, is found in all classes and orders of the vegetable kingdom, and this extension of it alone indicates that it is an adaptation useful for the maintenance of the most different species; thus we find diœcism in many Algæ (e.g. most Fucaceæ), in most Characeæ, many Muscineæ, in the prothallia of some Ferns, and most Equisetaceæ, and further in many Gymnosperms and Angiosperms

If the vegetative body which produces the sexual organs is itself large, or at any rate much segmented, a distant relationship of the two kinds of sexual cells is attained by male cells being produced on different branches from the female ones; this case also, which may be denominated generally as *monœcism*, is very widely distributed in the vegetable kingdom (some Algæ, many Muscineæ, very many Gymnosperms and Angiosperms)

But even the apparently most unfavourable condition as regards the principle laid down above, that the sexual cells arise close beside one another, is frequently realised in the vegetable kingdom, the sexual cells being thus of close though not always of the closest descent. thus the same cell-filament of the algal genus *Œdogonium* produces male and female cells, the same vesicle of *Vaucheria* forms antheridia and oogonia close together, the same receptacle of *Fucus platycarpus* gives rise to oospheres and zoosperms, the oogonium of most Characeæ arises close beside the antheridium on the same leaf, the archegonia and antheridia of some Mosses (species of *Bryum*) are collected together in one 'flower,' and the prothallia of many Ferns produce both kinds of sexual organs in close proximity to one another. In the flowers of Angiosperms the androgynous sexual apparatus is typical and very general. But in all these cases where the object is apparently to promote the union of sexual cells which are closely allied, mechanisms exist at the same time which prevent the male cells coming into contact with the female ones produced close beside them, or at any rate care is taken that this need not always occur, a fact which was first recognised by Kolreuter (1761) and Conrad Sprengel (1793), and more recently extended by Darwin, Hildebrand and others It is just in the case of the hermaphrodite flowers and the similar distributions of sexes in the Cryptogams, that it is most conspicuously shown that the co-operation of the sexual cells of near relationship must be injurious for the existence of most plants, since such various and often perfectly astounding means are employed for avoiding fertilisation within a hermaphrodite sexual apparatus.

One of the commonest and simplest means is *Dichogamy*—i. e. the non-simultaneous development of the two sexual organs in one and the same androgynous sexual apparatus, so that the closely related sexual cells produced side by side, compelled to exercise their functions at different times, and thus cannot act together. The male cells must therefore unite with the female ones of another androgynous sexual apparatus. This is very generally the case with the flowers of Angiosperms, as well as with most Fern-prothallia and those Characeæ which are not diœcious, where, although the oogonium arises close beside the antheridium, it attains sexual maturity later than the latter (very conspicuous for example in *Nitella flexilis*).

In the case of the dichogamous flowers of Phanerogams, insects are employed for the transference of the pollen on to the stigma of other flowers, and for this purpose special mechanisms exist in the floral organs: we shall examine these later on. In the dichogamous Nitellas and Fern-prothallia the movement of the antherozoids suffices, the close growth of the plants promoting their access to archegonia of neighbouring prothallia, or to the oogonia on other leaves of the Nitella,· or even of other plants. Whether dichogamy exists in the case of the Algæ above mentioned, and some Muscineæ, is questionable, but at any rate the possibility is given, by means of the motility of the antherozoids and other conditions which here prevail, that they come in contact with the oospheres of other plants or of other branches of the same plant.

In the Angiosperms however, in addition to the frequent dichogamy, quite other arrangements also occur which have exclusively the object of accomplishing the transference of the pollen of hermaphrodite plants with the aid of insects to the stigma of other flowers, or even of the flowers of other plants. In most Orchideæ, Asclepiadeæ, *Viola*, &c., the sexual organs of each individual flower are developed simultaneously, it is true, but at the time of sexual maturity there are mechanical arrangements which prevent the pollen coming on to the stigma of the same flower (*Herkogamy*): it must be transferred to other flowers by insects.

In other cases, as in *Corydalis cava* (pointed out by Hildebrand) the pollen actually falls on the stigma of the same flower, but it is here without effect, and it is only effectual in fertilisation when it is transferred to the stigma of another flower, and only completely so if it is carried to the flowers of another plant of the same species. This plant, therefore, is only morphologically androgynous physiologically it is diœcious. The Orchid *Oncidium microchilum* behaves similarly, according to John Scott, in so far as the pollen placed on the stigma of the same flower does not fertilise it, while it is able to fertilise another individual, and also that the female organ is fertilised by foreign pollen. Pollen and stigma of the same flower are thus functionally capable, but only for the organs of a foreign flower. Similar relations were observed by Gartner in *Lobelia fulgens* and *Verbascum nigrum*, and by Fritz Müller in Bignonias.

No less remarkable is *Heterostylism*, in connection with the mutual fertilisation of different plants of the same species with androgynous flowers. The individuals of the same plant in this case differ as regards their sexual organs: the one individual forms exclusively flowers with a long style (elevated stigma), and short filaments (depressed anthers), the other individual on the contrary, flowers with depressed stigma and elevated anthers; we have in this case, then, in the same species of plant individuals with macrostylous and others with microstylous flowers. Examples are *Linum perenne, Primula sinensis* and other Primulaceæ. The case also occurs, however, as in many species of *Oxalis* and in *Lythrum Salicaria*, that three degrees of length of the sexual organs are met with in the flowers of three specimens of the same species, in addition to those with macrostylous and those with microstylous flowers, there is found also one with mesostylous flowers. Now in these cases of heterostylism Darwin and Hildebrand have demonstrated that fertilisation is only possible (*Linum perenne*), or at any rate only has the best result, when the pollen of the macrostylous flowers is transferred to the microstylous stigma of another plant, and the pollen of the microstylous flowers to the macrostylous stigma of another plant. Where three lengths of the styles occur, fertilisation is most successful, according to the same rule extended, when the pollen is transferred to that stigma which, in another flower, stands at the same level as the anthers from which the pollen is derived.

While in the numerous diclinous and dichogamous Phanerogams, and in those to be mentioned below, insects carry the pollen of one flower to the stigma of another, it occurs but relatively seldom that the pollination of one flower by another is also accomplished without the aid of insects; e.g. in some Urticaceæ, such as *Pilea*, and Moreæ, such as *Broussonetia*, where the anthers flying suddenly from the bud scatter their light pollen in the air as delicate clouds of dust, which is blown to the female organs of other flowers. Still more simple is the case of the Rye; the flowers in the ears of the Rye open singly, mostly in the morning, and the rapidly elongating filaments thrust the mature anthers out of the glumes; the anthers then hang down on the long filaments, and at once open and let the heavy pollen fall. It falls on to the stigmas of flowers standing lower down on the same spike or on neighbouring spikes, the swinging of the haulms in the wind promoting the process. Rimepau has shown, moreover, that the Rye is 'self-sterile,' that the individual flower can fertilise neither itself nor the different flowers of an ear, nor can the different ears of one and the same plant pollinate one another with success, although no mechanical hindrance to this exists.

Considering the effort so clearly expressed among the Cryptogams, and still more among the Phanerogams, to avoid fertilisation within the same bi-sexual apparatus (self-fertilisation) it is a very striking fact that among the Angiosperms several plants occur which form two kinds of androgynous flowers, namely, large ones which are generally accessible to fertilisation by the pollen of other flowers, and small, more or less abortive and occasionally subterranean (*cleistogamous*) flowers, which never open, and the pollen of which sends its tubes directly from the anthers to the stigma and fertilises the ovules; we have here, therefore, on the same individual plant, flowers of which the one kind are accessible to foreign pollination, the others exclusively to self-pollination. This is the case, for example in *Oxalis acetosella*, where the small flowers concealed in the soil appear when the large flowers are already ripening their fruits; further in *Impatiens noli me tangere*, *Lamium amplexicaule, Specularia perfoliata* and many species of *Viola* (*V. odorata, elatior, canina, mirabilis*, &c), *Ruellia clandestina*, in several Papilionaceæ (*Amphicarpæa, Voandzeia*), *Commelina bengalensis*, &c Where in these cases the large typically developed flowers are fertile, crossings with other flowers of the same species can and must occur at least occasionally in the course of the generation, and then the small aborted self-fertilising flowers appear more as an accessory arrangement, the purpose and importance of which is quite unknown; but it is remarkable and apparently contradictory to the general rule that the large typical flowers have occasionally a tendency to be barren (species of *Viola*) or are entirely infertile (*Voandzeia*), so that the reproduction in such cases depends chiefly or alone on the self-fertilising abnormal flowers.

In other cases, as in most Fumariaceæ, *Canna indica, Salvia hirta, Linum usitatissimum, Draba verna, Brassica Rapa, Oxalis micrantha* and *O. sensitiva*, the pollen, in virtue of the position of the sexual organs, comes (according to Hildebrand) directly on to the stigma of the same flower, and is also effective; but in such cases, since the flowers are visited by insects, an occasional crossing with other flowers is at least not avoided. Even among the Orchideæ, where the most astonishing mechanisms for the avoidance of self-fertilisation occur, the case is found in *Cephalanthera grandiflora*, according to Darwin, that the pollen-grains send their tubes out from the anther into the stigma, from Darwin's experiments, however, the yield of good seeds is smaller when the plants are left to this self-fertilisation alone, than when they are exposed to crossing, to pollination with foreign pollen, by the aid of insects.

It comes out in the fertilisation of flowers more than in any other case, how closely the structure of the organ is adapted to perfectly definite vital relations of the plant, and to the fulfilment of perfectly definite functions. Each plant has its own special mechanisms to ensure the transference of the pollen to the stigma of another flower. It is thus impossible to say much of a general nature; but the following points may be noticed.

In the first place it is to be observed that the insects effect the transference of the pollen involuntarily and unknowingly, as they seek the nectar of the flowers which is (for this purpose) secreted deep down in the base of the flower, flowers which are not visited by insects, and the Cryptogams which do not need them, excrete no nectar.

The position of the nectaries, usually deep down in the base of the flower, as well as the size, form, position, and often also the movements of the floral organs during the period of pollination, are always so calculated that the insect, and this often of a particular species, must assume a particular position and make definite movements when seeking the nectar, so that the pollen-masses hang on to its hairs, feet or proboscis, and it then, by assuming the same positions in another flower is bound to wipe it off on to the stigma. In the case of dichogamous flowers, the movements of the stamens and the style or stigmatic lobes come in as additional aids. These movements are often of such a kind that at a certain time the opened anthers assume the same position in the flower which the stigmas in a receptive condition have at another time, so that the insect, by the same movement, brings the same part of its body in the one flower into contact with the opened anthers, in the other with the receptive stigmas, and wipes off on to the latter the pollen which hangs on to that part of its body. The same principle is also employed in the case of heterostylous flowers, in so far that here the pollination is most successful when anthers and stigmas which occupy the same (permanent) position in the different flowers, co-operate with the aid of insects.

In addition, however, there are most manifold, often perfectly astounding mechanical adaptations to ensure the transference of the pollen by the aid of insects. A few examples may now be cited in illustration.

(1) Dichogamous plants are either protandrous or protogynous. In the former the stamens are developed first, and their anthers dehisce at a time when the stigmas are still undeveloped and not yet receptive for pollination: the stigmatic surfaces do not open until later, mostly not until the pollen from the anthers of the same flower has been borne away by insects, so that they can only then be pollinated by the pollen of younger flowers. This is true of species of *Geranium*, *Pelargonium*, *Epilobium*, *Malva*, the Umbelliferæ, Compositæ, Campanulaceæ, Lobeliaceæ, *Digitalis* and others. The observation of these points, and also of the movements of stamens and stigmas mentioned above, is so easily accomplished in these cases, e. g. *Geranium*, *Althæa*, that a detailed description scarcely appears necessary. In the case of protogynous dichogamous flowers, the stigma is receptive at a time when the anthers of the same flower are not yet ripe, when these dehisce later, and allow the pollen to escape, the stigma has been already pollinated by pollen from a distance, or has even already withered and fallen off (e. g *Parietaria diffusa*). The pollen of this flower can therefore only be employed for younger flowers, this is the case in *Scrophularia nodosa*, *Mandragora vernalis*, *Scopolia atropoides*, *Plantago media*, *Luzula pilosa*, *Anthoxanthum odoratum*, and others (Hildebrand). Among protogynous dichogamous flowers *Aristolochia Clematitis* is distinguished by specially conspicuous and peculiar adaptations

Fig. 451 *A* shows a young flower in longitudinal section; the stigmatic surface *n* is just ready for fertilisation, but the anthers are still closed A small fly *i*, which has brought on its back a heap of pollen from an older flower, has just penetrated through the narrow throat of the flower, and is roaming about in the flask-like enlargement *k*. Not uncommonly six to ten such flies may be found in a flower. they are imprisoned and cannot escape, because the throat *r* of the flower is beset like a trap with long motile hairs, which offer no hindrance to the entrance of the flies, but bar the passage out as in a weir-basket While the insect is thus wandering around the cavity, it brings its pollen-laden back in contact with the stigmatic surface, and pollinates it, in consequence of which the stigmatic lobes curve upwards, as in Fig. 451 *B n*. As soon as this has taken place, the anthers, which have been closed hitherto, dehisce, and become freely accessible, at the same time, by the change in the stigma, and by the collapse of the hairs at the base of the enlargement, which now widens; the flies, having deposited on the stigmatic surface the pollen which they brought with them, can now therefore creep under to the open anthers where the pollen of the latter becomes attached to them. About this time, moreover, the throat *r* of the flower has also become passable from within; the trap-like hairs in it having perished and dried up as a result of the pollination of the stigma. The insect, laden with the pollen of this flower, can now escape, and, in spite of its late experience, it again forces its way into a younger flower, there to give up to the

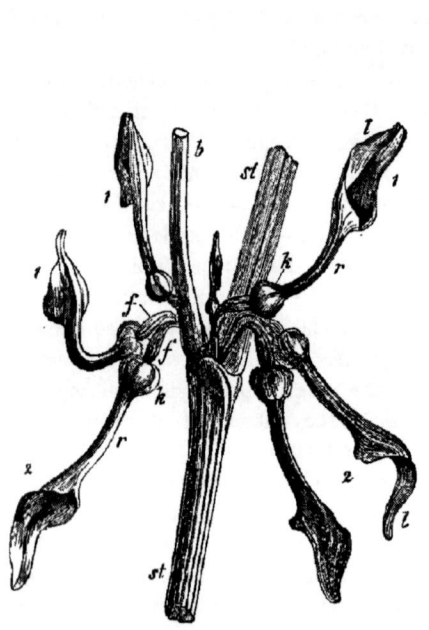

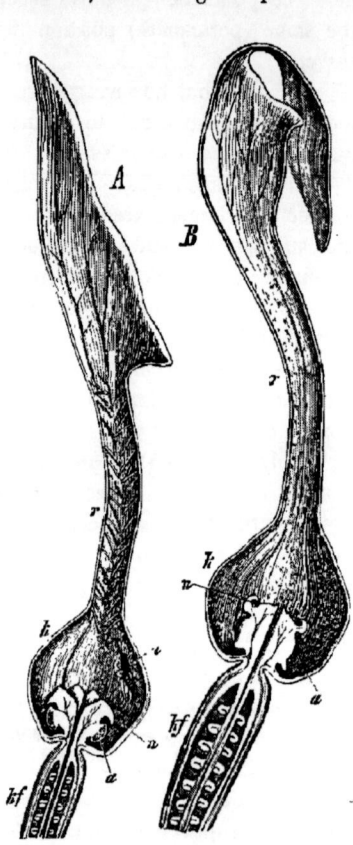

FIG. 450.—*Aristolochia Clematitis.* Portion of stem *st*, with petiole *b*, in the axil of which are flowers of various ages. *1, 1* young and as yet unfertilised flowers; *2, 2* flowers which have been fertilised and bent downwards; *k* flask-like enlargement of the flower-tube *r*; *f* the inferior ovaries (nat. size).

FIG. 451.—*Aristolochia Clematitis.* Flowers in longitudinal section; *A* before, and *B* after fertilisation (enlarged—see text).

still receptive stigma the pollen it has brought with it. While the above changes are going on in the interior of the flower, the latter, moreover, alters its position. So long as the stigma in the young flower is still receptive, the pedicel is erect, and the perianth open outwards (Fig. 450 1, 1,), presenting to the flies a hospitably open door; but as soon as they have accomplished the pollination of the stigma, the pedicel bends sharply downwards at the base of the ovary, and when the flies, again laden with pollen, have flown away from the flower, the banner-like lobe of the corolla (*B*, Fig 451) closes over the mouth of the throat, stopping the entrance to the flies, which have now nothing more to do here.

(2) Flowers with simultaneous dehiscence of stigmas and anthers, but in which self-pollination is rendered impossible or difficult by the position of the organs, and by mechanical obstructions. The transference of the pollen on to the stigma is here also usually dependent upon insects, mostly so that a stigma can only be pollinated by the pollen of another flower; occasionally however, (as in the Asclepiadeæ) pollination by the pollen of the same flower, in addition to that from a distance, is not excluded entirely. The adaptations here are extraordinarily manifold, and sometimes so complicated that their explanation can only be detected by means of close research. To this sub-division, for instance, belong the species of *Iris, Crocus, Pedicularis,* many Labiates; also Melastomaceæ, Passifloreæ, and Papilionaceæ. Among the most interesting are the Asclepiadeæ, where these relations, however, can only be explained with the aid of numerous figures and prolix descriptions.

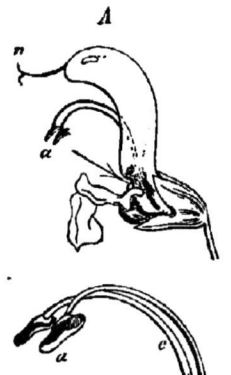

FIG 452

The mechanism for the avoidance of self-fertilisation and for the ensuring of crossing between different flowers of the same species is unusually elegant and easily comprehended in the case of *Salvia pratensis* (the Meadow Sage) and some other species of this genus. Fig 452 *A* shows a flower of this species seen from the side, *n* being the bilobed receptive stigma, and the position of one of the two stamens being indicated by means of a dotted line within the upper lip of the corolla. If a needle is pushed in the direction of the arrow into the throat of the flower, both the stamens spring forward as at *A a*. If a Bee does the same with its proboscis, striving to obtain honey thence, the dehiscing anthers strike it on the back and there deposit their pollen at a definite spot; on the insect coming into the same position on another flower, it rubs its pollen-laden back against the stigma and pollinates it. The cause of the springing forward of the anther is sufficiently clear from Fig. 452 *B*, here are shown the short true filaments *f f* fixed by their bases on to the sides of the throat of the flower, and supporting the long connectives *c x*, which can be swung to and fro about the points of attachment. Only the upper long thin arm of each connective *c* bears a half-anther *a*, the lower short arm at *x* being devoid of any anther, and so connected with that of the other stamen, that the two together form a sort of lounging-chair. If then the honey-seeking proboscis of a Bee strikes this apparatus in the direction of the arrow, the short arm of the connective is driven down and the upper arm *c* is moved forwards.

The impossibility of self-fertilisation in *Viola tricolor* depends upon mechanical arrangements of quite a different kind. Fig. 453 *A* and *B* illustrate the position and arrangement of the floral parts in this case. The base of the flower is invested by the floral leaves, and completely filled up by the anthers and the ovary which they surround, with the exception of the saccate appendage (spur) of the lower petal, in which the nectar excreted by the appendages of the two lower stamens collects. The entrance to this nectary thus situated behind the sexual organs is only accessible through a deep furrow beset with hairs, in the lower petal; the lateral and upper petals converge in front of the ovary surrounded by the anthers, and over this channel in such a way that the entrance is quite blocked by the head of the, stigma *n* (in *B*). This head is situated on a flexible style (*gr* in *C*) and is hollow, and it opens by means of a hole turned towards the hairy channel on the lower petal: the posterior lower margin of this opening is provided with a lip-like appendage. The anthers dehisce spontaneously, and the pollen collects below and behind the head of the stigma, and forms a yellow dust between the hairs of the channel mentioned above. An insect carrying pollen from another flower on its proboscis, pushes the latter beneath the stigma-head, through the channel and behind into the nectary in order to suck the honey; by this means the foreign pollen hanging to the proboscis is wiped off on to the lip of the stigma-head, and it at once sticks to the viscid stigmatic fluid filling the cavity of the stigma-head, and subsequently sends its pollen-tubes down the canal of the style. Meanwhile, as the insect is sucking the nectar in the spur behind, the pollen of this flower lying in the canal behind the stigma-head becomes attached to the proboscis, and when the latter is withdrawn this attached pollen does not come in contact with the stigmatic fluid, because the lip is drawn forwards by the movement of the proboscis, and covers the opening of the stigma-head from behind and below. The pollen which it takes with it from this flower is then wiped off in the manner already indicated (by the pushing in of the proboscis) on the opening of the stigma-head in another

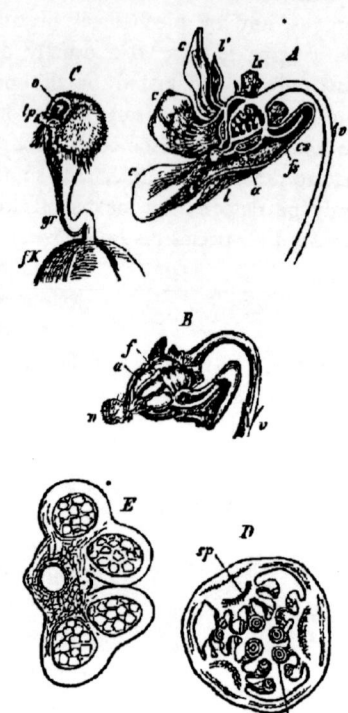

FIG 453.—*Viola tricolor A* longitudinal section of flower (nat. size) *B* the freed ovary and anthers, the former already fertilised and swollen, the filaments are ruptured and the anthers carried forward by the growing ovary *C* the capitate stigma with its opening *o* and lip *lp*, *gr* the style (magnified) *l* sepal, *ls* appendage at base of sepal, *c* petal, *cs* hollow spur of the lower petal—it acts as a receptacle for the nectar, *ft* the appendages on the two lower stamens—they project into the spur and according to Hildebrand secrete the nectar *a* anthers, *n* stigma, *v* bract on flower peduncle. *D* transverse section of ovary with three placentas *sp* and the ovules *sk E* transverse section of an immature anther

flower. If the insect were to insert its proboscis repeatedly into the nectary of the same flower the pollen of the latter would thus come into the opening of its own stigma; but insects, as Hildebrand noticed, generally do not do this (and the same elsewhere) but only enter once, suck the nectar, and then visit another flower. It is easy to imitate the manipulations of the insects, and to fill the stigmatic cavity with pollen (from its own or another flower) by pushing a sharp thin needle into the channel under the stigma-head and then withdrawing it

The adaptations for cross-pollination in most Orchids, as various as they are complicated and ingenious, have been described in detail by Darwin in the book cited above. One of the simpler, and, in its main features, commoner cases is presented by *Epipactis latifolia*, and may be here shortly described. At the time when the sexual organs are mature, the flower, in consequence of a twisting of the pedicel, stands so that what is properly the posterior of the six perianth-leaves hangs forwards and downwards; its basal portion is deepened like a bowl and thus transformed into a receptacle for the nectar which it produces itself (Fig 454 *B, D, l*) The sexual apparatus, borne by the Gynostemium *S* (in *C*) projects obliquely over this nectary; the stigma forms a disk with several lobes and is deepened and viscid in the centre, its surface being bent obliquely over the depression of the labellum. Right and left, above, to the sides and behind the stigma, are situated the two aborted glandular stamens *x x*; above the stigma, hanging over like a roof, is the single fertile anther, which is rather large and is in its turn roofed over by its cushion-like connective (*cn*). The side-walls of the two halves of the anther spring open longitudinally to the right and left, so that the pollen-masses are partially freed; the pollen-grains are connected together by means of a viscid material. In the middle in front of the anther and above the stigmatic surface is found the so-called rostellum *h*, a peculiarly metamorphosed portion of the body of the stigma (cf. *A*); the tissue of the rostellum is converted into a viscid substance which is covered only by a thin membrane. The flower of *Epipactis* left to itself does not get fertilised, for the pollen-masses do not spontaneously fall out of the anthers, and even if they did would not come on to the stigmatic surface: they must be removed by insects and transferred to the stigma of another flower. The manner in which this is accomplished may be rendered clear with the aid of a sharp-pointed lead-pencil On pushing the point under the stigmatic surface in the direction of the base of the labellum, and then pressing it a little on the rostellum, and again withdrawing it slowly, in the same position (*D*), the viscid mass of the rostellum—the adhesive-disc—remains sticking to the pencil, with the adherent pollen-masses. These latter are now completely extracted from the two anther-halves on the withdrawal of the pencil, as shown in *E* and *F*. If the pencil-point together with the pollinia are again pushed into another flower in the direction of the base of the labellum, the pollinia necessarily come in contact with the viscid portion of the stigmatic surface and stick

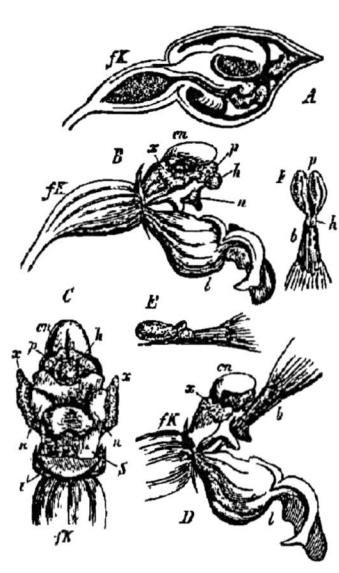

FIG 454.—*Epipactis latifolia* (an Orchid) *A* longitudinal section of a flower bud. *B* newly-opened flower after removal of the perianth except the labellum *l* *C* sexual apparatus after the removal of all the perianth lobes—seen from in front and below *D* as *B* the point of a pencil is inserted after the manner of the proboscis of an insect, *E* and *F* pencil point with pollinia attached *f K* ovary, *l* labellum, the bag-like depression of which functions as a nectary, *n* the broad stigma, *m* the connective of the one fertile anther, *p* pollinia, *h* the rostellum, *x x* the two abortive lateral gland like stamens, *t* insertion of the excised labellum. *S* (in *C*) the gynostemium.

fast there ; on again withdrawing they remain fixed there, wholly or partly torn away from the pencil. In virtue of the form and position of the parts of the flower, then, an insect which settles on the anterior portion of the labellum can creep down into the base of the nectary without touching the rostellum; on creeping out after sucking the nectar it strikes against it and takes away the pollinia with it. On creeping into a second flower these pollinia come on to the viscid stigmatic surface and there remain fixed   In some other Orchids the relations are far more complicated.

(3) In flowers which are pollinated by insects, the mature pollen must often remain lying in the already dehisced anthers for some time before it is removed ; during this period it must neither be dispersed by the wind nor moistened by rain or dew   Numerous and very various adaptations therefore exist for the protection of the pollen, further details as to which are given by Kerner in his work ' *Die Schutzmittel des Pollens*,' (Innsbruck, 1873).

LECTURE XLVI.

THE OBJECT OF FERTILISATION. APOGAMY[1]

THERE are many plants which, like Mammals, Birds, and other highly organised animals, reproduce themselves exclusively in the sexual way because, in the normal course of life at least, no other mode of reproduction is open to them, these comprise the majority of the Conifers, especially the Firs and Araucarieæ, and among the flowering-plants probably also many Palms, our cereals, Flax, Hemp, Gourd, and many others, and some are certainly to be found among the Cryptogams.

The great majority of plants, however, have abundant opportunity of multiplying and reproducing themselves otherwise than by means of sexual organs. Among the Cryptogams indeed we may leave the spores proper out of consideration, since it is very generally the case that gemmæ, conidia, or other segregating portions of the shoot are formed in the alternation of generations both before and after fertilisation, and a very large number of Phanerogams, especially those provided with runners, bulbs, tubers, subaerial gemmæ of the most various kinds, for though they produce seeds regularly by the sexual mode, almost none of these ever succeeds in germinating. It is only here necessary to think of the Potato, which has for hundreds of years continually been propagated by its tubers, and thus by the asexual mode. There are in fact, as we shall see, a somewhat large number of cryptogamic and phanerogamic plants which have in the course of time either entirely lost their sexual organs or have let them become functionless, but which, nevertheless, and sometimes in perfectly astounding numbers, multiply and propagate themselves; and on the other hand, in some cases with common ubiquitous plants, the development of sexual organs depends upon favourable conditions rarely met with, while vegetative propagation occurs abundantly. In addition to less known examples the commonest of all moulds, *Penicillium glaucum*, may be quoted as an instance; and even in the case of the largest of all the Fungi, the Hymenomycetes and Gasteromycetes it is, according to

---

[1] The most important publications on Apogamy are —

Anton De Bary. '*Über apogame Farne und die Erscheinung der Apogamie im Allgemeinen*' (Bot. Zeitg, 1878)

De Bary. '*Beitrage zur Morphologie und Physiologie der Pilze*' (by De Bary and Woronin in Abhandlungen der Senkenbergischen naturforsch Ges B XII, pp. 225-370, IV Reihe, 1881, section 14, '*Entstehung und Wachsthumsursachen von Antheridien und Nebenasten*' is particularly worthy of note.

Strasburger. '*Über die Befruchtung und Zelltheilung*' (Jena, 1878, p 63).

the view of the most prominent mycologists, very probable that they possess no sexual organs whatever.

The consideration of this fact, which we could easily make good by numerous other examples, leads directly to the question, what is the precise object which Nature attains by the production of sexual organs and by sexual propagation?

This question appears the more pertinent when we see, on the other hand, with what care (if this picturesque expression is allowable) Nature proceeds in very many cases to ensure the union of the sexual cells, and the production of sexually produced descendants all the marvellous adaptations of Dichogamy, Heterostylism, Herkogamy, and other arrangements, which we have studied with the aid of examples in the preceding lecture, may be looked upon in this sense.

Meanwhile, as De Bary has already stated elsewhere, we shall probably have to concede that, as matter of fact, we simply know that fertilisation is in many cases demonstrated by experience to be an indispensable process to the plants concerned, in many other cases this is simply not so, and we have in the meantime no ground for assuming that all organisms must behave similarly in this respect. This somewhat unsatisfactory conclusion, however, does not prevent the assumption that in the many cases where reproduction is regularly attained by fertilisation, special advantages are connected with it, which in the contrary case are simply attained in some other manner, or perhaps in certain cases are even not attained. A few of such probable advantages may here be brought forward.

Darwin, on the basis of the comprehensive results of the artificial breeding of animals and plants, has demonstrated to realisation the idea already expressed by Sprengel, that in all sexual reproduction the chief point is to ensure the crossing of individuals of the same species, of which detailed illustrations have been given in the preceding lecture It also results from the experimental investigations of Darwin, Hildebrand, and others, that just as so-called incest among some domestic animals results in the production of few or feeble descendants, so also does the continued self-fertilisation of androgynous flowers, whereas in like species of plants the crossing of different individuals results in the production of vigorous seeds Supported by Darwin's authority, one is now very ready to suppose that incidental abnormalities or diseased conditions are equilibrated by means of the sexual intermixture, and are rendered uninjurious in the descendants. In addition to some other considerations, mention should here be made, however, of the very large number of plants which certainly maintain themselves asexually through hundreds and thousands of generations without the slightest ground existing for supposing that they are gradually degenerated by the process.

On the other hand, we may here think of the fact, established by artificial hybridisation, that, by means of the sexual intermingling of individuals from different sources, the variability of the descendants is increased, and that in this way the number of the different organic forms may have gradually been multiplied: though even here also it is not to be forgotten that the formation of varieties sometimes occurs also during asexual reproduction; at any rate the majority of the varieties of Potato have probably been produced asexually

And nevertheless in all the suppositions there again exists the perception that, with increasing complexity of organisation both in the animal and vegetable kingdoms, the sexual organs become more and more developed, and the sexual reproduction gains more and more over the vegetative, or even becomes the predominating one. It would be possible to believe that with increasing perfection of the organisation a corresponding division of physiological labour also is given, by which the vegetative mode of reproduction is limited and the sexual one simply promoted.

I may finally notice yet another observation, which I have already expressed in my 'Textbook' (Ed. IV, p. 877). Those Cryptogams which possess pronounced alternation of generations, particularly the Mosses and Vascular Cryptogams, although in other respects belonging to entirely different types, nevertheless illustrate repeatedly and in every class the fact that the highest development of the organisation is always attained only by means of fertilisation In the case of the Equisetums, Ferns and Lycopodiaceæ this is at once obvious on remembering that the first generation produced from the asexual spore, the prothallium, is usually a minute, very simple, and transitory structure, the life and importance of which are closed with the fertilisation of the oosphere; whereas the embryo, originating from this act of fertilisation, developes into a highly organised plant, a Tree-fern, for instance, &c. In the case of the Mosses, it is true, matters are different, in as far as here it is the generation which has originated from the asexual spore itself which we are in the habit of regarding as the proper plant; but on comparing the forms of cells and tissues and the histological structure generally of the 'Moss-fruit' produced by fertilisation with that of the Moss-plant, there can be no doubt that the former is more perfectly organised than the asexually produced Moss-plant itself In the case of the Algæ and Fungi it is the same, although the fact is not so easily made out as in these cases. In those Fungi in which a sexual apparatus is known, the most perfect product of the whole development proceeds from the fertilisation. The asexual spore of the Ascomycetes gives rise to the very simply organised mycelium, and it is only after the act of fertilisation on this that the Fungus-fructification with its complicated structure and high organisation arises (see Fig. 409, p. 726), and similarly may be said of many Algæ, even in the case where the result of fertilisation is only a single cell, an oospore or zygospore (zygote), this tends to exhibit, at least in the development of its wall-layers, a more perfect organisation than the vegetative parts of the same plant.

Moreover the Phanerogams or Spermaphytes only apparently contradict the above observation; in reality they confirm it in the most astounding manner. As we have seen, the embryo-sac in the ovule is the true macrospore, in which the first structure to arise is what is termed the prothallium in the Vascular Cryptogams: the endosperm is a physiologically and histologically reduced and degenerated prothallium, of which, strictly speaking, only the oosphere and synergidæ survive in the Angiosperms. What we designate generally the plant among the Spermaphyta is the sexually-produced product, which also here has sprung from the fertilised oosphere, while the preceding stage of development, corresponding to the prothallium, no longer exists at all as an independent organism.

In conclusion I may return to the phenomena of Apogamy already referred to. With this word De Bary distinguishes the case, partly discovered by himself, where asexual reproduction occurs in the place of sexual reproduction. this may happen in very different ways—for example, by oospheres, which under normal conditions require fertilisation, proceeding to form embryos without it, of which the highly-developed Alga *Chara crinita* affords the only established (first by Alexander Braun) example. This plant, which lives at the bottom of stagnant water, is met with throughout the whole of North Europe exclusively as female individuals, which, however, and thus without fertilisation, yield abundant and normal germinating fruits. Male plants of this species are known as isolated specimens from Transylvania, the south of France, and the neighbourhood of the Caspian Sea, though their generative power has not been investigated. It is evident that *Chara crinita*, like all other Charas, was formerly sexually propagated, and that the power to give rise to progeny from the existing female apparatus even without fertilisation can only have appeared subsequently.

To a second category belong three cases of Ferns, discovered and investigated by De Bary himself and his pupil Farlow, which have long been known as common garden plants, and possess the remarkable property of giving rise to new Fern plants directly from the tissue of the prothallium by means of simple budding. In two of these Ferns (*Pteris cretica* and a garden-variety of *Asplenium filix-femina-cristatum*) no archegonia whatever are developed on the prothallium, although antheridia occur occasionally. In *Asplenium falcatum*, on the other hand, there are found pro-thallia completely devoid of sexual organs and still capable of propagation by means of budding, as well as others with a few antheridia, and finally prothallia which bear antheridia and archegonia, but nevertheless give rise to the Fern by simple budding. There is still to be added that in the three Ferns mentioned this asexual propagation by budding

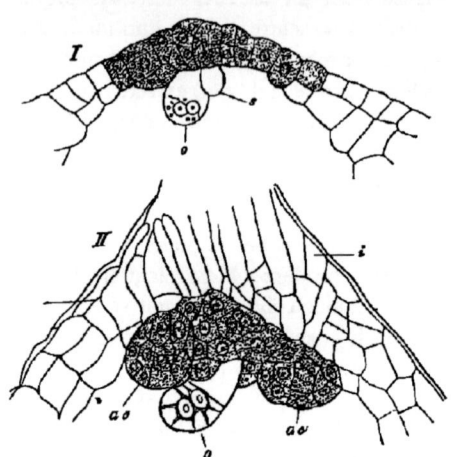

FIG. 455.—Development of the adventitious embryos in *Funkia ovata* (after Strasburger × about 150) *I* apical region of nucellus of ovule with the oosphere *o* and one of the synergidæ *s*. *II* the cells shaded in *I* have developed into the adventitious embryos *a e*, the oosphere remaining sterile. The tissue *i* belongs to the micropyle portion of the integument.

from the prothallium is the only mode, and that no example of them was found with the embryo formed from an oosphere, whereas in very many other ferns which De Bary investigated with this object not a single one exhibited apogamy. All the facts considered, there can be no doubt whatever even in the case of these apogamous Ferns that the prothallia formerly gave rise to normal sexual organs and propagated themselves in the ordinary way, and that Apogamy, the loss of sexuality, was only, as physicians say, 'acquired' subsequently, and perhaps in this case it depends upon the fact that the three Ferns in question have been cultivated plants for a long time.

A point worthy of notice in the case of the Ferns just mentioned is that the leafy shoot which really replaces the actual embryo, arises at that spot on the prothallium where the archegonia would be formed in the normal case. In this respect the cases of apogamy in some flowering-plants observed by Strasburger resemble them. In

Funkia ovata and *Allium fragrans*, two common garden plants, according to his investigations, no embryo is developed from the actual oosphere in the embryo-sac, not even when a pollen-tube may have happened to penetrate into the micropyle; but close to it cells of the nucellus of the ovule grow out into the embryo-sac and embryos arise from these cell-proliferations. It is very probable that matters are quite similar in the case of the Orange-tree also, and in the case of one of the Euphorbiaceæ from Australia, *Cœlebogyne,* of which female specimens alone occur with us   In all these plants several embryos are produced in the interior of the embryo-sac by budding from the surrounding tissue.

Among the phenomena of apogamy are also to be counted those cases in the flowering-plants where, though flowers are developed, they are devoid of true sexual organs, or where no flowers at all are developed.   Here again the plants in question are chiefly cultivated plants.   Thus Müller designates certain Scitamineæ and Dioscoreæ and also the Horse-radish (*Armoracia*) as entirely seedless, and De Bary remarks in this connection that also our (of course not cultivated) *Ficaria* and *Dentaria bulbifera* but rarely produce seeds; among the species of the genus *Allium* (Garlic) there are several in which small bulbils arise in place of the flowers, and among these is also *Allium sativum* (the Garlic) in which no seeds whatever are developed.

The view that such apogamous species are undergoing extinction is opposed, and correctly, by De Bary, with the remark that it is just among most apogamous plants that an excessive production of asexually produced descendants tends to occur.   Sexual propagation is more than sufficiently replaced by asexual productivity.

INDEX.

The figures in large type refer to illustrations.

THE END.

Lightning Source UK Ltd.
Milton Keynes UK
174086UK00006B/22/P